www.wadsworth.com

www.wadsworth.com is the World Wide Web site for Thomson Wadsworth and is your direct source to dozens of online resources.

At *www.wadsworth.com* you can find out about supplements, demonstration software, and student resources. You can also send e-mail to many of our authors and preview new publications and exciting new technologies.

www.wadsworth.com
Changing the way the world learns®

CLASSIC READINGS
and
CONTEMPORARY DEBATES
in
INTERNATIONAL RELATIONS

THIRD EDITION

Edited by
PHIL WILLIAMS
DONALD M. GOLDSTEIN
JAY M. SHAFRITZ
Graduate School of Public and International Affairs
University of Pittsburgh

THOMSON
™
WADSWORTH

Australia • Brazil • Canada • Mexico • Singapore • Spain
United Kingdom • United States

THOMSON

✳ ™

WADSWORTH

Classic Readings and Contemporary Debates in International Relations
Third Edition
Phil Williams, Donald M. Goldstein, Jay M. Shafritz

Publisher: *Clark Baxter*
Executive Editor: *David Tatom*
Development Editor: *Drake Bush*
Associate Development Editor: *Rebecca Green*
Editorial Assistant: *Eva Dickerson*
Technology Project Manager:
  Michelle Vardeman
Marketing Manager: *Janise Fry*
Marketing Assistant: *Teresa Jessen*
Project Manager, Editorial Production:
  Marti Paul
Creative Director: *Rob Hugel*
Art Director: *Maria Epes*

Print Buyer: *Judy Inouye*
Permissions Editor: *Kiely Sisk*
Production Service: *Scratchgravel Publishing
  Services*
Copy Editor: *Carol Lombardi*
Cover Design: *Jeanette Barber/Silver Valley
  Graphic Design*
Cover Image: © *The Studio Dog/Getty
  Images*
Cover Printer: *Transcontinental
  Printing/Louiseville*
Compositor: *Cadmus*
Printer: *Transcontinental Printing/Louiseville*

© 2006 Thomson Wadsworth, a part of The
Thomson Corporation. Thomson, the Star
logo, and Wadsworth are trademarks used
herein under license.

ALL RIGHTS RESERVED. No part of this
work covered by the copyright hereon may
be reproduced or used in any form or by any
means—graphic, electronic, or mechanical,
including photocopying, recording, taping, Web
distribution, information storage and retrieval
systems, or in any other manner—without the
written permission of the publisher.

Printed in Canada
1 2 3 4 5 6 7 09 08 07 06 05

Library of Congress Control Number:
2005923121

ISBN 0-534-63189-4

Thomson Higher Education
10 Davis Drive
Belmont, CA 94002-3098
USA

For more information about our products,
contact us at:
**Thomson Learning Academic Resource
Center
1-800-423-0563**
For permission to use material from this
text or product, submit a request online at
http://www.thomsonrights.com.
Any additional questions about permissions
can be submitted by e-mail to
thomsonrights@thomson.com.

ABOUT THE EDITORS

Phil Williams is a professor in the Graduate School of Public and International Affairs at the University of Pittsburgh. He has previously taught at the University of Southampton and Aberdeen and was formerly director of the International Security Program, Royal Institute of International Affairs. He has written extensively for such journals as *Washington Quarterly, International Affairs, Survival, Defense Nationale,* and *Journal for Arms Control.* His major publications include *Crisis Management, Contemporary Strategy, The Senate and the U.S. Troops in Europe,* and *Superpower Detente: A Reappraisal.* Since the early 1990s Dr. Williams has focused on transnational threats and has edited or co-edited books on trafficking in women and such books as *The United Nations and Transnational Crime* and *Combating Transnational Crime.* He has also published extensively on transnational organized crime, including articles on organized crime in Russia, Ukraine, and central Asia as well as on money laundering, criminal networks, and nuclear material trafficking. In addition, Dr. Williams has researched terrorist finances and attacking terrorist networks. Dr. Williams received his Ph.D. from the University of Southampton.

Donald M. Goldstein is a professor in the Graduate School of Public and International Affairs at the University of Pittsburgh. A retired U.S. Air Force officer, he formerly taught history and international affairs at the Air Force Academy, the Air Command and Staff College, the Air War College, and Troy State University. Dr. Goldstein is the winner of two Peabody Awards for his work on the television productions "Pearl Harbor: Two Hours That Changed the World" and "D-Day: A Soldier's Story." He is the coauthor, along with K. V. Dillon and Gordon W. Prange, of the bestsellers *At Dawn We Slept: The Untold Story of Pearl Harbor, Miracle at Midway, Target Tokyo,* and *The Williwaw War.* Dr. Goldstein received his Ph.D. in history from the University of Denver.

Jay M. Shafritz is a professor in the Graduate School of Public and International Affairs at the University of Pittsburgh. Previously he has taught at the University of Colorado in Denver, the University of Houston in Clear Lake City, the State University of New York in Albany, and Rensselaer Polytechnic Institute. He is the author, coauthor, or editor of more than three dozen books on government including the *HarperCollins Dictionary of American Government and Politics,* 1992, and the *Dictionary of Twentieth-Century World Politics,* 1993. Dr. Shafritz received his Ph.D. from Temple University.

BRIEF CONTENTS

Contents

Terrorism

Sovereignty and Intervention, Deterrence and Pre-Emption

Unipolarity and the U.S. Role in the World

FOREWORD

International relations scholars were appalled by the ending of the Cold War. Their failure to predict the biggest event in the second half of the twentieth century seemed to cast an unforgiving light on this branch of the social sciences. They have been too hard on themselves. Intelligence agencies, military staffs, and chancelleries around the world similarly fell short. And the entire global fraternity of computer software designers failed to predict the end of the century—an event a good deal more certain than anything in international affairs.

There have been four kinds of responses within the academic discipline of international relations. The first is to continue the fresh work being done before 1989, incorporating new ideas within international relations, such as the communications revolution, international crime, gender, ethnic, and environmental studies. This has narrowed the focus for individual scholars but, broadly, the agenda here is to suggest that the discipline will be better placed in the future to accommodate shifts within the system if a wider range of issues is added to the subject. The second response is postmodernism, frequently the favored path for those who might be said to have "lost" the Cold War. The thrust here is that what is thought to have been East–West issues about power and strategic absolutes now need to be reexamined. So-called facts and ideas that had (and have) intellectual currency were (and are) merely conventions of knowledge supported by prevailing assumptions and particular power structures. Look at it this way, they say, and it seems like this; look at it another way and it appears like that—and both views are held to be equally valid. The third response is to move closer to current affairs commentary and away somewhat from academic and theoretical rigor. This is not necessarily abandonment of intellectual rectitude; rather it is an acceptance that the discipline is in transition. Social sciences should be distinctly modest about prediction and should focus on theoretical development shifts away from vast and relevant developments. It is as though they are casting themselves in the role of the first drafters of history.

The fourth response is represented by this new edition of *Classic Readings and Contemporary Debates in International Relations*. It is to reestablish, for the new generation of students, the intellectual credentials of international relations from the writing of its best exponents now supplemented by new work on areas into which the discipline is moving. Everyone will have slightly different views about which of the most recent pieces should be included—how old does a "classic" have to be? What is on offer is a fair representation of the post–Cold War synthesis. This is easily summarized. Security needs careful redefinition if it is to carry its new conceptual burdens. Questions about the centrality of the nation state in the international system have yet to be answered. Non-state actors, with varying legitimacy, are now given greater academic respect. Military power, relative to other instruments of power, has probably less utility than formerly, but worries persist about proliferation. Scholars are divided, for example, as to whether the war to liberate Kuwait in 1990 through 1991 was the last of the old wars or the first of the new. Ethnic and religious tensions, often fueling nationalist fervor, so long bottled up in many parts of the world, suggest clear challenges to regional order. The conjunction of resource shortages and population growth has produced a new crop of neo-Malthusians. A clear consensus exists that international economic developments, influenced in all probability by environmental change, will profoundly shape the future, even if there is less agreement on quite how and when. Few ignore the communications revolution.

This third edition therefore supplies students with the excellent service that the editors offered with the first: a comprehensive and effective way into the discipline. My own students found the first and second editions most helpful in charting the post–Cold War changes; the third is broader in scope and thus even more academically valuable. It provides a brilliant array of ideas about how people have tried to deal with the complexity of collective human experience in an international setting under constant stress. Defining the world we want is usually a positive and active, if perhaps somewhat innocent, exercise. Positing what world we expect is a more complex thing to achieve, tending toward the negative and passive—more prejudiced by current experience masquerading as prediction. The most difficult task is to shape what actually happens so as to avoid what is expected and to produce something close to what we want. If the first law of politics is not to make things any worse, the first law of any academic discipline must be to help make things better. This compilation shows how generations of international relations analysts, political practitioners, lawyers, historians, strategists, and political scientists have attempted this larger ambition. The whole point of being a student is to carry on that task. The point of this book is to make that possible.

Peter Foot
Deputy Dean of Academic Studies
Joint Services Command and Staff College
Bracknell
United Kingdom

PREFACE

The classic selections in this volume are intended to provide international relations students with an understanding of the diversity of approaches to the study of international relations and an appreciation of the key concepts and frameworks. These readings better enable us to understand a subject that is not only complex, exciting, full of controversy and debate, but also a matter of great importance in the contemporary world. The introductions to each section, which were written by Phil Williams, are designed to provide an overview and guide and also reflect the author's own assessment on particular issues.

In the post–Cold War international system, the familiar issues of peace and war, conflict and cooperation, independence and interdependence, order and disorder, anarchy and society, sovereignty and intervention, power and hierarchy remain as significant as they have always been. Many of these fundamental issues are as salient in the twenty-first century as they were for Thucydides, Machiavelli, Hobbes, and Rousseau in earlier centuries.

The analyses of these issues by the great philosophers and historians have a profundity, depth, and universality that ensure their continued relevance. This is evident, for example, in Thucydides' *History of the Peloponnesian War*, especially in his discussion of the debate between the Athenians and the Melians about whether the island of Melos should surrender to Athenian forces or fight. The subsequent debate is full of ideas about the respective roles of power and justice in international politics and about relations between large and small states. It is necessary only to think of the Iraqi invasion of Kuwait in August 1990, the wars in Yugoslavia through the 1990s, and the U.S. invasion of Iraq in 2003 to see the continued relevance of the issues and questions raised by Thucydides.

In a period when scholars and students alike are groping for understanding of a newly ordered world, therefore, revisiting classic analyses of international relations is a rewarding enterprise. Consequently, one purpose of this volume is to identify themes and issues that have enduring importance rather than those that are simply matters of the moment. Yet, as the reader will see, many of the selections facilitate an understanding of the changing international system and provide a solid basis from which to think about the future of world politics.

There are several reasons for this current relevance.

- This book identifies some of the main ways in which analysts and scholars have understood and explained relations among states. Although huge changes are now taking place, part of the challenge for the student of international relations is to determine which approaches remain appropriate and which are less helpful.

◆ Consideration of the actors in international relations has never been more pertinent than in a period when the states of Eastern Europe and the former Soviet Union have reasserted their sovereignty and independence and are attempting to make the dual transition to democracies and market economies, and when the states of the Third World are seeking a greater sense of identity and a more equitable distribution of global resources.

◆ Closely related to this, the end of the Cold War has had little impact on issues of development. The problems of economic inequality remain acute. This is reflected in the inclusion of selections offering analyses of imperialism and the relations between the core and the periphery of the international economic system.

◆ This book contains several selections that focus on the distribution of power in the international system. Although this appears to be changing fundamentally, the direction and consequences of change remain uncertain.

These selections on the international system help the reader to formulate more clearly some of the crucial questions about international relations in the twenty-first century. The bipolar international system of the postwar period has disappeared, but what kind of system is replacing it? What are the prospects for stability in a unipolar international system? How enduring is such a system? The selections here do not necessarily provide clear and easy answers to such questions, but they do offer a sense of the possibilities and encourage the reader to consider issues such as the relationship between the distribution of power and the problems of maintaining international order and stability.

Another goal of this volume is to provide insights into the proliferation of actors in international relations. These range from nongovernmental organizations, which seek to promote positive change in the world, to transnational criminal and terrorist networks, which pose new security challenges. Indeed, one of the themes that emerges, especially in the later sections, is that international relations is no longer simply about the relations among states. A multiplicity of other actors pose new and intractable problems for efforts to develop global governance mechanisms in an era of globalization. Indeed, Part VI (on contemporary issues and debates) contains for the most part a new set of excerpts that revolve around key themes and can either be juxtaposed with one another in the form of a debate or can be seen as complementing or supplementing each other. In some cases, as on the issue of global chaos, we have three selections, each of which offers a very distinct perspective. Two of these excerpts emphasize the notion of conflict and chaos, whereas the third contends that global chaos is a myth. Indeed, in this section we have focused on a variety of issues and challenges that are likely to be of enduring importance. We have also provided material that we believe will both stimulate and inform.

In choosing the readings for this volume, we used seven criteria:

1. the seminal importance of each selection in the evolution of thinking about international relations
2. comprehensive representation of divergent approaches and schools of thought with which students should be familiar
3. the utility of each selection for students
4. the continued relevance of each reading
5. the need for balance between selections to reflect some of the great debates in the study of international relations
6. accessibility
7. the provision of important insights into contemporary issues in global politics

In the event that some of the commentaries on contemporary global politics become the classics of the future, then we will have chosen well. Even if they do not achieve this status, they will still provide a basis for debate and discussion and encourage further reading.

We avoided selections that are particularly jargon-ridden or arcane in their approach. Although this volume makes clear that the language, concepts, and great debates in international relations are intellectually demanding, it also attempts to make them both accessible and interesting.

In sum, the selections in the book have been chosen to introduce students to many of the classic analyses, basic themes, and enduring problems of international relations. The readers will not find in the following pages many references to current events. But they will find concepts, ideas, and analyses that will greatly assist them as they try to give meaning, order, and interpretation to these events.

ACKNOWLEDGMENTS

Putting together a volume of classic readings of this kind is not an easy task, especially in a subject as rich as international relations. During the course of this endeavor, therefore, it is hardly surprising that the editors incurred large debts to a number of people. In the early stages of the first edition, Dr. Hanna Freij was particularly helpful both in thinking about choices of material and in assisting the editors in tracking down references. In the later stages Dr. Simon Reich, of the Graduate School of Public and International Affairs, University of Pittsburgh, reviewed the selections, pointed out important omissions, and provided advice as to how the gaps could best be filled. He was particularly helpful regarding the literature on international political economy.

A number of students in the Graduate School of Public and International Affairs also assisted, and we would like to thank Anita Caivara, Douglas Brooks, and Nathanial Herman for their help. Students in the classes in international relations have also offered many insights and ideas. For the third edition our thanks go to Brant Hahn, who provided invaluable assistance in tracking down and organizing material for us.

During the preparation for this volume, we also benefited from discussions with other colleagues in the Graduate School of Public and International Affairs, especially Michael Brenner, Paul Hammond, Martin Staniland, and Davis Bobrow.

We would also like to thank the following reviewers for their helpful comments during the development of this book: Richard Foster, Idaho State University; Dennis R. Gordon, Santa Clara University; Forest Grieves, University of Montana; Timothy J. Lomperis, Duke University; Michael Mastanduno, Dartmouth College; Stephen R. Newlin, California State University, Chico; and Neil Richardson, University of Wisconsin–Madison. The anonymous reviewers of the third edition also gave us many good suggestions, and we have followed as many of them as possible. All of these people have made our task easier, but the responsibility for the sins of commission and omission that remain is clearly that of the editors themselves.

Classic Readings
and
Contemporary Debates
in
International Relations

INTRODUCTION

This volume not only emphasizes the value of classic readings in international relations but also presents insightful commentary on contemporary developments. It thereby challenges the notion that, during periods of great change in world politics, the only analyses worth reading are those that take account of the most recent developments. In periods of change and turmoil, analyses that offer the latest and most up-to-date summary of events need to be complemented by more reflective and detached studies that locate contemporary change amidst a wide historical panorama. Such approaches allow the reader to discern patterns of continuity as well as change, facilitate the identification of analogies that can be illuminating without being exact, and encourage the recognition that neither the historical upheaval that marked the end of the Cold War, nor the legacy of problems that policymakers and citizens had to confront in the 1990s, nor those that they face in the first decade of the twenty-first century are unique or wholly novel. The disintegration of the Soviet bloc, for example, was not the first occasion on which an empire founded on military coercion rather than political legitimacy fell apart. Similarly, the rise of ethnic tensions in Europe during the 1990s was a reversion to a phenomenon that was very obvious throughout the first half of the twentieth century. Recognizing that contemporary changes are not without precedent or pattern, therefore, provides both a broader perspective and deeper insight into the direction and possible destination of these changes.

At the same time, we acknowledge that the period since the end of the Cold War has been marked by profound changes. These have resulted not in a "new world order" (as conceived by the first President Bush) but a new world disorder in which the forces of conflict and turbulence are more diverse and more salient than in the Cold War. The dynamics of globalization, for example, have had profound and often unforeseen consequences—both positive and negative—and the rise of non-state actors has challenged the traditional dominance of states. The terrorist attacks on the World Trade Center and the Pentagon on September 11, 2001, were orchestrated not by a state but by a transnational Islamic terrorist network with a safe haven in Afghanistan. The fact that the first major challenge to U.S. hegemony did not come from a rival state exemplified the changes that had occurred since the end of the Cold War and pointed to what could easily become a pattern for the future. In other words, where the Cold War was rigid, predictable, and dominated by military and strategic considerations; the post–Cold War international system is more fluid, the factors of state power more indeterminate, the imponderables much greater, the cast of significant actors more diverse, and the capacity to pose threats to national and international security more diffused.

In this uncertain and complex environment, many controversial issues and debates arise. Consequently, this edition includes readings that, in our judgment, do not necessarily meet the criteria for classics, but do help to illuminate some of the contemporary issues. Where possible, we have juxtaposed competing assessments that can be used as the basis for class debates.

In the first section of this book, we focus primarily on the development of the discipline of international relations, highlighting the antecedents of the contemporary approaches and theories and showing how the traditions are represented in more recent analyses. The section contains readings representing divergent approaches to understanding and studying international relations. Excerpts are taken from those who emphasize international cooperation, the significance of international law, and the norms of international society; from those who emphasize international anarchy and the struggle for power in the international system; and from those who believe that international relations can best be studied through a focus on economic processes and interactions.

The second section focuses on structural characteristics of the international system, with particular attention to the distribution of power among the constituent units and how this impinges on patterns of cooperation, conflict, and alignment. It contains readings that highlight competing assessments of the impact on stability of different power configurations. Several selections also note that, although the international system of the postwar period was predominantly bipolar, with two great powers providing the main focus for conflict and alignment within the system, other levels of activity also had to be considered.

The third section focuses on the nature of the actors in international relations. It looks at the state as the primary actor and considers characteristics of the state, such as the notions of territoriality and sovereignty. In addition, it also looks at two challenges to the predominance of the state-centric model.

The first of these stems from the rise of other actors, including international organizations and transnational actors. In one sense, of course, transnational actors are nothing new: The Papacy has long been a non-state actor in international relations. And even the multinational corporation is not new: The activities of the famous East India Company, which was such an important part of British colonial expansion, would almost certainly be reassuringly familiar to analysts of modern multinational corporations. Nevertheless, it is hard to deny that, as national economies have become more intertwined and interdependent, non-state actors have also become more important. Many non-governmental organizations have even developed transnational advocacy networks, which are discussed in one of the readings. Another new selection looks at international organizations from a novel perspective, highlighting both their power and their pathologies.

The second challenge to the dominance of the state-centric approach has come from those who argue that the state is simply an abstraction, and rather than abstracting it and treating it as a distinct autonomous actor, we would do far better to look at those individuals, governments, and organizations that act on behalf of the state in international relations. This is reflected in selections that deal with the decision-making approach, with the beliefs and perceptions of policymakers, and with bureaucratic and organizational politics.

The fourth section of the book examines the sources of conflict and the incentives for cooperation in the international system. The selections dealing with international anarchy focus on the way in which international politics is defined by the lack of a central overriding authority and show how this provides an environment in which insecurity is endemic. Particular emphasis is placed on the security dilemma in which actions taken by one state to enhance its security create insecurity in others. Attention is also given to the way in which states attempt to manage anarchy and the attendant search for security and to the struggle for power through such mechanisms as the balance of power, collective security, and the balance of terror. This section also includes readings that show how states can cooperate despite the security dilemma and how they have developed mechanisms and procedures to mitigate the effects of international anarchy. Particular attention is given to the notion of regimes—an idea that has been developed primarily in relation to the international economy but is sometimes discussed in relation to international security—and to theories of integration. We also include in this section readings that represent new approaches that have developed in recent years—especially constructivism and feminism—as well as provide some of the responses from more traditional scholars to these approaches.

The focus of the fifth section is on international conflict and its various manifestations. Here the selections cover several interrelated themes: nuclear deterrence, coercive diplomacy, and the nature and origins of war. Most of these selections are helpful in terms of both clarifying the key concepts and illuminating the dynamics of conflict. We also include a selection highlighting the possibility that states will not always behave rationally—a concept that takes on particular salience as more states develop and deploy weapons of mass destruction.

Section six, the final section of the book, focuses on current and future developments that seem likely to have a profound impact on the evolution of international relations. Given that most of the selections are recent, it is difficult to regard them as "classics" in the same way as many of the earlier readings. Consequently, we have chosen readings that, in our judgment, help us think in imaginative and stimulating ways about international relations in the twenty-first century. Among the themes we include in this section are unipolarity and the future of U.S. power, the United States' preventive war in Iraq, order versus disorder in world politics, intervention versus sovereignty, and both the rise and the potential impact of terrorism. The aim here is to spark discussion and analysis by highlighting divergent assessments of contemporary problems and help students to think about alternative futures. This is fitting: Although the volume focuses primarily on classic contributions, it is designed to look forward as much as backward.

Our main hope, in fact, is that the selections we have made will allow the reader to look ahead not only with greater insight and understanding but also with a sense of excitement about what is one of the most fascinating, if often frustrating, facets of human activity. If this volume provides a sense of the richness and diversity of international relations in the twenty-first century as well as the analytical rigor with which we need to approach the subject, then it will have fulfilled its purpose.

I

THEORIES AND TRADITIONS

12. Theotonio Dos Santos
    The Structure of Dependence

INTELLECTUAL FOUNDATIONS

International relations as an academic discipline is a product of the twentieth century. Perhaps the most important reason for this is that political philosophers traditionally focused more on the principles and practices of governance within political units than on the relationships among these units. Even Thomas Hobbes, whose characterizations of the relations between sovereigns have given rise to the dominant school of thought about international relations, devoted only a few pages to international political philosophy, focusing far more on the role of the state or the Leviathan in establishing order and stability within domestic society. To argue this point, however, is not to deny the importance of the philosophical writings that did deal with relations among independent political entities, whether city-states, feudal baronies, or states. The works of Grotius, Rousseau, Clausewitz, and Kant, for example, offer immense insights into various aspects of these relationships, as do the few pages by Hobbes that deal with the interaction of sovereigns. Moreover, although these insights reflect the observations of specific individuals rather than the collective output of an academic discipline, they are both timeless and profound. Not surprisingly, therefore, they also provide much of the basis for the various intellectual traditions underpinning the contemporary study of international relations. These intellectual traditions include: (1) liberal institutionalism, which has several diverse strands of origin; (2) Hobbesian realism and its contemporary variant of neo-realism; and (3) Marxist and neo-Marxist thinking, which were crucial both to Cold War revisionism and to the development of dependency theory. Each of these is reflected in pertinent selections in this section.

LIBERAL THEORIES
OF INTERNATIONAL RELATIONS

One of the strands in liberal thinking about international relations—what might be the termed the legalistic—can be traced back to the work of Hugo Grotius and his contention that there is a society of states bound by common rules, customs, and shared norms. Based at the outset on natural law thinking, this strand of thought is represented here by a selection from the famous work by Hugo Grotius (1583–1645), *The Rights of War and Peace Including the Law of Nature and of Nations*. This volume provided the basis for international law in the European state system. Indeed, Grotius has been widely considered the key figure in the development of international jurisprudence and been described as the father of international law. Using natural law as his starting point, Grotius emphasized that there was a law of war as well as a law of peace. In the selection included here, he distinguishes between public and private war and also discusses the nature of sovereign power.

A second strand of liberal thinking is represented by the work of Immanuel Kant. Although some of Kant's ideas contributed enormously to the notion of global cosmopolitanism, which is currently manifested in ideas about global civil society, he also provided many of the intellectual antecedents for contemporary liberal institutionalism as well as a series of propositions that are currently articulated in the idea of the liberal peace—the notion that liberal democratic states, if not inherently pacifist, are very unlikely to fight other liberal democracies. Rather than going directly to the body of Kant's work, however, we thought it more useful to provide excerpts from the work of Michael Doyle, one of the major democratic peace theorists, whose commentaries on Kant are far more accessible than Kant's own philosophic writings. Doyle provides an incisive commentary on Kant's First, Second, and Third Definitive Articles: The First Article requires that states have a republican constitution, representative government, and juridical freedom. The Second Article covers the creation and expansion of a federation of free states, and the Third seeks to establish what Doyle describes as "a cosmopolitan law to operate in conjunction with the pacific union." The end state envisaged by Kant is a state of perpetual peace.

Although much of the liberal tradition was initially based on perceptive insights into the nature of behavior of sovereigns, the liberal tradition became much more divorced from the actual behavior of states during the period between World Wars I and II. It is little exaggeration to suggest, in fact, that this tradition was hijacked by a kind of idealism presupposing that international relations could be fundamentally transformed so long as the right formula was found. The idealists of this period, particularly in Great Britain and the United States, believed drastic change was crucial to avoiding war. This was a direct response to World War I, which also provided the main stimulus to the development of the discipline of international relations. The slaughter on the Western Front resulted in a "never again" philosophy reflected in the emergence of idealism as the dominant approach to international relations, especially in Great Britain.

Consequently, interwar studies of international relations were predominantly prescriptive pieces aiming to reform the international system and ensure that further destructive wars were avoided. These ideas were enshrined in Woodrow Wilson's "Fourteen Points" (which is reproduced here), and in the philosophy, structure, and organization of the League of Nations. They were developed particularly fully in Great Britain and the United States. Enjoying the luxury of relative security provided by the English Channel in one case and by the Atlantic Ocean in the other, British and American thinkers could offer prescriptions for reform of the international system that were far less compelling for states surrounded by potential enemies.[1]

---

[1] This is discussed more fully in Arnold Wolfers, *The Anglo-American Tradition in Foreign Affairs* (New Haven, Conn.: Yale University Press, 1956).

The starting point for many liberals and idealists was the Enlightenment notion that human society could be perfected. This had important implications for assessing why war occurred and what needed to be done to prevent it. Many liberals and idealists saw war stemming not from human nature but from imperfect political institutions that an advancing civilization could eliminate. They also assumed that a natural harmony of interests existed among peoples but that this harmony was disrupted by imperfect arrangements and practices—at both the national and international levels. The crucial task, therefore, was to identify the causes of war and to eradicate them. Many analysts saw the main causes of World War I as international anarchy and the balance of power. Others saw the prime cause as the arms race; yet others emphasized secret diplomacy. The prescriptions followed the diagnoses: international anarchy should be replaced by international organization, with the League of Nations playing the primary role in ensuring the rule of law; arms races would be prevented by general disarmament; and secret diplomacy was to be replaced by public diplomacy and democratic control—a notion that can be traced back directly to Kant's First Definitive Article.

There were, of course, differences of emphasis: Some liberals and idealists focused on reform of the international system, whereas others wanted to start with reform at the state level. Members of this latter group believed that democracies were inherently less aggressive and less likely to go to war than were authoritarian states. This belief was perhaps best reflected in Wilson's "Fourteen Points" and still finds many echoes in much contemporary thinking. During the 1990s, arguments about the promotion of democratic forms of government in Eastern Europe and the former Soviet Union were based on the fear that the alternative to democracy was a re-emergence of ultra-nationalist regimes that would pursue aggressive and expansionist foreign policies. More recently, the United States' intervention in Iraq was justified, in part at least, in terms of the need to replace authoritarian leadership in the Middle East with liberal democracies. The liberal argument—which, ironically, was embraced by many conservatives and neo-conservatives in the Bush administration prior to U.S. military action in Iraq—is that creating democracy in the country will have a domino effect throughout the region, and that the spread of democracy in turn will greatly increase the opportunities for peace and stability.

In effect, this reflects the sheer persistence of one of the major characteristics of the liberal tradition—a faith in reform. The idealists who emerged after World War I believed that they had the solutions to the problems of international politics and war; their only remaining task was to educate governments and peoples so that they would carry out the actions necessary to achieve those solutions. The problem was that much of this approach was characterized by wishful thinking rather than a hard-headed appraisal of the possibilities for reform and the obstacles that would have to be overcome if it was to succeed.

If the idealists of the interwar period were in the Kantian and Grotian tradition, they allowed their desire to transform international relations to hinder their understanding of state practice. Their aspirations for reform encountered two main difficulties. The first was that similar sentiments were not fully shared by the states of Continental Europe, which did not have the English Channel or the Atlantic Ocean to protect them from security threats—and were therefore reluctant to put their faith in new and untried institutions as opposed to their own efforts to enhance their security and power. The second and closely related problem was that the arguments for reform of the international system presumed that all major states in the system saw peace and security as their main goal. This was a particularly inappropriate assumption in the 1930s, with the emergence of Fascist dictatorships that pursued policies of internal terror and external expansion—a development that should have raised immediate red flags for liberals who, following Kant, emphasized the pacific nature of democracies and the aggressive nature of other forms of government. The aggressions of Nazi Germany and Japan underlined the fact that, as Henry Kissinger subsequently noted, when peace becomes the primary goal of most states in the international system, the system itself is soon at the mercy of its most ruthless members.[2]

Although the idealists' remoteness from the harsh realities of international relations in the 1930s discredited some of the ideas about international institutions and the rule of law, the Grotian component of the liberal tradition has been revitalized in the writings of Hedley Bull. One of the foremost authorities on nuclear arms control and at one point the director of the Arms Control and Disarmament Research Unit of the British Foreign Office, Bull approached contemporary problems within a framework of traditional philosophy. Although he placed himself within the Grotian tradition, however, Bull was careful to differentiate his position from that of the idealists of the interwar period. He was very critical of what he termed the "twentieth century emphasis upon ideas of a reformed or improved international society, as distinct from the elements of society in actual practice" arguing that this has "led to a treatment of the League of Nations, the United Nations and other general international organizations as the chief institutions of international society, to the neglect of those institutions whose role in the maintenance of international order is the central one."[3] Bull believed that "the Wilsonian rejection of the balance of power" and "the denigration of diplomacy" were particularly unfortunate as both the balance of power and diplomacy are crucial to maintaining order in the international system.[4]

A compelling component of Bull's approach to international relations was his recognition that relations among states were, in many respects, anarchical, but that there were nonetheless elements of society in the international system. In his desire not to claim too much for the notion of international

---

[2] Henry A. Kissinger, *A World Restored* (New York: Grosset and Dunlap, 1964), esp. pp. 1–6.

[3] H. Bull, *The Anarchical Society* (London: Macmillan, 1977), p. 40.

[4] H. Bull, *The Anarchical Society*, p. 40.

society, Bull reflected the influence of the realist tradition, even while rejecting many of its tenets. Unlike the idealists who believed that the forces of disorder could be dispelled through the transformation of the international system, Bull recognized the power of these forces and claimed only that they could be contained rather than abolished. As is evident in the excerpt from *The Anarchical Society* reproduced here, he also argued that the elements of international society, though often precarious, generally provide important components of order in the international system. The essential point for Bull is that states form an international society, which, although it differs in important respects from domestic society, is a society nonetheless. It is a society that is regulated and has distinct institutions. One of the most important regulatory devices is international law; another is the balance of power; a third is diplomacy; and a fourth is the use of force.

REALIST AND NEO-REALIST THEORIES OF INTERNATIONAL RELATIONS

Bull's work reflected the Grotian tradition and was also influenced by the realist tradition. Realism as a distinct approach to international relations grew out of the reaction against idealism in the interwar period. Its roots, however, go back to Thucydides, Machiavelli, Hobbes, and Rousseau.

Thucydides, in particular, can be understood as the intellectual godfather of both realism and neo-realism. His famous study of the Peloponnesian War was not only a graphic portrayal of the roots of conflict seen from the vantage point of ancient Greece, but also a treatise on the more fundamental causes of war. In a famous and oft-quoted statement, Thucydides argued that it was necessary to go beyond the obvious and superficial causes of the war between Athens and Sparta and to identify the real reason for the conflict. In his view, "What made war inevitable was the growth of Athenian power and the fear this caused in Sparta." In essence, he says that insecurity as well as the quest for power might be the cause of war—in effect, combining later variants of realism and neo-realism. Also included here is Thucydides' account of the dialogue between the Athenians and the Melians about whether Melos can be left in peace. Perhaps more than any other excerpt, this highlights the tension between principles of order and justice on the one side and international practice on the other. As well as emphasizing that might is more important than right, the Athenians provide an early version of the domino theory, arguing that if they allow Melos to remain independent, this will encourage other states to disregard or challenge the power of Athens. The importance of power and security considerations is evident in the writings of Thucydides, and his work combines many of the insights later elucidated in both realism and neo-realism.

Ironically, the distinction of being the first important realist was given by E. H. Carr, not to Thucydides, but to Niccolo Machiavelli (1469–1527). In some ways this was understandable. Machiavelli was one of the first political philosophers to emphasize the use of force to obtain desired objectives, He was also concerned with amassing, maintaining, and using power—and offered explicit advice to rulers about how best to do all this. Machiavelli's *The Prince* (1532) emphasized the need to acquire skill in warfare. It also displayed a real appreciation of the role of power—understood as the capacity to make someone do something he would not otherwise do—which is best exemplified in Machiavelli's comment that "there is simply no comparison between a man who is armed and one who is not, It is unreasonable to expect that an armed man should obey one who is not or that an unarmed man should remain safe and secure when his servants are armed." A similar kind of thinking was evident in Machiavelli's advice to princes that they should endeavor to be feared rather than loved, that they should honor their word only when it does not place them at a disadvantage, and that they should appear to have many virtuous qualities even when they do not. What counts, Machiavelli argued, was the result.

Machiavelli developed an appreciation for the role of power in political life, and the same sense is evident in the writings of Thomas Hobbes (1588–1679), one of the great English philosophers and political theorists of the seventeenth century. Hobbes shares with Machiavelli a pessimism about human nature. Yet perhaps Hobbes's most important contribution to thinking about international politics, and the one contained here from *Leviathan* (1651), was his contrast between relations among persons in a society controlled by the state (or "Leviathan") and the relations among persons, and more particularly sovereigns, where no Leviathan exists to maintain order. For Hobbes, the relationship among kings or persons in sovereign authority is akin to that in the state of nature (before the formation of the state) in which life is "solitary, poor, nasty, brutish and short." As he contends, sovereigns are in a state of continual jealousies and in the posture of gladiators with their weapons pointing toward one another. This comment illustrates perhaps better than any other single statement the suspicion and sense of insecurity characterizing the relations among states in a system without a central overriding authority.

The analyses of Machiavelli and Hobbes provide the intellectual antecedents for the development of realism. However, as mentioned above, the main stimulus to the rise of contemporary realism came out of a sense of frustration with the idealism of the interwar period. Although World War II was to provide the death knell for the naive idealism of the 1920s and 1930s, British historian E. H. Carr contributed to the demise of idealism in his book *The Twenty Years Crisis*. Carr offered an important and devastating critique of untempered idealist thinking, part of which is reproduced in this section. Although Carr was not wholly uncritical of realism either, he argued that notions of the harmony of interest—fundamental to idealism—were simply a disguise for the vested interests of the predominant powers and their desire to maintain the status quo.

If Carr pointed the way to the realist tradition, this tradition was perhaps best exemplified by the father of the realist school and one of the most influential analysts in international relations, Hans Morgenthau, who taught for many years at the University of Chicago. Morgenthau's *Politics Among Nations* was an immensely important study that influenced successive generations of scholars and analysts and, occasionally, national decision makers. During the early 1970s, in particular, the foreign policy of Richard Nixon and his National Security Adviser, Henry Kissinger, was based on considerations of realpolitik and geopolitics of the kind emphasized by Morgenthau. Indeed, Morgenthau started from the premise that international politics, like all politics, was a struggle for power and that states defined their national interest in terms of power. His basic thesis is enshrined in his famous statement of the principles of political realism, reprinted here. A careful reading of this excerpt will illustrate Morgenthau's view of human nature as essentially unchanging and as exhibiting a lust for power; his emphasis on rational choice by statesmen, accompanied by a dismissive attitude toward motives other than the search for power; his assessment of the central importance of the balance of power; his contention that politics is a distinct and autonomous sphere of action; and his desire to establish a theory of international politics.

Critics were not slow to point out the shortcomings of *Politics Among Nations*. They argued that Morgenthau relied too heavily for his starting point on a concept of human nature that was very elusive, that his core concepts such as power and interest were vague and ill-defined, and that it was not clear whether he had developed a prescriptive or a descriptive theory. They also noted inconsistencies between Morgenthau's contention that state behavior could be understood as the pursuit of interests defined in terms of power and his criticisms of U.S. foreign policymakers for acting according to ideological principles rather than according to the principles he had set forth as the basic determinants of behavior. This ambivalence about whether he was being prescriptive or descriptive, however, did not prevent Morgenthau from having a major impact.

Although many subsequent analysts rejected key parts of Morgenthau's analysis, his idea of international politics as a struggle for power became the basis for much later theorizing. Robert Keohane, one of the first analysts to write about the growing trend toward the interdependence of states and a trenchant critic of Morgenthau, has pointed out that even many of those who followed in the tradition of power politics did not share all of Morgenthau's assumptions.[5] Perhaps the most important difference was that subsequent theorists focused less on the inherent lust for power and more on the anarchical nature of the international system as a basic determinant of international political behavior.

This view was most evident in the writings of Kenneth Waltz, who placed unprecedented emphasis on the structure of the system, a term that Waltz used

---

[5] See Robert Keohane, ed., *Neorealism and Its Critics* (New York: Columbia University Press, 1986).

to cover both anarchy (in the sense that a central overriding authority was absent) and the distribution of power or capabilities within the system.[6] Waltz argues that the distribution of power or the shape of the international hierarchy has crucial implications for the stability of the system and is the key to theorizing about international politics. This provided the basis for what is generally described as structural realism or neo-realism. The selection by Waltz included in this section is valuable because it summarizes the main elements of the neo-realist approach to international politics and also because Waltz differentiates his approach from the realism of Morgenthau. One of these crucial differences is that, whereas Morgenthau sees states as striving for power, Waltz sees them as searching for security. States in Morgenthau's world are driven by ambition; those in Waltz's world are motivated by fear about the possible ambitions of others.

One of the ways in which Waltz's work does resemble that of Morgenthau, however, is in the criticism it has attracted. Critics have claimed that neo-realism is far too deterministic, that it cannot predict change in the international system, and that Waltz, like Morgenthau, disregards the internal attributes of states. Yet others contend that by emphasizing the autonomy of international politics, Waltz overlooks or dismisses crucial elements of the international system such as economic processes, international political institutions, and growing interdependence among states.[7]

One criticism perhaps not made often enough, however, is that Waltz conflates several distinct aspects of the international system under the term *structure*. International anarchy, which is a key element in his thinking, is better described in terms of the *nature* of the system rather than its *structure*. The lack of a central overriding authority and the fact that states consequently have to rely on self-help for security are permanent features of international politics and characteristics that endure, whatever the precise distribution of power in the system. A world containing two great powers and a world containing many great powers are very different in structural terms; yet, in terms of the anarchical nature of the system, they are essentially the same. In both systems, insecurity is endemic—although there are likely to be major differences in terms of who is afraid of whom and why. In other words, although patterns of insecurity will differ along with variations in the distribution of power, insecurity is pervasive and endemic. To the extent that this is accepted—and Waltz himself argues that anarchy is unchanging whereas the distribution of power among the units and the number of great powers vary greatly—the notion of structure should be used to refer only to the distribution of power within the system and not to international anarchy, which is best conceived and understood in terms of the essential and irreducible nature of the system.

---

[6] See Kenneth N. Waltz, *Theory of International Politics* (London: Addison-Wesley, 1979).

[7] These criticisms are developed more fully in many of the selections in Keohane, *Neorealism and Its Critics*.

If Waltz can be criticized for lumping together distinct elements of the international system, he can also be attacked for ignoring patterns of cooperation. This is not surprising. The divide between those who focus on cooperation in international society and those who emphasize conflict in international anarchy has provided the basis for perhaps the most important single debate in the discipline. Yet it would be a serious mistake to ignore other approaches toward international relations simply because of the centrality of this debate.

THE ROOTS OF INTERNATIONAL POLITICAL ECONOMY

One of the most obvious alternatives to Waltz's approach or to realist theories in general is the economic approach, encompassing, but not confined to, Marxist and neo-Marxist theories. Radical and neo-Marxist theories not only offer alternative explanations for the outbreak of war from those offered by neo-realism but also focus on inequality or underdevelopment, which are ignored in more traditional, state-centric approaches. Marxist approaches to international relations are characterized by an emphasis not so much on state conflict as on class conflict. The crucial divisions are not those between states but those between the exploiters and the exploited, the oppressors and the oppressed within societies and between them. And where conflict arises among states, this occurs because these states embody particular kinds of economic structures and ideologies.

For Karl Marx (1818–1883), history was not about the rise and fall of nations or about patterns of security and cooperation among states; rather, it was about societies' changing system of economic production, which determined the ownership of wealth. Marx developed a theory of history based on the dialectics of the class struggle. His writings traced the transition from feudalism to capitalism and predicted the transition from capitalism to socialism—a development he saw as preordained by the weaknesses or contradictions of capitalism. The rise of capitalism itself was inextricably bound up with the rise of the bourgeoisie, or new capitalists. The bourgeoisie controlled the means of production in society and exploited the workers, or proletariat, who were the actual producers but benefited very little from the results of their labor. By selling products for much more than was paid to the workers, the capitalists were able to accrue even more wealth. Profit widened the gap between the bourgeoisie and the proletariat. Marx argued, however, that this system contained the seeds of its own destruction—that the alienation of the proletariat would lead eventually to revolution and the replacement of the capitalist system by a socialist system. He provided a theory of history and of revolution rather than a theory of international relations. Yet those who either followed in the intellectual tradition he established or were influenced by it (even though they rejected some of its precepts) were to develop Marxist ideas in ways that helped to explain crucial aspects of state behavior and some characteristics of the international system.

In the late nineteenth and early twentieth centuries, one of the most obvious aspects of great power behavior was overseas expansion. The European states engaged in a "scramble for Africa," and even the United States became involved in Asia, taking control of the Philippines. Like other imperialist powers, the United States provided a self-serving rationale that explained imperialism in terms of honor and duty. The Leninist view, however, characterized imperialism as exploitative and as leading to war between the capitalist powers. Lenin's interpretation built not only on Marx but also on the writings of John Hobson (1858–1940), an English non-Marxist economist who went to the Boer War as a correspondent for the Manchester *Guardian* and whose work *Imperialism: A Study* (1902) was crucial in changing attitudes toward imperialism.

Hobson was one of the first commentators to point to the exploitative nature of imperialism. The basis of his argument was that, in the capitalist system, those who had surplus capital preferred to invest it abroad rather than to redistribute it at home. They sought to "broaden the channel for the flow of their surplus wealth by seeking foreign markets and foreign investments to take off the goods and capital they cannot sell or use at home."[8] In Hobson's view, financial interests were the dynamic force in imperial expansion and manipulated the other forces of society for their economic ends. This emerges very clearly in the excerpt from Hobson contained here.

This emphasis on economic motivations provided the basis for the Leninist interpretation, which saw imperialism as the highest form of capitalism and argued that war between imperialist powers was inevitable. Indeed, Lenin's greatest contribution to the neo-Marxist tradition may be this linkage between imperialism and war. For Lenin, imperialist policies were a means of staving off domestic revolution. The problem for the capitalist states, however, was that both markets and raw materials were finite. Consequently, conflict among them was inevitable—hence World War I.

An interesting point of similarity between neo-Marxism and neo-realism is an emphasis on international conflict. Moreover, although the explanations for conflict are very different, both approaches see the roots of conflict in terms of system characteristics: neo-Marxists emphasize the nature and structure of capitalist economic systems; neo-realists the nature and structure of the international system. In other respects, however, radical or neo-Marxist approaches are very distinctive. In neo-Marxist thinking, for example, the state has a very different role than is attributed to it in either of the other traditions outlined above: The state is important primarily as a reflection of underlying economic forces. Conversely, the horizontal linkages that cut across states and are reflected in such notions as international class solidarity highlight the limit of a state-centric approach. Indeed, the focus on horizontal linkages in neo-Marxist thinking gives it something in common with contemporary proponents of international society who emphasize the growing interdependence among states.

One of the most important elements differentiating the two approaches, however, is that neo-Marxism also focuses on horizontal divisions and the asymmetric nature of economic relationships: The key theme is not so much

---

[8] J. A. Hobson, *Imperialism: A Study* (London: Allen and Unwin, 1938), p. 85.

interdependence as dependence—and exploitation. Some of these differences emerge more forcefully from a careful reading of the piece by Stephen Krasner, a non-Marxist scholar who has done important work on the economic dimensions of U.S. foreign policy. In the selection we have chosen, Krasner identifies some of the ways in which Marxism differs from other approaches to international politics and distinguishes between what he calls instrumental and structural Marxists. The article by Theotonio Dos Santos elaborates on the notion of economic dependence, identifying three different forms such dependence takes and elucidating the ways in which dependence is perpetuated.

Despite some apparent similarities or points of convergence, therefore, the fundamental nature of the differences among the three perspectives—Hobbesian realism; the Kantian and Grotian emphasis on an international society of liberal democracies; and the neo-Marxist emphasis on inequality, exploitation, and dependence—needs to be understood. Indeed, these differences of approach are woven throughout this volume, the better to illustrate our challenging yet fascinating discipline.

Understanding international relations is a massive and complex undertaking, and diversity of approach and scholarship can illuminate its many facets. International relations involves conflict and cooperation, anarchy and society, independence, interdependence, and dependence. All are different elements of a complex reality that poses formidable problems of analysis and understanding but is also one of the most distinctive and engrossing areas of human activity.

I

HUGO GROTIUS

THE RIGHTS OF WAR AND PEACE

THE DIVISION OF WAR INTO PUBLIC AND PRIVATE AND THE NATURE OF SOVEREIGN POWER

I. The first and most necessary divisions of war are into one kind called private, another public, and another mixed. Now public war is carried on by the person holding the sovereign power. Private war is that which is carried on by private persons without authority from the state. A mixed war is that which is carried

SOURCE: From *The Rights of War and Peace*, Hugo Grotius, A. C. Campbell, A. M., trans. (New York: M. Walter Dunne, 1901), pp. 55–57, 62.

on, on one side by public authority, and on the other by private persons. But private war, from its greater antiquity, is the first subject for inquiry.

The proofs that have been already produced, to shew that to repel violence is not repugnant to natural law, afford a satisfactory reason to justify private war, as far as the law of nature is concerned. But perhaps it may be thought that since public tribunals have been erected, private redress of wrongs is not allowable. An objection which is very just. Yet although public trials and courts of justice are not institutions of nature, but erected by the invention of men, yet as it is much more conducive to the peace of society for a matter in dispute to be decided by a disinterested person, than by the partiality and prejudice of the party aggrieved, natural justice and reason will dictate the necessity and advantage of every one's submitting to the equitable decisions of public judges. Paulus, the Lawyer, observes that "what can be done by a magistrate with the authority of the state, should never be intrusted to individuals; as private redress would give rise to greater disturbance." And "the reason, *says King Theodoric,* why laws were invented, was to prevent any one from using personal violence, for wherein would peace differ from all the confusion of war, if private disputes were terminated by force?" And the law calls it force for any man to seize what he thinks his due, without seeking a legal remedy.

II. It is a matter beyond all doubt that the liberty of private redress, which once existed, was greatly abridged after courts of justice were established. Yet there may be cases, in which private redress must be allowed, as for instance, if the way to legal justice were not open. For when the law prohibits any one from redressing his own wrongs, it can only be understood to apply to circumstances where a legal remedy exists. Now the obstruction in the way to legal redress may be either temporary or absolute. Temporary, where it is impossible for the injured party to wait for a legal remedy, without imminent danger and even destruction. As for instance, if a man were attacked in the night, or in a secret place where no assistance could be procured. Absolute, either as the right, or the fact may require. Now there are many situations, where the right must cease from the impossibility of supporting it in a legal way, as in unoccupied places, on the seas, in a wilderness, or desert island, or any other place, where there is no civil government. All legal remedy too ceases by fact, when subjects will not submit to the judge, or if he refuses openly to take cognizance of matters in dispute. The assertion that all private war is not made repugnant to the law of nature by the erection of legal tribunals, may be understood from the law given to the Jews, wherein God thus speaks by the mouth of Moses, Exod. xxii. 2. "If a thief be found breaking up, that is, by night, and be smitten that he dies, there shall no blood be shed for him, but if the sun be risen upon him, there shall be blood shed for him." Now this law, making so accurate a distinction in the merits of the case, seems not only to imply impunity for killing any one, in self-defence, but to explain a natural right, founded not on any special divine command, but on the common principles of justice. From whence other nations have plainly followed the same rule. The passage of the twelve tables is well known, undoubtedly taken from the old Athenian Law, "If a thief commit a robbery in the night, and a man kill him, he is killed lawfully." Thus by the laws of all known and civilized nations, the person is judged innocent, who kills another, forcibly attempting or endangering his life; a conspiring and universal testimony, which proves that in justifiable homicide, there is nothing repugnant to the law of nature. . . .

IV. Public war, according to the law of nations, is either SOLEMN, that is FORMAL, or LESS SOLEMN, that is INFORMAL. The name of lawful war is commonly given to what is here called formal, in the same sense in which a regular will is opposed to a codicil, or a lawful marriage to the cohabitation of slaves. This opposition by no means implies that it is not allowed to any man, if he pleases, to make a codicil, or to slaves to cohabit in matrimony, but only, that, by the civil law, FORMAL WILLS and SOLEMN MARRIAGES, were attended with peculiar privileges and effects. These observations were the more necessary; because many, from a misconception of the word just or lawful, think that all wars, to which those epithets do not apply, are condemned as unjust and unlawful. Now to give a war the formality required by the law of nations, two things are necessary. In the first place it must be made on both sides, by the sovereign power of the state, and in the next place it must be accompanied with certain formalities. Both of which are so essential that one is insufficient without the other.

Now a public war, LESS SOLEMN, may be made without those formalities, even against private persons, and by any magistrate whatever. And indeed, considering the thing without respect to the civil law, every magistrate, in case of resistance, seems to have a right to take up arms, to maintain his authority in the execution of his office; as well as to defend the people committed to his protection. But as a whole state is by war involved in danger, it is an established law in almost all nations that no war can be made but by the authority of the sovereign in each state. . . .

VII. That power is called sovereign, whose actions are not subject to the control of any other power, so as to be annulled at the pleasure of any other human will. The term ANY OTHER HUMAN WILL exempts the sovereign himself from this restriction, who may annul his own acts, as may also his successor, who enjoys the same right, having the same power and no other. We are to consider then what is the subject in which this sovereign power exists. Now the subject is in one respect common, and in another proper, as the body is the common subject of sight, the eye the proper, so the common subject of sovereign power is the state, which has already been said to be a perfect society of men.

Now those nations, who are in a state of subjugation to another power, as the Roman provinces were, are excluded from this definition. For those nations are not sovereign states of themselves, in the present acceptation of the word; but are subordinate members of a great state, as slaves are members of a household.

2

MICHAEL W. DOYLE

KANT'S PERPETUAL PEACE

LIBERAL INTERNATIONALISM

Modern liberalism carries with it two legacies. They do not affect liberal states separately, according to whether they are pacifistic or imperialistic, but simultaneously.

The first of these legacies is the pacification of foreign relations among liberal states.[1] During the nineteenth century, the United States and Great Britain engaged in nearly continual strife; however, after the Reform Act of 1832 defined actual representation as the formal source of the sovereignty of the British parliament, Britain and the United States negotiated their disputes. They negotiated despite, for example, British grievances during the Civil War against the North's blockade of the South, with which Britain had close economic ties. Despite severe Anglo-French colonial rivalry, liberal France and liberal Britain formed an entente against illiberal Germany before World War I. And from 1914 to 1915, Italy, the liberal member of the Triple Alliance with Germany and Austria, chose not to fulfill its obligations under that treaty to support its allies. Instead, Italy joined in an alliance with Britain and France, which prevented it from having to fight other liberal states and then declared war on Germany and Austria. Despite generations of Anglo-American tension and Britain's wartime restrictions on American trade with Germany, the United States leaned toward Britain and France from 1914 to 1917 before entering World War I on their side.

Beginning in the eighteenth century and slowly growing since then, a zone of peace, which Kant called the "pacific federation" or "pacific union," has begun to be established among liberal societies. More than 40 liberal states currently make up the union. Most are in Europe and North America, but they can be found on every continent. . . .

Here the predictions of liberal pacifists (and President Reagan) are borne out: liberal states do exercise peaceful restraint, and a separate peace exists among them. This separate peace provides a solid foundation for the United States' crucial alliances with the liberal powers, e.g., the North Atlantic Treaty Organization and our Japanese alliance. This foundation appears to be

SOURCE: From Michael W. Doyle, "Kant's Perpetual Peace," *The American Political Science Review,* Vol. 80, No. 4 (Dec. 1986), 1115–1169.

impervious to the quarrels with our allies that bedeviled the Carter and Reagan administrations. It also offers the promise of a continuing peace among liberal states, and as the number of liberal states increases, it announces the possibility of global peace this side of the grave or world conquest.

Of course, the probability of the outbreak of war in any given year between any two given states is low. The occurrence of a war between any two adjacent states, considered over a long period of time, would be more probable. The apparent absence of war between liberal states, whether adjacent or not, for almost 200 years thus may have significance. Similar claims cannot be made for feudal, fascist, communist, authoritarian, or totalitarian forms of rule (Doyle, 1983a, pp. 222), nor for pluralistic or merely similar societies. More significant perhaps is that when states are forced to decide on which side of an impending world war they will fight, liberal states all wind up on the same side despite the complexity of the paths that take them there. These characteristics do not prove that the peace among liberals is statistically significant nor that liberalism is the sole valid explanation for the peace.[2] They do suggest that we consider the possibility that liberals have indeed established a separate peace—but only among themselves.

Liberalism also carries with it a second legacy: international "imprudence" (Hume, 1963, pp. 346–47). Peaceful restraint only seems to work in liberals' relations with other liberals. Liberal states have fought numerous wars with nonliberal states. . . .

Many of these wars have been defensive and thus prudent by necessity. Liberal states have been attacked and threatened by nonliberal states that do not exercise any special restraint in their dealings with the liberal states. Authoritarian rulers both stimulate and respond to an international political environment in which conflicts of prestige, interest, and pure fear of what other states might do all lead states toward war. War and conquest have thus characterized the careers of many authoritarian rulers and ruling parties, from Louis XIV and Napoleon to Mussolini's fascists, Hitler's Nazis, and Stalin's communists.

Yet we cannot simply blame warfare on the authoritarians or totalitarians, as many of our more enthusiastic politicians would have us do.[3] Most wars arise out of calculations and miscalculations of interest, misunderstandings, and mutual suspicions, such as those that characterized the origins of World War I. However, aggression by the liberal state has also characterized a large number of wars. Both France and Britain fought expansionist colonial wars throughout the nineteenth century. The United States fought a similar war with Mexico from 1846 to 1848, waged a war of annihilation against the American Indians, and intervened militarily against sovereign states many times before and after World War II. Liberal states invade weak nonliberal states and display striking distrust in dealings with powerful nonliberal states (Doyle, 1983b).

Neither realist (statist) nor Marxist theory accounts well for these two legacies. While they can account for aspects of certain periods of international stability (Aron, 1974, pp. 151–54; Russett, 1985), neither the logic of the balance of power nor the logic of international hegemony explains the separate peace maintained for more than 150 years among states sharing one particular form of governance—liberal principles and institutions. Balance-of-power theory expects—indeed is premised upon—flexible arrangements of geostrategic rivalry that include preventive war. Hegemonies wax and wane, but the liberal peace holds. Marxist "ultra-imperialists" expect a form of peaceful rivalry among capitalists, but only liberal capitalists maintain peace. Leninists expect liberal capitalists to be aggressive toward nonliberal states, but they also (and especially) expect them to be imperialistic toward fellow liberal capitalists.

Kant's theory of liberal internationalism helps us understand these two legacies. The importance of Immanuel Kant as a theorist of international ethics has been well appreciated (Armstrong, 1931; Friedrich, 1948; Gallie, 1978, chap. 1; Galston, 1975; Hassner, 1972; Hinsley, 1967, chap. 4; Hoffmann, 1965; Waltz, 1962; Williams, 1983), but Kant also has an important analytical theory of international politics. *Perpetual Peace,* written in 1795 (Kant, 1970, pp. 93–130), helps us understand the interactive nature of international relations. Kant tries to teach us methodologically that we can study neither the systemic relations of states nor the varieties of state behavior in isolation from each other. Substantively, he anticipates for us the ever-widening pacification of a liberal pacific union, explains this pacification, and at the same time suggests why liberal states are not pacific in their relations with nonliberal states. Kant argues that perpetual peace will be guaranteed by the ever-widening acceptance of three "definitive articles" of peace. When all nations have accepted the definitive articles in a metaphorical "treaty" of perpetual peace he asks them to sign, perpetual peace will have been established.

The First Definitive Article requires the civil constitution of the state to be republican. By *republican* Kant means a political society that has solved the problem of combining moral autonomy, individualism, and social order. A private property and market-oriented economy partially addressed that dilemma in the private sphere. The public, or political, sphere was more troubling. His answer was a republic that preserved juridical freedom—the legal equality of citizens as subjects—on the basis of a representative government with a separation of powers. Juridical freedom is preserved because the morally autonomous individual is by means of representation a self-legislator making laws that apply to all citizens equally, including himself or herself. Tyranny is avoided because the individual is subject to laws he or she does not also administer (Kant, *PP,* pp. 99–102; Riley, 1983, chap. 5).[4]

Liberal republics will progressively establish peace among themselves by means of the pacific federation, or union *(foedus pacificum),* described in Kant's Second Definitive Article. The pacific union will establish peace within a federation of free states and securely maintain the rights of each state. The world will not have achieved the "perpetual peace" that provides the ultimate guarantor of republican freedom until "a late stage and after many unsuccessful attempts" (Kant, *UH*, p. 47). At that time, all nations will have learned the lessons of peace through right conceptions of the appropriate constitution, great and sad experience, and good will. Only then will individuals enjoy perfect republican rights or the full guarantee of a global and just peace. In the meantime, the "pacific federation" of liberal republics—"an enduring and gradually expanding federation likely to prevent war"—brings within it more and more republics—despite republican collapses, backsliding, and disastrous wars—creating an ever-expanding separate peace (Kant, *PP*, p. 105).[5] Kant emphasizes that

> it can be shown that this idea of federalism, extending gradually to encompass all states and thus leading to perpetual peace, is practicable and has objective reality. For if by good fortune one powerful and enlightened nation can form a republic (which is by nature inclined to seek peace), this will provide a focal point for federal association among other states. These will join up with the first one, thus securing the freedom of each state in accordance with the idea of international right, and the whole will gradually spread further and further by a series of alliances of this kind. (Kant, *PP*, p. 104)

The pacific union is not a single peace treaty ending one war, a world state, nor a state of nations. Kant finds the first insufficient. The second and third are impossible or potentially tyrannical. National sovereignty precludes reliable subservience to a state of nations; a world state destroys the civic freedom on which the development of human capacities rests (Kant, *UH*, p. 50). Although Kant obliquely refers to various classical interstate confederations and modern diplomatic congresses, he develops no systematic organizational embodiment of this treaty and presumably does not find institutionalization necessary (Riley, 1983, chap. 5; Schwarz, 1962, p. 77). He appears to have in mind a mutual non-aggression pact, perhaps a collective security agreement, and the cosmopolitan law set forth in the Third Definitive Article.[6]

The Third Definitive Article establishes a cosmopolitan law to operate in conjunction with the pacific union. The cosmopolitan law "shall be limited to conditions of universal hospitality." In this Kant calls for the recognition of the "right of a foreigner not to be treated with hostility when he arrives on someone else's territory." This "does not extend beyond those conditions which make it possible for them [foreigners] to attempt to enter into relations [commerce] with the native inhabitants" (Kant, *PP*, p. 106). Hospitality does not require extending to foreigners either the right to citizenship or the right to settlement, unless the foreign visitors would perish if they were expelled. Foreign conquest and plunder also find no justification under this right. Hospitality does appear to include the right of access and the obligation of maintaining the opportunity for citizens to exchange goods and ideas without imposing the obligation to trade (a voluntary act in all cases under liberal constitutions).

Perpetual peace, for Kant, is an epistemology, a condition for ethical action, and, most importantly, an explanation of how the "mechanical process of nature visibly exhibits the purposive plan of producing concord among men, even against their will and indeed by means of their very discord" (Kant, *PP,* p. 108; *UH,* pp. 44–45). Understanding history requires an epistemological foundation, for without a teleology, such as the promise of perpetual peace, the complexity of history would overwhelm human understanding (Kant, *UH,* pp. 51–53). Perpetual peace, however, is not merely a heuristic device with which to interpret history. It is guaranteed, Kant explains in the "First Addition" to *Perpetual Peace* ("On the Guarantee of Perpetual Peace"), to result from men fulfilling their ethical duty or, failing that, from a hidden plan.[7] Peace is an ethical duty because it is only under conditions of peace that all men can treat each other as ends, rather than means to an end (Kant, *UH,* p. 50; Murphy, 1970, chap. 3). In order for this duty to be practical, Kant needs, of course, to show that peace is in fact possible. The widespread sentiment of approbation that he saw aroused by the early success of the French revolutionaries showed him that we can indeed be moved by ethical sentiments with a cosmopolitan reach (Kant, *CF,* pp. 181–82; Yovel, 1980, pp. 153–54). This does not mean, however, that perpetual peace is certain ("prophesiable"). Even the scientifically regular course of the planets could be changed by a wayward comet striking them out of orbit. Human freedom requires that we allow for much greater reversals in the course of history. We must, in fact, anticipate the possibility of backsliding and destructive wars— though these will serve to educate nations to the importance of peace (Kant, *UH,* pp. 47–48).

In the end, however, our guarantee of perpetual peace does not rest on ethical conduct. As Kant emphasizes,

> we now come to the essential question regarding the prospect of perpetual peace. What does nature do in relation to the end which man's own reason prescribes to him as a duty, i.e. how does nature help to promote his *moral purpose?* And how does nature guarantee that what man ought to do by the laws of his freedom (but does not do) will in fact be done through nature's compulsion, without prejudice to the free agency of man? . . . This does not mean that nature imposes on us a *duty* to do it, for duties can only be imposed by practical reason. On the contrary, nature does it herself, whether we are willing or not: *facta volentem ducunt, nolentem tradunt. (PP,* p. 112)

The guarantee thus rests, Kant argues, not on the probable behavior of moral angels, but on that of "devils, so long as they possess understanding" (PP, p. 112). In explaining the sources of each of the three definitive articles of the perpetual peace, Kant then tells us how we (as free and intelligent devils) could be motivated by fear, force, and calculated advantage to undertake a course of action whose outcome we could reasonably anticipate to be perpetual peace. Yet while it is possible to conceive of the Kantian road to peace in these terms, Kant himself recognizes and argues that social evolution also makes the conditions of moral behavior less onerous and hence more likely *(CF,* pp. 187–89; Kelly, 1969, pp. 106–13). In tracing the effects of both political and moral development, he builds an account of why liberal states do maintain peace among themselves and of how it will (by implication, has) come about that the pacific union will expand. He also explains how these republics would engage in wars with nonrepublics and therefore suffer the "sad experience" of wars that an ethical policy might have avoided.

The first source of the three definitive articles derives from a political evolution—from a constitutional law. Nature (providence) has seen to it that human beings can live in all the regions where they have been driven to settle by wars. (Kant, who once taught geography, reports on the Lapps, the Samoyeds, the Pescheras.) "Asocial sociability" draws men together to fulfill needs for security and material welfare as it drives them into conflicts over the distribution and control of social products (Kant, *UH*, pp. 44–45; *PP*, pp. 110–11). This violent natural evolution tends towards the liberal peace because "asocial sociability" inevitably leads toward republican governments, and republican governments are a source of the liberal peace.

Republican representation and separation of powers are produced because they are the means by which the state is "organized well" to prepare for and meet foreign threats (by unity) and to tame the ambitions of selfish and aggressive individuals (by authority derived from representation, by general laws, and by nondespotic administration) (Kant, *PP*, pp. 112–13). States that are not organized in this fashion fail. Monarchs thus encourage commerce and private property in order to increase national wealth. They cede rights of representation to their subjects in order to strengthen their political support or to obtain willing grants of tax revenue (Hassner, 1972, pp. 583–86).

Kant shows how republics, once established, lead to peaceful relations. He argues that once the aggressive interests of absolutist monarchies are tamed and the habit of respect for individual rights engrained by republican government, wars would appear as the disaster to the people's welfare that he and the other liberals thought them to be. The fundamental reason is this:

> If, as is inevitably the case under this constitution, the consent of the citizens is required to decide whether or not war should be declared, it is very natural that they will have a great hesitation in embarking on so dangerous an enterprise. For this would mean calling down on themselves all the miseries of war, such as doing the fighting themselves, supplying the costs of the war from their own resources, painfully making good the ensuing devastation, and, as the crowning evil, having to take upon themselves a burden of debts which will embitter peace itself and which can never be paid off on account of the constant threat of new wars. But under a constitution where the subject is not a citizen, and which is therefore not republican, it is the simplest thing in the world to go to war. For the head of state is not a fellow citizen, but the owner of the state, and war will not force him to make the slightest sacrifice so far as his banquets, hunts, pleasure palaces and court festivals are concerned. He can thus decide on war, without any significant reason, as a kind of amusement, and unconcernedly leave it to the diplomatic corps (who are always ready for such proposes) to justify the war for the sake of propriety. (Kant, *PP*, p. 100)

Yet these domestic republican restraints do not end war. If they did, liberal states would not be warlike, which is far from the case. They do introduce republican caution—Kant's "hesitation"—in place of monarchical caprice. Liberal wars are only fought for popular, liberal purposes. The historical liberal legacy is laden with popular wars fought to promote freedom, to protect private property, or to support liberal allies against nonliberal enemies. Kant's position is ambiguous. He regards these wars as unjust and warns liberals of their susceptibility to them (Kant, *PP*, p. 106). At the same time, Kant argues that each nation "can and ought to" demand that its neighboring nations enter into the pacific union of liberal states (*PP*, p. 102). Thus to see how the pacific union removes the occasion of wars among liberal states and not wars between liberal and nonliberal states, we need to shift our attention from constitutional law to international law, Kant's second source.

Complementing the constitutional guarantee of caution, international law adds a second source for the definitive articles: a guarantee of respect. The separation of nations that asocial sociability encourages is reinforced by the development of separate languages and religions. These further guarantee a world of separate states—an essential condition needed to avoid a "global, soul-less despotism." Yet, at the same time, they also morally integrate liberal states: "as culture grows and men gradually move towards greater agreement over their principles, they lead to mutual understanding and peace" (Kant, *PP*, p. 114). As republics emerge (the first source) and as culture progresses, an understanding of the legitimate rights of all citizens and of all republics comes into play; and this, now that caution characterizes policy, sets up the moral foundations for the liberal peace. Correspondingly, international law highlights the importance of Kantian publicity. Domestically, publicity helps ensure that the officials of republics act according to the principles they profess to hold just and according to the interests of the electors they claim to represent. Internationally, free speech and the effective communication of accurate conceptions of the political life of foreign peoples is essential to establishing and preserving the understanding on which the guarantee of respect depends. Domestically just republics, which rest on consent, then presume foreign republics also to be consensual, just, and therefore deserving of accommodation. The experience of cooperation helps engender further cooperative behavior when the consequences of state policy are unclear but (potentially) mutually beneficial. At the same time, liberal states assume that nonliberal states, which do not rest on free consent, are not just. Because nonliberal governments are in a state of aggression with their own people, their foreign relations become for liberal governments deeply suspect. In short, fellow liberals benefit from a presumption of amity; nonliberals suffer from a presumption of enmity. Both presumptions may be accurate; each, however, may also be self-confirming.

Lastly, cosmopolitan law adds material incentives to moral commitments. The cosmopolitan right to hospitality permits the "spirit of commerce" sooner or later to take hold of every nation, thus impelling states to promote peace and to try to avert war. Liberal economic theory holds that these cosmopolitan ties derive from a cooperative international division of labor and free trade according to comparative advantage. Each economy is said to be better off than it would have been under autarky; each thus acquires an incentive to avoid policies that would lead the other to break these economic ties. Because keeping open markets rests upon the assumption that the next set of transactions will also be determined by prices rather than coercion, a sense of mutual security is vital to avoid security-motivated searches for economic autarky. Thus, avoiding a challenge to another liberal state's security or even enhancing each other's security by means of alliance naturally follows economic interdependence.

A further cosmopolitan source of liberal peace is the international market's removal of difficult decisions of production and distribution from the direct sphere of state policy. A foreign state thus does not appear directly responsible for these outcomes, and states can stand aside from, and to some degree above, these contentious market rivalries and be ready to step in to resolve crises. The interdependence of commerce and the international contacts of state officials help create crosscutting transnational ties that serve as lobbies for mutual accommodation. According to modern liberal scholars, international financiers and transnational and transgovernmental organizations create interests in favor of accommodation. Moreover, their variety has ensured that no single conflict sours an entire relationship by setting off a spiral of reciprocated retaliation (Brzezinski and Huntington, 1963, chap. 9; Keohane and Nye, 1977, chap. 7; Neustadt, 1970; Polanyi, 1944, chaps. 1–2). Conversely, a sense of suspicion, such as that characterizing relations between liberal and nonliberal governments, can lead to restrictions on the range of contacts between societies, and this can increase the prospect that a single conflict will determine an entire relationship.

No single constitutional, international, or cosmopolitan source is alone sufficient, but together (and only together) they plausibly connect the characteristics of liberal polities and economies with sustained liberal peace. Alliances founded on mutual strategic interest among liberal and nonliberal states have been broken; economic ties between liberal and nonliberal states have proven fragile; but the political bonds of liberal rights and interests have proven a remarkably firm foundation for mutual nonaggression. A separate peace exists among liberal states.

In their relations with nonliberal states, however, liberal states have not escaped from the insecurity caused by anarchy in the world political system considered as a whole. Moreover, the very constitutional restraint, international respect for individual rights, and shared commercial interests that establish grounds for peace among liberal states establish grounds for additional conflict in relations between liberal and nonliberal societies.

CONCLUSION

Kant's liberal internationalism, Machiavelli's liberal imperialism, and Schumpeter's liberal pacifism rest on fundamentally different views of the nature of the human being, the state, and international relations.[8]

Schumpeter's humans are rationalized, individualized, and democratized. They are also homogenized, pursuing material interests "monistically." Because their material interests lie in peaceful trade, they and the democratic state that these fellow citizens control are pacifistic. Machiavelli's citizens are splendidly diverse in their goals but fundamentally unequal in them as well, seeking to rule or fearing being dominated. Extending the rule of the dominant elite or avoiding the political collapse of their state, each calls for imperial expansion.

Kant's citizens, too, are diverse in their goals and individualized and rationalized, but most importantly, they are capable of appreciating the moral equality of all individuals and of treating other individuals as ends rather than as means. The Kantian state thus is governed publicly according to law, as a republic. Kant's is the state that solves the problem of governing individualized equals, whether they are the "rational devils" he says we often find ourselves to be or the ethical agents we can and should become. Republics tell us that

> in order to organize a group of rational beings who together require universal laws for their survival, but of whom each separate individual is secretly inclined to exempt himself from them, the constitution must be so designed so that, although the citizens are opposed to one another in their private attitudes, these opposing views may inhibit one another in such a way that the public conduct of the citizens will be the same as if they did not have such evil attitudes. (Kant, *PP.* p. 113)

Unlike Machiavelli's republics, Kant's republics are capable of achieving peace among themselves because they exercise democratic caution and are capable of appreciating the international rights of foreign republics. These international rights of republics derive from the representation of foreign individuals, who are our moral equals. Unlike Schumpeter's capitalist democracies, Kant's republics—including our own—remain in a state of war with nonrepublics. Liberal republics see themselves as threatened by aggression from nonrepublics that are not constrained by representation. Even though wars often cost more than the economic return they generate, liberal republics also are prepared to protect and promote—sometimes forcibly—democracy, private property, and the rights of individuals overseas against nonrepublics, which, because they do not authentically represent the rights of individuals, have no rights to noninterference. These wars may liberate oppressed individuals overseas; they also can generate enormous suffering.

Preserving the legacy of the liberal peace without succumbing to the legacy of liberal imprudence is both a moral and a strategic challenge. The bipolar stability of the international system, and the near certainty of mutual devastation resulting from a nuclear war between the superpowers, have created a "crystal ball effect" that has helped to constrain the tendency toward miscalculation present at the outbreak of so many wars in the past (Carnesale, Doty, Hoffmann, Huntington, Nye, and Sagan, 1983, p. 44; Waltz, 1964). However, this "nuclear peace" appears to be limited to the superpowers. It has not curbed military interventions in the Third World. Moreover, it is subject to a desperate technological race designed to overcome its constraints and to crises that have pushed even the superpowers to the brink of war. We must still reckon with the war fevers and moods of appeasement that have almost alternately swept liberal democracies.

Yet restraining liberal imprudence, whether aggressive or passive, may not be possible without threatening liberal pacification. Improving the strategic acumen of our foreign policy calls for introducing steadier strategic calculations of the national interest in the long run and more flexible responses to changes in the international political environment. Constraining the indiscriminate meddling of our foreign interventions calls for a deeper appreciation of the "particularism of history, culture, and membership" (Walzer, 1983, p. 5), but both the improvement in strategy and the constraint on intervention seem, in turn, to require an executive freed from the restraints of a representative legislature in the management of foreign policy and a political culture indifferent to the universal rights of individuals. These conditions, in their turn, could break the chain of constitutional guarantees, the respect for representative government, and the web of transnational contact that have sustained the pacific union of liberal states.

Perpetual peace, Kant says, is the end point of the hard journey his republics will take. The promise of perpetual peace, the violent lessons of war, and the experience of a partial peace are proof of the need for and the possibility of world peace. They are also the grounds for moral citizens and statesmen to assume the duty of striving for peace. . . .

NOTES

I would like to thank Marshall Cohen, Amy Gutmann, Ferdinand Hermens, Bonnie Honig, Paschalis Kitromilides, Klaus Knorr, Diana Meyers, Kenneth Oye, Jerome Schneewind, and Richard Ullman for their helpful suggestions. One version of this paper was presented at the American Section of the International Society for Social and Legal Philosophy, Notre Dame, Indiana, November 2–4, 1984, and will appear in *Realism and Morality,* edited by Kenneth Kipnis and Diana Meyers. Another version was presented on March 19, 1986, to the Avoiding Nuclear War Project, Center for Science and International Affairs, The John F. Kennedy School of Government, Harvard University. This essay draws on research assisted by a MacArthur Fellowship in International Security awarded by the Social Science Research Council. . . .

1. Clarence Streit (1938, pp. 88, 90–92) seems to have been the first to point out (in contemporary foreign relations) the empirical tendency of democracies to maintain peace among themselves, and he made this the foundation of his proposal for a (non-Kantian) federal union of the 15 leading democracies of the 1930s. In a very interesting

book, Ferdinand Hermens (1944) explored some of the policy implications of Streit's analysis. D. V. Babst (1972, pp. 55–58) performed a quantitative study of this phenomenon of "democratic peace," and R. J. Rummel (1983) did a similar study of "libertarianism" (in the sense of laissez faire) focusing on the postwar period that drew on an unpublished study (Project No. 48) noted in Appendix 1 of his *Understanding Conflict and War* (1979, p. 386). I use the term *liberal* in a wider, Kantian sense in my discussion of this issue (Doyle, 1983a). In that essay, I survey the period from 1790 to the present and find no war among liberal states.

2. Babst (1972) did make a preliminary test of the significance of the distribution of alliance partners in World War I. He found that the possibility that the actual distribution of alliance partners could have occurred by chance was less than 1% (Babst, 1972, p. 56). However, this assumes that there was an equal possibility that any two nations could have gone to war with each other, and this is a strong assumption. Rummel (1983) has a further discussion of the issue of statistical significance as it applies to his libertarian thesis.

3. There are serious studies showing that Marxist regimes have higher military spending per capita than non-Marxist regimes (Payne, n.d.), but this should not be interpreted as a sign of the inherent aggressiveness of authoritarian or totalitarian governments or of the inherent and global peacefulness of liberal regimes. Marxist regimes, in particular, represent a minority in the current international system; they are strategically encircled, and due to their lack of domestic legitimacy, they might be said to "suffer" the twin burden of needing defenses against both external and internal enemies. Andreski (1980), moreover, argues that (purely) military dictatorships, due to their domestic fragility, have little incentive to engage in foreign military adventures. According to Walter Clemens (1982, pp. 117–18), the United States intervened in the Third World more than twice as often during the period 1946–1976 as the Soviet Union did in 1946–79. Relatedly, Posen and VanEvera (1980, p. 105; 1983, pp. 86–89) found that the United States devoted one quarter and the Soviet Union one tenth of their defense budgets to forces designed for Third World interventions (where responding to perceived threats would presumably have a less than purely defensive character).

4. All citations from Kant are from *Kant's Political Writings* (Kant, 1970), the H. B. Nisbet translation edited by Hans Reiss. The works discussed and the abbreviations by which they are identified in the text are as follows:

PP Perpetual Peace (1795)
UH The Idea for a Universal History with a Cosmopolitan Purpose (1784)

CF   *The Contest of Faculties* (1798)
MM *The Metaphysics of Morals* (1797)

5. I think Kant meant that the peace would be established among liberal regimes and would expand by ordinary political and legal means as new liberal regimes appeared. By a process of gradual extension the peace would become global and then perpetual; the occasion for wars with nonliberals would disappear as nonliberal regimes disappeared.

6. Kant's *foedus pacificum* is thus neither a *pactum pacis* (a single peace treaty) nor a *civitas gentium* (a world state). He appears to have anticipated something like a less formally institutionalized League of Nations or United Nations. One could argue that in practice, these two institutions worked for liberal states and only for liberal states, but no specifically liberal "pacific union" was institutionalized. Instead, liberal states have behaved for the past 180 years as if such a Kantian pacific union and treaty of perpetual peace had been signed.

7. In the *Metaphysics of Morals* (the *Rechtslehre*) Kant seems to write as if perpetual peace is only an epistemological device and, while an ethical duty, is empirically merely a "pious hope" (*MM,* pp. 164–75)—though even here he finds that the pacific union is not "impracticable" (*MM,* p. 171). In the *Universal History (UH),* Kant writes as if the brute force of physical nature drives men toward inevitable peace. Yovel (1980, pp. 168 ff.) argues that from a post-critical (*post–Critique of Judgment*) perspective, *Perpetual Peace* reconciles the two views of history. "Nature" is human-created nature (culture or civilization). Perpetual peace is the "*a priori* of the *a posteriori*"—a critical perspective that then enables us to discern causal, probabilistic patterns in history. Law and the "political technology" of republican constitutionalism are separate from ethical development, but both interdependently lead to perpetual peace—the first through force, fear, and self-interest; the second through progressive enlightenment—and both together lead to perpetual peace through the widening of the circumstances in which engaging in right conduct poses smaller and smaller burdens.

8. For a comparative discussion of the political foundations of Kant's ideas, see Shklar (1984, pp. 232-38).

REFERENCES

Andreski, Stanislav. 1980. On the Peaceful Disposition of Military Dictatorships. *Journal of Strategic Studies,* 3:3–10.

Armstrong, A. C. 1931. Kant's Philosophy of Peace and War. *The Journal of Philosophy.* 28:197–204.

Aron, Raymond. 1966. *Peace and War: A Theory of International Relations.* Richard Howard and Annette Baker Fox, trans. Garden City, NY: Doubleday.

Aron, Raymond. 1974. *The Imperial Republic.* Frank Jellinek, trans. Englewood Cliffs, NJ: Prentice Hall.

Babst, Dean V. 1972. A Force for Peace. *Industrial Research.* 14 (April): 55–58.

Banks, Arthur, and William Overstreet, eds. 1983. *A Political Handbook of the World; 1982–1983.* New York: McGraw Hill.

Barnet, Richard. 1968. *Intervention and Revolution.* Cleveland: World Publishing Co.

Brzezinski, Zbigniew, and Samuel Huntington. 1963. *Political Power: USA/USSR.* New York: Viking Press.

Carnesale, Albert, Paul Doty, Stanley Hoffmann, Samuel Huntington, Joseph Nye, and Scott Sagan. 1983. *Living With Nuclear Weapons.* New York. Bantam.

Chan, Steve. 1984. Mirror, Mirror on the Wall. . .: Are Freer Countries More Pacific? *Journal of Conflict Resolution,* 28:617–48.

Clemens, Walter C. 1982. The Superpowers and the Third World. In Charles Kegley and Pat McGowan, eds., *Foreign Policy; USA/USSR.* Beverly Hills: Sage. pp. 111–35.

Doyle, Michael W. 1983a. Kant, Liberal Legacies, and Foreign Affairs: Part 1. *Philosophy and Public Affairs,* 12:205–35.

Doyle, Michael W. 1983b. Kant, Liberal Legacies, and Foreign Affairs: Part 2. *Philosophy and Public Affairs,* 12:323–53.

Doyle, Michael W. 1986. *Empires.* Ithaca: Cornell University Press.

The Europa Yearbook for 1985. 1985. 2 vols. London. Europa Publications.

Friedrich, Karl. 1948. *Inevitable Peace.* Cambridge, MA: Harvard University Press.

Gallie, W. B. 1978. *Philosophers of Peace and War.* Cambridge: Cambridge University Press.

Galston, William. 1975. *Kant and the Problem of History.* Chicago: Chicago University Press.

Gastil, Raymond. 1985. The Comparative Survey of Freedom 1985. *Freedom at Issue,* 82:3–16.

Haas, Michael. 1974. *International Conflict.* New York: Bobbs-Merrill.

Hassner, Pierre. 1972. Immanuel Kant. In Leo Strauss and Joseph Cropsey, eds., *History of Political Philosophy.* Chicago: Rand McNally. pp. 554–93.

Hermens, Ferdinand A. 1944. *The Tyrants' War and the People's Peace.* Chicago: University of Chicago Press.

Hinsley, F. H. 1967. *Power and the Pursuit of Peace.* Cambridge: Cambridge University Press.

Hoffmann, Stanley. 1965. Rousseau on War and Peace. In Stanley Hoffmann, ed. *The State of War.* New York: Praeger. pp. 45–87.

Holmes, Stephen. 1979. Aristippus in and out of Athens. *American Political Science Review,* 73:113–28.

Huliung, Mark. 1983. *Citizen Machiavelli.* Princeton: Princeton University Press.

Hume, David. 1963. Of the Balance of Power. *Essays: Moral, Political, and Literary.* Oxford: Oxford University Press.

Kant, Immanuel. 1970. *Kant's Political Writings.* Hans Reiss, ed. H. B. Nisbet, trans. Cambridge: Cambridge University Press.

Kelly, George A. 1969. *Idealism, Politics, and History.* Cambridge: Cambridge University Press.

Keohane, Robert, and Joseph Nye. 1977. *Power and Interdependence.* Boston: Little Brown.

Langer, William L., ed. 1968. *The Encylopedia of World History.* Boston: Houghton Mifflin.

Mansfield, Harvey C. 1970. Machiavelli's New Regime. *Italian Quarterly,* 13:63–95.

Montesquieu, Charles de. 1949 *Spirit of the Laws*. New York: Hafner. (Originally published in 1748.)

Murphy, Jeffrie. 1970. *Kant: The Philosophy of Right*. New York: St. Martins.

Neustadt, Richard. 1970. *Alliance Politics*. New York: Columbia University Press.

Payne, James L. n.d. Marxism and Militarism. *Polity*. Forthcoming.

Pocock, J. G. A. 1975. *The Machiavellian Moment*. Princeton: Princeton University Press.

Polanyi, Karl. 1944. *The Great Transformation*. Boston: Beacon Press.

Posen, Barry, and Stephen VanEvera. 1980. Overarming and Underwhelming. *Foreign Policy*, 40:99–118.

Posen, Barry, and Stephen VanEvera. 1983. Reagan Administration Defense Policy. In Kenneth Oye, Robert Lieber, and Donald Rothchild, eds., *Eagle Defiant*. Boston: Little Brown. pp. 67–104.

Powell, G. Bingham. 1982. *Contemporary Democracies*. Cambridge, MA: Harvard University Press.

Reagan, Ronald. June 9, 1982. Address to Parliament. *New York Times*.

Riley, Patrick. 1983. *Kant's Political Philosophy*. Totowa, NJ: Rowman and Littlefield.

Rummel, Rudolph J. 1979. *Understanding Conflict and War*, 5 vols. Beverly Hills: Sage Publications.

Rummel, Rudolph J. 1983. Libertarianism and International Violence. *Journal of Conflict Resolution*, 27:27–71.

Russett, Bruce. 1985. The Mysterious Case of Vanishing Hegemony. *International Organization*, 39:207–31.

Schumpeter, Joseph. 1950. *Capitalism, Socialism, and Democracy*. New York: Harper Torchbooks.

Schumpeter, Joseph. 1955. The Sociology of Imperialism. In *Imperialism and Social Classes*. Cleveland: World Publishing Co. (Essay originally published in 1919.)

Schwarz, Wolfgang. 1962. Kant's Philosophy of Law and International Peace. *Philosophy and Phenomenonological Research*, 23:71–80.

Shell, Susan. 1980. The Rights of Reason. Toronto: University of Toronto Press.

Shklar, Judith. 1984. *Ordinary Vices*. Cambridge, MA: Harvard University Press.

Skinner, Quentin. 1981. *Machiavelli*. New York: Hill and Wang.

Small, Melvin, and J. David Singer. 1976. The War-Proneness of Democratic Regimes. *The Jerusalem Journal of International Relations*, 1(4):50–69.

Small, Melvin, and J. David Singer. 1982. *Resort to Arms*. Beverly Hills: Sage Publications.

Streit, Clarence. 1938. *Union Now: A Proposal for a Federal Union of the Leading Democracies*. New York: Harpers.

Thucydides. 1954. *The Peloponnesian War*. Rex Warner, ed. and trans. Baltimore: Penguin.

U.K. Foreign and Commonwealth Office. 1980. *A Yearbook of the Commonwealth 1980*. London: HMSO.

U.S. Congress. Senate. Select Committee to Study Governmental Operations with Respect to Intelligence Activities. 1975. *Covert Action in Chile, 1963–74*. 94th Cong., 1st sess., Washington, D.C.: U.S. Government Printing Office.

U.S. Department of State. 1981. *Country Reports on Human Rights Practices*. Washington, D.C.: U.S. Government Printing Office.

Waltz, Kenneth. 1962. Kant, Liberalism, and War. *American Political Science Review*, 56:331–40.

Waltz, Kenneth. 1964. The Stability of a Bipolar World. *Daedalus,* 93:881–909.

Walzer, Michael. 1983. *Spheres of Justice.* New York: Basic Books.

Weede, Erich. 1984. Democracy and War Involvement. *Journal of Conflict Resolution,* 28:649–64.

Wilkenfeld, Jonathan. 1968. Domestic and Foreign Conflict Behavior of Nations. *Journal of Peace Research,* 5:56–69.

Williams, Howard. 1983. *Kant's Political Philosophy.* Oxford: Basil Blackwell.

Wright, Quincy. 1942. *A Study of History.* Chicago: Chicago University Press.

Yovel, Yirmiahu. 1980. *Kant and the Philosophy of History.* Princeton: Princeton University Press.

3

WOODROW WILSON

THE FOURTEEN POINTS

Gentlemen of the Congress:

. . . It will be our wish and purpose that the processes of peace, when they are begun, shall be absolutely open and that they shall involve and permit henceforth no secret understandings of any kind. The day of conquest and aggrandizement is gone by, so is also the day of secret covenants entered into in the interest of particular governments and likely at some unlooked-for moment to upset the peace of the world. It is this happy fact, now clear to the view of every public man whose thoughts do not still linger in an age that is dead and gone, which makes it possible for every nation whose purposes are consistent with justice and the peace of the world to avow now or at any other time the objects it has in view.

We entered this war because violations of right had occurred which touched us to the quick and made the life of our own people impossible unless they were corrected and the world secured once for all against their recurrence. What we demand in this war, therefore, is nothing peculiar to ourselves. It is that the world be made fit and safe to live in; and particularly that it be made safe for every peace-loving nation which, like our own, wishes to live its own life, determine its own institutions, be assured of justice and fair dealing by the other peoples of the world as against force and selfish aggression. All

SOURCE: From The Fourteen Points, Wilson's Address to Congress, Woodrow Wilson, January 8, 1918.

the peoples of the world are in effect partners in this interest, and for our own part we see very clearly that unless justice be done to others it will not be done to us. The program of the world's peace, therefore, is our program; and that program, the only possible program, as we see it, is this:

I. Open covenants of peace, openly arrived at, after which there shall be no private international understandings of any kind but diplomacy shall proceed always frankly and in the public view.

II. Absolute freedom of navigation upon the seas, outside territorial waters, alike in peace and in war, except as the seas may be closed in whole or in part by international action for the enforcement of international covenants.

III. The removal, so far as possible, of all economic barriers and the establishment of an equality of trade conditions among all the nations consenting to the peace and associating themselves for its maintenance.

IV. Adequate guarantees given and taken that national armaments will be reduced to the lowest point consistent with domestic safety.

V. A free, open-minded, and absolutely impartial adjustment of all colonial claims, based upon a strict observance of the principle that in determining all such questions of sovereignty the interests of the populations concerned must have equal weight with the equitable claims of the government where title is to be determined.

VI. The evacuation of all Russian territory and such a settlement of all questions affecting Russia as will secure the best and freest cooperation of the other nations of the world in obtaining for her an unhampered and unembarrassed opportunity for the independent determination of her own political development and national policy and assure her of a sincere welcome into the society of free nations under institutions of her own choosing; and, more than a welcome, assistance also of every kind that she may need and may herself desire. The treatment accorded Russia by her sister nations in the months to come will be the acid test of their good will, of their comprehension of her needs as distinguished from their own interests, and of their intelligent and unselfish sympathy.

VII. Belgium, the whole world will agree, must be evacuated and restored, without any attempt to limit the sovereignty which she enjoys in common with all other free nations. No other single act will serve as this will serve to restore confidence among the nations in the laws which they have themselves set and determined for the government of their relations with one another. Without this healing act the whole structure and validity of international law is forever impaired.

VIII. All French territory should be freed and the invaded portions restored, and the wrong done to France by Prussia in 1871 in the matter of Alsace-Lorraine, which has unsettled the peace of the world for nearly fifty years, should be righted, in order that peace may once more be made secure in the interest of all.

IX. A readjustment of the frontiers of Italy should be effected along clearly recognizable lines of nationality.

X. The people of Austria-Hungary, whose place among the nations we wish to see safe guarded and assured, should be accorded the freest opportunity of autonomous development.

XI. Rumania, Serbia, and Montenegro should be evacuated; occupied territories restored; Serbia accorded free and secure access to the sea; and the relations of the several Balkan states to one another determined by friendly counsel along historically established lines of allegiance and nationality; and international guarantees of the political and economic independence and territorial integrity of the several Balkan states should be entered into.

XII. The Turkish portions of the present Ottoman Empire should be assured a secure sovereignty, but the other nationalities which are now under Turkish rule should be assured an undoubted security of life and an absolutely unmolested opportunity of autonomous development, and the Dardanelles should be permanently opened as a free passage to the ships and commerce of all nations under international guarantees.

XIII. An independent Polish state should be erected which should include the territories inhabited by indisputably Polish populations, which should be assured a free and secure access to the sea, and whose political and economic independence and territorial integrity should be guaranteed by international covenant.

XIV. A general association of nations must be formed under specific covenants for the purpose of affording mutual guarantees of political independence and territorial integrity to great and small states alike.

In regard to these essential rectifications of wrong and assertions of right we feel ourselves to be intimate partners of all the governments and peoples associated together against the Imperialists. We cannot be separated in interest or divided in purpose. We stand together until the end.

For such arrangements and covenants we are willing to fight and to continue to fight until they are achieved; but only because we wish the right to prevail and desire a just and stable peace such as can be secured only by removing the chief provocations to war, which this program does not remove. We have no jealousy of German greatness, and there is nothing in this program that impairs it. We grudge her no achievement or distinction of learning or of pacific enterprise such as have made her record very bright and very enviable. We do not wish to injure her or to block in any way her legitimate influence or power. We do not wish to fight her either with arms or with hostile arrangements of trade if she is willing to associate herself with us and the other peace-loving nations of the world in covenants of justice and law and fair dealing. We wish her only to accept a place of equality among the peoples of the world,—the new world in which we now live,—instead of a place of mastery.

Neither do we presume to suggest to her any alteration or modification of her institutions. But it is necessary, we must frankly say, and necessary as a preliminary to any intelligent dealings with her on our part, that we should know whom her spokesmen speak for when they speak to us, whether for the Reichstag majority or for the military party and the men whose creed is imperial domination.

We have spoken now, surely, in terms too concrete to admit of any further doubt or question. An evident principle runs through the whole program I have outlined. It is the principle of justice to all peoples and nationalities, and their right to live on equal terms of liberty and safety with one another, whether they be strong or weak. Unless this principle be made its foundation no part of the structure of international justice can stand. The people of the United States could act upon no other principle; and to the vindication of this principle they are ready to devote their lives, their honor, and everything that they possess. The moral climax of this the culminating and final war for human liberty has come, and they are ready to put their own strength, their own highest purpose, their own integrity and devotion to the test.

4

HEDLEY BULL

THE IDEA OF INTERNATIONAL SOCIETY

DOES ORDER EXIST IN WORLD POLITICS?

THE IDEA OF INTERNATIONAL SOCIETY

Throughout the history of the modern states system there have been three competing traditions of thought: the Hobbesian or realist tradition, which views international politics as a state of war; the Kantian or universalist tradition, which sees at work in international politics a potential community of mankind; and the Grotian or internationalist tradition, which views international politics as taking place within an international society.[1] Here I shall state what is essential to the Grotian or internationalist idea of international society, and what divides it from the Hobbesian or realist tradition on the one hand, and from the Kantian or universalist tradition on the other. Each of

SOURCE: From *The Anarchical Society: A Study of World Politics,* Hedley Bull (London: The Macmillan Press Ltd., 1977), pp. 24–27, 41, 51–52. © Columbia University Press, New York. Reprinted with permission of Columbia University Press.

these traditional patterns of thought embodies a description of the nature of international politics and a set of prescriptions about international conduct.

The Hobbesian tradition describes international relations as a state of war of all against all, an arena of struggle in which each state is pitted against every other. International relations, on the Hobbesian view, represent pure conflict between states and resemble a game that is wholly distributive or zero-sum: the interests of each state exclude the interests of any other. The particular international activity that, on the Hobbesian view, is most typical of international activity as a whole, or best provides the clue to it, is war itself. Thus peace, on the Hobbesian view, is a period of recuperation from the last war and preparation for the next.

The Hobbesian prescription for international conduct is that the state is free to pursue its goals in relation to other states without moral or legal restrictions of any kind. Ideas of morality and law, on this view, are valid only in the context of a society, but international life is beyond the bounds of any society. If any moral or legal goals are to be pursued in international politics, these can only be the moral or legal goals of the state itself. Either it is held (as by Machiavelli) that the state conducts foreign policy in a kind of moral and legal vacuum, or it is held (as by Hegel and his successors) that moral behaviour for the state in foreign policy lies in its own self-assertion. The only rules or principles which, for those in the Hobbesian tradition, may be said to limit or circumscribe the behaviour of states in their relations with one another are rules of prudence or expediency. Thus agreements may be kept if it is expedient to keep them, but may be broken if it is not.

The Kantian or universalist tradition, at the other extreme, takes the essential nature of international politics to lie not in conflict among states, as on the Hobbesian view, but in the transnational social bonds that link the individual human beings who are the subjects or citizens of states. The dominant theme of international relations, on the Kantian view, is only apparently the relationship among states, and is really the relationship among all men in the community of mankind—which exists potentially, even if it does not exist actually, and which when it comes into being will sweep the system of states into limbo.[2]

Within the community of all mankind, on the universalist view, the interests of all men are one and the same; international politics, considered from this perspective, is not a purely distributive or zero-sum game, as the Hobbesians maintain, but a purely cooperative or non-zero-sum game. Conflicts of interest exist among the ruling cliques of states, but this is only at the superficial or transient level of the existing system of states; properly understood, the interests of all peoples are the same. The particular international activity which, on the Kantian view, most typifies international activity as a whole is the horizontal conflict of ideology that cuts across the boundaries of states and divides human society into two camps—the trustees of the immanent community of mankind and those who stand in its way, those who are of the true faith and the heretics, the liberators and the oppressed.

The Kantian or universalist view of international morality is that, in contrast to the Hobbesian conception, there are moral imperatives in the field of international relations limiting the action of states, but that these imperatives enjoin not coexistence and cooperation among states but rather the overthrow of the system of states and its replacement by a cosmopolitan society. The community of mankind, on the Kantian view, is not only the central reality in international politics, in the sense that the forces able to bring it into being are present; it is also the end or object of the highest moral endeavour. The rules that sustain coexistence and social intercourse among states should be ignored if the imperatives of this higher morality require it. Good faith with heretics has no meaning, except in terms of tactical convenience; between the elect and the damned, the liberators and the oppressed, the question of mutual acceptance of rights to sovereignty or independence does not arise.

What has been called the Grotian or internationalist tradition stands between the realist tradition and the universalist tradition. The Grotian tradition describes international politics in terms of a society of states or international society.[3] As against the Hobbesian tradition, the Grotians contend that states are not engaged in simple struggle, like gladiators in an arena, but are limited in their conflicts with one another by common rules and institutions. But as against the Kantian or universalist perspective the Grotians accept the Hobbesian premise that sovereigns or states are the principal reality in international politics; the immediate members of international society are states rather than individual human beings. International politics, in the Grotian understanding, expresses neither complete conflict of interest between states nor complete identity of interest: it resembles a game that is partly distributive but also partly productive. The particular international activity which, on the Grotian view, best typifies international activity as a whole is neither war between states, nor horizontal conflict cutting across the boundaries of states, but trade—or, more generally, economic and social intercourse between one country and another.

The Grotian prescription for international conduct is that all states, in their dealings with one another, are bound by the rules and institutions of the society they form. As against the view of the Hobbesians, states in the Grotian view are bound not only by rules of prudence of expediency but also by imperatives of morality and law. But, as against the view of the universalists, what these imperatives enjoin is not the overthrow of the system of states and its replacement by a universal community of mankind, but rather acceptance of the requirements of coexistence and cooperation in a society of states.

Each of these traditions embodies a great variety of doctrines about international politics, among which there exists only a loose connection. In different periods each pattern of thought appears in a different idiom and in relation to different issues and preoccupations. This is not the place to explore further the connections and distinctions within each tradition. Here we have only to take account of the fact that the Grotian idea of international society has always been present in thought about the states system, and to indicate in broad terms the metamorphoses which, in the last three to four centuries, it has undergone. . . .

The Element of Society

My contention is that the element of a society has always been present, and remains present, in the modern international system, although only as one of the elements in it, whose survival is sometimes precarious. The modern international system in fact reflects all three of the elements singled out, respectively, by the Hobbesian, the Kantian and the Grotian traditions: the element of war and struggle for power among states, the element of transnational solidarity and conflict, cutting across the divisions among states, and the element of cooperation and regulated intercourse among states. In different historical phases of the states system, in different geographical theatres of its operation, and in the policies of different states and statesmen, one of these three elements may predominate over the others. . . .

Because international society is no more than one of the basic elements at work in modern international politics, and is always in competition with the elements of a state of war and of transnational solidarity or conflict, it is always erroneous to interpret international events as if international society were the sole or the dominant element. This is the error committed by those who speak or write as if the Concert of Europe, the League of Nations or the United Nations were the principal factors in international politics in their respective times; as if international law were to be assessed only in relation to the function it has of binding states together, and not also in relation to its function as an instrument of state interest and as a vehicle of transnational purposes; as if attempts to maintain a balance of power were to be interpreted only as endeavours to preserve the system of states, and not also as manoeuvres on the part of particular powers to gain ascendancy; as if great powers were to be viewed only as "great responsibles" or "great indispensables," and not also as great predators; as if wars were to be construed only as attempts to violate the law or to uphold it, and not also simply as attempts to advance the interests of particular states or of transnational groups. The element of international society is real, but the elements of a state of war and of transnational loyalties and divisions are real also, and to reify the first element, or to speak as if it annulled the second and third, is an illusion.

Moreover, the fact that international society provides some element of order in international politics should not be taken as justifying an attitude of complacency about it, or as showing that the arguments of those who are dissatisfied with the order provided by international society are without foundation. The order provided within modern international society is precarious and imperfect. To show that modern international society has provided some degree of order is not to have shown that order in world politics could not be provided more effectively by structures of a quite different kind.

NOTES

1. This concept of the "protection" of the rules may seem to carry the sinister implica-
   tion of justifying conduct that is contrary to the rules, or of placing persons "above"
   them, but I have not been able to think of a better term.
2. See, for example, M. Fortes and E. E. Evans-Pritchard, *African Political Systems*
   (Oxford University Press, 1940); John Middleton and David Tait (eds.), *Tribes
   Without Rulers, Studies in African Segmentary Systems* (London: Routledge &
   Kegan Paul, 1958); and I. Southall, "Stateless Societies," in *Encyclopaedia of the
   Social Sciences,* ed. David L. Sills (New York: Free Press, 1968). I am also indebted
   to Roger D. Masters's penetrating article "World Politics as a Primitive Political
   System," *World Politics,* vol. xvi, no. 4 (July 1964).
3. Masters, "World Politics as a Primitive Political System," p. 607.

5

THUCYDIDES

THE PELOPONNESIAN WAR AND THE MELIAN DEBATE

BOOK ONE

CHAPTER I: THE IMPORTANCE OF THE WAR. RELATIVE INSIGNIFICANCE OF THE ANCIENT PAST. IMPORTANCE OF SEA POWER. METHODS AND AIMS OF HISTORY

I began my history at the very outbreak of the war, in the belief that it was
going to be a great war and more worth writing about than any of those which
had taken place in the past. My belief was based on the fact that the two sides
were at the very height of their power and preparedness, and I saw, too, that
the rest of the Hellenic world was committed to one side or the other; even
those who were not immediately engaged were deliberating on the courses
which they were to take later. This was the greatest disturbance in the history
of the Hellenes, affecting also a large part of the non-Hellenic world, and
indeed, I might almost say, the whole of mankind. For though I have found it
impossible, because of its remoteness in time, to acquire a really precise
knowledge of the distant past or even of the history preceding our own period,
yet, after looking back into it as far as I can, all the evidence leads me to

conclude that these periods were not great periods either in warfare or in anything else. . . .

For a long time the state of affairs everywhere in Hellas was such that nothing very remarkable could be done by any combination of powers and that even the individual cities were lacking in enterprise.

Finally, however, the Spartans put down tyranny in the rest of Greece, most of which had been governed by tyrants for much longer than Athens. From the time when the Dorians first settled in Sparta there had been a particularly long period of political disunity; yet the Spartan constitution goes back to a very early date, and the country has never been ruled by tyrants. For rather more than 400 years they have had the same system of government, and this has been not only a source of internal strength, but has enabled them to intervene in the affairs of other states.

Not many years after the end of tyrannies in Hellas the battle of Marathon was fought between the Persians and the Athenians. Ten years later the foreign enemy returned with his vast armada for the conquest of Hellas, and at this moment of peril the Spartans, since they were the leading power, were in command of the allied Hellenic forces. In face of the invasion the Athenians decided to abandon their city; they broke up their homes, took to their ships, and became a people of sailors. It was by a common effort that the foreign invasion was repelled; but not long afterwards the Hellenes—both those who had fought in the war together and those who later revolted from the King of Persia—split into two divisions, one group following Athens and the other Sparta. These were clearly the two most powerful states, one being supreme on land, the other on the sea. For a short time the war-time alliance held together, but it was not long before quarrels took place and Athens and Sparta, each with her own allies, were at war with each other, while among the rest of the Hellenes states that had their own differences now joined one or other of the two sides. So from the end of the Persian War till the beginning of the Peloponnesian War, though there were some intervals of peace, on the whole these two Powers were either fighting with each other or putting down revolts among their allies. They were consequently in a high state of military preparedness and had gained their military experience in the hard school of danger.

The Spartans did not make their allies pay tribute, but saw to it that they were governed by oligarchies who would work in the Spartan interest. Athens, on the other hand, had in the course of time taken over the fleets of her allies (except for those of Chios and Lesbos) and had made them pay contributions of money instead. Thus the forces available to Athens alone for this war were greater than the combined forces had ever been when the alliance was still intact. . . .

The greatest war in the past was the Persian War; yet in this war the decision was reached quickly as a result of two naval battles and two battles on land. The Peloponnesian War, on the other hand, not only lasted for a long time, but throughout its course brought with it unprecedented suffering for

Hellas. Never before had so many cities been captured and then devastated, whether by foreign armies or by the Hellenic Powers themselves; never had there been so many exiles; never such loss of life—both in the actual warfare and in internal revolutions. Old stories of past prodigies, which had not found much confirmation in recent experience, now became credible. Wide areas, for instance, were affected by violent earthquakes; there were more frequent eclipses of the sun than had ever been recorded before; in various parts of the country there were extensive droughts followed by famine; and there was the plague which did more harm and destroyed more life than almost any other single factor. All these calamities fell together upon the Hellenes after the outbreak of the war.

War began when the Athenians and the Peloponnesians broke the Thirty Years Truce which had been made after the capture of Euboea. As to the reasons why they broke the truce, I propose first to give an account of the causes of complaint which they had against each other and of the specific instances where their interests clashed: this is in order that there should be no doubt in anyone's mind about what led to this great war falling upon the Hellenes. But the real reason for the war is, in my opinion, most likely to be disguised by such an argument. What made war inevitable was the growth of Athenian power and the fear which this caused in Sparta. As for the reasons for breaking the truce and declaring war which were openly expressed by each side, they are as follows. . . .

BOOK FIVE

THE MELIAN DEBATE

Next summer Alcibiades sailed to Argos with twenty ships and seized 300 Argive citizens who were still suspected of being pro-Spartan. These were put by the Athenians into the nearby islands under Athenian control.

The Athenians also made an expedition against the island of Melos. They had thirty of their own ships, six from Chios, and two from Lesbos; 1,200 hoplites, 300 archers, and twenty mounted archers, all from Athens; and about 1,500 hoplites from the allies and the islanders.

The Melians are a colony from Sparta. They had refused to join the Athenian empire like the other islanders, and at first had remained neutral without helping either side; but afterwards, when the Athenians had brought force to bear on them by laying waste their land, they had become open enemies of Athens.

Now the generals Cleomedes, the son of Lycomedes, and Tisias, the son of Tisimachus, encamped with the above force in Melian territory and, before doing any harm to the land, first of all sent representatives to negotiate. The Melians did not invite these representatives to speak before the people, but asked them to make the statement for which they had come in front of the governing body and the few. The Athenian representatives then spoke as follows:

Athenians: So we are not to speak before the people, no doubt in case the mass of the people should hear once and for all and without interruption an argument from us which is both persuasive and incontrovertible, and should so be led astray. This, we realize, is your motive in bringing us here to speak before the few. Now suppose that you who sit here should make assurance doubly sure. Suppose that you, too, should refrain from dealing with every point in detail in a set speech, and should instead interrupt us whenever we say something controversial and deal with that before going on to the next point? Tell us first whether you approve of this suggestion of ours.

The Council of the Melians replied as follows:

Melians: No one can object to each of us putting forward our own views in a calm atmosphere. That is perfectly reasonable. What is scarcely consistent with such a proposal is the present threat, indeed the certainty, of your making war on us. We see that you have come prepared to judge the argument yourselves, and that the likely end of it all will be either war, if we prove that we are in the right, and so refuse to surrender, or else slavery.

Athenians: If you are going to spend the time in enumerating your suspicions about the future, or if you have met here for any other reason except to look the facts in the face and on the basis of these facts to consider how you can save your city from destruction, there is no point in our going on with this discussion. If, however, you will do as we suggest, then we will speak on.

Melians: It is natural and understandable that people who are placed as we are should have recourse to all kinds of arguments and different points of view. However, you are right in saying that we are met together here to discuss the safety of our country and, if you will have it so, the discussion shall proceed on the lines that you have laid down.

Athenians: Then we on our side will use no fine phrases saying, for example, that we have a right to our empire because we defeated the Persians, or that we have come against you now because of the injuries you have done us—a great mass of words that nobody would believe. And we ask you on your side not to imagine that you will influence us by saying that you, though a colony of Sparta, have not joined Sparta in the war, or that you have never done us any harm. Instead we recommend that you should try to get what it is possible for you to get, taking into consideration what we both really do think; since you know as well as we do that, when these matters are discussed by practical people, the standard of justice depends on the equality of power to compel and that in fact the strong do what they have the power to do and the weak accept what they have to accept.

Melians: Then in our view (since you force us to leave justice out of account and to confine ourselves to self-interest)—in our view it is at any rate useful that you should not destroy a principle that is to the general good of all men—namely, that in the case of all who fall into danger there should be such a thing as fair play and just dealing, and that such people should be allowed to use and to profit by arguments that fall short of a mathematical accuracy. And this is a principle which affects you as much as anybody, since your own fall would be visited by the most terrible vengeance and would be an example to the world.

Athenians: As for us, even assuming that our empire does come to an end, we are not despondent about what would happen next. One is not so much frightened by being conquered by a power which rules over others, as Sparta does (not that we are concerned with Sparta now), as of what would happen if a ruling power is attacked and defeated by its own subjects. So far as this point is concerned, you can leave it to us to face the risks involved. What we shall do now is to show you that it is for the good of our own empire that we are here and that it is for the preservation of your city that we shall say what we are going to say. We do not want any trouble in bringing you into our empire, and we want you to be spared for the good both of yourselves and of ourselves.

Melians: And how could it be just as good for us to be the slaves as for you to be the masters?

Athenians: You, by giving in, would save yourselves from disaster; we, by not destroying you, would be able to profit from you.

Melians: So you would not agree to our being neutral, friends instead of enemies, but allies of neither side?

Athenians: No, because it is not so much your hostility that injures us; it is rather the case that, if we were on friendly terms with you, our subjects would regard that as a sign of weakness in us, whereas your hatred is evidence of our power.

Melians: Is that your subjects' idea of fair play—that no distinction should be made between people who are quite unconnected with you and people who are mostly your own colonists or else rebels whom you have conquered?

Athenians: So far as right and wrong are concerned they think that there is no difference between the two, that those who still preserve their independence do so because they are strong, and that if we fail to attack them it is because we are afraid. So that by conquering you we shall increase not only the size but the security of our empire. We rule the sea and you are islanders, and weaker islanders too than the others; it is therefore particularly important that you should not escape.

Melians: But do you think there is no security for you in what we suggest? For here again, since you will not let us mention justice, but tell us to give in to your interests, we, too, must tell you what our interests are and, if yours and ours happen to coincide, we must try to persuade you of the fact. Is it not certain that you will make enemies of all states who are at present neutral, when they see what is happening here and naturally conclude that in course of time you will attack them too? Does not this mean that you are strengthening the enemies you have already and are forcing others to become your enemies even against their intentions and their inclinations?

Athenians: As a matter of fact we are not so much frightened of states on the continent. They have their liberty, and this means that it will be a long time before they begin to take precautions against us. We are more concerned about islanders like yourselves, who are still unsubdued, or subjects who have already become embittered by the constraint which our empire imposes on them. These are the people who are most likely to act in a reckless manner and to bring themselves and us, too, into the most obvious danger.

Melians: Then surely, if such hazards are taken by you to keep your empire and by your subjects to escape from it, we who are still free would show ourselves great cowards and weaklings if we failed to face everything that comes rather than submit to slavery.

Athenians: No, not if you are sensible. This is no fair fight, with honour on one side and shame on the other. It is rather a question of saving your lives and not resisting those who are far too strong for you.

Melians: Yet we know that in war fortune sometimes makes the odds more level than could be expected from the difference in numbers of the two sides. And if we surrender, then all our hope is lost at once, whereas, so long as we remain in action, there is still a hope that we may yet stand upright.

Athenians: Hope, that comforter in danger! If one already has solid advantages to fall back upon, one can indulge in hope. It may do harm, but will not destroy one. But hope is by nature an expensive commodity, and those who are risking their all on one cast find out what it means only when they are already ruined; it never fails them in the period when such a knowledge would enable them to take precautions. Do not let this happen to you, you who are weak and whose fate depends on a single movement of the scale. And do not be like those people who, as so commonly happens, miss the chance of saving themselves in a human and practical way, and, when every clear and distinct hope has left them in their adversity, turn to what is blind and vague, to prophecies and oracles and such things which by encouraging hope lead men to ruin.

Melians: It is difficult, and you may be sure that we know it, for us to oppose your power and fortune, unless the terms be equal. Nevertheless we trust that the gods will give us fortune as good as yours, because we are standing for what is right against what is wrong; and as for what we lack in power, we trust that it will be made up for by our alliance with the Spartans, who are bound, if for no other reason, then for honour's sake, and because we are their kinsmen, to come to our help. Our confidence, therefore, is not so entirely irrational as you think.

Athenians: So far as the favour of the gods is concerned, we think we have as much right to that as you have. Our aims and our actions are perfectly consistent with the beliefs men hold about the gods and with the principles which govern their own conduct. Our opinion of the gods and our knowledge of men lead us to conclude that it is a general and necessary law of nature to rule wherever one can. This is not a law that we made ourselves, nor were we the first to act upon it when it was made. We found it already in existence, and we shall leave it to exist for every among those who come after us. We are merely acting in accordance with it, and we know that you or anybody else with the same power as ours would be acting in precisely the same way. And therefore, so far as the gods are concerned, we see no good reason why we should fear to be at a disadvantage. But with regard to your views about Sparta and your confidence that she, out of a sense of honour, will come to your aid, we must say that we congratulate you on your simplicity but do not envy you your folly. In matters that concern themselves or their own constitution the Spartans are quite remarkably good; as for their relations with others, that is a long story, but it can be expressed shortly and clearly by saying that of all people we know the Spartans are most conspicuous for believing that what they like doing is honourable and what suits their interests is just. And this kind of attitude is not going to be of much help to you in your absurd quest for safety at the moment.

Melians: But this is the very point where we can feel most sure. Their own self-interest will make them refuse to betray their own colonists, the Melians, for that would mean losing the confidence of their friends among the Hellenes and doing good to their enemies.

Athenians: You seem to forget that if one follows one's self-interest one wants to be safe, whereas the path of justice and honour involves one in danger. And, where danger is concerned, the Spartans are not, as a rule, very venturesome.

Melians: But we think that they would even endanger themselves for our sake and count the risk more worth taking than in the case of others, because we are so close to the Peloponnese that they could operate more easily, and because they can depend on us more than on others, since we are of the same race and share the same feelings.

Athenians: Goodwill shown by the party that is asking for help does not mean security for the prospective ally. What is looked for is a positive preponderance of power in action. And the Spartans pay attention to this point even more than others do. Certainly they distrust their own native resources so much that when they attack a neighbour they bring a great army of allies with them. It is hardly likely therefore that, while we are in control of the sea, they will cross over to an island.

Melians: But they still might send others. The Cretan sea is a wide one, and it is harder for those who control it to intercept others than for those who want to slip through to do so safely. And even if they were to fail in this, they would turn against your own land and against those of your allies left unvisited by Brasidas. So, instead of troubling about a country which has nothing to do with you, you will find trouble nearer home, among your allies, and in your own country.

Athenians: It is a possibility, something that has in fact happened before. It may happen in your case, but you are well aware that the Athenians have never yet relinquished a single siege operation through fear of others. But we are somewhat shocked to find that, though you announced your intention of discussing how you could preserve yourselves, in all this talk you have said absolutely nothing which could justify a man in thinking that he could be preserved. Your chief points are concerned with what you hope may happen in the future, while your actual resources are too scanty to give you a chance of survival against the forces that are opposed to you at this moment. You will therefore be showing an extraordinary lack of common sense if, after you have asked us to retire from this meeting, you still fail to reach a conclusion wiser than anything you have mentioned so far. Do not be led astray by a false sense of honour—a thing which often brings men to ruin when they are faced with an obvious danger that somehow affects their pride. For in many cases men have still been able to see the dangers ahead of them, but this thing called dishonour, this word, by its own force of seduction, has drawn them into a state where they have surrendered to an idea, while in fact they have fallen voluntarily into irrevocable disaster, in dishonour that is all the more dishonourable because it has come to them from their own folly rather than their misfortune. You, if you take the right view, will be careful to avoid this. You will see that there is nothing disgraceful in giving way to the greatest city in Hellas when she is offering you such reasonable terms— alliance on a tribute-paying basis and liberty to enjoy your own property. And, when you are allowed to choose between war and safety, you will not be so insensitively arrogant as to make the wrong choice. This is the safe rule—to stand up to one's equals, to behave with deference towards one's superiors, and to treat one's inferiors with moderation. Think it over again, then, when we have withdrawn from the meeting, and let this be a point that constantly recurs to your minds—that you are discussing the fate of your country, that you have only one country, and that its future for good or ill depends on this one single decision which you are going to make.

The Athenians then withdrew from the discussion. The Melians, left to themselves, reached a conclusion which was much the same as they had indicated in their previous replies. Their answer was as follows:

Melians: Our decision, Athenians, is just the same as it was at first. We are not prepared to give up in a short moment the liberty which our city has enjoyed from its foundation for 700 years. We put our trust in the fortune that the gods will send and which has saved us up to now, and in the help of men—that is, of the Spartans; and so we shall try to save ourselves. But we invite you to allow us to be friends of yours and enemies to neither side, to make a treaty which shall be agreeable to both you and us, and so to leave our country.

The Melians made this reply, and the Athenians, just as they were breaking off the discussion, said:

Athenians: Well, at any rate, judging from this decision of yours, you seem to us quite unique in your ability to consider the future as something more certain than what is before your eyes, and to see uncertainties as realities, simply because you would like them to be so. As you have staked most on and trusted most in Spartans, luck, and hopes, so in all these you will find yourselves most completely deluded.

The Athenian representatives then went back to the army, and the Athenian generals, finding that the Melians would not submit, immediately commenced hostilities and built a wall completely around the city of Melos, dividing the work out among the various states. Later they left behind a garrison of some of their own and some allied troops to blockade the place by land and sea, and with the greater part of their army returned home. The force left behind stayed on and continued with the siege.

About the same time the Argives invaded Phliasia and were ambushed by the Phliasians and the exiles from Argos, losing about eighty men.

Then, too, the Athenians at Pylos captured a great quantity of plunder from Spartan territory. Not even after this did the Spartans renounce the treaty and make war, but they issued a proclamation saying that any of their people who wished to do so were free to make raids on the Athenians. The Corinthians also made some attacks on the Athenians because of private quarrels of their own, but the rest of the Peloponnesians stayed quiet.

Meanwhile the Melians made a night attack and captured the part of the Athenian lines opposite the market-place. They killed some of the troops, and then, after bringing in corn and everything else useful that they could lay their hands on, retired again and made no further move, while the Athenians took measures to make their blockade more efficient in future. So the summer came to an end.

In the following winter the Spartans planned to invade the territory of Argos, but when the sacrifices for crossing the frontier turned out unfavourably, they gave up the expedition. The fact that they had intended to invade made the Argives suspect certain people in their city, some of whom they arrested, though others succeeded in escaping.

About this same time the Melians again captured another part of the Athenian lines where there were only a few of the garrison on guard. As a result of this, another force came out afterwards from Athens under the command of Philocrates, the son of Demeas. Siege operations were now carried on vigorously and, as there was also some treachery from inside, the Melians surrendered unconditionally to the Athenians, who put to death all the men of military age whom they took, and sold the women and children as slaves. Melos itself they took over for themselves, sending out later a colony of 500 men.

6

THOMAS HOBBES

RELATIONS AMONG SOVEREIGNS

OF THE NATURAL CONDITION OF MANKIND, AS CONCERNING THEIR FELICITY, AND MISERY

MEN BY NATURE EQUALL

Nature hath made men so equall, in the faculties of body, and mind; as that though there bee found one man sometimes manifestly stronger in body, or of quicker mind then another; yet when all is reckoned together, the difference between man, and man, is not so considerable, as that one man can thereupon claim to himselfe any benefit, to which another may not pretend, as well as he. For as to the strength of body, the weakest has strength enough to kill the strongest, either by secret machination, or by confederacy with others, that are in the same danger with himselfe.

And as to the faculties of the mind, (setting aside the arts grounded upon words, and especially that skill of proceeding upon generall, and infallible rules, called Science; which very few have, and but in few things; as being not a native faculty, born with us; nor attained, (as Prudence,) while we look after somewhat els,) I find yet a greater equality amongst men, than that of strength. For Prudence, is but Experience; which equall time, equally bestowes on all men, in those things they equally apply themselves unto. That which may perhaps make such equality incredible, is but a vain conceipt of ones owne wisdome, which almost all men think they have in a greater degree, than the Vulgar; that is, than all men but themselves, and a few others, whom by Fame, or for concurring with themselves, they approve. For such is the nature of men, that howsoever they may acknowledge many others to be more witty, or more eloquent, or more learned; Yet they will hardly believe there be many so wise as themselves: For they see their own wit at hand, and other mens at a distance. But this proveth rather that men are in that point equall, than unequall. For there is not ordinarily a greater signe of the equall distribution of any thing, than that every man is contented with his share.

SOURCE: From *Leviathan*, Thomas Hobbes, (Oxford: The Clarendon Press, 1909), pp. 94–98.

FROM EQUALITY PROCEEDS DIFFIDENCE

From this equality of ability, ariseth equality of hope in the attaining of our Ends. And therefore if any two men desire the same thing, which neverthelesse they cannot both enjoy, they become enemies; and in the way to their End, (which is principally their owne conservation, and sometimes their delectation only,) endeavour to destroy, or subdue one an other. And from hence it comes to passe, that where an Invader hath no more to feare, than an other mans single power; if one plant, sow, build, or possesse a convenient Seat, others may probably be expected to come prepared with forces united, to dispossesse, and deprive him, not only of the fruit of his labour, but also of his life, or liberty. And the Invader again is in the like danger of another.

FROM DIFFIDENCE WARRE

And from this diffidence of one another, there is no way for any man to secure himselfe, so reasonable, as Anticipation; that is, by force, or wiles, to master the persons of all men he can, so long, till he see no other power great enough to endanger him: And this is no more than his own conservation requireth, and is generally allowed. Also because there be some, that taking pleasure in contemplating their own power in the acts of conquest, which they pursue farther than their security requires; if others, that otherwise would be glad to be at ease within modest bounds, should not by invasion increase their power, they would not be able, long time, by standing only on their defence, to subsist. And by consequence, such augmentation of dominion over men, being necessary to a mans conservation, it ought to be allowed him.

Againe, men have no pleasure, (but on the contrary a great deale of griefe) in keeping company, where there is no power able to over-awe them all. For every man looketh that his companion should value him, at the same rate he sets upon himselfe: And upon all signes of contempt, or undervaluing, naturally endeavours, as far as he dares (which amongst them that have no common power to keep them in quiet, is far enough to make them destroy each other,) to extort a greater value from his contemners, by dommage; and from others, by the example.

So that in the nature of man, we find three principall causes of quarrell. First, Competition; Secondly, Diffidence; Thirdly, Glory.

The first, maketh men invade for Gain; the second, for Safety; and the third, for Reputation. The first use Violence, to make themselves Masters of other mens persons, wives, children, and cattell; the second, to defend them; the third, for trifles, as a word, a smile, a different opinion, and any other signe of undervalue, either direct in their Persons, or by reflexion in their Kindred, their Friends, their Nation, their Profession, or their Name.

OUT OF CIVIL STATES, THERE IS ALWAYES WARRE OF EVERY ONE AGAINST EVERY ONE

Hereby it is manifest, that during the time men live without a common Power to keep them all in awe, they are in that condition which is called Warre; and such a warre, as is of every man, against every man. For WARRE, consisteth not in Battell onely, or the act of fighting; but in a tract of time, wherein the Will to contend by Battell is sufficiently known: and therefore the notion of *Time,* is to be considered in the nature of Warre; as it is in the nature of Weather. For as the nature of Foule weather, lyeth not in a showre or two of rain; but in an inclination thereto of many dayes together: So the nature of War, consisteth not in actuall fighting; but in the known disposition thereto, during all the time there is no assurance to the contrary. All other time is PEACE.

THE INCOMMODITIES OF SUCH A WAR

Whatsoever therefore is consequent to a time of Warre, where every man is Enemy to every man; the same is consequent to the time, wherein men live without other security, than what their own strength, and their own invention shall furnish them withall. In such condition, there is no place for Industry; because the fruit thereof is uncertain: and consequently no Culture of the Earth; no Navigation, nor use of the commodities that may be imported by Sea; no commodious Building; no Instruments of moving, and removing such things as require much force; no Knowledge of the face of the Earth; no account of Time; no Arts; no Letters; no Society; and which is worst of all, continuall feare, and danger of violent death; And the life of man, solitary, poore, nasty, brutish, and short.

It may seem strange to some man, that has not well weighed these things; that Nature should thus dissociate, and render men apt to invade, and destroy one another: and he may therefore, not trusting to this Inference, made from the Passions, desire perhaps to have the same confirmed by Experience. Let him therefore consider with himselfe, when taking a journey, he armes himselfe, and seeks to go well accompanied; when going to sleep, he locks his dores; when even in his house he locks his chests; and this when he knowes there bee Lawes, and publike Officers, armed, to revenge all injuries shall bee done him; what opinion he has of his fellow subjects, when he rides armed; of his fellow Citizens, when he locks his dores; and of his children, and servants, when he locks his chests. Does he not there as much accuse mankind by his actions, as I do by my words? But neither of us accuse mans nature in it. The Desires, and other Passions of man, are in themselves no Sin. No more are the Actions, that proceed from those Passions, till they know a Law that forbids them: which till Lawes be made they cannot know: nor can any Law be made, till they have agreed upon the Person that shall make it.

It may peradventure be thought, there was never such a time, nor condition of warre as this; and I believe it was never generally so, over all the world: but there are many places, where they live so now. For the savage people in many places of *America*, except the government of small Families, the concord whereof dependeth on naturall lust, have no government at all; and live at this day in that brutish manner, as I said before. Howsoever, it may be perceived what manner of life there would be, where there were no common Power to feare; by the manner of life, which men that have formerly lived under a peacefull government, use to degenerate into, in a civill Warre.

But though there had never been any time, wherein particular men were in a condition of warre one against another; yet in all times, Kings, and Persons of Soveraigne authority, because of their Independency, are in continuall jealousies, and in the state and posture of Gladiators; having their weapons pointing, and their eyes fixed on one another; that is, their Forts, Garrisons, and Guns upon the Frontiers of their Kingdomes; and continuall Spyes upon their neighbours; which is a posture of War. But because they uphold thereby, the Industry of their Subjects; there does not follow from it, that misery, which accompanies the Liberty of particular men.

IN SUCH A WARRE, NOTHING IS UNJUST

To this warre of every man against every man, this also is consequent; that nothing can be Unjust. The notions of Right and Wrong, Justice and Injustice have there no place. Where there is no common Power, there is no Law: where no Law, no Injustice. Force, and Fraud, are in warre the two Cardinall vertues. Justice, and Injustice are none of the Faculties neither of the Body, nor Mind. If they were, they might be in a man that were alone in the world, as well as his Senses, and Passions. They are Qualities, that relate to men in Society, not in Solitude. It is consequent also to the same condition, that there be no Propriety, no Dominion, no *Mine* and *Thine* distinct; but onely that to be every mans, that he can get; and for so long, as he can keep it. And thus much for the ill condition, which man by meer Nature is actually placed in; though with a possibility to come out of it, consisting partly in the Passions, partly in his Reason.

THE PASSIONS THAT INCLINE MEN TO PEACE

The Passions that encline men to Peace, are Feare of Death; Desire of such things as are necessary to commodious living; and a Hope by their Industry to obtain them. And Reason suggesteth convenient Articles of Peace, upon which men may be drawn to agreement. These Articles, are they, which otherwise are called the Lawes of Nature. . . .

7

EDWARD HALLETT CARR

The Realist Critique and the Limitations of Realism

THE REALIST CRITIQUE

The Foundations of Realism

Realism enters the field far behind utopianism and by way of reaction from it. The thesis that "justice is the right of the stronger" was, indeed, familiar in the Hellenic world. But it never represented anything more than the protest of an uninfluential minority, puzzled by the divergence between political theory and political practice. Under the supremacy of the Roman Empire, and later of the Catholic Church, the problem could hardly arise; for the political good, first of the empire, then of the church, could be regarded as identical with moral good. It was only with the breakup of the mediaeval system that the divergence between political theory and political practice became acute and challenging. Machiavelli is the first important political realist.

Machiavelli's starting-point is a revolt against the utopianism of current political thought:

> It being my intention to write a thing which shall be useful to him who apprehends it, it appears to me more appropriate to follow up the real truth of a matter than the imagination of it; for many have pictured republics and principalities which in fact have never been seen and known, because how one lives is so far distant from how one ought to live that he who neglects what is done for what ought to be done sooner effects his ruin than his preservation.

The three essential tenets implicit in Machiavelli's doctrine are the foundation-stones of the realist philosophy. In the first place, history is a sequence of cause and effect, whose course can be analysed and understood by intellectual effort, but not (as the utopians believe) directed by "imagination." Secondly, theory does not (as the utopians assume) create practice, but practice theory.

Source: From *The Twenty Years' Crisis 1919–1939: An Introduction to the Study of International Relations*, Edward Hallett Carr (New York: Harper and Row, Publishers, 1964), pp. 63–64, 75–76, 80–82, 87–89, 93. Reprinted with permission of St. Martin's Press, Incorporated.

In Machiavelli's words, "good counsels, whencesoever they come, are born of the wisdom of the prince, and not the wisdom of the prince from good counsels." Thirdly, politics are not (as the utopians pretend) a function of ethics, but ethics of politics. Men "are kept honest by constraint." Machiavelli recognised the importance of morality, but thought that there could be no effective morality where there was no effective authority. Morality is the product of power.[1] . . .

NATIONAL INTEREST AND THE UNIVERSAL GOOD

The realist should not . . . linger over the infliction of . . . pin-pricks through chinks in the utopian defences. His task is to bring down the whole cardboard structure of utopian thought by exposing the hollowness of the material out of which it is built. The weapon of the relativity of thought must be used to demolish the utopian concept of a fixed and absolute standard by which policies and actions can be judged. If theories are revealed as a reflexion of practice and principles of political needs, this discovery will apply to the fundamental theories and principles of the utopian creed, and not least to the doctrine of the harmony of interests which is its essential postulate.

It will not be difficult to show that the utopian, when he preaches the doctrine of the harmony of interests, is innocently and unconsciously adopting Walewski's maxim, and clothing his own interest in the guise of a universal interest for the purpose of imposing it on the rest of the world. "Men come easily to believe that arrangements agreeable to themselves are beneficial to others," as Dicey observed[2]; and theories of the public good, which turn out on inspection to be an elegant disguise for some particular interest, are as common in international as in national affairs. The utopian, however eager he may be to establish an absolute standard, does not argue that it is the duty of his country, in conformity with that standard, to put the interest of the world at large before its own interest; for that would be contrary to his theory that the interest of all coincides with the interest of each. He argues that what is best for the world is best for his country, and then reverses the argument to read that what is best for his country is best for the world, the two propositions being, from the utopian standpoint, identical. . . .

THE REALIST CRITIQUE OF THE HARMONY OF INTERESTS

The doctrine of the harmony of interests yields readily to analysis in terms of this principle. It is the natural assumption of a prosperous and privileged class, whose members have a dominant voice in the community and are therefore naturally prone to identify its interest with their own. In virtue of this identification, any assailant of the interests of the dominant group is made to incur the odium of assailing the alleged common interest of the whole community, and is told that in making this assault he is attacking his own higher interests. The doctrine of the harmony of interests thus serves as an ingenious moral device invoked, in perfect sincerity, by privileged groups in order to justify and maintain their dominant position. But a further point requires notice. The supremacy within the community of the privileged group may be, and often is, so overwhelming that there is, in fact, a sense in which its interests are those of the community, since its well-being necessarily carries with it some measure of well-being for other members of the community, and its collapse would entail the collapse of the community as a whole. In so far, therefore, as the alleged natural harmony of interests has any reality, it is created by the overwhelming power of the privileged group, and is an excellent illustration of the Machiavellian maxim that morality is the product of power. . . .

British nineteenth-century statesmen, having discovered that free trade promoted British prosperity, were sincerely convinced that, in doing so, it also promoted the prosperity of the world as a whole. British predominance in world trade was at that time so overwhelming that there was a certain undeniable harmony between British interests and the interests of the world. British prosperity flowed over into other countries, and a British economic collapse would have meant world-wide ruin. British free traders could and did argue that protectionist countries were not only egotistically damaging the prosperity of the world as a whole, but were stupidly damaging their own, so that their behaviour was both immoral and muddle headed. In British eyes, it was irrefutably proved that international trade was a single whole, and flourished or slumped together. Nevertheless, this alleged international harmony of interests seemed a mockery to those under-privileged nations whose inferior status and insignificant stake in international trade were consecrated by it. The revolt against it destroyed that overwhelming British preponderance which had provided a plausible basis for the theory. Economically, Great Britain in the nineteenth century was dominant enough to make a bold bid to impose on the world her own conception of international economic morality. When competition of all against all replaced the domination of the world market by a single Power, conceptions of international economic morality necessarily became chaotic.

Politically, the alleged community of interest in the maintenance of peace, whose ambiguous character has already been discussed, is capitalised in the same way by a dominant nation or group of nations. Just as the ruling class in a community prays for domestic peace, which guarantees its own security and predominance, and denounces class-war, which might threaten them, so international peace becomes a special vested interest of predominant Powers. In the past, Roman and British imperialism were commended to the world in the guise of the *pax Romana* and the *pax Britannica*. To-day, when no single Power is strong enough to dominate the world, and supremacy is vested in a group of nations, slogans like "collective security" and "resistance to aggression" serve the same purpose of proclaiming an identity of interest between the dominant group and the world as a whole in the maintenance of peace. . . .

The exposure of the real basis of the professedly abstract principles commonly invoked in international politics is the most damning and most convincing part of the realist indictment of utopianism. The nature of the charge is frequently misunderstood by those who seek to refute it. The charge is not that human beings fail to live up to their principles. It matters little that Wilson, who thought that the right was more precious than peace, and Briand, who thought that peace came even before justice, and Mr. Eden, who believed in collective security, failed themselves, or failed to induce their countrymen, to apply these principles consistently. What matters is that these supposedly absolute and universal principles were not principles at all, but the unconscious reflexions of national policy based on a particular interpretation of national interest at a particular time. There is a sense in which peace and co-operation between nations or classes or individuals is a common and universal end irrespective of conflicting interests and politics. There is a sense in which a common interest exists in the maintenance of order, whether it be international order or "law and order" within the nation. But as soon as the attempt is made to apply these supposedly abstract principles to a concrete political situation, they are revealed as the transparent disguises of selfish vested interests. The bankruptcy of utopianism resides not in its failure to live up to its principles, but in the exposure of its inability to provide any absolute and disinterested standard for the conduct of international affairs. . . .

THE LIMITATIONS OF REALISM

The exposure by realist criticism of the hollowness of the utopian edifice is the first task of the political thinker. It is only when the sham has been demolished that there can be any hope of raising a more solid structure in its place. But we cannot ultimately find a resting place in pure realism; for realism, though logically overwhelming, does not provide us with the springs of action which are necessary even to the pursuit of thought. Indeed, realism itself, if we attack it with its own weapons, often turns out in practice to be just as much conditioned as any other mode of thought. In politics, the belief that certain facts are unalterable or certain trends irresistible commonly reflects a lack of desire or lack of interest to change or resist them. The impossibility of being a consistent and thorough-going realist is one of the most certain and most curious lessons of political science. Consistent realism excludes four things which appear to be essential ingredients of all effective political thinking: a finite goal, an emotional appeal, a right of moral judgment and a ground for action. . . .

We return therefore to the conclusion that any sound political thought must be based on elements of both utopia and reality. Where utopianism has become a hollow and intolerable sham, which serves merely as a disguise for the interests of the privileged, the realist performs an indispensable service in unmasking it. But pure realism can offer nothing but a naked struggle for power which makes any kind of international society impossible. Having demolished the current utopia with the weapons of realism, we still need to build a new utopia of our own, which will one day fall to the same weapons. The human will will continue to seek an escape from the logical consequences of realism in the vision of an international order which, as soon as it crystallises itself into concrete political form, becomes tainted with self-interest and hypocrisy, and must once more be attacked with the instruments of realism.

Here, then, is the complexity, the fascination and the tragedy of all political life. Politics are made up of two elements—utopia and reality—belonging to two different planes which can never meet. There is no greater barrier to clear political thinking than failure to distinguish between ideals, which are utopia, and institutions, which are reality.

NOTES

1. Machiavelli, *The Prince*, chs. 15 and 23 (Engl. transl., Everyman's Library, pp. 121, 193).
2. Dicey, *Law and Opinion in England* (2nd ed.), pp. 14–15.

8

HANS J. MORGENTHAU

SIX PRINCIPLES OF POLITICAL REALISM

. . . SIX PRINCIPLES OF POLITICAL REALISM

1. Political realism believes that politics, like society in general, is governed by objective laws that have their roots in human nature. In order to improve society it is first necessary to understand the laws by which society lives. The operation of these laws being impervious to our preferences, men will challenge them only at the risk of failure.

Realism, believing as it does in the objectivity of the laws of politics, must also believe in the possibility of developing a rational theory that reflects, however imperfectly and one-sidedly, these objective laws. It believes also, then, in the possibility of distinguishing in politics between truth and opinion—between what is true objectively and rationally, supported by

SOURCE: From *Politics Among Nations: The Struggle for Power and Peace*, 5th ed. Hans J. Morgenthau (New York, NY: Alfred A. Knopf, 1973), pp. 4–6, 8–12. Copyright © 1948, 1954, 1960, 1967, 1972 by Alfred A. Knopf, Inc. Reprinted by permission of Alfred A. Knopf, Inc.

evidence and illuminated by reason, and what is only a subjective judgment, divorced from the facts as they are and informed by prejudice and wishful thinking.

Human nature, in which the laws of politics have their roots, has not changed since the classical philosophies of China, India, and Greece endeavored to discover these laws. Hence, novelty is not necessarily a virtue in political theory, nor is old age a defect. The fact that a theory of politics, if there be such a theory, has never been heard of before tends to create a presumption against, rather than in favor of, its soundness. Conversely, the fact that a theory of politics was developed hundreds or even thousands of years ago—as was the theory of the balance of power—does not create a presumption that it must be outmoded and obsolete. A theory of politics must be subjected to the dual test of reason and experience. To dismiss such a theory because it had its flowering in centuries past is to present not a rational argument but a modernistic prejudice that takes for granted the superiority of the present over the past. To dispose of the revival of such a theory as a "fashion" or "fad" is tantamount to assuming that in matters political we can have opinions but no truths.

For realism, theory consists in ascertaining facts and giving them meaning through reason. It assumes that the character of a foreign policy can be ascertained only through the examination of the political acts performed and of the foreseeable consequences of these acts. Thus we can find out what statesmen have actually done, and from the foreseeable consequences of their acts we can surmise what their objectives might have been.

Yet examination of the facts is not enough. To give meaning to the factual raw material of foreign policy, we must approach political reality with a kind of rational outline, a map that suggests to us the possible meanings of foreign policy. In other words, we put ourselves in the position of a statesman who must meet a certain problem of foreign policy under certain circumstances, and we ask ourselves what the rational alternatives are from which a statesman may choose who must meet this problem under these circumstances (presuming always that he acts in a rational manner), and which of these rational alternatives this particular statesman, acting under these circumstances, is likely to choose. It is the testing of this rational hypothesis against the actual facts and their consequences that gives meaning to the facts of international politics and makes a theory of politics possible.

2. The main signpost that helps political realism to find its way through the landscape of international politics is the concept of interest defined in terms of power. This concept provides the link between reason trying to understand international politics and the facts to be understood. It sets politics as an autonomous sphere of action and understanding apart from other spheres, such as economics (understood in terms of interest defined as wealth), ethics, aesthetics, or religion. Without such a concept a theory of politics, international or domestic, would be altogether impossible, for without it we could not distinguish between political and nonpolitical facts, nor could we bring at least a measure of systematic order to the political sphere.

We assume that statesmen think and act in terms of interest defined as power, and the evidence of history bears that assumption out. That assumption allows us to retrace and anticipate, as it were, the steps a statesman—past, present, or future—has taken or will take on the political scene. We look over his shoulder when he writes his dispatches; we listen in on his conversation with other statesmen; we read and anticipate his very thoughts. Thinking in terms of interest defined as power, we think as he does, and as disinterested observers we understand his thoughts and actions perhaps better than he, the actor on the political scene, does himself.

The concept of interest defined as power imposes intellectual discipline upon the observer, infuses rational order into the subject matter of politics, and thus makes the theoretical understanding of politics possible. On the side of the actor, it provides for rational discipline in action and creates that astounding continuity in foreign policy which makes American, British, or Russian foreign policy appear as an intelligible, rational continuum, by and large consistent within itself, regardless of the different motives, preferences, and intellectual and moral qualities of successive statesmen. A realist theory of international politics, then, will guard against two popular fallacies: the concern with motives and the concern with ideological preferences.

To search for the clue to foreign policy exclusively in the motives of statesmen is both futile and deceptive. It is futile because motives are the most illusive of psychological data, distorted as they are, frequently beyond recognition, by the interests and emotions of actor and observer alike. Do we really know what our own motives are? And what do we know of the motives of others?

Yet even if we had access to the real motives of statesmen, that knowledge would help us little in understanding foreign policies, and might well lead us astray. It is true that the knowledge of the statesman's motives may give us one among many clues as to what the direction of his foreign policy might be. It cannot give us, however, the one clue by which to predict his foreign policies. History shows no exact and necessary correlation between the quality of motives and the quality of foreign policy. This is true in both moral and political terms. . . .

3. Realism assumes that its key concept of interest defined as power is an objective category which is universally valid, but it does not endow that concept with a meaning that is fixed once and for all. The idea of interest is indeed of the essence of politics and is unaffected by the circumstances of time and place. Thucydides' statement, born of the experiences of ancient Greece, that "identity of interests is the surest of bonds whether between states or individuals" was taken up in the nineteenth century by Lord Salisbury's remark that "the only bond of union that endures" among nations is "the absence of all clashing interests." It was erected into a general principle of government by George Washington:

> A small knowledge of human nature will convince us, that, with far the greatest part of mankind, interest is the governing principle; and that almost every

man is more or less, under its influence. Motives of public virtue may for a time, or in particular instances, actuate men to the observance of a conduct purely disinterested; but they are not of themselves sufficient to produce persevering conformity to the refined dictates and obligations of social duty. Few men are capable of making a continual sacrifice of all views of private interest, or advantage, to the common good. It is vain to exclaim against the depravity of human nature on this account; the fact is so, the experience of every age and nation has proved it and we must in a great measure, change the constitution of man, before we can make it otherwise. No institution, not built on the presumptive truth of these maxims can succeed.[1]

It was echoed and enlarged upon in our century by Max Weber's observation:

Interests (material and ideal), not ideas, dominate directly the actions of men. Yet the "images of the world" created by these ideas have very often served as switches determining the tracks on which the dynamism of interests kept actions moving.[2]

Yet the kind of interest determining political action in a particular period of history depends upon the political and cultural context within which foreign policy is formulated. The goals that might be pursued by nations in their foreign policy can run the whole gamut of objectives any nation has ever pursued or might possibly pursue.

The same observations apply to the concept of power. Its content and the manner of its use are determined by the political and cultural environment. Power may comprise anything that establishes and maintains the control of man over man. Thus power covers all social relationships which serve that end, from physical violence to the most subtle psychological ties by which one mind controls another. Power covers the domination of man by man, both when it is disciplined by moral ends and controlled by constitutional safeguards, as in Western democracies, and when it is that untamed and barbaric force which finds its laws in nothing but its own strength and its sole justification in its aggrandizement.

Political realism does not assume that the contemporary conditions under which foreign policy operates, with their extreme instability and the ever present threat of large-scale violence, cannot be changed. The balance of power, for instance, is indeed a perennial element of all pluralistic societies, as the authors of *The Federalist* papers well knew; yet it is capable of operating, as it does in the United States, under the conditions of relative stability and peaceful conflict. If the factors that have given rise to these conditions can be duplicated on the international scene, similar conditions of stability and peace will then prevail there, as they have over long stretches of history among certain nations.

What is true of the general character of international relations is also true of the nation state as the ultimate point of reference of contemporary foreign policy. While the realist indeed believes that interest is the perennial standard by which political action must be judged and directed, the contemporary connection between interest and the nation state is a product of history, and is therefore bound to disappear in the course of history. Nothing in the realist position militates against the assumption that the present division of the political world into nation states will be replaced by larger units of a quite different character, more in keeping with the technical potentialities and the moral requirements of the contemporary world.

The realist parts company with other schools of thought before the all-important question of how the contemporary world is to be transformed. The realist is persuaded that this transformation can be achieved only through the workmanlike manipulation of the perennial forces that have shaped the past as they will the future. The realist cannot be persuaded that we can bring about that transformation by confronting a political reality that has its own laws with an abstract ideal that refuses to take those laws into account.

4. Political realism is aware of the moral significance of political action. It is also aware of the ineluctable tension between the moral command and the requirements of successful political action. And it is unwilling to gloss over and obliterate that tension and thus to obfuscate both the moral and the political issue by making it appear as though the stark facts of politics were morally more satisfying than they actually are, and the moral law less exacting than it actually is.

Realism maintains that universal moral principles cannot be applied to the actions of states in their abstract universal formulation, but that they must be filtered through the concrete circumstances of time and place. . . . Realism, then, considers prudence—the weighing of the consequences of alternative political actions—to be the supreme virtue in politics. Ethics in the abstract judges action by its conformity with the moral law; political ethics judges action by its political consequences. Classical and medieval philosophy knew this, and so did Lincoln when he said:

> I do the very best I know how, the very best I can, and I mean to keep doing so until the end. If the end brings me out all right, what is said against me won't amount to anything. If the end brings me out wrong, ten angels swearing I was right would make no difference.

5. Political realism refuses to identify the moral aspirations of a particular nation with the moral laws that govern the universe. As it distinguishes between truth and opinion, so it distinguishes between truth and idolatry. All nations are tempted—and few have been able to resist the temptation for long—to clothe their own particular aspirations and actions in the moral purposes of the universe. To know that nations are subject to the moral law is one thing, while to pretend to know with certainty what is good and evil in the relations among nations is quite another. There is a world of difference between the belief that all nations stand under the judgment of God, inscrutable to the human mind, and the blasphemous conviction that God is always on one's side and that what one wills oneself cannot fail to be willed by God also.

The lighthearted equation between a particular nationalism and the counsels of Providence is morally indefensible, for it is that very sin of pride against which the Greek tragedians and the Biblical prophets have warned rulers and ruled. That equation is also politically pernicious, for it is liable to engender the distortion in judgment which, in the blindness of crusading frenzy, destroys nations and civilizations—in the name of moral principle, ideal, or God himself.

On the other hand, it is exactly the concept of interest defined in terms of power that saves us from both that moral excess and that political folly. For if we look at all nations, our own included, as political entities pursuing their respective interests defined in terms of power, we are able to do justice to all of them. And we are able to do justice to all of them in a dual sense: We are able to judge other nations as we judge our own and, having judged them in this fashion we are then capable of pursuing policies that respect the interests of other nations, while protecting and promoting those of our own. Moderation in policy cannot fail to reflect the moderation of moral judgment.

6. The difference, then, between political realism and other schools of thought is real, and it is profound. However much the theory of political realism may have been misunderstood and misinterpreted, there is no gainsaying its distinctive intellectual and moral attitude to matters political.

Intellectually, the political realist maintains the autonomy of the political sphere, as the economist, the lawyer, the moralist maintain theirs. He thinks in terms of interest defined as power, as the economist thinks in terms of interest defined as wealth; the lawyer, of the conformity of action with legal rules; the moralist, of the conformity of action with moral principles. The economist asks: "How does this policy affect the wealth of society, or a segment of it?" The lawyer asks: "Is this policy in accord with the rules of law?" The moralist asks: "Is this policy in accord with moral principles?" And the political realist asks: "How does this policy affect the power of the nation?" (Or of the federal government, of Congress, of the party, of agriculture, as the case may be.)

The political realist is not unaware of the existence and relevance of standards of thought other than political ones. As political realist, he cannot but subordinate these other standards to those of politics. And he parts company with other schools when they impose standards of thought appropriate to other spheres upon the political sphere.

NOTES

1. *The Writings of George Washington,* edited by John C. Fitzpatrick (Washington: United States Printing Office, 1931–44), Vol. X, p. 363.
2. Marianne Weber, *Max Weber* (Tuebingen: J. C. B. Mohr, 1926), pp. 347–8. See also Max Weber, *Gesammelte Aufsätze zur Religionssociologie* (Tuebingen: J. C. B. Mohr, 1920), p. 252.

9

KENNETH N. WALTZ

THE ORIGINS OF WAR IN NEOREALIST THEORY

Like most historians, many students of international politics have been skeptical about the possibility of creating a theory that might help one to understand and explain the international events that interest us. Thus Morgenthau, foremost among traditional realists, was fond of repeating Blaise Pascal's remark that "the history of the world would have been different had Cleopatra's nose been a bit shorter" and then asking "How do you systemize that?"[1] His appreciation of the role of the accidental and the occurrence of the unexpected in politics dampened his theoretical ambition.

The response of neorealists is that, although difficulties abound, some of the obstacles that seem most daunting lie in misapprehensions about theory. Theory obviously cannot explain the accidental or account for unexpected events; it deals in regularities and repetitions and is possible only if these can be identified. A further difficulty is found in the failure of realists to conceive of international politics as a distinct domain about which theories can be fashioned. Morgenthau, for example, insisted on "the autonomy of politics," but he failed to apply the concept to international politics. A theory is a depiction of the organization of a domain and of the connections among its parts. A theory indicates that some factors are more important than others and specifies relations among them. In reality, everything is related to everything else, and one domain cannot be separated from others. But theory isolates one realm from all others in order to deal with it intellectually. By defining the structure of international political systems, neorealism establishes the autonomy of international politics and thus makes a theory about it possible.[2]

In developing a theory of international politics, neorealism retains the main tenets of *realpolitik*, but means and ends are viewed differently, as are causes and effects. Morgenthau, for example, thought of the "rational" statesman as ever striving to accumulate more and more power. He viewed power as an end in itself. Although he acknowledged that nations at times act out of considerations other than power, Morgenthau insisted that, when they do so,

SOURCE: Reprinted from *The Journal of Interdisciplinary History,* Vol. 18, No. 4 (Spring, 1988), pp. 39–52. With the permission of the editors of *The Journal of Interdisciplinary History* and the MIT Press, Cambridge, Massachusetts. © 1988 by the Massachusetts Institute of Technology and the editors of *The Journal of Interdisciplinary History.*

their actions are not "of a political nature."[3] In contrast, neorealism sees power as a possibly useful means, with states running risks if they have either too little or too much of it. Excessive weakness may invite an attack that greater strength would have dissuaded an adversary from launching. Excessive strength may prompt other states to increase their arms and pool their efforts against the dominant state. Because power is a possibly useful means, sensible statesmen try to have an appropriate amount of it. In crucial situations, however, the ultimate concern of states is not for power but for security. This revision is an important one.

An even more important revision is found in a shift of causal relations. The infinite materials of any realm can be organized in endlessly different ways. Realism thinks of causes as moving in only one direction, from the interactions of individuals and states to the outcomes that their acts and interactions produce. Morgenthau recognized that, when there is competition for scarce goods and no one to serve as arbiter, a struggle for power will ensue among the competitors and that consequently the struggle for power can be explained without reference to the evil born in men. The struggle for power arises simply because men want things, not because of the evil in their desires. He labeled man's desire for scarce goods as one of the two roots of conflict, but, even while discussing it, be seemed to pull toward the "other root of conflict and concomitant evil"—"the *animus dominandi,* the desire for power." He often considered that man's drive for power is more basic than the chance conditions under which struggles for power occur. This attitude is seen in his statement that "in a world where power counts, no nation pursuing a rational policy has a choice between renouncing and wanting power; *and, if it could,* the lust for power for the individual's sake would still confront us with its less spectacular yet no less pressing moral defects."[4]

Students of international politics have typically inferred outcomes from salient attributes of the actors producing them. Thus Marxists, like liberals, have linked the outbreak of war or the prevalence of peace to the internal qualities of states. Governmental forms, economic systems, social institutions, political ideologies—these are but a few examples of where the causes of war have been found. Yet, although causes are specifically assigned, we know that states with widely divergent economic institutions, social customs, and political ideologies have all fought wars. More striking still, many different sorts of organizations fight wars, whether those organizations be tribes, petty principalities, empires, nations, or street gangs. If an identified condition seems to have caused a given war, one must wonder why wars occur repeatedly even though their causes vary. Variations in the characteristics of the states are not linked directly to the outcomes that their behaviors produce, nor are variations in their patterns of interaction. Many historians, for example, have claimed that World War I was caused by the interaction of two opposed and closely balanced coalitions. But then many have claimed that World War II was caused by the failure of some states to combine forces in an effort to right an imbalance of power created by an existing alliance.

Neorealism contends that international politics can be understood only if the effects of structure are added to the unit-level explanations of traditional realism. By emphasizing how structures affect actions and outcomes, neorealism rejects the assumption that man's innate lust for power constitutes a sufficient cause of war in the absence of any other. It reconceives the causal link between interacting units and international outcomes. According to the logic of international politics, one must believe that some causes of international outcomes are the result of interactions at the unit level, and, since variations in presumed causes do not correspond very closely to variations in observed outcomes, one must also assume that others are located at the structural level. Causes at the level of units interact with those at the level of structure, and, because they do so, explanation at the unit level alone is bound to be misleading. If an approach allows the consideration of both unit-level and structural-level causes, then it can cope with both the changes and the continuities that occur in a system.

Structural realism presents a systemic portrait of international politics depicting component units according to the manner of their arrangement. For the purpose of developing a theory, states are cast as unitary actors wanting at least to survive, and are taken to be the system's constituent units. The essential structural quality of the system is anarchy—the absence of a central monopoly of legitimate force. Changes of structure and hence of system occur with variations in the number of great powers. The range of expected outcomes is inferred from the assumed motivation of the units and the structure of the system in which they act.

A systems theory of international politics deals with forces at the international, and not at the national, level. With both systems-level and unit-level forces in play, how can one construct a theory of international politics without simultaneously constructing a theory of foreign policy? An international-political theory does not imply or require a theory of foreign policy any more than a market theory implies or requires a theory of the firm. Systems theories, whether political or economic, are theories that explain how the organization of a realm acts as a constraining and disposing force on the interacting units within it. Such theories tell us about the forces to which the units are subjected. From them, we can draw some inferences about the expected behavior and fate of the units: namely, how they will have to compete with and adjust to one another if they are to survive and flourish. To the extent that the dynamics of a system limit the freedom of its units, their behavior and the outcomes of their behavior become predictable. How do we expect firms to respond to differently structured markets, and states to differently structured international-political systems? These theoretical questions require us to take firms as firms, and states as states, without paying attention to differences among them. The questions are then answered by reference to the placement of the units in their system and not by reference to the internal qualities of the units. Systems theories explain why different units behave similarly and, despite their variations, produce outcomes that fall within expected ranges.

Conversely, theories at the unit level tell us why different units behave differently despite their similar placement in a system. A theory about foreign policy is a theory at the national level. It leads to expectations about the responses that dissimilar politics will make to external pressures. A theory of international politics bears on the foreign policies of nations although it claims to explain only certain aspects of them. It can tell us what international conditions national policies have to cope with.

From the vantage point of neorealist theory, competition and conflict among states stem directly from the twin facts of life under conditions of anarchy: States in an anarchic order must provide for their own security, and threats or seeming threats to their security abound. Preoccupation with identifying dangers and counteracting them become a way of life. Relations remain tense; the actors are usually suspicious and often hostile even though by nature they may not be given to suspicion and hostility. Individually, states may only be doing what they can to bolster their security. Their individual intentions aside, collectively their actions yield arms races and alliances. The uneasy state of affairs is exacerbated by the familiar "security dilemma," wherein measures that enhance one state's security typically diminish that of others.[5] In an anarchic domain, the source of one's own comfort is the source of another's worry. Hence a state that is amassing instruments of war, even for its own defense, is cast by others as a threat requiring response. The response itself then serves to confirm the first state's belief that it had reason to worry. Similarly an alliance that in the interest of defense moves to increase cohesion among its members and add to its ranks inadvertently imperils an opposing alliance and provokes countermeasures.

Some states may hunger for power for power's sake. Neorealist theory, however, shows that it is not necessary to assume an innate lust for power in order to account for the sometimes fierce competition that marks the international arena. In an anarchic domain, a state of war exists if all parties lust for power. But so too will a state of war exist if all states seek only to ensure their own safety.

Although neorealist theory does not explain why particular wars are fought, it does explain war's dismal recurrence through the millennia. Neorealists point not to the ambitions or the intrigues that punctuate the outbreak of individual conflicts but instead to the existing structure within which events, whether by design or accident, can precipitate open clashes of arms. The origins of hot wars lie in cold wars, and the origins of cold wars are found in the anarchic ordering of the international arena.

The recurrence of war is explained by the structure of the international system. Theorists explain what historians know: War is normal. Any given war is explained not by looking at the structure of the international-political system but by looking at the particularities within it: the situations, the characters, and the interactions of states. Although particular explanations are found at the unit level, general explanations are also needed. Wars vary in frequency, and in other ways as well. A central question for a structural theory is this: How do changes of the system affect the expected frequency of war?

KEEPING WARS COLD: THE STRUCTURAL LEVEL

In an anarchic realm, peace is fragile. The prolongation of peace requires that potentially destabilizing developments elicit the interest and the calculated response of some or all of the system's principal actors. In the anarchy of states, the price of inattention or miscalculation is often paid in blood. An important issue for a structural theory to address is whether destabilizing conditions and events are managed better in multipolar or bipolar systems.

In a system of, say, five great powers, the politics of power turns on the diplomacy by which alliances are made, maintained, and disrupted. Flexibility of alignment means both that the country one is wooing may prefer another suitor and that one's present alliance partner may defect. Flexibility of alignment limits a state's options because, ideally, its strategy must please potential allies and satisfy present partners. Alliances are made by states that have some but not all of their interests in common. The common interest is ordinarily a negative one: fear of other states. Divergence comes when positive interests are at issue. In alliances among near equals, strategies are always the product of compromise since the interests of allies and their notions of how to secure them are never identical.

If competing blocs are seen to be closely balanced, and if competition turns on important matters, then to let one's side down risks one's own destruction. In a moment of crisis the weaker or the more adventurous party is likely to determine its side's policy. Its partners can afford neither to let the weaker member be defeated nor to advertise their disunity by failing to back a venture even while deploring its risks.

The prelude to World War I provides striking examples of such a situation. The approximate equality of partners in both the Triple Alliance and Triple Entente made them closely interdependent. This interdependence, combined with the keen competition between the two camps, meant that, although any country could commit its associates, no one country on either side could exercise control. If Austria-Hungary marched, Germany had to follow; the dissolution of the Austro-Hungarian Empire would have left Germany alone in the middle of Europe. If France marched, Russia had to follow; a German victory over France would be a defeat for Russia. And so the vicious circle continued. Because the defeat or the defection of a major ally would have shaken the balance, each state was constrained to adjust its strategy and the use of its forces to the aims and fears of its partners.

In alliances among equals, the defection of one member threatens the security of the others. In alliances among unequals, the contributions of the lesser members are at once wanted and of relatively small importance. In alliances among unequals, alliance leaders need worry little about the faithfulness of their followers, who usually have little choice anyway. Contrast the situation in 1914 with that of the United States and Britain and France in 1956. The United States could dissociate itself from the Suez adventure of its two principal allies and subject one of them to heavy financial pressure. Like Austria-Hungary in 1914, Britain and France tried to commit or at least immobilize their ally by presenting a fait accompli. Enjoying a position of predominance, the United States could continue to focus its attention on the major adversary while disciplining its two allies. Opposing Britain and France endangered neither the United States nor the alliance because the security of Britain and France depended much more heavily on us than our security depended on them. The ability of the United States, and the inability of Germany, to pay a price measured in intra-alliance terms is striking.

In balance-of-power politics old style, flexibility of alignment led to rigidity of strategy or the limitation of freedom of decision. In balance-of-power politics new style, the obverse is true: Rigidity of alignment in a two-power world results in more flexibility of strategy and greater freedom of decision. In a multipolar world, roughly equal parties engaged in cooperative endeavors must look for the common denominator of their policies. They risk finding the lowest one and easily end up in the worst of all possible worlds. In a bipolar world, alliance leaders can design strategies primarily to advance their own interests and to cope with their main adversary and less to satisfy their own allies.

Neither the United States nor the Soviet Union has to seek the approval of other states, but each has to cope with the other. In the great-power politics of a multipolar world, who is a danger to whom and who can be expected to deal with threats and problems are matters of uncertainty. In the great-power politics of a bipolar world, who is a danger to whom is never in doubt. Any event in the world that involves the fortunes of either of the great powers automatically elicits the interest of the other. President Harry S. Truman, at the time of the Korean invasion, could not very well echo Neville Chamberlain's words in the Czechoslovakian crisis by claiming that the Americans knew nothing about the Koreans, a people living far away in the east of Asia. We had to know about them or quickly find out.

In a two-power competition, a loss for one is easily taken to be a gain for the other. As a result, the powers in a bipolar world promptly respond to unsettling events. In a multipolar world, dangers are diffused, responsibilities unclear, and definitions of vital interests easily obscured. Where a number of states are in balance, the skillful foreign policy of a forward power is designed to gain an advantage without antagonizing other states and frightening them into united action. At times in modern Europe, the benefits of possible gains have seemed to outweigh the risks of likely losses. Statesmen have hoped to push an issue to the limit without causing all of the potential opponents to unite. When there are several possible enemies, unity of action among them is difficult to achieve. National leaders could therefore think—or desperately hope, as did Theobald von Bethmann Hollweg and Adolf Hitler before two world wars—that a united opposition would not form.

If interests and ambitions conflict, the absence of crises is more worrisome than their presence. Crises are produced by the determination of a state to resist a change that another state tries to make. As the leaders in a bipolar system, the United States and the Soviet Union are disposed to do the resisting, for in important matters they cannot hope that their allies will do it for them. Political action in the postwar world has reflected this condition. Communist guerrillas operating in Greece prompted the Truman Doctrine. The tightening of Soviet control over the states of Eastern Europe led to the Marshall Plan and the Atlantic Defense Treaty, and these in turn gave rise to the Cominform and the Warsaw Pact. The plan to create a West German government produced the Berlin blockade. During the past four decades, our responses have been geared to the Soviet Union's actions, and theirs to ours.

Miscalculation by some or all of the great powers is a source of danger in a multipolar world; overreaction by either or both of the great powers is a source of danger in a bipolar world. Which is worse: miscalculation or overreaction? Miscalculation is the greater evil because it is more likely to permit an unfolding of events that finally threatens the status quo and brings the powers to war. Overreaction is the lesser evil because at worst it costs only money for unnecessary arms and possibly the fighting of limited wars. The dynamics of a bipolar system, moreover, provide a measure of correction. In a world in which two states united in their mutual antagonism overshadow any others, the benefits of a calculated response stand out most clearly, and the sanctions against irresponsible behavior achieve their greatest force. Thus two states, isolationist by tradition, untutored in the ways of international politics, and famed for impulsive behavior, have shown themselves—not always and everywhere, but always in crucial cases—to be wary, alert, cautious, flexible, and forbearing.

Moreover, the economies of the great powers in a bipolar world are less interdependent than those of the great powers of a multipolar one. The size of great powers tends to increase as their numbers fall, and the larger a state is, the greater the variety of its resources. States of continental size do proportionately less of their business abroad than, for example, Britain, France, and Germany did in their heydays. Never before in modern history have the great powers depended so little on the outside world, and been so uninvolved in one another's economic affairs, as the United States and the Soviet Union have been since the war. The separation of their interests reduces the occasions for dispute and permits them, if they wish, to leave each other alone even though each defines its security interests largely in terms of the other.

Interdependence of parties, diffusion of dangers, confusion of responses: These are the characteristics of great-power politics in a multipolar world. Self-dependence of parties, clarity of dangers, certainty about who has to face them: These are the characteristics of great-power politics in a bipolar world.

KEEPING WARS COLD: THE UNIT LEVEL

A major reason for the prolongation of the postwar peace is the destruction of the old multipolar world in World War II and its replacement by a bipolar one. In a bipolar world, we expect competition to be keen, yet manageable. But to believe that bipolarity alone accounts for the "long peace" between the

United States and the Soviet Union is difficult. Given the depth and extent of the distrust felt by both parties, one may easily believe that one or another of the crises that they have experienced would, in earlier times, have drawn them into war. For a fuller explanation of why that did not happen, we must look to that other great force for peace: nuclear weapons.

States continue to coexist in an anarchic order. Self-help is the principle of action in such an order, and the most important way in which states must help themselves is by providing for their own security. Therefore, in weighing the chances of peace, the first questions to ask are questions about the ends for which states use force and about the strategies and weapons they employ. The chances of peace rise if states can achieve their most important ends without actively using force. War becomes less likely as the costs of war rise in relation to the possible gains. Realist theory, old and new alike, draws attention to the crucial role of military technology and strategy among the forces that fix the fate of states and their systems.

Nuclear weapons dissuade states from going to war much more surely than conventional weapons do. In a conventional world, states can believe both that they may win and that, should they lose, the price of defeat will be bearable, although World Wars I and II called the latter belief into question even before atomic bombs were dropped. If the United States and the Soviet Union were now armed only with conventional weapons, the lessons of those wars would be clearly remembered, especially by the Soviet Union, which suffered more in war than the United States. Had the atom never been split, those two nations would still have much to fear from each other. Armed with increasingly destructive conventional weapons, they would be constrained to strive earnestly to avoid war. Yet, in a conventional world, even sad and strong lessons like those of the two world wars have proved exceedingly difficult for states to learn. Throughout modern history, one great power or another has looked as though it might become dangerously strong: for example, France under Louis XIV and Napoleon Bonaparte, and Germany under Wilhelm II and Hitler. In each case, an opposing coalition formed and turned the expansive state back. The lessons of history would seem to be clear: In international politics, success leads to failure. The excessive accumulation of power by one state or coalition of states elicits the opposition of others. The leaders of expansionist states have nevertheless been able to persuade themselves that skillful diplomacy and clever strategy would enable them to transcend the normal processes of balance-of-power politics.

The experience of World War II, bipolarity, and the increased destructiveness of conventional weapons would make World War III more difficult to start than earlier wars were; and the presence of nuclear weapons dramatically increases that difficulty. Nuclear weapons reverse or negate many of the conventional causes of war. Wars can be fought in the face of nuclear weapons, but the higher the stakes and the closer a country comes to winning them, the more surely that country invites retaliation and risks its own destruction. The accumulation of significant power through conquest, even if only conventional weapons are used, is no longer possible in the world of nuclear powers. Those individuals who believe that the Soviet Union's leaders are so bent on world domination that they may be willing to run catastrophic risks for problematic gains fail to understand bow governments behave. Do we expect to lose one city or two? Two cities or ten? When these are the pertinent questions, political leaders stop thinking about running risks and start worrying about how to avoid them.

Deterrence is more easily achieved than most military strategists would have us believe. In a conventional world, a country can sensibly attack if it believes that success is probable. In a nuclear world, a country cannot sensibly attack unless it believes that success is assured. A nation will be deterred from attacking even if it believes that there is only a possibility that its adversary will retaliate. Uncertainty of response, not certainty, is required for deterrence because, if retaliation occurs, one risks losing all. As Clausewitz wrote: If war approaches the absolute, it becomes imperative "not to take the first step without thinking what may be the last." [6]

Nuclear weapons make the implications even of victory too horrible to contemplate. The problem that the nuclear powers must solve is how to perpetuate peace when it is not possible to eliminate all of the causes of war. The structure of international politics has not been transformed; it remains anarchic in form. Nuclear states continue to compete militarily. With each state striving to ensure its own security, war remains constantly possible. In the anarchy of states, improving the means of defense and deterrence relative to the means of offense increases the chances of peace. Weapons and strategies that make defense and deterrence easier, and offensive strikes harder to mount, decrease the likelihood of war. [7]

Although the possibility of war remains, the probability of a war involving states with nuclear weapons has been drastically reduced. Over the centuries great powers have fought more wars than minor states, and the frequency of war has correlated more closely with a structural characteristic—their international standing—than with unit-level attributes. Yet, because of a change in military technology, a change at the unit level, waging war has increasingly become the privilege of poor and weak states. Nuclear weapons have banished war from the center of international politics. A unit-level change has dramatically reduced a structural effect.

The probability of major war among states having nuclear weapons approaches zero. But the "real war" may, as James claimed, lie in the preparations for waging it. The logic of a deterrent strategy, if it is followed, also circumscribes the causes of "real wars." [8] In a conventional world, the structure of international politics encourages states to arm competitively. In a nuclear world, deterrent strategies offer the possibility of dampening the competition. Conventional weapons are relative. With conventional weapons, competing countries must constantly compare their strengths. How secure a country is depends on how it compares to others in the quantity and quality of its weaponry, the suitability of its strategy, the resilience of its society and economy, and the skill of its leaders.

Nuclear weapons are not relative but absolute weapons. [9] They make it possible for a state to limit the size of its strategic forces so long as other states are unable to achieve disarming first-strike capabilities by improving their forces. If no state can launch a disarming attack with high confidence, comparing the size of strategic forces becomes irrelevant. For deterrence, one asks how much is enough, and enough is defined as a second-strike capability. This interpretation does not imply that a deterrent force can deter everything, but rather that, beyond a certain level, additional forces provide no additional security for one party and pose no additional threat to others. The two principal powers in the system have long had second-strike forces, with neither able to launch a disarming strike against the other. That both nevertheless continue to pile weapon upon unneeded weapon is a puzzle whose solution can be found only within the United States and the Soviet Union.

Wars, Hot and Cold

Wars, hot and cold, originate in the structure of the international political system. Most Americans blame the Soviet Union for creating the Cold War, by the actions that follow necessarily from the nature of its society and government. Revisionist historians, attacking the dominant view, assign blame to the United States. Some American error, or sinister interest, or faulty assumption about Soviet aims, they argue, is what started the Cold War. Either way, the main point is lost. In a bipolar world, each of the two great powers is bound to focus its fears on the other, to distrust its motives, and to impute offensive intentions to defensive measures. The proper question is what, not who, started the Cold War. Although its content and virulence vary as unit-level forces change and interact, the Cold War continues. It is firmly rooted in the structure of postwar international politics, and will last as long as that structure endures.

In any closely competitive system, it may seem that one is either paranoid or a loser. The many Americans who ascribe paranoia to the Soviet Union are saying little about its political elite and much about the international-political system. Yet, in the presence of nuclear weapons, the Cold War has not become a hot one, a raging war among major states. Constraints on fighting big wars have bound the major nuclear states into a system of uneasy peace. Hot wars originate in the structure of international politics. So does the Cold War, with its temperature kept low by the presence of nuclear weapons.

Notes

1. Hans J. Morgenthau, "International Relations: Quantitative and Qualitative Approaches," in Norman D. Palmer (ed.), *A Design for International Relations Research: Scope, Theory, Methods, and Relevance* (Philadelphia, 1970), 78.

2. Morgenthau, *Politics among Nations* (New York, 1973; 5th ed.), 11. Ludwig Boltzman (trans. Rudolf Weingartner), "Theories as Representations," excerpted in Arthur Danto and Sidney Morgenbesser (eds.), *Philosophy of Science* (Cleveland, 1960), 245–252. Neorealism is sometimes dubbed structural realism. I use the terms interchangeably and, throughout this article, refer to my own formulation of neorealist theory. See Waltz, *Theory of International Politics* (Reading, Mass., 1979); Robert Keohane (ed.), *Neorealism and its Critics* (New York, 1986).

3. Morgenthau, *Politics among Nations,* 27.
4. *Idem, Scientific Man vs. Power Politics* (Chicago, 1946), 192, 200. Italics added.
5. See John H. Herz, "Idealist Internationalism and the Security Dilemma," *World Politics,* II (1950), 157–180.
6. Karl von Clausewitz (ed. Anatol Rapaport; trans. J. J. Graham), *On War* (Hammondsworth, 1968), V. 374.
7. See Malcolm W. Hoag, "On Stability in Deterrent Races," in Morton A. Kaplan (ed.), *The Revolution in World Politics* (New York, 1962), 388–410; Robert Jervis, "Cooperation under the Security Dilemma," *World Politics,* XXX (1978), 167–214.
8. Williams James, "The Moral Equivalent of War," in Leon Bramson and George W. Goethals (eds.), *War: Studies from Psychology, Sociology, and Anthropology* (New York, 1968; rev. ed.), 23.
9. Cf. Bernard Brodie, *The Absolute Weapon: Atomic Power and World Order* (New York, 1946), 75–76.

10

JOHN A. HOBSON

THE ECONOMIC TAPROOTS OF IMPERIALISM

. . . American Imperialism was the natural product of the economic pressure of a sudden advance of capitalism which could not find occupation at home and needed foreign markets for goods and for investments.

The same needs existed in European countries, and, as is admitted, drove Governments along the same path. Overproduction in the sense of an excessive manufacturing plant, and surplus capital which could not find sound investments within the country, forced Great Britain, Germany, Holland, France to place larger and larger portions of their economic resources outside the area of their present political domain, and then stimulate a policy of political expansion so as to take in the new areas. The economic sources of this movement are laid bare by periodic trade-depressions due to an inability of producers to find adequate and profitable markets for what they can produce. The Majority Report of the Commission upon the Depression of Trade in 1885 put the matter in a nutshell. "That, owing to the nature of the times, the demand for our commodities does not increase at the same rate as formerly;

SOURCE: From *Imperialism,* John A. Hobson (London: George Allen & Unwin, 1954). Reprinted with permission of the publisher.

that our capacity for production is consequently in excess of our requirements, and could be considerably increased at short notice; that this is due partly to the competition of the capital which is being steadily accumulated in the country." The Minority Report straightly imputed the condition of affairs to "overproduction." Germany was in the early 1900's suffering severely from what is called a glut of capital and of manufacturing power: she had to have new markets; her Consuls all over the world were "hustling" for trade; trading settlements were forced upon Asia Minor; in East and West Africa, in China and elsewhere the German Empire was impelled to a policy of colonization and protectorates as outlets for German commercial energy.

Every improvement of methods of production, every concentration of ownership and control, seems to accentuate the tendency. As one nation after another enters the machine economy and adopts advanced industrial methods, it becomes more difficult for its manufacturers, merchants, and financiers to dispose profitably of their economic resources, and they are tempted more and more to use their Governments in order to secure for their particular use some distant undeveloped country by annexation and protection.

The process, we may be told, is inevitable, and so it seems upon a superficial inspection. Everywhere appear excessive powers of production, excessive capital in search of investment. It is admitted by all businessmen that the growth of the powers of production in their country exceeds the growth in consumption, that more goods can be produced than can be sold at a profit, and that more capital exists than can find remunerative investment.

It is this economic condition of affairs that forms the taproot of Imperialism. If the consuming public in this country raised its standard of consumption to keep pace with every rise of productive powers, there could be no excess of goods or capital clamorous to use Imperialism in order to find markets: foreign trade would indeed exist, but there would be no difficulty in exchanging a small surplus of our manufactures for the food and raw material we annually absorbed, and all the savings that we made could find employment, if we chose, in home industries. . . .

The fallacy of the supposed inevitability of imperial expansion as a necessary outlet for progressive industry is now manifest. It is not industrial progress that demands the opening up of new markets and areas of investment, but maldistribution of consuming power which prevents the absorption of commodities and capital within the country. The oversaving which is the economic root of Imperialism is found by analysis to consist of rents, monopoly profits, and other unearned or excessive elements of income, which, not being earned by labour of head or hand, have no legitimate *raison d'être*. Having no natural relation to effort of production, they impel their recipients to no corresponding satisfaction of consumption: they form a surplus wealth, which, having no proper place in the normal economy of production and consumption, tends to accumulate as excessive savings. Let any turn in the tide of politico-economic forces divert from these owners their excess of income and make it flow, either to the workers in higher wages, or to the community in taxes, so that it will be spent instead of being saved, serving in either of these ways to swell the tide of consumption—there will be no need to fight for foreign markets or foreign areas of investment.

. . . The controlling and directing agent of the whole process is the pressure of financial and industrial motives, operated for the direct, short-range, material interests of small, able, and well-organized groups in a nation. These groups secure the active co-operation of statesmen and of political cliques who wield the power of "parties," partly by associating them directly in their business schemes, partly by appealing to the conservative instincts of members of the possessing classes, whose vested interest and class dominance are best preserved by diverting the currents of political energy from domestic on to foreign politics. The acquiescence, even the active and enthusiastic support, of the body of a nation in a course of policy fatal to its own true interests is secured partly by appeals to the mission of civilization, but chiefly by playing upon the primitive instincts of the race.

The psychology of these instincts is not easy to explore, but certain prime factors easily appear. The passion which a French writer describes as kilometritis,[1] or milo-mania, the instinct for control of land, drives back to the earliest times when a wide range of land was necessary for a food supply for men or cattle, and is linked on to the "trek" habit, which survives more powerfully than is commonly supposed in civilized peoples. The "nomadic" habit bred of necessity survives as a chief ingredient in the love of travel, and merges into "the spirit of adventure" when it meets other equally primitive passions. This "spirit of adventure," especially in the Anglo-Saxon, has taken the shape of "sport," which in its stronger or "more adventurous" forms involves a direct appeal to the lust of slaughter and the crude struggle for life involved in pursuit. The animal lust of struggle, once a necessity, survives in the blood, and just in proportion as a nation or a class has a margin of energy and leisure from the activities of peaceful industry, it craves satisfaction through "sport," in which hunting and the physical satisfaction of striking a blow are vital ingredients. The leisured classes in Great Britain, having most of their energy liberated from the necessity of work, naturally specialize on "sport," the hygienic necessity of a substitute for work helping to support or coalescing with the survival of a savage instinct.

. . . The sporting and military aspects of Imperialism form, therefore, a very powerful basis of popular appeal. The desire to pursue and kill either big game or other men can only be satisfied by expansion and militarism. It may indeed be safely said that the reason why our army is so inefficient in its officers, as compared with its rank and file, is that at a time when serious scientific preparation and selection are required for an intellectual profession, most British officers choose the army and undertake its work in the spirit of "sport." While the average "Tommy" is perhaps actuated in the main by similar motives, "science" matters less in his case, and any lack of serious professional purpose is more largely compensated by the discipline imposed on him.

But still more important than these supports of militarism in the army is the part played by "war" as a support of Imperialism in the non-combatant body of the nation. Though the active appeal of sport is still strong, even among townsmen, clear signs are visible of a degradation of this active interest of the participant into the idle excitement of the spectator. How far sport has thus degenerated may be measured by the substitution everywhere of a specialized professionalism for a free amateur exercise, and by the growth of the attendant vice of betting, which everywhere expresses the worst form of sporting excitement, drawing all disinterested sympathy away from the merits of the competition, and concentrating it upon the irrational element of chance in combination with covetousness and low cunning. The equivalent of this degradation of interest in sport is Jingoism in relation to the practice of war. Jingoism is merely the lust of the spectator, unpurged by any personal effort, risk, or sacrifice, gloating over the perils, pains, and slaughter of fellow-men whom he does not know, but whose destruction he desires in a blind and artificially stimulated passion of hatred and revenge. In the Jingo all is concentrated on the hazard and blind fury of the fray. . . .

Whether such expensive remedies are really effectual or necessary we are not called on to decide, but it is quite evident that the spectatorial lust of Jingoism is a most serious factor in Imperialism. The dramatic falsification both of war and of the whole policy of imperial expansion required to feed this popular passion forms no small portion of the art of the real organizers of imperialist exploits, the small groups of business men and politicians who know what they want and how to get it.

NOTE

1. M. Novicov, *La Federation de l'Europe*, p. 158.

11

STEPHEN D. KRASNER

TWO ALTERNATIVE PERSPECTIVES: MARXISM AND LIBERALISM

The basic approach taken in this study can better be understood by contrasting its assumptions with those of two other prominent perspectives on the political process: Marxism and liberalism. These paradigms involve different arguments about policymaking and the objectives of official action.

SOURCE: *Defending the National Interest*. Stephen D. Krasner. Copyright 1978 Princeton University Press. Reprinted with permission.

MARXISM

Scholars in the Marxist tradition have presented the most extensive analysis of foreign economic policy. Marx himself was primarily concerned with developments within national economies, although he did not entirely ignore international problems. With Lenin's *Imperialism* the international aspects of capitalism assumed a place of first importance for Marxist scholars. The analytic assumptions of this paradigm differ in a number of fundamental ways from the state-centric approach of this study.

Marxist theories can be divided into two basic types: instrumental and structural.[1] Instrumental Marxist theories view governmental behavior as the product of direct societal pressure. In its most primitive form, this kind of argument emphasizes personal ties between leading capitalists and public officials.[2] In its more sophisticated form, instrumental Marxist arguments analyze the general ties between the capitalist sector and public officials. Ralph Miliband is the leading recent exponent of this kind of argument. He maintains that there is a cohesive capitalist class. This class controls the state because public officials are heavily drawn from the middle and upper classes, are in frequent contact with businessmen, and depend on the cooperation of private firms to carry out public policy. In addition, cultural institutions such as the media and churches reflect the dominant conservative ideology. Harold Laski took a very similar position, arguing that "historically, we always find that any system of government is dominated by those who at the time wield economic power; and what they mean by 'good' is, for the most part, the preservation of their own interests."[3] From an instrumental Marxist perspective, the state is the executive committee of the bourgeoisie.[4]

Structural Marxist arguments take a different tack. They do not attempt to trace the behavior of the state to the influence of particular capitalists or the capitalist class. Instead, they see the state playing an independent role within the overall structure of a capitalist system. Its task is to maintain the cohesion of the system as a whole. At particular times this may require adopting policies opposed by the bourgeoisie, but generally official action and the preferences of leading elements in the capitalist class will coincide.

For structural Marxism, the behavior of the state involves an effort to deal with economic and political contradictions that are inherent in a capitalist system. Economically, capitalism is not seen as a self-sustaining system tending toward equilibrium. Rather, over the long-term profit rates decline because capitalists can only secure profit through the exploitation of labor, but technological innovation reduces the long-term equilibrium ratio of labor to capital. This process also leads to underconsumption: the system produces more goods than its members can consume. It promotes concentration because weaker firms are driven out of the market. Excess capital is accumulated because there is no market for the goods that would be produced by more investment.

Politically, concentration—what Marxists call the increased socialization of the production process—produces tensions. As societies develop, they become more complex and interdependent. However, control is increasingly concentrated in the hands of an ever smaller group of the owners or managers of capital. At the same time, the working class grows and workers come into more intimate and constant contact with each other. The increased socialization of the production process itself and the continued private appropriation of power and profit produce political and social tensions that threaten the stability of the system.

From a structural Marxist perspective, policy analysis can be viewed as a catalogue of state efforts to cope with these tensions. In the area of foreign economic policy the major conclusion is that the state must follow an expansionary, an imperialist, foreign policy. Early Marxist writers elaborated the relationship between colonialism and expanded opportunities for trade and investment. The opening of new areas could help alleviate underconsumption because capitalists could find new markets by eliminating local artisans. Colonies also offered opportunities for surplus capital. This is the major argument presented by Lenin. These contentions have not been sustained by empirical investigations, however. Even in the heyday of empire only a small proportion of goods and capital moved from the mother country to colonial areas.[5] Recent radical analyses have suggested somewhat different motivations for expansion, including protection of the oligopolistic position of large firms, militarism, and the quest for raw materials.

The relationship between advanced capitalist societies, giant firms, and foreign activity has been emphasized by two recent Marxist analysts, Harry Magdoff and James O'Connor. Using arguments from the behavioral theory of the firm, Magdoff suggests that corporations are systems of power. Each firm strives to control its own market. This objective could not be realized during the early stages of capitalism because the level of competition was too high. As concentration increases, however, "the exercise of controlling power becomes not only possible but increasingly essential for the security of the firm and its assets."[6] Businesses seek to maximize control over actual and potential sources of raw materials and over foreign markets. Foreign investment is a particularly effective device for guaranteeing such control, although trading opportunities are not ignored. If control is lost, either to competitors or to socialist regimes, the oligopoly can be destroyed. Since these corporations are the foundation of the American capitalist system, their political power is great, and their collapse would precipitate a deep economic crisis. There are impelling reasons for the United States, the world's leading capitalist nation, to maintain an international economic system with minimum constraints on the operations of giant multinational firms.[7]

James O'Connor has taken an even more classical Marxist position. He maintains that the monopoly sector in modern capitalist systems is the most important source of profits. However, there is an inherent tendency for the productive capacity of the monopoly sector to expand more quickly than demand or employment. This leads to pressure for an aggressive foreign economic policy. Overseas activity can increase sales and profit, and offer opportunities for new investment. The purpose of foreign assistance and more direct military intervention is to keep foreign client states within the capitalist order.

Magdoff, O'Connor, and other structural Marxist analysts have also postulated an intimate relationship between the economic needs of the capitalist system, military expenditure, and imperialism. Military expenditures are a primary source of revenue for some major firms in the monopoly sector. Such expenditures help maintain the stability of the system because they are not subject to the rational calculations of profit and loss that are an inherent part of the capitalist ideology. Finally, militarism is important in a direct sense because the use of force may be necessary to keep foreign areas open to trade and investment.[8]

An argument directly related to the empirical concerns of this study, which has received new emphasis from Marxists, is that capitalists must have foreign raw materials. This aim was not ignored by classical Marxist writers. Lenin stated that capitalists were driven to control ever increasing amounts of even apparently worthless land because it might contain some unknown material that could lead to economic disaster if it were to fall into the hands of a competitor. Cheap raw materials also contributed to staving off the inevitable tendency toward declining rates of profits: new and rich discoveries could, at least temporarily, provide high profits. Magdoff has maintained that the search for raw materials is part of the general quest of giant corporations for security and oligopolistic profits. Only through vertical integration from mine to final sale can these firms assure themselves of tight market control. Furthermore, the United States and other capitalist states are seen as being vitally dependent on foreign sources for some commodities that are essential for industrial operations and advanced military equipment.[9] One author has argued that all American foreign policy can be explained by the need "to insure that the flow of raw materials from the Third World is never interrupted."[10]

While Marxist writers have dropped some arguments, modified others, and found new ones, there is a central thread that runs through their position. Foreign economic expansion is a necessity. It is not a matter of the preferences of particular enterprises. It is not a policy that has a marginal effect on profits. It is an issue that touches the very core of capitalism's continued viability. Cut off from the rest of the world, the economies of advanced capitalist states would confront problems of great severity. "For Marxism," Tom Kemp avers, "imperialism is not a political or ideological phenomenon but expresses the imperative necessities of advanced capitalism."[11]

For structural Marxists, the state can be treated as having autonomy, not from the needs of the system as a whole, but from direct political pressure from the capitalist class. Indeed, such autonomy is necessary because internal divisions preclude effective bourgeois political organization. To maintain cohesion the state must mitigate the social and political pressures arising from the increasing socialization of the production process coupled with the continuing private appropriation of profits and control. Carrying out this task requires it to pose as a representative of all the people. To appear to follow the explicit preferences of powerful capitalists too slavishly would weaken the stability of the whole system. Compromises, such as the recognition of unions and higher social welfare payments, are essential, even if they are opposed by the capitalist class. Such policies protect the existing structure of economic relationships by disarming and disuniting potential opposition from the oppressed.[12]

The analytic assumptions of Marxist theories, whether of the instrumental or structural variety, differ from the statist approach in at least three ways. First, the notion of national interest is rejected by Marxists. The aims pursued by the state mirror the preferences of the capitalist class or some of its elements, or the needs of the system as a whole. State behavior does not reflect either autonomous power drives or the general well-being of the society. Second, the behavior of the state is taken by them to be intimately related to economic goals; other objectives are instrumental, not consummatory. In particular, ideological objectives cannot be independent of economic considerations. Ideology is a mask that hides the reality of exploitation and thus helps mislead and mollify those who have no real power. Third, even though structural Marxists may view the state as relatively autonomous, they do not believe that it can really be understood outside of its societal context. The state has peculiar tasks within the structure of a capitalist system, but they are ultimately associated with the interests of a particular class.

NOTES

1. Gold, Lo, and Wright, "Recent Developments in Marxist Theories of the Capitalist State." This excellent essay also discusses a third approach, Marxist Hegelianism. A similar distinction is made in Wolfe, "New Directions in the Marxist Theory of Politics," pp. 133–36. Nicos Poulantzas, who is generally described as one of the leading proponents of the structuralist position, has argued that the distinction does not make sense. However, Poulantzas defines structuralism as either the view that does "not grant sufficient importance to the role of concrete individuals . . ." or the view that "neglects the importance and weight of the class struggle in history. . . ." See his essay "The Capitalist State," pp. 70 and 71. This is hardly what those who have described Poulantzas as a structuralist have in mind. Poulantzas dismisses his American Marxist critics with the statement that "the academic and ideologico-political conjuncture in the United States" is responsible for their misreading (p. 76).

2. For examples of such reasoning in the area of raw materials see Engler, *Brotherhood of Oil;* Goff and Locker, "The Violence of Domination"; and the much more sophisticated argument of Lipson, "Corporate Preferences and Public Choices."

3. *Foundations of Sovereignty,* p. 289, and *The State in Theory and Practice.*

4. See Kolko, *Roots of American Foreign Policy,* and Miliband, *The State in Capitalist Society,* for applications of instrumental Marxism to the concerns of the study. Recently, Miliband has taken a more structuralist position.

5. Barratt Brown, "A Critique of Marxist Theories of Imperialism," p. 44; Fieldhouse, "Imperialism"; Cohen, *The Questions of Imperialism,* Ch. 2.

6. "Imperialism Without Colonies," p. 157.

7. *Age of Imperialism,* pp. 34–35 and Ch. 5.

8. O'Connor, *Fiscal Crisis,* Ch. 6.

9. Lenin, *Imperialism,* pp. 83–84; Magdoff, *Age of Imperialism,* pp. 52, 156; Kolko, *Roots of American Foreign Policy,* pp. 50–54.

10. Dean, "Scarce Resources," p. 149.

11. "The Marxist Theory of Imperialism," p. 17. See also Mack, "Comparing Theories of Economic Imperialism," p. 40.

12. Poulantzas, *Political Power and Social Classes;* O'Connor, *Fiscal Crisis,* esp. Ch. 1; Poulantzas, "The Capitalist State," p. 73; and Gough, "State Expenditure in Advanced Capitalism," pp. 64–65. It is not my purpose here to critique a structural Marxist position, but it is important to note that granting the state the kind of autonomy imputed to it by this approach weakens any dialectical analysis of capitalism. The state appears to be so independent and prescient that it can save capitalism from its own infirmities.

1 2

THEOTONIO DOS SANTOS

THE STRUCTURE OF DEPENDENCE

This paper attempts to demonstrate that the dependence of Latin American countries on other countries cannot be overcome without a qualitative change in their internal structures and external relations. We shall attempt to show that the relations of dependence to which these countries are subjected conform to a type of international and internal structure which leads them to underdevelopment or more precisely to a dependent structure that deepens and aggravates the fundamental problems of their peoples.

I. WHAT IS DEPENDENCE?

By dependence we mean a situation in which the economy of certain countries is conditioned by the development and expansion of another economy to which the former is subjected. The relation of interdependence between two or more economies, and between these and world trade, assumes the form of

Note: This work expands on certain preliminary work done in a research project on the relations of dependence in Latin America, directed by the author at the Center for Socio-Economic Studies of the Faculty of Economic Science of the University of Chile. In order to abridge the discussion of various aspects, the author was obliged to cite certain of his earlier works. The author expresses his gratitude to the researcher Orlando Caputo and Roberto Pizarro for some of the data utilized and to Sergio Ramos for his critical comments on the paper.

SOURCE: "The Structure of Dependence." Theotonio Dos Santos. *American Economic Review,* 1970, vol. 60, issue 2, pages 231–236.

dependence when some countries (the dominant ones) can expand and can be self-sustaining, while other countries (the dependent ones) can do this only as a reflection of that expansion, which can have either a positive or a negative effect on their immediate development [7, p. 6].

The concept of dependence permits us to see the internal situation of these countries as part of world economy. In the Marxian tradition, the theory of imperialism has been developed as a study of the process of expansion of the imperialist centers and of their world domination. In the epoch of the revolutionary movement of the Third World, we have to develop the theory of laws of internal development in those countries that are the object of such expansion and are governed by them. This theoretical step transcends the theory of development which seeks to explain the situation of the underdeveloped countries as a product of their slowness or failure to adopt the patterns of efficiency characteristic of developed countries (or to "modernize" or "develop" themselves). Although capitalist development theory admits the existence of an "external" dependence, it is unable to perceive underdevelopment in the way our present theory perceives it, as a consequence and part of the process of the world expansion of capitalism—a part that is necessary to and integrally linked with it.

In analyzing the process of constituting a world economy that integrates the so-called "national economies" in a world market of commodities, capital, and even of labor power, we see that the relations produced by this market are unequal and combined—unequal because development of parts of the system occurs at the expense of other parts. Trade relations are based on monopolistic control of the market, which leads to the transfer of surplus generated in the dependent countries to the dominant countries; financial relations are, from the viewpoint of the dominant powers, based on loans and the export of capital, which permit them to receive interest and profits; thus increasing their domestic surplus and strengthening their control over the economies of the other countries. For the dependent countries these relations represent an export of profits and interest which carries off part of the surplus generated domestically and leads to a loss of control over their productive resources. In order to permit these disadvantageous relations, the dependent countries must generate large surpluses, not in such a way as to create higher levels of technology but rather superexploited manpower. The result is to limit the development of their internal market and their technical and cultural capacity, as well as the moral and physical health of their people. We call this combined development because it is the combination of these inequalities and the transfer of resources from the most backward and dependent sectors to the most advanced and dominant ones which explains the inequality, deepens it, and transforms it into a necessary and structural element of the world economy.

II. Historic Forms of Dependence

Historic forms of dependence are conditioned by: (1) the basic forms of this world economy which has its own laws of development; (2) the type of economic relations dominant in the capitalist centers and the ways in which the latter expand outward; and (3) the types of economic relations existing inside the peripheral countries which are incorporated into the situation of dependence within the network of international economic relations generated by capitalist expansion. It is not within the purview of this paper to study these forms in detail but only to distinguish broad characteristics of development.

Drawing on an earlier study, we may distinguish: (1) Colonial dependence, trade export in nature, in which commercial and financial capital in alliance with the colonialist state dominated the economic relations of the Europeans and the colonies, by means of a trade monopoly complemented by a colonial monopoly of land, mines, and manpower (serf or slave) in the colonized countries. (2) Financial-industrial dependence which consolidated itself at the end of the nineteenth century, characterized by the domination of big capital in the hegemonic centers, and its expansion abroad through investment in the production of raw materials and agricultural products for consumption in the hegemonic centers. A productive structure grew up in the dependent countries devoted to the export of these products (which Levin labeled export economies [11]; other analysis in other regions [12] [13]), producing what ECLA has called "foreign-oriented development" *(desarrollo hacia afuera)* [4]. (3) In the postwar period a new type of dependence has been consolidated, based on multinational corporations which began to invest in industries geared to the internal market of underdeveloped countries. This form of dependence is basically technological-industrial dependence [6].

Each of these forms of dependence corresponds to a situation which conditioned not only the international relations of these countries but also their internal structures: the orientation of production, the forms of capital accumulation, the reproduction of the economy, and, simultaneously, their social and political structure.

III. THE EXPORT ECONOMIES

In forms (1) and (2) of dependence, production is geared to those products destined for export (gold, silver, and tropical products in the colonial epoch; raw materials and agricultural products in the epoch of industrial-financial dependence); i.e., production is determined by demand from the hegemonic centers. The internal productive structure is characterized by rigid specialization and monoculture in entire regions (the Caribbean, the Brazilian Northeast, etc.). Alongside these export sectors there grew up certain complementary economic activities (cattle-raising and some manufacturing, for example) which were dependent, in general, on the export sector to which they sell their products. There was a third, subsistence economy which provided manpower for the export sector under favorable conditions and toward which excess population shifted during periods unfavorable to international trade.

Under these conditions, the existing internal market was restricted by four factors: (1) Most of the national income was derived from export, which was used to purchase the inputs required by export production (slaves, for example) or luxury goods consumed by the hacienda- and mine-owners, and by the more prosperous employees. (2) The available manpower was subject to very arduous forms of superexploitation, which limited its consumption. (3) Part of the consumption of these workers was provided by the subsistence economy, which served as a complement to their income and as a refuge during periods of depression. (4) A fourth factor was to be found in those countries in which land and mines were in the hands of foreigners (cases of an enclave economy): a great part of the accumulated surplus was destined to be sent abroad in the form of profits, limiting not only internal consumption but also possibilities of reinvestment [1]. In the case of enclave economies the relations of the foreign companies with the hegemonic center were even more exploitative and were complemented by the fact that purchases by the enclave were made directly abroad.

IV. THE NEW DEPENDENCE

The new form of dependence, (3) above, is in process of developing and is conditioned by the exigencies of the international commodity and capital markets. The possibility of generating new investments depends on the existence of financial resources in foreign currency for the purchase of machinery and processed raw materials not produced domestically. Such purchases are subject to two limitations: the limit of resources generated by the export sector (reflected in the balance of payments, which includes not only trade but also service relations); and the limitations of monopoly on patents which leads monopolistic firms to prefer to transfer their machines in the form of capital rather than as commodities for sale. It is necessary to analyze these relations of dependence if we are to understand the fundamental structural limits they place on the development of these economies.

1. Industrial development is dependent on an export sector for the foreign currency to buy the inputs utilized by the industrial sector. The first consequence of this dependence is the need to preserve the traditional export sector, which limits economically the development of the internal market by the conservation of backward relations of production and signifies, politically, the maintenance of power by traditional decadent oligarchies. In the countries where these sectors are controlled by foreign capital, it signifies the remittance abroad of high profits, and political dependence on those interests. Only in rare instances does foreign capital not control at least the marketing of these products. In response to these limitations, dependent countries in the 1930's and 1940's developed a policy of exchange restrictions and taxes on the national and foreign export sector; today they tend toward the gradual nationalization of production and toward the imposition of certain timid limitations on foreign control of the marketing of exported products. Furthermore, they seek, still somewhat timidly, to obtain better terms for the sale of their products. In recent decades, they have created mechanisms for international price

agreements, and today UNCTAD and ECLA press to obtain more favorable tariff conditions for these products on the part of the hegemonic centers. It is important to point out that the industrial development of these countries is dependent on the situation of the export sector, the continued existence of which they are obliged to accept.

2. Industrial development is, then, strongly conditioned by fluctuations in the balance of payments. This leads toward deficit due to the relations of dependence themselves. The causes of the deficit are three:

a) Trade relations take place in a highly monopolized international market, which tends to lower the price of raw materials and to raise the prices of industrial products, particularly inputs. In the second place, there is a tendency in modern technology to replace various primary products with synthetic raw materials. Consequently the balance of trade in these countries tends to be less favorable (even though they show a general surplus). The overall Latin American balance of trade from 1946 to 1968 shows a surplus for each of those years. The same thing happens in almost every underdeveloped country. However, the losses due to deterioration of the terms of trade (on the basis of data from ECLA and the International Monetary Fund), excluding Cuba, were $26,383 million for the 1951–66 period, taking 1950 prices as a base. If Cuba and Venezuela are excluded, the total is $15,925 million.

b) For the reasons already given, foreign capital retains control over the most dynamic sectors of the economy and repatriates a high volume of profit; consequently, capital accounts are highly unfavorable to dependent countries. The data show that the amount of capital leaving the country is much greater than the amount entering; this produces an enslaving deficit in capital accounts. To this must be added the deficit in certain services which are virtually under total foreign control—such as freight transport, royalty payments, technical aid, etc. Consequently, an important deficit is produced in the total balance of payments; thus limiting the possibility of importation of inputs for industrialization.

c) The result is that "foreign financing" becomes necessary, in two forms: to cover the existing deficit, and to "finance" development by means of loans for the stimulation of investments and to "supply" an internal economic surplus which was decapitalized to a large extent by the remittance of part of the surplus generated domestically and sent abroad as profits.

Foreign capital and foreign "aid" thus fill up the holes that they themselves created. The real value of this aid, however, is doubtful. If overcharges resulting from the restrictive terms of the aid are subtracted from the total amount of the grants, the average net flow, according to calculations of the Inter-American Economic and Social Council, is approximately 54 percent of the gross flow [5].

If we take account of certain further facts—that a high proportion of aid is paid in local currencies, that Latin American countries make contributions to international financial institutions, and that credits are often "tied"—we find a "real component of foreign aid" of 42.2 percent on a very favorable hypothesis and of 38.3 percent on a more realistic one [5, 11-33]. The gravity of the situation becomes even clearer if we consider that these credits are used in large part to finance North American investments, to subsidize foreign imports which compete with national products, to introduce technology not adapted to the needs of underdeveloped countries, and to invest in low-priority sectors of the national economies. The hard truth is that the underdeveloped countries have to pay for all of the "aid" they receive. This situation is generating an enormous protest movement by Latin American governments seeking at least partial relief from such negative relations.

3. Finally, industrial development is strongly conditioned by the technological monopoly exercised by imperialist centers. We have seen that the underdeveloped countries depend on the importation of machinery and raw materials for the development of their industries. However, these goods are not freely available in the international market; they are patented and usually belong to the big companies. The big companies do not sell machinery and processed raw materials as simple merchandise: they demand either the payment of royalties, etc., for their utilization or, in most cases, they convert these goods into capital and introduce them in the form of their own investments. This is how machinery which is replaced in the hegemonic centers by more advanced technology is sent to dependent countries as capital for the installation of affiliates. Let us pause and examine these relations, in order to understand their oppressive and exploitative character.

The dependent countries do not have sufficient foreign currency, for the reasons given. Local businessmen have financing difficulties, and they must pay for the utilization of certain patented techniques. These factors oblige the national bourgeois governments to facilitate the entry of foreign capital in order to supply the restricted national market, which is strongly protected by high tariffs in order to promote industrialization. Thus, foreign capital enters with all the advantages: in many cases, it is given exemption from exchange controls for the importation of machinery; financing of sites for installation of industries is provided; government financing agencies facilitate industrialization; loans are available from foreign and domestic banks, which prefer such clients; foreign aid often subsidizes such investments and finances complementary public investments; after installation, high profits obtained in such favorable circumstances can be reinvested freely. Thus it is not surprising that the data of the U.S. Department of Commerce reveal that the percentage of capital brought in from abroad by these companies is but a part of the total amount of invested capital. These data show that in the period from 1946 to 1967 the new entries of capital into Latin America for direct investment amounted to $5,415 million, while the sum of reinvested profits was $4,424 million. On the other hand, the transfers of profits from Latin America to the United States amounted to $14,775 million. If we estimate total profits as approximately equal to transfers plus reinvestments we have the sum of $18,983 million. In spite of enormous transfers of profits to the United States, the book value of the United States's direct investment in Latin America went from $3,045 million in 1946 to $10,213 million in 1967. From these data it is clear that: (1) Of the new investments made by U.S. companies in Latin America for the period 1946–67, 55 percent corresponds to new entries of capital and 45 percent to reinvestment of profits; in recent years, the trend is more marked, with reinvestments between 1960 and 1966 representing more than 60 percent of new investments. (2) Remittances remained at about 10 percent of book value throughout the period. (3) The ratio of remitted capital to new flow is around 2.7 for the period 1946–67; that is, for each dollar that enters $2.70 leaves. In the 1960's this ratio roughly doubled, and in some years was considerably higher.

The *Survey of Current Business* data on sources and uses of funds for direct North American investment in Latin America in the period 1957–64 show that, of the total sources of direct investment in Latin America, only 11.8 percent came from the United States. The remainder is in large part, the result of the activities of North American firms in Latin America (46.4 percent net income, 27.7 percent under the heading of depreciation), and from "sources located abroad" (14.1 percent). It is significant that the funds obtained abroad that are external to the companies are greater than the funds originating in the United States.

V. EFFECTS ON THE PRODUCTIVE STRUCTURE

It is easy to grasp, even if only superficially, the effects that this dependent structure has on the productive system itself in these countries and the role of this structure in determining a specified type of development, characterized by its dependent nature.

The productive system in the underdeveloped countries is essentially determined by these international relations. In the first place, the need to conserve the agrarian or mining export structure generates a combination between more advanced economic centers that extract surplus value from the more backward sectors, and also between internal "metropolitan" centers and internal interdependent "colonial" centers [10]. The unequal and combined character of capitalist development at the international level is reproduced internally in an acute form. In the second place the industrial and technological structure responds more closely to the interests of the multinational corporations than to internal developmental needs (conceived of not only in terms of the overall interests of the population, but also from the point of view of the interests of a national capitalist development). In the third place, the same technological and economic-financial concentration of the hegemonic economies is transferred without substantial alteration to very different economies and societies, giving rise to a highly unequal productive structure, a high concentration of incomes, underutilization of installed capacity, intensive exploitation of existing markets concentrated in large cities, etc.

The accumulation of capital in such circumstances assumes its own characteristics. In the first place, it is characterized by profound differences among domestic wage-levels, in the context of a local cheap labor market, combined with a capital-intensive technology. The result, from the point of view of relative surplus value, is a high rate of exploitation of labor power. (On measurements of forms of exploitation, see [3].)

This exploitation is further aggravated by the high prices of industrial products enforced by protectionism, exemptions and subsidies given by the national governments, and "aid" from hegemonic centers. Furthermore, since dependent accumulation is necessarily tied into the international economy, it is profoundly conditioned by the unequal and combined character of international capitalist economic relations, by the technological and financial control of the imperialist centers by the realities of the balance of payments, by the economic policies of the state, etc. The role of the state in the growth of national and foreign capital merits a much fuller analysis than can be made here.

Using the analysis offered here as a point of departure, it is possible to understand the limits that this productive system imposes on the growth of the internal markets of these countries. The survival of traditional relations in the countryside is a serious limitation on the size of the market, since industrialization does not offer hopeful prospects. The productive structure created by dependent industrialization limits the growth of the internal market.

First, it subjects the labor force to highly exploitative relations which limit its purchasing power. Second, in adopting a technology of intensive capital use, it creates very few jobs in comparison with population growth, and limits the generation of new sources of income. These two limitations affect the growth of the consumer goods market. Third, the remittance abroad of profits carries away part of the economic surplus generated within the country. In all these ways limits are put on the possible creation of basic national industries which could provide a market for the capital goods this surplus would make possible if it were not remitted abroad.

From this cursory analysis we see that the alleged backwardness of these economies is not due to a lack of integration with capitalism but that, on the contrary, the most powerful obstacles to their full development come from the way in which they are joined to this international system and its laws of development.

VI. SOME CONCLUSIONS: DEPENDENT REPRODUCTION

In order to understand the system of dependent reproduction and the socioeconomic institutions created by it, we must see it as part of a system of world economic relations based on monopolistic control of large-scale capital, on control of certain economic and financial centers over others, on a monopoly of a complex technology that leads to unequal and combined development at a national and international level. Attempts to analyze backwardness as a failure to assimilate more advanced models of production or to modernize are nothing more than ideology disguised as science. The same is true of the attempts to analyze this international economy in terms of relations among elements in free competition, such as the theory of comparative costs which seeks to justify the inequalities of the world economic system and to conceal the relations of exploitation on which it is based [14].

In reality we can understand what is happening in the underdeveloped countries only when we see that they develop within the framework of a process of dependent production and reproduction. This system is a dependent one because it reproduces a productive system whose development is limited by those world relations which necessarily lead to the development of only certain economic sectors, to trade under unequal conditions [9], to domestic competition with international capital under unequal conditions, to the imposition of relations of superexploitation of the domestic labor force with a view to dividing the economic surplus thus generated between internal and external forces of domination. (On economic surplus and its utilization in the dependent countries, see [1].)

In reproducing such a productive system and such international relations, the development of dependent capitalism reproduces the factors that prevent it from reaching a nationally and internationally advantageous situation; and it thus reproduces backwardness, misery, and social marginalization within its borders. The development that it produces benefits very narrow sectors, encounters unyielding domestic obstacles to its continued economic growth (with respect to both internal and foreign markets), and leads to the progressive accumulation of balance-of-payments deficits, which in turn generate more dependence and more superexploitation.

The political measures proposed by the developmentalists of ECLA, UNCTAD, BID, etc., do not appear to permit destruction of these terrible chains imposed by dependent development. We have examined the alternative forms of development presented for Latin America and the dependent countries under such conditions elsewhere [8]. Everything now indicates that what can be expected is a long process of sharp political and military confrontations and of profound social radicalization which will lead these countries to a dilemma: governments of force which open the way to facism, or popular revolutionary governments, which open the way to socialism. Intermediate solutions have proved to be, in such a contradictory reality, empty and utopian.

REFERENCES

1. Paul Baran, *Political Economy of Growth* (Monthly Review Press, 1967).
2. Thomas Baloch, *Unequal Partners* (Basil Blackwell, 1963).
3. Pablo Gonzalez Casanova, *Sociología de la explotación,* Siglo XXI (México, 1969).
4. CEPAL, *La CEPAL y el Análisis del Desarrollo Latinoamericano* (1968, Santiago, Chile).
5. Consejo Interamericano Economico Social (CIES) O.A.S., Interamerican Economic and Social Council, External Financing for Development in LA. *El Financiamiento Externo para el Desarrollo de América Latina* (Pan-American Union, Washington, 1969).

6. Theotonio Dos Santos, *El nuevo carácter de la dependencia*, CESO (Santiago de Chile, 1968).
7. ———, *La crisis de la teoría del desarrollo y las relaciones de dependencia en América Latina*, Boletín del CESO, 3 (Santiago, Chile, 1968).
8. ———, *La dependencia económica y las alternativas de cambio en América Latina*, Ponencia al IX Congreso Latinoamericano de Sociología (México, Nov., 1969).
9. A. Emmanuel, *L'Echange Inégal* (Maspero, Paris, 1969).
10. Andre G. Frank, *Development and Underdevelopment in Latin America* (Monthly Review Press, 1968).
11. I. V. Levin, *The Export Economies* (Harvard Univ. Press, 1964).
12. Gunnar Myrdal, *Asian Drama* (Pantheon, 1968).
13. K. Nkrumah, *Neocolonialismo, última etapa del imperialismo*, Siglo XXI (México, 1966).
14. Cristian Palloix, *Problemes de la Croissance en Economie Ouverte* (Maspero, Paris, 1969).

II

THE STRUCTURE OF THE INTERNATIONAL SYSTEM

DEFINING THE SYSTEM

A key concept used by analysts of international relations is the notion of an international system. As defined by K. J. Holsti, the term refers to "any system of independent political entitles . . . which interact with one another frequently and according to regularized processes."[1] These units can be tribes,

---

[1] See K. J. Holsti, *International Politics: A Framework for Analysis*, 2nd ed. (Englewood Cliffs, N.J.: Prentice-Hall, 1972), p. 29.

city-states, nations, or empires. The crucial point about them, however, is that they are formally independent of one another. Independence, of course, is not an absolute: in practice, the systems includes degrees of dependence as the weaker members of the system rely on the stronger for protection, and as the poorer look to the rich for economic aid and assistance. Nevertheless, even weaker units have some discretion and, unless they are assimilated within larger and more powerful units, are able to initiate policies of their own—policies that, on occasion, can cause problems for major powers. Sometimes the weak are able to manipulate the strong; often they are the objects or casualties of policies pursued by the stronger members of the system who engage in a mix of cooperative and competitive behavior with each other.

These patterns of interaction—specially but not exclusively among the great powers—are a primary focus of attention for students of international politics who are concerned with "describing the typical or characteristic behavior of these political units towards each other and explaining major changes in these patterns of interaction."[2]

In trying to explain particular kinds of occurrences (such as crises or war) within the international system, the analyst can ask similar questions about relations among the players, whether these be city-states in Renaissance Italy, Chinese warlords, Japanese daimyo, baronial fiefdoms in medieval Europe, or contemporary states. This is not to discount the importance of the units themselves. Nor is it to ignore the obvious point that the characteristics of the units have changed dramatically over time—in terms of size, political structures, degree of participation and centralization, technological and military capabilities, and many other attributes.

In this connection, one of the most significant developments in the period since the Treaty of Westphalia in 1648 has been the rise of the modern nation-state system. The European state system of the eighteenth and nineteenth centuries, based on the principles of national sovereignty and nonintervention, became the basis for a global system in the second half of the twentieth century—even though some new states of the Third World that evolved out of the decolonization process did not always exhibit a neat congruence between nation and state. In such instances, nation-building became the top priority of the state, dominating the agenda in both domestic and foreign policies. Even these states, however, have the requisites of formal sovereignty and are represented at the United Nations.

Although all states are formally sovereign, immense disparities in wealth and power exist. An important characteristic of the contemporary international system, therefore, is that it is very hierarchical—a hierarchy that ranges from the superpower or hegemonic status of the United States to a series of micro-states that possess less wealth and power than some of the city-states of

---

[2] Holsti, *International Politics*, p. 29.

earlier eras. Yet, even large and powerful states find themselves constrained and limited by the international system. The system provides the environment in which all states have to operate.[3] Consequently, the distribution of power, norms of behavior, and patterns of alignment and enmity that operate at the system level exert an important influence on the foreign policies of individual states. Indeed, a large element in foreign policy involves the efforts to adapt to the pressures, demands, and opportunities that arise at the level of the international system.

These pressures, demands, and opportunities vary in intensity in different kinds of international systems. In fact, one of the most important controversies about international politics has focused on the extent to which the interactions are determined by the distribution of power among the states in the system. Those who emphasize the importance of structural factors tend to argue, for example, that the Cold War was an inevitable consequence of bipolarity: in a two-power world, the two powers are preordained to be adversaries.[4] The implication is that whereas competing ideologies, misperceptions, and misunderstandings might have contributed to the Cold War, the distribution of power at the end of World War II made it inevitable that the Soviet Union and the United States would become adversaries.

Although the bipolar system is very familiar because of its salience during the Cold War years, it is not the only, nor even the most common, configuration of power. Analysts have identified other configurations of power, ranging from world empire through a bipolar world, a tripolar system of three great powers, to a multipolar system of five or more great powers.[5] In the sense that international systems are distinguished from one another by the number of great powers they contain, then the distribution of power is clearly a defining characteristic—and one that imposes its own particular requirements of system management and maintenance.

BIPOLAR AND MULTIPOLAR SYSTEMS

There is also an important distinction between change within an existing international system and more fundamental system transformations, which are characterized by major shifts in the distribution of power and in the number of great powers in the system. The end of World War II saw the dominance of

---

[3] This theme is developed by Arnold Wolfers, *Discord and Collaboration* (Baltimore: Johns Hopkins University Press, 1962), esp. pp. 13–16.

[4] This theme is developed in Louis J. Halle, *The Cold War as History* (New York: Harper and Row, 1967).

[5] One of the most comprehensive discussions of different kinds of international system is Morton A. Kaplan, *System and Process in International Politics* (New York: Wiley, 1957). See also Richard Rosecrance, *International Relations: Peace or War?* (New York: McGraw-Hill, 1973).

a bipolar system in which the United States and the Soviet Union developed rival alliance systems and competed for power and influence. In the 1970s, the Nixon administration enunciated the proposition that a new pentagonal or multipolar system was emerging in which the United States and the Soviet Union would be joined by Japan, China, and Western Europe as the dominant powers. Although this was premature, it remains a long-term possibility—albeit with Russia taking the place of the Soviet Union. The nature of the interactions and the prevailing patterns of conflict and cooperation or alignment and defection in such a system remain uncertain.

Questions about the stability of a pentagonal world are part of a broader and more fundamental issue facing analysts of international systems—that is, whether some systems or configurations of power are more prone than others to lead to war. This issue is generally cast in terms of the stability of the system and has become a particularly important theme now that the bipolar system of the Cold War world has disappeared. Accordingly, the initial selections in this section focus on the question of how different types of power configurations and the number of major powers impinge on patterns of cooperation, conflict, and alignment. In the first reading, Kenneth Waltz, the leading figure in the neo-realist school and author of the classic work *The Man, The State and War*, argues that a bipolar international system is one of the most stable kinds of international system. Although it can be argued that in a bipolar world the security dilemma—in which actions taken for defensive purposes are construed by others as offensive or threatening in character—that characterizes relations in anarchy is more intense than usual, in Waltz's view the system has a number of characteristics that make it relatively easy to manage. Most important, it is simple, with the result that the prospects for miscalculation are minimal. Multipolar systems, in contrast, suffer from several destabilizing factors, not the least of which is that they are much more complex and offer greater opportunity for war through miscalculation or misperception.

This thesis is juxtaposed with the contrary argument by Karl Deutsch and J. David Singer, two leading political scientists who have pioneered the use of quantitative techniques for the study of international relations. In their view, multipolarity is a relatively stable system largely because the greater the number of actors, the greater the number of interactions. Although, in the article from which this selection is taken, Singer and Deutsch acknowledge that multipolar systems may tend toward instability, their analysis nevertheless provides a useful counterpoint to that of Waltz.

A third important contribution to this debate was made by Morton Kaplan, whose earlier work identified six possible kinds of international system, including tight and loose bipolar systems. Although Kaplan's contribution was sometimes criticized as too abstract—and he acknowledged that only two of his six systems had historical counterparts—the part of his analysis we have excerpted focuses on a multipolar system with at least five "essential national actors," or great powers, and elucidates the rules or modes of behavior necessary for the functioning of this system. Kaplan's rules are normative in the sense that, if states want to maintain equilibrium, then these are the rules they have to follow. At the same time, Kaplan acknowledges the possibility of what he terms deviant behavior as well as the likelihood of the eventual breakdown of the system itself in the event that the rules are systematically violated. He also notes that all six of the rules he identifies are essential: a breakdown of one rule would significantly undermine the other rules. One conclusion that can be drawn from Kaplan's analysis concerns the sheer complexity of the balance of power system. In contrast, the bipolar system's simplicity made it much easier to manage.

Even so, it is difficult to derive unequivocal conclusions from an analysis of the bipolar system that existed during the Cold War. Stability during the Cold War years was a function not only of the system structure but also of the fear imposed by the possibility of nuclear war. This has particular relevance to the issue of nuclear proliferation, one of the key items on the post–Cold War security agenda. There are diametrically opposed views about the impact of the spread of nuclear capabilities to more and more states—what was known in the 1960s as the Nth power problem. One view of nuclear proliferation is that it is likely to enhance stability, by turning each state that possesses nuclear weapons into an inviolable sanctuary.[6] Ironically, Kenneth Waltz, the leading proponent of the argument that stability is a function of bipolarity, has argued that, so far as proliferation is concerned, more nuclear weapons states may be better than fewer.[7]

The other, and more common, view is that the more states that have nuclear weapons, the greater the potential for miscalculation, accident, or even deliberate use. New nuclear powers are unlikely to have the resources to build the kind of invulnerable retaliatory systems that were developed and deployed by the two nuclear superpowers and are an indispensable contribution to crisis stability. Nor are they likely to have the resources to build the elaborate command, control, communications, and safeguards systems necessary to reduce the prospects of accidental use. A major question to consider for the future, therefore, is at what point the diffusion of nuclear weapons introduces fundamentally new instabilities into the international system. Such an assessment is unlikely to be easy, but the discussions of the international system in this section provide many insights applicable to the problems of instability in an increasingly nuclear world.

If particular attention has to be paid to the distribution of power among the constituent units, other questions about the international system also have to be addressed. It is important, for example, to consider whether the system is divided by ideological conflicts or by the states—or at least the major powers—sharing

---

[6] This view was put forward in the 1950s by the French strategist Pierre Gallois in *The Balance of Terror* (Boston: Houghton Mifflin, 1961).

[7] Kenneth Waltz, *The Spread of Nuclear Weapons: More May Be Better*, Adelphi Paper 171 (London: International Institute for Strategic Studies).

the same basic values about the rules of permissible behavior. It is important to know the extent to which the great powers share fundamentally similar outlooks and values. Indeed, conflict in a homogeneous international system is likely to be easier to manage than the clash of values and ideologies in a heterogeneous system.[8]

UNDERLYING COMPLEXITIES

Another aspect of the international system to be considered is the notion of system change—whether through evolution or more rapid and often violent upheaval. In this connection, one of the most interesting characteristics of the bipolar international system of the period from 1945 to the late 1980s is that, even before the demise of the Soviet Union removed one of the poles, a series of gradual and subtle changes had transformed it into a much more complex multilevel system.[9] Underneath the strategic and geopolitical competition between the United States and the Soviet Union there developed other, more complex layers of relations. The two blocs were fractured in the one case by the development of the Sino-Soviet rift and in the other by French aspirations to greater status and independence, aspirations that led de Gaulle to challenge American dominance of the Atlantic Alliance. Indeed, during the 1960s the problems of alliance management became in some ways even more complex than those involved in managing the central strategic relationship between Moscow and Washington.

Many of the more complex formulations of the international system, however, still focused primarily on interstate relations. Some argue that such an exclusive focus is too narrow. Many critics—both liberals who emphasize the growth of economic interdependence and analysts who identify and highlight patterns of economic dependence—contend that concentrating solely on states offers only a partial and in some ways distorted assessment of international relations. States are, after all, only one of many actors, and focusing on issues such as system structure or system stability obscures other equally important dimensions of international activity. Seeing the international system solely in terms of states underestimates the importance of transnational actors and forces and ignores the development of various interdependencies that, in crucial respects, have altered the nature of the system and have had an impact on the foreign policies of even large, powerful states. Before moving from the system level to the level of the actors in international relations, therefore, we

---

[8] Raymond Aron, the famous French commentator on international relations, dealt with homogeneous and heterogeneous international systems in his work *Peace and War: A Theory of International Relations* (New York: Praeger Publishers, 1968).

[9] This theme was developed in Stanley Hoffmann, *Gulliver's Troubles* (New York: McGraw-Hill, 1968).

have included a selection from James Rosenau, University Professor of International Affairs at George Washington University and one of the most imaginative and pioneering analysts in the field of international relations. Rosenau has provided a very compelling analysis that goes well beyond the traditional state-dominated models of international relations. He has argued that there are in fact two worlds of world politics—the state-centric system and the multi-centric system. The former is the traditional one, long the focus of realism and neo-realism. The latter is a much more diverse grouping of actors who vary considerably in nature, size, focus, and influence but have in common their lack of statehood and all its attributes. Rather than focus on the "non-state" nature of these entities (which suggests that they lack something important), Rosenau contends that we should view them as "sovereignty-free" and recognize that this endows them with certain advantages. The selection elucidates the key elements in these two worlds, highlights the differences in their functioning, and looks at possible patterns of interaction between them. It is supplemented with an important analysis done by Robert Keohane and Joseph Nye in the 1970s that highlighted the growing interdependencies among states and elaborated upon the characteristics of what the authors termed complex interdependence.

More radical critics argue that the traditional focus on states obscures underlying political and economic patterns of exploitation and dependence. Their emphasis is not on the power hierarchy but on a worldwide system in which there are economically rich and powerful interests at the center of the global economy and poor and exploited populations on the periphery. This world systems approach presents an even more fundamental challenge to the traditional emphasis of the realists and neo-realists than does the analysis of Rosenau. With its roots in neo-Marxism, world systems theory traces patterns of the evolution of the international system, not only in traditional terms of the rise and fall of nations but in terms of dominance and exploitation. Immanuel Wallerstein, one of the leading figures in the world systems approach, traced the rise of the world capitalist system to sixteenth-century Europe, distinguishing between three economic areas: the core, the periphery, and the semi-periphery.[10] It should be emphasized, however, that Wallerstein does not ignore states—he simply argues that the economic and political development of states has to be seen in terms of their function and role in the world economy. What this has in common with neo-realism and the analysis of Kenneth Waltz is an emphasis on structure. The difference is that Waltz focuses on the structure of the international system whereas world systems theorists focus on the structure of the world economy. As we see in Section III, however, those who focus on actors tend to see this concern with structure, of whatever kind, as overly determinist.

---

[10] See Immanuel Wallerstein, *The Capitalist World Economy* (New York: Cambridge University Press, 1979).

13

KENNETH N. WALTZ

THE STABILITY OF A
BIPOLAR WORLD

There is a conventional wisdom, accumulated over the centuries, upon which statesmen and students often draw as they face problems in international politics. One part of the conventional wisdom is now often forgotten. Many in Europe, and some in America, have come to regard an alliance as unsatisfactory if the members of it are grossly unequal in power. "Real partnership," one hears said in a variety of ways, "is possible only between equals." [1] If this is true, an addendum should read: Only unreal partnerships among states have lasted beyond the moment of pressing danger. Where states in association have been near equals, some have voluntarily abdicated the leadership to others, or the alliance has become paralyzed by stalemate and indecision, or it has simply dissolved. One may observe that those who are less than equal are often dissatisfied without thereby concluding that equality in all things is good. As Machiavelli and Bismarck well knew, an alliance requires an alliance leader; and leadership can be most easily maintained where the leader is superior in power. Some may think of these two exemplars as unworthy; even so, where the unworthy were wise, their wisdom should be revived.

A second theorem of the conventional wisdom is still widely accepted. It reads: A world of many powers is more stable than a bipolar world, with stability measured by the peacefulness of adjustment within the international system and by the durability of the system itself. While the first element of the conventional wisdom might well be revived, the second should be radically revised.

Pessimism about the possibility of achieving stability in a two-power world was reinforced after the war by contemplation of the character of the two major contenders. The Soviet Union, led by a possibly psychotic Stalin, and the United States, flaccid, isolationist by tradition, and untutored in the ways of international relations, might well have been thought unsuited to the task of finding a route to survival. How could either reconcile itself to coexistence when ideological differences were great and antithetical interests provided constant occasion for conflict? Yet the bipolar world of the postwar period has shown a remarkable stability. Measuring time from the termination

SOURCE: From Kenneth Waltz, "The Stability of a Bipolar World," *Daedalus*, 93:3 (Summer, 1964), pp. 881–909. © 1964 by the American Academy of Arts and Sciences. Reprinted with permission.

of war, 1964 corresponds to 1937. Despite all of the changes in the nineteen years since 1945 that might have shaken the world into another great war, 1964 somehow looks and feels safer than 1937. Is this true only because we now know that 1937 preceded the holocaust by just two years? Or is it the terror of nuclear weapons that has kept the world from major war? Or is the stability of the postwar world intimately related to its bipolar pattern?

STABILITY WITHIN A BIPOLAR SYSTEM

Within a bipolar world, four factors conjoined encourage the limitation of violence in the relations of states. First, with only two world powers there are no peripheries. The United States is the obsessing danger for the Soviet Union, and the Soviet Union for us, since each can damage the other to an extent that no other state can match. Any event in the world that involves the fortunes of the Soviet Union or the United States automatically elicits the interest of the other. Truman, at the time of the Korean invasion, could not very well echo Chamberlain's words in the Czechoslovakian crisis and claim that the Koreans were a people far away in the east of Asia of whom Americans knew nothing. We had to know about them or quickly find out. In the 1930's, France lay between England and Germany. England could believe, and we could too, that their frontier and ours lay on the Rhine. After World War II, no third power could lie between the United States and the Soviet Union, for none existed. The statement that peace is indivisible was controversial, indeed untrue, when it was made by Litvinov in the 1930's. It became a truism in the 1950's. Any possibility of maintaining a general peace required a willingness to fight small wars. With the competition both serious and intense, a loss to one could easily appear as a gain to the other, a conclusion that follows from the very condition of a two-power competition. Political action has corresponded to this assumption. Communist guerrillas operating in Greece prompted the Truman doctrine. The tightening of Soviet control over the states of Eastern Europe led to the Marshall Plan and the Atlantic Defense Treaty, and these in turn gave rise to the Cominform and the Warsaw Pact. The plan to form a West German government produced the Berlin blockade. Our response in a two-power world was geared to Soviet action, and theirs to ours, which produced an increasingly solid bipolar balance.

Not only are there no peripheries in a bipolar world but also, as a second consideration, the range of factors included in the competition is extended as the intensity of the competition increases. Increased intensity is expressed in a reluctance to accept small territorial losses, as in Korea, the Formosa Strait, and Indo-China. Extension of range is apparent wherever one looks. Vice President Nixon hailed the Supreme Court's desegregation decision as our greatest victory in the cold war. When it became increasingly clear that the Soviet economy was growing at a rate that far exceeded our own, many began to worry that falling behind in the economic race would lead to our losing the cold war without a shot being fired. Disarmament negotiations have most often been taken as an opportunity for propaganda. As contrasted with the 1930's, there is now constant and effective concern lest military preparation fall below the level necessitated by the military efforts of the major antagonist. Changes between the wars affected different states differently, with adjustment to the varying ambitions and abilities of states dependent on cumbrous mechanisms of compensation and realignment. In a multipower balance, who is a danger to whom is often a most obscure matter: the incentive to regard all disequilibrating changes with concern and respond to them with whatever effort may be required is consequently weakened. In our present world changes may affect each of the two powers differently, and this means all the more that few changes in the national realm or in the world at large are likely to be thought irrelevant. Policy proceeds by imitation, with occasional attempts to outflank.

The third distinguishing factor in the bipolar balance, as we have thus far known it, is the nearly constant presence of pressure and the recurrence of crises. It would be folly to assert that repeated threats and recurring crises necessarily decrease danger and promote stability. It may be equally wrong to assert the opposite, as Khrushchev seems to appreciate. "They frighten us with war," he told the Bulgarians in May of 1962, "and we frighten them back bit by bit. They threaten us with nuclear arms and we tell them: 'Listen, now only fools can do this, because we have them too, and they are not smaller than yours but, we think, even better than yours. So why do you do foolish things and frighten us? This is the situation, and this is why we consider the situation to be good.' " [2] Crises, born of a condition in which interests and ambitions conflict, are produced by the determination of one state to effect a change that another state chooses to resist. With the Berlin blockade, for example, as with Russia's emplacement of missiles in Cuba, the United States decided that to resist the change the Soviet Union sought to bring about was worth the cost of turning its action into a crisis. If the condition of conflict remains, the absence of crisis be comes more disturbing than their recurrence. Rather a large crisis now than a small war later is an axiom that should precede the statement, often made, that to fight small wars in the present may be the means of avoiding large wars later.

Admittedly, crises also occur in a multipower world, but the dangers are diffused, responsibilities unclear, and definition of vital interests easily obscured. The skillful foreign policy, where many states are in balance, is designed to gain an advantage over one state without antagonizing others and frightening them into united action. Often in modern Europe, possible gains have seemed greater than likely losses. Statesmen could thus hope in crises to push an issue to the limit without causing all the potential opponents to unite. When possible enemies are several in number, unity of action among states is difficult to secure. One could therefore think—or hope desperately, as did Bethmann Hollweg and Adolf Hitler—that no united opposition would form.

In a bipolar world, on the other hand, attention is focused on crises by both of the major competitors, and especially by the defensive state. To move piecemeal and reap gains serially is difficult, for within a world in confusion there is one great certainty, namely, the knowledge of who will oppose whom. One's motto may still be, "push to the limit," but *limit* must be emphasized as heavily as *push*. Caution, moderation, and the management of crisis come to be of great and obvious importance.

Many argue, nonetheless, that caution in crises, and resulting bipolar stability, is accounted for by the existence of nuclear weapons, with the number of states involved comparatively inconsequent. That this is a doubtful deduction can be indicated by a consideration of how nuclear weapons may affect reactions to crises. In the postwar world, bipolarity preceded the construction of two opposing atomic weapons systems. The United States, with some success, substituted technological superiority for expenditure on a conventional military system as a deterrent to the Soviet Union during the years when we had first an atomic monopoly and then a decisive edge in quantity and quality of weapons. American military policy was not a matter of necessity but of preference based on a calculation of advantage. Some increase in expenditure and a different allocation of monies would have enabled the United States to deter the Soviet Union by posing credibly the threat that any Soviet attempt, say, to overwhelm West Germany would bring the United States into a large-scale conventional war.* For the Soviet Union, war against separate European states would have promised large gains; given the bipolar balance, no such war could be undertaken without the clear prospect of American entry. The Russians' appreciation of the situation is perhaps best illustrated by the structure of their military forces. The Soviet Union has concentrated heavily on medium-range bombers and missiles and, to our surprise, has built relatively few intercontinental weapons. The country of possibly aggressive intent has assumed a posture of passive deterrence vis-à-vis her major adversary, whom she quite sensibly does not want to fight. Against European and other lesser states, the Soviet Union has a considerable offensive capability.† Hence nuclear capabilities merely reinforce a condition that would exist in their absence: without nuclear technology both the United States and the Soviet Union have the ability to develop weapons of considerable destructive power. Even had the atom never been split, each would lose heavily if it were to engage in a major war against the other.

If number of states is less important than the existence of nuclear power, then one must ask whether the world balance would continue to be stable were three or more states able to raise themselves to comparable levels of nuclear potency. For many reasons one doubts that the equilibrium would be so secure. Worries about accidents and triggering are widespread, but a still greater danger might well arise. The existence of a number of nuclear states would increase the temptation for the more virile of them to maneuver, with defensive states paralyzed by the possession of military forces the use of which would mean their own destruction. One would be back in the 1930's, with the addition of a new dimension of strength which would increase the pressures upon status quo powers to make piecemeal concessions.

Because bipolarity preceded a two-power nuclear competition, because in the absence of nuclear weapons destructive power would still be great, because the existence of a number of nuclear states would increase the range of difficult political choices, and finally, as will be discussed below, because nuclear weapons must first be seen as a product of great national capabilities rather than as their cause, one is led to the conclusion that nuclear weapons cannot by themselves be used to explain the stability—or the instability—of international systems.

Taken together, these three factors—the absence of peripheries, the range and intensity of competition, and the persistence of pressure and crisis—are among the most important characteristics of the period since World War II. The first three points combine to produce an intense competition in a wide arena with a great variety of means employed. The constancy of effort of the two major contenders, combined with a fourth factor, their preponderant power, have made for a remarkable ability to comprehend and absorb within the bipolar balance the revolutionary political, military, and economic changes that have occurred. . . .

The effects of American-Soviet preponderance are complex. Its likely continuation and even its present existence are subjects of controversy. The stability of a system has to be defined in terms of its durability, as well as of the peacefulness of adjustment within it. . . .

SOME DISSENTING OPINIONS

The fact remains that many students of international relations have continued to judge bipolarity unstable as compared to the probable stability of a multi-power world. Why have they been so confident that the existence of a number of powers, moving in response to constantly recurring variations in national power and purpose, would promote the desired stability? According to Professors Morgenthau and Kaplan, the uncertainty that results from flexibility of alignment generates a healthy caution in the foreign policy of every country.[3] Concomitantly, Professor Morgenthau believes that in the present bipolar world, "the flexibility of the balance of power and, with it, its restraining influence upon the power aspirations of the main protagonists on the international scene have disappeared."[4] One may agree with his conclusion and yet draw from his analysis another one unstated by him: The inflexibility of a bipolar world, with the appetite for power of each major competitor at once whetted and checked by the other, may promote a greater stability than flexible balances of power among a larger number of states.

What are the grounds for coming to a diametrically different conclusion? The presumed double instability of a bipolar world, that it easily erodes or explodes, is to a great extent based upon its assumed bloc character. A bloc improperly managed may indeed fall apart. The leader of each bloc must be concerned at once with alliance management, for the defection of an allied state might be fatal to its partners, and with the aims and capabilities of the opposing bloc. The system is more complex than is a multipower balance, which in part accounts for its fragility.[‡] The situation preceding World War I provides a striking example. The dissolution of the Austro-Hungarian Empire would have left Germany alone in the center of Europe. The approximate equality of alliance partners, or their relation of true interdependence, plus the closeness of competition between the two camps, meant that while any country could commit its associates, no one country on either side could exercise control. By contrast, in 1956 the United States could dissociate itself from the Suez adventure of its two principal allies and even subject them to pressure. Great Britain, like Austria in 1914, tried to commit, or at least immobilize, its alliance partner by presenting him with a *fait accompli*. Enjoying a position of predominance, the United States could, as Germany could not, focus its attention on the major adversary while disciplining its ally. The situations are in other respects different, but the ability of the United States, in contrast to Germany, to pay a price measured in intraalliance terms is striking.

It is important, then, to distinguish sharply a bipolarity of blocs from a bipolarity of countries. Fénelon thought that of all conditions of balance the opposition of two states was the happiest. Morgenthau dismisses this judgment with the comment that the benefits Fénelon had hoped for had not accrued in our world since the war, which depends, one might think, on what benefits had otherwise been expected.[§]

The conclusion that a multipower balance is relatively stable is reached by overestimating the system's flexibility, and then dwelling too fondly upon its effects.[¶] A constant shuffling of alliances would be as dangerous as an unwillingness to make new combinations. Neither too slow nor too fast: the point is a fine one, made finer still by observing that the rules should be followed not merely out of an immediate interest of the state but also for the sake of preserving the international system. The old balance-of-power system here looks suspiciously like the new collective-security system of the League of Nations and the United Nations. Either system depends for its maintenance and functioning upon a "neutrality of alignment" at the moment of serious threat. To preserve the system, the powerful states must overcome the constraints of previous ties and the pressures of both ideological preferences and conflicting present interests in order to confront the state that threatens the system.[5]

In the history of the modern state system, flexibility of alignment has been conspicuously absent just when, in the interest of stability, it was most highly desirable.[6] A comparison of flexibility within a multipower world with the ability of the two present superpowers to compensate for changes by their internal efforts is requisite, for comparison changes the balance of optimism and pessimism as customarily applied to the two different systems. In the world of the

1930's, with a European grouping of three, the Western democracies, out of lassitude, political inhibition, and ideological distaste, refrained from acting or from combining with others at the advantageous moment. War provided the pressure that forced the world's states into two opposing coalitions. In peacetime the bipolar world displays a clarity of relations that is ordinarily found only in war. Raymond Aron has pointed out that the international "système depend de ce que sont, concrètement, les deux pôles, non pas seulement du fait qu'ils sont deux." [7] Modifying Aron's judgment and reversing that of many others, we would say that in a bipolar world, as compared to one of many powers, the international system is more likely to dominate. External pressures, if clear and great enough, force the external combination or the internal effort that interest requires. The political character of the alliance partner is then most easily overlooked and the extent to which foreign policy is determined by ideology is decreased.

The number of great states in the world has always been so limited that two acting in concert or, more common historically, one state driving for hegemony could reasonably conclude that the balance would be altered by their actions. In the relations of states since the Treaty of Westphalia, there have never been more than eight great powers, the number that existed, if one is generous in admitting doubtful members to the club, on the eve of the First World War. Given paucity of members, states cannot rely on an equilibrating tendency of the system. Each state must instead look to its own means, gauge the likelihood of encountering opposition, and estimate the chances of successful cooperation. The advantages of an international system with more than two members can at best be small. A careful evaluation of the factors elaborated above indicates that the disadvantages far outweigh them.

NOTES

* The point has been made by Raymond Aron, among others. "Even if it had not had the bomb, would the United States have tolerated the expansion of the Soviet empire as far as the Atlantic? And would Stalin have been ready to face the risk of general war?" Raymond Aron, *The Century of Total War* (Boston: Beacon Press, 1955), p. 151.

† Hanson W. Baldwin, from information supplied by Strategic Air Command headquarters, estimates that Russian intercontinental missiles are one-fourth to one-fifth as numerous as ours, though Russian warheads are larger. The Russians have one-sixth to one-twelfth the number of our long-range heavy bombs, with ours having a greater capability (*New York Times,* November 21, 1963). In medium range ballistic missiles Russia has been superior. A report of the Institute of Strategic Studies estimated that as of October, 1962, Russia had 700 such missiles, the West a total of 250 (*New York Times,* November 9, 1962). British sources tend to place Russian capabilities in the medium range higher than do American estimates. Cf. P. M. S. Blackett, "The Real Road to Disarmament: The Military Background to the Geneva Talks," *New Statesman* (March 2, 1962), pp. 295–300, with Hanson W. Baldwin, *New York Times,* November 26, 1961.

‡Morton A. Kaplan, *System and Process in International Politics* (New York: Wiley, 1957), p. 37; and "Bipolarity in a Revolutionary Age," in Kaplan, ed., *The Revolution in World Politics* (New York: Wiley, 1962), p. 254. The difficulties and dangers found in a bipolar world by Kaplan are those detected by Hans J. Morgenthau in a system of opposing alliances. It is of direct importance in assessing the stability of international systems to note that Morgenthau finds "the opposition of two alliances . . . the most frequent configuration within the system of the balance of power" (*Politics Among Nations* [3d ed.; New York: Knopf, 1961, part 4], p. 189). Kaplan, in turn, writes that "the most likely transformation of the 'balance of power' system is to a bipolar system" (*System and Process*, p. 36).

§Kaplan, though he treats the case almost as being trivial, adds a statement that is at least suggestive: "The tight bipolar system is stable only when both bloc actors are hierarchically organized" (*System and Process*, p. 43).

¶Kaplan, e.g., by the fourth and sixth of his rules of a balance-of-power system, requires a state to oppose any threatening state and to be willing to ally with any other (*System and Process*, p. 23).

REFERENCES

1. Henry Kissinger, "Strains on the Alliance," *Foreign Affairs,* XI.I (January, 1963), 284. Cf. Max Kohnstamm, "The European Tide," *Daedalus,* XCIII (Winter, 1964), 101–102; McGeorge Bundy's speech to the Economic Club of Chicago, *New York Times,* December 7, 1961; John F. Kennedy, "Address at Independence Hall," Philadelphia, July 4, 1962. *Public Papers of the Presidents of the United States* (Washington, D.C.: Government Printing Office, 1963), pp. 537–539.

2. Quoted in V. D. Sokolovskii, ed., *Soviet Military Strategy,* Herbert S. Dinerstein, Leon Gouré, and Thomas W. Wolfe, translators and English editors (Englewood Cliffs: Prentice-Hall, 1963), p. 43.

3. Hans J. Morgenthau, *Politics Among Nations* (3d ed.; New York: Knopf, 1961), part 4. Morton A. Kaplan, *System and Process in International Politics* (New York: Wiley, 1957), pp. 22–36. I shall refer only to Morgenthau and Kaplan, for their writings are widely known and represent the majority opinion of students in the field.

4. Morgenthau, *Politics Among Nations,* p. 350. Cf. Kaplan, *System and Process,* pp. 36–43; and Kaplan, "Bipolarity in a Revolutionary Age," in Kaplan, ed., *The Revolution in World Politics* (New York: Wiley, 1963), pp. 251–266.

5. The point is nicely made in an unpublished paper by Wolfram F. Hanrieder, "Actor Objectives and International Systems" (Center of International Studies, Princeton University, February, 1964), pp. 43.

6. For a sharp questioning of "the myth of flexibility," see George Liska's review article "Continuity and Change in International Systems," *World Politics,* XVI (October, 1963), 122–123.

7. Raymond Aron, *Paix et Guerre entre les Nations* (Paris: Calmann-Lévy, 1962), p. 156.

14

KARL W. DEUTSCH AND
J. DAVID SINGER

MULTIPOLAR POWER SYSTEMS AND INTERNATIONAL STABILITY

In the classical literature of diplomatic history, the balance-of-power concept occupies a central position. Regardless of one's interpretation of the term or one's preference for or antipathy to it, the international relations scholar cannot escape dealing with it. The model is, of course, a multifaceted one, and it produces a fascinating array of corollaries; among these, the relationship between the number of actors and the stability of the system is one of the most widely accepted and persuasive. That is, as the system moves away from bipolarity toward multipolarity, the frequency and intensity of war should be expected to diminish.

To date, however, that direct correlation has not been subjected to rigorous scrutiny by either abstract or empirical test. For the most part, it has seemed so intuitively reasonable that a few historical illustrations have been accepted as sufficient. This is, on balance, not enough to support a lawful generaliza-tion; it must eventually be put to the historical test. This will be done eventually,[1] but in the interim this hypothesis should at least be examined on formal, abstract grounds. The purpose of this article, therefore, is to present two distinct—but related—lines of formal, semi-quantitative, argument as to why the diffusion-stability relationship should turn out as the theoretician has generally assumed and as the historian has often found to be the case.

I. A PROBABILISTIC CONCEPT OF INTERNATIONAL POLITICAL STABILITY

Stability may, of course, be considered from the vantage point of both the total system and the individual states comprising it. From the broader, or systemic, point of view, we shall define stability as the probability that the system retains all of its essential characteristics; that no single nation becomes dominant; that

SOURCE: From *World Politics,* Vol. 16, No. 3 (April 1964), pp. 390–400, 404–406. Reprinted with permission of The Johns Hopkins University Press and J. David Singer.

most of its members continue to survive; and that large-scale war does not occur. And from the more limited perspective of the individual nations, stability would refer to the probability of their continued political independence and territorial integrity without any significant probability of becoming engaged in a "war for survival." The acceptable level of this probability—such as 90, or 95, or 99 per cent—seems to be intuitively felt by political decision-makers, without necessarily being made explicit, but it could be inferred by investigators in the analysis of particular cases. A more stringent definition of stability would require also a low probability of the actors' becoming engaged even in limited wars. . . .

II. THE ACCELERATED RISE OF INTERACTION OPPORTUNITIES

The most obvious effect of an increase in the number of independent actors is an increase in the number of possible pairs or dyads in the total system. This assumes, of course, that the number of independent actors is responsive to the general impact of coalition membership, and that as a nation enters into the standard coalition it is much less of a free agent than it was while non-aligned. That is, its alliance partners now exercise an inhibiting effect—or perhaps even a veto—upon its freedom to interact with non-alliance nations.

This reduction in the number of possible dyadic relations produces, both for any individual nation and for the totality of those in the system, a corresponding diminution in the number of opportunities for interaction with other actors. Although it must be recognized at the outset that, in the international system of the nineteenth and twentieth centuries, such opportunities are as likely to be competitive as they are to be cooperative, the overall effect is nevertheless destabilizing. The argument is nothing more than a special case of the widely employed pluralism model.

In that model, our focus is on the degree to which the system exhibits negative feedback as well as cross-pressuring. By negative—as distinguished from positive or amplifying—feedback, we refer to the phenomenon of self-correction: as stimuli in one particular direction increase, the system exhibits a decreasing response to those stimuli, and increasingly exhibits tendencies that counteract them. This is the self-restraining system, manifested in the automatic pilot, the steam-engine governor, and most integrated social systems, and it stands in contrast to the self-aggravating system as seen in forest fires, compound interest, nuclear fission, runaway inflation or deflation, and drug addiction.[2]

The pluralistic model asserts that the amplifying feedback tendency is strengthened, and the negative feedback tendency is weakened, to the extent that conflict positions are superimposed or reinforcing. Thus, if all clashes and incompatibilities in the system produce the same divisions and coalitions—if all members in class Blue line up *with* one another and *against* all or most of those in class Red—the line of cleavage will be wide and deep, with positive feedback operating both within and between the two classes or clusters. But if some members of class Blue have some incompatible interests with others in their class, and an overlap of interests with some of those in Red, there will be some degree of negative or self-correcting feedback both within and between the two classes.

This notion is analogous to that of cross-cutting pressure familiar to the student of politics. Here we observe that every individual plays a fairly large number of politically relevant roles and that most of these pull him in somewhat different attitudinal, behavioral, and organizational directions. For example, if an individual is (1) a loving parent, (2) a member of a militant veterans organization, (3) owner of a factory, and (4) a Catholic, the first and third factors will tend to deflect him toward a "coexistence" foreign policy, the second will pull him toward a "holy war" orientation, and his religious affiliation will probably (in the 1960's) produce a deep ambivalence. Likewise, following Ralf Dahrendorf's formulation, if status difference is a major determinant of conflict exacerbation, and an individual is head of a family, a bank teller, and president of the lodge, he will coalesce with and against different people on different issues.[3] In each of these cases, his relatively large number of interaction opportunities produces a set of cross-pressures such as largely to inhibit any superimposition or reinforcement. The consequence would seem to favor social stability and to inhibit social cleavage; increasing differentiation and role specialization in industrial society has, in a sense, counteracted the Marxian expectation of class warfare.

Thus, in any given bilateral relationship, a rather limited range of possible interactions obtains, even if the relationship is highly symbiotic. But as additional actors are brought into the system, the range of possible interactions open to each—and hence to the total system—increases. In economics, this accretion produces the transformation from barter to market, and in any social setting it produces a comparable increase in the range and flexibility of possible interactions. Traditionally, social scientists have believed—and observed—that as the number of possible exchanges increases, so does the probability that the "invisible hand" of pluralistic interests will be effective. One might say that one of the greatest threats to the stability of any impersonal social system is the shortage of alternative partners.

NOTES

* Research used in this article has been supported in part by the Carnegie Corporation.
  1. Data-gathering on this topic is currently being carried on by David Singer.
  2. For an application of these and related concepts to a range of political questions, see Karl W. Deutsch, *The Nerves of Government* (New York, 1963).
  3. Ralf Dahrendorf, "Toward a Theory of Social Conflict," *Journal of Conflict Resolution,* 11 (June, 1958), 176–77.

15

MORTON KAPLAN
_____

RULES FOR THE BALANCE
OF POWER SYSTEM

. . .The "balance of power" international system is an international social system that does not have as a component a political sub-system. The actors within the system are exclusively national actors, such as France, Germany, Italy, etc. Five national actors—as a minimum—must fall within the classification "essential national actor"[1] to enable the system to work.

The "balance of power" international system is characterized by the operation of the following essential rules, which constitute the characteristic behavior of the system: (1) increase capabilities, but negotiate rather than fight; (2) fight rather than fail to increase capabilities; (3) stop fighting rather than eliminate an essential actor; (4) oppose any coalition or single actor that tends to assume a position of predominance within the system; (5) constrain actors who subscribe to supranational organizational principles; and (6) permit defeated or constrained essential national actors to re-enter the system as acceptable role partners, or act to bring some previously inessential actor within the essential actor classification. Treat all essential actors as acceptable role partners.

The first two rules of the "balance of power" international system reflect the fact that no political sub-system exists within the international social system. Therefore, essential national actors must rely upon themselves or upon their allies for protection. However, if they are weak, their allies may desert them. Therefore, an essential national actor must ultimately be capable of protecting its own national values. The third essential rule illustrates the fact that other nations are valuable as potential allies. In addition, nationality may set limits on potential expansion.

The fourth and fifth rules give recognition to the fact that a predominant coalition or national actor would constitute a threat to the interests of other national actors. Moreover, if a coalition were to become predominant, then the largest member of that coalition might also become predominant over the lesser members of its own coalition. For this reason members of a successful coalition may be alienated; they may also be able to bargain for more from the losers than from their own allies.

_____

SOURCE: From Morton A. Kaplan, "Some Problems of International Systems Research," in *International Political Communities: An Anthology* (Garden City and New York: Doubleday and Company, 1966), pp. 469–501. Reprinted with permission of the author.

The sixth rule states that membership in the system is dependent upon only behavior that corresponds with the essential rules or norms of the "balance of power" system. If the number of essential actors is reduced, the "balance of power" international system will become unstable. Therefore, maintaining the number of essential national actors above a critical lower bound is a necessary condition for the stability of the system. This is best done by returning to full membership in the system defeated actors or reformed deviant actors.

Although any particular action or alignment may be the product of "accidents," i.e., of the set of specific conditions producing the action or alignment, including such elements as chance meetings or personality factors, a high correlation between the pattern of national behavior and the essential rules of the international system would represent a confirmation of the predictions of the theory.

Just as any particular molecule of gas in a gas tank may travel in any direction, depending upon accidental bumpings with other molecules, particular actions of national actors may depend upon chance or random conjunctions. Yet, just as the general pattern of behavior of the gas may represent its adjustment to pressure and temperature conditions within the tank, the set of actions of national actors may correspond to the essential rules of the system when the other variables take the appropriate specified values.

By shifting the focus of analysis from the particular event to the type of event, seemingly accidental events may become part of a meaningful pattern. In this way, the historical loses its quality of uniqueness and is translated into the universal language of science.

The number of essential rules cannot be reduced. The failure of any rule to operate will result in the failure of at least one other rule. Moreover, at this level of abstraction, there does not seem to be any other rule that is interrelated with the specified set in this fashion.

Any essential rule of the system is in equilibrium[2] with the remaining rules of the set. This does not imply that particular rules can appear only in one kind of international system. The first two rules, for instance, also apply to bloc leaders in the bipolar system. However, they are necessary to each of the systems and, in their absence, other rules of the two systems will be transformed.

The rules of the system are interdependent. For instance, the failure to restore or to replace defeated essential national actors eventually will interfere with the formation of coalitions capable of constraining deviant national actors or potentially predominant coalitions.

The equilibrium of the set of rules is not a continuous equilibrium but one that results from discrete actions over periods of time. Therefore, the possibility of some change operating to transform the system becomes great if sufficient time is allowed.

Apart from the equilibrium within the set of essential rules, there are two other kinds of equilibrium characteristic of the international system: the equilibrium between the set of essential rules and the other variables of the international system and the equilibrium between the international system and its environment or setting.

If the actors do not manifest the behavior indicated by the rules, the kind and numbers of actors will change. If the kind or number of actors changes, the behavior called for in the rules cannot be maintained. Some changes in capabilities and information, for instance, may be compatible with the rules of the system, while others may not. If the value of one variable changes—for instance, the capabilities of a given coalition—the system may not maintain itself unless the information of some of the actors changes correspondingly. Otherwise a necessary "counter-balancing" shift in alignment may not take place. Some shifts in the pattern of alliance may be compatible with the rules of the system and others may not.

The rules, in short, are equilibrium rules for the system. This does not, however, imply that the rules will be followed by the actors because they are equilibrium rules, unless an actor has an interest in maintaining the equilibrium of the system. The constraints on the actor must motivate it to behave consonantly with the rules; or, if one or more actors are not so motivated, the others must be motivated to act in a way which forces the deviant actors back to rule-consonant behavior.[3] Thus the rules may be viewed normatively, that is, as describing the behavior which will maintain the equilibrium of the system or as predictive, that is, as predicting that actors will so behave if the other variables of the system and the environment are at their equilibrium settings. If the other variables of the system and the environment are not at their equilibrium settings, deviant behavior is expected.

It is relatively easy to find historical examples illustrating the operation of the "balance of power" system. The European states would have accepted Napoleon had he been willing to play according to the rules of the game.[4] The restoration of the Bourbons permitted the application of rule three. Had this not been possible, the international system would immediately have become unstable. Readmission of France to the international system after restoration fulfilled rule six.

The European concert, so ably described by Mowat, illustrates rule one. The *entente cordiale* illustrates rule four and the history of the eighteenth and nineteenth centuries rule two. Perhaps the best example of rule three, however, can be found in the diplomacy of Bismarck at Sadowa, although his motivation was more complex than the rule alone would indicate. It is not the purpose of this essay to multiply historical illustrations. The reader can make his own survey to determine whether international behavior tended to correspond to these rules during the eighteenth and nineteenth centuries.

The changes in conditions that may make the "balance of power" international system unstable are: the existence of an essential national actor who does not play according to the rules of the game, such as one who acts contrary to the essential rules of the system; in the example discussed, a player who seeks hegemony; failures of information which prevent a national actor from taking the required measures to protect its own international position; capability changes that become cumulative and thus increase an initial disparity between the capabilities of essential national actors; conflicts between the prescriptions of different rules under some conditions; difficulties arising from the logistics of the "balancing" process, the small number of essential actors, or an inflexibility of the "balancing" mechanism.

An important condition for stability concerns the number of essential national actors. If there are only three, and if they are relatively equal in capability, the probability that two would combine to eliminate the third is relatively great. Although the two victorious nations would have an interest in limiting the defeat of the third and in restoring it to the system as an acceptable role partner, they might not do so. Since this might not happen, the penalty for being left out of an alliance would be high and even the hazards of being in an alliance relatively great. Even if a nation were in one alliance, it might be left out of the next. Therefore this would be a system in which each victorious nation might attempt to gain as much as it could from the war as a protection against what might happen in the next round. Moreover, each victorious nation would attempt to double-cross the other in order to obtain a differential advantage. There would be a premium upon deceit and dishonesty. On the other hand, the addition of some other nations to the system would remove many of the pressures and add to the stability of the system.

Coalitions with many members may thus regard loosely attached members with equanimity. The role of the non-member of the coalition will also be tolerated. When there are a large number of loosely attached actors or non-members of an alliance any change of alliance or addition to an alliance can be "counter-balanced" by the use of an appropriate reward or by the cognition by some national actor of danger to its national interest.

When, however, there are very few loosely attached or non-member actors, a change in or an addition to an alignment introduces considerable tension into the international system. Under these circumstances, it becomes difficult to make the necessary compensatory adjustments.

For the same reasons, coalition members will have more tolerance for the role of "balancer," i.e., the actor who implements rule four, if the international system has a large number of members and the alignments are fluid. Under these conditions, the "balancer" does not constitute a lethal threat to the coalition against which it "balances." If, however, there are only a few essential actors, the very act of "balancing" may create a permanent "unbalance." In these circumstances the tolerance of the system for the "balancing" role will be slight and the "balance of power" system will become unstable.

Instability may result, although the various national actors have no intention of overthrowing the "balance of power" system. The wars against Poland corresponded to the rule directing the various national actors to increase their capabilities. Since Poland was not an essential national actor, it did not violate the norms of the system to eliminate Poland as an actor. The Polish spoils were divided among the victorious essential national actors. Nevertheless, even this co-operation among the essential national actors had an "unbalancing" effect. Since the acquisitions of the victorious actors could not be equal—unless some exact method were found for weighting geographic, strategic, demographic, industrial, material factors, etc., and determining accurately how the values of these factors would be projected into the future—a differential factor making the system unstable could not easily be avoided.

Even the endeavor to defeat Napoleon and to restrict France to her historic limits had some effects of this kind. This effort, although conforming to rules four, five, and six, also aggrandized Prussia and hence upset the internal equilibrium among the German actors. This episode may have triggered the process which later led to Prussian hegemony within Germany and to German hegemony within Europe. Thus, a dynamic process was set off for which shifts within alignments or coalitions were not able to compensate.

The logistical or environmental possibilities for "balancing" may be decisive in determining whether the "balancing" role within the "balance of power" international system will be filled effectively. For example, even had it so desired, the Soviet Union could not have "balanced" Nazi pressure against Czechoslovakia without territorial access to the zone of potential conflict. In addition, the intervening actors—Poland and Rumania—and possibly also Great Britain and France regarded Soviet intervention as a threat to their national interests. Therefore, they refused to co-operate.

It is possible that a major factor accounting for British success in the "balancing" role in the nineteenth century lay in the fact that Great Britain was predominantly a naval power and had no territorial ambitions on the European continent. These facts increased the tolerance of other national actors for Britain's "balancing" role. As a preponderant maritime power, Great Britain could interfere with the shipping of other powers and could transport its small army; it also was able to use its naval capabilities to dispel invading forces. Even so, Palmerston discovered occasions on which it was difficult to play the "balancing" role either because it was difficult to make effective use of Britain's limited manpower or because other powers displayed little tolerance for the role.

The "balance of power" system has the following consequences. Alliances tend to be specific, of short duration, and to shift according to advantage and not according to ideology (even within war). Wars tend to be limited in objectives. There is a wide range of international law that applies universally within the system. Among the most significant rules of applicable law are those dealing with the rules of war and the doctrine of non-intervention.[5]

The "balance of power" system in its ideal form is a system in which any combination of actors within alliances is possible so long as no alliance gains a marked preponderance in capabilities. The system tends to be maintained by the fact that even should any nation desire to become predominant itself, it must, to protect its own interests, act to prevent any other nation from accomplishing such an objective. Like Adam Smith's "unseen hand" of competition, the international system is policed informally by self-interest, without the necessity of a political sub-system. . .

NOTES

1. The term "essential actor" refers roughly to "major power" as distinguished from "minor power."

2. This kind of equilibrium is not mechanical like the equilibrium of the seesaw, which re-establishes itself mechanically after a disturbance. Instead, it is a "steady state" or homeostatic equilibrium which maintains the stability of selected variables as the consequence of changes in other variables. For instance, the body maintains the temperature of blood in a "steady state" by perspiring in hot weather and by flushing the skin in cold weather. The international system is not simply stable but in Ashby's sense is ultrastable. That is, it acts selectively toward states of its internal variables and rejects those which lead to unstable states. See W. Ross Ashby, *Design for a Brain*, p. 99, New York: John Wiley and Sons, 1952, for a precise treatment of the concept of ultrastability (and also of multistability).

3. See Morton Kaplan, Arthur Burns, and Richard Quandt, "Theoretical Analysis of the 'Balance of Power,'" *Behavioral Science*, Vol. V, No. 3, July 1960, pp. 240–52, for an account of why consonant motivation is expected.

4. It is nevertheless true that since Napoleon threatened the principle of dynastic legitimacy, the system would have been strained. The principle of legitimacy, for quite some time, reduced the suspicions that are natural to a "balance of power" system.

5. For an explication at greater length of the hypothetical relationship between system structure and system of norms, see Morton A. Kaplan, and Nicholas deB. Katzenbach, *The Political Foundations of International Law*, New York: John Wiley and Sons, 1961.

16

JAMES N. ROSENAU

THE TWO WORLDS
OF WORLD POLITICS

By sapping the authority of the centralized state, the new technologies have shifted the locus of decisive action to the more modest concentrations of intellect and will. These smaller organizations can be defined as the transnational

SOURCE: From *Turbulence In World Politics,* James N. Rosenau (Princeton, NJ: Princeton University Press, 1991). Copyright © 1991 Princeton University Press. Reprinted by permission of the publisher.

corporation, as the merchant city-state (Singapore, Taiwan, Hong Kong), as militant causes (the PLO or the IRA), even as individuals as intransigent as Manuel Noriega or Muammar Qaddafi, Israeli tank commanders, Colombian drug dealers, African despots, Turkish assassins, and Lebanese terrorists. . . . As yet nobody has drawn a map that reflects the new order.

— LEWIS H. LAPHAM[1]

Modern society has no single designer nor an overall, coherent design. There are multiple sources of organizing principles, rules and policies, many of which compete with and contradict one another. The pressures for change are many and varied. Diverse rule-making groups and institutions pursue their own particular interests, visions, and modes of knowledge development. Coordination and integration among different rule-making processes, and the agents involved, tends to be weak. We refer to this condition as "structural incoherence."

—TOM R. BURNS AND HELENA FLAM[2]

Together these two observations, one an empirical description and the other an abstract formulation, foreshadow the central themes of this [article]. The aim is to sketch the map of the new order called for in the first observation and to do so along the lines suggested in the second observation. For the multi-centric world, while not a society, also lacks an overall design, derives from multiple sources, and is marked by high degrees of diversity, decentralization, and dynamism that render coordination difficult.

However, the label offered for this condition is misleading. It suggests that a system lacking coherence lacks structure as well. But structural incoherence lies at one extreme on a continuum, at that end beyond which randomness prevails and structure collapses into formlessness. Inchoate as it may be, structural incoherence is a form of structure. The various collectivities encompassed by it do persist and they interact in repeated, patterned ways. If they did not, if complexity and dynamism were to overwhelm all structure, actors would have difficulty adapting, and their activities would be at such cross-purposes that they could hardly be called a society or a world.

Given that it encompasses collectivities most of which do manage to adapt, the multi-centric world can be presumed to have an underlying structure accessible to study. To explore this structure, we have thus far relied only on a series of anomalies and examples as the basis for discerning the emergence of a new global structure for the first time since the advent of the Western state system. Obviously, however, anomalies and examples can be neither proof of change nor a guide to assessing its sources and dynamics. They do serve as indicators of greater complexity and dynamism, and they provoke a search for the appearance of new structural arrangements. Still, they present no clear picture of what the foundations of a bifurcated global order might be.

To support the conception of a bifurcated world, therefore, the anomalies need to be located in a theoretical perspective that is internally consistent and empirically compelling. Such is the task of this [article]: to set forth a basis for stepping outside the state-system paradigm and framing an alternative one through which to assess the early indicators of a new, if structurally incoherent, form of world order.

AN OLD PARADIGM

Abandoning existing assumptions is no easy matter. . . . Students of world politics, like politicians, are prisoners of their paradigms, unwilling or unable to escape the premise of state predominance and constantly tempted to cling to familiar assumptions about hierarchy, authority, and sovereignty.

Those who adhere to a realist perspective are illustrative of these difficulties. Forced to acknowledge that profound socioeconomic changes have marked the latter half of the twentieth century, many realists contend that these have nonetheless taken place in an unchanging political context, that the socio-economic transformations have not had an appreciable impact on the long-established international system in which states predominate and seek to solve their security problems through the maximization of power. While conceding that transnational processes and actors other than states have become increasingly conspicuous in world politics, they preserve their paradigm by insisting that this conspicuousness acquires meaning only in the context of an international environment controlled by states.

The work of Kenneth Waltz exemplifies this position. He argues that while states "may choose to interfere little in the affairs of nonstate actors for long periods of time," they "nevertheless set the terms of the intercourse. . . . When the crunch comes, states remake the rules by which other actors operate." As Waltz sees it, this structural predominance of states is sufficient to obviate the need for theorizing afresh: "A theory that denies the central role of states will be needed only if nonstate actors develop to the point of rivaling or surpassing the great powers, not just a few of the minor ones. They show no sign of doing that." Similarly, transnational processes are posited as "among those that go on within" the state-centric structure. Waltz contends that "the 'state-centric' phrase suggests something about the system's structure," and to question its existence by citing nonstate actors and transnational movements "merely reflects the difficulty political scientists have in keeping the distinction between structures and processes clearly and constantly in mind."[3]

A variant of this response to the conditions of the postindustrial era involves locating the new actors and transnational processes in the context of "international regimes," which are conceived to be sets of norms, principles, rules, and procedures that operate in particular issue-areas to guide the interactions among all the actors who may have interests at stake.[4] An international regime thus brings states and transnational entities into the same analytic setting, where they are seen as bargaining and conflicting with each other through non-hierarchical processes. While the regime concept offers some valuable insights into world politics,[5] it does not confront directly the possibility that the state-centric system is being bounded within a more encompassing universe. Rather, it merely grafts additional institutions and processes onto the state system without allowing for the possibility of its diminution. As Waltz sees it, for example, the advent of international regimes merely illustrates that the state system is flexible enough to "passively [permit] informal rules to develop," a flexibility that also enables states to intervene "to change rules that no longer suit them."[6] In effect, the regime concept updates the realist paradigm without altering its fundamental premises, producing a synthesis of long-standing assumptions and modern realities that some call "neorealism."[7]

TOWARD A NEW PARADIGM

But there are limits beyond which a theory cannot be preserved by grafting and patching. As indicated by the myriad anomalies and the evidence of change in the micro and relational parameters, which have been previously noted, there are reasons to suspect that the structural parameter is evolving in ways that neither the regime concept nor neorealism adequately explains. If it is the case that the profound socioeconomic changes of the post-industrial era necessarily have comparable consequences for world politics, and if existing paradigms are insufficient to account for these dynamics, some new organizing principles for understanding the political bases of global life are needed.

We begin with the assumption that the dynamics of postindustrialism are simultaneously fostering centralizing and decentralizing tendencies in global life, some of which cancel each other out but many of which progressively circumscribe nation-states and the international system they have sustained for several centuries. From there, we proceed on the basis of the five guidelines for an escape from the realist jail that were set forth earlier. It will be recalled that these guidelines focus on authority, hierarchy, issue agenda, and systems as they relate to the identity, conduct, and interaction of the actors who produce outcomes in global politics. They depart sufficiently from long-standing presumptions to permit the delineation of parametric changes in which a new multi-centric world is discerned as challenging, rivaling, ignoring, and otherwise coexisting alongside—neither superordinate nor subordinate to—the historic state-centric world. The result is a paradigm that neither circumvents nor negates the state-centric model, but preserves it in a larger context, one that posits sovereignty-bound and sovereignty-free actors as inhabitants of separate worlds that interact in such a way as to make their coexistence possible.

It might be argued that the integrity of the new paradigm has already been compromised: that a potential for backtracking is created by the proposition that the multi-centric system has come to coexist with, rather than to replace, the state-centric system, that retention of the latter represents a failure to engineer a thoroughgoing jailbreak, or a means of keeping open an escape hatch through which to beat a hasty retreat back to the neorealist paradigm in the event the multi-centric world proves too chaotic for incisive theorizing. Either states dominate world affairs or they do not, such an argument would hold, so that positing them as dominant in one world and merely active in the other is yielding to old analytic habits and avoiding a full, unqualified break with realist premises.

There is much to be said for this charge of timidity and compromise. After all, if states are still powerful, why have they not done a better job in managing world affairs? Why do world politics so often seem out of control, propelling communities and continents in directions that nobody wants? Has not the combination of dynamic technologies and global decentralization overwhelmed the state system and made it subservient to the multi-centric world? If so, is it not a distortion to continue to give conceptual importance to the state-centric world? Indeed, might it not even be the case that the state system is already well along the road to decay, so that the coexistence of the two worlds of world politics may be merely a transitional phase in global development?

All of these doubts notwithstanding, it is difficult to ignore the present capacity of states to control the instruments of coercive force and the publics needed to support their use. The range of issues on which these instruments can be used effectively has narrowed considerably in recent decades, but not yet to the point where it is reasonable to presume that states and their world are dissolving into the multi-centric environment. Instead, states must be regarded as still capable of maintaining the norms and practices of their own international system, and consequently, the interaction between the state-centric and multi-centric worlds emerges as the focus of important theoretical questions.

This two-world conception of global politics runs counter to the prevailing analytic mode, which presumes that, over time, the state-centric system either subsumes alternatives to it or fragments and collapses as the rival alternatives come to prevail. That both the system and the alternatives can co-exist is thus not viewed as a meaningful possibility: a momentary and transitional condition, to be sure, but highly improbable as an enduring form of world order.

Hedley Bull's work is illustrative of this tendency. In a lengthy analysis, he delineates four structural arrangements—a disarmed world, a UN-dominated world of states, a world of many nuclear powers, and a world marked by ideological homogeneity—that "would be radically different from what exists now," but, he adds, they "would represent a new phase of the states system, not its replacement by something different."[8] He also considers the possibility that international politics will move beyond the state system to one of four alternative arrangements: a number of states forming a system but not an international society, a situation in which there are states but no system, a world government, or a new "mediaeval system" of nonsovereign actors. Nowhere, however, does he envision the development of another world operating alongside the existing political universe rather than superseding it. At one point in identifying the prospects for "a new mediaevalism," he seems on the verge of positing a two-world universe, when he asserts that "it is not fanciful to imagine that there might develop a modern and secular counterpart of [the mediaeval model] that embodies its central characteristic: a system of overlapping authority and multiple loyalty." Indeed, his account of this alternative comes close to the conception of the multi-centric world to be developed below:

> It is familiar that sovereign states today share the stage of world politics with "other actors" just as in mediaeval times the state had to share the stage with "other associations" (to use the mediaevalists' phrase). If modern states were to come to share their authority over their citizens, and their ability to command their loyalties, on the one hand with regional and world authorities, and on the other hand, with sub-state or sub-national authorities, *to such an extent that the concept of sovereignty ceased to be applicable,* then a neo-mediaeval form of universal political order might be said to have emerged.[9]

The italicized phrase is crucial. It takes Bull's formulation well beyond the conception of a two-world universe. He allows for the emergence of a multi-centric world, but at the same time suggests that it will culminate in the irrelevance of state sovereignty. . . .

THE TWO WORLDS OF WORLD POLITICS

The main features of the two worlds are contrasted in table 1. Here it can be seen that the state-centric world is much more coherent and structured than is its multi-centric counterpart. It is to some degree anarchic and decentralized, because of the lack of an over-arching world government,[10] but that anarchy is minimal compared to the chaos that results from the much greater decentralization that marks the multi-centric system. Not only are there many fewer points at which action originates in the state-centric than in the multi-centric system, but action and interaction in the former is also considerably more subject to formal procedures and hierarchical precepts than in the latter. In the multi-centric world, relations among actors are on more equal footing, are more temporary and ad hoc, and more susceptible to change, but are less symmetrical and less constrained by power differentials, formal authority, and established institutions.

TABLE 1 **Structure and Process in the Two Worlds of World Politics**

	STATE-CENTRIC WORLD	MULTI-CENTRIC WORLD
Number of essential actors	Fewer than 200	Hundreds of thousands
Prime dilemma of actors	Security	Autonomy
Principal goals of actors	Preservation of territorial integrity, and physical security	Increase in world market shares, maintenance of integration of subsystems
Ultimate resort for realizing goals	Armed force	Withholding of cooperation or compliance
Normative priorities	Processes, especially those that preserve sovereignty and the rule of law	Outcomes, especially those that expand human rights, justice, and wealth
Modes of collaboration	Formal alliances whenever possible	Temporary coalitions
Scope of agenda	Limited	Unlimited
Rules of governing interactions among actors	Diplomatic practices	Ad hoc, situational
Distribution of power among actors	Hierarchical by amount of power	Relative equality as far as initiating action is concerned
Interaction patterns among actors	Symmetrical	Asymmetrical
Locus of leadership	Great powers	Innovative actors with extensive resources
Institutionalization	Well established	Emergent
Susceptibility to change	Relatively low	Relatively high
Control over outcomes	Concentrated	Diffused
Bases of decisional structures	Formal authority, law	Various types of authority, effective leadership

Given these features of the multi-centric world, especially the unavailability and the disutility of physical coercion as means of pursuing goals, the question is raised of how the multi-centric world can remain independent in the face of the greater coherence and capabilities of its state-centric counterpart.

One response to this question is that many actors of the multi-centric world are able to ignore or evade the demands of the state system. To be sure, with few exceptions the actors of the multi-centric world are located within the jurisdiction of a counterpart in the state-centric world and, accordingly, must abide by its rules. But their adherence to these rules is often formalistic. In their scenarios, they are the subjects of action and states are merely objects; they may sometimes, even frequently, have to work through and with the rules of states, but they do so in order to procure the resources or the other forms of support needed to attain their goals. . . .

Needless to say, neither the multi-centric nor the state-centric world is marked by as much uniformity as this formulation implies. In the multi-centric world, the actors vary widely from culture to culture and in terms of their goals, orientations, capabilities, and modes of organization. In the state-centric world, there are such obvious distinctions as those between countries with democratic institutions and those with authoritarian regimes. Without minimizing the importance of such differences, however, here the emphasis is upon the uniformities induced by the dynamics of postindustrial interdependence. Business firms, political parties, ethnic groups, and the other types of sovereignty-free actors tend to share an aspiration to maintain their autonomy with respect to each other and to any states that may jeopardize their prerogatives. Authoritarian states may control their citizens more thoroughly than do their democratic counterparts, but even they have been compelled to acknowledge the advent of a multi-centric world of diverse—and effective—sovereignty-free actors. For authoritarian states, the relevant comparison is not with nonauthoritarian actors, but with their own situations in earlier eras.

In sum, it is in the sense that both sovereignty-bound and sovereignty-free actors have come to define themselves as the subjects of world politics, while viewing the other as its objects, that global life can be said to consist of two worlds. Or, if the word "worlds" connotes a completeness and orderliness not fully substantiated by everyday observation, they can be thought of as two "domains" (as empirical theorists might say), "texts" (as critical theorists might prefer), or "projects" (as postmodernists might put it). Whatever the labels, the point is to distinguish between two separate sets of complex actors that overlap and interact even as they also maintain a high degree of independence.

NOTES

1. "Notebook: Leviathan in Trouble," *Harper's*, September 1988, pp. 8–9.
2. "Political Transactions and Regime Structuring: The Perspective of Actor-Systems Dynamics" (manuscript prepared for the Workshop on Political Exchange: Between Governance and Ideology, Florence, December 1986), p. 209.
3. Kenneth N. Waltz, *Theory of International Politics* (Reading, Mass.: Addison-Wesley, 1979), pp. 94, 95.
4. Stephen D. Krasner, ed., *International Regimes* (Ithaca, N.Y.: Cornell University Press, 1983), esp. p. 2.
5. These insights are elaborated in James N. Rosenau, "Before Cooperation: Hegemons, Regimes, and Habit-Driven Actors in World Politics," *International Organization* 40 (Autumn 1986): 879–84.
6. Waltz, *Theory of International Politics*, p. 94.
7. See, for example, Robert O. Keohane, "Realism, Neorealism, and the Study of World Politics," in R. O. Keohane, ed., *Neorealism and Its Critics* (New York: Columbia University Press, 1986), p. 15.
8. Hedley Bull, *The Anarchical Society: A Study of Order in World Politics* (New York: Columbia University Press, 1977), p. 238.
9. Bull, *Anarchical Society*, pp. 254–55 (italics added).
10. On the conception of anarchy in international politics, see the essays in Kenneth A. Oye, ed., *Cooperation under Anarchy* (Princeton: Princeton University Press, 1986).

17

ROBERT O. KEOHANE AND
JOSEPH S. NYE

THE CHARACTERISTICS OF COMPLEX
INTERDEPENDENCE

. . . In common parlance, *dependence* means a state of being determined or significantly affected by external forces. *Interdependence,* most simply defined, means *mutual* dependence. Interdependence in world politics refers to situations characterized by reciprocal effects among countries or among actors in different countries.

These effects often result from international transactions—flows of money, goods, people, and messages across international boundaries. Such transactions have increased dramatically since World War II: "Recent decades reveal a general tendency for many forms of human interconnectedness across national boundaries to be doubling every ten years." Yet this interconnectedness is not the same as interdependence. The effects of transactions on interdependence will depend on the constraints, or costs, associated with them. A country that imports all of its oil is likely to be more dependent on a continual flow of petroleum than a country importing furs, jewelry, and perfume (even of equivalent monetary value) will be on uninterrupted access to these luxury goods. Where there are reciprocal (although not necessarily symmetrical) costly effects of transactions, there is interdependence. Where interactions do not have significant costly effects, there is simply interconnectedness. The distinction is vital if we are to understand the *politics* of interdependence.

Costly effects may be imposed directly and intentionally by another actor—as in Soviet-American strategic interdependence, which derives from the mutual threat of nuclear destruction. But some costly effects do not come directly or intentionally from other actors. For example, collective action may be necessary to prevent disaster for an alliance (the members of which are interdependent), for an international economic system (which may face chaos because of the absence of coordination, rather than through the malevolence of any actor), or for an ecological system threatened by a gradual increase of industrial effluents.

We do not limit the term *interdependence* to situations of mutual benefit. Such a definition would assume that the concept is only useful analytically

SOURCE: From *Power and Interdependence*, Robert O. Keohane and Joseph S. Nye. Copyright © 1977 Scott, Foresman and Company. Reprinted by permission of HarperCollins Publishers.

where the modernist view of the world prevails: where threats of military force are few and levels of conflict are low. It would exclude from interdependence cases of mutual dependence, such as the strategic interdependence between the United States and the Soviet Union. Furthermore, it would make it very ambiguous whether relations between industrialized countries and less developed countries should be considered interdependent or not. Their inclusion would depend on an inherently subjective judgment about whether the relationships were "mutually beneficial."

Because we wish to avoid sterile arguments about whether a given set of relationships is characterized by interdependence or not, and because we seek to use the concept of interdependence to integrate rather than further to divide modernist and traditional approaches, we choose a broader definition. Our perspective implies that interdependent relationships will always involve costs, since interdependence restricts autonomy; but it is impossible to specify *a priori* whether the benefits of a relationship will exceed the costs. This will depend on the values of the actors as well as on the nature of the relationship. Nothing guarantees that relationships that we designate as "interdependent" will be characterized by mutual benefit.

Two different perspectives can be adopted for analyzing the costs and benefits of an interdependent relationship. The first focuses on the joint gains or joint losses to the parties involved. The other stresses *relative* gains and distributional issues. Classical economists adopted the first approach in formulating their powerful insight about comparative advantage: that undistorted international trade will provide overall net benefits. Unfortunately, an exclusive focus on joint gain may obscure the second key issue: how those gains are divided. Many of the crucial political issues of interdependence revolve around the old question of politics, "who gets what?"

It is important to guard against the assumption that measures that increase joint gain from a relationship will somehow be free of distributional conflict. Governments and nongovernmental organizations will strive to increase their shares of gains from transactions, even when they both profit enormously from the relationship. Oil-exporting governments and multinational oil companies, for instance, share an interest in high prices for petroleum; but they have also been in conflict over shares of the profits involved.

We must therefore be cautious about the prospect that rising interdependence is creating a brave new world of cooperation to replace the bad old world of international conflict. As every parent of small children knows, baking a larger pie does not stop disputes over the size of the slices. An optimistic approach would overlook the uses of economic and even ecological interdependence in competitive international politics.

The difference between traditional international politics and the politics of economic and ecological interdependence is *not* the difference between a world of "zero-sum" (where one side's gain is the other side's loss) and "nonzero-sum" games. Military interdependence need not be zero-sum. Indeed, military allies actively seek interdependence to provide enhanced security for all. Even balance of power situations need not be zero-sum. If one side seeks to upset the status quo, then its gain is at the expense of the other. But if most or all participants want a stable status quo, they can jointly gain by preserving the balance of power among them. Conversely, the politics of economic and ecological interdependence involve competition even when large net benefits can be expected from cooperation. There are important continuities, as well as marked differences, between the traditional politics of military security and the politics of economic and ecological interdependence.

We must also be careful not to define interdependence entirely in terms of situations of *evenly balanced* mutual dependence. It is *asymmetries* in dependence that are most likely to provide sources of influence for actors in their dealings with one another. Less dependent actors can often use the interdependent relationship as a source of power in bargaining over an issue and perhaps to affect other issues. At the other extreme from pure symmetry is pure dependence (sometimes disguised by calling the situation interdependence); but it too is rare. Most cases lie between these two extremes. And that is where the heart of the political bargaining process of interdependence lies.

THE CHARACTERISTICS OF COMPLEX INTERDEPENDENCE

Complex interdependence has three main characteristics: . . .

1. *Multiple channels* connect societies, including: informal ties between governmental elites as well as formal foreign office arrangements; informal ties among nongovernmental elites (face-to-face and through telecommunications); and transnational organizations (such as multinational banks or corporations). These channels can be summarized as interstate, transgovernmental, and transnational relations. *Interstate* relations are the normal channels assumed by realists. *Transgovernmental* applies when we relax the realist assumption that states act coherently as units; *transnational* applies when we relax the assumption that states are the only units.

2. The agenda of interstate relationships consists of multiple issues that are not arranged in a clear or consistent hierarchy. This *absence of hierarchy among issues* means, among other things, that military security does not consistently dominate the agenda. Many issues arise from what used to be considered domestic policy, and the distinction between domestic and foreign issues becomes blurred. These issues are considered in several government departments (not just foreign offices), and at several levels. Inadequate policy coordination on these issues involves significant costs. Different issues generate different coalitions, both within governments and across them, and involve different degrees of conflict. Politics does not stop at the waters' edge.

3. Military force is not used by governments toward other governments within the region, or on the issues, when complex interdependence prevails.

It may, however, be important in these governments' relations with governments outside that region, or on other issues. Military force could, for instance, be irrelevant to resolving disagreements on economic issues among members of an alliance, yet at the same time be very important for that alliance's political and military relations with a rival bloc. For the former relationships this condition of complex interdependence would be met; for the latter, it would not.

III

THE ACTORS IN INTERNATIONAL POLITICS

DEFINING THE OPERATING UNITS

One of the perennial issues facing scholars of international relations concerns their focus of attention. Should it be on the macro-level of the international system or the micro-level of the national state? The answer will, of course, vary both for different scholars and for the same scholars at different times. Each approach, however, has certain advantages and weaknesses. These are outlined in J. David Singer's classic examination of the level-of-analysis problem in international relations. As well as warning of the dangers of moving too easily from one level to another, Singer—whose subsequent work has included a long-term project (the correlates of war) employing quantitative approaches to the study of war—identifies some problems that occur when focusing at each level.

Keeping Singer's warning in mind, this section focuses not on the international system as a whole but on the units operating within the system. Even when one focuses on the unit level, however, several issues remain outstanding, the most important of which concern the nature of the major units or actors. One possible focus is on the state and its major attributes as an actor in international relations. It is equally important, however, to focus on the decision-making process within states and on the rise of non-state actors.

THE STATE AS ACTOR

Although the nation-state emerged as the dominant actor in the international system, to do so it had to triumph over several other forms of social and political organization: the city-state, the empire, and feudalism.[1] The contemporary nation-state is characterized by jurisdiction over territory, a political and administrative apparatus, and the acknowledgment by others that it is a sovereign entity. The essence of sovereignty is that the state recognizes no higher constitutional authority than itself.[2] Although sovereignty is often treated as synonymous with independence, there is an important difference: sovereignty is essentially a legal concept, whereas independence is a political matter. States can be formally sovereign even though they may heavily depend on others in practice. At the same time, the principle of sovereignty is essential to the functioning of the society of states and the maintenance of international order. Once a state is recognized as a sovereign entity, then others are obligated to refrain from intervention in its affairs. Indeed, the counterpart to the notion of sovereignty is the norm of non-intervention.[3] And although this norm is frequently breached,

---

[1] For a fuller analysis, see Robert Gilpin, *War and Change in World Politics* (Cambridge: Cambridge University Press, 1981).

[2] Alan James, *Sovereign Statehood* (London: Allen and Unwin, 1986)

[3] This is developed in John Vincent, *Nonintervention and International Order* (Princeton: Princeton University Press, 1974).

this cannot be done unless extraordinary justifications or rationales are provided. Sovereignty does not prevent intervention or interference in the internal affairs of states, but it does at least inhibit this kind of activity.

The idea of the state as the dominant actor in international relations also has an intellectual appeal—it leads to a focus on the capabilities of the state and the interactions of states with one another. This approach is sometimes termed the billiard ball approach.[4] One of the great strengths of the billiard ball approach is parsimony; another is that it captures the constants in state behavior—the concern with power and security—that transcend the particular political incumbents at any one time. Yet, these considerations are also seen as the main weakness of an exclusive focus on states as actors. Indeed, the most important source of the challenge to state dominance as the primary mode of discourse in international relations has been a fundamental dissatisfaction with analysis that treats the state as a unitary, monolithic actor.

INSTITUTIONS AND INDIVIDUALS AS ACTORS

One difficulty with an exclusive focus on the state is that this encourages reification and ignores the existence of decision makers who act on behalf of the state. Certain actions are attributed to France, to the United States, to Russia, to Nigeria, or to Israel, for example, rather than to the governments and individuals who made the decisions and the organizations that implemented them. One reaction to this focus was the development of the foreign policy decision-making approach to the study of international politics. This began in the 1950s with the work of Snyder, Bruck, and Sapin.[5] By focusing not on the state as actor, but on those acting on behalf of the state, this approach opened the way was open for a much fuller examination of political, psychological, and sociological variables.

The following selections illustrate this fuller examination. The analysis by Ole R. Holsti, a distinguished political scientist, highlights several challenges to the dominant state-as-actor approach (which is also embedded in realism and neo-realism). Holsti looks at liberal theories, which emphasize that the issue areas facing states have broadened beyond the traditional issues of war and peace; surveys world systems theory, which emphasizes the capitalist economy rather than the nation-state as the focus of attention; and highlights decision-making perspectives that offer a more finely granulated approach to foreign policy than does the state-as-actor perspective. As he puts it, "Decision-making

---

[4] This theory was elaborated most succinctly by Arnold Wolfers, one of the major theorists of international relations in the 1950s and early 1960s, in his book *Discord and Collaboration* (Baltimore: Johns Hopkins University Press, 1962).

[5] R. C. Snyder, H. W. Bruck, and B. M. Sapin, *Foreign Policy Decision-Making: An Approach to the Study of International Politics* (New York: Free Press, 1962).

models challenge the premise that it is fruitful to conceptualize the nation as a unitary rational actor whose behavior can adequately be explained by reference to the system structure . . . because individuals, groups, and organizations acting in the name of the state are also sensitive to pressures and constraints other than international ones, including elite maintenance, electoral politics, public opinion, pressure group activities, ideological preferences, and bureaucratic politics." Holsti subsequently surveys three models of decision making—individual, group dynamics, and bureaucratic politics. Significantly, in some of his other work, he focused on cognitive dynamics and other psychological variables highlighting the ways in which they affected foreign policy.[6]

The emphasis by Holsti and others on cognitive and psychological variables challenged the idea that states or governments act rationally and according to simple calculations of costs and gains, and this notion was contested even more vigorously by Graham Allison, in a famous and often-quoted article published in the *American Political Science Review* in 1969 (parts of which are reproduced here) and in his subsequent book, *Essence of Decision*.[7] In both of these studies, Allison (who subsequently became dean of the John F. Kennedy School of Government at Harvard) disaggregated government, suggesting that concepts based on the presumption of a single monolithic actor in rational pursuit of a coherent set of objectives were fundamentally flawed. As an alternative to the rational actor model of state behavior, Allison suggested two approaches. The first was the organizational process model, which focused on organizational routines and argued that the implementation of policy could often be understood only in terms of standard operational procedures developed and carried out by large, complex bureaucratic organizations. The second was a governmental politics model that emphasized that government consisted of multiple players in particular positions in the bureaucracy. From this perspective, decisions are reached as a result of an intense bargaining process in which participants' stances are determined largely by their governmental or bureaucratic responsibilities. Consequently, foreign policy decisions are not the product of rational calculation about what is good for the state; rather, they are a compromise—and sometimes compromised—product of the internal bargaining process.

---

[6] Holsti showed how the views of the Soviet Union held by Eisenhower's Secretary of State, John Foster Dulles, led Dulles to dismiss Soviet overtures as tricks rather than as serious offers to negotiate in Holsti's "Cognitive Dynamics and Images of the Enemy," in *Image and Reality in World Politics*, edited by John C. Farrell and Asa P. Smith (New York: Columbia University Press, 1968). A similar approach was also used to study other decision makers. See, for example, Harvey Starr, *Henry Kissinger: Perceptions of International Politics* (Lexington: University Press of Kentucky, 1984).

[7] Graham Allison, *Essence of Decision: Explaining the Cuban Missile Crisis* (Boston: Little, Brown, 1971).

THE RISE OF NON-STATE ACTORS

One of the underlying premises of the decision-making approach in its various manifestations concerned the necessity of efforts to un-package the "black box" of the state as actor. Yet another challenge to the dominance of the state-centric model came from critics who saw the focus on the state as missing many aspects of international activity and ignoring not only non-state actors but also other dimensions of international relations. Some of the selections we have reproduced here develop this theme.

Those who point to the emergence of non-state actors also tend to emphasize the interconnections between the international economic system and the international political system. They also argue that many of the new transnational actors in international relations, whether terrorist groups or economic corporations, are rarely under the control of nation-states. This is not to ignore the support that terrorist groups receive from certain states; nor is it to deny that many of the corporations with far-flung economic activities are based predominantly in the United States, Japan, and Western Europe. It is simply to note that such groups and corporations act not only independently of the host government but, on occasion, even against the will of this government.

The rise of non-state actors such as multinational corporations is part of a broader pattern discussed by Mansbach, Ferguson, and Lampert largely in terms of the growth of complex interdependencies in the international system. As the selection makes clear, the basic premise of these authors is that "individuals and groups become functionally linked as they discover that they share common interests and common needs that transcend existing organizational frontiers." From this, they go on to argue that the inability of nation-states to satisfy the demands of their populations or to cope with problems not solely under their jurisdiction, is partly the result of the growing expectations of these populations and "partly the result of the growing complexity and specialization of functional systems. . . ." Not surprisingly, therefore, other actors have emerged to complement and supplement the activities of the nation-state. In this selection, six types of international actor are identified by the authors, who contend that the traditional state-centric model of the international system needs to be replaced by what they call the "complex conglomerate system."

One of the categories identified by Mansbach, Ferguson, and Lampert is that of the "interstate governmental actor." This encompasses such regional security organizations as the North Atlantic Treaty Organization as well as global actors like the United Nations. International organizations are the subject of the article by Michael N. Barnett and Martha Finnemore, parts of which we have excerpted in this section. In some respects, the analysis by Barnett and Finnemore incorporates an imaginative extension of the bureaucratic politics model enunciated by Graham Allison and develops a novel and unconventional approach to the analysis of international organizations. Unlike many analysts of international relations, they do not simply extol the virtues of organizations such as the United Nations. On the contrary, they use an approach based on sociological institutionalism to explain the power of international organizations—which they see as far greater than do most liberal institutionalists—as well as their capacity for dysfunctional or pathological behavior. In their view, international organizations can exercise power independently of the states that created them. Yet some of the things that help to endow international organizations with power also create pathologies that inhibit or distort the way power is exercised.

Another kind of non-state actor—the transnational advocacy network—is discussed in the excerpt from the work of Margaret Keck and Kathryn Sikkink. These authors focus on what they describe as a subset of issues "characterized by the prominence of principled ideas and a central role for nongovernmental organizations" that tend to form transnational networks to maximize their impact. The global movement to ban land-mines, the work of NGOs to combat trafficking in women and children, and the transnational activities of environmental activists are all examples of the kind of networks on which Keck and Sikkink focus. They explain why these transnational networks have emerged and explore the techniques and strategies they use.

Overall, this section highlights the diversity of approaches and key controversies about what the primary focus of attention should be in terms of identifying and analyzing international actors. Several observations can be made about this issue. First, diversity of approach should be regarded primarily as a sign of intellectual health in the discipline. International relations is a vast and complex subject that can be fully understood only through a variety of analyses with different approaches and emphases.

Second, and following on from this, different approaches should not be regarded as mutually exclusive. International relations continues to be dominated both by states and by a variety of non-state actors. Many transnational interactions are not under the control of states but will nevertheless be affected by decisions taken by states. Conversely, the state in turn will be affected by the actions of other actors and by the complex web of transnational interactions that has become an increasingly important element in international relations.

Third, it is worth emphasizing that not all these non-state actors are benign. Keck and Sikkink focus on transnational advocacy networks that are part of global civil society; it is equally important to focus on transnational criminal and terrorist networks, which are part of an uncivil society, are malevolent in intent, and have an adverse affect on international security and stability. Not all Hobbesian or Machiavellian actors are states, and not all non-state actors adhere to Kantian or Grotian principles. It would be a mistake, therefore, for liberal institutionalists to assume that non-state or sovereignty-free actors are always positive in intent or effect. Indeed the impact of the transnational advocacy networks could well be outweighed by the impact of subterranean networks that challenge global norms, undermine global governance, and seek to neutralize rather than mobilize the power of states.

The fourth observation concerns the other challenge to the state-centric model: a focus on decision making by governments and policymakers.

Although this approach has illuminated both psychological and organizational variables, which often have a profound impact on foreign policy, it is worth emphasizing that those who act on behalf of states are compelled to fulfill certain roles and responsibilities. One difficulty with the governmental politics model of Graham Allison is that it largely ignores the imperatives that propel decision-making groups toward agreement. Moreover, Allison's bureaucratic politics model, in effect, replaces the rational statesperson who attempts to maximize the interests of the state in the international game with a rational bureaucrat who attempts to maximize personal and organizational interests in the domestic governmental game. Whereas it would be foolish to deny that calculations of domestic political advantage often intrude into the foreign policy process, it is equally foolish to ignore the pressures from the international system or the responsibility upon policymakers to act as the custodians of state interests in the international strategic game. Policymakers in international politics, for example, cannot be oblivious to challenges to national security. This imposes a degree of uniformity on states or those who act on their behalf regardless of their personal preferences and predilections.[8] As the reader examines the selections dealing with the nature of the actors in international relations, the extent to which these actors have to respond to their environment should be borne in mind. The nature of that environment and the patterns of conflict and cooperation within it are explored more fully in Part IV.

18

J. DAVID SINGER

THE LEVEL-OF-ANALYSIS PROBLEM IN INTERNATIONAL RELATIONS

In any area of scholarly inquiry, there are always several ways in which the phenomena under study may be sorted and arranged for purposes of systemic analysis. Whether in the physical or social sciences, the observer may choose to focus upon the parts or upon the whole, upon the components or upon the

---

[8] This issue is examined in a very interesting way in Arnold Wolfers, *Discord and Collaboration*, pp. 3–24.

SOURCE: From *The International System: Theoretical Essays*, David J. Singer, Klaus Knorr, and Sidney Verba, eds. (Princeton, NJ: Princeton University Press, 1961), pp. 77–92. Reprinted by permission of the Johns Hopkins University Press.

system. He may, for example, choose between the flowers or the garden, the rocks or the quarry, the trees or the forest, the houses or the neighborhood, the cars or the traffic jam, the delinquents or the gang, the legislators or the legislative, and so on.[1] Whether he selects the micro- or macro-level of analysis is ostensibly a mere matter of methodological or conceptual convenience. Yet the choice often turns out to be quite difficult, and may well become a central issue within the discipline concerned. The complexity and significance of these level-of-analysis decisions are readily suggested by the long-standing controversies between social psychology and sociology, personality-oriented and culture-oriented anthropology, or micro- and macroeconomics, to mention but a few. In the vernacular of general systems theory, the observer is always confronted with a system, its sub-systems, and their respective environments, and while he may choose as his system any cluster of phenomena from the most minute organism to the universe itself, such choice cannot be merely a function of whim or caprice, habit or familiarity.[2] The responsible scholar must be prepared to evaluate the relative utility—conceptual and methodological—of the various alternatives open to him, and to appraise the manifold implications of the level of analysis finally selected. So it is with international relations.

But whereas the pros and cons of the various possible levels of analysis have been debated exhaustively in many of the social sciences, the issue has scarcely been raised among students of our emerging discipline.[3] Such tranquillity may be seen by some as a reassuring indication that the issue is not germane to our field, and by others as evidence that it has already been resolved, but this writer perceives the quietude with a measure of concern. He is quite persuaded of its relevance and certain that it has yet to be resolved. Rather, it is contended that the issue has been ignored by scholars still steeped in the intuitive and artistic tradition of the humanities or enmeshed in the web of "practical" policy. We have, in our texts and elsewhere, roamed up and down the ladder of organizational complexity with remarkable abandon, focusing upon the total system, international organizations, regions, coalitions, extra-national associations, nations, domestic pressure groups, social classes, elites, and individuals as the needs of the moment required. And though most of us have tended to settle upon the nation as our most comfortable resting place, we have retained our propensity for vertical drift, failing to appreciate the value of a stable point of focus.[4] Whether this lack of concern is a function of the relative infancy of the discipline or the nature of the intellectual traditions from whence it springs, it nevertheless remains a significant variable in the general sluggishness which characterizes the development of theory in the study of relations among nations. It is the purpose of this paper to raise the issue, articulate the alternatives, and examine the theoretical implications and consequences of two of the more widely employed levels of analysis: the international system and the national sub-systems.

I. THE REQUIREMENTS OF AN ANALYTICAL MODEL

Prior to an examination of the theoretical implications of the level of analysis or orientation employed in our model, it might be worthwhile to discuss the uses to which any such model might be put, and the requirements which such uses might expect of it.

Obviously, we would demand that it offer a highly accurate *description* of the phenomena under consideration. Therefore the scheme must present as complete and undistorted a picture of these phenomena as is possible; it must correlate with objective reality and coincide with our empirical referents to the highest possible degree. Yet we know that such accurate representation of a complex and wide-ranging body of phenomena is extremely difficult. Perhaps a useful illustration may be borrowed from cartography; the oblate spheroid which the planet earth most closely represents is not transferable to the two-dimensional surface of a map without *some* distortion. Thus, the Mercator projection exaggerates distance and distorts direction at an increasing rate as we move north or south *from* the equator, while the polar gnomonic projection suffers from these same debilities as we move *toward* the equator. Neither offers therefore a wholly accurate presentation, yet each is true enough to reality to be quite useful for certain specific purposes. The same sort of tolerance is necessary in evaluating any analytical model for the study of international relations; if we must sacrifice total representational accuracy, the problem is to decide where distortion is least dysfunctional and where such accuracy is absolutely essential.

These decisions are, in turn, a function of the second requirement of any such model—a capacity to *explain* the relationships among the phenomena under investigation. Here our concern is not so much with accuracy of description as with validity of explanation. Our model must have such analytical capabilities as to treat the causal relationships in a fashion which is not only valid and thorough, but parsimonious; this latter requirement is often overlooked, yet its implications for research strategy are not inconsequential.[5] It should be asserted here that the primary purpose of theory is to explain, and when descriptive and explanatory requirements are in conflict, the latter ought to be given priority, even at the cost of some representational inaccuracy.

Finally, we may legitimately demand that any analytical model offer the promise of reliable *prediction*. In mentioning this requirement last, there is no implication that it is the most demanding or difficult of the three. Despite the popular belief to the contrary, prediction demands less of one's model than does explanation or even description. For example, any informed layman can predict that pressure on the accelerator of a slowly moving car will increase its speed; that more or less of the moon will be visible tonight than last night; or that the normal human will flinch when confronted with an impending blow. These *predictions* do not require a particularly elegant or sophisticated model of the universe, but their *explanation* demands far more than most of us carry around in our minds. Likewise, we can predict with impressive reliability that any nation will respond to military attack in kind, but a description and understanding of the processes and factors leading to such a response are considerably more elusive, despite the gross simplicity of the acts themselves.

Having articulated rather briefly the requirements of an adequate analytical model, we might turn now to a consideration of the ways in which one's choice of analytical focus impinges upon such a model and affects its descriptive, explanatory, and predictive adequacy.

II. THE INTERNATIONAL SYSTEM
AS LEVEL OF ANALYSIS

Beginning with the systemic level of analysis, we find in the total international system a partially familiar and highly promising point of focus. First of all, it is the most comprehensive of levels available, encompassing the totality of interactions which take place within the system and its environment. By focusing on the system, we are enabled to study the patterns of interaction which the system reveals, and to generalize about such phenomena as the creation and dissolution of coalitions, the frequency and duration of specific power configurations, modifications in its stability, its responsiveness to changes in formal political institutions, and the norms and folklore which it manifests as a societal system. In other words, the systemic level of analysis, and only this level, permits us to examine international relations in the whole, with a comprehensiveness that is of necessity lost when our focus is shifted to a lower, and more partial, level. For descriptive purposes, then, it offers both advantages and disadvantages; the former flow from its comprehensiveness, and the latter from the necessary dearth of detail.

As to explanatory capability, the system-oriented model poses some genuine difficulties. In the first place, it tends to lead the observer into a position which exaggerates the impact of the system upon the national actors and, conversely, discounts the impact of the actors on the system. This is, of course, by no means inevitable; one could conceivably look upon the system as a rather passive environment in which dynamic states act out their relationships rather than as a socio-political entity with a dynamic of its own. But there is a natural tendency to endow that upon which we focus our attention with somewhat greater potential than it might normally be expected to have. Thus, we tend to move, in a system-oriented model, away from notions implying much national autonomy and independence of choice and toward a more deterministic orientation.

Secondly, this particular level of analysis almost inevitably requires that we postulate a high degree of uniformity in the foreign policy operational codes of our national actors. By definition, we allow little room for divergence in the behavior of our parts when we focus upon the whole. It is no coincidence that our most prominent theoretician—and one of the very few text writers focusing upon the international system—should "assume that [all] statesmen think and act in terms of interest defined as power."[6] If this single-minded behavior be interpreted literally and narrowly, we have a simplistic image comparable to economic man or sexual man, and if it be defined broadly, we are no better off than the psychologist whose human model pursues "self-realization" or "maximization of gain"; all such gross models suffer from the same fatal weakness as the utilitarian's "pleasure-pain" principle. Just as individuals differ widely in what they deem to be pleasure and pain, or gain and loss, nations may differ widely in what they consider to be the national interest, and we end up having to break down and refine the larger category. Moreover, Professor Morgenthau finds himself compelled to go still further and disavow the relevance of both motives and ideological preferences in national behavior, and these represent two of the more useful dimensions in differentiating among the several nations in our international system. By eschewing any empirical concern with the domestic and internal variations within the separate nations, the system-oriented approach tends to produce a sort of "black box" or "billiard ball" concept of the national actors.[7] By discounting—or denying—the differences among nations, or by positing the near-impossibility of observing many of these differences at work within them,[8] one concludes with a highly homogenized image of our nations in the international system. And though this may be an inadequate foundation upon which to base any *causal* statements, it offers a reasonably adequate basis for *correlative* statements. More specifically, it permits us to observe and measure correlations between certain forces or stimuli which seem to impinge upon the nation and the behavior patterns which are the apparent consequence of these stimuli. But one must stress the limitations implied in the word "apparent"; what is thought to be the consequence of a given stimulus may only be a coincidence or artifact, and until one investigates the major elements in the causal link—no matter how persuasive the deductive logic—one may speak only of correlation, not of consequence.

Moreover, by avoiding the multitudinous pitfalls of intra-nation observation, one emerges with a singularly manageable model, requiring as it does little of the methodological sophistication or onerous empiricism called for when one probes beneath the behavioral externalities of the actor. Finally, as has already been suggested in the introduction, the systemic orientation should prove to be reasonably satisfactory as a basis for prediction, even if such prediction is to extend beyond the characteristics of the system and attempt anticipatory statements regarding the actors themselves; this assumes, of course, that the actors are characterized and their behavior predicted in relatively gross and general terms.

These, then, are some of the more significant implications of a model which focuses upon the international system as a whole. Let us turn now to the more familiar of our two orientations, the national state itself.

III. THE NATIONAL STATE AS
LEVEL OF ANALYSIS

The other level of analysis to be considered in this paper is the national state—our primary actor in international relations. This is clearly the traditional focus among Western students, and is the one which dominates almost all of the texts employed in English-speaking colleges and universities.

Its most obvious advantage is that it permits significant differentiation among our actors in the international system. Because it does not require the attribution of great similarity to the national actors, it encourages the observer to examine them in greater detail. The favorable results of such intensive analysis cannot be overlooked, as it is only when the actors are studied in some depth that we are able to make really valid generalizations of a comparative nature. And though the systemic model does not necessarily preclude comparison and contrast among the national sub-systems, it usually eventuates in rather gross comparisons based on relatively crude dimensions and characteristics. On the other hand, there is no assurance that the nation-oriented approach will produce a sophisticated model for the comparative study of foreign policy; with perhaps the exception of the Haas and Whiting study,[9] none of our major texts makes a serious and successful effort to describe and explain national behavior in terms of most of the significant variables by which such behavior might be comparatively analyzed. But this would seem to be a function, not of the level of analysis employed, but of our general unfamiliarity with the other social sciences (in which comparison is a major preoccupation) and of the retarded state of comparative government and politics, a field in which most international relations specialists are likely to have had some experience.

But just as the nation-as-actor focus permits us to avoid the inaccurate homogenization which often flows from the systemic focus, it also may lead us into the opposite type of distortion—a marked exaggeration of the differences among our sub-systemic actors. While it is evident that neither of these extremes is conducive to the development of a sophisticated comparison of foreign policies, and such comparison requires a balanced preoccupation with both similarity and difference, the danger seems to be greatest when we succumb to the tendency to overdifferentiate; comparison and contrast can proceed only from observed uniformities.[10]

One of the additional liabilities which flow in turn from the pressure to overdifferentiate is that of Ptolemaic parochialism. Thus, in over-emphasizing the differences among the many national states, the observer is prone to attribute many of what he conceives to be virtues to his own nation and the vices to others, especially the adversaries of the moment. That this ethnocentrism is by no means an idle fear is borne out by perusal of the major international relations texts published in the United States since 1945. Not only is the world often perceived through the prism of the American national interest, but an inordinate degree of attention (if not spleen) is directed toward the

Soviet Union; it would hardly be amiss to observe that most of these might qualify equally well as studies in American foreign policy. The scientific inadequacies of this sort of "we-they" orientation hardly require elaboration, yet they remain a potent danger in any utilization of the national actor model.

Another significant implication of the sub-systemic orientation is that it is only within its particular framework that we can expect any useful application of the decision-making approach.[11] Not all of us, of course, will find its inapplicability a major loss; considering the criticism which has been leveled at the decision-making approach, and the failure of most of us to attempt its application, one might conclude that it is no loss at all. But the important thing to note here is that a system-oriented model would not offer a hospitable framework for such a detailed and comparative approach to the study of international relations, no matter what our appraisal of the decision-making approach might be.

Another and perhaps more subtle implication of selecting the nation as our focus or level of analysis is that it raises the entire question of goals, motivation, and purpose in national policy.[12] Though it may well be a peculiarity of the Western philosophical tradition, we seem to exhibit, when confronted with the need to explain individual or collective behavior, a strong proclivity for a goal-seeking approach. The question of whether national behavior is purposive or not seems to require discussion in two distinct (but not always exclusive) dimensions.

Firstly, there is the more obvious issue of whether those who act on behalf of the nation in formulating and executing foreign policy consciously pursue rather concrete goals. And it would be difficult to deny, for example, that these role-fulfilling individuals envisage certain specific outcomes which they hope to realize by pursuing a particular strategy. In this sense, then, nations may be said to be goal-seeking organisms which exhibit purposive behavior.

However, purposiveness may be viewed in a somewhat different light, by asking whether it is not merely an intellectual construct that man imputes to himself by reason of his vain addiction to the free-will doctrine as he searches for characteristics which distinguish him from physical matter and the lower animals. And having attributed this conscious goal-pursuing behavior to himself as an individual, it may be argued that man then proceeds to project this attribute to the social organizations of which he is a member. The question would seem to distill down to whether man and his societies pursue goals of their own choosing or are moved toward those imposed upon them by forces which are primarily beyond their control.[13] Another way of stating the dilemma would be to ask whether we are concerned with the ends which men and nations strive for or the ends toward which they are impelled by the past and present characteristics of their social and physical milieu. Obviously, we are using the terms "ends," "goals," and "purpose" in two rather distinct ways; one refers to those which are consciously envisaged and more or less rationally pursued, and the other to those of which the actor has little knowledge but toward which he is nevertheless propelled.

Taking a middle ground in what is essentially a specific case of the free will vs. determinism debate, one can agree that nations move toward outcomes of which they have little knowledge and over which they have less control, but that they nevertheless do prefer, and therefore select, particular outcomes and *attempt* to realize them by conscious formulation of strategies.

Also involved in the goal-seeking problem when we employ the nation-oriented model is the question of how and why certain nations pursue specific sorts of goals. While the question may be ignored in the system-oriented model or resolved by attributing identical goals to all national actors, the nation-as-actor approach demands that we investigate the processes by which national goals are selected, the internal and external factors that impinge on those processes, and the institutional framework from which they emerge. It is worthy of note that despite the strong predilection for the nation-oriented model in most of our texts, empirical or even deductive analyses of these processes are conspicuously few.[14] Again, one might attribute these lacunae to the methodological and conceptual inadequacies of the graduate training which international relations specialists traditionally receive.[15] But in any event, goals and motivations are both dependent and independent variables, and if we intend to explain a nation's foreign policy, we cannot settle for the mere postulation of these goals; we are compelled to go back a step and inquire into their genesis and the process by which they become the crucial variables that they seem to be in the behavior of nations.

There is still another dilemma involved in our selection of the nation-as-actor model, and that concerns the phenomenological issue: do we examine our actor's behavior in terms of the objective factors which allegedly influence that behavior, or do we do so in terms of the actor's *perception* of these "objective factors"? Though these two approaches are not completely exclusive of one another, they proceed from greatly different and often incompatible assumptions, and produce markedly divergent models of national behavior.[16]

The first of these assumptions concerns the broad question of social causation. One view holds that individuals and groups respond in a quasi-deterministic fashion to the realities of physical environment, the acts or power of other individuals or groups, and similar "objective" and "real" forces or stimuli. An opposite view holds that individuals and groups are not influenced in their behavior by such objective forces, but by the fashion in which these forces are perceived and evaluated, however distorted or incomplete such perceptions may be. For adherents of this position, the only reality is the phenomenal—that which is discerned by the human senses; forces that are not discerned do not exist for that actor, and those that do exist do so only in the fashion in which they are perceived. Though it is difficult to accept the position that an individual, a group, or a nation is affected by such forces as climate, distance, or a neighbor's physical power only insofar as they are recognized and appraised, one must concede that perceptions will certainly affect the manner in which such forces are responded to. As has often been pointed out, an individual will fall to the ground when he steps out of a tenth-story window regardless of his perception of gravitational forces, but on the other hand such perception is a major factor in whether or not he steps out of the window in the first place.[17] The point here is that if we embrace a phenomenological view of causation, we will tend to utilize a phenomenological model for explanatory purposes.

The second assumption which bears on one's predilection for the phenomenological approach is more restricted, and is primarily a methodological one. Thus, it may be argued that any description of national behavior in a given international situation would be highly incomplete were it to ignore the link between the external forces at work upon the nation and its general foreign policy behavior. Furthermore, if our concern extends beyond the mere description of "what happens" to the realm of explanation, it could be contended that such omission of the cognitive and the perceptual linkage would be ontologically disastrous. How, it might be asked, can one speak of "causes" of a nation's policies when one has ignored the media by which external conditions and factors are translated into a policy decision? We may observe correlations between all sorts of forces in the international system and the behavior of nations, but their causal relationship must remain strictly deductive and hypothetical in the absence of empirical investigation into the causal chain which allegedly links the two. Therefore, even if we are satisfied with the less-than-complete descriptive capabilities of a non-phenomenological model, we are still drawn to it if we are to make any progress in explanation.

The contrary view would hold that the above argument proceeds from an erroneous comprehension of the nature of explanation in social science. One is by no means required to trace every perception, transmission, and receipt between stimulus and response or input and output in order to explain the behavior of the nation or any other human group. Furthermore, who is to say that empirical observation—subject as it is to a host of errors—is any better a basis of explanation than informed deduction, inference, or analogy? Isn't an explanation which flows logically from a coherent theoretical model just as reliable as one based upon a misleading and elusive body of data, most of which is susceptible to analysis only by techniques and concepts foreign to political science and history?

This leads, in turn, to the third of the premises relevant to one's stand on the phenomenological issue: are the dimensions and characteristics of the policy-makers' phenomenal field empirically discernible? Or, more accurately, even if we are convinced that their perceptions and beliefs constitute a crucial variable in the explanation of a nation's foreign policy, can they be observed in an accurate and systematic fashion?[18] Furthermore, are we not required by the phenomenological model to go beyond a classification and description of such variables, and be drawn into the tangled web of relationships out of which they emerge? If we believe that these phenomenal variables are systematically observable, are explainable, and can be fitted into our explanation of a nation's behavior in the international system, then there is a further tendency to embrace the phenomenological approach. If not, or if we are convinced that the gathering of such data is inefficient or uneconomical, we will tend to shy clear of it.

The fourth issue in the phenomenological dispute concerns the very nature of the nation as an actor in international relations. Who or what is it that we study? Is it a distinct social entity with well-defined boundaries—a unity unto itself? Or is it an agglomeration of individuals, institutions, customs, and procedures? It should be quite evident that those who view the nation or the state as an integral social unit could not attach much utility to the phenomenological approach, particularly if they are prone to concretize or reify the abstraction. Such abstractions are incapable of perception, cognition, or anticipation (unless, of course, the reification goes so far as to anthropomorphize and assign to the abstraction such attributes as will, mind, or personality). On the other hand, if the nation or state is seen as a group of individuals operating within an institutional framework, then it makes perfect sense to focus on the phenomenal field of those individuals who participate in the policy-making process. In other words, *people* are capable of experiences, images, and expectations, while institutional abstractions are not, except in the metaphorical sense. Thus, if our actor cannot even have a phenomenal field, there is little point in employing a phenomenological approach.[19]

These, then, are some of the questions around which the phenomenological issue would seem to revolve. Those of us who think of social forces as operative regardless of the actor's awareness, who believe that explanation need not include all of the steps in a causal chain, who are dubious of the practicality of gathering phenomenal data, or who visualize the nation as a distinct entity apart from its individual members, will tend to reject the phenomenological approach.[20] Logically, only those who disagree with each of the above four assumptions would be compelled to adopt the approach. Disagreement with any one would be *sufficient* grounds for so doing.

The above represent some of the more significant implications and fascinating problems raised by the adoption of our second model. They seem to indicate that this sub-systemic orientation is likely to produce richer description and more satisfactory (from the empiricist's point of view) explanation of international relations, though its predictive power would appear no greater than the systemic orientation. But the descriptive and explanatory advantages are achieved only at the price of considerable methodological complexity.

IV. CONCLUSION

Having discussed some of the descriptive, explanatory, and predictive capabilities of these two possible levels of analysis, it might now be useful to assess the relative utility of the two and attempt some general statement as to their prospective contributions to greater theoretical growth in the study of international relations.

In terms of description, we find that the systemic level produces a more comprehensive and total picture of international relations than does the national or sub-systemic level. On the other hand, the atomized and less coherent image produced by the lower level of analysis is somewhat balanced by its richer detail, greater depth, and more intensive portrayal.[21] As to explanation, there seems little doubt that the sub-systemic or actor orientation is considerably more fruit-ful, permitting as it does a more thorough investigation of the processes by which foreign policies are made. Here we are enabled to go beyond the limita-tions imposed by the systemic level and to replace mere correlation with the more significant causation. And in terms of prediction, both orientations seem to offer a similar degree of promise. Here the issue is a function of what we seek to predict. Thus the policy-maker will tend to prefer predictions about the way in which nation x or y will react to a contemplated move on his own nation's part, while the scholar will probably prefer either generalized predictions regard-ing the behavior of a given class of nations or those regarding the system itself.

Does this summary add up to an overriding case for one or another of the two models? It would seem not. For a staggering variety of reasons the scholar may be more interested in one level than another at any given time and will undoubtedly shift his orientation according to his research needs. So the prob-lem is really not one of deciding which level is most valuable to the discipline as a whole and then demanding that it be adhered to from now unto eternity.[22] Rather, it is one of realizing that there *is* this preliminary conceptual issue and that it must be temporarily resolved prior to any given research undertaking. And it must also be stressed that we have dealt here only with two of the more common orientations, and that many others are available and perhaps even more fruitful potentially than either of those selected here. Moreover, the international system gives many indications of prospective change, and it may well be that existing institutional forms will take on new characteristics or that new ones will appear to take their place. As a matter of fact, if incapacity to perform its functions leads to the transformation or decay of an institution, we may expect a steady deterioration and even ultimate disappearance of the national state as a significant actor in the world political system.

However, even if the case for one or another of the possible levels of analy-sis cannot be made with any certainty, one must nevertheless maintain a con-tinuing awareness as to their use. We may utilize one level here and another there, but we cannot afford to shift our orientation in the midst of a study. And when we do in fact make an original selection or replace one with another at appropriate times, we must do so with a full awareness of the descriptive, explanatory, and predictive implications of such choice.

A final point remains to be discussed. Despite this lengthy exegesis, one might still be prone to inquire whether this is not merely a sterile exercise in verbal gymnastics. What, it might be asked, is the difference between the two levels of analysis if the empirical referents remain essentially the same? Or, to put it another way, is there any difference between international relations and comparative foreign policy? Perhaps a few illustrations will illuminate the subtle but important differences which emerge when one's level of analysis shifts. One might, for example, postulate that when the international system is characterized by political conflict between two of its most powerful actors, there is a strong tendency for the system to bipolarize. This is a systemic-oriented proposition. A sub-systemic proposition, dealing with the same general empirical referents, would state that when a powerful actor finds itself in political conflict with another of approximate parity, it will tend to exert pressure on its weaker neighbors to join its coalition. Each proposition, assuming it is true, is theoretically useful by itself, but each is verified by a different intellectual operation. Moreover—and this is the crucial thing for theoretical development—one could not add these two kinds of statements together to achieve a cumulative growth of empirical generalizations.

To illustrate further, one could, at the systemic level, postulate that when the distribution of power in the international system is highly diffused, it is more stable than when the discernible clustering of well-defined coalitions occurs. And at the sub-systemic or national level, the same empirical phenomena would produce this sort of proposition: when a nation's decision-makers find it difficult to categorize other nations readily as friend or foe, they tend to behave toward all in a more uniform and moderate fashion. Now, taking these two sets of propositions, how much cumulative usefulness would arise from attempting to merge and codify the systemic proposition from the first illustration with the sub-systemic proposition from the second, or vice versa? Representing different levels of analysis and couched in different frames of reference, they would defy theoretical integration; one may well be a corollary of the other, but they are not immediately combinable. A prior translation from one level to another must take place.

This, it is submitted, is quite crucial for the theoretical development of our discipline. With all of the current emphasis on the need for more empirical and data-gathering research as a prerequisite to theory-building, one finds little concern with the relationship among these separate and discrete data-gathering activities. Even if we were to declare a moratorium on deductive and speculative research for the next decade, and all of us were to labor diligently in the vineyards of historical and contemporary data, the state of international relations theory would probably be no more advanced at that time than it is now, unless such empirical activity becomes far more systematic. And "systematic" is used here to indicate the cumulative growth of inductive and deductive generalizations into an impressive array of statements conceptually related to one another and flowing from some common frame of reference. What that frame of reference should be, or will be, cannot be said with much certainty, but it does seem clear that it must exist. As long as we evade some of these crucial *a priori* decisions, our empiricism will amount to little more than an ever-growing potpourri of discrete, disparate, non-comparable, and isolated bits of information or extremely low-level generalizations. And, as such, they will make little contribution to the growth of a theory of international relations.

NOTES

1. As Kurt Lewin observed in his classic contribution to the social sciences: "The first prerequisite of a successful observation in any science is a definite understanding about what size of unit one is going to observe at a given time." *Field Theory in Social Science*, New York, 1951, I, p. 157.

2. For a useful introductory statement on the definitional and taxonomic problems in a general systems approach, see the papers by Ludwig von Bertalanffy, "General System Theory," and Kenneth Boulding, "General System Theory: The Skeleton of Science," in Society for the Advancement of General Systems Theory, *General Systems,* Ann Arbor, Mich., 1956, I, part I.

3. An important pioneering attempt to deal with some of the implications of one's level of analysis, however, is Kenneth N. Waltz, *Man, the State, and War,* New York, 1959. But Waltz restricts himself to a consideration of these implications as they impinge on the question of the causes of war. See also this writer's review of Waltz, "International Conflict: Three Levels of Analysis," *World Politics,* XII (April 1960), pp. 453–461.

4. Even during the debate between "realism" and "idealism" the analytical implications of the various levels of analysis received only the scantiest attention; rather the emphasis seems to have been at the two extremes of pragmatic policy and speculative metaphysics.

5. For example, one critic of the decision-making model formulated by Richard C. Snyder, H. W. Bruck, and Burton Sapin, in *Decision-Making as an Approach to the Study of International Politics* (Princeton, N.J., 1954), points out that no single researcher could deal with all the variables in that model and expect to complete more than a very few comparative studies in his lifetime. See Herbert McClosky, "Concerning Strategies for a Science of International Politics," *World Politics,* VIII (January 1956), pp. 281–295. In defense, however, one might call attention to the relative ease with which many of Snyder's categories could be collapsed into more inclusive ones, as was apparently done in the subsequent case study (see note 11 below). Perhaps a more telling criticism of the monograph is McClosky's comment that "Until a greater measure of theory is introduced into the proposal and the relations among variables are specified more concretely, it is likely to remain little more than a setting-out of categories and, like any taxonomy, fairly limited in its utility" (p. 291).

6. Hans J. Morgenthau, *Politics Among Nations,* 3rd ed., New York, 1960, pp. 5–7. Obviously, his model does not preclude the use of power as a dimension for the differentiation of nations.

7. The "black box" figure comes from some of the simpler versions of S-R psychology, in which the observer more or less ignores what goes on within the individual and concentrates upon the correlation between stimulus and response; these are viewed as empirically verifiable, whereas cognition, perception, and other mental processes have to be imputed to the individual with a heavy reliance on these assumed "intervening variables." The "billiard ball" figure seems to carry the same sort of connotation, and is best employed by Arnold Wolfers in "The Actors in International Politics" in William T. R. Fox, ed., *Theoretical Aspects of International Relations,* Notre Dame, Ind., 1959, pp. 83–106. See also, in this context, Richard C. Snyder, "International Relations Theory—Continued," *World Politics* (January 1961), pp. 300–312; and J. David Singer, "Theorizing About Theory in International Politics," *Journal of Conflict Resolution,* IV (December 1960), pp. 431–442. Both are review articles dealing with the Fox anthology.

8. Morgenthau observes, for example, that it is "futile" to search for motives because they are "the most illusive of psychological data, distorted as they are, frequently beyond recognition, by the interests and emotions of actor and observer alike" (*op.cit.,* p. 6).

9. Ernst B. Haas and Allen S. Whiting, *Dynamics of International Relations,* New York, 1956.

10. A frequent by-product of this tendency to overdifferentiate is what Waltz calls the "second-image fallacy," in which one explains the peaceful or bellicose nature of a nation's foreign policy exclusively in terms of its domestic economic, political, or social characteristics (*op.cit.,* chs. 4 and 5).

11. Its most well-known and successful statement is found in Snyder *et al., op.cit.* Much of this model is utilized in the text which Snyder wrote with Edgar S. Furniss, Jr., *American Foreign Policy: Formulation, Principles, and Programs,* New York, 1954. A more specific application is found in Snyder and Glenn D. Paige, "The United States Decision to Resist Aggression in Korea: The Application of an Analytical Scheme," *Administrative Science Quarterly,* III (December 1958), pp. 341–378. For those interested in this approach, very useful is Paul Wasserman and Fred S. Silander, *Decision-Making: An Annotated Bibliography,* Ithaca, N.Y., 1958.

12. And if the decision-making version of this model is employed, the issue is unavoidable. See the discussion of motivation in Snyder, Bruck, and Sapin, *op.cit.,* pp. 92–117; note that 25 of the 49 pages on "The Major Determinants of Action" are devoted to motives.

13. A highly suggestive, but more abstract treatment of this teleological question is in Talcott Parsons, *The Structure of Social Action,* 2nd ed., Glencoe, Ill., 1949, especially in his analysis of Durkheim and Weber. It is interesting to note that for Parsons an act implies, *inter alia,* "a future state of affairs toward which the process of action is oriented," and he therefore comments that "in this sense and this sense only, the schema of action is inherently teleological" (p. 44).

14. Among the exceptions are Haas and Whiting, *op.cit.,* chs. 2 and 3; and some of the chapters in Roy C. Macridis, ed., *Foreign Policy in World Politics,* Englewood Cliffs, N.J., 1958, especially that on West Germany by Karl Deutsch and Lewis Edinger.

15. As early as 1934, Edith E. Ware noted that ". . . the study of international relations is no longer entirely a subject for political science or law, but that economics, history, sociology, geography—all the social sciences—are called upon to contribute towards the understanding . . . of the international system." See *The Study of International Relations in the United States,* New York, 1934, p. 172. For some contemporary suggestions, see Karl Deutsch, "The Place of Behavioral Sciences in Graduate Training in International Relations," *Behavioral Science,* III (July 1958), pp. 278–284; and J. David Singer, "The Relevance of the Behavioral Sciences to the Study of International Relations," *ibid.,* VI (October 1961), pp. 324–335.

16. The father of phenomenological philosophy is generally acknowledged to be Edmund Husserl (1859–1938), author of *Ideas: General Introduction to Pure Phenomenology,* New York, 1931, trans. by W. R. Boyce Gibson; the original was published in 1913 under the title *Ideen zu einer reinen Phänomenologie und Phänomenologischen Philosophie.* Application of this approach to social psychology has come primarily through the work of Koffka and Lewin.

17. This issue has been raised from time to time in all of the social sciences, but for an excellent discussion of it in terms of the present problem, see Harold and Margaret Sprout, *Man-Milieu Relationship Hypotheses in the Context of International Politics,* Princeton University, Center of International Studies, 1956, pp. 63–71.

18. This is another of the criticisms leveled at the decision-making approach which, almost by definition, seems compelled to adopt some form of the phenomenological

model. For a comprehensive treatment of the elements involved in human perception, see Karl Zener *et al.,* eds., "Inter-relationships Between Perception and Personality: A Symposium," *Journal of Personality,* XVIII (1949), pp. 1–266.

19. Many of these issues are raised in the ongoing debate over "methodological individualism," and are discussed cogently in Ernest Nagel, *The Structure of Science,* New York, 1961, pp. 535–546.

20. Parenthetically, holders of these specific views should also be less inclined to adopt the national or sub-systemic model in the first place.

21. In a review article dealing with two of the more recent and provocative efforts toward theory (Morton A. Kaplan, *System and Process in International Politics,* New York, 1957, and George Liska, *International Equilibrium,* Cambridge, Mass., 1957), Charles P. Kindleberger adds a further—if not altogether persuasive— argument in favor of the lower, sub-systemic level of analysis: "The total system is infinitely complex with everything interacting. One can discuss it intelligently, therefore, only bit by bit." "Scientific International Politics," *World Politics,* XI (October 1958), p. 86.

22. It should also be kept in mind that one could conceivably develop a theoretical model which successfully embraces both of these levels of analysis without sacrificing conceptual clarity and internal consistency. In this writer's view, such has not been done to date, though Kaplan's *System and Process in International Politics* seems to come fairly close.

19

OLE R. HOLSTI

MODELS OF INTERNATIONAL RELATIONS AND FOREIGN POLICY

Scholars and statesmen, philosophers and reformers have long debated the question of how best to understand relations among nations, but discussions among proponents of alternative theories have always gained intensity in times of profound turmoil and change. In our own century, the cataclysm of World War I resurfaced and intensified the dialogue between such liberals as Woodrow Wilson, who sought to create a new world order anchored in the League of Nations, and realists, exemplified by Georges Clemenceau, who sought to use more traditional means to assure their nations' security. World War II renewed that debate, but the events leading up to that conflict and the

SOURCE: *Controversies in International Relations Theory: Realism and the Neoliberal Challenge,* Ed. Charles W. Kegley Jr, pp. 35–65. Copyright 1995 St. Martin Press.

Cold War that emerged almost immediately after the guns had stopped firing in 1945 seemed to provide ample evidence to tip the balance strongly in favor of the realist vision of international relations.

In the meanwhile, the growth of Soviet power, combined with the disintegration of the great colonial empires that gave rise to the emergence of some one hundred newly independent nations, gave prominence to still another perspective on world affairs, most variants of which drew to some extent on the writings of Marx and Lenin. More recent events, including the disintegration of the Soviet Union, the end of the Cold War, the reemergence of inter- and intranational ethnic conflicts that had been suppressed during the Cold War, the Persian Gulf War, the continuing economic integration of Europe, and the declining international economic position of the United States, have stimulated new debates . . . on theories of international relations and foreign policy. This [reading] summarizes three prominent schools of thought that place primary explanatory emphasis on features of the international system. The following section discusses several "decision-making" approaches, all of which share a skepticism about the adequacy of theories that focus on the structure of the international system while neglecting political processes within units that comprise the system. A speculative conclusion assesses the impact of recent events on the several theoretical positions.

Three limitations should be stated at the outset. Each of the systemic and decision-making approaches described below is a composite of several models; limitations of space have made it necessary to focus on the common denominators rather than on subtle differences among them. This discussion will also avoid purely methodological issues and debates, for example, what Stanley Hoffmann (1977: 54) calls "the battle of the literates versus the numerates." Finally, "formal" or mathematical approaches of international relations (Richardson, 1960a, 1960b; Rapoport, 1957; Bueno de Mesquita, 1981, 1985; Niou et al., 1989) are neglected here, as are recent "postmodern" approaches (P. Rosenau, 1990).

Because "classical realism" is the most venerable and persisting model of international relations, it provides a good starting point and base line for comparison with competing models. Robert Gilpin (1981) may have been engaging in hyperbole when he questioned whether our understanding of international relations has advanced significantly since Thucydides, but one must acknowledge that the latter's analysis of the Peloponnesian War includes concepts that are not foreign to contemporary students of balance-of-power politics. There have always been Americans such as Alexander Hamilton who viewed international relations from a realist perspective, but its contemporary intellectual roots are largely European. Three important figures probably had the greatest impact on American scholarship: the historian E. H. Carr (1939), the geographer Nicholas Spykman (1942), and the political theorist Hans J. Morgenthau (1973). Other Europeans who have contributed significantly to realist thought include John Herz (1959), Raymond Aron (1966), Hedley Bull (1977), and Martin Wight (1973), while notable Americans of this school include scholars Arnold Wolfers (1962) and

Norman Graebner (1984), as well as diplomat George F. Kennan (1951), journalist Walter Lippmann (1943), and theologian Reinhold Niebuhr (1945).

Although realists do not constitute a homogeneous school—any more than do any of the others discussed in this essay—most of them share at least five core premises about international relations. To begin with, they consider the central questions to be the causes of war and the conditions of peace. They also regard the structure of the system as a necessary if not always sufficient explanation for many aspects of international relations. According to classical realists, "structural anarchy," or the absence of a central authority to settle disputes, is the essential feature of the contemporary system. It gives rise to the "security dilemma": In a self-help system, one nation's search for security often leaves its current and potential adversaries insecure; any nation that strives for absolute security leaves all others in the system absolutely insecure; and it can provide a powerful incentive for arms races and other types of hostile interactions. Consequently, the question of *relative* capabilities is a crucial factor. Efforts to deal with this central element of the international system constitute the driving force behind the relations of units within the system; those that fail to cope will not survive. Thus, unlike "idealists" or "liberals," classical realists view conflict as a natural state of affairs rather than a consequence that can be attributed to historical circumstances, evil leaders, flawed sociopolitical systems, or inadequate international understanding and education.

A third premise that unites classical realists is their focus on geographically based groups as the central actors in the international system. During other periods the primary entities may have been city-states or empires, but at least since the Treaties of Westphalia (1648), nation-states have been the dominant units.

Classical realists also agree that state behavior is rational. The assumption behind this fourth premise is that states are guided by the logic of the "national interest," usually defined in terms of survival, security, power, and relative capabilities. To Morgenthau (1973: 5, 3), for example, "rational foreign policy minimizes risks and maximizes benefits." Although the national interest may vary according to specific circumstances, the similarity of motives among nations permits the analyst to reconstruct the logic of policymakers in their pursuit of national interests—what Morgenthau called the "rational hypothesis"—and to avoid the fallacies of "concern with motives and concern with ideological preferences."

Finally, the nation-state can also be conceptualized as a unitary actor. Because the central problems for states are starkly defined by the nature of the international system, their actions are primarily a response to external rather than domestic political forces. At best, the latter provide very weak explanations for external policy. According to Stephen Krasner (1978: 33), for example, the state "can be treated as an autonomous actor pursuing goals associated with power and the general interest of the society." However, classical realists sometimes use domestic politics to explain deviations from rational policies.

Realism has been the dominant model of international relations during recent decades, perhaps in part because it seemed to provide a useful framework for understanding World War II and the Cold War. Nevertheless, the classical versions articulated by Morgenthau and others have received a good deal of critical scrutiny. The critics have included scholars who accept the basic premises of realism but who found that in at least four important respects these theories lacked sufficient precision and rigor.

CRITIQUES OF CLASSICAL REALISM

Classical realism has usually been grounded in a pessimistic theory of human nature, either a theological version (e.g., St. Augustine and Reinhold Niebuhr) or a secular one (e.g., Machiavelli, Hobbes, and Morgenthau). Egoism and self-interested behavior are not limited to a few evil or misguided leaders, as the idealists would have it, but are basic to *homo politicus* and thus are at the core of a realist theory. But because human nature, if it means anything, is a constant rather than a variable, it is an unsatisfactory explanation for the full range of international relations. If human nature explains war and conflict, what accounts for peace and cooperation? In order to avoid this problem, most modern realists have turned their attention from human nature to the structure of the international system to explain state behavior. In addition, critics have noted a lack of precision and even contradictions in the way classical realists use such concepts as "power," "national interest," and "balance of power" (Claude, 1962; Rosenau, 1968; George and Keohane, 1980; Haas, 1953; and Zinnes, 1967). They also see possible contradictions between the central descriptive and prescriptive elements of classical realism. On the one hand, nations and their leaders "think and act in terms of interests defined as power," but, on the other, statesmen are urged to exercise prudence and self-restraint, as well as to recognize the legitimate national interests of other nations (Morgenthau, 1973: 5). Obviously, then, power plays a central role in classical realism. But the correlation between the relative power balance and political outcomes is often less than compelling, suggesting the need to enrich analyses with other variables. Moreover, the distinction between "power as capabilities" and "usable options" is especially important in the nuclear age.

While classical realists have typically looked to history, philosophy, and political science for insights and evidence, the search for greater precision has led many modern realists to look elsewhere for appropriate models, analogies, metaphors, and insights. The discipline of choice is often economics, from which modern realists have borrowed such tools and concepts as rational choice, expected utility, theories of firms and markets, bargaining theory, and game theory. Contrary to the assertion of some critics (Ashley, 1984), however, modern realists *share* rather than reject the core premises of their classical predecessors.

The quest for precision has yielded a rich harvest of theories and models, and a somewhat less bountiful crop of supporting empirical applications. Drawing in part on game theory, Morton Kaplan described several types of international systems—for example, balance of power, loose bipolar, tight bipolar, universal, hierarchical, and a unit-veto system in which any action requires the unanimous approval of all its members. He then outlined the essential rules that constitute these systems. For example, the rules for a balance of power system are:

> (1) Increase capabilities, but negotiate rather than fight. (2) Fight rather than fail to increase capabilities. (3) Stop fighting rather than eliminate an essential actor. (4) Oppose any coalition or single actor that tends to assume a position of predominance within the system. (5) Constrain actors who subscribe to supranational organizational principles. (6) Permit defeated or constrained essential actors to reenter the system. (Kaplan, 1957: 23)

Richard Rosecrance (1963, 1966), J. David Singer (1963), Karl Deutsch and Singer (1964), Bruce Russett (1963), and many others (Waltz, 1964; Scott, 1967), although not necessarily realists, also have developed models that seek to understand international relations by virtue of system-level explanations. Andrew M. Scott's (1967) survey of the literature, which yielded a catalog of propositions about the international system, also illustrates the quest for greater precision in systemic models.

Kenneth Waltz's *Theory of International Politics* (1979), the most prominent effort to develop a rigorous and parsimonious model of "modern" or "structural" realism, has tended to define the terms of recent theoretical debates. It follows and builds upon another enormously influential book in which Waltz (1959) developed the Rousseauian position that a theory of war must include the system level (the "third image") and not just first (theories of human nature) or second (state attributes) images. Why war? Because there is nothing in the system to prevent it. *Theory of International Politics* is grounded in analogies from microeconomics: International politics and foreign policy are analogous to markets and firms. Oligopoly theory is used to illuminate the dynamics of interdependent choice in a self-help anarchical system. Waltz explicitly limits his attention to a structural theory of international systems, eschewing the task of linking it to a theory of foreign policy. Indeed, he doubts that the two can be joined in a single theory and is highly critical of many system-level analysts, including Morton Kaplan, Stanley Hoffmann, Richard Rosecrance, Karl Deutsch and J. David Singer, and others, charging them with various errors, including "reductionism"; that is, defining the system in terms of the attributes or interactions of the units.

In order to avoid reductionism and to gain rigor and parsimony, Waltz (1979: 82–101) erects his theory on the foundations of three core propositions that define the structure of the international system. The first concentrates on the principles by which the system is ordered. The contemporary system is anarchic and decentralized rather than hierarchical; although differing in many respects, each unit (state) is formally equal. Because Waltz strives for a universal theory that is not limited to any era, he uses the term "unit" to refer to the constituent members of the system; in the contemporary system these are states, but in order to reflect Waltz's intent more faithfully, the term "unit" is used here. A second defining proposition is the character of the units. An anarchic system is composed of similar sovereign units and therefore the functions that they perform are also similar rather than different; for example, all have the task of providing for their own security. In contrast, a hierarchical system would be characterized by some type of division of labor, as is the case in domestic politics. Finally, there is the distribution of capabilities among units in the system. Although capabilities are a unit-level attribute, the distribution of capabilities is a system-level concept.

A change in any of these elements constitutes a change in system structure. The first element of structure as defined by Waltz is a quasi-constant because the ordering principle rarely changes, and the second element drops out of the analysis because the functions of units are similar as long as the system remains anarchic. Thus, the last of the three attributes, the distribution of capabilities, plays the central role in Waltz's model.

Waltz (1970, 1981) uses his theory to deduce the central characteristics of international relations. These include some nonobvious propositions about the contemporary international system. For example, with respect to system stability (defined as maintenance of its anarchic character and no consequential variation in the number of major actors) he concludes that (1) because the bipolar system reduces uncertainty, it is more stable than alternative structures; (2) interdependence has declined rather than increased during the twentieth century, a tendency that has actually contributed to stability; and (3) the proliferation of nuclear weapons may contribute to rather than erode system stability.

Unlike some system-level models, Waltz's effort to bring rigor and parsimony to realism has stimulated a good deal of further research, but it has not escaped controversy and criticism (Grieco, 1990; Walt, 1987; Keohane, 1986). Leaving aside highly charged polemics—for example, that Waltz and his supporters are guilty of engaging in a "totalitarian project of global proportions" (Ashley, 1984: 228)—most of the vigorous debate has centered on four alleged deficiencies relating to interests and preferences, system change, misallocation of variables between the system and unit levels, and an ability to explain outcomes in generalities only.

Specifically, a spare structural approach suffers from an inability to identify adequately the nature and sources of interests and preferences because these are unlikely to derive solely from the structure of the system. Ideology or domestic considerations may often be at least as important. Consequently, the model is also unable to specify how interests and preferences may change. The three defining characteristics of system structure are too general, moreover, and thus they are not sufficiently sensitive to specify the sources and dynamics of system change. The critics buttress their claim that the model is too static by pointing to Waltz's assertion that there has been only a single structural change in the international system during the past three centuries.

Another drawback is the restrictive definition of system properties, which leads Waltz to misplace, and therefore neglect, elements of international relations that properly belong at the system level. Critics have focused on his treatment of the destructiveness of nuclear weapons and interdependence. Waltz labels these as unit-level properties, whereas some of his critics assert that they are in fact attributes of the system.

Finally, the distribution of capabilities explains outcomes in international affairs only in the most general way, falling short of answering the questions that are of central interest to many analysts. For example, the distribution of power at the end of World War II would have enabled one to predict the rivalry that emerged between the United States and the Soviet Union (as de Tocqueville did more than a century earlier), but it would have been inadequate for explaining the pattern of relations between these two nations—the Cold War rather than withdrawal into isolationism by either or both, a division of the world into spheres of influence, or World War III. In order to do so, it is necessary to explore political processes *within* states—at minimum within the United States and the USSR—as well as *between* them.

Robert Gilpin (1981: 10–11) shares with Waltz the core assumptions of modern realism, but his study of *War and Change in World Politics* also attempts to cope with some of the criticism leveled at Waltz's theory by focusing on the dynamics of system change. Drawing upon both economic and sociological theory, his model is based on five core propositions. The first is that the international system is stable—in a state of equilibrium—if no state believes that it is profitable to attempt to change it. Secondly, a state will attempt to change the status quo of the international system if the expected benefits outweigh the costs; that is, if there is an expected net gain for the revisionist state. Related to this is the proposition that a state will seek change through territorial, political, and economic expansion until the marginal costs of further change equal or exceed the marginal benefits. Moreover, when an equilibrium between the costs and benefits of further change and expansion is reached, the economic costs of maintaining the status quo (expenditures for military forces, support for allies, etc.) tend to rise faster than the resources needed to do so. An equilibrium exists when no powerful state believes that a change in the system would yield additional net benefits. Finally, if the resulting disequilibrium between the existing governance of the international system and the redistribution of power is not resolved, the system will be changed and a new equilibrium reflecting the distribution of relative capabilities will be established.

Unlike Waltz, Gilpin (1981, chap. 4) includes state-level processes in order to explain change. Differential economic growth rates among nations (a structural–systemic-level variable) play a vital role in his explanation for the rise and decline of great powers, but his model also includes propositions about the law of diminishing returns on investments, the impact of affluence on martial spirits and on the ratio of consumptions to investment, and structural change in the economy (see also Kennedy, 1987). Table 1 summarizes some key elements of realism. It also contrasts them to two other system-level models of international relations—the liberal and the World System models, to which we now turn our attention.

TABLE 1 **Three Models of the International System**

	Realism	Liberalism	World System
Type of model	Classical: descriptive and normative Modern: deductive	Descriptive and normative	Descriptive and normative
Central problems	Causes of war Conditions of peace	Broad agenda of social, economic, and environmental issues arising from gap between demands and resources	Inequality and exploitation Uneven development
Conception of current international system	Structural anarchy	Global society Complex interdependence (structure varies by issue-area)	World capitalist system
Key actors	Geographically based units (tribes, city-states, nation-states, etc.)	Highly permeable nation-states *plus* a broad range of nonstate actors, including IOs, IGOs, NGOs, and individuals[a]	Classes and their agents
Central motivations	National interest Security Power	Human needs and wants	Class interests
Loyalties	To geographically based groups (from tribes to nation-states)	Loyalties to nation-state declining To emerging global values and institutions that transcend those of the nation-state and/or to subnational groups	To class values and interests that transcend those of the nation-state

Central processes	Search for security and survival	Aggregate effects of decisions by national and nonnational actors How units (not limited to nation-states) cope with a growing agenda of threats and opportunities arising from human wants	Modes of production and exchange International division of labor in a world capitalist system
Likelihood of system transformation	Low (basic structural elements of system have revealed an ability to persist despite many other kinds of changes)	High in the direction of the model (owing to the rapid pace of technological change, etc.)	High in the direction of the model (owing to inherent contradictions within the world capitalist system)
Sources of theory, insights, and evidence	Politics History Economics (especially "modern" realists)	Broad range of social sciences Natural and technological sciences	Marxist–Leninist theory (several variants)

[a] IO = International Organization; IGO = Intergovernmental Organization; NGO = Nongovernmental Organization.

LIBERAL THEORIES

Just as there are variants of realism, there are several liberal theories, but this discussion focuses on two common denominators. They all challenge the first and third core propositions of realism identified earlier, asserting that inordinate attention to the war/peace issue and the nation-state renders it an increasingly anachronistic model of global relations (Keohane and Nye, 1977; Morse, 1976; Rosenau, 1980; Mansbach and Vasquez, 1981; Scott, 1982; and J. Rosenau, 1990).

The agenda of critical problems confronting states has been vastly expanded during the twentieth century. Attention to the issues of war and peace is by no means misdirected according to proponents of a liberal perspective, but concerns for welfare, modernization, the environment, and the like are today no less potent sources of motivation and action. Indeed many liberals define security in terms that are broader than the geopolitical–military spheres, and they emphasize the potential for cooperative relations among nations. Institution building to reduce uncertainty and fears of perfidy; improved international education and communication to ameliorate fears and antagonisms based on misinformation and misperceptions; and the positive-sum possibilities of such activities as trade are but a few of the ways, according to liberals, by which nations may jointly gain and thus mitigate, if not eliminate, the harshest features of international relations emphasized by the realists. Finally, the diffusion of knowledge and technology, combined with the globalization of communications, has vastly increased popular expectations. The resulting demands have outstripped resources and the ability of existing institutions—notably the nation-state—to cope effectively with them. Interdependence arises from an inability of even the most powerful states to cope, or to do so unilaterally or at acceptable levels of cost and risk, with issues ranging from trade to AIDS and immigration to environmental threats.

Paralleling the widening agenda of critical issues is the expansion of actors whose behavior can have a significant impact beyond national boundaries; indeed, the cumulative effects of their actions can have profound consequences for the international system. Thus, although nation-states continue to be important international actors, they possess a declining ability to control their own destinies. The aggregate effect of actions by multitudes of nonstate actors can have potent effects that transcend political boundaries. These may include such powerful or highly visible nonstate organizations as Exxon, the Organization of Petroleum Exporting Countries, or the Palestine Liberation Organization. On the other hand, the cumulative effects of decisions by less powerful or less visible actors may also have profound international consequences. For example, decisions by thousands of individuals, mutual funds, banks, pension funds, and other financial institutions to sell securities on 19 October 1987 not only resulted in an unprecedented "crash" on Wall Street, but within hours its consequences were felt throughout the entire global financial system. Governments might take such actions as loosening credit or even closing exchanges, but they were largely unable to contain the effects of the panic.

The widening agenda of critical issues, most of which lack a purely national solution, has also led to creation of new actors that transcend political boundaries; for example, international organizations, transnational organizations, nongovernment organizations, multinational corporations, and the like. Thus, not only does an exclusive focus on the war/peace issue fail to capture the complexities of contemporary international life but it blinds the analyst to the institutions, processes, and norms that permit cooperation and significantly mitigate some features of an anarchic system. In short, according to liberal perspectives, an adequate understanding of the emergent global system must recognize that no single model is likely to be sufficient for all issues and that if it restricts attention to the manner in which states deal with traditional security concerns, it is more likely to obfuscate rather than clarify the realities of contemporary world affairs.

The liberal models have several important virtues. They recognize that international behavior and outcomes arise from a multiplicity of motives, not merely security, at least if security is defined solely in military or strategic terms. They also alert us to the fact that important international processes and conditions originate not only in the actions of nation-states but also in the aggregated behavior of other actors. These models not only enable the analyst to deal with a broader agenda of critical issues but, more importantly, they force one to contemplate a much richer menu of demands, processes, and outcomes than would be derived from power-centered realist models. Stated differently, liberal theories are more sensitive to the possibility that politics of trade, currency, immigration, health, the environment, and the like may significantly and systematically differ from those typically associated with security issues.

On the other hand, some liberal analysts underestimate the potency of nationalism and the durability of the nation-state. Almost three decades ago one of them wrote that "the nation is declining in its importance as a political unit to which allegiances are attached" (Rosenau, 1968: 39; see also Rosecrance, 1986; Herz, 1957, 1968). Objectively, nationalism may be an anachronism but, for better or worse, powerful loyalties are still attached to nation-states. The suggestion that, because even some well-established nations have experienced independence movements among ethnic, cultural, or religious minorities, the sovereign territorial state may be in decline is not wholly persuasive. Indeed, that evidence perhaps points to precisely the opposite conclusion: In virtually every region of the world there are groups that seek to create or restore geographically based entities in which their members may enjoy the status and privileges associated with sovereign territorial statehood. Evidence from Poland to Palestine, Serbia to Sri Lanka, Estonia to Eritrea, Armenia to Afghanistan, and elsewhere seem to indicate that obituaries for nationalism may be somewhat premature.

The notion that such powerful non-national actors as major multinational corporations (MNCs) will soon transcend the nation-state seems equally premature (Vernon, 1971, 1991). International drug rings do appear capable of dominating such states as Colombia and Panama. However, the pattern of outcomes in confrontations between MNCs and states, including cases involving major expropriations of corporate properties, indicates that even relatively weak nations are not always the hapless pawns of the MNCs. Case studies by Joseph Grieco (1984) and Gary Gereffi (1983), among others, indicate that MNC–state relations yield a wide variety of outcomes.

Underlying the liberal critique of realist models is that the latter are too wedded to the past and are thus incapable of dealing adequately with change. For the present, however, even if global dynamics arise from multiple sources (including nonstate actors), the actions of nation-states and their agents would appear to remain the major sources of change in the international system. However, the last group of systemic models, the Marxist/World System/Dependency models—hereafter cited as World System models—downplay the role of the nation-state even further.

As in other parts of this essay, many of the distinctions among World System models are inevitably lost by treating them together and by focusing on their common features. These models challenge both the war/peace and state-centered features of realism, but they do so in ways that differ sharply from challenges of liberal theories (Galtung, 1971; Cockroft, Frank, and Johnson, 1972; Wallerstein, 1974a, 1974b; Chase-Dunn, 1979, 1981; Kubalkova and Cruickshank, 1985; and Denemark and Thomas, 1988). Rather than focusing on war and peace, World System models direct attention to quite different issues, including uneven development, poverty, and exploitation within and between nations. These conditions, arising from the dynamics of the modes of production and exchange, are basic, and they must be incorporated into any analysis of intra- and inter-nation conflict.

At a superficial level, according to adherents of these models, what exists today may be described as a system of nation-states. More fundamentally, however, the key groups within and between nations are classes and their agents: As Immanuel Wallerstein (1974a: 390) put it, "in the nineteenth and twentieth centuries there has been only one world system in existence, the world capitalist world economy." The "world capitalist system" is characterized by a highly unequal division of labor between the periphery and core. Those at the periphery are essentially the drawers of water and the hewers of wood whereas the latter appropriate the surplus of the entire world economy. This critical feature of the World System not only gives rise to and perpetuates a widening rather than narrowing gap between the wealthy core and poor periphery but also to a dependency relationship from which the latter are unable to break loose. Moreover, the class structure within the core, characterized by a growing gap between capital and labor, is faithfully reproduced in the periphery so that elites there share with their counterparts in the core an interest in perpetuating the system. Thus, in contrast to realist theories, World System models encompass and integrate theories of both the global and domestic arenas.

As has been the case with other systemic theories, World System models have been subjected to trenchant critiques (Smith, 1979; Zolberg, 1981). The state, nationalism, security dilemmas, and related concerns essentially drop out of these analyses; they are at the theoretical periphery rather than at the core: "Capitalism was from the beginning an affair of the world economy," Wallerstein (1974a: 401) asserts, "not of nation-states." A virtue of many World System models is that they take a long historical perspective on world affairs rather than merely focusing on contemporary issues. However, by neglecting nation-states and the dynamics arising from their efforts to deal with security in an anarchical system—or at best relegating these actors and motivations to a minor role—these models lose much of their appeal. Models of world affairs during the past few centuries that fail to give the nation-state a central role seem as incomplete as analyses *of Hamlet* that neglect the central character and his motivations.

Second, the concept of "world capitalist system" is central to these models, but its relevance for much of the twentieth century can be questioned. Whether this term accurately describes the world of the 1880s could be debated, but its declining analytical utility or even descriptive accuracy for international affairs of the post–World War II period seems clear. Thus, one could question Wallerstein's assertion (1974a: 412) two decades ago that "there are today no socialist systems in the world economy any more than there are feudal systems because there is only *one world system*. It is a world economy and it is *by definition capitalist* in form." Where within a system so defined would we have located the USSR or Eastern Europe? During the Cold War this area included enough industrial nations that it hardly seems to belong in the periphery. Yet to place these states in the core of a "world capitalist system" would require conceptual gymnastics of a high order. Would it have increased our analytical capabilities to have described the USSR and East European countries as "state capitalists"? Where would we have located China? How do we explain dynamics within the "periphery," or the differences between rapid-growth Asian nations such as South Korea, Taiwan, or Singapore and their slow-growth neighbors in Bangladesh, North Korea, and the Philippines? The inclusion of a third structural position—the "semiperiphery"— does not wholly answer these questions.

Third, World System models have considerable difficulty in explaining relations between noncapitalist nations during the Cold War—for example, between the USSR and its East European neighbors or China—much less outright conflict between them. Indeed, advocates of these models have usually restricted their attention to West–South relations, eschewing analyses of East–East or East–South relations. Would one have gained greater and more general analytical power by using the lenses and language of marxism or of realism to describe relations between the USSR and Eastern Europe, the USSR and Third World nations, China and Vietnam, India and Sri Lanka, or Vietnam and Kampuchea? Were these relationships better described and understood in terms of such World System categories as "class" or such realist ones as "relative capabilities"?

Finally, the earlier observations about the persistence of nationalism as an element of international relations seem equally appropriate here. Perhaps national loyalties can be dismissed as prime examples of "false consciousness," but even in areas that experienced almost two generations of one-party Communist rule, as in Poland, evidence that feelings of transnational solidarity with workers in other socialist nations have replaced nationalist sentiments is in short supply.

DECISION-MAKING CHALLENGES TO REALISM

Many advocates of realism recognize that it cannot offer fine-grained analyses of foreign policy behavior, and, as noted earlier, Waltz denies that it is desirable or even possible to combine theories of international relations and foreign policy. Decision-making models challenge the premise that it is fruitful to conceptualize the nation as a unitary rational actor whose behavior can adequately be explained by reference to the system structure—the second, fourth, and fifth realist propositions identified earlier—because individuals, groups, and organizations acting in the name of the state are also sensitive to pressures and constraints other than international ones, including elite maintenance, electoral politics, public opinion, pressure group activities, ideological preferences, and bureaucratic politics. Such core concepts as "the national interest" are not defined solely by the international system, much less by its structure alone, but they are also likely to reflect elements within the domestic political arena. Thus, rather than assuming with the realists that the state can be conceptualized as a "black box"—that the domestic political processes are both hard to comprehend and generally superfluous for explaining its external behavior—decision-making analysts believe one must indeed take these internal processes into account, with special attention directed at decision makers and their "definitions of the situation" (Snyder, Bruck, and Sapin, 1962). In order to reconstruct how nations deal with each other, it is necessary to view the situation through the eyes of those who act in the name of the nation-state: decision makers, and the group and bureaucratic-organizational contexts within which they act. Table 2 provides an overview of three major types of decision-making models.

Traditional models of complex organizations and bureaucracy emphasize the positive contributions to be expected from a division of labor, hierarchy, and centralization, coupled with expertise, rationality, and obedience. Such models assume that clear boundaries should be maintained between politics and decision making, on the one hand, and administration and implementation on the other. Following pioneering works by Chester I. Barnard (1938), Herbert Simon (1957), James G. March and Simon (1958), and others, more recent theories depict organizations quite differently. The central premise is that decision making in bureaucratic organizations is not constrained only by the legal and formal norms that are intended to enhance the rational and eliminate the capricious aspects of bureaucratic behavior. Rather, most complex organizations are seen as generating serious "information pathologies" (Wilensky, 1967). There is an *emphasis* upon rather than a denial of the political character of bureaucracies,

TABLE 2 Three Models of Decision Making

	BUREAUCRATIC POLITICS	GROUP DYNAMICS	INDIVIDUAL DECISION MAKING
Conceptualization of decision making	Decision making as the result of bargaining within bureaucratic organizations	Decision making as the product of group interaction	Decision making as the result of individual choice
Premises	Central organizational values are imperfectly internalized Organizational behavior is political behavior Structure and standard operating procedures affect substance and quality of decisions	Most decisions are made by small elite groups Group is different than the sum of its members Group dynamic affect substance and quality of decisions	Importance of subjective appraisal (definition of the situation) and cognitive processes (information processing, etc.)
Constraints on rational decision making	Imperfect information, resulting from centralization, hierarchy, and specialization Organizational inertia Conflict between individual and organizational utilities Bureaucratic politics and bargaining dominate decision making and implementation of decisions	Groups may be more effective for some tasks, less for others Pressures for conformity Risk-taking propensity of groups (controversial) Quality of leadership "Groupthink"	Cognitive limits on rationality Information processing distorted by cognitive consistency dynamics (unmotivated biases) Systematic and motivated biases in causal analysis Individual differences in abilities related to decision making (e.g., problem-solving ability, tolerance of ambiguity, defensiveness and anxiety, information seeking, etc.)
Sources of theory, insights, and evidence	Organization theory Sociology of bureaucracies Bureaucratic politics	Social psychology Sociology of small groups	Cognitive dissonance Cognitive psychology Dynamic psychology

as well as on other "informal" aspects of organizational behavior. Complex organizations are composed of individuals and units with conflicting perceptions, values, and interests that may arise from parochial self-interest ("what is best for my bureau is also best for my career") and also from different perceptions of issues arising ineluctably from a division of labor ("where you stand depends on where you sit"). Organizational norms and memories, prior policy commitments, normal organizational inertia, routines, and standard operating procedures may shape and perhaps distort the structuring of problems, channeling of information, use of expertise, and implementation of executive decisions. The consequences of bureaucratic politics within the executive branch or within the government as a whole may significantly constrain the manner in which issues are defined, the range of options that may be considered, and the manner in which executive decisions are implemented by subordinates. Consequently, organizational decision making is essentially political in character, dominated by bargaining for resources, roles, and missions, and by compromise rather than analysis (Kissinger, 1960; Allison, 1971; Allison and Halperin, 1972; and Halperin, 1974).

Perhaps because of the dominant position of the realist perspective, most students of foreign policy have only recently incorporated bureaucratic–organizational models and insights into their analyses. An ample literature on budgeting, weapons acquisitions, military doctrine, and similar situations confirms that foreign and defense policy bureaucracies rarely conform to the Weberian "ideal type" of rational organization (see for example, Williamson, 1969; Lauren, 1975; and Posen, 1984). Some analysts assert that crises may provide the motivation and means for reducing some of the nonrational aspects of bureaucratic behavior. Crises are likely to push decisions to the top of the organization where higher quality of intelligence is available; information is more likely to enter the top of the hierarchy directly, reducing the distorting effects of information processing through several levels of the organization; and broader, less parochial values may be invoked. Short decision time in crises reduces the opportunities for decision making by bargaining, log rolling, incrementalism, lowest-common-denominator values, "muddling through," and the like (Wilensky, 1967; Lowi, 1969; and Verba, 1961).

However, even studies of international crises from a bureaucratic–organizational perspective are not uniformly sanguine about decision making in such circumstances (Hermann, 1963). Graham T. Allison's (1971) analysis of the Cuban missile crisis identified several critical bureaucratic malfunctions concerning dispersal of American aircraft in Florida, the location of the naval blockade, and grounding of weather-reconnaissance flights from Alaska that might stray over the Soviet Union. Richard Neustadt's (1970) study of two crises involving the United States and Great Britain revealed significant misperceptions of each other's interests and policy processes. And an examination of three American nuclear alerts found substantial gaps in understanding and communication between policymakers and the military leaders who were responsible for implementing the alerts (Sagan, 1985).

Critics of some organizational–bureaucratic models and the studies employing them have focused on several points (Rothstein, 1972; Krasner, 1972; Art, 1973; Ball, 1974; and Perlmutter, 1974). They point out, for instance, that the emphasis on bureaucratic bargaining fails to differentiate adequately between the positions of the participants. In the American system, the president is not just another player in a complex bureaucratic game. Not only must he ultimately decide but he must also select who the other players will be, a process that may be crucial in shaping the ultimate decisions. If General Matthew Ridgway and Attorney General Robert Kennedy played key roles in the American decisions not to intervene in Indochina in 1954 or not to bomb Cuba in 1962, it was because Presidents Eisenhower and Kennedy chose to accept their advice rather than that of other officials. Also the conception of bureaucratic bargaining tends to emphasize its nonrational elements to the exclusion of genuine intellectual differences that may be rooted in broader concerns—including disagreements on what national interests, if any, are at stake in a situation—rather than narrow parochial interests. Indeed, properly managed, decision processes that promote and legitimize "multiple advocacy" among officials may facilitate high-quality decisions (George, 1972).

These models may be especially useful for understanding the slippage between executive decisions and foreign policy actions that may arise during *implementation*, but they may be less valuable for explaining the decisions themselves. Allison's (1971) study of the Cuban missile crisis does not indicate an especially strong correlation between bureaucratic roles and evaluations of the situation or policy recommendations, as predicted by his "Model III" (bureaucratic politics), and recent evidence about deliberations during the crisis does not offer more supporting evidence for that model (Welch and Blight, 1987-1988; Bundy and Blight, 1987–1988; and Blight and Welch, 1989). On the other hand, Allison does present some compelling evidence concerning policy implementation that casts considerable doubt on the adequacy of "Model I" (the realist conception of the unitary rational actor).

Another decision-making model supplements bureaucratic–organizational models by narrowing the field of view to top policymakers. This approach lends itself well to investigations of foreign policy decisions, which are usually made in a small-group context. Some analysts have drawn upon sociology and social psychology to assess the impact of various types of group dynamics on decision making (de Rivera, 1968; Paige, 1968; Janis, 1972, 1982). Underlying these models are the premises that the group is not merely the sum of its members (thus decisions emerging from the group are likely to be different than what a simple aggregation of individual preferences and abilities might suggest), and that group dynamics, the interactions among its members, can have a significant impact on the substance and quality of decisions.

Groups often perform better than individuals in coping with complex tasks due to diverse perspectives and talents, an effective division of labor, and high-quality debates centering on evaluations of the situation and policy recommendations for dealing with it. Groups may also provide decision makers with emotional and other types of support that may facilitate coping with complex problems. On the other hand, they may exert pressures for conformity to group norms, thereby inhibiting the search for information and policy options or cutting it off prematurely, ruling out the legitimacy of some options, curtailing independent evaluation, and suppressing some forms of intragroup conflict that might serve to clarify goals, values, and options. Classic experiments by the psychologist Solomon Asch revealed the extent to which group members will suppress their beliefs and judgments when faced with a majority adhering to the contrary view, even a counterfactual one (Festinger, 1965; Asch, 1953, 1965).

Drawing upon a series of historical case studies, social psychologist Irving L. Janis (1972, 1982, and a critique in Etheredge, 1985) has identified a different variant of group dynamics, which he labeled "groupthink" to distinguish it from the more familiar type of conformity pressure on "deviant" members of the group. Janis challenged the conventional wisdom that strong cohesion among the members of a group invariably enhances performance. Under certain conditions, strong cohesion can markedly degrade the group's performance in decision making. Thus, the members of a cohesive group may, as a means of dealing with the stresses of having to cope with consequential problems and in order to bolster self-esteem, increase the frequency and intensity of face-to-face interaction. This results in a greater identification with the group and less competition within it. The group dynamics of what Janis called "concurrence seeking" may displace or erode reality testing and sound information processing and judgment. As a consequence, groups may be afflicted by unwarranted feelings of optimism and invulnerability, stereotyped images of adversaries, and inattention to warnings. Janis's analyses (1982: 260–76) of both "successful" (the Marshall Plan, the Cuban missile crisis) and "unsuccessful" (The Munich Conference of 1938, Pearl Harbor, the Bay of Pigs invasion) cases indicate that "groupthink" or other decision-making pathologies are not inevitable, and he developed some guidelines for avoiding them.

Still other decision-making analysts focus on the individual. Many approaches to the policymaker emphasize the gap between the demands of the: classical model of rational decision making and the substantial body of theory and evidence about various constraints that come into play in even relatively simple choice situations (Abelson and Levi, 1985; Jervis, 1976; Steinbruner, 1974; and Axelrod, 1976). The more recent perspectives, drawing upon cognitive psychology, go well beyond some of the earlier formulations that drew upon psychodynamic theories to identify various types of psychopathologies among political leaders: paranoia, authoritarianism, and the displacement of private motives on public objects, among others (Lasswell, 1930). These more recent efforts to include the information-processing behavior of the decision maker in foreign policy analyses have been directed at the cognitive and motivational constraints that, in varying degrees, affect the decision-making performance of "normal" rather than pathological subjects.

Thus, attention is directed to all leaders, not merely those, such as Hitler or Stalin, who display evidence of clinical abnormalities.

The major challenges to the classical model have focused on limited human capabilities for performing the tasks required by objectively rational decision making. The cognitive constraints on rationality include limits on the individual's capacity to receive, process, and assimilate information about the situation; an inability to identify the entire set of policy alternatives; fragmentary knowledge about the consequences of each option; and an inability to order preferences on a single utility scale (March and Simon, 1958: 113). These have given rise to several conceptions of the decision maker's strategies for dealing with complexity, uncertainty, incomplete or contradictory information, and, paradoxically, information overload. They variously characterize the individual as a problem solver, naive or intuitive scientist, cognitive balancer, dissonance avoider, information seeker, cybernetic information processor, and reluctant decision maker.

Three of these conceptions seem especially relevant for foreign policy analysis. The first views the decision maker as a "bounded rationalist" who seeks satisfactory rather than optimal solutions. As Herbert Simon (1957: 198) has put it, "The capacity of the human mind for formulating and solving complex problems is very small compared with the size of the problem whose solution is required for objectively rational behavior in the real world—or even a reasonable approximation of such objective rationality." Moreover, it is not practical for the decision maker to seek optimal choices; for example, because of the costs of searching for information. Related to this is the more recent concept of the individual as a "cognitive miser," one who seeks to simplify complex problems and to find short cuts to problem solving and decision making.

Another approach is to look at the decision maker as an "error-prone intuitive scientist" who is likely to commit a broad range of inferential mistakes. Thus, rather than emphasizing the limits on the search for policy options, information processing, and the like, this conception views the decision maker as the victim of flawed heuristics or decision rules who uses data poorly. There are tendencies to underuse rate data in making judgments, believe in the "law of small numbers," underuse diagnostic information, overweight low probabilities and underweight high ones, and violate other requirements of consistency and coherence. These deviations from classical decision theory are traced to the psychological principles that govern perceptions of problems and evaluations of options (Tversky and Kahneman, 1981; Kahneman and Tversky, 1973; and Kahneman, Slovic, and Tversky, 1982).

The final perspective emphasizes the motivational forces that will not or cannot be controlled (Janis and Mann, 1977; Steiner, 1983; and Lebow, 1987). Decision makers are not merely rational calculators; important decisions generate conflict, and a reluctance to make irrevocable choices often results in behavior that reduces quality of decisions. These models direct the analyst's attention to policymakers' belief systems, images of relevant actors' perceptions, information processing strategies, heuristics, certain personality traits (ability to tolerate ambiguity, cognitive complexity, etc.), and their impact on decision making.

Despite this diversity of perspectives and the difficulty of choosing between cognitive and motivational models, there has been some convergence on several types of constraints that may affect decision processes (Kinder and Weiss, 1978; Holsti, 1976). One involves the consequences of efforts to achieve cognitive consistency on perceptions and information processing. Several kinds of systematic bias have been identified in both experimental and historical studies. Policymakers have a propensity to assimilate and interpret information in ways that conform to rather than challenge existing beliefs, preferences, hopes, and expectations. They may deny the need to confront tradeoffs between values by persuading themselves that an option will satisfy all of them, or they may indulge in rationalizations to bolster the selected option while denigrating those that were not selected.

An extensive literature on styles of attribution has revealed several types of systematic bias in causal analysis. Perhaps the most important for foreign policy analysis is the basic attribution error—a tendency to explain the adversary's behavior in terms of his characteristics (for example, inherent aggressiveness or hostility) rather than in terms of the context or situation, while attributing one's own behavior to the latter (for example, legitimate security needs arising from a dangerous and uncertain environment) rather than to the former. A somewhat related type of double standard has been noted by George Kennan (1978: 87–88): "Now is it our view that we should take account only of their [Soviet] capabilities, disregarding their intentions, but we should expect them to take account only for our supposed intentions, disregarding our capabilities?"

Analysis also have illustrated the effect on decisions of policymakers assumptions about order and predictability in the environment. Whereas a policymaker may have an acute appreciation of the disorderly environment in which he or she operates (arising, for example, from domestic political processes), there is a tendency to assume that others, especially adversaries, are free of such constraints. Graham T. Allison (1971), Robert Jervis (1976), and others have demonstrated that decision makers tend to believe that the realist "unitary rational actor" is the appropriate representation of the opponent's decision processes and, thus, whatever happens is the direct result of deliberate choices. For example, the hypothesis that the Soviet destruction of KAL flight 007 may have resulted from intelligence failures or bureaucratic foul-ups, rather than from a calculated decision to murder civilian passengers, was either not given serious consideration or it was suppressed for strategic reasons (Hersh, 1986).

Drawing on a very substantial experimental literature, several models linking crisis-induced stress to decision processes have been developed and used in foreign policy studies (Hermann, 1972; Hermann and Hermann, 1975; Hermann, 1979; Holsti, 1972; and Holsti and George, 1975). Irving L. Janis and Leon Mann (1977:3) have developed a more general conflict-theory model that conceives of man as a "reluctant decision maker" and focuses upon "when, how and why psychological stress generated by decisional cor imposes limitations on the rationality of a person's decisions." One may employ five strategies for coping with a situation requiring a decision: unconflicted adherence to existing policy, unconflicted change, defensive avoidance, hypervigliance, and vigilant decision making. The first four strategies are likely to yield low-quality decisions due to incomplete search for information, inadequate appraisal of the situation and options, and poor contingency planning, whereas vigilant decision making, characterized by a more adequate performance of vital tasks, is more likely to result in a high-quality choice. Decision styles are affected by information about risks, expectations of finding a better option, and time for adequate search and deliberation.

A final approach attempts to show the impact of personal traits on decision making. There is no shortage of typologies linking leadership traits to decision-making behavior, but systematic research demonstrating such links is in much shorter supply. Still, some efforts have borne fruit. Margaret G. Hermann (1980, 1984) has developed a scheme for analyzing leaders' public statements of unquestioned authorship for eight variables: nationalism, belief in one's ability to control the environment, need for power, need for affiliation, ability to differentiate environments, distrust of others, self-confidence, and task emphasis. The scheme has been tested with impressive results on a broad range of contemporary leaders. Alexander L. George (1969) has reformulated Nathan Leites's (1951) concept of "operational code" into five philosophical and five instrumental beliefs that are intended to describe politically relevant core beliefs, stimulating a number of empirical studies and, more recently, further significant conceptual revisions (Walker, 1977, 1983). Finally several psychologists have developed and tested the concept of "integrative complexity," defined as the ability to make subtle distinction along multiple dimensions, flexibility, and the integration of large amounts of diverse information to make coherent judgments. A standard content analysis technique has been used for research on documentary materials generated by top decision makers in a wide range of international crises, including World War I, Cuba (1962), Morocco (1911), Berlin (1948–1949 and 1961), Korea, and the Middle East wars of 1948, 1956, 1967, and 1973 (Suedfeld and Tetlock, 1977; Suedfeld, Tetlock, and Ramirez, 1977; Raphael, 1982; and Tetlock, 1985).

Decision-making approaches clearly permit the analyst to overcome many limitations of the systemic models described earlier, but not without costs. Those described here impose increasingly heavy data burdens on the analyst. Moreover, there is a danger that adding levels of analysis may result in an undisciplined proliferation of variables with at least two adverse consequences: It may become increasingly difficult to determine which are more or less important, and ad hoc explanations for individual cases erode the possibilities for broader generalizations across cases. However, well-designed, multicase, decision-making studies indicate that these and other traps are avoidable (George and Smoke, 1974; Smoke, 1977; Snyder and Diesing, 1977; Brecher and Geist, 1980; Lebow, 1981; Eckstein, 1975; and George, 1979).

The study of international relations and foreign policy has always been an eclectic undertaking, with extensive borrowing from disciplines other than political science and history (Wright, 1955). The primary differences today tend to be between two broad approaches. Analysts of the first school focus on the structure of the international system, often borrowing from economics for models, analogies, insights, and metaphors, with an emphasis on *rational preferences and strategy* and how these tend to be shaped and constrained by the structure of the international system. Decision-making analysts, meanwhile, display a concern for domestic political processes and tend to borrow from social psychology and psychology in order to understand better the *limits and barriers* to information processing and rational choice. For many purposes both approaches are necessary and neither is sufficient. Neglect of the system structure and its constraints may result in analyses that depict policymakers as relatively free agents with an almost unrestricted menu of choices, limited only by the scope of their ambitions and the resources at their disposal. At worst, this type of analysis can degenerate into Manichean explanations that depict foreign policies of the "bad guys" as the external manifestation of flawed leaders or domestic structures, whereas the "good guys" only react from necessity. Radical-right explanations of it the Cold War usually depicted Soviet policies as driven by inherently aggressive totalitarian communism and the United States as its blameless victim; radical-left explanations tended to be structurally similar, with the roles of aggressor and victim reversed (Holsti, 1974).

Conversely, neglect of foreign policy decision making not only leaves one unable to explain the dynamics of the international relations, but many important aspects of a nation's external behavior will be inexplicable. Advocates of realism have often argued its superiority for understanding the "high" politics of deterrence, containment, alliances, crises, and wars, if not necessarily for "low" politics. But there are several rejoinders to this line of reasoning first the low politics of trade, currencies, and other issues that are almost always highly sensitive to domestic pressures are becoming an increasingly important element of international relations. Second, the growing literature in the putative domain par excellence of realism—security issues—raises substantial doubts about the universal validity of the realist model even for these issues (in addition to the previously cited literature on war, crises, and deterrence, see Betts, 1987; Jervis, Lebow, and Stein, 1985; and Lebow, 1987). Finally, exclusive reliance on realist models and their assumptions of rationality may lead to unwarranted complacency about dangers in the international system. Nuclear weapons and other features of the system have no doubt contributed to the "long peace" among major powers (Gaddis, 1986). At the same time, however, a narrow focus on power balances, "correlations of forces," and other features of the international system will result in neglect of dangers—for example, the command, communication, control, intelligence problem or inadequate information processing—that can only be identified and analyzed by a decision-making perspective (Bracken, 1983; Blair, 1985; Steinbruner, 1981–1982; Sagan, 1985; and George, 1980).

This observation parallels that made three decades ago by the foremost contemporary proponent of realism: The third image (system structure) is necessary for understanding the context of international behavior, whereas the first and second images (decision makers and domestic political processes) are needed to understand dynamics within the system (Waltz, 1959: 238). But to acknowledge the existence of various levels of analysis is not enough. *What* the investigator wants to explain and the *level of specificity and comprehensiveness* to be sought should determine which level(s) of analysis are relevant and necessary. In this connection, it is essential to distinguish two different dependent variables: foreign policy decisions by states, on the one hand, and the outcomes of policy and interactions between two or more states, on the other. If the goal is to understand the former—foreign policy decisions—Harold and Margaret Sprout's (1957) notion of "psychological milieu" is relevant and sufficient; that is, the objective structural variables influence the decisions via the decision maker's perception and evaluation of those "outside" variables. However, if the goal is to explain outcomes, the "psychological milieu" is quite inadequate; the objective factors, even if misperceived or misjudged by the decision maker, will influence the outcome. Students of international relations are increasingly disciplining their use of multiple levels of analysis in studying outcomes that cannot be adequately explained via only a single level (for example, Yoffie, 1983; Odell, 1982; Larson, 1985; Snyder, 1984; Aggarwal, 1985; Posen, 1984; and Walt, 1987).

CONCLUSION

A renowned diplomatic historian has asserted that most theories of international relations flunked a critical test by failing to forecast the end of the Cold War (Gaddis, 1992–1993). This conclusion speculates on the related question of how well the theories discussed above might help us to understand international politics in the post–Cold War world. Dramatic events since the late 1980s would appear to have posed serious challenges for several theories, but one should be wary about writing premature obituaries for any of them. The importance of recent developments notwithstanding, one should avoid "naive (single case) falsification" of major theories. Further, less than six years after the Berlin Wall came down and less than four years after dissolution of the Soviet Union, some caution about declaring that major events and trends are irreversible seems warranted.

Because recent debates on the theories of international politics have often centered on realism, especially structural realism, most of these comments will focus on that approach. However, a few comments on the other two systemic theories may also be in order. Events of the past decade have not been kind to theories that draw at least in part from the works of Marx and Lenin, including World System approaches. This is not the place to engage in detailed analyses of the relative performance of centrally planned and market economics, either in the developed or developing worlds, but recent trends would appear to favor the latter by a wide margin. Moreover, we may gain greater leverage for understanding inter- and intrastate conflict in much of the "second" and "third" worlds by focusing on ethnic, nationalist, and religious passions rather than on the clash of class-based material interests. Nevertheless, we may expect materialist interpretations of world politics to persist, if only because their adherents may justly argue that theirs is a long-term perspective that should not be judged merely by specific events or short-term trends.

Liberal theories have generally fared better, at least for explaining relations among the industrial democracies. Progress toward economic unification of Europe, although not without detours and setbacks, would appear to provide significant support for the liberal view that, even in an anarchic world, major powers may find ways of cooperating and overcoming the constraint of the "relative gains" problem. Moreover, Wilson's thesis that a world of democratic nations will be more peaceful has stood the test of time rather well, at least in the sense that democratic nations don't go to war with each other (Doyle, 1983, 1986). His diagnosis that self-determination also supports peace may be correct in the abstract, but universal application of that principle is neither possible nor desirable, if only because it would result in immense bloodshed; the peaceful divorces of Norway and Sweden in 1905 and of the Czech Republic and Slovakia in 1992 are unfortunately not the norm. Although it appears that economic interests have come to dominate nationalist, ethnic, or religious passions among the industrial democracies, the evidence is far less assuring in other areas, including parts of the former Soviet Union, Central Europe, the Middle East, South Asia, and elsewhere.

Recent events appear to have created an especially acute challenge to structural realism. Although structural realism provides a parsimonious and elegant theory, its deficiencies are likely to become more rather than less apparent in the post–Cold War world. Its weaknesses in dealing with questions of system change and in specifying policy preferences other than survival and security are likely to be magnified. Moreover, whereas classical realism espouses a number of attractive prescriptive features (caution, humility, warnings against mistaking one's preferences for the moral laws of the universe), neorealism is an especially weak source of policy-relevant theory (George, 1993). Indeed some of the prescriptions put forward by neorealists seem reckless; for example, the suggestion to let Germany join the nuclear club (Mearsheimer, 1990). In addition to European economic cooperation, specific events that seem inexplicable by structural realism include Soviet acquiescence in the collapse of its empire and peaceful transformation of the system structure. These developments are especially telling because structural realism is explicitly touted as a theory of major powers (Waltz, 1979). Consequently, even as distinguished a realist as Robert Tucker (1992–1993: 36) has characterized the structural version of realism as "more questionable than ever."

More important, even though the international system remains anarchic, the possibility of war among major powers cannot wholly be dismissed, and proliferation may place nuclear weapons in the hands of leaders with little stake in maintaining the status quo, the constraints imposed by systemic imperatives on foreign policy choices are clearly eroding. National interests and even national security increasingly have come to be defined in ways that transcend the military/strategic concerns that are at the core of realist theory. Well before the disintegration of the Soviet Union, an Americans Talk Security survey revealed that the perceived threat to national security from "Soviet aggression around the world" ranked in a seventh-place tie with the "green-house effect" and well behind a number of post–Cold War, nonmilitary threats (ATS, 1988). Trade, drug trafficking, immigration, the environment, and AIDS are among the nonmilitary issues that regularly appear on lists of top national security threats as perceived by both mass publics and elites.

The expanded agenda of national interests, combined with the trend toward greater democracy in many parts of the world, suggests that we are entering an era in which the balance between the relative potency of systemic and domestic forces in shaping and constraining foreign policies is moving toward the latter. Such issues as trade, immigration, and others can be expected to enhance the impact of domestic actors—including public opinion and ethnic, religious, economic, and perhaps even regional pressure groups—while reducing the ability of executives to dominate policy process on the grounds, so frequently invoked during the Cold War, that the adept pursuit of national security requires secrecy, flexibility, and the ability to all with speed. In short, we are likely to see the increasing democratization of foreign policy in the post–Cold War era. And that brings us back to the point at which we started, for the relationship between democracy and foreign policy is another of the issues on which realists and liberals are in sharp disagreement. Realists such as de Tocqueville, Morgenthau, Lippmann, Kennan, and many others share a profound skepticism about the impact of demo cratic political processes, and especially of public opinion, on the quality and continuity of foreign policy. In contrast, liberals in the Kant–Wilson tradition maintain that more democratic foreign policy processes contribute to peace and stability in international politics. Thus, if domestic politics does in fact come to play an increasingly important role in shaping post–Cold War era foreign policies, that development will ensure continuation of the venerable debate between realists and liberals.

NOTE

This chapter draws heavily on my essay "Models of International Relations and Foreign Policy," *Diplomatic History* (Winter, 1989). Alexander L. George, Joseph Grieco, Michael J. Hogan, Timothy Lomperis, Roy Melbourne, James N. Rosenau, and Andrew M. Scott kindly provided very helpful comments and suggestions on early drafts of that essay.

REFERENCES

Abelson, Robert, and A. Levi. (1985) "Decision Making and Decision Theory," in Gardner Lindzey and Elliott Aronson, eds., *Handbook of Social Psychology*, 3rd ed., vol. 1. New York: Random House.

Aggarwal, Vinod K. (1985) *Liberal Protectionism: The International Politics of Organized Textile Trade*. Berkeley: University of California Press.

Allison, Graham T. (1971). *Essence of Decision: Explaining the Cuban Missile Crisis*. Boston: Little, Brown.

Allison, Graham T., and Morton Halperin. (1972) "Bureaucratic Politics: A Paradigm and Some Policy Implications," *World Politics* 24: 40–79.

Americans Talk Security. (1988) *Attitudes Concerning National Security: National Survey No. 9*. Winchester, Mass.: ATS.

Aron, Raymond. (1966) *Peace and War*. Garden City, N.Y.: Doubleday.

Art, Robert J. (1973) "Bureaucratic Politics and American Foreign Policy: A Critique," *Policy Sciences* 4: 467–90.

Asch, Solomon. (1965) "Opinions and Social Pressure," in A. Paul Hare, Edgar G. Borgotta, and Robert F. Bates, eds., *Small Groups: Studies in Social Interaction*. New York: Knopf.

_____. (1953) "Effects of Group Pressures upon Modification and Distortion of Judgment," in Dorwin Cartwright and A. Zander, eds., *Group Dynamics: Research and Theory*. Evanston, Ill.: Row, Peterson.

Ashley, Richard K. (1984) "The Poverty of Neo-Realism," *International Organization* 38: 225–86.

Axelrod, Robert. (1976) *The Structure of Decision*. Princeton, N.J.: Princeton University Press.

Ball, Desmond J. (1974) "The Blind Men and the Elephant: A Critique of Bureaucratic Politics Theory," *Australian Outlook* 28: 71–92.

Barnard, Chester. (1938) *Functions of the Executive*. Cambridge, Mass.: Harvard University Press.

Betts, Richard. (1987) *Nuclear Blackmail and Nuclear Balance*. Washington D.C.: Brookings Institution.

Blair, Bruce. (1985) *Strategic Command and Control*. Washington, D.C.: Brookings Institution.

Blight, James, and David Welch. (1989) *On the Brink*. New York: Hill and Wang.

Bracken, Paul. (1983) *Command and Control of Nuclear Forces*. New Haven, Conn.:, Yale University Press.

Brecher, Michael, and Barbara Geist. (1980) *Decisions in Crisis: Israel, 1967 and 1973*. Berkeley: University of California Press.

Bueno de Mesquita, Bruce. (1985) "The War Trap Revisited: A Revised Expected Utility Model," *American Political Science Review* 79: 156–77.

_____, (1981) *The War Trap*. New Haven, Conn.: Yale University Press.

Bull, Hedley. (1977) *The Anarchical Society: A Study of Order In World Politics*. London: Macmillan.

Bundy, McGeorge, and James G. Blight. (1987–1988) "October 27, 1962: Transcripts of the Meetings of the ExComm," *International Security* 12: 30–92.

Carr, E. H. (1939). *Twenty Year Crisis*. London: Macmillan.

Chase-Dunn, Christopher. (1981) "Interstate System and Capitalist World-Economy: One Logic or Two?" *International Studies Quarterly* 25: 19–42.

_____. (1979) "Comparative Research on World System Characteristics," *International Studies Quarterly* 23: 601–23.

Claude, Inis L. (1962) *Power and International Relations.* New York: Random House.

Cockroft, James, Andre Gunder Frank, and Dale L. Johnson. (1972) *Dependence and Under-Development.* New York: Anchor Books.

de Rivera, Joseph. (1968) *The Psychological Dimension of Foreign Policy.* Columbus, Ohio: C. E. Merrill.

Denemark, Robert A., and Kenneth O. Thomas. (1988) "The Brenner–Wallerstein Debates," *International Studies Quarterly* 28: 47–66.

Deutsch, Karl, and J. David Singer. (1964) "Multipolar Power Systems and Interntional Stability," *World Politics* 16: 390–406.

Doyle, Michael. (1986) "Liberalism and World Politics," *American Political Science Review* 80: 1151–70.

_____. (1983) "Kant, Liberal Legacies, and Foreign Affairs," *Philosophy and Public Affairs* 12: 205–35.

Eckstein, Harry. (1975) "Case Study and Theory in Political Science," in Fred I. Greenstein and Nelson W. Polsby, eds., *Handbook of Political Science.* Reading, Mass.: Addison-Wesley.

Etheredge, Lloyd. (1985) *Can Governments Learn?* New York: Pergamon Press.

Festinger, Leon. (1965) "A Theory of Social Comparison Processes," in A. Paul Hare, Edgar F. Borgatta, and Robert F. Bales, eds., *Small Groups: Studies in Social Interaction.* New York: Knopf.

Gaddis, John Lewis. (1992–1993) "International Relations Theory and the End of the Cold War," *International Security* 17: 5–58.

_____. (1986) "The Long Peace: Elements of Stability in the Postwar International System," *International Security* 10: 99–142.

Galtung, John. (1971) "A Structural Theory of Imperialism," *Journal of Peace Research* 8: 81–117.

George, Alexander I. (1993) *Bridging the Gap: Theory and Practice in Foreign Policy.* Washington, D.C.: U.S. Institute of Peace.

_____. (1980) *Presidential Decision Making in Foreign Policy: The Effective Use of Information and Advice.* Boulder, Colo.: Westview.

_____. (1979) "Case Studies and Theory Development: The Method of Structured Focused Comparison," in Paul Gordon Lauren, ed. *Diplomacy.* New York: Free Press.

_____. (1972) "The Case for Multiple Advocacy in Making Foreign Policy," *American Political Science Review* 66: 751–85.

_____. (1969) "The 'Operational Code': A Neglected Approach to the Study of Political Leaders and Decision Making," *International Studies Quarterly* 13: 190–222.

George, Alexander L., and Robert Keohane. (1980) "The Concept of National Interest: Uses and. Limitations," in Alexander L. George, *Presidential Decision Making in Foreign Policy: The Effective Use of Information and Advice.* Boulder, Colo.: Westview.

George, Alexander L., and Richard Smoke. (1974) *Deterrence in American Foreign Policy.* New York: Columbia University Press.

Gereffi, Gary. (1983) *The Pharmaceutical Industry and Dependency in the Third World.* Princeton, N.J.: Princeton University Press.

Gilpin, Robert. (1981) *War and Change in World Politics.* Cambridge: Cambridge University Press.

Graebner, Norman A. (1984) *America as a World Power: A Realist Appraisal from Wilson to Reagan*. Wilmington, Del.: Scholarly Resources.

Grieco, Joseph. (1990) *Cooperation among Nations*. Ithaca, N.Y.: Cornell University Press.

_____. (1988) "Anarchy and the Limits of Cooperation: A Realist Critique of Neoliberal Institutionalism," *International Organization* 42: 485–507.

_____. (1984) *Between Dependence and Autonomy*. Berkeley: University of California Press.

Haas, Ernst B. (1953) "The Balance of Power: Prescription, Concept or Propaganda?" *World Politics* 5: 442–77.

Halperin, Morton. (1974) *Bureaucratic Politics and Foreign Policy*. Washington, D.C.: Brookings Institution.

Hermann, Charles F. (1972) *International Crises: Insights from Behavioral Research*. New York: Free Press.

_____. (1963) "Some Consequences of Crises Which Limit the Viability of Organizations," *Administrative Science Quarterly* 8: 61–82.

Hermann, Margaret G. (1984) "Personality and Foreign Policy Decision Making," in Donald Sylvan and Steve Chan, eds., *Foreign Policy Decision Making: Perception, Cognition, and Artificial Intelligence*. New York: Praeger.

_____. (1980) "Explaining Foreign Policy Behavior Using Personal Characteristics of Political Leaders," *International Studies Quarterly* 24: 7–46.

_____. (1979) "Indicators of Stress in Policy-makers during Foreign Policy Crises," *Political Psychology* 1: 27–46.

Hermann, Charles F., and Margaret G. Hermann. (1987) "Who Makes Foreign Policy Decisions and How: An Initial Test of Model." Paper presented to the Annual Meeting of the American Political Science Association, Chicago.

Hermann, Margaret G., and Charles F. Hermann. (1975) "Maintaining the Quality of Decision Making in Foreign Policy Crises," in *Report of the Commission on the Organization of the Government for the Conduct in Foreign Policy*, vol. 2. Washington, D.C.: U.S. Government Printing Office.

Hermann, Margaret G., Charles F. Hermann, and Joe D. Hagan. (1987) "How Decision Units Shape Foreign Policy Behavior," in Charles F. Hermann, Charles W. Kegley Jr., and James N. Rosenau, eds., *New Directions in the Study of Foreign Policy*. London: HarperCollins Academic.

Hersh, Seymour M. (1986) *The Target Is Destroyed*. New York: Random House.

Herz, John H. (1968) "The Territorial State Revisited: Reflections on the Future of the Nation-State," *Polity* 1: 12–34.

_____. (1959) *International Politics in the Atomic Age*. New York: Columbia University Press.

_____. (1957) "The Rise and Demise of the Territorial State," *World Politics* 9: 473–93.

Hoffmann, Stanley. (1977) "An American Social Science: International Relations," *Daedalus* 106: 41–60.

Holsti, Ole R. (1976) "Foreign Policy Formation Viewed Cognitively," in Robert Axelrod, ed., *Structure of Decision*. Princeton, N.J.: Princeton University Press.

_____. (1974) "The Study of International Politics Makes Strange Bedfellows," American *Political Science Review* 68: 217–42.

_____. (1972) *Crisis, Escalation, War*. Montreal: Queen's University Press.

Holsti, Ole R., and Alexander L. George. (1975) "The Effects of Stress on the Performance of Foreign Policy-Makers," *Political Science Annual*, vol. 6. Indianapolis: Bobbs-Merrill.

Janis, Irving L. (1982) *Groupthink*. Boston: Houghton Mifflin.

———. (1972) *Victims of Groupthink: A Psychological Study of Foreign Policy Decisions and Fiascos*. Boston: Houghton Mifflin.

Janis, Irving L., and Leon Mann. (1977) *Decision Making*. New York: Free Press.

Jervis, Robert. (1976) *Perception and Misperception in International Politics*. Princeton, N.J.: Princeton University Press.

Jervis, Robert, Richard Ned Lebow, and Janice G. Stein. (1985) *Psychology and Deterrence*. Baltimore: Johns Hopkins University Press.

Kahneman, Daniel, Paul Slovic, and Amos Tversky. (1982) *Judgment under Uncertainty: Heuristics and Biases*. Cambridge: Cambridge University Press.

Kahneman, Daniel, and Amos Tversky. (1973) "On the Psychology of Prediction," *Psychology Review* 80: 251–73.

Kaplan, Morton. (1957) *System and Process in International Politics*. New York: Wiley.

Kennan, George F. (1978) *The Cloud of Danger*. London: Hutchinson.

———. (1951) *American Diplomacy, 1900–1950*. Chicago: University of Chicago Press.

Kennedy, Paul. (1987) *The Rise and Fall of the Great Powers*. New York: Random House.

Keohane, Robert, ed. (1986) *Neorealism and Its Critics*. New York: Columbia University Press.

Keohane, Robert, and Joseph S. Nye Jr. (1977) *Power and Interdependence*. Boston: Little, Brown.

Kinder, Donald, and J. R. Weiss. (1978) "In Lieu of Rationality: Psychological Perspectives on Foreign Policy," *Journal of Conflict Resolution* 22: 707–35.

Kissinger, Henry A. (1960) "Conditions of World Order," *Daedalus* 95: 503–29.

Krasner, Stephen. (1978) *Defending the National Interest*. Princeton, N.J.: Princeton University Press.

———. (1972) "Are Bureaucracies Important?" *Foreign Policy* 7: 159-70.

Kubalkova, Vendulka, and A. A. Cruickshank. (1985) *Marxism and International Relations*. Oxford: Clarendon.

Larson, Deborah. (1985) *Origins of Containment: A Psychological Explanation*. Princeton, N.J.: Princeton University Press.

Lasswell, Harold. (1930) *Psychopathology and Politics*. Chicago: University of Chicago Press.

Lauren, Paul Gordon. (1975) *Diplomats and Bureaucrats*. Stanford, Calif.: Hoover Institute Press.

———. ed. (1979) *Diplomacy: New Approaches to History, Theory and Policy*. New York: Free Press.

Lebow, Richard Ned. (1987) *Nuclear Crisis Management: A Dangerous Illusion*. Ithaca, N.Y.: Cornell University Press.

———. (1981) *Between Peace and War*. Baltimore: Johns Hopkins University Press.

Leites, Nathan. (1951) *The Operational Code of the Politburo*. New York: McGraw-Hill.

Lippmann, Walter. (1943) U.S. *Foreign Policy: Shield of the Republic*. Boston: Little, Brown and Co.

Lowi, Theodore. (1969) *The End of Liberalism: Ideology, Policy and the Crisis of Public Authority*. New York: Norton.

Mansbach, Richard, and John Vasquez. (1981) *In Search of Theory: A New Paradigm for Global Politics*. New York: Columbia University Press.

March, James G., and Herbert Simon. (1958) *Organizations*. New York: Wiley.

Mearsheimer, John. (1990) "Back to the Future: Instability in Europe after the Cold War," *International Security* 15: 5–56.

Morgenthau, Hans J. (1973) *Politics among Nations,* 5th ed. New York: Knopf.

Morse, Edward. (1976) *Modernization and the Transformation of International Relations.* New York: Free Press.

Neustadt, Richard. (1970). *Alliance Politics.* New York: Columbia University Press.

Niebuhr, Reinhold. (1945) *The Children of Light and the Children of Darkness.* New York: Scribner.

Niou, Emerson, Peter C. Ordeshook, and G. F. Rose (1989). *The Balance of Power.* Cambridge: Cambridge University Press.

Nye, Joseph S., Jr. (1988) "Neorealism and Neoliberalism," *World Politics* 40: 235–51.

Odell, John. (1982). *U.S. International Monetary Policy: Markets, Power and Ideas as Sources of Change.* Princeton, N.J.: Princeton University Press.

Paige, Glenn D. (1968) *The Korean Decision.* New York: Free Press.

Perlmutter, Amos. (1974) "Presidential Political Center and Foreign Policy," *World Politics* 27: 87-106.

Posen, Barry. (1984) *The Sources of Military Doctrine.* Ithaca, N.Y.: Cornell University Press.

Rapoport, Anatol. (1957) "L. F. Richardson's Mathematical Theory of War," *Journal of Conflict Resolution* 1: 249-99.

Raphael, Theodore D. (1982) "Integrative Complexity Theory and Forecasting International Crises: Berlin 1946-1962," *Journal of Conflict Resolution* 26: 433–50.

Richardson, Lewis Fry. (1960a) *Arms and Insecurity.* Chicago: Quadrangle Press.

_____. (1960b) *Statistics of Deadly Quarrels.* Chicago: Quadrangle Press.

Rosecrance, Richard. (1986) *The Rise of the Trading State.* New York: Basic Books.

_____. (1966) "Bipolarity, Multipolarity, and the Future," *Journal of Conflict Resolution* 10: 314–27.

_____. (1963) *Action and Reaction in International Politics.* Boston: Little, Brown.

Rosenau, James N. (1990) *Turbulence in World Politics.* Princeton, N.J.: Princeton University Press.

_____. (1980) *The Study of Global Interdependence.* London: F. Pinter.

_____. (1968) "National Interest," *International Encyclopedia of the Social Sciences,* vol. 11: 34–40. New York: Macmillan.

Rosenau, Pauline. (1990) "Once Again into the Breach: International Relations Confronts the Humanities," *Millenium* 19: 83–110.

Rothstein, Robert. (1972) *Planning, Prediction, and Policy-making in Foreign Affairs: Theory and Practice.* Boston: Little, Brown.

Rummel, Rudolph J. (1983) "Libertarianism and Violence, "*Journal of Conflict Resolution* 27: 27–71.

Russett, Bruce M. (1963) "Toward a Model of Competitive International Politics," *Journal of Politics* 25: 226–47.

Sagan, Scott. (1985) "Nuclear Alerts and Crisis Management," *International Security* 9: 99–139.

Scott, Andrew M. (1982) *The Dynamics of Interdependence.* Chapel Hill: University of North Carolina Press.

_____. (1967) *The Functioning, of the International Political System.* New York: Macmillan.

Simon, Herbert. (1957) *Administrative Behavior.* New York: Macmillan.

Singer, J. David. (1963) "Inter-Nation Influence: A Formal Model," *American Political Science Review* 57: 420–30.

Smith, Tony. (1979) "The Underdevelopment of Development Literature: The Case of Dependency Theory," *World Politics* 31: 247–88.

Smoke, Richard. (1977) *War: Controlling Escalation*. Cambridge, Mass.: Harvard University Press.

Snyder, Glenn H., and Paul Diesing. (1977) *Conflict among Nations: Bargaining, Decision Making and System Structure in International Crises*. Princeton, N.J.: Princeton University Press.

Snyder, Jack. (1984) *The Ideology of the Offensive: Military Decision Making and the Disaster of 1914*. Ithaca, N.Y.: Cornell University Press.

Snyder, Richard C, H. W. Bruck, and Burton Sapin, eds. (1962) *Foreign Policy Decision Making*. New York: Free Press.

Sprout, Harold, and Margaret Sprout. (1957) "Environmental Factors in the Study of International Politics," *Journal of Conflict Resolution* 1: 309–28.

Spykman, Nicholas. (1942) *America's Strategy in World Politics*. New York: Harcourt, Brace and Co.

Steinbruner, John. (1974) *The Cybernetic Theory of Decision*. Princeton, N. J.: Princeton University Press.

_____. (1981–1982) "Nuclear Decapitation," *Foreign Policy* 45: 16–28.

Steiner, Miriam. (1983) "World of Foreign Policy," *International Organization* 37: 373–414.

Stewart, Philip D., Margaret G. Hermann, and Charles F. Hermann. (1986) "The Politburo and Foreign Policy: Toward a Model of Soviet Decision Making." Paper presented to the Annual Meeting of International Society for Political Psychology, Amsterdam.

Suedfeld, Peter, and Philip Tetlock. (1977) "Integrative Complexity of Communications in International Crises," *Journal of Conflict Resolution* 21: 169–86.

Suedfeld, Peter, Philip Tetlock, and Carmenza Ramirez. (1977) "War, Peace and Integrative Complexity," *Journal of Conflict Resolution* 21: 427–42.

Tetlock Philip. (1985) "Integrative Complexity of American and Soviet Foreign Policy Rhetoric: A Time Series Analysis," *Journal of Personality and Social Psychology* 49: 1565–85.

_____. (1979) "Identifying Victims of Groupthink from Public Statements of Decision Makers," *Journal of Personality and Social Psychology* 37: 1314–24. Tucker, Robert W. (1992–1993) "Realism and the New Consensus," *National Interest* 30: 33–36.

Tversky, Amos, and Daniel Kahneman. (1981) "Judgment under Uncertainty," *Science* 211: 453–55.

Verba, Sidney. (1961) "Assumptions of Rationality and Non-Rationality in Models of the International System," *World Politics* 14: 93–117.

Vernon, Raymond. (1991) "Sovereignty at Bay: Twenty Years After," *Millenium* 20: 191–95.

_____. (1971) *Sovereignty at Bay*. New York Basic Books.

Walker, Stephen G. (1983) 'The Motivational Foundations of Political Belief Systems: A Re-Analysis of the Operational Code Construct," *International Studies Quarterly* 27: 179–202.

_____. (1977) "The Interface between Beliefs and Behavior: Henry Kissinger's Operational Code and the Vietnam War," *Journal of Conflict Resolution* 21: 129–68.

Wallerstein, Immanuel. (1974a) *The Modern World-System*. New York: Academic Press.

_____. (1974b) "The Rise and Future Demise of the World Capitalist System: Concepts for Comparative Analysis," *Comparative Studies in Society and History* 16: 387–415.

Walt, Steven M. (1987) *The Origin of Alliances*. Ithaca, N.Y.: Cornell University Press.

Waltz, Kenneth W. (1981) "The Spread of Nuclear Weapons: More May Be Better," *Adelphi Papers*, No. 171.

_____. (1979) *Theory of International Politics*. Reading, Mass.: Addison-Wesley.

_____. (1970) "The Myth of National Interdependence," in Charles P. Kindleberger, ed., *The International Corporation*. Cambridge, Mass.: M.I.T. Press.

_____. (1964) "The Stability of a Bipolar World," *Daedalus* 93: 881–909.

_____. (1959) *Man, the State, and War*. New York: Columbia University Press.

Welch, David A., and James G. Blight. (1987–1988) "An Introduction to the ExComm Transcripts," *International Security* 12: 5–29.

Wight, Martin. (1973) "The Balance of Power and International Order," in Alan James, ed., *The Bases of International Order*. London: Oxford University Press.

Wilensky, Harold. (1967) *Organizational Intelligence: Knowledge and Policy in Government and Industry*. New York: Basic Books.

Williamson, Samuel R., Jr. (1969) *The Politics of Grand Strategy: Britain and France Prepare for War, 1904–1914*. Cambridge, Mass.: Harvard University Press.

Wolfers, Arnold. (1962) *Discord and Collaboration*. Baltimore: Johns Hopkins University Press.

Wright, Quincy. (1955) *The Study of International Relations*. New York: Appleton-Century-Crofts.

Yoffie, David B. (1983) *Power and Protectionism: Strategies of the Newly Industrializing Countries*. New York: Columbia University Press.

Zinnes, Dina A. (1967) "An Analytical Study of the Balance of Power," *Journal of Peace Research* 3: 270–88.

Zolberg, Aristide. (1981) "Origins of the Modern World System: A Missing Link," *World Politics* 33: 253–81.

20

GRAHAM T. ALLISON

CONCEPTUAL MODELS AND THE CUBAN MISSILE CRISIS

The Cuban missile crisis is a seminal event. For thirteen days of October 1962, there was a higher probability that more human lives would end suddenly than ever before in history. Had the worst occurred, the death of 100 million Americans, over 100 million Russians, and millions of Europeans as well would make previous natural calamities and inhumanities appear

SOURCE: Reprinted with permission from *American Political Science Review*, Vol. LXIII, No. 3 (September, 1969), pp. 698–703, 707–712, 715–718.

insignificant. Given the probability of disaster—which President Kennedy estimated as "between 1 out of 3 and even"—our escape seems awesome.[1] This event symbolizes a central, if only partially thinkable, fact about our existence. That such consequences could follow from the choices and actions of national governments obliges students of government as well as participants in governance to think hard about these problems.

Improved understanding of this crisis depends in part on more information and more probing analyses of available evidence. To contribute to these efforts is part of the purpose of this study. But here the missile crisis serves primarily as grist for a more general investigation. This study proceeds from the premise that marked improvement in our understanding of such events depends critically on more self-consciousness about what observers bring to the analysis. What each analyst sees and judges to be important is a function not only of the evidence about what happened but also of the "conceptual lenses" through which he looks at the evidence. The principal purpose of this essay is to explore some of the fundamental assumptions and categories employed by analysts in thinking about problems of governmental behavior, especially in foreign and military affairs.

The general argument can be summarized in three propositions:

1. Analysts think about problems of foreign and military policy in terms of largely implicit conceptual models that have significant consequences for the content of their thought.[2]

   Though the present product of foreign policy analysis is neither systematic nor powerful, if one carefully examines explanations produced by analysts, a number of fundamental similarities emerge. Explanations produced by particular analysts display quite regular, predictable features. This predictability suggests a substructure. These regularities reflect an analyst's assumptions about the character of puzzles, the categories in which problems should be considered, the types of evidence that are relevant, and the determinants of occurrences. The first proposition is that clusters of such related assumptions constitute basic frames of reference or conceptual models in terms of which analysts both ask and answer the questions: What happened? Why did the event happen? What will happen?[3] Such assumptions are central to the activities of explanation and prediction, for in attempting to explain a particular event, the analyst cannot simply describe the full state of the world leading up to that event. The logic of explanation requires that he single out the occurrence.[4] Moreover, as the logic of prediction underscores, the analyst must summarize the various determinants as they bear on the event in question. Conceptual models both fix the mesh of the nets that the analyst drags through the material in order to explain a particular action or decision and direct casting that net in select ponds, at certain depths, in order to catch the desired fish.

2. Most analysts explain (and predict) the behavior of national governments in terms of various forms of one basic conceptual model, here
   entitled the Rational Policy Model.[5]

   In terms of this conceptual model, analysts attempt to understand
   happenings as the more or less purposive acts of unified national governments. For these analysts, the point of an explanation is to show
   how the nation or government could have chosen the action in question, given the strategic problem that it faced. For example, in confronting the problem posed by the Soviet installation of missiles in
   Cuba, rational policy model analysts attempt to show how this was a
   reasonable act from the point of view of the Soviet Union, given Soviet
   strategic objectives.
3. Two "alternative" conceptual models, here labeled an Organizational
   Process model (model II) and a Bureaucratic Politics model (model III)
   provide a base for improved explanation and prediction. . . .

MODEL I: RATIONAL POLICY

RATIONAL POLICY MODEL ILLUSTRATED

Where is the pinch of the puzzle raised by the *New York Times* over Soviet
deployment of an antiballistic missile system?[6] The question, as the *Times* states
it, concerns the Soviet Union's objective in allocating such large sums of money
for this weapon system while at the same time seeming to pursue a policy of
increasing détente. In former President Johnson's words, "the paradox is that
this [Soviet deployment of an antiballistic missile system] should be happening
at a time when there is abundant evidence that our mutual antagonism is beginning to ease."[7] This question troubles people primarily because Soviet antiballistic missile deployment, and evidence of Soviet actions towards détente, when
juxtaposed in our implicit model, produce a question. With reference to what
objective could the Soviet government have rationally chosen the simultaneous
pursuit of these two courses of action? This question arises only when the analyst attempts to structure events as purposive choices of consistent actors.

How do analysts attempt to explain the Soviet emplacement of missiles in
Cuba? The most widely cited explanation of this occurrence has been produced by two RAND Sovietologists, Arnold Horelick and Myron Rush.[8] They
conclude that "the introduction of strategic missiles into Cuba was motivated
chiefly by the Soviet leaders' desire to overcome . . . the existing large margin
of US strategic superiority."[9] How do they reach this conclusion? In Sherlock
Holmes style, they seize several salient characteristics of this action and use
these features as criteria against which to test alternative hypotheses about
Soviet objectives. For example, the size of the Soviet deployment, and the
simultaneous emplacement of more expensive, more visible intermediate-range
missiles as well as medium-range missiles, it is argued, exclude an explanation

of the action in terms of Cuban defense—since the objective could have been secured with a much smaller number of medium-range missiles alone. Their explanation presents an argument for one objective that permits interpretation of the details of Soviet behavior as a value-maximizing choice.

How do analysts account for the coming of the First World War? According to Hans Morgenthau, "the first World War had its origin exclusively in the fear of a disturbance of the European balance of power." [10] In the period preceding World War I, the Triple Alliance precariously balanced the Triple Entente. If either power combination could gain a decisive advantage in the Balkans, it would achieve a decisive advantage in the balance of power. "It was this fear," Morgenthau asserts, "that motivated Austria in July 1914 to settle its accounts with Serbia once and for all, and that induced Germany to support Austria unconditionally. It was the same fear that brought Russia to the support of Serbia, and France to the support of Russia." [11] How is Morgenthau able to resolve this problem so confidently? By imposing on the data a "rational outline." [12] The value of this method, according to Morgenthau, is that "it provides for rational discipline in action and creates astounding continuity in foreign policy which makes American, British, or Russian foreign policy appear as an intelligent, rational continuum . . . regardless of the different motives, preferences, and intellectual and moral qualities of successive statesmen." [13] . . .

Most contemporary analysts (as well as laymen) proceed predominantly—albeit most often implicitly—in terms of this model when attempting to explain happenings in foreign affairs. Indeed, that occurrences in foreign affairs are the *acts* of *nations* seems so fundamental to thinking about such problems that this underlying model has rarely been recognized: to explain an occurrence in foreign policy simply means to show how the government could have rationally chosen that action. [14] These brief examples illustrate five uses of the model. To prove that most analysts think largely in terms of the rational policy model is not possible. In this limited space it is not even possible to illustrate the range of employment of the framework. Rather, my purpose is to convey to the reader a grasp of the model and a challenge: let the readers examine the literature with which they are most familiar and make a judgment.

The general characterization can be sharpened by articulating the rational policy model as an "analytic paradigm" in the technical sense developed by Robert K. Merton for sociological analyses. [15] Systematic statement of basic assumptions, concepts, and propositions employed by model I analysts highlights the distinctive thrust of this style of analysis. To articulate a largely implicit framework is of necessity to caricature. But caricature can be instructive.

RATIONAL POLICY PARADIGM

Basic Unit of Analysis: Policy as National Choice

Happenings in foreign affairs are conceived as actions chosen by the nation or national government. [16] Governments select the action that will maximize strategic goals and objectives. These "solutions" to strategic problems are the fundamental categories in terms of which the analyst perceives what is to be explained.

Organizing Concepts

NATIONAL ACTOR

The nation or government, conceived as a rational, unitary decision-maker, is the agent. This actor has one set of specified goals (the equivalent of a consistent utility function), one set of perceived options, and a single estimate of the consequences that follow from each alternative.

THE PROBLEM

Action is chosen in response to the strategic problem which the nation faces. Threats and opportunities arising in the "international strategic market place" move the nation to act.

STATIC SELECTION

The sum of activity of representatives of the government relevant to a problem constitutes what the nation has chosen as its "solution." Thus the action is conceived as a steady-state choice among alternative outcomes (rather than, for example, a large number of partial choices in a dynamic stream).

ACTION AS RATIONAL CHOICE

The components include:

1. *Goals and Objectives.* National security and national interests are the principal categories in which strategic goals are conceived. Nations seek security and a range of further objectives. (Analysts rarely translate strategic goals and objectives into an explicit utility function; nevertheless, analysts do focus on major goals and objectives and trade off side effects in an intuitive fashion.)
2. *Options.* Various courses of action relevant to a strategic problem provide the spectrum of options.
3. *Consequences.* Enactment of each alternative course of action will produce a series of consequences. The relevant consequences constitute benefits and costs in terms of strategic goals and objectives.
4. *Choice.* Rational choice is value-maximizing. The rational agent selects the alternative whose consequences rank highest in terms of his goals and objectives.

Dominant Inference Pattern

This paradigm leads analysts to rely on the following pattern of inference: if a nation performed a particular action, that nation must have had ends towards which the action constituted an optimal means. The rational policy model's explanatory power stems from this inference pattern. Puzzlement is relieved by revealing the purposive pattern within which the occurrence can be located as a value-maximizing means.

General Propositions

The disgrace of political science is the infrequency with which propositions of any generality are formulated and tested. "Paradigmatic analysis" argues for explicitness about the terms in which analysis proceeds, and seriousness about the logic of explanation. Simply to illustrate the kind of propositions on which analysts who employ this model rely, the formulation includes several.

The basic assumption of value-maximizing behavior produces propositions central to most explanations. The general principle can be formulated as follows: the likelihood of any particular action results from a combination of the nation's (1) relevant values and objectives, (2) perceived alternative courses of action, (3) estimates of various sets of consequences (which will follow from each alternative), and (4) net valuation of each set of consequences. This yields two propositions.

(1) An increase in the cost of an alternative, i.e., a reduction in the value of the set of consequences which will follow from that action, or a reduction in the probability of attaining fixed consequences, reduces the likelihood of that alternative being chosen.

(2) A decrease in the costs of an alternative, i.e., an increase in the value of the set of consequences which will follow from that alternative, or an increase in the probability of attaining fixed consequences, increases the likelihood of that action being chosen.[17]

Specific Propositions

DETERRENCE

The likelihood of any particular attack results from the factors specified in the general proposition. Combined with factual assertions, this general proposition yields the propositions of the subtheory of deterrence.

(1) A stable nuclear balance reduces the likelihood of nuclear attack. This proposition is derived from the general proposition plus the asserted fact that a second-strike capability affects the potential attacker's calculations by increasing the likelihood and the costs of one particular set of consequences which might follow from attack—namely, retaliation.

(2) A stable nuclear balance increases the probability of limited war. This proposition is derived from the general proposition plus the asserted fact that though increasing the costs of a nuclear exchange, a stable nuclear balance nevertheless produces a more significant reduction in the probability that such consequences would be chosen in response to a limited war. Thus this set of consequences weighs less heavily in the calculus.

SOVIET FORCE POSTURE

The Soviet Union chooses its force posture (i.e., its weapons and their deployment) as a value-maximizing means of implementing Soviet strategic objectives and military doctrine. A proposition of this sort underlies Secretary of Defense Laird's inference from the fact of 200 SS-9s (large intercontinental missiles) to the assertion that, "the Soviets are going for a first-strike capability, and there's no question about it."[18]

VARIANTS OF THE RATIONAL POLICY MODEL

This paradigm exhibits the characteristics of the most refined version of the rational model. The modern literature of strategy employs a model of this sort. Problems and pressures in the "international strategic marketplace" yield probabilities of occurrence. The international actor, which could be any national actor, is simply a value-maximizing mechanism for getting from the strategic problem to the logical solution. But the explanations and predictions pro-duced by most analysts of foreign affairs depend primarily on variants of this "pure" model. The point of each is the same: to place the action within a value-maximizing framework, given certain constraints. Nevertheless, it may be helpful to identify several variants, each of which might be exhibited similarly as a paradigm. The first focuses upon the national actor and his choice in a particular situation, leading analysts to further constrain the goals, alternatives, and consequences considered. Thus, (1) national propensities or personality traits reflected in an "operational code," (2) concern with certain objectives, or (3) special principles of action, narrow the "goals" or "alternatives" or "consequences" of the paradigm. For example, the Soviet deployment of ABMs is sometimes explained by reference to the Soviets' "defense-mindedness." Or a particular Soviet action is explained as an instance of a special rule of action in the Bolshevik operational code.[19] A second, related, cluster of variants focuses on the individual leader or leadership group as the actor whose preference function is maximized and whose personal (or group) characteristics are allowed to modify the alternatives, consequences and rules of choice. Explanations of the US involvement in Vietnam as a natural consequence of the Kennedy-Johnson administration's axioms of foreign policy rely on this variant. A third, more complex variant of the basic model recognizes the existence of several actors within a government, for example, hawks and doves or military and civilians, but attempts to explain (or predict) an occurrence by reference to the objectives of the victorious actor. Thus, for example, some revisionist histories of the cold war recognize the forces of light and the forces of darkness within the US government, but explain American actions as a result of goals and perceptions of the victorious forces of darkness.

Each of these forms of the basic paradigm constitutes a formalization of what analysts typically rely upon implicitly. In the transition from implicit conceptual model to explicit paradigm much of the richness of the best employment of this model has been lost. But the purpose in raising loose, implicit conceptual models to an explicit level is to reveal the basic logic of analysts' activity. Perhaps some of the remaining artificiality that surrounds the statement of the paradigm can be erased by noting a number of the standard additions and modifications employed by analysts who proceed *predominantly* within the rational policy model. First, in the course of a document, analysts shift from one variant of the basic model to another, occasionally appropriating in an ad hoc fashion aspects of a situation which are logically incompatible with the basic model. Second, in the course of explaining a number of occurrences, analysts sometimes pause over a particular event about which they have a great deal of information and unfold it in such detail that an impression of randomness is created. Third, having employed other assumptions and categories in deriving an explanation or prediction, analysts will present their product in a neat, convincing rational policy model package. (This accommodation is a favorite of members of the intelligence community whose association with the details of a process is considerable, but who feel that by putting an occurrence in a larger rational framework, it will be more comprehensible to their audience.) Fourth, in attempting to offer an explanation—particularly in cases where a prediction derived from the basic model has failed—the notion of a "mistake" is invoked. Thus, the failure in the prediction of a "missile gap" is written off as a Soviet mistake in not taking advantage of their opportunity. Both these and other modifications permit model I analysts considerably more variety than the paradigm might suggest. But such accommodations are essentially appendages to the basic logic of these analyses. . . .

MODEL II: ORGANIZATIONAL PROCESS

For some purposes, governmental behavior can be usefully summarized as action chosen by a unitary, rational decision-maker: centrally controlled, completely informed, and value maximizing. But this simplification must not be allowed to conceal the fact that a "government" consists of a conglomerate of semifeudal, loosely allied organizations, each with a substantial life of its own. Government leaders do sit formally, and to some extent in fact, on top of this conglomerate. But governments perceive problems through organizational sensors. Governments define alternatives and estimate consequences as organizations process information. Governments act as these organizations enact routines. Government behavior can therefore be understood according to a second conceptual model, less as deliberate choices of leaders and more as *outputs* of large organizations functioning according to standard patterns of behavior.

To be responsive to a broad spectrum of problems, governments consist of large organizations among which primary responsibility for particular areas is divided. Each organization attends to a special set of problems and acts in quasi-independence on these problems. But few important problems fall exclusively within the domain of a single organization. Thus government behavior relevant to any important problem reflects the independent output of several organizations, partially coordinated by government leaders. Government leaders can substantially disturb, but not substantially control, the behavior of these organizations.

To perform complex routines, the behavior of large numbers of individuals must be coordinated. Coordination requires standard operating procedures: rules according to which things are done. Assured capability for reliable performance of action that depends upon the behavior of hundreds of persons requires established "programs." Indeed, if the eleven members of a football team are to perform adequately on any particular down, each player must not "do what he thinks needs to be done" or "do what the quarterback tells him to do." Rather, each player must perform the maneuvers specified by a previously established play which the quarterback has simply called in this situation.

At any given time, a government consists of *existing* organizations, each with a *fixed* set of standard operating procedures and programs. The behavior of these organizations—and consequently of the government—relevant to an issue in any particular instance is, therefore, determined primarily by routines established in these organizations prior to that instance. But organizations do change. Learning occurs gradually, over time. Dramatic organizational change occurs in response to major crises. Both learning and change are influenced by existing organizational capabilities.

Borrowed from studies of organizations, these loosely formulated propositions amount simply to *tendencies*. Each must be hedged by modifiers like "other things being equal" and "under certain conditions." In particular instances, tendencies hold—more or less. In specific situations, the relevant question is: more or less? But this is as it should be. For, on the one hand, "organizations" are no more homogeneous a class than "solids." When scientists tried to generalize about "solids," they achieved similar results. Solids tend to expand when heated, but some do and some don't. More adequate categorization of the various elements now lumped under the rubric "organizations" is thus required. On the other hand, the behavior of particular organizations seems considerably more complex than the behavior of solids. Additional information about a particular organization is required for further specification of the tendency statements. In spite of these two caveats, the characterization of government action as organizational output differs distinctly from model I. Attempts to understand problems of foreign affairs in terms of this frame of reference should produce quite different explanations.[20]

ORGANIZATIONAL PROCESS PARADIGM[21]

Basic Unit of Analysis: Policy as Organizational Output

The happenings of international politics are, in three critical senses, outputs of organizational processes. First, the actual occurrences are organizational outputs. For example, Chinese entry into the Korean War—that is, the fact that Chinese soldiers were firing at UN soldiers south of the Yalu in 1950—is an organizational action: the action of men who are soldiers in platoons which are in companies, which in turn are in armies, responding as privates to lieutenants who are responsible to captains and so on to the commander, moving into Korea, advancing against enemy troops, and firing according to fixed routines of the Chinese Army. Government leaders' decisions trigger organizational routines. Government leaders can trim the edges of this output and exercise some choice in combining outputs. But the mass of behavior is determined by previously established procedures. Second, existing organizational routines for employing present physical capabilities constitute the effective options open to government leaders confronted with any problem. Only the existence of men, equipped and trained as armies and capable of being transported to North Korea, made entry into the Korean War a live option for the Chinese leaders. The fact that fixed programs (equipment, men, and routines which exist at the particular time) exhaust the range of buttons that leaders can push is not always perceived by these leaders. But in every case it is critical for an understanding of what is actually done. Third, organizational outputs structure the situation within the narrow constraints of which leaders must contribute their "decision" concerning an issue. Outputs raise the problem, provide the information, and make the initial moves that color the face of the issue that is turned to the leaders. As Theodore Sorensen has observed: "Presidents rarely, if ever, make decisions—particularly in foreign affairs—in the sense of writing their conclusions on a clean slate . . . The basic decisions, which confine their choices, have all too often been previously made."[22] If one understands the structure of the situation and the face of the issue—which are determined by the organizational outputs—the formal choice of the leaders is frequently anticlimactic.

Organizing Concepts

ORGANIZATIONAL ACTORS

The actor is not a monolithic "nation" or "government" but rather a constellation of loosely allied organizations on top of which government leaders sit. This constellation acts only as component organizations perform routines.[23]

FACTORED PROBLEMS AND FRACTIONATED POWER

Surveillance of the multiple facets of foreign affairs requires that problems be cut up and parceled out to various organizations. To avoid paralysis, primary power must accompany primary responsibility. But if organizations are permitted to do anything, a large part of what they do will be determined within the organization. Thus each organization perceives problems, processes information, and performs a range of actions in quasi-independence (within broad guidelines of national policy). Factored problems and fractionated power are two edges of the same sword. Factoring permits more specialized attention to particular facets of problems than would be possible if government leaders tried to cope with these problems by themselves. But this additional attention must be paid for in the coin of discretion for *what* an organization attends to, and *how* organizational responses are programmed.

PAROCHIAL PRIORITIES, PERCEPTIONS, AND ISSUES

Primary responsibility for a narrow set of problems encourages organizational parochialism. These tendencies are enhanced by a number of additional factors: (1) selective information available to the organization, (2) recruitment of personnel into the organization, (3) tenure of individuals in the organization, (4) small group pressures within the organization, and (5) distribution of rewards by the organization. Clients (e.g., interest groups), government allies (e.g., Congressional committees), and extranational counterparts (e.g., the British Ministry of Defense for the Department of Defense, ISA, or the British Foreign Office for the Department of State, EUR) galvanize this parochialism. Thus organizations develop relatively stable propensities concerning operational priorities, perceptions, and issues.

ACTION AS ORGANIZATIONAL OUTPUT

The preeminent feature of organizational activity is its programmed character: the extent to which behavior in any particular case is an enactment of preestablished routines. In producing outputs, the activity of each organization is characterized by:

1. *Goals: Constraints Defining Acceptable Performance.* The operational goals of an organization are seldom revealed by formal mandates. Rather, each organization's operational goals emerge as a set of constraints defining acceptable performance. Central among these constraints is organizational health, defined usually in terms of bodies assigned and dollars appropriated. The set of constraints emerges from a mix of expectations and demands of other organizations in the government, statutory authority, demands from citizens and special interest groups, and bargaining within the organization. These constraints represent a quasi-resolution of conflict—the constraints are relatively stable, so there is some resolution. But conflict among alternative goals is always latent; hence, it is a quasi-resolution. Typically, the constraints are formulated as imperatives to avoid roughly specified discomforts and disasters.[24]

2. *Sequential Attention to Goals.* The existence of conflict among operational constraints is resolved by the device of sequential attention. As a

problem arises, the subunits of the organization most concerned with that problem deal with it in terms of the constraints they take to be most important. When the next problem arises, another cluster of subunits deals with it, focusing on a different set of constraints.

3. *Standard Operating Procedures.* Organizations perform their "higher" functions, such as attending to problem areas, monitoring information, and preparing relevant responses for likely contingencies, by doing "lower" tasks, for example, preparing budgets, producing reports, and developing hardware. Reliable performance of these tasks requires standard operating procedures (hereafter SOPs). Since procedures are "standard" they do not change quickly or easily. Without these standard procedures, it would not be possible to perform certain concerted tasks. But because of standard procedures, organizational behavior in particular instances often appears unduly formalized, sluggish, or inappropriate.

4. *Programs and Repertoires.* Organizations must be capable of performing actions in which the behavior of large numbers of individuals is carefully coordinated. Assured performance requires clusters of rehearsed SOPs for producing specific actions, e.g., fighting enemy units or answering an embassy's cable. Each cluster comprises a "program" (in the terms both of drama and computers) which the organization has available for dealing with a situation. The list of programs relevant to a type of activity, e.g., fighting, constitutes an organizational repertoire. The number of programs in a repertoire is always quite limited. When properly triggered, organizations execute programs; programs cannot be substantially changed in a particular situation. The more complex the action and the greater the number of individuals involved, the more important are programs and repertoires as determinants of organizational behavior.

5. *Uncertainty Avoidance.* Organizations do not attempt to estimate the probability distribution of future occurrences. Rather, organizations avoid uncertainty. By arranging a *negotiated environment,* organizations regularize the reactions of other actors with whom they have to deal. The primary environment, relations with other organizations that comprise the government, is stabilized by such arrangements as agreed budgetary splits, accepted areas of responsibility, and established conventional practices. The secondary environment, relations with the international world, is stabilized between allies by the establishment of contracts (alliances) and "club relations" (US State and UK Foreign Office and US Treasury and UK Treasury). Between enemies, contracts and accepted conventional practices perform a similar function, for example, the rules of the "precarious status quo" which President Kennedy referred to in the missile crisis. Where the international environment cannot be negotiated, organizations deal with remaining uncertainties by establishing a set of *standard scenarios* that constitute the contingencies for which they prepare. For example, the standard scenario for Tactical Air Command of the US Air Force involves combat with enemy aircraft. Planes are designed and pilots trained to meet this problem. That these preparations are less relevant

to more probable contingencies, e.g., provision of close-in ground support in limited wars like Vietnam, has had little impact on the scenario.

6. *Problem-directed Search.* Where situations cannot be construed as standard, organizations engage in search. The style of search and the solution are largely determined by existing routines. Organizational search for alternative courses of action is problem-oriented: it focuses on the atypical discomfort that must be avoided. It is simple-minded: the neighborhood of the symptom is searched first; then, the neighborhood of the current alternative. Patterns of search reveal biases which in turn reflect such factors as specialized training or experience and patterns of communication.

7. *Organizational Learning and Change.* The parameters of organizational behavior mostly persist. In response to nonstandard problems, organizations search and routines evolve, assimilating new situations. Thus learning and change follow in large part from existing procedures. But marked changes in organizations do sometimes occur. Conditions in which dramatic changes are more likely include: (1) Periods of budgetary feast. Typically, organizations devour budgetary feasts by purchasing additional items on the existing shopping list. Nevertheless, if commmitted to change, leaders who control the budget can use extra funds to effect changes. (2) Periods of prolonged budgetary famine. Though a single year's famine typically results in few changes in organizational structure but a loss of effectiveness in performing some programs, prolonged famine forces major retrenchment. (3) Dramatic performance failures. Dramatic change occurs (mostly) in response to major disasters. Confronted with an undeniable failure of procedures and repertoires, authorities outside the organization demand change, existing personnel are less resistant to change, and critical members of the organization are replaced by individuals committed to change.

CENTRAL COORDINATION AND CONTROL

Action requires decentralization of responsibility and power. But problems lap over the jurisdictions of several organizations. Thus the necessity for decentralization runs headlong into the requirement for coordination. (Advocates of one horn or the other of this dilemma—responsive action entails decentralized power versus coordinated action requires central control—account for a considerable part of the persistent demand for government reorganization.) Both the necessity for coordination and the centrality of foreign policy to national welfare guarantee the involvement of government leaders in the procedures of the organizations among which problems are divided and power shared. Each organization's propensities and routines can be disturbed by government leaders' intervention. Central direction and persistent control of organizational activity, however, are not possible. The relation among organizations, and between organizations and the government leaders depends critically on a number of structural variables including: (1) the nature of the job, (2) the measures and information available to government leaders, (3) the system of rewards and punishments for organizational members, and (4) the procedures by which human and material resources get committed. For example, to the extent that rewards and punishments for the members of an organization are distributed by higher authorities, these authorities can exercise some control by specifying criteria in terms of which organizational output is to be evaluated. These criteria become constraints within which organizational activity proceeds. But constraint is a crude instrument of control.

Intervention by government leaders does sometimes change the activity of an organization in an intended direction. But instances are fewer than might be expected. As Franklin Roosevelt, the master manipulator of government organizations, remarked:

> The Treasury is so large and far-flung and ingrained in its practices that I find it is almost impossible to get the action and results I want . . . But the Treasury is not to be compared with the State Department. You should go through the experience of trying to get any changes in the thinking, policy, and action of the career diplomats and then you'd know what a real problem was. But the Treasury and the State Department put together are nothing compared with the Na-a-vy . . . To change anything in the Na-a-vy is like punching a feather bed. You punch it with your right and you punch it with your left until you are finally exhausted, and then you find the damn bed just as it was before you started punching.[25]

John Kennedy's experience seems to have been similar: "The State Department," he asserted, "is a bowl full of jelly." [26] And lest the McNamara revolution in the Defense Department seem too striking a counterexample, the Navy's recent rejection of McNamara's major intervention in Naval weapons procurement, the F-111B, should be studied as an antidote.

DECISIONS OF GOVERNMENT LEADERS

Organizational persistence does not exclude shifts in governmental behavior. For government leaders sit atop the conglomerate of organizations. Many important issues of governmental action require that these leaders decide what organizations will play out which programs where. Thus stability in the parochialisms and SOPs of individual organizations is consistent with some important shifts in the behavior of governments. The range of these shifts is defined by existing organizational programs.

Dominant Inference Pattern

If a nation performs an action of this type today, its organizational components must yesterday have been performing (or have had established routines for performing) an action only marginally different from this action. At any specific point in time, a government consists of an established conglomerate of organizations, each with existing goals, programs, and repertoires. The characteristics of a government's action in any instance follow from those established routines, and from the choice of government leaders—on the basis of information and estimates provided by existing routines—among existing programs. The best explanation of an organization's behavior at t is $t - 1$; the prediction of $t + 1$ is t. Model II's explanatory power is achieved by uncovering the organizational routines and repertoires that produced the outputs that comprise the puzzling occurrence.

General Propositions

A number of general propositions have been stated above. In order to illustrate clearly the type of proposition employed by model II analysts, this section formulates several more precisely.

ORGANIZATIONAL ACTION

Activity according to SOPs and programs does not constitute farsighted, flexible adaptation to "the issue" (as it is conceived by the analyst). Detail and nuance of actions by organizations are determined predominantly by organizational routines, not government leaders' directions.

SOPs constitute routines for dealing with *standard* situations. Routines allow large numbers of ordinary individuals to deal with numerous instances, day after day, without considerable thought, by responding to basic stimuli. But this regularized capability for adequate performance is purchased at the price of standardization. If the SOPs are appropriate, average performance, i.e., performance averaged over the range of cases, is better than it would be if each instance were approached individually (given fixed talent, timing, and resource constraints). But specific instances, particularly critical instances that typically do not have "standard" characteristics, are often handled sluggishly or inappropriately.

A program, i.e., a complex action chosen from a short list of programs in a repertoire, is rarely tailored to the specific situation in which it is executed. Rather, the program is (at best) the most appropriate of the programs in a previously developed repertoire.

Since repertoires are developed by parochial organizations for standard scenarios defined by that organization, programs available for dealing with a particular situation are often ill-suited.

LIMITED FLEXIBILITY AND INCREMENTAL CHANGE

Major lines of organizational action are straight, i.e., behavior at one time is marginally different from that behavior at $t - 1$. Simpleminded predictions work best: Behavior at $t + 1$ will be marginally different from behavior at the present time.

Organizational budgets change incrementally—both with respect to totals and with respect to intraorganizational splits. Though organizations could divide the money available each year by carving up the pie anew (in the light of changes in objectives or environment), in practice, organizations take last year's budget as a base and adjust incrementally. Predictions that require large budgetary shifts in a single year between organizations or between units within an organization should be hedged.

Once undertaken, an organizational investment is not dropped at the point where "objective" costs outweigh benefits. Organizational stakes in adopted projects carry them quite beyond the loss point.

ADMINISTRATIVE FEASIBILITY

Adequate explanation, analysis, and prediction must include administrative feasibility as a major dimension. A considerable gap separates what leaders choose (or might rationally have chosen) and what organizations implement.

Organizations are blunt instruments. Projects that require several organizations to act with high degrees of precision and coordination are not likely to succeed.

Projects that demand that existing organizational units depart from their accustomed functions and perform previously unprogrammed tasks are rarely accomplished in their designed form.

Government leaders can expect that each organization will do its "part" in terms of what the organization knows how to do.

Government leaders can expect incomplete and distorted information from each organization concerning its part of the problem.

Where an assigned piece of a problem is contrary to the existing goals of an organization, resistance to implementation of that piece will be encountered.

Specific Propositions

DETERRENCE

The probability of nuclear attack is less sensitive to balance and imbalance, or stability and instability (as these concepts are employed by model I strategists) than it is to a number of organizational factors. Except for the special case in which the Soviet Union acquires a credible capability to destroy the US with a disarming blow, US superiority or inferiority affects the probability of a nuclear attack less than do a number of organizational factors.

First, if a nuclear attack occurs, it will result from organizational activity: the firing of rockets by members of a missile group. The enemy's *control system,* i.e., physical mechanisms and standard procedures which determine who can launch rockets when, is critical. Second, the enemy's programs for bringing his strategic forces to *alert status* determine probabilities of accidental firing and momentum. At the outbreak of World War I, if the Russian tsar had understood the organizational processes which his order of full mobilization triggered, he would have realized that he had chosen war. Third, organizational repertoires fix the range of effective choice open to enemy leaders. The menu available to Tsar Nicholas in 1914 has two entrees: full mobilization and no mobilization. Partial mobilization was not an organizational option. Fourth, since organizational routines set the chessboard, the training and deployment of troops and nuclear weapons is crucial. Given that the outbreak of hostilities in Berlin is more probable than most scenarios for nuclear war, facts about deployment, training, and tactical nuclear equipment of Soviet troops stationed in East Germany—which will influence the face of the issue seen by Soviet leaders at the outbreak of hostilities and the manner in which choice is implemented—are as critical as the question of "balance."

SOVIET FORCE POSTURE

Soviet Force posture, i.e., the fact that certain weapons rather than others are procured and deployed, is determined by organizational factors such as the goals and procedures of existing military services and the goals and processes of research and design labs, within budgetary constraints that emerge from the government leader's choices. The frailty of the Soviet Air Force within the Soviet military establishment seems to have been a crucial element in the Soviet failure to acquire a large bomber force in the 1950s (thereby faulting American intelligence predictions of a "bomber gap"). The fact that missiles were controlled until 1960 in the Soviet Union by the Soviet Ground Forces, whose goals and procedures reflected no interest in an intercontinental mission, was not irrelevant to the slow Soviet buildup of ICBMs (thereby faulting US intelligence predictions of a "missile gap"). These organizational factors (Soviet Ground Forces' control of missiles and that service's fixation with European scenarios) make the Soviet deployment of so many MRBMs that European targets could be destroyed three times over, more understandable. Recent weapon developments, e.g., the testing of a Fractional Orbital Bombardment System (FOBS) and multiple warheads for the SS-9, very likely reflect the activity and interests of a cluster of Soviet research and development organizations, rather than a decision by Soviet leaders to acquire a first-strike weapon system. Careful attention to the organizational components of the Soviet military establishment (Strategic Rocket Forces, Navy, Air Force, Ground Forces, and National Air Defense), the missions and weapons systems to which each component is wedded (an independent weapon system assists survival as an independent service), and existing budgetary splits (which probably are relatively stable in the Soviet Union as they tend to be everywhere) offer potential improvements in medium- and longer-term predictions. . . .

MODEL III: BUREAUCRATIC POLITICS

The leaders who sit on top of organizations are not a monolithic group. Rather, each is, in his own right, a player in a central, competitive game. The name of the game is bureaucratic politics: bargaining along regularized channels among players positioned hierarchically within the government.

Government behav-ior can thus be understood according to a third conceptual model not as organizational outputs, but as outcomes of bargaining games. In contrast with model I, the bureaucratic politics model sees no unitary actor but rather many actors as players, who focus not on a single strategic issue but on many diverse intranational problems as well, in terms of no consistent set of strategic objectives but rather according to various conceptions of national, organizational, and personal goals, making government decisions not by rational choice but by the pulling and hauling that is politics.

The apparatus of each national government constitutes a complex arena for the intranational game. Political leaders at the top of this apparatus plus the men who occupy positions on top of the critical organizations form the circle of central players. Ascendancy to this circle assures some independent standing. The necessary decentralization of decisions required for action on the broad range of foreign policy problems guarantees that each player has considerable discretion. Thus power is shared.

The nature of problems of foreign policy permits fundamental disagreement among reasonable men concerning what ought to be done. Analyses yield conflicting recommendations. Separate responsibilities laid on the shoulders of individual personalities encourage differences in perceptions and priorities. But the issues are of first-order importance. What the nation does really matters. A wrong choice could mean irreparable damage. Thus responsible men are obliged to fight for what they are convinced is right.

Men share power. Men differ concerning what must be done. The differences matter. This milieu necessitates that policy be resolved by politics. What the nation does is sometimes the result of the triumph of one group over others. More often, however, different groups pulling in different directions yield a result distinct from what anyone intended. What moves the chess pieces is not simply the reasons which support a course of action, nor the routines of organizations which enact an alternative, but the power and skill of proponents and opponents of the action in question.

This characterization captures the thrust of the bureaucratic politics orientation. If problems of foreign policy arose as discrete issues, and decisions were determined one game at a time, this account would suffice. But most "issues," e.g., Vietnam or the proliferation of nuclear weapons, emerge piecemeal, over time, one lump in one context, a second in another. Hundreds of issues compete for players' attention every day. Each player is forced to fix upon his issues for that day, fight them on their own terms, and rush on to the next. Thus the character of emerging issues and the pace at which the game is played converge to yield government "decisions" and "actions" as collages. Choices by one player, outcomes of minor games, outcomes of central games, and "foul-ups"—these pieces, when stuck to the same canvas, constitute government behavior relevant to an issue.

The concept of national security policy as political outcome contradicts both public imagery and academic orthodoxy. Issues vital to national security, it is said, are too important to be settled by political games. They must be "above" politics. To accuse someone of "playing politics with national security" is a most serious charge. What public conviction demands, the academic penchant for intellectual elegance reinforces. Internal politics is messy; moreover, according to prevailing doctrine, politicking lacks intellectual content. As such, it constitutes gossip for journalists rather than a subject for serious investigation. Occasional memoirs, anecdotes in historical accounts, and several detailed case studies to the contrary, most of the literature of foreign policy avoids bureaucratic politics. The gap between academic literature and the experience of participants in government is nowhere wider than at this point.

BUREAUCRATIC POLITICS PARADIGM [27]

Basic Unit of Analysis: Policy as Political Outcome

The decisions and actions of governments are essentially intranational political outcomes: outcomes in the sense that what happens is not chosen as a solution to a problem but rather results from compromise, coalition, competition, and confusion among government officials who see different faces of an issue; political in the sense that the activity from which the outcomes emerge is best characterized as bargaining. Following Wittgenstein's use of the concept of a "game," national behavior in international affairs can be conceived as outcomes of intricate and subtle, simultaneous, overlapping games among players located in positions, the hierarchical arrangement of which constitutes the government.[28] These games proceed neither at random nor at leisure. Regular channels structure the game. Deadlines force issues to the attention of busy players. The moves in the chess game are thus to be explained in terms of the bargaining among players with separate and unequal power over particular pieces and with separable objectives in distinguishable subgames.

Organizing Concepts

PLAYERS IN POSITIONS

The actor is neither a unitary nation, nor a conglomerate of organizations, but rather a number of individual players. Groups of these players constitute the agent for particular government decisions and actions. Players are men in jobs.

Individuals become players in the national security policy game by occupying a critical position in an administration. For example, in the US government the players include "Chiefs": the president, secretaries of state, defense, and treasury, director of the CIA, Joint Chiefs of Staff, and, since 1961, the special assistant for national security affairs,[29] "Staffer": the immediate staff of each Chief, "Indians": the political appointees and permanent government officials within each of the departments and agencies; and "Ad Hoc Players": actors in the wider government game (especially "Congressional Influentials"), members of the press, spokesmen for important interest groups (especially the "bipartisan foreign policy establishment" in and out of Congress), and surrogates for each of these groups. Other members of the Congress, press, interest groups, and public form concentric circles around the central arena—circles which demarcate the permissive limits within which the game is played.

Positions define what players both may and must do. The advantages and handicaps with which each player can enter and play in various games stems from his position. So does a cluster of obligations for the performance of certain tasks. The two sides of this coin are illustrated by the position of the modern secretary of state. First, in form and usually in fact, he is the primary repository of political judgment on the political-military issues that are the stuff of contemporary foreign policy; consequently, he is a senior personal adviser to the president. Second, he is the colleague of the president's other senior advisers on the problems of foreign policy, the secretaries of defense and treasury, and the special assistant for national security affairs. Third, he is the ranking US diplomat for serious negotiation. Fourth, he serves as an administration voice to Congress, the country, and the world. Finally, he is "Mr. State Department" or "Mr. Foreign Office," "leader of officials, spokesman for their causes, guardian of their interests, judge of their disputes, superintendent of their work, master of their careers." [30] But he is not first one, and then the other. All of these obligations are his simultaneously. His performance in one affects his credit and power in the others. The perspective stemming from the daily work which he must oversee—the cable traffic by which his department maintains relations with other foreign offices—conflicts with the president's requirement that he serve as a generalist and coordinator of contrasting perspectives. The necessity that he be close to the president restricts the extent to which, and the force with which, he can front for his department. When he defers to the secretary of defense rather than fighting for his department's position—as he often must—he strains the loyalty of his officialdom. The secretary's resolution of these conflicts depends not only upon the position, but also upon the player who occupies the position.

For players are also people. Men's metabolisms differ. The core of the bureaucratic politics mix is personality. How each man manages to stand the heat in his kitchen, each player's basic operating style, and the complementarity or contradiction among personalities and styles in the inner circles are irreducible pieces of the policy blend. Moreover, each person comes to his position with baggage in tow, including sensitivities to certain issues, commitments to various programs, and personal standing and debts with groups in society.

PAROCHIAL PRIORITIES, PERCEPTIONS AND ISSUES

Answers to the questions: "What is the issue?" and "What must be done?" are colored by the position from which the questions are considered. For the factors which encourage organizational parochialism also influence the players who occupy positions on top of (or within) these organizations. To motivate members of his organization, a player must be sensitive to the organization's orientation. The games into which the player can enter and the advantages with which he plays enhance these pressures. Thus propensities of perception stemming from position permit reliable prediction about a player's stances in many cases. But these propensities are filtered through the baggage which players bring to positions. Sensitivity to both the pressures and the baggage is thus required for many predictions.

INTERESTS, STAKES, AND POWER

Games are played to determine outcomes. But outcomes advance and impede each player's conceptions of the national interest, specific programs to which he is committed, the welfare of his friends, and his personal interests. These overlapping interests constitute the stakes for which games are played. Each player's ability to play successfully depends upon his power. Power, i.e., effective influence on policy outcomes, is an elusive blend of at least three elements: bargaining advantages (drawn from formal authority and obligations, institutional backing, constituents, expertise, and status), skill and will in using bargaining advantages, and other players' perceptions of the first two ingredients. Power wisely invested yields an enhanced reputation for effectiveness. Unsuccessful investment depletes both the stock of capital and the reputation. Thus each player must pick the issues on which he can play with a reasonable probability of success. But no player's power is sufficient to guarantee satisfactory outcomes. Each player's needs and fears run to many other players. What ensues is the most intricate and subtle of games known to man.

THE PROBLEM AND THE PROBLEMS

"Solutions" to strategic problems are not derived by detached analysts focusing coolly on *the* problem. Instead, deadlines and events raise issues in games, and demand decisions of busy players in contexts that influence the face the issue wears. The problems for the players are both narrower and broader than *the* strategic problem. For each player focuses not on the total strategic problem but rather on the decision that must be made now. But each decision has critical consequences not only for the strategic problem but for each player's organizational, reputational, and personal stakes. Thus the gap between the problems the player was solving and the problem upon which the analyst focuses is often very wide.

ACTION-CHANNELS

Bargaining games do not proceed randomly. Action-channels, i.e., regularized ways of producing action concerning types of issues, structure the game by preselecting the major players, determining their points of entrance into the game, and distributing particular advantages and disadvantages for each game. Most critically, channels determine "who's got the action," that is, which department's Indians actually do whatever is chosen. Weapon procurement decisions are made within the annual budgeting process; embassies' demands for action cables are answered according to routines of consultation and clearance from State to Defense and White House; requests for instructions from military groups (concerning assistance all the time, concerning operations during war) are composed by the military in consultation with the Office of the Secretary of Defense, State, and White House; crisis responses are debated among White House, State, Defense, CIA, and Ad Hoc players; major political speeches, especially by the President but also by other Chiefs, are cleared through established channels.

ACTION AS POLITICS

Government decisions are made, and government actions emerge neither as the calculated choice of a unified group, nor as a formal summary of leaders' preferences. Rather the context of shared power but separate judgments concerning important choices, determines that politics is the mechanism of choice. Note the *environment* in which the game is played: inordinate uncertainty about what must be done, the necessity that something be done, and crucial consequences of whatever is done. These features force responsible men to become active players. The *pace of the game*—hundreds of issues, numerous games, and multiple channels—compels players to fight to "get others' attention," to make them "see the facts," to assure that they "take the time to think seriously about the broader issue." The *structure of the game*—power shared by individuals with separate responsibilities—validates each player's feeling that "others don't see my problem," and "others must be persuaded to look at the issue from a less parochial perspective." The *rules of the game*—he who hesitates loses his chance to play at that point, and he who is uncertain about his recommendation is overpowered by others who are sure—pressures players to come down on one side of a 51–49 issue and play. The *rewards of the game*—effectiveness, i.e., impact on outcomes, as the immediate measure of performance—encourages hard play. Thus, most players come to fight to "make the government do what is right." The strategies and tactics employed are quite similar to those formalized by theorists of international relations.

STREAMS OF OUTCOMES

Important government decisions or actions emerge as collages composed of individual acts, outcomes of minor and major games, and foul-ups. Outcomes which could never have been chosen by an actor and would never have emerged from bargaining in a single game over the issue are fabricated piece by piece. Understanding of the outcome requires that it be disaggregated.

Dominant Inference Pattern

If a nation performed an action, that action was the *outcome* of bargaining among individuals and groups within the government. That outcome included *results* achieved by groups committed to a decision or action, *resultants* which emerged from bargaining among groups with quite different positions and *foul-ups*. Model III's explanatory power is achieved by revealing the pulling and hauling of various players, with different perceptions and priorities, focusing on separate problems, which yielded the outcomes that constitute the action in question.

General Propositions

ACTION AND INTENTION

Action does not presuppose intention. The sum of behavior of representatives of a government relevant to an issue was rarely intended by any individual or group. Rather separate individuals with different intentions contributed pieces which compose an outcome distinct from what anyone would have chosen.

WHERE YOU STAND DEPENDS ON WHERE YOU SIT[31]

Horizontally, the diverse demands upon each player shape his priorities, perceptions, and issues. For large classes of issues, e.g., budgets and procurement decisions, the stance of a particular player can be predicted with high reliability from information concerning his seat. In the notorious B-36 controversy, no one was surprised by Admiral Radford's testimony that "the B-36 under any theory of war, is a bad gamble with national security," as opposed to Air Force Secretary Symington's claim that "a B-36 with an A-bomb can destroy distant objectives which might require ground armies years to take." [32]

CHIEFS AND INDIANS

The aphorism "where you stand depends on where you sit" has vertical as well as horizontal application. Vertically, the demands upon the president, Chiefs, Staffers, and Indians are quite distinct.

The foreign policy issues with which the president can deal are limited primarily by his crowded schedule: the necessity of dealing first with what comes next. His problem is to probe the special face worn by issues that come to his attention, to preserve his leeway until time has clarified the uncertainties, and to assess the relevant risks.

Foreign policy Chiefs deal most often with the hottest issue *de jour*, though they can get the attention of the president and other members of the government for other issues which they judge important. What they cannot guarantee is that "the President will pay the price" or that "the others will get on board." They must build a coalition of the relevant powers that be. They must "give the President confidence" in the right course of action.

Most problems are framed, alternatives specified, and proposals pushed, however, by Indians. Indians fight with Indians of other departments; for example, struggles between International Security Affairs of the Department of Defense and Political-Military of the State Department are a microcosm of the action at higher levels. But the Indian's major problem is how to get the *attention* of Chiefs, how to get an issue decided, how to get the government "to do what is right."

In policymaking then, the issue looking *down* is options: how to preserve my leeway until time clarifies uncertainties. The issue looking *sideways* is commitment: how to get others committed to my coalition. The issue looking *upwards* is confidence: how to give the boss confidence in doing what must be done. To paraphrase one of Neustadt's assertions which can be applied down the length of the ladder, the essence of a responsible official's task is to induce others to see that what needs to be done is what their own appraisal of their own responsibilities requires them to do in their own interests.

Specific Propositions

DETERRENCE

The probability of nuclear attack depends primarily on the probability of attack emerging as an outcome of the bureaucratic politics of the attacking government. First, which players can decide to launch an attack? Whether the effective power over action is controlled by an individual, a minor game, or the central game is critical. Second, though model I's confidence in nuclear deterrence stems from an assertion that, in the end, governments will not commit suicide, model III recalls historical precedents. Admiral Yamamoto, who designed the Japanese attack on Pearl Harbor, estimated accurately: "In the first six months to a year of war against the US and England I will run wild, and I will show you an uninterrupted succession of victories; I must also tell you that, should the war be prolonged for two or three years, I have no confidence in our ultimate victory."[33] But Japan attacked. Thus, three questions might be considered. One: could any member of the government solve his problem by attack? What patterns of bargaining could yield attack as an outcome? The major difference between a stable balance of terror and a questionable balance may simply be that in the first case most members of the government appreciate fully the consequences of attack and are thus on guard against the emergence of this outcome. Two: what stream of outcomes might lead to an attack? At what point in that stream is the potential attacker's politics? If members of the US government had been sensitive to the stream of decisions from which the Japanese attack on Pearl Harbor emerged, they would have been aware of a considerable probability of that attack. Three: how might miscalculation and confusion generate foul-ups that yield attack as an outcome? For example, in a crisis or after the beginning of conventional war, what happens to the information available to, and the effective power of, members of the central game. . . .

CONCLUSION

This essay has obviously bitten off more than it has chewed. For further developments and synthesis of these arguments the reader is referred to the larger study.[34] In spite of the limits of space, however, it would be inappropriate to stop without spelling out several implications of the argument and addressing the question of relations among the models and extensions of them to activity beyond explanation.

At a minimum, the intended implications of the argument presented here are four. First, formulation of alternative frames of reference and demonstration that different analysts, relying predominantly on different models, produce quite different explanations should encourage the analyst's self-consciousness about the nets he employs. The effect of these "spectacles" in sensitizing him to particular aspects of what is going on—framing the puzzle in one way rather than another, encouraging him to examine the problem in terms of certain categories rather than others, directing him to particular kinds of evidence, and relieving puzzlement by one procedure rather than another—must be recognized and explored.

Second, the argument implies a position on the problem of "the state of the art." While accepting the commonplace characterization of the present condition of foreign policy analysis—personalistic, noncumulative, and sometimes insightful—this essay rejects both the counsel of despair's justification of this condition as a consequence of the character of the enterprise, and the "new frontiersmen's" demand for a priori theorizing on the frontiers and ad hoc appropriation of "new techniques."[35] What is required as a first step is noncasual examination of the present product: inspection of existing explanations, articulation of the conceptual models employed in producing them, formulation of the propositions relied upon, specification of the logic of the various intellectual enterprises, and reflection on the questions being asked. Though it is difficult to overemphasize the need for more systematic processing of more data, these preliminary matters of formulating questions with clarity and sensitivity to categories and assumptions so that fruitful acquisition of large quantities of data is possible are still a major hurdle in considering most important problems.

Third, the preliminary, partial paradigms presented here provide a basis for serious reexamination of many problems of foreign and military policy. Model II and model III cuts at problems typically treated in model I terms can permit significant improvements in explanation and prediction.[36] Full model II and III analyses require large amounts of information. But even in cases where the information base is severely limited, improvements are possible. Consider the problem of predicting Soviet strategic forces. In the mid-1950s, model I style calculations led to predictions that the Soviets would rapidly deploy large numbers of long-range bombers. From a model II perspective, both the frailty of the Air Force within the Soviet military establishment and the budgetary implications of such a buildup, would have led analysts to hedge this prediction. Moreover, model II would have pointed to a sure, visible indicator of such a buildup: noisy struggles among the Services over major budgetary shifts. In the late 1950s and early 1960s, model I calculations led to the prediction of immediate, massive Soviet deployment of ICBMs. Again, a model II cut would have reduced this number because, in the earlier period, strategic rockets were controlled by the Soviet Ground Forces rather than an independent service, and in the later period, this would have necessitated massive shifts in budgetary splits. Today, model I considerations lead many analysts both to recommend that an agreement not to deploy ABMs be a major American objective in upcoming strategic negotiations with the USSR, and to predict success. From a model II vantage point, the existence of an on-going Soviet ABM program, the strength of the organization (National Air Defense) that controls ABMs, and the fact that an agreement to stop ABM deployment would force the virtual dismantling of this organization, make a viable agreement of this sort much less likely. A model III cut suggests that (a) there must be significant differences among perceptions and priorities of Soviet leaders over strategic negotiations, (b) any agreement will affect some players' power bases, and (c) agreements that do not require extensive cuts in the sources of some major players' power will prove easier to negotiate and more viable.

Fourth, the present formulation of paradigms is simply an initial step. As such it leaves a long list of critical questions unanswered. Given any action, an imaginative analyst should always be able to construct some rationale for the government's choice. By imposing, and relaxing, constraints on the parameters of rational choice (as in variants of model I) analysts can construct a large number of accounts of any act as a rational choice. But does a statement of reasons why a rational actor would choose an action constitute an explanation of the *occurrence* of that action? How can model I analysis be forced to make more systematic contributions to the question of the determinants of occurrences? Model II's explanation of t in terms of $t - 1$ is explanation. The world is contiguous. But governments sometimes make sharp departures. Can an organizational process model be modified to suggest where change is likely? Attention to organizational change should afford greater understanding of why particular programs and SOPs are maintained by identifiable types of organizations and also how a manager can improve organizational performance. Model III tells a fascinating "story." But its complexity is enormous, the information requirements are often overwhelming, and many of the details of the bargaining may be superfluous. How can such a model be made parsimonious? The three models are obviously not exclusive alternatives. Indeed, the paradigms highlight the partial emphasis of the framework—what each emphasizes and what it leaves out. Each concentrates on one class of variables, in effect, relegating other important factors to a *ceteris paribus* clause. Model I concentrates on "market factors": pressures and incentives created by the "international strategic marketplace." Models II and III focus on the internal mechanism of the government that chooses in this environment. But can these relations be more fully specified? Adequate synthesis would require a typology of decisions and actions, some of which are more amenable to treatment in terms of one model and some to another. Government behavior is but one cluster of factors relevant to occurrences in foreign affairs. Most students of foreign policy adopt this focus (at least when explaining and predicting). Nevertheless, the dimensions of the chess board, the character of the pieces, and the rules of the game—factors considered by international systems theorists— constitute the context in which the pieces are moved. Can the major variables in the full function of determinants of foreign policy outcomes be identified?

Both the outline of a partial, ad hoc working synthesis of the models, and a sketch of their uses in activities other than explanation can be suggested by generating predictions in terms of each. Strategic surrender is an important problem of international relations and diplomatic history. War termination is a new, developing area of the strategic literature. Both of these interests lead scholars to address a central question: *Why* do nations surrender *when?* Whether implicit in explanations or more explicit in analysis, diplomatic historians and strategists rely upon propositions which can be turned forward to produce predictions. Thus at the risk of being timely—and in error—the present situation (August, 1968) offers an interesting test case: Why will North Vietnam surrender when? [37]

In a nutshell, analysis according to model I asserts: nations quit when costs outweigh the benefits. North Vietnam will surrender when it realizes "that continued fighting can only generate additional costs without hope of compensating gains, this expectation being largely the consequence of the previous application of force by the dominant side." [38] US actions can increase or decrease Hanoi's strategic costs. Bombing North Vietnam increases the pain and thus increases the probability of surrender. This proposition and prediction are not without meaning. That—"other things being equal"—nations are more likely to surrender when the strategic cost-benefit balance is negative, is true. Nations rarely surrender when they are winning. The proposition specifies a range within which nations surrender. But over this broad range, the relevant question is: why do nations surrender?

Models II and III focus upon the government machine through which this fact about the international strategic marketplace must be filtered to produce a surrender. These analysts are considerably less sanguine about the possibility of surrender *at the point* that the cost-benefit calculus turns negative. Never in history (i.e., in none of the five cases I have examined) have nations surrendered at that point. Surrender occurs sometime thereafter. *When* depends on process of organizations and politics of players within these governments—as they are affected by the opposing government. Moreover, the effects of the victorious power's action upon the surrendering nation cannot be adequately summarized as increasing or decreasing strategic costs. Imposing additional costs by bombing a nation may increase the probability of surrender. But it also may reduce it. An appreciation of the impact of the acts of one nation upon another thus requires some understanding of the machine which is being influenced. For more precise prediction, models II and III require considerably more information about the organizations and politics of North Vietnam than is publicly available. On the basis of the limited public information, however, these models can be suggestive.

Model II examines two subproblems. First, to have lost is not sufficient. The government must know that the strategic cost-benefit calculus is negative. But neither the categories, nor the indicators, of strategic costs and benefits are clear. And the sources of information about both are organizations whose parochial priorities and perceptions do not facilitate accurate information or estimation. Military evaluation of military performance, military estimates of factors like "enemy morale," and military predictions concerning when "the tide will turn" or "the corner will have been turned" are typically distorted. In cases of highly decentralized guerrilla operations, like Vietnam, these problems are exacerbated. Thus strategic costs will be underestimated. Only highly *visible* costs can have direct impact on leaders without being filtered through organizational channels. Second, since organizations define the details of options and execute actions, surrender (and negotiation) is likely to entail considerable bungling in the early stages. No organization can define options or prepare programs for this treasonous act. Thus, early overtures will be uncoordinated with the acts of other organizations, e.g., the fighting forces, creating contradictory "signals" to the victor.

Model III suggests that surrender will not come at the point that strategic costs outweigh benefits, but that it will not wait until the leadership group concludes that the war is lost. Rather the problem is better understood in terms of four additional propositions. First, strong advocates of the war effort, whose careers are closely identified with the war, rarely come to the conclusion that costs outweigh benefits. Second, quite often from the outset of a war, a number of members of the government (particularly those whose responsibilities sensitize them to problems other than war, e.g., economic planners or intelligence experts) are convinced that the war effort is futile. Third, surrender is likely to come as the result of a political shift that enhances the effective power of the latter group (and adds swing members to it). Fourth, the course of the war, particularly actions of the victor, can influence the advantages and disadvantages of players in the loser's government. Thus, North Vietnam will surrender not when its leaders have a change of heart, but when Hanoi has a change of leaders (or a change of effective power within the central circle). How US bombing (or pause), threats, promises, or action in the South affect the game in Hanoi is subtle but nonetheless crucial.

That these three models could be applied to the surrender of governments other than North Vietnam should be obvious. But that exercise is left for the reader.

NOTES

1. Theodore Sorensen, *Kennedy* (New York: Harper and Row, 1965), p. 705.
2. In attempting to understand problems of foreign affairs, analysts engage in a number of related, but logically separable enterprises: (a) description, (b) explanation, (c) prediction, (d) evaluation, and (e) recommendation. This essay focuses primarily on explanation (and by implication, prediction).

3. In arguing that explanations proceed in terms of implicit conceptual models, this essay makes no claim that foreign policy analysts have developed any satisfactory, empirically tested theory. In this essay, the use of the term "model" without qualifiers should be read "conceptual scheme."

4. For the purpose of this argument we shall accept Carl G. Hempel's characterization of the logic of explanation: an explanation "answers the question, '*Why did the explanadum-phenomenon occur?*' by showing that the phenomenon resulted from particular circumstances, specified in C_1, C_2, . . . C_x, in accordance with laws L_1, L_2, . . . L_r. By pointing this out, the argument shows that, given the particular circumstances and the laws in question, the occurrence of the phenomenon was to be *expected;* and it is in this sense that the explanation enables us to understand why the phenomenon occurred." *Aspects of Scientific Explanation* (New York: Harcourt, Brace and World, 1961), p. 337. While various patterns of explanation can be distinguished, *viz.,* Ernest Nagel, *The Structure of Science: Problems in the Logic of Scientific Explanation* (New York: Harcourt, Brace and World, 1961), satisfactory scientific explanations exhibit this basic logic. Consequently prediction is the converse of explanation.

5. Earlier drafts of this argument have aroused heated arguments concerning proper names for these models. To choose names from ordinary language is to court confusion, as well as familiarity. Perhaps it is best to think of these models as I, II, and III.

6. *New York Times,* 18 Feb. 1967.

7. Ibid.

8. Arnold Horelick and Myron Rush, *Strategic Power and Soviet Foreign Policy* (Chicago: University of Chicago Press, 1965). Based on A. Horelick, "The Cuban Missile Crisis: An Analysis of Soviet Calculations and Behavior," *World Politics* 16 (Apr. 1964).

9. Horelick and Rush, *Strategic Power,* p. 154.

10. Hans Morgenthau, *Politics among Nations* 3d ed. (New York: Knopf, 1960), p. 191.

11. Ibid., p. 192.

12. Ibid., p. 5.

13. Ibid., pp. 5–6.

14. The larger study examines several exceptions to this generalization. Sidney Verba's excellent essay "Assumptions of Rationality and Non-Rationality in Models of the International System" is less an exception than it is an approach to a somewhat different problem. Verba focuses upon models of rationality and irrationality of *individual* statesmen: in Knorr and Verba, *International System.*

15. Robert K. Merton, *Social Theory and Social Structures,* rev. and enl. ed. (New York: Free Press, 1957), pp. 12–16. Considerably weaker than a satisfactory theoretical model, paradigms nevertheless represent a short step in that direction from looser, implicit conceptual models. Neither the concepts nor the relations among the variables are sufficiently specified to yield propositions deductively. "Paradigmatic Analysis" nevertheless has considerable promise for clarifying and codifying styles of analysis in political science. Each of the paradigms stated here can be represented rigorously in mathematical terms. For example, model I lends itself to mathematical formulation along the lines of Herbert Simon's "Behavioral Theory of Rationality," *Models of Man* (New York: Wiley, 1957). But this does not solve the most difficult problem of "measurement and estimation."

16. Though a variant of this model could easily be stochastic, this paradigm is stated in nonprobabilistic terms. In contemporary strategy, a stochastic version of this model is sometimes used for predictions; but it is almost impossible to find an explanation of an occurrence in foreign affairs that is consistently probabilistic.

    Analogies between model I and the concept of explanation developed by R. G. Collingwood, William Dray, and other "revisionists" among philosophers concerned with the critical philosophy of history are not accidental. For a summary of the "revisionist position" see Maurice Mandelbaum, "Historical Explanation: The Problem of Covering Laws," *History and Theory* 1 (1960).

17. This model is an analogue of the theory of the rational entrepreneur which has been developed extensively in economic theories of the firm and the consumer. These two propositions specify the "substitution effect." Refinement of this model and specification of additional general propositions by translating from the economic theory is straightforward.

18. *New York Times,* 22 Mar. 1969.

19. See Nathan Leites, *A Study of Bolshevism* (Glencoe, Ill.: Free Press, 1953).

20. The influence of organizational studies upon the present literature of foreign affairs is minimal. Specialists in international politics are not students of organization theory. Organization theory has only recently begun to study organizations as decision-makers and has not yet produced behavioral studies of national security organizations from a decision-making perspective. It seems unlikely, however, that these gaps will remain unfilled much longer. Considerable progress has been made in the study of the business firm as an organization. Scholars have begun applying these insights to government organizations, and interest in an organizational perspective is spreading among institutions and individuals concerned with actual government operations. The "decision-making" approach represented by Richard Snyder, R. Bruck, and B. Sapin, *Foreign Policy Decision-Making* (Glencoe, Ill.: Free Press, 1962), incorporates a number of insights from organization theory.

21. The formulation of this paradigm is indebted both to the orientation and insights of Herbert Simon and to the behavioral model of the firm stated by Richard Cyert and James March, *A Behavioral Theory of the Firm* (Englewood Cliffs, N.J.: Prentice-Hall, 1963). Here, however, one is forced to grapple with the less routine, less quantified functions of the less differentiated elements in government organizations.

22. Theodore Sorensen, "You Get to Walk to Work," *New York Times Magazine,* 19 Mar. 1967.

23. Organizations are not monolithic. The proper level of disaggregation depends upon the objectives of a piece of analysis. This paradigm is formulated with reference to the major organizations that constitute the US government. Generalization to the major components of each department and agency should be relatively straight forward.

24. The stability of these constraints is dependent on such factors as rules for promotion and reward, budgeting and accounting procedures, and mundane operating procedures.

25. Marriner Eccles, *Beckoning Frontiers* (New York: A. A. Knopf, 1951), p. 336.

26. Arthur Schlesinger, *A Thousand Days* (Boston: Houghton-Mifflin, 1965), p. 406.

27. This paradigm relies upon the small group of analysts who have begun to fill the gap. My primary source is the model implicit in the work of Richard E. Neustadt, though his concentration on presidential action has been generalized to a concern with policy as the outcome of political bargaining among a number of independent

players, the president amounting to no more than a "superpower" among many lesser but considerable powers. As Warner Schilling argues, the substantive problems are of such inordinate difficulty that uncertainties and differences with regard to goals, alternatives, and consequences are inevitable. This necessitates what Roger Hilsman describes as the process of conflict and consensus building. The techniques employed in this process often resemble those used in legislative assemblies, though Samuel Huntington's characterization of the process as "legislative" overemphasizes the equality of participants as opposed to the hierarchy which structures the game. Moreover, whereas for Huntington, foreign policy (in contrast to military policy) is set by the executive, this paradigm maintains that the activities which he describes as legislative are characteristic of the process by which foreign policy is made.

28. The theatrical metaphor of stage, roles, and actors is more common than this metaphor of games, positions, and players. Nevertheless, the rigidity connotated by the concept of "role" both in the theatrical sense of actors reciting fixed lines and in the sociological sense of fixed responses to specified social situations makes the concept of names, positions, and players more useful for this analysis of active participants in the determination of national policy. Objections to the terminology on the grounds that "game" connotes nonserious play overlook the concept's application to most serious problems both in Wittgenstein's philosophy and in contemporary game theory. Game theory typically treats more precisely structured games, but Wittgenstein's examination of the "language game" wherein men use words to communicate is quite analogous to this analysis of the less specified game of bureaucratic politics. See Ludwig Wittgenstein, *Philosophical Investigations*, 3d. ed. (New York: Macmillan, 1968), and Thomas Schelling, "What Is Game Theory?" in James Charlesworth, *Contemporary Political Analysis* (New York: Free Press, 1967).

29. Inclusion of the president's special assistant for national security affairs in the tier of "Chiefs" rather than among the "Staffers" involves a debatable choice. In fact he is both super-staffer and near-chief. His position has no statutory authority. He is especially dependent upon good relations with the president and the secretaries of defense and state. Nevertheless, he stands astride a genuine action-channel. The decision to include this position among the Chiefs reflects my judgment that the Bundy function is becoming institutionalized.

30. Richard E. Neustadt, Testimony, United States Senate, Committee on Government Operations, Subcommittee on National Security Staffing, *Administration of National Security,* 26 Mar. 1963, pp. 82–83.

31. This aphorism was stated first, I think, by Don K. Price.

32. Paul Y. Hammond, "Super Carriers and B-36 Bombers," in Harold Stein, ed., *American Civil-Military Decisions* (Birmingham: University of Alabama Press, 1963).

33. Roberta Wohlstetter, *Pearl Harbor* (Stanford: Stanford University Press, 1962), p. 350.

34. Graham T. Allison, *Essence of Decision* (Boston: Little, Brown, 1971).

35. Thus my position is quite distinct from both poles in the recent "great debate" about international relations. While many "traditionalists" of the sort Kaplan attacks adopt the first posture and many "scientists" of the sort attacked by Bull adopt the second, this third posture is relatively neutral with respect to whatever is in substantive dispute, See Hedley Bull, "International Theory: The Case for a Classical Approach," *World Politics* 18 (Apr. 1966); and Morton Kaplan, "The New Great Debate: Traditionalism vs. Science in International Relations," *World Politics* 19 (Oct. 1966).

36. A number of problems are now being examined in these terms both in the Bureaucracy Study Group on Bureaucracy and Policy of the Institute of Politics at Harvard University and at the RAND Corporation.
37. In response to several readers' recommendations, what follows is reproduced verbatim from the paper delivered at the Sept. 1968 Association meetings (RAND P-3919). The discussion is heavily indebted to Ernest R. May.
38. Richard Snyder, *Deterrence and Defense* (Princeton: Princeton University Press, 1961), p. 11. For a more general presentation of this position see Paul Kecskemeti, *Strategic Surrender* (New York: Stanford University Press, 1964).

2 1

RICHARD MANSBACH,
YALE H. FERGUSON, AND
DONALD E. LAMPERT

Towards a New Conceptualization of Global Politics

THE EMERGENCE AND DISAPPEARANCE OF ACTORS

Individuals and groups become functionally linked as they discover that they share common interests and common needs that transcend existing organizational frontiers. They may then develop common views and even cooperative approaches to the problems that they confront. The complexity of contemporary modes of industrial production, for example, may generate a linkage between business firms in different countries that depend upon each other for raw materials, parts, expertise, or marketing facilities. Industrialists in several countries may discover that they share problems with which they can cope more effectively by pooling their resources; they may seek, for instance, common tax and pricing policies from the governments of the states in which they reside. In the course of collaborating, their common or complementary interests may grow and deepen beyond mere economic expediency. "There is," argues Werner Feld, "an emotive side to such efforts which produces in the

SOURCE: From *The Web of World Politics: Nonstate Actors in the Global System* (Englewood Cliffs, NJ: Prentice-Hall, Inc., 1976), pp. 32–45. © 1976. Reprinted by permission of Prentice-Hall, Englewood Cliffs, New Jersey.

staff members concerned with collaboration a distinct feeling of being involved in a 'united or cooperative' endeavor."[1]

When one begins to identify the many functional systems that link men, the world appears "like millions of cobwebs superimposed one upon another, covering the whole globe."[2] Functional systems themselves tend to be interdependent and related to each other in complex ways. Each system requires the existence of others to perform effectively; in this respect systems, too, may be said to be linked. In J. W. Burton's words:

> Linked systems create clusters that tend to be concentrated geographically. . . . Linked systems tend to consolidate into administrative units. . . . Once consolidated . . . linked systems and their administrative controls acquire an identity and a legitimized status within their environment.[3]

From this perspective, governments of nation-states may be seen as functional (administrative) systems whose central function since the seventeenth century has been to regulate and manage clusters of other functional systems. More accurately perhaps, in their function as administrators for many functional systems, states have been essentially multifunctional actors organizing collective efforts toward objectives which could not be realized by individuals in their private capacity. The boundaries of nation-states have tended to coincide with the boundaries of other functional systems, and therefore political frontiers have seemed to represent "marked discontinuities in the frequency of transactions and marked discontinuities in the frequency of responses."[4] States were able to control and limit the transactions which crossed their frontiers as well as those that occurred within their borders. As long as states remained relatively impermeable, they were able, for example, to regulate the economic or cultural relations of their citizens with those living abroad and with foreign nationals.

In theory, however, it is *not necessary* that the governments of nation-states be the umbrella administrative systems through which all other systems are regulated. The boundaries of such systems coincide with nation-state frontiers only insofar as national governments can control them and can independently open or close their state borders to transnational influences. Consider the situation of many states whose political or historical frontiers do *not* coincide with the national boundaries of groups residing within them. Ties may develop across borders, and loyalties may shift away from governments. There are many historical cases of such phenomena; the Austro-Hungarian Empire, for example, consisted of a patchwork of different national groups, and Serbian, Italian, and Croatian nationals tended to reserve their highest loyalties for fellow-nationals living outside the Empire and for the idea of "their nation." In recent years violence in areas as diverse as Cyprus, the Congo (Zaire), Nigeria, Canada, and Ireland suggest the way in which the loyalties of national groups may transcend the borders of states and lead to conflict.

The question of human loyalties is not one that can be settled once and for all; loyalties constantly shift as men perceive that their interests and aspirations are more fully represented by new groups. As Arnold Wolfers noted some years ago, "attention must be focused on the individual human beings for whom identification is a psychological event."[5] To the degree that human loyalties are divided between states and other groups, the latter can become significant global actors.

This is, in fact, what has happened. As Burton reminds us, "there is in contemporary world society an increasing number of systems—some basically economic, scientific, cultural, ideological, or religious—that have little relationship to State boundaries," and "whatever significance geographically drawn boundaries had, has been and is being greatly reduced by these developments."[6] Of the various transnational exchanges, some of the more important and well-known include teaching and research abroad, study abroad, overseas religious missions, military service abroad, tourism, work in multinational corporations, and participation in nongovernmental and international organizations.

Functional systems have spilled across nation-state boundaries and in some cases have defied the efforts of governments to regulate them. Citizens of many states find themselves linked in horizontal fashion, working together regardless of the wishes of governments. Thus, Jews in the United States, Israel, the Soviet Union, and Europe are linked by loyalties that transcend the interests of the states in which they reside. Leftist revolutionaries, industrial managers, international civil servants and others are linked in similar fashion though for different purposes. Individuals have become increasingly aware of the interests that they share with others in different states, have communicated these interests, and have developed new loyalties. In some cases these transnational affiliations have been organized and have acquired their own administrative hierarchies, thereby becoming nonstate actors in a more formal sense.[7]

Several major trends have contributed to these developments. The proliferation and increasing potential destructiveness of thermonuclear weapons have made the prospect of war between the superpowers "unthinkable" and have contributed to the erosion of the great postwar ideological blocs. Conventional military force and intervention have become less effective in coping with certain problems, as evidenced by the French defeat in Algeria and the American debacle in Vietnam. As nuclear and conventional warfare have become more expensive to contemplate and less effective, new means of gaining influence, including guerrilla warfare, political terrorism, economic boycott, and political propaganda, have become more common, thereby permitting actors lacking the traditional instruments of power to exercise considerable influence and enjoy considerable autonomy. Even more frightening is the possibility that such actors may gain access to modern technology.

In addition, the diminution of the central ideological cleavage, the resurgence of Europe, China, and Japan, and the independence of a multitude of small and poor nation-states in Africa and Asia have led to the emergence of other cleavages, some global and many of a regional and local scope, and have therefore encouraged the "regionalization" or "localization" of international conflict. "The structure of the international system," Jorge Domínguez declares, "has been transformed through a process of fragmentation of the linkages of the center of the system to its peripheries and of those between the continental subsystems of the peripheries."[8] The new conflicts that have surfaced revolve around questions such as national self-determination, local border adjustment, economic inequality and exploitation, and racial or ethnic discrimination. These are questions that encourage the shifting of people's loyalties away from institutions that formerly held their affections.

At root, the twentieth-century emergence of new actors in the global system reflects the inability of territorially-limited nation-states to respond to, cope with, or suppress changing popular demands. Popular demands can be suppressed (and often are) by existing authorities; they can be fulfilled by them; or they can lead to the emergence of new political structures designed to fulfill them. Thus, when a state can no longer guarantee the defense of its subjects, it may be conquered and eliminated as happened to eighteenth-century Poland. Conversely, the integration of existing units, like the merger of two corporations, or the creation of new nation-state actors such as the United States in 1776, Biafra (temporarily) in 1968, and Bangladesh in 1971, are partly the consequence of demands for a more capable and responsive performance of certain tasks—demands that were neither suppressed nor fulfilled.

Today the global system is complexly interdependent owing in part to improved communications and transportation. People's lives are being touched and affected ever more profoundly by decisions made outside their own national states. Their demands for justice, equality, prosperity, and independence tend to increase and further tax the capacity of existing nation-states. We are in the midst of a revolution of "rising expectations" in which the achievements of people in one corner of the system generate demands for similar achievements elsewhere. When these demands remain unanswered, they may lead to intense frustration. Thus, the frustration of large numbers of Arabs at continued Israeli occupation of Palestine and the failure of Arab governments to satisfy their claims have led to the creation of Palestinian terrorist and liberation groups, the organization and behavior of which are in part patterned after successful movements in Algeria, Cuba, and Vietnam.

In the contemporary world demands such as those for defense, full employment, or social reform place overwhelming burdens on the resources of poor states. Others, increasingly, are beyond the capacity of *any* single nation-state to fulfill. As Robert Keohane and Joseph Nye observe:

> It is clear that most if not all governments will find it very difficult to cope with many aspects of transnational relations in the decade of the 1970s and thereafter. . . . Outer space, the oceans, and the internationalization of production are only three of the most obvious areas in which intergovernmental control may be demanded in the form of new international laws or new organizations or both.[9]

One way in which national governments may seek to deal with transnational pressures is through the creation of specialized intergovernmental actors which acquire limited global roles. The emergence of regional agencies and organizations and those associated with the United Nations attests to the growth of large-scale functional systems with their own administrative over-seers. Such organizations reinforce pre-existing linkages or create new ones.[10] Intergovernmental organizations that have achieved some measure of auton-omy, however, are often engaged in highly technical and relatively nonpoliti-cal tasks. In those areas where governments resist transnational pressures, other groups may emerge.

GLOBAL TASKS

There are at least four general types of tasks that can be performed by actors:

1. *Physical protection* or security which involves the protection of men and their values from coercive deprivation either by other members within the group or by individuals or groups outside it.
2. *Economic development and regulation* which comprise activities that are intended to overcome the constraints imposed on individual or col-lective capacity for self-development and growth by the scarcity or dis-tribution of material resources.
3. *Residual public interest tasks* which involve activities that are designed to overcome constraints other than economic, such as disease or igno-rance, that restrict individual or collective capacity for self-development and growth.
4. *Group status* which refers to the provision of referent identification through collective symbols that bind the individual to others, provide him with psychological and emotional security, and distinguish him in some manner from others who are not members of the group. Such symbols are often grounded in ethnicity, nationality, class, religion, and kinship.

The behavior of actors in the global system involves the performance of one or more of the foregoing tasks in cooperation or competition with other actors responding to the actual or anticipated demands of their "constituen-cies." Although governments of nation-states customarily perform these tasks "domestically," tasks become relevant at the "international" level when a government acts to protect its citizens from externally-imposed change or to adapt them to such change. For example, the regulation of the domestic econ-omy to create and sustain full employment is not itself an internationally-relevant task. When, however, tariffs are imposed on imports or the currency is devalued, the behavior acquires significance for the global system. Others outside the state are affected and made to bear the burdens of the "domestic" economic adjustment.

The suggested categories of tasks are, of course, in the nature of analytic pigeonholes, and many activities involve more than a single category. Most actors tend to perform several tasks for their members, but an actor may be specialized and perform only one type. The World Health Organization (WHO), for example, is largely concerned with upgrading global health standards (a residual public interest task). Armed mercenaries, on the other hand, are generally involved only in offering physical protection to those who require it and can pay for it. In practice different categories of tasks are often perceived as mutually supportive. Hence, national groups may believe that only by unifying their "nation" can they protect themselves, yet at the same time unification depends on self-protection.

Actors may add and drop tasks or enlarge and restrict them over a period of time. For example, only recently many "welfare state" policies have been initiated by nation-states or intergovernmental organizations, thereby enlarging the scope of activities involved in the residual public interest category. Previously, such services were offered, if at all, by groups such as the family, church, or political party. Technological change, the behavior of others, and the solution of old problems encourage demands for the performance of new tasks. Thus, modern technology and medicine, while solving problems that have bedeviled people for centuries, are partly responsible for growing global pollution and population pressures. If nation-states continue to cope only sporadically with these burgeoning problems, demands for pollution and population control may lead to the creation of significant intergovernmental and nongovernmental political structures. Indeed, in 1972 the United Nations for the first time began to turn its attention seriously to questions of world pollution control, and two years later it addressed itself to the specter of world hunger.

The increasing inability of modern nation-states to satisfy the demands of their citizens or to cope with problems that transcend their boundaries is partly the result of the growing complexity and specialization of functional systems as well as of the increase in the number of collective goods and benefits desired by individuals.[11] In contrast, states in the eighteenth century were concerned principally with providing physical protection for members and insulating subjects from externally-imposed change. Individuals were able to provide for their own economic and social needs either privately or through small groups such as the extended family. Only peripherally and sporadically was the larger collectivity called upon to undertake economic and social service tasks or even to provide group status. Political philosophers were largely preoccupied with identifying the areas in which collective action was called for, and they tended to agree that these areas were narrowly circumscribed.

The increasing size and complexity of systems and institutions threaten individuals with a sense of helplessness in a world dominated by large impersonal forces where rapid change and "future shock" are common. Many small and new nation-states are only barely (if at all) able to provide physical security, economic satisfaction, or social welfare for their citizens. On the other hand, often they do provide their citizens with an emotionally-comforting sense of national identity and "in-group" unity. In this respect these states (as well as some nonstate units) can be seen as rather specialized actors in an increasingly interdependent world.[12]

THE PANOPLY OF GLOBAL ACTORS

We can identify at least six types of actors in the contemporary global system.

The first type is the *interstate governmental actor* (IGO) composed of governmental representatives from more than one state. Sometimes known as "international" or "supranational" organizations, depending upon their degree of autonomy, they include as members two or more national governments. Since the beginning of the nineteenth century, the number of such organizations has increased even more rapidly than has the number of nation-states.[13] Examples of this type of actor include military alliances such as NATO and the Warsaw Pact, universal organizations such as the League of Nations or the United Nations, and special purpose organizations such as the European Economic Community (EEC) and the Universal Postal Union (UPU). In 1972 there were at least 280 such actors in the international system.[14]

A second type is the *interstate nongovernmental actor.* Sometimes referred to as "transnational" or "crossnational," this type of actor encompasses individuals who reside in several nation-states but who do not represent any of the governments of these states. According to the *Yearbook of International Organizations,* there were at least 2,190 such organizations in 1972 as compared to under 1,000 in 1958.[15] These groups are functionally diverse and include religious groups such as the International Council of Jewish Women, the Salvation Army, and the World Muslim Congress; trade unions such as the Caribbean Congress of Labor and the World Confederation of Labor; and social welfare organizations such as the International Red Cross or Kiwanis International. (*The Yearbook* may, in fact, not include the most significant of these groups because it omits multinational corporations and terrorist and revolutionary groups.) While many of these actors seek to avoid involvement in politically-sensitive questions, some behave autonomously and do become so embroiled. This is illustrated by the role of the International Red Cross in the Nigerian-Biafran civil war[16] and the conflict culminating in 1968 between Standard of New Jersey's subsidiary, the International Petroleum Corporation, and the government of Peru. The multinational corporation in particular is becoming a major transnational actor, rendering more obsolete the state-centric model of international interaction.[17]

A third type of actor is commonly known as the *nation-state.* It consists of personnel from the agencies of a single central government. Though often regarded as unified entities, national governments are often more usefully identified in terms of their parts such as ministries and legislatures. On occasion, the "parts" may behave autonomously with little reference to other government bureaucracies. "The apparatus of each national government," declares Graham Allison, "constitutes a complex arena for the intranational game."[18] The ministries that make up large governments bargain with each other and regularly approach "national questions with parochial or particularist views; each may view the "national interest" from a different standpoint. For instance, it has been alleged that the American Central Intelligence Agency has, on occasion, formulated and carried out policy independently and without the complete knowledge or approval of elected officials.

Fourth, there is the *governmental noncentral* actor composed of personnel from regional, parochial, or municipal governments within a single state or of colonial officials representing the state. Such parochial bureaucracies and officials generally are only peripherally concerned with world politics or, at most, have an indirect impact on the global political system. Occasionally, however, they have a direct impact when they serve as the core of secessionist movements or when they establish and maintain direct contact with other actors. In this context, the provincial officials of Katanga, Biafra, and in the 1860's the American South come to mind.

A fifth type is the *intrastate nongovernmental* actor consisting of nongovernmental groups or individuals located primarily within a single state. Again, this type of actor is generally thought of as subject to the regulation of a central government, at least in matters of foreign policy. Yet, such groups, ranging from philanthropic organizations and political parties to ethnic communities, labor unions, and industrial corporations may, from time to time, conduct relations directly with autonomous actors other than their own government. In this category, we find groups as disparate as the Ford Foundation, Oxfam, the Turkish and Greek Cypriot communities, the Communist Party of the Soviet Union, the Jewish Agency, and the Irish Republican Army.

Finally, *individuals* in their private capacity are, on occasion, able to behave autonomously in the global arena. Such "international" individuals were more common before the emergence of the nation-state, particularly as diplomatic or military mercenaries. More recently, one might think of the American industrialist Andrew Carnegie who willed ten million dollars for "the speedy abolition of war between the so-called civilized nations," the Swedish soldier Count Gustaf von Rosen who was responsible for creating a Biafran air force during the Nigerian civil war, or the Argentine revolutionary Ché Guevara.

Figure 1 relates actors to the tasks mentioned above and suggests the range of actors that exist in the global system and the principal tasks they perform. The entries in the matrix are illustrative and indicate that these actors at some point in time have performed these functions in ways relevant for the global system. Some categories may have many representatives; others only a few.

THE COMPLEX CONGLOMERATE SYSTEM

Our analysis up to this point enables us to return to the question of the structure and processes of the global political system. The contemporary global system defies many conventional descriptions of its structure as bipolar, multipolar, or balance of power.[19] These descriptions account only for the number

FIGURE I Actors Defined by Membership and Principal Task

	PHYSICAL PROTECTION	ECONOMIC	PUBLIC INTEREST	GROUP STATUS
INTERSTATE GOVERNMENTAL	NATO	GATT	WHO	British Commonwealth
INTERSTATE NONGOVERNMENTAL	Al Fatah	Royal Dutch Petroleum	International	Comintern
NATION-STATE	Turkish Cypriot Government Officials	U. S. Dept. of Commerce	HEW	Biafra
GOVERNMENTAL NONCENTRAL	Confederacy	Katanga	New York City	Quebec
INTRASTATE NONGOVERNMENTAL	Jewish Defense League	CARE	Ford Foundation	Ibo tribe
INDIVIDUAL	Gustav von Rosen	Jean Monnet	Andrew Carnegie	Dalai Lama

of states and their distribution of power. "In particular," declares Oran Young, "it seems desirable to think increasingly in terms of world systems that are heterogeneous with respect to types of actor (i.e. mixed actor systems) in the analysis of world politics." [20]

We propose an alternative model of the contemporary global system which we shall call the *complex conglomerate system*.[21] The concept of "conglomerate" refers to "a mixture of various materials or elements clustered together without assimilation." [22] In economics the term is used to describe the grouping of firms of different types under a single umbrella of corporate leadership.

The principal feature of the complex conglomerate system is the formation of situationally-specific alignments of different types of actors using a variety of means to achieve complementary objectives. It is significant that many of these alignment "conglomerates" lack the formal structure of traditional alliances such as NATO and tend to be flexible and ideologically diffuse.

For example, until recently one could identify conglomerate alignments that are essentially adversarial on the issue of Angolan independence. On one side were the Angolan rebel groups, the U.N. General Assembly, Black African states like Tanzania, the Soviet bloc of states, and even the World Council of Churches; on the other side were Portugal, the United States, and several major international corporations. Another illustrative pair of alignments has formed over the question of the pricing of petroleum products and the ownership of petroleum-production and exploitation facilities in the Middle East.

FIGURE 2

	INTERSTATE GOVERNMENTAL	INTERSTATE NON-GOVERNMENTAL	NATION-STATE	GOVERNMENTAL NON-CENTRAL	INTRASTATE NON-GOVERNMENTAL	INDIVIDUAL
INTERSTATE GOVERNMENTAL	UN–NATO (1950)	UN–International Red Cross (Palestine)	EEC–Francophone African states	OAU–Biafra	Arab League–Al Fatah	Grand Mufti of Jerusalem–Arab League
INTERSTATE NON-GOVERNMENTAL	UN–International Red Cross (Palestine)	Shell Oil–ESSO (1972)	USSR–Comintern (1920's)	IBM–Scotland	ITT–Allende opposition (Chile)	Sun-Yat sen–Comintern
NATION-STATE	EEC–Francophone African states	USSR–Comintern (1920's)	"traditional alliances" (NATO)	Belgium–Katanga (1960)	North Vietnam–Viet Cong	U.S.–James Donovan
GOVERNMENTAL NON-CENTRAL	OAU–Biafra	IBM–Scotland	Belgium–Katanga (1960)	N.Y. Mayor–Moscow Mayor (1973)	Algerian rebels–French Socialists (1954)	South African mercenaries–Katanga
INTRASTATE NON-GOVERNMENTAL	Arab League–Al Fatah	ITT–Allende Opposition (Chile)	North Vietnam–Viet Cong	Ulster–Protestant Vanguard (1970)	Communist Party-USSR–Communist Party-German Democratic Republic	George Grivas–Greek Cypriots
INDIVIDUAL	Grand Mufti of Jerusalem–Arab League	Sun-Yat-sen–Comintern	U.S.–James Donovan	South African mercenaries–Katanga (1960)	George Grivas–Greek Cypriots	Louis of Conde–Gaspard de Coligny (1562)

On one side in favor of the *status quo* are the major Western powers and the principal petroleum corporations, sometimes called "the seven sisters"; on the other side are the major oil producing states of the Middle East and elsewhere organized in a group called OPEC (Organization of Petroleum Exporting Countries), along with various Palestinian liberation groups, Egypt, and the Eastern bloc of states which perceive the oil question as linked to the Arab-Israeli conflict.

Figure 2 further suggests the range of alignments that characterize the complex conglomerate system.

In summary, we should stress that the complex conglomerate system exhibits several other characteristics in addition to the primary one relating to the existence of many autonomous actors of different types and their grouping into diffuse, flexible, and situationally-specific alignments:

1. The global system in traditional terms is steadily moving in the direction of multipolarity, with the breakup of the great postwar ideological blocs and the assumption of new global roles by Europe, Japan, and China. Concurrently, many new states have joined the system and the gap between the living standards of "haves" and "have nots" continues to widen. In addition, the Third World has begun to divide into resource-rich and resource-deprived states (the "Fourth World").

2. Weapons with the greatest destructive capacity are deemed unusable, and military intervention by nation-states is becoming increasingly expensive. Economic adjustment among the developed countries is rapidly joining security as a major preoccupation of developed-country policy-makers. Additional conflicts involve questions like national self-determination, local border adjustment, economic inequality and exploitation, and racial or ethnic discrimination.

3. Many poor and small nation-states are unable to perform the tasks demanded of them by their populations.

4. Global problems such as oceanic pollution are emerging that transcend national boundaries and overwhelm the capacities of individual nation-states.

5. Many means are available and are used to exert influence including conventional military force (nation-states), control of marketing facilities, pricing, and technology (multinational corporations), clandestine military force (terrorist and revolutionary groups), moral suasion (Roman Catholic Church), money and expertise (Ford Foundation), voting strength (Jewish community in the United States), and so forth.

6. Functional linkages creates transnational perceptions of mutual interest and lead to regularized communication among status groups across state frontiers.

7. A high level of interdependence links diffuse groups in different nation-states and is fostered by modern communication and transportation facilities and complex production processes.

8. Nation-states are becoming increasingly permeable, that is, subject to external penetration.

9. The loyalties of peoples are increasingly divided among many actors and tend to shift depending upon the nature of the issue.

10. Discontinuities exist which are directly related to the salience of local issues and the level of political development of various regional systems.

Notes

1. Werner Feld, "Political Aspects of Transnational Business Collaboration in the Common Market," *International Organization* 24:2 (Spring 1970), p. 210. For

an elaboration of the thesis that transnationalism promotes complementary views among elites, see Robert C. Angell, *Peace on the March* (New York: Van Nostrand, 1969).

2. J. W. Burton, *Systems, States, Diplomacy and Rules* (New York: Cambridge University Press, 1968), pp. 8–9.

3. *Ibid.,* p. 8.

4. Karl W. Deutsch, "External Influences on the Internal Behavior of States," in R. Barry Farrell, ed., *Approaches to Comparative and International Politics* (Evanston, Ill.: Northwestern University Press, 1966), p. 15.

5. Arnold Wolfers, *Discord and Collaboration* (Baltimore: Johns Hopkins Press, 1962), p. 23.

6. Burton, *Systems,* p. 10.

7. See Oran R. Young, "The Actors in World Politics," in James N. Rosenau, Vincent Davis, and Maurice A. East, eds., *The Analysis of International Politics* (New York: Free Press, 1972), p. 132.

8. Jorge I. Domínguez, "Mice that Do Not Roar: Some Aspects of International Politics in the World's Peripheries," *International Organization* 25:2 (Spring 1971), p. 208.

9. Robert O. Keohane and Joseph S. Nye, Jr., "Transnational Relations and World Politics: An Introduction," in Keohane and Nye, eds. "Transnational Relations and World Politics," special edition of *International Organization* 25:3 (Summer 1971), p. 348.

10. For a summary of many contemporary intergovernmental organizations, see John Paxton, ed., *The Statesman's Yearbook 1973–1974* (London: Macmillan, 1973), pp. 3–61; and Richard P. Stebbins and Alba Amoia, eds., *Political Handbook and Atlas of the World 1970* (New York: Simon & Schuster, 1970), pp. 437–513.

11. For an explanation of the difference between "collective" and "private" goods, see Mancur Olson, Jr., *The Logic of Collective Action* (Cambridge: Harvard University Press, 1965).

12. Occasionally, states may fail to provide even group status for inhabitants. Thus, in 1969–1970, it appeared that guerrilla organizations such as Al Fatah were largely providing physical protection and group states for many Palestinians in Jordan. When one prominent guerrilla leader was asked why his commandos permitted Jordan's King Hussein to remain on the throne and did not themselves seize the reins of government, he replied: "We don't want to have to take care of sewers and stamp the passports." Eric Pace, "The Violent Men of Amman," *The New York Times Magazine,* 19 July 1970, p. 42.

13. See J. David Singer and Michael D. Wallace, "Intergovernmental Organization in the Global System, 1815–1964: A Quantitative Description," *International Organization* 24:2 (Spring 1970), p. 277.

14. E. S. Tew, ed., *Yearbook of International Organizations* 14th ed. (Brussels: Union of International Associations, 1972), p. 879.

15. *Ibid.,* see also Angell, *Peace on the March,* pp. 129–46.

16. For a description of the rich variety of actors and actor-types involved in the Nigerian-Biafran war, see M. Davis, "The Structuring of International Communications About the Nigeria-Biafra War," paper delivered at the 8th European Conference, Peace Research Society (International).

17. See, for example, *infra.,* Chap. 8: Jonathan F. Galloway, "Multi-national Enterprises as Worldwide Interest Groups," paper delivered to the 1970 Meeting of

the American Political Science Association; Galloway, "Worldwide Corporations and International Integration: The Case of INTELSAT," *International Organization* 24:3 (Summer 1970), pp. 503–19; Raymond F. Hopkins and Richard W. Mansbach, *Structure and Process in International Politics* (New York: Harper & Row, 1973), Chap. 12.

18. Graham Allison, *Essence of Decision* (Boston: Little, Brown and Co., 1971), p. 144.
19. See Morton Kaplan, *System and Process in International Politics* (New York: John Wiley & Sons, 1957).
20. Young, "The Actors in World Politics," p. 136.
21. See Hopkins and Mansbach, *Structure and Process,* p. 128.
22. *The Compact Edition of the Oxford English Dictionary* (New York: Oxford University Press, 1971), p. 516.

22

MICHAEL N. BARNETT AND
MARTHA FINNEMORE

THE POLITICS, POWER AND PATHOLOGIES OF INTERNATIONAL ORGANIZATIONS

Do international organizations really do what their creators intend them to do? In the past century the number of international organizations (IOs) has increased exponentially, and we have a variety of vigorous theories to explain why they have been created. Most of these theories explain IO creation as a response to problems of incomplete information, transaction costs, and other barriers to Pareto efficiency and welfare improvement for their members. Research flowing from these theories, however, has paid little attention to how IOs actually behave after they are created. Closer scrutiny would reveal that many IOs stray from the efficiency goals these theories impute and that many IOs exercise power autonomously in ways unintended and unanticipated by states at their creation. Understanding how this is so requires a reconsideration of IOs and what they do.

SOURCE: From Michael N. Barnett and Martha Finnemore, "The Politics, Power, and Pathologies of International Organizations," *International Organizations,* 53:4 (Autumn, 1999), pp. 699–732. © 1999 by the IO Foundation and Massachusetts Institute of Technology.

In this article we develop a constructivist approach rooted in sociological institutionalism to explain both the power of IOs and their propensity for dysfunctional, even pathological, behavior. Drawing on long-standing Weberian arguments about bureaucracy and sociological institutionalist approaches to organizational behavior, we argue that the rational-legal authority that IOs embody gives them power independent of the states that created them and channels that power in particular directions. Bureaucracies, by definition, make rules, but in so doing they also create social knowledge. They define shared international tasks (like "development"), create and define new categories of actors (like "refugee"), create new interests for actors (like "promoting human rights"), and transfer models of political organization around the world (like markets and democracy). However, the same normative valuation on impersonal, generalized rules that defines bureaucracies and makes them powerful in modern life can also make them unresponsive to their environments, obsessed with their own rules at the expense of primary missions, and ultimately lead to inefficient, self-defeating behavior. We are not the first to suggest that IOs are more than the reflection of state preferences and that they can be autonomous and powerful actors in global politics.[1] Nor are we the first to note that IOs, like all organizations, can be dysfunctional and inefficient.[2] However, our emphasis on the way that characteristics of bureaucracy as a generic cultural form shape IO behavior provides a different and very broad basis for thinking about how IOs influence world politics.[3]

Developing an alternative approach to thinking about IOs is only worthwhile if it produces significant insights and new opportunities for research on major debates in the field. Our approach allows us to weigh in with new perspectives on at least three such debates. First, it offers a different view of the power of IOs and whether or how they matter in world politics. This issue has been at the core of the neoliberal-institutionalists' debate with neorealists for years.[4] We show in this article how neoliberal-institutionalists actually disadvantage themselves in their argument with realists by looking at only one facet of IO power. Global organizations do more than just facilitate cooperation by helping states to overcome market failures, collective action dilemmas, and problems associated with interdependent social choice. They also create actors, specify responsibilities and authority among them, and define the work these actors should do, giving it meaning and normative value. Even when they lack material resources, IOs exercise power as they constitute and construct the social world.[5]

Second and related, our perspective provides a theoretical basis for treating IOs as autonomous actors in world politics and thus presents a challenge to the statist ontology prevailing in international relations theories. Despite all their attention to international institutions, one result of the theoretical orientation of neoliberal institutionalists and regimes theorists is that they treat IOs the way pluralists treat the state. IOs are mechanisms through which others (usually states) act; they are not purposive actors. The regimes literature is particularly clear on this point. Regimes are "principles, norms, rules, and decision-making procedures"; they are not actors.[6] Weber's insights about the normative power of the rational-legal authority that bureaucracies embody and its implications for the ways bureaucracies produce and control social knowledge provide a basis for challenging this view and treating IOs as agents, not just as structure.

Third, our perspective offers a different vantage point from which to assess the desirability of IOs. While realists and some policymakers have taken up this issue, surprisingly few other students of IOs have been critical of their performance or desirability.[7] Part of this optimism stems from central tenets of classical liberalism, which has long viewed IOs as a peaceful way to manage rapid technological change and globalization, far preferable to the obvious alternative—war.[8] Also contributing to this uncritical stance is the normative judgment about IOs that is built into the theoretical assumptions of most neoliberal and regimes scholars and the economic organization theories on which they draw. IOs exist, in this view, only because they are Pareto improving and solve problems for states. Consequently, if an IO exists, it must be because it is more useful than other alternatives since, by theoretical axiom, states will pull the plug on any IO that does not perform. We find this assumption unsatisfying. IOs often produce undesirable and even self-defeating outcomes repeatedly, without punishment much less dismantlement, and we, as theorists, want to understand why. International relations scholars are familiar with principal-agent problems and the ways in which bureaucratic politics can compromise organizational effectiveness, but these approaches have rarely been applied to IOs. Further, these approaches by no means exhaust sources of dysfunction. We examine one such source that flows from the same rational-legal characteristics that make IOs authoritative and powerful. Drawing from research in sociology and anthropology, we show how the very features that make bureaucracies powerful can also be their weakness.

The claims we make in this article flow from an analysis of the "social stuff" of which bureaucracy is made. We are asking a standard constructivist question about what makes the world hang together or, as Alexander Wendt puts it, "how are things in the world put together so that they have the properties they do."[9] In this sense, our explanation of IO behavior is constitutive and differs from most other international relations approaches. This approach does not make our explanation "mere description," since understanding the constitution of things does essential work in explaining how those things behave and what causes outcomes. Just as understanding how the double-helix DNA molecule is constituted materially makes possible causal arguments about genetics, disease, and other biological processes, so understanding how bureaucracies are constituted socially allows us to hypothesize about the behavior of IOs and the effects this social form might have in world politics. This type of constitutive explanation does not allow us to offer law-like statements such as "if X happens, then Y must follow." Rather, by providing a more complete understanding of what bureaucracy is, we can provide explanations of how certain kinds of bureaucratic behavior are possible, or even probable, and why.[10]

We begin by examining the assumptions underlying different branches of organization theory and exploring their implications for the study of IOs. We argue that assumptions drawn from economics that undergird neoliberal and neorealist treatments of IOs do not always reflect the empirical situation of most IOs commonly studied by political scientists. Further, they provide research hypotheses about only some aspects of IOs (like why they are created) and not others (like what they do). We then introduce sociological arguments that help remedy these problems.

In the second section we develop a constructivist approach from these sociological arguments to examine the power wielded by IOs and the sources of their influence. Liberal and realist theories only make predictions about, and consequently only look for, a very limited range of welfare-improving effects caused by IOs. Sociological theories, however, expect and explain a much broader range of impacts organizations can have and specifically highlight their role in constructing actors, interests, and social purpose. We provide illustrations from the UN system to show how IOs do, in fact, have such powerful effects in contemporary world politics. In the third section we explore the dysfunctional behavior of IOs, which we define as behavior that undermines the stated goals of the organization. International relations theorists are familiar with several types of theories that might explain such behavior. Some locate the source of dysfunction in material factors, others focus on cultural factors. Some theories locate the source of dysfunction outside the organization, others locate it inside. We construct a typology, mapping these theories according to the source of dysfunction they emphasize, and show that the same internally generated cultural forces that give IOs their power and autonomy can also be a source of dysfunctional behavior. We use the term *pathologies* to describe such instances when IO dysfunction can be traced to bureaucratic culture. We conclude by discussing how our perspective helps to widen the research agenda for IOs.

THEORETICAL APPROACHES TO ORGANIZATIONS

Within social science there are two broad strands of theorizing about organizations. One is economistic and rooted in assumptions of instrumental rationality and efficiency concerns; the other is sociological and focused on issues of legitimacy and power."[The different assumptions embedded within each type of theory focus attention on different kinds of questions about organizations and provide insights on different kinds of problems.

The economistic approach comes, not surprisingly, out of economics departments and business schools for whom the fundamental theoretical problem, laid out first by Ronald Coase and more recently by Oliver Williamson, is why we have business firms. Within standard microeconomic logic, it should be much more efficient to conduct all transactions through markets rather than "hierarchies" or organizations. Consequently, the fact that economic life is dominated by huge organizations (business firms) is an anomaly. The body of theory developed to explain the existence and power of firms focuses on organizations as efficient solutions to contracting problems, incomplete information, and other market imperfections.[12]

This body of organization theory informs neoliberal and neorealist debates over international institutions. Following Kenneth Waltz, neoliberals and neorealists understand world politics to be analogous to a market filled with utility-maximizing competitors.[13] Thus, like the economists, they see organizations as welfare-improving solutions to problems of incomplete information and high transaction costs.[14] Neoliberals and realists disagree about the degree to which constraints of anarchy, an interest in relative versus absolute gains, and fears of cheating will scuttle international institutional arrangements or hobble their effectiveness, but both agree, implicitly or explicitly, that IOs help states further their interests where they are allowed to work.[15] State power may be exercised in political battles inside IOs over where, on the Pareto frontier, political bargains fall, but the notion that IOs are instruments created to serve state interests is not much questioned by neorealist or neoliberal scholars.[16] After all, why else would states set up these organizations and continue to support them if they did not serve state interests?

Approaches from sociology provide one set of answers to this question. They provide reasons why, in fact, organizations that are not efficient or effective servants of member interests might exist. In so doing, they lead us to look for kinds of power and sources of autonomy in organizations that economists overlook. Different approaches within sociology treat organizations in different ways, but as a group they stand in sharp contrast to the economists' approaches in at least two important respects: they offer a different conception of the relationship between organizations and their environments, and they provide a basis for understanding organizational autonomy.

IOs and Their Environment

The environment assumed by economic approaches to organizations is socially very thin and devoid of social rules, cultural content, or even other actors beyond those constructing the organization. Competition, exchange, and consequent pressures for efficiency are the dominant environmental characteristics driving the formation and behavior of organizations. Sociologists, by contrast, study organizations in a wider world of nonmarket situations, and, consequently, they begin with no such assumptions. Organizations are treated as "social facts" to be investigated; whether they do what they claim or do it efficiently is an empirical question, not a theoretical assumption of these approaches. Organizations respond not only to other actors pursuing material interests in the environment but also to normative and cultural forces that shape how organizations see the world and conceptualize their own missions. Environments can "select" or favor organizations for reasons other than efficient or responsive behavior. For example, organizations may be created and supported for reasons of legitimacy and normative lit rather than efficient output; they may be created not for what they do but for what they are—for what they represent symbolically and the values they embody.[17]

Empirically, organizational environments can lake many forms. Some organizations exist in competitive environments that create strong pressures for efficient or responsive behavior, but many do not. Some organizations operate with clear criteria for "success" (like firms that have balance sheets), whereas others (like political science departments) operate with much vaguer missions, with few clear criteria for success or failure and no serious threat of elimination. Our point is simply that when we choose a theoretical framework, we should choose one whose assumptions approximate the empirical conditions of the IO we are analyzing, and that we should be aware of the biases created by those assumptions. Economistic approaches make certain assumptions about the environment in which IOs are embedded that drive researchers who use them to look for certain kinds of effects and not others. Specifying different or more varied environments for IOs would lead us to look for different and more varied effects in world politics.[18]

IO AUTONOMY

Following economistic logic, regime theory and the broad range of scholars working within it generally treat IOs as creations of states designed to further state interests.[19] Analysis of subsequent IO behavior focuses on processes of aggregating member state preferences through strategic interaction within the structure of the IO. IOs, then, are simply epiphenomena of state interaction; they are, to quote Waltz's definition of reductionism, "understood by knowing the attributes and the interactions of [their] parts."[20]

These theories thus treat IOs as empty shells or impersonal policy machinery to be manipulated by other actors. Political bargains shape the machinery at its creation, states may politick hard within the machinery in pursuit of their policy goals, and the machinery's norms and rules may constrain what states can do, but the machinery itself is passive. IOs are not purposive political actors in their own right and have no ontological independence. To the extent that IOs do, in fact, take on a life of their own, they breach the "limits of realism" as well as of neoliberalism by violating the ontological structures of these theories.[21]

The regimes concept spawned a huge literature on interstate cooperation that is remarkably consistent in its treatment of IOs as structure rather than agents. Much of the neoliberal institutionalist literature has been devoted to exploring the ways in which regimes (and IOs) can act as intervening variables, mediating between states' pursuit of self-interest and political outcomes by changing the structure of opportunities and constraints facing states through their control over information, in particular.[22] Although this line of scholarship accords IOs some causal, status (since they demonstrably change outcomes), it does not grant them autonomy and purpose independent of the states that comprise them. Another branch of liberalism has recently divorced itself from the statist ontology and focuses instead on the preferences of social groups as the causal engine of world politics, but, again, this view simply argues for attention to a different group of agents involved in the construction of IOs and competing for access to IO mechanisms. It does not offer a fundamentally different conception of IOs.[23]

The relevant question to ask about this conceptualization is whether it is a reasonable approximation of the empirical condition of most IOs. Our reading of detailed empirical case studies of IO activity suggests not. Yes, IOs are constrained by states but the notion that they are passive mechanisms with no independent agendas of their own is not borne out by any detailed empirical study of an IO that we have found. Field studies of the European Union provide evidence of independent roles for "eurocrats."[24] Studies of the World Bank consistently identify an independent culture and agendas for action.[25] Studies of recent UN peacekeeping and reconstruction efforts similarly document a UN agenda that frequently leads to conflict with member states.[26] Accounts of the UN High Commission on Refugees (UNHCR) routinely note how its autonomy and authority has grown over the years. Not only are IOs independent actors with their own agendas, but they may embody multiple agendas and contain multiple sources of agency—a problem we take up later.

Principal-agent analysis, which has been increasingly employed by students of international relations to examine organizational dynamics, could potentially provide a sophisticated approach to understanding IO autonomy.[27] Building on theories of rational choice and of representation, these analysts understand IOs as "agents" of states ("principals"). The analysis is concerned with whether agents are responsible delegates of their principals, whether agents smuggle in and pursue their own preferences, and how principals can construct various mechanisms to keep their agents honest.[28] This framework provides a means of treating IOs as actors in their own right with independent interests and capabilities. Autonomous action by IOs is to be expected in this perspective. It would also explain a number of the nonresponsive and pathological behaviors that concern us because we know that monitoring and shirking problems are pervasive in these principal-agent relationships and that these relationships can often get stuck at suboptimal equilibria.

The problem with applying principal-agent analysis to the study of IOs is that it requires a priori theoretical specification of what IOs want. Principal-agent dynamics are fueled by the disjuncture between what agents want and what principals want. To produce any insights, those two sets of interests cannot be identical. In economics this type of analysis is usually applied to preexisting agents and principals (clients hiring lawyers, patients visiting doctors) whose ongoing independent existence makes specification of independent interests relatively straightforward. The lawyer or the doctor would probably be in business even if you and I did not take our problems to them. IOs, on the other hand, are often created by the principals (states) and given mission statements written by the principals. How, then, can we impute independent preferences a priori?

Scholars of American politics have made some progress in producing substantive theoretical propositions about what U.S. bureaucratic agencies want. Beginning with the pioneering work of William Niskanen, scholars theorized that bureaucracies had interests defined by the absolute or relative size of their budget and the expansion or protection of their turf. At first these interests were imputed, and later they became more closely investigated, substantiated, and in some cases modified or rejected altogether.[29]

Realism and liberalism, however, provide no basis for asserting independent utility functions for IOs. Ontologically, these are theories about states. They provide no basis for imputing interests to IOs beyond the goals states (that is, principals) give them. Simply adopting the rather battered Niskanen hypothesis seems less than promising given the glaring anomalies—for example, the opposition of many NATO and OSCE (Organization for Security and Cooperation in Europe) bureaucrats to those organizations' recent expansion and institutionalization. There are good reasons to assume that organizations care about their resource base and turf, but there is no reason to presume that such matters exhaust or even dominate their interests. Indeed, ethnographic studies of IOs describe a world in which organizational goals are strongly shaped by norms of the profession that dominate the bureaucracy and in which interests themselves are varied, often in flux, debated, and worked out through interactions between the staff of the bureaucracy and the world in which they are embedded.[30]

Various strands of sociological theory can help us investigate the goals and behavior of IOs by offering a very different analytical orientation than the one used by economists. Beginning with Weber, sociologists have explored the notion that bureaucracy is a peculiarly modern cultural form that embodies certain values and can have its own distinct agenda and behavioral dispositions. Rather than treating organizations as mere arenas or mechanisms through which other actors pursue interests, many sociological approaches explore the social content of the organization—its culture, its legitimacy concerns, dominant norms that govern behavior and shape interests, and the relationship of these to a larger normative and cultural environment. Rather than assuming behavior that corresponds to efficiency criteria alone, these approaches recognize that organizations also are bound up with power and social control in ways that can eclipse efficiency concerns.

THE POWER OF IOS

IOs can become autonomous sites of authority, independent from the state "principals" who may have created them, because of power flowing from at, least two sources: (1) the legitimacy of the rational-legal authority they embody, and (2) control over technical expertise and information. The first of these is almost entirely neglected by the political science literature, and the second, we argue, has been conceived of very narrowly, leading scholars to overlook some of the most basic and consequential forms of IO influence. Taken together, these two features provide a theoretical basis for treating IOs as autonomous actors in contemporary world politics by identifying sources of support for them, independent of states, in the larger social environment. Since rational-legal authority and control over expertise are part of what defines and constitutes any bureaucracy (a bureaucracy would not be a bureaucracy without them), the autonomy that flows from them is best understood as a constitutive effect, an effect of the way bureaucracy is constituted, which, in turn, makes possible (and in that sense causes) other processes and effects in global politics. . . .

If IOs have autonomy and authority in the world, what do they do with it? A growing body of research in sociology and anthropology has examined ways in which IOs exercise power by virtue of their culturally constructed status as sites of authority; we distill from this research three broad types of IO power. We examine how IOs (1) classify the world, creating categories of actors and action; (2) fix meanings in the social world; and (3) articulate and diffuse new norms, principles, and actors around the globe. All of these sources of power flow from the ability of IOs to structure knowledge.[31] . . .

THE FIXING OF MEANINGS

IOs exercise power by virtue of their ability to fix meanings, which is related to classification.[32] Naming or labeling the social context establishes the parameters, the very boundaries, of acceptable action. Because actors are oriented toward objects and objectives on the basis of the meaning that they have for them, being able to invest situations with a particular meaning constitutes an important source of power.[33] IOs do not act alone in this regard, but their organizational resources contribute mightily to this end. . . .

DIFFUSION OF NORMS

Having established rules and norms, IOs are eager to spread the benefits of their expertise and often act as conveyor belts for the transmission of norms and models of "good" political behavior.[34] There is nothing accidental or unintended about this role. Officials in IOs often insist that part of their mission is to spread, inculcate, and enforce global values and norms. They are the "missionaries" of our time. Armed with a notion of progress, an idea of how to create the better life, and some understanding of the conversion process, many IO elites have as their stated purpose a desire to shape state practices by establishing, articulating, and transmitting norms that define what constitutes acceptable and legitimate state behavior. To be sure, their success depends on more than their persuasive capacities, for their rhetoric must be supported by power, sometimes (but not always) state power. But to overlook how state power and organizational missionaries work in tandem and the ways in which IO officials channel and shape states' exercise of power is to disregard a fundamental feature of value diffusion.[35] . . .

THE PATHOLOGIES OF IOS

. . . IOs, too, are prone to dysfunctional behaviors, but international relations scholars have rarely investigated this, in part, we suspect, because the theoretical apparatus they use provides few grounds for expecting undesirable IO behavior.[36] The state-centric utility-maximizing frameworks most international relations scholars have borrowed from economics simply assume that IOs are reasonably responsive to state interests (or, at least, more responsive than alternatives), otherwise slates would withdraw from them. This assumption, however, is a necessary theoretical axiom of these frameworks; it is rarely treated as a hypothesis subject to empirical investigation.[37] With little theoretical reason to expect suboptimal or self-defeating behavior in IOs, these scholars do not look for it and have had little to say about it. Policymakers, however, have been quicker to perceive and address these problems and are putting them on the political agenda. It is time for scholars, too, to begin to explore these issues more fully.

In this section we present several bodies of theorizing that might explain dysfunctional IO behavior, which we define as behavior that undermines the IO's stated objectives. Thus our vantage point for judging dysfunction (and later pathology) is the publicly proclaimed mission of the organization. There may be occasions when overall organizational dysfunction is, in fact, functional for certain members or others involved in the IO's work, but given our analysis of the way claims of efficiency and effectiveness act to legitimate rational-legal authority in our culture, whether organizations actually do what they claim and accomplish their missions is a particularly important issue to examine. Several bodies of theory provide some basis for understanding dysfunctional behavior by IOs, each of which emphasizes a different locus of causality for such behavior. Analyzing these causes, we construct a typology of these explanations that locates them in relation to one another. Then, drawing on the work of James March and Johan Olsen, Paul DiMaggio and Walter Powell, and other sociological institutionalists, we elaborate how the same sources of bureaucratic power, sketched earlier, can cause dysfunctional behavior. We term this particular type of dysfunction *pathology*.[38] We identify five features of bureaucracy that might produce pathology, and using examples from the UN system we illustrate the way these might work in IOs.

Extant theories about dysfunction can be categorized in two dimensions: (1) whether they locate the cause of IO dysfunction inside or outside the

FIGURE 1 **Theories of International Organization Dysfunction**

	Internal	External
Material	Bureaucratic politics	Realism/ neoliberal institutionalism
Cultural	Bureaucratic culture	World polity model

organization, and (2) whether they trace the causes to material or cultural forces. Mapping theories on these dimensions creates the typology shown in Figure 1.

Within each cell we have identified a representative body of theory familiar to most international relations scholars. Explanations of IO dysfunction that emphasize the pursuit of material interests within an organization typically examine how competition among subunits over material resources leads the organization to make decisions and engage in behaviors that are inefficient or undesirable as judged against some ideal policy that would better allow the IO to achieve its stated goals. Bureaucratic politics is the best-known theory here, and though current scholars of international politics have not widely adopted this perspective to explain IO behavior, it is relatively well developed in the older IO literature.[39] Graham Allison's central argument is that the "name of the game is politics: bargaining along regularized circuits among players positioned hierarchically within the government. Government behavior can thus be understood as . . . results of these bargaining games."[40] In this view, decisions are not made after a rational decision process but rather through a competitive bargaining process over turf, budgets, and staff that may benefit parts of the organization at the expense of overall goals.

Another body of literature traces IO dysfunctional behavior to the material forces located outside the organization. Realist and neoliberal theories might posit that state preferences and constraints are responsible for understanding IO dysfunctional behavior. In this view IOs are not to blame for bad outcomes, states are. IOs do not have the luxury of choosing the optimal policy but rather are frequently forced to chose between the bad and the awful because more desirable policies are denied to them by states who do not agree among themselves and/or do not wish to see the IO fulfill its mandate in some particular instance. As Robert Keohane observed, IOs often engage in policies not because they are strong and have autonomy but because they are weak and have none.[41] The important point of these theories is that they trace IO dysfunctional behavior back to the environmental conditions established by, or the explicit preferences of, states.

Cultural theories also have internal and external variants. We should note, that many advocates of cultural theories would reject the claim that an organization can be understood apart from its environment or that culture is separable from the material world. Instead they would stress how the organization is permeated by that environment, defined in both material and cultural terms, in which it is embedded. Many are also quite sensitive to the ways in which resource constraints and the material power of important actors will shape organizational culture. That said, these arguments clearly differ from the previous two types in their emphasis on ideational and cultural factors and clearly differ among themselves in the motors of behavior emphasized. For analytical clarity we divide cultural theories according to whether they see the primary causes of the IO's dysfunctional behavior as deriving from the culture of the organization (internal) or of the environment (external).

The world polity model exemplifies theories that look to external culture to understand an IO's dysfunctional behavior. There are two reasons to expect dysfunctional behavior here. First, because IO practices reflect a search for symbolic legitimacy rather than efficiency, IO behavior might be only remotely connected in the efficient implementation of its goals and more closely coupled to legitimacy criteria that come from the cultural environment.[42] For instance, many arms-export control regimes now have a multilateral character not because of any evidence that this architecture is the most efficient way to monitor mid prevent arms exports but rather because multilateralism has attained a degree of legitimacy that is not empirically connected to any efficiency criteria.[43] Second, the world polity is full of contradictions; for instance, a liberal world polity has several defining principles, including market economics and human equality, that might conflict at any one moment. Thus, environments are often ambiguous about missions and contain varied, often conflicting, functional, normative, and legitimacy imperatives.[44] Because they are embedded in that cultural environment, IOs can mirror and reproduce those contradictions, which, in turn, can lead to contradictory and ultimately dysfunctional behavior.

Finally, organizations frequently develop distinctive internal cultures that can promote dysfunctional behavior, behavior that we call "pathological." The basic logic of this argument flows directly from our previous observations about the nature of bureaucracy as a social form. Bureaucracies are established as rationalized means to accomplish collective goals and to spread particular values. To do this, bureaucracies create social knowledge and develop expertise as they act upon the world (and thus exercise power). But the way bureaucracies are constituted to accomplish these ends can, ironically, create a cultural disposition toward undesirable and ultimately self-defeating behavior.[45] Two features of the modern bureaucratic form are particularly important in this regard. The first is the simple fact that bureaucracies are organized around rules, routines, and standard operating procedures designed to trigger a standard and predictable response to environmental stimuli. These rules can be formal or informal, but in either case they tell actors which action is appropriate in response to a specific stimuli, request, or demand. This kind of routinization is, after all, precisely what bureaucracies are supposed to exhibit—it is what makes them effective and competent in performing complex social tasks. However, the presence of such rules also compromises the extent to which means-ends rationality drives organizational behavior. Rules and routines may come to obscure overall missions and larger social goals. They may create "ritualized behavior" in bureaucrats and construct a very parochial normative environment within the organization whose connection to the larger social environment is tenuous at best.[46]

Second, bureaucracies specialize and compartmentalize. They create a division of labor on the logic that because individuals have only so much time, knowledge, and expertise, specialization will allow the organization to emulate a rational decision-making process.[47] Again, this is one of the virtues of bureaucracy in that it provides a way of overcoming the limitations of individual rationality and knowledge by embedding those individuals in a structure that lakes advantage of their competencies without having to rely on their weaknesses. However, it, too, has some negative consequences. Just as rules can eclipse goals, concentrated expertise and specialization can (and perhaps must) limit bureaucrats' field of vision and create, subcultures within bureaucracy that are distinct from those of the larger environment. Professional training plays a particularly strong role here since this is one widespread way we disseminate specialized knowledge and credential "experts." Such training often gives experts, indeed is designed to give them, a distinctive worldview and normative commitments, which, when concentrated in a subunit of an organization, can have pronounced effects on behavior.[48]

Once in place, an organization's culture, understood as the rules, rituals, and beliefs that are embedded in the organization (and its subunits), has important consequences for the way individuals who inhabit that organization make sense of the world. It provides interpretive frames that individuals use to generate meaning.[49] This is more than just bounded rationality; in this view, actors' rationality itself, the very means and ends that they value, are shaped by the organizational culture.[50] Divisions and subunits within the organization may develop their own cognitive frameworks that are consistent with but still distinct from the larger organization, further complicating this process.

All organizations have their own culture (or cultures) that shape their behavior. The effects of bureaucratic culture, however, need not be dysfunctional. Indeed, specific organizational cultures may be valued and actively promoted as a source of "good" behavior, as students of business culture know very well. Organizational culture is tied to "good" and "bad" behavior, alike, and the effects of organizational culture on behavior are an empirical question to be researched.

To further such research, we draw from studies in sociology and anthropology to explore five mechanisms by which bureaucratic culture can breed pathologies in IOs: the irrationality of rationalization, universalism, normalization of deviance, organizational insulation, and cultural contestation. The first three of these mechanisms all flow from defining features of bureaucracy itself. Consequently, we expect them to be present in any bureaucracy to a limited degree. Their severity may be increased, however, by specific empirical conditions of the organization. Vague mission, weak feedback from the environment, and strong professionalism all have the potential to exacerbate these mechanisms and to create two others, organizational insulation and cultural contestation, through processes we describe later. Our claim, therefore, is that the very nature of bureaucracy—the "social stuff" of which it is made—creates behavioral predispositions that make bureaucracy prone to these kinds of behaviors.[51] But the connection between these mechanisms and pathological behavior is probabilistic, not deterministic, and is consistent with our constitutive analysis. Whether, in fact, mission-defeating behavior occurs depends on empirical conditions. We identify three such conditions that are particularly important (mission, feedback, and professionals) and discuss how they intensify these inherent predispositions and activate or create additional ones.

IRRATIONALITY OF RATIONALIZATION

Weber recognized that the "rationalization" processes at which bureaucracies excelled could be taken to extremes and ultimately become irrational if the rules and procedures that enabled bureaucracies to do their jobs became ends in themselves. Rather than designing the most appropriate and efficient rules and procedures to accomplish their missions, bureaucracies often tailor their missions to fit the existing, well-known, and comfortable rulebook.[52] Thus, means (rules and procedures) may become so embedded and powerful that they determine ends and the way the organization defines its goals. One observer of the World Bank noted how, at an operational level, the bank did not decide on development goals and collect data necessary to pursue them. Rather, it continued to use existing data-collection procedures and formulated goals and development plans from those data alone.[53] UN-mandated elections may be another instance where means become ends in themselves. The "end" pursued in the many troubled states where the UN has been involved in reconstruction is presumably some kind of peaceful, stable, just government. Toward that end, the UN has developed a repertoire of instruments and responses that are largely intended to promote something akin to a democratic government. Among those various repertoires, elections have become privileged as a measure of "success" and a signal of an operation's successful conclusion. Consequently, UN (and other IO) officials have conducted elections even when evidence suggests that such elections are either premature or perhaps even counterproductive (frequently acknowledged as much by state and UN officials).[54] In places like Bosnia elections have ratified precisely the outcome the UN and outside powers had intervened to prevent—ethnic cleansing—and in places like Africa elections are criticized as exacerbating the very ethnic tensions they were ostensibly designed to quell. . . .

BUREAUCRATIC UNIVERSALISM

A second source of pathology in IOs derives from the fact that bureaucracies "orchestrate numerous local contexts at once."[55] Bureaucracies necessarily flatten diversity because they are supposed to generate universal rules and categories that are, by design, inattentive to contextual and particularistic concerns. Part of the justification for this, of course, is the bureaucratic view that technical knowledge is transferable across circumstances. Sometimes this is a good assumption, but not always; when particular circumstances are not appropriate to the generalized knowledge being applied, the results can be disastrous.[56]

Many critics of the IMF's handling of the Asian financial crises have argued that the IMF inappropriately applied a standardized formula of budget cuts plus high interest rates to combat rapid currency depreciation without appreciating the unique and local causes of this depreciation. These governments were not profligate spenders, and austerity policies did little to reassure investors, yet the IMF prescribed roughly the same remedy that it had in Latin America. The result, by the IMF's later admission, was to make matters worse.[57]

Similarly, many of those who worked in peacekeeping operations in Cambodia were transferred to peacekeeping operations in Bosnia or Somalia on the assumption that the knowledge gained in one location would be applicable to others. Although some technical skills can be transferred across contexts, not all knowledge and organizational lessons derived from one context are appropriate elsewhere. The UN has a longstanding commitment to neutrality, which operationally translates into the view that the UN should avoid the use of force and the appearance of partiality. This knowledge was employed with some success by UN envoy Yasushi Akashi in Cambodia. After his stint in Cambodia, he became the UN Special Representative in Yugoslavia. As many critics of Akashi have argued, however, his commitment to these rules, combined with his failure to recognize that Bosnia was substantially different from Cambodia, led him to fail to use force to defend the safe havens when it was appropriate and likely to be effective.[58]

NORMALIZATION OF DEVIANCE

We derive a third type of pathology from Diane Vaughan's study of the space shuttle *Challenger* disaster in which she chronicles the way exceptions to rules (deviance) over time become routinized and normal parts of procedures.[59] Bureaucracies establish rules to provide a predictable response to environmental stimuli in ways that safeguard against decisions that might lead to accidents and faulty decisions. At times, however, bureaucracies make small, calculated deviations from established rules because of new environmental or institutional developments, explicitly calculating that bending the rules in this instance does not create excessive risk of policy failure. Over time, these exceptions can become the rule—they become normal, not exceptions at all: they can become institutionalized to the point where deviance is "normalized." The result of this process is that what at time t_1 might be weighed seriously and debated as a potentially unacceptable risk or dangerous procedure comes to be treated as normal at time t_n. Indeed, because of staff turnover, those making decisions at a later point in time might be unaware that the now-routine behavior was ever viewed as risky or dangerous. . . .

INSULATION

Organizations vary greatly in the degree to which they receive and process feedback from their environment about performance. Those insulated from such feedback often develop internal cultures and worldviews that do not promote the goals and expectations of those outside the organization who created it and whom it serves. These distinctive worldviews can create the conditions for pathological behavior when parochial classification and categorization schemes come to define reality—how bureaucrats understand the world—such that they routinely ignore information that is essential to the accomplishment of their goals.[60]

Two causes of insulation seem particularly applicable to IOs. The first is professionalism. Professional training does more than impart technical knowledge. It actively seeks to shape the normative orientation and worldviews of those who are trained. Doctors are trained to value life above all else, soldiers are trained to sacrifice life for certain strategic objectives, and economists are trained to value efficiency. Bureaucracies, by their nature, concentrate professionals inside organizations, and concentrations of people with the same expertise or professional training can create an organizational worldview distinct from the larger environment. Second, organizations for whom "successful performance" is difficult to measure—that is, they are valued for what they represent rather than for what they do and do not "compete" with other organizations on the basis of output—are protected from selection and performance pressures that economistic models simply assume will operate. The absence of a competitive environment that selects out inefficient practices coupled with already existing tendencies toward institutionalization of rules and procedures insulates the organization from feedback and increases the likelihood of pathologies. . . .

Insulation contributes to and is caused by another well-known feature of organizations—the absence of effective feedback loops that allow the organization to evaluate its efforts and use new information to correct established routines. This is surely a "rational" procedure in any social task but is one that many organizations, including IOs, fail to perform.[61] Many scholars and journalists, and even the current head of the World Bank, have noticed that the bank has accumulated a rather distinctive record of "failures" but continues to operate with the same criteria and has shown a marked lack of interest in evaluating the effectiveness of its own projects.[62] The same is true of other IOs. Jarat Chopra observes that the lessons-learned conferences that were established after Somalia were structurally arranged so that no information could' come out that would blemish the UN's record. Such attempts at face saving, Chopra cautions, make it more likely that these maladies will go uncorrected.[63] Sometimes new evaluative criteria are hoisted in order to demonstrate that the failures were not really failures but successes.

CULTURAL CONTESTATION

Organizational coherence is an accomplishment rather than a given. Organizational control within a putative hierarchy is always incomplete, creating pockets of autonomy and political battles within the bureaucracy.[64] This is partly a product of the fact that bureaucracies are organized around the principle of division-of-labor, and different divisions tend to be staffed by individuals who are "experts" in their assigned tasks. These different divisions may battle over budgets or material resources and so follow the bureaucratic politics model, but they may also clash because of distinct internal cultures that grow up inside different parts of the organization. Different segments of the organization may develop different ways of making sense of the world, experience different local environments, and receive different stimuli from outside; they may also be populated by different mixes of professions or shaped by different historical experiences. All of these would contribute to the development of different local cultures within the organization and different ways of perceiving the environment and the organization's overall mission. Organizations may try to minimize complications from these divisions by arranging these demands hierarchically, but to the extent that hierarchy resolves conflict by squelching input from some subunits in favor of others, the organization loses the benefits of a division of labor that it was supposed to provide. More commonly, though, attempts to reconcile competing worldviews hierarchically are simply incomplete. Most organizations develop overlapping and contradictory sets of preferences among subgroups.[65] Consequently, different constituencies representing different normative views will suggest different tasks and goals for the organization, resulting in a clash of competing perspectives that generates pathological tendencies. . . .

NOTES

We are grateful to John Boli, Raymond Duvall, Ernst Haas, Peter Haas, Robert Keohane, Keith Krause, Jeffrey Legro, John Malley, Craig Murphy, M. J. Peterson, Mark Pollack, Andrew Moravcsik, Thomas Risse, Duncan Snidal, Steve Weber, Thomas Weiss, and two anonymous referees for their comments. We are especially grateful for the careful attention of the editors of *International Organization*. Earlier versions of this article were presented at the 1997 APSA meeting, the 1997 ISA meeting, and at various fora. We also acknowledge financial assistance, from the Smith Richardson Foundation and the United States Institute of Peace.

1. For Gramscian approaches, see Cox 1980, 1992, and 1996; and Murphy 1995. For Society of States approaches, see Hurrell and Woods 1995. For the epistemic communities literature, see Haas 1992. For IO decision-making literature, see

Cox et al. 1974; Cox and Jacobson 1977; Cox 1996; and Ness and Brechin 1988. For a rational choice perspective, see Snidal 1996.

2. Haas 1990.
3. Because the neorealist and neoliberal arguments we engage have focused on inter-governmental organizations rather than nongovernmental ones, and because Weberian arguments from which we draw deal primarily with public bureaucracy, we too focus on intergovernmental organizations in this article and use the term *international organizations* in that way.
4. Baldwin 1993.
5. See Finnemore 1993 and 1996b; and McNeely 1995.
6. Krasner 1983b.
7. See Mearsheimer 1994; and Helms 1996.
8. See Commission on Global Governance 1995; Jacobson 1979, 1; and Doyle 1997.
9. See Ruggie 1998; and Wendt 1998.
10. Wendt 1998.
11. See Powell and DiMaggio 1991, chap. 1; and Grandori 1993.
12. See Williamson 1975 and 1985; and Coase 1937.
13. Waltz 1979.
14. See Vaubel 1991, 27; and Dillon, Ilgen, and Willett 1991.
15. Baldwin 1993.
16. Krasner 1991.
17. See DiMaggio and Powell 1983; Scott 1992; Meyer and Scott 1992, 1–5; Powell and DiMaggio 1991; Weber 1994; and Finnemore 1996a.
18. Researchers applying these economistic approaches have become increasingly aware of the mismatch between the assumptions of their models and the empirics of IOs. See Snidal 1996.
19. Note that empirically this is not the case; most IOs now are created by other IOs. See Shanks, Jacobson, and Kaplan 1996.
20. Waltz 1979, 18.
21. Krasner 1983a, 355–68; but see Finnemore 1996b; and Rittberger 1993.
22. See Keohane 1984; and Baldwin 1993.
23. Moravcsik 1997.
24. See Pollack 1997; Ross 1995; and Zabusky 1995; but see Moravcsik 1999.
25. See Ascher 1983; Ayres 1983; Ferguson 1990; Escobar 1995; Wade 1996; Nelson 1995; and Finnemore 1996a.
26. Joint Evaluation of Emergency Assistance to Rwanda 1996.
27. See Pollack 1997; Lake 1996; Vaubel 1991; and Dillon, Ilgen, and Willett 1991.
28. See Pratt and Zeckhauser 1985; and Kiewit and McCubbins 1991.
29. See Niskanen 1971; Miller and Moe 1983; Weingast and Moran 1983; Moe 1984; and Sigelman 1986.
30. See Ascher l983; Zabusky 1995; Barnett 1997b; and Wade 1996.
31. See Foucault 1977, 27; and Clegg 1994b, 156–59. International relations theory typically disregards the negative side of the knowledge and power equation. For an example, see Haas 1992.
32. See Williams 1996; Clegg 1994b; Bourdieu 1994; Carr [1939] 1964; and Keeley 1990.
33. Blumer 1969.
34. See Katzenstein 1996; Finnemore 1996b; and Legro 1997.
35. See Alger 1963, 425; and Claude 1966, 373.

36. Two exceptions are Galaroti 1991; and Snidal 1996.
37. Snidal 1996.
38. Karl Deutsch used the concept of pathology in a way similar to our usage. We thank Hayward Alker for this point. Deutsch 1963, 170.
39. See Allison 1971; Haas 1990; Cox et al. 1974; and Cox and Jacobson 1977.
40. See Allison 1971, 144; and Bendor and Hammond 1992.
41. Personal communication to the authors.
42. See Meyer and Rowan 1977; Meyer and Zucker 1989; Weber 1994; and Finnemore 1996a.
43. Lipson 1999.
44. McNeely 1995.
45. See Vaughan 1996; and Lipartilo 1995.
46. See March and Olsen 1989, 21–27; and Meyer and Rowan 1977.
47. See March and Olsen 1989, 26–27; and March 1997.
48. See DiMaggio and Powell 1983; and Schien 1996.
49. See Starr 1992, 160; Douglas 1986; and Berger and Luckman 1966, chap. 1.
50. See Campbell 1998, 378; Alvesson 1996; Burrell and Morgan 1979; Dobbin 1994; and Immergnt 1998, 14–19.
51. Wendt 1998.
52. Beetham 1985, 76.
53. See Ferguson 1990; and Nelson 1995.
54. Paris 1997.
55. Heyman 1995, 262.
56. Haas 1990, chap. 3.
57. See Feldstein 1998; Radelet and Sachs 1999; and Kapur 1998.
58. Rieff 1996.
59. Vaughan 1996.
60. See Berger and Luckman 1967, chap. 1; Douglas 1986; Burner 1990; March and Olsen 1989; and Starr 1992.
61. March and Olsen 1989, chap. 5; Haas 1990.
62. See Wade 1996, 14–17; Nelson 1995, chaps. 6, 7; and Richard Stevenson, "The Chief Banker for the Nations at the Bottom of the Heap," *New York Times*, 14 September 1997, sec. 3, pp. 12–14.
63. Chopra 1996.
64. See Clegg 1994a, 30; Vaughan 1996, 64; and Martin 1992.
65. Haas 1990, 188.

REFERENCES

Alger, Chadwick. 1963. United Nations Participation as a Learning Process. *Public Opinion Quarterly* 27 (3):411–26.

Allison, Graham. 1971. *Essence of Decision.* Boston: Little, Brown.

Alvesson, Mats. 1996. *Cultural Perspectives on Organizations.* New York: Cambridge University Press.

Ascher, William. 1983. New Development Approaches and the Adaptability of International Agencies: The Case of the World Bank. *International Organization* 37 (3):415–39.

Ayres, Robert L. 1983. *Banking on the Poor: The World Bank and World Poverty.* Cambridge. Mass.: MIT Press.

Baldwin, David, ed. 1993. *Neorealisim and Neoliberalism*. New York: Columbia University Press.

Barnett, Michael. 1997a. The Politics of Indifference at the United Nations and Genocide in Rwanda and Bosnia. In *This Time We Knew: Western Responses to Genocide in Bosnia,* edited by Thomas Cushman and Stjepan Mestrovic, 128–62. New York: New York University Press.

_____. 1997b. The UN Security Council, Indifference, and Genocide in Rwanda. *Cultural Anthropology* 12 (4):551–78.

Beetham, David. 1985. *Max Weber and the Theory of Modern Politics*. New York: Polity.

_____. 1996. *Bureaucracy.* 2d ed. Minneapolis: University of Minnesota Press.

Bendor, Jonathan, and Thomas Hammond. 1992. Rethinking Allison's Models. *American Political Science Review* 82 (2):301–22.

Berger, Peter, and Thomas Luckmann. 1966. *The Social Construction of Reality.* New York: Doubleday.

Blumer, Herbert. 1969. *Symbolic Interactionism: Perspective and Method.* Englewood Cliffs. N.J.: Prentice-Hall.

Bruner, Jerome. 1990. *Acts of Meaning.* Cambridge, Mass.: Harvard University Press.

Burley, Anne-Marie, and Walter Mattli. 1993. Europe Before the Court: A Political Theory of Integration. *International Organization* 47 (1):41–76.

Burrell, Gibson, and Gareth Morgan. 1979. *Sociological Paradigms and Organizational Analysis.* London: Heinemann.

Campbell, John. 1988. Institutional Analysis and the Role of Ideas Political Economy. *Theory and Society* 27:377–409.

Carr, Edward H. [1939] 1964. The Twenty Year's Crisis. New York: Harper Torchbooks.

Chopra, Jarat. 1996. Fighting for Truth at the UN. *Crosslines Global Report,* 26 November, 7–9.

Chopra, Jara, Age Eknes, and Toralv Nordbo. 1995. *Fighting for Hope in Somalia.* Oslo: NUPI.

Claude, Inis L., Jr. 1966. Collective Legitimization as a Political Function of the United Nations. *International Organization* 20 (3):337—67.

Clegg, Stewart. 1994a. Power and Institutions in the Theory of Organizations. In *Toward a New Theory of Organizations,* edited by John Hassard and Martin Parker, 24–49. New York: Routledge.

_____. 1994b. Weber and Foucault: Social Theory for the Study of Organizations. *Organization* 1 (1): 149–78.

Coase, Ronald. 1937. The Nature of the Firm. *Economica* 4 (November):386–405.

Commission on Global Governance. 1995. *Our Global Neighborhood.* New York: Oxford University Press.

Cox, Robert. 1980. The Crisis of World Order and the Problem of International Organization in the 1980s. *International Journal* 35 (2):370–95.

_____. 1992. Multilateralism and World Order. *Review of International Studies* 18 (2): 161–80.

_____. 1996. The Executive Head: An Essay on Leadership in International Organization. In *Approaches to World Order,* edited by Robert Cox, 317–48. New York: Cambridge University Press.

Cox, Robert, and Harold Jacobson. 1977. Decision Making. *International Social Science Journal* 29 (1):115–33.

Cox, Robert, Harold Jacobson, Gerard Curzon, Victoria Curzon, Joseph Nye, Lawrence Scheinman, James Sewell, and Susan Strange. 1974. *The Anatomy of Influence: Decision Making in International Organization.* New Haven, Conn.: Yale University Press.

Deutsch, Karl. 1963. *The Nerves of Government: Models of Political Communication and Control.* Glencoe, Ill.: Free Press.

Dillon, Patricia, Thomas Ilgen, and Thomas Willett. 1991. Approaches to the Study of International Organizations: Major Paradigms in Economics and Political Science. In *The Political Economy of International Organizations: A Public Choice Approach,* edited by Ronald Vaubel and Thomas Willett, 79–99. Boulder, Colo.: Westview Press.

DiMaggio, Paul J., and Walter W. Powell. 1983. The Iron Cage Revisited: Institutional Isomorphism and Collective Rationality in Organizational Fields. *American Sociological Review* 48:147–60.

Dobbin, Frank. 1994. Cultural Models of Organization: The Social Construction of Rational Organizing Principles. In *The Sociology of Culture,* edited by Diana Crane, 117–42. Boston: Basil Blackwell.

Douglas, Mary. 1986. *How Institutions Think.* Syracuse, N.Y.: Syracuse University Press.

Doyle, Michael. 1997. *Ways of War and Peace.* New York: Norton.

Escobar, Arturo. 1995. *Encountering Development: The Making and Unmaking of the Third World.* Princeton, N.J.: Princeton University Press.

Feldstein, Martin. 1998. Refocusing the IMF. *Foreign Affairs* 77 (2):20–33.

Ferguson, James. 1990. *The Anti-Politics Machine: "Development," Depoliticization, and Bureaucratic Domination in Lesotho.* New York: Cambridge University Press.

Finnemore, Martha. 1993. International Organizations as Teachers of Norms: The United Nations Educational, Scientific, and Cultural Organization and Science Policy. *International Organization* 47:565–97.

_____.1996a. Norms, Culture, and World Politics: Insights from Sociology's Institutionalism. *International Organization* 50 (2):325–47.

_____.1996b. *National Interests in International Society.* Ithaca, N.Y.: Cornell University Press.

Fisher, William. 1997. Doing Good? The Politics and Antipolitics of NGO Practices. *Annual Review of Anthropology* 26:439–64.

Foucault, Michel. 1977. *Discipline and Punish.* New York: Vintage Press.

Gallaroti, Guilio. 1991. The Limits of International Organization. *International Organization* 45 (2):183–220.

Grandori, Anna. 1993. Notes on the Use of Power and Efficiency Constructs in the Economics and Sociology of Organizations. In *Interdisciplinary Perspectives on Organizational Studies,* edited by S. Lindenberg and H. Schreuder, 61–78. New York: Pergamon.

Haas, Ernst. 1990. *When Knowledge Is Power.* Berkeley: University of California Press.

Haas, Ernst, and Peter Haas. 1995. Learning to Learn: Improving International Governance. *Global Goverance* 1 (3):255–85.

Haas, Peter, ed. 1992. Epistemic Communities. *International Organization* 46 (1). Special issue.

Helms, Jesse. 1996. Saving the UN. *Foreign Affairs* 75 (5):2–7.

Heyman, Josiah McC. 1995. Putting Power in the Anthropology of Bureaucracy. *Current Anthropology* 36 (2):261–77.

Hurrell, Andrew, and Ngaire Woods. 1995. Globalisation and Inequality. *Millennium* 24 (3):447–70.

Immergut, Ellen. 1998. The Theoretical Core of the New Institutionalism. *Politics and Society* 26 (1):5–34.

Jacobson, Harold. 1979. *Networks of Interdependence.* New York: Alfred A. Knopf.

Joint Evaluation of Emergency Assistance to Rwanda. 1996. *The International Response to Conflict and Genocide: Lessons from the Rwanda Experience.* 5 vols. Copenhagen: Steering Committee of the Joint Evaluation of Emergency Assistance to Rwanda.

Kapur, Devesh. 1998. The IMF: A Cure or a Curse? *Foreign Policy* 111:114–29.

Katzenstein, Peter J., ed. 1996. *The Culture of National Security: Identity and Norms in World Politics.* New York: Columbia University Press.

Keeley, James. 1990. Toward a Foucauldian Analysis of International Regimes. *International Organization* 44 (1):83–105.

Keohane, Robert O. 1984. *After Hegemony.* Princeton, N.J.: Princeton University Press.

Kiewiet, D. Roderick, and Matthew McCubbins. 1991. *The Logic of Delegation.* Chicago: University of Chicago Press.

Krasner, Stephen D. 1991. Global Communications and National Power: Life on the Pareto Frontier. *World Politics* 43 (3):336–66.

———. 1983a. Regimes and the Limits of Realism: Regimes as Autonomous Variables. In *International Regimes,* edited by Stephen Krasner, 355–68. Ithaca, N.Y.: Cornell University Press.

Krasner, Stephen D., ed. 1983b. *International Regimes.* lthaca, N.Y.: Cornell University Press.

Krause, Keith, and Michael Williams. 1996. Broadening the Agenda of Security Studies: Politics and Methods. *Mershon International Studies Review* 40 (2):229–54.

Lake, David. 1996. Anarchy, Hierarchy, and the Variety of International Relations. *International Organization* 50 (1):1–34.

Legro, Jeffrey. 1997. Which Norms Matter? Revisiting the "Failure" of Internationalism. *International Organization* 51(1):31–64.

Lipartito, Kenneth. 1995. Culture and the Practice of Business History. *Business and Economic History* 24 (2):1–41.

Lipson, Michael. 1999. International Cooperation on Export Controls: Nonproliferation, Globalization, and Multilateralism. Ph.D. diss., University of Wisconsin, Madison.

March, James. 1988. *Decisions and Organizations.* Boston: Basil Blackwell.

———. 1997. Understanding How Decisions Happen in Organizations. In *Organizational Decision Making,* edited by Z. Shapira, 9–33. New York: Cambridge University Press.

March, James, and Johan P. Olsen. 1989. *Rediscovering Institutions: The Organizational Basis of Politics.* New York: Free Press.

McNeely, Connie. 1995. *Constructing the Nation-State: International Organization and Prescriptive Action.* Westport, Conn.: Greenwood Press.

Mearsheimer, John. 1994. The False Promise of International Institutions. *International Security* 19 (3):5–49.

Meyer, John W., and Brian Rowan. 1977. Institutionalized Organizations: Formal Structure as Myth and Ceremony. *American Journal of Sociology* 83:340–63.

Meyer, John W., and W. Richard Scott. 1992. *Organizational Environments: Ritual and Rationality.* Newbury Park, Calif.: Sage.

Miller, Gary, and Terry M. Moe. 1983. Bureaucrats, Legislators, and the Size of Government. *American Political Science Review* 77 (June):297–322.

Moe, Terry M. 1984. The New Economics of Organization. *American Journal of Political Science* 28:739–77.

Moravcsik, Andrew. 1997. Taking Preferences Seriously: Liberal Theory and International Politics. *International Organization* 51 (4):513–54.

_____. 1999. A New Statecraft? Supranational Entrepreneurs and International Cooperation. *International Organization* 53 (2):267–306.

Nelson, Paul 1995. *The World Bank and Non-Governmental Organizations.* New York: St. Martin's Press.

Ness, Gayl, and Steven Brechin. 1988. Bridging the Gap: International Organization as Organizations. *International Organization* 42 (2):245–73.

Niskanen, William A. 1971. *Bureaucracy and Representative Government.* Chicago: Aldine.

Paris, Roland. 1997. Peacebuilding the Limits of Liberal Internationalism, *International Security* 22 (2):54–89.

Perry, William A. 1996. Defense in an Age of Hope. *Foreign Affairs* 75 (6):64–79.

Pollack, Mark. 1997. Delegation, Agency, and Agenda-Setting in the European Community. *International Organization* 51 (1):99–134.

Powell, Walter W., and Paul J. DiMaggio, eds. 1991. *The New Institutional in Organizational Analysis.* Chicago: University of Chicago Press.

Pratt, John, and Richard J. Zeckhauser. 1985. *Prinicipals and Agents: The Structure of Business.* Boston: Harvard Bussiness School Press.

Radelet, Steven, and Jeffrey Sach. 1999. What Have We Learned, So Far, From the Asian Financial Crisis? Harvard Institute for International Development, 4 January. Available from <ww.hiid.harvard.edu/pub/other/aea122.pdf>.

Rittberger, Volker, ed. 1993. *Regime Theory and International Relations.* Oxford: Clarendon Press.

Ross, Geoorge. 1995. *Jacques Delors and European Integration.* New York: Oxford University Press.

Ruggie, John. 1996. *Winning the Peace.* New York: Columbia University Press.

_____. 1998. What Makes the World Hang Together. *International Organization* 52(3):855–86.

Sandholtz, Wayne. 1993. Choosing Union: Monetary Politics and Maastricht. *International Organization* 47:1–40.

Schien, Edgar. 1996. Culture: The Missing Concept in Organization Studies. *Administrative Studies Quarterly* 41:229–40.

Scott, W. Richard. 1992. *Organizations: Rational, Natural, and Open Systems.* 3d ed. Englewood Cliffs, N.J.: Prentice-Hall.

Shanks, Cheryl, Harold K. Jacobson, and Jeffery H. Kaplan. 1996. Inertia and Change in the Constellation of Intergovernmental Organizations, 1981–1992. *International Organization* 50 (4):593–627.

Sigelman, Lee. 1986. The Bureaucratic Budget Maximizer: An Assumption Examined. *Public Budgeting and Finance* (spring):50–59.

Snidal, Duncan. 1996. Political Economy and International Institutions. *International Review of Law and Economics* 16:121–37.

Star, Paul. 1992. Social Categories and Claims in the Liberal State. In *How Classification Works: Nelson Goodman Among the Social Sciences*, edited by Mary Douglas and David Hall, 154–79. Edinburgh: Edinburgh University Press.

Vaubel, Roland. 1991. A Public Choice View of International Organization. In *The Political Economy of International Organizations*, edited by Roland Vaubel and Thomas Willett, 27–45. Boulder. Colo.: Westview Press.

Vaughan, Diane. 1996. *The Challenger Launch Decision*. Chicago: University of Chicago Press.

Wade, Robert. 1996. Japan, the World Bank, and the Art of Paradigm Maintenance: The East Asian Miracle in Political Perspective. *New Left Review* 217:3–36.

Waltz, Kenneth. 1979. *Theory of International Politics*. Reading, Mass.: Addison-Wesley.

Weingast, Barry R., and Mark Moran. 1983. Bureaucratic Discretion or Congressional Control: Regulatory Policymaking by the Federal Trade Commission. *Journal of Political Economy* 91 (October):765–800.

Wendt, Alexander. 1995. Constructing International Politics. *International Security* 20 (1):71–81

____. 1998. Constitution and Causation in International Relations. *Review of International Studies* 24 (4):101–17. Special issue.

Williams, Michael. 1996. Hobbes and International Relations: A Reconsideration. *International Organization* 50 (2):213–37.

Zabusky, Stacia. 1995. *Launching Europe*. Princeton, N.J.: Princeton University Press.

23

MARGARET E. KECK AND
KATHRYN SIKKINK

ADVOCACY NETWORKS IN INTERNATIONAL POLITICS

World politics at the end of the twentieth century involves, alongside states, many nonstate actors that interact with each other, with states, and with international organizations. These interactions are structured in terms of networks, and transnational networks are increasingly visible in international politics. Some involve economic actors and firms. Some are networks of scientists and experts whose professional ties and shared causal ideas underpin their efforts to influence policy.[1] Others are networks of activists, distinguishable largely

SOURCE: Reprinted from *Activists Beyond Borders: Advocacy Networks in International Politics*, by Margaret E. Keck and Kathryn Sikkink. Copyright © 1998 by Cornell University. Used by permission of Cornell University Press.

by the centrality of principled ideas or values in motivating their formation.[2] We will call these *transnational advocacy networks.*

Advocacy networks are significant transnationally and domestically. By building new links among actors in civil societies, states, and international organizations, they multiply the channels of access to the international system. In such issue areas as the environment and human rights, they also make international resources available to new actors in domestic political and social struggles. By thus blurring the boundaries between a state's relations with its own nationals and the recourse both citizens and states have to the international system, advocacy networks are helping to transform the practice of national sovereignty.

To explore these issues, we first look at four historical forerunners to modern advocacy networks, including the antislavery movement and the campaign for woman suffrage, and we examine in depth three contemporary cases in which transnational organizations are very prominent: human rights, environment, and women's rights. We also refer to transnational campaigns around indigenous rights, labor rights, and infant formula. Despite their differences, these networks are similar in several important respects: the centrality of values or principled ideas, the belief that individuals can make a difference, the creative use of information, and the employment by nongovernmental actors of sophisticated political strategies in targeting their campaigns.

Scholars have been slow to recognize either the rationality or the significance of activist networks. Motivated by values rather than by material concerns or professional norms, these networks fall outside our accustomed categories. More than other kinds of transnational actors, advocacy networks often reach beyond policy change to advocate and instigate changes in the institutional and principled basis of international interactions. When they succeed, they are an important part of an explanation for changes in world politics. A transnational advocacy network includes those relevant actors working internationally on an issue, who are bound together by shared values, a common discourse, and dense exchanges of information and services.[3] Such networks are most prevalent in issue areas characterized by high value content and informational uncertainty. At the core of the relationship is information exchange. What is novel in these networks is the ability of nontraditional international actors to mobilize information strategically to help create new issues and categories and to persuade, pressure, and gain leverage over much more powerful, organizations and governments. Activists in networks try not only to influence policy outcomes, but to transform the terms and nature of the debate. They are not always successful in their efforts, but they are increasingly relevant players in policy debates.

Transnational advocacy networks are proliferating, and their goal is to change the behavior of states and of international organizations. Simultaneously principled and strategic actors, they "frame" issues to make them comprehensible to target audiences, to attract attention and encourage action, and to "fit" with favorable institutional venues.[4] Network actors bring new ideas, norms, and discourses into policy debates, and serve as sources of information and testimony. Norms, here, follows the usage given by Peter Katzenstein,

> to describe collective expectations for the proper behavior of actors with a given identity. In some situations norms operate like rules that define the identity of an actor, thus having "constitutive effects" that specify what actions will cause relevant others to recognize a particular identity.[5]

They also promote norm implementation, by pressuring target actors to adopt new policies, and by monitoring compliance with international standards. Insofar as is possible, they seek to maximize their influence or leverage over the target of their actions. In doing so they contribute to changing perceptions that both state and societal actors may have of their identities, interests, and preferences, to transforming their discursive positions, and ultimately to changing procedures, policies, and behavior.[6]

Networks are communicative structures. To influence discourse, procedures, and policy, activists may engage and become part of larger policy communities that group actors working on an issue from a variety of institutional and value perspectives. Transnational advocacy networks must also be understood as political spaces, in which differently situated actors negotiate—formally or informally—the social, cultural, and political meanings of their joint enterprise.

. . . ADVOCACY NETWORKS AND INTERNATIONAL SOCIETY

Scholars theorizing about transnational relations must grapple with the multiple interactions of domestic and international politics as sources of change in the international system.[7] The blurring of boundaries between international and domestic arenas has long been evident in international and comparative political economy, but its relevance for other forms of politics is less well theorized. Our work on transnational advocacy networks highlights a subset of international issues, characterized by the prominence of principled ideas and a central role for nongovernmental organizations. In this subset of issues, complex global networks carry and re-frame ideas, insert them in policy debates, pressure for regime formation, and enforce existing international norms and rules, at the same time that they try to influence particular domestic political issues. . . . We have tried to achieve greater theoretical clarity in a number of areas. First, we specify how, why, among whom, and to what end transnational relations occur. Second, we discuss the characteristic content of such relations—what kinds of ideas and issues seem to require or be amenable to these linkages—and the strategies and tactics networks use. Finally, we consider the implications for world politics of forms of organization that are neither hierarchical nor reducible to market relations.

We suggest that scholars of international relations should pay more attention to network forms of organization—characterized by voluntary, reciprocal, and horizontal exchanges of information and services. Theorists have highlighted the role of networks in the domestic polity and economy. What is distinctive about the networks we describe here is their transnational nature, and the way they are organized around shared values and discourses. Networks are difficult to organize transnationally, and have emerged around a particular set of issues with high value content and transcultural resonance. But the agility and fluidity of networked forms of organization make them particularly appropriate to historical periods characterized by rapid shifts in problem definition. Thus we expect the role of networks in international politics to grow.

Both technological and cultural change have contributed to the emergence of transnational advocacy networks. Faster, cheaper, and more reliable international information and transportation technologies have speeded their growth and helped to break government monopolies over information. New public receptivity arose partly from the cultural legacy of the 1960s and drew upon the shared normative basis provided by the international human rights instruments created after the Second World War. Transnational value-based advocacy networks are particularly useful where one state is relatively immune to direct local pressure and linked activists elsewhere have better access to their own governments or to international organizations. Linking local activists with media and activists abroad can then create a characteristic "boomerang" effect, which curves around local state indifference and repression to put foreign pressure on local policy elites. Activists may "shop" the entire global scene for the best venues to present their issues, and seek points of leverage at which to apply pressure. Thus international contacts amplify voices to which domestic governments are deaf, while the local work of target country activists legitimizes efforts of activists abroad.

Transnational networks have developed a range of increasingly sophisticated strategies and techniques. We highlight four: *information politics; symbolic politics; leverage politics;* and *accountability politics.* Networks stress gathering and reporting reliable information, but also dramatize facts by using testimonies of specific individuals to evoke commitment and broader understanding. Activists use important symbolic events and conferences to publicize issues and build networks. In addition to trying to persuade through information and symbolic politics, networks also try to pressure targets to change policies by making an implied or explicit threat of sanctions or leverage if the gap between norms and practices remains too large. Material leverage comes from linking the issue of concern to money, trade, or prestige, as more powerful institutions or governments are pushed to apply pressure. Moral leverage pushes actors to change their practices by holding their behavior up to international scrutiny, or by holding governments or institutions accountable to previous commitments and principles they have endorsed.

Issues involving core values—ideas about right and wrong—arouse strong feelings and stimulate network formation among activists, who see their task as meaningful. Activists capture attention where their issues resonate with existing ideas and ideologies. To motivate action, however, network activists must also innovate, by identifying particular social issues as problematic, attributing blame, proposing a solution, and providing a rationale for action, or by making new connections within accepted value frames. . . .

NOTES

1. Peter Haas has called these "knowledge-based" or "epistemic communities." See Peter Haas, "Introduction: Epistemic Communities and International Policy Coordination," *Knowledge, Power and International Policy Coordination,* special issue. *International Organization* 46 (Winter 1992), pp. 1–36.

2. Ideas that specify criteria for determining whether actions are right and wrong and whether outcomes are just or unjust are shared principled beliefs or values. Beliefs about cause-effect relationships are shared causal beliefs. Judith Goldstein and Robert Keohane, eds., *Ideas and Foreign Policy: Beliefs, Institutions, and Political Change* (Ithaca: Cornell University Press, 1993), pp. 8–10.

3. See also J. Clyde Mitchell, "Networks, Norms, and Institutions," in *Network Analysis,* ed. Jeremy Boissevain and J. Clyde Mitchell (The Hague: Mouton, 1973), p. 23. A "common discourse" was suggested by Stewart Lawrence in "The Role of International 'Issue Networks' in Refugee Repatriation: The Case of El Salvador" (Columbia University, mimeo).

4. David Snow and his colleagues have adapted Erving Goffman's concept of framing. We use it to mean "conscious strategic efforts by groups of people to fashion shared understandings of the world and of themselves that legitimate and motivate collective action." Definition from Doug McAdam, John D. McCarthy, and Mayer N. Zald, "Introduction," *Comparative Perspectives on Social Movements: Political Opportunities, Mobilizing Structures, and Cultural Framings,* ed. McAdam, McCarthy, and Zald (New York: Cambridge University Press, 1996), p. 6. See also Frank Baumgartner and Bryan Jones, "Agenda Dynamics and Policy Subsystems," *Journal of Politics* 53:4 (1991): 1044–74.

5. Peter J. Katzenstein, "Introduction," in *The Culture of National Security: Norms and Identity in World Politics,* ed. Katzenstein (New York: Columbia University Press, 1966), p. 5. See also Friedrich Kratochwil, *Rules, Norms, and Decisions: On the Conditions of Practical and Legal Reasoning in International Relations and Domestic Affairs* (Cambridge: Cambridge University Press, 1989); David H. Lumsdaine, *Moral Vision in International Politics: The Foreign Aid Regime, 1949–1989* (Princeton: Princeton University Press, 1993); Audie Klotz, *Norms in International Relations: The Struggle against Apartheid* (Ithaca: Cornell University Press, 1995); Janice E. Thomson, "State Practices, International Norms, and the Decline of Mercenarism," *International Studies Quarterly* 34 (1990): 23–47; and Martha Finnemore, "International Organizations as Teachers of Norms," *International Organization* 47 (August 1993): 565–97.

6. With the "constructivists" in international relations theory, we take actors and interests to be constituted in interaction. See Martha Finnemore, *National Interests in International Society* (Ithaca: Cornell University Press, 1996), who argues that "states are embedded in dense networks of transnational and international social relations that shape their perceptions of the world and their role in that world. States are *socialized* to want certain things by the international society in which they and the people in them live" (p. 2).

7. For example, see Robert Putnam, "Diplomacy and Domestic Politics: The Logic of Two-Level Games," *International Organization* 42 (Summer 1988): 427–60; David H. Lumsdaine, *Moral Vision in International Politics: The Foreign Aid Regime, 1949–1989* (Princeton: Princeton University Press, 1993); Peter Haas, ed., *Knowledge, Power, and International Policy Coordination* special issue, *International Organization* 46 (Winter 1992); James Rosenau, *Turbulence in World Politics: Non-State Actors, Domestic Structures, and International Institutions* (Cambridge: Cambridge University Press, 1995); Thomas Risse-Kappen, ed., *Bringing Transnational Relations Back In* (Princeton: Princeton University Press, 1990); Douglas Chalmers, "Internationalized Domestic Politics in Latin America," Studies, Princeton University, April 1993; Ronnie Lipschutz, "Reconstructing World Politics: The Emergence of Global Civil Society," *Millennium* 21:3 (1992): 389–420; and on transnational social movement organizations see Jackie G. Smith, Charles Chatfield, and Ron Pagnucco, *Transnational Social Movements and World Politics: Solidarity beyond the State* (New York: Syracuse University Press, forthcoming 1997).

IV

ANARCHY AND SOCIETY IN THE INTERNATIONAL SYSTEM

A DELICATE BALANCE

Considerable insight into the functioning of the international system can be gleaned by focusing on the tension between the forces of anarchy and disorder on the one side and those of society and order on the other. Both elements are usually present, and Hedley Bull's characterization of world politics as an "an anarchical society" is appropriate. The notion of anarchy as used by Bull does not mean disorder, but simply the lack of a central overriding authority. Without government, of course, relations among states exhibit an inherent potential to move toward disorder. But this is not preordained. The balance between the elements of anarchy and the elements of society can alter within a particular international system and from one kind of system to another. The focus of this section, however, is on both elements, thus highlighting and illustrating some of the themes previously identified in Part II.

POWER AND ANARCHY

The first group of readings concentrates on the elements of anarchy and conflict. It begins with a selection from Kenneth Waltz's famous study, *Man, the State and War,* in which Waltz examines the causes of war from different perspectives. In this study, Waltz looks at arguments that war is inherent in human nature, then at the contention that certain kinds of state are inherently aggressive. The most compelling part of his analysis examines the nature of international anarchy. The basic thesis Waltz develops is that the lack of a central overriding authority and the self-help nature of the international system provide a very permissive environment for war. As he puts it in the excerpt we have chosen: "Because any state may at any time use force, all states must constantly be ready either to counter force with force or to pay the cost of weakness. The requirements of state action are, in this view, imposed by the circumstances in which all states exist."

The next article, by Robert Gilpin, amplifies the notions of countering force and develops some of the themes laid out in the excerpt from *History of the Peloponnesian War* contained in Section I. Gilpin focuses on a particular kind of war within the anarchical international system: hegemonic war, in which the fundamental structure of the system is at stake. He finds the roots of such wars in changes in the underlying distribution of power in the international system and the growing disconnect between these changes and the existing system structure. In effect, hegemonic wars either reaffirm the existing structure or change the structure to accord more with the new realities of power and influence. The wars result from a mix of power and fear. Indeed, Thucydides himself noted that the real cause of the war was the rise of Athenian power and the fear this inspired in Sparta. In effect, hegemonic wars provide some of the most dramatic manifestations of the self-help system of international relations.

The argument that states exist in an environment in which fear and insecurity are endemic is also the key theme in the next selection, in which John Herz provides the classic statement of the security dilemma. According to Herz, states existing in an anarchical system are driven by the need to find more security. The problem is that actions taken by one state to enhance its security may inadvertently create insecurity in other states. This constant fear not only is one of the basic features of life in the international system but also is immensely difficult to transcend. In the following selection, however, Robert Jervis—one of the leading scholars in the field and author of works on signaling, perception, and misperception, as well as on the impact of nuclear weapons on international politics—develops the argument that the security dilemma is partly a function of offensive military strategies and capabilities. As a result, he suggests, the problems associated with the security dilemma, under certain circumstances, can be greatly eased.

Although Jervis's analysis predated the winding down of the Cold War (which took place in the latter half of the 1980s), it is worth noting that one of the changes Gorbachev made was to initiate a restructuring of Soviet forces away from offensive capabilities and toward what was sometimes termed defensive defense. This had considerable impact in Europe. Not only did it help to reduce the longstanding fears about Soviet power and potential aggression, but it also made it easier to achieve a significant agreement on conventional arms reductions. Although this suggests that states can transcend the security dilemma, as opposed simply to mitigating its consequences, many analysts, especially neo-realists, believe that insecurity remains one of the defining characteristics of the international system.

For many observers, the problems of security and those of power are inextricably related. Not surprisingly, therefore, one major approach to managing international relations has been through the management of power. This has taken several forms, one of which is the balance of power system. The nature of this system is enunciated in the selection from Hans J. Morgenthau. According to Morgenthau, the balance of power system—and the notion of equilibrium that is central to it—is not confined to international politics but is evident in many other walks of life. Morgenthau emphasizes that the key element in maintaining stability is equilibrium among the great powers, although he also acknowledges that each state will attempt to over-ensure and obtain more power than is really needed.

The next selection, by A. F. K. Organski, seeks both to challenge and to modify Morgenthau's analysis. Organski provides a valuable critique of balance of power theory, questioning many of its assumptions and arguing that it contains a basic ambiguity about whether stability is better maintained through equilibrium or through an obvious preponderance of power. He also argues that the balance of power theorists are selective in their assumptions—and implicitly treat the state, which maintains the balance, as being different from other powers.

It is partly because of the inadequacies of a balance of power system that both policymakers and analysts have focused on alternative approaches to managing power in the international system. One of the most important alternatives is a collective security system. This notion is covered in a selection by Inis Claude, whose books on power and on international organizations have been widely acclaimed. In this excerpt, Claude defines collective security in terms of "the proposition that aggressive and unlawful use of force by any nation against any nation will be met by the combined force of all other nations." He also locates a collective security system somewhere between traditional alliances and the chimera of world government and highlights the presence of certain components reminiscent of the balance of power system. In addition, Claude examines the requirements of an effective collective security system, one of which is that national leaders must be prepared to subordinate immediate national interests to the overall good of the system. In essence, he argues that, for such an approach to be effective, states must pursue a policy of what Robert Keohane in a later study described as "enlightened or farsighted—as opposed to myopic—self-interest."[1] The proposition that states often behave in this way is the basis for the second set of readings in this chapter, which deal with cooperation and international society.

---

[1] Robert O. Keohane, *After Hegemony: Cooperation and Discord in the World Political Economy* (Princeton, N.J.: Princeton University Press, 1984).

COOPERATION AND
INTERNATIONAL SOCIETY

The extent to which states pursue cooperative behavior or abide by rules in international relations will depend on their calculation of the long-term benefits of rule maintenance or continued cooperation as opposed to the short-term benefits of breaching the rules or defecting from cooperation. Yet it is clear that all states have a vested interest in some kind of cooperative structures in international relations. One of these cooperative structures is international law. William Coplin's selection on this topic challenges the notion that international law is an instrument of control or of coercive restraint in the international system. He argues instead that it is better understood as "an institutional device for communicating to the policymakers of various states a consensus on the nature of the international system." Although he acknowledges that international law is only "quasi-authoritative" because the norms of international law reflect an imperfect consensus among states, it nevertheless is important in communicating to governments both "the reasons for state actions and the requisites for international order."

International law is only one form that rules of the game can take in international relations. Many others exist, ranging from tacit codes of conduct for managing international crises and conflicts, through the spirit of agreements to formal treaties and written obligations.[2] Since the early 1970s, considerable attention also has been given to the notion of international regimes that encompass rules and norms. The next selection, by Robert Keohane, deals with this concept of regimes.

Although regime theory was introduced into the literature on international relations in the mid-1970s by John Ruggie,[3] the leading figure in its subsequent development was Robert Keohane, a principal figure in the field of international political economy. We have chosen a selection from Keohane's *After Hegemony* as one of the clearest and most concise statements both of the nature of cooperation in international relations and of the concept of regimes. Keohane starts his analysis of regimes with a definition by Stephen Krasner in which regimes are understood as "sets of implicit or explicit principles, norms, rules and decision-making procedures around which actors' expectations converge in a given area of international relations."[4] Keohane elaborates various elements in the definition and also suggests that regimes are not inconsistent with realist theory because, even in realism, states cooperate

---

[2] These rules and their impact are dissected in the excellent study by Raymond Cohen, *International Politics: The Rules of the Game* (London: Longman, 1981).

[3] John C. Ruggie, "International Responses to Technology: Concepts and Trends," *International Organization* 29, no. 3 (Summer 1975): 557–584.

[4] Stephen D. Krasner, ed., *International Regimes* (Ithaca, N.Y.: Cornell University Press, 1983), p. 2.

when it is advantageous to do so. His argument is that enlightened self-interest helps to maintain regimes, although the myopic self-interest of states may lead to efforts to seek unilateral advantage.

Regime theory can be understood as a contemporary variant of some of the older ideas of international society and, in many respects, is very attractive as a way of understanding crucial aspects of international relations. The broader issue of cooperation is dealt with in an excerpt from *The Evolution of Cooperation* by Robert Axelrod, a prominent political scientist who has had a major impact on our understanding of cooperation and how it evolves. In the excerpt we have chosen, Axelrod emphasizes the importance of reciprocity and the "shadow of the future," which inhibits defection for short-term gain. He also highlights the importance of tit-for-tat strategies, which reciprocate both cooperation and defection.

The ultimate form of cooperation is integration. Accordingly, the next selection, by Donald J. Puchala, focuses on integration and the different approaches that have been taken toward it. One of the mainsprings of integration theory was the concept of functional cooperation (or functionalism, as it became known). The principle of functionalism is that states can cooperate in areas wherein they have common needs and that are essentially technical and nonpolitical in nature. The classic statement of functionalism was presented in David Mitrany, *A Working Peace System,* which was initially published in 1943 and reprinted two decades later. Mitrany saw functionalism as a dynamic process. He expected "ramification" to occur whereby cooperation in one area would produce a need for cooperation in other sectors and would lead eventually to political agreement.

Functionalist theory was both an approach to peace and an approach to integration. Indeed, the prevailing assumption was that areas of functional cooperation would gradually be expanded. As James Dougherty and Robert Pfaltzgraff have noted, "Functionalism is based upon the hypothesis that national loyalties can be diffused and redirected into a framework for international cooperation in place of national competition and war. . . . Because the state is inadequate for solving many problems because of the interdependent nature of the modern world, the obvious answer is said to lie in international organizations, and perhaps eventually in more tightly knit management and resolution of technical issues at the regional or global level."[5]

Functionalist theory presents many problems, however, not the least of which is that it downplays power considerations and ignores the difficulty of separating the technical from the political. Nevertheless, it provided the basis for much theorizing about integration and for the development of neo-functionalist theories. One of the leading figures in the replacement of

---

[5] Robert Pfaltzgraff and James Dougherty, *Contending Theories of International Relations* (New York: Harper and Row, 1981), p. 419.

functionalism by neo-functionalism was Ernst Haas. In both *The Uniting of Europe* and *Beyond the Nation-State: Functionalism and International Organization,* Haas identified and elaborated many of the concepts of neo-functionalism.[6] Central to his thinking was the notion that integration stems from the beliefs and actions of elites who see the process as having certain specific advantages. He emphasized functionally specific international programs, which he saw as maximizing national welfare and the integration process—a task that was facilitated by the learning that took place in government and by the process of spillover, as those who had benefited from supranational organizations in one sector extended their cooperation to other sectors. By the 1970s, however, Haas had identified certain conditions under which, he believed, the integration process was likely to be halted or even reversed.[7] Actors could change their views about the advantages of regional cooperation or could decide that the problems they were trying to solve through regional integration were not in fact regional problems.

The approach taken by Haas focused on government policies as the key to integration, but this was not the only approach. Karl Deutsch (mentioned in Part II as one of the pioneers in the application of quantitative techniques to the study of international relations) developed an approach to integration based on the actions of societies rather than governments and focused not on policies, but on transaction flows—that is, communications that flow from one political system to another. These transactions—including mail, trade, tourism, student exchanges, migration, and telephone traffic—can be measured and, according to Deutsch and his colleagues, assist in assessing the degree of integration among states.[8]

These two approaches to integration have very different roots and emphases. In both cases, however, the focus has been primarily on Western Europe, where the integration process has been most pronounced. Rather than offer excerpts from either neo-functionalist or transaction analysis, though, we have chosen the article by Donald Puchala because it not only highlights the main elements in both of these approaches but also offers a balanced and concise assessment of their strengths and weaknesses. In addition to providing a succinct and extremely helpful overview of integration theory, Puchala looks at the ways it has challenged and modified political realism. This work fits in perfectly with the approach adopted in this volume, in that it accentuates

---

[6] Ernst B. Haas, *The Uniting of Europe: Political, Social and Economic Forces 1950–57* (Stanford, Calif.: Stanford University Press, 1958), and *Beyond the Nation-State: Functionalism and International Organization* (Stanford, Calif.: Stanford University Press, 1964).

[7] See Ernst B. Haas, "Turbulent Fields and the Theory of Regional Integration," *International Organization* 30, no. 2 (Spring 1976): 173–212.

[8] Karl W. Deutsch et al., *Political Community and the North Atlantic Area* (Princeton, N.J.: Princeton University Press, 1957).

some of the major distinctions and debates running through our choices of material. The following set of readings provides even more of a flavor of this debate.

DEBATING RIVAL THEORIES

This volume emphasizes readings that reflect major intellectual traditions in international relations. Most readers will see very clearly that these traditions conflict with one another. Moreover, the discipline of international relations is far from static. New approaches and strands of thinking have arisen to challenge, to modify, and to accompany the more enduring approaches. The rise of constructivist and feminist approaches to international relations marks two of the newest schools of international relations, and both are represented in our excerpts.

The constructivist school is represented by Alexander Wendt, one of the leading theorists of this non-traditional approach to international relations. Wendt challenges one of the fundamental tenets of realist and neo-realist approaches to international relations—the notion of international anarchy as the dominant feature of world politics. Starting from a concern with identity and interest formation, Wendt argues that neither self-help nor power politics are logical or causal consequences of anarchy. The corollary to this is that the self-help system is a result of process, not structure. As he puts it, "There is no 'logic' of anarchy apart from the practices that create and instantiate one structure of identities and interests rather than another; structure has no existence or causal powers apart from process. Self-help and power politics are institutions, not essential features of anarchy. *Anarchy is what states make of it.*" Wendt goes on to argue that anarchy is a permissive factor in processes that give rise to self-help, but the interaction itself gives rise to the meanings in terms of which action is organized.

The feminist school of thought is represented here by J. Ann Tickner, whose work on gendering world politics has added another important component to the assault on realism and neo-realism. The feminist approach shares certain characteristics with constructivism, not the least of which is the contention that "an examination of states' identities is crucial for understanding their security-seeking behavior." Indeed, feminists challenge the role of states as security providers, adopting instead a multidimensional, multilevel approach to security. Tickner also argues that war is a deeply gendered concept. In the excerpt we have included, she also discusses feminist redefinitions of security.

The next excerpt is from a distinguished realist scholar, Joseph Grieco, who challenges both the liberal critiques of realism and neo-realism and the tenets of what he calls the new liberalism. One of Grieco's key themes is that liberal institutionalists focus on the absolute gains that result from cooperative behavior but ignore the fact that states are concerned about relative gains.

One of the main targets of his criticisms is Robert Keohane, a leading scholar in the modernization and adaptation of liberal theories to contemporary international relations.[9]

The next excerpt is by John Mearsheimer, the leading contemporary proponent of realism, and focuses on critical theory—a term that embraces the constructivist approach of Wendt and is also directly relevant to the desire of the feminists to redefine security and, thus international relations. In his usual trenchant style and with ruthlessly compelling logic, Mearsheimer highlights some of the tensions and problems inherent in the constructivist approach and its attack on realism.

This is not to suggest that realism and neo-realism are themselves sufficient to explain contemporary international relations. In this section's final excerpt, Jack Snyder, a distinguished political scientist at Columbia University, provides an excellent summary of the major traditions and some of the key figures representing them before he examines their relevance and utility to the interpretation and understanding of the world since September 11, 2001. In his analysis Snyder looks at realism, liberalism, and idealism, contending very persuasively that constructivism is merely a new version of the idealist tradition discussed in the Introduction to Part I of this volume. Snyder identifies the core beliefs of each of the theories, the key actors each focuses on, and the main instruments each school believes is important. He also identifies the blind spots in each theory before examining what each theory explains and fails to explain about the world since September 11. Naturally, Snyder's analysis contains some points about which one may disagree. The omission of the dark side of globalization and the consequent focus on transnational networks as something that comes under the idealist or constructivist school are serious shortcomings—although understandable, given the way in which neither liberalism nor realism explains the rise of malevolent transnational social and political networks. Nevertheless, Snyder's overview is particularly helpful in assessing the contemporary relevance of the main theories. Moreover, by highlighting the difficulties that these theories have in explaining some of the characteristics of contemporary international relations, Snyder, in effect, challenges the theories' major proponents to modify and develop them in ways that enhance their relevance and utility. (We return to this challenge in Part VI, which deals with contemporary issues.)

---

[9] Keohane's articulation of liberal institutionalism was one of the major targets in "The False Promise of International Institutions," by John Mearsheimer, in *International Security* 19, no. 3 (Winter 1994/95): 5–49.

24

KENNETH N. WALTZ

INTERNATIONAL CONFLICT AND INTERNATIONAL ANARCHY: THE THIRD IMAGE

For what can be done against force without force?
CICERO, *The Letters to his Friends*

With many sovereign states, with no system of law enforceable among them, with each state judging its grievances and ambitions according to the dictates of its own reason or desire—conflict, sometimes leading to war, is bound to occur. To achieve a favorable outcome from such conflict a state has to rely on its own devices, the relative efficiency of which must be its constant concern. This, the idea of the third image, is to be examined in the present chapter. It is not an esoteric idea; it is not a new idea. Thucydides implied it when he wrote that it was "the growth of the Athenian power, which terrified the Lacedaemonians and forced them into war."[1] John Adams implied it when he wrote to the citizens of Petersburg, Virginia, that "a war with France, if just and necessary, might wean us from fond and blind affections, which no Nation ought ever to feel towards another, as our experience in more than one instance abundantly testifies."[2] There is an obvious relation between the concern over relative power position expressed by Thucydides and the admonition of John Adams that love affairs between states are inappropriate and dangerous. This relation is made explicit in Frederick Dunn's statement that "so long as the notion of self-help persists, the aim of maintaining the power position of the nation is paramount to all other considerations."[3]

In anarchy there is no automatic harmony. The three preceding statements reflect this fact. A state will use force to attain its goals if, after assessing the prospects for success, it values those goals more than it values the pleasures of peace. Because each state is the final judge of its own cause, any state may at any time use force to implement its policies. Because any state may at any time use force, all states must constantly be ready either to counter force with force or to pay the cost of weakness. The requirements of state action are, in this view, imposed by the circumstances in which all states exist.

. . . In the early state of nature, men were sufficiently dispersed to make any pattern of cooperation unnecessary. But finally the combination of

SOURCE: From *Man, The State and War: A Theoretical Analysis* (New York, NY: Columbia University Press, 1959), pp. 159–160, 167–170, 183–184. © Columbia University Press, New York. Reprinted with permission of the publisher.

increased numbers and the usual natural hazards posed, in a variety of situations, the proposition: cooperate or die. Rousseau illustrates the line of reasoning with the simplest example. The example is worth reproducing, for it is the point of departure for the establishment of government and contains the basis for his explanation of conflict in international relations as well. Assume that five men who have acquired a rudimentary ability to speak and to understand each other happen to come together at a time when all of them suffer from hunger. The hunger of each will be satisfied by the fifth part of a stag, so they "agree" to cooperate in a project to trap one. But also the hunger of any one of them will be satisfied by a hare, so, as a hare comes within reach, one of them grabs it. The defector obtains the means of satisfying his hunger but in doing so permits the stag to escape. His immediate interest prevails over consideration for his fellows.[4]

The story is simple; the implications are tremendous. In cooperative action, even where all agree on the goal and have an equal interest in the project, one cannot rely on others. . . .

In the stag-hunt example the tension between one man's immediate interest and the general interest of the group is resolved by the unilateral action of the one man. To the extent that he was motivated by a feeling of hunger, his act is one of passion. Reason would have told him that his long-run interest depends on establishing, through experience, the conviction that cooperative action will benefit all of the participants. But reason also tells him that if he foregoes the hare, the man next to him might leave his post to chase it, leaving the first man with nothing but food for thought on the folly of being loyal.

The problem is now posed in more significant terms. If harmony is to exist in anarchy, not only must I be perfectly rational but I must be able to assume that everyone else is too. Otherwise there is no basis for rational calculation. To allow in my calculation for the irrational acts of others can lead to no determinate solutions, but to attempt to act on a rational calculation without making such an allowance may lead to my own undoing. The latter argument is reflected in Rousseau's comments on the proposition that "a people of true Christians would form the most perfect society imaginable." In the first place he points out that such a society "would not be a society of men." Moreover, he says, "For the state to be peaceable and for harmony to be maintained, *all* the citizens *without exception* would have to be [equally] good Christians; if by ill hap there should be a single self-seeker or hypocrite . . . he would certainly get the better of his pious compatriots."[5]

If we define cooperative action as rational and any deviation from it irrational, we must agree with Spinoza that conflict results from the irrationality of men. But if we examine the requirements of rational action, we find that even in an example as simple as the stag-hunt we have to assume that the reason of each leads to an identical definition of interest, that each will draw the same conclusion as to the methods appropriate to meet the original situation, that all will agree instantly on the action required by any chance incidents that raise the question of altering the original plan, and that each can rely completely on the steadfastness of purpose of all the others. Perfectly rational action requires not only the perception that our welfare is tied up with the welfare of others but also a perfect appraisal of details so that we can answer the question: Just *how* in each situation is it tied up with everyone else's? Rousseau agrees with Spinoza in refusing to label the act of the rabbit-snatcher either good or bad; unlike Spinoza, he also refuses to label it either rational or irrational. He has noticed that the difficulty is not only in the actors but also in the situations they face. While by no means ignoring the part that avarice and ambition play in the birth and growth of conflict, Rousseau's analysis makes clear the extent to which conflict appears inevitably in the social affairs of men. . . .

In the stag-hunt example, the will of the rabbit-snatcher was rational and predictable from his own point of view. From the point of view of the rest of the group, it was arbitrary and capricious. So of any individual state, a will perfectly good for itself may provoke the violent resistance of other states.[6] The application of Rousseau's theory of international politics is stated with eloquence and clarity in his commentaries on Saint-Pierre and in a short work entitled *The State of War.* His application bears out the preceding analysis. The states of Europe, he writes, "touch each other at so many points that no one of them can move without giving a jar to all the rest; their variances are all the more deadly, as their ties are more closely woven." They "must inevitably fall into quarrels and dissensions at the first changes that come about." And if we ask why they must "inevitably" clash, Rousseau answers: because their union is "formed and maintained by nothing better than chance." The nations of Europe are willful units in close juxtaposition with rules neither clear nor enforceable to guide them. The public law of Europe is but "a mass of contradictory rules which nothing but the right of the stronger can reduce to order: so that in the absence of any sure clue to guide her, reason is bound, in every case of doubt, to obey the promptings of self-interest— which in itself would make war inevitable, even if all parties desired to be just." In this condition, it is foolhardy to expect automatic harmony of interest and automatic agreement and acquiescence in rights and duties.

Notes

1. Thucydides, *History of the Peloponnesian War,* tr. Jowett, Book I, par. 23.
2. Letter of John Adams to the citizens of the town of Petersburg, dated June 6, 1798, and reprinted in the program for the visit of William Howard Taft, Petersburg, Va., May 19, 1909.
3. Dunn, *Peaceful Change,* p. 13.
4. Rousseau, *Inequality,* p. 238.
5. *Social Contract,* pp. 135–36 (Book IV, ch. viii). Italics added. The word "equally" is necessary for an accurate rendering of the French text but does not appear in the translation cited.
6. *A Lasting Peace,* tr. Vaughan, p. 72. On p. 91 Rousseau refers to men as "unjust, grasping and setting their own interest above all things." This raises the question of the relation of the third image to the first, which will be discussed in ch. viii, below.

25

ROBERT GILPIN

THE THEORY OF HEGEMONIC WAR

. . . In the introduction to his history of the great war between the Spartans and the Athenians, Thucydides wrote that he was addressing "those inquirers who desire an exact knowledge of the past as an aid to the interpretation of the future, which in the course of human things must resemble if it does not reflect it. . . . In fine, I have written my work, not as an essay which is to win the applause of the moment, but as a possession for all time."[1] Thucydides, assuming that the behavior and phenomena that he observed would repeat themselves throughout human history, intended to reveal the underlying and unalterable nature of what is today called international relations.

In the language of contemporary social science, Thucydides believed that he had uncovered the general law of the dynamics of international relations. Although differences exist between Thucydides' conceptions of scientific law and methodology and those of present-day students of international relations, it is significant that Thucydides was the first to set forth the idea that the dynamic of international relations is provided by the differential growth of power among states. This fundamental idea—that the uneven growth of power among states is the driving force of international relations—can be identified as the theory of hegemonic war.

This essay argues that Thucydides' theory of hegemonic war constitutes one of the central organizing ideas for the study of international relations. The following pages examine and evaluate Thucydides' theory of hegemonic war and contemporary variations of that theory. To carry out this task, it is necessary to make Thucydides' ideas more systematic, expose his basic assumptions, and understand his analytical method. Subsequently, this article discusses whether or not Thucydides' conception of international relations has proved to be a "possession for all time." Does it help explain wars in the modern era? How, if at all, has it been modified by more modern scholarship? What is its relevance for the contemporary nuclear age?

Robert Gilpin is Eisenhower Professor of International Affairs at Princeton University. He is the author of *The Political Economy of International Relations* (Princeton, 1987).

SOURCE: "The Theory of Hegemonic War" by Robert Gilpin. *Journal of Interdisciplinary History*, Vol. 18, No. 4, *The Origin and Prevention of Major Wars* (Spring, 1988), 591–613. © 1988 by The Massachusetts Institute of Technology and the editors of the *The Journal of Interdisciplinary History*.

THUCYDIDES' THEORY OF HEGEMONIC WAR

The essential idea embodied in Thucydides' theory of hegemonic war is that fundamental changes in the international system are the basic determinants of such wars. The structure of the system or distribution of power among the states in the system can be stable or unstable. A stable system is one in which changes can take place if they do not threaten the vital interests of the dominant states and thereby cause a war among them. In his view, such a stable system has an unequivocal hierarchy of power and an unchallenged dominant or hegemonic power. An unstable system is one in which economic, technological, and other changes are eroding the international hierarchy and undermining the position of the hegemonic state. In this latter situation, untoward events and diplomatic crises can precipitate a hegemonic war among the states in the system. The outcome of such a war is a new international structure.

Three propositions are embedded in this brief summary of the theory. The first is that a hegemonic war is distinct from other categories of war; it is caused by broad changes in political, strategic, and economic affairs. The second is that the relations among individual states can be conceived as a system; the behavior of states is determined in large part by their strategic interaction. The third is that a hegemonic war threatens and transforms the structure of the international system; whether or not the participants in the conflict are initially aware of it, at stake is the hierarchy of power and relations among states in the system. Thucydides' conception and all subsequent formulations of the theory of hegemonic war emerge from these three propositions.

Such a structural theory of war can be contrasted with an escalation theory of war. According to this latter theory, as Waltz has argued in *Man, the State, and War,* war occurs because of the simple fact that there is nothing to stop it.[2] In the anarchy of the international system, statesmen make decisions and respond to the decisions of others. This action-reaction process in time can lead to situations in which statesmen deliberately provoke a war or lose control over events and eventually find themselves propelled into a war. In effect, one thing leads to another until war is the consequence of the interplay of foreign policies.

Most wars are the consequence of such an escalatory process. They are not causally related to structural features of the international system, but rather are due to the distrust and uncertainty that characterizes relations among states in what Waltz has called a self-help system.[3] Thus, the history of ancient times, which introduces Thucydides' history, is a tale of constant warring. However, the Peloponnesian War, he tells us, is different and worthy of special attention because of the massive accumulation of power in Hellas and its implications for the structure of the system. This great war and its underlying causes were the focus of his history.

Obviously, these two theories do not necessarily contradict one another; each can be used to explain different wars. But what interested Thucydides was a particular type of war, what he called a great war and what this article calls a hegemonic war—a war in which the overall structure of an international system is at issue. The structure of the international system at the outbreak of such a war is a necessary, but not a sufficient cause of the war. The theory of hegemonic war and international change that is examined below refers to those wars that arise from the specific structure of an international system and in turn transform that structure.

ASSUMPTIONS OF THE THEORY

Underlying Thucydides' view that he had discovered the basic mechanism of a great or hegemonic war was his conception of human nature. He believed that human nature was unchanging and therefore the events recounted in his history would be repeated in the future. Since human beings are driven by three fundamental passions—interest, pride, and, above all else, fear—they always seek to increase their wealth and power until other humans, driven by like passions, try to stop them. Although advances in political knowledge could contribute to an understanding of this process, they could not control or arrest it. Even advances in knowledge, technology, or economic development would not change the fundamental nature of human behavior or of international relations. On the contrary, increases in human power, wealth, and technology would serve only to intensify conflict among social groups and enhance the magnitude of war. Thucydides the realist, in contrast to Plato the idealist, believed that reason would not transform human beings, but would always remain the slave of human passions. Thus, uncontrollable passions would again and again generate great conflicts like the one witnessed in his history. . . .

CONCEPTION OF SYSTEMIC CHANGE

Underlying this analysis and the originality of Thucydides' thought was his novel conception of classical Greece as constituting a system, the basic components of which were the great powers—Sparta and Athens. Foreshadowing later realist formulations of international relations, he believed that the structure of the system was provided by the distribution of power among states; the hierarchy of power among these states defined and maintained the system and determined the relative prestige of states, their spheres of influence, and their political relations. The hierarchy of power and related elements thus gave order and stability to the system.

Accordingly, international political change involved a transformation of the hierarchy of the states in the system and the patterns of relations dependent upon that hierarchy. Although minor changes could occur and lesser states could move up and down this hierarchy without necessarily disturbing the stability of the system, the positioning of the great powers was crucial. Thus, as he tells us, it was the increasing power of the second most powerful state in the system, Athens, that precipitated the conflict and brought about what I have elsewhere called systemic change, that is, a change in the hierarchy or control of the international political system.[4]

Searching behind appearances for the reality of international relations, Thucydides believed that he had found the true causes of the Peloponnesian War, and by implication of systemic change, in the phenomenon of the uneven growth of power among the dominant states in the system. "The real cause," he concluded in the first chapter, "I consider to be the one which was formally most kept out of sight. The growth of the power of Athens, and the alarm which this inspired in Lacedaemon [Sparta], made war inevitable."[5] In a like fashion and in future ages, he reasoned, the differential growth of power in a state system would undermine the status quo and lead to hegemonic war between declining and rising powers.

In summary, according to Thucydides, a great or hegemonic war, like a disease, follows a discernible and recurrent course. The initial phase is a relatively stable international system characterized by hierarchical ordering of states with a dominant or hegemonic power. Over time, the power of one subordinate state begins to grow disproportionately; as this development occurs, it comes into conflict with the hegemonic state. The struggle between these contenders for preeminence and their accumulating alliances leads to a bipolarization of the system. In the parlance of game theory, the system becomes a zero-sum situation in which one side's gain is by necessity the other side's loss. As this bipolarization occurs the system becomes increasingly unstable, and a small event can trigger a crisis and precipitate a major conflict; the resolution of that conflict will determine the new hegemon and the hierarchy of power in the system. . . .

In brief, it was the combination of significant environmental changes and the contrasting natures of the Athenian and Spartan societies that precipitated the war. Although the underlying causes of the war can be traced to geographical, economic, and technological factors, the major determinant of the foreign policies of the two protagonists was the differing character of their domestic regimes. Athens was a democracy; its people were energetic, daring, and commercially disposed; its naval power, financial resources, and empire were expanding. Sparta, the traditional hegemon of the Hellenes, was a slavocracy; its foreign policy was conservative and attentive merely to the narrow interests of preserving its domestic status quo. Having little interest in commerce or overseas empire, it gradually declined relative to its rival. In future ages, in Thucydides' judgment, situations similar to that of Athens and Sparta would arise, and this fateful process would repeat itself eternally. . . .

The theory's fundamental contribution is the conception of hegemonic war itself and the importance of hegemonic wars for the dynamics of international relations. The expression hegemonic war may have been coined by Aron; certainly he has provided an excellent definition of what Thucydides called a great war. Describing World War I as a hegemonic war, Aron writes that such a war "is characterized less by its immediate causes or its explicit purposes than by its extent and the stakes involved. It affect[s] all the political units inside one system of relations between sovereign states. Let us call it, for want of a better term, a war of hegemony, hegemony being, if not the conscious motive, at any rate the inevitable consequence of the victory of at least one of the states or groups." Thus, the outcome of a hegemonic war, according to Aron, is the transformation of the structure of the system of interstate relations.[6]

In more precise terms, one can distinguish a hegemonic war in terms of its scale, the objectives at stake, and the means employed to achieve those objectives. A hegemonic war generally involves all of the states in the system; it is a world war. Whatever the immediate and conscious motives of the combatants, as Aron points out, the fundamental issues to be decided are the leadership and structure of the international system. Its outcome also profoundly affects the internal composition of societies because, as the behavior of Athens and Sparta revealed, the victor remolds the vanquished in its image. Such wars are at once political, economic, and ideological struggles. Because of the scope of the war and the importance of the issues to be decided, the means employed are usually unlimited. In Clausewitzian terms, they become pure conflicts or clashes of society rather than the pursuit of limited policy objectives.

Thus, in the Peloponnesian War the whole of Hellas became engaged in an internecine struggle to determine the economic and political future of the Greek world. Although the initial objectives of the two alliances were limited, the basic issue in the contest became the structure and leadership of the emerging international system and not merely the fate of particular city-states. Ideological disputes, that is, conflicting views over the organization of domestic societies, were also at the heart of the struggle; democratic Athens and aristocratic Sparta sought to reorder other societies in terms of their own political values and socioeconomic systems. As Thucydides tells us in his description of the leveling and decimation of Melos, there were no constraints on the means employed to reach their goals. The war released forces of which the protagonists had previously been unaware; it took a totally unanticipated course. As the Athenians had warned the Spartans in counseling them against war, "consider the vast influence of accident in war, before you are engaged in it."[7] Furthermore, neither rival anticipated that the war would leave both sides exhausted and thereby open the way to Macedonian imperialism.

The central idea embodied in the hegemonic theory is that there is incompatibility between crucial elements of the existing international system and the changing distribution of power among the states within the system. The elements of the system—the hierarchy of prestige, the division of territory, and the international economy—became less and less compatible with the shifting distribution of power among the major states in the system. The resolution of the disequilibrium between the superstructure of the system and the underlying distribution of power is found in the outbreak and intensification of what becomes a hegemonic war. . . .

NOTES

1. Thucydides (trans. John H. Finley, Jr.), *The Peloponnesian War* (New York, 1951), 14–15.
2. Kenneth N. Waltz, *Man, the State, and War: A Theoretical Analysis* (New York, 1959).
3. *Idem, Theory of International Relations* (Reading, Mass., 1979).
4. Robert Gilpin, *War and Change in World Politics* (New York, 1981), 40.
5. Thucydides, *Peloponnesian War,* 15.
6. Raymond Aron, "War and Industrial Society," in Leon Bramson and George W. Goethals (eds.), *War—Studies from Psychology, Sociology, Anthropology* (New York, 1964), 359.
7. Thucydides, *Peloponnesian War,* 45.

26

JOHN H. HERZ

THE SECURITY DILEMMA IN THE ATOMIC AGE

The "security dilemma," or "power and security dilemma," is a social constellation in which units of power (such as states or nations in international relations) find themselves whenever they exist side by side without higher authority that might impose standards of behavior upon them and thus protect them from attacking each other. In such a condition, a feeling of insecurity, deriving from mutual suspicion and mutual fear, compels these units to compete for ever more power in order to find more security, an effort which proves self-defeating because complete security remains ultimately unobtainable. I believe that this dilemma, and not such (possibly additional) factors as "aggressiveness," or desire to acquire the wealth of others, or general depravity of human nature, constitutes the basic cause of what is commonly referred to as the "urge for power" and resulting "power politics."

This constellation and its effects can be observed at the primitive as well as the higher levels of human organization. As I have observed before, "the fact that is decisive for his (i.e., man's) social and political attitudes and ideas

SOURCE: From *International Politics in the Atomic Age,* John H. Herz. (New York, NY: Columbia University Press, 1959), pp. 231–235. © Columbia University Press, New York. Reprinted with the permission of the publisher.

is that other human beings are able to inflict death upon him. This very realization that his own brother may play the role of Cain makes his fellow men appear to him as potential foes. Realization of this fact by others, in turn, makes him appear to them as their potential mortal enemy. Thus there arises a fundamental social constellation, a mutual suspicion and a mutual dilemma: the dilemma of 'kill or perish,' of attacking first or running the risk of being destroyed. There is apparently no escape from this vicious circle. Whether man is 'by nature' peaceful and cooperative, or aggressive and domineering, is not the question. The condition that concerns us here is not an anthropological or biological, but a social one. It is his uncertainty and anxiety as to his neighbors' intentions that places man in this basic dilemma, and makes the 'homo homini lupus' a primary fact of the social life of man." And further: "Politically active groups and individuals are concerned about their security from being attacked, subjected, dominated, or annihilated by other groups and individuals. Because they strive to attain security from such attack, and yet can never feel entirely secure in a world of competing units, they are driven toward acquiring more and more power for themselves, in order to escape the impact of the superior power of others. It is important to realize that such competition for security, and hence for power, is a basic situation which is unique with men and their social groups. At any rate, it has nothing to do with a hypothetical 'power urge' or 'instinct of pugnacity' of the race, and even less, since the competition is intraspecific, with the biological 'big fish eats small fish' situation."[1]

The power and security dilemma, in principle, affects relationships between all groups, but how it does so within units where some sort of government exists does not concern us here. Rather, we are concerned with its impact on those relations which are characterized by the absence of any kind of "government" over and above the coexisting power units, and in particular, international relations since the dawn of the modern era. For it is in this area that the dilemma reveals itself as a prime mover in a more clear-cut—one is inclined to say, more brutal—way than anywhere else. "Because this is the realm where the ultimate power units have faced, and still are facing each other as 'monades' irreducible to any further, higher ruling or coordinating power, the vicious circle of the power and security dilemma works here with more drastic force than in any other field. Power relationships and the development of the means of exercising power in the brutal form of force have dominated the field here to the almost complete exclusion of the more refined 'governmental' relationships which prevail in 'internal politics.' Marxism maintains that political relations and developments form the 'superstructure' over the system and the development of the means of *production*. Within the sphere of international relations, it might rather be said that political developments constitute a superstructure over the system and the development of the means of *destruction*."[2] The elaboration . . . on the developments in the defense (or offense) systems of nation-states and on their impact upon the policies and relationships of "powers" has been sufficient, I hope, to illustrate the influence which considerations of "security," concern for protection from outside aggression and interference, mutual fear and suspicion, have exercised on their "power politics" as well as on their efforts to mitigate these effects through systems and organizations like the balance of power and collective security. But before inquiring how the dilemma applies to the present situation in world politics, further clarification may be gained by reference to another author, whose analysis closely parallels my own.

When I first claimed primary importance for the security dilemma, I was not aware that a similar thesis had been powerfully put forth by a British historian and student of power politics, Herbert Butterfield.[3] What I have termed "security dilemma" is called "predicament of Hobbesian fear" by Mr. Butterfield, and for obvious reasons.[4] The "Hobbesian" dilemma, he states, constitutes "a grand dialectical jam of a kind that exasperates men"; indeed, he claims for it such fundamental importance as to talk of it as "the absolute predicament," the "irreducible dilemma," which, lying in "the very geometry of human conflict," is "the basis of all the tensions of the present day, representing even now the residual problem that the world has not solved, the hard nut that we still have to crack."[5] To illustrate this "predicament," Butterfield asks us to imagine two enemies, armed with pistols, locked in one room. "Both of you would like to throw the pistols out of the window, yet it defeats the intelligence to find a way of doing it. . . . In international affairs it is this situation of Hobbesian fear which, so far as I can see, has hitherto defeated all the endeavor of the human intellect."[6] He then elucidates the role which suspicion and countersuspicion, and the inability to enter the other fellow's mind, play in this respect: "You cannot enter into the other man's counter-fear. . . . It is never possible for you to realize or remember properly that since he cannot see the inside of your mind, he can never have the same assurance of your intentions that you have."[7] And—it may be added, transferring this argument to the plane of international affairs—even if a nation could do so, how could it trust in the continuance of good intentions in the case of collective entities with leaders and policies forever changing? How could it, then, afford not to be prepared for "the worst"?

If mutual suspicion and the security dilemma thus constitute the basic underlying condition in a system of separate, independent power units, one would assume that history must consist of one continual race for power and armaments, an unadulterated rush into unending wars, indeed, a chain of "preventive wars." This obviously has not been the case. There have unquestionably been periods in which units have been less suspicious of each other than at other times, periods in which they have felt more secure and have been able to work out systems that gave them even a certain feeling of protection. The security dilemma, in its acute form, was then "mitigated." Thus, while it has confronted units of international politics throughout history, it has done so in various degrees of acuity, depending on the circumstances.

NOTES

1. *Political Realism and Political Idealism* (Chicago, 1951), pp. 3, 14. Reducing the "power urge" to "power competition," "power competition" to concern with "security," and the latter to a social constellation called "security dilemma" constitutes what has been characterized as "pragmatic realism," as distinguished from the "doctrinaire realism" (I would call it more politely "anthropological" or "metaphysical" realism) of the Niebuhr-Morgenthau school of thought, which bases power phenomena ultimately on the corruption of human nature (for this distinction see Wilham T. R. Fox, "Les fondements moraux et juridiques de la politique étrangère américaine," in J. B. Duroselle [ed.], *La politique étrangère et ses fondements* [Paris, 1954], p. 288 f.). For a similar distinction of two kinds of "realism" see Arnold Wolfers, "The Pole of Power and the Pole of Indifference," *World Politics,* 4: 41 f. (1961–62).
2. *Political Realism and Political Idealism,* p. 200.
3. *Christianity and History* (New York, 1950): *History and Human Relations* (New York, 1952). See also his essay "The Tragic Element in Modern International Conflict," *Review of Politics,* 12: 147 ff. (1950).
4. My own book has been called purely "Hobbesian" by some reviewers. It is perhaps so in the first part and so far as the exposition of the security dilemma goes: it hardly is so in the less analytical and more constructive second part, which deals with what I have called "realist liberalism" and which, if historical antecedents are desired, is more indebted to Burke than to either Hobbes or Locke. Certain reviewers have thus charged me with neglecting what I meticulously dealt with in the second half of my book.
5. *History and Human Relations,* pp. 19, 20. Similarly, in his essay quoted above, he terms it "a standing feature of mankind in world history" (p. 161). "Here is the basic pattern of all narrative of human conflict, whatever other patterns may be superimposed upon it later" (p. 154). I cannot go along with him quite that far. To consider the dilemma the basis of *all* past and present conflict seems to me an exaggeration. We shall attempt to show that there is a difference between "security policies" and policies motivated by interests that go beyond security proper. Consider the world conflict provoked by Hitler's policy of world domination. It can hardly be maintained that it was a German security dilemma which lay at the heart of that conflict, but rather one man's, or one regime's ambition to master the world.
6. *Christianity and History,* pp. 96 t.
7. *History and Human Relations,* p. 21.

27

ROBERT JERVIS

COOPERATION UNDER THE
SECURITY DILEMMA

Unless each person thinks that the others will cooperate, he himself will not. And why might he fear that any other person would do something that would sacrifice his own first choice? The other might not understand the situation, or might not be able to control his impulses if he saw a rabbit, or might fear that some other member of the group is unreliable. If the person voices any of these suspicions, others are more likely to fear that he will defect, thus making them more likely to defect, thus making it more rational for him to defect. Of course in this simple case—and in many that are more realistic—there are a number of arrangements that could permit cooperation. But the main point remains: although actors may know that they seek a common goal, they may not be able to reach it.

Even when there is a solution that is everyone's first choice, the international case is characterized by three difficulties not present in the Stag Hunt. First, to the incentives to defect given above must be added the potent fear that even if the other state now supports the status quo, it may become dissatisfied later. No matter how much decision makers are committed to the status quo, they cannot bind themselves and their successors to the same path. Minds can be changed, new leaders can come to power, values can shift, new opportunities and dangers can arise.

The second problem arises from a possible solution. In order to protect their possessions, states often seek to control resources or land outside their own territory. Countries that are not self-sufficient must try to assure that the necessary supplies will continue to flow in wartime. This was part of the explanation for Japan's drive into China and Southeast Asia before World War II. If there were an international authority that could guarantee access, this motive for control would disappear. But since there is not, even a state that would prefer the status quo to increasing its area of control may pursue the latter policy.

When there are believed to be tight linkages between domestic and foreign policy or between the domestic politics of two states, the quest for security may drive states to interfere pre-emptively in the domestic politics of

---

SOURCE: From *World Politics*, Vol. 30, No. 2 (January, 1978). Reprinted with permission of The Johns Hopkins University Press and Robert Jervis.

others in order to provide an ideological buffer zone. Thus, Metternich's justification for supervising the politics of the Italian states has been summarized as follows:

> Every state is absolutely sovereign in its internal affairs. But this implies that every state must do nothing to interfere in the internal affairs of any other. However, any false or pernicious step taken by any state in its internal affairs may disturb the repose of another state, and this consequent disturbance of another state's repose constitutes an interference in that state's internal affairs. Therefore, every state—or rather, every sovereign of a great power—has the duty, in the name of the sacred right of independence of every state, to supervise the governments of smaller states and to prevent them from taking false and pernicious steps in their internal affairs.[1]

More frequently, the concern is with direct attack. In order to protect themselves, states seek to control, or at least to neutralize, areas on their borders. But attempts to establish buffer zones can alarm others who have stakes there, who fear that undesirable precedents will be set, or who believe that their own vulnerability will be increased. When buffers are sought in areas empty of great powers, expansion tends to feed on itself in order to protect what is acquired, as was often noted by those who opposed colonial expansion. Balfour's complaint was typical: "Every time I come to a discussion—at intervals of, say, five years—I find there is a new sphere which we have got to guard, which is supposed to protect the gateways of India. Those gateways are getting further and further away from India, and I do not know how far west they are going to be brought by the General Staff."[2]

Though this process is most clearly visible when it involves territorial expansion, it often operates with the increase of less tangible power and influence. The expansion of power usually brings with it an expansion of responsibilities and commitments; to meet them, still greater power is required. The state will take many positions that are subject to challenge. It will be involved with a wide range of controversial issues unrelated to its core values. And retreats that would be seen as normal if made by a small power would be taken as an index of weakness inviting predation if made by a large one.

The third problem present in international politics but not in the Stag Hunt is the security dilemma: many of the means by which a state tries to increase its security decrease the security of others . . .

OFFENSE, DEFENSE, AND THE SECURITY DILEMMA

Another approach starts with the central point of the security dilemma—that an increase in one state's security decreases the security of others—and examines the conditions under which this proposition holds. Two crucial variables are involved: whether defensive weapons and policies can be distinguished from offensive ones, and whether the defense or the offense has the advantage. The definitions are not always clear, and many cases are difficult to judge, but these two variables shed a great deal of light on the question of whether status-quo powers will adopt compatible security policies. All the variables discussed so far leave the heart of the problem untouched. But when defensive weapons differ from offensive ones, it is possible for a state to make itself more secure without making others less secure. And when the defense has the advantage over the offense, a large increase in one state's security only slightly decreases the security of the others, and status-quo powers can all enjoy a high level of security and largely escape from the state of nature.

OFFENSE-DEFENSE BALANCE

When we say that the offense has the advantage, we simply mean that it is easier to destroy the other's army and take its territory than it is to defend one's own. When the defense has the advantage, it is easier to protect and to hold than it is to move forward, destroy, and take. If effective defenses can be erected quickly, an attacker may be able to keep territory he has taken in an initial victory. Thus, the dominance of the defense made it very hard for Britain and France to push Germany out of France in World War I. But when superior defenses are difficult for an aggressor to improvise on the battlefield and must be constructed during peacetime, they provide no direct assistance to him.

The security dilemma is at its most vicious when commitments, strategy, or technology dictate that the only route to security lies through expansion. Status-quo powers must then act like aggressors; the fact that they would gladly agree to forego the opportunity for expansion in return for guarantees for their security has no implications for their behavior. Even if expansion is not sought as a goal in itself, there will be quick and drastic changes in the distribution of territory and influence. Conversely, when the defense has the advantage, status-quo states can make themselves more secure without gravely endangering others.[3] Indeed, if the defense has enough of an advantage and if the states are of roughly equal size, not only will the security dilemma cease to inhibit status-quo states from cooperating, but aggression will be next to impossible, thus rendering international anarchy relatively unimportant. If states cannot conquer each other, then the lack of sovereignty, although it presents problems of collective goods in a number of areas, no longer forces states to devote their primary attention to self-preservation. Although, if force were not usable, there would be fewer restraints on the use of nonmilitary instruments, these are rarely powerful enough to threaten the vital interests of a major state.

Two questions of the offense-defense balance can be separated. First, does the state have to spend more or less than one dollar on defensive forces to offset each dollar spent by the other side on forces that could be used to attack? If the state has one dollar to spend on increasing its security, should it put it into offensive or defensive forces? Second, with a given inventory of forces, is it better to attack or to defend? Is there an incentive to strike first or to absorb the other's blow? These two aspects are often linked: if each dollar spent on offense can overcome each dollar spent on defense, and if both sides have the same defense budgets, then both are likely to build offensive forces and find it attractive to attack rather than to wait for the adversary to strike.

These aspects affect the security dilemma in different ways. The first has its greatest impact on arms races. If the defense has the advantage, and if the status-quo powers have reasonable subjective security requirements, they can probably avoid an arms race. Although an increase in one side's arms and security will still decrease the other's security, the former's increase will be larger than the latter's decrease. So if one side increases its arms, the other can bring its security back up to its previous level by adding a smaller amount to its forces. And if the first side reacts to this change, its increase will also be smaller than the stimulus that produced it. Thus a stable equilibrium will be reached. Shifting from dynamics to statics, each side can be quite secure with forces roughly equal to those of the other. Indeed, if the defense is much more potent than the offense, each side can be willing to have forces much smaller than the other's, and can be indifferent to a wide range of the other's defense policies.

The second aspect—whether it is better to attack or to defend—influences short-run stability. When the offense has the advantage, a state's reaction to international tension will increase the chances of war. The incentives for pre-emption and the "reciprocal fear of surprise attack" in this situation have been made clear by analyses of the dangers that exist when two countries have first-strike capabilities.[4] There is no way for the state to increase its security without menacing, or even attacking, the other. Even Bismarck, who once called preventive war "committing suicide from fear of death," said that "no government, if it regards war as inevitable even if it does not want it, would be so foolish as to leave to the enemy the choice of time and occasion and to wait for the moment which is most convenient for the enemy."[5] In another arena, the same dilemma applies to the policeman in a dark alley confronting a suspected criminal who appears to be holding a weapon. Though racism may indeed be present, the security dilemma can account for many of the tragic shootings of innocent people in the ghettos.

Beliefs about the course of a war in which the offense has the advantage further deepen the security dilemma. When there are incentives to strike first, a successful attack will usually so weaken the other side that victory will be relatively quick, bloodless, and decisive. It is in these periods when conquest is possible and attractive that states consolidate power internally—for instance, by destroying the feudal barons—and expand externally. There are several consequences that decrease the chance of cooperation among status-quo states. First, war will be profitable for the winner. The costs will be low and the benefits high. Of course, losers will suffer; the fear of losing could induce states to try to form stable cooperative arrangements, but the temptation of victory will make this particularly difficult. Second, because wars are expected to be both frequent and short, there will be incentives for high levels of arms, and quick and strong reaction to the other's increases in arms. The state cannot afford to wait until there is unambiguous evidence that the other is building new weapons. Even large states that have faith in their economic strength cannot wait, because the war will be over before their products can reach the army. Third, when wars are quick, states will have to recruit allies in advance.[6] Without the opportunity for bargaining and re-alignments during the opening stages of hostilities, peacetime diplomacy loses a degree of the fluidity that facilitates balance-of-power policies. Because alliances must be secured during peacetime, the international system is more likely to become bipolar. It is hard to say whether war therefore becomes more or less likely, but this bipolarity increases tension between the two camps and makes it harder for status-quo states to gain the benefits of cooperation. Fourth, if wars are frequent, statemen's perceptual thresholds will be adjusted accordingly and they will be quick to perceive ambiguous evidence as indicating that others are aggressive. Thus, there will be more cases of status-quo powers arming against each other in the incorrect belief that the other is hostile.

When the defense has the advantage, all the foregoing is reversed. The state that fears attack does not pre-empt—since that would be a wasteful use of its military resources—but rather prepares to receive an attack. Doing so does not decrease the security of others, and several states can do it simultaneously; the situation will therefore be stable, and status-quo powers will be able to cooperate. When Herman Kahn argues that ultimatums "are vastly too dangerous to give because . . . they are quite likely to touch off a pre-emptive strike,"[7] he incorrectly assumes that it is always advantageous to strike first.

More is involved than short-run dynamics. When the defense is dominant, wars are likely to become stalemates and can be won only at enormous cost. Relatively small and weak states can hold off larger and stronger ones, or can deter attack by raising the costs of conquest to an unacceptable level. States then approach equality in what they can do to each other. Like the .45-caliber pistol in the American West, fortifications were the "great equalizer" in some periods. Changes in the status quo are less frequent and cooperation is more common wherever the security dilemma is thereby reduced. . . .

The other major variable that affects how strongly the security dilemma operates is whether weapons and policies that protect the state also provide the capability for attack. If they do not, the basic postulate of the security dilemma no longer applies. A state can increase its own security without decreasing that of others. The advantage of the defense can only ameliorate the security dilemma. A differentiation between offensive and defensive stances comes close to abolishing it. Such differentiation does not mean, however, that all security problems will be abolished. If the offense has the advantage, conquest and aggression will still be possible. And if the offense's advantage is great enough, status-quo powers may find it too expensive to protect themselves by defensive forces and decide to procure offensive weapons even though this will menace others. Furthermore, states will still have to worry that even if the other's military posture shows that it is peaceful now, it may develop aggressive intentions in the future. . . .

FOUR WORLDS

The two variables we have been discussing—whether the offense or the defense has the advantage, and whether offensive postures can be distinguished from defensive ones—can be combined to yield four possible worlds.

The first world is the worst for status-quo states. There is no way to get security without menacing others, and security through defense is terribly difficult to obtain. Because offensive and defensive postures are the same, status-quo states acquire the same kind of arms that are sought by aggressors. And because the offense has the advantage over the defense, attacking is the best route to protecting what you have; status-quo states will therefore behave like aggressors. The situation will be unstable. Arms races are likely. Incentives to strike first will turn crises into wars. Decisive victories and conquests will be common. States will grow and shrink rapidly, and it will be hard for any state to maintain its size and influence without trying to increase them. Cooperation among status-quo powers will be extremely hard to achieve.

There are no cases that totally fit this picture, but it bears more than a passing resemblance to Europe before World War I. Britain and Germany, although in many respects natural allies, ended up as enemies. Of course much of the explanation lies in Germany's ill-chosen policy. And from the perspective of our theory, the powers' ability to avoid war in a series of earlier crises cannot be easily explained. Nevertheless, much of the behavior in this period was the product of technology and beliefs that magnified the security dilemma.

	OFFENSE HAS THE ADVANTAGE	DEFENSE HAS THE ADVANTAGE
OFFENSIVE POSTURE NOT DISTINGUISHABLE FROM DEFENSIVE ONE	1 Doubly dangerous.	2 Security dilemma, but security requirements may be compatible.
OFFENSIVE POSTURE DISTINGUISHABLE FROM DEFENSIVE ONE	3 No security dilemma, but aggression possible. Status-quo states can follow different policy than aggressors. Warning given.	4 Doubly stable.

Decision makers thought that the offense had a big advantage and saw little difference between offensive and defensive military postures. The era was characterized by arms races. And once war seemed likely, mobilization races created powerful incentives to strike first.

In the nuclear era, the first world would be one in which each side relied on vulnerable weapons that were aimed at similar forces and each side understood the situation. In this case, the incentives to strike first would be very high—so high that status-quo powers as well as aggressors would be sorely tempted to pre-empt. And since the forces could be used to change the status quo as well as to preserve it, there would be no way for both sides to increase their security simultaneously. Now the familiar logic of deterrence leads both sides to see the dangers in this world. Indeed, the new understanding of this situation was one reason why vulnerable bombers and missiles were replaced. Ironically, the 1950's would have been more hazardous if the decision makers had been aware of the dangers of their posture and had therefore felt greater pressure to strike first. This situation could be recreated if both sides were to rely on MIRVed ICBM's.

In the second world, the security dilemma operates because offensive and defensive postures cannot be distinguished; but it does not operate as strongly as in the first world because the defense has the advantage, and so an increment in one side's strength increases its security more than it decreases the other's. So, if both sides have reasonable subjective security requirements, are of roughly equal power, and the variables discussed earlier are favorable, it is quite likely that status-quo states can adopt compatible security policies. Although a state will not be able to judge the other's intentions from the kinds of weapons it procures, the level of arms spending will give important evidence. Of course a state that seeks a high level of arms might be not an aggressor but merely an insecure state, which if conciliated will reduce its arms, and if confronted will reply in kind. To assume that the apparently excessive level of arms indicates aggressiveness could therefore lead to a response that would deepen the dilemma and create needless conflict. But empathy and skillful statesmanship can reduce this danger. Furthermore, the advantageous position of the defense means that a status-quo state can often maintain a high degree of security with a level of arms lower than that of its expected adversary. Such a state demonstrates that it lacks the ability or desire to alter the status quo, at least at the present time. The strength of the defense also allows states to react slowly and with restraint when they fear that others are menacing them. So, although status-quo powers will to some extent be threatening to others, that extent will be limited.

This world is the one that comes closest to matching most periods in history. Attacking is usually harder than defending because of the strength of fortifications and obstacles. But purely defensive postures are rarely possible because fortifications are usually supplemented by armies and mobile guns which can support an attack. In the nuclear era, this world would be one in which both sides relied on relatively invulnerable ICBM's and believed that limited nuclear war was impossible. Assuming no MIRV's, it would take more than one attacking missile to destroy one of the adversary's. Pre-emption is therefore unattractive. If both sides have large inventories, they can ignore all but drastic increases on the other side. A world of either ICBM's or SLBM's in which both sides adopted the "Schlesinger Doctrine" would probably fit in this category too. The means of preserving the status quo would also be the means of changing it, as we discussed earlier. And the defense usually would have the advantage, because compellence is more difficult than deterrence. Although a state might succeed in changing the status quo on issues that matter much more to it than to others, status-quo powers could deter major provocations under most circumstances.

In the third world there may be no security dilemma, but there are security problems. Because states can procure defensive systems that do not threaten others, the dilemma need not operate. But because the offense has the advantage, aggression is possible, and perhaps easy. If the offense has enough of an advantage, even status-quo states may take the initiative rather than risk being attacked and defeated. If the offense has less of an advantage, stability and cooperation are likely because the status-quo states will procure defensive forces. They need not react to others who are similarly armed, but can wait for the warning they would receive if others started to deploy offensive weapons. But each state will have to watch the others carefully, and there is room for false suspicions. The costliness of the defense and the allure of the offense can lead to unnecessary mistrust, hostility, and war, unless some of the variables discussed earlier are operating to restrain defection.

A hypothetical nuclear world that would fit this description would be one in which both sides relied on SLBM's, but in which ASW techniques were very effective. Offense and defense would be different, but the former would have the advantage. This situation is not likely to occur; but if it did, a status-quo state could show its lack of desire to exploit the other by refraining from threatening its submarines. The desire to have more protecting you than merely the other side's fear of retaliation is a strong one, however, and a state that knows that it would not expand even if its cities were safe is likely to believe that the other would not feel threatened by its ASW program. It is easy to see how such a world could become unstable, and how spirals of tensions and conflict could develop.

The fourth world is doubly safe. The differentiation between offensive and defensive systems permits a way out of the security dilemma; the advantage of the defense disposes of the problems discussed in the previous paragraphs. There is no reason for a status-quo power to be tempted to procure offensive forces, and aggressors give notice of their intentions by the posture they adopt. Indeed, if the advantage of the defense is great enough, there are no security problems. The loss of the ultimate form of the power to alter the status quo would allow greater scope for the exercise of nonmilitary means and probably would tend to freeze the distribution of values.

This world would have existed in the first decade of the 20th century if the decision makers had understood the available technology. In that case, the European powers would have followed different policies both in the long run and in the summer of 1914. Even Germany, facing powerful enemies on both sides, could have made herself secure by developing strong defenses. France could also have made her frontier almost impregnable. Furthermore, when crises arose, no one would have had incentives to strike first. There would have been no competitive mobilization races reducing the time available for negotiations.

In the nuclear era, this world would be one in which the superpowers relied on SLBM's, ASW technology was not up to its task, and limited nuclear options were not taken seriously. We have discussed this situation earlier; here we need only add that, even if our analysis is correct and even if the policies and postures of both sides were to move in this direction, the problem of violence below the nuclear threshold would remain. On issues other than defense of the homeland, there would still be security dilemmas and security problems. But the world would nevertheless be safer than it has usually been.

NOTES

1. Paul Schroeder, *Metternich's Diplomacy at Its Zenith, 1820–1823* (Westport, Conn.: Greenwood Press 1969), 126.
2. Quoted in Michael Howard, *The Continental Commitment* (Harmondsworth, England: Penguin 1974), 67.
3. Thus, when Wolfers, *Discord and Collaboration* (Baltimore: Johns Hopkins University Press 1962), 126, argues that a status-quo state that settles for rough equality of power with its adversary, rather than seeking preponderance, may be able to convince the other to reciprocate by showing that it wants only to protect itself, not menace the other, he assumes that the defense has an advantage.
4. Thomas Schelling, *The Strategy of Conflict* (New York: Columbia University Press 1963), chap. 9.
5. Quoted in Fritz Fischer, *War of Illusions* (New York: Norton 1975), 377, 461.
6. George Quester, *Offense and Defense in the International System* (New York: John Wiley 1977), 105–06.
7. Herman Kahn, *On Thermonuclear War* (Princeton, N.J.: Princeton University Press 1960), 211 (also see 144).

28

HANS J. MORGENTHAU

THE BALANCE OF POWER

THE BALANCE OF POWER

The aspiration for power on the part of several nations, each trying either to maintain or overthrow the status quo, leads of necessity to a configuration that is called the balance of power[1] and to policies that aim at preserving it. We say "of necessity" advisedly. For here again we are confronted with the basic misconception that has impeded the understanding of international politics and has made us the prey of illusions. This misconception asserts that men have a choice between power politics and its necessary outgrowth, the balance of power, on the one hand, and a different, better kind of international relations on the other. It insists that a foreign policy based on the balance of power is one among several possible foreign policies and that only stupid and evil men will choose the former and reject the latter.

It will be shown in the following pages that the international balance of power is only a particular manifestation of a general social principle to which all societies composed of a number of autonomous units owe the autonomy of their component parts; that the balance of power and policies aiming at its preservation are not only inevitable but are an essential stabilizing factor in a society of sovereign nations; and that the instability of the international balance of power is due not to the faultiness of the principle but to the particular conditions under which the principle must operate in a society of sovereign nations.

SOCIAL EQUILIBRIUM

BALANCE OF POWER AS UNIVERSAL CONCEPT

The concept of "equilibrium" as a synonym for "balance" is commonly employed in many sciences—physics, biology, economics, sociology, and political science. It signifies stability within a system composed of a number of autonomous forces. Whenever the equilibrium is disturbed either by an

SOURCE: From *Politics Among Nations: The Struggle for Power and Peace,* 5th ed. Hans J. Morgenthau (New York, NY: Alfred Knopf, 1973), pp. 167–169, 193–194, 207–208. Copyright © 1948, 1954, 1960, 1967, 1972 Alfred A. Knopf, Inc. Reprinted by permission of Alfred A. Knopf, Inc.

outside force or by a change in one or the other elements composing the system, the system shows a tendency to re-establish either the original or a new equilibrium. Thus equilibrium exists in the human body. While the human body changes in the process of growth, the equilibrium persists as long as the changes occurring in the different organs of the body do not disturb the body's stability. This is especially so if the quantitative and qualitative changes in the different organs are proportionate to each other. When, however, the body suffers a wound or loss of one of its organs through outside interference, or experiences a malignant growth or a pathological transformation of one of its organs, the equilibrium is disturbed, and the body tries to overcome the disturbance by reestablishing the equilibrium either on the same or a different level from the one that obtained before the disturbance occurred.[2]

The same concept of equilibrium is used in a social science, such as economics, with reference to the relations between the different elements of the economic system, e.g., between savings and investments, exports and imports, supply and demand, costs and prices. Contemporary capitalism itself has been described as a system of "countervailing power."[3] It also applies to society as a whole. Thus we search for a proper balance between different geographical regions, such as the East and the West, the North and the South; between different kinds of activities, such as agriculture and industry, heavy and light industries, big and small businesses, producers and consumers, management and labor; between different functional groups, such as city and country, the old, the middle-aged, and the young, the economic and the political sphere, the middle classes and the upper and lower classes.

Two assumptions are at the foundation of all such equilibriums: first, that the elements to be balanced are necessary for society or are entitled to exist and, second, that without a state of equilibrium among them one element will gain ascendancy over the others, encroach upon their interests and rights, and may ultimately destroy them. Consequently, it is the purpose of all such equilibriums to maintain the stability of the system without destroying the multiplicity of the elements composing it. If the goal were stability alone, it could be achieved by allowing one element to destroy or overwhelm the others and take their place. Since the goal is stability plus the preservation of all the elements of the system, the equilibrium must aim at preventing any element from gaining ascendancy over the others. The means employed to maintain the equilibrium consist in allowing the different elements to pursue their opposing tendencies up to the point where the tendency of one is not so strong as to overcome the tendency of the others, but strong enough to prevent the others from overcoming its own. . . .

THE "HOLDER" OF THE BALANCE

Whenever the balance of power is to be realized by means of an alliance—and this has been generally so throughout the history of the Western world—two possible variations of this pattern have to be distinguished. To use the metaphor of the balance, the system may consist of two scales, in each of which are to be found the nation or nations identified with the same policy of the status quo or of imperialism. The continental nations of Europe have generally operated the balance of power in this way.

2) The system may, however, consist of two scales plus a third element, the "holder" of the balance or the "balancer." The balancer is not permanently identified with the policies of either nation or group of nations. Its only objective within the system is the maintenance of the balance, regardless of the concrete policies the balance will serve. In consequence, the holder of the balance will throw its weight at one time in this scale, at another time in the other scale, guided only by one consideration—the relative position of the scales. Thus it will put its weight always in the scale that seems to be higher than the other because it is lighter. The balancer may become in a relatively short span of history consecutively the friend and foe of all major powers, provided they all consecutively threaten the balance by approaching predominance over the others and are in turn threatened by others about to gain such predominance. To paraphrase a statement of Palmerston: While the holder of the balance has no permanent friends, it has no permanent enemies either; it has only the permanent interest of maintaining the balance of power itself. The balancer is in a position of "splendid isolation." It is isolated by its own choice; for, while the two scales of the balance must vie with each other to add its weight to theirs in order to gain the overweight necessary for success, it must refuse to enter into permanent ties with either side. The holder of the balance waits in the middle in watchful detachment to see which scale is likely to sink. Its isolation is "splendid"; for, since its support or lack of support is the decisive factor in the struggle for power, its foreign policy, if cleverly managed, is able to extract the highest price from those whom it supports. But since this support, regardless of the price paid for it, is always uncertain and shifts from one side to the other in accordance with the movements of the balance, its policies are resented and subject to condemnation on moral grounds. Thus it has been said of the outstanding balancer in modern times, Great Britain, that it lets others fight its wars, that it keeps Europe divided in order to dominate the continent, and that the fickleness of its policies is such as to make alliances with Great Britain impossible. "Perfidious Albion" has become a byword in the mouths of those who either were unable to gain Great Britain's support, however hard they tried, or else lost it after they had paid what seemed to them too high a price.

The holder of the balance occupies the key position in the balance-of-power system, since its position determines the outcome of the struggle for power. It has, therefore, been called the "arbiter" of the system, deciding who will win and who will lose. By making it impossible for any nation or combination of nations to gain predominance over the others, it preserves its own independence as well as the independence of all the other nations, and is thus a most powerful factor in international politics.

The holder of the balance can use this power in three different ways. It can make its joining one or the other nation or alliance dependent upon certain conditions favorable to the maintenance or restoration of the balance. It can make its support of the peace settlement dependent upon similar conditions. It can, finally, in either situation see to it that the objectives of its own national policy, apart from the maintenance of the balance of power, are realized in the process of balancing the power of others. . . .

THE UNREALITY OF THE BALANCE OF POWER

This uncertainty of all power calculations not only makes the balance of power incapable of practical application but leads also to its very negation in practice. Since no nation can be sure that its calculation of the distribution of power at any particular moment in history is correct, it must at least make sure that, whatever errors it may commit, they will not put the nation at a disadvantage in the contest for power. In other words, the nation must try to have at least a margin of safety which will allow it to make erroneous calculations and still maintain the balance of power. To that effect, all nations actively engaged in the struggle for power must actually aim not at a balance—that is, equality—of power, but at superiority of power in their own behalf. And since no nation can foresee how large its miscalculations will turn out to be, all nations must ultimately seek the maximum of power obtainable under the circumstances. Only thus can they hope to attain the maximum margin of safety commensurate with the maximum of errors they might commit. The limitless aspiration for power, potentially always present, as we have seen, in the power drives of nations, finds in the balance of power a mighty incentive to transform itself into an actuality.

Since the desire to attain a maximum of power is universal, all nations must always be afraid that their own miscalculations and the power increases of other nations might add up to an inferiority for themselves which they must at all costs try to avoid. Hence all nations who have gained an apparent edge over their competitors tend to consolidate that advantage and use it for changing the distribution of power permanently in their favor. This can be done through diplomatic pressure by bringing the full weight of that advantage to bear upon the other nations, compelling them to make the concessions that will consolidate the temporary advantage into a permanent superiority. It can also be done by war. Since in a balance-of-power system all nations live in constant fear lest their rivals deprive them, at the first opportune moment, of their power position, all nations have a vital interest in anticipating such a development and doing unto the others what they do not want the others to do unto them.

NOTES

1. The term "balance of power" is used in the text with four different meanings: (1) as a policy aimed at a certain state of affairs, (2) as an actual state of affairs, (3) as an approximately equal distribution of power, (4) as any distribution of power. Whenever the term is used without qualification, it refers to an actual state of affairs in which power is distributed among several nations with approximate equality.

2. Cf., for instance, the impressive analogy between the equilibrium in the human body and in society in Walter B. Cannon, *The Wisdom of the Body* (New York: W. W. Norton and Company, 1932), pp. 293, 294.
3. John K. Galbraith, *American Capitalism, the Concept of Countervailing Power* (Boston: Houghton Mifflin, 1952).

29

A. F. K. ORGANSKI

CRITICISM OF BALANCE OF POWER THEORY

The idea of a balance of power is certainly plausible and surely interesting. Indeed, it has been proclaimed so many times and by such august authorities that it has entered into that realm of ideas that people almost take for granted. In view of this, it is shocking how badly the theory stands up under even the most cursory critical examination. The sad truth is that the balance of power is neither a logical abstraction nor an accurate description of empirical fact. . . .

The major ambiguity of the theory lies in the key definition of what constitutes a "balance." How is power distributed among the nations of the world when a "balance of power" exists? Given the analogy of the scales, one would think that this was perfectly clear. The power of two nations or two groups of nations ought to be "balanced" when it is roughly equal, when neither side is noticeably stronger than the other. But this is not the case. Through most of the nineteenth century, England and her allies enjoyed a tremendous preponderance of power over their rivals, and yet England is said to have been maintaining the balance of power. How can this be? Is a balance an equal distribution of power or an unequal distribution of power?

Martin Wight has pointed out that one must distinguish between an objective and a subjective view of the balance of power:

> The historian will say that there is a balance when the opposing groups seem to him to be equal in power. The statesman will say that there is a balance when he thinks that his side is stronger than the other. And he will say that his country *holds* the balance, when it has freedom to join one side or the other according to its own interests.[1]

SOURCE: From *World Politics*, 2nd ed., A. F. K. Organski (New York, NY: Alfred Knopf, 1968), pp. 282–283, 286–290. Reprinted with permission of McGraw-Hill, Inc.

This is a useful distinction. The difficulty is that at least two of these three definitions of a balance are mutually exclusive. We cannot accept them all as equally valid and then erect a theory around a word which means sometimes one thing and sometimes another. Yet this is exactly what has been done. In reading any discussion of the balance of power, the reader must keep his wits about him, for he will find that sometimes the term balance of power is used to refer to an equal distribution of power, sometimes to a preponderance of power, sometimes to the *existing* distribution of power *regardless* of whether it is balanced or not, sometimes to *any* stable distribution of power. Worst of all, the term is sometimes used as a synonym for power politics in general. The balance is all things to all men.[2]

When it comes to the concept of the balancer, we encounter still other ambiguities. Indeed, the very need for a balancer contradicts many of the assumptions of the theory. If the system is self-regulated, no balancer should be required. Even if we assume that a balancer is necessary, there are difficulties. If we are going to look at history and see whether the balance of power does in fact operate, we must know just what it is that the balancer does. What is the distribution of power before it intervenes, and what is it after it intervenes? Again the theory is far from clear.

When the system is working correctly, a balance of power is supposed to exist in the normal run of events. If the balance is upset, the balancer intervenes and restores it. We gather, then, that the distribution of power is initially balanced (equally distributed) among the major nations or groups of nations. The balancer itself apparently does not count in this calculation, because it remains aloof.

Then events change, and the balance is upset. One side becomes stronger than the other, but the difference in power cannot be very great, for the balancer is supposed to intervene immediately to rectify the balance. The balancer, then, intervenes when the scales are just beginning to tip, throwing its weight on the lighter side. This is supposed to redress the balance (restore an equal distribution of power). But does it? The balancer is always a major nation (England, for example, is said to be too weak to act as a balancer today), and if a major nation moves to either side of the scales, the result should be a great preponderance of power on its side, not a balance. Thus, intervention by the balancer brings about the very thing it is said to be designed to prevent. This is the point where it becomes useful to call a preponderance a balance, for otherwise the balancer is not a balancer at all. Thus, the ambiguity as to what constitutes a balance obscures a basic contradiction in the theory.

It also seems that the balancer is somehow different from all the other nations. All other states are said to be bent on maximizing their power and thus would make use of a preponderance of power to upset peace and conquer their neighbors, certainly a state of affairs to be avoided. This quest for maximum power is a universal law, but it apparently does not apply to the balancer (another contradiction, alas), for the balancer is different. The balancer is aloof, derives its power from outside the balance, and uses it only to maintain the balance. Unlike its fellow nations, the balancer does not strive to maximize its power and so will not press the advantage it gains by having a preponderance of power. The balancer derives full satisfaction from rebuilding and maintaining the balance. The balancer is reserved, self-restrained, humane, moderate, and wise. . . .

ERRONEOUS ASSUMPTIONS

Once the ambiguities are penetrated, the basic errors of the balance of power theory become apparent. To begin with, it is based upon two erroneous assumptions: (1) that nations are fundamentally static units whose power is not changed from within and (2) that nations have no permanent ties to each other but move about freely, motivated primarily by considerations of power.

Unchanging Units

The concept of the balance of power is said to be dynamic, and yet the units involved in the balancing are strangely static. The system described assumes a number of nations of roughly equal strength. Furthermore, it assumes that the strength of each nation remains about the same unless it increases its armaments, conquers new territory, or wins new allies. Apparently, a nation can suddenly become ambitious and aggressive and can prepare to fight, but it cannot actually gain in power without infringing upon the rights of other nations, and the other nations, of course, will act to prevent this. Two nations can ally themselves against a third creating a bloc of greater power, but this does not change the power of each individual nation involved. It merely adds their power together for certain common purposes.

In such a world, international politics becomes a giant chess game or quadrille, to use two of the figures of speech that are often applied. The pieces are of a given power, but they are skillfully manipulated in various ways as the game is played. The dancers remain the same but the figures of the dance change. In such a world, skill in political intrigue and in manipulation is of crucial importance. In the last analysis, the outcome may depend upon victory in warfare, but war is viewed as a breakdown of the system. When the balance is working, success in international politics depends primarily upon the skillful formation of alliances and counteralliances. The dynamism of the system is provided by occasional wars and peace settlements that redistribute territory and by the constant shifting of allies.

It is possible that these were in fact the major dynamic factors in international politics until about the middle of the eighteenth century, but as we have observed repeatedly, the nature of international politics has changed considerably since then. Back in the dynastic period in Europe, "nations" were kings and their courts, and politics was indeed a sport. A king could increase his power by raising an army, by conquering a province, by marrying a queen, or by allying himself with a powerful neighbor but all of this was considerably removed from the daily life of ordinary citizens, who cared little about kings and their wars.

Two modern forces, nationalism and industrialism, have transformed the nature of international politics. Under the influence of nationalism, the hundreds of principalities and city-states that lay scattered across Central Europe were collected into nations, and more recently the same thing has happened in other parts of the world. These unifications have not merely created new and larger units; they have created a new kind of unit—nations whose citizens can be mobilized into an awesome instrument of power by the ruler who is skilled in new techniques. Napoleon was perhaps the first of these new national leaders, but we have seen many since. The time-honored defenses of the balance of power do not stop these men, for their initial power stems from within the nations they rule, from a place beyond the reach of jealous and fearful neighbors.

And if this is true of the power springing from nationalism, how much truer is it of the power that comes with industrialization. The theory of the balance of power takes no account whatever of the tremendous spurt of power that occurs when a nation first industrializes. It was England's factories, not her diplomats that let her dominate the nineteenth-century world. Until the nations of the world are all industrialized, the distribution of power among nations will continue to shift, and any momentary equilibrium will be upset. A theory which assumes that the major road to national power lies in the waging of wars and in the formation of alliances has missed the most important development of modern times.

No Permanent Ties

A second major assumption underlying the whole concept of the balance of power is that nations have freedom of movement, that they are free to switch sides from one coalition to another whenever they desire and that in so doing they are motivated primarily by considerations of power. This applies particularly to the nation acting as the balancer, since this nation *must* be free to join the weaker side in order to redress the balance.

Such an assumption appears to divorce power considerations from the rest of life, in particular from the hard facts of economic life. Again, this assumption may have been more true of preindustrial, dynastic Europe. In those days, subsistence agriculture occupied the great majority of people, trade was mostly local, and although international trade existed and was growing in importance, economic relations between nations were not of great importance. However, the assumption surely does not hold for the present-day world, or even for nineteenth-century Europe. England was the center of an international economy, much as the United States is today, and she could no more switch to the side of those who sought to upset the order she headed than she could move to Mars. Sixteenth-century monarchs might make or break alliances through a royal marriage or in a fit of royal temper, but modern rulers cannot. Years of propaganda are required before a population will believe that a former enemy is a friend or vice versa. A democratic government may be unable to switch sides in some cases, and even a totalitarian government may find its efforts embarrassed by popular resistance to too sudden a switch. Nor is a government likely to want to shift sides suddenly when its economy as well as its sentiments are intricately meshed with those of other nations.

NOTES

1. Martin Wight, *Power Politics* (London: Royal Institute of International Affairs, 1946), "Looking Forward," pamphlet no. 8, p. 45.
2. See Inis Claude, *Power and International Relations* (New York: Random House, 1962), chap. 2; Ernst Haas, "The Balance of Power: Prescription, Concept, or Propaganda," in James Rosenau (ed.), *International Politics and Foreign Policy* (New York: Free Press, 1961), pp. 318–29.

30

INIS L. CLAUDE, JR.

COLLECTIVE SECURITY AS AN APPROACH TO PEACE

If the movement for international organization in the twentieth century can be said to have a preoccupation, a dominant purpose, a supreme ideal, it is clear that the achievement of collective security answers that description. Other objectives have figured prominently in the development of international organization, but the hope of establishing a successful collective security system has been the primary motivating force behind the organizational enterprises of our time. *Security* represents the end; *collective* defines the nature of the means; *system* denotes the institutional component of the effort to make the means serve the end. It is doubtful whether international organization can properly be evaluated exclusively in terms of its success or failure in realizing

SOURCE: From *Swords Into Plowshares,* Inis L. Claude, Jr. (New York, NY: Random House, Inc., 1964), pp. 223–225, 227–238. Copyright © 1956, 1959, 1964 by Inis L. Claude, Jr. Reprinted by permission of Random House, Inc.

this ideal, but it is certain that this criterion applies in judging the extent to which the aspirations of its creative spirits have been satisfied.

While collective security has been the central concern of the builders of international agencies, it has not been regarded as an exclusivistic approach to peace. It has, for instance, been intimately related to pacific settlement. Collective security is necessary because pacific settlement cannot always succeed; it is feasible, if at all, only because pacific settlement succeeds most of the time; and its existence increases the probability that pacific settlement will succeed more of the time. Hence, the creators of the League and the United Nations have sought to combine the techniques of moral inducement and coercive threat for the preservation of peace.

Collective security has generally been regarded as a halfway house between the terminal points of international anarchy and world government. Given the assumption that the former has become intolerable and the latter remains, at least for the foreseeable future, unattainable, collective security is conceived as an alternative, far enough from anarchy to be useful and far enough from world government to be feasible. Advocates of collective security have differed as to whether it should be envisaged as a temporary expedient, contributing to the ultimate possibility of world government, or a permanent solution to the problem of order, eliminating the ultimate necessity of world government. But, regardless of their differing expectations concerning the probability that collective security will yield ideal results, they have been united in the belief that its requirements are less revolutionary than those posed by world government, and that it is therefore within the realm of possibility in an age dominated by the basic values of a multistate system.

It should be noted in the beginning that collective security is a specialized concept, a technical term in the vocabulary of international relations. Its definition may be approached by the process of elimination: it represents the means for achieving national security and world order which remain when security through isolation is discarded as an anachronism, security through self-help is abandoned as a practical impossibility, security through alliance is renounced as a snare and a delusion, and security through world government is brushed aside as a dream irrelevant to reality. The concept of collective security may be stated in deceptively simple terms: it is the principle that, in the relations of states, everyone is his brother's keeper; it is an international translation of the slogan, "one for all and all for one"; [1] it is the proposition that aggressive and unlawful use of force by any nation against any nation will be met by the combined force of all other nations.

Emphasis upon the specific character of collective security is particularly essential because in recent years the term has been so loosely used that it has virtually lost its original meaning. The kind of semantic debasement which collective security has undergone cannot be prevented, and it may be argued that it should not be resented, in accordance with the precept of tolerance that every man has as good a right as any other to use whatever words he pleases to express whatever meaning he wants to convey. Yet, just as a considerable medical literature would be invalidated if doctors fell into the habit of using the word "penicillin" for what has previously been called "insulin," a substantial body of international thought is confused by the tendency to use "collective security" to refer to concepts alien to its original meaning.

The term *collective security* is now being generally applied to arrangements of virtually any sort which involve the probability of joint military action in a crisis by two or more states. Thus, it has come to be a synonym, used for euphemistic purposes, for the policy of creating alliances to function in a balance of power system. For instance, an editorial in the *New York Times* interpreted the development of NATO as both a necessary return to the system of balance of power and a symbolic recognition by Western nations "that their only salvation lies in standing together in a system of collective security."[2] Senator McMahon defined collective security as "the attempt to weld together a military alliance to keep the peace such as we have attempted to do in the North Atlantic Pact,"[3] and General Omar Bradley described that treaty as "our collective-security alliance."[4] An official American publication in 1952 asserted that a treaty of alliance, signed by the United States, Australia, and New Zealand, "pledges these three nations to a program of collective security."[5]

Such statements ignore the fact that collective security was originally set out not only as something different from an alliance system, but as a consciously contrived substitute for such a system, based upon the supposition that the latter was, as Wilson put it, "forever discredited."[6] Wilson, the chief spokesman for the concept of collective security as the fundamental principle of the League of Nations, made it absolutely clear that the new concept was incompatible with, and antithetical to, a policy of alliances.[7] . . .

THE THEORY OF COLLECTIVE SECURITY

Collective security depends less heavily than pacific settlement upon the precise accuracy of a set of assumptions about the nature and causes of war. By the same token, it purports to be applicable to a wider variety of belligerent situations, assuming that not all wars arise from the same type of causation. It is at once a second line of defense against the wars which pacific settlement should but does not prevent, and a supplementary defense, on the flanks of pacific settlement, against the wars which are not within the range of the latter; thus, it adds to the protective system of world peace the benefits of both defense in depth and defense in breadth.

The necessary assumption of collective security is simply that wars are likely to occur and that they ought to be prevented. The conflicts may be the fruit of unreflective passion or of deliberate planning; they may represent efforts to settle disputes, effects of undefinably broad situations of hostility, or calculated means to realize ambitious designs of conquest. They may be launched by the irresponsible dictate of cynical autocrats or the democratic will of a chauvinistic people—although the champions of collective security have frequently evinced the conviction that most wars are likely to stem from the former type of initiative. The point is that the theory of collective security is not invalidated by the discovery that the causes, functional purposes, and initiatory mechanisms of war are varied.

However, the basic assumption about the problem of war is more precise in certain important respects. Collective security is a specialized instrument of international policy in the sense that it is intended only to forestall the arbitrary and aggressive use of force, not to provide enforcement mechanisms for the whole body of international law; it assumes that, so far as the problem of world order is concerned, the heart of the matter is the restraint of military action rather than the guarantee of respect for all legal obligations. Moreover, it assumes that this ideal may be realized, or at least approximated, by a reformation of international policy, without the institution of a revolution in the structure of the international system.

To some degree, collective security shares with pacific settlement the belief that governments, or the peoples who may be in a position to influence their governments, are amenable to moral appeals against the misuse of force, and it may also be described as a rationalistic approach to peace. But the rational appeal directed by collective security to potential belligerents is not so much a suggestion of a decent and sensible alternative to violence, which characterizes pacific settlement, as a threat of dire consequences if the warning against violence is imprudently ignored. The stock in trade of pacific settlement is investigation, conciliation, arbitration, and the like—equipment for inducing rational decision to follow a morally respectable course; the stock in trade of collective security is diplomatic, economic, and military sanctions—equipment for inducing rational decision to avoid threatened damage to the national self-interest. Pacific settlement assumes, at least for tactical purposes, the moral ambiguity of a situation of conflict; avoiding an initial judgment on the moral merits of the positions held by disputants, it applies pressure equally to the two parties to adopt positive moral attitudes conducive to an agreed solution. Collective security, on the other hand, assumes the moral clarity of a situation, the assignability of guilt for a threat to or breach of the peace; starting by tagging one state as the culpable party, it then discards primary concern with the factor of international morality in favor of the principle of power. Whereas pacific settlement fails if it proves impossible to make states rationally calm enough to behave morally, collective security falls down if either of two assumptions proves invalid: that blame can be confidently assessed for international crises, and that states are rationally calculating enough to behave prudently.

Collective security may be described as resting upon the proposition that war can be prevented by the deterrent effect of overwhelming power upon states which are too rational to invite certain defeat. In this respect, it is fundamentally similar to a balance of power system involving defensive alliances. However, as we shall see, collective security has other essential aspects which are its distinguishing marks, and which validate the Wilsonian claim that collective security is basically different from the system of policy which it was explicitly designed to replace.

However simple the collective security approach may seem upon superficial acquaintance, the truth is that it assumes the satisfaction of an extraordinarily complex network of requirements. The first group of prerequisites includes those of a *subjective* character, related to the general acceptability of the responsibilities of collective security; the second group may be characterized as a category of *objective* requirements, related to the suitability of the global situation to the operation of collective security.

Subjective Requirements of Collective Security

In contrast to pacific settlement, which is mainly concerned to evoke peaceful attitudes from quarreling states, collective security depends upon a positive commitment to the value of world peace by the great mass of states. Its basic requirement is that the premise of the "indivisibility of peace" should be deeply established in the thinking of governments and peoples. Collective security rests upon the assumption that it is true, and that governments and peoples can be expected to act upon the truth, that the fabric of human society has become so tightly woven that a breach anywhere threatens disintegration everywhere. Unchecked aggression in one direction emboldens and helps to empower its perpetrator to penetrate in other directions, or, more abstractly, successful use of lawless force in one situation contributes to the undermining of respect for the principle of order in all situations. The geographical remoteness of aggression is irrelevant; Kant's prophetic insight that "The intercourse . . . which has been everywhere steadily increasing between the nations of the earth, has now extended so enormously that a violation of right in one part of the world is felt all over it,"[8] must be universally acknowledged. The world's thinking must undergo the transformation that was exemplified by British Prime Minister Neville Chamberlain, when he switched from sighing, in the fall of 1938, "How horrible, fantastic, incredible it is that we should be digging trenches and trying on gas-masks here, because of a quarrel in a far-away country between people of whom we know nothing," to asserting, one year later, that "If, in spite of all, we find ourselves forced to embark upon a struggle . . . we shall not be fighting for the political future of a faraway city in a foreign land; we shall be fighting for the preservation of those principles, the destruction of which would involve the destruction of all possibility of peace and security for the peoples of the world."[9] Collective security requires rejection of the isolationist ideal of localizing wars, in terms of both its possibility and its desirability, and recommends to all the classic advice proffered by Alfred Nemours, the representative of Haiti, in the League debate concerning Italian aggression against Ethiopia: "Great or small, strong or weak, near or far, white or coloured, let us never forget that one day we may be somebody's Ethiopia."[10]

In requiring conviction of the indivisibility of peace, collective security demands what is essentially a factual agreement; it then imposes a related normative requirement: loyalty to the world community. The system will work only if the peoples of the world identify their particular interests so closely with the general interest of mankind that they go beyond mere recognition of interdependence to a feeling of involvement in the destiny of all nations. The responsibilities of participation in a collective security system are too onerous to be borne by any but a people actuated by genuine sympathy for any and all victims of aggression, and loyalty to the values of a global system of law and order. The operation of a collective security system must always be precarious unless the conviction that what is good for world peace is necessarily good for the nation is deeply engrained in governments and peoples.

The leaders of nations and their constituents must be prepared to subordinate to the requirements of the collective security system their apparent and immediate national interest—to incur economic loss and run the risk of war, even in situations when the national interest does not seem to be involved, or when this policy seems to conflict with the national interest or to undermine established national policies. This means that states must renounce both pacifism and the right to use war as an instrument of national policy, while standing ready to resort to force for the fulfillment of their international obligations. As Arnold J. Toynbee has put it: "We have got to give up war for all the purposes for which sovereign communities have fought since war has been in existence, but we have still got to be willing to accept the risks and the losses of war for a purpose for which hitherto people have never thought of fighting." [11] It means that states must abandon as illusions any convictions they may have traditionally held that they are peculiarly safe against aggression, overcome the temptation to regard any specific conflict as immaterial to or even favorable to their interests, and dedicate themselves to the performance of duties which may upset the equilibrium of their national life and disrupt relationships which they have laboriously constructed. All this theoretically takes place within a system which assumes the maintenance of the basic multistate character of international society, and demands not that national loyalties be abandoned, but that they merely be harmonized by the enlightened conception that national interests are identifiable with the global interest. What it really requires is that a state adopt this conception once and for all, and thereafter act on the assumption that it is valid, despite contrary appearances that may arise from time to time.

Collective security is a design for providing the certainty of collective action to frustrate aggression—for giving to the potential victim the reassuring knowledge, and conveying to the potential law-breaker the deterring conviction, that the resources of the community will be mobilized against any abuse of national power. This ideal permits no *ifs* or *buts*. If it merely encourages states to hope for collective support in case they are victims of attack, it must fail to stimulate the revisions of state behavior at which it aims and upon which its ultimate success depends; if the hope which it encourages should prove illusory, it stands convicted of contributing to the downfall of states whose security it purported to safeguard. If it merely warns potential aggressors that they may encounter concerted resistance, it fails to achieve full effectiveness in its basic function, that of discouraging resort to violence, and if its warning should be revealed as a bluff, it stimulates the contempt for international order which it is intended to eradicate. The theory of collective security is replete with absolutes, of which none is more basic than the requirement of certainty.

In accordance with this essential of the collective security system, the states which constitute the system must be willing to accept commitments which involve the sacrifice of their freedom of action or inaction in the most crucial of future situations. They must say in advance what they will do; they must agree to dispense with *ad hoc* national judgments, and bind themselves to a pattern of action from which they will not be at liberty to deviate. This pattern may be prescribed, at least in part, by the explicit terms of a multilateral treaty. It may, additionally or alternatively, be determined by the decision of an international agency. What is essential, in either case, is that the states upon which the operation of collective security depends should clearly renounce the right to withhold their support from a collective undertaking against whatever aggressions may arise.

Moreover, the renunciation of national decision-making capacity necessarily includes surrender of discretionary competence to resort to forcible action in the absence of international authorization. Collective security can tolerate the maintenance of a carefully restricted right of self-defense, to be exercised within the bounds of international supervision, but it is a fundamental requirement of a full-fledged system that an international authority should be the master of all situations involving the use of coercive instruments. Basically, the state must abdicate its traditional control over the elements of national power, accepting the responsibility to act or to refrain from acting in accordance with the stipulations of a multilateral agreement and the dictates of an international agency. Thus, the state exposes itself to obligations determined by the community for dealing with situations which may be created by the action and policy of other states.

It is very clear that the acceptance of this kind of commitment is a drastic if not a revolutionary act for a national state. It involves a relinquishment of sovereignty in the most crucial area of policy; "To all intents and purposes a state's right of disposal of its military potential is the most sensitive segment of national sovereignty, and that part which traditionally is impervious to foreign decision or control."[12] For constitutional democracies, it implies a transfer of power to make vital decisions which is likely to collide with established concepts of the distribution of governmental functions and powers, and a rigidification of national policy which is difficult to reconcile with the democratic principle that the people have an inalienable right to change their minds through the continuous operation of the mechanism of majority rule. It requires democratic statesmen, as democrats, to follow policies which their people may not approve in the circumstances, and, as statesmen, to abjure the exercise of the most cherished virtue of statesmanship, that of demonstrating empirical wisdom by making sound decisions in the light of the unique characteristics of a given situation. Thus, the good politician is required to betray the democratic ideal of doing what the people want, the shrewd politician is required to violate his vote-getting instincts, and the wise statesman is required to follow the rule book in a manner befitting an automaton. Finally, it means that governments and peoples must develop an unprecedented degree of confidence in the judgment and good will of foreigners, for the discretionary authority which is subtracted from the competence of the democratic majority and the national leadership is added to that of an international organization. Indeed, it is ultimately transferred to unidentifiable foreign states—those whose policy may be so obtuse that they provoke aggression against themselves, and those whose policy may be so cynical that they deliberately resort to aggression.

The essential commitments of a collective security system necessitate the willingness of nations to fight for the status quo. Collective security is not inherently an attempt to perpetuate an existing state of affairs; it is entirely compatible with a system of peaceful change, and such a system is in fact absolutely necessary for producing the kind of status quo and the kind of attitudes toward the status quo that are required if the ideal of collective security is to be realized. But at any given moment, the function of collective security is to combat assaults upon the currently legitimate pattern of national rights, and the responsibility of participating peoples is to cooperate in that enterprise without regard to any underlying sympathies they may have for claims of frustrated justice that may be enunciated by the assailants. As a general proposition, peace through justice must be the watchword of collective security. However, its provisional rule of action can hardly be any other than peace *over* justice, and the member states of the system must be prepared to go to war to preserve the system which keeps the peace, even though this involves injury to innocent people and the squelching of valid objections to the moral legitimacy of the legally established state of things.

A basic requirement of collective security is that it function impartially. It is a design for preserving the integrity of the anonymous victim of attack by the anonymous aggressor; it is no respecter of states, but an instrument to be directed against any aggressor, on behalf of any violated state. This description points to one of the significant differences between a balance of power system and a collective security system: in the former, collaborative activity is directed against *undue power,* as such, while in the latter it is turned against *aggressive policy,* whether that policy be pursued by a giant which threatens to grow to earth-shaking proportions or by a pygmy which has scant prospect of becoming a major factor in world politics.[13]

The demands imposed by the principle of anonymity upon the states which form a collective security system provide further indications of the distinction between the new and the old regimes for the management of international relations. If collective security is to operate impartially, governments and peoples must exhibit a fundamental flexibility of policy and sentiment. France must be as ready to defend Germany as Belgium against aggression, and Britain must be equally willing to join in collective sanctions against the United States or the Soviet Union. In short, collective security recognizes no traditional friendships and no inveterate enmities, and permits no alliances *with* or alliances *against*. It is true that a balance of power system, in the long run, requires similar changes of partners and redefinition of villains, but in the short run, such a system operates through the basic mechanism of alliances. For the purposes of collective security, an alliance is either superfluous—since every state is already committed to the defense of every other state—or it is incompatible with the system—since it implies that its members will defend each other but not outsiders, and raises doubt that they will join in international sanctions as readily against one of their number as against other states. The principle of alliance tends to inject into international relations a concept of the advance identification of friends and enemies that is alien to the basic proposition of collective security: whoever commits aggression is everybody's enemy; whoever resists aggression is everybody's friend.

All of this adds up to the fundamental subjective requirement that all states be willing to entrust their destinies to collective security. Confidence is the quintessential condition of the success of the system; states must be prepared to rely upon its effectiveness and impartiality. If they are so prepared, they are likely to behave in such a way as to maximize the probability that this confidence will prove justified. If they are not, they are almost certain to resort to policies which undermine the system and make it unworthy of the confidence which they declined to bestow upon it. The familiar dilemma of circularity appears here: collective security cannot work unless the policies of states are inspired by confidence in the system, but it requires an extraordinary act of political faith for states to repose confidence in the system without previous demonstration that collective security works. The stakes are high in the world of power politics, and states do not lightly undertake experiments in the critical field of national security.

This analysis of the subjective requirements of collective security proves nothing if not that the realization of the ideal first institutionally espoused by the League makes singularly stringent demands upon the human beings of the twentieth century. It calls for a moral transformation of political man. It offends the most pacific and the most bellicose of men; it challenges neutralism and isolationism as well as militarism and imperialism; it clashes with the views of the most conservative supporters of national sovereignty and the most liberal proponents of democratic control of foreign policy; it demands alike the dissolution of ancient national hatreds and the willingness to abandon traditional national friendships. Indeed, the question inexorably arises whether the demands imposed upon the human mind and will by collective security are in truth less rigorous than those imposed by the ideal of world government. Is collective security really a halfway house? If human beings were fully prepared to meet the subjective requirements of collective security, would they be already prepared for world government?

Objective Requirements of Collective Security

The prerequisites thus far discussed have to do with the human situation. Collective security also depends upon the satisfaction of a number of basic conditions in the external sphere—in the power situation, the legal situation, and the organizational situation.

The ideal setting for a collective security system is a world characterized by a considerable diffusion of power. The most favorable situation would be one in which all states commanded approximately equal resources, and the least favorable, one marked by the concentration of effective power in a very few major states. The existence of several great powers of roughly equal strength is essential to collective security.

Given a power configuration meeting this minimal requirement, a collective security system next demands substantial universality of membership. It might be argued that potential aggressors might just as well be omitted, since they presumably will dishonor both the negative obligations and the positive responsibilities incumbent upon members, or that they might better be left out, since their absence will facilitate the planning and initiation of collective measures to restrain their misbehavior. This is a plausible view, even though it ignores the value for an organized community of having lawless elements clearly subject to the local regime—surely, criminals are the last persons who ought to be formally exempted from the bonds of the law. The basic objection to this position is that it misses the point that collective security knows no "probable aggressor" but assumes that *any* state may become an aggressor. In a sense, this is an expression of the *abstractness* which is a leading characteristic of collective security; for better or for worse, collective security is not an expedient for dealing with a concrete threat to world peace, but a design for a system of world order. In another sense, however, this is an implication of the *generality* of collective security. The system is intended to provide security for every state against the particular threat which arouses its national anxiety, and if every potential aggressor, every state which is the source of the misgivings of another state, were excluded, the system would have very sparse membership indeed.

In any event, a workable system of collective security can hardly afford the exclusion or abstention of a major power. It is particularly damaging to have an important commercial and naval power on the outside, for the danger of its refusal to co-operate and to acquiesce in the infringement of its normal rights is sufficient to render improbable the effective application of economic sanctions to an aggressor. The doctrine of collective security relies heavily upon the proposition that nonmilitary measures will normally be adequate to stifle aggression—its military commitments are acceptable only because of the presumption that they will rarely be invoked—but economic sanctions are peculiarly dependent upon universal application for their efficacy.

The basic importance of the objective conditions of power diffusion and organizational comprehensiveness lies in the fact that collective security assumes the possibility of creating such an imbalance of power in favor of the upholders of world order that aggression will be prevented by the certainty of defeat or defeated by the minimal efforts of collective forces. This assumption may be invalidated by the inadequate diffusion of power. If the power configuration is such that no state commands more than, say, ten per cent of the world's strength, the possibility is open for collective security to mobilize up to ninety per cent against it, a very comfortable margin of superiority. If, however, one state controls a very substantial portion of global power resources, forty-five per cent, for instance, the collective matching of its strength is doubtful and the massing of overwhelming power against it is manifestly impossible. The importance of universality is also clarified by this analysis; as a collective security system approaches all-inclusiveness, the possibility of its disposing of sufficient resources to outclass any aggressor grows; as it moves in the opposite direction, that possibility is correspondingly diminished.

The point is that collective security is not a design for organizing coalition warfare in the twentieth-century sense, but a plan for organizing international police action in an unprecedented sense. Its aim is not to sponsor the winning team in a free-for-all, but to eliminate international brawls by forcing aggressive states to forfeit their matches before being decisively beaten. It purports to require of participating states not that they should consent to compulsory involvement in major wars, but that they should accept obligatory service in a system for preventing major wars, and it can expect to retain their loyal support only if it succeeds in reducing, rather than increasing, their exposure to the perils of military involvement. All this is dependent upon the existence of a power situation and the achievement of an organizational situation making the massive overpowering of potential aggressors a feasible objective. The first essential of a police force is that its power should be so considerable, and that of its possible opponents so negligible, that any contest will be virtually won before it has begun; otherwise, its function will be that of conducting warfare, no matter how it may be described.

The intrinsic disadvantages of a collective security force are so great that its margin of superiority is always smaller than any purely objective standard of measurement would reveal. Since it confronts an anonymous aggressor, its capacity for formulating advance plans of action is severely limited. Since it is by definition a coalition force, its strength is very likely to be less than that of the sum of its parts. Its value depends heavily upon its ability to act quickly, so as to forestall threatened aggression, and yet its very inability to concentrate on plans for defeating a specific enemy and its complex structure militate against promptness in the effective mobilization of its potential strength. Collective security can command little confidence if it promises to become effective only after an aggressor has ravaged a country. Given the nature of modern war, a military campaign cannot be organized overnight, and the power of an aggressive state is maximized by preparatory measures. The collaborative force required for the implementation of collective security must be overwhelmingly preponderant in theory if it is to be even somewhat preponderant in practice.

The situation envisaged by collective security is marked not only by the wide distribution of power among states and the possibility of the near-monopolization of power by the community, but also by the general reduction of power, as embodied in military instruments. That is to say, collective security is based upon the assumption of partial disarmament. In strict theoretical terms, the system might work as well at a high level of armament as at a low level, but the intrusion of the subjective factor makes it virtually essential that collective security have a substantially demilitarized world to work in. This is because collective security is fundamentally an attempt to mobilize the world's antiwar forces for the prevention of war by the threat to make war; the ambiguity of the system is underlined by the fact that it relies for its initiation upon recognition that the risk of war is intolerable, and for its operation upon willingness to accept the risk of war. Its army of pacifists is tentatively willing to use force only because it abhors the use of force. Being precariously founded upon this psychological and moral paradox, collective security requires a power situation which permits it to do its job with a minimum of military exertion. If every state is reduced to military weakness, no aggressor will be strong enough to make a catastrophic war out of an encounter with the community's forces, and no member of the enforcement team will be tempted to feel that its joining up has been a jump from the military frying pan into the military fire. Just as the peaceful citizen may be less inclined to volunteer as a policeman if potential criminals are equipped with machine guns rather than mere fists, the willingness of peacefully-inclined states to participate in the venture of collective security is dependent upon the magnitude of the military involvement prospectively required; they are prepared to serve as whistle-blowing and nightstick-wielding policemen, but they reserve decision about becoming full-fledged soldiers.

At this point, we again encounter the troublesome problem of circularity. Collective security cannot work unless states disarm, but states will not disarm until collective security has clearly shown that it merits confidence. The maintenance of national military strength is an indication that states are unwilling to entrust their fate to a community agency, but their armament policy, born of lack of confidence in collective security, prevents the development of an effective collective security system.

Another significant objective requirement might be described as the universality of economic vulnerability. Collective security assumes that the states of the world are as interdependent for their strength as for their peace, and that its restraining function can be exercised in large part by the imposition of isolation, the organization of deprivation, without resort to collective measures of suppression. It envisages a world in which every state is not only susceptible to the impact of organized force, but also vulnerable to the squeeze of organized boycott, and it accordingly regards economic sanctions as its first line of attack. It recognizes the vital importance of holding the military weapon in reserve, but it offers to its participating members the reassuring possibility that they may be able to discharge their responsibilities by the relatively painless and humane method of denying to aggressors the benefits of normal intercourse, rather than by running the risks involved in the resort to arms.

In summary, collective security assumes the existence of a world in which every state is so limited by the distribution of power, the reduction of military power levels by a disarmament program, and the lack of economic self-sufficiency, that any state which may develop aggressive inclinations can be held in check by methods which probably need not include the large-scale use of force. It assumes the possibility of securing the acceptance by states of theoretically formidable responsibilities for enforcing the peace, only because it assumes the improbability that it will be necessary to invoke the performance of the most drastic enforcement duties.

Finally, collective security requires the creation of a legal and structural apparatus capable of giving institutional expression to its basic principles. This involves the legal establishment of the prohibition of aggression, the commitment of states to collaborate in the suppression of aggression, and the endowment of an international organization with authority to determine when and against what state sanctions are to be initiated, to decide upon the nature of the inhibitory measures, to evoke the performance of duties to which states have committed themselves, and to plan and direct the joint action which it deems necessary for the implementation of collective security. The meaningfulness of the system is dependent upon the capacity of the organizational mechanism to exercise these vital functions without obstruction. In specific terms, this means that the decision to set the system into operation against a particular state must not be subject to the veto of an obstinate minority, and that no state can be permitted to nullify its commitment to act on behalf of the community by withholding its assent from a decision to call for the performance of that obligation. The elaboration of an adequate supervisory agency is no less important to collective security than the satisfaction of the subjective requirements and the realization of the prerequisite conditions in the global power situation.

NOTES

1. Hans J. Morgenthau, *Politics Among Nations* (1st ed.; New York: Knopf, 1949), p. 331.
2. January 6, 1951.
3. *Military Situation in the Far East, Hearings before the Committee on Armed Services and the Committee on Foreign Relations, United States Senate, 82nd Congress, 1st Session* (Washington: Government Printing Office, 1951), Part I, p. 87.

4. *United States News and World Report,* March 28, 1952, p. 84.

5. *Our Foreign Policy: 1952,* Department of State Publication 4466, General Foreign Policy Series 56 (Washington: Government Printing Office, 1952), p. 39.

6. Address to Congress, February 11, 1918, cited in Green H. Hackworth, *Digest of International Law* (Washington: Government Printing Office, 1940), I, 424.

7. See the quotations from Wilson in Hans J. Morgenthau, *In Defense of the National Interest* (New York: Knopf, 1951), pp. 24–25, 27–28.

8. *Perpetual Peace,* p. 21.

9. Cited in Alan Bullock, *Hitler: A Study in Tyranny* (New York: Harper, 1953), p. 499.

10. Cited in Walters, *A History of the League of Nations,* II, 653.

11. Royal Institute of International Affairs, *The Future of the League of Nations,* p. 14. Cf. Werner Levi, *Fundamentals of World Organization* (Minneapolis: University of Minnesota Press, 1950), p. 77; Morgenthau, *Politics Among Nations,* p. 333.

12. Karl Loewenstein, "Sovereignty and International Co-operation," *American Journal of International Law,* April 1954, p. 235.

13. Cf. Wright, *Problems of Stability and Progress in International Relations,* p. 355.

31

WILLIAM D. COPLIN

INTERNATIONAL LAW AND ASSUMPTIONS ABOUT THE STATE SYSTEM

Most writers on international relations and international law still examine the relationship between international law and politics in terms of the assumption that law either should or does function only as a coercive restraint on political action. Textbook writers on general international politics like Morgenthau,[1] and Lerche and Said,[2] as well as those scholars who have specialized in international law like J. L. Brierly[3] and Charles De Visscher,[4] make the common assumption that international law should be examined as a system of coercive norms controlling the actions of states. Even two of the newer works, *The Political Foundations of International Law* by Morton A. Kaplan and Nicholas deB. Katzenbach[5] and *Law and Minimum World Public Order* by

SOURCE: From *World Politics,* Vol. XVIII No. 4 (July 1965), pp. 615–634. Reprinted with permission of the Johns Hopkins University Press and William D. Coplin.

Myres S. McDougal and Florentino P. Feliciano,[6] in spite of an occasional reference to the non-coercive aspects of international law, are developed primarily from the model of international law as a system of restraint. Deriving their conception of the relationship between international law and political action from their ideas on the way law functions in domestic communities, most modern writers look at international law as an instrument of direct control. The assumption that international law is or should be a coercive restraint on state action structures almost every analysis, no matter what the school of thought or the degree of optimism or pessimism about the effectiveness of the international legal system.[7] With an intellectual framework that measures international law primarily in terms of constraint on political action, there is little wonder that skepticism about international law continues to increase while creative work on the level of theory seems to be diminishing.[8]

Therefore, it is desirable to approach the relationship between international law and politics at a different functional level, not because international law does not function at the level of coercive restraint, but because it also functions at another level. In order to illustrate a second functional level in the relationship between international law and politics, it is necessary to examine the operation of domestic law. In a domestic society, the legal system as a series of interrelated normative statements does more than direct or control the actions of its members through explicit rules backed by a promise of coercion. Systems of law also act on a more generic and pervasive level by serving as authoritative (i.e., accepted as such by the community) modes of communicating or reflecting the ideals and purposes, the acceptable roles and actions, as well as the very processes of the societies. The legal system functions on the level of the individual's perceptions and attitudes by presenting to him an image of the social system—an image which has both factual and normative aspects and which contributes to social order by building a consensus on procedural as well as on substantive matters. In this sense, law in the domestic situation is a primary tool in the "socialization"[9] of the individual.

International law functions in a similar manner: namely, as an institutional device for communicating to the policy-makers of various states a consensus on the nature of the international system. The purpose of this article is to approach the relationship between international law and politics not as a system of direct restraints on state action, but rather as a system of quasi-authoritative communications to the policy-makers concerning the reasons for state actions and the requisites for international order. It is a "quasi-authoritative" device because the norms of international law represent only an imperfect consensus of the community of states, a consensus which rarely commands complete acceptance but which usually expresses generally held ideas. Given the decentralized nature of law-creation and law-application in the international community, there is no official voice of the states as a collectivity. However, international law taken as a body of generally related norms is the closest thing to such a voice. Therefore, in spite of the degree of uncertainty about the authority of international law, it may still be meaningful to examine international law as a means for expressing the commonly held assumptions about the state system.

The approach advocated in this article has its intellectual antecedents in the sociological school, since it seeks to study international law in relation to international politics. Furthermore, it is similar to that of the sociological school in its assumption that there is or should be a significant degree of symmetry between international law and politics on the level of intellectual constructs—that is, in the way in which international law has expressed and even shaped ideas about relations between states. It is hoped that this approach will contribute to a greater awareness of the interdependence of international law and conceptions of international politics.

Before analyzing the way in which international law has in the past and continues today to reflect common attitudes about the nature of the state system, let us discuss briefly the three basic assumptions which have generally structured those attitudes.[10] First, it has been assumed that the state is an absolute institutional value and that its security is the one immutable imperative for state action. If there has been one thing of which policy-makers could always be certain, it is that their actions must be designed to preserve their state. Second, it has been assumed that international politics is a struggle for power, and that all states seek to increase their power. Although the forms of power have altered during the evolution of the state system, it has been generally thought that states are motivated by a drive for power, no matter what the stakes. The third basic assumption permeating ideas about the international system has to do with maintaining a minimal system of order among the states. This assumption, symbolized generally by the maxim "Preserve the balance of power," affirms the necessity of forming coalitions to counter any threat to hegemony and of moderating actions in order to avoid an excess of violence that could disrupt the system.

It is necessary at this point to note that an unavoidable tension has existed between the aim of maintaining the state and maximizing power, on the one hand, and of preserving the international system, on the other. The logical extension of either aim would threaten the other, since complete freedom of action by the state would not allow for the limitation imposed by requirements to maintain the system, and a strict regularization of state action inherent in the idea of the system would curtail the state's drive for power. However, the tension has remained constant, with neither norm precluding the other except when a given state was in immediate danger of destruction. At those times, the interests of the system have been subordinated to the drive for state survival, but with no apparent long-range effect on the acceptance by policy-makers of either set of interests, despite their possible incompatibility. The prescriptions that states should be moderate, flexible, and vigilant[11] have been a manifestation of the operation of the system. Together, the three basic assumptions about the state system have constituted the conceptual basis from which the policy-makers have planned the actions of their state.

I. CLASSICAL INTERNATIONAL LAW AND THE IMAGE OF THE STATE SYSTEM

Almost every legal aspect of international relations from 1648 to 1914 reinforced and expressed the assumptions of the state system. State practices in regard to treaties, boundaries, neutrality, the occupation of new lands, freedom of the seas, and diplomacy, as well as classical legal doctrines, provide ample illustration of the extent to which the basic assumptions of the state were mirrored in international law.

The essential role of treaties in international law reflected the three assumptions of the state system. First, treaty practices helped to define the nature of statehood. Emanating from the free and unfettered will of states, treaties were the expression of their sovereign prerogatives. Statehood itself was defined in part as the ability to make treaties, and that ability presupposed the equality and independence usually associated with the idea of the state. Moreover, certain definitive treaties, like those written at the Peace of Augsburg (1515) and the Peace of Westphalia (1648), actually made explicit the attributes of statehood. The former treaty affirmed the idea that the Prince had complete control over the internal affairs of the state, while the latter emphasized that states were legally free and equal in their international relationships.[12] Even the actual wording of treaties expressed the classical assumption about the sanctity of the state. Whether in the formal references to the "high contracting parties" or in the more vital statements about the agreement of sovereigns not to interfere with the actions of other sovereigns, treaties were clear expressions of the classical idea of the state.[13]

Treaty law also contributed to the evolution of the classical assumption regarding the maintenance of the international system. Both explicitly and implicitly, treaties affirmed the necessity of an international system. Whether or not they contained such phrases as "balance of power, "Just equilibrium," universal and perpetual peace,"[14] "common and public safety and tranquillity,"[15] "public tranquillity on a lasting foundation,"[16] or "safety and interest of Europe,"[17] the most important treaties during the classical period affirmed the desirability of maintaining the international system.[18] Also, many treaties reaffirmed earlier treaty agreements, contributing to the idea that the international system was a continuing, operative unity.[19] Therefore, treaties usually reminded the policy-maker that the maintenance of the international system was a legitimate and necessary objective of state policy.

Finally, treaties affirmed the necessity and, in part, the legality of the drive for power. The constant juggling of territory, alliances, and other aspects of capability was a frequent and rightful subject of treaty law. Treaties implicitly confirmed that power was the dynamic force in relations between states by defining the legal criteria of power and, more important, by providing an institutional means, subscribed to by most of the members of the system, which legalized certain political transactions, such as territorial acquisition and dynastic exchange.

A second state practice which contributed to the classical assumptions about the state system was the legal concept of boundaries. Inherent in the very idea of the boundary were all three assumptions of the classical system. First, the boundary marked off that most discernible of all criteria of a state's existence—territory.[20] A state was sovereign within its territory, and the boundary was essential to the demarcation and protection of that sovereignty. Freedom and equality necessitated the delineation of a certain area of complete control; the boundary as conceptualized in international law was the institutional means through which that necessity was fulfilled. Second, the boundary was essential for the preservation of the international system.[21] After every war the winning powers set up a new or revised set of boundaries which aided them in maintaining order by redistributing territory. More important, the boundary also provided a criterion by which to assess the intentions of other states. Change of certain essential boundaries signified a mortal threat to the whole system, and signaled the need for a collective response.[22] Finally, the legal concept of boundaries provided a means through which the expansion and contraction of power in the form of territory could be measured. Since the boundary was a legal means of measuring territorial changes, international law in effect reinforced the idea that the struggle for power was an essential and accepted part of international politics. All three assumptions of the state system, therefore, were mirrored in the classical legal concept of boundaries.

Another international legal concept which reflected the assumptions about the state system was the idea of neutrality. The primary importance of neutrality law lay in its relation to the classical emphasis on the preservation of the international system. The practice of neutrality was an essential element in the mitigation of international conflict because it provided a legitimate means of lessening the degree of violence in any given war (by reducing the number of belligerents) and also made those involved in a war aware of the possibility of hostile actions from outside should the conflict weaken the participants too greatly. In short, the legal concept of neutrality implied that the actions of states must remain moderate and flexible in order to preserve the state system.[23]

There were other aspects of international legal practice which substantiated the assumptions of the state system. For instance, since the sixteenth century the law pertaining to the occupation of new lands and to freedom of the high seas constituted a vital aspect of international law, and provided "legitimate" areas in which the struggle for power could take place.

From the outset, most of the non-European areas of the world were considered by the great powers to be acceptable arenas for the struggle for power. International legal practice made it easy for states to gain control of land overseas by distinguishing between the laws of occupation and the laws of subjugation. This distinction made it easier for powers to extend control over non-European territorial expanses because it enabled states to "occupy" territory legally without actually controlling it.[24] Through the laws of occupation, international law confirmed the assumption that colonial expansion was part of the struggle for power.

The law of the high seas also contributed to the idea of the struggle for power. The expansion of trade, military power, and territorial domain was, throughout almost the entire history of the state system, greatly dependent upon the free use of the high seas. The laws of the sea were designed so that maximum use could be made of this relatively cheap mode of transportation. Like the laws of occupation of non-European territory, sea law helped to keep the distribution of power among European states in continuous flux.[25]

Therefore, both the laws of the seas and the laws governing the occupation of new lands were instrumental in "legalizing" areas for conflict. Given the assumption that states always maximize their power, a free sea and the easy acquisition of non-European lands provided the fluidity needed for the states to struggle for power. Moreover, both sets of laws removed the area of conflict from the home territory, thus enabling states to increase the scope of their struggle without proportionately increasing its intensity.[26]

A final category of international law which reinforced the assumptions about the state system was the law of diplomacy. The legal rationalization behind the rights and duties of diplomats (i.e., since diplomats represent sovereign states, they owe no allegiance to the receiving state) emphasized the inviolability of the state which was an essential aspect of the classical assumptions.[27] At the same time, the very fact that even semi-hostile states could exchange and maintain ambassadors emphasized that all states were part of a common international system.[28] Finally, the classical functions of a diplomat—to make sure that conditions are not changing to the disadvantage of his state and, if they are, to suggest and even implement policies to rectify the situation—exemplified the rule of constant vigilance necessary in a group of states struggling for power. Therefore, in their own way, the laws of diplomacy expressed all three of the assumptions of the state systems.

The assumptions of the state system were reinforced not only by the legal practices of states but also by the major international legal theories of the classical period. Three general schools of thought developed: the naturalists, the eclectics or Grotians, and the positivists.[29] In each school, there was a major emphasis on both the state and the state system as essential institutional values. Whether it was Pufendorf's insistence on the "natural equality of state,"[30] the Grotians' concept of the sovereign power of state,[31] or Bynkershoek and the nineteenth-century positivists' point that treaties were the prime, if not the only, source of international law,[32] the state was considered by most classical theorists to be the essential institution protected by the legal system. At the same time, almost every classical writer on international law either assumed or argued for the existence of an international system of some kind.[33] Along with Grotians, the naturalists maintained that a system of states existed, since man was a social animal. Vattel, probably the most famous international lawyer in the classical period, asserted that a balance of power and a state system existed.[34] Even the positivists of the nineteenth century assumed that there was an international system of some kind. This is apparent from their emphasis on the balance of power,[35] as well as from their assumption that relations between nations could be defined in terms of legal rights and duties.[36]

Therefore, there was a consensus among the classical theorists of international law that international politics had two structural elements: the state, with its rights of freedom and self-preservation; and the system, with its partial effectiveness in maintaining a minimal international order. That the theorists never solved the conflict between the idea of the unfettered sovereign state, on the one hand, and a regulating system of law, on the other, is indicative of a conflict within the assumptions of the state system,[37] but a conflict which neither prevented international lawyers from writing about an international legal order nor kept policy-makers from pursuing each state's objectives without destroying the state system.

Although the norms of classical international law sometimes went unheeded, the body of theory and of state practice which constituted "international law as an institution" nonetheless expressed in a quasi-authoritative manner the three assumptions about international politics. It legalized the existence of states and helped to define the actions necessary for the preservation of each state and of the system as a whole. It reinforced the ideas that vigilance, moderation, and flexibility are necessary for the protection of a system of competing states. And finally, international law established a legalized system of political payoffs by providing a means to register gains and losses without creating a static system. In fact, this last aspect was essential to the classical state system. With international law defining certain relationships (territorial expansion, empire-building, etc.) as legitimate areas for political competition, other areas seemed, at least generally in the classical period, to be removed from the center of the political struggle. By legitimizing the struggle as a form of political competition rather than as universal conflict, international law sanctioned a form of international system that was more than just an anarchic drive for survival.

II. CONTEMPORARY INTERNATIONAL LAW AND THE ASSUMPTIONS OF THE STATE SYSTEM

As a quasi-authoritative system of communicating the assumptions of the state system to policy-makers, contemporary international law no longer presents a clear idea of the nature of international politics. This is in part a result of the tension, within the structure of contemporary international law itself, between the traditional legal concepts and the current practices of states. International law today is in a state of arrested ambiguity—in a condition of unstable equilibrium between the old and the new. As a result, it no longer contributes as it once did to a consensus on the nature of the state system. In fact, it adds to the growing uncertainty and disagreement as to how the international political system itself is evolving. The following discussion will attempt to assess the current developments in international law in terms of the challenges those developments make to the three assumptions of the state system. It is realized that the three assumptions themselves have already undergone change, but our purpose is to show where contemporary international legal practice and theory stand in relation to that change.

THE CHALLENGE TO THE STATE AND THE SYSTEM

The current legal concept of the state is a perfect example of the arrested ambiguity of contemporary international law and of the threat that this condition represents to the assumptions of the state system. On the one hand, most of the traditional forms used to express the idea of statehood are still employed. Treaty-makers and statesmen still write about "respect for territorial integrity," the "right of domestic jurisdiction," and the "sovereign will of the high contracting parties." Moreover, most of the current substantive rights and duties, such as self-defense, legal equality, and territorial jurisdiction, that are based on the assumption that states as units of territory are the irreducible institutional values of the system continue to be central to international legal practice.[38] On the other hand, certain contemporary developments contrast sharply with the traditional territory-oriented conceptions of international law.[39] With the growth of international entities possessing supranational powers (e.g., ECSC), the legal idea of self-contained units based on territorial control lacks the clear basis in fact that it once enjoyed. Many of the traditional prerogatives of the sovereign state, such as control over fiscal policy,[40] have been transferred in some respects to transnational units. While the development of supranational powers is most pronounced in Europe, there is reason to believe, especially concerning international cooperation on technical matters, that organizations patterned on the European experience might occur elsewhere.

Another significant manifestation of ambiguity in the territorial basis of international law is found in the post-World War II practice of questioning the validity of the laws of other states. The "act of state doctrine" no longer serves as the guideline it once did in directing the national courts of one state to respect the acts promulgated in another.[41] Once based on the assumption of the "inviolability of the sovereign," the "act of state doctrine" today is the source of widespread controversy. The conflicting views of the doctrine are symptomatic of the now ambiguous role of territoriality in questions of jurisdictional and legal power. Although these developments in current legal practice are only now emerging, they nonetheless can be interpreted as a movement away from the strictly and clearly defined legal concept of the state that appeared in classical international law.

Other developments in contemporary international law represent, theoretically at least, a challenge to the assumption that the state and its freedom of action are an absolute necessity for the state system. Most noticeable has been the attempt to develop an international organization which would preserve a minimal degree of order. Prior to the League of Nations, there had been attempts to institutionalize certain aspects of international relations, but such attempts either did not apply to the political behavior of states (e.g., the Universal Postal Union) or did not challenge the basic assumptions of the state system (as the very loosely defined Concert of Europe failed to do). As it was formulated in the Covenant and defined by the intellectuals, the League represented a threat to the assumptions of the state system because it sought to settle once and for all the tension between the policy-maker's commitment to preserve his state and his desire to maintain the state system by subordinating his state to it through a formal institution.

Proponents of the League saw it as a means to formalize a system of maintaining international order by committing states in advance to a coalition against any state that resorted to war without fulfilling the requirements of the Covenant. If it had been operative, such a commitment would have represented a total revolution in the legal concept of the state as an independent entity, since it would have abolished the most essential of all sovereign prerogatives, the freedom to employ coercion. However, the ideal purpose of the League, on the one hand, and the aims of politicians and the actual constitutional and operational aspects of the League, on the other, proved to be quite different. Owing to certain legal formulations within the Covenant (Articles 10, 15, 21) and the subsequent application of the principles (e.g., in Manchuria and Ethiopia), the hoped-for subordination of the state to the system was not realized.[42]

Like the League, the United Nations was to replace the state as the paramount institutional value by establishing a constitutional concert of powers. However, it has succeeded only in underscoring the existing tension between the drive to maintain the state and the goal of maintaining the system. In the Charter itself, the tension between the state and the system remains unresolved.[43] Nor does the actual operation of the United Nations provide a very optimistic basis for the hope that tension will be lessened in the future.

In terms of international law, regional organizations constitute a mixed challenge to the traditional relationship between the state and the system. Although certain organizations represent an attempt to transcend the traditional bounds of their constituent members on functional grounds, this does not necessarily mean that those members have rejected the state as a political form. In reality, if regional organizations represent any transformation at all in the structural relationship between the state and the system, they constitute an attempt to create a bigger and better state, an attempt which is not contrary to the traditional assumptions of the state system. In spite of the fact that some organizations are given supranational power and present a challenge in that sense, most of the organizations are as protective of the sovereign rights of the state as is the United Nations Charter (e.g., the OAS Charter) or are not regional organizations at all, but military alliances.[44]

A more serious challenge, but one somewhat related to the challenge by regional organizations, is the changing relation of the individual in the international legal order. In the classical system, international law clearly relegated the individual to the position of an object of the law. Not the individual, but the state had the rights and duties of the international legal order.[45] This legal formulation was in keeping with the classical emphasis on the sanctity of the state. Today, however, the development of the concepts of human rights, international and regional organizations, and the personal responsibility of policy-makers to a higher law not only limit the scope of legally permissible international action but, more important, limit the traditional autonomy of the leaders of the state over internal matters.[46] The idea that the individual rather than the state is the unit of responsibility in the formulation of policy has a long intellectual tradition;[47] however, it is only recently that the norms associated with that idea have become a part of international law.

Although the role of the individual in international law is small and the chances for its rapid development in the near future slight, it represents a more vital challenge to traditional international law and to the assumptions of the state system than either international or regional organizations. Since the principle of collective responsibility (of the state) rather than individual responsibility has traditionally served as the infrastructure for the rights and duties of states,[48] the development of a place for the individual in the international legal system that would make him personally responsible would completely revolutionize international law. At the same time, by making the individual a higher point of policy reference than the state, the development of the role of the individual represents a challenge to the assumption once reflected in classical international law that the preservation and maximization of state power is an absolute guideline for policy-makers. The evolving place of the individual in the contemporary international legal system, then, is contrary to the traditional tendency of international law to reaffirm the absolute value of the state.

THE CHALLENGE TO THE CONCEPT OF POWER

One of the most significant developments in international law today relates to the assumption that states do and should compete for power. In the classical period, international law, through the legal concepts of neutrality, rules of warfare, occupation of new lands, rules of the high seas, and laws of diplomacy, reinforced the idea that a struggle for power among states was normal and necessary. Today, many of these specific legal norms still apply, but the overall permissible range of the struggle for military power[49] has been limited by the concept of the just war.

The idea of the just war is not new to international law. Most of the classical writers discussed it, but they refused to define the concept in strict legal terms and usually relegated it to the moral or ethical realm.[50] The nineteenth-century positivists completely abandoned the doctrine with the formulation that "wars between nations must be considered as just on both sides with respect to treatment of enemies, military arrangements, and peace."[51]

However, with the increased capability of states to destroy each other, a movement has grown to regulate force by legal means.

This movement developed through the Hague Conventions and the League of Nations and, in some respects, culminated in the Kellogg-Briand Pact of 1928. Today, the just war is a more or less accepted concept in international law. Most authors write, and most policy-makers state, that aggression is illegal and must be met with the sanction of the international community. The portent of this formulation of the assumption regarding power is great since, theoretically at least, it deprives the states of the range of action which they once freely enjoyed in maximizing their power and in protecting themselves. If the only legal justification for war is self-defense, or authorization of action in accordance with the Charter of the United Nations,[52] then a war to preserve the balance of power or to expand in a limited fashion is outlawed. While the traditional formulation of international law provided a broad field upon which the game of power politics could be played, the new formulations concerning the legal use of force significantly limit and, one could argue, make illegal the military aspects of the game of power politics.[53] The freedom to use military power, once an essential characteristic of sovereignty and an integral part of international law, is no longer an accepted international legal norm.

The concept of the just war directly challenges the assumptions of the state system, because it implies that the military struggle for power is no longer a normal process of international politics. No longer does international law legitimize the gains of war, and no longer do policy-makers look upon war as a rightful tool of national power.[54] This is not to say that states do not use force in their current struggles or that the doctrine of the just war would deter them in a particular case. However, the doctrine does operate on the conceptual level by expressing to the policy-makers the idea that the use of force is no longer an everyday tool of international power politics. In terms of the traditional assumption about the state's natural inclination to maximize power, the contemporary legal commitment to the just-war doctrine represents a profound and historic shift.

III. INTERNATIONAL LAW AND THE REALITY OF CONTEMPORARY INTERNATIONAL POLITICS

Contemporary international legal practice, then, is developing along lines which represent a threat not only to traditional concepts of international law but also to the assumptions of the state system. The sporadic developments in international and regional organizations, the evolving place of the individual in the international legal system, and the doctrine of the just war are manifestations of the transformation occurring today both in the structure of international law and in attitudes about the state system. Actually, of course, the traditional conceptions of international law and the classical assumptions about international politics are not extinct.[55] Rather, there is in both international law and politics a perplexing mixture of past ideas and current developments. The only thing one can be sure of is that behind the traditional legal and political symbols which exist today in a somewhat mutated form, a subtle transformation of some kind is taking place.

It is not possible to evaluate the line of future development of the assumptions about the state system or the international legal expression of those assumptions from the work of contemporary theorists of international law. The most apparent new expressions are those that propose increased formalizations of world legal and political processes.[56] On the other hand, much international legal theory today seems to be dedicated to an affirmation of the traditional assumptions of international politics. Political analysts like Hans Morgenthau,[57] E. H. Carr,[58] and George F. Kennan,[59] and legal theorists like Julius Stone,[60] P. E. Corbett,[61] and Charles De Visscher,[62] are predisposed to "bring international law back to reality."

This trend toward being "realistic" occupies the mainstream of current international legal theory,[63] and to identify its exact nature is therefore crucial. Many writers who express this viewpoint seem to fear being labeled as overly "idealistic." They utter frequent warnings that international law cannot restore international politics to order, but, on the contrary, can exist and flourish only after there is a political agreement among states to maintain order. In short, it is assumed that international law cannot shape international political reality, but can merely adjust to it. Although there are complaints of too much pessimism in current legal theory,[64] most writers, given the initial predisposition to avoid "idealism," do not heed them.

The desire of contemporary theorists to be "realistic" has been crucial to the relationship between contemporary international law and the assumptions of the state system. In their effort to achieve realism, current theorists have not examined their traditional assumptions about international politics. When they talk about adjusting international law to the realities of power, they usually have in mind the traditional reality of international politics. Today, a large share of the theoretical writing on international law that is designed to adapt law to political reality is in effect applying it to an image of international politics which itself is rapidly becoming outmoded. Much contemporary international legal theory, then, has not contributed to the development of a new consensus on the nature of international politics but instead has reinforced many of the traditional ideas.

In order to understand more fully the relation of international law to world politics, it is necessary to do more than examine law merely as a direct constraint on political action. The changes in the conceptual basis of international law that are manifested in current practice and, to a lesser extent, in current legal theory are symptomatic of a series of social and institutional revolutions that are transforming all of international politics. To conclude that international law must adjust to political reality, therefore, is to miss the point, since international law is part of political reality and serves as an institutional means of developing and reflecting a general consensus on the nature of international reality. In the contemporary period, where the international legal system is relatively decentralized, and international politics is subject to rapid and profound development, it is necessary to avoid a conceptual framework of international law which breeds undue pessimism because it demands too much. If international law does not contribute directly and effectively to world order by forcing states to be peaceful, it does prepare the conceptual ground on which that order could be built by shaping attitudes about the nature and promise of international political reality.

NOTES

1. Hans J. Morgenthau, *Politics Among Nations* (New York 1961), 275–311. The entire evaluation of the "main problems" of international law is focused on the question of what rules are violated and what rules are not.
2. Charles O. Lerche, Jr., and Abdul A. Said, *Concepts of International Politics* (Englewood Cliffs, N.J., 1963), 167–87. That the authors have employed the assumption that international law functions as a system of restraint is evident from the title of their chapter which examines international law, "Limitations on State Actions."
3. J. L. Brierly, *The Law of Nations* (New York 1963), 1. Brierly defines international law as "the body of rules and principles of action which are binding upon civilized states in their relations. . . ."
4. Charles De Visscher, *Theory and Reality in Public International Law* (Princeton 1957), 99–100.
5. Morton A. Kaplan and Nicholas deB. Katzenbach, *The Political Foundations of International Law* (New York 1961), 5. In a discussion of how the student should observe international law and politics, the authors write: "To understand the substance and limits of such constraining rules (international law), it is necessary to examine the interests which support them in the international system, the means by which they are made effective, and the functions they perform. Only in this way is it possible to predict the areas in which rules operate, the limits of rules as effective constraints, and the factors which underlie normative change." Although the authors are asking an important question—"Why has international law been binding in some cases?"—they still assume that international law functions primarily as a direct restraint on state action. For an excellent review of this book, see Robert W. Tucker, "Resolution," *Journal of Conflict Resolution,* VII (March 1963), 69–75.
6. Myers S. McDougal and Florentino P. Feliciano, *Law and Minimum World Public Order* (New Haven 1961), 10. The authors suggest that if any progress in conceptualizing the role of international law is to be made, it is necessary to distinguish between the "factual process of international coercion and the process of authoritative decision by which the public order of the world community endeavors to regulate such process of coercion." This suggestion is based on the assumption that international law promotes order primarily through the establishment of restraints on state actions.

7. There are a few writers who have tried to approach international law from a different vantage point. For a survey of some of the other approaches to international law and politics, see Michael Barkun, "International Norms: An Interdisciplinary Approach," *Background*, VIII (August 1964), 121–29. The survey shows that few "new" approaches to international law have developed beyond the preliminary stages, save perhaps for the writings of F. S. C. Northrop. Northrop's works (e.g., *Philosophical Anthropology and Practical Politics* [New York 1960], 326–30) are particularly significant in their attempt to relate psychological, philosophical, and cultural approaches to the study of law in general, although he has not usually been concerned with the overall relationship of international law to international political action. Not mentioned in Barkun's survey but important in the discussion of international law and politics is Stanley Hoffmann, "International Systems and International Law," in Klaus Knorr and Sidney Verba, eds., *The International System* (Princeton 1961), 205–38. However, Hoffmann's essay is closer in approach to the work by Kaplan and Katzenbach than to the approach developed in this article. Finally, it is also necessary to point to an article by Edward McWhinney, "Soviet and Western International Law and the Cold War in a Nuclear Era of Bipolarity: Inter Bloc Law in a Nuclear Age," *Canadian Yearbook of International Law*, I (1963), 40–81. Professor McWhinney discusses the relationship between American and Russian structures of action, on the one hand, and their interpretations of international law, on the other. While McWhinney's approach is basically similar to the one proposed in this article in its attempt to relate international law to politics on a conceptual level, his article is focused on a different set of problems, the role of national attitudes in the contemporary era on ideas of international law. Nevertheless, it is a significant contribution to the task of analyzing more clearly the relationship between international law and politics.

8. See Richard A. Falk, "The Adequacy of Contemporary International Law: Gaps in Legal Thinking," *Virginia Law Review*, 1 (March 1964), 231–65, for a valuable but highly critical analysis of contemporary international legal theory.

9. See Gabriel A. Almond and James S. Coleman, eds., *The Politics of the Developing Areas* (Princeton 1960), 26–31, for an explanation of the concepts of socialization.

10. The following discussion of the assumptions of the state system is brief, since students of international politics generally agree that the three assumptions listed have structured most of the actions of states. This agreement is most complete concerning the nature of the "classical" state system. The author is also of the opinion that these assumptions continue to operate today in a somewhat mutated form. (See his unpublished manuscript "The Image of Power Politics: A Cognitive Approach to the Study of International Politics," chaps. 2, 4, 8.) Note also the agreement on the nature of classical ideas about international politics in the following: Ernst B. Haas, "The Balance of Power as a Guide to Policy Making," *Journal of Politics*, xv (August 1953), 370–97; Morton A. Kaplan, *System and Process in International Politics* (New York 1957), 22–36; and Edward Vose Gulick, *Europe's Classical Balance of Power* (Ithaca, N.Y., 1955).

11. See Gulick, 34; and for a discussion of the principles of moderation, flexibility, and vigilance, *ibid.*, 11–16.

12. For the effects of the two treaties, see Charles Petrie, *Diplomatic History, 1713–1939* (London 1949), 111; David Jayne Hill, *A History of Diplomacy in*

the International Development of Europe (New York 1924), 6036; and Arthur Nussbaum, *A Concise History of the Law of Nations* (New York 1961), 116.

13. E.g., *The Treaty of Ryswick, 1697* in Andrew Browning, ed., *English History Documents,* VIII (New York 1963), 881–83.
14. *Treaty of Ryswick,* Article 1, in *ibid.*
15. *Barrier Treaty of 1715,* Article 1, in *ibid.,* Vol. II.
16. *Treaty of Vienna, 1713,* in *ibid.,* Vol. VIII.
17. *Treaty of Quadruple Alliance, 1815,* in *ibid.,* Vol. XI.
18. Leo Gross, "The Peace of Westphalia, 1648–1948," *American Journal of International Law,* XLII (January 1948), 20–40.
19. For a treaty which expressed the necessity of keeping prior obligations, see *Treaty of Aix-la-Chapelle, 1748,* in Browning, ed., Vol. X.
20. See John H. Herz, *International Politics in the Atomic Age* (New York 1963), 53, for a discussion of the role of territory in the classical state system and the international legal system.
21. See Hoffmann, 212, 215, for a discussion of the way in which territorial settlements in treaties aided stability within the system. He calls this function part of the law of political framework.
22. E.g., the English and French attitude toward Belgium.
23. For a discussion of the role of neutrality in the balance of power system, see McDougal and Feliciano, 391–413.
24. L. Oppenheim, in H. Lauterpacht, ed., *International Law* (New York 1948), 507.
25. The attempt to control a "closed sea" was sometimes a bid by a powerful state to freeze the status quo—e.g., Portugal's control of the Indian Ocean in the sixteenth and seventeenth centuries (Nussbaum, 111).
26. Analysts have argued over whether colonialism reduced or exacerbated international antagonism. Without settling the argument, it seems safe to say that the struggle for colonies was a more spectacular and relatively less dangerous system of conflict than was competition for European land.
27. For the relationship of the assumption of statehood and the functioning of diplomatic immunities, see a discussion of the theoretical underpinnings of diplomatic immunities in Ernest L. Kesey, "Some Aspects of the Vienna Conference on Diplomatic Intercourse and Immunities," *American Journal of International Law,* LXXXVIII (January 1962), 92–94.
28. Morgenthau, 547.
29. For a discussion of the precise meaning of these classifications, see Nussbaum.
30. *Ibid.,* 149.
31. Hugo Grotius, *The Rights of War and Peace,* ed. with notes by A. C. Campbell (Washington 1901), 62.
32. Cornelius Van Bynkershoek, *De dominio maris dissertatio,* trans. by Ralph Van Deman Mogoffin (New York 1923), 35.
33. De Visscher, 88. For similar interpretations of classical and pre-twentieth century theorists, see Walter Schiffer, *The Legal Community of Mankind* (New York 1951), chap 1; or Percy E. Corbett, *Law and Society in the Relations of States* (New York 1951).
34. Emeric de Vattel, *The Laws of Nations* (Philadelphia 1867), 412–14.
35. G. F. Von Martens, *The Law of Nations: Being the Science of National Law, Covenants, Power & Founded upon the Treaties and Custom of Modern Nations in Europe,* trans. by William Cobbett (4th ed., London, 1829), 123–24.

36. Almost all of the nineteenth-century positivists assumed that relations between nations were systematized enough to allow for a system of rights and duties. E.g., William Edward Hall, *A Treatise on International Law* (Oxford 1904), 43–59. Henry Wheaton, *Elements of International Law* (Oxford 1936), 75. Wheaton does not discuss duties as such, but when he talks about legal rights he distinguishes between "absolute" and "conditional" rights. According to Wheaton, the "conditional" rights are those resulting from membership in the international legal system. This formulation implies the existence of corresponding duties.

37. See Von Martens, 123–34, for the intellectual and legal problems growing out of the assumption that states may legally maximize power but that they also have a responsibility "to oppose by alliances and even by force of arms" a series of aggrandizements which threaten the community.

38. E.g., Charles G. Fenwick, *International Law* (New York 1952), chap. 11.

39. For a survey of current challenges to traditional international law, see Wolfgang Friedmann, "The Changing Dimensions of International Law," *Columbia Law Review*, LXII (November 1962), 1147–65. Also, see Richard A. Falk, *The Role of the Domestic Courts in the International Legal Order* (Syracuse 1964), 14–19, for a discussion of the fact that while there is a growing "functional obsolescence" of the state system, the assumptions of the state system continue to operate for psychological and political reasons.

40. E.g., Articles 3 and 4 of the *Treaty Establishing the European Coal and Steel Community* (April 18, 1951).

41. For an excellent discussion of the legal and political problems related to the question of the "act of state doctrine" in particular, and of territorial supremacy as a concept in general, see Kenneth S. Carlston, *Law and Organization in World Society* (Urbana, Ill., 1962), 191–93, 266–69. Also, for a discussion of the problem in a larger framework, see Falk, *Role of the Domestic Courts*. Since World War II, states, especially on the European continent, have found increasingly broader bases to invalidate the effect of foreign laws. Traditionally, states have refused to give validity to the laws of other lands for a small number of narrowly constructed reasons (e.g., refusal to enforce penal or revenue laws). Today many states have declared foreign laws invalid for a variety of reasons, the most important being the formulation that the national court cannot give validity to a foreign law that is illegal in terms of international law (see *"The Rose Mary Case," International Law Report* [1953], 316ff.), and the most frequent being a broad interpretation of "sense of public order" (see Martin Domke, "Indonesian Nationalization Measures Before Foreign Courts," *American Journal of International Law*, LIV [April 1960], 305–23). The most recent case in American practice, the *Sabbatino* decision (Supplement, *International Legal Materials*, III, No. 2 [March 1964], 391), appears to reaffirm the traditional emphasis on the territorial supremacy of the national legal order in these matters, but is actually ambiguous. On the one hand, the Opinion of the Court applied the "act of state doctrine" in declaring the Cuban law valid, but on the other hand, the Court stated that "international law does not require application of the doctrine."

42. For a useful discussion of the relationship between the idea of collective security and the assumption of the balance of power system, see Inis L. Claude, *Swords into Plowshares* (New York 1962), 255–60; and Herz, chap. 5. It is necessary to make a distinction between the theory of collective security, which certainly would challenge the basic assumptions of the state system, and its operation, which would not.

43. Compare Articles 25–51 , or paragraphs 2–7 in Article 2, for the contrast between system-oriented and state-oriented norms.

44. This is not to say that regional organizations do not represent a challenge to the concept of the state on psychological or social grounds. Obviously, the type of allegiance to a United Europe would be different in kind and degree from the traditional allegiance to a European state. However, in terms of the challenge to the legal concept of the state, regional organizations still adhere to the idea that the constituent members are sovereign in their relationship with states outside the organization.

45. See Corbett, 51–56, for a discussion of the place of the individual in classical international law.

46. Most modern writers have noted that the individual no longer stands in relation to international law solely as the object (e.g., Corbett, 133–35, or Friedmann, 1160–62), though they are agreed that, to use Friedmann's words, "the rights of the individual in international law are as yet fragmentary and uncertain."

47. According to Guido de Ruggiero, *The History of European Liberalism* (Boston 1959), 363–70, the liberal conception of the state has always assumed that the individual was the absolute value, though this idea has not always been operative.

48. For an excellent discussion of the role of collective responsibility in international law, see Hans Kelsen, *Principles of International Law* (New York 1959), 9–13, 114–48.

49. Although the military struggle today is considered to be only one aspect of the struggle for power, it is the one most closely related to the problem of order in both the classical and the contemporary system, and therefore the most crucial in the relationship between law and politics.

50. See D. W. Bowett, *Self Defense in International Law* (Manchester 1958), 156–57, and Nussbaum, 137, 153–55, 171.

51. See Nussbaum, 182–83. Also see Ian Brownlie, *International Law and the Use of Force by States* (Oxford 1963), 15–18.

52. Actually, the range of action provided by the contemporary formulation, especially regarding the authorization in accordance with the United Nations Charter, could be broad and could conceivably take in "balancing" action if the deadlock in the Security Council were broken. The reason for this is the very ambiguous mandate for Security Council action spelled out in the Charter. It is possible under this mandate to call the limited "balancing" action, typical of the eighteenth century, an action taken to counter a "threat to the peace." Nonetheless, given the current stalemate within the Security Council, and the nature of the General Assembly actions to date, it is safe to conclude that contemporary international law has greatly limited the wide-ranging legal capacity that states once had in deciding on the use of force.

53. See Brownlie, 251–80, for a discussion of the contemporary legal restrictions on the use of force. Also see Kaplan and Katzenbach, 205, for a discussion of the just war doctrine and its compatibility with the balance of power system.

54. Certainly, technological developments have been primarily responsible for the rejection of war as a typical tool of international power. In this case, as in most, international legal doctrine mirrors the existing attitudes and helps to reinforce them.

55. As in the past, international lawyers are still concerned with definitions and applications of concepts of territorial integrity, self-defense, and domestic jurisdiction,

and policy-makers are still motivated by the traditional ideas of state security and power. However, the traditional political and legal symbols have been "stretched" to apply to current conditions. For a development of this position see Coplin, chaps. 4 and 8.

56. E.g., Arthur Larson, *When Nations Disagree* (Baton Rouge, La., 1961); or Grenville Clark and Louis B. Sohn, *World Peace Through World Law* (Cambridge, Mass., 1960). These theorists and others who fall under this classification are "radical" in the sense that what they suggest is antithetical to the assumptions of the state system as traditionally developed. These writers are not necessarily utopian in their radicalism. This is especially true since adherence today to the traditional assumptions might itself be considered a form of (reactionary) radicalism. However, the radical scholars, in the sense used here, are very scarce, especially among American students of international law. Today there is a very thin line separating the few radical scholars from the more numerous radical polemicists of world government.

57. Morgenthau writes (277): "To recognize that international law exists is, however, not tantamount to assessing that . . . it is effective in regulating and restraining the struggle for power on the international scene."

58. E. H. Carr, in *The Twenty Years' Crisis, 1919–1939* (London 1958), 170, writes: "We are exhorted to establish 'the rule of law' . . . and the assumption is made that, by so doing, we shall transfer our differences from the turbulent political atmosphere of self interest to the purer, serener air of impartial justice." His subsequent analysis is designed to disprove this assumption.

59. George F. Kennan, *Realities of American Foreign Policy* (Princeton 1954), 16.

60. Julius Stone, *Legal Control of International Conflict* (New York, 1954), introduction.

61. Corbett, 68–70, 201–06.

62. De Visscher writes (xiv): "International law cannot gather strength by isolating itself from the political realities with which international relations are everywhere impregnated. It can only do so by taking full account of the place that these realities occupy and measuring the obstacle which they present."

63. The programs of the last two annual meetings of the American Society of International Law exemplify the way in which the concern for reality (as power) has come to dominate international legal theory. In the 1963 program, the relationship between international law and the use of force was not discussed by international legal theorists but by two well known writers on the role of conflict in international politics. The 1964 program manifested the same tendency. It centered on the question of compliance with transnational law, a topic treated in a sociopolitical framework by most panelists. This point is not to be taken as a criticism of the two programs, both of which were excellent and very relevant, but as proof of the assertion that the mainstream of contemporary theory of international law is significantly oriented to the role of power.

64. Many writers, even realists like Morgenthau (*op.cit.*, 275) and others like McDougal and Feliciano (*op.cit.*, 2–4), decry the modern tendency toward "cynical disenchantment with law," but it is obvious from their subsequent remarks that they are reacting more against the "utopianism" of the past than the cynicism of the present. There have been a few who have attacked the "realist" position on international law (e.g., A. H. Feller, "In Defense of International Law and Morality," *Annals of the Academy of Political and Social Science*, vol. 282 [July

1951], 77–84). However, these attacks have been infrequent and generally inef-
fective in starting a concerted action to develop more constructive theory.
For another evaluation of the "realist" trend, see Covey T. Oliver, "Thoughts
on Two Recent Events Affecting the Function of Law in the International
Community," in George A. Lipsky, ed., *Law and Politics in the World Community*
(Berkeley 1953).

32

R O B E R T   O.   K E O H A N E

COOPERATION AND
INTERNATIONAL REGIMES

HARMONY, COOPERATION, AND DISCORD

Cooperation must be distinguished from harmony. Harmony refers to a situation in which actors' policies (pursued in their own self-interest without regard
for others) *automatically* facilitate the attainment of others' goals. The classic
example of harmony is the hypothetical competitive-market world of the classical economists, in which the Invisible Hand ensures that the pursuit of self-
interest by each contributes to the interest of all. In this idealized, unreal
world, no one's actions damage anyone else; there are no "negative externalities," in the economists' jargon. Where harmony reigns, cooperation is unnecessary. It may even be injurious, if it means that certain individuals conspire
to exploit others. Adam Smith, for one, was very critical of guilds and other
conspiracies against freedom of trade (1776/1976). Cooperation and harmony
are by no means identical and ought not to be confused with one another.

Cooperation requires that the actions of separate individuals or organizations—which are not in pre-existent harmony—be brought into conformity
with one another through a process of negotiation, which is often referred to
as "policy coordination." Charles E. Lindblom has defined policy coordination as follows (1965, p. 227):

> A set of decisions is coordinated if adjustments have been made in them,
> such that the adverse consequences of any one decision for other decisions

SOURCE: From *After Hegemony: Cooperation and Discord in the World Economy*, Robert O.
Keohane (Princeton, NJ: Princeton University Press, 1984), pp. 49, 51–64. Copyright © 1984 by
Princeton University Press. Reprinted by permission of the publisher.

are to a degree and in some frequency avoided, reduced, or counterbalanced or overweighed.

Cooperation occurs when actors adjust their behavior to the actual or anticipated preferences of others, through a process of policy coordination. To summarize more formally, *intergovernmental cooperation takes place when the policies actually followed by one government are regarded by its partners as facilitating realization of their own objectives, as the result of a process of policy coordination.*

With this definition in mind, we can differentiate among cooperation, harmony, and discord, as illustrated by Figure 1. First, we ask whether actors' policies automatically facilitate the attainment of others' goals. If so, there is harmony: no adjustments need to take place. Yet harmony is rare in world politics. Rousseau sought to account for this rarity when he declared that even two countries guided by the General Will in their internal affairs would come into conflict if they had extensive contact with one another, since the General Will of each would not be general for both. Each would have a

FIGURE 1 **Harmony, Cooperation, and Discord**

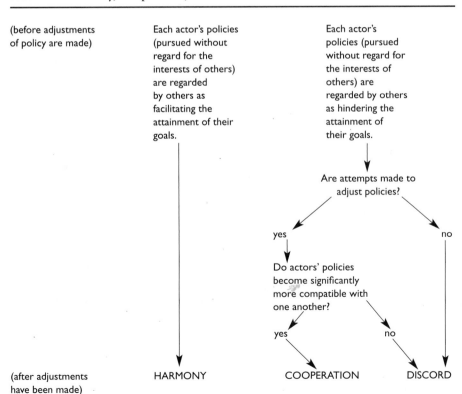

partial, self-interested perspective on their mutual interactions. Even for Adam Smith, efforts to ensure state security took precedence over measures to increase national prosperity. In defending the Navigation Acts, Smith declared: "As defence is of much more importance than opulence, the act of navigation is, perhaps, the wisest of all the commercial regulations of England" (1776/1976, p. 487). Waltz summarizes the point by saying that "in anarchy there is no automatic harmony" (1959, p. 182).

Yet this insight tells us nothing definitive about the prospects for cooperation. For this we need to ask a further question about situations in which harmony does not exist. Are attempts made by actors (governmental or nongovernmental) to adjust their policies to each others' objectives? If no such attempts are made, the result is discord: a situation in which governments regard each others' policies as hindering the attainment of their goals, and hold each other responsible for these constraints.

Discord often leads to efforts to induce others to change their policies; when these attempts meet resistance, policy conflict results. Insofar as these attempts at policy adjustment succeed in making policies more compatible, however, cooperation ensues. The policy coordination that leads to cooperation need not involve bargaining or negotiation at all. What Lindblom calls "adaptive" as opposed to "manipulative" adjustment can take place: one country may shift its policy in the direction of another's preferences without regard for the effect of its action on the other state, defer to the other country, or partially shift its policy in order to avoid adverse consequences for its partner. Or nonbargained manipulation—such as one actor confronting another with a *fait accompli*—may occur (Lindblom, 1965, pp. 33–34 and ch. 4). Frequently, of course, negotiation and bargaining indeed take place, often accompanied by other actions that are designed to induce others to adjust their policies to one's own. Each government pursues what it perceives as its self-interest, but looks for bargains that can benefit all parties to the deal, though not necessarily equally.

Harmony and cooperation are not usually distinguished from one another so clearly. Yet, in the study of world politics, they should be. Harmony is apolitical. No communication is necessary, and no influence need be exercised. Cooperation, by contrast, is highly political: somehow, patterns of behavior must be altered. This change may be accomplished through negative as well as positive inducements. Indeed, studies of international crises, as well as game-theoretic experiments and simulations, have shown that under a variety of conditions strategies that involve threats and punishments as well as promises and rewards are more effective in attaining cooperative outcomes than those that rely entirely on persuasion and the force of good example (Axelrod, 1981, 1984; Lebow, 1981; Snyder and Diesing, 1977).

Cooperation therefore does not imply an absence of conflict. On the contrary, it is typically mixed with conflict and reflects partially successful efforts to overcome conflict, real or potential. Cooperation takes place only in situations in which actors perceive that their policies are actually or potentially in conflict, not where there is harmony. Cooperation should not be viewed as the absence of conflict, but rather as a reaction to conflict or potential conflict. Without the specter of conflict, there is no need to cooperate.

The example of trade relations among friendly countries in a liberal international political economy may help to illustrate this crucial point. A naive observer, trained only to appreciate the overall welfare benefits of trade, might assume that trade relations would be harmonious: consumers in importing countries benefit from cheap foreign goods and increased competition, and producers can increasingly take advantage of the division of labor as their export markets expand. But harmony does not normally ensue. Discord on trade issues may prevail because governments do not even seek to reduce the adverse consequences of their own policies for others, but rather strive in certain respects to increase the severity of those effects. Mercantilist governments have sought in the twentieth century as well as the seventeenth to manipulate foreign trade, in conjunction with warfare, to damage each other economically and to gain productive resources themselves (Wilson, 1957; Hirschman, 1945/1980). Governments may desire "positional goods," such as high status (Hirsch, 1976), and may therefore resist even mutually beneficial cooperation if it helps others more than themselves. Yet even when neither power nor positional motivations are present, and when all participants would benefit in the aggregate from liberal trade, discord tends to predominate over harmony as the initial result of independent governmental action.

This occurs even under otherwise benign conditions because some groups or industries are forced to incur adjustment costs as changes in comparative advantage take place. Governments often respond to the ensuing demands for protection by attempting, more or less effectively, to cushion the burdens of adjustment for groups and industries that are politically influential at home. Yet unilateral measures to this effect almost always impose adjustment costs abroad, and discord continually threatens. Governments enter into international negotiations in order to reduce the conflict that would otherwise result. Even substantial potential common benefits do not create harmony when state power can be exercised on behalf of certain interests and against others. In world politics, harmony tends to vanish: attainment of the gains from pursuing complementary policies depends on cooperation.

Observers of world politics who take power and conflict seriously should be attracted to this way of defining cooperation, since my definition does not relegate cooperation to the mythological world of relations among equals in power. Hegemonic cooperation is not a contradiction in terms. Defining cooperation in contrast to harmony should, I hope, lead readers with a Realist orientation to take cooperation in world politics seriously rather than to dismiss it out of hand. . . . One way to study cooperation and discord would be to focus on particular actions as the units of analysis. This would require the systematic compilation of a data set composed of acts that could be regarded as comparable and coded according to the degree of cooperation that they reflect. Such a strategy has some attractive features. The problem with it, however, is that instances of cooperation and discord could all too easily be isolated from the context of beliefs and behavior within which they are embedded. This book does not view cooperation atomistically as a set of discrete, isolated acts, but rather seeks to understand patterns of cooperation in the world political economy. Accordingly, we need to examine actors' expectations about future patterns of interaction, their assumptions about the proper nature of economic arrangements, and the kinds of political activities they regard as legitimate. That is, we need to analyze cooperation within the context of international institutions, broadly defined in terms of practices and expectations. Each act of cooperation or discord affects the beliefs, rules, and practices that form the context for future actions. Each act must therefore be interpreted as embedded within a chain of such acts and their successive cognitive and institutional residues.

This argument parallels Clifford Geertz's discussion of how anthropologists should use the concept of culture to interpret the societies they investigate. Geertz sees culture as the "webs of significance" that people have created for themselves. On their surface, they are enigmatical; the observer has to interpret them so that they make sense. Culture, for Geertz, "is a context, something within which [social events] can be intelligibly described" (1973, p. 14). It makes little sense to describe naturalistically what goes on at a Balinese cock-fight unless one understands the meaning of the event for Balinese culture. There is not a world culture in the fullest sense, but even in world politics, human beings spin webs of significance. They develop implicit standards for behavior, some of which emphasize the principle of sovereignty and legitimize the pursuit of self-interest, while others rely on quite different principles. Any act of cooperation or apparent cooperation needs to be interpreted within the context of related actions, and of prevailing expectations and shared beliefs, before its meaning can be properly understood. Fragments of political behavior become comprehensive when viewed as part of a larger mosaic.

The concept of international regime not only enables us to describe patterns of cooperation; it also helps to account for both cooperation and discord. Although regimes themselves depend on conditions that are conducive to interstate agreements, they may also facilitate further efforts to coordinate policies.

DEFINING AND IDENTIFYING REGIMES

When John Ruggie introduced the concept of international regimes into the international politics literature in 1975, he defined a regime as "a set of mutual expectations, rules and regulations, plans, organizational energies and financial commitments, which have been accepted by a group of states" (p. 570). More recently, a collective definition, worked out at a conference on the subject, defined international regimes as "sets of implicit or explicit principles, norms, rules and decision-making procedures around which actors' expectations converge in a given area of international relations. Principles are beliefs of fact, causation, and rectitude. Norms are standards of behavior defined in terms of rights and obligations. Rules are specific prescriptions or proscriptions for action. Decision-making procedures are prevailing practices for making and implementing collective choice" (Krasner, 1983, p. 2).

This definition provides a useful starting-point for analysis, since it begins with the general conception of regimes as social institutions and explicates it further. The concept of norms, however, is ambiguous. It is important that we understand norms in this definition simply as standards of behavior defined in terms of rights and obligations. Another usage would distinguish norms from rules and principles by stipulating that participants in a social system regard norms, but not rules and principles, as morally binding regardless of considerations of narrowly defined self-interest. But to include norms, thus defined, in a definition of necessary regime characteristics would be to make the conception of regimes based strictly on self-interest a contradiction in terms. Since this book regards regimes as largely based on self-interest, I will maintain a definition of norms simply as standards of behavior, whether adopted on grounds of self-interest or otherwise. . . .

The principles of regimes define, in general, the purposes that their members are expected to pursue. For instance, the principles of the postwar trade and monetary regimes have emphasized the value of open, nondiscriminatory patterns of international economic transactions; the fundamental principle of the nonproliferation regime is that the spread of nuclear weapons is dangerous. Norms contain somewhat clearer injunctions to members about legitimate and illegitimate behavior, still defining responsibilities and obligations in relatively general terms. For instance, the norms of the General Agreement on Tariffs and Trade (GATT) do not require that members resort to free trade immediately, but incorporate injunctions to members to practice nondiscrimination and reciprocity and to move toward increased liberalization. Fundamental to the nonproliferation regime is the norm that members of the regime should not act in ways that facilitate nuclear proliferation.

The rules of a regime are difficult to distinguish from its norms; at the margin, they merge into one another. Rules are, however, more specific: they indicate in more detail the specific rights and obligations of members. Rules can be altered more easily than principles or norms, since there may be more than one set of rules that can attain a given set of purposes. Finally, at the same level of specificity as rules, but referring to procedures rather than substances, the decision-making procedures of regimes provide ways of implementing their principles and altering their rules.

An example from the field of international monetary relations may be helpful. The most important principle of the international balance-of-payments regime since the end of World War II has been that of liberalization of trade and payments. A key norm of the regime has been the injunction to states not to manipulate their exchange rates unilaterally for national advantage. Between 1958 and 1971 this norm was realized through pegged exchange rates and procedures for consultation in the event of change, supplemented with a variety of devices to help governments avoid exchange-rate changes through a combination of borrowing and internal adjustment. After 1973 governments have subscribed to the same norm, although it has been implemented more informally and probably less effectively under a system of floating exchange rates. Ruggie (1983b) has argued that the abstract principle of liberalization, subject to constraints imposed by the acceptance of the welfare state, has been maintained throughout the postwar period: "embedded liberalism" continues, reflecting a fundamental element of continuity in the international balance-of-payments regime. The norm of nonmanipulation has also been maintained, even though the specific rules of the 1958–71 system having to do with adjustment have been swept away.

The concept of international regime is complex because it is defined in terms of four distinct components: principles, norms, rules, and decision-making procedures. It is tempting to select one of these levels of specificity— particularly, principles and norms or rules and procedures—as *the* defining characteristic of regimes (Krasner, 1983; Ruggie, 1983b). Such an approach, however, creates a false dichotomy between principles on the one hand and rules and procedure on the other. As we have noted, at the margin norms and rules cannot be sharply distinguished from each other. It is difficult if not impossible to tell the difference between an "implicit rule" of broad significance and a well-understood, relatively specific operating principle. Both rules and principles may affect expectations and even values. In a strong international regime, the linkages between principles and rules are likely to be tight. Indeed, it is precisely the linkages among principles, norms, and rules that give regimes their legitimacy. Since rules, norms, and principles are so closely intertwined, judgments about whether changes in rules constitute changes *of* regime or merely changes *within* regimes necessarily contain arbitrary elements.

Principles, norms, rules, and procedures all contain injunctions about behavior: they prescribe certain actions and proscribe others. They imply obligations, even though these obligations are not enforceable through a hierarchical legal system. It clarifies the definition of regime, therefore, to think of it in terms of injunctions of greater or lesser specificity. Some are far-reaching and extremely important. They may change only rarely. At the other extreme, injunctions may be merely technical, matters of convenience that can be altered without great political or economic impact. In-between are injunctions that are both specific enough that violations of them are in principle identifiable and that changes in them can be observed, and sufficiently significant that changes in them make a difference for the behavior of actors and the nature of the international political economy. It is these intermediate injunctions—politically consequential but specific enough that violations and changes can be identified—that I take as the essence of international regimes.[1]

A brief examination of international oil regimes, and their injunctions, may help us clarify this point. The pre-1939 international oil regime was dominated by a small number of international firms and contained explicit injunctions about where and under what conditions companies could produce oil, and where and how they should market it. The rules of the Red Line and Achnacarry or "As-Is" agreements of 1928 reflected an "anticompetitive ethos": that is, the basic principle that competition was destructive to the system and the norm that firms should not engage in it (Turner, 1978, p. 30). This principle and this norm both persisted after World War II, although an intergovernmental regime with explicit rules was not established, owing to the failure of the Anglo-American Petroleum Agreement. Injunctions against price-cutting were reflected more in the practices of companies than in formal rules. Yet expectations and practices of major actors were strongly affected by these injunctions, and in this sense the criteria for a regime—albeit a weak one—were met. As governments of producing countries became more assertive, however, and as formerly domestic independent companies entered international markets, these arrangements collapsed; after the mid-to-late 1960s, there was no regime for the issue-area as a whole, since no injunctions could be said to be accepted as obligatory by all influential actors. Rather, there was a "tug of war" (Hirschman, 1981) in which all sides resorted to self-help. The Organization of Petroleum Exporting Countries (OPEC) sought to create a producers' regime based on rules for prorationing oil production, and consumers established an emergency oil-sharing system in the new International Energy Agency to counteract the threat of selective embargoes.

If we were to have paid attention only to the principle of avoiding competition, we would have seen continuity: whatever the dominant actors, they have always sought to cartelize the industry one way or another. But to do so would be to miss the main point, which is that momentous changes have occurred. At the other extreme, we could have fixed our attention on very specific particular arrangements, such as the various joint ventures of the 1950s and 1960s or the specific provisions for controlling output tried by OPEC after 1973, in which case we would have observed a pattern of continual flux. The significance of the most important events—the demise of old cartel arrangements, the undermining of the international majors' positions in the 1960s, and the rise of producing governments to a position of influence in the 1970s—could have been missed. Only by focusing on the intermediate level of relatively specific but politically consequential injunctions, whether we call them rules, norms, or principles, does the concept of regime help us identify major changes that require explanation.

As our examples of money and oil suggest, we regard the scope of international regimes as corresponding, in general, to the boundaries of issue-areas, since governments establish regimes to deal with problems that they regard as so closely linked that they should be dealt with together. Issue-areas are best defined as sets of issues that are in fact dealt with in common negotiations and by the same, or closely coordinated, bureaucracies, as opposed to issues that are dealt with separately and in uncoordinated fashion. Since issue-areas depend on actors' perceptions and behavior rather than on inherent qualities of the subject-matters, their boundaries change gradually over time. Fifty years ago, for instance, there was no oceans issue-area, since particular questions now grouped under that heading were dealt with separately; but there was an international monetary issue-area even then (Keohane and Nye, 1977, ch. 4). Twenty years ago trade in cotton textiles had an international regime of its own—the Long-Term Agreement on Cotton Textiles—and was treated separately from trade in synthetic fibers (Aggarwal, 1981). Issue-areas are defined and redefined by changing patterns of human intervention; so are international regimes.

SELF-HELP AND INTERNATIONAL REGIMES

The injunctions of international regimes rarely affect economic transactions directly: state institutions, rather than international organizations, impose tariffs and quotas, intervene in foreign exchange markets, and manipulate oil prices through taxes and subsidies. If we think about the impact of the principles, norms, rules, and decision-making procedures of regimes, it becomes clear that insofar as they have any effect at all, it must be exerted on national controls, and especially on the specific interstate agreements that affect the exercise of national controls (Aggarwal, 1981). International regimes must be distinguished from these specific agreements; a major function of regimes is to facilitate the making of specific cooperative agreements among governments.

Superficially, it could seem that since international regimes affect national controls, the regimes are of superior importance—just as federal laws in the United States frequently override state and local legislation. Yet this would be a fundamentally misleading conclusion. In a well-ordered society, the units of action—individuals in classic liberal thought—live together within a framework of constitutional principles that define property rights, establish who may control the state, and specify the conditions under which subjects must obey governmental regulations. In the United States, these principles establish the supremacy of the federal government in a number of policy areas, though not in all. But world politics is decentralized rather than hierarchic: the prevailing principle of sovereignty means that states are subject to no superior government (Ruggie, 1983a). The resulting system is sometimes referred to as one of "self-help" (Waltz, 1979).

Sovereignty and self-help mean that the principles and rules of international regimes will necessarily be weaker than in domestic society. In a civil society, these rules "specify terms of exchange" within the framework of constitutional principles (North, 1981, p. 203). In world politics, the principles, norms, and rules of regimes are necessarily fragile because they risk coming into conflict with the principle of sovereignty and the associated norm of self-help. They may promote cooperation, but the fundamental basis of order on which they would rest in a well-ordered society does not exist. They drift around without being tied to the solid anchor of the state.

Yet even if the principles of sovereignty and self-help limit the degree of confidence to be placed in international agreements, they do not render cooperation impossible. Orthodox theory itself relies on mutual interests to explain forms of cooperation that are used by states as instruments of competition. According to balance-of-power theory, cooperative endeavors such as political-military alliances necessarily form in self-help systems (Waltz, 1979). Acts of cooperation are accounted for on the grounds that mutual interests are sufficient to enable states to overcome their suspicions of one another. But since even orthodox theory relies on mutual interests, its advocates are on weak ground in objecting to interpretations of system-wide cooperation along these lines. There is no logical or empirical reason why mutual interests in world politics should be limited to interests in combining forces against adversaries. As economists emphasize, there can also be mutual interests in securing efficiency gains from voluntary exchange or oligopolistic rewards from the creation and division of rents resulting from the control and manipulation of markets.

International regimes should not be interpreted as elements of a new international order "beyond the nation-state." They should be comprehended chiefly as arrangements motivated by self-interest: as components of systems in which sovereignty remains a constitutive principle. This means that, as Realists emphasize, they will be shaped largely by their most powerful members, pursuing their own interests. But regimes can also affect state interests, for the notion of self-interest is itself elastic and largely subjective. Perceptions of self-interest depend both on actors' expectations of the likely consequences that will follow from particular actions and on their fundamental values. Regimes can certainly affect expectations and may affect values as well. Far from being contradicted by the view that international behavior is shaped largely by power and interests, the concept of international regime is consistent both with the importance of differential power and with a sophisticated view of self-interest. Theories of regimes can incorporate Realist insights about the role of power and interest, while also indicating the inadequacy of theories that define interests so narrowly that they fail to take the role of institutions into account.

Regimes not only are consistent with self-interest but may under some conditions even be necessary to its effective pursuit. They facilitate the smooth operation of decentralized international political systems and therefore perform an important function for states. In a world political economy characterized by growing interdependence, they may become increasingly useful for governments that wish to solve common problems and pursue complementary purposes without subordinating themselves to hierarchical systems of control.

CONCLUSIONS

In this chapter international cooperation has been defined as a process through which policies actually followed by governments come to be regarded by their partners as facilitating realization of their own objectives, as the result of policy coordination. Cooperation involves mutual adjustment and can only arise from conflict or potential conflict. It must therefore be distinguished from harmony. Discord, which is the opposite of harmony, stimulates demands for policy adjustments, which can either lead to cooperation or to continued, perhaps intensified, discord.

Since international regimes reflect patterns of cooperation and discord over time, focusing on them leads us to examine long-term patterns of behavior, rather than treating acts of cooperation as isolated events. Regimes consist of injunctions at various levels of generality, ranging from principles to norms to highly specific rules and decision-making procedures. By investigating the evolution of the norms and rules of a regime over time, we can use the concept of international regime both to explore continuity and to investigate change in the world political economy.

From a theoretical standpoint, regimes can be viewed as intermediate factors, or "intervening variables," between fundamental characteristics of world politics such as the international distribution of power on the one hand and the behavior of states and nonstate actors such as multinational corporations on the other. The concept of international regime helps us account for cooperation and discord. To understand the impact of regimes, it is not necessary to posit idealism on the part of actors in world politics. On the contrary, the norms and rules of regimes can exert an effect on behavior even if they do not embody common ideals but are used by self-interested states and corporations engaging in a process of mutual adjustment.

NOTE

1. Some authors have defined "regime" as equivalent to the conventional concept of international system. For instance, Puchala and Hopkins (1983) claim that "a regime exists in every substantive issue-area in international relations where there is discernibly patterned behavior" (p. 63). To adopt this definition would be to make either "system" or "regime" a redundant term. At the opposite extreme, the concept of regime could be limited to situations with genuine normative content, in which governments followed regime rules *instead of* pursuing their own self-interests when the two conflicted. If this course were chosen, the concept of regime would be just another way of expressing ancient "idealist" sentiments in international relations. The category of regime would become virtually empty. This dichotomy poses a false choice between using "regime" as a new label for old patterns and defining regimes as utopias. Either strategy would make the term irrelevant.

33

ROBERT AXELROD

THE EVOLUTION OF COOPERATION

The main results of Cooperation Theory are encouraging. They show that cooperation can get started by even a small cluster of individuals who are prepared to reciprocate cooperation, even in a world where no one else will cooperate. The analysis also shows that the two key requisites for cooperation to thrive are that the cooperation be based on reciprocity, and that the shadow of the future is important enough to make this reciprocity stable. But once cooperation based on reciprocity is established in a population, it can protect itself from invasion by uncooperative strategies.

It is encouraging to see that cooperation can get started, can thrive in a variegated environment, and can protect itself once established. But what is most interesting is how little had to be assumed about the individuals or the social setting to establish these results. The individuals do not have to be rational: the evolutionary process allows the successful strategies to thrive, even if the players do not know why or how. Nor do the players have to exchange messages or commitments: they do not need words, because their deeds speak for them. Likewise, there is no need to assume trust between the players: the use of reciprocity can be enough to make defection unproductive. Altruism is not needed: successful strategies can elicit cooperation even from an egoist. Finally, no central authority is needed: cooperation based on reciprocity can be self-policing.

The emergence, growth, and maintenance of cooperation do require some assumptions about the individuals and the social setting. They require an individual to be able to recognize another player who has been dealt with before. They also require that one's prior history of interactions with this player can be remembered, so that a player can be responsive. Actually, these requirements for recognition and recall are not as strong as they might seem. Even bacteria can fulfill them by interacting with only one other organism and using a strategy (such as Tit for Tat) which responds only to the recent behavior of the other player. And if bacteria can play games, so can people and nations.

For cooperation to prove stable, the future must have a sufficiently large shadow. This means that the importance of the next encounter between the same two individuals must be great enough to make defection an unprofitable strategy when the other player is provocable. It requires that the players have a

SOURCE: *The Evolution of Cooperation* by Robert Axelrod, pp. 173–179, 181–182, 189–191. Copyright 1984 Basic Books.

large enough chance of meeting again and that they do not discount the significance of their next meeting too greatly. For example, what made cooperation possible in the trench warfare of World War I was the fact that the same small units from opposite sides of no-man's-land would be in contact for long periods of time, so that if one side broke the tacit understandings, then the other side could retaliate against the same unit.

Finally, the evolution of cooperation requires that successful strategies can thrive and that there be a source of variation in the strategies which are being used. These mechanisms can be classical Darwinian survival of the fittest and the mutation, but they can also involve more deliberate processes such as imitation of successful patterns of behavior and intelligently designed new strategic ideas.

In order for cooperation to get started in the first place, one more condition is required. The problem is that in a world of unconditional defection, a single individual who offers cooperation cannot prosper unless others are around who will reciprocate. On the other hand, cooperation can emerge from small clusters of discriminating individuals as long as these individuals have even a small proportion of their interactions with each other. So there must be some clustering of individuals who use strategies with two properties: the strategies will be the first to cooperate, and they will discriminate between those who respond to the cooperation and those who do not.

The conditions for the evolution of cooperation tell what is necessary, but do not, by themselves, tell what strategies will be most successful. For this question, the tournament approach has offered striking evidence in favor of the robust success of the simplest of all discriminating strategies: Tit for Tat. By cooperating on the first move, and then doing whatever the other player did on the previous move, Tit for Tat managed to do well with a wide variety of more or less sophisticated decision rules. It not only won the first round of the Computer Prisoner's Dilemma Tournament when facing entries submitted by professional game theorists, but it also won the second round which included over sixty entries designed by people who were able to take the results of the first round into account. It was also the winner in five of the six major variants of the second round (and second in the sixth variant). And most impressive, its success was not based only upon its ability to do well with strategies which scored poorly for themselves. This was shown by an ecological analysis of hypothetical future rounds of the tournament. In this simulation of hundreds of rounds of the tournament, Tit for Tat again was the most successful rule, indicating that it can do well with good and bad rules alike.

Tit for Tat's robust success is due to being nice, provocable, forgiving, and clear. Its niceness means that it is never the first to defect, and this property prevents it from getting into unnecessary trouble. Its retaliation discourages the other side from persisting whenever defection is tried. Its forgiveness helps restore mutual cooperation. And its clarity makes its behavioral pattern easy to recognize; and once recognized, it is easy to perceive that the best way of dealing with Tit for Tat is to cooperate with it.

Despite its robust success, Tit for Tat cannot be called the ideal strategy to play in the iterated Prisoner's Dilemma. For one thing, Tit for Tat and other nice rules require for their effectiveness that the shadow of the future be sufficiently great. But even then there is no ideal strategy independent of the strategies used by the others. In some extreme environments, even Tit for Tat would do poorly—as would be the case if there were not enough others who would ever reciprocate its initial cooperative choice. And Tit for Tat does have its strategic weaknesses as well. For example, if the other player defects once, Tit for Tat will always respond with a defection, and then if the other player does the same in response, the result would be an unending echo of alternating defections. In this sense, Tit for Tat is not forgiving enough. But another problem is that Tit for Tat is too forgiving to those rules which are totally unresponsive, such as a completely random rule. What can be said for Tit for Tat is that it does indeed perform well in a wide variety of settings where the other players are all using more or less sophisticated strategies which themselves are designed to do well.

If a nice strategy, such as Tit for Tat, does eventually come to be adopted by virtually everyone, then individuals using this nice strategy can afford to be generous in dealing with any others. In fact, a population of nice rules can also protect itself from clusters of individuals using any other strategy just as well as they can protect themselves against single individuals.

These results give a chronological picture for the evolution of cooperation. Cooperation can begin with small clusters. It can thrive with rules that are nice, provocable, and somewhat forgiving. And once established in a population, individuals using such discriminating strategies can protect themselves from invasion. The overall level of cooperation tends to go up and not down. In other words, the machinery for the evolution of cooperation contains a ratchet. . . .

Ordinary business transactions are also based upon the idea that a continuing relationship allows cooperation to develop without the assistance of a central authority. Even though the courts do provide a central authority for the resolution of business disputes, this authority is usually not invoked. A common business attitude is expressed by a purchasing agent who said that "if something comes up you get the other man on the telephone and deal with the problem. You don't read legalistic contract clauses at each other if you ever want to do business again" (Macaulay 1963, p. 61). This attitude is so well established that when a large manufacturer of packaging materials inspected its records it found that it had failed to create legally binding contracts in two-thirds of the orders from its customers (Macaulay 1963). The fairness of the transactions is guaranteed not by the threat of a legal suit, but rather by the anticipation of mutually rewarding transactions in the future.

It is precisely when this anticipation of future interaction breaks down that an external authority is invoked. According to Macaulay, perhaps the most common type of business contracts case fought all the way to the appellate courts is an action for a wrongful termination of a dealer's franchise by a parent company. This pattern of conflict makes sense because once a franchise is ended, there is no prospect for further mutually rewarding transactions between the franchiser and the parent company. Cooperation ends, and costly court battles are often the result.

In other contexts, mutually rewarding relations become so commonplace that the separate identities of the participants can become blurred. For example, Lloyd's of London began as a small group of independent insurance brokers. Since the insurance of a ship and its cargo would be a large undertaking for one dealer, several brokers frequently made trades with each other to pool their risks. The frequency of the interactions was so great that the underwriters gradually developed into a federated organization with a formal structure of its own. . . .

The potential for attaining cooperation without formal agreements has its bright side in other contexts. For example, it means that cooperation on the control of the arms race does not have to be sought entirely through the formal mechanism of negotiated treaties. Arms control could also evolve tacitly. Certainly, the fact that the United States and the Soviet Union know that they will both be dealing with each other for a very long time should help establish the necessary conditions. The leaders may not like each other, but neither did the soldiers in World War I who learned to live and let live.

Occasionally a political leader gets the idea that cooperation with another major power should not be sought because a better plan would be to drive them into bankruptcy. This is an extraordinarily risky enterprise because the target need not limit its response to the withholding of normal cooperation, but would also have a strong incentive to escalate the conflict before it was irreversibly weakened. Japan's desperate gamble at Pearl Harbor, for example, was a response to powerful American economic sanctions aimed at stopping Japanese intervention in China (Ike 1967; Hosoya 1968). Rather than give up what it regarded as a vital sphere, Japan decided to attack America before becoming even further weakened. Japan understood that America was much more powerful, but decided that the cumulative effects of the sanctions made it better to attack rather than to wait for the situation to get even more desperate.

Trying to drive someone bankrupt changes the time perspective of the participants by placing the future of the interaction very much in doubt. And without the shadow of the future, cooperation becomes impossible to sustain. Thus, the role of time perspectives is critical in the maintenance of cooperation. When the interaction is likely to continue for a long time, and the players care enough about their future together, the conditions are ripe for the emergence and maintenance of cooperation.

The foundation of cooperation is not really trust, but the durability of the relationship. When the conditions are right, the players can come to cooperate with each other through trial-and-error learning about possibilities for mutual rewards, through imitation of other successful players, or even through a blind process of selection of the more successful strategies with a weeding out of the less successful ones. Whether the players trust each other or not is less important in the long run than whether the conditions are ripe for them to build a stable pattern of cooperation with each other.

Just as the future is important for the establishment of the conditions for cooperation, the past is important for the monitoring of actual behavior. It is essential that the players are able to observe and respond to each other's prior choices. Without this ability to use the past, defections could not be punished, and the incentive to cooperate would disappear. . . .

Once the word gets out that reciprocity works, it becomes the thing to do. If you expect others to reciprocate your defections as well as your cooperations, you will be wise to avoid starting any trouble. Moreover, you will be wise to defect after someone else defects, showing that you will not be exploited. Thus you too will be wise to use a strategy based upon reciprocity. So will everyone else. In this manner the appreciation of the value of reciprocity becomes self-reinforcing. Once it gets going, it gets stronger and stronger. . . .

We might come to see more clearly that there is a lesson in the fact that Tit for Tat succeeds without doing better than anyone with whom it interacts. It succeeds by eliciting cooperation from others, not by defeating them. We are used to thinking about competitions in which there is only one winner, competitions such as football or chess. But the world is rarely like that. In a vast range of situations mutual cooperation can be better for *both* sides than mutual defection. The key to doing well lies not in overcoming others, but in eliciting their cooperation.

Today, the most important problems facing humanity are in the arena of international relations, where independent, egoistic nations face each other in a state of near anarchy. Many of these problems take the form of an iterated Prisoner's Dilemma. Examples can include arms races, nuclear proliferation, crisis bargaining, and military escalation. Of course, a realistic understanding of these problems would have to take into account many factors not incorporated into the simple Prisoner's Dilemma formulation, such as ideology, bureaucratic politics, commitments, coalitions, mediation, and leadership. Nevertheless, we can use all the insights we can get. . . .

The advice . . . to players of the Prisoner's Dilemma might serve as good advice to national leaders as well: don't be envious, don't be the first to defect, reciprocate both cooperation and defection, and don't be too clever. Likewise, the techniques . . . for promoting cooperation in the Prisoner's Dilemma might also be useful in promoting cooperation in international politics.

The core of the problem of how to achieve rewards from cooperation is that trial and error in learning is slow and painful. The conditions may all be favorable for long-run developments, but we may not have the time to wait for blind processes to move us slowly toward mutually rewarding strategies based upon reciprocity. Perhaps if we understand the process better, we can use our foresight to speed up the evolution of cooperation.

REFERENCE

Macaulay, Stewart. "Non-Contractual Relations in Business: A Preliminary Study." *American Sociological Review* 28, no. 1: 55–67, 1963.

34

DONALD J. PUCHALA

THE INTEGRATION THEORISTS AND THE STUDY OF INTERNATIONAL RELATIONS

When the intellectual history of twentieth-century social science is written, there is likely to be at least one chapter on "the study of international integration." Somewhere in that chapter there may be a rather long, but not especially prominent, footnote that will explain how a series of events in Western Europe[1] after World War II prompted two generations of scholars to proliferate abstract explanations of what was happening.[2] It will further tell how the European experience and forthcoming explanations inspired some of these scholars to ask whether what was happening on the Old Continent was also happening elsewhere.[3] The early consensus among these scholars was to label the phenomenon under consideration "international integration" (although, as it turned out, there was little consensus about what this label meant). Under the influence of the prevailing social "scientism" of the 1950s and 1960s, newly generated abstractions about international integration were clustered and elevated to the status of "integration theories."[4] There ensued a prolonged debate among scholars concerning the power and accuracy of the various theories, and schools of analysis consequently emerged, all mutually critical and highly self-critical as well, and each claiming exclusive insight, almost as in the parable of the blind men and the elephant.[5]

As this debate among theorists gathered momentum, and indeed as it was beginning to yield some imaginative efforts to "integrate" integration theory,[6] whatever had been happening in Western Europe apparently stopped happening. It stopped happening elsewhere as well, and to the intellectual embarrassment of scholars involved, integration theory offered no satisfactory explanation for these turns of events.[7] At this juncture some suggested that the so-called integration theories were probably not theories at all but simply *post hoc* generalizations about current events. Others suggested that the integration theories had been moralizations and utopian prescriptions only. Still others held that they were accurate generalizations, but that since they were

SOURCE: From *The Global Agenda: Issues and Perspectives*. 2nd Ed., Charles W. Kegley, Jr. and Eugene R. Wittkopf, eds. (New York, NY: Random House, Inc., 1988), pp. 198–215. Reprinted with permission of McGraw-Hill, Inc. and Donald J. Puchala.

addressed to explaining time-bound, nonrecurrent events, they were prone to obsolescence as theories.[8]

INTEGRATION THEORIES

It is true that integration theories formulated during the 1950s and 1960s did not provide complete answers to the theorists' main question: *Within what environment, under what conditions, and by what processes does a new transnational political unit peacefully emerge from two or more initially separate and different ones?* The theories had to be incomplete because the cases available for investigation—the Western European Common Market, Latin American and African customs unions and various other regional ventures—were themselves incomplete. Little could therefore be learned about processes leading to an end state because no end states were attained. It was supposed that integration would ultimately produce something like a nation-state or multinational federation, but empirically there was no way to tell. History could have been mined for more cases, and it was to a certain extent, but this left other unanswerable questions about the comparability of conditions across eras.[9]

The main point of this [essay] is that the findings of the integration theorists specifically concerning international political unification are, in retrospect, less important than their broader contributions to the contemporary study of international relations. This point will be elaborated in a moment. However, the integration theories per se should not be dismissed out of hand, because they reveal a good deal about the process of peaceful international merger. We will therefore examine these first before taking up their implications. Most of the lasting work was done within the intellectual confines of two distinct theoretical schools, transactionalism and neo-functionalism, led by two American political scientists, Karl W. Deutsch and Ernst B. Haas, respectively.

TRANSACTIONALISM

Karl Deutsch's approach to the study of international integration came to be labeled *transactionalism* because members of the theoretical school tested propositions concerning community formation among peoples by examining frequencies of intra- and intergroup transactions.[10] However, Deutsch's most direct statements concerning international integration are set forth in *Political Community and the North Atlantic Area*, written in collaboration with colleagues at Princeton University between 1952 and 1956.[11] Here Deutsch specifies that integration is to be distinguished from amalgamation, in that the former has to do with the formation of communities, and the latter with the establishment of organizations, associations, or political institutions. Communities are groups of people who have attributes in common, who display mutual responsiveness, confidence, and esteem, and who self-consciously self-identify. A minimum condition of community is a shared expectation among members that their conflicts will be peacefully resolved.[12] This minimum community is called a security community.[13]

International communities may be either amalgamated or pluralistic. If amalgamated, the community would look very much like a federation or nation-state, with institutions of central government regulating the internal and external relations of an integrated population. (A fully amalgamated community would in fact be indistinguishable from a federation or nation-state.) By contrast, the pluralistic international community is a population integrated into at least a security community, but politically fragmented into two or more separate sovereign states. Typical of the various kinds of international communities would be the thirteen American states in 1781, as an example of a newly amalgamated international community, Americans and Canadians at present, as an example of a pluralistic international community, and the Benelux Union, as an example of an entity intermediate between a pluralistic and an amalgamated community.

It should be underlined that for the transactionalists, both integration and amalgamation are quantitative concepts. Both are to be measured with regard to degree or intensity and both range along continua that extend from incipience to fulfillment. Notably, this gives rise to an almost infinite variety of entities defined by the combination of their degrees of integration and amalgamation. Many of these exist empirically. What is fascinating here is that the behavioral properties of the various entities created by combination of integration and amalgamation tend to differ markedly with regard to both their internal and external relations. Compare, for example, differences in internal and external relations between Scotland, the United Kingdom, the British Empire, and the British Commonwealth of Nations, each of which can be located at a different integration-amalgamation intersect. What is theoretically challenging is to determine precisely the behavioral properties of the various bi-variately defined entities, and to explain whether and exactly why variations in behavior relate to varying degrees of integration and amalgamation in combination.

Deutsch and his colleagues took up this theoretical challenge by nominally distinguishing between amalgamated and pluralistic communities (and implicitly between amalgamated and pluralistic noncommunities). But the more refined theorizing suggested by the quantitative conceptualization of amalgamation and integration never reached fruition in either Deutsch's work or that of his students, because the metrics that would permit accurate assessment of degrees of amalgamation and integration could not be devised. Operationalization proved insuperable.[14] "Integration," for example, is in one sense an attitudinal phenomenon having to do in the broadest way with people's degrees of feelings of "we-ness." In another sense, integration is a process of attitudinal change that creates or culminates in such feelings of "we-ness." In neither sense is "integration" readily observable or measurable, except perhaps in the very limited number of very recent cases where mass opinion data are available, accurate, and appropriate.[15]

Amalgamation similarly defies precise quantification, partly because it has no precise definition. Deutsch defines it as "the formal merger of two or more independent units into a larger unit, with some type of common government after amalgamation." [16] But what does "formal merger" mean in an operational sense, and how does one know it when one sees it? A number of historical cases, and all of the contemporary ones, intuitively suggest that "formal merger" tends to take place in piecemeal fashion, one institution or one institutional task at a time. But, empirically, it remains extremely difficult to determine whether there is more of it or less of it in evidence [17] in particular cases at particular times. These became crucial concerns for the analysis of Western European unification during the 1960s, and a considerable effort was invested in index construction, with the result that "amalgamation" became "institutionalization," which then became a multivariate concept embodying degrees of authority, scope of authority, and resources available to authorities. Measures of institutionalization were then questioned as indices of amalgamation because they ignored "political system" attributes on the input side. [18] Amalgamation then became the "coming into being of a political system" as this was variously defined by leading theorists in comparative politics. [19] Indicators and metrics were sought for degrees of political socialization, interest articulation, demand and support, and the like. By this time "amalgamation" operationally defined had become a matrix of attributes. But their indicators tended to vary in different directions at different rates in different contexts and hence to render confusing (and fruitless) any attempts to devise composite measures of amalgamation. Of course, too, as soon as one moved from contemporary cases to historical ones, measurement problems were exacerbated by data problems.

None of this is to suggest that the methodological problems generated in attempts to operationalize and measure integration and amalgamation should detract from the heuristic value of the concepts. Even rather primitive measurement, at the level of nominal typology or simple dichotomy, often opens the way to productive research and theorizing. As alluded to above, in terms of Deutsch's concepts, we can develop an interesting typology by distinguishing between integrated and non-integrated international communities, and between amalgamated and non-amalgamated ones. From this classification, we get four entities: (1) state systems (non-integrated and non-amalgamated), (2) empires (non-integrated but amalgamated), (3) pluralistic security communities (integrated but non-amalgamated), and (4) amalgamated security communities (integrated and amalgamated). The first two have been the foci of traditional research and theorizing in international relations for many years; number 4 was the particular object of integration theorizing, and number 3 is the threshold for a number of recent departures in international relations theory discussed later.

Examining the amalgamated security community and the forces that produce and maintain it is tantamount to examining international political unification. For Deutsch, as for others, the principal empirical focus for the investigation of the amalgamated security community was the Western Europe of the Six. Here his work and that of his students and colleagues was directed toward ascertaining the existence of a security community among the peoples of the Six, ascertaining the degree of political amalgamation in evidence, and projecting both integration and amalgamation into the future in order to draw conclusions about European unification. Deutsch's most ambitious efforts at analyzing developments in Western Europe appear in his book with Merritt, Macridis, and Edinger, *France, Germany and the Western Alliance*.[20]

Aside from their substantive importance as attempts to better understand the course of European unification, these exercises were also a test of a developmental model of political unification devised by Deutsch and initially contained in his work on nationalism.[21] In this model, international political unification, or the coming into being of amalgamated security communities, is a phenomenon similar to the coming into being of nation-states. Therefore, what one would observe at the international level as political unification occurs is comparable to what one would observe at the national level when nation-states are born. First, functional links develop between separate communities. Such ties in trade, migration, mutual services, or military collaboration prompted by necessity or profit generate flows of transactions between communities and enmesh people in transcommunity communications networks. Under appropriate conditions of high volume, expanding substance, and continuing reward, over extended periods of time, intercommunity interactions generate social-psychological processes that lead to the assimilation of peoples, and hence to their integration into larger communities. Such assimilatory processes are essentially learning experiences of the stimulus-response variety.[22] Once such community formation has taken place, the desires of members and the efforts of the elites may be directed toward institutionalizing, preserving, and protecting the community's integrity and distinctiveness and regulating transactions through the establishment of institutions of government. In overview, then, the model posits that political unification—national or international—consists in moving first from communities to community, and then from community to state. This follows from initial functional link, increased transaction, social assimilation, community formation, and ultimately political amalgamation. Integration therefore precedes amalgamation; sentimental change precedes institutional change; social change precedes political change. At the core of this formulation rests the assumption that peaceful change in international relations has its origins in the perceptions and identification of people.

As an *integration theory,* in the sense that the term is being used here, Deutsch's formulation is valuable in that it focuses attention on international community formation during unification. This sentimental dimension is largely ignored in other integration theories.[23] Deutsch's formulations allow for a number of possible end-products, as noted, but to the extent that international political unification is under investigation, the postulated end-product looks like a nation-state, and attaining this implies that both integration and amalgamation have occurred, most likely in sequence.

For all its elegance and intuitive promise, Deutsch's developmental model of the unification process has some rather serious shortcomings. For one thing, the conditions under which people in newly integrated communities will or will not initiate drives for political amalgamation are never specified. Therefore, one cannot predict future amalgamation from evidence of present integration. The relationship between integration and amalgamation is certainly not causal. Otherwise the pluralistic community could never exist for any length of time. But there is a contingency link between the two that is never exactly specified in either Deutsch's work or that of his students. In short, the motivational dynamics are missing from Deutsch's process model, and this opens a serious gap.[24]

Political dynamics are similarly missing from Deutsch's model and this too seriously affects its explanatory and predictive power. The underemphasis on political dynamics—that is, decision-making, organizational behavior, coalition behavior, and so on—in the Deutsch model is essentially a level-of-analysis problem. His formulation makes statements about people's attitudes and sentiments, individually and in the aggregate, and it also makes statements about governments' policies (that is, to amalgamate or not). Therefore, as far as the theory informs us, we can believe that changes in people's attitudes and sentiments may prompt changes in governments' policies. This is reasonable, but not very helpful. What remains undisclosed is how, when, and why changes at the social-psychological level are converted into changes at the governmental level. There are no social or political structures or processes in Deutsch's integration models—no groups or classes (except elites and masses, and even these are seldom differentiated analytically), no decision makers, no decisions, very little voluntaristic behavior, and no politics. Without these social-political variables the Deutsch model forces unguided inferential leaps of considerable magnitude.

These criticisms of Deutsch's model of political unification suggest that it is incomplete, not inaccurate. Its strengths lie precisely in the fact that its explanatory and predictive power can be improved through further research into clearly definable problems. Much could be accomplished, for example, by filling the gap between integration and amalgamation with some of the neo-functionalists' findings (explained below) concerning the politics of unification, the conditions for "spillover," and the influence of international bureaucracies. If political structure and dynamics were added in this manner the power of the model would be greatly enhanced. Similarly, the gap between integration and amalgamation could be further filled by modeling the motivational dynamics of the unification process from the findings of the literatures of ideology and integration, liberal and Marxist political economy, domestic politics and integration, and the management of interdependence.[25]

NEO-FUNCTIONALISM

As contemporaries, Karl Deutsch and Ernst Haas exchanged relatively few insights concerning international integration because their foci of analytical attention and conceptual vocabularies were very different. Where Deutsch paid scant attention to the role of international institutions during political unification, Haas dwelt upon this. Moreover, Deutsch's concepts and analytical vocabulary came largely from communications theory and his earlier work on nationalism, whereas Haas drew some of his concepts from David

Mitrany's functionalism,[26] created many of his own, and wrote using a vocabulary tailored for his specific purposes. It also appeared for a time that Deutsch and Haas differed rather fundamentally on a principal causal relationship in the political unification process. As noted, Deutsch saw the mutual identification of peoples or "community" preceding, and creating favorable conditions for, institutional amalgamation. But Haas' work, by contrast, suggested that institutional amalgamation precedes and leads to community because effective institutionalization at the international level invites a refocusing of people's political attentions and a shifting of their loyalties. Community among peoples, Haas contended, follows sometime after these political and cultural shifts have occurred.[27]

Research ultimately stilled much of the controversy about the sequencing of community formation and institutional amalgamation, as both turned out to be more complex than either Deutsch or Haas supposed, and each partially caused the other in homeostatic fashion.[28] Moreover, while it may have appeared to contemporaries that Haas and Deutsch and their respective colleagues were laboring in separate intellectual vineyards, reviewing their work a decade later reveals striking complementarities in their ideas and findings. Most important, Haas explained the political dynamics of international institutionalization and policy-making and consequently linked the learning and assimilatory experiences that Deutsch observed in community formation to the political-decisional processes that occurred as governments decided to amalgamate.

Haas' work, contained in *The Uniting of Europe* and in a series of articles that refined his theory,[29] came to be called *neo-functionalism* partly, we would suppose, because it was a revision of Mitrany's work and partly because it generalized about the theories of people like Jean Monnet and Walter Hallstein who called themselves "neo-functionalists."[30] In his book Haas sought to determine the extent to which the architects of European unity were correct in assuming that they could move from piecemeal international mergers in particular sectors, such as coal and steel, to ultimately arrive at the full-blown political union of formerly separate nation-states. Even more ambitiously, in his articles Haas sought to determine whether there were general conditions and dynamics in functional amalgamation that could set integration into motion anywhere.

Haas discovered that there is an "expansive logic" in sector integration that operates, under appropriate conditions, to continually extend the range of activities under international jurisdiction. Therefore, once the international amalgamation process is initiated it could, again under appropriate conditions, "spill over" to broaden and deepen the international policy realm until ultimately most functions normally performed by national governments were transferred to international authorities. This happens because each functional step toward greater international authority sets into motion political processes that generate demands for further steps. At each step, and in the face of demands for new ones, national governments are forced to choose between surrendering additional autonomy or refusing to do so and risking the collapse of their initial effort at sectoral amalgamation. At higher levels of amalgamation, where many sectors have been internationalized, further movement comes to require major cessions of national autonomy, but, at these levels, failure to move forward, or sliding backward, may also impose great costs. Neo-functionalism posits that, other things being equal, political pressures mounted at key decision points will cause governments to choose to move toward greater amalgamation.

Spillover follows from several causes, all having to do with the politicization of issues in pluralistic societies. First, because modern industrial societies are highly interdependent it is impossible to internationalize one functional sector, say, steel production, without affecting numerous other sectors, as for example mining, transport, and labor organization and representation. Because other sectors are affected and because elites within them are organized to bring pressure on national governments, their concerns become subjects of international discussion and questions arise about granting further authority to international agencies to handle matters in affected cognate sectors. At such points governments must decide to either grant the extended international authority or court failure in the initial sector integration. If the balance of perceived rewards and penalties favors moving toward greater amalgamation, as it frequently does, governments will grant extended authority to international agencies.

Sometimes spillover follows from failures to appreciate the true magnitude or implications of tasks assigned to international agencies, so that initial conservative grants of authority prove unfeasible and must be extended. For example, when Western European attempts to promote free trade in pharmaceutical products began, the European Commission was empowered only to ask national governments to remove obstacles like tariffs. But before the free flow of pharmaceuticals could be fully facilitated it proved necessary to involve the Commission in everything pertaining to the drug industry, up to and including the education of pharmacists.[31] Then too, international bureaucrats can, and do, deliberately engineer links among tasks and sectors in efforts to enhance their own authority and to push toward the complete political unification of countries to which they are committed.[32]

Haas and his colleagues uncovered considerable evidence of spillover in the progressive integration of the European Communities during the 1960s, but very little elsewhere. In fact, in most other regions, "functional encapsulation" was the most frequent result of sector amalgamation, as no expansion of international authority followed initial grants.[33] As a result Haas was prompted to elaborate and enrich his theory by specifying conditions under which spillover would and would not occur. Most important among these was societal pluralism, which contributed to the politicization of integration issues that forced governmental decisions at pivotal points. Also crucial were the nature of sectors selected for amalgamation, links between international and national bureaucracies, prevailing incremental styles in national and international decision-making, and general value complementarity among national elites.[34]

The great strength of Haas' work was his accurate portrayal of international integration as an intensely political phenomenon. It has to do with numerous political actors, pursuing their own interests, pressuring governments, or, if they are governments, pressuring one another to negotiate toward international policies that are collectively beneficial because they are individually beneficial for all concerned. Like politics more generally, the politics of international integration is a game of bargaining—tugging, hauling, logrolling, and horse-trading that eventuates in transnationally applicable policies. A distinctive element in the politics of integration, however, is that there are always some actors who perceive that they cannot accept diminutions of national prerogative and others who insist that they will not accept the undoing of amalgamation already attained. Therefore the fate of the union itself is a constant political consideration.

Neo-functionalism naturally had some weaknesses. For one thing, the theory is limited in applicability. It concerns only international mergers that proceed in sectoral fashion, and only under appropriate conditions. In addition, it says little about the initiation of the amalgamation process. On this the neo-functionalists are as sketchy as the transactionalists. Surely, if political forces and processes drive amalgamation once it is underway, they must also have something to do with first steps. Yet neo-functionalism offers little insight into the politics of this matter. With regard to the progressive merger of sectors, moreover, neo-functionalism never produced a complete process model. The spillover dynamic is stipulated and conditioning factors are inventoried, but these factors are not related to the dynamic directly or clearly enough to show the "whens," "hows," and "whys" of their speeding, slowing, starting, or stopping effects. Some of the neo-functionalist theorists were moving toward such sophisticated modeling about the time that the effort began to peter out.[35]

The neo-functionalist effort to understand and model international integration stalled about the time that Western European movement toward greater unity encountered difficulties in the 1970s. By this time, a number of other potentially promising regional schemes in East Africa, West Africa, Central America, the Caribbean, and Latin America had also collapsed. Cases for investigation by students of international integration were therefore vanishing and this was happening before any had reached the end-state of political union that the theorists aspired to explain. At this point Haas pronounced integration theory obsolete.[36] He concluded that with some effort the theories could be improved, but he questioned the worth of making the effort, given the unlikelihood of significant international political unification during the remainder of our century. Though Haas' notice about the demise of Western European integration was exaggerated, his sense that integration theorizing had run its course was largely correct.

INTEGRATION STUDIES AND THE DISCIPLINE OF INTERNATIONAL RELATIONS

I began this essay by relegating the efforts of twenty years of formal theorizing about international integration to the status of a "footnote" to intellectual history because in a broader and more meaningful context explaining political unification was neither the most enduring nor the most significant accomplishment of the integration theorists. To understand why this is so we must make two distinctions, first between the *theories* of the integrationists and their *philosophies,* and second between *integration theory,* as represented by the generalizations of the transactionalists, neo-functionalists and others, and *integration studies* as represented by the full range of concerns, questions, observations and findings of all of those scholars who undertook to discover in the broadest sense "what was happening" within customs unions, common markets and other regional associations.

THE ATTAINABILITY OF PEACE

Though the integration theorists differed in their approaches and foci of attention and at times questioned one another's findings, their philosophies, or the values that prompted them to try to better understand international unification, were similar. Most fundamentally, the integration theorists sought to explain the conditions and dynamics of peaceful change in international relations. They were convinced that lasting peace and peaceful change were attainable, that integration processes were somehow involved in accounting for these, and that to shed light on the causes and conditions of peace was the principal goal of the study of international relations.

But, in their assumptions about the promise in international collaboration and the attainability of peace, the integration theorists, in the 1960s, were a small minority among students of international relations. Their works were injected into a scholarly community preoccupied with questions of strategic balancing in a world dominated by cold warfare. It was therefore the integrationists, and almost the integrationists alone among American scholars, who kept alive an idealism that made peace worth studying because it was assumed to be attainable. The assumption was not a flight of idealistic fancy, because the integrationists' subject matter demonstrated that peaceful change could take place and that peace could last.

THE CHALLENGE TO POLITICAL REALISM

The integrationists' studies also demonstrated that the legitimate and theoretically significant subject matter of international relations was more extensive, varied, and complex than allowed for in the disciplinary paradigm that prevailed during the first two postwar decades. Students of international integration probed into realms of postwar international relations where productive collaboration among governments was actually taking place—regional theaters, customs unions, and common markets. The patterns of behavior turned up by their research not only enlightened the understanding of integration, but also shook a number of orthodox assumptions about the nature of international relations. According to conventional wisdom in the discipline of International Relations at that time, much of the behavior and many of the outcomes and events that the integrationists were reporting *either were not supposed to happen or were not supposed to be very consequential if and when they did happen.* That is, from the very beginning of their investigations in the early 1950s students of integration were making observations and reporting discoveries that directly contradicted the prevailing political realist or "power politics" paradigm of the discipline of International Relations.[37] With emphases on conflict and coercion, states as unitary actors, and state security as an end, this paradigm conditioned the philosophical assumptions of scholars and their research priorities in studying international relations from the early 1940s onward. By the 1950s, with the eclipse of early idealism about the United Nations, political realism also became the prevailing paradigm for the study of international organization, thus leaving integration studies as a distinct, rather isolated, philosophically unorthodox subculture within International Relations. As Table 1 shows, there was no place in political realist thinking for the kinds of findings that the integrationists were making. For one thing, in the 1950s and early 1960s the integrationists were virtually alone in holding that international collaboration for welfare ends was an important aspect of contemporary international relations. They were also alone in arguing that, in terms of quantity and intensity, such collaboration was something new in the post-World War II world.

Of course the new findings of the integrationists were no more representative of the total substance of international relations than were the more traditional ones of the realists. But they were valid findings arrived at by focusing upon cases of collaborative behavior. For example:

- widespread and consequential collaboration does occur in international relations;
- supranationality is both practicable and practiced in international relations;
- international pursuits of welfare ends tend often to be highly, or more highly, politicized than international pursuits of security ends;
- transnationally organized non-governmental organizations are consequential actors in international relations;
- transgovernmentally linked bureaucrats and officials coordinate foreign policies and foreign policy-making;
- interdependence constrains states' autonomy and it complicates determinations of relative power;
- to the extent to which they serve welfare ends, the domestic and foreign policies of modern states, both industrialized and less developed, are integrally and inextricably linked.

TABLE 1 **The Realist Paradigm and Integrationist Findings**

ASSUMPTIONS OF POLITICAL REALISM AS APPLIED TO INTERNATIONAL RELATIONS	FINDINGS OF INTEGRATION STUDIES IN THE 1950S AND 1960S	IMPACTS ON THE DISCIPLINE OF INTERNATIONAL RELATIONS
(1) States and nation-states are the only consequential actors in international relations, and therefore the study of international relations should be focused upon the motives and behavior of states and nation-states or their representatives. Other actors exist but they are consequential only as agents or instruments of states.	(1) States and nation-states are not the only consequential actors in international relations. Indeed, some outcomes in international relations can be understood only in terms of the motives and behavior of international public organizations and bureaucracies, formal and *ad hoc* coalitions of officials transnationally grouped, transnationally organized non-governmental associations, multinational business enterprises, international social classes, and other actors traditionally deemed inconsequential.	(1) Orthodoxy was brought into question, and theoretical and empirical inquiries were initiated that led eventually to theories of transnational relations.
(2) International relations result from foreign policies directed toward enhancing national security, defined in terms of military might and territorial and ideological domain. Other goals are pursued by international actors, but these are "low politics" and hence command little priority in foreign policy and are of little consequence to international relations.	(2) International relations result from foreign policies directed toward enhancing national welfare defined in terms of per capital income, employment, and general well-being. The importance which governments attach to such goals and the domestic penalties and rewards surrounding their attainment or sacrifice render their pursuit "high politics."	(2) Orthodoxy was brought into question and theoretical analyses were initiated that led to the emergence and prominence of international political economy as a central disciplinary concern.
(3) International relations are fundamentally conflict processes played out in zero-sum matrices, i.e. all significant outcomes take the form of aggrandizement for one actor or coalition at the expense of other actors or coalitions. Conflict is the international mode.	(3) International relations are fundamentally collaborative processes played out in positive sum matrices, i.e. all significant outcomes take the form of realizing and distributing rewards among collaborating actors or coalitions. Cooperation is the international mode.	(3) Orthodoxy was brought into question and theoretical and empirical inquiries were initiated that led to the emergence and prominence of bargaining theory as applied to international relations.
(4) Influence in international relations follows from the application of power defined as military or economic capability, actual or potential. Coercion is the modal means to influence.	(4) Influence in international relations follows from the manipulation of bonds of interdependence that connect actors. Persuasion is the modal means to influence.	(4) Orthodoxy was brought into question and theoretical and empirical inquiries were initiated that led ultimately to theories of interdependence.

SOURCE: From R. L. Merritt and Bruce M. Russett (eds.), *From National Development to Global Community* (London: George Allen and Unwin, 1981), p. 149.

Because these new findings were valid, they opened the way and lent academic legitimacy to the study of international cooperation at a time when the world seemed engulfed in all-pervading, protracted conflict, and when the discipline of International Relations seemed fixed in the notion that conflict was the beginning and the end of its subject matter. Although it was not clearly articulated until the 1970s, integration studies in the 1950s and 1960s embodied the conceptual elements of an alternative disciplinary paradigm that contrasted sharply with the *Weltanschauung* of political realism. Later this came to be labeled post-realism.[38] In the light of this, it is small wonder that integrationist writings were greeted with incredulity by the more realist-oriented, whose frequent criticisms were either that politics within common markets were basically competitions for national power, like all international politics, or that they were not really politics at all but technocratic dealings of little international political consequence.[39] Interestingly, and ironically, at the time that the findings of integrationists were so engaged in intellectual conflict with one another that they largely ignored what their work was doing to their discipline.[40]

Enlightened by twenty years of hindsight, and cognizant of recent developments in the study of international relations, one can say with some confidence that the lasting impact of the study of international integration was the confrontation with disciplinary orthodoxy that it fomented in the 1950s and 1960s. This is its contribution to the history of social science. . . .

There are more fundamental questions about pluralistic international communities that need to be confronted and answered. When, where, and why do such entities form? How durable are they, and what affects this durability? Under what conditions do they deteriorate? Methodologically, how are we to observe the emergence of such communities, what indexes their durability, and what signals their deterioration? Except for the fascinating study of the Anglo-American security community by Russett and the fine doctoral dissertation on the same subject by Richard Storatz, very little research has been directed toward answering these questions in theoretical terms.[41] And yet they are crucial to understanding the foundations of the international relations of the contemporary Western world! We presently have no theory of international pluralism; Deutsch and other integration theorists left this work unfinished and no one has carried it forward.

Whatever the future of integration theory, integration studies and their progeny in transnational relations and interdependence studies will likely remain prominent in international relations into the foreseeable future. So too will the "post-realist" paradigm that integration studies thrust upon the discipline. Whether peaceful problem-solving and peaceful change will ever become prevailing features of international relations is uncertain. But they have apparently become more frequent in our part of the twentieth century. If understanding these better could have anything to do with further increasing their frequency, then there is much to be said for heightening our understanding.

NOTES

1. See, for example, Ernst B. Haas, *The Uniting of Europe: Political, Social and Economic Forces, 1950–1957* (Stanford: Stanford University Press, 1958).

2. Ernst B. Haas, "International Integration: The European and the Universal Process," *International Organization,* Vol. 15, no. 3 (Summer 1961), pp. 366–392; Leon N. Lindberg and Stuart A. Scheingold, *Europe's Would-Be Polity: Patterns of Change in the European Community* (Englewood Cliffs, N.J.: Prentice-Hall, 1970).

3. Ernst B. Haas and Philippe C. Schmitter, "Economics and Differential Patterns of Political Integration: Projections About Unity in Latin America," *International Organization,* Vol. 18, no. 4 (Autumn 1964), pp. 705–737; Philippe C. Schmitter, "Central American Integration: Spillover, Spill-Around or Encapsulation?" *Journal of Common Market Studies,* Vol. 9, no. 1 (September 1970), pp. 1–48; Joseph S. Nye, Jr., "East African Economic Integration," in *International Political Communities: An Anthology* (Garden City, N.Y.: Doubleday/Anchor Books, 1966), pp. 405–436; and Andrzej Korbonski, "Theory and Practice of Regional Integration: The Case of COMECON," *International Organization,* Vol. 24, no. 4 (Autumn 1970), pp. 942–977.

4. For a comparative sampling of these theories, see Leon N. Lindberg and Stuart A. Scheingold, eds., *Regional Integration: Theory and Research* (Cambridge, Mass.: Harvard University Press, 1971); Charles Pentland, *International Theory and European Integration* (N.Y.: Free Press, 1973); Roger D. Hansen, "Regional Integration: Reflections on a Decade of Theoretical Efforts," *World Politics,* Vol. 21, no. 2 (January 1969), pp. 242–271; Ronn D. Kaiser, "Toward the Copernican Phase of Regional Integration Theory," *Journal of Common Market Studies,* Vol. 10, no. 2 (March 1972), pp. 207–232; *Pour l'Etude de l'Integration Europeenne* (Montreal, Que.: Université de Montreal, Centre d'Etudes et de Documentation Europeennes, 1977), pp. 3–91; and Marie-Elisabeth de Bussy, Helene Delorme, and Françoise de la Serre, "Approches theoriques de l'integration europeenne," *Revue Française de Science Politique,* Vol. 20, no. 3 (June 1971), pp. 615–653.

5. Donald J. Puchala, "Of Blind Men, Elephants and International Integration," *Journal of Common Market Studies,* Vol. 10, no. 3 (March 1972), pp. 267–284.

6. See, for example, Pentland, *International Theory and European Integration;* and Lindberg and Scheingold, eds., *Regional Integration.*

7. Ernst B. Haas, "The Uniting of Europe and the Uniting of Latin America," *Journal of Common Market Studies,* Vol. 5, no. 4 (June 1967), pp. 315–343.

8. Ernst B. Haas, "Turbulent Fields and the Theory of Regional Integration," *International Organization,* Vol. 30, no. 2 (Spring 1976), pp. 173–212; and Ernst B. Haas, *The Obsolescence of Regional Integration Theory* (Berkeley Calif.: University of California, Institute of International Studies, 1975).

9. See Karl W. Deutsch et al., *Political Community and the North Atlantic Area: International Organization in the Light of Historical Experience* (Princeton, N.J.: Princeton University Press, 1957); Robert A. Kann, *The Hapsburg Empire: A Study in Integration and Disintegration* (N.Y.: Praeger, 1957); Raymond E. Lindgren, *Norway-Sweden: Union, Disunion and Scandinavian Integration* (Princeton, N.J.: Princeton University Press, 1959).

10. Donald J. Puchala, "International Transactions and Regional Integration," *International Organization,* Vol. 24, no. 4 (Autumn 1970), pp. 732–764.

11. Deutsch et al., op. cit.

12. Ibid., pp. 5–7.
13. The concept "security community" was introduced by Richard W. Van Wagenen in his *Research in the International Organization Field: Some Notes on a Possible Focus* (Princeton, N.J.: Princeton University, Center for Research on World Political Institutions, 1952).
14. For attempts at such operationalization, see Donald J. Puchala, "Patterns in West European Integration," *Journal of Common Market Studies,* Vol. 9, no. 2 (December 1970), pp. 117–142; Donald J. Puchala, "Integration and Disintegration in Franco-German Relations, 1954–1965," *International Organization,* Vol. 24, no. 2 (Spring 1970), pp. 183–208; and Leon N. Lindberg, "Political Integration as a Multidimensional Phenomenon Requiring Multivariate Measurement," *International Organization,* Vol. 24, no. 4 (Autumn 1970), pp. 649–731.
15. Karl W. Deutsch et al., *France, Germany and the Western Alliance: A Study of Elite Attitudes on European Integration and World Politics* (N.Y.: Charles Scribner's Sons, 1967); Ronald A. Inglehart, "Ongoing Changes in West European Political Cultures," *Integration,* Vol. 1, no. 4 (1970), pp. 250–273; Ronald A. Inglehart, "Public Opinion and Regional Integration," *International Organization,* Vol. 24, no. 4 (Autumn 1970), pp. 764–795; Ronald A. Inglehart, "Cognitive Mobilization and European Identity," *Comparative Politics,* Vol. 3, no. 1 (October 1970), pp. 45–70; Donald J. Puchala, "The Common Market and Political Federation in Western European Public Opinion," *International Studies Quarterly,* Vol. 14, no. 1 (March 1970), pp. 32–59.
16. Deutsch et al., *Political Community and the North Atlantic Area,* p. 6.
17. Lindberg and Scheingold, eds., *Regional Integration;* Puchala, "Patterns in West European Integration"; Karl W. Deutsch, "Integration and Arms Control in the European Political Environment: A Summary Report," *American Political Science Review,* Vol. 60, no. 2 (June 1966), pp. 354–365.
18. James A. Caporaso, *The Structure and Function of European Integration* (Pacific Palisades, Calif.: Goodyear, 1974).
19. Gabriel A. Almond, "Introduction: A Functional Approach to Comparative Politics," in *The Politics of the Developing Areas,* ed. Gabriel A. Almond and James S. Coleman (Princeton, N.J.: Princeton University Press, 1960), pp. 364; and David Easton, *A Systems Analysis of Political Life* (New York: Wiley, 1965).
20. Deutsch et al., *France, Germany, and the Western Alliance.*
21. Karl W. Deutsch, *Nationalism and Social Communication: An Inquiry into the Foundations of Nationality* (Cambridge, Mass., and N.Y.: M.I.T. Press and John Wiley & Sons, 1953); and Puchala, "International Transactions and Regional Integration."
22. Donald J. Puchala, "The Pattern of Contemporary Regional Integration," *International Studies Quarterly,* Vol. 12, no. 1 (March 1968), pp. 38–64.
23. The work of Amitai Etzioni is an exception; see his *Political Unification: A Comparative Study of Leaders and Forces* (N.Y.: Holt, Rinehart & Winston, 1965).
24. Peter J. Katzenstein takes important steps toward filling this gap in his *Disjoined Partners: Austria and Germany Since 1815* (Berkeley, Calif.: University of California Press, 1976); Cf. also, Katzenstein, "Domestic Structures and Political Strategies: Austria in an Interdependent World," in Merritt and Russett, eds., op. cit., pp. 252–278.
25. Joseph S. Nye, Jr., *Pan-Africanism and East African Integration* (Cambridge, Mass.: Harvard University Press, 1965); Richard N. Cooper, *The Economics of Interdependence: Economic Policy in the Atlantic Community* (N.Y.: McGraw-Hill,

1968); Johan Galtung, *The European Community: A Superpower in the Making* (Oslo: Universitetsforlaget; London: Allen & Unwin, 1973); and Robert Keohane and Joseph S. Nye Jr., *Power and Interdependence: World Politics in Transition* (Boston: Little, Brown, 1977).

26. David Mitrany, *A Working Peace System* (Chicago: Quadrangle Books, 1966).

27. Ernst B. Haas, "The Challenge of Regionalism," in *Contemporary Theory in International Relations,* Stanley Hoffmann, ed. (Englewood Cliffs, N.J.: Prentice-Hall, 1960), pp. 223–240.

28. Lindberg and Scheingold, op. cit., Chs. 3, 8, and 9.

29. See Haas, "International Integration: The European and the Universal Process"; Haas and Schmitter, op. cit.; and Haas, "The Uniting of Europe and the Uniting of Latin America."

30. See Walter Hallstein, *Europe in the Making* (N.Y.: Norton, 1972), pp. 24–28, 292–303.

31. Donald J. Puchala, "Domestic Politics and Regional Harmonization in the European Communities," *World Politics,* Vol. 27, no. 4 (July 1975), pp. 496–520.

32. Leon N. Lindberg, *The Political Dynamics of European Economic Integration* (Stanford: Stanford University Press, 1963), pp. 284–285.

33. Philippe C. Schmitter, "Central American Integration."

34. Ernst B. Haas and Philippe C. Schmitter, op. cit.

35. Joseph S. Nye, Jr., *Peace in Parts: Integration and Conflict in Regional Organization* (Boston: Little, Brown, 1971), pp. 21–107.

36. See Haas, *The Obsolescence of Regional Integration Theory,* and Haas, "Turbulent Fields and the Theory of Regional Integration."

37. Robert O. Keohane and Joseph S. Nye, Jr., "Interdependence and Integration," in *Handbook of Political Science,* Fred I. Greenstein and Nelson Polsby, eds. (Reading, Mass.: Addison-Wesley, 1975), Vol. 8, pp. 363–414; Keohane and Nye, *Power and Interdependence,* pp. 3–62; Donald J. Puchala and Stuart I. Fagan, "International Politics in the 1970s: The Search for a Perspective," *International Organization,* Vol. 28, no. 2 (Spring 1974), pp. 247–266.

38. Puchala and Fagan, op. cit., pp. 247–250.

39. Stanley Hoffmann, "Obstinate or Obsolete? The Fate of the Nation-State and the Case of Western Europe," in *International Regionalism,* Joseph S. Nye, Jr., ed. pp. 177–231; Stanley Hoffmann, "Europe's Identity Crisis: Between Past and America," *Daedalus,* Vol. 93, no. 4 (Fall 1964), pp. 1244–1297; Raymond Aron, *Peace and War: A Theory of International Relations* (Garden City, N.Y.: Doubleday, 1966), pp. 21–176, 643–666; Hans J. Morgenthau, *Politics Among Nations: The Struggle for Power and Peace,* 4th ed. (N.Y.: Alfred A. Knopf, 1967), pp. 511–516.

40. Ernst B. Haas, "The Challenge of Regionalism"; Karl W. Deutsch, "Towards Western European Integration: An Interim Assessment," *Journal of International Affairs,* Vol. 16, no. 1 (1962), pp. 89–101; Ronald A. Inglehart, "An End to European Integration?" *American Political Science Review,* Vol. 61, no. 1 (March 1967), pp. 91–105; and William E. Fisher, "An Analysis of the Deutsch Sociocausal Paradigm of Political Integration," *International Organization,* Vol. 23, no. 2 (Spring 1969), pp. 254–290.

41. Bruce M. Russett, *Community and Contention: Britain and America in the Twentieth Century* (Cambridge, Mass.: M.I.T. Press, 1963); Richard Storatz, "Anglo-American Relations: A Theory and History of Political Integration," unpublished doctoral dissertation, Department of Political Science, Columbia University, 1981.

35

ALEXANDER WENDT

ANARCHY IS WHAT
STATES MAKE OF IT

The debate between realists and liberals has reemerged as an axis of contention in international relations theory.[1] Revolving in the past around competing theories of human nature, the debate is more concerned today with the extent to which state action is influenced by "structure" (anarchy and the distribution of power) versus "process" (interaction and learning) and institutions. Does the absence of centralized political authority force states to play competitive power politics? Can international regimes overcome this logic, and under what conditions? What in anarchy is given and immutable, and what is amenable to change?

The debate between "neorealists" and "neoliberals" has been based on a shared commitment to "rationalism."[2] Like all social theories, rational choice directs us to ask some questions and not others, treating the identities and interests of agents as exogenously given and focusing on how the behavior of agents generates outcomes. As such, rationalism offers a fundamentally behavioral conception of both process and institutions: they change behavior but not identities and interests.[3] In addition to this way of framing research problems, neorealists and neoliberals share generally similar assumptions about agents: states are the dominant actors in the system, and they define security in "self-interested" terms. Neorealists and neoliberals may disagree about the extent to which states are motivated by relative versus absolute gains, but both groups take the self-interested state as the starting point for theory.

This starting point makes substantive sense for neorealists, since they believe anarchies are necessarily "self-help" systems, systems in which both

This article was negotiated with many individuals. If my records are complete (and apologies if they are not), thanks are due particularly to John Aldrich, Mike Barnett, Lea Brilmayer, David Campbell, Jim Caporaso, Simon Dalby, David Dessler, Bud Duvall, Jean Elshtain, Kanyn Ertel, Lloyd Etheridge, Ernst Haas, Martin Hollis, Naeem Inayatullah, Stewart Johnson, Frank Klink, Steve Krasner, Friedrich Kratochwil, David Lumsdaine, M. J. Peterson, Spike Peterson, Thomas Risse-Kappen, John Ruggie, Bruce Russett, Jim Scott, Rogers Smith, David Sylvan, Jan Thomson, Mark Warren, and Jutta Weldes. The article also benefited from presentations and seminars at the American University, the University of Chicago, the University of Massachusetts at Amherst, Syracuse University, the University of Washington at Seattle, the University of California at Los Angeles, and Yale University.

SOURCE: From Alexander Wendt, "Anarchy Is What States Make of It: The Social Construction of Power Politics," *International Organization*, 46:2 (Spring, 1992), pp. 391–425. © 1992 by the World Peace Foundation and the Massachusetts Institute of Technology.

central authority and collective security are absent. The self-help corollary to anarchy does enormous work in neorealism, generating the inherently competitive dynamics of the security dilemma and collective action problem. Self-help is not seen as an "institution" and as such occupies a privileged explanatory role vis-à-vis process, setting the terms for, and unaffected by, interaction. Since states failing to conform to the logic of self-help will be driven from the system, only simple learning or behavioral adaptation is possible; the complex learning involved in redefinitions of identity and interest is not.[4] Questions about identity- and interest-formation are therefore not important to students of international relations. A rationalist problématique, which reduces process to dynamics of behavioral interaction among exogenously constituted actors, defines the scope of systemic theory.

By adopting such reasoning, liberals concede to neorealists the causal powers of anarchic structure, but they gain the rhetorically powerful argument that process can generate cooperative behavior, even in an exogenously given, self-help system. Some liberals may believe that anarchy does, in fact, constitute states with self-interested identities exogenous to practice. Such "weak" liberals concede the causal powers of anarchy both rhetorically and substantively and accept rationalism's limited, behavioral conception of the causal powers of institutions. They are realists before liberals (we might call them "weak realists"), since only if international institutions can change powers and interests do they go beyond the "limits" of realism.[5]

Yet some liberals want more. When Joseph Nye speaks of "complex learning," or Robert Jervis of "changing conceptions of self and interest," or Robert Keohane of "sociological" conceptions of interest, each is asserting an important role for transformations of identity and interest in the liberal research program and, by extension, a potentially much stronger conception of process and institutions in world politics.[6] "Strong" liberals should be troubled by the dichotomous privileging of structure over process, since transformations of identity and interest through process are transformations of structure. Rationalism has little to offer such an argument,[7] which is in part why, in an important article, Friedrich Kratochwil and John Ruggie argued that its individualist ontology contradicted the intersubjectivist epistemology necessary for regime theory to realize its full promise.[8] Regimes cannot change identities and interests if the latter are taken as given. Because of this rationalist legacy, despite increasingly numerous and rich studies of complex learning in foreign policy, neoliberals lack a systematic theory of how such changes occur and thus must privilege realist insights about structure while advancing their own insights about process.

The irony is that social theories which seek to explain identities and interests do exist. Keohane has called them "reflectivist";[9] because I want to emphasize their focus on the social construction of subjectivity and minimize their image problem, following Nicholas Onuf I will call them "constructivist."[10] Despite important differences, cognitivists, poststructuralists, standpoint and postmodern feminists, rule theorists, and structurationists share a concern with the basic "sociological" issue bracketed by rationalists—namely, the issue of identity- and interest-formation. Constructivism's potential contribution to a strong liberalism has been obscured, however, by recent epistemological debates between modernists and postmodernists, in which Science disciplines Dissent for not defining a conventional research program, and Dissent celebrates its liberation from Science.[11] Real issues animate this debate, which also divides constructivists. With respect to the substance of international relations, however, both modern and postmodern constructivists are interested in how knowledgeable practices constitute subjects, which is not far from the strong liberal interest in how institutions transform interests. They share a cognitive, intersubjective conception of process in which identities and interests are endogenous to interaction, rather than, a rationalist-behavioral one in which they are exogenous.

My objective in this article is to build a bridge between these two traditions (and, by extension, between the realist-liberal and rationalist-reflectivist debates) by developing a constructivist argument, drawn from structurationist and symbolic interactionist sociology, on behalf of the liberal claim that international institutions can transform state identities and interests.[12] In contrast to the "economic" theorizing that dominates mainstream systemic international relations scholarship, this involves a "sociological social psychological" form of systemic theory in which identities and interests are the dependent variable.[13] Whether a "communitarian liberalism" is still liberalism does not interest me here. What does is that constructivism might contribute significantly to the strong liberal interest in identity- and interest-formation and thereby perhaps itself be enriched with liberal insights about learning and cognition which it has neglected.

My strategy for building this bridge will be to argue against the neorealist claim that self-help is given by anarchic structure exogenously to process. Constructivists have not done a good job of taking the causal powers of anarchy seriously. This is unfortunate, since in the realist view anarchy justifies disinterest in the institutional transformation of identities and interests and thus building systemic theories in exclusively rationalist terms; its putative causal powers must be challenged if process and institutions are not to be subordinated to structure. I argue that self-help and power politics do not follow either logically or causally from anarchy and that if today we find ourselves in a self-help world, this is due to process, not structure. There is no "logic" of anarchy apart from the practices that create and instantiate one structure of identities and interests rather than another; structure has no existence or causal powers apart from process. Self-help and power politics are institutions, not essential features of anarchy. *Anarchy is what states make of it.*

In the subsequent sections of this article, I critically examine the claims and assumptions of neorealism, develop a positive argument about how self-help and power politics are socially constructed under anarchy, and then explore three ways in which identities and interests are transformed under anarchy: by the institution of sovereignty, by an evolution of cooperation, and by intentional efforts to transform egoistic identities into collective identities.

ANARCHY AND POWER POLITICS

Classical realists such as Thomas Hobbes, Reinhold Niebuhr, and Hans Morgenthau attributed egoism and power politics primarily to human nature, whereas structural realists or neorealists emphasize anarchy. The difference stems in part from different interpretations of anarchy's causal powers. Kenneth Waltz's work is important for both. In *Man, the State, and War,* he defines anarchy as a condition of possibility for or "permissive" cause of war, arguing that "wars occur because there is nothing to prevent them."[14] It is the human nature or domestic politics of predator states, however, that provide the initial impetus or "efficient" cause of conflict which forces other states to respond in kind.[15] Waltz is not entirely consistent about this, since he slips without justification from the permissive causal claim that in anarchy war is always possible to the active causal claim that "war may at any moment occur."[16] But despite Waltz's concluding call for third-image theory, the efficient causes that initialize anarchic systems are from the first and second images. This is reversed in Waltz's *Theory of International Politics,* in which first- and second-image theories are spurned as "reductionist," and the logic of anarchy seems by itself to constitute self-help and power politics as necessary features of world politics.[17]

This is unfortunate, since whatever one may think of first- and second-image theories, they have the virtue of implying that practices determine the character of anarchy. In the permissive view, only if human or domestic factors cause A to attack B will B have to defend itself. Anarchies may contain dynamics that lead to competitive power politics, but they also may not, and we can argue about when particular structures of identity and interest will emerge. In neorealism, however, the role of practice in shaping the character of anarchy is substantially reduced, and so there is less about which to argue: self-help and competitive power politics are simply given exogenously by the structure of the state system.

I will not here contest the neorealist description of the contemporary state system as a competitive, self-help world;[18] I will only dispute its explanation. I develop my argument in three stages. First, I disentangle the concepts of self-help and anarchy by showing that self-interested conceptions of security are not a constitutive property of anarchy. Second, I show how self-help and competitive power politics may be produced causally by processes of interaction between states in which anarchy plays only a permissive role. In both of these stages of my argument, I self-consciously bracket the first- and second-image determinants of state identity, not because they are unimportant (they are indeed important), but because like Waltz's objective, mine is to clarify the "logic" of anarchy. Third, I reintroduce first- and second-image determinants to assess their effects on identity-formation in different kinds of anarchies.

ANARCHY, SELF-HELP, AND INTERSUBJECTIVE KNOWLEDGE

Waltz defines political structure on three dimensions: ordering principles (in this case, anarchy), principles of differentiation (which here drop out), and the distribution of capabilities.[19] By itself, this definition predicts little about state behavior. It does not predict whether two states will be friends or foes, will recognize each other's sovereignty, will have dynastic ties, will be revisionist or status quo powers, and so on. These factors, which are fundamentally intersubjective, affect states' security interests and thus the character of their interaction under anarchy. In an important revision of Waltz's theory, Stephen Walt implies as much when he argues that the "balance of threats," rather than the balance of power, determines state action, threats being socially constructed.[20] Put more generally, without assumptions about the structure of identities and interests in the system, Waltz's definition of structure cannot predict the content or dynamics of anarchy. Self-help is one such intersubjective structure and, as such, does the decisive explanatory work in the theory. The question is whether self-help is a logical or contingent feature of anarchy. In this section, I develop the concept of a "structure of identity and interest" and show that no particular one follows logically from anarchy.

A fundamental principle of constructivist social theory is that people act toward objects, including other actors, on the basis of the meanings that the objects have for them.[21] States act differently toward enemies than they do toward friends because enemies are threatening and friends are not. Anarchy and the distribution of power are insufficient to tell us which is which. U.S. military power has a different significance for Canada than for Cuba, despite their similar "structural" positions, just as British missiles have a different significance for the United States than do Soviet missiles. The distribution of power may always affect states' calculations, but how it does so depends on the intersubjective understandings and expectations, on the "distribution of knowledge," that constitute their conceptions of self and other.[22] If society "forgets" what a university is, the powers and practices of professor and student cease to exist; if the United States and Soviet Union decide that they are no longer enemies, "the cold war is over." It is collective meanings that constitute the structures which organize our actions.

Actors acquire identities—relatively stable, role-specific understandings and expectations about self—by participating in such collective meanings.[23] Identities are inherently relational: "Identity, with its appropriate attachments of psychological reality, is always identity within a specific, socially constructed world," Peter Berger argues.[24] Each person has many identities linked to institutional roles, such as brother, son, teacher, and citizen. Similarly, a state may have multiple identities as "sovereign," "leader of the free world," "imperial power," and so on.[25] The commitment to and the salience of particular identities vary, but each identity is an inherently social definition of the actor grounded in the theories which actors collectively hold about themselves and one another and which constitute the structure of the social world.

Identities are the basis of interests. Actors do not have a "portfolio" of interests that they carry around independent of social context; instead, they define their interests in the process of defining situations.[26] As Nelson Foote puts it: "Motivation . . . refer[s] to the degree to which a human being, as a participant in the ongoing social process in which he necessarily finds himself, defines a problematic situation as calling for the performance of a particular act, with more or less anticipated consummations and consequences, and thereby his organism releases the energy appropriate to performing it."[27] Sometimes situations are unprecedented in our experience, and in these cases we have to construct their meaning, and thus our interests, by analogy or invent them de novo. More often they have routine qualities in which we assign meanings on the basis of institutionally defined roles. When we say that professors have an "interest" in teaching, research, or going on leave, we are saying that to function in the role identity of "professor," they have to define certain situations as calling for certain actions. This does not mean that they will necessarily do so (expectations and competence do not equal performance), but if they do not, they will not get tenure. The absence or failure of roles makes defining situations and interests more difficult, and identity confusion may result. This seems to be happening today in the United States and the former Soviet Union: without the cold war's mutual attributions of threat and hostility to define their identities, these states seem unsure of what their "interests" should be.

An institution is a relatively stable set or "structure" of identities and interests. Such structures are often codified in formal rules and norms, but these have motivational force only in virtue of actors' socialization to and participation in collective knowledge. Institutions are fundamentally cognitive entities that do not exist apart from actors' ideas about how the world works.[28] This does not mean that institutions are not real or objective, that they are "nothing but" beliefs. As collective knowledge, they are experienced as having an existence "over and above the individuals who happen to embody them at the moment."[29] In this way, institutions come to confront individuals as more or less coercive social facts, but they are still a function of what actors collectively "know." Identities and such collective cognitions do not exist apart from each other; they are "mutually constitutive."[30] On this view, institutionalization is a process of internalizing new identities and interests, not something occurring outside them and affecting only behavior; socialization is a cognitive process, not just a behavioral one. Conceived in this way, institutions may be cooperative or conflictual, a point sometimes lost in scholarship on international regimes, which tends to equate institutions with cooperation. There are important differences between conflictual and cooperative institutions to be sure, but all relatively stable self-other relations—even those of "enemies"—are defined intersubjectively.

Self-help is an institution, one of various structures of identity and interest that may exist under anarchy. Processes of identity-formation under anarchy are concerned first and foremost with preservation or "security" of the self. Concepts of security therefore differ in the extent to which and the manner in which the self is identified cognitively with the other,[31] and, I want to suggest, it is upon this cognitive variation that the meaning of anarchy and the distribution of power depends. Let me illustrate with a standard continuum of security systems.[32]

At one end is the "competitive" security system, in which states identify negatively with each other's security so that ego's gain is seen as alter's loss. Negative identification under anarchy constitutes systems of "realist" power politics: risk-averse actors that infer intentions from capabilities and worry about relative gains and losses. At the limit—in the Hobbesian war of all against all—collective action is nearly impossible in such a system because each actor must constantly fear being stabbed in the back.

In the middle is the "individualistic" security system, in which states are indifferent to the relationship between their own and others' security. This constitutes "neoliberal" systems: states are still self-regarding about their security but are concerned primarily with absolute gains rather than relative gains. One's position in the distribution of power is less important, and collective action is more possible (though still subject to free riding because states continue to be "egoists").

Competitive and individualistic systems are both "self-help" forms of anarchy in the sense that states do not positively identify the security of self with that of others but instead treat security as the individual responsibility of each. Given the lack of a positive cognitive identification on the basis of which to build security regimes, power politics within such systems will necessarily consist of efforts to manipulate others to satisfy self-regarding interests.

This contrasts with the "cooperative" security system, in which states identify positively with one another so that the security of each is perceived as the responsibility of all. This is not self-help in any interesting sense, since the "self" in terms of which interests are defined is the community; national interests are international interests.[33] In practice, of course, the extent to which states' identification with the community varies, from the limited form found in "concerts" to the full-blown form seen in "collective security" arrangements.[34] Depending on how well developed the collective self is, it will produce security practices that are in varying degrees altruistic or prosocial. This makes collective action less dependent on the presence of active threats and less prone to free riding.[35] Moreover, it restructures efforts to advance one's objectives, or "power politics," in terms of shared norms rather than relative power.[36]

On this view, the tendency in international relations scholarship to view power and institutions as two opposing explanations of foreign policy is therefore misleading, since anarchy and the distribution of power only have meaning for state action in virtue of the understandings and expectations that constitute institutional identities and interests. Self-help is one such institution, constituting one kind of anarchy but not the only kind. Waltz's three-part definition of structure therefore seems underspecified. In order to go from structure to action, we need to add a fourth: the intersubjectively constituted structure of identities and interests in the system.

This has an important implication for the way in which we conceive of states in the state of nature before their first encounter with each other. Because states do not have conceptions of self and other, and thus security interests, apart from or prior to interaction, we assume too much about the state of nature if we concur with Waltz that, in virtue of anarchy, "international political systems, like economic markets, are formed by the coaction of self-regarding units."[37] We also assume too much if we argue that, in virtue of anarchy, states in the state of nature necessarily face a "stag hunt" or "security dilemma."[38] These claims presuppose a history of interaction in which actors have acquired "selfish" identities and interests; before interaction (and still in abstraction from first- and second-image factors) they would have no experience upon which to base such definitions of self and other. To assume otherwise is to attribute to states in the state of nature qualities that they can only possess in society.[39] Self-help is an institution, not a constitutive feature of anarchy.

What, then, *is* a constitutive feature of the state of nature before interaction? Two things are left if we strip away those properties of the self which presuppose interaction with others. The first is the material substrate of agency, including its intrinsic capabilities. For human beings, this is the body; for states, it is an organizational apparatus of governance. In effect, I am suggesting for rhetorical purposes that the raw material out of which members of the state system are constituted is created by domestic society before states enter the constitutive process of international society,[40] although this process implies neither stable territoriality nor sovereignty, which are internationally negotiated terms of individuality. . . . The second is a desire to preserve this material substrate, to survive. This does not entail "self-regardingness," however, since actors do not have a self prior to interaction with an other; how they view the meaning and requirements of this survival therefore depends on the processes by which conceptions of self evolve.

This may all seem very arcane, but there is an important issue at stake: are the foreign policy identities and interests of states exogenous or endogenous to the state system? The former is the answer of an individualistic or undersocialized systemic theory for which rationalism is appropriate; the latter is the answer of a fully socialized systemic theory. Waltz seems to offer the latter and proposes two mechanisms, competition and socialization, by which structure conditions state action.[41] The content of his argument about this conditioning, however, presupposes a self-help system that is not itself a constitutive feature of anarchy. As James Morrow points out, Waltz's two mechanisms condition behavior, not identity and interest.[42] This explains how Waltz can be accused of both "individualism" and "structuralism."[43] He is the former with respect to systemic constitutions of identity and interest, the latter with respect to systemic determinations of behavior.

ANARCHY AND THE SOCIAL CONSTRUCTION OF POWER POLITICS

If self-help is not a constitutive feature of anarchy, it must emerge causally from processes in which anarchy plays only a permissive role.[44] This reflects a second principle of constructivism: that the meanings in terms of which action is organized arise out of interaction.[45] This being said, however, the situation facing states as they encounter one another for the first time may be such that only self-regarding conceptions of identity can survive; if so, even if these conceptions are socially constructed, neorealists may be right in holding identities and interests constant and thus in privileging one particular meaning of anarchic structure over process. In this case, rationalists would be right to argue for a weak, behavioral conception of the difference that institutions make, and realists would be right to argue that any international institutions which are created will be inherently unstable, since without the power to transform identities and interests they will be "continuing objects of choice" by exogenously constituted actors constrained only by the transaction costs of behavioral change.[46] Even in a permissive causal role, in other words, anarchy may decisively restrict interaction and therefore restrict viable forms of systemic theory. I address these causal issues first by showing how self-regarding ideas about security might develop and then by examining the conditions under which a key efficient cause—predation—may dispose states in this direction rather than others.

Conceptions of self and interest tend to "mirror" the practices of significant others over time. This principle of identity-formation is captured by the symbolic interactionist notion of the "looking-glass self," which asserts that the self is a reflection of an actor's socialization.

Consider two actors—ego and alter—encountering each other for the first time.[47] Each wants to survive and has certain material capabilities, but neither actor has biological or domestic imperatives for power, glory, or conquest (still bracketed), and there is no history of security or insecurity between the two. What should they do? Realists would probably argue that each should act on the basis of worst-case assumptions about the other's intentions, justifying such an attitude as prudent in view of the possibility of death from making a mistake. Such a possibility always exists, even in civil society; however, society would be impossible if people made decisions purely on the basis of worst-case possibilities. Instead, most decisions are and should be made on the basis of probabilities, and these are produced by interaction, by what actors *do*.

In the beginning is ego's gesture, which may consist, for example, of an advance, a retreat, a brandishing of arms, a laying down of arms, or an attack.[48] For ego, this gesture represents the basis on which it is prepared to respond to alter. This basis is unknown to alter, however, and so it must make an inference or "attribution" about ego's intentions and, in particular, given that this is anarchy, about whether ego is a threat.[49] The content of this inference will largely depend on two considerations. The first is the gesture's and ego's physical qualities, which are in part contrived by ego and which include the direction of movement, noise, numbers, and immediate consequences of the gesture.[50] The second consideration concerns what alter would intend by such qualities were it to make such a gesture itself. Alter may make an attributional "error" in its inference about ego's intent, but there is also no reason for it to assume a priori—before the gesture—that ego is threatening, since it is only through a process of signaling and interpreting that the costs and probabilities of being wrong can be determined.[51] Social threats are constructed, not natural.

Consider an example. Would we assume, a priori, that we were about to be attacked if we are ever contacted by members of an alien civilization?

I think not. We would be highly alert, of course, but whether we placed our military forces on alert or launched an attack would depend on how we interpreted the import of their first gesture for our security—if only to avoid making an immediate enemy out of what may be a dangerous adversary. The possibility of error, in other words, does not force us to act on the assumption that the aliens are threatening: action depends on the probabilities we assign, and these are in key part a function of what the aliens do; prior to their gesture, we have no systemic basis for assigning probabilities. If their first gesture is to appear with a thousand spaceships and destroy New York, we will define the situation as threatening and respond accordingly. But if they appear with one spaceship, saying what seems to be "we come in peace," we will feel "reassured" and will probably respond with a gesture intended to reassure them, even if this gesture is not necessarily interpreted by them as such.[52]

This process of signaling, interpreting, and responding completes a "social act" and begins the process of creating intersubjective meanings. It advances the same way. The first social act creates expectations on both sides about each other's future behavior: potentially mistaken and certainly tentative, but expectations nonetheless. Based on this tentative knowledge, ego makes a new gesture, again signifying the basis on which it will respond to alter, and again alter responds, adding to the pool of knowledge each has about the other, and so on over time. The mechanism here is reinforcement; interaction rewards actors for holding certain ideas about each other and discourages them from holding others. If repeated long enough, these "reciprocal typifications" will create relatively stable concepts of self and other regarding the issue at stake in the interaction.[53]

It is through reciprocal interaction, in other words, that we create and instantiate the relatively enduring social structures in terms of which we define our identities and interests. Jeff Coulter sums up the ontological dependence of structure on process this way: "The parameters of social organization themselves are reproduced only in and through the orientations and practices of members engaged in social interactions over time. ... Social configurations are not 'objective' like mountains or forests, but neither are they 'subjective' like dreams or flights of speculative fancy. They are, as most social scientists concede at the theoretical level, intersubjective constructions."[54]

The simple overall model of identity- and interest-formation proposed in Figure 1 applies to competitive institutions no less than to cooperative ones. Self-help security systems evolve from cycles of interaction in which each party acts in ways that the other feels are threatening to the self, creating expectations that the other is not to be trusted. Competitive or egoistic identities are caused by such insecurity; if the other is threatening, the self is forced to "mirror" such behavior in its conception of the self's relationship to that other.[55] Being treated as an object for the gratification of others precludes the positive identification with others necessary for collective security; conversely, being treated by others in ways that are empathic with respect to the security of the self permits such identification.[56]

Competitive systems of interaction are prone to security "dilemmas," in which the efforts of actors to enhance their security unilaterally threatens the security of the others, perpetuating distrust and alienation. The forms of

FIGURE 1 **The Codetermination of Institutions and Process**

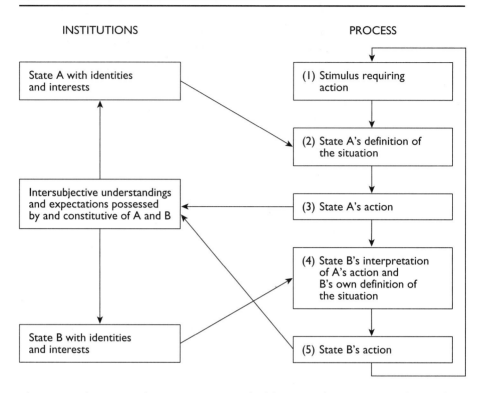

identity and interest that constitute such dilemmas, however, are themselves ongoing effects of, not exogenous to, the interaction; identities are produced in and through "situated activity."[57] We do not *begin* our relationship with the aliens in a security dilemma; security dilemmas are not given by anarchy or nature. Of course, once institutionalized such a dilemma may be hard to change . . . but the point remains: identities and interests are constituted by collective meanings that are always in process. As Sheldon Stryker emphasizes, "The social process is one of constructing and reconstructing self and social relationships."[58] If states find themselves in a self-help system, this is because their practices made it that way. Changing the practices will change the intersubjective knowledge that constitutes the system.

PREDATOR STATES AND ANARCHY AS PERMISSIVE CAUSE

The mirror theory of identity-formation is a crude account of how the process of creating identities and interests might work, but it does not tell us why a system of states—such as, arguably, our own—would have ended up with self-regarding and not collective identities. In this section, I examine an efficient cause, predation, which, in conjunction with anarchy as a permissive cause, may generate a self-help system. In so doing, however, I show the key role that the structure of identities and interests plays in mediating anarchy's explanatory role.

The predator argument is straightforward and compelling. For whatever reasons—biology, domestic politics, or systemic victimization—some states may become predisposed toward aggression. The aggressive behavior of these predators or "bad apples" forces other states to engage in competitive power politics, to meet fire with fire, since failure to do so may degrade or destroy them. One predator will best a hundred pacifists because anarchy provides no guarantees. This argument is powerful in part because it is so weak: rather than making the strong assumption that all states are inherently power-seeking (a purely reductionist theory of power politics), it assumes that just one is power-seeking and that the others have to follow suit because anarchy permits the one to exploit them.

In making this argument, it is important to reiterate that the possibility of predation does not in itself force states to anticipate it a priori with competitive power politics of their own. The possibility of predation does not mean that "war may at any moment occur"; it may in fact be extremely unlikely. Once a predator emerges, however, it may condition identity- and interest-formation in the following manner.

In an anarchy of two, if ego is predatory, alter must either define its security in self-help terms or pay the price. This follows directly from the above argument, in which conceptions of self mirror treatment by the other. In an anarchy of many, however, the effect of predation also depends on the level of collective identity already attained in the system. If predation occurs right after the first encounter in the state of nature, it will force others with whom it comes in contact to defend themselves, first individually and then collectively *if* they come to perceive a common threat. The emergence of such a defensive alliance will be seriously inhibited if the structure of identities and interests has already evolved into a Hobbesian world of maximum insecurity, since potential allies will strongly distrust each other and face intense collective action problems; such insecure allies are also more likely to fall out amongst themselves once the predator is removed. If collective security identity is high, however, the emergence of a predator may do much less damage. If the predator attacks any member of the collective, the latter will come to the victim's defense on the principle of "all for one, one for all," even if the predator is not presently a threat to other members of the collective. If the predator is not strong enough to withstand the collective, it will be defeated and collective security will obtain. But if it is strong enough, the logic of the two-actor case (now predator and collective) will activate, and balance-of-power politics will reestablish itself.

The timing of the emergence of predation relative to the history of identity-formation in the community is therefore crucial to anarchy's explanatory role as a permissive cause. Predation will always lead victims to defend themselves, but whether defense will be collective or not depends on the history of interaction within the potential collective as much as on the ambitions of the predator. Will the disappearance of the Soviet threat renew old insecurities among the members of the North Atlantic Treaty Organization? Perhaps, but not if they have reasons independent of that threat for identifying their security with one another. Identities and interests are relationship-specific, not intrinsic attributes of a "portfolio"; states may be competitive in some relationships and solidary in others. "Mature" anarchies are less likely than "immature" ones to be reduced by predation to a Hobbesian condition, and maturity, which is a proxy for structures of identity and interest, is a function of process.[59]

The source of predation also matters. If it stems from unit-level causes that are immune to systemic impacts (causes such as human nature or domestic politics taken in isolation), then it functions in a manner analogous to a "genetic trait" in the constructed world of the state system. Even if successful, this trait does not select for other predators in an evolutionary sense so much as it teaches other states to respond in kind, but since traits cannot be unlearned, the other states will continue competitive behavior until the predator is either destroyed or transformed from within. However, in the more likely event that predation stems at least in part from prior systemic interaction—perhaps as a result of being victimized in the past (one thinks here of Nazi Germany or the Soviet Union)—then it is more a response to a learned identity and, as such, might be transformed by future social interaction in the form of appeasement, reassurances that security needs will be met, systemic effects on domestic politics, and so on. In this case, in other words, there is more hope that process can transform a bad apple into a good one.

The role of predation in generating a self-help system, then, is consistent with a systematic focus on process. Even if the source of predation is entirely exogenous to the system, it is what states *do* that determines the quality of their interactions under anarchy. In this respect, it is not surprising that it is classical realists rather than structural realists who emphasize this sort of argument. The former's emphasis on unit-level causes of power politics leads more easily to a permissive view of anarchy's explanatory role (and therefore to a processual view of international relations) than does the latter's emphasis on anarchy as a "structural cause";[60] neorealists do not need predation because the system is given as self-help.

This raises anew the question of exactly how much and what kind of role human nature and domestic politics play in world politics. The greater and more destructive this role, the more significant predation will be, and the less amenable anarchy will be to formation of collective identities. Classical realists, of course, assumed that human nature was possessed by an inherent lust for power or glory. My argument suggests that assumptions such as this were made for a reason: an unchanging Hobbesian man provides the powerful efficient cause necessary for a relentless pessimism about world politics that anarchic structure alone, or even structure plus intermittent predation, cannot supply. One can be skeptical of such an essentialist assumption, as I am, but it does produce determinate results at the expense of systemic theory. A concern with systemic process over structure suggests that perhaps it is time to revisit the debate over the relative importance of first-, second-, and third-image theories of state identity-formation.[61]

Assuming for now that systemic theories of identity-formation in world politics are worth pursuing, let me conclude by suggesting that the realist-rationalist alliance "reifies" self-help in the sense of treating it as something separate from the practices by which it is produced and sustained. Peter Berger and Thomas Luckmann define reification as follows: "[It] is the apprehension of the products of human activity *as if* they were something else than human products—such as facts of nature, results of cosmic laws, or manifestations of divine will. Reification implies that man is capable of forgetting his own authorship of the human world, and further, that the dialectic between man, the producer, and his products is lost to consciousness. The reified world is . . . experienced by man as a strange facticity, an *opus alienum* over which he has no control rather than as the *opus proprium* of his own productive activity."[62] By denying or bracketing states' collective authorship of their identities and interests, in other words, the realist-rationalist alliance denies or brackets the fact that competitive power politics help create the very "problem of order" they are supposed to solve—that realism is a self-fulfilling prophecy. Far from being exogenously given, the intersubjective knowledge that constitutes competitive identities and interests is constructed every day by processes of "social will formation."[63] It is what states have made of themselves.

INSTITUTIONAL TRANSFORMATIONS OF POWER POLITICS

Let us assume that processes of identity- and interest-formation have created a world in which states do not recognize rights to territory or existence—a war of all against all. In this world, anarchy has a "realist" meaning for state action: be insecure and concerned with relative power. Anarchy has this meaning only in virtue of collective, insecurity-producing practices, but if those practices are relatively stable, they do constitute a system that may resist change. The fact that worlds of power politics are socially constructed, in other words, does not guarantee they are malleable, for at least two reasons.

The first reason is that once constituted, any social system confronts each of its members as an objective social fact that reinforces certain behaviors and discourages others. Self-help systems, for example, tend to reward competition and punish altruism. The possibility of change depends on whether the exigencies of such competition leave room for actions that deviate from the prescribed script. If they do not, the system will be reproduced and deviant actors will not.[64]

The second reason is that systemic change may also be inhibited by actors' interests in maintaining relatively stable role identities. Such interests are rooted not only in the desire to minimize uncertainty and anxiety, manifested in efforts to confirm existing beliefs about the social world, but also in the desire to avoid the expected costs of breaking commitments made to others—notably domestic constituencies and foreign allies in the case of states—as part of past practices. The level of resistance that these commitments induce will depend on the "salience" of particular role identities to the actor.[65] The United States, for example, is more likely to resist threats to its identity as "leader of anticommunist crusades" than to its identity as "promoter of human rights." But for almost any role identity, practices and information that challenge it are likely to create cognitive dissonance and even perceptions of threat, and these may cause resistance to transformations of the self and thus to social change.[66]

For both systemic and "psychological" reasons, then, intersubjective understandings and expectations may have a self-perpetuating quality, constituting path-dependencies that new ideas about self and other must transcend. This does not change the fact that through practice agents are continuously producing and reproducing identities and interests, continuously "choosing now the preferences [they] will have later."[67] But it does mean that choices may not be experienced with meaningful degrees of freedom. This could be a constructivist justification for the realist position that only simple learning is possible in self-help systems. The realist might concede that such systems are socially constructed and still argue that after the corresponding identities and interests have become institutionalized, they are almost impossible to transform.

NOTES

1. See, for example, Joseph Grieco, "Anarchy and the Limits of Cooperation: A Realist Critique of the Newest Liberal Institutionalism," *International Organization* 42 (Summer 1988), pp. 485–507; Joseph Nye, "Neorealism and Neoliberalism," *World Politics* 40 (January 1988), pp. 235–51; Robert Keohane, "Neoliberal Institutionalism: A Perspective on World Politics," in his collection of essays entitled *International Institutions and State Power* (Boulder, Colo.: Westview Press, 1989), pp. 1–20; John Mearsheimer, "Back to the Future: Instability in Europe After the Cold War," *International Security* 13 (Summer 1990), pp. 5–56, along with subsequent published correspondence regarding Mearsheimer's article; and Emerson Niou and Peter Ordeshook, "Realism Versus Neoliberalism: A Formulation," *American Journal of Political Science* 35 (May 1991), pp. 481–511.

2. See Robert Keohane, "International Institutions: Two Approaches," *International Studies Quarterly* 32 (December 1988), pp. 379–96.

3. Behavioral and rationalist models of man and institutions share a common intellectual heritage in the materialist individualism of Hobbes, Locke, and Bentham. On the relationship between the two models, see Jonathan Turner, *A Theory of Social Interaction* (Stanford, Calif.: Stanford University Press, 1988), pp. 24–31; and George Homans, "Rational Choice Theory and Behavioral Psychology," in Craig Calhoun et al., eds., *Structures of Power and Constraint* (Cambridge: Cambridge University Press, 1991), pp. 77–89.

4. On neorealist conceptions of learning, see Philip Tetlock, "Learning in U.S. and Soviet Foreign Policy," in George Breslauer and Philip Tetlock, eds., *Learning in U.S. and Soviet Foreign Policy* (Boulder, Colo.: Westview Press, 1991), pp. 24–27. On the difference between behavioral and cognitive learning, see ibid., pp. 20–61;

Joseph Nye, "Nuclear Learning and U.S.–Soviet Security Regimes," *International Organization* 41 (Summer 1987), pp. 371–402; and Ernst Haas, *When Knowledge Is Power* (Berkeley: University of California Press, 1990), pp. 17–49.

5. See Stephen Krasner, "Regimes and the Limits of Realism: Regimes as Autonomous Variables," in Stephen Krasner, ed., *International Regimes* (Ithaca, N.Y.: Cornell University Press, 1983), pp. 355–68.

6. See Nye, "Nuclear Learning and U.S.–Soviet Security Regimes"; Robert Jervis, "Realism, Game Theory, and Cooperation," *World Politics* 40 (April 1988), pp. 340–44; and Robert Keohane, "International Liberalism Reconsidered," in John Dunn, ed., *The Economic Limits to Modern Politics* (Cambridge: Cambridge University Press, 1990), p. 183.

7. Rationalists have given some attention to the problem of preference-formation, although in so doing they have gone beyond what I understand as the characteristic parameters of rationalism. See, for example, Jon Elster, "Sour Grapes: Utilitarianism and the Genesis of Wants," in Amartya Sen and Bernard Williams, eds., *Utilitarianism and Beyond* (Cambridge: Cambridge University Press, 1982), pp. 219–38; and Michael Cohen and Robert Axelrod, "Coping with Complexity: The Adaptive Value of Changing Utility," *American Economic Review* 74 (March 1984), pp. 30–42.

8. Friedrich Kratochwil and John Ruggie, "International Organization: A State of the Art on an Art of the State," *International Organization* 40 (Autumn 1986), pp. 753–75.

9. Keohane, "International Institutions."

10. See Nicholas Onuf, *World of Our Making* (Columbia: University of South Carolina Press, 1989).

11. On Science, see Keohane, "International Institutions"; and Robert Keohane, "International Relations Theory: Contributions of a Feminist Standpoint," *Millennium* 18 (Summer 1989), pp. 245–53. On Dissent, see R. B. J. Walker, "History and Structure in the Theory of International Relations," *Millennium* 18 (Summer 1989), pp. 163–83; and Richard Ashley and R. B. J. Walker, "Reading Dissidence/Writing the Discipline: Crisis and the Question of Sovereignty in International Studies," *International Studies Quarterly* 34 (September 1990), pp. 367–416. For an excellent critical assessment of these debates, see Yosef Lapid, "The Third Debate: On the Prospects of International Theory in a Post-Positivist Era," *International Studies Quarterly* 33 (September 1989), pp. 235–54.

12. The fact that I draw on these approaches aligns me with modernist constructivists, even though I also draw freely on the substantive work of postmodernists, especially Richard Ashley and Rob Walker. For a defense of this practice and a discussion of its epistemological basis, see my earlier article, "The Agent-Structure Problem in International Relations Theory," *International Organization* 41 (Summer 1987), pp. 335–70; and Ian Shapiro and Alexander Wendt, "The Difference That Realism Makes: Social Science and the Politics of Consent," forthcoming in *Politics and Society*. Among modernist constructivists, my argument is particularly indebted to the published work of Emanuel Adler, Friedrich Kratochwil, and John Ruggie, as well as to an unpublished paper by Naeem Inayatullah and David Levine entitled "Politics and Economics in Contemporary International Relations Theory," Syracuse University, Syracuse, N.Y., 1990.

13. See Viktor Gecas, "Rekindling the Sociological Imagination in Social Psychology," *Journal for the Theory of Social Behavior* 19 (March 1989), pp. 97–115.

14. Kenneth Waltz, *Man, the State, and War* (New York: Columbia University Press, 1959), p. 232.
15. Ibid., pp. 169–70.
16. Ibid., p. 232. This point is made by Hidemi Suganami in "Bringing Order to the Causes of War Debates," *Millennium* 19 (Spring 1990), p. 34, fn. 11.
17. Kenneth Waltz, *Theory of International Politics* (Boston: Addison-Wesley, 1979).
18. The neorealist description is not unproblematic. For a powerful critique, see David Lumsdaine, *Ideals and Interests: The Foreign Aid Regime, 1949–1989* (Princeton, N.J.: Princeton University Press, forthcoming).
19. Waltz, *Theory of International Politics*, pp. 79–101.
20. Stephen Walt, *The Origins of Alliances* (Ithaca, N.Y.: Cornell University Press, 1987).
21. See, for example, Herbert Blumer, "The Methodological Position of Symbolic Interactionism," in his *Symbolic Interactionism: Perspective and Method* (Englewood Cliffs, N.J.: Prentice-Hall, 1969), p. 2. Throughout this article, I assume that a theoretically productive analogy can be made between individuals and states. There are at least two justifications for this anthropomorphism. Rhetorically, the analogy is an accepted practice in mainstream international relations discourse, and since this article is an immanent rather than external critique, it should follow the practice. Substantively, states are collectivities of individuals that through their practices constitute each other as "persons" having interests, fears, and so on. A full theory of state identity- and interest-formation would nevertheless need to draw insights from the social psychology of groups and organizational theory, and for that reason my anthropomorphism is merely suggestive.
22. The phrase "distribution of knowledge" is Barry Barnes's, as discussed in his work *The Nature of Power* (Cambridge: Polity Press, 1988); see also Peter Berger and Thomas Luckmann, *The Social Construction of Reality* (New York: Anchor Books, 1966). The concern of recent international relations scholarship on "epistemic communities" with the cause-and-effect understandings of the world held by scientists, experts, and policymakers is an important aspect of the role of knowledge in world politics; see Peter Haas, "Do Regimes Matter? Epistemic Communities and Mediterranean Pollution Control," *International Organization* 43 (Summer 1989), pp. 377–404; and Ernst Haas, *When Knowledge Is Power.* My constructivist approach would merely add to this an equal emphasis on how such knowledge also *constitutes* the structures and subjects of social life.
23. For an excellent short statement of how collective meanings constitute identities, see Peter Berger, "Identity as a Problem in the Sociology of Knowledge," *European Journal of Sociology,* vol. 7, no. 1,1966, pp. 32–40. See also David Morgan and Michael Schwalbe, "Mind and Self in Society: Linking Social Structure and Social Cognition," *Social Psychology Quarterly* 53 (June 1990), pp. 148–64. In my discussion, I draw on the following interactionist texts: George Herbert Mead, *Mind, Self, and Society* (Chicago: University of Chicago Press, 1934); Berger and Luckmann, *The Social Construction of Reality;* Sheldon Stryker, *Symbolic Interactionism: A Social Structural Version* (Menlo Park, Calif.: Benjamin/Cummings, 1980); R. S. Perinbanayagam, *Signifying Acts: Structure and Meaning in Everyday Life* (Carbondale: Southern Illinois University Press, 1985); John Hewitt, *Self and Society: A Symbolic Interactionist Social Psychology* (Boston: Allyn & Bacon, 1988); and Turner, *A Theory of Social Interaction.* Despite some differences, much the same points are made by structurationists such

as Bhaskar and Giddens. See Roy Bhaskar, *The Possibility of Naturalism* (Atlantic Highlands, N.J.: Humanities Press, 1979); and Anthony Giddens, *Central Problems in Social Theory* (Berkeley: University of California Press, 1979).

24. Berger, "Identity as a Problem in the Sociology of Knowledge," p. 111.

25. While not normally cast in such terms, foreign policy scholarship on national role conceptions could be adapted to such identity language. See Kal Holsti, "National Role Conceptions in the Study of Foreign Policy," *International Studies Quarterly* 14 (September 1970), pp. 233–309; and Stephen Walker, ed., *Role Theory and Foreign Policy Analysis* (Durham, N.C: Duke University Press, 1987). For an important effort to do so, see Stephen Walker, "Symbolic Interactionism and International Politics: Role Theory's Contribution to International Organization," in C. Shih and Martha Cottam, eds., *Contending Dramas: A Cognitive Approach to Post-War International Organizational Processes* (New York: Praeger, forthcoming).

26. On the "portfolio" conception of interests, see Barry Hindess, *Political Choice and Social Structure* (Aldershot, U.K.: Edward Elgar, 1989), pp. 2–3. The "definition of the situation" is a central concept in interactionist theory.

27. Nelson Foote, "Identification as the Basis for a Theory of Motivation," *American Sociological Review* 16 (February 1951), p. 15. Such strongly sociological conceptions of interest have been criticized, with some justice, for being "oversocialized"; see Dennis Wrong, "The Oversocialized Conception of Man in Modern Sociology," *American Sociological Review* 26 (April 1961), pp. 183-93. For useful correctives, which focus on the activation of presocial but nondetermining human needs within social contexts, see Turner, *A Theory of Social Interaction,* pp. 23–69; and Viktor Gecas, "The Self-Concept as a Basis for a Theory of Motivation," in Judith Howard and Peter Callero, eds., *The Self-Society Dynamic* (Cambridge: Cambridge University Press, 1991), pp. 171–87.

28. In neo-Durkheimian parlance, Institutions are "social representations." See Serge Moscovici, "The Phenomenon of Social Representations," in Rob Farr and Serge Moscovici, eds., *Social Representations* (Cambridge: Cambridge University Press, 1984), pp. 3–69. See also Barnes, *The Nature of Power.* Note that this is a considerably more socialized cognitivism than that found in much of the recent scholarship on the role of "ideas" in world politics, which tends to treat ideas as commodities that are held by individuals and intervene between the distribution of power and outcomes. For a form of cognitivism closer to my own, see Emanuel Adler, "Cognitive Evolution: A Dynamic Approach for the Study of International Relations and Their Progress," in Emanuel Adler and Beverly Crawford, eds., *Progress in Postwar International Relations* (New York: Columbia University Press, 1991), pp. 43–88.

29. Berger and Luckmann, *The Social Construction of Reality,* p. 58.

30. See Giddens, *Central Problems in Social Theory;* and Alexander Wendt and Raymond Duvall, "Institutions and International Order," in Ernst-Otto Czempiel and James Rosenau, eds., *Global Changes and Theoretical Challenges* (Lexington, Mass.: Lexington Books, 1989), pp. 51–74.

31. Proponents of choice theory might put this in terms of "interdependent utilities." For a useful overview of relevant choice-theoretic discourse, most of which has focused on the specific case of altruism, see Harold Hochman and Shmuel Nitzan, "Concepts of Extended Preference," *Journal of Economic Behavior and Organization* 6 (June 1985), pp. 161–76. The literature on choice theory usually

does not link behavior to issues of identity. For an exception, see Amartya Sen, "Goals, Commitment, and Identity," *Journal of Law, Economics, and Organization* 1 (Fall 1985), pp. 341–55; and Robert Higgs, "Identity and Cooperation: A Comment on Sen's Alternative Program," *Journal of Law, Economics, and Organization* 3 (Spring 1987), pp. 140–42.

32. Security systems might also vary in the extent to which there is a functional differentiation or a hierarchical relationship between patron and client, with the patron playing a hegemonic role within its sphere of influence in defining the security interests of its clients. I do not examine this dimension here; for preliminary discussion, see Alexander Wendt, "The States System and Global Militarization," Ph.D. diss., University of Minnesota, Minneapolis, 1989; and Alexander Wendt and Michael Bamett, "The International System and Third World Militarization," unpublished manuscript, 1991.

33. This amounts to an "internationalization of the state." For a discussion of this subject, see Raymond Duvall and Alexander Wendt, "The International Capital Regime and the Internationalization of the State," unpublished manuscript, 1987. See also R. B. J. Walker, "Sovereignty, Identity, Community: Reflections on the Horizons of Contemporary Political Practice," in R. B. J. Walker and Saul Mendlovitz, eds., *Contending Sovereignties* (Boulder, Colo.: Lynne Rienner, 1990), pp. 159–85.

34. On the spectrum of cooperative security arrangements, see Charles Kupchan and Clifford Kupchan, "Concerts, Collective Security, and the Future of Europe," *International Security* 16 (Summer 1991), pp. 114–61; and Richard Smoke, "A Theory of Mutual Security," in Richard Smoke and Andrei Kortunov, eds., *Mutual Security* (New York: St. Martin's Press, 1991), pp. 59–111. These may be usefully set alongside Christopher Jencks' "Varieties of Altruism," in Jane Mansbridge, ed., *Beyond Self-Interest* (Chicago: University of Chicago Press, 1990), pp. 53–67.

35. On the role of collective identity in reducing collective action problems, see Bruce Fireman and William Gamson, "Utilitarian Logic in the Resource Mobilization Perspective," in Mayer Zald and John McCarthy, eds., *The Dynamics of Social Movements* (Cambridge, Mass.: Winthrop, 1979), pp. 8–44; Robyn Dawes et al., "Cooperation for the Benefit of Us—Not Me, or My Conscience," in Mansbridge, *Beyond Self-Interest*, pp. 97–110; and Craig Calhoun, "The Problem of Identity in Collective Action," in Joan Huber, ed., *Macro-Micro Linkages in Sociology* (Beverly Hills, Calif.: Sage, 1991), pp. 51–75.

36. See Thomas Risse-Kappen, "Are Democratic Alliances Special?" unpublished manuscript, Yale University, New Haven, Conn., 1991. This line of argument could be expanded usefully in feminist terms. For a useful overview of the relational nature of feminist conceptions of self, see Paula England and Barbara Stanek Kilbourne, "Feminist Critiques of the Separative Model of Self: Implications for Rational Choice Theory," *Rationality and Society* 2 (April 1990), pp. 156–71. On feminist conceptualizations of power, see Ann Tickner, "Hans Morgenthau's Principles of Political Realism: A Feminist Reformulation," *Millennium* 17 (Winter 1988), pp. 429–40; and Thomas Wartenberg, "The Concept of Power in Feminist Theory," *Praxis International* 8 (October 1988), pp. 301–16.

37. Waltz, *Theory of International Politics,* p. 91.

38. See Waltz, *Man, the State, and War;* and Robert Jervis, "Cooperation Under the Security Dilemma," *World Politics* 30 (January 1978), pp. 167–214.

39. My argument here parallels Rousseau's critique of Hobbes. For an excellent critique of realist appropriations of Rousseau, see Michael Williams, "Rousseau,

Realism, and Realpolitik," *Millennium* 18 (Summer 1989), pp. 188–204. Williams argues that far from being a fundamental starting point in the state of nature, for Rousseau the stag hunt represented a stage in man's fall. On p. 190, Williams cites Rousseau's description of man prior to leaving the state of nature: "Man only knows himself; he does not see his own well-being to be identified with or contrary to that of anyone else; he neither hates anything nor loves anything; but limited to no more than physical instinct, he is no one, he is an animal." For another critique of Hobbes on the state of nature that parallels my constructivist reading of anarchy, see Charles Landesman, "Reflections on Hobbes: Anarchy and Human Nature," in Peter Caws, ed., *The Causes of Quarrel* (Boston: Beacon, 1989), pp. 139–48.

40. Empirically, this suggestion is problematic, since the process of decolonization and the subsequent support of many Third World states by international society point to ways in which even the raw material of "empirical statehood" is constituted by the society of states. See Robert Jackson and Carl Rosberg, "Why Africa's Weak States Persist: The Empirical and the Juridical in Statehood," *World Politics* 35 (October 1982), pp. 1–24.

41. Waltz, *Theory of International Politics*, pp. 74–77.

42. See James Morrow, "Social Choice and System Structure in World Politics," *World Politics* 41 (October 1988), p. 89. Waltz's behavioral treatment of socialization may be usefully contrasted with the more cognitive approach taken by Ikenberry and the Kupchans in the following articles: G. John Ikenberry and Charles Kupchan, "Socialization and Hegemonic Power," *International Organization* 44 (Summer 1989), pp. 283–316; and Kupchan and Kupchan, "Concerts, Collective Security, and the Future of Europe." Their approach is close to my own, but they define socialization as an elite strategy to induce value change in others, rather than as a ubiquitous feature of interaction in terms of which all identities and interests get produced and reproduced.

43. Regarding individualism, see Richard Ashley, "The Poverty of Neorealism," *International Organization* 38 (Spring 1984), pp. 225–86; Wendt, "The Agent-Structure Problem in International Relations Theory"; and David Dessler, "What's at Stake in the Agent-Structure Debate?" *International Organization* 43 (Summer 1989), pp. 441–74. Regarding structuralism, see R. B. J. Walker, "Realism, Change, and International Political Theory," *International Studies Quarterly* 31 (March 1987), pp. 65–86; and Martin Hollis and Steven Smith, *Explaining and Understanding International Relations* (Oxford: Clarendon Press, 1989). The behavioralism evident in neorealist theory also explains how neorealists can reconcile their structuralism with the individualism of rational choice theory. On the behavioral-structural character of the latter, see Spiro Latsis, "Situational Determinism in Economics," *British Journal for the Philosophy of Science* 23 (August 1972), pp. 207–45.

44. The importance of the distinction between constitutive and causal explanations is not sufficiently appreciated in constructivist discourse. See Wendt, "The Agent-Structure Problem in International Relations Theory," pp. 362–65; Wendt, "The States System and Global Militarization," pp. 110–13; and Wendt, "Bridging the Theory/Meta-Theory Gap in International Relations," *Review of International Studies* 17 (October 1991), p. 390.

45. See Blumer, "The Methodological Position of Symbolic Interactionism," pp. 2–4.

46. See Robert Grafstein, "Rational Choice: Theory and Institutions," in Kristen Monroe, ed., *The Economic Approach to Politics* (New York: Harper Collins,

1991), pp. 263–64. A good example of the promise and limits of transaction cost approaches to institutional analysis is offered by Robert Keohane in his *After Hegemony* (Princeton, N.J.: Princeton University Press, 1984).

47. This situation is not entirely metaphorical in world politics, since throughout history states have "discovered" each other, generating an instant anarchy as it were. A systematic empirical study of first contacts would be interesting.

48. Mead's analysis of gestures remains definitive. See Mead's *Mind, Self, and Society.* See also the discussion of the role of signaling in the "mechanics of interaction" in Turner's *A Theory of Social Interaction,* pp. 74–79 and 92–115.

49. On the role of attribution processes in the interactionist account of identity-formation, see Sheldon Stryker and Avi Gottlieb, "Attribution Theory and Symbolic Interactionism," in John Harvey et al., eds., *New Directions in Attribution Research,* vol. 3 (Hillsdale, N.J.: Lawrence Erlbaum, 1981), pp. 425–58; and Kathleen Crittenden, "Sociological Aspects of Attribution," *Annual Review of Sociology,* vol. 9, 1983, pp. 425–46. On attributional processes in international relations, see Shawn Rosenberg and Gary Wolfsfeld, "International Conflict and the Problem of Attribution," *Journal of Conflict Resolution* 21 (March 1977), pp. 75–103.

50. On the "stagecraft" involved in "presentations of self," see Erving Goffman, *The Presentation of Self in Everyday Life* (New York: Doubleday, 1959). On the role of appearance in definitions of the situation, see Gregory Stone, "Appearance and the Self," in Arnold Rose, ed., *Human Behavior and Social Processes* (Boston: Houghton Mifflin, 1962), pp. 86–118.

51. This discussion of the role of possibilities and probabilities in threat perception owes much to Stewart Johnson's comments on an earlier draft of my article.

52. On the role of "reassurance" in threat situations, see Richard Ned Lebow and Janice Gross Stein, "Beyond Deterrence," *Journal of Social Issues,* vol. 43, no. 4, 1987, pp. 5–72.

53. On "reciprocal typifications," see Berger and Luckmann, *The Social Construction of Reality,* pp. 54–58.

54. Jeff Coulter, "Remarks on the Conceptualization of Social Structure," *Philosophy of the Social Sciences* 12 (March 1982), pp. 42–43.

55. The following articles by Noel Kaplowitz have made an important contribution to such thinking in international relations: "Psychopolitical Dimensions of International Relations: The Reciprocal Effects of Conflict Strategies," *International Studies Quarterly* 28 (December 1984), pp. 373–406; and "National Self-Images, Perception of Enemies, and Conflict Strategies: Psychopolitical Dimensions of International Relations," *Political Psychology* 11 (March 1990), pp. 39–82.

56. These arguments are common in theories of narcissism and altruism. See Heinz Kohut, *Self-Psychology and the Humanities* (New York: Norton, 1985); and Martin Hoffmann, "Empathy, Its Limitations, and Its Role in a Comprehensive Moral Theory," in William Kurtines and Jacob Gewirtz, eds., *Morality, Moral Behavior, and Moral Development* (New York: Wiley, 1984), pp. 283–302.

57. See C. Norman Alexander and Mary Glenn Wiley, "Situated Activity and Identity Formation," in Morris Rosenberg and Ralph Turner, eds., *Social Psychology: Sociological Perspectives* (New York: Basic Books, 1981), pp. 269–89.

58. Sheldon Stryker, "The Vitalization of Symbolic Interactionism," *Social Psychology Quarterly* 50 (March 1987), p. 93.

59. On the "maturity" of anarchies, see Barry Buzan, *People, States, and Fear* (Chapel Hill: University of North Carolina Press, 1983).

60. A similar intuition may lie behind Ashley's effort to reappropriate classical realist discourse for critical international relations theory. See Richard Ashley, "Political Realism and Human Interests," *International Studies Quarterly* 38 (June 1981), pp. 204–36.

61. Waltz has himself helped open up such a debate with his recognition that systemic factors condition but do not determine state actions. See Kenneth Waltz, "Reflections on *Theory of International Politics*: A Response to My Critics," in Robert Keohane, ed., *Neorealism and Its Critics* (New York: Columbia University Press, 1986), pp. 322–45. The growing literature on the observation that "democracies do not fight each other" is relevant to this question, as are two other studies that break important ground toward a "reductionist" theory of state identity: William Bloom's *Personal Identity, National Identity and International Relations* (Cambridge: Cambridge University Press, 1990) and Lumsdaine's *Ideals and Interests*.

62. See Berger and Luckmann, *The Social Construction of Reality*, p. 89. See also Douglas Maynard and Thomas Wilson, "On the Reification of Social Structure," in Scott McNall and Gary Howe, eds., *Current Perspectives in Social Theory*, vol. 1 (Greenwich, Conn.: JAI Press, 1980), pp. 287–322.

63. See Richard Ashley, "Social Will and International Anarchy," in Hayward Alker and Richard Ashley, eds., *After Realism*, Massachusetts Institute of Technology, Cambridge, and Arizona State University, Tempe, 1992.

64. See Ralph Turner, "Role-Taking: Process Versus Conformity," in Rose, *Human Behavior and Social Processes*, pp. 20–40; and Judith Howard, "From Changing Selves Toward Changing Society," in Howard and Callero, *The Self-Society Dynamic*, pp. 209–37.

65. On the relationship between commitment and identity, see Foote, "Identification as the Basis for a Theory of Motivation"; Howard Becker, "Notes on the Concept of Commitment," *American Journal of Sociology* 66 (July 1960), pp. 32–40; and Stryker, *Symbolic Interactionism*. On role salience, see Stryker, ibid.

66. On threats to identity and the types of resistance that they may create, see Glynis Breakwell, *Coping with Threatened Identities* (London: Methuen, 1986); and Terrell Northrup, "The Dynamic of Identity in Personal and Social Conflict," in Louis Kreisberg et al., eds., *Intractable Conflicts and Their Transformation* (Syracuse, N.Y.: Syracuse University Press, 1989), pp. 55–82. For a broad overview of resistance to change, see Timur Kuran, "The Tenacious Past: Theories of Personal and Collective Conservatism," *Journal of Economic Behavior and Organization* 10 (September 1988), pp. 143–71.

67. James March, "Bounded Rationality, Ambiguity, and the Engineering of Choice," *Bell Journal of Economics* 9 (Autumn 1978), p. 600.

36

J . A N N   T I C K N E R

A GENDERED PERSPECTIVE ON NATIONAL SECURITY

FEMINIST PERSPECTIVES ON SECURITY

Critical-security studies challenges realism on both ontological and epistemological grounds. Many of its adherents argue for a broader definition of security, linked to justice and emancipation; a concept of security that starts with the individual allows for a global definition of security that moves beyond hierarchical binary distinctions between order and anarchy and inside and outside. Although not all critical-security scholars are willing to dispense with state-centric analysis, all agree that an examination of states' identities is crucial for understanding their security-seeking behavior.

Most feminist scholarship on security also employs a different ontology and epistemology from conventional security studies. Reluctant to be associated with either side of the realist/idealist debate, . . . and generally skeptical of rationalist, scientific claims to universality and objectivity, most feminist scholarship on security is compatible with the critical side of the third debate. Questioning the role of states as adequate security providers, many feminists have adopted a multidimensional, multilevel approach, similar to some of the efforts to broaden the definition of security described above. Feminists' commitment to the emancipatory goal of ending women's subordination is consistent with a broad definition of security that takes the individual, situated in broader social structures, as its starting point. Feminists seek to understand how the security of individuals and groups is compromised by violence, both physical and structural, at all levels.

Feminists generally share the view of other critical scholars that culture and identity and interpretive "bottom up" modes of analysis are crucial for understanding security issues and that emancipatory visions of security must get beyond statist frameworks. They differ, however, in that they adopt gender as a central category of analysis for understanding how unequal social structures, particularly gender hierarchies, negatively impact the security of individuals and groups.

Challenging the myth that wars are fought to protect women, children, and others stereotypically viewed as "vulnerable," feminists point to the high level of civilian casualties in contemporary wars. Feminist scholarship has been

SOURCE: From *Gendering World Politics* by J. Ann Tickner, pp. 47–55. Copyright 2001 Columbia University Press.

particularly concerned with what goes on during wars, especially the impact of war on women and civilians more generally. Whereas conventional security studies has tended to look at causes and consequences of wars from a top-down, or structural, perspective, feminists have generally taken a bottom-up approach, analyzing the impact of war at the microlevel. By so doing, as well as adopting gender as a category of analysis, feminists believe they can tell us something new about the causes of war that is missing from both conventional and critical perspectives. By crossing what many feminists believe to be mutually constitutive levels of analysis, we get a better understanding of the interrelationship between all forms of violence and the extent to which unjust social relations, including gender hierarchies, contribute to insecurity, broadly defined.

Claiming that the security-seeking behavior of states is described in gendered terms, feminists have pointed to the masculinity of strategic discourse and how this may impact on understanding of and prescriptions for security; it may also help to explain why women's voices have so often been seen as inauthentic in matters of national security. Feminists have examined how states legitimate their security-seeking behavior through appeals to types of "hegemonic" masculinity. They are also investigating the extent to which state and national identities, which can lead to conflict, are based on gendered constructions. The valorization of war through its identification with a heroic kind of masculinity depends on a feminized, devalued notion of peace seen as unattainable and unrealistic. Since feminists believe that gender is a variable social construction, they claim that there is nothing inevitable about these gendered distinctions; thus, their analyses often include the emancipatory goal of postulating a different definition of security less dependent on binary and unequal gender hierarchies. . . .

However, war makes it harder for women to fulfill their reproductive and core behavior in the international system. But, as Rebecca Grant asserts, this is a male, rather than a universal, model: were life to go on in the state of nature for more than one generation, other activities such as childbirth and child rearing, typically associated with women, must also have taken place. Grant also claims that Rousseau's stag hunt, which realists have used to explain the security dilemma, ignores the deeper social relations in which the activities of the hunters are embedded. When women are absent from these foundational myths, a source of gender bias is created that extends into international-relations theory.[1]

Feminists are also questioning the use of more scientifically based rational-choice theory, based on the instrumentally rational behavior of individuals in the marketplace that neorealists have used to explain states' security-seeking behavior. According to this model, states are unproblematically assumed to be instrumental profit maximizers pursuing power and autonomy in an anarchic international system. Where international cooperation exists, it is explained not in terms of community but, rather, in terms of enlightened self-interest. Feminists suggest that rational-choice theory is based on a partial representation of human behavior that, since women in the West have historically been confined to reproductive activities, has been more typical of certain men.[2] Characteristics such as self-help, autonomy, and power maximizing that are prescribed by realists as security-enhancing behavior are very similar to the hegemonic, masculine-gendered characteristics. The instrumentally competitive behavior of states, which results in power balancing, is similar to equilibrium theory, or the market behavior of rational-economic man. Therefore, it tends to privilege certain types of behaviors over others. While states do indeed behave in these ways, these models offer us only a partial understanding of their behavior. As other IR scholars, too, have pointed out, states engage in cooperative as well as conflictual behavior; privileging these masculinist models tends to delegitimate other ways of behaving and make them appear less "realistic." . . .

GENDERING WAR

The association between masculinity and war has been central to feminist investigations. While the manliness of war is rarely denied, militaries must work hard to turn men into soldiers, using misogynist training that is thought necessary to teach men to fight. Importantly, such training depends on the denigration of anything that could be considered feminine; to act like a soldier is not to be "womanly." "Military manhood," or a type of heroic masculinity that goes back to the Greeks, attracts recruits and maintains self-esteem in institutions where subservience and obedience are the norm.[3]

Another image of a soldier is a just warrior, self-sacrificially protecting women, children, and other vulnerable people. The notion that (young) males fight wars to protect vulnerable groups, such as women and children, who cannot be expected to protect themselves, has been an important motivator for the recruitment of military forces. The concept of the "protected" is essential to the legitimation of violence; it has been an important myth that has sustained support for war and its legitimation for both women and men. In wartime, the heroic, just warrior is sometimes contrasted with a malignant, often racialized, masculinity attributed to the enemy that serves as further justification for protection.[4]

These images of the masculinities of war depend on rendering women invisible. Yet women have been part of armies—as cooks, laundresses, and nurses—throughout history. Since the late nineteenth century, military nursing has involved women serving close to the front lines; such women have been vital to war efforts, although stories about their activities are rarely told, perhaps because they speak of death, injury, and vulnerability, rather than heroism.[5] More recently, in certain states, women are beginning to be incorporated into the armed forces. . . .

FEMINIST REDEFINITIONS OF SECURITY

At the International Congress of Women at The Hague during World War I, a meeting called to protest the war, Jane Addams spoke of the need for a new internationalism that could replace the kind of nationalism that was fostering such a devastating war. She claimed that, since civilians could no longer be protected during war, war was becoming an obsolete instrument of national policy; the congress passed a resolution to end warfare.[6] After the congress, Addams met with Woodrow Wilson; as is frequently the case when women write about security issues or offer policy advice, the president never cited Addams, but there was a remarkable similarity between Wilson's Fourteen Points and the congress's proposals.[7] Although Addams was branded at the time as a hysterical woman, her proposals were actually quite similar to the "common security" proposals of the 1980s that defined security as interdependent rather than zero-sum.

Feminists are suspicious of statist ontologies that define security in zero-sum terms associated with binary distinctions between anarchy and order; they are also aware of the dangers of identities that, in their quest for unifying symbols that can themselves be a source of conflict, mask social relations of inequality and insecurity. Many feminists, therefore, like certain critical-security scholars, define security broadly in multidimensional and multilevel terms—as the diminution of all forms of violence, including physical, structural, and ecological.[8] Since women have been marginal to the power structures of most states, and since feminist perspectives on security take human security as their central concern, most of these definitions start at the bottom, with the individual or community rather than the state or the international system. According to Christine Sylvester, security is elusive and partial and involves struggle and contention; it is a process, rather than an ideal in which women must act as agents in the provision of their own security.[9] It is important to emphasize that women must be (and are) involved in providing for their own security; notions of security that rely on protection reinforce gender hierarchies that, in turn, diminish women's (and certain men's) real security. Speaking from the margins, feminists are sensitive to the various ways in which social hierarchies manifest themselves across societies and history. Striving for an emancipatory type of security involves exposing these different social hierarchies, understanding how they construct and are constructed by the international order, and working to denaturalize and dismantle them.

Questioning the role of states as adequate security providers, but being aware of their continuing importance as the political category within which security is defined by policymakers and scholars alike, leads feminists to analyze power and military capabilities differently from conventional security studies. Rather than seeing military capability as an assurance against outside threats to the state, militaries are seen as frequently antithetical to individuals' (particularly women's) security—as winners in the competition for resources, as definers of an ideal type of militarized citizenship, usually denied to women,[10] and as legitimators of a kind of social order that can sometimes even valorize state violence. Simona Sharoni has suggested that, in states torn by conflict, the more government is preoccupied with national security, the less its citizens, especially women, experience physical security.[11] State violence is a particular problem in certain states, but it must also be emphasized that many states, although formally at peace, sustain huge military budgets at the same time as social spending is being cut; this, too, can be a form of violence.

These feminist definitions of security grow out of the centrality of social relations, particularly gender relations, for feminist theorizing. Feminists claim that structural inequalities, which are central contributors to the insecurity of individuals, are built into the historical legacy of the modern state and the international system of which it is a part. Calling into question realist boundaries between anarchy and danger on the outside and order and security on the inside, feminists point out that state-centric and structural analyses miss the interrelation of insecurity across levels of analysis. Since "women's space" inside households has also been beyond the reach of law in most states, feminists are often quite suspicious of boundaries that mark states as security providers. Although, in nationalist ideologies, family metaphors are used to evoke a safe space or sense of belonging, families are not always considered a safe space for women. In most societies, families, frequently beyond the reach of law, have too often been the site of unsanctioned violence against women and children.[12] Violence, therefore, runs across levels of analysis. While these types of issues have not normally been considered within the subject matter of security studies, feminists are beginning to show how all of these issues and levels are interrelated.

In this [essay], I have shown how feminist perspectives on security come out of different ontologies and epistemologies from those in conventional security studies. Believing that the culture and identity of states is important for understanding their security-seeking behavior, feminists are closer to some of the work in critical-security studies than to the mainstream; their goal of thinking about security as emancipation is also closer to certain critical perspectives. Questioning state-centric frameworks of conventional security analysis, feminists have tried to get beyond boundaries between inside and outside to construct a more comprehensive definition of security. Nevertheless, it is important to remember that states are fundamental to the way we think about security. Feminists have pointed out how often the security-seeking behavior of states is legitimated by its association with certain types of hegemonic masculinity. Besides narrowing the range of permissible or legitimate ways for states to act, this can also contribute to the subordination of women and the perceived inauthenticity of their voices in matters of policymaking. Claiming that the personal cannot be separated from the political and the international, feminists have suggested that issues of personal and international insecurity are not unrelated. This is a question that deserves further empirical investigation.

Feminists have generally rejected rationalist models when seeking to understand states' security-seeking behavior. They believe that the claim to universality and objectivity made by these models is problematic since it is based on male models of human behavior. Such a search for universalistic laws may miss the ways in which gender hierarchies manifest themselves in a variety of ways across time and culture. Claiming that theory cannot be separate from practice, feminists have investigated strategic language and foreign-policy discourse to see how they shape, legitimate, and constrain certain policy options. Starting at the microlevel and listening to the experiences of women, feminists base their understanding of security on situated knowledge, rather than knowledge that is decontextualized and universalized. Speaking from the experiences of those on the margins of national security, feminists are sensitive to the various ways in which social hierarchies are variably constructed. Striving for security involves exposing these different social hierarchies, understanding how they construct and are constructed by the international order, and working to denaturalize and dismantle them. . . .

NOTES

1. Grant, "Sources of Gender Bias," pp. 9–17.
2. For further elaboration on this issue, see Tickner, *Gender in International Relations,* p. 82.
3. Segal, *Is the Future Female?* p. 187.
4. Ruddick, "Toward a Feminist Peace Politics," p. 112.
5. For a discussion of military nursing, see Enloe, *Maneuvers,* chapter 6.
6. Addams, Balch, and Hamilton, *Women at the Hague.*
7. Washburn, "Women and the Peace Movement," p. 140.
8. For examples, see Peterson and Runyan, *Global Gender Issues;* Sharoni, "Gender and Middle East Politics"; Tickner, *Gender in International Relations*; and Pettman, *Worlding Women,* p. 105.
9. Sylvester, *Feminist Theory and International Relations in a Postmodern Era,* p. 183.
10. Tobias, "Shifting Heroisms," p. 164.
11. Sharoni, "Gender and Middle East Politics," p. 65.
12. The issue of family violence is a global one. In the United States, ten women are killed by batterers every day, 74 percent of them after they have left the relationship or sought a divorce or restraining order against the batterer. Seager, *The State of Women,* p. 26. In the United States in 1998, women were victims in 876,340 violent crimes committed by an intimate partner. Women were victims at a rate about five times that of males. Rennison and Welchans, *Intimate Partner Violence,* p. 2.

37

JOSEPH M. GRIECO

ANARCHY AND THE LIMITS TO COOPERATION

. . . THE NEW LIBERAL INSTITUTIONALISM

In contrast to earlier presentations of liberal institutionalism, the newest liberalism accepts realist arguments that states are the major actors in world affairs and are unitary–rational agents. It also claims to accept realism's emphasis on anarchy to explain state motives and actions. Robert Axelrod, for example, seeks to address this question: "Under what conditions will cooperation

SOURCE: From Joseph M. Grieco, "Anarchy and the Limits of Cooperation: A Realist Critique of the Newest Liberal Institutionalism," *International Organization*, 42:3 (Summer, 1988), pp. 485–507. © 1988 by the World Peace Foundation and the Massachusetts Institute of Technology.

emerge in a world of egoists without central authority?"[1] Similarly, Axelrod and Robert Keohane observe of world politics that "there is no common government to enforce rules, and by the standards of domestic society, international institutions are weak."[2]

Yet neoliberals argue that realism is wrong to discount the possibilities for international cooperation and the capacities of international institutions. Neoliberals claim that, contrary to realism and in accordance with traditional liberal views, institutions can help states work together.[3] Thus, neoliberals argue, the prospects for international cooperation are better that realism allows.[4] These points of convergence and divergence among the three perspectives are summarized in Table 1.

Neoliberals begin with assertions of acceptance of several key realist propositions; however, they end with a rejection of realism and with claims of affirmation of the central tenets of the liberal institutionalist tradition. To develop this argument, neoliberals first observe that states in anarchy often face mixed interests and, in particular, situations which can be depicted by Prisoner's Dilemma.[5] In the game, each state prefers mutual cooperation to mutual noncooperation (CC>DD), but also successful cheating to mutual cooperation (DC>CC) and mutual defection to victimization by another's cheating (DD>CD); overall, then, DC>CC>DD>CD. In these circumstances, and in the absence of a centralized authority or some other countervailing force to bind states to their promises, each defects regardless of what it expects the other to do.

However, neoliberals stress that countervailing forces often do exist—forces that cause states to keep their promises and thus to resolve the Prisoner's Dilemma. They argue that states may pursue a strategy of tit-for-tat and cooperate on a conditional basis—that is, each adheres to its promises so long as partners do so. They also suggest that conditional cooperation is more likely to occur in Prisoner's Dilemma if the game is highly iterated, since states that interact repeatedly in either a mutually beneficial or harmful manner are likely to find that mutual cooperation is their best long-term strategy. Finally, conditional cooperation is more attractive to states if the costs of verifying one another's compliance, and of sanctioning cheaters, are low compared to the benefits of joint action. Thus, conditional cooperation among states may evolve in the face of international anarchy and mixed interests through strategies of reciprocity, extended time horizons, and reduced verification and sanctioning costs.

Neoliberals find that one way states manage verification and sanctioning problems is to restrict the number of partners in a cooperative arrangement.[6] However, neoliberals place much greater emphasis on a second factor—international institutions. In particular, neoliberals argue that institutions reduce verification costs, create iterativeness, and make it easier to punish cheaters. As Keohane suggests, "in general, regimes make it more sensible to cooperate by lowering the likelihood of being double-crossed."[7] Similarly, Keohane and Axelrod assert that "international regimes do not substitute for reciprocity;

TABLE 1 **Liberal Institutionalism, Neoliberal Institutionalism, and Realism: Summary of Major Propositions**

PROPOSITION	LIBERAL INSTITUTIONALISM	NEOLIBERAL INSTITUTIONALISM	REALISM
States are the only major actors in world politics	No; other actors include: —specialized international agencies —supranational authorities —interest groups —transgovernmental policy networks —transnational actors (MNCs, etc.)	Yes (but international institutions play a major role)	Yes
States are unitary–rational actors	No; state is fragmented	Yes	Yes
Anarchy is a major shaping force for state preferences and actions	No; forces such as technology, knowledge, welfare-orientation of domestic interests are also salient	Yes (apparently)	Yes
International institutions are an independent force facilitating cooperation	Yes	Yes	No
Optimistic/pessimistic about prospects for cooperation	Optimistic	Optimistic	Pessimistic

rather, they reinforce and institutionalize it. Regimes incorporating the norm of reciprocity delegitimize defection and thereby make it more costly."[8] In addition, finding that "coordination conventions" are often an element of conditional cooperation in Prisoner's Dilemma, Charles Lipson suggests that "in international relations, such conventions, which are typically grounded in ongoing reciprocal exchange, range from international law to regime rules."[9] Finally, Arthur Stein argues that, just as societies "create" states to resolve collective action problems among individuals, so too "regimes in the international arena are also created to deal with the collective suboptimality that can emerge from individual [state] behavior."[10] Hegemonic power may be necessary to establish cooperation among states, neoliberals argue, but it may endure after hegemony with the aid of institutions. As Keohane concludes, "When we think about cooperation after hegemony, we need to think about institutions."[11]

. . . REALISM AND THE FAILURE OF THE NEW LIBERAL INSTITUTIONALISM

The new liberals assert that they can accept key realist views about states and anarchy and still sustain classic liberal arguments about institutions and international cooperation. Yet, in fact, realist and neoliberal perspectives on states and anarchy differ profoundly, and the former provides a more complete understanding of the problem of cooperation than the latter.

Neoliberals assume that states have only one goal in mixed-interest interactions: to achieve the greatest possible individual gain. For example, Axelrod suggests that the key issue in selecting a "best strategy" in Prisoner's Dilemma—offered by neoliberals as a powerful model of the problem of state cooperation in the face of anarchy and mixed interests—is to determine "what strategy will yield a player the highest possible score."[12] Similarly, Lipson observes that cheating is attractive in a single play of Prisoner's Dilemma because each player believes that defecting "can maximize his own reward," and, in turning to iterated plays, Lipson retains the assumption that players seek to maximize individual payoffs over the long run.[13] Indeed, reliance upon conventional Prisoner's Dilemma to depict international relationships and upon iteration to solve the dilemma unambiguously requires neoliberalism to adhere to an individualistic payoff maximization assumption, for a player responds to an iterated conventional Prisoner's Dilemma with conditional cooperation *solely out of a desire to maximize its individual long-term total payoffs*.

Moreover, neoliberal institutionalists assume that states define their interests in strictly individualistic terms. Axelrod, for example, indicates that his objective is to show how actors "who pursue their own interests" may nevertheless work together.[14] He also notes that Prisoner's Dilemma is useful to study states in anarchy because it is assumed in the game that "the object is to do as well as possible, regardless of how well the other player does."[15] Similarly, Lipson suggests that Prisoner's Dilemma "clearly parallels the

Realist conception of sovereign states in world politics" because each player in the game "is assumed to be a self-interested, self-reliant maximizer of his own utility."[16]

Finally, Keohane bases his analysis of international cooperation on the assumption that states are basically atomistic actors. He suggests that states in an anarchical context are, as microeconomic theory assumes with respect to business firms, "rational egoists." Rationality means that states possess "consistent, ordered preferences, and . . . calculate costs and benefits of alternative courses of action in order to maximize their utility in view of these preferences." In turn, he defines utility maximization atomistically; egoism, according to Keohane, "means that their [i.e., state] utility functions are independent of one another: they do not gain or lose utility simply because of the gains or losses of others."[17]

Neoliberalism finds that states attain greater utility—that is, a higher level of satisfaction—as they achieve higher individual payoffs. Also, in keeping with the concept of rational egoism, a utility function specified by the new theory for one state would not be "linked" to the utility functions of others. Hence, if a state enjoys utility, U, in direct proportion to its payoff, V, then the neoliberal institutionalist specification of that state's utility function would be $U = V$.[18]

Overall, "rational egoist" states care only about their own gains. They do not care whether partners achieve or do not achieve gains, or whether those gains are large or small, or whether such gains are greater or less than the gains they themselves achieve. The major constraint on their cooperation in mixed interest international situations is the problem of cheating.

And yet, realist theory rejects neoliberalism's exclusive focus on cheating. Differences in the realist and neoliberal understanding of the problem of cooperation result from a fundamental divergence in their interpretations of the basic meaning of international anarchy. Neoliberal institutionalism offers a well-established definition of anarchy, specifying that it means "the lack of common government in world politics."[19] Neoliberalism then proceeds to identify one major effect of international anarchy. Because of anarchy, according to neoliberals, individuals or states believe that no agency is available to "enforce rules," or to "enact or enforce rules of behavior," or to "force them to cooperate with each other."[20] As a result, according to neoliberal theory, "cheating and deception are endemic" in international relations.[21] Anarchy, then, means that states may wish to cooperate, but, aware that cheating is both possible and profitable, *lack a central agency to enforce promises*. Given this understanding of anarchy, neoliberal institutional theory correctly identifies the problem of cheating and then proceeds to investigate how institutions can ameliorate that particular problem.

For realists, as for neoliberals, international anarchy means the absence of a common inter-state government. Yet, according to realists, states do not believe that the lack of a common government only means that no agency can reliably enforce promises. Instead, realists stress, states recognize that, in anarchy, *there is no overarching authority to prevent others from using violence, or the threat of violence, to destroy or enslave them.* As Kenneth Waltz suggests, in anarchy, wars can occur "because there is nothing to prevent them," and therefore "in international politics force serves, not only as the *ultima ratio,* but indeed as the first and constant one."[22] Thus, some states may sometimes be driven by greed or ambition, but anarchy and the danger of war cause all states always to be motivated in some measure by fear and distrust.[23]

Given its understanding of anarchy, realism argues that individual well-being is not the key interest of states; instead, it finds that *survival* is their core interest. Raymond Aron, for example, suggested that "politics, insofar as it concerns relations among states, seems to signify—in both ideal and objective terms—simply the survival of states confronting the potential threat created by the existence of other states."[24] Similarly, Robert Gilpin observes that individuals and groups may seek truth, beauty, and justice, but he emphasizes that "all these more noble goals will be lost unless one makes provision for one's security in the power struggle among groups."[25]

Driven by an interest in survival, states are acutely sensitive to any erosion of their relative capabilities, which are the ultimate basis for their security and independence in an anarchical, self-help international context. Thus, realists find that the major goal of states in any relationship is not to attain the highest possible individual gain or payoff. Instead, *the fundamental goal of states in any relationship is to prevent others from achieving advances in their relative capabilities.* For example, E. H. Carr suggested that "the most serious wars are fought in order to make one's own country militarily stronger or, *more often,* to prevent another from becoming militarily stronger."[26] Along the same lines, Gilpin finds that the international system "stimulates; and may compel, a state to increase its power; at the least, it necessitates that the prudent state prevent relative increases in the power of competitor states."[27] Indeed, states may even forgo increases in their absolute capabilities if doing so prevents others from achieving even greater gains. This is because, as Waltz suggests, "the first concern of states is not to maximize power but to maintain their position in the system."[28]

States seek to prevent increases in others' relative capabilities. As a result, states always assess their performance in any relationship in terms of the performance of others.[29] Thus, I suggest that states are positional, not atomistic, in character. Most significantly, *state positionality may constrain the willingness of states to cooperate.* States fear that their partners will achieve relatively greater gains; that, as a result, the partners will surge ahead of them in relative capabilties; and, finally, that their increasingly powerful partners in the present could become all the more formidable foes at some point in the future.[30]

State positionality, then, engenders a "relative gains problem" for cooperation. That is, a state will decline to join, will leave, or will sharply limit its commitment to a cooperative arrangement if it believes that partners are achieving, or are likely to achieve, relatively greater gains. It will eschew cooperation even though participation in the arrangement was providing it, or would have provided it, with large absolute gains. Moreover, a state concerned about relative gains may decline to cooperate even if it is confident that partners will keep their commitments to a joint arrangement. Indeed, if a state believed that a proposed arrangement would provide all parties absolute gains, but would also generate gains favoring partners, then greater certainty that partners would adhere to the terms of the arrangement would only accentuate its relative gains concerns. Thus, a state worried about relative gains might respond to greater certainty that partners would keep their promises with a lower, rather than a higher, willingness to cooperate.

I must stress that realists do not argue that positionality causes all states to possess an offensively oriented desire to maximize the difference in gains arising from cooperation to their own advantage. They do not, in other words, attribute to states what Stein correctly calls a mercantilist definition of self-interest.[31] Instead, realists argue that states are more likely to concentrate on the danger that relative gains may advantage partners and thus may foster the emergence of a more powerful potential adversary.[32] Realism, then, finds that states are positional, but it also finds that state positionality is more defensive than offensive in nature.

In addition, realists find that defensive state positionality and the relative gains problem for cooperation essentially reflect the persistence of uncertainty in international relations. States are uncertain about one another's future *intentions;* thus, they pay close attention to how cooperation might affect relative *capabilities* in the future.[33] This uncertainty results from the inability of states to predict or readily to control the future leadership or interests of partners. As Robert Jervis notes, "Minds can be changed, new leaders can come to power, values can shift, new opportunities and dangers can arise."[34]

Thus, realism expects a state's utility function to incorporate *two distinct terms*. It needs to include the state's individual payoff, V, reflecting the realist view that states are motivated by absolute gains. Yet it must also include a term integrating both the state's individual payoff and the partner's payoff, W, in such a way that gaps favoring the state add to its utility while, more importantly, gaps favoring the partner detract from it. One function that depicts this realist understanding of state utility is $U = V - k (W - V)$, with k representing the state's coefficient of sensitivity to gaps in payoffs either to its advantage or disadvantage.[35] . . .

Faced with both problems—cheating and relative gains—states seek to ensure that partners in common endeavors comply with their promises and that their collaboration produces "balanced" or "equitable" achievements of gains. According to realists, states define balance and equity as distributions of gains that roughly maintain pre-cooperation balances of capabilities. To attain this balanced relative achievement of gains, according to Hans

Morgenthau, states offer their partners "concessions"; in exchange, they expect to receive approximately equal "compensations." As an example of this balancing tendency, Morgenthau offers the particular case of "cooperation" among Prussia, Austria, and Russia in their partitions of Poland in 1772, 1793, and 1795. He indicates that in each case, "the three nations agreed to divide Polish territory in such a way that the distribution of power among themselves would be approximately the same after the partitions as it had been before."[36] For Morgenthau, state balancing of joint gains is a universal characteristic of the diplomacy of cooperation. He attributes this to the firmly grounded practice of states to balance power, and argues that "given such a system, no nation will agree to concede political advantages to another nation without the expectation, which may or may not be well founded, of receiving *proportionate* advantages in return."[37]

In sum, neoliberals find that anarchy impedes cooperation through its generation of uncertainty in states about the compliance of partners. For neoliberals, the outcome a state most fears in mixed interest situations is to be cheated. Yet, successful unilateral cheating is highly unlikely, and the more probable neoliberal "worst case" is for all states to defect and to find themselves less well off than if they had all cooperated. For neoliberal institutionalists, then, anarchy and mixed interests often cause states to suffer the opportunity costs of not achieving an outcome that is mutually more beneficial. Keohane and Axelrod argue that games like Prisoner's Dilemma, Stag Hunt, Chicken, and Deadlock illustrate how many international relationships offer both the danger that "the myopic pursuit of self-interest can be disastrous" and the prospect that "both sides can potentially benefit from cooperation—if they can only achieve it."[38]

Realists identify even greater uncertainties for states considering cooperation: which among them could achieve the greatest gains, and would imbalanced achievements of gains affect relative capabilities? In addition, a state that knows it will not be cheated still confronts another risk that is at least as formidable: perhaps a partner will achieve disproportionate gains, and, thus strengthened, might someday be a more dangerous enemy than if they had never worked together. For neoliberal theory, the problem of cooperation in anarchy is that states may fail to achieve it; in the final analysis, the worst possible outcome is a lost opportunity. For realist theory, state efforts to cooperate entail these dangers plus the much greater risk, for some states, that cooperation might someday result in lost independence or security.

Realism and neoliberal institutionalism offer markedly different views concerning the effects of international anarchy on states. These differences are summarized in Table 2. Compared to realist theory, neoliberal institutionalism understates the range of uncertainties and risks states believe they must overcome to cooperate with others. Hence, realism provides a more comprehensive theory of the problem of cooperation than does neoliberal institutionalism. . . .

TABLE 2 **Anarchy, State Properties, and State Inhibitions about Cooperation: Summary of Neoliberal and Realist Views**

BASIS OF COMPARISON	NEOLIBERAL INSTITUTIONALISM	POLITICAL REALISM
Meaning of anarchy	No central agency is available to enforce promises	No central agency is available to enforce promises *or* to provide protection
State properties		
Core interest	To advance in utility defined individualistically	To enhance prospects for survival
Main goal	To achieve greatest possible absolute gains	To achieve greatest gains *and* smallest gap in gains favoring partners
Basic character	Atomistic ("rational egoist")	Defensively positional
Utility function	Independent: U = V	Partially interdependent: $U = V - k\,(W - V)$
State inhibitions concerning cooperation		
Range of uncertainties associated with cooperation	Partners' compliance	Compliance *and* relative achievement of gains *and* uses to which gaps favoring partners may be employed
Range of risks associated with cooperation	To be cheated and to receive a low payoff	To be cheated *or* to experience decline in relative power if others achieve greater gains
Barriers to cooperation	State concerns about partners' compliance	State concerns about partners' compliance *and* partners' relative gains

NOTES

1. Axelrod, *Evolution of Cooperation,* p. 3; also see pp. 4, 6.
2. Axelrod and Keohane, "Achieving Cooperation," p. 226. Stein argues that his theory of international regimes "is rooted in the classic characterization of international politics as relations between sovereign entities dedicated to their own self-preservation, ultimately able to depend only upon themselves, and prepared to resort to force"; see Stein, "Coordination and Collaboration," p. 116. Lipson notes that Axelrod's ideas are important because they "obviously bear on a central issue in international relations theory: the emergence and maintenance of cooperation among sovereign, self-interested states, operating without any centralized authority"; see Lipson, "International Cooperation," p. 6.

3. Keohane notes in *After Hegemony* (p. 9) that "I begin with Realist insights about the role of power and the effects of hegemony" but that "my central arguments draw more on the Institutionalist tradition, arguing that cooperation can under some conditions develop on the basis of complementary interests, and that institutions, broadly defined, affect the patterns of cooperation that emerge." Keohane also notes (p. 26) that "what distinguishes my argument from structural Realism is my emphasis on the effects of international institutions and practices on state behavior."

4. Keohane indicates in *After Hegemony* (pp. 14, 16) that he does not seek the wholesale rejection of realism. However, on the issue of the prospects for cooperation, like the question of international institutions, he does seek to refute realism's conclusions while employing its assumptions. He notes (p. 29) that "[s]tarting with similar premises about motivations, I seek to show that Realism's pessimism about welfare-increasing cooperation is exaggerated," and he proposes (p. 67) "to show, on the basis of their own assumptions, that the characteristic pessimism of Realism does not follow." Keohane also suggests (p. 84) that rational-choice analysis "helps us criticize, in its own terms, Realism's bleak picture of the inevitability of either hegemony or conflict." Finally, he asserts (p. 84) that rational-choice theory, "combined with sensitivity to the significance of international institutions," allows for an awareness of both the strengths and weaknesses of realism, and in so doing "[w]e can strip away some of the aura of verisimilitude that surrounds Realism and reconsider the logical and empirical foundations of its claims to our intellectual allegiance."

5. On the importance of Prisoner's Dilemma in neoliberal theory, see Axelrod, *Evolution of Cooperation*, p. 7; Keohane, *After Hegemony*, pp. 66–69; Axelrod and Keohane, "Achieving Cooperation," p. 231; Lipson, "International Cooperation," p. 2; and Stein, "Coordination and Collaboration," pp. 120–24.

6. See Keohane, *After Hegemony*, p. 77; Axelrod and Keohane, "Achieving Cooperation," pp. 234–38. For a demonstration, see Lipson, "Bankers' Dilemmas."

7. Keohane, *After Hegemony*, p. 97.

8. Axelrod and Keohane, "Achieving Cooperation," p. 250.

9. Lipson, "International Cooperation," p. 6.

10. Stein, "Coordination and Collaboration," p. 123.

11. Keohane, *After Hegemony*, p. 246.

12. Axelrod, *Evolution of Cooperation*, pp. 6, 14. Stein acknowledges that he employs an absolute-gains assumption and that the latter "is very much a liberal, not mercantilist, view of self-interest; it suggests that actors focus on their own returns and compare different outcomes with an eye to maximizing their own gains." See Stein, "Coordination and Collaboration," p. 134. It is difficult to see how Stein can employ a "liberal" assumption of state interest and assert that his theory of regimes, as noted earlier in note 2, is based on the "classic [realist?] characterization" of international politics.

13. Lipson, "International Cooperation," pp. 2, 5.

14. Axelrod, *Evolution of Cooperation*, p. 9.

15. Ibid., p. 22.

16. Lipson, "International Cooperation," p. 2.

17. Keohane, *After Hegemony*, p. 27.

18. On payoffs and utility functions, see Anatol Rapoport, *Fights, Games and Debates* (Ann Arbor: University of Michigan Press, 1960), p. 121, and Michael Taylor, *Anarchy and Cooperation* (London: Wiley, 1976), pp. 70–74.

19. Axelrod and Keohane, "Achieving Cooperation," p. 226; see also Keohane, *After Hegemony*, p. 7; Lipson, "International Cooperation," pp. 1–2; Axelrod, *Evolution of Cooperation*, pp. 3–4; and Stein, "Coordination and Collaboration," p. 116.
20. See Axelrod and Keohane, "Achieving Cooperation," p. 226; Keohane, *After Hegemony*, p. 7; and Axelrod, *Evolution of Cooperation*, p. 6.
21. Axelrod and Keohane, "Achieving Cooperation," p. 226. Similarly, Lipson notes that while institutionalized mechanisms (such as governments) that guarantee the enforcement of contracts are available in civil society, "the absence of reliable guarantees is an essential feature of international relations and a major obstacle to concluding treaties, contracts, and agreements." The resulting problem, according to Lipson, is that "constraints on opportunism are weak." See Lipson, "International Cooperation," p. 4. Also see Keohane, *After Hegemony*, p. 93, and Stein, "Coordination and Collaboration," p. 116.
22. See Waltz, *Man, State, and War*, p. 232; and Waltz, *Theory of International Politics*, p. 113. Similarly, Carr suggests that war "lurks in the background of international politics just as revolution lurks in the background of domestic politics." See Carr, *Twenty Years Crisis*, p. 109. Finally, Aron observes that international relations "present one original feature which distinguishes them from all other social relations: they take place within the shadow of war." See Aron, *Peace and War*, p. 6.
23. See Gilpin, "Political Realism," pp. 304–5.
24. Aron, *Peace and War*, p. 7; also see pp. 64–65.
25. Gilpin, "Political Realism," p. 305. Similarly, Waltz indicates that "in anarchy, security is the highest end. Only if survival is assured can states safely seek such other goals as tranquility, profit, and power." See Waltz, *Theory of International Politics*, p. 126; also see pp. 91–92, and Waltz, "Reflections," p. 334.
26. Carr, *Twenty-Years Crisis*, p. 111, emphasis added.
27. Gilpin, *War and Change*, pp. 87–88.
28. Waltz, *Theory of International Politics*, p. 126; see also Waltz, "Reflections," p. 334.
29. On the tendency of states to compare performance levels, see Oran Young, "International Regimes: Toward a New Theory of Institutions," *World Politics* 39 (October 1989), p. 118. Young suggests that realists assume that states are "status maximizers" and attribute to states the tendency to compare performance levels because each seeks "to attain the highest possible rank in the hierarchy of members of the international community." The present writer offers a different understanding of realism: while realism acknowledges that *some* states may be positional in the sense noted by Young, its fundamental insight is that *all* states are positional and compare performance levels because they fear that *others* may attain a higher ranking in an issue-area.
30. As Waltz suggests, "When faced with the possibility of cooperating for mutual gains, states that feel insecure must ask how the gain will be divided. They are compelled to ask not 'Will both of us gain?' but 'Who will gain more?' If an expected gain is to be divided, say, in the ratio of two to one, one state may use its disproportionate gain to implement a policy intended to damage or destroy the other." See Waltz, *Theory of International Politics*, p. 105.
31. Stein, "Coordination and Collaboration," p. 134.
32. In her review of Axelrod, Joanne Gowa cites the 1979 Waltz passage employed in note 62 and, following Taylor's terminology in *Anarchy and Cooperation* (pp. 73–74), suggests that a state may display "negative altruism." Furthermore,

according to Gowa, a state "may seek to maximize a utility function that depends both on increases in its own payoffs *and* on increases in the difference between its payoffs and those of another state." See Joanne Gowa, "Anarchy, Egoism, and Third Images: *The Evolution of Cooperation* and International Relations," *International Organization* 40 (Winter 1986), p. 178. This portrays realist thinking in a manner similar to that suggested by Young and cited above in note 61. However, this understanding of state utility cannot be readily based on Waltz, for his core insight, and that of the realist tradition, is not that all states necessarily seek a balance of advantages in their favor (although some may do this) but rather that all fear that relative gains may favor and thus strengthen others. From a realist viewpoint, some states may be negative altruists, but *all* states will be "defensive positionalists." Waltz emphasizes that he does not believe that all states necessarily seek to maximize their power: see his statement cited in note 28 and see especially his "Response to My Critics," p. 334.

33. Waltz, for example, observes that "the impediments to collaboration may not lie in the character and the immediate intention of either party. Instead, the condition of insecurity—at the least, the uncertainty of each about the other's future intentions and actions—works against their cooperation." See Waltz, *Theory of International Politics,* p. 105.

34. Robert Jervis, "Cooperation Under the Security Dilemma," *World Politics* 30 (January 1978), p. 168.

35. Similar to the concept of a state "sensitivity coefficient" to gaps in jointly produced gains is the concept of a "defense coefficient" in Lewis Richardson's model of arms races. The latter serves as an index of one state's fear of another: the greater the coefficient, the stronger the state's belief that it must match increases in the other's weapons inventory with increases in its own. See Lewis F. Richardson, *Arms and Insecurity: A Mathematical Study of the Causes and Origins of War,* eds. Nicolas Rachevsky and Ernesto Trucco (Pittsburgh and Chicago: Boxwood Press and Quadrangle Books, 1960), pp. 14–15.

36. Morgenthau, *Politics Among Nations,* 5th ed. (New York: Alfred Knopf, 1973), p. 179.

37. Ibid., p. 180, emphasis added.

38. Axelrod and Keohane, "Achieving Cooperation," p. 231; see also Stein, "Coordination and Collaboration," pp. 123–24.

38

JOHN J. MEARSHEIMER

CRITIQUE OF CRITICAL THEORY

CRITICAL THEORY

Critical theorists[1] directly address the question of how to bring about peace, and they make bold claims about the prospects for changing state behavior.[2] Specifically, they aim to transform the international system into a "world society," where states are guided by "norms of trust and sharing." Their goal is to relegate security competition and war to the scrap heap of history, and create instead a genuine "peace system."[3]

Critical theorists take ideas very seriously. In fact, they believe that discourse, or how we think and talk about the world, largely shapes practice. Roughly put, ideas are the driving force of history. Furthermore, they recognize that realism has long been the dominant theory of international politics, and therefore, according to their account of reality, has had substantial influence on state behavior. But critical theorists intend to change that situation by challenging realism and undermining it. Richard Ashley graphically describes their intentions: "Let us then play havoc with neorealist concepts and claims. Let us neither admire nor ignore the orrery of errors, but let us instead fracture the orbs, crack them open, crack them and see what possibilities they have enclosed. And then, when we are done, let us not cast away the residue. Let us instead sweep it into a jar, shine up the glass, and place it high on the bookshelf with other specimens of past mistakes."[4] With realism shattered, the way would presumably be open to a more peaceful world.

Critical theory is well-suited for challenging realism because critical theory is, by its very nature, concerned with criticizing "hegemonic" ideas like realism, not laying out alternative futures. The central aim is "to seek out the contradictions within the existing order, since it is from these contradictions that change could emerge."[5] It is called "critical" theory for good reason. Very significantly, however, critical theory *per se* has little to say about the future shape of international politics. In fact, critical theory emphasizes that, "It is impossible to predict the future."[6] Robert Cox explains this point: "Critical awareness of potentiality for change must be distinguished from utopian planning, i.e., the laying out of the design of a future society that is to

SOURCE: From John Mearsheimer, "The False Promise of International Institutions," *International Security*, 19:3 (Winter, 1994), pp. 5–49. © 1955 by the President and Fellows of Harvard College and the Massachusetts Institute of Technology.

be the end goal of change. Critical understanding focuses on the process of change rather than on its ends; it concentrates on the possibilities of launching a social movement rather than on what that movement might achieve."[7]

Nevertheless, international relations scholars who use critical theory to challenge and subvert realism certainly expect to create a more harmonious and peaceful international system. But the theory itself says little about either the desirability or feasibility of achieving that particular end.

CAUSAL LOGIC

Institutions are at the core of critical theory, as its central aim is to alter the constitutive and regulative norms of the international system so that states stop thinking and acting according to realism. Specifically, critical theorists hope to create "pluralistic security communities," where states behave according to the same norms or institutions that underpin collective security.[8] States would renounce the use of military force, and there would instead be "a generally shared expectation of peaceful change."[9] Furthermore, states would "identify positively with one another so that the security of each is perceived as the responsibility of all."[10] States would not think in terms of self-help or self-interest, but would instead define their interests in terms of the international community. In this new world, "national interests are international interests."[11]

Critical theorists have a more ambitious agenda than proponents of collective security. Critical theorists aim to create a world in which all states consider war an unacceptable practice, and are not likely to change their minds about the matter. There do not appear to be any troublemaker states in a pluralistic security community, as there might be in a collective security system. In fact, military power seems to be largely irrelevant in the critical theorists' post-realist world, which has the earmarks of a true "peace system."[12]

For critical theorists, the key to achieving a "postmodern international system" is to alter state identity radically, or more specifically, to transform how states think about themselves and their relationship with other states.[13] In the jargon of the theory, "intersubjective understandings and expectations" matter greatly.[14] In practice, this means that states must stop thinking of themselves as solitary egoists, and instead develop a powerful communitarian ethos.[15] Critical theorists aim to create an international system characterized not by anarchy, but by community. States must stop thinking of themselves as separate and exclusive—i.e., sovereign—actors, and instead see themselves as mutually conditioned parts of a larger whole.[16] States, or more precisely, their inhabitants and leaders, should be made to care about concepts like "rectitude," "rights," and "obligations." In short, they should have a powerful sense of responsibility to the broader international community.

A realist might argue that this goal is desirable in principle, but not realizable in practice, because the structure of the international system forces states to behave as egoists. Anarchy, offensive capabilities, and uncertain intentions combine to leave states with little choice but to compete aggressively with each other. For realists, trying to infuse states with communitarian norms is a hopeless cause.

Critical theory, however, directly challenges the realist claim that structural factors are the main determinants of state behavior. In contrast to realism, critical theory assumes that ideas and discourse are the driving forces that shape the world, although it recognizes that structural factors have some, albeit minor, influence.[17] How individuals think about and talk about the world matters greatly for determining how states act in the international system. Ideas matter so much, according to critical theorists, because the world is socially constructed by individual human beings whose behavior is mediated by their thoughts; these thoughts, in turn, are shared by the members of a larger culture. Individuals bear responsibility for shaping the world they inhabit. The world around them is not a given that forces itself upon them. On the contrary, critical theorists argue that ideational forces or "institutions often can change environments."[18] Markus Fischer sums up this crucial point: "In essence, critical theory holds that social reality is constituted by intersubjective consciousness based on language and that human beings are free to change their world by a collective act of will."[19]

Robert Cox's description of the state illustrates how this process of thinking about the world determines how it is structured. "The state," he writes, "has no physical existence, like a building or a lamp-post; but it is nevertheless a real entity. It is a real entity because everyone acts as though it were."[20] Alexander Wendt's discussion of anarchy provides another good example: "Structure," he writes, "has no existence or causal powers apart from process."[21] States, in fact, can think about anarchy in a number of different ways. "Anarchy is what states make of it." Moreover, "self-help and power politics are institutions . . . not essential features of anarchy."

This discussion of how critical theorists think about the state and anarchy points up the fact that realism and critical theory have fundamentally different epistemologies and ontologies, which are the most basic levels at which theories can be compared.[22] Realists maintain that there is an objective and knowable world, which is separate from the observing individual. Critical theorists, on the other hand, "see subject and object in the historical world as a reciprocally interrelated whole," and they deny the possibility of objective knowledge.[23] Where realists see a fixed and knowable world, critical theorists see the possibility of endless interpretations of the world before them. For critical theorists, "there are no constants, no fixed meanings, no secure grounds, no profound secrets, no final structures or limits of history . . . there is only interpretation. . . . History itself is grasped as a series of interpretations imposed upon interpretation—none primary, all arbitrary."[24]

Nevertheless, critical theorists readily acknowledge that realism has been the dominant interpretation of international politics for almost seven hundred years. "Realism is a name for a discourse of power and rule in modern global life."[25] Still, critical theory allows for change, and there is no reason, according to the theory anyway, why a communitarian discourse of peace and harmony cannot supplant the realist discourse of security competition and war. In fact, change is always possible with critical theory because it allows for an unlimited number of discourses, and it makes no judgment about the merit or staying power of any particular one. Also, critical theory makes no judgment about whether human beings are "hard-wired" to be good or bad, but instead treats people as infinitely changeable. The key to how they think and behave is the particular "software program" that individuals carry around in their heads, and those can be changed. In essence, critical theorists hope to replace the widely used realist software package with new software that emphasizes communitarian norms. Once that switch has been made, states will cooperate with each other and world politics will be more peaceful.

Most critical theorists do not see ideas and discourses forming at the grass roots and then percolating up to the elites of society. Rather, theirs is a top-down theory, whereby elites play the key role in transforming language and discourse about international relations. Experts, especially scholars, determine the flow of ideas about world politics. It is especially useful, however, if this intellectual vanguard consists of individuals from different states. These transnational elites, which are sometimes referred to as "epistemic communities," are well-suited for formulating and spreading the communitarian ideals that critical theorists hope will replace realism.[26]

Finally, it is worth noting that critical theorists are likely to be quite intolerant of other discourses about international politics, especially realism.[27] Four factors combine to account for this situation. The theory is based on the belief that ideas matter greatly for shaping international politics. Also, it recognizes that particular theories triumph in the marketplace of ideas, and the result is hegemonic discourse. Moreover, although the theory itself does not distinguish between good and bad ideas, critical theorists themselves certainly make that distinction. Furthermore, critical theorists have no historical guarantee that hegemonic discourse will move toward ideas about world politics that they consider sound. Realism, for example, has been the dominant discourse in the international arena for many centuries. Therefore, it makes sense for critical theorists to try to eliminate ideas they do not like, thus maximizing the prospects that their favorite discourse will triumph. Realist thinking, in this view, is not only dangerous, but is the main obstacle critical theorists face in their effort to establish a new and more peaceful hegemonic discourse.[28]

FLAWS IN THE CAUSAL LOGIC

The main goal of critical theorists is to change state behavior in fundamental ways, to move beyond a world of security competition and war and establish a pluralistic security community. However, their explanation of how change occurs is at best incomplete, and at worst, internally contradictory.[29]

Critical theory maintains that state behavior changes when discourse changes. But that argument leaves open the obvious and crucially important question: what determines why some discourses become dominant and others lose out in the marketplace of ideas? What is the mechanism that governs the rise and fall of discourses? This general question, in turn, leads to three more specific questions: 1) Why has realism been the hegemonic discourse in world politics for so long? 2) Why is the time ripe for its unseating? 3) Why is realism likely to be replaced by a more peaceful communitarian discourse?

Critical theory provides few insights on why discourses rise and fall. Thomas Risse-Kappen writes, "Research on . . . 'epistemic communities' of knowledge-based transnational networks has failed so far to specify the conditions under which specific ideas are selected and influence policies while others fall by the wayside."[30] Not surprisingly, critical theorists say little about why realism has been the dominant discourse, and why its foundations are now so shaky. They certainly do not offer a well-defined argument that deals with this important issue. Therefore, it is difficult to judge the fate of realism through the lens of critical theory.

Nevertheless, critical theorists occasionally point to particular factors that might lead to changes in international relations discourse. In such cases, however, they usually end up arguing that changes in the material world drive changes in discourse. For example, when Ashley makes surmises about the future of realism, he claims that "a crucial issue is whether or not changing historical conditions have disabled longstanding realist rituals of power." Specifically, he asks whether "developments in late capitalist society," like the "fiscal crisis of the state," and the "internationalization of capital," coupled with "the presence of vastly destructive and highly automated nuclear arsenals [has] deprived statesmen of the latitude for competent performance of realist rituals of power?"[31] Similarly, Cox argues that fundamental change occurs when there is a "disjuncture" between "the stock of ideas people have about the nature of the world and the practical problems that challenge them." He then writes, "Some of us think the erstwhile dominant mental construct of neorealism is inadequate to confront the challenges of global politics today."[32]

It would be understandable if realists made such arguments, since they believe there is an objective reality that largely determines which discourse will be dominant. Critical theorists, however, emphasize that the world is socially constructed, and not shaped in fundamental ways by objective factors. Anarchy, after all, is what we make of it. Yet when critical theorists attempt to explain why realism may be losing its hegemonic position, they too point to objective factors as the ultimate cause of change. Discourse, so it appears, turns out not to be determinative, but mainly a reflection of developments in the objective world. In short, it seems that when critical theorists who study international politics offer glimpses of their thinking about the causes of change in the real world, they make arguments that directly contradict their own theory, but which appear to be compatible with the theory they are challenging.[33]

There is another problem with the application of critical theory to international relations. Although critical theorists hope to replace realism with a discourse that emphasizes harmony and peace, critical theory *per se* emphasizes that it is impossible to know the future. Critical theory, according to its own logic, can be used to undermine realism and produce change, but it cannot serve as the basis for predicting which discourse will replace realism, because the theory says little about the direction change takes. In fact, Cox argues that although "utopian expectations may be an element in stimulating people to act . . . such expectations are almost never realized in practice."[34] Thus, in a sense, the communitarian discourse championed by critical theorists is wishful thinking, not an outcome linked to the theory itself. Indeed, critical theory cannot guarantee that the new discourse will not be more malignant than the discourse it replaces. Nothing in the theory guarantees, for example, that a fascist discourse far more violent than realism will not emerge as the new hegemonic discourse.

PROBLEMS WITH THE EMPIRICAL RECORD

Critical theorists have offered little empirical support for their theory.[35] It is still possible to sketch the broad outlines of their account of the past. They appear to concede that realism was the dominant discourse from about the start of the late medieval period in 1300 to at least 1989, and that states and other political entities behaved according to realist dictates during these seven centuries. However, some critical theorists suggest that both the discourse and practice of international politics during the preceding five centuries of the feudal era or central medieval period (800–1300) was not dominated by realism and, therefore, cannot be explained by it.[36] They believe that European political units of the feudal era did not think and therefore did not act in the exclusive and selfish manner assumed by realism, but instead adopted a more communitarian discourse, which guided their actions. Power politics, so the argument goes, had little relevance in these five hundred years.

Furthermore, most critical theorists see the end of the Cold War as an important watershed in world politics. A few go so far as to argue that "the revolutions of 1989 transformed the international system by changing the rules governing superpower conflict and, thereby, the norms underpinning the international system."[37] Realism, they claim, is no longer the hegemonic discourse. "The end of the Cold War . . . undermined neorealist theory."[38] Other critical theorists are more tentative in their judgment about whether the end of the Cold War has led to a fundamental transformation of international politics.[39] For these more cautious critical theorists, the revolutions of 1989 have created opportunities for change, but that change has not yet been realized.

Three points are in order regarding the critical theorists' interpretation of history. First, one cannot help but be struck by the sheer continuity of realist behavior in the critical theorists' own account of the past. Seven centuries of security competition and war represents an impressive span of time, especially when you consider the tremendous political and economic changes that have taken place across the world during that lengthy period. Realism is obviously a human software package with deep-seated appeal, although critical theorists do not explain its attraction.

Second, a close look at the international politics of the feudal era reveals scant support for the claims of critical theorists: Markus Fischer has done a detailed study of that period, and he finds "that feudal discourse was indeed distinct, prescribing unity, functional cooperation, sharing, and lawfulness."[40]

More importantly, however, he also finds "that while feudal actors observed these norms for the most part on the level of form, they in essence behaved like modern states." Specifically, they "strove for exclusive territorial control, protected themselves by military means, subjugated each other, balanced against power, formed alliances and spheres of influence, and resolved their conflicts by the use and threat of force."[41] Realism, not critical theory, appears best to explain international politics in the five centuries of the feudal era.

Third, there are good reasons to doubt that the demise of the Cold War means that the millennium is here. It is true that the great powers have been rather tame in their behavior towards each other over the past five years. But that is usually the case after great-power wars. Moreover, although the Cold War ended in 1989, the Cold War order that it spawned is taking much longer to collapse, which makes it difficult to determine what kind of order or disorder will replace it. For example, Russian troops remained in Germany until mid-1994, seriously impinging on German sovereignty, and the United States still maintains a substantial military presence in Germany. Five years is much too short a period to determine whether international relations has been fundamentally transformed by the end of the Cold War, especially given that the "old" order of realist discourse has been in place for at least twelve centuries.

A close look at the sources of this purported revolutionary change in world politics provides further cause for skepticism. For critical theorists, "the Cold War was fundamentally a discursive, not a material, structure."[42] Thus, if the United States and the Soviet Union had decided earlier in the Cold War that they were no longer enemies, it would have been over sooner.[43] Mikhail Gorbachev, critical theorists argue, played the central role in ending the Cold War. He challenged traditional Soviet thinking about national security, and championed ideas about international security that sounded like they had been scripted by critical theorists.[44] In fact, critical theorists argue that Gorbachev's "new thinking" was shaped by a "transnational liberal internationalist community [epistemic community] comprising the U.S. arms control community, Western European scholars and center-left policy makers, as well as Soviet institutchiks."[45] These new ideas led Gorbachev to end the Soviet Union's "imperial relationship with Eastern Europe," which led to a fundamental change in "the norms of bloc politics and thereby the rules governing superpower relations."[46] In essence, "the changed practices of one of the major actors . . . [had] system-wide repercussions."[47] Both superpowers "repudiated the notion of international relations as a self-help system and . . . transcended the consequences of anarchy as depicted by realism."[48]

Gorbachev surely played the key role in ending the Cold War, but there are good reasons to doubt that his actions fundamentally transformed international politics. His decision to shut down the Soviet empire in Eastern Europe can very well be explained by realism. By the mid-1980s, the Soviet Union was suffering an economic and political crisis at home that made the costs of empire prohibitive, especially since nuclear weapons provided the Soviets with a cheap and effective means of defense. Many empires collapsed and many states broke apart before 1989, and many of them sought to give to dire necessity the appearance of virtue. But the basic nature of international politics remained unchanged. It is not clear why the collapse of the Soviet Union is a special case.

Furthermore, now that Gorbachev is out of office and has little political influence in Russia, the Russians have abandoned his "new thinking."[49] In fact, they now have an offensively-oriented military doctrine that emphasizes first use of nuclear weapons. More importantly, since the end of 1992, the Russians have been acting like a traditional great power toward their neighbors. The former Soviet Union seems to be an arena for power politics, and Boris Yeltsin's Russia appears to be fully engaged in that enterprise.[50]

Regarding the more modest claim that the end of the Cold War presents an opportunity to move to a world where states are guided by norms of trust and sharing, perhaps this is true. But since critical theorists acknowledge that their theory cannot predict the future, why should we believe their claim, especially when it means choosing against realism, a theory that has at least 1200 years of staying power?

Critical theorists have ambitious aims. However, critical theory also has important flaws, and therefore it will likely remain in realism's shadow. Specifically, critical theory is concerned with affecting fundamental change in state behavior, but it says little about how it comes about. Critical theorists do occasionally point to particular causes of change, but when they do, they make arguments that are inconsistent with the theory itself. Finally, there is little empirical evidence to support the claims of critical theorists, and much to contradict them. . . .

NOTES

1. Critical theory is an approach to studying the human condition that is not tied to a particular discipline. In fact, critical theory was well-developed and employed widely in other disciplines before it began to penetrate the international relations field in the early 1980s. This article does not focus on critical theory *per se,* but examines the scholarly literature where critical theory is applied to international relations. I treat those works as a coherent whole, although there are differences, especially of emphasis, among them. For a general discussion of critical theory, see David Held, *Introduction to Critical Theory: Horkheimer to Habermas* (Berkeley: University of California Press, 1980); and Pauline M. Rosenau, *Post-Modernism And The Social Sciences: Insights, Inroads, and Intrusions* (Princeton, N.J.: Princeton University Press, 1992). Also see Pauline Rosenau, "Once Again Into the Fray: International Relations Confronts the Humanities," *Millennium: Journal of International Studies,* Vol. 19, No. 1 (Spring 1990), pp. 83–110.

2. Among the key works applying critical theory to international relations are: Richard K. Ashley, "The Poverty of Neorealism," *International Organization,* Vol. 38, No. 2 (Spring 1984), pp. 225–286; Ashley, "The Geopolitics of Geopolitical Space: Toward a Critical Social Theory of International Politics," *Alternatives,* Vol. 12, No. 4 (October 1987), pp. 403–434; Robert W. Cox,

"Gramsci, Hegemony and International Relations: An Essay in Method," *Millennium: Journal of International Studies,* Vol. 12, No. 2 (Summer 1983), pp. 162–175; Cox, "Social Forces, States and World Orders: Beyond International Relations Theory," *Millennium: Journal of International Studies,* Vol. 10, No. 2 (Summer 1981), pp. 126–155; Cox, "Towards A Post-Hegemonic Conceptualization of World Order: Reflections on the Relevancy of Ibn Khaldun," in James N. Rosenau, and Ernst-Otto Czempiel, eds., *Governance Without Government: Order and Change in World Politics* (New York: Cambridge University Press, 1992), pp. 132–159; Rey Koslowski and Friedrich V. Kratochwil, "Understanding Change in International Politics: The Soviet Empire's Demise and the International System," *International Organization,* Vol. 48, No. 2 (Spring 1994), pp. 215–247; Friedrich Kratochwil and John G. Ruggie, "International Organization: A State of the Art on an Art of the State," *International Organization,* Vol. 40, No. 4 (Autumn 1986), pp. 753–775; Ruggie, "Continuity and Transformation in the World Polity: Toward a Neorealist Synthesis," *World Politics,* Vol. 35, No. 2 (January 1983), pp. 261–285; Ruggie, "Territoriality And Beyond: Problematizing Modernity in International Relations," *International Organization,* Vol. 47, No. 1 (Winter 1993), pp. 139–174; Alexander Wendt, "The Agent-Structure Problem in International Relations Theory," *International Organization,* Vol. 41, No. 3 (Summer 1987), pp. 335–370; Wendt, "Anarchy Is What States Make of It: The Social Construction of Power Politics," *International Organization,* Vol. 46, No. 2. (Spring 1992), pp. 391–425; and Wendt, "Collective Identity Formation and the International State," *American Political Science Review,* Vol. 88, No. 2 (June 1994), pp. 384–396. I use the label "critical theory" to describe this body of literature; other labels are sometimes used, among them constructivism, reflectivism, post-modernism, and post-structuralism.

3. The quotations in this paragraph are from Ashley, "Poverty of Neorealism," p. 285; and Wendt, "Anarchy Is What States Make of It," p. 431.
4. Ashley, "Poverty of Neorealism," p. 286.
5. Robert W. Cox, *Production, Power, and World Order: Social Forces in the Making of World History* (New York: Columbia University Press, 1987), p. 393.
6. Cox, "Post-Hegemonic Conceptualization," p. 139.
7. Cox, *Production, Power, and World Order,* p. 393. The young Karl Marx summed up this approach in 1844: "the advantage of the new trend [is] that we do not attempt dogmatically to prefigure the future, but want to find the new world only through criticism of the old." Karl Marx, "For a Ruthless Criticism of Everything Existing," in Robert C. Tucker, ed., *The Marx-Engels Reader,* 2nd ed. (New York: Norton, 1978), p. 13. Marx's early writings have markedly influenced critical theory. See, for example, Ashley, "Poverty of Neorealism," pp. 226–230; and Cox, "Social Forces," p. 133. Critical theorists, however, disparage Marx's later writings, which lay out a structural theory of politics that has much in common with realism.
8. Emanuel Adler, "Arms Control, Disarmament, and National Security: A Thirty Year Retrospective and a New Set of Anticipations," *Daedalus,* Vol. 120, No. 1 (Winter 1991), pp. 11–18; Ashley, "Geopolitics of Geopolitical Space," pp. 428, 430; and Richard Ned Lebow, "The Long Peace, the End of the Cold War, and the Failure of Realism," *International Organization,* Vol. 48, No. 2 (Spring 1994), pp. 269–277. Wendt uses the term "cooperative security system" in place of "pluralistic security community." See "Anarchy Is What States Make of It," pp. 400–401. Karl Deutsch invented the concept of a pluralistic security community.

See Karl W. Deutsch, et al., *Political Community and the North Atlantic Area: International Organization in the Light of Historical Experience* (Princeton, N.J.: Princeton University Press, 1957), pp. 5–9.

9. Ashley, "Geopolitics of Geopolitical Space," p. 430. Also see Adler, "Arms Control, Disarmament, and National Security," p. 11.

10. Wendt, "Anarchy Is What States Make of It," p. 400.

11. Ibid.

12. This outcome is fully consistent with Deutsch's definition of a pluralistic security community: "there is real assurance that the members of that community will not fight each other physically, but will settle their disputes in some other way. If the entire world were integrated as a security community, wars would be automatically eliminated." Deutsch, *Political Community*, p. 5.

13. John G. Ruggie, "International Structure and International Transformation: Space, Time, and Method," in Ernst-Otto Czempiel and James N. Rosenau, eds., *Global Changes and Theoretical Challenges: Approaches to World Politics for the 1990s* (Lexington, Mass.: Lexington Books, 1989), p. 30.

14. Wendt, "Anarchy Is What States Make of It," p. 397.

15. "Critical social scientific approaches," as Ashley notes, "are inherently communitarian." See Ashley, "Geopolitics of Geopolitical Space," p. 403; also see pp. 404–407.

16. In a recent article, Alexander Wendt discusses the "emergence of 'international states,' which would constitute a structural transformation of the Westphalian states system." Wendt, "Collective Identity Formation," p. 385.

17. It is important to emphasize that critical theorists do not make a case for pure idealism, where realist structure has little bearing on state behavior. Their argument is much more sophisticated, as they maintain that structure and discourse are inextricably linked together and constantly interact in a dialectical fashion. Structure, they emphasize, both enables and constrains individual behavior. Nevertheless, the key point for critical theorists is that structure is ultimately shaped and reshaped by discourse. In other words, structure may shape our thinking about the world, but structure is ultimately shaped by our discourse. Structure is not an independent material force that shapes how we think and talk about the world. Social reality, in the end, is ultimately a construction of our minds.

18. Koslowski and Kratochwil, "Understanding Change," p. 226.

19. Markus Fischer, "Feudal Europe, 800–1300: Communal Discourse and Conflictual Practices," *International Organization*, Vol. 46, No. 2 (Spring 1992), p. 430.

20. Cox, "Post-Hegemonic Conceptualization," p. 133.

21. Wendt, "Anarchy Is What States Make of It," p. 395. The subsequent quotations in this paragraph are from ibid. Also see Richard K. Ashley, "Untying the Sovereign State: A Double Reading of the Anarchy Problematique," *Millennium: Journal of International Studies*, Vol. 17, No. 2 (Summer 1988), pp. 227–262.

22. See Cox, "Post-Hegemonic Conceptualization," pp. 132–139; Kratochwil and Ruggie, "International Organization," pp. 763–775; Yosef Lapid, "The Third Debate: On the Prospects of International Theory in a Post-Positivist Era," *International Studies Quarterly*, Vol. 33, No. 3 (September 1989), pp. 235–254; Wendt, "The Agent-Structure Problem," pp. 335–370.

23. Cox, "Post-Hegemonic Conceptualization," p. 135.

24. Ashley, "Geopolitics of Geopolitical Space," pp. 408–409.

25. Ibid., p. 422.

26. See Adler, "Arms Control"; and Peter M. Haas, ed., *Knowledge, Power, and International Policy Coordination,* special issue of *International Organization,* Vol. 46, No. 1 (Winter 1992).

27. For example, see Ashley, "Poverty of Neorealism," *passim.*

28. Lebow, for example, writes that "Contemporary realists' . . . theories and some of the policy recommendations based on them may now stand in the way of the better world we all seek." Lebow, "The Long Peace," p. 277.

29. My thinking on this matter has been markedly influenced by Hein Goemans.

30. Thomas Risse-Kappen, "Ideas Do Not Float Freely: Transnational Coalitions, Domestic Structures, and the End of the Cold War," *International Organization,* Vol. 48, No. 2 (Spring 1994), p. 187. Also see Koslowski and Kratochwil, "Understanding Change," p. 225.

31. Ashley, "Geopolitics of Geopolitical Space," pp. 426–427.

32. Cox, "Post-Hegemonic Conceptualization," p. 138. Also see Cox, "Social Forces," pp. 138–149. For other examples, see Ruggie, "Continuity and Transformation," pp. 281–286; and Wendt, "Collective Identity Formation," pp. 389–390.

33. Cox is apparently aware of this problem. After spending eleven pages outlining various objective factors that might shape a new world order, he notes, "It would, of course, be *logically inadmissible,* as well as imprudent, to base predictions of future world order upon the foregoing considerations." Cox, "Social Forces," p. 149, emphasis added. Nevertheless, he then emphasizes in the next few sentences how important those objective considerations are for understanding future world order prospects. He writes: "Their utility is rather in drawing attention to factors which could incline an emerging world order in one direction or another. The social forces generated by changing production processes are the starting point for thinking about possible futures. These forces may combine in different configurations, and as an exercise one could consider the hypothetical configurations most likely to lead to three different outcomes as to the future of the state system. The focus on these three outcomes is not, of course, to imply that no other outcomes or configurations of social forces are possible." In other words, Cox does rely heavily on objective factors to explain possible future world orders.

34. Cox, *Production, Power, And World Order,* p. 393.

35. Wendt, for example, acknowledges that, "Relatively little empirical research has been explicitly informed by structuration [critical] theory, which might illustrate its implications for the explanation of state action." Wendt, "The Agent-Structure Problem," p. 362.

36. Ruggie, "Continuity and Transformation," pp. 273–279. Also see Robert W. Cox, "Postscript 1985," in Robert O. Keohane, ed., *Neorealism and Its Critics* (New York: Columbia University Press, 1986), pp. 244–245.

37. Koslowski and Kratochwil, "Understanding Change," p. 215. Also see Lebow, "The Long Peace"; Risse-Kappen, "Ideas Do Not Float Freely"; and Janice Gross Stein, "Political Learning By Doing: Gorbachev As Uncommitted Thinker and Motivated Learner," *International Organization,* Vol. 48, No. 2 (Spring 1994), pp. 155–183. All four of these articles are published together as a symposium on "The End of the Cold War and Theories of International Relations," in the Spring 1994 *International Organization.*

38. Koslowski and Kratochwil, "Understanding Change," p. 217.

39. See, for example, Ruggie, "Territoriality and Beyond," pp. 173–174; Wendt, "Anarchy Is What States Make of It," p. 422; and Wendt, "Collective Identity Formation," p. 393.

40. Fischer, "Feudal Europe," p. 428. Also see the subsequent exchange between Fischer and Rodney Hall and Friedrich Kratochwil in *International Organization*, Vol. 47, No. 3 (Summer 1993), pp. 479–500.

41. Fischer, "Feudal Europe," p. 428.

42. Wendt, "Collective Identity Formation," p. 389.

43. This sentence is a paraphrase of Wendt, "Anarchy Is What States Make of It," p. 397.

44. See Koslowski and Kratochwil, "Understanding Change," p. 233.

45. Risse-Kappen, "Ideas Do Not Float Freely," p. 213. Also see ibid., pp. 195–214; and Stein, "Political Learning By Doing," pp. 175–180.

46. Koslowski and Kratochwil, "Understanding Change," pp. 228, 239.

47. Ibid., p. 227.

48. Lebow, "The Long Peace," p. 276.

49. See Charles Dick, "The Military Doctrine of the Russian Federation," in *Jane's Intelligence Review*, Special Report No. 1, January 1994, pp. 1–5; Michael C. Desch, "Why the Soviet Military Supported Gorbachev and Why the Russian Military Might Only Support Yeltsin for a Price," *Journal of Strategic Studies*, Vol. 16, No. 4 (December 1993), pp. 467–474; and Stephen Foye, "Updating Russian Civil-Military Relations," *RFE/RL Research Report*, Vol. 2, No. 46 (November 19, 1993), pp. 44–50.

50. See, for example, Thomas Goltz, "Letter from Eurasia: The Hidden Russian Hand," *Foreign Policy*, No. 92, pp. 92–116; Steven E. Miller, "Russian National Interests," in Robert D. Blackwill and Sergei A. Karaganov, eds., *Damage Limitation or Crisis? Russia and the Outside World*, CSIA Studies in International Security No. 5 (Washington, D.C.: Brassey's, 1994), pp. 77–106; Alexei K. Pushkov, "Russia and America: The Honeymoon's Over," *Foreign Policy*, No. 93 (Winter 1993–1994), pp. 77–90; and Bruce D. Porter and Carol R. Saivetz, "The Once and Future Empire: Russia and the 'Near Abroad'," *Washington Quarterly*, Vol. 17, No. 3 (Summer 1994), pp. 75–90.

39

JACK SNYDER

ONE WORLD, RIVAL THEORIES

The U.S. government has endured several painful rounds of scrutiny as it tries to figure out what went wrong on Sept. 11, 2001. The intelligence community faces radical restructuring; the military has made a sharp pivot to face a new

Jack Snyder is the Robert and Renée Belfer professor of international relations at Columbia University.

SOURCE: FOREIGN POLICY by JACK SNYDER. Copyright 2004 by FOREIGN POLICY. Reproduced with permission of FOREIGN POLICY.

enemy; and a vast new federal agency has blossomed to coordinate homeland security. But did September 11 signal a failure of theory on par with the failures of intelligence and policy? Familiar theories about how the world works still dominate academic debate. Instead of radical change, academia has adjusted existing theories to meet new realities. Has this approach succeeded? Does international relations theory still have something to tell policymakers?

Six years ago, political scientist Stephen M. Walt published a much-cited survey of the field in these pages ("One World, Many Theories," Spring 1998). He sketched out three dominant approaches: realism, liberalism, and an updated form of idealism called "constructivism." Walt argued that these theories shape both public discourse and policy analysis. Realism focuses on the shifting distribution of power among states. Liberalism highlights the rising number of democracies and the turbulence of democratic transitions. Idealism illuminates the changing norms of sovereignty, human rights, and international justice, as well as the increased potency of religious ideas in politics.

The influence of these intellectual constructs extends far beyond university classrooms and tenure committees. Policymakers and public commentators invoke elements of all these theories when articulating solutions to global security dilemmas. President George W. Bush promises to fight terror by spreading liberal democracy to the Middle East and claims that skeptics "who call themselves 'realists'. . . . have lost contact with a fundamental reality" that "America is always more secure when freedom is on the march." Striking a more eclectic tone, National Security Advisor Condoleezza Rice, a former Stanford University political science professor, explains that the new Bush doctrine is an amalgam of pragmatic realism and Wilsonian liberal theory. During the recent presidential campaign, Sen. John Kerry sounded remarkably similar: "Our foreign policy has achieved greatness," he said, "only when it has combined realism and idealism."

International relations theory also shapes and informs the thinking of the public intellectuals who translate and disseminate academic ideas. During the summer of 2004, for example, two influential framers of neoconservative thought, columnist Charles Krauthammer and political scientist Francis Fukuyama, collided over the implications of these conceptual paradigms for U.S. policy in Iraq. Backing the Bush administration's Middle East policy, Krauthammer argued for an assertive amalgam of liberalism and realism, which he called "democratic realism." Fukuyama claimed that Krauthammer's faith in the use of force and the feasibility of democratic change in Iraq blinds him to the war's lack of legitimacy, a failing that "hurts both the realist part of our agenda, by diminishing our actual power, and the idealist portion of it, by undercutting our appeal as the embodiment of certain ideas and values."

Indeed, when realism, liberalism, and idealism enter the policymaking arena and public debate, they can sometimes become intellectual window dressing for simplistic worldviews. Properly understood, however, their policy implications are subtle and multifaceted. Realism instills a pragmatic appreciation of the role of power but also warns that states will suffer if they overreach. Liberalism highlights the cooperative potential of mature democracies, especially when working together through effective institutions, but it also notes democracies' tendency to crusade against tyrannies and the propensity of emerging democracies to collapse into violent ethnic turmoil. Idealism stresses that a consensus on values must underpin any stable political order, yet it also recognizes that forging such a consensus often requires an ideological struggle with the potential for conflict.

Each theory offers a filter for looking at a complicated picture. As such, they help explain the assumptions behind political rhetoric about foreign policy. Even more important, the theories act as a powerful check on each other. Deployed effectively, they reveal the weaknesses in arguments that can lead to misguided policies.

IS REALISM STILL REALISTIC?

At realism's core is the belief that international affairs is a struggle for power among self-interested states. Although some of realism's leading lights, notably the late University of Chicago political scientist Hans J. Morgenthau, are deeply pessimistic about human nature, it is not a theory of despair. Clearsighted states can mitigate the causes of war by finding ways to reduce the danger they pose to each other. Nor is realism necessarily amoral; its advocates emphasize that a ruthless pragmatism about power can actually yield a more peaceful world, if not an ideal one.

In liberal democracies, realism is the theory that everyone loves to hate. Developed largely by European émigrés at the end of World War II, realism claimed to be an antidote to the naive belief that international institutions and law alone can preserve peace, a misconception that this new generation of scholars believed had paved the way to war. In recent decades, the realist approach has been most fully articulated by U.S. theorists, but it still has broad appeal outside the United States as well. The influential writer and editor Josef Joffe articulately comments on Germany's strong realist traditions. (Mindful of the overwhelming importance of U.S. power to Europe's development, Joffe once called the United States "Europe's pacifier.") China's current foreign policy is grounded in realist ideas that date back millennia. As China modernizes its economy and enters international institutions such as the World Trade Organization, it behaves in a way that realists understand well: developing its military slowly but surely as its economic power grows, and avoiding a confrontation with superior U.S. forces.

Realism gets some things right about the post-9/11 world. The continued centrality of military strength and the persistence of conflict, even in this age of global economic interdependence, does not surprise realists. The theory's most obvious success is its ability to explain the United States' forceful military response to the September 11 terrorist attacks. When a state grows vastly more powerful than any opponent, realists expect that it will eventually use that power to expand its sphere of domination, whether for security, wealth, or other motives. The United States employed its military power in what some deemed an imperial fashion in large part because it could.

It is harder for the normally state-centric realists to explain why the world's only superpower announced a war against al Qaeda, a nonstate terrorist organization. How can realist theory account for the importance of powerful and violent individuals in a world of states? Realists point out that the central battles in the "war on terror" have been fought against two states (Afghanistan and Iraq), and that states, not the United Nations or Human Rights Watch, have led the fight against terrorism.

Even if realists acknowledge the importance of nonstate actors as a challenge to their assumptions, the theory still has important things to say about the behavior and motivations of these groups. The realist scholar Robert A. Pape, for example, has argued that suicide terrorism can be a rational, realistic strategy for the leadership of national liberation movements seeking to expel democratic powers that occupy their homelands. Other scholars apply standard theories of conflict in anarchy to explain ethnic conflict in collapsed states. Insights from political realism—a profound and wide-ranging intellectual tradition rooted in the enduring philosophy of Thucydides, Niccolò Machiavelli, and Thomas Hobbes—are hardly rendered obsolete because some nonstate groups are now able to resort to violence.

Post-9/11 developments seem to undercut one of realism's core concepts: the balance of power. Standard realist doctrine predicts that weaker states will ally to protect themselves from stronger ones and thereby form and reform a balance of power. So, when Germany unified in the late 19th century and became Europe's leading military and industrial power, Russia and France (and later, Britain) soon aligned to counter its power. Yet no combination of states or other powers can challenge the United States militarily, and no balancing coalition is imminent. Realists are scrambling to find a way to fill this hole in the center of their theory. Some theorists speculate that the United States' geographic distance and its relatively benign intentions have tempered the balancing instinct. Second-tier powers tend to worry more about their immediate neighbors and even see the United States as a helpful source of stability in regions such as East Asia. Other scholars insist that armed resistance by U.S. foes in Iraq, Afghanistan, and elsewhere, and foot-dragging by its formal allies actually constitute the beginnings of balancing against U.S. hegemony. The United States' strained relations with Europe offer ambiguous evidence: French and German opposition to recent U.S. policies could be seen as classic balancing, but they do not resist U.S. dominance militarily. Instead, these states have tried to undermine U.S. moral legitimacy and constrain the superpower in a web of multilateral institutions and treaty regimes—not what standard realist theory predicts.

These conceptual difficulties notwithstanding, realism is alive, well, and creatively reassessing how its root principles relate to the post-9/11 world. Despite changing configurations of power, realists remain steadfast in stressing that policy must be based on positions of real strength, not on either empty bravado or hopeful illusions about a world without conflict. In the run-up to the recent Iraq war, several prominent realists signed a public letter criticizing what they perceived as an exercise in American hubris. And in the continuing aftermath of that war, many prominent thinkers called for a return to realism. A group of scholars and public intellectuals (myself included) even formed the Coalition for a Realistic Foreign Policy, which calls for a more modest and prudent approach. Its statement of principles argues that "the move toward empire must be halted immediately." The coalition, though politically diverse, is largely inspired by realist theory. Its membership of seemingly odd bedfellows—including former Democratic Sen. Gary Hart and Scott McConnell, the executive editor of the *American Conservative* magazine—illustrates the power of international relations theory to cut through often ephemeral political labels and carry debate to the underlying assumptions.

THE DIVIDED HOUSE OF LIBERALISM

The liberal school of international relations theory, whose most famous proponents were German philosopher Immanuel Kant and U.S. President Woodrow Wilson, contends that realism has a stunted vision that cannot account for progress in relations between nations. Liberals foresee a slow but inexorable journey away from the anarchic world the realists envision, as trade and finance forge ties between nations, and democratic norms spread. Because elected leaders are accountable to the people (who bear the burdens of war), liberals expect that democracies will not attack each other and will regard each other's regimes as legitimate and nonthreatening. Many liberals also believe that the rule of law and transparency of democratic processes make it easier to sustain international cooperation, especially when these practices are enshrined in multilateral institutions.

Liberalism has such a powerful presence that the entire U.S. political spectrum, from neoconservatives to human rights advocates, assumes it as largely self-evident. Outside the United States, as well, the liberal view that only elected governments are legitimate and politically reliable has taken hold. So it is no surprise that liberal themes are constantly invoked as a response to today's security dilemmas. But the last several years have also produced a fierce tug-of-war between disparate strains of liberal thought. Supporters and critics of the Bush administration, in particular, have emphasized very different elements of the liberal canon.

For its part, the Bush administration highlights democracy promotion while largely turning its back on the international institutions that most liberal theorists champion. The U.S. National Security Strategy of September 2002, famous for its support of preventive war, also dwells on the need to promote democracy as a means of fighting terrorism and promoting peace. The Millennium Challenge program allocates part of U.S. foreign aid according to how well countries improve their performance on several measures of democratization and the rule of law. The White House's steadfast support for promoting democracy in the Middle East—even with turmoil in Iraq and rising anti-Americanism in the Arab world—demonstrates liberalism's emotional and rhetorical power.

In many respects, liberalism's claim to be a wise policy guide has plenty of hard data behind it. During the last two decades, the proposition that democratic institutions and values help states cooperate with each other is among the most intensively studied in all of international relations, and it has held up reasonably well. Indeed, the belief that democracies never fight wars against each other is the closest thing we have to an iron law in social science.

But the theory has some very important corollaries, which the Bush administration glosses over as it draws upon the democracy-promotion element of liberal thought. Columbia University political scientist Michael W. Doyle's articles on democratic peace warned that, though democracies never fight each other, they are prone to launch messianic struggles against warlike authoritarian regimes to "make the world safe for democracy." It was precisely American democracy's tendency to oscillate between self-righteous crusading and jaded isolationism that prompted early Cold War realists' call for a more calculated, prudent foreign policy.

Countries transitioning to democracy, with weak political institutions, are more likely than other states to get into international and civil wars. In the last 15 years, wars or large-scale civil violence followed experiments with mass electoral democracy in countries including Armenia, Burundi, Ethiopia, Indonesia, Russia, and the former Yugoslavia. In part, this violence is caused by ethnic groups' competing demands for national self-determination, often a problem in new, multiethnic democracies. More fundamental, emerging democracies often have nascent political institutions that cannot channel popular demands in constructive directions or credibly enforce compromises among rival groups. In this setting, democratic accountability works imperfectly, and nationalist politicians can hijack public debate. The violence that is vexing the experiment with democracy in Iraq is just the latest chapter in turbulent story that began with the French Revolution.

Contemporary liberal theory also points out that the rising democratic tide creates the presumption that all nations ought to enjoy the benefits of self-determination. Those left out may undertake violent campaigns to secure democratic rights. Some of these movements direct their struggles against democratic or semidemocratic states that they consider occupying powers—such as in Algeria in the 1950s, or Chechnya, Palestine, and the Tamil region of Sri Lanka today. Violence may also be directed at democratic supporters of oppressive regimes, much like the U.S. backing of the governments of Saudi Arabia and Egypt. Democratic regimes make attractive targets for terrorist violence by national liberation movements precisely because they are accountable to a cost-conscious electorate.

Nor is it clear to contemporary liberal scholars that nascent democracy and economic liberalism can always cohabitate. Free trade and the multifaceted globalization that advanced democracies promote often buffet transitional societies. World markets' penetration of societies that run on patronage and protectionism can disrupt social relations and spur strife between potential winners and losers. In other cases, universal free trade can make separatism look attractive, as small regions such as Aceh in Indonesia can lay claim to lucrative natural resources. So far, the trade-fueled boom in China has created incentives for improved relations with the advanced democracies, but it has also set the stage for a possible showdown between the relatively wealthy coastal entrepreneurs and the still impoverished rural masses.

While aggressively advocating the virtues of democracy, the Bush administration has shown little patience for these complexities in liberal though—or for liberalism's emphasis on the importance of international institutions. Far from trying to assure other powers that the United States would adhere to a constitutional order, Bush "unsigned" the International Criminal Court statute, rejected the Kyoto environmental agreement, dictated take-it-or-leave-it arms control changes to Russia, and invaded Iraq despite opposition at the United Nations and among close allies.

Recent liberal theory offers a thoughtful challenge to the administration's policy choices. Shortly before September 11, political scientist G. John Ikenberry studied attempts to establish international order by the victors of hegemonic struggles in 1815, 1919, 1945, and 1989. He argued that even the most powerful victor needed to gain the willing cooperation of the vanquished and other weak states by offering a mutually attractive bargain, codified in an international constitutional order. Democratic victors, he found, have the best chance of creating a working constitutional order, such as the Bretton Woods system after World War II, because their transparency and legalism make their promises credible.

Does the Bush administration's resistance to institution building refute Ikenberry's version of liberal theory? Some realists say it does, and that recent events demonstrate that international institutions cannot constrain a hegemonic power if its preferences change. But international institutions can nonetheless help coordinate outcomes that are in the long-term mutual interest of both the hegemon and the weaker states. Ikenberry did not contend that hegemonic democracies are immune from mistakes. States can act in defiance of the incentives established by their position in the international system, but they will suffer the consequences and probably learn to correct course. In response to Bush's unilateralist stance, Ikenberry wrote that the incentives for the United States to take the lead in establishing a multilateral constitutional order remain powerful. Sooner or later, the pendulum will swing back.

IDEALISM'S NEW CLOTHING

Idealism, the belief that foreign policy is and should be guided by ethical and legal standards, also has a long pedigree. Before World War II forced the United States to acknowledge a less pristine reality, Secretary of State Henry

Stimson denigrated espionage on the grounds that "gentlemen do not read each other's mail." During the Cold War, such naive idealism acquired a bad name in the Kissingerian corridors of power and among hardheaded academics. Recently, a new version of idealism—called constructivism by its scholarly adherents—returned to a prominent place in debates on international relations theory. Constructivism, which holds that social reality is created through debate about values, often echoes the themes that human rights and international justice activists sound. Recent events seem to vindicate the theory's resurgence; a theory that emphasizes the role of ideologies, identities, persuasion, and transnational networks is highly relevant to understanding the post-9/11 world.

The most prominent voices in the development of constructivist theory have been American, but Europe's role is significant. European philosophical currents helped establish constructivist theory, and the *European Journal of International Relations* is one of the principal outlets for constructivist work. Perhaps most important, Europe's increasingly legalistic approach to international relations, reflected in the process of forming the European Union out of a collection of sovereign states, provides fertile soil for idealist and constructivist conceptions of international politics.

Whereas realists dwell on the balance of power and liberals on the power of international trade and democracy, constructivists believe that debates about ideas are the fundamental building blocks of international life. Individuals and groups become powerful if they can convince others to adopt their ideas. People's understanding of their interests depends on the ideas they hold. Constructivists find absurd the idea of some identifiable and immutable "national interest," which some realists cherish. Especially in liberal societies, there is overlap between constructivists and liberal approaches, but the two are distinct. Constructivists contend that their theory is deeper than realism and liberalism because it explains the origins of the forces that drive those competing theories.

For constructivists, international change results from the work of intellectual entrepreneurs who proselytize new ideas and "name and shame" actors whose behavior deviates from accepted standards. Consequently, constructivists often study the role of transnational activist networks—such as Human Rights Watch or the International Campaign to Ban Landmines—in promoting change. Such groups typically uncover and publicize information about violations of legal or moral standards at least rhetorically supported by powerful democracies, including "disappearances" during the Argentine military's rule in the late 1970s, concentration camps in Bosnia, and the huge number of civilian deaths from land mines. This publicity is then used to press governments to adopt specific remedies, such as the establishment of a war crimes tribunal or the adoption of a landmine treaty. These movements often make pragmatic arguments as well as idealistic ones, but their distinctive power comes from the ability to highlight deviations from deeply held norms of appropriate behavior.

Progressive causes receive the most attention from constructivist scholars, but the theory also helps explain the dynamics of illiberal transnational forces, such as Arab nationalism or Islamist extremism. Professor Michael N. Barnett's 1998 book *Dialogues in Arab Politics: Negotiations in Regional Order* examines how the divergence between state borders and transnational Arab political identities requires vulnerable leaders to contend for legitimacy with radicals throughout the Arab world—a dynamic that often holds moderates hostage to opportunists who take extreme stances.

Constructivist thought can also yield broader insights about the ideas and values in the current international order. In his 2001 book, *Revolutions in Sovereignty: How Ideas Shaped Modern International Relations,* political scientist Daniel Philpott demonstrates how the religious ideas of the Protestant Reformation helped break down the medieval political order and provided a conceptual basis for the modern system of secular sovereign states. After September 11, Philpott focused on the challenge to the secular international order posed by political Islam. "The attacks and the broader resurgence of public religion," he says, ought to lead international relations scholars to "direct far more energy to understanding the impetuses behind movements across the globe that are reorienting purposes and policies." He notes that both liberal human rights movements and radical Islamic movements have transnational structures and principled motivations that challenge the traditional supremacy of self-interested states in international politics. Because constructivists believe that ideas and values helped shape the modern state system, they expect intellectual constructs to be decisive in transforming it—for good or ill.

When it comes to offering advice, however, constructivism points in two seemingly incompatible directions. The insight that political orders arise from shared understanding highlights the need for dialogue across cultures about the appropriate rules of the game. This prescription dovetails with liberalism's emphasis on establishing an agreed international constitutional order. And, yet, the notion of cross-cultural dialogue sits awkwardly with many idealists' view that they already know right and wrong. For these idealists, the essential task is to shame rights abusers and cajole powerful actors into promoting proper values and holding perpetrators accountable to international (generally Western) standards. As with realism and liberalism, constructivism can be many things to many people.

STUMPED BY CHANGE

None of the three theoretical traditions has a strong ability to explain change—a significant weakness in such turbulent times. Realists failed to predict the end of the Cold War, for example. Even after it happened, they tended to assume that the new system would become multipolar ("back to the future," as the scholar John J. Mearsheimer put it). Likewise, the liberal theory of democratic peace is stronger on what happens after states become democratic than in predicting the timing of democratic transitions, let alone prescribing how to make transitions happen peacefully. Constructivists are good at describing changes in norms and ideas, but they are weak on the material and institutional circumstances necessary to support the emergence of consensus about new values and ideas.

With such uncertain guidance from the theoretical realm, it is no wonder that policymakers, activists, and public commentators fall prey to simplistic or wishful thinking about how to effect change by, say, invading Iraq or setting up an International Criminal Court. In lieu of a good theory of change, the most prudent course is to use the insights of each of the three theoretical traditions as a check on the irrational exuberance of the others. Realists should have to explain whether policies based on calculations of power have sufficient legitimacy to last. Liberals should consider whether nascent democratic institutions can fend off powerful interests that oppose them, or how international institutions can bind a hegemonic power inclined to go its own way. Idealists should be asked about the strategic, institutional, or material conditions in which a set of ideas is likely to take hold.

Theories of international relations claim to explain the way international politics works, but each of the currently prevailing theories falls well short of that goal. One of the principal contributions that international relations theory can make is not predicting the future but providing the vocabulary and conceptual framework to ask hard questions of those who think that changing the world is easy.

WANT TO KNOW MORE?

Stephen M. Walt's **"International Relations: One World, Many Theories"** (FOREIGN POLICY, Spring 1998) is a valuable survey of the field. For a more recent survey, see Robert Jervis, **"Theories of War in an Era of Leading Power Peace"** (*American Political Science Review,* March 2002).

Important recent realist contributions include John J. Mearsheimer's *The Tragedy of Great Power Politics* (New York: Norton, 2001) and Fareed Zakaria, *From Wealth to Power: The Unusual Origins of America's World Role* (Princeton: Princeton University Press, 1998). Important realist inspired analyses of post 9/11 issues include. **"The Strategic Logic of Suicide Terrorism"** (*American Political Science Review,* August 2003), by Robert A. Pape; **"The Compulsive Empire"** (FOREIGN POLICY, July/August 2003), by Robert Jervis; and **"An Unnecessary War"** (FOREIGN POLICY, January/February 2003), by John Mearsheimer and Stephen Walt. Read about a current effort to inject realism into U.S. foreign policy at the Web site of the **Coalition for a Realistic Foreign Policy**. For a worried look at the realist resurgence, see Lawrence F. Kaplan, **"Springtime for Realism"** (*The New Republic,* June 21, 2004).

Recent additions to the liberal canon are Bruce Russett and John R. Oneal's *Triangulating Peace: Democracy, Interdependence, and International Organizations* (New York: Norton, 2001) and G. John Ikenberry's *After*

Victory: Institutions, Strategic Restraint, and the Rebuilding of Order After Major Wars (Princeton: Princeton University Press, 2001). To read about the dangers of democratization in countries with weak institutions, see Edward D. Mansfield and Jack Snyder, *Electing to Fight: Why Emerging Democracies Go to War* (Cambridge: MIT Press, 2005) and Zakaria's *The Future of Freedom: Illiberal Democracy at Home and Abroad* (New York: W.W. Norton & Co., 2003). Charles Krauthammer and Francis Fukuyama tussle over strains of liberalism in a recent exchange. Krauthammer makes the case for spreading democracy in **"Democratic Realism: An American Foreign Policy for a Unipolar World,"** an address to the American Enterprise Institute, and Fukuyama responds in **"The Neoconservative Moment,"** (*The National Interest,* Summer 2004). Krauthammer's rejoinder, **"In Defense of Democratic Realism"** (*The National Interest,* Fall 2004), counters Fukuyama's claims.

Read more on constructivism in Alexander Wendt, *Social Theory of International Politics* (New York: Cambridge University Press, 1999). Margaret E. Keck and Kathryn Sikkink look at constructivism at work in *Activists Beyond Borders: Advocacy Networks in International Politics* (Ithaca: Cornell University Press, 1998). More focused works include Sikkink's *Mixed Messages: U.S. Human Rights Policy and Latin America* (Ithaca: Cornell University Press, 2004) and Michael N. Barnett's *Dialogues in Arab Politics: Negotiations in Regional Order* (New York: Columbia University Press, 1998).

For links to relevant Web sites, access to the *FP* Archive, and a comprehensive index of related FOREIGN POLICY articles, go to **www.foreignpolicy.com.**

V

DETERRENCE, COERCION, AND WAR

THE ROLE OF FORCE

One of the most important features distinguishing international politics from domestic politics is the role of force. In domestic affairs, the state has a monopoly on the legitimate use of force; in international politics, where self-help is emphasized and considerations relating to power and security are pervasive, the use of force is much more widespread. In fact, a perennial problem in international politics is how to control and regulate military force. This has become increasingly important as military capabilities have expanded.

In eighteenth-century Europe, wars were fought for limited objectives using limited means. This system was initially challenged by the French Revolution and Napoleonic Wars, which were wars of nations rather than simple engagements between mercenary armies. After the Napoleonic Wars, the old system was temporarily re-established, at least in part, and the participants once more placed emphasis on war limitation. If the nineteenth century was a period of limited war in Europe, however, it was also a period in which the forces of democracy, nationalism, and industrialization were developing in ways that would undermine all efforts at restraint.

These trends culminated in World War I, in which nationalist passions were aroused, peoples and industries were mobilized for the war effort, and objectives were expanded to include the total defeat of the enemy. The massive and unprecedented slaughter of World War I led to efforts to eradicate war and to establish more effective ways of managing the state system. Although this antiwar sentiment initially appeared to be universal, problems arose in the 1930s with the emergence of totalitarian, militaristic regimes in Germany and Japan. Far from finding war abhorrent, these regimes saw it as a legitimate means of achieving their objectives. Initially, Nazi Germany, in particular, was able to get what it wanted in Europe simply through the threat of war—a threat that led the democracies to make strenuous efforts to appease Germany by yielding to its demands. Eventually, though, it became clear that Germany was making a bid for total domination in Europe, and when Britain and France reluctantly accepted that they would have to resort to force for self-preservation, the stage was set for the second total war of the twentieth century.

The end of this war not only resulted in the unconditional surrender of both Germany and Japan but also ushered in the beginning of the nuclear age. The atomic bombs dropped on Hiroshima and Nagasaki made clear that destructive power had reached new levels. As the atomic bomb was superseded by the hydrogen bomb, it was even more obvious that the means of destruction had become virtually unlimited. One consequence of this was that, in relations between the two superpowers, the emphasis moved from open conflict to threat-based relations in which deterrence and coercive diplomacy were central.

NUCLEAR DETERRENCE

During the 1950s, U.S.–Soviet relations were increasingly dominated by the notion of nuclear deterrence. The idea of deterrence itself is a simple one: preventing an adversary from taking actions one regards as undesirable by threatening to inflict unacceptable costs on the adversary if the action is taken. What caused more uncertainty was not the purpose of deterrence but what might be termed its scope—what actions could be deterred? Analysts also held many discussions about the requirements of deterrence. This is reflected in the selections we have made. One is by Bernard Brodie, who was perhaps the first scholar to appreciate fully the nature of the nuclear revolution—an appreciation evident in his landmark volume, *The Absolute Weapon,* which appeared in 1946. The selection we have reprinted is from *Strategy in the Missile Age* and discusses the impact of the nuclear revolution. Although Brodie was not oblivious to specific military requirements, he was acutely aware of the profoundly inhibiting effect of nuclear weapons. In some ways, he can be regarded as the forerunner of the notion of "existential deterrence," which presumes that nuclear weapons, rather than strategies of nuclear deterrence, are the key to deterrence. The basic argument of "existentialism" is that the nuclear component of the U.S.–Soviet relationship inhibited both superpowers from high-risk action against each other. The Soviet installation of missiles in Cuba could be regarded as the exception to this argument, although it is clear that Khrushchev underestimated the risks and backed down when it became apparent how serious these risks were. In this view, deterrence has been relatively easy.

Albert Wohlstetter, another important strategic analyst from the 1950s through the 1970s, had a more stringent assessment of the requirements of deterrence. Wohlstetter was probably the single most critical figure in the effort to ensure that the nuclear balance between the United States and the Soviet Union remained stable and provided no incentives for a Soviet first-strike attack. Although he may have overestimated the delicacy of the balance of terror, Wohlstetter's emphasis on the need for invulnerable retaliatory or second-strike forces rightly achieved the status of strategic orthodoxy from the late 1950s onward. The selection reprinted here, which is taken from a famous article in *Foreign Affairs,* highlights the requirement for a second-strike capability as the basis for force planning for effective deterrence. Indeed, Wohlstetter's emphasis on the survivability of retaliatory forces was enshrined in the triad of strategic capabilities—manned bombers, land-based missiles, and submarine-launched ballistic missiles—that would ensure the failure of any attempt at a strategic disarming attack and became the basis for what was subsequently known as mutual assured destruction.

Although deterrence appeared to be very robust, one of its potential shortcomings was that some participants in deterrence relationships might not have the capacity or will to perform the kind of cost-gain calculations that made deterrence work. The idea of dealing with crazy states has never been comfortable for U.S. strategists. This possibility, however, was raised in an unorthodox but compelling article by Yehezkel Dror, an Israeli political scientist and decision-making analyst. In the excerpt we have chosen, Dror argues that the notion of craziness has several dimensions. He also suggests that, although crazy states have a low probability of emerging, they cannot be ruled out completely. Originally intended to challenge some of the complacency of Cold War deterrence in an era of mutual assured destruction, Dror's ideas are even more relevant to the contemporary international system.

Although the Soviet Union and the United States behaved in ways that were very different from Dror's crazy states, their prudential calculations did not prevent them from probing each other to detect any sign of weakness that might be exploited as part of the Cold War competition. It is therefore not surprising that, alongside the literature on deterrence, a body of literature emerged on other threat-based strategies—what can be termed coercion.

COERCION

Coercive tactics are many and varied. They have been explored in a highly systematic and very imaginative way in the writings of Thomas Schelling, an economist by training and one of the first scholars to write not only about deterrence but also about compellence and compliance. Schelling's book *The Strategy of Conflict* is one of the landmark studies in strategic analysis.[1] The reading by Schelling that we have chosen, however, is from his later work, *Arms and Influence,* and deals with coercive bargaining tactics that exploit risk and uncertainty. Schelling discusses how brinkmanship and "the threat that leaves something to chance" can be used to intimidate an adversary. Although Schelling's analysis is full of brilliant ideas, he was essentially a theoretical rather than an empirical strategist. As a result, he did not focus sufficiently on either the difficulties of implementing some of the coercive strategies or on questions about the conditions under which these strategies were likely to succeed or fail.

The next reading, by Alexander L. George, (now professor emeritus at Stanford University) and two collaborators, David Hall and William Simons, remedies this deficiency. It is taken from an examination of the attempts at coercive diplomacy by the United States during the crisis in Laos in 1961, the Cuban missile crisis in 1962, and the Vietnam War in 1965. Basing their ideas on this series of case studies the authors use a method that subsequently became known as "focused comparison" to delineate the conditions under

---

[1] Thomas C. Schelling, *The Strategy of Conflict* (New York: Oxford University Press, 1963).

which coercive diplomacy is likely to succeed or fail.[2] One of the problems, for example, is that some kinds of adversary are likely to be much more resistant to the strategy than others.

Another difficulty with coercive diplomacy or coercive bargaining is that it is only one aspect of the overall task of crisis management. Other analysts point out the many cross pressures inherent in crisis situations as decision makers attempt to "coerce prudently" and "accommodate cheaply."[3] Whereas Schelling emphasized the value of exploiting or manipulating the risks inherent in crises, others suggest that policymakers will be more inclined to minimize these risks.

These differences between Schelling on the one side and analysts such as George on the other stem in part from different approaches to the subject. Schelling was more concerned with an exploration of theoretical possibilities whereas George focused more on empirical behavior. The same kind of distinction is evident in discussions about escalation. The notion of escalation was developed most fully by Herman Kahn, one of the early scholars in the field. Kahn wrote candidly about nuclear war actually being fought in his classic but highly controversial study, *Thinking about the Unthinkable*.[4] In this analysis, Kahn conceptualized escalation in terms of a ladder, a theme he subsequently developed in *On Escalation: Metaphors and Scenarios*. One of the implications of the ladder metaphor is the presumption that it is possible to take small discrete steps; another is the expectation that the direction can be reversed almost at will. Richard Smoke, in a study that examined how war can be controlled, suggested that, in certain respects, the ladder analogy was inappropriate and that it might be more appropriate to see escalation in terms of a slide that was not fully under the control of the actors.[5] These different conceptions of escalation are always implicit and sometimes explicit in the analyses of Kahn on the one side and George on the other.

THE NATURE AND ORIGINS OF WAR

The last group of readings in this section looks at war. Much of our contemporary thinking about warfare has been influenced by Carl von Clausewitz, a Prussian military officer who wrote about war in the aftermath of the Napoleonic Wars. Clausewitz, one of the most frequently quoted (although

---

[2] The focused comparison methodology is developed more fully in Alexander L. George and Richard Smoke, *Deterrence in American Foreign Policy* (New York: Columbia University Press, 1974).

[3] Glenn Snyder, "Crisis Bargaining," in *International Crises: Insights from Behavioral Research*, edited by Charles H. Hermann (New York: The Free Press, 1972). Snyder also argues that policymakers are more concerned with maintaining freedom of action than with making the kind of irrevocable commitments that look so attractive in bargaining theory.

[4] Herman Kahn, *Thinking about the Unthinkable* (London: Weidenfeld and Nicolson, 1962).

[5] Richard Smoke, *War: Controlling Escalation* (Cambridge, Mass.: Harvard University Press, 1977).

perhaps less frequently read) writers about war, has had an enormous effect on thinking about military strategy and tactics, even though much of his analysis was conceptual rather than practical. Clausewitz developed his understanding of war in both philosophical and empirical terms. He claimed that, philosophically, war was like a large duel without any limits or restraints. The result was that it developed toward what he called "absolute war," that is, a war without limits. In practice, though there were limits that, he suggested, stemmed partly from the existence of "frictions" but, more important, from the fact that war was a continuation of policy by other means. It was the political objectives of the parties that, ideally, would determine the level of violence.

As well as being concerned about the nature of war, many analysts have also written about its causes. Some of these will be familiar to the reader from the selections on international anarchy and the security dilemma in Part III. We have chosen two selections that complement the emphasis on the permissive conditions for war and broaden the discussion of the causes. The reading by Dean Pruitt and Richard Snyder provides a useful summary of the various theories developed to explain the outbreak of war. The authors survey the literature, provide an inventory of goals that can be advanced through war, and hold up the various explanations to critical analysis. They look at imperialism, perceptions of threat, and hostility toward other states as the possible causes of war. They acknowledge the limits of an analysis "based on speculation rather than empirical methodology," but they nevertheless provide a succinct and effective overview of different interpretations.

In the next selection, by Robert Jervis, one of the pioneers in applying political psychology to international relations and foreign policy, looks in more detail at how misperceptions can lead to war. Jervis (who discussed the security dilemma in Part IV) is careful not to claim too much for his analysis. He does, however, highlight some of the ways in which "inaccurate inferences, miscalculations of consequences, and misjudgments about how others will react to one's policies" can lead governments into war. He identifies two different models of how misperception can have a serious impact: the first is the World War II model, in which the aggressive power underestimates the willingness of governments defending the status quo to fight; the second is the World War I, or spiral, model, in which the states involved exaggerate each other's hostility.

During the Cold War, much of the debate, in the United States at least, concerned the relative applicability of these two models to U.S.–Soviet relations. Hawks emphasized the need to avoid a Soviet underestimation of United States power and will, whereas doves focused on the dangers of a superpower confrontation getting out of control. One could argue that the Cold War was managed in ways designed to avoid both dangers. Although some assessments of the Cold War suggest that the United States and the Soviet Union managed to avoid nuclear war through good luck rather than good judgment or skill, John Lewis Gaddis, a prominent diplomatic historian who has produced the definitive study on the strategies of containment, offers a different assessment.

In an article evoking some of the earlier readings on system structure, deterrence, and crisis management, Gaddis argues that the Cold War is best seen as a period of long peace. He identifies both the structural and the behavioral reasons why the Cold War did not result in a hot war. In his view, there was a mix of objective conditions—such as the fact that the superpowers were not neighbors—as well as very effective management techniques, including the development of certain norms of behavior or "rules of prudence."[6] The result was that, throughout the Cold War, U.S. and Soviet forces did not meet in combat; wars in what were sometimes referred to as grey areas were limited; and direct confrontations were managed and defused. In addition, the arms race between the United States and the Soviet Union was subject to restraints or controls that became increasingly stringent as the Cold War continued into the 1980s.

Indeed, some would argue that the security challenges of the Cold War pale in comparison to those that challenge the United States and the international community in the early years of the twenty-first century. Others believe that, although uncertainties and complexities have increased, the dangers of nuclear holocaust have been significantly reduced. This is a theme for Part VI of this volume.

---

[6] Also very illuminating on these rules is Alexander L. George et al., *Managing U.S.–Soviet Rivalry* (Boulder, Colo.: Westview Press, 1983).

40

Bernard Brodie

Nuclear Weapons and Strategy

Few people were unexcited or unimpressed by the first atomic weapons. That something tremendously important had happened was immediately understood by almost everyone. Interpretations of the military significance of the new weapons naturally varied greatly, but even the most conservative saw nothing inappropriate or extravagant in such extraordinary consultations and decisions as resulted in the Truman-Attlee-King Declaration of November 15, 1945, or the Baruch Proposals before the United Nations in the following year. Then the MacMahon Act set up the Atomic Energy Commission, an autonomous government agency hedged about by all sorts of special provisions, for the manufacture and development of atomic weapons. Nothing of the sort had ever happened before; but photographs of the destruction wrought at Hiroshima and Nagasaki had been spread across the land, and few persons were unaffected. . . .

In an age that had grown used to taking rapid advances in military technology for granted, how remarkable was this immediate and almost universal consensus that the atomic bomb was different and epochal! Equally striking was the fact that the invention caused the greatest forebodings in the hearts of the people who first possessed it and benefited from it. The thought that it represented a fabulous and mostly American scientific and engineering accomplishment, that it had apparently helped to end World War II, and that the United States had for the time being a monopoly on it seemed to cause no exhilaration among Americans.

Subsequent events did not undermine the early consensus on the importance of the new weapon, nor did they qualify the misgivings. On the contrary, the first decade of the atomic age saw the collapse of the American monopoly, of the myth of inevitable scarcity, and of reasonable hopes for international atomic disarmament. It saw also the development of the thermonuclear weapon in both major camps. If at the end of that decade one looked back at the opinions expressed so voluminously at the beginning of it, one found almost none that had proved too extravagant. Only the conservative guesses had proved to be hopelessly wrong.

It is no longer possible to distinguish between the new weapons on the one hand and the "battle-tested" or "tried and true" ones on the other,

Source: From *Strategy in the Missile Age*, Bernard Brodie (Princeton, New Jersey: Princeton University Press, 1959), pp. 150–158. Reprinted with permission of RAND.

because in this new world no weapons are tried and tested. The hand rifle, the field gun, and the tank, as well as the infantry division or combat team that uses them, are at least as much on trial in the age of atomic warfare as is the atomic bomb itself; indeed, they are more so.

THE THERMONUCLEAR BOMB

Since we are now well launched into the thermonuclear age, we might first ask what differences, if any, the thermonuclear or fusion or hydrogen bomb must make for our strategic predictions. We have been living with the fission bomb for more than a decade, and it may well be that the fusion type introduces nothing essentially new other than a greater economy of destruction along patterns already established. Unfortunately, that is not the case.

No doubt the strategic implications of the first atomic bombs were radical in the extreme, and it was right at the time to stress the drastic nature of the change.[1] The effectiveness of strategic bombing as a way of war could no longer be questioned. It at once became, incontrovertibly, the dominant form of war. A strategic-bombing program could be carried through entirely with air forces existing at the outset of a war, and at a speed which, however variously estimated, would be phenomenal by any previous standard. Also, because any payload sufficient to include one atomic bomb was quite enough to justify any sortie, strategic bombing could be carried out successfully over any distance that might separate the powers involved. If the limited ranges of the aircraft made a refueling necessary, it was worthwhile. These conclusions represented change enough from the conditions of World War II. They served, among other things, to end completely American invulnerability.

Nevertheless, fission bombs were sufficiently limited in power to make it appear necessary that a substantial number would have to be used to achieve decisive and certain results. That in turn made it possible to visualize a meaningful even if not wholly satisfactory air defense, both active and passive. It was therefore still necessary to think in terms of a struggle for command of the air in the old Douhet sense, hardly shorter in duration than what he imagined. It was also still necessary to apply, though in much modified form, the lore so painfully acquired in World War II concerning target selection for a strategic-bombing campaign. Even with fission weapons numbering in the hundreds, there was still a real—and difficult—analytical problem in choosing targets that would make the campaign decisive rather than merely hurtful. It was possible also to distinguish between attacks on population and attacks on the economy. Finally, the functions of ground and naval forces, though clearly and markedly affected by the new weapons, still appeared vital.

Even these tenuous ties with the past were threatened when it became known that thermonuclear bombs were not only feasible but apparently also inexpensive enough to justify their manufacture in substantial numbers.[2] Possibly the feeling that the H-bomb was distinctively new and significantly different from the A-bomb argued in part an underestimation of the A-bomb. But when one has to confront a basic change in circumstances, it helps if it is unequivocal. . . .

One immediate result of the new development was the realization that questions inherited from World War II concerning appropriate selection among industrial target-systems were now irrelevant. Only a few industries tend to have important manufacturing facilities outside cities, these being notably in steel and oil production. Since a large thermonuclear bomb exploded over a city would as a rule effectively eliminate all its industrial activities, there is hardly much point in asking which industries should be hit and in what order, or which particular facilities within any industry. New and important kinds of discrimination are still possible—for example, between disarming the enemy and destroying him—but henceforward attacking his industrial economy is practically indistinguishable from hitting his cities, with obvious consequences for populations. Cities are in any case the easiest targets to find and hit. Of course the enemy's strategic retaliatory force must be the first priority target in time, and possibly also in weight of bombs, but destroying that force, if it can be done, is essentially a disarming move which seems to await some kind of sequential action.

There is nothing in logic to require such a sequence. It is likely, however, in view of traditional attitudes, to be considered a practical necessity. The attacker may feel he cannot count with high confidence on fully eliminating the enemy air force, even if he strikes first. He might, therefore, feel obliged to begin the counter-economy competition before he knew the results of the counter-air-force strike. At any rate, decisions of the sort we are implying would have to be made well before hostilities began. The plan which goes into effect at the beginning of a war, insofar as circumstances permit its going into effect, is the emergency war plan, which is prepared in peacetime and periodically revised. In view of existing habits of thinking, one would expect that even where a counter-air-force attack was given top priority in such a war plan, a counter-economy attack would probably be to some degree integrated with it.

There could indeed be a significant difference in ultimate results between a strategy aimed primarily at the enemy air force and one aimed chiefly at population, even if a lot of people were killed in both. However, it must be remembered that in striking at an enemy strategic air force, an attacker will normally feel obliged to hit many more airfields than those indicated to be major strategic air bases, because he must assume in advance that some dispersion of enemy aircraft will have taken place as a result either of warning or of routine operating procedures. In striking at airfields near cities, he might, especially if he entertained conventional attitudes about maximizing effects, choose to use some quite large thermonuclear weapons.

Thus the distinction in priority could turn out to be an academic one. It is idle to talk about our strategies being counter-force strategies, as distinct from counter-economy or counter-population strategies, *unless* planners were actually to take deliberate restrictive measures to refrain from injuring cities. They would have to conclude that it is desirable to avoid such damage, which would be a reversal of the traditional attitude that damage done to enemy installations or populations in the vicinity of the primary target is a "bonus." Otherwise it can hardly matter much to the populations involved whether the destruction of cities is a by-product of the destruction of airfields or vice versa.

The number of cities that account for the so-called economic war potential of either the U.S. or the U.S.S.R. is small: possibly fifty or less, and certainly not over two hundred. The range in these figures is the result of the varying weight that can be given to certain tangible but difficult-to-measure factors, such as interdependence. The leading fifty-four American "metropolitan areas" (as defined by the Census Bureau) contain over 60 per cent of the nation's industrial capital, and a population of over 80,000,000, including a disproportionate number of the people whose special skills are associated with large-scale production.[3] Altogether the Census Bureau lists 170 metropolitan areas in the United States, which together contain over 75 per cent of industrial capital and 55 per cent of the nation's population. We must note that by far the greater portion of these cities are concentrated in the eastern and especially the northeastern part of the United States, where urban and non-urban populations alike may be subject to overlapping patterns of radioactive fallout.[4] The concentration of industry in Russian cities, and the concentration of cities and populations in the western part of their national area, make of the Soviet Union a target complex roughly comparable to the United States, though less urbanized. The Soviet Union has only four cities of over a million population, as compared with fourteen such cities in the United States.

The great Hamburg raids of July 1943, which were so tremendous a shock to the whole German nation, caused the destruction of about 50 per cent of the city's housing and resulted in casualties amounting to about three per cent of its population. A single H-bomb of anything above one megaton yield bursting within the confines of a city such as Hamburg would cause a degree of housing destruction much higher than 50 per cent; and unless the city had been evacuated in advance the proportion of casualties to housing destroyed would certainly be far greater than it was at Hamburg.

The latter fact underlines one of the distinctive features of nuclear weapons. There are at least four reasons why casualty rates with nuclear weapons are likely to be far greater in relation to property destroyed than was true of nonatomic bombing: (1) warning time is likely to be less, or nonexistent, unless the attacker deliberately offers it before attacking; (2) the *duration* of an attack at any one place will be literally a single instant, in contrast to the several hours' duration of a World War II attack; (3) shelters capable of furnishing good protection against high-explosive bombs might be of no use at all within the fireball radius of a large ground-burst nuclear weapon, or within the oxygen-consuming fire-storm that such a detonation would cause; and (4) nuclear weapons have the distinctive effect of producing radioactivity, which can be lingering as well as instantaneous, and which causes casualties but not property injury.[5]

NOTES

1. See Part I: "The Weapon," in *The Absolute Weapon: Atomic Power and World Order,* ed. by Bernard Brodie, Harcourt, Brace, New York, 1946, pp. 21–110. See also Bernard Brodie and Eilene Galloway, *The Atomic Bomb and the Armed Services,* Library of Congress: Legislative Reference Service, Public Affairs Bulletin No. 55 (May 1947).
2. Information which was first officially revealed in the many references to Dr. Edward Teller's special contributions to H-bomb technology in the published transcript of the Oppenheimer hearings—an investigation designed to tighten security. See *In the Matter of J. Robert Oppenheimer: Transcript of Hearing before Personnel Security Board,* U.S. Government Printing Office, Washington, 1954.
3. See Margaret B. Rowan and Harry V. Kincaid, *The Views of Corporation Executives on the Probable Effect of the Loss of Company Headquarters in Wartime,* The RAND Corporation, Research Memorandum RM-1723 (ASTIA No. AD 105967), May 1, 1956, p. 86.
4. See S. M. Greenfield, R. R. Rapp, and P. A. Walters, *A Catalog of Fallout Patterns,* The RAND Corporation, Research Memorandum RM-1676-AEC, April 16, 1956, p. 91.
5. The direct gamma radiation of any nuclear detonation is of extremely brief duration, and its lethal radius depends roughly on the size of the explosion and on the amount of shielding . . . in the target area.

41

ALBERT WOHLSTETTER

THE DELICATE BALANCE OF TERROR

. . . Because of its crucial role in the Western strategy of defense, I should like to examine the stability of the thermonuclear balance which, it is generally supposed, would make aggression irrational or even insane. The balance, I believe, is in fact precarious, and this fact has critical implications for policy. Deterrence in the 1960s is neither assured nor impossible but will be the product of sustained intelligent effort and hard choices, responsibly made. As a major illustration important both for defense and foreign policy, I shall treat the particularly stringent conditions for deterrence which affect forces based close to the enemy, whether they are U.S. forces or those of our allies, under

SOURCE: Reprinted by permission of *Foreign Affairs,* Vol. 37, No. 1–4 (October 1958–July 1959), pp. 211–213, 215–216, 219–221. Copyright 1959 by the Council on Foreign Affairs, Inc.

single or joint control. I shall comment also on the inadequacy as well as the necessity of deterrence, on the problem of accidental outbreak of war, and on disarmament.[1]

THE PRESUMED AUTOMATIC BALANCE

I emphasize that requirements for deterrence are stringent. We have heard so much about the atomic stalemate and the receding probability of war which it has produced that this may strike the reader as something of an exaggeration. Is deterrence a necessary consequence of both sides having a nuclear delivery capability, and is all-out war nearly obsolete? Is mutual extinction the only outcome of a general war? This belief, frequently expressed by references to Mr. Oppenheimer's simile of the two scorpions in a bottle, is perhaps the prevalent one. It is held by a very eminent and diverse group of people—in England by Sir Winston Churchill, P. M. S. Blackett, Sir John Slessor, Admiral Buzzard and many others; in France by such figures as Raymond Aron, General Gallois and General Gazin; in this country by the titular heads of both parties as well as almost all writers on military and foreign affairs, by both Henry Kissinger and his critic, James E. King, Jr., and by George Kennan as well as Dean Acheson. Mr. Kennan refers to American concern about surprise attack as simply obsessive;[2] and many people have drawn the consequence of the stalemate as has Blackett, who states: "If it is in fact true, as most current opinion holds, that strategic air power has abolished global war, then an urgent problem for the West is to assess how little effort must be put into it to keep global war abolished."[3] If peace were founded firmly on mutual terror, and mutual terror on symmetrical nuclear capabilities, this would be, as Churchill has said, "a melancholy paradox;" none the less a most comforting one.

Deterrence, however, is not automatic. While feasible, it will be much harder to achieve in the 1960s than is generally believed. One of the most disturbing features of current opinion is the underestimation of this difficulty. This is due partly to a misconstruction of the technological race as a problem in matching striking forces, partly to a wishful analysis of the Soviet ability to strike first.

Since sputnik, the United States has made several moves to assure the world (that is, the enemy, but more especially our allies and ourselves) that we will match or overmatch Soviet technology and, specifically, Soviet offense technology. We have, for example, accelerated the bomber and ballistic missile programs, in particular the intermediate-range ballistic missiles. The problem has been conceived as more or better bombers—or rockets; or sputniks; or engineers. This has meant confusing deterrence with matching or exceeding the enemy's ability to strike first. Matching weapons, however, misconstrues the nature of the technological race. Not, as is frequently said, because only a few bombs owned by the defender can make aggression fruitless, but because even many might not. One outmoded A-bomb dropped from an obsolete bomber might destroy a great many supersonic jets and ballistic missiles. To deter an attack means being able to strike back in spite of it. It means, in other words, a capability to strike second. In the last year or two there has been a growing awareness of the importance of the distinction between a "strike-first" and a "strike-second" capability, but little, if any, recognition of the implications of this distinction for the balance of terror theory. . . .

Perhaps the first step in dispelling the nearly universal optimism about the stability of deterrence would be to recognize the difficulties in analyzing the uncertainties and interactions between our own wide range of choices and the moves open to the Soviets. On our side we must consider an enormous variety of strategic weapons which might compose our force, and for each of these several alternative methods of basing and operation. . . .

Some of the complexities can be suggested by referring to the successive obstacles to be hurdled by any system providing a capability to strike second, that is, to strike back. Such deterrent systems must have (a) a stable, "steady-state" peacetime operation within feasible budgets (besides the logistic and operational costs there are, for example, problems of false alarms and accidents). They must have also the ability (b) to survive enemy attacks, (c) to make and communicate the decision to retaliate, (d) to reach enemy territory with fuel enough to complete their mission, (e) to penetrate enemy active defenses, that is, fighters and surface-to-air missiles, and (f) to destroy the target in spite of any "passive" civil defense in the form of dispersal or protective construction or evacuation of the target itself.

The first hurdle to be surmounted is the attainment of a stable, steady-state peacetime operation. Systems which depend for their survival on extreme decentralization of controls, as may be the case with large-scale dispersal and some of the mobile weapons, raise problems of accidents and over a long period of peacetime operation this leads in turn to serious political problems. Systems relying on extensive movement by land, perhaps by truck caravan, are an obvious example; the introduction of these on European roads, as is sometimes suggested, would raise grave questions for the governments of some of our allies. Any extensive increase in the armed air alert will increase the hazard of accident and intensify the concern already expressed among our allies. Some of the proposals for bombardment satellites may involve such hazards of unintended bomb release as to make them out of the question.

The cost to buy and operate various weapons systems must be seriously considered. Some systems buy their ability to negotiate a given hurdle—say, surviving the enemy attack—only at prohibitive cost. Then the number that can be bought out of a given budget will be small and this will affect the relative performance of competing systems at various other hurdles, for example penetrating enemy defenses. Some of the relevant cost comparisons, then, are between competing systems; others concern the extra costs to the enemy of canceling an additional expenditure of our own. For example, some dispersal is essential, though usually it is expensive; if the dispersed bases are within a warning net, dispersal can help to provide warning against some sorts of attack, since it forces the attacker to increase the size of his raid and so makes it more liable to detection as well as somewhat harder to coordinate. But as the sole or principal defense of our offensive force, dispersal has only a brief useful life and can be justified financially only up to a point. For against our costs of construction, maintenance and operation of an additional base must beset the enemy's much lower costs of delivering one extra weapon. And, in general, any feasible degree of dispersal leaves a considerable concentration of value at a single target point. For example, a squadron of heavy bombers costing, with their associated tankers and penetration aids, perhaps $500,000,000 over five years, might be eliminated, if it were otherwise unprotected, by an enemy intercontinental ballistic missile costing perhaps $16,000,000. After making allowance for the unreliability and inaccuracy of the missile, this means a ratio of some ten for one or better. To achieve safety by *brute* numbers in so unfavorable a competition is not likely to be viable economically or politically. However, a viable peacetime operation is only the first hurdle to be surmounted.

At the second hurdle—surviving the enemy offense—ground alert systems placed deep within a warning net look good against a manned bomber attack, much less good against ballistic intercontinental ballistic missiles, and not good at all against missiles launched from the sea. In the last case, systems such as the Minuteman, which may be sheltered and dispersed as well as alert, would do well. Systems involving launching platforms which are mobile and concealed, such as Polaris submarines, have particular advantage for surviving an enemy offense.

However, there is a third hurdle to be surmounted—namely that of making the decision to retaliate and communicating it. Here, Polaris, the combat air patrol of B-52s, and in fact all of the mobile platforms—under water, on the surface, in the air and above the air—have severe problems. Long distance communication may be jammed and, most important, communication centers may be destroyed.

At the fourth hurdle—ability to reach enemy territory with fuel enough to complete the mission—several of our short-legged systems have operational problems such as coordination with tankers and using bases close to the enemy. For a good many years to come, up to the mid-1960s in fact, this will be a formidable hurdle for the greater part of our deterrent force.

The fifth hurdle is the aggressor's long-range interceptors and close-in missile defenses. To get past these might require large numbers of planes and missiles. (If the high cost of overcoming an earlier obstacle—using extreme dispersal or airborne alert or the like—limits the number of planes or missiles bought, our capability is likely to be penalized disproportionately here.) Or getting through may involve carrying heavy loads of radar decoys, electronic jammers and other aids to defense penetration. For example, vehicles like Minuteman and Polaris, which were made small to facilitate dispersal or mobility, may suffer here because they can carry fewer penetration aids.

At the final hurdle—destroying the target in spite of the passive defenses that may protect it—low-payload and low-accuracy systems, such as Minuteman and Polaris, may be frustrated by blast-resistant shelters. For example, five half-megaton weapons with an average inaccuracy of two miles might be expected to destroy half the population of a city of 900,000, spread over 40 square miles, provided the inhabitants are without shelters. But if they are provided with shelters capable of resisting over-pressures of 100 pounds per square inch, approximately 60 such weapons would be required; and deep rock shelters might force the total up to over a thousand.

Prizes for a retaliatory capability are not distributed for getting over one of these jumps. A system must get over all six. I hope these illustrations will suggest that assuring ourselves the power to strike back after a massive thermonuclear surprise attack is by no means as automatic as is widely believed.

In counteracting the general optimism as to the ease and, in fact, the inevitability of deterrence, I should like to avoid creating the extreme opposite impression. Deterrence demands hard, continuing, intelligent work, but it can be achieved. The job of deterring rational attack by guaranteeing great damage to an aggressor is, for example, very much less difficult than erecting a nearly airtight defense of cities in the face of full-scale thermonuclear surprise attack. Protecting manned bombers and missiles is much easier because they may be dispersed, sheltered or kept mobile, and they can respond to warning with greater speed. Mixtures of these and other defenses with complementary strengths can preserve a powerful remainder after attack. Obviously not all our bombers and missiles need to survive in order to fulfill their mission. To preserve the majority of our cities intact in the face of surprise attack is immensely more difficult, if not impossible. (This does not mean that the aggressor has the same problem in preserving his cities from retaliation by a poorly-protected, badly-damaged force. And it does not mean that *we* should not do more to limit the extent of the catastrophe to our cities in case deterrence fails. I believe we should.) Deterrence, however, provided we work at it, is feasible, and, what is more, it is a crucial objective of national policy.

NOTES

1. I want to thank C. J. Hitch, M. W. Hoag, W. W. Kaufman, A. W. Marshall, H. S. Rowen and W. W. Taylor for suggestions in preparation of this article.
2. George F. Kennan, "A Chance to Withdraw Our Troops in Europe," *Harper's Magazine,* February 1958, p. 41.
3. P. M. S. Blackett, "Atomic Weapons and East-West Relations" (New York: Cambridge University Press, 1956), p. 32.

42

YEHEZKEL DROR

CRAZY STATES

The concept of crazy states as defined by me is critical for my analysis. It contradicts most of common sense, many accepted perceptions, widespread expectations, and . . . strategic fallacies. . . . It also somewhat differs from the meanings of the term crazy as used in common discourse or in psychology. Therefore, the concept of crazy states must be carefully considered.

Aggressive religious movements such as the Christian Crusaders or the Islam Holy Warriors; anarchists after the First World War and before it; contemporary terrorist groups in the United States, in Canada, in the Middle East, and in some South American countries; Nazi Germany; and—to a more limited extent—Japan before the Second World War—these are some illustration of what I call crazy states. While . . . a small number of prototype[1] constructs serve as main subjects for analysis, nevertheless the prototypes must meet the variety of historical reality and of future potential realization. This precludes any simple conception of crazy states. Rather, the concept of craziness must be broken down into several dimensions and a number of prototypes must be constructed on the basis of different combinations of those dimensions. In this way, an initial set of different prototypes of crazy states can be arrived at, some of which have been approximated by historical reality, and some of which have some probability of approximated realization in the future.

Before taking up construction of these prototypes, I want to point out my value-free use of the term crazy states—a term which I use as a technical concept, as defined and explained in this [essay.][2] While the constructed and discussed prototypes are by contemporary Western culture and United States culture in particular, crazy, this a culturally given and timebound value judgment. Viewed from a perspective of one or another crazy state, the United States would be discussed and analyzed in terms of supercrazy features and behaviors. From some moral points of view, some may in fact regard one or another of the crazy prototypes as superior to the United States: readiness to sacrifice oneself and to take high risks for collectively shared and believed in values, may appear to some as morally superior to looking after individual goals, abstract rules of law and achievement of a well-adjusted life of aggregation

SOURCE: From *Crazy States* by Y. Dror, pp. 23–31. Copyright 1971 D. C. Heath & Company.

of material goods and routinized relations with other individuals, who are equally missing deep commitment to collective transcendental values. To make an even more extreme illustration, if someone deeply and sincerely believed that other people are better off dead than to live as nonbelievers, then one will be ready and indeed feel oneself obligated to kill others for deep moral purposes. In such a case, we have what I in this [essay] call an extreme case of craziness, even though it may be accompanied by deep and sincere feelings of moral obligations which—were they only directed at some other goal and a different type of belief—we would all admire and respect very much.

Because of the subjective basis of all beliefs, intrinsic values, transcendental obligations and commitments, most of the dimensions by which some states are classified as crazy (or normal) are arbitrary from a scientific point of view. In order to avoid mixing up moral judgment with analytical discourse, I want to make this point absolutely clear. While I regard several types of crazy states as highly dangerous for the world and therefore recommend a number of countermeasures, including some extreme ones, this may or may not involve moral condemnation. We may understand a terrorist, sympathize with some of the reasons which brought about his present state, and sometimes even appreciate the moral purposes he may have in mind. Nevertheless, it may be necessary to make sure he cannot cause any damage.

Clarification of the concept of craziness as used in this [essay] requires differentiation between five main dimensions as described below[3]

Goal Contents This quality can be expressed in various ways, ranging from official and semiofficial pronouncements by the leaders of a country to concrete types of behavior, and including various artifacts of culture and media, such as literature and drama, news reporting, and activities of youth organizations. Within the strategic context, we are interested in goals which involve aggressive activities abroad (or, when the crazy state is a noncountry unit—aggressive activities against other groups). Such goals can range in content from slight revisions of the border up to conversion of the world to a new dogma.

I will use the terms reasonable, unreasonable, and counterreasonable as referent to the goal-contents dimension.

Goal Commitment No less important in some respects than the contents of goals is the intensity with which they are held, that is, the degree of goal commitment. This concept can be overrationalized in terms of the price that a state, as led by a given group, is willing to pay for achievement of those goals. Goal commitment can range in intensity from daydreaming to complete commitment, leading up to a readiness for martyrdom.

I will use the terms low intensity, medium intensity, and high intensity as referent to the goal-commitment dimension.

Risk Propensity This quality is a dimension of particular importance for the concept of crazy states. Risk propensities may range from an extreme dislike of any risks, to a preference for low-risk policies, up to an extreme preference for taking high risks—regarded by American standards as recklessness and brinkmanship.[4]

I will use the terms low risk, medium risk, and high risk as referents to the risk-propensity dimension, while ignoring the negative extreme of strong fear of even minimum risk, which is abnormal in the opposite direction from crazy states.

Means-Goals Relation   This dimension, as contrasted with all other dimensions here, has an objective criteria (if some metaphysical assumptions of positivistic philosophy are taken for granted). It is possible to make an objective judgment on how far given goals are served by certain means or not. We may lack the knowledge and information for making this judgment, but in principle, means-goals relation can be dealt with on the intellectual level. Therefore, it is sometimes possible to identify clearly counterproductive means and means based on absurd reasons (such as astrology, unless it is a randomizer or a cover for tacit knowledge in the absence of applicable objective criteria).

In addition to objective instrumental rationality, irrationality, and counter-rationality, there may also be cases of subjective instrumental rationality, irrationality, and counterrationality. Subjective instrumental irrationality and counterrationality exist where the decision-makers do not even claim that any relations obtain between the means and the goals. Much as such a view may appear not only absurd but nearly impossible to persons brought up in Western culture, it is one which should not be ignored. Actions which are explicitly justified in terms of satisfying passing moods or which are represented proudly as taken under the influence of altered states of consciousness illustrate such a possibility. Actual cases of action not even nominally justified in terms of any means-goals relation are illustrated, for instance, by ritualistic killings committed under the influence of psychotic drugs. To avoid seemingly contradictory terms such as crazy rational states, I will use the terms instrumental, noninstrumental and counterinstrumental as referents to the means-goals relation dimension, including its objective and subjective facets.

Style   When we focus our intentions on style—as contrasted with goal contents, risk propensity and means-goals relation—it is possible to distinguish between two deviations relevant to the crazy states issue from what is regarded normal behavior within the international context. One deviation is a strong ritualistic-dogmatic fixation on specific types of behavior and expressions. It is a stylistic feature separate from goal contents, risk propensity, or means-goals relation. (Some Communist and Asian patterns of communication illustrate this stylistic feature and are hard for Western negotiators to understand.) The second deviation is the propensity and preference for stylistic innovations which are not bound by accepted opinions and which are not regulated by accepted patterns. Aircraft hijacking, taking diplomats as hostages, and selective assassinations are illustrations of such stylistic innovations already in existence. Hypothetical illustrations are only limited by our imagination, by our inability to think of the unthinkable, and by the undesirability of supplying ideas to crazy states.[5] I will use the terms accepted, unaccepted, and counteraccepted—with or without the adjective ritualistic—as referents to the style dimension.

Possibilities for classification, subclassifications, fine distinctions, and subdistinctions in respect to all these dimensions of normality versus craziness are infinite. But elaboration of a detailed breakdown of the dimensions would be a pure exercise in taxonomy, which would detract rather than add to the basic line of analysis of this [essay]. Analysis of the main problems of crazy states at the present state of study of this subject requires a few clear-cut prototypes rather than a range of shady distinctions. Therefore, I will limit myself to an ordinal three-step classification of these dimensions, as presented in Table 1.

These dimensions of craziness can be used for behavioral study of reality, that is, description and dissection of historic situations. It is possible to take real cases of crazy international behavior and analyze them in terms of dimensions. Thus, Nazi Germany, the Crusaders, Holy Wars, imperialistic states, terror groups, and so on can be classified, described, and analyzed with the help of the dimensions of craziness. Such an endeavor would be much more than an exercise in classification. It may provide better understanding of crazy states, permit inductive validation of general patterns and relationships, provide a basis for reliable predictions concerning the emergence of crazy states in the future and—ultimately—derivation of a theory of crazy states and modeling of their relationships with the environment.

However interesting and worthwhile such an endeavor may be, my approach in this [essay] is different. For a definite treatment of crazy states which wants to arrive at general theories of such phenomena, historic study in which the dimensions of craziness are used as one of the conceptual tools is essential. But for a policy-oriented exploration, a different utilization of the dimensions of craziness is preferable, namely, the synthesis of prototypes.

Hypothetically, different combinations of goals contents, goal commitments, risk propensity, means-goals relation, and styles may occur and form a large number of possible conditions. Some of these combinations may be less probable than others, and some may even appear to us, with present knowledge, to be impossible because of inherent contradictions—though this is an *a priori* assumption which should not be taken as completely reliable. By breaking down the dimensions into subdimensions and considering different possible mixes of subdimensions in respect to different issues within any one state, many more combinations can be made. But for purposes of analyzing crazy states and their strategic implications, a smaller number of sharper and more extreme prototypes is preferable. Reality will move on the ranges between the various prototypes, but for clarification of the basic issues involved, sharper and fewer prototypes are most useful. A set of main prototypes, based on combinations of the three-step scale, together with some initial comments on their features . . . is represented in Table 2. . . .

To complete initial circumscription of the concept of crazy states, we must now add the unit to which the various dimensions of craziness apply, that is, the societies and countries involved. These can be classified as (a) countries

TABLE 1 Dimensions of Craziness

DIMENSIONS	DEGREES OF CRAZINESS		
	(1) LOW	(2) MEDIUM	(3) HIGH
(a) Goal Contents	(1) Reasonable Status quo or minor external goals, such as: voluntary commercial trade activities; minor influence on policies of other states; no or very limited diffusion of ideology; no territorial change or very minor border adjustments.	(2) Unreasonable Extensive external goals, such as economic hegemony over other states; much control over some policies of other states; significant export of ideology; medium changes in borders.	(3) Counterreasonable Very extensive external goals, such as full control over economic activities of other states; full control of all policies of other states; total conversion of others to ideology; radical changes in borders; up to destruction of other states and absorption or liquidation of their population.
(b) Goal Commitment	(1) Low Intensity Devotion of minor parts of budget and limited manpower to external goals; no readiness to sacrifice internal goals for external goals.	(2) Medium Intensity Devotion of large parts of budget, GNP, and manpower to external goals; readiness to sacrifice internal goals for external goals.	(3) High Intensity Devotion of most of budget, GNP, and manpower to external goals; the internal goals regarded only as means for external goals; external goals accepted as national mission, up to readiness to sacrifice self-existence to achieve external goals.
(c) Risk Propensity	(1) Low Risk Strong tendency to reduce risks by avoiding risky policies.	(2) Medium Risk Acceptance of risk, with a mix between more risky and less risky policies.	(3) High Risk Preference for very risky policies, up to ideological commitment to adventurism and risk-taking as a preferable lifestyle.
(d) Means-Goals Relation	(1) Instrumental Full formal desire to be rational; justification of means in terms of goals; usually means do not obviously contradict goals; efforts to develop and use methodologies to improve means-goals relations (such as systems analysis, PPBS, and policy sciences); where easily usable criteria are available, means tend to fit goals.	(2) Noninstrumental Limited lip service to rationality; little justification of means in terms of goals; some means obviously contradict goals; no interest in means-goals relation-improving methodology; even where easily usable criteria are available, means often do not fit goals.	(3) Counterinstrumental Ideology completely ignores or rejects rationality; no justification of means in terms of goals; many means obviously contradict goals; explicit resistance to means-goals relation-improving methodology and explicit preference for nonrational methods, such as astrology and arbitrary leader myths; even where easily usable criteria are available, means very often do not fit goals.
(e) Style	(1) Accepted Nearly full compliance with present styles, even under provocation; some deviations themselves take place in stylized forms within special and isolated units, such as the CIA. Some elasticity, incremental change capacity, and adjustment to context.	(2) Unaccepted Much deviation from present styles, such as: extensive insurgence activities formally engaged in; some use of terror, execution of hostages, blackmail, sabotage, etc.; some unannounced use of biochemical weapons. Some elasticity, incremental change capacity, and adjustment to context.	(3) Counteraccepted Extreme deviation from present styles (and morals) such as: genocide (here as a style of operation, not as goal content); mass assassination of leaders; food poisoning; systematic sabotage of civilian peaceful facilities; counter-value terror against schools, hospitals, recreation areas, civil transportation, etc.; extensive killing of diplomats; full biochemical warfare. Some elasticity, incremental change capacity, and adjustment to context.
	(1a) Accepted Ritualistic Fixation and rigidity in respect to more or less accepted styles.	(2a) Unaccepted Ritualistic Fixation and rigidity in respect to specific unaccepted styles.	(3a) Counteraccepted Ritualistic Fixation and rigidity in respect to specific counter-accepted styles.

Note: As explained in the text, the classification is based on contemporary Western, and especially United States standards. Therefore, the classification is culture-bound and time-bound and does not presume any universal, absolute, or intrinsic validity.

TABLE 2 Main Prototypes of Craziness

COMBINATION OF DIMENSIONS

(A) GOAL CONTENTS	(B) GOAL COMMITMENT	(C) RISK PROPENSITY	(D) MEANS-GOALS RELATION	(E) STYLE	NAME
Reasonable (1) some unreasonable (2)	Low intensity (1) some medium intensity (2)	Low risk (1), some medium risk (2)	Instrumental (1), some noninstrumental (2)	Accepted (1), some unaccepted (2) with or without some accepted ritualism (1a)	Normal state
Unreasonable (2)	Medium intensity (2)	Medium risk (2)	Instrumental (1), some noninstrumental (2)	Unaccepted (2), with or without some unaccepted ritualism (2a)	Somewhat crazy state
Counterreasonable (3)	High intensity (3)	Medium risk (2) and some high risk (3)	Instrumental (1), some noninstrumental (2)	Counteraccepted (3)	Crazy state
Counterreasonable (3)	High intensity (3)	Medium risk (2) and some high risk (3)	Counterinstrumental (3)	Counteraccepted (3)	Crazy noninstrumental state
Counterreasonable (3)	High intensity (3)	Medium risk (2) and some high risk (3)	Counterinstrumental (3)	Counteraccepted ritualistic (3a)	Crazy noninstrumental ritualistic state
Counterreasonable (3)	High intensity (3)	Extreme high risk (extreme 3)	Instrumental (1), some noninstrumental (2)	Counteraccepted (3)	Crazy martyr state
Counterreasonable (3)	High intensity (3)	Extreme high risk (extreme 3)	Counterinstrumental (3)	Counteraccepted (3) or counteraccepted ritualistic (3a)	Crazy noninstrumental martyr state

Note: This table presents only some possible combinations of dimensions of craziness (referred to by the numbers used in Table 1 above), with special attention to construction of prototypes of extreme crazy states.

and (b) noncountries. Most attention in strategic studies still goes to countries, and indeed, countries are the most important multiactor. But this was not always the case in the past and may not always be the case in the future. At different periods, multiactors which were not countries fulfilled critical strategic roles. Sufficient to mention the Catholic Church, moving nomads, medieval cities, and Chinese secret societies to illustrate the security implications on noncountry multiactors. In the future, with expected changes in weapons technology and possible changes in postsaturation societies, noncountry units may become more important as security issues than they are now (even on the international scene)—and thus they may become a main theme for strategic studies. This possibility begins to be recognized in the growing attention to what is called subversion, guerrilla warfare, internal warfare and international terrorism.

These phenomena involve subcountry units ranging from very small groups up to large movements, or even country-within-country structures. Less recognized are other noncountry multiactors, some of which are intercountry, and some of which do not belong to any country at all. Units which cross national borders and have significant memberships in a number of countries, such as a religious movement or—as some times—the Communist movement, illustrate the case of intercountry units. Units which regard themselves as outside the domain of any existing country, such as some of the medieval orders and, nowadays, some of the Palestinian movements, illustrate the category of belonging-to-no-country units. I am including all these forms of multiactors which are not countries under the term noncountry units.

. . . The strategic problems that may be posed by noncountry multiactors (and perhaps even by crazy individuals) may become growing ones—with such units becoming more probable and with their capacities to cause significant trouble being on the increase. For purposes of conceptual economy, I am including country, subcountry, and intercountry units within the concept of crazy states, using the double meaning of states as referring (a) to countries; and (b) to situations. Often, when speaking about crazy states, I refer mainly to crazy countries, as will be made clear by the context, But noncountry units are very important for the problem of states-of-craziness. . . .

Policy analysis must be justified by more than intellectual curiosity and theoretical fascination. Therefore, before proceeding with our study of crazy states, we must demonstrate its significance for the real world. In other words, we must face the question, What are the probabilities of crazy states?

Even if crazy states have low probability, the study of them as a counterfactual construct (that is, a construct contradicting all known phenomena— though not theoretically impossible) would be beneficial. It could, for example, help repudiate the fallacies which result from the tacit theory of most American strategic studies . . . and thus help improve these studies on realistic issues. But I do not think that crazy states are counterfactual constructs; rather, I think they are possible future occurrences of history-shaping impact.

My reasons for this belief can be summed up in the following statements.

1. Crazy states have happened in the past. This at least, shows that they are possible in the sense that they do not contradict basic patterns of human and social behavior.

2. While present knowledge is too limited to allow us to construct a theory on the causes of crazy states, accelerated societal transformation—by definition—involves appearance of infrequent and even completely new, social phenomena. Some of the latter can be crazy states. Therefore, the contemporary rate of social change must be regarded as a factor which may contribute to the emergence of crazy states.

3. It is possible to diagnose a contemporary trend toward the emergence of crazy states. While they appear as isolated instances and mainly on the noncountry level, their imitation and diffusion may be encouraged by the characteristics of present mass communication which can reinforce underlying (and unknown) reasons and accelerate a possible trend toward craziness. Even if the present occurrences do not become as yet a trend, they may indicate the possibility of such a trend beginning in the future.

4. Historically, crazy states occurred from time to time. But many of them were localized and easily repressed. Modern technology changes this situation, permitting incipient crazy states both to (1) build up significant external-action capabilities; and (2) achieve stature thanks to their fascination for the mass media. These possibilities make crazy states more probable and more dangerous if realized. . . .

NOTES

1. From a methodological point of view, these prototypes are pure types or ideal types, as used by Max Weber.

2. Alternative concepts which I could have used are fanatic state, extreme state, ideologically agressive state, missionary state, terror state, etc. Each one of these terms and other possible concepts would be open to misunderstanding, as is the concept of crazy states itself. One possibility was to coin a new term, such as X-type state, but this would have made this [essay] hard to read and even more abstract than it is. The reader is strongly urged to try to keep in mind my exposition of the meaning of craziness as used [here] — a meaning somewhat different from common usage of the term. Thus, as will be explained later, a crazy state can behave rationally in the instrumental sense, that is, it can pick instruments which are highly effective for achievement of its (crazy) goals.

3. All Five dimensions can be regarded as parts of a multidimensional objective function, crazy states being characterized by the particular shape of their objective function.

4. It is important to note that risk propensity relates to the evaluation of risks *per se*, separate analytically from the expected value of particular outcomes.

5. This is an important consideration which I confronted in writing this [work]. Because of it, I use illustrations more sparsely than would otherwise be desirabe.

43

THOMAS C. SCHELLING

THE MANIPULATION OF RISK

If all threats were fully believable (except for the ones that were completely unbelievable) we might live in a strange world—perhaps a safe one, with many of the marks of a world based on enforceable law. Countries would hasten to set up their threats; and if the violence that would accompany infraction were confidently expected, and sufficiently dreadful to outweigh the fruits of transgression, the world might get frozen into a set of laws enforced by what we could figuratively call the Wrath of God. If we could threaten world inundation for any encroachment on the Berlin corridor, and everyone believed it and understood precisely what crime would bring about the deluge, it might not matter whether the whole thing were arranged by human or supernatural powers. If there were no uncertainty about what would and would not set off the violence, and if everyone could avoid accidentally overstepping the bounds, and if we and the Soviets (and everybody else) could avoid making simultaneous and incompatible threats, every nation would have to live within the rules set up by its adversary. And if all the threats depended on some kind of physical positioning of territorial claims, trip-wires, troop barriers, automatic alarm systems, and other such arrangements, and all were completely infallible and fully credible, we might have something like an old fashioned western land rush, at the end of which—as long as nobody tripped on his neighbor's electric fence and set the whole thing off—the world would be carved up into a tightly bound status quo. The world would be full of literal and figurative frontiers and thresholds that nobody in his right mind would cross.

But uncertainty exists. Not everybody is always in his right mind. Not all the frontiers and thresholds are precisely defined, fully reliable, and known to be so beyond the least temptation to test them out, to explore for loopholes, or to take a chance that they may be disconnected this time. Violence, especially war, is a confused and uncertain activity, highly unpredictable, depending on decisions made by fallible human beings organized into imperfect governments, depending on fallible communications and warning systems and on the untested performance of people and equipment. It is furthermore a hotheaded activity, in which commitments and reputations can develop a momentum of their own.

SOURCE: From *Arms and Influence*, Thomas C. Schelling (London: Yale University Press, 1966), pp. 92–94, 96–99, 103–105, 116–121. Reprinted by permission of the publisher.

This last is particularly true, because what one does today in a crisis affects what one can be expected to do tomorrow. A government never knows just how committed it is to action until the occasion when its commitment is challenged. Nations, like people, are continually engaged in demonstrations of resolve, tests of nerve, and explorations for understandings and misunderstandings.

One never quite knows in the course of a diplomatic confrontation how opinion will converge on signs of weakness. One never quite knows what exits will begin to look cowardly to oneself or to the bystanders or to one's adversary. It would be possible to get into a situation in which either side felt that to yield now would create such an asymmetrical situation, would be such a gratuitous act of surrender, that whoever backed down could not persuade anybody that he wouldn't yield again tomorrow and the day after.

This is why there is a genuine risk of major war not from "accidents" in the military machine but through a diplomatic process of commitment that is itself unpredictable. The unpredictability is not due solely to what a destroyer commander might do at midnight when he comes across a Soviet (or American) freighter at sea, but to the psychological process by which particular things become identified with courage or appeasement or how particular things get included in or left out of a diplomatic package. Whether the removal of their missiles from Cuba while leaving behind 15,000 troops is a "defeat" for the Soviets or a "defeat" for the United States depends more on how it is construed than on the military significance of the troops, and the construction placed on the outcome is not easily foreseeable.

The resulting international relations often have the character of a competition in risk taking, characterized not so much by tests of force as by tests of nerve. Particularly in the relations between major adversaries—between East and West—issues are decided not by who *can* bring the most force to bear in a locality, or on a particular issue, but by who is eventually *willing* to bring more force to bear or able to make it appear that more is forthcoming. . . .

There was nothing about the blockade of Cuba by American naval vessels that could have led straightforwardly into general war. Any *foreseeable* course of events would have involved steps that the Soviets or the Americans—realizing that they would lead straightforwardly to general war—would not have taken. But the Soviets could be expected to take steps that, though not leading directly to war, could further compound risk; they might incur some risk of war rather than back down completely. The Cuban crisis was a contest in risk taking, involving steps that would have made no sense if they led predictably and ineluctably to a major war, yet would also have made no sense if they were completely without danger. Neither side needed to believe the other side would deliberately and knowingly take the step that would raise the possibility to a certainty.

What deters such crises and makes them infrequent is that they are genuinely dangerous. Whatever happens to the danger of deliberate premeditated war in such a crisis, the danger of inadvertent war appears to go up. This is why they are called "crises." The essence of the crisis is its unpredictability.

The "crisis" that is confidently believed to involve no danger of things getting out of hand is no crisis; no matter how energetic the activity, as long as things are believed safe there is no crisis. And a "crisis" that is known to entail disaster or large losses, or great changes of some sort that are completely foreseeable, is also no crisis; it is over as soon as it begins, there is no suspense. It is the essence of a crisis that the participants are not fully in control of events; they take steps and make decisions that raise or lower the danger, but in a realm of risk and uncertainty.

Deterrence has to be understood in relation to this uncertainty. We often talk as though a "deterrent threat" was a credible threat to launch a disastrous war coolly and deliberately in response to some enemy transgression. People who voice doubts, for example, about American willingness to launch war on the Soviet Union in case of Soviet aggression against some ally, and people who defend American resolve against those doubts, both often tend to argue in terms of a once-for-all decision. The picture is drawn of a Soviet attack, say, on Greece or Turkey or Western Germany, and the question is raised, would the United States then launch a retaliatory blow against the Soviet Union. Some answer a disdainful no, some answer a proud yes, but neither seems to be answering the pertinent question. The choice is unlikely to be one between everything and nothing. The question is really: is the United States likely to do something that is fraught with the danger of war, something that could lead—through a compounding of actions and reactions, of calculations and miscalculations, of alarms and false alarms, of commitments and challenges—to a major war?

This is why deterrent threats are often so credible. They do not need to depend on a willingness to commit anything like suicide in the face of a challenge. A response that carries some risk of war can be plausible, even reasonable, at a time when a final, ultimate decision to *have* a general war would be implausible or unreasonable. A country can threaten to stumble into a war even if it cannot credibly threaten to invite one. In fact, though a country may not be able with absolute credibility to threaten general war, it may be equally unable with absolute credibility to forestall a major war. The Russians would have been out of their minds at the time of the Cuban crisis to incur deliberately a major nuclear war with the United States; their missile threats were far from credible, there was nothing that the United States wanted out of the Cuban crisis that the Russians could have rationally denied at the cost of general war. Yet their implicit threat to behave in a way that might—that just might, in spite of all their care and all our care—lead up to the brink and over it in a general war, had some substance. If we were anywhere near the brink of war on that occasion, it was a war that neither side wanted but that both sides might have been unable to forestall.

The idea, expressed by some writers, that such deterrence depends on a "credible first strike capability," and that a country cannot plausibly threaten to engage in a general war over anything but a mortal assault on itself unless it has an appreciable capacity to blunt the other side's attack, seems to depend on the clean-cut notion that war results—or is expected to result—only from a deliberate yes–no decision. But if war tends to result from a *process,* a dynamic process in which both sides get more and more deeply involved, more and more expectant, more and more concerned not to be a slow second in case the war starts, it is not a "credible first strike" that one threatens, but just plain war. The Soviet Union can indeed threaten us with war: they can even threaten us with a war that *we* eventually start, by threatening to get involved with us in a process that blows up into war. And some of the arguments about "superiority" and "inferiority" seem to imply that one of the two sides, being weaker, must absolutely fear war and concede while the other, being stronger, may confidently expect the other to yield. There is undoubtedly a good deal to the notion that the country with the less impressive military capability may be less feared, and the other may run the riskier course in a crisis; other things being equal, one anticipates that the strategically "superior" country has some advantage. But this is a far cry from the notion that the two sides just measure up to each other and one bows before the other's superiority and acknowledges that he was only bluffing. Any situation that scares one side will scare both sides with the danger of a war that neither wants, and both will have to pick their way carefully through the crisis, never quite sure that the other knows how to avoid stumbling over the brink.

BRINKMANSHIP: THE MANIPULATION OF RISK

If "brinkmanship" means anything, it means *manipulating the shared risk of war.* It means exploiting the danger that somebody may inadvertently go over the brink, dragging the other with him. If two climbers are tied together, and one wants to intimidate the other by seeming about to fall over the edge, there has to be some uncertainty or anticipated irrationality or it won't work. If the brink is clearly marked and provides a firm footing, no loose pebbles underfoot and no gusts of wind to catch one off guard, if each climber is in full control of himself and never gets dizzy, neither can pose any risk to the other by approaching the brink. There is no danger in approaching it; and while either can deliberately jump off, he cannot credibly pretend that he is about to. Any attempt to intimidate or to deter the other climber depends on the threat of slipping or stumbling. With loose ground, gusty winds, and a propensity toward dizziness, there is some danger when a climber approaches the edge; one can credibly threaten to fall off *accidentally* by standing near the brink. . . .

In this way uncertainty imports tactics of intimidation into the game. One can incur a moderate probability of disaster, sharing it with his adversary, as a deterrent or compellent device, where one could not take, or persuasively threaten to take, a deliberate last clear step into certain disaster.[1]

The route by which major war might actually be reached would have the same kind of unpredictability. Either side can take steps—engaging in a limited war would usually be such a step—that genuinely raise the probability of a blow-up. This would be the case with intrusions, blockades, occupations of third areas, border incidents, enlargement of some small war, or any incident that involves a challenge and entails a response that may in turn have to be risky. Many of these actions and threats designed to pressure and intimidate would be nothing but noise, if it were reliably known that the situation could not get out of hand. They would neither impose risk nor demonstrate willingness to incur risk. And if they definitely would lead to major war, they would not be taken. (If war were desired, it would be started directly.) What makes them significant and usable is that they create a genuine risk—a danger that can be appreciated—that the thing will blow up for reasons not fully under control.[2]

It has often been said, and correctly, that a general nuclear war would not liberate Berlin and that local military action in the neighborhood of Berlin could be overcome by Soviet military forces. But that is not all there is to say. What local military forces can do, even against very superior forces, is to initiate this uncertain process of escalation. One does not have to be able to win a local military engagement to make the threat of it effective. Being able to lose a local war in a dangerous and provocative manner may make the risk—not the sure consequences, but the possibility of this act—outweigh the apparent gains to the other side. . . .

FACE, NERVE, AND EXPECTATIONS

Cold war politics have been likened, by Bertrand Russell and others, to the game of "chicken." This is described as a game in which two teen-age motorists head for each other on a highway—usually late at night, with their gangs and girlfriends looking on—to see which of the two will first swerve aside. The one who does is then called "chicken."

The better analogy is with the less frivolous contest of chicken that is played out regularly on streets and highways by people who want their share of the road, or more than their share, or who want to be first through an intersection or at least not kept waiting indefinitely.

"Chicken" is not just a game played by delinquent teen-agers with their hot-rods in southern California; it is a universal form of adversary engagement. It is played not only in the Berlin air corridor but by Negroes who want to get their children into schools and by whites who want to keep them out; by rivals at a meeting who both raise their voices, each hoping the other will yield the floor to avoid embarrassment; as well as by drivers of both sexes and all ages at all times of day. Children played it before they were old enough to drive and before automobiles were invented. The earliest instance I have come across, in a race with horse-drawn vehicles, antedates the auto by some time:

> The road here led through a gully, and in one part the winter flood had broken down part of the road and made a hollow. Menelaos was driving in the middle of the road, hoping that no one would try to pass too close to his

wheel, but Antilochos turned his horses out of the track and followed him a little to one side. This frightened Menelaos, and he shouted at him:

"What reckless driving Antilochos! Hold in your horses. This place is narrow, soon you will have more room to pass. You will foul my car and destroy us both!"

But Antilochos only plied the whip and drove faster than ever, as if he did not hear. They raced about as far as the cast of quoit . . . and then [Menelaos] fell behind: he let the horses go slow himself, for he was afraid that they might all collide in that narrow space and overturn the cars and fall in a struggling heap.

This game of chicken took place outside the gates of Troy three thousand years ago. Antilochos won, though Homer says—somewhat ungenerously— "by trick, not by merit."[3]

Even the game in its stylized teen-age automobile form is worth examining. Most noteworthy is that the game virtually disappears if there is no uncertainty, no unpredictability. If the two cars, instead of driving continuously, took turns advancing exactly fifty feet at a time toward each other, a point would be reached when the next move would surely result in collision. Whichever driver has that final turn will not, and need not, drive deliberately into the other. This is no game of nerve. The lady who pushes her child's stroller across an intersection in front of a car that has already come to a dead stop is in no particular danger as long as she sees the driver watching her: even if the driver prefers not to give her the right of way she has the winning tactic and gets no score on nerve. The more instructive automobile form of the game is the one people play as they crowd each other on the highway, jockey their way through an intersection, or speed up to signal to a pedestrian that he'd better not cross yet. These are the cases in which, like Antilochos' chariot, things may get out of control; no one can trust with certainty that someone will have the "last clear chance" to avert tragedy and will pull back in time.

These various games of chicken—the genuine ones that involve some real unpredictability—have some characteristics that are worth noting. One is that, unlike those sociable games it takes two to play, with chicken it takes two *not* to play. If you are publicly invited to play chicken and say you would rather not, you have just played.

Second, what is in dispute is usually not the issue of the moment, but everyone's expectations about how a participant will behave in the future. To yield may be to signal that one can be expected to yield; to yield often or continually indicates acknowledgement that that is one's role. To yield repeatedly up to some limit and then to say "enough" may guarantee that the first show of obduracy loses the game for both sides. If you can get a reputation for being reckless, demanding, or unreliable—and apparently hot-rods, taxis, and cars with "driving school" license plates sometimes enjoy this advantage—you may find concessions made to you. (The driver of a wide American car on a narrow European street is at less of a disadvantage than a static calculation would indicate. The smaller cars squeeze over to give him room.) Between these extremes, one can get a reputation for being firm in demanding an appropriate share of the road but not aggressively challenging about the other's half. Unfortunately, in less stylized games than the highway version, it is often hard to know just where the central or fair or expected division should lie, or even whether there should be any recognition of one contestant's claim.[4]

Another important characteristic is that, though the two players are cast as adversaries, the game is somewhat collaborative. Even in the stylized version in which they straddle the white line, there is at least an advantage in understanding that, when a player does swerve, he will swerve to the right and not to the left! And the players may try to signal each other to try to coordinate on a tie; if each can swerve a little, indicating that he will swerve a little more if the other does too, and if their speeds are not too great to allow some bargaining, they may manage to turn at approximately the same time, neither being proved chicken.

They may also collaborate in declining to play the game. This is a little harder. When two rivals are coaxed by their friends to have it out in a fight, they may manage to shrug it off skillfully, but only if neither comes away looking exclusively responsible for turning down the opportunity. Both players can appreciate a rule that forbids play; if the cops break up the game before it starts, so that nobody plays and nobody is proved chicken, many and perhaps all of the players will consider it a great night, especially if their ultimate willingness to play was not doubted.

In fact, one of the great advantages of international law and custom, or an acknowledged code of ethics, is that a country may be obliged *not* to engage in some dangerous rivalry when it would actually prefer not to but might otherwise feel obliged to for the sake of its bargaining reputation. The boy who wears glasses and can't see without them cannot fight if he wants to; but if he wants to avoid the fight it is not so obviously for lack of nerve. (Equally good, if he'd prefer not to fight but might feel obliged to, is to have an adversary who wears glasses. Both can hope that at least one of them is honorably precluded from joining the issue.) One of the values of laws, conventions, or traditions that restrain participation in games of nerve is that they provide a graceful way out. If one's motive for declining is manifestly not lack of nerve, there are no enduring costs in refusing to compete.

Since these tests of nerve involve both antagonism and cooperation, an important question is how these two elements should be emphasized. Should we describe the game as one in which the players are adversaries, with a modest admixture of common interest? Or should we describe the players as partners, with some temptation toward doublecross?

This question arises in real crises, not just games. Is a Berlin crisis—or a Cuban crisis, a Quemoy crisis, a Hungarian crisis, or a crisis in the Gulf of Tonkin—mainly bilateral competition in which each side should be motivated mainly toward winning over the other? Or is it a shared danger—a case of both being pushed to the brink of war—in which statesmanlike forbearance, collaborative withdrawal, and prudent negotiation should dominate?

It is a matter of emphasis, not alternatives, but in distributing emphasis between the antagonistic and the collaborative motives, a distinction should be made. The distinction is between a game of chicken to which one has been deliberately challenged by an adversary, with a view to proving his superior nerve, and a game of chicken that events, or the activities of bystanders, have compelled one into along with one's adversary. If one is repeatedly challenged, or expected to be, by an *opponent* who wishes to impose dominance or to cause one's allies to abandon him in disgust, the choice is between an appreciable loss and a fairly aggressive response. If one is repeatedly forced by *events* into a test of nerve along with an opponent, there is a strong case for developing techniques and understandings for minimizing the mutual risk.[5]

NOTES

1. To clarify the theoretical point it may be worth observing that the uncertainty and unpredictability need not arise from a genuine random mechanism like the dice. It is unpredictability, not "chance," that makes the difference; it could as well arise in the clumsiness of the players, some uncertainty about the rules of the game or the scoring system, bad visibility or moves made in secret, the need to commit certain moves invisibly in advance, meddling by a third party, or errors made by the referee. Dice are merely a convenient way to introduce unpredictability into an artificial example.

2. The purest real-life example I can think of in international affairs is "buzzing" an airplane, as in the Berlin air corridor or when a reconnaissance plane intrudes. The *only* danger is that of an *unintended* collision. The pilot who buzzes obviously wants no collision. (If he did, he could proceed to do it straightforwardly.) The danger is that he may not avoid accident, through mishandling his aircraft, or misjudging distance, or failure to anticipate the movements of his victim. He has to fly close enough, or recklessly enough, to create an appreciated risk that he may— probably won't, but nevertheless may—fail in his mission and actually collide, to everyone's chagrin including his own.

3. *The Iliad*, W. H. D. Rouse, transl. (Mentor Books, 1950), p. 273.

4. Analytically there appear to be at least three different motivational structures in a contest of "chicken." One is the pure "test case," in which nothing is at stake but reputations, expectations, and precedents. That is, accommodation or obstinacy, boldness or surrender, merely establishes who is an accommodator, who is obstinate or bold, who tends to surrender or what order of precedence is to be observed. A second, not easily distinguished in practice, occurs when something is consciously *put* at stake (as in a gambling game or trial by ordeal) such as leadership, deference, popularity, some agreed tangible prize, or the outcome of certain issues in dispute. (The duel between David and Goliath . . . is an example of putting something at stake.) The third, which might be called the "real" in contrast to the "conventional," is the case in which yielding or withdrawing yields something that the dispute is about, as in road-hogging or military probes; that is, the gains and losses are part of the immediate structure of the contest, not attached by convention nor resulting entirely from expectations established for future events. The process of putting something at stake—if what is at stake involves third parties—may not be within the control of the participants; nor, in the second and third cases, can future expectations be disassociated (unless, as in momentary road-hogging, the participants are

anonymous). So most actual instances are likely to be mixtures. (The same distinctions can be made for tests of *endurance* rather than risk: wealthy San Franciscans were reported to settle disputes by a "duel" that involved throwing gold coins into the bay, one after the other, until one was ready to quit; and the "potlatch" in both its primitive and its contemporary forms is a contest for status and reputation.) A fourth and a fifth case may also deserve recognition: the case of sheer play for excitement, which is probably not confined to teen-agers, and the case of "joint ordeal" in which the contest, though nominally between two (or among more than two) contestants, involves no adversary relation between them, and each undergoes a unilateral test or defends his honor independently of the other's.

5. "Brinkmanship" has few friends, "chicken" even fewer, and I can see why most people are uneasy about what, in an earlier book, I called "the threat that leaves something to chance." There is, though, at least one good word to be said for threats that intentionally involve some loss of control or some generation of "crisis." It is that this kind of threat may be more impersonal, more "external" to the participants; the threat becomes part of the environment rather than a test of will between two adversaries. The adversary may find it easier—less costly in prestige or self-respect—to back away from a risky situation, even if we created the situation, than from a threat that is backed exclusively by our resolve and determination. He can even, in backing away, blame us for irresponsibility, or take credit for saving us both from the consequences.

44

ALEXANDER L. GEORGE, DAVID K. HALL, AND WILLIAM E. SIMONS

THE LIMITS OF COERCIVE DIPLOMACY

Two variables that have not always been clearly identified in theory determine what is necessary to successfully coerce an opponent: first, what is demanded of the opponent and, second, how strongly disinclined the opponent is to comply. These two variables are not independent and must not be treated by the coercing power as if they were. Rather, the strength of the opponent's motiva-

SOURCE: From *The Limits of Coercive Diplomacy: Laos, Cuba, Vietnam,* Alexander L. George, David K. Hall and William E. Simons (Boston, MA: Little Brown and Co., 1971), pp. 22–30, 32–35, 215–216, 227–232, 250–253. Reprinted by permission of Alexander L. George. Footnotes partially omitted.

tion not to comply is highly dependent on what is demanded of him. In order
to determine how difficult the task of coercive diplomacy will be in any specific
situation the coercing power must take into account the strength of the opponent's disinclination to yield. But this cannot be calculated without reference
to what precisely the coercing power is demanding or plans to demand of its
opponent, and how the opponent perceives the demand.

Two types of demands can be made on the opponent. The opponent may
be asked to *stop* what he is doing; or he may be asked to *undo* what he has
been doing or to reverse what he has already accomplished.[1] This distinction
applies to many, though not all, types of behavior to which the defending power
may decide to respond by means of coercive diplomacy. The distinction is of
considerable importance for the theory and practice of coercive diplomacy in
view of the fact that the first type of demand asks appreciably less of the opponent than the second type. To ask the opponent to stop the encroachment in
which he is engaged constitutes a more modest objective for the strategy of
coercive diplomacy than to ask him to undo what he has already done.
Because it asks less of the opponent, the first type of demand is easier to comply with and easier to enforce. The opponent's disinclination to yield is maximized, on the other hand, by a demand that he undo whatever his action has
already accomplished—for example, to give up territory he has occupied.
Stronger threats and greater pressure may be needed, therefore, to enforce the
second type of demand.

This distinction has been found useful in our case studies. In Laos, as we
shall see, Kennedy demanded merely that the opposing forces halt their forward progress against vital Royal Lao territory. He was also interested, it is
true, in obtaining a reversal of some of the gains already made by the Pathet
Lao, but, and this is critical, he left this question to be taken up later via negotiations at the conference table. His coercive diplomacy in this case focussed
exclusively on the more modest and easier objective of getting the opponent
to halt his forward progress and agree to negotiations. In the Cuban missile
crisis, on the other hand, Kennedy made both types of demands on
Khrushchev. The blockade, an example of the first type of demand, was
designed to halt Soviet moves in progress, i.e. the shipment of additional missiles and bombers to Cuba. In addition, Kennedy also demanded that
Khrushchev undo the fait accompli he had already accomplished by removing
the missiles already in Cuba. The same distinction, while logically applicable
in the Vietnam case, was blurred somewhat because of the nature of the situation and the way in which Johnson chose to formulate his demands on Hanoi.

We can argue that the first type of demand is similar to deterrence, insofar
as it is a matter of persuading the opponent not to do something he has not
yet done. Thus, we might say, Kennedy's demand in the Laos case was perhaps as much an example of deterrence strategy as it was an example of coercive diplomacy. It seems preferable, however, to limit the concept of deterrence
strategy to its original and more familiar meaning, namely the effort to dissuade an opponent from doing something he has not yet started to do. What

FIGURE I

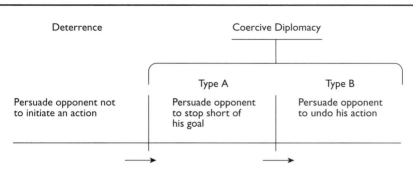

(Increasing difficulty from standpoint of the "defender," in terms of pressure on "aggressor" necessary to achieve the desired effect)

emerges, then, is a continuum in which deterrence may be attempted before the opponent has initiated an action, and coercive diplomacy employed afterwards either to persuade him merely to halt or to undo his action. This is depicted in Figure 1.

So far we have depicted only the defensive uses of coercive diplomacy in which it is employed to persuade an opponent to stop doing something he is already doing that is distasteful or harmful to the defender, or to undo what he has already accomplished. In contrast to this defensive use of the strategy, coercion may also be employed offensively to get the opponent to do something he has not done and does not want to do—to make him pay a price, give up territory—in order to avoid the threatened sanctions. An analogy here is the robber who persuades his victim to turn over his money peacefully. The term "diplomatic blackmail" is often applied to this offensive use of the strategy. This study considers only defensive uses of coercive diplomacy.

What we have been emphasizing, essentially, is that the task of coercion is determined or set by the magnitude of the opponent's motivation not to comply and that this, in turn, is a function of his perception of what is demanded of him. Thus, asking very little of an opponent makes it easier for him to permit himself to be coerced. Conversely, demanding a great deal of an opponent— and even asking him merely to stop may be asking a great deal—makes the task of coercing him all the more difficult. In this event, it may be difficult for the coercing power to threaten sanctions sufficiently potent and sufficiently credible to overcome the opponent's strong disinclination to comply with what is demanded of him.

This leads to another major proposition in the theory of coercive diplomacy. The feasibility of this strategy in any particular case may depend on whether one relies solely on negative sanctions or whether one combines threats with positive inducements in order to reduce the opponent's disinclination to comply with what is demanded of him. This point is of considerable practical as well as theoretical significance. Some theorists and practitioners subscribe to an oversimplified, crude notion of coercive strategy that relies exclusively on threats. Their version of coercive diplomacy makes no provision for use of the carrot as well as the stick. Or, to put it somewhat differently, their theory envisages that one offers an opponent only face-saving gestures on trivial or peripheral matters. This theory overlooks the possibility that coercive diplomacy in any given situation may be facilitated by, if indeed it does not require, genuine concessions to an opponent as part of a quid pro quo that secures one's essential demands. Coercive diplomacy, therefore, needs to be distinguished from pure coercion; it includes the possibility of bargains, negotiations. and compromises as well as coercive threats.

What the stick cannot achieve by itself, unless it is a very formidable one, can possibly be achieved by combining a carrot with the stick. Thus, a proper reading either of Kennedy's modest success in Laos or of his more spectacular success in coercing the Soviets to withdraw the missiles from Cuba would call attention not only to the threats Kennedy made but also to the willingness he conveyed to give the opponent a substantial quid pro quo. Thus, the inducement offered the opponent for this purpose must be viewed as credible by him. Finding a way of making the quid pro quo offered the opponent plausible and binding, of committing oneself to it in a way that removes the suspicion that it will not be honored after the crisis is over, is very important.[2]

Earlier we pointed out that in devising a coercive strategy the defending power must calculate the strength of the opponent's motivation to resist what is demanded of him. We emphasized that the opponent's motivation is a variable that is dependent upon his perception of the nature and magnitude of what is demanded of him. The coercing power's own motivation is also an important factor that must enter into the calculus of a coercive strategy. Moreover, the coercing power's motivation, too, is a variable that is affected by the nature and magnitude of the demand it chooses to make on the opponent.

The choice of the demand to be made on the opponent, therefore, affects the strength of motivation of both sides. This takes on special importance because the relative motivation of the two sides in a conflict can exert critical leverage on the outcome.[3] There is often an important strategic dimension, therefore, to the choice of the objective on behalf of which coercive diplomacy will be employed. The chances that coercive diplomacy will be successful will be appreciably greater if the objective selected—and the demand made—by the coercing power reflects only the most important of its interests that are at stake, for this is more likely to create an asymmetry of motivation favoring the coercing power. Thus, for example, if Kennedy had chosen as his objective in the Cuban missile crisis the removal of all Soviet military and political influence from Cuba, the Soviet motivation to resist would have been appreciably greater than it was. Instead, Kennedy limited his objective—and his demand on the Soviets—to the removal of offensive missiles. Such a limited, focussed objective not only concentrated and maximized motivation on the United States side; it also delimited what was at stake for the Soviets and helped to create an asymmetry of motivation favoring the United States. This facilitated the president's effort to exert unrelenting, eventually successful pressure on behalf of his demand on Khrushchev.

Let us turn now to the central task of a coercive strategy: how to create in the opponent the expectation of unacceptable costs of sufficient magnitude to erode his motivation to continue what he is doing. Success may depend upon whether the initial military action directed towards the opponent stands by itself or is part of a credible threat to escalate the conflict further, if necessary, and to do so within a short period of time. Even without this additional threat, a quite limited military action or even a mere alert or deployment of one's forces may suffice to alter the opponent's expectations and his policy. But against a determined opponent or one who feels he is on the verge of an important success, even a stronger coercive threat may not be effective.

This leads us to introduce an important distinction in the theory of coercive diplomacy between weaker and stronger variants of the strategy. Oversimplifying to make the point, we can distinguish between two basic variants of coercive strategy:

1. The try-and-see approach, the weak variant, and
2. The tacit-ultimatum, the strong variant.

These two variants represent the endpoints of a continuum; intermediate variants are also possible.

In the try-and-see approach, the defending power in an attempt to persuade its opponent to call off or curtail its encroachment takes only one step at a time. It deliberately postpones the decision to take additional action until it becomes clear whether the steps already taken will have a sufficient coercive impact on the opponent. When employing a try-and-see approach, the coercing power may make a more or less specific demand on the opponent to stop his encroachment or to pull back altogether; but it does not create a sense of urgency for his compliance with the demand. In contrast, in the tacit-ultimatum variant of the strategy, at the same time the defending power takes its initial actions it communicates to the opponent that other, more damaging steps will follow in short order if he does not comply with the demand made on him.

"Tacit-ultimatum"[4] is an appropriate designation for the strong variant of coercive diplomacy, for it utilizes all three elements of a classical ultimatum:

1. a *specific demand* on the opponent;
2. a *time limit* (explicit or implicit) for compliance;
3. a *threat of punishment* for noncompliance that is *sufficiently strong and credible.*

To the extent that one or more of these three elements of an ultimatum are not conveyed by the power that is attempting to coerce, the coercive impact of what it says and does on the opponent is weakened. Nonetheless, coercive diplomacy may succeed in the absence of a full-fledged ultimatum, and a weaker variant of the strategy, resembling the try-and-see approach, may suffice in some circumstances. Still another possibility, as we shall see, is that the coercing power may start with the try-and-see approach and resort at some point to an ultimatum.

Even a relatively small increment of force can have a disproportionately large coercive impact if it is part of the tacit-ultimatum rather than the try-and-see approach. The coercive effect of what little is actually done can be magnified substantially by linking it with a credible threat of additional action. This is the essence of any form of intimidation.

Intimidation, of course, does not always require a formal, explicit ultimatum. Coercive diplomacy may succeed without it in some situations. The defending power may not need to state a specific time limit or define the threat of punishment for noncompliance to reinforce its demand on the opponent. Either or both may be sufficiently implicit in the structure of a situation and, in particular, in the way that situation is developing. Thus, a sense of urgency may spring from the way events unfold to lead one or both sides to believe that the crisis is approaching a critical threshold. That the opponent is continuing his activity and thereby threatening to create a fait accompli may imbue the defending power with an increasing sense of urgency to act or to accept the consequences. In this kind of developing situation the defender may not need to articulate a full-fledged ultimatum. A demand that the opponent stop or undo what he is doing may generate sufficient pressure, especially if the defender also makes visible preparations to employ the sanctions at his disposal. As a result, the opponent may believe that the situation will now head towards a clearly identifiable climax unless he halts or slows down the activity to which the defending power is objecting. The time limit for compliance with the defender's demand may spring from the structure of the situation itself, from the actions and postures being taken by one or both sides that point them towards a possible collision within a short period of time unless one or both alter their behavior.[5]

Certain similarities exist between what has been described here and the game of chicken. Some writers have drawn upon the model of this game to illuminate a class of real-life crisis situations.[6] But the model ignores both the importance and intricacy of crisis management in many international crises. It also overlooks the flexibility inherent in the strategy of coercive diplomacy that makes it possible to adapt to a variety of situations. The game of chicken, in brief, encompasses only the crudest form and extreme methods of intimidation; it shrinks the role of diplomacy in this strategy to the vanishing point and ignores the possibility (and, oftentimes, the necessity) of combining a carrot with the stick. The analogy of the game of chicken, therefore, is imperfect as either a description or an explanation of the behavior of the two sides in the historical crises we examine here. Moreover the analogy with the game of chicken would be positively dangerous if used as a basis for offering advice on how a defending power may employ coercive diplomacy to halt the opponent's encroachment. This is not to deny that elements of an externally imposed time limit, or sense of urgency, were present in both the Laos crisis of 1961 and the Cuban missile case. In both crises, the structure of the developing situation that was set into motion by the actions of the opponent generated a sense of urgency for the defender which he then managed to transmit back to the advancing opponent. In neither case, however, did Kennedy rely exclusively on the structure of the situation itself to transmit a sense of urgency and the threat of credible punishment for noncompliance. Particularly in the Cuban crisis, Kennedy eventually felt himself obliged to reinforce the message implicit in the structure of the situation by delivering a verbal ultimatum which contained a time limit and a threat of punishment for noncompliance.

As the preceding discussion has indicated, coercive diplomacy may operate on two levels of communication; in addition to what is said, significant non-verbal communication may emerge from the structure of the developing situation. Therefore, analysis of coercive diplomacy cannot be restricted to the verbal communications that the defending power transmits to the opponent. Coercive persuasion depends not merely on whether the defending power includes all three components of a classical ultimatum in its verbal messages to the opponent. The structure of the situation, as it develops and is expected to develop, must also be taken into account. The defending power can shape the opponent's expectations in this respect by means other than, or in addition to, a verbal ultimatum. The actions it takes—for example, deploying and alerting its military forces, making political and diplomatic preparations of the kind needed to back its demand and enforce it, if necessary—can reinforce and make credible the verbal communications employed to coerce the opponent.

Actions, then, may reinforce strong words and make them more credible. But, as we have suggested, actions may also compensate for weak words; that is, something less than a classical explicit ultimatum may be strengthened by the actions the defender is taking. Still another aspect of the relationship between words and actions should be described. Contrary to the conventional wisdom on these matters, actions do not always speak louder than words. Actions may be perceived by the opponent as equivocal, as not excluding the possibility that the coercing power is bluffing and is not prepared to act if its demand is not accepted. Words, then, may be needed in some situations to clarify the meaning of the actions taken and to reinforce the credibility of the threat implied by the preparatory actions. If, then, actions may be needed in some situations to reinforce strong words, in other situations strong words, explicit ultimata, may be needed to reinforce and to define the meaning and credibility of the threatening actions the defender is taking as part of his attempt to make coercive diplomacy work.

We conclude, therefore, that while the relationship between words and actions—the two levels of communication—is likely to be very important in the strategy of coercive diplomacy, there is no single way of stating what that relationship must be to ensure the success of this strategy. Accordingly, such situations are replete with opportunities for miscommunication and miscalculation. This, then, is another aspect of coercive diplomacy that makes it an elusive, problematical strategy to employ effectively as an instrument of foreign policy. . . .

PRE-CONDITIONS FOR COERCIVE DIPLOMACY

Overlooking the profound differences between the Cuban and Vietnam cases, some critics have tried to argue that a stronger variant of coercive strategy should have been applied in the latter case. The hawks in the controversy over Vietnam policy, by no means confined to members of the military services, have been critical of the way in which Johnson initially used airpower against North Vietnam. They argue that he dissipated its potential coercive impact by engaging in too slow and too weak a form of graduated air escalation in February–April 1965.[7]

The question is: Could Johnson have employed airpower as part of the stronger variant of coercive diplomacy? The hawks assume this was a viable option and that the administration is to be blamed for not resorting to it. This assumption is quite dubious. The strong form of coercive diplomacy cannot be considered to have been a real alternative because the pre-conditions for its adoption and success were lacking in this case. This emerges more clearly if we compare the situation surrounding Johnson's effort to coerce Hanoi with the contexts of the earlier Laos and Cuban cases.

Before proceeding with the comparison, it will be useful to state the major conclusion we will draw: *Only seldom—only when a special set of conditions is present, as in the Laos and Cuban cases—is it feasible for United States leaders to undertake and to succeed with the strong variant of coercive strategy,* what has been called the ultimatum approach.

What, then, are these special conditions? They emerge from comparative analysis of these three cases and of two other historical cases that we have not examined in as much detail. We have identified eight conditions which seem to have causal importance. To the extent that these conditions are present in a crisis—and *all eight were present in the Cuban and Laos crises*—they favor adoption and successful implementation of the strong tacit-ultimatum form of coercive diplomacy. On the other hand, to the extent that the eight conditions are absent—and perhaps as many as six of them were missing in 1965 when Johnson attempted to coerce Hanoi, or were present in relatively weak form—then it is difficult and imprudent for American leaders to adopt the strong form of coercive diplomacy. If, nonetheless, they try to employ this strategy, as Johnson did in Vietnam, they risk having their bluff called or having to settle for the weak try-and-see form of the strategy, which may not suffice for the purpose and which may then degenerate into an attrition strategy. . . .

The judgments made in the preceding pages as to whether the eight conditions were present or absent in the three cases are summarized in Table 1.

TABLE 1 **Presence of Conditions Favoring Successful Outcome of Coercive Diplomacy in Three Crises**

	Laos 1961	Cuba 1962	Vietnam 1965
1. Strength of United States motivation	+	+	+
2. Asymmetry of motivation favoring United States	+	+	
3. Clarity of American objectives	+	+	
4. Sense of urgency to achieve American objective	+	+	
5. Adequate domestic political support	+	+	
6. Usable military options	+	+	+
7. Opponent's fear of unacceptable escalation	+	+	
8. Clarity concerning the precise terms of settlement	+	+	

Not all of these conditions would appear to be equally important for coercive diplomacy. Three seem particularly significant in affecting the outcome: asymmetry of motivation favoring the United States; a sense of urgency behind the demand made on the opponent; and the opponent's fear that unacceptable escalation may take place. The perceptions of these three variables, particularly by the opponent, appear to be critical in shaping the success or failure of coercive diplomacy. The possibility of misperception by either or both sides is present and can affect the outcome in either direction. Thus, American leaders may misperceive the asymmetry of motivation as operating in their favor. While an erroneous perception that this condition is satisfied would favor adoption of coercive diplomacy, the fact that the opponent's motivation was really stronger relative to that of American leaders would increase the likelihood that coercive diplomacy would fail.

Misperception of a condition could operate in the opposite direction. Thus, the opponent might attribute to American leaders a stronger sense of urgency to achieve their objective in the crisis than was, in fact, the case. Such a misperception of this variable could affect the opponent's behavior in such a way as to contribute to the success of the United States effort at coercing him.

Thus, while American leaders' perceptions of the presence of these three conditions are most directly relevant in accounting for the adoption of the strategy, the opponent's perceptions of them become more important in determining the success or failure of the effort at coercive diplomacy. The numerous possibilities for misperception in coercive diplomacy enormously complicate the task for both the policy-maker and the investigator.

Thus far in our analysis we have identified and discussed eight conditions whose presence in a situation favors the adoption and success of the strategy of coercive diplomacy. But by no means does the presence of these conditions guarantee success. Other requirements, having to do with additional variables, must also be met. We turn to these in the next section.

PROBLEMS OF OPERATIONALIZING
COERCIVE DIPLOMACY

We emphasized . . . the limited utility for policy-making of even a well-formulated theory of coercive diplomacy. Any theory is necessarily stated in somewhat abstract, generalized terms. A theoretical, textbook model of coercive diplomacy is useful up to a point. It identifies critical variables and factors and depicts the general relationships among them. But it does not and cannot say very much about the feasibility of applying the textbook model in particular cases. The limitations of a theoretical model are particularly severe in the case of coercive diplomacy. For, more so than any other strategy for using force as an instrument of diplomacy, the strategy of coercive diplomacy is highly context-dependent. The meaning and full implications of this fact require discussion.

No theory, of course, can provide blueprints either to ensure good judgment in deciding whether coercive diplomacy is a viable strategy in any particular situation or to ensure skillful implementation of the strategy in the variety of complex situations where it seems applicable. Being highly context-dependent, coercive diplomacy must be tailored in a rather exacting manner to fit the unique configuration of each individual situation. Tailoring force to diplomacy is a difficult enough skill to begin with; it is also a skill that is not easily acquired. Even if that skill is available within the presidential circle and even if it survives the clash that typically occurs among competing viewpoints and judgments within the policy-making group, the skill of tailoring the strategy of coercive diplomacy to a given situation cannot be exercised successfully unless the special configuration of that situation is clearly understood.

But it is precisely the special configuration of the crisis situation—the values of the various critical variables identified in the theory—that is seldom clearly visible to the policy-maker. As a result, the policy-maker must tailor somewhat in the dark, guessing at some of the dimensions that must be fitted by the strategy being developed, hoping for but not certain of having opportunities for correcting one's initial errors and first approximations by successive fittings and alterations—all the while with an uncooperative subject who quite rightly regards what is being tailored for him as a straitjacket rather than an attractive suit of clothes.

For these reasons, again more so than with other strategies, the effort to devise and employ coercive diplomacy rests heavily upon the skill at improvisation. . . . We must add, however, that skill can contribute to the successful application of the strategy only if the conditions that favor it are present in that situation. Skillful tactics can only capitalize on favorable conditions already latent in the situation; skill cannot compensate for the absence of these favorable conditions. This is certainly one of the major lessons and warnings to be drawn from this study. . . .

To regard skill as the most critical factor on which the success of coercive diplomacy depends would be superficial and misleading. Too sharp a focus on skill in policy implementation encourages a narrow, technocratic approach to strategy, one that emphasizes the importance of techniques of manipulation as if to imply that one can hope to overcome more fundamental contextual dis-advantages in a conflict situation by sheer virtuosity of technique in signalling and bargaining. Accordingly, the basic criticism of the Johnson administra-tion's handling of coercive diplomacy against Hanoi concerns not its inept implementation of the strategy but rather its failure to recognize that the situ-ation was intrinsically wrong for it.

For this reason we have thought it particularly important to identify more sharply the specific kinds of problems encountered when one attempts to oper-ationalize the strategy of coercive diplomacy, that is, tailor it to the special, always somewhat unique configuration of a particular crisis. We have identified six problems or tasks of this kind that may be expected to arise in every case in which this strategy is employed:

1. Risks of an ultimatum	Will ultimatum be provocative?
2. Conflict between crisis management and coercive diplomacy	Will adherence to requirements of crisis management dilute sense of urgency needed for coercion?
3. Timing of strong coercive threats	Has opponent been sufficiently impressed with your determination to regard coercive threat as credible?
4. Timing of negotiations	Can negotiations be delayed until opponent is sufficiently impressed with your determination?
5. Content of carrot and stick	Are the carrot and stick adequate to overcome opponent's disinclination to accept demand?
6. Timing of carrot and stick	Can the carrot and stick be applied before military actions harden opponent's determination? . . .

THE LIMITS OF POWER AND WILL

Coercive diplomacy is understandably attractive when compared to the alter-native strategies. . . . [It] offers the leaders of a country an opportunity to achieve their objectives in a crisis with much greater economy than strategies that rely more directly and exclusively on use of force. If the coercive strategy can be made to work successfully, it is a less costly, less risky way of achieving one's objectives than traditional military strategy.

But the attractiveness of coercive diplomacy must not be allowed to pre-judge the question of its feasibility in any particular situation. The beguiling character of the strategy may easily distort the judgment of policy-makers who are confronted by a difficult crisis that poses damage to national interests they would like to avoid. The problems of operationalizing the strategy of coercive diplomacy, as we have discussed, are many. Skill is certainly necessary to deal with these problems adequately, but even an unusually skillful policy-maker can accomplish little when the basic pre-conditions favoring this strategy are lacking. Adding to the risks is the fact that it is often not self-evident whether these basic conditions are present in a crisis situation; the policy-maker can easily err in assuming that the fundamental configuration of the situation is more favorable to coercive diplomacy than is in fact the case. Further, the informational requirements of the strategy are complex and also difficult to meet. A particularly good knowledge of the opponent is necessary in order to estimate properly his motivation and his cost-benefit calculations on the basis of the fragmentary and equivocal information typically available on these matters.

For all these reasons, there will be few crises in which coercive diplomacy—and particularly the strong variant of it that attempts to meet all three components of a classical ultimatum—will constitute a feasible and useful strategy. The reasons for this conclusion, we have emphasized, are many and complex. One can disagree as to the relative importance of the various constraints on the strategy that we have mentioned; and one can also quarrel with the role we have assigned to some of these factors in trying to account for the success or failure of this strategy in the crises we have examined. It is too soon to write definitive histories of every aspect of these crises; indeed that may never be possible. At the same time, it is urgent to learn the lessons that recent history holds for policy-making. We have attempted, therefore, to draw such lessons from plausible interpretations of the historical cases. Whatever the scope of scholarly disagreement in this respect, it surely excludes the simple-minded proposition that to coerce an opponent successfully is, as some imply, merely a matter of the president exercising our national resolution or guts to threaten, and use if need be, the ample military capabilities at our disposal.

NOTES

1. Both types of demands, it may be noted, satisfy Thomas Schelling's definition of "compellence" and indeed are discussed by him without being explicitly differentiated. (*Arms and Influence*, pp. 72, 77.) I am indebted to David Hall for pointing out the value of distinguishing between them and for the major points made in the discussion here.
2. I am indebted to David Hall for calling attention to the fact that the requirements of credibility and potency apply to the carrot as well as the stick.
3. The importance of relative motivation has been emphasized recently by several writers, for example by Stephen Maxwell "Rationality in Deterrence," Adelphi Paper No. 50, Institute of Strategic Studies, London; and Jervis's *The Logic of Images*.
4. Although many have attempted to define the Latin word "ultimatum," past definitions have been noted for either their narrowness or their overly general assertions about the nature of ultimata. Definitional shortcomings, however, have not

prevented ultimata from being incorporated into the strategy of coercive diplomacy and into the rules of war and international law. The Hague Convention III (1907), for example, intending to prevent "surprise" and "equivocation" in the beginning of war, provided in Article I that the Contracting Powers "recognize that hostilities between them are not to commence without a previous unequivocal warning, which shall take the form either of a declaration of war, giving reasons, or of an ultimatum with a conditional declaration of war." Yet, now under the United Nations Charter such threats of war are legal only in self-defense or in collective defense of the Charter, which, under other circumstances, prohibits not only acts of force but also threats of force. See H. Lauterpacht, ed., *Oppenheim's International Law, A Treatise* (7th ed.) (London: Longmans, Green and Co.), Vol. II, *Disputes, War, and Neutrality* (London: Longmans, Green and Co., 1952), pp. 133 and 295–297; Sir Ernest Satow, *A Guide to Diplomatic Practice* (4th ed.) (London: Longmans, Green and Co., 1957), pp. 105–107; James Brown Scott (ed.), *Proceedings of the Hague Peace Conference of 1907*, Vol. III (New York: Oxford University Press, 1921), p. 43; Norman Hill, "Was There an Ultimatum Before Pearl Harbor?" in *The American Journal of International Law*, Vol. XLII (1948), pp. 355–367; *Dictionnaire Diplomatique, Académie Diplomatique Internationale,* Vol. II (Paris: Associates, Académie Diplomatique Internationale, 1933), pp. 999–1000; and Hans Asbeck, *Das Ultimatum im modernen Volkerrecht* (Berlin: Walter Rothchild, 1933). In preparing this footnote I have drawn on the valuable paper on the nature and uses of ultimata since the middle of the nineteenth century written for my seminar by Paul Gordon Lauren, a graduate student in the History Department, Stanford University.

5. Discussions with Robert Jervis and Robert Weinland have helped me to clarify the importance of the structure of the situation in which coercive diplomacy takes place.

6. See, for example, Herman Kahn, *On Escalation* (New York: Praeger, 1965); Anatol Rapoport, *Fights, Games, and Debates* (Ann Arbor: University of Michigan Press, 1960); and Karl W. Deutsch, *The Analysis of International Relations* (Englewood Cliffs, N.J.: Prentice-Hall, 1968).

7. These arguments were drawn together and forcefully stated in "Gradualism—Fuel of Wars," prepared by the Task Force on National Security, for the Republican National Committee, March 1968.

45

CARL VON CLAUSEWITZ

WAR AS AN INSTRUMENT OF POLICY

INFLUENCE OF THE POLITICAL OBJECT ON THE MILITARY OBJECT

We never find that a State joining in the cause of another State takes it up with the same earnestness as its own. An auxiliary Army of moderate strength is sent; if it is not successful, then the Ally looks upon the affair as in a manner ended, and tries to get out of it on the cheapest terms possible.

In European politics it has been usual for States to pledge themselves to mutual assistance by an alliance offensive and defensive, not so far that the one takes part in the interests and quarrels of the other, but only so far as to promise one another beforehand the assistance of a fixed, generally very moderate, contingent of troops, without regard to the object of the War or the scale on which it is about to be carried on by the principals. In a treaty of alliance of this kind the Ally does not look upon himself as engaged with the enemy in a War properly speaking, which should necessarily begin with a declaration of War and end with a treaty of peace. Still, this idea also is nowhere fixed with any distinctness, and usage varies one way and another.

The thing would have a kind of consistency, and it would be less embarrassing to the theory of War if this promised contingent of ten, twenty, or thirty thousand men was handed over entirely to the State engaged in War, so that it could be used as required; it might then be regarded as a subsidised force. But the usual practice is widely different. Generally the auxiliary force has its own Commander, who depends only on his own Government, and to whom it prescribes an object such as best suits the shilly-shally measures it has in view.

But even if two States go to War with a third, they do not always both look in like measure upon this common enemy as one that they must destroy or be destroyed by themselves. The business is often settled like a commercial transaction; each, according to the amount of the risk he incurs or the advantage to be expected, takes shares in the concern to the extent of 30,000 or 40,000 men, and acts as if he could not lose more than the amount of his investment.

SOURCE: From *On War*, Carl Von Clausewitz. Colonel J. J. Graham, trans. (London: Kegan Paul, Trench, Trubner and Company Limited, 1911), pp. 118–130.

Not only is this the point of view taken when a State comes to the assistance of another in a cause in which it has, in a manner, little concern, but even when both have a common and very considerable interest at stake nothing can be done except under diplomatic reservation, and the contracting parties usually only agree to furnish a small stipulated contingent, in order to employ the rest of the forces according to the special ends to which policy may happen to lead them.

This way of regarding Wars entered into by reason of alliances was quite general, and was only obliged to give place to the natural way in quite modern times, when the extremity of danger drove men's minds into the natural direction (as in the Wars *against* Bonaparte), and when the most boundless power compelled them to it (as *under* Bonaparte). It was an abnormal thing, an anomaly, for War and Peace are ideas which in their foundation can have no gradations; nevertheless it was no mere diplomatic offspring which the reason could look down upon, but deeply rooted in the natural limitedness and weakness of human nature.

Lastly, even in Wars carried on without Allies, the political cause of a War has a great influence on the method in which it is conducted.

If we only require from the enemy a small sacrifice, then we content ourselves with aiming at a small equivalent by the War, and we expect to attain that by moderate efforts. The enemy reasons in very much the same way. Now, if one or the other finds that he has erred in his reckoning—that in place of being slightly superior to the enemy, as he supposed, he is, if any thing, rather weaker, still, at that moment, money and all other means, as well as sufficient moral impulse for greater exertions, are very often deficient: in such a case he just does what is called "the best he can"; hopes better things in the future, although he has not the slightest foundation for such hope, and the War in the meantime drags itself feebly along, like a body worn out with sickness.

Thus it comes to pass that the reciprocal action, the rivalry, the violence and impetuosity of War lose themselves in the stagnation of weak motives, and that both parties move with a certain kind of security in very circumscribed spheres.

If this influence of the political object is once permitted, as it then must be, there is no longer any limit, and we must be pleased to come down to such warfare as consists in a *mere threatening of the enemy* and in *negotiating*.

That the theory of War, if it is to be and to continue a philosophical study, finds itself here in a difficulty is clear. All that is essentially inherent in the conception of War seems to fly from it, and it is in danger of being left without any point of support. But the natural outlet soon shows itself. According as a modifying principle gains influence over the act of War, or rather, the weaker the motives to action become, the more the action will glide into a passive resistance, the less eventful it will become, and the less it will require guiding principles. All military art then changes itself into mere prudence, the principal object of which will be to prevent the trembling balance from suddenly turning to our disadvantage, and the half War from changing into a complete one.

WAR AS AN INSTRUMENT OF POLICY

Having made the requisite examination on both sides of that state of antagonism in which the nature of War stands with relation to other interests of men
individually and of the bond of society, in order not to neglect any of the
opposing elements—an antagonism which is founded in our own nature, and
which, therefore, no philosophy can unravel—we shall now look for that
unity into which, in practical life, these antagonistic elements combine themselves by partly neutralising each other. We should have brought forward this
unity at the very commencement if it had not been necessary to bring out this
contradiction very plainly, and also to look at the different elements separately. Now, this unity is *the conception that War is only a part of political
intercourse, therefore by no means an independent thing in itself.*

We know, certainly, that War is only called forth through the political
intercourse of Governments and Nations; but in general it is supposed that
such intercourse is broken off by War, and that a totally different state of
things ensues, subject to no laws but its own.

We maintain, on the contrary, that War is nothing but a continuation of
political intercourse, with a mixture of other means. We say mixed with other
means in order thereby to maintain at the same time that this political intercourse does not cease by the War itself, is not changed into something quite
different, but that, in its essence, it continues to exist, whatever may be the
form of the means which it uses, and that the chief lines on which the events
of the War progress, and to which they are attached, are only the general features of policy which run all through the War until peace takes place. And
how can we conceive it to be otherwise? Does the formation of diplomatic
notes stop the political relations between different Nations and Governments?
Is not War merely another kind of writing and language for political thoughts?
It has certainly a grammar of its own, but its logic is not peculiar to itself.

Accordingly, War can never be separated from political intercourse, and
if, in the consideration of the matter, this is done in any way, all the threads of
the different relations are, to a certain extent, broken, and we have before us
a senseless thing without an object.

This kind of idea would be indispensable even if War was perfect War, the
perfectly unbridled element of hostility, for all the circumstances on which it
rests, and which determine its leading features, viz., our own power, the
enemy's power, Allies on both sides, the characteristics of the people and their
Governments respectively, &c., . . . —are they not of a political nature, and
are they not so intimately connected with the whole political intercourse that
it is impossible to separate them? But this view is doubly indispensable if we
reflect that real War is no such consistent effort tending to an extreme, as it
should be according to the abstract idea, but a half-and-half thing, a contradiction in itself; that, as such, it cannot follow its own laws, but must be
looked upon as a part of another whole—and this whole is policy.

Policy in making use of War avoids all those rigorous conclusions which
proceed from its nature; it troubles itself little about final possibilities, confining

its attention to immediate probabilities. If such uncertainty in the whole action ensues therefrom, if it thereby becomes a sort of game, the policy of each Cabinet places its confidence in the belief that in this game it will surpass its neighbor in skill and sharpsightedness.

Thus policy makes out of the all-overpowering element of War a mere instrument, changes the tremendous battlesword, which should be lifted with both hands and the whole power of the body to strike once for all, into a light handy weapon, which is even sometimes nothing more than a rapier to exchange thrusts and feints and parries.

Thus the contradictions in which man, naturally timid, becomes involved by War may be solved, if we choose to accept this as a solution.

If War belongs to policy, it will naturally take its character from thence. If policy is grand and powerful, so also will be the War, and this may be carried to the point at which War attains to *its absolute form*.

In this way of viewing the subject, therefore, we need not shut out of sight the absolute form of War, we rather keep it continually in view in the background.

Only through this kind of view War recovers unity; only by it can we see all Wars as things of *one* kind; and it is only through it that the judgment can obtain the true and perfect basis and point of view from which great plans may be traced out and determined upon.

It is true the political element does not sink deep into the details of War. Vedettes are not planted, patrols do not make their rounds from political considerations; but small as is its influence in this respect, it is great in the formation of a plan for a whole War, or a campaign, and often even for a battle.

For this reason we were in no hurry to establish this view at the commencement. While engaged with particulars, it would have given us little help, and, on the other hand, would have distracted our attention to a certain extent; in the plan of a War or campaign it is indispensable.

There is, upon the whole, nothing more important in life than to find out the right point of view from which things should be looked at and judged of, and then to keep to that point; for we can only apprehend the mass of events in their unity from *one* standpoint; and it is only the keeping to one point of view that guards us from inconsistency.

If, therefore, in drawing up a plan of a War, it is not allowable to have a two-fold or three-fold point of view, from which things may be looked at, now with the eye of a soldier, then with that of an administrator, and then again with that of a politician, &c., then the next question is, whether *policy* is necessarily paramount and everything else subordinate to it.

That policy unites in itself, and reconciles all the interests of internal administrations, even those of humanity, and whatever else are rational subjects of consideration is presupposed, for it is nothing in itself, except a mere representative and exponent of all these interests towards other States. That policy may take a false direction, and may promote unfairly the ambitious ends, the private interests, the vanity of rulers, does not concern us here; for, under no circumstances can the Art of War be regarded as its preceptor, and we can only look at policy here as the representative of the interests generally of the whole community.

The only question, therefore, is whether in framing plans for a War the political point of view should give way to the purely military (if such a point is conceivable), that is to say, should disappear altogether, or subordinate itself to it, or whether the political is to remain the ruling point of view and the military to be considered subordinate to it.

That the political point of view should end completely when War begins is only conceivable in contests which are Wars of life and death, from pure hatred: as Wars are in reality, they are, as we before said, only the expressions or manifestations of policy itself. The subordination of the political point of view to the military would be contrary to common sense, for policy has declared the War; it is the intelligent faculty, War only the instrument, and not the reverse. The subordination of the military point of view to the political is, therefore, the only thing which is possible.

If we reflect on the nature of real War, and call to mind . . . *that every War should be viewed above all things according to the probability of its character, and its leading features as they are to be deduced from the political forces and proportions,* and that often—indeed we may safely affirm, in our days, *almost* always—War is to be regarded as an organic whole, from which the single branches are not to be separated, in which therefore every individual activity flows into the whole, and also has its origin in the idea of this whole, then it becomes certain and palpable to us that the superior standpoint for the conduct of the War, from which its leading lines must proceed, can be no other than that of policy.

From this point of view the plans come, as it were, out of a cast; the apprehension of them and the judgment upon them become easier and more natural, our convictions respecting them gain in force, motives are more satisfying, and history more intelligible.

At all events from this point of view there is no longer in the nature of things a necessary conflict between the political and military interests, and where it appears it is therefore to be regarded as imperfect knowledge only.

That policy makes demands on the War which it cannot respond to, would be contrary to the supposition that it knows the instrument which it is going to use, therefore, contrary to a natural and indispensable supposition. But if policy judges correctly of the march of military events, it is entirely its affair to determine what are the events and what the direction of events most favourable to the ultimate and great end of the War.

In one word, the Art of War in its highest point of view is policy, but, no doubt, a policy which fights battles instead of writing notes.

According to this view, to leave a great military enterprise, or the plan for one, to *a purely military judgment and decision* is a distinction which cannot be allowed, and is even prejudicial; indeed, it is an irrational proceeding to consult professional soldiers on the plan of a War, that they may give a *purely military opinion* upon what the Cabinet ought to do; but still more absurd is the demand of Theorists that a statement of the available means of War should be laid before the General, that he may draw out a purely military plan for the War or for a campaign in accordance with those means. Experience in general also teaches us that notwithstanding the multifarious branches and scientific character of military art in the present day, still the leading outlines of a War are always determined by the Cabinet, that is, if we would use technical language, by a political not a military organ.

This is perfectly natural. None of the principal plans which are required for a War can be made without an insight into the political relations; and, in reality, when people speak, as they often do, of the prejudicial influence of policy on the conduct of a War, they say in reality something very different to what they intend. It is not this influence but the policy itself which should be found fault with. If policy is right, that is, if it succeeds in hitting the object, then it can only act with advantage on the War. If this influence of policy causes a divergence from the object, the cause is only to be looked for in a mistaken policy.

It is only when policy promises itself a wrong effect from certain military means and measures, an effect opposed to their nature, that it can exercise a prejudicial effect on War by the course it prescribes. Just as a person in a language with which he is not conversant sometimes says what he does not intend, so policy, when intending right, may often order things which do not tally with its own views.

This happened times without end, and it shows that a certain knowledge of the nature of War is essential to the management of political intercourse.

But before going further, we must guard ourselves against a false interpretation of which this is very susceptible. We are far from holding the opinion that a War Minister smothered in official papers, a scientific engineer, or even a soldier who has been well tried in the field, would, any of them, necessarily make the best Minister of State where the Sovereign does not act for himself; or, in other words, we do not mean to say that this acquaintance with the nature of War is the principal qualification for a War Minister; elevation, superiority of mind, strength of character, these are the principal qualifications which he must possess; a knowledge of War may be supplied in one way or the other. France was never worse advised in its military and political affairs than by the two brothers Belleisle and the Duke of Choiseul, although all three were good soldiers.

If War is to harmonise entirely with the political views and policy, to accommodate itself to the means available for War, there is only one alternative to be recommended when the statesman and soldier are not combined in one person, which is, to make the Commander-in-Chief a member of the Cabinet, that he may take part in its councils and decisions on important occasions. But then, again, this is only possible when the Cabinet, that is, the Government itself, is near the theatre of War, so that things can be settled without a serious waste of time.

This is what the Emperor of Austria did in 1809, and the allied Sovereigns in 1813, 1814, 1815, and the arrangement proved completely satisfactory.

The influence of any military man except the General-in-Chief in the Cabinet is extremely dangerous; it very seldom leads to able vigorous action. The example of France in 1793, 1794, 1795, when Carnot, while residing in Paris, managed the conduct of the War, is to be avoided, as a system of terror is not at the command of any but a revolutionary government.

We shall now conclude with some reflections derived from history.

In the last decade of the past century, when that remarkable change in the Art of War in Europe took place by which the best Armies found that a part of their method of War had become utterly unserviceable, and events were brought about of a magnitude far beyond what any one had any previous conception of, it certainly appeared that a false calculation of everything was to be laid to the charge of the Art of War. It was plain that while confined by habit within a narrow circle of conceptions, she had been surprised by the force of a new state of relations, lying, no doubt, outside that circle, but still not outside the nature of things.

Those observers who took the most comprehensive view ascribed the circumstance to the general influence which policy had exercised for centuries on the Art of War, and undoubtedly to its very great disadvantage, and by which it had sunk into a half-measure, often into mere sham-fighting. They were right as to fact, but they were wrong in attributing it to something accidental, or which might have been avoided.

Others thought that everything was to be explained by the momentary influence of the particular policy of Austria, Prussia, England, &c., with regard to their own interests respectively.

But is it true that the real surprise by which men's minds were seized was confined to the conduct of War, and did not rather relate to policy itself? That is: Did the ill success proceed from the influence of policy on the War, or from a wrong policy itself?

The prodigious effects of the French Revolution abroad were evidently brought about much less through new methods and views introduced by the French in the conduct of War than through the changes which it wrought in state-craft and civil administration, in the character of Governments, in the condition of the people, &c. That other Governments took a mistaken view of all these things; that they endeavored, with their ordinary means, to hold their own against forces of a novel kind and overwhelming in strength—all that was a blunder in policy.

Would it have been possible to perceive and mend this error by a scheme for the War from a purely military point of view? Impossible. For if there had been a philosophical strategist, who merely from the nature of the hostile elements had foreseen all the consequences, and prophesied remote possibilities, still it would have been practically impossible to have turned such wisdom to account.

If policy had risen to a just appreciation of the forces which had sprung up in France, and of the new relations in the political state of Europe, it might have foreseen the consequences which must follow in respect to the great features of War, and it was only in this way that it could arrive at a correct view of the extent of the means required as well as of the best use to make of those means. We may therefore say, that the twenty years' victories after the Revolution are chiefly to be ascribed to the erroneous policy of the Governments by which it was opposed.

It is true these errors first displayed themselves in the War, and the events of the War completely disappointed the expectations which policy entertained.

But this did not take place because policy neglected to consult its military advisers. That Art of War in which the politician of the day could believe, namely, that derived from the reality of War at that time, that which belonged to the policy of the day, that familiar instrument which policy had hitherto used—*that* Art of War, I say, was naturally involved in the error of policy, and therefore could not teach it anything better. It is true that War itself underwent important alterations both in its nature and forms, which brought it nearer to its absolute form; but these changes were not brought about because the French Government had, to a certain extent, delivered itself from the leading-strings of policy; they arose from an altered policy, produced by the French Revolution, not only in France, but over the rest of Europe as well. This policy had called forth other means and other powers, by which it became possible to conduct War with a degree of energy which could not have been thought of otherwise.

Therefore, the actual changes in the Art of War are a consequence of alterations in policy; and, so far from being an argument for the possible separation of the two, they are, on the contrary, very strong evidence of the intimacy of their connection.

Therefore, once more: War is an instrument of policy: it must necessarily bear its character, it must measure with its scale: the conduct of War, in its great features, is therefore policy itself, which takes up the sword in place of the pen, but does not on that account cease to think according to its own laws.

46

DEAN G. PRUITT AND
RICHARD C. SNYDER

MOTIVES AND PERCEPTIONS UNDERLYING ENTRY INTO WAR

INTRODUCTION

Most theories of the forces (factors) that impel states toward war can be reduced to formulations about the motives that lead men to involve their states in war, or to place them on the road toward war, and the perceptions underlying such motives. This introduction will be organized around three motivational and

SOURCE: From *Theory and Research on the Causes of War*, Dean G. Pruitt and Richard C. Snyder. (Englewood Cliffs, NJ: Prentice-Hall, Inc., 1969), pp. 15–34. © 1969. Reprinted by permission of Prentice Hall, Englewood Cliffs, New Jersey.

perceptual concepts that have received particular attention: (a) goals that can be advanced through war, (b) the perception of threat, and (c) hostility toward other states.

All three of these concepts are admittedly psychological in nature, and a question naturally arises concerning whose psychology is at stake, i.e., whose goals, perceptions, and hostility lead states into war? Answers to this question differ markedly, depending on the "unit of analysis" favored by a writer. Some writers avoid the question altogether, taking as their unit of analysis the state as a whole with its "national goals and capabilities." Others prefer a more analytical approach and refer, often rather vaguely, to the motives of "decision makers" or the "public." A third group of authors implicate specific interest groups, such as investors or munitions makers. Despite these differences in unit of analysis, all three kinds of authors share a concern with motivational and perceptual concepts and, hence, can be classed together for purposes of exposition.

Most of the literature in this area is speculative, so that little empirical evidence can be presented in this introduction.

GOALS THAT CAN BE ADVANCED THROUGH WAR

AN INVENTORY OF GOALS

Most authors who have written about the motives underlying the resort to war have been content to describe or list goals that appear to have played a part in the origin of historical wars. No wholly reliable method as yet exists for identifying such goals. One cannot fully trust the public statements of policy makers because they usually try to dress their actions in the most acceptable garments. Instead, one must mainly rely on inferential analysis and base one's conclusions on the "feeling that the argument somehow makes sense" (Rapoport, 1964, p. 13). Nevertheless, some writers probably have come close enough to the truth at times to make it worth reviewing their conclusions.

A distinction can be drawn between two kinds of goals that motivate conflict: *success-oriented* and *conflict-oriented* goals. Conflict that is produced by a desire for the fruits of victory, e.g., booty or dominion over the vanquished, can be said to have success-oriented goals. Conflict-oriented goals are satisfied by engaging in conflict, per se, whether victory is achieved or not, e.g., the desire for adventure or glory. Conflict that has its origins in success-oriented goals has sometimes been called "real" conflict in contrast to "induced" conflict, which has its origins in conflict-oriented goals (Mack and Snyder, 1957).

Success-Oriented Goals

War has been traced to a variety of *economic* goals, e.g., the desire for treasure, raw materials, means of production, trade routes, markets, outlets for investment, and places to settle population. *Political* goals have also been cited, e.g., the wish to regain territories formerly controlled, to achieve independence, to free oppressed groups in other countries, and to install or restore friendly governments in neighboring countries. Other authors have stressed *ideological* goals, e.g., spreading or destroying a religion, political philosophy, or economic system. *Punishment* motives are sometimes implicated, e.g., revenging an injury or insult, teaching another state a "lesson." Sometimes, violence appears to be initiated for the purpose of achieving greater *military security,* as in the Soviet war against Finland in 1939. Occasionally, a state fights a war in order to maintain or increase the *credibility* of its guarantees or threats in other areas. This appears to be one motive underlying American participation in the Vietnam War.

Many writers (e.g., Morgenthau, 1960; Organski, 1958; and Levi, 1960) have stressed the importance of the search for *power* in their explanations of war and lesser forms of international conflict. Various definitions have been given of power, but in this context it seems to mean the capacity to destroy, injure, deprive, thwart, or otherwise control another state, in short, the capacity to resolve future conflict in one's own favor. Thus present-day conflict is explained as a search for the capacity to win future conflict. "Elements" of power that can be achieved through international conflict include such things as economic resources, alliances, control of military strategic regions, and destruction of enemy resources.

To explain war as an effort to achieve the means to win future conflict is simply to push the search for causes one step backward. One must then account for the concern about future conflict. On this issue, a controversy has developed. Some authors (e.g., Van Dyke, 1957, and Levi, 1960) have argued that the search for power is motivated by the desire to achieve other kinds of goals in the future, such as economic and ideological goals. Others (Dunn, 1937, and Morgenthau, 1960) maintain that the search for power becomes an autonomous motive, i.e. that the capacity to win future conflict becomes a goal in itself, not subordinated to other goals. Both positions probably fit the facts under certain circumstances, but the nature of these circumstances is not well understood.

Conflict-Oriented Goals

Success-oriented goals can only be satisfied by the fruits of victory, while conflict-oriented goals are satisfied by the struggle, per se. Hence, to identify the conflict-oriented goals that can underlie war, one must look for the byproducts of war that may have positive value to society as a whole or to powerful groups within society. For example, war, at least in its early stages, generally intensifies *national dynamism.* Morale improves, people work harder for the common good, internal conflicts and rivalries diminish. The anticipation of such results may provide a rationale for supporting the entry of one's state into war. Fighting a war may also be a way of maintaining or regaining the *national honor,* a sense that one's nation is respectable. In addition, certain groups within a state always benefit from war. *Jobs* are available for workers in defense industries and *profits* for their owners. The *position* and *influence* of military and related governmental elites are likely to be strengthened in time of war. The anticipation of such outcomes may produce demands from certain groups for greater use of violence in relations with other states (Engelbrecht and Hanighen, 1934). Such demands may lead to war or may contribute to a movement toward war that is also impelled by success-oriented goals.

THEORIES OF IMPERIALISM

A list, such as the one just given, of the goals that contribute to the use of violence in international affairs is only the first step toward a motivational theory of war. A sound theory must also embody propositions about two issues: (a) the ways in which such goals develop and (b) the conditions under which war is elected as a method for achieving such goals. Little theory exists on the second issue other than the commonsense recognition that few goals in and of themselves produce war but that war grows out of a realization on the part of decision makers that violence is the most workable approach to a goal and that other alternatives are less attractive. A variety of theories have developed concerning the first issue, the roots of goals that can lead to war. Among the best known are those that attempt to account for *imperialism.*

Imperialism can be defined as a policy of unlimited geographical expansion. Most theories of imperialism have focused on the historical period in the late nineteenth century when the more powerful states of Europe annexed, by a series of military actions, most areas of the underdeveloped world. Only one of the major theorists, Schumpeter, has drawn his evidence from a broader historical spectrum.

The three most famous theories of imperialism will be summarized in this section. Fuller details on these and other theories can be found in Strachey (1960) and Winslow (1948).

Hobson's Theory

Hobson (1938, first published in 1902) based his theory on an analysis of British imperialism. He argued that in his day the British Empire imposed a heavy drain on England's economic, social, and moral resources. Since the nation as a whole did not benefit from the existence of the Empire, he assumed that special interest groups must have foisted the Empire on the body politic. The most likely suspects were those who derived benefit from the Empire, among them investors, financiers, certain manufacturers, exporters, shippers, members of the armed services and the Indian Civil Service, and educated groups whose sons might be able to find administrative jobs in the territories composing the Empire. Among these groups, he assigned a leading role to business interests seeking outlets for capital and goods.

Following up the last point, he suggested conditions under which the goal of unlimited expansion develops. He reasoned that imperialism develops during a period of economic imbalance, in which there is an *oversupply of both capital and goods* at home. Such an imbalance forces businessmen to seek outlets abroad; and, since foreign investments and markets generally need protection, these businessmen prevail on their government to seize and administer the territories in which they are conducting their operations.

As a solution to the problem of imperialism, Hobson recommended a reform of capitalism to prevent the development of an oversupply of capital and goods. His solution boiled down to placing the surplus capital in the hands of people at home who would use it to purchase the surplus goods, i.e., in the hands of workers and the government. Thus he recommended strengthening unions and imposing higher taxes on certain kinds of income.

Lenin's Theory

Lenin (1950, first published in 1917) leaned heavily on Hobson and on several earlier Marxist writers but added his own systematization. Like Hobson, he traced imperialism to an oversupply of capital. But he went beyond Hobson in asserting that imperialism would ultimately lead to major war between the great capitalist powers. He reasoned that the competition for colonies between these states would increase as the supply of underdeveloped regions of the world diminished. A major war might develop out of this competition, although it was possible instead that the states who were most powerful in any given period might come to an agreement about who possessed what. However, such an agreement could not last forever, since other capitalist nations who were outside of the agreement would eventually develop sufficient strength to challenge it. Major war would surely develop out of such a challenge. Lenin explained the First World War in terms of his theory, identifying the challenger as Germany.

Unlike Hobson, Lenin believed that imperialism was an inevitable outcome of capitalism in its mature stages and saw no cure for imperialism and world war other than the triumph of socialism. He argued that capitalism could not be reformed because the capitalists were so fully in control of their governments that they would be able to block all efforts at reform.

Schumpeter's Theory

Schumpeter (1955, first published in 1919; reviewed by Knorr, 1952) based his theory on a careful analysis and comparison of several past societies, including precapitalist societies, in which policies of imperialism developed. Like Hobson, he traced the support of this policy to a coalition of powerful political groups, including economic interests. But he argued that the major pressure for imperialism came from military and governmental circles whose authority and position in society depended on continued warfare. Thus he traced war to conflict-oriented rather than success-oriented goals.

For Schumpeter, the critical conditions that foster imperialism are those which create a large military machine and corresponding political organization, whose members then seek to maintain their position. Such institutions may have their origin in success-oriented conflicts, such as a war for independence.

Once established, they tend to become self-perpetuating by constantly engaging their state in new war.

Schumpeter's solution to the problem of imperialism was markedly different from Lenin's. Schumpeter claimed that imperialism was an atavism (holdover) from precapitalist society and would eventually disappear as capitalism matured. He claimed that the spirit of capitalism is individualistic, democratic, and rational and that these traits would eventually make imperialism unwelcome in capitalist societies.

Critique of the Theories of Imperialism

The theories of imperialism just described have the defects of all single-factor approaches. They overstate the case for a particular explanation by ignoring other important factors. Hence, they are easily "refuted" by citing negative instances. For example, Lenin's claim to have explained the origin of the First World War has been seriously questioned by writers like Aron (1954) who show that the ferocity of competition for colonies among the major European states *declined* in the period just preceding the outbreak of this war. Schumpeter's picture of a military elite, spawned in one war and instrumental in producing the next, does not provide a close fit to German expansionism in the Second World War, which was guided by a political elite that came to power in peacetime.

On the other hand, if we are willing to look beyond the obvious defects in these theories, it may be possible to derive some useful ideas from them. For example, the causal mechanisms which they describe may be important in the case of certain kinds of wars. Thus, Schumpeter's picture of a governing elite whose position in society depends on preparation for and engagement in war is not inconsistent with what is known about roots of the Japanese war in Southeast Asia which culminated in an attack on the United States. Further theoretical advances are needed to specify the conditions under which such mechanisms operate.

OTHER THEORIES ABOUT THE SOURCES OR GOALS UNDERLYING WAR

Among the major rivals to the theories of imperialism described above are theories that trace violence-inducing goals to the *form of government* possessed by a state. Waltz (1959, pp. 120–121) presents the following summary statement about this diverse and contradictory literature:

> A world full of democracies would be a world forever at peace, but autocratic governments are warlike. . . . Monarchies are peaceful; democracies are irresponsible and impulsive, and consequently foment war. . . . Each of these formulations has claimed numerous adherents, and each adherent has in turn been called to task by critics and by history.

The development of goals that lead to war has also been traced to *uncertainty about tenure of power* among ruling elites. For example,

Rosecrance (1963, p. 255) argues for the period between 1890 and 1918, "In Austro-Hungary, Germany and Russia where the position of the ruling elite was in jeopardy, aggressive military and political personalities came to the fore." Such goals are, presumably, in part conflict-oriented; i.e., elite groups assume that the preparation for and the conduct of war will cause the citizenry to rally around its government. In part, they may also be success-oriented; i.e., elite groups assume that they will gain internal prestige if they succeed in making conquests abroad. While the desire to resolve political instability may sometimes motivate elites to enter a war, the national dislocation resulting from political instability may also at times cause elites to feel that their state is too weak to succeed in war and hence cause them to shy away from involvement in it. In other words, there is no simple relationship between political instability and the likelihood of military involvement. Rosecrance (1963) argues that a positive relationship between instability and belligerence will only be found in those states that have a "measure of social cohesion" (p. 305) and will be stronger in those cases where elites foresee a short, successful (and, hence, politically nondisruptive) military campaign.

Rosecrance also stresses the importance of ideological differences between states in the genesis of war. He argues, "the most violent forms of international conflict have usually been associated with divergences in elite ethos" (p. 280), citing in particular the period in European history between 1789 and 1814. Such divergences arouse both missionary zeal and the fear of internal ideological subversion, both of which can lead to the goal of overturning the political leadership of other states and thereby altering the religious, political, or economic systems in these states.

The development of national goals whose pursuit leads to war has also sometimes been traced to the perception of new opportunities for influence and conquest abroad. The concept of *power vacuum* is important in this regard. A power vacuum describes a geographical region that is militarily or politically weak and, hence, invites military or subversive incursion from abroad. Greece in 1946, South Korea in 1951, and the Congo in 1962 are possible examples. Power vacuums encourage ambition for control on the part of other states, either because control looks easy to establish or because it is feared that still other states will seek control. Power vacuums have often become the tinder boxes of war as states have vied for control over them.

Growth in perceived military and economic capability can also create among national leaders a sense of new opportunities for influence and conquest and, thereby, produce ambitions that set their state on a collision course with other states. Organski (1958) has cited this mechanism as a major determinant of both world wars, with German and Japanese industrialization heightening the ambitions of the leaders of these states and causing them to adopt expansionist policies. Past military success can also, of course, enhance perceived capability and raise ambitions.

If the perception of new opportunity can heighten national ambition, it seems reasonable to suppose that reduction in perceived opportunity will cause ambition to wane. Military deterrents are sometimes justified on this basis. For example, in his famous article advocating a policy of containing Russian expansionism, Kennan (1947) argued that the eventual outcome of the containment policy would be a reduction in Soviet aspirations for greater power in Europe. More recently, the United States has been making an effort to hold the line against communist takeovers in South Vietnam and Laos at least partially in an effort to reduce the motivation for war and revolution among communists in Asia and other parts of the underdeveloped world. . . .

While subscribing to the notion that increased military capacity can cause a state to become more ambitious for influence over other states, Burton (1962) has questioned the companion assumption embraced by Kennan that blocking such ambitions will cause aggressive motivation to decline. He argues that resistance to a limited challenge from a state whose capabilities are growing will produce frustration and anger in that state and cause it to develop less-limited power needs that may make it more aggressive and dangerous in the long run. Thus, international instability results from an international system that provides no mechanisms for peaceful change to accommodate the desires of states whose military and economic capability is increasing.

To the present authors, it seems reasonable to suppose that Burton's theory is right under some circumstances and Kennan's containment theory is right under others. The most effective response to a challenge from a newly powerful state depends on the circumstances. Under some circumstances, peace is best preserved by giving in to the demands of an adversary to prevent the development of more dangerous goals in the future. Under other circumstances, one should oppose these demands so that the motives underlying them will disappear. But what are the appropriate circumstances for each kind of policy? There is clearly a theoretical gap at this point.

THE PERCEPTION OF THREAT

The theories discussed in the last section attempt to account for the existence of certain success-oriented and conflict-oriented goals. For success-oriented goals to cause involvement in war, it is also necessary that they be seen by decision makers as *incompatible with* the goals of another state. Otherwise, there is no basis for conflict. There are two kinds of perceived incompatibility. The other state may be seen as an *obstacle* to the attainment of new goals; i.e., if we are intent on conquering one state, its ally may be seen as an obstacle to the attainment of our goal. Or the other state may be seen as a *threat* to continued achievement of an old, already realized goal; e.g., its military activity may be seen as a threat to our national security.

The first kind of incompatibility is prominent in theories that trace war to a scarcity of resources. Thus, as mentioned earlier, Lenin (1950) argued that war between the major European states became more likely as the supply of uncaptured potential colonies diminished. Rosecrance (1963, p. 234) argues, "The existence of large expanses still available [in the 18th century] for major actor appropriation helped to make extra-European expansion a safety value for European conflict."

The latter kind of incompatibility has received particular attention in recent years in discussions of the role of the *perception of threat* in the etiology of war. A synopsis of some of these discussions will now be presented.

THEORIES OF PRE-EMPTIVE AND PREVENTIVE ATTACK

When the perception of threat leads directly to violence, we speak of *pre-emptive* or *preventive attack*. The purpose of such an attack is to deal the first blow before the other side has a chance to attack. The distinction between pre-emptive and preventive attack is relatively minor: a pre-emptive attack is based on the notion that the other side is about to begin a war, while a preventive attack is based on the assumption that war will begin at some time in the more distant future.

There is evidence that important wars of the past were initiated on a pre-emptive or preventive basis. For example, the German attack on Belgium and France in 1914, which came as a response to Russian mobilization, seems to have been based on the assumption that England, France, and Russia were about to initiate hostilities. Some writers have argued in recent years that a third world war, if it comes, is likely to have its beginning in a pre-emptive or preventive strike.

A number of recent books and articles (e.g., Kahn, 1960; Singer, 1962; Snyder, 1961; Schelling, 1960; and Schelling and Halperin, 1961) have discussed the mechanisms underlying pre-emptive and preventive attack. The basic pre-condition for such an attack is the belief that the other party is going to start a war sometime in the future, i.e., that war is inevitable. Such a belief can lead to military action because it nullifies the most important restraints against the use of violence, fear of the cost of war and fear that a war will not be won. When war is seen as inevitable, questions of feasibility and cost do not militate against the use of violence.

If, in addition, it appears that the cost or likelihood of winning a war can be materially improved by early launching of a surprise attack, such an attack becomes even more likely. The extent to which early, surprise attack is seen as advantageous depends in part on the vulnerability of one's own or the other party's military forces. The more vulnerable the other's forces, the more can be gained by surprise action. The more vulnerable one's own forces, the more can be lost by waiting for the other to attack. The perceived advantage of early military action also depends on the direction in which the distribution of military capability seems to be moving. The more rapidly the other party is gaining militarily, the greater is the apparent danger of delay and, therefore, the more attractive is preventive attack.

PREPARATION FOR WAR AS AN ANTECEDENT TO WAR

Perception of threats of a lesser magnitude than those just described often leads to defensive preparations, e.g., mobilizing troops, converting industries to the production of war materials, seeking allies, etc. Such preparations are usually heralded as efforts to avoid war by deterring the adversary and often have this effect. But, under some circumstances, military preparations in themselves can increase the probability of war.

There are various ways in which this can come about. The need to justify the expenditure on arms may through "psychologie" cause an increase in the perceived magnitude of threat to the point where a pre-emptive or preventive war is launched (Noel-Baker, 1958). Or preparation for war may elevate the social status of a military elite, which may then, according to Schumpeter's analysis, strive to preserve its status by stirring up foreign conflicts.

In addition, preparation for war usually changes goal priorities. Weakening the adversary becomes an important objective. Attempts must be made to block his procurement of goods, discredit him with potential allies, etc. Such action generally elicits resistance from the adversary, and the resulting conflict may eventually touch off a war that neither side really wants. The goal of weakening the adversary also usually stands in the way of developing functional and emotional ties with him that might otherwise act as restraints on violence.

Finally, defensive preparations may be seen by citizens of the *other* state as evidence of threat, and so lead to all of the reactions just described on their side. If each side reacts to the other's military preparations with a new perception of threat and further military preparations, a vicious circle is born.

DETERMINANTS OF THE PERCEPTION OF THREAT

The discussion in this section will be based on an analysis of the determinants of threat perception in international affairs published by . . . [D. G.] Pruitt (1965). This analysis rests on established psychological principles regarding perception, but supporting evidence from the realm of international affairs is admittedly scanty at present. The analysis postulates two sorts of antecedents for threat perception: evidence of threat and predispositions to perceive threat.

Evidence of Threat

For another state to be perceived as a threat, it must be seen as having both the *capability* and the *intent* to interfere with goal attainment (Singer, 1958). Such perceptions are usually based, at least to some extent, on objective evidence.

Evidence of capability consists of such things as the possession of a large army. Such evidence is a two-edged sword. Not only does it contribute directly to threat perception, but it also is sometimes regarded as evidence of intent and thus contributes indirectly. The argument linking capability to intent usually goes as follows; "Why would they have all those arms if they didn't intend to attack us?" It seems to be very difficult for people to conclude that an adversary is arming out of fear of *their* armed forces.

Evidence of intent is also found in the circumstances surrounding the other state. During periods of controversy, the other state is usually assumed to have greater incentives for engaging in violence. The same is true during periods in which one's own or the other's military forces are highly vulnerable. For the reasons given above, such circumstances may be seen as raising the probability of pre-emptive or preventive war from the other side and hence as evidence of threat from the other side. Schelling (1960) has also suggested that knowledge that the other side expects an attack from us may be interpreted as evidence that the other side is likely to launch a pre-emptive or preventive attack.

Actions and statements from other states are also, of course, taken as evidence of intent. A number of writers (e.g., Phelps, 1963; Schelling and Halperin, 1961; and Singer, 1962) have been concerned about the danger of *accidental war* based on mistaken intelligence about another state's actions or misinterpretation of such actions. Incidents that might falsely lead to the conclusion that the other side is about to launch (or is in the process of launching) an attack include such things as misinterpretation of objects on a radar screen, unauthorized or unintended launching of rockets from the other side, and actions of third parties aimed at throwing the blame on the other side (*catalytic war*).

Predispositions to Perceive Threat

Threat perception is often grounded in unambiguous and unassailable evidence; e.g., an army is approaching the border. But there are also many cases in which the evidence is not so clear-cut and in which the perception of threat is an inference, with all of the usual fallibility of inferences. Whether ambiguous evidence will lead to threat perception is determined by the *predispositions* of the perceiver. Predispositions to perceive threat take many forms. Some are general, embracing all sources and all types of threat; others are specific to one kind of threat, e.g., military attack; still others are specific to one source of threat, e.g., a certain foreign country.

Gladstone (1955) has shown through empirical research that some people have a general tendency to perceive threat, which leads them to be overly suspicious of other people and other states. Gladstone and Taylor (1958) suggest that such people may be making greater than average use of the defense mechanism of projection to protect themselves from recognizing their own hostile impulses. It is conceivable that some cultures may make greater use of projection than others and hence be more predisposed to the perception of threat.

The predisposition to perceive a certain kind of threat is probably enhanced by past experience with this kind of threat; e.g., people who have lived through bombing tend to overreact to minimal evidence that more bombs are coming. In addition, preparation for certain kinds of threat may, through a process of psychological justification, produce a predisposition to perceive such threats (Lerner, 1965; de Rivera, 1968). Hence, one might speculate that people or societies which engage in a great deal of military contingency planning or build elaborate military defenses tend to be especially alert to evidence of military threat. People who have a vested interest in institutions for coping with threats, e.g., Schumpeter's military elites, may be especially likely to find evidence of the existence of such threats.

The concept *distrust* is used when a predisposition is specific to a certain source of threat, e.g., a certain foreign country. Distrust of another state is usually based on unfavorable past experience with that state. The more acute and recent this experience, the greater the distrust is likely to be. This means that conflict with another state is a common source of distrust and, hence, of renewed conflict. By heightening distrust, conflict can engender conflict.

The notion that conflict can engender conflict is implicit in a concern that has frequently been voiced (e.g., Phelps, 1963, and Russett, 1962) that a political or conventional military crisis involving the great powers will heighten distrust to the point at which one side interprets minimal evidence as indicating that the other is about to launch a nuclear attack. A pre-emptive or preventive attack might result from such a situation.

Favorable experiences with another state often create trust, but this is not always the case. Conciliatory behavior by a distrusted adversary is sometimes, instead, treated as a sign of weakness. Holsti (1962) has demonstrated the operation of such logic in the results of a content analysis of six years of speeches by John Foster Dulles, former United States Secretary of State.

Trust is most likely to develop out of circumstances that cause states to become positively oriented toward each other's welfare (M. Deutsch, 1962), i.e., out of mutual dependence that motivates states to seek one another's good will. Such interdependence may be based upon a trade agreement, a joint development plan, or a common enemy.

Ambiguity of Evidence

Two propositions can be stated about the relationships between predispositions and threat perception (Pruitt, 1965): (a) The stronger the predisposition to perceive threat, the more likely it is that threat will be perceived, and (b) the more *ambiguous* the evidence concerning another state's capabilities or intentions, the more impact will predispositions have on the perception of threat from that state. What determines the ambiguity of such evidence?

Some *kinds of evidence* are inherently more ambiguous than others. For example, as evidence of intent, military capability is often quite ambiguous, since a state may be arming for a variety of reasons.

A number of *conditions* increase the ambiguity of actions and statements and thereby increase the likelihood that threat will be falsely perceived. Ambiguity is greater, (a) the smaller the number of highly placed people who are well acquainted with the state being observed, (b) the poorer the capacity to empathize with citizens of the state being observed, and (c) the fewer and less adequate channels of communication that exist with members of the other state (Frank, 1968). Installation of the "hot line" between Washington and Moscow in 1962 is an example of an attempt to increase the number of channels of communication through which a seemingly threatening event (e.g., the accidental launching of a rocket) can be explained and hopefully made less ambiguous and, therefore, less liable to be misinterpreted under the pressure of cold-war mistrust.

HOSTILITY TOWARD OTHER STATES

TRADITIONAL THEORIES OF WAR AS THE RESULTANT OF HOSTILITY

In the 1930's and early 1940's, a group of behavioral scientists under the spell of psychoanalytic theory (Durbin and Bowlby, 1939; Tolman, 1942; Kluckhohn, 1944; May, 1943) began writing about the causes of war. Their analysis was based on an analogy to interpersonal violence, which is often an expression of hostile emotions even when it can be rationalized as goal-seeking behavior. On the basis of this analogy, they reasoned that international violence must have expressive roots, i.e., must arise from hostility toward other states.[1] They condemned as naive those theorists who traced war to rational (goal-oriented) considerations.[2]

These writers were never particularly explicit about whose emotions are responsible for war or how emotions become transformed into the decision to employ violence. But one gets the impression that they viewed hostility as a mass phenomenon permeating most levels of society and forcing national policy makers to launch an attack, willing or not.

The traditional psychoanalytic theory of scapegoating was employed by these theorists to explain the development of hostility toward other states. According to this theory, hostility develops whenever a person is frustrated, i.e., prevented from attaining his goals (Dollard et al., 1939). Ordinarily, hostility is expressed toward the agent of frustration. But, if this agent is protected by social norms, hostility will be *displaced* (redirected) onto other, safer objects, the scapegoats. Thus, a man who is denied a pay raise by his employer may come home and yell at his wife. This theory of scapegoating has received considerable support in laboratory and field research on interpersonal relations (Berkowitz, 1962).

The extension of this theory to international relations is quite straightforward. Instead of being displaced onto another person, hostility may sometimes be displaced onto another state. Thus, hostility originating in frustrations experienced by the individual becomes translated into antagonism toward another state, which can contribute to a decision to employ violence against that state.

In some versions of this theory (e.g., Durbin and Bowlby, 1939), war seems nearly inescapable since it is attributed to the normal and presumably inescapable frustrations of everyday life. Other versions offer greater hope by tracing war to especially frustrating periods in the life of society as a whole, when "social and economic relations of life have been disrupted so that people feel bewildered, confused, uncertain, and insecure" (Duvall, 1947). Such frustrations can presumably be avoided if man can learn how to control the business cycle or solve other problems that produce mass frustration.

Criticism of "Hostility" Theories

A certain amount of evidence can be found to support the assumption that mass hostility produces war. In a number of historical cases, popular hostility toward another state has risen abruptly just prior to an attack on that state, a phenomenon that has sometimes been called *war fever*. However, a number of writers (e.g., Abel, 1941, and Bernard, 1958) have suggested that this evidence is misleading. On the basis of an empirical study of twenty-five past wars, the details of which are unfortunately not reported, Abel concluded that the decision to go to war is typically made by governmental elites well in advance of the outbreak of war and war fever. Abel argues that war fever results from propaganda produced by governmental elites to prepare their people for war and is not causally antecedent to war. The elites, not the masses, carry their states into war.

Even if we reject the role of *mass* hostility, it is still possible to assert with the psychologists that hostility *among elite decision makers* predisposes them to involve their nation in war. However, this position has also been attacked by authors who view war as rational behavior. On the basis of his twenty-five cases, Abel concludes that the decision to fight is always based on a careful weighing of probabilities and anticipation of consequences. "In no case," he writes (p. 855), "is the decision precipitated by emotional tensions, sentimentality . . . or other irrational motivations." Levi (1960) adds to this criticism the observation (for what it is worth) that Anthony Eden's memoirs reveal that the British campaign against Egypt in the Suez crisis was "undertaken on the basis of a fairly unemotional conclusion that British interests in the Suez Canal made it worthwhile" (p. 418).

A MODERN VERSION OF THE EXPRESSIVE THEORY OF WAR

One must be sympathetic with the critics just cited when they attack the traditional assumption that hostility is the *only* cause of war. One-factor theories are inherently mistaken. Furthermore, these critics are undoubtedly on sound ground in asserting that war seldom erupts out of mass anger the way a fistfight erupts from a fit of temper and that mass anger is *often* a response to governmental manipulations. But to deny altogether the role of mass and elite hostility in the genesis of war seems to throw out the baby with the bath. What is needed instead is a more subtle version of the relationship between hostility and war and the source of hostility toward other states. Such a version has been developing in the literature of recent years. Empirical evidence for it . very insufficient, but it is in line with modern psychological theory.

Hostility and War

Hostility presumably works more subtly in the case of international conflict than in the case, say, of a fistfight between two gangs of boys. Rather than erupting in an angry display, hostility toward another state gently prods a decision maker toward a choice of harsher tactics and sharper words than he would otherwise use in dealing with that state. Hostility may close off certain alternatives that involve contributing to the other state's welfare. Hostility may reduce the capacity to empathize with the other state and the amount of communication with that state (Newcomb, 1947), both of which increase the ambiguity of the evidence concerning the other state and, therefore, the likelihood of perceiving it as a threat. Hostility may also prevent the development of an alliance with another state that would otherwise deter a third party from aggressive military action. These mechanisms can contribute to the likelihood of an eventual outbreak of violence as well as to the likelihood that a war will develop at any given time.[3]

The question of mass versus elite participation in national policy making is no longer posed as an "either-or." Both masses and elites are assumed to play a role, and the relevant question concerns the determinants of their relative weight. K. W. Deutsch (1957) has suggested that their relative weight may differ from era to era. At times, public opinions may be quite pliable, permitting national leaders to encourage mass hostility toward another state "in order to marshal public support for [an] effective but costly foreign policy" (p. 201). However, once the enemy has been identified in the public thinking, public opinion sometimes becomes so inflexibly hostile that the government is forced to adopt harsher tactics toward the other state than are warranted by the situation.[4] The psychology of enemy identification has also been discussed by Gladstone (1959).

The role of hostility in elite decision making is easier to accept if it is realized that emotion and rational deliberation can operate side by side. A man who is influenced by emotion need not be livid and raging; he may seem cool and collected. Most of his behavior may be guided by rational deliberation while, at the same time, as was described above, hostility may be gently nudging him toward the adoption of harsher, less compromising tactics than he would otherwise adopt. He may rationalize such tactics by invoking quite reasonable goals such as "defending the national honor" or "punishing aggression." Such a subtle input of emotion, if continued over a period of time, can have an important impact on the course of events, especially if, as is likely to happen, it is magnified by the other side's reactions and the first side's counterreactions to those reactions.

Furthermore, despite what the critics have written, historical examples can be found in which it is reasonable to believe that emotion played a role in the decision to go to war. For example, in examining the private notes made by the German Kaiser in 1914 at the point of his decision to go to war, North and his collaborators (North et al., 1963, p. 174) found the following highly emotional statement:

> The net has been suddenly thrown over our head and England sneeringly reaps the brilliant success of her persistently prosecuted purely anti-German world policy, against which we have proved ourselves helpless, while she twists the noose of our political and economic destruction out of our fidelity to Austria, as we squirm isolated in the net.

Sources of Hostility toward Another State

The traditional displacement theory of the sources of international hostility is probably still worthy of some attention, but it needs updating. This theory has always been weak on the issue of why certain states are chosen as targets for displacing hostility and others are not. For example, if we accept the argument that German aggression in the 1930's arose in part from frustrations experienced by the average German as a result of the depression, we must still explain why this aggression was channeled toward England and France rather than Italy and Spain.

Recent laboratory research has provided some general information on the choice of target in interpersonal relations that is probably applicable to the special case of attitudes toward states. Berkowitz (1962) has shown that people tend to choose as the object on which to displace new hostility an individual or group toward which some hostility is already felt. Hence traditions of antagonism or a history of past conflict with another state probably increase the likelihood that it will become the target of displacement.

In addition, Duvall (1947) has suggested that the choice of a scapegoat can be directed by statements from national leaders, just as Hitler was able to channel German hostilities onto the Jews.

Although, as was just said, the displacement mechanism may be worthy of some attention, it can certainly not be considered the most important source of hostility toward another state. Considerably more important is perceived provocation from the other state, i.e., frustration *at the hands of that state* and the perception of that state as a threat.

An important question arises from this formulation: What determines the amount of hostility generated by a given level of perceived provocation? We can certainly assume that hostility is a positive function of the level of frustration or threat perceived. But what determines the steepness of this function? In some cases, the reaction to a given level of provocation is mild; in other cases, acute.

Some speculation exists on this issue, and also some empirical evidence, arising out of studies of personality correlates of individual differences in the way people feel their states should react to provocation from abroad. Such evidence is relevant to the issue of why states go to war to the extent that (a) people with certain personality structures tend to inhabit powerful positions in society or (b) states differ in the dominant personality makeup of their citizenry.

A number of writers, including Lerche (1956), have stressed the importance of *nationalism* as a determinant of the reaction to perceived provocation from other states. Nationalism can be defined as the love of one's state or "a focussing of attention, drive and positive emotion on the symbols of the nation" (Stagner, 1946, p. 404). The stronger this sentiment, the more hostility will be generated by experiences of frustration or threat from another state. Empirical evidence for this assertion has been found by Christiansen (1959) in a study of the relationship between personality and attitude toward foreign affairs in Norway. It follows that citizens of the newer states, where nationalism is often stronger, should react more violently to provocation from abroad.

Prior sentiment toward the other state may also determine the amount of hostility resulting from a given level of perceived provocation. Coleman (1957) has suggested that old hostility remaining from earlier incidents tends to interact with new hostility and cause an overreaction to what may sometimes seem a trivial provocation. Conversely, it is probable that frustration or threat from a state toward whom there are strong positive feelings will produce less hostility than would otherwise be expected. The hypotheses just stated are not directly supported by empirical evidence but are consonant with modern psychological theory.

To come back to the displacement theory of hostility toward other states, it seems reasonable to suppose that the reaction to perceived provocation is a function of the general level of frustration experienced by an individual. Provocative behavior identifies the other state as an appropriate target for displacement of hostility. The greater an individual's general level of frustration, the greater will be his potential for displacement once a target is found. Evidence supporting this supposition has also been developed by Christiansen (1959 and 1965). Christiansen found a correlation in Norwegian subjects between the extent to which an individual favors harsh reactions to provocation from other states and the extent to which he is in conflict about basic psychosexual impulses, an index of underlying frustration. It is interesting to note that the strength of this correlation was a function of nationalism. Hence, the more nationalistic an individual, the more likely he is to displace his anger onto other states when they have created a provocation.

These findings suggest that, in times of national crisis when many citizens are experiencing acute frustration, a state is likely to overreact to provocation from abroad and that this overreaction is particularly likely to occur if the citizens of the state are strongly nationalistic. However, as yet, no direct evidence has been developed concerning this proposition.

CONCLUSIONS

A number of motivational and perceptual factors (various goals, the perception of threat, and hostility) have been cited in this [article], each of which conceivably plays a part in moving states toward war. Various propositions have also been stated about the antecedents of these motivational factors—the conditions under which they develop. Some of these propositions come from a study of war itself, others from parallels with well-documented research on human behavior in other situations.

Although provocative and hopefully important, the contents of this [article] fall considerably short of the ideal theory. . . . Three deficiences can be cited in the field of knowledge reflected [herein]. First, the basic presentation of motivational factors lacks coherence. A list of factors that can contribute to the evolution of war is not a theory until something is said about how these factors interrelate and about the conditions that govern the relative importance of each factor as a cause of war. Second, our understanding of the antecedents of these motivational factors is clearly rudimentary; much theoretical elaboration is obviously needed here. Third, and most important because it is a key to the other two deficiencies, it is clear that very little *empirical research* has been done on the motives underlying war. Most of the research cited in this [article] is based on speculation rather than empirical methodology. Yet empirical investigations are by no means out of the question in this area. Many of the propositions stated above could serve as the initial basis for an empirical study.

As an example, take Burton's (1962) proposition that blocking limited challenges from a state with newly developed military capabilities typically causes it to embrace less-limited power goals, which causes it to become more aggressive in the long run than it would otherwise be. If this proposition were explored with historical data, the investigator might construct a population of historical states whose economic and military capabilities, at one time or another, increased rapidly. An analysis of public pronouncements in that state and diplomatic notes from that state might then be made to assess changes in international goals, and an index might be made of the rapidity and extent to which these goals were satisfied by other states. Those states whose new goals were satisfied might then be compared with those whose new goals were frustrated. Comparisons could be made on such variables as the extent to which more general power needs emerge and such related phenomena as increased militancy and nationalism (as measured by content analysis of the mass media), diplomatic intractability (from analysis of diplomatic records), and military preparation (from analysis of budgetary records). Alternatively, a simulation method might be used in which systematic variations were made in economic and military capability and the willingness of other states to make concessions.[5] In both kinds of studies, as much interest would be centered on the cases in which the hypothesized relationship failed to develop as on the cases in which it developed, in an effort to determine the conditions under which the hypothesis is true and those under which it is false.

REFERENCES

Abel, T., "The element of decision in the pattern of war," *American Sociological Review*, 6(6), 853–859, 1941.

Aron, R., *The Century of Total War*. Boston: Beacon Press, 1954.

Berkowitz, L., *Aggression: A Social Psychological Analysis*. New York: McGraw-Hill Book Company, 1962.

Bernard, J., "The sociological study of conflict," in UNESCO, *The Nature of Conflict*. Paris: UNESCO, 1958.

Bramson, L., and G. W. Goethals, eds., *War: Studies from Psychology, Sociology and Anthropology*. New York: Basic Books, Inc., 1964.

Burton, J. W., *Peace Theory*. New York: Alfred A. Knopf, Inc., 1962.

Christiansen, B., *Attitudes towards Foreign Affairs as a Function of Personality*. Oslo: Oslo University Press, 1959.

Christiansen, B., "Attitudes towards foreign affairs as a function of personality," *in* H. Proshansky and B. Seidenberg, eds., *Basic Studies in Social Psychology*, New York: Holt, Rinehart and Winston, Inc., 1965.

Coleman, J. S., *Community Conflict*. New York: The Free Press, 1957.

de Rivera, J. H., *The Psychological Dimension of Foreign Policy*. Columbus, Ohio: Charles E. Merrill Publishing Co., 1968.

Deutsch, K. W., "Mass communications and the loss of freedom in national decision-making: a possible research approach to interstate conflict," *Journal of Conflict Resolution*, 1(2), 200–211, 1957.

Deutsch, M., "Psychological alternatives to war," *Journal of Social Issues*, 18(2), 97–119, 1962.

Dollard, J., L. Doob, N. E. Miller, O. H. Mowrer, and R. R. Sears, *Frustration and Aggression*. New Haven, Conn.: Yale University Press, 1939.

Dunn, F. S., *Peaceful Change*. New York: Council on Foreign Relations, 1937.

Durbin, E. F. M., and J. Bowlby, *Personal Aggressiveness and War*. New York: Columbia University Press, 1939.

Duvall, S. M., *War and Human Nature*. Public Affairs Pamphlet 125, 1947.

Engelbrecht, H. C., and F. C. Hanighen, *Merchants of Death*. New York: Dodd, Mead and Co., 1934.

Frank, J. D., *Sanity and Survival: Psychological Aspects of War and Peace*. New York: Vintage Books, 1968.

Gladstone, A. I., "The possibility of predicting reactions to international events," *Journal of Social Issues*, 11(1), 21–28, 1955.

Gladstone, A. I., "The concept of the enemy," *Journal of Conflict Resolution*, 3(2), 132–137, 1959.

Gladstone, A. I., and M. A. Taylor, "Threat-related attitudes as reactions to communications about international events," *Journal of Conflict Resolution*, 2(1), 17–28, 1958.

Hobson, J. A., *Imperialism: A Study* (rev. ed.). London: George Allen and Unwin, 1938.

Holsti, O. R., "The belief system and national images: a case study," *Journal of Conflict Resolution*, 6(3), 244–252, 1962.

Kahn, H., *On Thermonuclear War*. Princeton, N. J.: Princeton University Press, 1960.

Kennan, G. F., "The Sources of Soviet Conduct," *Foreign Affairs*, 25(4), 566–582, 1947.

Kluckhohn, C., "Anthropological research and world peace," *in* L. Bryson, L. Finkelstein, and R. M. MacIver, eds., *Approaches to World Peace: A Symposium*, Conference on Science, Philosophy and Religion, New York, 1944.

Knorr, K., "Theories of imperialism," *World Politics*, 4(3), 402–421, 1952.

Lenin, V. I., *Imperialism: The Highest Form of Capitalism*. Moscow: Foreign Languages Publishing House, 1950.

Lerche, C. O., *Principles of International Politics*. New York: Oxford University Press, Inc., 1956.

Lerner, M., "The effect of preparatory action on beliefs concerning nuclear war," *Journal of Social Psychology,* 65(2), 225–231, 1965.

Levi, W., "On the causes of war and the conditions of peace." *Journal of Conflict Resolution,* 4(4), 411–420, 1960.

Mack, R. W., and R. C. Snyder, "An analysis of social conflict—toward an overview and synthesis," *Journal of Conflict Resolution,* 1(2), 212–248, 1957.

May, Mark A., *A Social Psychology of War and Peace.* New Haven, Conn.: Yale University Press, 1943.

Morgenthau, H. J., *Politics among Nations.* New York: Alfred A. Knopf, Inc., 1960.

Newcomb, T. M., "Autistic hostility and social reality," *Human Relations,* 1(1), 3–20, 1947.

Noel-Baker, P., *The Arms Race.* London: John Calder Publishers, Ltd., 1958.

North, R. C., O. R. Holsti, M. G. Zaninovich, and D. A. Zinnes, *Content Analysis.* Evanston, Ill.: Northwestern University Press, 1963.

Organski, A. F. K., *World Politics.* New York: Alfred A. Knopf, Inc., 1958.

Phelps, J., *Military Stability and Arms Control: A Critical Survey.* China Lake, Calif.: U.S. Naval Ordinance Test Station, 1963.

Pruitt, D. G., "Definition of the situation as a determinant of international action," *in* H. C. Kelman, ed., *International Behavior.* New York: Holt, Rinehart and Winston, Inc., 1965.

Rapoport, A., "Perceiving the cold war," *in* R. Fisher, ed., *International Conflict and Behavioral Science.* New York: Basic Books, Inc., 1964.

Rosecrance, R. N., *Action and Reaction in World Politics.* Boston: Little, Brown and Co., 1963.

Russett, B. M., "Cause, surprise, and no escape," *The Journal of Politics,* 24(1), 3–22, 1962.

Schelling, T. C., "Arms control, proposal for a special surveillance force," *World Politics,* 13(1), 1–18, 1960.

Schelling, T. C., and M. H. Halperin, *Strategy and Arms Control.* New York: Twentieth Century Fund, 1961.

Schumpeter, J., *The Sociology of Imperialism.* New York: Meridian Books, 1955.

Singer, J. D., "Threat perception and the armament-tension dilemma," *Journal of Conflict Resolution,* 2(1), 90–105, 1958.

Singer, J. D., *Deterrence, Arms Control and Disarmament: Toward a Synthesis in National Security Policy.* Columbus, Ohio: Ohio State University Press, 1962.

Snyder, G. H., *Deterrence and Defense. Toward a Theory of National Security.* Princeton, N.J.: Princeton University Press, 1961.

Stagner, R., "Nationalism," *in* P. L. Harriman, ed., *The Encyclopedia of Psychology.* New York: Philosophical Library, 1946.

Strachey, J., *The End of Empire.* New York: Random House, 1960.

Tolman, E. C., *Drives toward War.* New York: D. Appleton-Century Co., Inc., 1942.

Van Dyke, V., *International Politics.* New York: Appleton-Century-Crofts, Inc., 1957.

Waltz, K. N., *Man, the State and War.* New York: Columbia University Press, 1959.

White, R. K., "Images in the context of international conflict: Soviet perceptions of the U.S. and the U.S.S.R.," *in* H. C. Kelman, ed., *International Behavior.* New York: Holt, Rinehart and Winston, Inc., 1965.

White, R. K., *Nobody Wanted War: Misperception in Vietnam and Other Wars.* Garden City, N.Y.: Doubleday and Co., Inc., 1968.

Winslow, E. M., *The Pattern of Imperialism.* New York: Columbia University Press, 1948.

Notes

1. The term actually used by these theorists was "aggressive impulses," but it seems to have the same meaning as "hostility" or "hostile emotions" (Berkowitz, 1962).
2. Excerpts from these and related writers can be found in Bramson and Goethals (1964).
3. A concept closely related to hostility as used here is White's "black and white image." (White, 1965, 1968). Many of the points made in this paragraph are also made by White.
4. Public opinion is by no means always of an emotional nature, but only the emotional elements are discussed in this section.
5. The studies briefly sketched here are illustrative of the kind of research that might be done rather than definitive of what should be done to test this hypothesis. Other approaches to measuring the variables or to the whole design might well prove more productive.

47

ROBERT JERVIS

WAR AND MISPERCEPTION

War has so many causes—in part because there are so many kinds of wars—and misperception has so many effects—again in part because there are so many kinds of misperceptions—that it is not possible to draw any definitive conclusions about the impact of misperception on war.[1] But we can address some conceptual and methodological problems, note several patterns, and try to see how misperceptions might lead to World War III. In this article, I use the term misperception broadly, to include inaccurate inferences, miscalculations of consequences, and misjudgments about how others will react to one's policies.

Although war can occur even when both sides see each other accurately, misperception often plays a large role. Particularly interesting are judgments and misjudgments of another state's intentions. Both overestimates and underestimates of hostility have led to war in the past, and much of the current debate about policy toward the Soviet Union revolves around different judgments about how that country would respond to American policies that were

SOURCE: Reprinted from *The Journal of Interdisciplinary History,* Vol. XVIII:4 (Spring, 1988), pp. 675–700, with the permission of the editors of *The Journal of Interdisciplinary History* and The MIT Press, Cambridge, Massachusetts. © 1988 by The Massachusetts Institute of Technology and the editors of *The Journal of Interdisciplinary History.*

either firm or conciliatory. Since statesmen know that a war between the United States and the Soviet Union would be incredibly destructive, however, it is hard to see how errors of judgment, even errors like those that have led to past wars, could have the same effect today. But perceptual dynamics could cause statesmen to see policies as safe when they actually were very dangerous or, in the final stages of deep conflict, to see war as inevitable and therefore to see striking first as the only way to limit destruction.

POSSIBLE AREAS OF MISPERCEPTION

Although this article will concentrate on misperceptions of intentions of potential adversaries, many other objects can be misperceived as well. Capabilities of course can be misperceived; indeed, as Blainey stresses, excessive military optimism is frequently associated with the outbreak of war.[2] Military optimism is especially dangerous when coupled with political and diplomatic pessimism. A country is especially likely to strike if it feels that, although it can win a war immediately, the chances of a favorable diplomatic settlement are slight and the military situation is likely to deteriorate. Furthermore, these estimates, which are logically independent, may be psychologically linked. Pessimism about current diplomatic and long-run military prospects may lead statesmen to exaggerate the possibility of current military victory as a way of convincing themselves that there is, in fact, a solution to what otherwise would be an intolerable dilemma.

Less remarked on is the fact that the anticipated consequences of events may also be incorrect. For example, America's avowed motive for fighting in Vietnam was not the direct goal of saving that country, but rather the need to forestall the expected repercussions of defeat. What it feared was a "domino effect" leading to a great increase in Communist influence in Southeast Asia and the perception that the United States lacked the resolve to protect its interests elsewhere in the world. In retrospect, it seems clear that neither of these possibilities materialized. This case is not unique; states are prone to fight when they believe that "bandwagoning" rather than "balancing" dynamics are at work—that is, when they believe that relatively small losses or gains will set off a self-perpetuating cycle. In fact, such beliefs are often incorrect. Although countries will sometimes side with a state which is gaining power, especially if they are small and can do little to counteract such a menace, the strength and resilience of balancing incentives are often underestimated by the leading powers. Statesmen are rarely fatalistic; they usually resist the growth of dominant powers.[3] A striking feature of the Cold War is how little each side has suffered when it has had to make what it perceived as costly and dangerous retreats.

At times we may need to distinguish between misperceptions of a state's predispositions—that is, its motives and goals—and misperceptions of the realities faced by the state. Either can lead to incorrect predictions, and, after the fact, it is often difficult to determine which kind of error was made. When the unexpected behavior is undesired, decision-makers usually think that they have misread the other state's motives, not the situation it faced.[4] Likewise, scholars generally focus on misjudgments of intentions rather than misjudgments of situations. We, too, shall follow this pattern, although it would be very useful to explore the proposition that incorrect explanations and predictions concerning other states' behaviors are caused more often by misperceptions concerning their situations than by misperceptions about their predispositions.

WAR WITHOUT MISPERCEPTION

It has often been argued that, by definition, the proposition is true that every war involves at least one serious misperception. If every war has a loser, it would seem to stand to reason that the defeated state made serious miscalculations when it decided to fight. But, whereas empirical investigations reveal that decisions to go to war are riddled with misperceptions, it is not correct that such a proposition follows by definition.

A country could rationally go to war even though it was certain it would lose. First, the country could value fighting itself, either as an ultimate goal or as a means for improving man and society. Second, faced with the choice of giving up territory to a stronger rival or losing it through a war, the state might choose war because of considerations of honor, domestic politics, or international reputation. Honor is self-explanatory, although, like the extreme form of Social Darwinism alluded to earlier, it sounds strange to modern ears. Domestic politics, however, are likely to remain with us and may have been responsible for at least some modern wars. It is a commonplace that leaders may seek "a quick and victorious war" in order to unify the country (this sentiment is supposed to have been voiced by Vyacheslav Plehve, the Russian minister of the interior on the eve of the Russo-Japanese War), but statesmen might also think that a short, unsuccessful war might serve the same function.

Although examples seem rare, international considerations could also lead a statesman to fight a war he knows he will lose. The object would be to impress third countries. Such a decision might appear particularly perverse because a loss would seem to show that the country is weak. But more important than the display of its lack of military capability could be the display of its resolve, if not foolhardiness. Other nations which had quarrels with the state might infer that it is willing to fight even when its position is weak, and such an inference might strengthen the state's bargaining position.[5]

Only rarely can statesmen be certain of a war's outcome, and once we take the probabilistic nature of judgments into consideration, it is even more clear that one can have wars without misperception. A state may believe that the chances of victory are small and yet rationally decide to fight if the gains of victory are large and the costs of losing are not much greater than those of making the concessions necessary to avoid war.

Although a state could start a war that it had little prospect of winning solely because of the attractions of victory, psychology and politics both conspire to make it much more likely that states go to war because of their gloomy prognostications of what will happen if they do not fight. Psychologically, losses hurt more than gains gratify. Both domestic and international politics produce a similar effect. Public opinion and partisan opposition are more easily turned against a government which seems to be sacrificing existing values than one which is not expanding the country's influence rapidly enough. Analyses of international politics reinforce these pressures. Statesmen are generally slower to believe that the domino effect will work for them than against them. They realize that other states will often respond to their gains by attempting to block further advances; by contrast, they also believe that any loss of their influence will lead to a further erosion of their power.

Because a state which finds the status quo intolerable or thinks it can be preserved only by fighting can be driven to act despite an unfavorable assessment of the balance of forces, it is neither surprising nor evidence of misperception that those who start wars often lose them. For example, Austria and Germany attacked in 1914 largely because they believed that the status quo was unstable and that the tide of events was moving against them. As Sagan shows, the Japanese made a similar calculation in 1941.[6] Although they overestimated the chance of victory because they incorrectly believed that the United States would be willing to fight—and lose—a limited war, the expectation of victory was not a necessary condition for their decision to strike. According to their values, giving up domination of China—which would have been required in order to avoid war—was tantamount to sacrificing their national survival. Victory, furthermore, would have placed them in the first rank of nations and preserved their domestic values. The incentives were somewhat similar in 1904, when they attacked Russia even though "the Emperor's most trusted advisers expressed no confidence as to the outcome of the war. . . . The army calculated that Japan had a fifty-fifty chance to win a war. The Navy expected that half its forces would be lost, but it hoped the enemy's naval forces would be annihilated with the remaining half."[7] Fighting was justified in light of Japan's deteriorating military position combined with the possibility of increasing its influence over its neighbors.

METHODOLOGICAL PROBLEMS

The most obvious way to determine the influence of misperception on war would be to employ the comparative method and contrast the effects of accurate and inaccurate perceptions. But several methodological problems stand in the way. First is the question of whether perceptions should be judged in terms of outcomes or processes—that is, whether we should compare them to what was later revealed to have been reality or whether we should ask how reasonable were the statesmen's inferences, given the information available at the time. The two criteria call for different kinds of evidence and often yield different conclusions.[8] People are often right for the wrong reasons and, conversely, good analyses may produce answers which later will be shown to have been incorrect. Shortly after Adolf Hitler took power, Robert Vansittart, the permanent undersecretary of the British Foreign Office, concluded that the Germans would increase their military power as rapidly as possible in order to overturn the status quo. In criticizing military officials, who generally disagreed with him, he said: "Prophecy is largely a matter of insight. I do not think the Service Departments have enough. On the other hand they might say I have too much. The answer is that I knew the Germans better."[9] His image of Hitler was quite accurate, but it is not clear that he reached it by better reasoning or supported it with more evidence than did those who held a different view.

A second difficulty is that historians and political scientists are drawn to the study of conflict more often than to the analysis of peaceful interactions. As a result, we know little about the degree to which harmonious relationships are characterized by accurate perceptions. I suspect, however, that they are the product of routinized and highly constrained patterns of interaction more often than the result of accurate perceptions.

A third problem lies in determining whether perceptions were accurate, which involves two subproblems. First, it is often difficult to determine what a statesman's—let alone a country's—perceptions are. We usually have to tease the person's views out of confused and conflicting evidence and try to separate his true beliefs from those he merely wants others to believe he holds. Indeed, in some cases the person initially may not have well-defined perceptions but may develop them to conform to the actions he has taken.[10] Second, even greater difficulties arise when the perceptions are compared with "reality." The true state of the military balance can be determined only by war; states' intentions may be impossible to determine, even after the fact and with all the relevant records open for inspection.

Our ability to determine whether statesmen's assessments are accurate is further reduced by the probabilistic nature of these assessments. Statesmen often believe that a given image is the one most likely to be correct or that a given outcome is the one most likely to occur. But the validity of such judgments is extremely hard to determine unless we have a large number of cases. If someone thinks that something will happen nine out of ten times, the fact that it does not happen once does not mean that the judgment was wrong. Thus if a statesman thinks that another country probably is aggressive and we later can establish that it was not, we cannot be sure that his probabilistic judgment was incorrect.[11]

MISPERCEPTIONS AND THE ORIGINS OF WORLD WARS I AND II

Tracing the impact of beliefs and perceptions in any given case might seem easy compared to the problems just presented. But it is not, although even a brief list of the misperceptions preceding the major conflicts of this century is impressive. Before World War I, all of the participants thought that the war would be short. They also seem to have been optimistic about its outcome, but there is conflicting evidence. (For example, both Edward Grey and Theobald von Bethmann Hollweg made well-known gloomy predictions, but it is unclear whether these statements accurately reflected their considered judgments. In addition, quantitative analysis of the available internal memoranda indicates pessimism, although there are problems concerning the methodology employed.[12])

May argues that the analyses of the intentions of the adversaries during this period were more accurate than the analyses of their capabilities, but even the former were questionable.[13] Some of the judgments of July 1914 were proven incorrect—for example, the German expectation that Britain would remain neutral and Germany's grander hopes of keeping France and even Russia out of the war. Furthermore, the broader assumptions underlying the diplomacy of the period may also have been in error. Most important on the German side was not an image of a particular country as the enemy, but its basic belief that the ensuing events would lead to either "world power or decline." For the members of the Triple Entente, and particularly Great Britain, the central question was German intentions, so brilliantly debated in Eyre Crowe's memorandum and Thomas Sanderson's rebuttal to it. We still cannot be sure whether the answer which guided British policy was correct.[14]

The list of misperceptions preceding World War II is also impressive. Capabilities again were misjudged, although not as badly as in the previous era.[15] Few people expected the blitzkrieg to bring France down; the power of strategic bombardment was greatly overestimated; the British exaggerated the vulnerability of the German economy, partly because they thought that it was stretched taut at the start of the war. Judgments of intention were even less accurate. The appeasers completely misread Hitler; the anti-appeasers failed to see that he could not be stopped without a war. For his part, Hitler underestimated his adversaries' determination. During the summer of 1939 he doubted whether Britain would fight and, in the spring of 1940, expected her to make peace.[16]

It might also be noted that in both cases the combatants paid insufficient attention to and made incorrect judgments about the behavior of neutrals. To a large extent, World War I was decided by the American entry and World War II by the involvement of the Soviet Union and the United States.[17] But we cannot generalize from these two examples to say that states are prone to make optimistic estimates concerning the role of neutrals; it may be equally true that pessimistic judgments may lead states to remain at peace, and we would have no way of determining the validity of such assessments.

DID THE MISPERCEPTIONS MATTER?

But did these misperceptions cause the wars? Which if any of them, had they been corrected, would have led to a peaceful outcome? In attempting to respond to such questions, we should keep in mind that they are hypothetical and so do not permit conclusive answers. As Stein has noted, not all misperceptions have significant consequences.[18]

If Britain and France had understood Hitler, they would have fought much earlier, when the balance was in their favor and victory could have been relatively quick and easy. (Managing the postwar world might have been difficult, however, especially if others—including the Germans—held a more benign image of Hitler.) If Hitler had understood his adversaries, the situation would have been much more dangerous since he might have devised tactics that would have allowed him to fight on more favorable terms. But on either of these assumptions, war still would have been inevitable; both sides preferred to fight rather than make the concessions that would have been necessary to maintain peace.[19]

The case of 1914 is not as clear. I suspect that the misperceptions of intentions in July, although fascinating, were not crucial. The Germans probably would have gone to war even if they had known that they would have had to fight all of the members of the Triple Entente. The British misjudgment of Germany—if it were a misjudgment—was more consequential, but even on this point the counterfactual question is hard to answer. Even if Germany did not seek domination, the combination of her great power, restlessness, and paranoia made her a menace. Perhaps a British policy based on a different image of Germany might have successfully appeased the Germans—to use the term in the older sense—but Britain could not have afforded to see Germany win another war in Europe, no matter what goals it sought.

Capabilities were badly misjudged, but even a correct appreciation of the power of the defense might not have changed the outcome of the July crisis. The "crisis instability" created by the belief that whoever struck first would gain a major advantage made the war hard to avoid once the crisis was severe, but may not have been either a necessary or a sufficient condition for the outbreak of the fighting. The Germans' belief that time was not on their side and that a quick victory would soon be beyond their reach was linked in part to the mistaken belief in the power of the offensive, but was not entirely driven by it. Thus, a preventive war might have occurred in the absence of the pressures for preemption.

Had the participants realized not only that the first offensive would not end the war, but also that the fighting would last for four punishing years, they might well have held back. Had they known what the war would bring, the kaiser, the emperor, and the czar presumably might have bluffed or sought a limited war, but they would have preferred making concessions to joining a general struggle. The same was probably true for the leaders of Britain and France, and certainly would have been true had they known the long-term consequences of the war. In at least one sense, then, World War I was caused by misperception.

MODELS OF CONFLICT

Two possible misperceptions of an adversary are largely the opposites of each other, and each is linked to an important argument about the causes of conflict. On the one hand, wars can occur if aggressors underestimate the willingness of status quo powers to fight (the World War II model); on the other hand, wars can also result if two states exaggerate each other's hostility when their differences are in fact bridgeable (the spiral or World War I model). These models only approximate the cases that inspired them. As noted earlier, World War II would have occurred even without this perceptual error, and the judgments of intentions before 1914 may have been generally accurate and, even if they were not, may not have been necessary for the conflict to have erupted. Nevertheless, the models are useful for summarizing two important sets of dynamics.

The World War II model in large part underlies deterrence theory. The main danger which is foreseen is that of an aggressive state which underestimates the resolve of the status quo powers. The latter may inadvertently encourage this misperception by errors of their own—for example, they may underestimate the aggressor's hostility and propose compromises that are taken as evidence of weakness. In the spiral model, by contrast, the danger is that each side will incorrectly see the other as a menace to its vital interests and will inadvertently encourage this belief by relying on threats to prevent war, thereby neglecting the pursuit of agreement and conciliation.

As I have stated elsewhere, the heated argument between the proponents of the two models is not so much a dispute between two rival theories as it is a dispute about the states' intentions.[20] The nature of the difference of opinion then points up both the importance and the difficulty of determining what states' motives and goals are, what costs and risks they are willing to run in order to expand, and the likely way in which they will respond to threats and conciliation. Determining others' intentions is so difficult that states have resorted to an approach that, were it suggested by an academic, would be seen as an example of how out of touch scholars are with international realities. On several occasions, states directly ask their adversaries what it is they want. The British frequently discussed directing such an inquiry to Hitler, and the United States did so to Joseph Stalin shortly after the end of World War II. Statesmen might be disabused of their misperceptions if they could listen in on their adversary's deliberations. Thus in his analysis of the Eastern crisis of 1887/88, Seton-Watson argues that Benjamin Disraeli's government greatly exaggerated the Russian ambitions, and points out that "it is difficult to believe that even the most confirmed Russophobe in the British Cabinet of those days could have failed to be reassured if it had been possible for him to [read the czar's telegrams to his ambassador in London]."[21] But of course were such access possible, it could be used for deception, and the information would therefore not be credible.

It is clear that states can either underestimate or overestimate the aggressiveness of their adversaries and that either error can lead to war. Although one issue raised by these twin dangers is not central to our discussion here, it is so important that it should at least be noted. If the uncertainty about others' intentions cannot be eliminated, states should design policies that will not fail disastrously even if they are based on incorrect assumptions. States should try to construct a policy of deterrence which will not set off spirals of hostility if existing political differences are in fact bridgeable; the policy should also be designed to conciliate without running the risk that the other side, if it is aggressive, will be emboldened to attack. Such a policy requires the state to combine firmness, promises, and a credible willingness to consider the other side's interests. But the task is difficult, and neither decision-makers nor academics have fully come to grips with it.[22]

The existence of a spiral process does not prove the applicability of the spiral model, for increasing tension, hostility, and violence can be a reflection of the underlying conflict, not a cause of it. For example, conflict between the United States and Japan increased steadily throughout the 1930s, culminating in the American oil embargo in 1941 and the Japanese attack on Pearl Harbor four months later. Misperceptions were common, but the spiral model should not be used to explain these events because the escalating exchange of threats and actions largely revealed rather than created the incompatibility of goals. Japan preferred to risk defeat rather than forego dominance of China; the United States preferred to fight rather than see Japan reach its goal.

Blainey advances similar arguments in his rebuttal of Higonnet's views on the origins of the Seven Years' War. Higonnet claims that "no one wanted to fight this war. It would never have occurred if, in their sincere efforts to resolve it, the French and English governments had not inadvertently magnified its insignificant original cause into a wide conflict."[23] Hostilities escalated as Britain and France attempted to counteract (and surpass) each other's moves. They became increasingly suspicious of their adversary's motives, and felt that the stakes were higher than originally had been believed. The cycle of action and threat perception eventually led both sides to believe that they had to fight a major war in order to protect themselves. Blainey's rebuttal is simple: what was at stake from the beginning was "mastery in North America." The initial moves were at a low level of violence because each side, having underestimated the other's willingness to fight, thought it was possible to prevail quickly and cheaply.[24] Resolving such differences would require detailed research and responses to a number of hypothetical questions. But it should be kept in mind that the existence of increasing and reciprocal hostility does not always mean that the participants have come to overestimate the extent to which the other threatens its vital interests.

Furthermore, even if the initial conflict of interest does not justify a war and it is the process of conflict itself which generates the impulse to fight, misperception may not be the crucial factor. The very fact that states contest an issue raises the stakes because influence and reputation are involved. To retreat after having expended prestige and treasure, if not blood, is psychologically more painful than retreating at the start; it is also more likely to have much stronger domestic and international repercussions.[25] The dilemmas which are created were outlined in 1953 by the American intelligence community in a paper which tried to estimate how the Russians and Chinese would react to various forms of American military pressure designed to produce an armistice in Korea:

> If prior to the onset of any UN/U.S. military course of action, the Communists recognized that they were faced with a clear choice between making the concessions necessary to reach an armistice, or accepting the likelihood that

UN/U.S. military operations would endanger the security of the Manchurian and Soviet borders, destroy the Manchurian industrial complex, or destroy the Chinese Communist armed forces, the Communists would probably agree to an armistice. However, it would be extremely difficult to present them with a clear choice of alternatives before such action was begun. Moreover, once such UN/U.S. action was begun, Communist power and prestige would become further involved, thereby greatly increasing the difficulties of making the choice between agreeing to [an] armistice or continuing the war.[26]

ASSESSING HOSTILE INTENT

On balance, it seems that states are more likely to overestimate the hostility of others than to underestimate it. States are prone to exaggerate the reasonableness of their own positions and the hostile intent of others; indeed, the former process feeds the latter. Statesmen, wanting to think well of themselves and their decisions, often fail to appreciate others' perspectives, and so greatly underestimate the extent to which their actions can be seen as threats.

When their intentions are peaceful, statesmen think that others will understand their motives and therefore will not be threatened by the measures that they are taking in their own self-defense. Richard Perle, former assistant secretary of defense, once said that if we are in doubt about Soviet intentions, we should build up our arms. He explained that if the Russians are aggressive, the buildup will be needed, and, if they are not, the only consequence will be wasted money. Similarly, when United States troops were moving toward the Yalu River, Secretary of State Dean Acheson said that there was no danger that the Chinese would intervene in an effort to defend themselves because they understood that we were not a threat to them. Exceptions, such as the British belief in the 1930s that German hostility was based largely on fear of encirclement and the Israeli view before the 1973 war that Egypt feared attack, are rare.[27] (The British and the Israeli perceptions were partly generated by the lessons they derived from their previous wars.)

This bias also operates in retrospect, when states interpret the other side's behavior after the fact. Thus American leaders, believing that China had no reason to be alarmed by the movement of troops toward the Yalu, assumed the only explanation for Chinese intervention in the Korean War was its unremitting hostility to the United States. India, although clearly seeing the Chinese point of view in 1950, saw the Chinese attack on her in 1962 as unprovoked, and so concluded that future cooperation was impossible. Similarly, although all Westerners, even those who could empathize with the Soviet Union, understand how the invasion of Afghanistan called up a strong reaction, Soviet leaders apparently did not and instead saw the Western response as part of a hostile design that would have led to the same actions under any circumstances."[28]

This problem is compounded by a second and better known bias—states tend to infer threatening motives from actions that a disinterested observer would record as at least partly cooperative. John Foster Dulles' view of Nikita Khrushchev's arms cuts in the mid-1950s is one such example and President Ronald Reagan's view of most Soviet arms proposals may be another.[29]

These two biases often operate simultaneously, with the result that both sides are likely to believe that they are cooperating and that others are responding with hostility. For example, when Leonid Brezhnev visited President Richard Nixon in San Clemente during 1973 and argued that the status quo in the Middle East was unacceptable, and when Andrei Gromyko later said that "the fire of war [in the Mid-East] could break out onto the surface at any time," they may well have thought that they were fulfilling their obligations under the Basic Principles Agreement to consult in the event of a threat to peace. The Americans, however, felt that the Soviets were making threats in the spring and violating the spirit of detente by not giving warning in the fall.[30]

People also tend to overperceive hostility because they pay closest attention to dramatic events. Threatening acts often achieve high visibility because they consist of instances like crises, occupation of foreign territory, and the deployment of new weapons. Cooperative actions, by contrast, often call less attention to themselves because they are not dramatic and can even be viewed as nonevents. Thus Larson notes how few inferences American statesmen drew from the Soviet's willingness to sign the Austrian State Treaty of 1955.[31] Similarly, their withdrawal of troops from Finland after World War II made little impact, and over the past few years few decision-makers or analysts have commented on the fact that the Soviets have *not* engaged in a strategic buildup.

MISPERCEPTION AND THE ORIGINS OF WORLD WAR III

Misperception could prove to be an underlying cause of World War III through either the overestimation or the underestimation of hostile intent. If the Soviet Union is highly aggressive—or if its subjective security requirements can be met only by making the West insecure—then war could result through a Soviet underestimation of American resolve. If the Soviet Union is driven primarily by apprehension that could be reduced by conciliation, then war could result through a spiral of threat-induced tensions and unwarranted fears. But, although it is easy to see how either of these misperceptions could increase conflict, it is hard to see how a nuclear war could start under current technology when both sides know how costly such a clash would be. To analyze this topic, concentrating on the role of misperception, we first examine the dynamics of the game of chicken and then discuss the psychological aspects of crisis stability and preemption.

MISPERCEPTION, COMMITMENT, AND CHANGE

In a situation that is similar to the game of chicken (that is, any outcome, including surrender, would be better than war), war should not occur as long as both sides are even minimally rational and maintain control over their own behavior.[32] Both sides may bluster and bluff, but it will make no sense for either of them to initiate all-out conflict. Each side will try to stand firm and so make the other back down; the most obvious danger would result from the mistaken belief that the other will retreat and that it is therefore safe to stand firm.

But if both sides maintain control, war can occur only if either or both sides become irrevocably committed to acting on their misperception. In other words, so long as either state retains its freedom of action, war can be avoided because that state can back down at the last minute. But commitment can inhibit this flexibility, and that, of course is its purpose. Standard bargaining logic shows that if one side persuades the other that it is committed to standing firm, the other will have no choice but to retreat.[33] What is of concern here is that this way of seeking to avoid war can make it more likely.

Whether a commitment—and indeed any message—is perceived as intended (or perceived at all) depends not only on its clarity and plausibility, but also on how it fits with the recipient's cognitive predispositions. Messages which are inconsistent with a person's beliefs about international politics and other actors are not likely to be perceived the way the sender intended. For example, shortly before the Spanish-American War President William McKinley issued what he thought was a strong warning to Spain to make major concessions over Cuba or face American military intervention. But the Spanish were worried primarily not about an American declaration of war, but about American aid for the Cuban rebels, and so they scanned the president's speech with this problem in mind. They therefore focused on sections of the speech that McKinley regarded as relatively unimportant and passed quickly over the paragraphs that he thought were vital.[34]

Furthermore, the state sending the message of commitment is likely to assume that it has been received. Thus one reason the United States was taken by surprise when the Soviet Union put missiles into Cuba was that it had assumed that the Soviets understood that such action was unacceptable. Statesmen, like people in their everyday lives, find it difficult to realize that their own intentions, which seem clear to them, can be obscure to others. The problem is magnified because the belief that the message has been received and understood as it was intended will predispose the state to interpret ambiguous information as indicating that the other side does indeed understand its commitment.

Psychological Commitment and Misperception

Misperception can lead to war not only through mistaken beliefs about the impact of the state's policy of commitment on others, but also through the impact of commitment on the state. We should not forget the older definition of the term commitment, which is more psychological than tactical. People and states become committed to policies not only by staking their bargaining reputations on them, but by coming to believe that their policies are morally justified and politically necessary. For example, the process of deciding that a piece of territory warrants a major international dispute and the effort that is involved in acting on this policy can lead a person to see the territory as even more valuable than he had originally thought. Furthermore, other members of the elite and the general public may become aroused, with the result that a post-commitment retreat will not only feel more costly to the statesman; it may actually be more costly in terms of its effect on his domestic power.

Commitment can also create misperceptions. As the decision-maker comes to see his policy as necessary, he is likely to believe that the policy can succeed, even if such a conclusion requires the distortion of information about what others will do. He is likely to come to believe that his threats will be credible and effective and that his opponents will ultimately cooperate and permit him to reach his objectives. Facing sharp value trade-offs is painful; no statesman wants to acknowledge that he may have to abandon an important foreign policy goal in order to avoid war or that he may have to engage in a bloody struggle if he is to reach his foreign policy goals. Of course, he will not embark on the policy in the first place if he thinks that the other will fight. Quite often, the commitment develops incrementally, without a careful and disinterested analysis of how others are likely to react. When commitments develop in this way, decision-makers can find themselves supporting untenable policies that others can and will challenge. The result could be war because the state behaves more recklessly than the chicken context would warrant.[35]

THE ULTIMATE SELF-FULFILLING PROPHECY

Even if the processes of commitment can entrap statesmen, it is hard to see how World War III could occur unless one or both sides concluded that it was inevitable in the near future. As long as both sides expect that all-out war will result in unlimited damage, they will prefer peace to war. But if either thinks that peace cannot be maintained, the choice is not between maintaining peace—even at a significant cost in terms of other values—and going to war, but between striking first or being struck first. Even under these circumstances, attacking would make sense only if the former alternative is preferable to the latter. Since strategic weapons themselves are relatively invulnerable, scholars, until recently, have believed that there were few incentives to strike first. But they are now aware of the vulnerability of command, control, and communication (C^3) systems which could lead decision-makers to believe that striking first would be at least marginally, and perhaps significantly, better than receiving the first blow.[36] Preemption would be advantageous, thereby creating what is called crisis instability.

Crisis instability is a large topic, and here it is addressed only in terms of the potential role of misperception.[37] First, perceptions create their own reality. Determinations about the inevitability of war are not objective, but instead are based on each side's perceptions of what the other will do, which in turn is influenced by what each side thinks its adversary thinks that it is going to do. To maintain the peace, a state would have to convince the adversary that it will not start a war and that it does not believe the other will either. This interaction would take place within the context of a crisis of unprecedented severity, probably involving military alerts, if not the limited use of force.

We know very little about how states in such circumstances would think about the problem, judge the adversary's behavior, try to reassure the adversary, and decide whether these reassurances had been believed. But however these analyses are carried out, they will constitute, not just describe, reality; the question of whether war is inevitable cannot be answered apart from the participants' beliefs about it.

War itself would provide an objective answer to the question of whether there would be a significant advantage to striking first. But even here beliefs would play a role—the military doctrine adopted by a state and its beliefs about the other side's doctrine would strongly influence a decision to strike first. On the one hand, the incentives to strike first would remain slight so long as each side believed that the war would be unlimited, or, if controlled, would concentrate on attacks against cities. On the other hand, if each side believed that it was crucial to deny the other any military advantage, first-strike incentives would be greater because attacks against weapons and C^3 systems might cripple the other's ability to fight a counterforce war, even if they could not destroy the other's second-strike capability.

The uncertainties here, and in other judgments of the advantages of striking first, are enormous. Furthermore, they cannot be resolved without war. Thus statesmen's perceptions will involve both guesswork and intuition. In such circumstances, many factors could lead to an exaggeration of the benefits of taking the offensive.[38] Military organizations generally seek to take the initiative; statesmen rarely believe that allowing the other to move first is beneficial; and the belief that war is inevitable could lead decision-makers to minimize psychological pain by concluding that striking first held out a significant chance of limiting damage.

If war is believed to be very likely but not inevitable, launching a first strike would be an incredible gamble. As noted at the start of this article, such gambles can be rational, but, even when they are not, psychological factors can lead people to take them. Although most people are risk-averse for gains, they are risk-acceptant for losses.[39] For example, given the choice between a 100 percent chance of winning $10 and a 20 percent chance of winning $55, most people will choose the former. But if the choice is between the certainty of losing $10 and a 20 percent chance of losing $55, they will gamble and opt for the latter. In order to increase the chance of avoiding any loss at all, people are willing to accept the danger of an even greater sacrifice. Such behavior is consistent with the tendency for people to be influenced by "sunk costs" which rationally should be disregarded and to continue to pursue losing ventures in the hope of recovering their initial investment when they would be better off simply cutting their losses.

This psychology of choice has several implications concerning crisis stability. First, because the status quo forms people's point of reference, they are willing to take unusual risks to recoup recent losses. Although a setback might be minor when compared to the total value of a person's holdings, he will see his new status in terms of where he was shortly before and therefore may risk an even greater loss in the hope of reestablishing his position. In a crisis, then, a decision-maker who had suffered a significant, but limited, loss might risk world war if he thought such a war held out the possibility of reversing the recent defeat. Where fully rational analysis would lead a person to cut his losses, the use of the status quo as the benchmark against which other results are measured could lead the statesman to persevere even at high risk. The danger would be especially great if both sides were to feel that they were losing, which could easily happen because they probably would have different perspectives and use different baselines. Indeed, if the Russians consider the status quo to be constant movement in their favor, they might be prone to take high risks when the United States thought that it was maintaining the status quo. Furthermore, it could prove dangerous to follow a strategy of making gains by fait accompli.[40] Unless the state which has been victimized quickly adjusts to and accepts the new situation, it may be willing to run unusually high risks to regain its previous position. The other side, expecting the first to be "rational," will in turn be taken by surprise by this resistance, with obvious possibilities for increased conflict.

A second consequence is that if a statesman thinks that war—and therefore enormous loss—is almost certain if he does not strike and that attacking provides a small chance of escaping unscathed, he may decide to strike even though a standard probability-utility calculus would call for restraint. Focusing on the losses that will certainly occur if his state is attacked can lead a decision-maker to pursue any course of action that holds out any possibility of no casualties at all. Similar and more likely are the dynamics which could operate in less severe crises, such as the expectation of a hostile coup in an important third-world country or the limited use of force by the adversary in a disputed area. Under such circumstances, the state might take actions which entailed an irrationally high chance of escalation and destruction in order to avoid the certain loss entailed by acquiescing.[41] With his attention riveted on the deterioration which will occur unless he acts strongly to reverse a situation, a statesman may accept the risk of even greater loss, thereby making these crises more dangerous.

The response can also be influenced by how the decision is framed. Although a powerful aversion to losses could lead a decision-maker to strike when the alternatives are posed as they were in the previous example, it also could lead him to hold back. For instance, he might choose restraint if he thought that striking first, although preferable to striking second, would lead to certain retaliation whereas not striking would offer some chance—even if small—of avoiding a war, although he risked much higher casualties if the other side attacked. If a decision-maker takes as his baseline not the existing situation, but the casualties that would be suffered in a war, his choice between the same alternatives might be different. He would then judge the policies according to lives that might be saved, not lost, with the result that he would choose a course of action that he believed would certainly save some lives rather than choose another that might save more, but might not save any. The obvious danger is that a first strike which would significantly reduce the other side's strategic forces would meet the former criterion whereas restraint could not provide the certainty of saving any lives and so would not seem as attractive as standard utility maximization theory implies.

But the picture is not one of unrelieved gloom. First, situations as bleak as those we are positing are extremely rare and probably will never occur. The Cuban missile crisis was probably as close as we have come to the brink of war, and even then President John F. Kennedy rated the chance of war at no more than 50 percent, and he seems to have been referring to the chances of armed conflict, not nuclear war. So American, and presumably Soviet, officials were far from believing that war was inevitable.

Second, the propensity for people to avoid value trade-offs can help to preserve peace. To face the choice between starting World War III and running a very high risk that the other side will strike first would be terribly painful, and decision-makers might avoid it by downplaying the latter danger. Of course to say that a decision-maker will try not to perceive the need for such a sharp value tradeoff does not tell us which consideration will guide him, but some evidence indicates that the dominating value may be the one which is most salient and to which the person was committed even before the possibility of conflict with another central value arose. Thus the very fact that decision-makers constantly reiterate the need to avoid war and rarely talk about the need to strike first if war becomes inevitable may contribute to restraint.

Finally, although exaggerating the danger of crisis instability would make a severe confrontation more dangerous than it would otherwise be, it also would serve the useful function of keeping states far from the brink of war. If decision-makers believed that crises could be controlled and manipulated, they would be less inhibited about creating them. The misperception may be useful: fear, even unjustified fear, may make the world a little more tranquil.

CONCLUSION

The methodological problems noted earlier make it impossible to draw firm generalizations about the relationships between war and misperception, but we tentatively offer a number of propositions. First, although war can occur in the absence of misperception, in fact misperception almost always accompanies it. To say that statesmen's beliefs about both capabilities and intentions are usually badly flawed is not to say that they are foolish. Rather, errors are inevitable in light of the difficulty of assessing technological and organizational capabilities, the obstacles to inferring others' intentions correctly, the limitations on people's abilities to process information, and the need to avoid excessively painful choices.

Second, to say that misperceptions are common is not to specify their content. Statesmen can either overestimate or underestimate the other side's capabilities and its hostility. Wars are especially likely to occur when a state simultaneously underestimates an adversary's strength and exaggerates its hostility. In many cases, however, estimates of capabilities are the product of a policy, not the foundation on which it is built. Policy commitments can influence evaluations as well as be driven by them. Others' hostility can also be overestimated or underestimated and, although exceptions abound, the former error seems more common than the latter. Similarly, more often than falling into the trap of incorrectly believing that other statesmen are just like themselves, decision-makers frequently fail to empathize with the adversary. That is, they tend to pay insufficient attention to constraints and pressures faced by their opponent, including those generated by the decision-maker's own state.

Third, objective analyses of the international system which are so popular among political scientists are not likely to provide a complete explanation for the outbreak of most wars. To historians who are accustomed to explanations which rely heavily on reconstructing the world as the statesmen saw it, this reality will not come as a surprise. But I would also argue that such reconstructions can both build and utilize generalizations about how people perceive information. Although some perceptions are random and idiosyncratic, many others are not. We know that decision-makers, like people in their everyday lives, are strongly driven by the beliefs that they hold, the lessons that they have learned from history, and the hope of being able to avoid painful choices.

Even if these generalizations are correct, any single case can be an exception. World War III, if it occurs, might not fit the dominant pattern. But, given the overwhelming destruction which both sides would expect such a war to bring, it seems hard to see how such a conflict could erupt in the absence of misperception. It would be particularly dangerous if either the United States or the Soviet Union or both believed that war was inevitable and that striking first was significantly preferable to allowing the other side to strike first. Since a number of psychological processes could lead people to overestimate these factors, it is particularly important for statesmen to realize the ways in which common perceptual processes can lead to conclusions that are not only incorrect, but also extremely dangerous.

NOTES

1. For a good typology of wars caused by misperception, see George H. Quester, "Six Causes of War," *Jerusalem Journal of International Relations*, VI (1982), 1–23.
2. For a discussion of the concept of intentions in international politics, see Jervis, *Perception and Misperception in International Politics* (Princeton, 1976), 48–57.

For a discussion of the meaning of that concept in general, see Gertrude E. M. Anscombe, *Intention* (Ithaca, 1969); Ernest May, "Conclusions: Capabilities and Proclivities," in *idem* (ed.), *Knowing One's Enemies* (Princeton, 1984), 503. A. Geoffrey Blainey, *The Causes of War* (New York, 1973).

3. See Arnold Wolfers, *Discord and Collaboration* (Baltimore, 1962), 122–24; Kenneth Waltz, *Theory of International Politics* (Reading, Mass., 1979); Stephen Walt, "Alliance Formation and the Balance of World Power," *International Security*, IX (1985), 3–43; *idem, The Origins of Alliances* (Ithaca, 1987).

4. For a good review, see Edward Jones, "How Do People Perceive the Causes of Behavior?" *American Scientist*, LXIV (1976), 300–305. For an analysis of related phenomena in international politics, see Jervis, *Perception and Misperception*, 343–354.

5. This concept is similar to the economist's notion of the "chain store paradox." It applies in cases in which the state can prevail in the conflict, but only at a cost which exceeds the immediate gains. The reason for fighting in this case is again to impress other potential challengers, and the analogy is the behavior of a large chain store toward small stores which challenge it by cutting prices. The chain store can respond by cutting prices even more, thus losing money but succeeding in driving the competitor out of business. The point of taking such action is to discourage other challengers, but the paradox is that in each particular case the chain store loses money and the tactic will be effective only if others believe it will be repeated. See Reinhard Selten, "The Chain Store Paradox," *Theory and Decision*, IX (1978), 127–159.

6. Scott D. Sagan, "The Origins of the Pacific War," *Journal of Interdisciplinary History*, XVIII (1988), 893–922.

7. Shumpei Okamoto, *The Japanese Oligarchy and the Russo-Japanese War* (New York, 1970), 101.

8. Processes which seem highly rational may yield less accurate perceptions than those which are more intuitive. See Kenneth Hammond, "A Theoretically Based Review of Theory and Research in Judgment and Decision Making," unpub. ms. (Boulder, 1986).

9. Quoted in Donald Watt, "British Intelligence and the Coming of the Second World War in Europe," in May (ed.), *Knowing One's Enemies*, 268.

10. Daryl Bem, "Self-Perception Theory," in Leonard Berkowitz (ed.), *Advances in Experimental Social Psychology* (New York, 1972), VI, 1–62. For an application to foreign policy, see Deborah Larson, *The Origins of Containment* (Princeton, 1985).

11. In politics, not only are situations rarely repeated, but the meaning of probabilistic judgments is not entirely clear. Are these statements merely indications of the degree to which the person feels he lacks important facts or an understanding of significant relationships? Or do they reflect the belief that politics is inherently uncertain and that, if somehow the same situation was repeated in all its details, behavior might be different on different occasions?

12. See Ole Holsti, Robert North, and Richard Brody, "Perception and Action in the 1914 Crisis," in J. David Singer (ed.), *Quantitative International Politics* (New York, 1968), 123–158.

13. May, "Conclusions," 504. For a more detailed discussion of May's argument, see Jervis, "Intelligence and Foreign Policy," *International Security*, XI (1986/87), 141–61.

14. This continuing debate also underlies the difficulty of determining when perceptions are misperceptions. Indeed, when we contemplate the task of avoiding World War III, it is disheartening to note that we cannot even be sure how the participants could have avoided World War I.

15. See May (ed.), *Knowing One's Enemies*, 237–301, 504–519.

16. This belief may not have been as foolish as it appears in retrospect. While France was falling, the British Cabinet spent two days debating whether to open talks with Germany. See Philip M. H. Bell, *A Certain Eventuality* (Farnborough, Eng., 1974), 31–54; Martin Gilbert, *Winston Churchill, VI: Finest Hour, 1939–1941* (London, 1983), 402–425. Given the situation Britain faced, seeking peace might have been reasonable. See David Reynolds, "Churchill and the British 'Decision' to Fight on in 1940: Right Policy, Wrong Reason," in Richard Langhorne (ed.), *Diplomacy and Intelligence during the Second World War* (Cambridge, 1985), 147–67.

17. The role of states which are not involved in the first stages of combat is stressed by Blainey, *Causes of War*, 57–67, 228–242; Bruce Bueno de Mesquita, *The War Trap* (New Haven, 1981).

18. Arthur Stein, "When Misperception Matters," *World Politics*, XXXIV (1982), 505–526.

19. Oddly enough, almost the only view of Hitler which indicates that he could have been deterred is that of Taylor, who paints a picture of the German leader as an opportunist, inadvertently misled by the acquiescence of Western statesmen (Alan J. P. Taylor, *The Origins of the Second World War* [New York, 1961]).

20. Jervis, *Perception and Misperception*, 58–113.

21. Robert W. Seton-Watson, *Disraeli, Gladstone, and the Eastern Question* (New York, 1972), 127, 192. It is interesting to note that during and after World War II the Soviet Union did have high-level spies who had good access to American thinking. The more recent penetrations of the American Embassy in Moscow may have duplicated this feat. The results may not have been entirely deleterious—both the United States and the Soviet Union may gain if the latter has convincing evidence that the former is driven by defensive motivations.

22. For a further discussion, see Jervis, *Perception and Misperception*, 109–113; *idem*, "Deterrence Theory Revisited," *World Politics*, XXXI (1979), 289–324; Richard Ned Lebow, "The Deterrence Deadlock: Is There a Way Out?" in Jervis, Lebow, and Janice Stein, *Psychology and Deterrence* (Baltimore, 1985), 180–202; Alexander George, David Hall, and William Simons, *Coercive Diplomacy* (Boston, 1971), 100–103, 238–244; George and Richard Smoke, *Deterrence in American Foreign Policy* (New York, 1974), 588–613; Glenn Snyder and Paul Diesing, *Conflict among Nations* (Princeton, 1977), 489–493.

23. Patrice Louis-René Higonnet, "The Origins of the Seven Years' War," *Journal of Modern History*, XL (1968), 57–58. See also Smoke, *War* (Cambridge, Mass., 1977), 195–236.

24. Blainey, *Causes of War*, 133–134.

25. One of the psychological mechanisms at work is cognitive dissonance. In order to justify the effort they are expending to reach a goal, people exaggerate its value.

26. Department of State, *Foreign Relations of the United States, 1952–54. XV: Korea* (Washington, D.C., 1984), Pt. 1, 888.

27. Daniel Yergin, " 'Scoop' Jackson Goes for Broke," *Atlantic Monthly*, CCXXIII (1974), 82. Perle, then an aide to Sen. Henry Jackson, is describing the latter's

views, but what he says seems to apply to his own beliefs as well. Acheson's views are presented in John Spanier, *The Truman-MacArthur Controversy and the Korean War* (New York, 1965), 97, Allen Whiting, *China Crosses the Yalu* (Stanford, 1968), 151. (Similar examples are discussed in Jervis, *Perception and Misperception,* 67–76.) The case of Israel in 1973 is analyzed in Janice Stein, "Calculation, Miscalculation, and Conventional Deterrence, 11. The View from Jerusalem," in Jervis, Lebow, and Stein, *Psychology and Deterrence,* 60–88. See also Richard Betts, *Surprise Attack* (Washington, D.C., 1982).

28. Raymond Garthoff, *Detente and Confrontation* (Washington, D.C., 1985), 1976.

29. See the classic essay by Holsti, "Cognitive Dynamics and Images of the Enemy: Dulles and Russia," in David Finlay, Holsti, and Richard Fagen, *Enemies in Politics* (Chicago, 1967), 25–96. Michael Sullivan, *International Relations: Theories and Evidence* (Englewood Cliffs, N.J., 1976), 45–46, questions the links between Dulles' beliefs and American behavior.

30. Gromyko is quoted in Galia Golan, *Yom Kippur and After* (London, 1977), 68. The treatment of the 1973 war is a good litmus test for one's views on detente: compare, for example, the discussions in Harry Gelman, *The Brezhnev Politburo and the Decline of Detente* (Ithaca, 1984), 135–139, 152–156; Garthoff, *Detente and Confrontation;* George, *Managing U.S.-Soviet Rivalry* (Boulder, 1983), 139–154.

31. Larson, "Crisis Prevention and the Austrian State Treaty," *International Organization,* XXXXI (1987), 27–60.

32. In fact, statesmen realize that large-scale conflict can result from confrontations even if they do not desire it. They then both fear and employ what Schelling calls "threats that leave something to chance" (Thomas Schelling, *Strategy of Conflict* [Cambridge, Mass., 1960], 187–203). Under current circumstances, control may be hard to maintain in a crisis if the decision-makers delegate the authority to fire nuclear weapons to local commanders.

33. *Ibid.,* 119–161.

34. May, *Imperial Democracy* (New York, 1961), 161. For an extended discussion of this problem, see Jervis, *Perception and Misperception,* 203–316; *idem,* "Deterrence Theory Revisited," 305–310. For a discussion of this problem in the context of the limited use of nuclear weapons, see Schelling, "The Role of War Games and Exercises," in Ashton Carter, John Steinbruner, and Charles Zraket (eds.), *Nuclear Operations and Command and Control* (Washington, D.C., 1987), 426–444.

35. The literature on these perceptual processes, which are a subcategory of what are known as "motivated biases" because of the important role played by affect, is large. The best starting place is Irving Janis and Leon Mann, *Decision Making* (New York, 1977). For applications to international politics, see Richard Cottam, *Foreign Policy Motivation* (Pittsburgh, 1977); Lebow, *Between Peace and War* (Baltimore, 1981); Jervis, "Foreign Policy Decision-Making: Recent Developments," *Political Psychology,* II (1980), 86–101; *idem,* Lebow, and Stein, *Psychology and Deterrence.* For earlier versions of the argument, see Holsti, North, and Brody, "Perception and Action," 123–158; Snyder, *Deterrence and Defense* (Princeton, 1961), 26–27. For a rebuttal to some points, see Sagan, "Origins of the Pacific War," 893–922. John Orme, "Deterrence Failures: A Second Look," *International Security,* XI (1987), 96–124. For further discussion of the tendency to avoid trade-offs, see Jervis, *Perception and Misperception.*

Quester points to the strategic value of commitment in making the other side retreat (Quester, "Crisis and the Unexpected," *Journal of Interdisciplinary History,* XVIII [1988], 701–719). He is correct, but such behavior can still lead to war if the other side does not gauge the situation accurately.

36. For further discussion of situations that could lead to World War III, see Warner Schilling et al., *American Arms and a Changing Europe* (New York, 1973), 172–174, and George, "Problems of Crisis Management and Crisis Avoidance in U.S.-Soviet Relations," unpub. paper (Oslo, 1985). C^3 is discussed by Desmond Ball, *Can Nuclear War Be Controlled?* (London, 1981); Paul Bracken, *The Command and Control of Nuclear Forces* (New Haven, 1983); Bruce Blair, *Strategic Command and Control* (Washington, D.C., 1985); Carter, Steinbruner, and Zraket (eds.), *Nuclear Operations.* The resulting dangers are analyzed in Graham Allison, Albert Carnesale, and Joseph Nye (eds.), *Hawks, Doves, and Owls* (New York, 1985). The fundamental argument about "the reciprocal fear of surprise attack" was developed by Schelling in *Strategy of Conflict,* 207–229.

37. For further discussion of some of the arguments being made here, see Jervis, *The Illogic of American Nuclear Strategy* (Ithaca, 1984); Lebow, *Nuclear Crisis Management* (Ithaca, 1987); Jervis, "Psychological Aspects of Crisis Instability," in *idem, The Implications of the Nuclear Revolution* (forthcoming); *idem, The Symbolic Nature of Nuclear Politics* (Urbana, 1987).

38. For a discussion of the operation of such factors in previous cases, see Jack Snyder, *The Ideology of the Offensive* (Ithaca, 1984); Barry Posen, *The Sources of Military Doctrine* (Ithaca, 1984). See also Sagan, "1914 Revisited: Allies, Offense, and Instability," *International Security,* XI (1986), 151–176, and the exchange between Sagan and Jack Snyder, "The Origins of Offense and the Consequences of Counterforce," in *International Security,* XI (1986/87), 187–198.

39. This discussion is drawn from Daniel Kahneman and Amos Tversky, "Prospect Theory. An Analysis of Decision Under Risk," *Econometrica,* LVII (1979), 263–291; Tversky and Kahneman, "The Framing of Decisions and the Psychology of Choice," *Science,* CCXI (1981), 453–458; Kahneman and Tversky, "Choices, Values, and Frames," *American Psychologist,* XXXIX (1984), 341–350; Tversky and Kahneman, "Rational Choice and the Framing of Decisions," *Journal of Business,* LIX (1986), S251–S278.

40. See George and Smoke, *Deterrence,* 536–540.

41. States may try to gain the bargaining advantages that come from seeming to be irrational, as Quester reminds us ("Crises and the Unexpected," 703–706).

48

JOHN LEWIS GADDIS

THE LONG PEACE: ELEMENTS OF STABILITY IN THE POSTWAR INTERNATIONAL SYSTEM

SYSTEMS THEORY AND INTERNATIONAL STABILITY

Anyone attempting to understand why there has been no third world war confronts a problem not unlike that of Sherlock Holmes and the dog that did not bark in the night: how does one account for something that did not happen? How does one explain why the great conflict between the United States and the Soviet Union, which by all past standards of historical experience should have developed by now, has not in fact done so? The question involves certain methodological difficulties, to be sure: it is always easier to account for what did happen than what did not. But there is also a curious bias among students of international relations that reinforces this tendency: "For every thousand pages published on the causes of wars," Geoffrey Blainey has commented, "there is less than one page directly on the causes of peace."[1] Even the discipline of "peace studies" suffers from this disproportion: it has given far more attention to the question of what we must do to avoid the apocalypse than it has to the equally interesting question of why, given all the opportunities, it has not happened so far.

It might be easier to deal with this question if the work that has been done on the causes of war had produced something approximating a consensus on why wars develop: we could then apply that analysis to the post-1945 period and see what it is that has been different about it. But, in fact, these studies are not much help. Historians, political scientists, economists, sociologists, statisticians, even meteorologists, have wrestled for years with the question of what causes wars, and yet the most recent review of that literature concludes that "our understanding of war remains at an elementary level. No widely accepted theory of the causes of war exists and little agreement has emerged on the methodology through which these causes might be discovered."[2]

Nor has the comparative work that has been done on international systems shed much more light on the matter. The difficulty here is that our actual

SOURCE: Reprinted from *International Security*, Vol. 10, No. 4 (Spring, 1986), The MIT Press, pp. 99–105, 108–114, 120–128, 131–132, 142. Reprinted by permission of the author.

experience is limited to the operations of a single system—the balance of power system—operating either within the "multipolar" configuration that characterized international politics until World War II, or the "bipolar" configuration that has characterized them since. Alternative systems remain abstract conceptualizations in the minds of theorists, and are of little use in advancing our knowledge of how wars in the real world do or do not occur.[3]

But "systems theory" itself is something else again: here one can find a useful point of departure for thinking about the nature of international relations since 1945. An "international system" exists, political scientists tell us, when two conditions are met: first, interconnections exist between units within the system, so that changes in some parts of it produce changes in other parts as well; and, second, the collective behavior of the system as a whole differs from the expectations and priorities of the individual units that make it up.[4] Certainly demonstrating the "interconnectedness" of post-World War II international relations is not difficult: one of its most prominent characteristics has been the tendency of major powers to assume that little if anything can happen in the world without in some way enhancing or detracting from their own immediate interests.[5] Nor has the collective behavior of nations corresponded to their individual expectations: the very fact that the interim arrangements of 1945 have remained largely intact for four decades would have astonished—and quite possibly appalled—the statesmen who cobbled them together in the hectic months that followed the surrender of Germany and Japan.[6]

A particularly valuable feature of systems theory is that it provides criteria for differentiating between stable and unstable political configurations: these can help to account for the fact that some international systems outlast others. Karl Deutsch and J. David Singer have defined "stability" as "the probability that the system retains all of its essential characteristics: that no single nation becomes dominant; that most of its members continue to survive; and that large-scale war does not occur." It is characteristic of such a system, Deutsch and Singer add, that it has the capacity for self-regulation: the ability to counteract stimuli that would otherwise threaten its survival, much as the automatic pilot on an airplane or the governor on a steam engine would do. "Self-regulating" systems are very different from what they call "self-aggravating" systems, situations that get out of control, like forest fires, drug addiction, runaway inflation, nuclear fission, and of course, although they themselves do not cite the example, all-out war.[7] Self-regulating mechanisms are most likely to function, in turn, when there exists some fundamental agreement among major states within the system on the objectives they are seeking to uphold by participating in it, when the structure of the system reflects the way in which power is distributed among its respective members, and when agreed-upon procedures exist for resolving differences among them.[8]

Does the post-World War II international system fit these criteria for "stability"? Certainly its most basic characteristic—bipolarity—remains intact, in that the gap between the world's two greatest military powers and their nearest rivals is not substantially different from what it was forty years ago.[9] At the same time, neither the Soviet Union nor the United States nor anyone else has been able wholly to dominate that system; the nations most active within it in 1945 are for the most part still active today. And of course the most convincing argument for "stability" is that, so far at least, World War III has not occurred. On the surface, then, the concept of a "stable" international system makes sense as a way of understanding the experience through which we have lived these past forty years.

But what have been the self-regulating mechanisms? How has an environment been created in which they are able to function? In what way do those mechanisms—and the environment in which they function—resemble or differ from the configuration of other international systems, both stable and unstable, in modern history? What circumstances exist that might impair their operation, transforming self-regulation into self-aggravation? These are questions that have not received the attention they deserve from students of the history and politics of the postwar era. What follows is a series of speculations—they can hardly be more than that, given present knowledge—upon these issues, the importance of which hardly needs to be stressed.

I should like to emphasize, though, that this essay's concentration on the way the world is and has been is not intended to excuse or to justify our current predicament. Nor is it meant to preclude the possibility of moving ultimately toward something better. We can all conceive of international systems that combine stability with greater justice and less risk than the present one does, and we ought to continue to think about these things. But short of war, which no one wants, change in international relations tends to be gradual and evolutionary. It does not happen overnight. That means that alternative systems, if they ever develop, probably will not be total rejections of the existing system, but rather variations proceeding from it. All the more reason, then, to try to understand the system we have, to try to distinguish its stabilizing from its destabilizing characteristics, and to try to reinforce the former as a basis from which we might, in time and with luck, do better.

THE STRUCTURAL ELEMENTS OF STABILITY

BIPOLARITY

Any such investigation should begin by distinguishing the structure of the international system in question from the behavior of the nations that make it up.[10] The reason for this is simple: behavior alone will not ensure stability if the structural prerequisites for it are absent, but structure can under certain circumstances impose stability even when its behavioral prerequisites are unpromising.[11] . . .

Now, bipolarity may seem to many today—as it did forty years ago—an awkward and dangerous way to organize world politics.[12] Simple geometric logic would suggest that a system resting upon three or more points of support would be more stable than one resting upon two. But politics is not geometry: the passage of time and the accumulation of experience has made clear certain structural elements of stability in the bipolar system of international relations that were not present in the multipolar systems that preceded it:

(1) The postwar bipolar system realistically reflected the facts of where military power resided at the end of World War II[13]—and where it still does today, for that matter. In this sense, it differed markedly from the settlement of 1919, which made so little effort to accommodate the interests of Germany and Soviet Russia. It is true that in other categories of power—notably the economic—states have since arisen capable of challenging or even surpassing the Soviet Union and the United States in the production of certain specific commodities. But as the *political* position of nations like West Germany, Brazil, Japan, South Korea, Taiwan, and Hong Kong suggests, the ability to make video recorders, motorcycles, even automobiles and steel efficiently has yet to translate into anything approaching the capacity of Washington or Moscow to shape events in the world as a whole.

(2) The post-1945 bipolar structure was a simple one that did not require sophisticated leadership to maintain it. The great multipolar systems of the 19th century collapsed in large part because of their intricacy: they required a Metternich or a Bismarck to hold them together, and when statesmen of that calibre were no longer available, they tended to come apart.[14] Neither the Soviet nor the American political systems have been geared to identifying statesmen of comparable prowess and entrusting them with responsibility; demonstrated skill in the conduct of foreign policy has hardly been a major prerequisite for leadership in either country. And yet, a bipolar structure of international relations—because of the inescapably high stakes involved for its two major actors—tends, regardless of the personalities involved, to induce in them a sense of caution and restraint, and to discourage irresponsibility. "It is not," Kenneth Waltz notes, "that one entertains the utopian hope that all future American and Russian rulers will combine in their persons . . . nearly perfect virtues, but rather that the pressures of a bipolar world strongly encourage them to act internationally in ways better than their characters may lead one to expect."[15]

(3) Because of its relatively simple structure, alliances in this bipolar system have tended to be more stable than they had been in the 19th century and in the 1919–1939 period. It is striking to consider that the North Atlantic Treaty Organization has now equaled in longevity the most durable of the pre-World War I alliances, that between Germany and Austria-Hungary; it has lasted almost twice as long as the Franco-Russian alliance, and certainly much longer than any of the tenuous alignments of the interwar period. Its principal rival, the Warsaw Treaty Organization, has been in existence for almost as long. The reason for this is simple: alliances, in the end, are the product of insecurity;[16] so long as the Soviet Union and the United States each remain for the other and for their respective clients the major source of insecurity in the world, neither superpower encounters very much difficulty in

maintaining its alliances. In a multipolar system, sources of insecurity can vary in much more complicated ways; hence it is not surprising to find alliances shifting to accommodate these variations.[17]

(4) At the same time, though, and probably because of the overall stability of the basic alliance systems, defections from both the American and Soviet coalitions—China, Cuba, Vietnam, Iran, and Nicaragua, in the case of the Americans; Yugoslavia, Albania, Egypt, Somalia, and China again in the case of the Russians—have been tolerated without the major disruptions that might have attended such changes in a more delicately balanced multipolar system. The fact that a state the size of China was able to reverse its alignment twice during the Cold War without any more dramatic effect upon the position of the superpowers says something about the stability bipolarity brings; compare this record with the impact, prior to 1914, of such apparently minor episodes as Austria's annexation of Bosnia and Herzegovina, or the question of who was to control Morocco. It is a curious consequence of bipolarity that although alliances are more durable than in a multipolar system, defections are at the same time more tolerable.[18]

In short, without anyone's having designed it, and without any attempt whatever to consider the requirements of justice, the nations of the postwar era lucked into a system of international relations that, because it has been based upon realities of power, has served the cause of order—if not justice—better than one might have expected.

INDEPENDENCE, NOT INTERDEPENDENCE

But if the structure of bipolarity in itself encouraged stability, so too did certain inherent characteristics of the bilateral Soviet-American relationship. . . .

It has long been an assumption of classical liberalism that the more extensive the contacts that take place between nations, the greater are the chances for peace. Economic interdependence, it has been argued, makes war unlikely because nations who have come to rely upon one another for vital commodities cannot afford it. Cultural exchange, it has been suggested, causes peoples to become more sensitive to each others' concerns, and hence reduces the likelihood of misunderstandings. "People to people" contacts, it has been assumed, make it possible for nations to "know" one another better; the danger of war between them is, as a result, correspondingly reduced.[19]

These are pleasant things to believe, but there is remarkably little historical evidence to validate them. As Kenneth Waltz has pointed out, "the fiercest civil wars and the bloodiest international ones are fought within arenas populated by highly similar people whose affairs are closely knit."[20] Consider, as examples, the costliest military conflicts of the past century and a half, using the statistics conveniently available now through the University of Michigan "Correlates of War" project: of the ten bloodiest interstate wars, every one of them grew out of conflicts between countries that either directly adjoined one another, or were involved actively in trade with one another.[21] Certainly economic interdependence did little to prevent Germany, France, Britain, Russia, and Austria-Hungary from going to war in 1914; nor did the fact that the United States was Japan's largest trading partner deter that country from attacking Pearl Harbor in 1941. Since 1945, there have been more civil wars than interstate wars;[22] that fact alone should be sufficient to call into question the proposition that interdependence necessarily breeds peace.

The Russian-American relationship, to a remarkable degree for two nations so extensively involved with the rest of the world, has been one of mutual independence. The simple fact that the two countries occupy opposite sides of the earth has had something to do with this: geographical remoteness from one another has provided little opportunity for the emergence of irredentist grievances comparable in importance to historic disputes over, say, Alsace-Lorraine, or the Polish Corridor, or the West Bank, the Gaza Strip, and Jerusalem. In the few areas where Soviet and American forces—or their proxies—have come into direct contact, they have erected artificial barriers like the Korean demilitarized zone, or the Berlin Wall, perhaps in unconscious recognition of an American poet's rather chilly precept that "good fences make good neighbors."

Nor have the two nations been economically dependent upon one another in any critical way. Certainly the United States requires nothing in the form of imports from the Soviet Union that it cannot obtain elsewhere. The situation is different for the Russians, to be sure, but even though the Soviet Union imports large quantities of food from the United States—and would like to import advanced technology as well—it is far from being wholly dependent upon these items, as the failure of recent attempts to change Soviet behavior by denying them has shown. The relative invulnerability of Russians and Americans to one another in the economic sphere may be frustrating to their respective policymakers, but it is probably fortunate, from the standpoint of international stability, that the two most powerful nations in the world are also its two most self-sufficient.[23] . . .

It may well be, then, that the extent to which the Soviet Union and the United States have been independent of one another rather than interdependent—the fact that there have been so few points of economic leverage available to each, the fact that two such dissimilar people have had so few opportunities for interaction—has in itself constituted a structural support for stability in relations between the two countries, whatever their respective governments have actually done. . . .

THE BEHAVIORAL ELEMENTS OF STABILITY

NUCLEAR WEAPONS

Stability in international systems is only partly a function of structure, though; it depends as well upon the conscious behavior of the nations that make them up. Even if the World War II settlement had corresponded to the distribution of power in the world, even if the Russian-American relationship had been one of minimal interdependence, even if domestic constraints had not created difficulties, stability in the postwar era still might not have resulted if there had been, among either of the dominant powers in the system, the same willingness to risk war that has existed at other times in the past. . . .

For whatever reason, it has to be acknowledged that the statesmen of the post-1945 superpowers have, compared to their predecessors, been exceedingly cautious in risking war with one another.[24] In order to see this point, one need only run down the list of crises in Soviet-American relations since the end of World War II: Iran, 1946; Greece, 1947; Berlin and Czechoslovakia, 1948; Korea, 1950; the East Berlin riots, 1953; the Hungarian uprising, 1956; Berlin again, 1958–59; the U-2 incident, 1960; Berlin again, 1961; the Cuban missile crisis, 1962; Czechoslovakia again, 1968; the Yom Kippur war, 1973; Afghanistan, 1979; Poland, 1981; the Korean airliner incident, 1983—one need only run down this list to see how many occasions there have been in relations between Washington and Moscow that in almost any other age, and among almost any other antagonists, would sooner or later have produced war.

That they have not cannot be chalked up to the invariably pacific temperament of the nations involved: the United States participated in eight international wars involving a thousand or more battlefield deaths between 1815 and 1980; Russia participated in nineteen.[25] Nor can this restraint be attributed to any unusual qualities of leadership on either side: the vision and competency of postwar Soviet and American statesmen does not appear to have differed greatly from that of their predecessors. Nor does weariness growing out of participation in two world wars fully explain this unwillingness to resort to arms in their dealings with one another: during the postwar era both nations have employed force against third parties—in the case of the United States in Korea and Vietnam; in the case of the Soviet Union in Afghanistan— for protracted periods of time, and at great cost.

It seems inescapable that what has really made the difference in inducing this unaccustomed caution has been the workings of the nuclear deterrent.[26] Consider, for a moment, what the effect of this mechanism would be on a statesman from either superpower who might be contemplating war. In the past, the horrors and the costs of wars could be forgotten with the passage of time. Generations like the one of 1914 had little sense of what the Napoleonic Wars—or even the American Civil War—had revealed about the brutality, expense, and duration of military conflict. But the existence of nuclear weapons— and, more to the point, the fact that we have direct evidence of what they can do when used against human beings[27]—has given this generation a painfully vivid awareness of the realities of war that no previous generation has had. It is difficult, given this awareness, to produce the optimism that historical experience tells us prepares the way for war; pessimism, it appears, is a permanent accompaniment to our thinking about war, and that, as Blainey reminds us, is a cause of peace.

That same pessimism has provided the superpowers with powerful inducements to control crises resulting from the risk-taking of third parties. It is worth recalling that World War I grew out of the unsuccessful management of a situation neither created nor desired by any of the major actors in the international system. There were simply no mechanisms to put a lid on escalation: to force each nation to balance the short-term temptation to exploit opportunities against the long-term danger that things might get out of hand.[28] The nuclear deterrent provides that mechanism today, and as a result the United States and the Soviet Union have successfully managed a whole series of crises—most notably in the Middle East—that grew out of the actions of neither but that could have involved them both.

None of this is to say, of course, that war cannot occur: if the study of history reveals anything at all it is that one ought to expect, sooner or later, the unexpected. Nor is it to say that the nuclear deterrent could not function equally well with half, or a fourth, or even an eighth of the nuclear weapons now in the arsenals of the superpowers. Nor is it intended to deprecate the importance of refraining from steps that might destabilize the existing stalemate, whether through the search for technological breakthroughs that might provide a decisive edge over the other side, or through so mechanical a duplication of what the other side has that one fails to take into account one's own probably quite different security requirements, or through strategies that rely upon the first use of nuclear weapons in the interest of achieving economy, forgetting the far more fundamental systemic interest in maintaining the tradition, dating back four decades now, of never actually employing these weapons for military purposes.

I am suggesting, though, that the development of nuclear weapons has had, on balance, a stabilizing effect on the postwar international system. They have served to discourage the process of escalation that has, in other eras, too casually led to war. They have had a sobering effect upon a whole range of statesmen of varying degrees of responsibility and capability. They have forced national leaders, every day, to confront the reality of what war is really like, indeed to confront the prospect of their own mortality, and that, for those who seek ways to avoid war, is no bad thing.

The Reconnaissance Revolution

But although nuclear deterrence is the most important behavioral mechanism that has sustained the post-World War II international system, it is by no means the only one. Indeed, the very technology that has made it possible to deliver nuclear weapons anywhere on the face of the earth has functioned also to lower greatly the danger of surprise attack, thereby supplementing the self-regulating features of deterrence with the assurance that comes from knowing a great deal more than in the past about adversary capabilities. I refer here to what might be called the "reconnaissance revolution," a development that may well rival in importance the "nuclear revolution" that preceded it, but one that rarely gets the attention it deserves.

. . . Nations tend to start wars on the basis of calculated assessments that they have the power to prevail. But it was suggested as well that they have often been wrong about this: they either have failed to anticipate the nature and the costs of war itself, or they have misjudged the intentions and the capabilities of the adversary they have chosen to confront.[29] . . . But both sides are able—and indeed have been able for at least two decades—to evaluate each other's *capabilities* to a degree that is totally unprecedented in the history of relations between great powers.

What has made this possible, of course, has been the development of the reconnaissance satellite, a device that if rumors are correct allows the reading of automobile license plates or newspaper headlines from a hundred or more miles out in space, together with the equally important custom that has evolved between the superpowers of allowing these objects to pass unhindered over their territories.[30] The effect has been to give each side a far more accurate view of the other's military capabilities—and, to some degree, economic capabilities as well—than could have been provided by an entire phalanx of the best spies in the long history of espionage. The resulting intelligence does not rule out altogether the possibility of surprise attack, but it does render it far less likely, at least as far as the superpowers are concerned. And that is no small matter, if one considers the number of wars in history—from the Trojan War down through Pearl Harbor—in the origins of which deception played a major role.[31] . . .

IDEOLOGICAL MODERATION

The relationship between the Soviet Union and the United States has not been free from ideological rivalries: it could be argued, in fact, that these are among the most ideological nations on the face of the earth.[32] Certainly their respective ideologies could hardly have been more antithetical, given the self-proclaimed intention of one to overthrow the other.[33] And yet, since their emergence as superpowers, both nations have demonstrated an impressive capacity to subordinate antagonistic ideological interests to a common goal of preserving international order. The reasons for this are worth examining.

If there were ever a moment at which the priorities *of* order overcame those of ideology, it would appear to be the point at which Soviet leaders decided that war would no longer advance the cause of revolution. That clearly had not been Lenin's position: international conflict, for him, was good or evil according to whether it accelerated or retarded the demise of capitalism.[34] Stalin's attitude on this issue was more ambivalent: he encouraged talk of an "inevitable conflict" between the "two camps" of communism and capitalism in the years immediately following World War II, but he also appears shortly before his death to have anticipated the concept of "peaceful coexistence."[35] It was left to Georgii Malenkov to admit publicly, shortly after Stalin's death, that a nuclear war would mean "the destruction of world civilization"; Nikita Khrushchev subsequently refined this idea (which he had initially condemned) into the proposition that the interests of world revolution, as well as those of the Soviet state, would be better served by working within the existing international order than by trying to overthrow it.[36] . . .

The effect was to transform a state which, if ideology alone had governed, should have sought a complete restructuring of the existing international system, into one for whom that system now seemed to have definite benefits, within which it now sought to function, and for whom the goal of overthrowing capitalism had been postponed to some vague and indefinite point in the future.[37] Without this moderation of ideological objectives, it is difficult to see how the stability that has characterized great power relations since the end of World War II could have been possible. . . .

American officials at no point during the history of the Cold War seriously contemplated, as a deliberate political objective, the elimination of the Soviet Union as a major force in world affairs. By the mid-1950s, it is true, war plans had been devised that, if executed, would have quite indiscriminately annihilated not only the Soviet Union but several of its communist and non-communist neighbors as well.[38] What is significant about those plans, though, is that they reflected the organizational convenience of the military services charged with implementing them, not any conscious policy decisions at the top. Both Eisenhower and Kennedy were appalled on learning of them; both considered them ecologically as well as strategically impossible; and during the Kennedy administration steps were initiated to devise strategies that would leave open the possibility of a surviving political entity in Russia even in the extremity of nuclear war.[39]

All of this would appear to confirm, then, the proposition that systemic interests tend to take precedence over ideological interests.[40] Both the Soviet ideological aversion to capitalism and the American ideological aversion to totalitarianism could have produced policies—and indeed had produced policies in the past—aimed at the complete overthrow of their respective adversaries. That such ideological impulses could be muted to the extent they have been during the past four decades testifies to the stake both Washington and Moscow have developed in preserving the existing international system: the moderation of ideologies must be considered, then, along with nuclear deterrence and reconnaissance, as a major self-regulating mechanism of postwar politics.

The Cold War, with all of its rivalries, anxieties, and unquestionable dangers, has produced the longest period of stability in relations among the great powers that the world has known in this century; it now compares favorably as well with some of the longest periods of great power stability in all of modern history. We may argue among ourselves as to whether or not we can legitimately call this "peace": it is not, I daresay, what most of us have in mind when we use that term. But I am not at all certain that the contemporaries of Metternich or Bismarck would have regarded their eras as "peaceful" either, even though historians looking back on those eras today clearly do.

Who is to say, therefore, how the historians of the year 2086—if there are any left by then—will look back on us? Is it not at least plausible that they will see our era, not as "the Cold War" at all, but rather, like those ages of Metternich and Bismarck, as a rare and fondly remembered "Long Peace"? Wishful thinking? Speculation through a rose-tinted word processor? Perhaps. But would it not behoove us to give at least as much attention to the question of how this might happen—to the elements in the contemporary international system that might make it happen—as we do to the fear that it may not?

NOTES

1. Geoffrey Blainey, *The Causes of War* (London: Macmillan, 1973), p. 3.
2. Jack S. Levy, *War in the Modern Great Power System, 1495–1975* (Lexington: University Press of Kentucky, 1983), p. 1. Other standard works on this subject, in addition to Blainey, cited above, include: Lewis F. Richardson, *Arms and Insecurity: A Mathematical Study of the Causes and Origins of War* (Pittsburgh: Quadrangle, 1960); Quincy Wright, *A Study of War,* 2nd ed. (Chicago: University of Chicago Press, 1965); Kenneth N. Waltz, *Man, the State and War: A Theoretical Analysis* (New York: Columbia University Press, 1959); Kenneth Boulding, *Conflict and Defense: A General Theory* (New York: Harper and Row, 1962); Raymond Aron, *Peace and War: A Theory of International Relations,* trans. Richard Howard and Annette Baker Fox (New York: Doubleday, 1966); Robert Gilpin, *War and Change in World Politics* (New York: Cambridge University Press, 1981); Melvin Small and J. David Singer, *Resort to Arms: International and Civil Wars, 1816–1980* (Beverly Hills, Calif.: Sage Publications, 1982); and Michael Howard, *The Causes of Wars,* 2nd ed. (Cambridge, Mass.: Harvard University Press, 1984). A valuable overview of conflicting explanations is Keith L. Nelson and Spencer C. Olin, Jr., *Why War? Ideology, Theory and History* (Berkeley: University of California Press, 1979).
3. The classic example of such abstract conceptualization is Morton A. Kaplan, *System and Process in International Politics* (New York: John Wiley, 1957). For the argument that 1945 marks the transition from a "multipolar" to a "bipolar" international system, see Glenn H. Snyder and Paul Diesing, *Conflict Among Nations: Bargaining, Decision Making, and System Structure in International Crises* (Princeton, N.J.: Princeton University Press, 1977), pp. 419–20; and Kenneth Waltz, *Theory of International Politics* (Reading, Mass.: Addison-Wesley, 1979), pp. 161–163. One can, of course, question whether the postwar international system constitutes true "bipolarity." Peter H. Beckman, for example, provides an elaborate set of indices demonstrating the asymmetrical nature of American and Soviet power after 1945 in his *World Politics in the Twentieth Century* (Englewood Cliffs, N.J.: Prentice Hall, 1984), pp. 207–209, 235–237, 282–285. But such retrospective judgments neglect the perceptions of policymakers *at the time,* who clearly saw their world as bipolar and frequently commented on the phenomenon. See, for example, David S. McLellan, *Dean Acheson:The State Department Years* (New York: Dodd, Mead, 1976), p. 116; and, for Soviet "two camp" theory, William Taubman, *Stalin's American Policy: From Entente to Detente to Cold War* (New York: Norton, 1982), pp. 176–178.
4. I have followed here the definition of Robert Jervis, "Systems Theories and Diplomatic History," in Paul Gordon Lauren, ed., *Diplomacy: New Approaches in History, Theory, and Policy* (New York: Free Press, 1979), p. 212. For a more rigorous discussion of the requirements of systems theory, and a critique of some

of its major practitioners, see Waltz, *Theory of International Politics*, pp. 38–78. Akira Iriye is one of the few historians who have sought to apply systems theory to the study of international relations. See his *After Imperialism: The Search for a New Order in the Far East, 1921–1931* (Cambridge: Harvard University Press, 1965); and *The Cold War in Asia: A Historical Introduction* (Englewood Cliffs, N.J.: Prentice Hall, 1974).

5. See, on this point, Robert Jervis, *Perception and Misperception in International Politics* (Princeton, N.J.: Princeton University Press, 1976), pp. 58–62. Jervis points out that "almost by definition, a great power is more tightly connected to larger numbers of other states than is a small power. . . . Growing conflict or growing cooperation between Argentina and Chile would not affect Pakistan, but it would affect America and American policy toward those states. . . ." Jervis, "Systems Theories and Diplomatic History," p. 215.

6. "A future war with the Soviet Union," retiring career diplomat Joseph C. Grew commented in May 1945, "is as certain as anything in this world." Memorandum of May 19, 1945, quoted in Joseph C. Grew, *Turbulent Era: A Diplomatic Record of Forty Years, 1904–1945* (Boston: Houghton Mifflin, 1952), Vol. 2, p. 1446. For other early expressions of pessimism about the stability of the postwar international system, see Walter Lippmann, *The Cold War: A Study in U.S. Foreign Policy* (New York: Harper Brothers, 1947), pp. 26–28, 37–39, 60–62. "There is, after all, something to be explained—about perceptions as well as events—when so much that has been written has dismissed the new state system as no system at all but an unstable transition to something else." A. W. DePorte, *Europe Between the Super-Powers: The Enduring Balance* (New Haven: Yale University Press, 1979), p. 167.

7. Karl W. Deutsch and J. David Singer, "Multipolar Power Systems and International Stability," in James N. Rosenau, ed., *International Politics and Foreign Policy: A Reader in Research and Theory*, rev. ed. (New York: Free Press, 1969), pp. 315–317. Deutsch and Singer equate "self-regulation" with "negative feedback": "By negative—as distinguished from positive or amplifying— feedback, we refer to the phenomenon of self-correction: as stimuli in one particular direction increase, the system exhibits a decreasing response to those stimuli, and increasingly exhibits the tendencies that counteract them." See also Jervis, "Systems Theories and Diplomatic History," p. 220. For Kaplan's more abstract definition of stability, see his *System and Process in International Politics*, p. 8. The concept of "stability" in international systems owes a good deal to "functionalist" theory; see, on this point, Charles Reynolds, *Theory and Explanation in International Politics* (London: Martin Robertson, 1973), p. 30.

8. I have followed here, in slightly modified form, criteria provided in Gordon A. Craig and Alexander L. George, *Force and Statecraft: Diplomatic Problems of Our Time* (New York: Oxford University Press, 1983), p. x, a book that provides an excellent discussion of how international systems have evolved since the beginning of the 18th century. But see also Gilpin, *War and Change in World Politics*, pp. 50–105.

9. See, on this point, Waltz, *Theory of International Politics*, pp. 180–181; also DePorte, *Europe Between the Super-Powers*, p. 167.

10. Waltz, *Theory of International Politics*, pp. 73–78; Gilpin, *War and Change in World Politics*, pp. 85–88.

11. ". . . [S]tructure designates a set of constraining conditions. . . . [It] acts as a selector, but it cannot be seen, examined, and observed at work. . . . Because structures

select by rewarding some behaviors and punishing others, outcomes cannot be inferred from intentions and behaviors." Waltz, *Theory of International Politics,* pp. 73–74.

12. Among those who have emphasized the instability of bipolar systems are Morgenthau, *Politics Among Nations,* pp. 350–354; and Wright, *A Study of War,* pp. 763–764. See also Blainey, *The Causes of War,* pp. 110–111.

13. ". . . [W]hat *was* dominant in their consciousness," Michael Howard has written of the immediate post-World War II generation of statesmen, "was the impotence, almost one might say the irrelevance, of ethical aspirations in international politics in the absence of that factor to which so little attention had been devoted by their more eminent predecessors, to which indeed so many of them had been instinctively hostile—military power." Howard, *The Causes of War,* p. 55.

14. Henry Kissinger has written two classic accounts dealing with the importance of individual leadership in sustaining international systems. See his *A World Restored* (New York: Grosset and Dunlap, 1957), on Metternich; and, on Bismarck, "The White Revolutionary: Reflections on Bismarck," *Daedalus,* Vol. 97 (Summer 1968), pp. 888–924. For a somewhat different perspective on Bismarck's role, see George F. Kennan, *The Decline of Bismarck's European Order: Franco-Russian Relations, 1875–1890* (Princeton, N.J.: Princeton University Press, 1979), especially pp. 421–422.

15. Waltz, *Theory of International Politics,* p. 176. On the tendency of unstable systemic structures to induce irresponsible leadership, see Ludwig Dehio, *The Precarious Balance: Four Centuries of the European Power Struggle,* trans. Charles Fullman (New York: Alfred A. Knopf, 1962), pp. 257–258.

16. See, on this point, Roger V. Dingman, "Theories of, and Approaches to, Alliance Politics," in Lauren, ed., *Diplomacy,* pp. 242–247.

17. My argument here follows that of Snyder and Diesing, *Conflict Among Nations,* pp. 429–445.

18. Waltz, *Theory of International Politics,* pp. 167–169.

19. The argument is succinctly summarized in Nelson and Olin, *Why War?,* pp. 35–43. Geoffrey Blainey labels the idea "Manchesterism" and satirizes it wickedly: "If those gifted early prophets of the Manchester creed could have seen Chamberlain—during the Czech crisis of September 1938—board the aircraft that was to fly him to Bavaria to meet Hitler at short notice they would have hailed aviation as the latest messenger of peace. If they had known that he met Hitler without even his own German interpreter they would perhaps have wondered whether the conversation was in Esperanto or Volapuk. It seemed that every postage stamp, bilingual dictionary, railway timetable and trade fair, every peace congress, Olympic race, tourist brochure and international telegram that had ever existed, was gloriously justified when Mr. Chamberlain said from the window of number 10 Downing Street on 30 September 1938: 'I believe it is peace for our time.' In retrospect the outbreak of war a year later seems to mark the failure and the end of the policy of appeasement, but the policy survived. The first British air raids over Germany dropped leaflets." *The Causes of War,* p. 28.

20. Waltz, *Theory of International Politics,* p. 138. For Waltz's general argument against interdependence as a necessary cause of peace, see pp. 138–160.

21. Small and Singer, *Resort to Arms,* p. 102. The one questionable case is the Crimean War, which pitted Britain and France against Russia, but that conflict began as a dispute between Russia and Turkey.

22. Small and Singer identify 44 civil wars as having been fought between 1945 and 1980; this compares with 30 interstate and 12 "extra-systemic" wars during the same period. Ibid., pp. 92–95, 98–99, 229–232.

23. Soviet exports and imports as a percentage of gross national product ranged between 4 and 7 percent between 1955 and 1975; for the United States the comparable figures were 7–14 percent. This compares with figures of 33–52 percent for Great Britain, France, Germany, and Italy in the four years immediately preceding World War I, and figures of 19–41 percent for the same nations plus Japan for the period 1949–1976. Waltz, *Theory of International Politics*, pp. 141, 212.

24. See Michael Howard's observations on the absence of a "bellicist" mentality among the great powers in the postwar era, in his *The Causes of War*, pp. 271–273.

25. Small and Singer, *Resort to Arms*, pp. 167, 169.

26. For a persuasive elaboration of this argument, with an intriguing comparison of the post-1945 "nuclear" system to the post-1815 "Vienna" system, see Michael Mandelbaum, *The Nuclear Revolution: International Politics Before and After Hiroshima* (New York: Cambridge University Press, 1981), pp. 58–77; also Morgan, *Deterrence*, p. 208; Craig and George, *Force and Statecraft*, pp. 117–120; Howard, *The Causes of War*, pp. 22, 278–279. It is interesting to speculate as to whether Soviet-American bipolarity would have developed if nuclear weapons had never been invented. My own view—obviously unverifiable— is that it would have, because bipolarity resulted from the way in which World War II had been fought; the condition was already evident at the time of Hiroshima and Nagasaki. Whether bipolarity would have lasted as long as it has in the absence of nuclear weapons is another matter entirely, though: it seems at least plausible that these weapons have perpetuated bipolarity beyond what one might have expected its normal lifetime to be by minimizing superpower risk-taking while at the same time maintaining an apparently insurmountable power gradient between the superpowers and any potential military rivals.

27. See, on this point, Mandelbaum, *The Nuclear Revolution*, p. 109; also the discussion of the "crystal ball effect" in Albert Carnesale et al., *Living With Nuclear Weapons* (New York: Bantam, 1983), p. 44.

28. For a brief review of the literature on crisis management, together with an illustrative comparison of the July 1914 crisis with the Cuban missile crisis, see Ole R. Holsti, "Theories of Crisis Decision Making," in Lauren, ed., *Diplomacy*, pp. 99–136; also Craig and George, *Force and Statecraft*, pp. 205–219.

29. Gilpin, *War and Change in World Politics*, pp. 202–203. Geoffrey Blainey, citing an idea first proposed by the sociologist Georg Simmel, has suggested that, in the past, war was the only means by which nations could gain an exact knowledge of each others' capabilities. Blainey, *The Causes of War*, p. 118.

30. A useful up-to-date assessment of the technology is David Hafemeister, Joseph J. Romm, and Kosta Tsipis, "The Verification of Compliance with Arms-Control Agreements," *Scientific American*, March 1985, pp. 38–45. For the historical evolution of reconnaissance satellites, see Gerald M. Steinberg, *Satellite Reconnaissance: The Role of Informal Bargaining* (New York: Praeger, 1983), pp. 19–70; Paul B. Stares, *The Militarization of Space: U.S. Policy, 1945–1984* (Ithaca, N.Y.: Cornell University Press, 1985), pp. 30–33, 47–57, 62–71; also Walter A. McDougall, *The Heavens and the Earth: A Political History of the Space Age* (New York: Basic Books, 1985), pp. 177–226.

31. The most recent assessment, but one whose analysis does not take into account examples prior to 1940. is Richard K. Betts, *Surprise Attack: Lessons for Defense Planning* (Washington, D.C.: Brookings, 1982). See also, on the problem of assessing adversary intentions, Ernest R. May, ed., *Knowing One's Enemies: Intelligence Assessment Before the Two World Wars* (Princeton, N.J.: Princeton University Press, 1984).

32. See, on this point, Halle, *The Cold War as History,* pp. 157–160.

33. Adam B. Ulam, *Expansion and Coexistence: The History of Soviet Foreign Policy, 1917–73,* 2nd ed. (New York: Praeger, 1974), pp. 130–131.

34. See, on this point, E. H. Carr, *The Bolshevik Revolution, 1917–1923* (New York: Macmillan, 1951–1953), Vol. 3, pp. 549–566; and Marshall D. Shulman, *Stalin's Foreign Policy Reappraised* (New York: Atheneum, 1969), p. 82. It is fashionable now, among Soviet scholars, to minimize the ideological component of Moscow's foreign policy; indeed Lenin himself is now seen as the original architect of "peaceful coexistence," a leader for whom the idea of exporting revolution can hardly have been more alien. See, for example, G. A. Trofimenko, "Uroki mirnogo so-sushestvovaniia," *Voprosy istorii,* Number 11 (November 1983), pp. 6–7. It seems not out of place to wonder how the great revolutionary would have received such perfunctory dismissals of the Comintern and all that it implied; certainly most Western students have treated more seriously than this the revolutionary implications of the Bolshevik Revolution.

35. For Stalin's mixed record on this issue, see Shulman, *Stalin's Foreign Policy Reappraised, passim;* also Taubman, *Stalin's American Policy,* pp. 128–227; and Adam B. Ulam, *Stalin: The Man and His Era* (New York: Viking, 1973), especially pp. 641–643, 654. It is possible, of course, that Stalin followed both policies intentionally as a means both of intimidating and inducing complacency in the West.

36. Herbert Dinerstein, *War and the Soviet Union: Nuclear Weapons and the Revolution in Soviet Military and Political Thinking* (New York: Praeger, 1959), pp. 65–90; William Zimmerman, *Soviet Perspectives on International Relations, 1956–1967* (Princeton: Princeton University Press, 1969), pp. 251–252.

37. ". . . [P]layers' goals may undergo very little change, but postponing their attainment to the indefinite future fundamentally transforms the meaning of . . . myth by revising its implications for social action. Exactly because myths are dramatic stories, changing their time-frame affects their character profoundly. Those who see only the permanence of professed goals, but who neglect structural changes—the incorporation of common experiences into the myths of both sides, shifts in the image of the opponent ('there are reasonable people also in the other camp'), and modifications in the myths' periodization—overlook the great effects that may result from such contextual changes." Friedrich V. Kratochwil, *International Order and Foreign Policy: A Theoretical Sketch of Post-War International Politics* (Boulder: Westview Press, 1978), p. 117.

38. David Alan Rosenberg, "'A Smoking, Radiating Ruin at the End of Two Hours': Documents on American Plans for Nuclear War with the Soviet Union, 1954–55," *International Security,* Vol. 6, No. 3 (Winter 1981/82), pp. 3–38, and "The Origins of Overkill: Nuclear Weapons and American Strategy, 1945–1960," *International Security,* Vol. 7, No. 3 (Spring 1983), pp. 3–71. For more general

accounts, see Fred Kaplan, *The Wizards of Armageddon* (New York: Simon and Schuster, 1983), especially pp. 263–270; and Gregg Herken, Counsels of War (New York: Alfred A. Knopf, 1985), pp. 137–140.

39. Rosenberg, "The Origins of Overkill," pp. 8, 69–71; Kaplan, *Wizards of Armageddon,* pp. 268–285; Herken, *Counsels of War,* pp. 140–165; and Stephen E. Ambrose, *Eisenhower: The President* (New York: Simon and Schuster, 1984), pp. 494, 523, 564.

40. See, on this point, John Spanier, *Games Nations Play: Analyzing International Politics,* 5th ed. (New York: Holt, Rinehart and Winston, 1984), p. 91.

VI

CONTEMPORARY ISSUES AND DEBATES

EFFECTS OF GLOBALIZATION

In the first decade of the twenty-first century, one of the most fundamental and important questions facing analysts of international relations is whether the future will be like the past. This question is deceptively simple; the answer is both complex and elusive. It depends in part on the continued dialectic in the international system between the impulses toward anarchy and the impulses toward the creation of a viable society of states with prescriptive and proscriptive rules that are widely accepted and observed. The nature of these competing impulses is a recurring theme throughout this volume. Yet, as September 11 vividly and tragically demonstrated, it has taken on several new dimensions. As a result, the traditional formulations that pitted realists and neo-realists against liberal institutionalists are no longer adequate to capture the diverse processes and pressures in international relations. The old tension between international anarchy and international society has morphed into a new dialectic between the forces of governance and the forces of disorder. This is evident in many of the readings in this portion of the volume—including assessments of globalization and the kind of governance mechanisms that are required for a globalized world.

GLOBALIZATION AND GOVERNANCE

The reading on globalization by David Held and Anthony McGrew, David Goldblatt and Jonathan Perraton comes from a widely used text on globalization. Emphasizing that globalization involves the widening, deepening, and speeding up of worldwide connectedness, the authors identify three approaches to the phenomenon: hyperglobalists, skeptics, and transformationalists. They then provide an excellent analysis of how the three approaches differ in terms of the conceptualization of globalization, its causation, its periodization, its impacts, and its likely trajectories. Overall they provide a very rich introduction to globalization and to the intellectual and policy debates it has precipitated. Their analysis helps to bring into focus some of the divisions and debates that have been woven through this volume.

Another approach to globalization and one that might also be helpful in a classroom setting is to consider two models of the process—benevolent and malevolent globalization. The notion of globalization as a positive force developed very clearly out of liberal institutionalism. In this interpretation, the globalization of trade, finance, information, and communications systems is a benevolent development and, even though the accruing benefits are not distributed evenly, benefits do accrue to all. The analogy is that of a high tide lifting all boats. The relative gains are less important than the absolute gains that are made by all countries. Moreover, it is not simply that technological advancement—from the Internet to the intermodal container—has reduced many of the transaction costs of global trade and finance; globalization involves the triumph of liberal democracy and the free market economy and in this sense is the natural result of the United States victory in the Cold War. Although the transition process in the former Soviet Union is taking longer than anticipated, the command economy and political totalitarianism of the Soviet era are gradually being replaced by free markets and liberal democracy. The market, it is assumed, will triumph in the end, taming the organized crime and corruption that have added unexpected discordance to the transition process. Similarly, the benefits of globalization for developing economies are very real: In the long term, connectivity to the global system is essential for development and prosperity; being disconnected is a recipe for continued poverty, despair, and instability. Moreover, being connected exposes states to the benefits of liberal democratic forms of governance and, as this form of government spreads, so the prospects for inter-state violence will diminish. In effect, benevolent globalization theory can be understood as a modern variant of the argument propounded by Norman Angell shortly before the First World War that economic interdependence reduces the prospects for war. This proposition is overlaid by democratic peace theory that has its roots in a Kantian vision of world politics. Put somewhat differently, the notion of benevolent globalization can be understood as the intellectual heir to a complex mix of Wilsonian idealism and economic functionalism. Although it is rarely made explicit, a globalized world from this perspective is the antithesis of a Hobbesian world: Life is pleasant, secure, and long—rather than nasty, brutish, and short.

This attractive vision does not claim that history has ended but does assert that it is heading in the right direction. Moreover, it presumes a rather orderly future in which more widespread material prosperity combines with political enfranchisement to create more sober and responsible national governments that are far less likely than in the past to resort to force against one another. This liberal institutionalist if not idealistic view of benevolent globalization is reflected in Thomas Barnett's analysis of the Pentagon's "New Map of the World." A provocative and stimulating analysis that initially appears very hardheaded about the use of force, Barnett's argument is based on assumptions about the positive benefits of globalization that are reflected in his emphasis on the importance of connectivity as the key to stability. In effect, Barnett argues that states that are part of globalization tend to be more stable and prosperous than those outside the globalization process and disconnected from the global economy.

In this analysis, Barnett argues that the United States, in effect, had to intervene in both Afghanistan and Iraq in order to reintegrate—that is, reconnect—these two countries into the global political and economic system. Afghanistan, in particular, he argues was one of the most isolated countries in the world and was almost completely absent from the global economy. The difficulty with this analysis is that it ignores the role of Afghanistan in the illicit global economy. During the 1990s, Afghanistan surpassed Burma as the world's major producer and supplier of opium and heroin. Although production declined in 2001 as a result of a Taliban-imposed opium cultivation ban, by 2002 and 2003, a major resurgence of production had occurred. From the drug problem perspective, the difficulty was not that Afghanistan was isolated but that it was too fully integrated. Indeed, the Afghan experience suggests that losers or bystanders in relation to licit globalization will develop compensatory mechanisms in the illicit world—and that these compensatory mechanisms and activities will also exploit the ease of global trade and travel. As suggested above, globalization facilitates illicit business as well as licit.

There are other difficulties with the vision of benevolent globalization. First, it presumes that absolute gains are always more important than relative gains; yet as realism has long argued, relative gains can become an important source of tension and conflict. Although this argument is generally applied to military power, it also has credence in relation to economic power. In this connection, one of the dangers, even with a benign view of globalization, is that the economic gap between the most developed and the least developed countries will increase rather than decrease. Although this will not necessarily (although it could) create tension in their political relationships, it will almost certainly have other adverse consequences, such as encouraging large-scale immigration—both legal and illegal—from developing to developed countries. Moreover, some aspects of globalization, such as the communications revolution, make continued disparities of wealth and power between developed and developing states even more obvious. Resentment and a desire to reduce the disparities could become a powerful impulse for groups in developing countries, sometimes combining with radical ideologies or fundamentalist religion, to create a radicalism of poverty and a desire to get rich or get even—whatever the methods or consequences. Globalization also has another dimension that suggests that, even if the benign assessment is accepted, not all the consequences will be benign because of the interrelatedness of developments in one part of the world with much of the rest of the world. Connectivity creates new sensitivities and new vulnerabilities. In a world that is highly connected, cascading effects and contagion are ever-present possibilities.

Even with the most optimistic view, therefore, it is only necessary to consider the multidimensional nature of globalization to acknowledge that some of its consequences might be profoundly destabilizing. Yet, a rather more somber assessment of globalization suggests that the adverse consequences of globalization are not merely qualifiers or additions to what is generally positive or beneficial but are inherent in the globalization process and likely to outweigh the benefits. This assessment agrees with those who emphasize the virtues of globalization in one important respect: the enormous significance of the process. In effect, it rejects the skeptical school (one of the three approaches outlined by Held, McGrew, Goldblatt and Perraton). It departs from the notion that globalization is benevolent, however, in several respects.

First, globalization has winners and losers, and the pain for the losers can be enormous. In effect, this is the NGO and protest movement critique of globalization. It sees globalization as having a disruptive impact on patterns of employment, on traditional cultures, and on state capacity to deal with the particular problems facing citizens in its jurisdiction. To take liberties with the analogy of the high tide, it suggests that some of the boats will be driven onto reefs and rocks.

Second, globalization is a great facilitator not only for the members of civil society and business but also for those who are part of an uncivil society and engaged in illicit business. Although notions of global citizenship have become popular, not all the new citizens are benign or upright. Globalization has provided a perfect environment for the growth of transnational criminal and terrorist organizations. It has also facilitated the expansion of dangerous and illegal commodity flows that pose a major challenge to regional stability, to governance at all levels, to international norms and regulations, and to aspirations to enhance what has become known as human security. Globalization has brought with it new problems, such as the capacity of diseases to spread rapidly along transportation vectors. The way in which SARS moved from China and Hong Kong to Toronto provided a vivid example of this. Not only does the emergence of transnational organized crime and global terrorism temper, if not confound, liberal optimism about the positive effects of globalization, but it also means that the traditional neo-realist focus on the state-system itself as the source of security threats has to be broadened. Arguably, there is a new form of transcendent geopolitics, in which threats to security are no longer as linked inextricably to territory as they were in the past—a theme that is picked up later in a selection from Robert Keohane. Similarly, security can no longer be understood in purely military terms.

Third, globalization is a major challenge to the dominance of the Westphalian state, contracting the domain of state authority and making it more difficult for the state to carry out its traditional functions in ways that meet the needs and demands of its citizens. In some cases, the level of public frustration and anger is exacerbated by the communications revolution, which has highlighted the gap between the prosperous developed nations and developing and transitional countries.

Emphasizing the dark side of globalization helps to balance overly enthusiastic and uncritical assessments by the proponents of globalization. Yet the difficulty with the notion of disruptive or malevolent globalization is that this too captures only one side of the process. It ignores the many positive benefits, which help to offset the negatives. Globalization has multiple facets and multiple consequences, which, not surprisingly, push and pull in several different and even contradictory directions: it is a multidimensional phenomenon that encompasses economic, political, social, cultural, and technological changes. The extent to which the benefits of globalization will be exploited and the dangers contained will depend in large part on the effectiveness of governance in a globalized world.

For an analysis of some of the major governance issues we have chosen another excerpt by James N. Rosenau. One of the keys to Rosenau's work during the last twenty years or so has been the way in which he has embraced paradox. This is reflected in the title of the volume—*Distant Proximities*—from which our selection is taken as well as in Rosenau's notion of fragmegration—a conflation of the competing tendencies toward fragmentation on the one side and integration on the other that stem from the tensions between localizing and globalizing forces. Rosenau argues that global governance requires accepting these tensions, going beyond the primacy of states and international institutions, and according centrality to micro-macro processes. He also acknowledges that "the prospects for effective governance on a worldwide scale are highly problematic, that progress in this respect may take decades, and that the probability of evolution towards a harmonious and progressive global order may not be any greater than the chance of deterioration toward a tension-filled and retrogressive disorder." Having examined some of the obstacles to global governance, Rosenau identifies six types of global governance depending on whether the structures of governance are formal, informal or mixed, and whether the processes are unidirectional (vertical or horizontal) or multidirectional (vertical and horizontal). He then suggests that the most appropriate to the world of fragmegration is a mixed formal and informal structure with vertical and horizontal processes—what he terms mobius-web governance—that intersect and overlap in complex ways. Rosenau recognizes that even this very complex form of governance might be inadequate to a complex world, but he also suggests that there are some grounds for being upbeat about the potential for governance. Others though are more pessimistic. Indeed, the next section focuses not on global governance but on the possibilities of global chaos.

GLOBAL CHAOS?

Samuel Huntington, a distinguished political scientist and international affairs analyst at Harvard, argues that the wars of the future are likely to be wars of civilizations rather than states. Huntington's analysis, which initially appeared in *Foreign Affairs,* has generated intense debate and controversy. Although Huntington subsequently developed the argument into a book entitled *The Clash of Civilizations and the Making of World Order,* we have chosen to include the initial analysis. According to Huntington, world politics is entering a new phase in which the fundamental sources of conflict will not be primarily ideological or economic, but cultural. Although Huntington concedes that nation-states will remain the most powerful actors in world affairs, he contends that the principal conflicts of global politics will occur between nations and groups of different civilizations. As he puts it, "the fault lines between civilizations will be the battle lines of the future." He suggests that the differences among the world's seven or eight major civilizations—Western, Confucian, Japanese, Islamic, Hindu, Slavic-Orthodox, Latin American, and possibly African—are fundamental in character. Because the world is becoming a smaller place, interactions among these civilizations are becoming more intense. Furthermore, this clash of civilizations appears at two distinct but related levels: "At the micro-level, adjacent groups along the fault lines between civilizations struggle, often violently, over the control of territory and each other. At the macro-level, states from different civilizations compete for relative military and economic power, struggle over the control of international institutions and third parties, and competitively promote their particular political and religious values." Particularly important in this connection is the clash between the West and Islam, a clash that, Huntington suggests, is likely to become more rather than less intense. Part of the reason for this is that the West is now at an extraordinary peak of power in relation to other civilizations. Not surprisingly, there has been a hostile reaction to Western dominance by the other civilizations. One facet of this, according to Huntington, is the growing Islamic-Confucian connection, which is manifested most obviously in the Chinese export of arms to countries such as Libya, Iraq, and Iran.

There are clearly problems with Huntington's thesis. At one level, he seems to be attributing civilization-related motives to actions that could equally well have a very different rationale. Chinese arms sales, for example, might have more to do with economic opportunity than with some kind of affinity or tacit alliance with Islamic states. Another problem is that Huntington ignores or downplays the potential for clashes among states that are part of the same civilization. For all its shortcomings, however, Huntington's analysis is an important contribution to the debate about the future of world politics. This was reflected in the way in which Huntington's analysis helped to frame the policy debate after September 11: Although many felt that Huntington had been prophetic, others argued that the United States response was in danger of creating the very clash between the West and Islam that Huntington had identified. The difference between supporters and critics of Huntington, therefore, was not over the importance of a clash of civilizations but about whether it had already taken place or was something to be avoided in the future.

Another important and controversial analysis is that presented by Robert Kaplan in his article, "The Coming Anarchy." Appearing first in *The Atlantic Monthly,* this was subsequently developed in a book entitled *The Ends of the Earth: A Journey at the Dawn of the 21st Century*. A contributing editor to the *Atlantic Monthly* and author of several books on travel and foreign affairs, Kaplan combines firsthand reporting with some bold generalizations. Developed on the basis of his visits to some of the key areas of conflict and instability,

Kaplan enunciates perhaps the most pessimistic diagnosis and prognosis of the global condition. The major problems on the global agenda include poverty, overcrowding, crime, disease, environmental degradation and the changing nature of warfare. In Kaplan's judgment, "West Africa is becoming *the* symbol of worldwide demographic, environmental, and societal stress, in which criminal anarchy emerges as the real 'strategic' danger. Disease, overpopulation, unprovoked crime, scarcity of resources, refugee migrations, the increasing erosion of nation-states and international borders, and the empowerment of private armies, security firms, and international drug cartels are now most tellingly demonstrated through a West African prism." Within West Africa, Kaplan focuses on Sierra Leone, which, he argues, "is a microcosm of what is occurring, albeit in a more tempered and gradual manner, throughout West Africa and much of the underdeveloped world: the withering away of central governments, the rise of tribal and regional domains, the unchecked spread of disease, and the growing pervasiveness of war." Part of the problem lies in the growing population in the region, the failure of the infrastructure to keep up with population growth, and the impact of population growth on the environment. According to Kaplan, Thomas Malthus (whom he describes as "the philosopher of demographic doomsday") is the "prophet of West Africa's future. And West Africa's future, eventually, will also be that of most of the rest of the world."

As well as this complex of problems in the developing world, Kaplan draws out some wider implications that are invariably highly provocative. He sees a major shift in governance mechanisms away from the state and toward a new post-modern cartography characterized by "themeless juxtapositions, in which the classificatory grid of nation-states is going to be replaced by a jagged-glass pattern of city-states, shanty-states, nebulous and anarchic regionalisms. . . . "

This shift is closely linked to new patterns of warfare that will generally occur in the poorest parts of the world. In a highly prescient passage Kaplan argues that "war-making entities will no longer be restricted to a specific territory. Loose and shadowy organisms such as Islamic terrorist organizations suggest why borders will mean increasingly little and sedimentary layers of tribalistic identity and control will mean more." He cites with approval the contention by Martin Van Creveld that "religious . . . fanaticisms will play a larger role in the motivation of armed conflict" in the future. He also agrees with Van Creveld, that "Once the legal monopoly of armed force, long claimed by the state, is wrested out of its hands, existing distinctions between war and crime will break down much as is already the case today in . . . Lebanon, Sri Lanka, El Salvador, Peru, or Colombia"—suggesting that, as a result of threats, "a pre-modern formlessness governs the battlefield, evoking the wars in medieval Europe prior to the 1648 Peace of Westphalia. . . ." National armies will become less important and private security companies and criminal organizations will both be involved in the provision of private protection, which the state can no longer provide. Most wars will be subnational rather than international and will be wars for "communal survival, aggravated or, in many cases, caused by environmental scarcity." Because states will be unable to protect their own citizens their legitimacy will be called into question and some will collapse, die, or simply be rendered irrelevant, exercising formal sovereignty and formal statehood but having little authority or function. The hollow state is likely to be a common feature of Kaplan's world.

The result of all this will be a new three-dimensional cartography resembling a hologram. "In this hologram would be the overlapping sediments of group and other identities atop the merely two-dimensional color markings of city-states and the remaining nations, themselves confused in places by shadowy tentacles, hovering overhead, indicating the power of drug cartels, mafias, and private security agencies. Instead of borders, there would be moving 'centers' of power, as in the Middle Ages. Many of these layers would be in motion. Replacing fixed and abrupt lines on a flat space would be a shifting pattern of buffer entities. . . . To this protean cartographic hologram one must add other factors, such as migrations of populations, explosions of birth rates, vectors of disease. Henceforward the map of the world will never be static. This future map—in a sense, the 'Last Map'—will be an ever-mutating representation of chaos."

This apocalyptic vision is alarming, but is not always persuasive, largely because of a lack of differentiation. In effect, Kaplan has taken one of the most anarchic, chaotic, and dysfunctional regions in the world—West Africa—and extrapolated from it to the rest of the world without acknowledging that this is a worst case analysis, or that there are regions and indeed continents where peace and stability are the norm and the horsemen of the apocalypse are nowhere in sight. By claiming that "West Africa's future, eventually, will also be that of most of the rest of the world" Kaplan damages his own credibility. Had he put the argument more cautiously and applied it merely to large parts of the world and especially the developing world, then it would have been more difficult to refute. Nonetheless, in spite of the hyperbole, Kaplan's analysis is never less than challenging and often compelling. His contention that the nation-state is becoming less powerful and less important, his view that traditional maps emphasizing static, impermeable, and immutable borders are being overtaken by a more complex and dynamic form of cartography, and his claim that war and crime are becoming less easy to distinguish from one another are highly persuasive. And if we take the coming anarchy not as a global anarchy but as a series of regions characterized by anarchy rather than order, by a vacuum of authority rather than the operation of governance, by the collapse of state structures, and by the fusion of war and crime, then it becomes less an apocalyptic vision of the future than a balanced description of the present—in those regions. Not all regions fit this pattern, of course, which suggests that the world is actually more varied and differentiated than Kaplan's vision suggests—and will remain so.

One of the more potent critics of Kaplan and Huntington is Yahya Sadowski, whose book the *Myth of Global Chaos* was published by the Brookings Institution. In the excerpts in this volume, Sadowski suggests that the emphasis on change has been overdrawn and that most of the analysts of change have failed to acknowledge the forces of continuity. This perspective is a cautionary yet optimistic one, suggesting that the notion of global anarchy is a myth; that modern wars, such as those in the Balkans in the 1990s, are not very different from the wars of the past; and that the major claims of what the author terms "global chaos theory" turn out to be false. Sadowski argues that the three components of this theory are (1) that globalization (which spreads Western cultural, political, and economic institutions around the world) forces more and more people to confront alien values; (2) "when the basic values of a culture are threatened, violence becomes more common and more savage" and more irrational; and (3) consequently, the world is "witnessing an explosion of irrational violence, manifest in the drug wars of Latin America, the tribal massacres of Africa, fundamentalist revolts in the Middle East, and ethnic cleansing in the Balkans. Crime, warfare, and genocide all seem to be not only proliferating but also spinning out of control." In addition, he argues that "the architects of global chaos theory . . . have erected a complex school of thought that deals with urbanization, narcoterrorism, immigration, humanitarian disasters, debates over military intervention, rogue states, collapsed states, the profusion of transnational organizations, terrorist networks, fundamentalism, ethnic conflict and so on." Close inspection, however, reveals that most conflicts in the world are the same as they have always been—"rational quarrels over the distribution of resources" rather than irrational outbreaks of anomic violence. Wars are fought for the same reasons they have always been fought and, although they are brutal and nasty, this is not new.

This thesis has much to say. Yet we note a strange disconnect between the general critique and the specific examples cited by Sadowski. Few if any observers claim that drug wars are a product (direct or indirect) of culture clashes, and careful analyses of at least some of the tribal massacres in Africa have suggested that control over diamonds was part of the reason for going to war and also provided resources that subsequently perpetuated the fighting. The main connection with globalization is that diamonds are integrated into the licit global diamond market—often by Lebanese diamond merchants who are part of the Lebanese diaspora. Similarly, nothing intrinsically relates collapsed states or rogue states to clashes of culture or civilization. The connection between the architects of global chaos theory and the specific components or manifestations of their theory identified by Sadowski is rather tenuous. Indeed, at least some of the proponents of global chaos theory have arrived at the theory as a result of empirical observation. Rather than starting with a grand theory of global chaos, they have started with specific problems, which, in total, indicate something new and different in the world. Indeed, it can be argued that the sheer diversity of contemporary problems makes the notion of global chaos (or at least zones of chaos) more compelling than Sadowski acknowledges.

Although it is appropriate to challenge some of the arguments about global chaos, it is important not to overlook the coterie of international and transnational problems that have to be managed and contained. Rejecting the clash of civilization thesis or the idea of the coming anarchy is one thing; discounting or dismissing a whole set of new problems such as terrorism, collapsed states, the negative consequences of globalization, and so on is quite another—and much more dangerous. Even if one dismisses the notion of global chaos theory, many of the problems that are typically incorporated or embraced in this theory are far less easy to ignore. The overall problem with Sadowski's analysis, therefore, is its under-estimation of the forces of change and its failure to see some problems as being qualitatively different. Underestimating continuity is a serious flaw in analyses that see only innovation and novelty; underestimating the impact of novelty and innovation is an even more serious flaw in analyses that emphasize continuity and conformity to traditional patterns.

TERRORISM

One area that both liberal institutionalists and political realists tended to ignore for too long was terrorism. For many international relations and security studies scholars whose focus was on nuclear weapons great power rivalry, terrorism was regarded as a secondary issue that required neither attention nor analytic rigor. This changed (although not completely) after September 11. Yet what is perhaps most interesting is that for several years prior to the attacks on the World Trade Center and the Pentagon, terrorism scholars had been warning of the emergence of new and more lethal forms of terrorism. Among those sounding the tocsin was Bruce Hoffman of the RAND Corporation, whose book, *Inside Terrorism,* from which our excerpt is taken, warned of the emergence of religious terrorist organizations far more intent than their predecessors on inflicting large-scale casualties. Hoffman's analysis suggested that religious motivations combined with enhanced terrorist capabilities "could portend an even bloodier and more destructive era of violence ahead than any we have seen before." His emphasis on the possibility of WMD terrorism is also something that needs to be taken very seriously.

If the events of September 11, 2001, vindicated Hoffman's assessment of the changing nature of terrorism, they also forced more traditional scholars to re-evaluate their thinking. One of the most interesting of these reappraisals was by Robert Keohane, parts of which are excerpted here. Emphasizing that the globalization of informal violence, symbolized by September 11, has changed geographic space from a barrier to a carrier, Keohane notes that this will make it much more difficult for the United States to differentiate between vital areas and interests demanding the use of forces and those that are non-vital. He also notes the failure "to understand that the most powerful state ever to exist on this planet could be vulnerable to small bands of terrorists due to patterns of asymmetrical interdependence. We have over-emphasized states and we have over-aggregated power."

This theme of asymmetrical interdependence is taken one step further in the excerpt from an article on "The Rise of Complex Terrorism" by Thomas Homer-Dixon, a scholar best known for his work on the environmental and security. Indeed, Homer-Dixon shows how sophistication can become a source of asymmetric vulnerability, especially when it involves dependence on complex, tightly coupled networks. The network theme is echoed in the reading by John Arquilla and David Ronfeldt—two of the leading proponents of network forms of warfare—which is taken from an afterword to a RAND book entitled *Networks and Netwars: The Future of Terror, Crime and Militancy*. In effect, Arquilla and Ronfeldt articulate the key elements of a strategy to combat al-Qaeda. They note that this strategy must be multilevel and include the creation of a global counter-terror network, the development of compelling narratives that generate support domestically and internationally, and the implementation of novel concepts such as netwar and novel strategies such as swarming. Although in the excerpt here, Arquilla and Ronfeldt do not deal with the obstacles and impediments to an effective counter-terrorism strategy, one of the most important of these is national sovereignty—which often inhibits international cooperation on security and intelligence matters and also presents terrorists with territorial sanctuaries. The issue of sovereignty is one of the themes of the next section.

SOVEREIGNTY AND INTERVENTION, DETERRENCE AND PRE-EMPTION

National sovereignty has always been an essential component of the Westphalian state system and has carried with it the notion of certain rights and obligations. As suggested in the Introduction to Part III of this volume, the principle of sovereignty is essential to the functioning of the society of states and the maintenance of international order—not least because the counterpart to respect for the sovereign rights of a state is the obligation not to interfere in the affairs of that state. For all its centrality to international relations, however, the concept of sovereignty is more problematic and contested than most observers acknowledge. Stephen Krasner of Stanford University, whose analysis of sovereignty is both incisive and provocative, provides an exception. According to Krasner, the term *sovereignty* has at least four different meanings. It is used to refer to domestic sovereignty (the exercise of public authority and jurisdictional control within a state), interdependence sovereignty (control over border flows), international legal sovereignty (mutual recognition of states), and Westphalian sovereignty (the exclusion of external actors from domestic authority configurations). This last meaning of sovereignty in particular has a concomitant of non-intervention by other states. Yet since the end of the Cold War, the idea of non-intervention has come under increasing challenge.

This is discussed in an excerpt from a book chapter by Stanley Hoffmann, a distinguished professor at Harvard and a prolific writer on both philosophical and empirical aspects of international relations and United States foreign policy. In a trenchant analysis, Hoffmann argues that most justifications for intervention in domestic conflicts in particular are either humanitarian justifications designed to reduce suffering or "just cause" arguments in response to egregious violations of human rights, such as genocide or ethnic cleansing. He also notes that realists tend to criticize such interventions, either because they involve altruism rather than self-interest or because of their adverse consequences. As Hoffmann puts it, "while the defenders of intervention are moved by a nightmare of human suffering spreading chaos, if each state is left, so to speak, in possession of the people under its jurisdiction, the opponents are inspired by a nightmare of interstate chaos if the pillars of state sovereignty and nonintervention are torn down." Whatever the merits of the arguments for and against any specific humanitarian or "just cause" intervention, it is noteworthy that realists are generally very prudent about the use of force.

This prudence is also evident in the debate over pre-emption—a strategy that has been central to the U.S. response to September 11. M. Elaine Bunn, a researcher in the Institute for National Strategic Studies at the National Defense University, provides a comprehensive assessment of the pre-emption strategy enunciated by the Bush administration. After demonstrating fairly convincingly that notions of pre-emption have been evident in previous administrations, Bunn explains why it has become so prominent in the Bush administration. She contends that the essence of pre-emption is action designed to preclude or forestall the actions of an adversary, and that as such, it can take many forms—of which military action is only one. Nevertheless, because of the concerns with terrorism and WMD proliferation, as well as the nexus between these two phenomena on the one side, and the administration's lack of faith in traditional deterrence strategies on the other, the notion of pre-emption has been elevated in significance. Bunn, however, recognizes the many remaining unanswered questions about pre-emption, including the what, when, and how. After considering these, along with the issues related to the impact of the strategy in practice, she considers whether it is simply an option for policymakers or has been elevated to the level of doctrine. In the final part of the paper, she outlines possible criteria for determining under what circumstances pre-emptive military action is likely to be an appropriate option.

Whereas Bunn provides a temperate treatment of a highly controversial issue, one of the sources of that controversy is the pre-emptive (or as some critics contend, preventive) attack on Iraq—an intervention that (in spring of 2005) had United States forces bogged down in Iraq with a continuing insurgency and no obvious exit strategy. The next selection—entitled "An Unnecessary War" and published in *Foreign Policy* prior to the war—two of the most prominent contemporary realists, John Mearsheimer and Stephen Walt, argue that the use of force in Iraq was unnecessary. Contending that Saddam Hussein could have been both deterred and contained by United States policy and that pre-emption was both unnecessary and undesirable, they enunciate a case that has subsequently been strengthened by the failure of United States forces to find weapons of mass destruction or any significant links between Saddam Hussein and al-Qaeda. Yet underlying the realist critique of war in Iraq is a broader concern with ensuring the continued legitimacy of the use of force. If resort to military force or military intervention is done carelessly or with insufficient and inadequate rationale, this can make it more difficult to use on future occasions—when it might be much more important. Indeed, it is not inconceivable that, in a world characterized by transnational terrorist networks and proliferation of weapons of mass destruction, pre-emption will under some circumstances prove to be critical for the United States in a way that was not the case with Iraq. And it is to the U.S. role in the world that attention must now be given.

UNIPOLARITY AND THE U.S. ROLE IN THE WORLD

Since the end of the Cold War, many observers of international relations have been preoccupied with the changed state system and in particular the question of what has replaced bipolarity.[1] Indeed, a broad consensus now holds that the United States has become by far the preponderant power in the international system. This is reflected in the excerpts we have chosen. In the first selection, Stephen Brooks and William Wohlforth emphasize that the United States "has no rival in any critical dimension of power." They also see this as a situation that is likely to endure, not least because the comprehensive nature of U.S. power, which "skews the odds against any major attempt at balancing, let alone a successful one." The lack of a hegemonic rival, it is argued, offers American policymakers enormous freedom. Joseph Nye's assessment, which is excerpted here, is more circumspect. It argues that the sources of American power go beyond military and economic power to include what he has termed soft power—the ability to co-opt rather than coerce others that rests in part on the attractiveness of American values and culture. In the last few years, however, the United States perception of itself as benevolent hegemon has not necessarily been shared by other states. Moreover, although the United States in the 1990s appeared to be making judicious use of multilateral institutions and providing a degree of order and predictability that helped to satisfy other states, the intervention in Iraq against the wishes of most other major powers casts doubt on the possibility that such an approach can be sustained for the medium and long term. From this perspective, it would certainly be unusual for hegemony not to be challenged. In the event that United States primacy is successfully challenged by other states, several possibilities can be identified.

The first is the re-emergence of a bipolar system with the dominant relationship being that between the United States and China. The key issue is whether this relationship will be friendly or hostile. For those who see the

---

[1] In "Why We Will Soon Miss the Cold War" (*Atlantic Monthly*, August 1990), John Mearsheimer contended that, as the world became multipolar, we would soon miss the stability of the bipolar Cold War international system. Ironically, the period since Mearsheimer's article has validated his concern about the loss of stability but not about the emergence of a multipolar system.

distribution of power in the international system as the major determinant of policy, bipolarity is inevitably characterized by competition and conflict between the two great powers. If this logic is accepted, then, as China becomes more ascendant during the twenty-first century, it will pose an inexorable challenge to U.S. hegemony, resulting in another Cold War and possibly even a hegemonic war.

A second possibility is a tripolar system in which the United States and China are joined by a resurgent Russia. Such a system would likely be highly competitive and unstable with the key imperative to be one of two in a world of three. The precedent for this was set during the 1970s, when the United States used the "China card" as a counterweight to an apparently ascendant Soviet Union. Most international system theorists believe tripolarity to be one of the least stable distributions of power.

A third possibility is the emergence of a classic multipolar system in which there are five major powers—the United States, China, Russia, Japan, and the European Union. Such a system might be reminiscent of the European state system of the nineteenth century, when as Bismarck noted, the important thing was to be one of three in a world of five. Balance of power diplomacy, however, might he complicated by the desire of the five great powers to obtain the allegiance of second-tier states such as Brazil or India. The key issue in this system would concern the ability of the five great powers to develop a multilateral capacity for system management along the lines of the nineteenth-century Concert of Europe.

Which of these patterns will emerge will depend critically upon domestic developments. Can Russia reverse its decline and re-emerge as a major actor in world politics? Can China remain a cohesive force in spite of regional and demographic splits within the country? Can the Europeans harmonize foreign and security policies sufficiently to act as a unified power? Can Japan complement economic power with enhanced military resources?

At the same time it is possible to argue that the precise configuration of power in the international system might be far less important in the future than it was in the past. Even if the United States remains the preponderant power in the state-centric world, for example, it might well be challenged by Rosenau's sovereignty-free actors (discussed in Reading 51). Indeed, it is arguable that September 11 represented a challenge to United States hegemony not by another state but by a transnational networked adversary. Furthermore, it is not clear that primacy in the state system translates into an equal level of power and influence in the interaction with the multi-centric system. Similarly, it is arguable that, if one accepts that the world is characterized by a clash of civilizations, then the key will be the capacity to transform soft power into effective narratives that appeal to moderates in the Islamic world and encourage the marginalization of radical fundamentalists. Yet there is little evidence so far that the United States has this capacity. And if the challenge is seen as one of coming anarchy, then most aspects of United States power appear irrelevant. In the simple power hierarchy the United States might be unrivalled, but its ability to deal with complex situations is much less impressive. Removing the Taliban in Afghanistan and Saddam Hussein in Iraq involved a traditional use of military power and was accomplished rapidly and very easily. The aftermath of these successful uses of military power was another story entirely. The United States proved unable—at least in the short term—to turn military victory into political stability and good governance.

One possible conclusion that can be drawn from all this is that one of the most important features of contemporary world politics is the challenge to the dominance of the state system. The message for liberal institutionalists is that developments such as globalization and interdependence, which have long been seen as positive in their impact, have a dark underside and are not leading inexorably to a more stable and harmonious world. For realists and neo-realists, the message is that challenges to security cannot be understood through a prism that focuses exclusively on states or that is confined to military challenges. Indeed, if scholars and analysts are to comprehend the complexities of international relations in the twenty-first century, they will have to transcend many of the traditions, approaches, categories, and intellectual disputes that have become the staple of the discipline but are increasingly irrelevant to the way in which the world has changed and is continuing to change.

49

THOMAS P. M. BARNETT

THE PENTAGON'S NEW MAP

Let me tell you why military engagement with Saddam Hussein's regime in Baghdad is not only necessary and inevitable, but good.

When the United States finally goes to war again in the Persian Gulf, it will not constitute a settling of old scores, or just an enforced disarmament of illegal weapons, or a distraction in the war on terror. Our next war in the Gulf will mark a historical tipping point—the moment when Washington takes real ownership of strategic security in the age of globalization.

That is why the public debate about this war has been so important: It forces Americans to come to terms with what I believe is the new security paradigm that shapes this age, namely, *Disconnectedness defines danger.*

SOURCE: "The Pentagon's New Map," by Thomas Barnett, *Esquire*, March 2003, pp. 174–179, 227–228.

Saddam Hussein's outlaw regime is dangerously disconnected from the globalizing world, from its rule sets, its norms, and all the ties that bind countries together in mutually assured dependence.

The problem with most discussion of globalization is that too many experts treat it as a binary outcome: Either it is great and sweeping the planet, or it is horrid and failing humanity everywhere. Neither view really works, because globalization as a historical process is simply too big and too complex for such summary judgments. Instead, this new world must be defined by where globalization has truly taken root and where it has not.

Show me where globalization is thick with network connectivity, financial transactions, liberal media flows, and collective security, and I will show you regions featuring stable governments, rising standards of living, and more deaths by suicide than murder. These parts of the world I call the Functioning Core, or Core. But show me where globalization is thinning or just plain absent, and I will show you regions plagued by politically repressive regimes, widespread poverty and disease, routine mass murder, and—most important— the chronic conflicts that incubate the next generation of global terrorists. These parts of the world I call the Non-Integrating Gap, or Gap.

Globalization's "ozone hole" may have been out of sight and out of mind prior to September 11, 2001, but it has been hard to miss ever since. And measuring the reach of globalization is not an academic exercise to an eighteen-year-old marine sinking tent poles on its far side. So where do we schedule the U.S. military's next round of away games? The pattern that has emerged since the end of the cold war suggests a simple answer: in the Gap.

The reason I support going to war in Iraq is not simply that Saddam is a cutthroat Stalinist willing to kill anyone to stay in power, nor because that regime has clearly supported terrorist networks over the years. The real reason I support a war like this is that the resulting long-term military commitment will finally force America to deal with the entire Gap as a strategic threat environment.

For most countries, accommodating the emerging global rule set of democracy, transparency, and free trade is no mean feat, which is something most Americans find hard to understand. We tend to forget just how hard it has been to keep the United States together all these years, harmonizing our own, competing internal rule sets along the way—through a Civil War, a Great Depression, and the long struggles for racial and sexual equality that continue to this day. As far as most states are concerned, we are quite unrealistic in our expectation that they should adapt themselves quickly to globalization's very American-looking rule set.

But you have to be careful with that Darwinian pessimism, because it is a short jump from apologizing for globalization-as-forced-Americanization to insinuating—along racial or civilization lines—that *those* people will simply never be like us." Just ten years ago, most experts were willing to write off poor Russia, declaring Slavs, in effect, genetically unfit for democracy and capitalism. Similar arguments resonated in most China-bashing during the 1990's, and you hear them today in the debates about the feasibility of imposing democracy on a post-Saddam Iraq—a sort of Muslims-are-from-Mars argument.

So how do we distinguish between who is really making it in globalization's Core and who remains trapped in the Gap? And how permanent is this dividing line?

Understanding that the line between the Core and Gap is constantly shifting, let me suggest that the direction of change is more critical than the degree. So, yes, Beijing is still ruled by a "Communist party" whose ideological formula is 30 percent Marxist-Leninist and 70 percent *Sopranos,* but China just signed on to the World Trade Organization, and over the long run, that is far more important in securing the country's permanent Core status. Why? Because it forces China to harmonize its internal rule set with that of globalization—banking, tariffs, copyright protection, environmental standards. Of course, working to adjust your internal rule sets to globalization's evolving rule set offers no guarantee of success. As Argentina and Brazil have recently found out, following the rules (in Argentina's case, *sort of* following) does not mean you are panicproof, or bubbleproof, or even recessionproof. Trying to adapt to globalization does not mean bad things will never happen to you. Nor does it mean all your poor will immediately morph into stable middle class. It just means your standard of living gets better over time.

In sum, it is always possible to fall off this bandwagon called globalization. And when you do, bloodshed will follow. If you are lucky, so will American troops.

So what parts of the world can be considered functioning right now? North America, much of South America, the European Union, Putin's Russia, Japan and Asia's emerging economies (most notably China and India), Australia and New Zealand, and South Africa, which accounts for roughly four billion out of a global population of six billion.

Whom does that leave in the Gap? It would be easy to say "everyone else," but I want to offer you more proof than that and, by doing so, argue why I think the Gap is a long-term threat to more than just your pocketbook or conscience.

If we map out U.S. military responses since the end of the cold war, . . . we find an overwhelming concentration of activity in the regions of the world that are excluded from globalization's growing Core—namely the Caribbean Rim, virtually all of Africa, the Balkans, the Caucasus, Central Asia, the Middle East and Southwest Asia, and much of Southeast Asia. That is roughly the remaining two billion of the world's population. Most have demographics skewed very young, and most are labeled, "low income" or "low middle income" by the World Bank (i.e., less than $3,000 annual per capita).

If we draw a line around the majority of those military interventions, we have basically mapped the Non-Integrating Gap. Obviously, there are outliers excluded geographically by this simple approach, such as an Israel isolated in the Gap, a North Korea adrift within the Core, or a Philippines straddling the line. But looking at the data, it is hard to deny the essential logic of the picture:

If a country is either losing out to globalization or rejecting much of the content flows associated with its advance, there is a far greater chance that the U.S. will end up sending forces at some point. Conversely, if a country is largely functioning within globalization, we tend not to have to send our forces there to restore order or eradicate threats.

Now, that may seem like a tautology—in effect defining any place that has not attracted U.S. military intervention in the last decade or so as "functioning within globalization" (and vice versa). But think about this larger point: Ever since the end of World War II, this country has assumed that the real threats to its security resided in countries of roughly similar size, development, and wealth—in other words, other great powers like ourselves. During the cold war, that other great power was the Soviet Union. When the big Red machine evaporated in the early 1990's, we flirted with concerns about a united Europe, a powerhouse Japan, and—most recently—a rising China.

What was interesting about all those scenarios is the assumption that only an advanced state can truly threaten us. The rest of the world? Those less-developed parts of the world have long been referred to in military plans as the "Lesser Includeds," meaning that if we built a military capable of handling a great power's military threat, it would always be sufficient for any minor scenarios we might have to engage in the less advanced world.

That assumption was shattered by September 11. After all, we were not attacked by a nation or even an army but by a group of—in Thomas Friedman's vernacular—Super-Empowered Individuals willing to die for their cause. September 11 triggered a system perturbation that continues to reshape our government (the new Department of Homeland Security), our economy (the de facto security tax we all pay), and even our society (*Wave to the camera!*). Moreover, it launched the global war on terrorism, the prism through which our government now views every bilateral security relationship we have across the world.

In many ways, the September 11 attacks did the U.S. national-security establishment a huge favor by pulling us back from the abstract planning of future high-tech wars against "near peers" into the here-and-now threats to global order. By doing so, the dividing lines between Core and Gap were highlighted, and more important, the nature of the threat environment was thrown into stark relief.

Think about it: Bin Laden and Al Qaeda are pure products of the Gap—in effect, its most violent feedback to the Core. They tell us how we are doing in exporting security to these lawless areas (not very well) and which states they would like to take "off line" from globalization and return to some seventh-century definition of the good life (any Gap state with a sizable Muslim population, especially Saudi Arabia).

If you take this message from Osama and combine it with our military-intervention record of the last decade, a simple security rule set emerges: *A country's potential to warrant a U.S. military response is inversely related to its globalization connectivity.* There is a good reason why Al Qaeda was based first in Sudan and then later in Afghanistan: These are two of the most disconnected countries in the world. Look at the other places U.S. Special Operations Forces have recently zeroed in on: northwestern Pakistan, Somalia, Yemen. We are talking about the ends of the earth as far as globalization is concerned.

But just as important as "getting them where they live" is stopping the ability of these terrorist networks to access the Core via the "seam states" that lie along the Gap's bloody boundaries. It is along this seam that the Core will seek to suppress bad things coming out of the Gap. Which are some of these classic seam states? Mexico, Brazil, South Africa, Morocco, Algeria, Greece, Turkey, Pakistan, Thailand, Malaysia, the Philippines, and Indonesia come readily to mind. But the U.S. will not be the only Core state working this issue. For example, Russia has its own war on terrorism in the Caucasus, China is working its western border with more vigor, and Australia was recently energized (or was it cowed?) by the Bali bombing.

If we step back for a minute and consider the broader implications of this new global map, then U.S. national-security strategy would seem to be: 1) Increase the Core's immune system capabilities for responding to September 11–like system perturbations; 2) Work the seam states to firewall the Core from the Gap's worst exports, such as terror, drugs, and pandemics; and, most important, 3) *Shrink the Gap*. Notice I did not just say *Mind the Gap*. The knee-jerk reaction of many Americans to September 11 is to say, "Let's get off our dependency on foreign oil, and then we won't have to deal with *those* people." The most naïve assumption underlying that dream is that reducing what little connectivity the Gap has with the Core will render it less dangerous to us over the long haul. Turning the Middle East into Central Africa will not build a better world for my kids. We cannot simply will *those* people away.

The Middle East is the perfect place to start. Diplomacy cannot work in a region where the biggest sources of insecurity lie not between states but within them. What is most wrong about the Middle East is the lack of personal freedom and how that translates into dead-end lives for most of the population—especially for the young. Some states like Qatar and Jordan are ripe for perestroika-like leaps into better political futures, thanks to younger leaders who see the inevitability of such change. Iran is likewise waiting for the right Gorbachev to come along—if he has not already.

What stands in the path of this change? Fear. Fear of tradition unraveling. Fear of the mullah's disapproval. Fear of being labeled a "bad" or "traitorous" Muslim state. Fear of becoming a target of radical groups and terrorist networks. But most of all, fear of being attacked from all sides for being different—the fear of becoming Israel.

The Middle East has long been a neighborhood of bullies eager to pick on the weak. Israel is still around because it has become—sadly—one of the toughest bullies on the block. The only thing that will change that nasty environment and open the floodgates for change is if some external power steps in and plays Leviathan full-time. Taking down Saddam, the region's bully-in-chief, will force the U.S. into playing that role far more fully than it has over the past several decades, primarily because Iraq is the Yugoslavia of the Middle East—a crossroads of civilizations that has historically required a dictatorship to keep the peace. As baby-sitting jobs go, this one will be a doozy, making our lengthy efforts in postwar Germany and Japan look simple in retrospect.

But it is the right thing to do, and now is the right time to do it, and we are the only country that can. Freedom cannot blossom in the Middle East without security, and security is this country's most influential public-sector export. By that I do not mean arms exports, but basically the attention paid by our military forces to any region's potential for mass violence. We are the only nation on earth capable of exporting security in a sustained fashion, and we have a very good track record of doing it.

Show me a part of the world that is secure in its peace and I will show you strong or growing ties between local militaries and the U.S. military. Show me regions where major war is inconceivable and I will show you permanent U.S. military bases and long-term security alliances. Show me the strongest investment relationships in the global economy and I will show you two postwar military occupations that remade Europe and Japan following World War II.

This country has successfully exported security to globalization's Old Core (Western Europe, Northeast Asia) for half a century and to its emerging New Core (Developing Asia) for a solid quarter century following our mishandling of Vietnam. But our efforts in the Middle East have been inconsistent—in Africa, almost nonexistent. Until we begin the systematic, long-term export of security to the Gap, it will increasingly export its pain to the Core in the form of terrorism and other instabilities.

Naturally, it will take a whole lot more than the U.S. exporting security to shrink the Gap. Africa, for example, will need far more aid than the Core has offered in the past, and the integration of the Gap will ultimately depend more on private investment than anything the Core's public sector can offer. But it all has to begin with security, because free markets and democracy cannot flourish amid chronic conflict.

Making this effort means reshaping our military establishment to mirror-image the challenge that we face. Think about it. Global war is not in the offing, primarily because our huge nuclear stockpile renders such war unthinkable—for anyone. Meanwhile, classic state-on-state wars are becoming fairly rare. So if the United States is in the process of "transforming" its military to meet the threats of tomorrow, what should it end up looking like? In my mind, we fight fire with fire. If we live in a world increasingly populated by Super-Empowered Individuals, we field a military of Super-Empowered-Individuals.

This may sound like additional responsibility for an already overburdened military, but that is the wrong way of looking at it, for what we are dealing with here are problems of success—not failure. It is America's continued success in deterring global war and obsolescing state-on-state war that allows us to stick our noses into the far more difficult subnational conflicts and the dangerous transnational actors they spawn. I know most Americans do not want to hear this, but the real battlegrounds in the global war on terrorism are still *over there*. If gated communities and rent-a-cops were enough, September 11 never would have happened.

History is full of turning points like that terrible day, *but no turning-back points*. We ignore the Gap's existence at our own peril, because it will not go away until we as a nation respond to the challenge of making globalization truly global.

Handicapping the Gap

My list of real trouble for the world in the 1990s, today, and tomorrow, starting in our own backyard:

(1) **Haiti** Efforts to build a nation in 1990s were disappointing. • We have been going into Haiti for about a century, and we will go back when boat people start flowing in during the next crisis—without fail.

(2) **Colombia** Country is broken into several lawless chunks, with private armies, rebels, narcos, and legit government all working the place over. • Drugs still flow. • Ties between drug cartels and rebels grew over decade, and now we know of links to international terror, too. • We get involved, keep promising more, and keep getting nowhere. Piecemeal, incremental approach is clearly not working.

(3) **Brazil and Argentina** Both on the bubble between the Gap and the Functioning Core. Both played the globalization game to hilt in nineties and both feel abused now. The danger of falling off the wagon and going self-destructively leftist or rightist is very real. • No military threats to speak of, except against their own democracies (the return of the generals). • South American alliance MERCOSUR tries to carve out its own reality while Washington pushes Free Trade of Americas, but we may have to settle for agreements with Chile or for pulling only Chile into bigger NAFTA. Will Brazil and Argentina force themselves to be left out and then resent it? • Amazon a large ungovernable area for Brazil, plus all that environmental damage continues to pile up. Will the world eventually care enough to step in?

(4) **Former Yugoslavia** For most of the past decade, served as shorthand for Europe's inability to get its act together even in its own backyard. • Will be long-term baby-sitting job for the West.

(5) **Congo and Rwanda/Burundi** Two to three million dead in central Africa from all the fighting across the decade. How much worse can it get before we try to do something, anything? Three million more dead? • Congo is a carrion state—not quite dead or alive, and everyone is feeding off it. • And then there's AIDS.

(6) **Angola** Never really has solved its ongoing civil war (1.5 million dead in past quarter century). • Basically at conflict with self since mid-seventies, when Portuguese "empire" fell. • Life expectancy right now is under forty!

(7) **South Africa** The only functioning Core country in Africa, but it's on the bubble. Lots of concerns that South Africa is a gateway country for terror networks trying to access Core through back door. • Endemic crime is biggest security threat. • And then there's AIDS.

(8) **Israel-Palestine** Terror will not abate—there is no next generation in the West Bank that wants anything but more violence. • Wall going up right now will be the Berlin Wall of twenty-first century. Eventually, outside powers will end up providing security to keep the two sides apart (this divorce is going to be very painful). • There is always the chance of somebody (Saddam in desperation?) trying to light up Israel with weapons of mass destruction (WMD) and triggering the counterpunch we all fear Israel is capable of.

(9) **Saudi Arabia** The let-them-eat-cake mentality of royal mafia will eventually trigger violent instability from within. • Paying terrorists protection money to stay away will likewise eventually fail, so danger will come from outside, too. • Huge young population with little prospects for future, and a ruling elite whose main source of income is a declining long-term asset. And yet the oil will matter to enough of the world far enough into the future that the United States will never let this place really tank, no matter what it takes.

(10) **Iraq** Question of when and how, not if. • Then there's the huge rehab job. We will have to build a security regime for the whole region.

(11) **Somalia** Chronic lack of governance. • Chronic food problems. • Chronic problem of terrorist-network infiltration. • We went in with Marines and Special Forces and left disillusioned—a poor man's Vietnam for the 1990s. Will be hard-pressed not to return.

(12) **Iran** Counterrevolution has already begun: This time the students want to throw the mullahs out. • Iran wants to be friends with U.S., but resurgence of fundamentalists may be the price we pay to invade Iraq. • The mullahs support terror, and their push for WMD is real: Does this make them inevitable target once Iraq and North Korea are settled?

(13) **Afghanistan** Lawless, violent place even before the Taliban stepped onstage and started pulling it back toward seventh century (short trip). • Government sold to Al Qaeda for pennies on the dollar. • Big source of narcotics (heroin). • Now U.S. stuck there for long haul, rooting out hardcore terrorists/rebels who've chosen to stay.

(14) **Pakistan** There is always the real danger of their having the bomb and using it out of weakness in conflict with India (very close call with December 13, 2001, New Delhi bombing). • Out of fear that Pakistan may fall to radical Muslims, we end up backing hard-line military types we don't

really trust. • Clearly infested with Al Qaeda. • Was on its way to being declared a rogue state by U.S. until September 11 forced us to cooperate again. Simply put, Pakistan doesn't seem to control much of its own territory.

(15) **North Korea** Marching toward WMD. • Bizarre recent behavior of Pyongyang (admitting kidnappings, breaking promises on nukes, shipping weapons to places we disapprove of and getting caught, signing agreements with Japan that seem to signal new era, talking up new economic zone next to China) suggests it is intent (like some mental patient) on provoking crises. • We live in fear of Kim's Götterdämmerung scenario (he is nuts). • Population deteriorating—how much more can they stand? • After Iraq, may be next.

(16) **Indonesia** Usual fears about breakup and "world's largest Muslim population." • Casualty of Asian economic crisis (really got wiped out). • Hot spot for terror networks, as we have discovered.

New/integrating members of Core I worry may be lost in coming years:

(17) **China** Running lots of races against itself in terms of reducing the unprofitable state-run enterprises while not triggering too much unemployment, plus dealing with all that growth in energy demand and accompanying pollution, plus coming pension crisis as population ages. • New generation of leaders looks suspiciously like unimaginative technocrats— big question if they are up to task. • If none of those macro pressures trigger internal instability, there is always the fear that the Communist party won't go quietly into the night in terms of allowing more political freedoms and that at some point, economic freedom won't be enough for the masses. Right now the CCP is very corrupt and mostly a parasite on the country, but it still calls the big shots in Beijing. • Army seems to be getting more disassociated from society and reality, focusing ever more myopically on countering U.S. threat to their ability to threaten Taiwan, which remains the one flash point that could matter. • And then there's AIDS.

(18) **Russia** Putin has long way to go in his dictatorship of the law; the mafia and robber barons still have too much power. • Chechnya and the near-abroad in general will drag Moscow into violence, but it will be kept within the federation by and large. • U.S. moving into Central Asia is a testy thing—a relationship that can sour if not handled just right. • Russia has so many internal problems (financial weakness, environmental damage, et cetera) and depends too much on energy exports to feel safe (does bringing Iraq back online after invasion kill their golden goose?). • And then there's AIDS.

(19) **India** First, there's always the danger of nuking it out with Pakistan. • Short of that, Kashmir pulls them into conflict with Pak, and that involves U.S. now in way it never did before due to war on terror. • India is microcosm of globalization: the high tech, the massive poverty, the islands of development, the tensions between cultures/civilizations/religions/et cetera.

It is too big to succeed, and too big to let fail. • Wants to be big responsible military player in region, wants to be strong friend of U.S., and also wants desperately to catch up with China in development (the self-imposed pressure to succeed is enormous). • And then there's AIDS.

50

DAVID HELD AND ANTHONY McGREW, DAVID GOLDBLATT AND JONATHAN PERRATON

THE GLOBALIZATION DEBATE

Globalization is an idea whose time has come. From obscure origins in French and American writings in the 1960s, the concept of globalization finds expression today in all the world's major languages (cf. Modelski, 1972). Yet, it lacks precise definition. Indeed, globalization is in danger of becoming, if it has not already become, the cliché of our times: the big idea which encompasses everything from global financial markets to the Internet but which delivers little substantive insight into the contemporary human condition.

Clichés, nevertheless, often capture elements of the lived experience of an epoch. In this respect, globalization reflects a widespread perception that the world is rapidly being moulded into a shared social space by economic and technological forces and that developments in one region of the world can have profound consequences for the life chances of individuals or communities on the other side of the globe. For many, globalization is also associated with a sense of political fatalism and chronic insecurity in that the sheer scale of contemporary social and economic change appears to outstrip the capacity of national governments or citizens to control, contest or resist that change. The limits to national politics, in other words, are forcefully suggested by globalization.

Although the popular rhetoric of globalization may capture aspects of the contemporary zeitgeist, there is a burgeoning academic debate as to whether globalization, as an analytical construct, delivers any added value in the search for a coherent understanding of the historical forces which, at the dawn of the

SOURCE: From Held, David, and Anthony McGrew, David Goldblatt and Jonathan Perraton, *Global Transformations: Politics, Economics, and Culture.* Copyright © 1999 David Held, Anthony McGrew, David Goldblatt, and Jonathan Perraton. All rights reserved. Used with permission of Stanford University Press, www.sup.org.

new millennium, are shaping the socio-political realities of everyday life. Despite a vast and expanding literature there is, somewhat surprisingly, no cogent theory of globalization nor even a systematic analysis of its primary features. Moreover, few studies of globalization proffer a coherent historical narrative which distinguishes between those events that are transitory or immediate and those developments that signal the emergence of a new conjuncture; that is, a transformation of the nature, form and prospects of human communities. In acknowledging the deficiencies of existing approaches, this volume seeks to develop a distinctive account of globalization which is both historically grounded and informed by a rigorous analytical framework. The framework is explicated in this introduction, while subsequent chapters use it to tell the story of globalization and to assess its implications for the governance and politics of nation-states today. In this respect, the introduction provides the intellectual foundation for addressing the central questions which animate the entire study:

- What is globalization? How should it be conceptualized?
- Does contemporary globalization represent a novel condition?
- Is globalization associated with the demise, the resurgence or the transformation of state power?
- Does contemporary globalization impose new limits to politics? How can globalization be "civilized" and democratized?

As will soon become apparent, these questions are at the root of the many controversies and debates which find expression in contemporary discussions about globalization and its consequences. The subsequent pages offer a way of thinking about how these questions might be addressed.

THE GLOBALIZATION DEBATE

Globalization may be thought of initially as the widening, deepening and speeding up of worldwide interconnectedness in all aspects of contemporary social life, from the cultural to the criminal, the financial to the spiritual. That computer programmers in India now deliver services in real time to their employers in Europe and the USA, while the cultivation of poppies in Burma can be linked to drug abuse in Berlin or Belfast, illustrate the ways in which contemporary globalization connects communities in one region of the world to developments in another continent. But beyond a general acknowledgement of a real or perceived intensification of global interconnectedness there is substantial disagreement as to how globalization is best conceptualized, how one should think about its causal dynamics, and how one should characterize its structural consequences, if any. A vibrant debate on these issues has developed in which it is possible to distinguish three broad schools of thought, which we will refer to as the *hyperglobalizers*, the *sceptics*, and the *transformationalists*. In essence each of these schools may be said to represent a distinctive account of globalization—an attempt to understand and explain this social phenomenon.

For the hyperglobalizers, such as Ohmae, contemporary globalization defines a new era in which peoples everywhere are increasingly subject to the disciplines of the global marketplace (1990; 1995). By contrast the sceptics, such
as Hirst and Thompson, argue that globalization is essentially a myth which
conceals the reality of an international economy increasingly segmented into
three major regional blocs in which national governments remain very
powerful (1996a; 1996b). Finally, for the transformationalists, chief among
them being Rosenau and Giddens, contemporary patterns of globalization are
conceived as historically unprecedented such that states and societies across
the globe are experiencing a process of profound change as they try to adapt
to a more interconnected but highly uncertain world (Giddens, 1990, 1996;
Rosenau, 1997).

Interestingly, none of these three schools map directly on to traditional ideological positions or worldviews. Within the hyperglobalist's camp orthodox
neoliberal accounts of globalization can be found alongside Marxist accounts,
while among the sceptics conservative as well as radical accounts share similar
conceptions of, and conclusions about, the nature of contemporary globalization. Moreover, none of the great traditions of social enquiry—liberal, conservative and Marxist—has an agreed perspective on globalization as a
socio-economic phenomenon. Among Marxists globalization is understood in
quite incompatible ways as, for instance, the extension of monopoly capitalist
imperialism or, alternatively, as a radically new form of globalized capitalism
(Callinicos et al., 1994; Gill, 1995; Amin, 1997). Similarly, despite their
broadly orthodox neoliberal starting points, Ohmae and Redwood produce
very different accounts of, and conclusions about, the dynamics of contemporary globalization (Ohmae, 1995; Redwood, 1993). Among the hyperglobalizers, sceptics and transformationalists there is a rich diversity of intellectual
approaches and normative convictions. Yet, despite this diversity, each of the
perspectives reflects a general set of arguments and conclusions about globalization with respect to its

- conceptualization
- causal dynamics
- socio-economic consequences
- implications for state power and governance
- and historical trajectory.

It is useful to dwell on the pattern of argument within and between approaches
since this will shed light on the fundamental issues at stake in the globalization
debate.[1]

THE HYPERGLOBALIST THESIS

For the hyperglobalizers, globalization defines a new epoch of human history in
which "traditional nation-states have become unnatural, even impossible
business units in a global economy" (Ohmae, 1995, p. 5; cf. Wriston, 1992;
Guéhenno, 1995). Such a view of globalization generally privileges an economic

logic and, in its neoliberal variant, celebrates the emergence of a single global market and the principle of global competition as the harbingers of human progress. Hyperglobalizers argue that economic globalization is bringing about a "denationalization" of economies through the establishment of transnational networks of production, trade and finance. In this "borderless" economy, national governments are relegated to little more than transmission belts for global capital or, ultimately, simple intermediate institutions sandwiched between increasingly powerful local, regional and global mechanisms of governance. As Strange puts it, "the impersonal forces of world markets . . . are now more powerful than the states to whom ultimate political authority over society and economy is supposed to belong . . . the declining authority of states is reflected in a growing diffusion of authority to other institutions and associations, and to local and regional bodies" (1996, p. 4; cf. Reich, 1991). In this respect, many hyperglobalizers share a conviction that economic globalization is constructing new forms of social organization that are supplanting, or that will eventually supplant, traditional nation-states as the primary economic and political units of world society.

Within this framework there is considerable normative divergence between, on the one hand, the neoliberals who welcome the triumph of individual autonomy and the market principle over state power, and the radicals or neo-Marxists for whom contemporary globalization represents the triumph of an oppressive global capitalism (cf. Ohmae, 1995; Greider, 1997). But despite divergent ideological convictions, there exists a shared set of beliefs that globalization is primarily an economic phenomenon; that an increasingly integrated global economy exists today; that the needs of global capital impose a neoliberal economic discipline on all governments such that politics is no longer the "art of the possible" but rather the practice of "sound economic management."

Furthermore, the hyperglobalizers claim that economic globalization is generating a new pattern of winners as well as losers in the global economy. The old North–South division is argued to be an increasing anachronism as a new global division of labour replaces the traditional core–periphery structure with a more complex architecture of economic power. Against this background, governments have to "manage" the social consequences of globalization, or those who "having been left behind, want not so much a chance to move forward as to hold others back" (Ohmae, 1995, p. 64). However, they also have to manage increasingly in a context in which the constraints of global financial and competitive disciplines make social democratic models of social protection untenable and spell the demise of associated welfare state policies (J. Gray, 1998). Globalization may be linked with a growing polarization between winners and losers in the global economy. But this need not be so, for, at least in the neoliberal view, global economic competition does not necessarily produce zero-sum outcomes. While particular groups within a country may be made worse off as a result of global competition, nearly all countries have a comparative advantage in producing certain goods which can be exploited in the long run. Neo-Marxists and radicals regard such an "optimistic view" as unjustified, believing that global capitalism creates and reinforces structural patterns of inequality within and between countries. But they agree at least with their neoliberal counterparts that traditional welfare options for social protection are looking increasingly threadbare and difficult to sustain.

Among the elites and "knowledge workers" of the new global economy tacit transnational "class" allegiances have evolved, cemented by an ideological attachment to a neoliberal economic orthodoxy. For those who are currently marginalized, the worldwide diffusion of a consumerist ideology also imposes a new sense of identity, displacing traditional cultures and ways of life. The global spread of liberal democracy further reinforces the sense of an emerging global civilization defined by universal standards of economic and political organization. This "global civilization" is also replete with its own mechanisms of global governance, whether it be the IMF or the disciplines of the world market, such that states and peoples are increasingly the subjects of new public and private global or regional authorities (Gill, 1995; Ohmae, 1995; Strange, 1996; Cox, 1997). Accordingly, for many neoliberals, globalization is considered as the harbinger of the first truly global civilization, while for many radicals it represents the first global "market civilization" (Perlmutter, 1991; Gill, 1995; Greider, 1997).

In this hyperglobalist account the rise of the global economy, the emergence of institutions of global governance, and the global diffusion and hybridization of cultures are interpreted as evidence of a radically new world order, an order which prefigures the demise of the nation-state (Luard, 1990; Ohmae, 1995; Albrow, 1996). Since the national economy is increasingly a site of transnational and global flows, as opposed to the primary container of national socio-economic activity, the authority and legitimacy of the nation-state are challenged: national governments become increasingly unable either to control what transpires within their own borders or to fulfil by themselves the demands of their own citizens. Moreover, as institutions of global and regional governance acquire a bigger role, the sovereignty and autonomy of the state are further eroded. On the other hand, the conditions facilitating transnational cooperation between peoples, given global infrastructures of communication and increasing awareness of many common interests, have never been so propitious. In this regard, there is evidence of an emerging "global civil society."

Economic power and political power, in this hyperglobalist view, are becoming effectively denationalized and diffused such that nation-states, whatever the claims of national politicians, are increasingly becoming "a transitional mode of organization for managing economic affairs" (Ohmae, 1995, p. 149). Whether issuing from a liberal or radical/socialist perspective, the hyperglobalist thesis represents globalization as embodying nothing less than the fundamental reconfiguration of the "framework of human action" (Albrow, 1996, p. 85).

THE SCEPTICAL THESIS

By comparison the sceptics, drawing on statistical evidence of world flows of trade, investment and labour from the nineteenth century, maintain that contemporary levels of economic interdependence are by no means historically unprecedented. Rather than globalization, which to the sceptics necessarily implies a perfectly integrated worldwide economy in which the "law of one price" prevails, the historical evidence at best confirms only heightened levels of internationalization, that is, interactions between predominantly national economies (Hirst and Thompson, 1996b). In arguing that globalization is a myth, the sceptics rely on a wholly economistic conception of globalization, equating it primarily with a perfectly integrated global market. By contending that levels of economic integration fall short of this "ideal type" and that such integration as there is remains much less significant than in the late nineteenth century (the era of the classical Gold Standard), the sceptics are free to conclude that the extent of contemporary "globalization" is wholly exaggerated (Hirst, 1997). In this respect, the sceptics consider the hyperglobalist thesis as fundamentally flawed and also politically naive since it underestimates the enduring power of national governments to regulate international economic activity. Rather than being out of control, the forces of internationalization themselves depend on the regulatory power of national governments to ensure continuing economic liberalization.

For most sceptics, if the current evidence demonstrates anything it is that economic activity is undergoing a significant "regionalization" as the world economy evolves in the direction of three major financial and trading blocs, that is, Europe, Asia-Pacific and North America (Ruigrok and Tulder, 1995; Boyer and Drache, 1996; Hirst and Thompson, 1996b). In comparison with the classical Gold Standard era, the world economy is therefore significantly less integrated than it once was (Boyer and Drache, 1996; Hirst and Thompson, 1996a). Among the sceptics, globalization and regionalization are conceived as contradictory tendencies. As both Gordon and Weiss conclude, in comparison with the age of world empires, the international economy has become considerably less global in its geographical embrace (Gordon, 1988; Weiss, 1998).

Sceptics tend also to discount the presumption that internationalization prefigures the emergence of a new, less state-centric world order. Far from considering national governments as becoming immobilized by international imperatives, they point to their growing centrality in the regulation and active promotion of cross-border economic activity. Governments are not the passive victims of internationalization but, on the contrary, its primary architects. Indeed, Gilpin considers internationalization largely a by-product of the US-initiated multilateral economic order which, in the aftermath of the Second World War, created the impetus for the liberalization of national economies (Gilpin, 1987). From a very different perspective, Callinicos and others explain the recent intensification of worldwide trade and foreign investment as a new phase of Western imperialism in which national governments, as the agents of monopoly capital, are deeply implicated (Callinicos et al., 1994).

However, despite such differences of emphasis, there is a convergence of opinion within the sceptical camp that, whatever its exact driving forces, internationalization has not been accompanied by an erosion of North–South inequalities but, on the contrary, by the growing economic marginalization of many "Third World" states as trade and investment flows within the rich North intensify to the exclusion of much of the rest of the globe (Hirst and Thompson, 1996b). Moreover, Krugman questions the popular belief that a new international division of labour is emerging in which deindustrialization in the North can be traced to the operation of multinational corporations exporting jobs to the South (Krugman, 1996). Similarly Ruigrok and Tulder, and Thompson and Allen seek to demolish the "myth" of the "global corporation," highlighting the fact that foreign investment flows are concentrated among the advanced capitalist states and that most multinationals remain primarily creatures of their home states or regions (Ruigrok and Tulder, 1995; Thompson and Allen, 1997). Accordingly, the sceptical thesis is generally dismissive of the notion that internationalization is bringing about a profound or even significant restructuring of global economic relations. In this respect, the sceptical position is an acknowledgement of the deeply rooted patterns of inequality and hierarchy in the world economy, which in structural terms have changed only marginally over the last century.

Such inequality, in the view of many sceptics, contributes to the advance of both fundamentalism and aggressive nationalism such that rather than the emergence of a global civilization, as the hyperglobalizers predict, the world is fragmenting into civilizational blocs and cultural and ethnic enclaves (Huntington, 1996). The notion of cultural homogenization and a global culture are thus further myths which fall victim to the sceptical argument. In addition, the deepening of global inequalities, the realpolitik of international relations and the "clash of civilizations" expose the illusory nature of "global governance" in so far as the management of world order remains, as it has since the last century, overwhelmingly the preserve of Western states. In this respect, the sceptical argument tends to conceive of global governance and economic internationalization as primarily Western projects, the main object of which is to sustain the primacy of the West in world affairs. As E. H. Carr once observed: "international order and 'international solidarity' will always be slogans of those who feel strong enough to impose them on others" (1981, p. 87).

In general the sceptics take issue with all of the primary claims of the hyperglobalizers pointing to the comparatively greater levels of economic interdependence and the more extensive geographical reach of the world economy at the beginning of the twentieth century. They reject the popular "myth" that the power of national governments or state sovereignty is being undermined today by economic internationalization or global governance (Krasner, 1993, 1995). Some argue that "globalization" more often than not reflects a politically convenient rationale for implementing unpopular orthodox neoliberal economic strategies (Hirst, 1997). Weiss, Scharpf and Armingeon, among others, argue that the available evidence contradicts the popular belief that there has been a convergence of macroeconomic and welfare policies across the globe (Weiss, 1998; Scharpf, 1991; Armingeon, 1997). While international economic conditions may constrain what governments can do, governments are by no means immobilized. The internationalization of capital may, as Weiss argues, "not merely restrict policy choices, but expand them as well" (1998, pp. 184ff.). Rather than the world becoming more interdependent, as the hyperglobalizers assume, the sceptics seek to expose the myths which sustain the globalization thesis.

THE TRANSFORMATIONALIST THESIS

At the heart of the transformationalist thesis is a conviction that, at the dawn of a new millennium, globalization is a central driving force behind the rapid social, political and economic changes that are reshaping modern societies and world order (Giddens, 1990; Scholte, 1993; Castells, 1996). According to the proponents of this view, contemporary processes of globalization are historically unprecedented such that governments and societies across the globe are having to adjust to a world in which there is no longer a clear distinction between international and domestic, external and internal affairs (Rosenau, 1990; Cammilleri and Falk, 1992; Ruggie, 1993; Linklater and MacMillan, 1995; Sassen, 1996). For Rosenau, the growth of "intermestic" affairs define a "new frontier," the expanding political, economic and social space in which the fate of societies and communities is decided (1997, pp. 4–5). In this respect, globalization is conceived as a powerful transformative force which is responsible for a "massive shake-out" of societies, economies, institutions of governance and world order (Giddens, 1996).

In the transformationalist account, however, the direction of this "shake-out" remains uncertain, since globalization is conceived as an essentially contingent historical process replete with contradictions (Mann, 1997). At issue is a dynamic and open-ended conception of where globalization might be leading and the kind of world order which it might prefigure. In comparison with the sceptical and hyperglobalist accounts, the transformationalists make no claims about the future trajectory of globalization; nor do they seek to evaluate the present in relation to some single, fixed ideal-type "globalized world," whether a global market or a global civilization. Rather, transformationalist accounts emphasize globalization as a long-term historical process which is inscribed with contradictions and which is significantly shaped by conjunctural factors.

Such caution about the exact future of globalization is matched, nonetheless, by the conviction that contemporary patterns of global economic, military, technological, ecological, migratory, political and cultural flows are historically unprecedented. As Nierop puts it, "virtually all countries in the world, if not all parts of their territory and all segments of their society, are now functionally part of that larger [global] system in one or more respects" (1994, p. 171). But the existence of a single global system is not taken as evidence of global convergence or of the arrival of single world society. On the contrary, for the transformationalists, globalization is associated with new patterns of global stratification in which some states, societies and communities are becoming increasingly enmeshed in the global order while others are becoming increasingly marginalized. A new configuration of global power relations is held to be crystallizing as the North–South division rapidly gives way to a new international division of labour such that the "familiar pyramid of the core–periphery hierarchy is no longer a geographic but a social division of the world economy" (Hoogvelt, 1997, p. xii). To talk of North and South, of First World and Third World, is to overlook the ways in which globalization has recast traditional patterns of inclusion and exclusion between countries by forging new hierarchies which cut across and penetrate all societies and regions of the world. North and South, First World and Third World, are no longer "out there" but nestled together within all the world's major cities. Rather than the traditional pyramid analogy of the world social structure, with a tiny top echelon and spreading mass base, the global social structure can be envisaged as a three-tier arrangement of concentric circles, each cutting across national boundaries, representing respectively the elites, the contented and the marginalized (Hoogvelt, 1997).

The recasting of patterns of global stratification is linked with the growing deterritorialization of economic activity as production and finance increasingly acquire a global and transnational dimension. From somewhat different starting points, Castells and Ruggie, among others, argue that national economies are being reorganized by processes of economic globalization such that national economic space no longer coincides with national territorial borders (Castells, 1996; Ruggie, 1996). In this globalizing economy, systems of transnational production, exchange and finance weave together ever more tightly the fortunes of communities and households on different continents.

At the core of the transformationalist case is a belief that contemporary globalization is reconstituting or "re-engineering" the power, functions and authority of national governments. While not disputing that states still retain the ultimate legal claim to "effective supremacy over what occurs within their own territories," the transformationalists argue that this is juxtaposed, to varying degrees, with the expanding jurisdiction of institutions of international governance and the constraints of, as well as the obligations derived from, international law. This is especially evident in the EU, where sovereign power is divided between international, national and local authorities, but it is also evident in the operation of the World Trade Organization (WTO) (Goodman, 1997). However, even where sovereignty still appears intact, states no longer, if they ever did, retain sole command of what transpires within their own territorial boundaries. Complex global systems, from the financial to the ecological, connect the fate of communities in one locale to the fate of communities in distant regions of the world. Furthermore, global infrastructures of communication and transport support new forms of economic and social organization which transcend national boundaries without any consequent diminution of efficiency or control. Sites of power and the subjects of power may be literally, as well as metaphorically, oceans apart. In these circumstances, the notion of the nation-state as a self-governing, autonomous unit appears to be more a normative claim than a descriptive statement. The modern institution of territorially circumscribed sovereign rule appears somewhat anomalous juxtaposed with the transnational organization of many aspects of contemporary economic and social life (Sandel, 1996). Globalization, in this account, is therefore associated with a transformation or, to use Ruggie's term, an "unbundling" of the relationship between sovereignty, territoriality and state power (Ruggie, 1993; Sassen, 1996).

Of course, few states have ever exercised complete or absolute sovereignty within their own territorial boundaries, as the practice of diplomatic immunity highlights (Sassen, 1996). Indeed the practice, as opposed to the doctrine, of sovereign statehood has always readily adapted to changing historical realities (Murphy, 1996). In arguing that globalization is transforming or reconstituting the power and authority of national governments, the transformationalists reject both the hyperglobalist rhetoric of the end of the sovereign nation-state and the sceptics' claim that "nothing much has changed." Instead, they assert that a new "sovereignty regime" is displacing traditional conceptions of statehood as an absolute, indivisible, territorially exclusive and zero-sum form of public power (Held, 1991). Accordingly, sovereignty today is, they suggest, best understood "less as a territorially defined barrier than a bargaining resource for a politics characterized by complex transnational networks" (Keohane, 1995).

This is not to argue that territorial boundaries retain no political, military or symbolic significance but rather to acknowledge that, conceived as the primary spatial markers of modern life, they have become increasingly problematic in an era of intensified globalization. Sovereignty, state power and territoriality thus stand today in a more complex relationship than in the epoch during which the modern nation-state was being forged. Indeed, the argument of the transformationalists is that globalization is associated not only with a new "sovereignty regime" but also with the emergence of powerful new non-territorial forms of economic and political organization in the global domain, such as multinational corporations, transnational social movements, international regulatory agencies, etc. In this sense, world order can no longer be conceived as purely state-centric or even primarily state governed, as authority has become increasingly diffused among public and private agencies at the local, national, regional and global levels. Nation-states are no longer the sole centres or the principal forms of governance or authority in the world (Rosenau, 1997).

Given this changing global order, the form and functions of the state are having to adapt as governments seek coherent strategies of engaging with a globalizing world. Distinctive strategies are being followed from the model of the neoliberal minimal state to the models of the developmental state (government as the central promoter of economic expansion) and the catalytic state (government as facilitator of coordinated and collective action). In addition, governments have become increasingly outward looking as they seek to pursue cooperative strategies and to construct international regulatory regimes to manage more effectively the growing array of cross-border issues which regularly surface on national agendas. Rather than globalization bringing about the "end of the state," it has encouraged a spectrum of adjustment strategies and, in certain respects, a more activist state. Accordingly, the power of national governments is not necessarily diminished by globalization but on the contrary is being reconstituted and restructured in response to the growing complexity of processes of governance in a more interconnected world (Rosenau, 1997).

The three dominant tendencies in the globalization debate are summarized in Table 1. To move beyond the debate between these three approaches requires a framework of enquiry through which the principal claims of each might be assessed. But to construct such a framework demands, as an initial condition, some understanding of the primary faultlines around which the debate itself revolves. Identifying the critical issues in the debate creates an intellectual foundation for thinking about how globalization might best be conceptualized and the particular grounds on which any assessment of competing claims about it might be pursued.

SOURCES OF CONTENTION IN THE GLOBALIZATION DEBATE

Five principal issues constitute the major sources of contention among existing approaches to globalization. These concern matters of

- conceptualization
- causation
- periodization
- impacts
- and the trajectories of globalization.

In exploring each of these in turn a cumulative picture will develop of the requirements of a rigorous account of globalization, a picture which will help move us beyond the debate between the three approaches outlined above.

CONCEPTUALIZATION

Among both the sceptics and hyperglobalizers there is a tendency to conceptualize globalization as prefiguring a singular condition or end-state, that is, a fully integrated global market with price and interest rate equalization. Accordingly, contemporary patterns of economic globalization are assessed, as previously noted, in relation to how far they match up to this ideal type (Hirst

TABLE 1 Conceptualizing Globalization: Three Tendencies

	HYPERGLOBALISTS	SCEPTICS	TRANSFORMATIONALISTS
What's new?	A global age	Trading blocs, weaker geogovernance than in earlier periods	Historically unprecedented levels of global inter-connectedness
Dominant features	Global capitalism, global governance, global civil society	World less inter-dependent than in 1890s	"Thick" (intensive and extensive) globalization
Power of national governments	Declining or eroding	Reinforced or enhanced	Reconstituted, restructured
Driving forces of globalization	Capitalism and technology	States and markets	Combined forces of modernity
Pattern of stratification	Erosion of old hierarchies	Increased marginal-ization of South	New architecture of world order
Dominant motif	McDonalds, Madonna, etc.	National interest	Transformation of political community
Conceptualization of globalization	As a reordering of the framework of human action	As internationalization and regionalization	As the reordering of interregional relations and action at a distance
Historical trajectory	Global civilization	Regional blocs/clash of civilizations	Indeterminate: global integration and fragmentation
Summary argument	The end of the nation-state	Internationalization depends on state acquiescence and support	Globalization transforming state power and world Politics

and Thompson, 1996b). But even on its own terms this approach is flawed, since there is no a priori reason to assume global markets need be "perfectly competitive" any more than national markets have ever been. National markets may well fall short of perfect competition but this does not prevent economists from characterizing them as markets, albeit markets with various forms of "imperfections." Global markets, as with domestic markets, can be problematic.

In addition, this "ideal type" approach is both unacceptably teleological and empiricist: unacceptably teleological in so far as the present is (and apparently should be) interpreted as the stepping stone in some linear progression towards a given future end-state, although there is no logical or empirical reason to assume that globalization—any more than industrialization or democratization—has one fixed end condition; and unacceptably empiricist in that the statistical evidence of global trends is taken by itself to confirm, qualify or reject the globalization thesis, even though such a methodology can generate considerable difficulties (Ohmae, 1990; R. J. B. Jones, 1995; Hirst and Thompson, 1996b). For instance, the fact that more people in the world speak (dialects of) Chinese than English as a first language does not necessarily confirm the thesis that Chinese is a global language. Likewise, even if it could be shown that trade–GDP ratios for Western states in the 1890s were similar to, or even higher than, those for the 1990s, this evidence by itself would reveal little about the social and political impacts of trade in either period. Caution and theoretical care are needed in drawing conclusions from seemingly clear global trends. Any convincing account of globalization must weigh the significance of relevant qualitative evidence and interpretative issues.

In comparison, socio-historical approaches to the study of globalization regard it as a process which has no single fixed or determinate historical "destination," whether understood in terms of a perfectly integrated global market, a global society or a global civilization (Giddens, 1990; Geyer and Bright, 1995; Rosenau, 1997). There is no a priori reason to assume that globalization must simply evolve in a single direction or that it can only be understood in relation to a single ideal condition (perfect global markets). Accordingly, for these transformationalists, globalization is conceived in terms of a more contingent and open-ended historical process which does not fit with orthodox linear models of social change (cf. Graham, 1997). Moreover, these accounts tend also to be sceptical of the view that quantitative evidence alone can confirm or deny the "reality" of globalization since they are interested in those qualitative shifts which it may engender in the nature of societies and the exercise of power; shifts which are rarely completely captured by statistical data.

Linked to the issue of globalization as a historical process is the related matter of whether globalization should be understood in singular or differentiated terms. Much of the sceptical and hyperglobalist literature tends to conceive globalization as a largely singular process equated, more often than not, with economic or cultural interconnectedness (Ohmae, 1990; Robertson, 1992; Krasner, 1993; Boyer and Drache, 1996; Cox, 1996; Hirst and Thompson, 1996b; Huntington, 1996; Strange, 1996; Burbach et al., 1997). Yet to conceive it thus ignores the distinctive patterns of globalization in different aspects of social life, from the political to the cultural. In this respect, globalization might be better conceived as a highly differentiated process which finds expression in all the key domains of social activity (including the political, the military, the legal, the ecological, the criminal, etc.). It is by no means clear why it should be assumed that it is a purely economic or cultural phenomenon (Giddens, 1991; Axford, 1995; Albrow, 1996). Accordingly, accounts of globalization which acknowledge this differentiation may be more satisfactory in explaining its form and dynamics than those which overlook it.

CAUSATION

One of the central contentions in the globalization debate concerns the issue of causation: what is driving this process? In offering an answer to this question existing accounts tend to cluster around two distinct sets of explanations: those which identify a single or primary imperative, such as capitalism or technological change; and those which explain globalization as the product of a combination of factors, including technological change, market forces, ideology and political decisions. Put simply, the distinction is effectively between monocausal and multicausal accounts of globalization. Though the tendency in much of the existing literature is to conflate globalization with the expansionary imperatives of markets or capitalism this has drawn substantial criticism on the grounds that such an explanation is far too reductionist. In response, there are a number of significant attempts to develop a more comprehensive explanation of globalization which highlights the complex intersection between a multiplicity of driving forces, embracing economic, technological, cultural and political change (Giddens, 1990; Robertson, 1992; Scholte, 1993; Axford, 1995; Albrow, 1996; Rosenau, 1990, 1997). Any convincing analysis of contemporary globalization has to come to terms with the central question of causation and, in so doing, offer a coherent view.

But the controversy about the underlying causes of globalization is connected to a wider debate about modernity (Giddens, 1991; Robertson, 1992; Albrow, 1996; Connolly, 1996). For some, globalization can be understood simply as the global diffusion of Western modernity, that is, Westernization. World systems theory, for instance, equates globalization with the spread of Western capitalism and Western institutions (Amin, 1996; Benton, 1996). By contrast, others draw a distinction between Westernization and globalization and reject the idea that the latter is synonymous with the former (Giddens, 1990). At stake in this debate is a rather fundamental issue: whether globalization today has to be understood as something more than simply the expanding reach of Western power and influence. No cogent analysis of globalization can avoid confronting this issue.

PERIODIZATION

Simply seeking to describe the "shape" of contemporary globalization necessarily relies (implicitly or explicitly) on some kind of historical narrative. Such narratives, whether they issue from grand civilizational studies or world historical studies, have significant implications for what conclusions are reached about the historically unique or distinctive features of contemporary globalization (Mazlish and Buultjens, 1993; Geyer and Bright, 1995). In particular, how world history is periodized is central to the kinds of conclusions which are deduced from any historical analysis, most especially, of course, with respect to the question of what's new about contemporary globalization. Clearly, in answering such a question, it makes a significant difference whether contemporary globalization is defined as the entire postwar era, the post-1970s era, or the twentieth century in general.

Recent historical studies of world systems and of patterns of civilizational interaction bring into question the commonly accepted view that globalization is primarily a phenomenon of the modern age (McNeill, 1995; Roudometof and Robertson, 1995; Bentley, 1996; Frank and Gills, 1996). The existence of world religions and the trade networks of the medieval era encourage a greater sensitivity to the idea that globalization is a process which has a long history. This implies the need to look beyond the modern era in any attempt to offer an explanation of the novel features of contemporary globalization. But to do so requires some kind of analytical framework offering a platform for contrasting and comparing different phases or historical forms of globalization over what the French historian Braudel refers to as the *longue durée*—that is, the passage of centuries rather than decades (Helleiner, 1997).

IMPACTS

There is an extensive literature implicating economic globalization in the demise of social democracy and the modern welfare state (Garrett and Lange, 1991; Banuri and Schor, 1992; Gill, 1995; Amin, 1996; J. Gray, 1996; Cox, 1997). Global competitive pressures have forced governments, according to this view, to curtail state spending and interventions; for, despite different partisan commitments, all governments have been pressed in the same direction. Underlying this thesis is a rather deterministic conception of globalization as an "iron cage" which imposes a global financial discipline on governments, severely constraining the scope for progressive policies and undermining the social bargain on which the post-Second World War welfare state rested. Thus there has apparently been a growing convergence of economic and welfare strategies among Western states, irrespective of the ideology of incumbent governments.

This thesis is contested vociferously by a plethora of recent studies which cast serious doubt on the idea that globalization effectively "immobilizes" national governments in the conduct of economic policy (Scharpf, 1991; R. J. B. Jones, 1995; Ruigrok and Tulder, 1995; Hirst and Thompson, 1996b). As Milner and Keohane observe, "the impact of the world economy on countries that are open to its influence does not appear to be uniform" (1996, p. 14). Such studies have delivered significant insights into how the social and political impact of globalization is mediated by domestic institutional structures, state strategies and a country's location in the global pecking order (Hurrell and Woods, 1995; Frieden and Rogowski, 1996; Garrett and Lange, 1996). A number of authors have also contributed to a greater awareness of the ways in which globalization is contested and resisted by states and peoples (Geyer and Bright, 1995; Frieden and Rogowski, 1996; Burbach et al., 1997). In so doing, such studies suggest the need for a sophisticated typology of how globalization impacts on national economies and national communities which acknowledges its differential consequences and the signal importance of the forms in which it is managed, contested and resisted (Axford, 1995).

TRAJECTORIES

Each of the three "schools" in the globalization debate has a particular conception of the dynamics and direction of global change. This imposes an overall shape on patterns of globalization and, in so doing, presents a distinctive account of globalization as a historical process. In this respect, the hyperglobalizers tend to represent globalization as a secular process of global integration (Ohmae, 1995; R. P. Clark, 1997). The latter is often associated with a linear view of historical change; globalization is elided with the relatively smooth unfolding of human progress. By comparison, the sceptical thesis tends to a view of globalization which emphasizes its distinct phases as well as its recurrent features. This, in part, accounts for the sceptics' preoccupation with evaluating contemporary globalization in relation to prior historical epochs, but most especially in relation to the supposedly "golden age" of global interdependence (the latter decades of the nineteenth century) (R. J. B. Jones, 1995; Hirst and Thompson, 1996b).

Neither of these models of historical change finds much support within the transformationalist camp. For the transformationalists tend to conceive history as a process punctuated by dramatic upheavals or discontinuities. Such a view stresses the contingency of history and how epochal change arises out of the confluence of particular historical conditions and social forces. And it informs the transformationalist tendency to describe the process of globalization as contingent and contradictory. For, according to this thesis, globalization pulls and pushes societies in opposing directions; it fragments as it integrates, engenders cooperation as well as conflict, and universalizes while it particularizes. Thus the trajectory of global change is largely indeterminate and uncertain (Rosenau, 1997).

Clearly, a convincing attempt to construct an analytical framework which moves the globalization debate beyond its present intellectual limits has to address the five major points of contention described above. For any satisfactory account of globalization has to offer: a coherent conceptualization; a justified account of causal logic; some clear propositions about historical periodization; a robust specification of impacts; and some sound reflections about the trajectory of the process itself. Confronting these tasks is central to devising and constructing fresh ways of thinking about globalization.

The five tasks inform the [sections] that follow, and we return to them again in the conclusion. What follows immediately is an attempt to address the first of the concerns—the nature and form of globalization.

RETHINKING GLOBALIZATION: AN ANALYTICAL FRAMEWORK

What is globalization? Although in its simplest sense globalization refers to the widening, deepening and speeding up of global interconnectedness, such a definition begs further elaboration. Despite a proliferation of definitions in contemporary discussion—among them "accelerating interdependence," "action at a distance" and "time-space compression"[2] (see, respectively, Ohmae, 1990; Giddens, 1990; Harvey, 1989)—there is scant evidence in the existing literature of any attempt to specify precisely what is "global" about globalization. For instance, all the above definitions are quite compatible with far more spatially confined processes such as the spread of national or regional interconnections. In seeking to remedy this conceptual difficulty, this study commences from an understanding of globalization which acknowledges its distinctive spatial attributes and the way these unfold over time.

Globalization can be located on a continuum with the local, national and regional.[3] At the one end of the continuum lie social and economic relations and networks which are organized on a local and/or national basis; at the other end lie social and economic relations and networks which crystallize on the wider scale of regional and global interactions. Globalization can be taken to refer to those spatio-temporal processes of change which underpin a transformation in the organization of human affairs by linking together and expanding human activity across regions and continents. Without reference to such expansive spatial connections, there can be no clear or coherent formulation of this term.

Accordingly, the concept of globalization implies, first and foremost, a *stretching* of social, political and economic activities across frontiers such that events, decisions and activities in one region of the world can come to have significance for individuals and communities in distant regions of the globe. In this sense, it embodies transregional interconnectedness, the widening reach of networks of social activity and power, and the possibility of action at a distance. Beyond this, globalization implies that connections across frontiers are not just occasional or random, but rather are regularized such that there is a detectable *intensification,* or growing magnitude, of interconnectedness, patterns of interaction and flows which transcend the constituent societies and states of the world order. Furthermore, growing extensity and intensity of global interconnectedness may also imply a *speeding up* of global interactions and processes as the development of worldwide systems of transport and communication increases the potential velocity of the global diffusion of ideas, goods, information, capital and people. And the growing *extensity, intensity* and *velocity* of global interactions may also be associated with a deepening enmeshment of the local and global such that the *impact* of distant events is magnified while even the most local developments may come to have enormous global consequences. In this sense, the boundaries between domestic matters and global affairs may be blurred. A satisfactory definition of globalization must capture each of these elements: extensity (stretching), intensity, velocity and impact. And a satisfactory account of globalization must examine them thoroughly. We shall refer to these four elements henceforth as the "spatio-temporal" dimensions of globalization.

By acknowledging these dimensions a more precise definition of globalization can be offered. Accordingly, globalization can be thought of as

> a process (or set of processes) which embodies a transformation in the spatial organization of social relations and transactions—assessed in terms of their

extensity, intensity, velocity and impact—generating transcontinental or inter-regional flows and networks of activity, interaction, and the exercise of power.

In this context, flows refer to the movements of physical artefacts, people, symbols, tokens and information across space and time, while networks refer to regularized or patterned interactions between independent agents, nodes of activity, or sites of power (Modelski, 1972; Mann, 1986; Castells, 1996).

This formulation helps address the failure of existing approaches to differentiate globalization from more spatially delimited processes—what we can call "localization," "nationalization," "regionalization" and "internationalization." For as it is defined above, globalization can be distinguished from more restricted social developments. Localization simply refers to the consolidation of flows and networks within a specific locale. Nationalization is the process whereby social relations and transactions are developed within the framework of fixed territorial borders. Regionalization can be denoted by a clustering of transactions, flows, networks and interactions between functional or geographical groupings of states or societies, while internationalization can be taken to refer to patterns of interaction and interconnectedness between two or more nation-states irrespective of their specific geographical location (see Nierop, 1994; Buzan, 1998). Thus contemporary globalization describes, for example, the flows of trade and finance between the major regions in the world economy, while equivalent flows within them can be differentiated in terms of local, national and regional clusters.

In offering a more precise definition of these concepts it is crucial to signal that globalization is not conceived here in opposition to more spatially delimited processes but, on the contrary, as standing in a complex and dynamic relationship with them. On the one hand, processes such as regionalization can create the necessary kinds of economic, social and physical infrastructures which facilitate and complement the deepening of globalization. In this regard, for example, economic regionalization (for instance, the European Union) has not been a barrier to the globalization of trade and production but a spur. On the other hand, such processes can impose limits to globalization, if not encouraging a process of deglobalization. However, there is no a priori reason to assume that localization or regionalization exist in an oppositional or contradictory relationship to globalization. . . .

HISTORICAL FORMS OF GLOBALIZATION

Sceptics of the globalization thesis alert us to the fact that international or global interconnectedness is by no means a novel phenomenon; yet they overlook the possibility that the particular form taken by globalization may differ between historical eras. To distinguish the novel features of globalization in any epoch requires some kind of analytical framework for organizing such comparative historical enquiry. For without such a framework it would be difficult to identify the most significant features, continuities or differences between epochs. Thus the approach developed here centres on the idea of *historical forms of globalization* as the basis for constructing a systematic comparative analysis of globalization over time. Utilizing this notion helps provide a mechanism for capturing and systematizing relevant differences and similarities. In this context, historical forms of globalization refer to

> the spatio-temporal and organizational attributes of global interconnectedness in discrete historical epochs.

To say anything meaningful about either the unique attributes or the dominant features of contemporary globalization requires clear analytical categories from which such descriptions can be constructed. Building directly on our earlier distinctions, historical forms of globalization can be described and compared initially in respect of the four spatio-temporal dimensions:

- the extensity of global networks
- the intensity of global interconnectedness
- the velocity of global flows
- the impact propensity of global interconnectedness.

Such a framework provides the basis for both a *quantitative* and a *qualitative* assessment of historical patterns of globalization. For it is possible to analyse (1) the extensiveness of networks of relations and connections; (2) the intensity of flows and levels of activity within these networks; (3) the velocity of speed of interchanges; and (4) the impact of these phenomena on particular communities. A systematic assessment of how these phenomena have evolved provides insights into the changing historical forms of globalization; and it offers the possibility of a sharper identification and comparison of the key attributes of, and the major disjunctures between, distinctive forms of globalization in different epochs. Such a historical approach to globalization avoids the current tendency to presume either that globalization is fundamentally new, or that there is nothing novel about contemporary levels of global economic and social interconnectedness since they appear to resemble those of prior periods. . . .

In Sum

The account of globalization developed in subsequent chapters reflects and builds on a number of points made so far in the introduction:

1. Globalization can best be understood as a process or set of processes rather than a singular condition. It does not reflect a simple linear developmental logic, nor does it prefigure a world society or a world community. Rather, it reflects the emergence of interregional networks and systems of interaction and exchange. In this respect, the enmeshment of national and societal systems in wider global processes has to be distinguished from any notion of global integration.

2. The spatial reach and density of global and transnational interconnectedness weave complex webs and networks of relations between communities, states, international institutions, non-governmental organizations and multinational corporations which make up the global order. These overlapping and interacting networks define an evolving structure which both imposes constraints on and empowers communities, states and social forces. In this respect, globalization is akin to a process of "structuration" in so far as it is a product of both the individual actions of, and the cumulative interactions between, countless agencies and institutions across the globe (Giddens, 1981; Buzan et al., 1993; Nierop, 1994; Jervis, 1997). Globalization is associated with an evolving dynamic global structure of enablement and constraint. But it is also a highly stratified structure since globalization is profoundly uneven: it both reflects existing patterns of inequality and hierarchy while also generating new patterns of inclusion and exclusion, new winners and losers (Hurrell and Woods, 1995). Globalization, thus, can be understood as embodying processes of structuration and stratification.

3. Few areas of social life escape the reach of processes of globalization. These processes are reflected in all social domains from the cultural through the economic, the political, the legal, the military and the environmental. Globalization is best understood as a multifaceted or differentiated social phenomenon. It cannot be conceived as a singular condition but instead refers to patterns of growing global interconnectedness within all the key domains of social activity. To understand the dynamics and consequences of globalization, therefore, demands some knowledge of the differential patterns of global interconnectedness in each of these domains. For instance, patterns of global ecological interconnectedness are quite different from the patterns of global cultural or military interaction. Any general account of the processes of globalization must acknowledge that, far from being a singular condition, it is best conceived as a differentiated and multifaceted process.

4. By cutting through and across political frontiers globalization is associated with both the deterritorialization and reterritorialization of socioeconomic and political space. As economic, social and political activities are increasingly "stretched" across the globe they become in a significant sense no longer primarily or solely organized according to a territorial principle. They may be rooted in particular locales but territorially disembedded. Under conditions of globalization, "local," "national" or even "continental" political, social and economic space is re-formed such that it is no longer necessarily coterminous with established legal and territorial boundaries. On the other hand, as globalization intensifies it generates pressures towards a reterritorialization of socioeconomic activity in the form of subnational, regional and supranational economic zones, mechanisms of governance and cultural complexes. It may also reinforce the "localization" and "nationalization" of societies. Accordingly, globalization involves a complex deterritorialization and

reterritorialization of political and economic power. In this respect, it is best described as being *aterritorial.*

5. Globalization concerns the expanding scale on which power is organized and exercised, that is, the extensive spatial reach of networks and circuits of power. Indeed, power is a fundamental attribute of globalization. In an increasingly interconnected global system, the exercise of power through the decisions, actions, or inactions, of agencies on one continent can have significant consequences for nations, communities and households on other continents. Power relations are deeply inscribed in the very processes of globalization. In fact, the stretching of power relations means that sites of power and the exercise of power become increasingly distant from the subjects or locales which experience their consequences. In this regard, globalization involves the structuring and restructuring of power relations at a distance. Patterns of global stratification mediate access to sites of power, while the consequences of globalization are unevenly experienced. Political and economic elites in the world's major metropolitan areas are much more tightly integrated into, and have much greater control over, global networks than do the subsistence farmers of Burundi.

NOTES

1. The approaches set out below present general summaries of different ways of thinking about globalization: they do not represent fully the particular positions and many differences among the individual theorists mentioned. The aim of the presentation is to highlight the main trends and faultlines in the current debate and literature.

2. By "accelerating interdependence" is understood the growing intensity of international enmeshment among national economies and societies such that developments in one country impact directly on other countries. "Action at a distance" refers to the way in which, under conditions of contemporary globalization, the actions of social agents (individuals, collectivities, corporations, etc.) in one locale can come to have significant intended or unintended consequences for the behaviour of "distant others." Finally, "time-space compression" refers to the manner in which globalization appears to shrink geographical distance and time; in a world of instantaneous communication, distance and time no longer seem to be a major constraint on patterns of human social organization or interaction.

3. Regions refer here to the geographical or functional clustering of states or societies. Such regional clusters can be identified in terms of their shared characteristics (cultural, religious, ideological, economic, etc.) and high level of patterned interaction relative to the outside world (Buzan, 1998).

REFERENCES

Albrow, M. (1996) *The Global Age,* Cambridge: Polity Press.

Amin, S. (1996) "The challenge of globalization," *Review of International Political Economy,* 2.

Amin, S. (1997) *Capitalism in the Age of Globalization,* London: Zed Press.

Armingeon, K. (1997) "Globalization as opportunity: two roads to welfare state reform," ECPR Conference Workshop 12, Bern.

Axford, B. (1995) *The Global System,* Cambridge: Polity Press.

Banuri, T. and Schor, J. (eds.) (1992) *Financial Openness and National Autonomy,* Oxford: Oxford University Press.

Bentley, J. H. (1996) "Cross-cultural interaction and periodization in world history," *American Historical Review,* 101, June.

Benton, L. (1996) "From the world systems perspective to institutional world history: culture and economy in global theory" *Journal of World History,* 7.

Boyer, R. and Drache, D. (eds.) (1996) *States against Markets,* London: Routledge.

Burbach, R. et al. (1997) *Globalization and its Discontents,* London: Pluto Press.

Buzan, B. (1998) "The Asia-Pacific: what sort of region, in what sort of world?," in McGrew and Brook 1998.

Buzan, B., Little, R., and Jones, C. (1993) *The Logic of Anarchy,* New York: Columbia University Press.

Callinicos, A. et al. (1994) *Marxism and the New Imperialism,* London: Bookmarks.

Cammilleri, J. A. and Falk, J. (1992) *The End of Sovereignty? The Politics of a Shrinking and Fragmented World,* Aldershot: Edward Elgar.

Carr, E. H. (1981) *The Twenty Years Crisis 1919–1939,* London: Papermac.

Castells, M. (1996) *The Rise of the Network Society,* Oxford: Blackwell.

Clark, R. P. (1997) *The Global Imperative: An Interpretative of the Spread of Mankind,* Boulder: Westview Press.

Connolly, W. E. (1996) *The Ethos of Pluralization,* Minneapolis: University of Minnesota Press.

Cox, R. (1996) "Economic globalization and the limits to liberal democracy," in McGrew 1997.

Cox, R. (1997) "Economic globalization and the limits to liberal democracy," in McGrew 1997.

Frank, A. G. and Gills, B. K. (eds.) (1996) *The World System,* London: Routledge.

Frieden, J. A. and Rogowski, R. (1996) "The impact of the international economy on national policies: an analytical overview," in Keohane and Milner 1996.

Garrett, G. and Lange, P. (1996) "Internationalization, institutions, and political change," in Keohane and Milner 1996.

Garrett, G. and Lange, P. (1991) "Political responses to interdependence: what's 'left' for the left?," *International Organization,* 45.

Geyer, M. and Bright, C. (1995) 'World history in a global age,' *American Historical Review,* 100.

Giddens, A. (1981) A *Contemporary Critique of Historical Materialism* vol. 1, London: Macmillan.

Giddens, A. (1990) *The Consequences of Modernity,* Cambridge: Polity Press.

Giddens, A. (1991) *Modernity and Self-identity,* Cambridge: Polity Press,

Giddens, A. (1995) *Beyond Left and Right,* Cambridge: Polity Press.

Giddens, A. (1996) "Globalization: a keynote address," *UNRISD News,* 15.

Gill, S. (1995) "Globalization, market civilization, and disciplinary neoliberalism," *Millennium,* 24.

Gilpin, R. (1987) *The Political Economy of International Relations,* Princeton: Princeton University Press.

Goodman, J. (1997) "The European Union: reconstituting democracy beyond the nation-state," in McGrew 1997.

Gordon, D. (1988) "The global economy: new edifice or crumbling foundations?," New *Left Review,* 168.

Graham, G. (1997) *The Shape of the Past: A Philosophical Approach to History,* Oxford: Oxford University Press.

Gray, J. (1996) *After Social Democracy,* London: Demos.

Gray, J. (1998) *False Dawn,* London: Granta.

Greider, W. (1997) *One World, Ready or Not: The Manic Logic of Global Capitalism,* New York: Simon and Schuster.

Guéhenno, J. M. (1995) *The End of the Nation-State,* Minneapolis: University of Minnesota Press.

Harvey, D. (1989) *The Condition of Postmodernity,* Oxford: Blackwell.

Held, D. (1991) "Democracy, the nation-state, and the global system," in D. Held (ed.), *Political Theory Today,* Cambridge: Polity Press.

Helleiner, E. (1997) "Braudelian reflections on economic globalization: the historian as pioneer," in S. Gill and J. Mittleman (eds.), *Innovation and Transformation in International Studies,* Cambridge: Cambridge University Press.

Hirst, P. (1997) "The global economy: myths and realities," *International Affairs, 73.*

Hirst, P. and Thompson, G. (1996a) "Globalization: ten frequently asked questions and some surprising answers," *Soundings, 4.*

Hirst, P. and Thompson, G. (1996b) *Globalization in Question: The International Economy and the Possibilities of Governance,* Cambridge: Polity Press.

Hoogvelt, A. (1997) *Globalization and the Postcolonial World: The New Political Economy of Development,* London: Macmillan.

Huntington, S. P. (1996) *The Clash of Civilizations and the Remaking of World Order,* New York: Simon and Schuster.

Hurrell, A. and Woods, N. (1995) "Globalization and inequality," *Millenium, 2.*

Jervis, R. (1997) *System Effects,* Princeton: Princeton University Press.

Jones, R. J. B. (1995) *Globalization and Interdependence in the International Political Economy,* London: Frances Pinter.

Keohane, R. O. (1995) "Hobbes' dilemma and institutional change in world politics: sovereignty in international society," in H. H. Holm and G. Sorensen (eds.), *Whose World Order?,* Boulder: Westview Press.

Keohane, R. O., Milner, H. et al. (1996) *Internationalization and Domestic Politics,* Cambridge: Cambridge University Press.

Krasner, S. (1993) "Economic interdependence and independent statehood," in R. H. Jackson and A. James (eds.), *States in a Changing World,* Oxford: Oxford University Press.

Krasner, S. (1995) "Compromising Westphalia," *International Security, 20, no. 3.*

Krugman, P. (1996) *Pop Internationalism,* Boston: MIT Press.

Linklater, A. and MacMillan, J. (1995) "Boundaries in question," in J. MacMillan and A. Linklater (eds.), *Boundaries in Question,* London: Frances Pinter.

Luard, E. (1990) *The Globalization of Politics,* London: Macmillan.

Mann, M. (1986) *The Sources of Social Power,* vol. 1: *A History of Power from the Beginning to AD 1760,* Cambridge: Cambridge University Press.

Mann, M. (1997) "Has globalization ended the rise of the nation-state?," *Review of International Political Economy, 4.*

Mazlish, B. and Buultjens, R. (eds.) (1993) *Conceptualizing Global History,* Boulder: Westview Press.

McGrew, A. and Brook, C. (eds.) (1998) *Asia-Pacific in the New World Order,* London and New York: Routledge.

McGrew, A. G. (ed.) (1997) *The Transformation of Democracy? Globalization and Territorial Democracy,* Cambridge: Polity Press.

McNeill, W. H. (1995) "The 'rise of the West' after twenty-five years," in S. K. Sanderson (ed.), *Civilizations and World Systems*, Walnut Creek: Altamira Press.

Milner, H. V. and R. O. Keohane (1996) "Internationalization and domestic politics," in Keohane and Milner (1996).

Modelski, G. (1972) *Principles of World Politics*, New York: Free Press.

Murphy, A. B. (1996) "The sovereign state system as a political-territorial ideal: historical and contemporary considerations," in T. J. Biersteker and C. Weber (eds.), *State Sovereignty as Social Construct*, Cambridge: Cambridge University Press.

Nierop, T. (1994) *Systems and Regions in Global Politics: An Empirical Study of Diplomacy, International Organization and Trade 1950–1991*, Chichester: John Wiley.

Ohmae, K. (1990) *The Borderless World*, London: Collins.

Ohmae, K. (1995) *The End of the Nation State*, New York: Free Press.

Perlmutter, H. V. (1991) "On the rocky road to the first global civilisation," *Human Relations*, 44.

Redwood, J. (1993) *The Global Marketplace*, London: HarperCollins.

Reich, R. (1991) *The Work of Nations: Preparing Ourselves for Twenty-First Century Capitalism*, New York: Simon and Schuster.

Robertson, R. (1992) *Globalization: Social Theory and Global Culture*, London: Sage.

Rogowski, R. (1989) *Commerce and Coalitions: How Trade Affects Domestic Political Alignments*, Princeton: Princeton University Press.

Rosenau, J. (1990) *Turbulence in World Politics*, Brighton: Harvester Wheatsheaf.

Rosenau, J. (1997) *Along the Domestic-Foreign Frontier*, Cambridge: Cambridge University Press.

Roudemetof, V. and Robertson, R. (1995) "Globalization, world-system theory, and the comparative study of civilizations," in S. K. Sanderson (ed.), *Civilizations and World Systems*, Walnut Creek: Altamira Press.

Ruggie, J. G. (1993) "Territoriality and beyond," *International Organization*, 41.

Ruggie, J. G. (1996) *Winning the Peace: America and World Order in the New Era*, New York: Columbia University Press.

Ruigrok, W. and Tulder, R. van (1995) *The Logic of International Restructuring*, London: Routledge.

Sandel, M. (1996) *Democracy's Discontent*, Cambridge: Harvard University Press.

Sassen, S. (1996) *Losing Control? Sovereignty in an Age of Globalization*, New York: Columbia University Press.

Scharpf, F. (1991) *Crisis and Choice in European Social Democracy*, New York: Cornell University Press.

Schiller, H. (1969) *Mass Communication and the American Empire*, New York: Augustus Kelly.

Scholte, J. A. (1993) *International Relations of Social Change*, Buckingham: Open University Press.

Strange, S. (1996) *The Retreat of the State: The Diffusion of Power in the World Economy*, Cambridge: Cambridge University Press.

Thompson, G. and Allen, J. (1997) "Think global, then think again: economic globalization in context," *Area*, 29, no. 3.

Weiss, L. (1998) *State Capacity: Governing the Economy in a Global Era*, Cambridge: Polity Press.

Wriston, W. (1992) *The Twilight of Sovereignty*, New York: Charles Scribners Sons.

51

JAMES N. ROSENAU

GOVERNANCE
IN FRAGMEGRATIVE SPACE

So dominant in contemporary consciousness is the assumption that authority must be centralized that scholars are just beginning to grapple with how decentralized authority might be understood. . . . [T]he question of how to think about a world that is becoming "domesticated" but not centralized, about a world after "anarchy," is one of the most important questions today facing not only students of international relations but of political theory as well.

—ALEXANDER WENDT[1]

We live in a messy world. There are far too many people who survive on or below the poverty line. There are far too many societies paralyzed by division. There is too much violence within and between countries. In many places there is too little water and too many overly populated, pollution-ridden cities. And, most conspicuously, there is all too little effective governance capable of ameliorating, if not resolving, these and numerous other problems that crowd high on the global agenda. Indeed, as distant proximities become ever less distant and ever more proximate, so do the problems of governance become ever more acute. Hardly less troubling, our generation lacks—as this [article's] epigraph implies—the orientations necessary to sound assessments of how the authority of governance can be brought to bear on the challenges posed by the prevailing disarray. Consequently, . . . the dynamics of fragmegration, and perhaps especially the complexities inherent in the extensive disaggregation of authority it has fostered, pose the question of whether governance on a global scale can be achieved in the emergent epoch.

To be sure, a vast and ever-growing literature on global governance has evolved in recent years, and much of it is imaginative and constructive,[2] suggesting that a variety of steering mechanisms and institutions have come into being as instruments of governance. But while some of the literature does allow for disaggregated authority, it suffers from three major limitations: it does not

SOURCE: From *Distant Proximities*, by James N. Rosenau, pp. 390–401. Copyright Princeton University Press.

focus on the tensions between localizing and globalizing forces and thus ignores the dynamics of fragmegration; second, it presumes that the primacy of states and that of their international institutions are the principal vehicles of governance on a global scale; and third, for these reasons it does not accord centrality to micro-macro processes.

It would be a mistake, however, to correct for these limitations by exploring the governance of fragmegration without reference to states and the international organizations they have fashioned to govern the course of events. If the times call for governance of a nonlinear world composed of endless feedback loops, contradictions, ambiguities, and uncertainties, then obviously states and the interactions of their governments need to be included in the exploration along with diverse, nongovernmental SOAs and micro-macro processes. If [analysts] are essentially accurate in depicting profound and deep-seated changes that are transforming the processes and structures of individual and collective life at the present moment in history, this does not mean that global governance, which is founded on a commitment to promoting a world that is at the same time peaceful, democratic, and orderly, and the governance of fragmegration, which focuses on resolving tensions between localizing and globalizing dynamics, should be treated as mutually exclusive undertakings. Instead, it seems imperative to view global governance and the governance of fragmegration as inextricably interrelated and possibly mutually reinforcing. While the types of conflict with which the two forms of governance are concerned differ somewhat, each seeks to minimize conflict and advance human well-being both within and across the borders that divide countries, cultures, and economies.

Accordingly, what is needed is a conception of governance that allows for the interplay of all the fragmegrative dynamics . . . and that does not shrink from the possibility that present generations, having matured in a world of states and fixed boundaries, may lack the experience—and possibly the political will—to cope with the many tensions, ambiguities, and contradictions to which fluid boundaries and diverse opposing forces give rise. Indeed, the governance of fragmegration must be conceived in broad enough terms to allow for Ashby's "Law of Requisite Variety," which asserts that for a system to survive it must be as complex as its environment.[3] The achievement of such a level of complexity in the present era requires learning and adaptation, else the global system will eventually collapse as a coherent whole. It remains to be seen whether the skill revolution, the organizational explosion, the mobility upheaval, and the other sources of transformation are powerful enough to foster the requisite learning, or whether the understanding and political will of elites and publics are insufficient to the tasks of adaptation.

Despite the enormous complexity that marks the emergent epoch, several of its features that underlie the potential for governance on a global scale are readily discernible. One is that the goals and interests of the individuals and collectivities on the global stage are so numerous, diverse, and disaggregated that a hierarchical global structure with a single mechanism for governance is not going to evolve in the foreseeable future. No hegemon, nor any cluster of like-minded powerful rule systems, nor the United Nations, is likely to evolve exclusive jurisdiction over the tasks of global governance. Some steering mechanisms may have wider scope for influencing the course of events than do others, but none is likely ever to be capable of alone dominating the processes of governance. A second characteristic of the current scene is that progress toward more effective governance must perforce be halting and accomplished in small increments, given the huge degree to which authority has been decentralized at every level of community. A third characteristic concerns the pervasiveness of authority crises in every part of the world, a pattern that seems bound to accelerate if Affirmative Locals and Globals persist in pursuing policies that can degrade the environment or promote poverty, or if system-wide circumstances such as a deep global recession lead individuals to greatly enlarge the ranks of the Resistant and Exclusionary Locals and join in collective actions designed to deter progress toward resolving global problems. In short, an overview suggests that the prospects for effective governance on a worldwide scale are highly problematic, that progress in this respect may take decades, and that the probability of evolution toward a harmonious and progressive global order may not be any greater than the chance of deterioration toward a tension-filled and retrogressive disorder.

THE PROLIFERATION OF GOVERNANCE

To meet the requirements of a broad conception, governance is here regarded as sustained by rule systems that serve as steering mechanisms through which leaders and collectivities frame and move toward their goals.[4] In the state-centric world some of the rule systems are presided over by states and their governments, while international institutions and regimes maintain others. In the multi-centric world numerous steering mechanisms are to be found in NGOs, and still others consist of informal SOAs that may never develop formal structures.

With the wide dispersion of authority at every level of community, in other words, recent decades have witnessed a vast expansion of rule systems and steering mechanisms. Nor is there a lack of variety in the extant systems of governance. On the contrary, . . . the era of fragmegration is both fostering and sustaining a world marked by a proliferation of all kinds of governance. And the organizational explosion is not confined to nongovernmental entities. New forms of government have been developed, and old ones have either added new layers or transferred their authority downward to subnational levels or upward to supranational levels. The result is an ever-widening realm in which governance is undertaken and implemented, a development that suggests the world may indeed be adapting to the ever-greater complexity of community, national, regional, and global life.

But how to probe the number and diversity of rule systems such that the governance of fragmegration can be assessed? And assuming that assessment is possible, what are the probabilities that the emergent disaggregated, diverse global system can achieve effective governance? In a world where groups and countries are simultaneously fragmenting and integrating, where the two contrary forces are pervasive, interactive, and feed on each other, are the resulting tensions subject to governance? Can mechanisms be developed that steer the tensions in constructive directions? If collapsed distance, time, and sequentiality are taken seriously, can they serve as stimuli to a renewal of creative thought about what governance may mean in the twenty-first century?

Except for the last, these questions serve as the focus of this [article], but the answers to them are far from clear. My response to the last question, however, is an unqualified yes. It is an unqualified response in the sense that the transformations at work in the world are so profound that a thoughtful observer cannot but experience a sense of renewal, an impulse to think afresh about how control might be achieved over the contradictions and changes that mark our emergent epoch.

But the task of thinking afresh involves more than sensitivity to profound transformations. A broad conception of governance also requires breaking out of the conceptual jails in which we have long been ensconced.[5] To do so it is useful to start at the beginning and treat politics and governance as social processes that transcend state and societal boundaries so thoroughly as to necessitate the invention of new wheels. What is needed are conveyances with many wheels that sometimes roll harmoniously in the same direction, that sometimes move crazily in contradictory directions, and that often lurch fitfully as some wheels turn while others are stationary. This is a metaphorical way of again asserting that, as the differences, overlaps, and contradictions that mark collectivities on the global stage have become ever more pervasive, rethinking is needed that allows for the possibility of new terminal entities emerging that serve as the focus of the most salient loyalties and affiliations of groups and individuals in the same ways states have.

One way to develop a broad conception that encompasses the micro-macro underpinnings of both global governance and the governance of fragmegration and allows for the vast proliferation of rule systems is to frame a typology that sorts out and juxtaposes the diverse horizontal and hierarchical actors and processes through which authority is exercised. While the greater number and variety of governance entities suggests that parsimonious classification may be unachievable, more than a few observers have undertaken to develop an appropriate typology. Two of these are illustrative of the difficulties involved. One is based on the movement of issues and labeled the "governance ladder."[6] The other differentiates five alternative models of state-society interactions in governance through "a continuum ranging from the most dominated by the State and those in which the State plays the least role and indeed one in which there is argued to be governance without government."[7]

THE GOVERNANCE LADDER AND
THE STATE-SOCIETY CONTINUUM

The governance ladder focuses on the movement of issues up and down the various rungs as they arrest the attention of officials and publics, thereby becoming governance issues. Issues that first generate widespread awareness at local levels get onto the ladder at the bottom rungs, while those that originate at the global level occupy the top rungs, just as those that get onto political agendas at the national level perch on the middle rungs. Some issues remain on the same rung throughout; some start at the bottom and move to the top; and some start at the top and percolate down. Such a scheme has been cogently framed with reference to environmental issues:

> If climate change has been introduced so-to-speak at a global level and is slowly moving down the governance ladder, biodiversity, on the other hand, . . . has mainly been introduced at a national level and is currently moving both upwards and downwards. Water . . . is clearly characterized by a bottom-up approach: awareness that it constitutes a governance issue has emerged first at a local level, tied as it is to livelihoods, and is currently moving to the national and the global levels. We propose here to use the term of comprehensive governance in order to account for the fact that governance occurs at all levels (from local to global), involves all stakeholders, and links at least the three issues together, i.e., water, biodiversity, and climate change.[8]

The state-society continuum is less hierarchical. At one extreme is the Etatist model based on "the assumption that government is the principal actor for all aspects of governance and can control the manner in which the society is permitted to be involved, if it is at all." Next to it on the continuum is the Liberal-Democratic model, which "accepts the role of the state as the principal actor in governance," but which allows for other actors competing to influence the state. There follows the State-Centric model, which "remains at the center of the process, but institutionalizes its relationships with social actors." The fourth is the Dutch Governance School that "depends heavily upon the role of social networks in governing, with the state being merely one among many actors involved in the process." Finally, at the other extreme of the continuum is the Governance without Government model, which argues that "the state has lost its capacity to govern and is at best an arena within which private actors play out their own governance arrangement."[9]

MOBIUS-WEB GOVERNANCE

Useful as such typologies may be, however, they do not adequately serve the need of analyzing the governance of fragmegration. With the exception of one extreme of the state-society continuum, both typologies differentiate governance undertaken within the state-centric system and do not extend the typology to the multi-centric system. And with the exception of links to livelihoods and stake-holders at the bottom rung of the governance ladder, neither typology explicitly includes micro-macro interactions as relevant to any form of governance.

Hence, a somewhat more elaborate conception needs to be framed if account is to be taken of micro-macro interactions as well as the diversity, the horizontality, the complexity, and the sheer number of SOAs that now mark the global stage and contribute to governance in both state-centric and multi-centric worlds. I have sought to meet this need through a more elaborate scheme that identifies six types of governance systems that, taken together, span the several dimensions of fragmegration that require the exercise of effective authority. The six types are set forth in table 1, with the distinctions between them being drawn in terms of the degree to which authority is formally established, the directions in which it may flow, and the eight kinds of actors principally involved in sustaining the flow. Since all six types have been analyzed elsewhere,[10] there is no need to probe each of them [here]. Rather, here the focus is on only one of them, what I call the *mobius-web* model of global governance.[11] If the mobius-web form does not presently subsume the other five, it is so fully expressive of the complexities of the emergent epoch that in the long run, if not the medium term, it is likely to encompass the other five. The underlying central tendency, in other words, is conceived to be one in which the mobius-web form is probably the end state toward which all other types of global governance are evolving.

Mobius-web governance is rooted in the impetus to employ rule systems that steer issues through both hierarchical and networked interactions across levels of aggregation that may encompass all the diverse collectivities and individuals who participate in the processes of governance. These interactions constitute a hybrid structure in which the dynamics of governance are so intricate and overlapping among the several levels as to I form a singular, weblike process that, like a mobius, neither begins nor culminates at any level or at any

TABLE 1 **Six Types of Global Governance**

STRUCTURES	PROCESSES (TYPE OF COLLECTIVITIES INVOLVED IN EACH FORM OF GOVERNANCE)	
	UNIDIRECTIONAL (VERTICAL OR HORIZONTAL)	MULTIDIRECTIONAL (VERTICAL AND HORIZONTAL)
Formal	Top-Down Governance *(governments, TNCs, IGOs)*	Network Governance *(governments, IGOs, NGOs, INGOs– e.g., business alliances)*
Informal	Bottom-Up Governance *(mass publics, NGOs, INGOs)*	Side-by-Side Governance *(NGO and INGO, governments)*
Mixed formal and informal	Market Governance *(governments, IGOs, elites, markets, mass publics, TNCs)*	Mobius-Web Governance *(governments, elites, mass publics, TNCs, IGOs, NGOs, INGOs)*

Note: TNC (Transnational Corporation); INGO (International Nongovernmental Organization)

point in time. Mobius-web governance I does not culminate with the passage of a law or compliance with its regulations. Rather, it is operative as long as the issues subjected to governance continue to be of concern.

The complexity of mobius-web governance suggests that fragmegrative dynamics pose perhaps the most difficult of all the challenges that face those who undertake to exercise authority. The difficulties are rooted in the nature of either the fragmenting forces that lead groups to resist the integrating forces they feel impinge on their well-being or the integrating forces that foster a sense of exclusion on the part of people and collectivities left out of the integrative process. The resistances tend to be deeply rooted in one or another kind of commitment to local practices, habits, and traditions, while resentments over exclusion tend to derive from aspirations for a better standard of living and other perquisites that may flow from integration.

Neither the resistant nor the resentful groups are readily amenable to the directives that stem from hierarchical authority. The governance of fragmegration, therefore, also requires authority that is dispersed and decentralized, that flows as much horizontally as vertically through participatory channels. Recent conflicts in Chechnya and Sri Lanka are extreme examples of how steering mechanisms founded on vertical authority do not result in effective governance, whereas the subsidiarity principle that has strengthened the European Union is illustrative of how various forms of horizontal authority can minimize, if not overcome, resistances to integration.

It follows that in mobius-web governance the relevant actors are closely linked, with the result that the relevant agencies are prone to cross the private-public divide by mobilizing mass publics as well as elites on behalf of the values at stake. The environmental issue area is illustrative. It encompasses intricate networks of actors at subnational, national, transnational, and international levels who interact in such diverse ways as to render fruitless any attempt to tease out the direction of causal processes. That is, IGOs and most states have often yielded to the pressures of NGOs and INGOs on issues pertaining to the environment and cooperatively formed both formal and informal networks through which the spreading norms get translated into mechanisms of governance.[12] Indeed, mobius-web governance may be marked by a cumulative sequencing in which the pressures generated by bottom-up governance give rise to top-down and side-by-side governance that, in turn, becomes a vast network encompassing all levels of governance and diverse flows of authority. One analyst disputes this possibility and, instead, estimates that in the course of these complex sequences the governance of issues will become more formalized under IGOs and states, thereby "eating into the realms of the INGOs/NGOs."[13]

Equally illustrative of mobius-web governance was the response to the challenges created by the terrorist attacks on the World Trade Center. The war on terrorism subsequently launched by the U.S. government; the anti-terrorist coalition of states it formed; the central role of protests by Islamic fundamentalists in Pakistan and elsewhere in the Middle East; the continued defiance of

Osama bin Laden and his Al Qaeda network; the intensified recognition of the rich-poor gap as a negative consequence of globalization; the involvement and coordination of national police forces; the anxieties that mushroomed in American society over fears of anthrax, smallpox, nuclear, and other mass terrorist attacks; and the redirection of the antiglobalization protests into an antiwar movement are only the more conspicuous aspects of the mobius-web governance with which the world reacted to the situation created by the attacks of September 11, 2001.

Mobius-web governance is not lacking in overlaps among the other types of governance outlined in table 1. Given the diversity of new forms of horizontal governance, however, the notion of authority being exercised horizontally as well as vertically through mobius webs brings a modicum of order to the subject even as it highlights the complexity of our fragmegrative epoch.

CONCLUSIONS

Of course, typologies are only aides in organizing thought. In themselves they do not in any way come close to answering the questions that need to be clarified: Will the weakening of states, the proliferation of rule systems, the disaggregation of authority, the clash between globalization and its opponents, the advent of mass terrorism, and the greater density of the global stage enhance or diminish the effectiveness of the overall system of governance on a global scale? While doubtless there will be pockets of ineffectiveness and breakdown, will the emergent system, on balance, make for more humane and sensitive governance? Are the tensions and conflicts fostered by the deleterious aspects of fragmegration likely to prove ungovernable?

It is not difficult to frame pessimistic answers to such questions. The gap between globalization's winners and losers persists as the skills of both groups continue to enlarge and their organizations continue to proliferate. And even if nonzero-sum solutions to fragmegrative dynamics do evolve, progress along such lines is likely to be so slow and intermittent as not to keep pace with the many tensions to which uncertainty is heir. The age of fragmegration, it can reasonably be concluded, will endure as far as one can see into the decades ahead.

On the other hand, upbeat responses to the foregoing questions strike me as plausible if one is able to look beyond the prevailing uncertainty. In the first place, sensitivity to the rich-poor gap and its deleterious potential is widening. The gulf between the Affirmative Globals and Locals on the one hand and their Resistant counterparts on the other may have narrowed as the realization of mutual interdependence has deepened since the hints of apocalypse were heightened by the mother of all distant proximities on September 11, 2001.

Second, more than a little truth attaches to the aphorism that there is safety in numbers. The more crowded the global stage gets with steering mechanisms, the less can any one of them, or any coalition of them, dominate the course of events, and the more will all of them have to be sensitive to how sheer numbers limit their influence. Every rule system, in other words, will be hemmed in by all the others, thus conducing to a growing awareness of the virtues of cooperation and the need to contain the worst effects of deleterious fragmegration.

Third, there is a consciousness of and intelligence about the processes of globalization that is spreading widely to every corner of the earth. What has been called "reflexivity"[14] and what I call the *globalization of globalization*[15] is accelerating at an extraordinary rate—from the halls of academe and government to the boardrooms of corporations, from the streets of urban cities to the rural homes of China (where the impact of the WTO is an intense preoccupation), people in all walks of life have begun to appreciate their interdependence with others as time and distance shrink. For some, maybe even many, the rush into a globalized world may be regrettable, but with perhaps only the Insular Locals and the Circumstantial Passives oblivious to the dynamics of change, there is likely to be a growing understanding of the necessity to confront the challenges of fragmegration and an openness to new ways of meeting them. Put more positively, there is substantial evidence that good minds in government, academe, journalism, and the business community in all parts of the world are turning, each in their own way, to the task of addressing and constructively answering the questions raised here. It is difficult to recall another period in history when so many thoughtful people concentrated their talents on the human condition from a worldwide perspective.

Fourth, the advent of networks and the flow of horizontal communications appear to have enlarged the local and global worlds, thereby bringing many more people into the political arena. The conditions for the emergence of a series of global consensuses never existed quite to the extent that they do today. The skills of individuals and the orientations of the organizations they support are increasingly conducive to convergence around shared values.

Fifth, as consensuses form, widen, and compete, so will expansion occur in the realm of governance. Increasingly, it seems clear, multilevel governance will be the dominant mode through which NGOs, communities, governments, regions, and the world attempt to exert a modicum of control over their affairs.

None of this is to suggest, however, that nirvana lies ahead. Surely it does not. Surely distant circumstances will become ever more proximate. Surely fragmegration will be with us for a long time, and surely many of its tensions will intensify. But inclinations to incorporate new, horizontal forms of authority into the panoply of governance mechanisms are not lacking, and that is not a trivial conclusion.

NOTES

1. *Social Theory of International Politics* (Cambridge: Cambridge University Press, 1999), p. 308.
2. See, for example, David Held, *Democracy and the Global Order: From the Modern State to Cosmopolitan Governance* (Cambridge, Mass.: Polity Press, 1995); Jon Pierre (ed.), *Debating Governance: Authority, Steering and Democracy* (Oxford:

Oxford University Press, 2000); Martin Hewson and Timothy J. Sinclair (eds.), *Approaches to Global Governance Theory* (Albany: State University of New York Press, 1999), pp. 287–301; Rahno Varyrynen (ed.), *Globalization and Global Governance* (Lanhan, Md.: Rowman and Littlefield, 1999); Oran Young, *International Governance: Protecting the Environment in a Stateless Society* (Ithaca, N.Y.: Cornell University Press, 1994); University of Victoria, *"Rethinking Governance" Handbook: An Inventory of Ideas to Enhance Accountability, Participation, and Transparency* (Victoria: Centre for Global Studies, 2001); and Heikki Patomaki, *Democratising Globalisation: The Leverage of the Tobin Tax* (London: Zed Books, 2001).

3. Ross Ashby, "Variety, Constraint, and the Law of Requisite Variety," in Walter Buckley (ed.), *Modern Systems Research for the Behavioral Scientist: A Sourcebook* (Chicago: Aldine, 1968), pp. 129–36.

4. This conception of the nature of governance is elaborated in James N. Rosenau, "Governance in the 21st Century," *Global Governance,* Vol. 1 (1995), pp. 13–43; and Rosenau, "Governance, Order, and Change in World Politics," in J. N. Rosenau and E. O. Czempiel (eds.), *Governance without Government: Order and Change in World Politics* (Cambridge: Cambridge University Press, 1992), Chap. 1.

5. Elsewhere I have elaborated at length on why we thrive entrapped in conceptual jails of our own making. See James N. Rosenau, *Turbulence in World Politics: Change and Continuity in World Politics* (Princeton, N.J.: Princeton University Press, 1990), Chap. 2.

6. In an agenda for the Workshop on Globalization and the Comprehensive Governance of Water, sponsored by the Commission on Economic, Environmental, and Social Policy of the World Conservation Union (Gland, Switzerland, May 26, 2000).

7. B. Guy Peters and Jon Pierre, "Is There a Governance Theory?" (paper presented at the XVIII Congress of the International Political Science Association, Quebec City, August 1–5, 2000), p. 4.

8. Agenda for the Workshop on Globalization and the Comprehensive Governance of Water, p. 1.

9. Peters and Pierre, "Is There a Governance Theory?" pp. 4–5.

10. This sixfold typology can be found in James N. Rosenau, "The Governance of Fragmegration: Neither a World Republic nor a Global Interstate System," *Studia Diplomatia,* Vol. 53, No. 5 (2000), pp. 15–39; and Rosenau, "Governance in a New Global Order," in David Held and Anthony McGrew (eds.), *Governing the Global Polity* (Cambridge, Mass.: Polity Press, 2002), pp. 70–86.

11. For another formulation that employs the mobius metaphor to assess the porosity of boundaries, see Didier Bigo, "The Mobius Ribbon of Internal and External Security(ies)," in Mathias Albert, David Jacobson, and Yosef Lapid (eds.), *Identities, Borders, Orders: Rethinking International Relations Theory* (Minneapolis: University of Minnesota Press, 2001), pp. 91–116.

12. David John Frank, Ann Hironaka, John W. Meyer, Evan Schofer, and Nancy Brandon Tuma, "The Rationalization and Organization of Nature in World Culture," in Boli and Thomas (eds.), *Constructing World Culture,* Chap. 3.

13. John Boli, personal correspondence, April 30, 1999.

14. Anthony Giddens and Christopher Pierson, *Conversations with Anthony Giddens: Making Sense of Modernity* (Cambridge, Mass.: Polity Press, 1998), pp. 115–17.

15. For a discussion of how concerns about globalization are spreading on a global scale, see James N. Rosenau, "The Globalization of Globalization," in Michael Brecher and Frank Harvey (eds.), *Millennium Reflections on International Studies* (Ann Arbor: University of Michigan Press, 2002), pp. 271–90.

52

SAMUEL P. HUNTINGTON

THE CLASH OF CIVILIZATIONS?

THE NEXT PATTERN OF CONFLICT

World politics is entering a new phase, and intellectuals have not hesitated to proliferate visions of what it will be—the end of history, the return of traditional rivalries between nation states, and the decline of the nation state from the conflicting pulls of tribalism and globalism, among others. Each of these visions catches aspects of the emerging reality. Yet they all miss a crucial, indeed a central, aspect of what global politics is likely to be in the coming years.

It is my hypothesis that the fundamental source of conflict in this new world will not be primarily ideological or primarily economic. The great divisions among humankind and the dominating source of conflict will be cultural. Nation states will remain the most powerful actors in world affairs, but the principal conflicts of global politics will occur between nations and groups of different civilizations. The clash of civilizations will dominate global politics. The fault lines between civilizations will be the battle lines of the future.

Conflict between civilizations will be the latest phase in the evolution of conflict in the modern world. For a century and a half after the emergence of the modern international system with the Peace of Westphalia, the conflicts of the Western world were largely among princes—emperors, absolute monarchs and constitutional monarchs attempting to expand their bureaucracies, their armies, their mercantilist economic strength and, most important, the territory they ruled. In the process they created nation states, and beginning with the French Revolution the principal lines of conflict were between nations rather than princes. In 1793, as R. R. Palmer put it, "The wars of kings were over; the wars of peoples had begun." This nineteenth-century pattern lasted until the end of World War I. Then, as a result of the Russian Revolution and the reaction against it, the conflict of nations yielded to the conflict of ideologies, first among communism, fascism-Nazism and liberal democracy, and then between communism and liberal democracy. During the Cold War, this latter conflict became embodied in the struggle between the two superpowers, neither of which was a nation state in the classical European sense and each of which defined its identity in terms of its ideology.

SOURCE: *Foreign Affairs* (Summer 1993).

These conflicts between princes, nation states and ideologies were primarily conflicts within Western civilization, "Western civil wars," as William Lind has labeled them. This was as true of the Cold War as it was of the world wars and the earlier wars of the seventeenth, eighteenth and nineteenth centuries. With the end of the Cold War, international politics moves out of its Western phase, and its centerpiece becomes the interaction between the West and non-Western civilizations and among non-Western civilizations. In the politics of civilizations, the peoples and governments of non-Western civilizations no longer remain the objects of history as targets of Western colonialism but join the West as movers and shapers of history.

THE NATURE OF CIVILIZATIONS

During the Cold War the world was divided into the First, Second and Third Worlds. Those divisions are no longer relevant. It is far more meaningful now to group countries not in terms of their political or economic systems or in terms of their level of economic development but rather in terms of their culture and civilization.

What do we mean when we talk of a civilization? A civilization is a cultural entity. Villages, regions, ethnic groups, nationalities, religious groups, all have distinct cultures at different levels of cultural heterogeneity. The culture of a village in southern Italy may be different from that of a village in northern Italy, but both will share in a common Italian culture that distinguishes them from German villages. European communities, in turn, will share cultural features that distinguish them from Arab or Chinese communities. Arabs, Chinese and Westerners, however, are not part of any broader cultural entity. They constitute civilizations. A civilization is thus the highest cultural grouping of people and the broadest level of cultural identity people have short of that which distinguishes humans from other species. It is defined both by common objective elements, such as language, history, religion, customs, institutions, and by the subjective self-identification of people. People have levels of identity: a resident of Rome may define himself with varying degrees of intensity as a Roman, an Italian, a Catholic, a Christian, a European, a Westerner. The civilization to which he belongs is the broadest level of identification with which he intensely identifies. People can and do redefine their identities and, as a result, the composition and boundaries of civilizations change.

Civilizations may involve a large number of people, as with China ("a civilization pretending to be a state," as Lucian Pye put it), or a very small number of people, such as the Anglophone Caribbean. A civilization may include several nation states, as is the case with Western, Latin American and Arab civilizations, or only one, as is the case with Japanese civilization. Civilizations obviously blend and overlap, and may include subcivilizations. Western civilization has two major variants, European and North American, and Islam has its Arab, Turkic and Malay subdivisions. Civilizations are nonetheless meaningful entities, and while the lines between them are seldom sharp, they are real. Civilizations are dynamic; they rise and fall; they divide and merge. And, as any student of history knows, civilizations disappear and are buried in the sands of time.

Westerners tend to think of nation states as the principal actors in global affairs. They have been that, however, for only a few centuries. The broader reaches of human history have been the history of civilizations. In *A Study of History*, Arnold Toynbee identified 21 major civilizations; only six of them exist in the contemporary world.

WHY CIVILIZATIONS WILL CLASH

Civilization identity will be increasingly important in the future, and the world will be shaped in large measure by the interactions among seven or eight major civilizations. These include Western, Confucian, Japanese, Islamic, Hindu, Slavic-Orthodox, Latin American and possibly African civilization. The most important conflicts of the future will occur along the cultural fault lines separating these civilizations from one another.

Why will this be the case?

First, differences among civilizations are not only real; they are basic. Civilizations are differentiated from each other by history, language, culture, tradition and, most important, religion. The people of different civilizations have different views on the relations between God and man, the individual and the group, the citizen and the state, parents and children, husband and wife, as well as differing views of the relative importance of rights and responsibilities, liberty and authority, equality and hierarchy. These differences are the product of centuries. They will not soon disappear. They are far more fundamental than differences among political ideologies and political regimes. Differences do not necessarily mean conflict, and conflict does not necessarily mean violence. Over the centuries, however, differences among civilizations have generated the most prolonged and the most violent conflicts.

Second, the world is becoming a smaller place. The interactions between peoples of different civilizations are increasing; these increasing interactions intensify civilization consciousness and awareness of differences between civilizations and commonalities within civilizations. North African immigration to France generates hostility among Frenchmen and at the same time increased receptivity to immigration by "good" European Catholic Poles. Americans react far more negatively to Japanese investment than to larger investments from Canada and European countries. Similarly, as Donald Horowitz has pointed out, "An Ibo may be . . . an Owerri Ibo or an Onitsha Ibo in what was the Eastern region of Nigeria. In Lagos, he is simply an Ibo. In London, he is a Nigerian. In New York, he is an African." The interactions among peoples of different civilizations enhance the civilization-consciousness of people that, in turn, invigorates differences and animosities stretching or thought to stretch back deep into history.

Third, the processes of economic modernization and social change throughout the world are separating people from longstanding local identities. They also weaken the nation state as a source of identity. In much of the world religion has moved in to fill this gap, often in the form of movements that are labeled "fundamentalist." Such movements are found in Western Christianity, Judaism, Buddhism and Hinduism, as well as in Islam. In most countries and most religions the people active in fundamentalist movements are young, college-educated, middle-class technicians, professionals and business persons. The "unsecularization of the world," George Weigel has remarked, "is one of the dominant social facts of life in the late twentieth century." The revival of religion, "la revanche de Dieu," as Gilles Kepel labeled it, provides a basis for identity and commitment that transcends national boundaries and unites civilizations.

Fourth, the growth of civilization-consciousness is enhanced by the dual role of the West. On the one hand, the West is at a peak of power. At the same time, however, and perhaps as a result, a return to the roots phenomenon is oc-curring among non-Western civilizations. Increasingly one hears references to trends toward a turning inward and "Asianization" in Japan, the end of the Nehru legacy and the "Hinduization" of India, the failure of Western ideas of socialism and nationalism and hence "re-Islamization" of the Middle East, and now a debate over Westernization versus Russianization in Boris Yeltsin's coun-try. A West at the peak of its power confronts non-Wests that increasingly have the desire, the will and the resources to shape the world in non-Western ways.

In the past, the elites of non-Western societies were usually the people who were most involved with the West, had been educated at Oxford, the Sorbonne or Sandhurst, and had absorbed Western attitudes and values. At the same time, the populace in non-Western countries often remained deeply imbued with the indigenous culture. Now, however, these relationships are being re-versed. A de-Westernization and indigenization of elites is occurring in many non-Western countries at the same time that Western, usually American, cul-tures, styles and habits become more popular among the mass of the people.

Fifth, cultural characteristics and differences are less mutable and hence less easily compromised and resolved than political and economic ones. In the for-mer Soviet Union, communists can become democrats, the rich can become poor and the poor rich, but Russians cannot become Estonians and Azeris cannot be-come Armenians. In class and ideological conflicts, the key question was "Which side are you on?" and people could and did choose sides and change sides. In conflicts between civilizations, the question is "What are you?" That is a given that cannot be changed. And as we know, from Bosnia to the Caucasus to the Sudan, the wrong answer to that question can mean a bullet in the head. Even more than ethnicity, religion discriminates sharply and exclusively among people. A person can be half-French and half-Arab and simultaneously even a citizen of two countries. It is more difficult to be half-Catholic and half-Muslim.

Finally, economic regionalism is increasing. The proportions of total trade that were intraregional rose between 1980 and 1989 from 51 percent to 59 percent in Europe, 33 percent to 37 percent in East Asia, and 32 percent to 36 percent in North America. The importance of regional economic blocs is likely to continue to increase in the future. On the one hand, successful economic regionalism will reinforce civilization-consciousness. On the other hand, economic regionalism may succeed only when it is rooted in a common civilization. The European Community rests on the shared foundation of European culture and Western Christianity. The success of the North American Free Trade Area depends on the convergence now underway of Mexican, Canadian and American cultures. Japan, in contrast, faces difficulties in creating a comparable economic entity in East Asia because Japan is a society and civilization unique to itself. However strong the trade and investment links Japan may develop with other East Asian countries, its cultural differences with those countries inhibit and perhaps preclude its promoting regional economic integration like that in Europe and North America.

Common culture, in contrast, is clearly facilitating the rapid expansion of the economic relations between the People's Republic of China and Hong Kong, Taiwan, Singapore and the overseas Chinese communities in other Asian countries. With the Cold War over, cultural commonalities increasingly overcome ideological differences, and mainland China and Taiwan move closer together. If cultural commonality is a prerequisite for economic integration, the principal East Asian economic bloc of the future is likely to be centered on China. This bloc is, in fact, already coming into existence. As Murray Weidenbaum has observed,

> Despite the current Japanese dominance of the region, the Chinese-based economy of Asia is rapidly emerging as a new epicenter for industry, commerce and finance. This strategic area contains substantial amounts of technology and manufacturing capability (Taiwan), outstanding entrepreneurial, marketing and services acumen (Hong Kong), a fine communications network (Singapore), a tremendous pool of financial capital (all three), and very large endowments of land, resources and labor (mainland China). . . . From Guangzhou to Singapore, from Kuala Lumpur to Manila, this influential network—often based on extensions of the traditional clans—has been described as the backbone of the East Asian economy.[1]

Culture and religion also form the basis of the Economic Cooperation Organization, which brings together ten non-Arab Muslim countries: Iran, Pakistan, Turkey, Azerbaijan, Kazakhstan, Kyrgyzstan, Turkmenistan, Tadjikistan, Uzbekistan and Afghanistan. One impetus to the revival and expansion of this organization, founded originally in the 1960s by Turkey, Pakistan and Iran, is the realization by the leaders of several of these countries that they had no chance of admission to the European Community. Similarly, Caricom, the Central American Common Market and Mercosur rest on common cultural foundations. Efforts to build a broader Caribbean-Central American economic entity bridging the Anglo-Latin divide, however, have to date failed.

As people define their identity in ethnic and religious terms, they are likely to see an "us" versus "them" relation existing between themselves and people of different ethnicity or religion. The end of ideologically defined states in Eastern Europe and the former Soviet Union permits traditional ethnic identities and animosities to come to the fore. Differences in culture and religion create differences over policy issues, ranging from human rights to immigration to trade and commerce to the environment. Geographical propinquity gives rise to conflicting territorial claims from Bosnia to Mindanao. Most important, the efforts of the West to promote its values of democracy and liberalism as universal values, to maintain its military predominance and to advance its economic interests engender countering responses from other civilizations. Decreasingly able to mobilize support and form coalitions on the basis of ideology, governments and groups will increasingly attempt to mobilize support by appealing to common religion and civilization identity.

The clash of civilizations thus occurs at two levels. At the micro-level, adjacent groups along the fault lines between civilizations struggle, often violently, over the control of territory and each other. At the macro-level, states from different civilizations compete for relative military and economic power, struggle over the control of international institutions and third parties, and competitively promote their particular political and religious values.

THE FAULT LINES BETWEEN CIVILIZATIONS

The fault lines between civilizations are replacing the political and ideological boundaries of the Cold War as the flash points for crisis and bloodshed. The Cold War began when the Iron Curtain divided Europe politically and ideologically. The Cold War ended with the end of the Iron Curtain. As the ideological division of Europe has disappeared, the cultural division of Europe between Western Christianity, on the one hand, and Orthodox Christianity and Islam, on the other, has reemerged. The most significant dividing line in Europe, as William Wallace has suggested, may well be the eastern boundary of Western Christianity in the year 1500. This line runs along what are now the boundaries between Finland and Russia and between the Baltic states and Russia, cuts through Belarus and Ukraine separating the more Catholic western Ukraine from Orthodox eastern Ukraine, swings westward separating Transylvania from the rest of Romania, and then goes through Yugoslavia almost exactly along the line now separating Croatia and Slovenia from the rest of Yugoslavia. In the Balkans this line, of course, coincides with the historic boundary between the Hapsburg and Ottoman empires. The peoples to the north and west of this line are Protestant or Catholic; they shared the common experiences of European history—feudalism, the Renaissance, the Reformation, the Enlightenment, the French Revolution, the Industrial Revolution; they are generally economically better off than the peoples to the east; and they may now look forward to increasing involvement in a common European economy and to the consolidation of democratic political systems. The peoples to the east and south of this line are Orthodox or Muslim; they historically belonged to the Ottoman or Tsarist empires and were only lightly touched by the shaping events in the rest of Europe; they are generally less advanced economically; they seem much less likely to develop stable democratic political systems. The Velvet Curtain of culture has replaced the Iron Curtain of ideology as the most significant dividing line in Europe. As the events in Yugoslavia show, it is not only a line of difference; it is also at times a line of bloody conflict.

Conflict along the fault line between Western and Islamic civilizations has been going on for 1,300 years. After the founding of Islam, the Arab and Moorish surge west and north only ended at Tours in 732. From the eleventh to the thirteenth century the Crusaders attempted with temporary success to bring Christianity and Christian rule to the Holy Land. From the fourteenth to the seventeenth century, the Ottoman Turks reversed the balance, extended their sway over the Middle East and the Balkans, captured Constantinople, and twice laid siege to Vienna. In the nineteenth and early twentieth centuries as Ottoman power declined Britain, France, and Italy established Western control over most of North Africa and the Middle East.

After World War II, the West, in turn, began to retreat; the colonial empires disappeared; first Arab nationalism and then Islamic fundamentalism manifested themselves; the West became heavily dependent on the Persian Gulf countries for its energy; the oil-rich Muslim countries became money-rich and, when they wished to, weapons-rich. Several wars occurred between Arabs and Israel (created by the West). France fought a bloody and ruthless war in Algeria for most of the 1950s; British and French forces invaded Egypt in 1956; American forces went into Lebanon in 1958; subsequently American forces returned to Lebanon, attacked Libya, and engaged in various military encounters with Iran; Arab and Islamic terrorists, supported by at least three Middle Eastern governments, employed the weapon of the weak and bombed Western planes and installations and seized Western hostages. This warfare between Arabs and the West culminated in 1990, when the United States sent a massive army to the Persian Gulf to defend some Arab countries against aggression by another. In its aftermath NATO planning is increasingly directed to potential threats and instability along its "southern tier."

This centuries-old military interaction between the West and Islam is unlikely to decline. It could become more virulent. The Gulf War left some Arabs feeling proud that Saddam Hussein had attacked Israel and stood up to the West. It also left many feeling humiliated and resentful of the West's military presence in the Persian Gulf, the West's overwhelming military dominance, and their apparent inability to shape their own destiny. Many Arab countries, in addition to the oil exporters, are reaching levels of economic and social development where autocratic forms of government become inappropriate and efforts to introduce democracy become stronger. Some openings in Arab political systems have already occurred. The principal beneficiaries of these openings have been Islamist movements. In the Arab world, in short, Western democracy strengthens anti-Western political forces. This may be a passing phenomenon, but it surely complicates relations between Islamic countries and the West.

Those relations are also complicated by demography. The spectacular population growth in Arab countries, particularly in North Africa, has led to increased migration to Western Europe. The movement within Western Europe toward minimizing internal boundaries has sharpened political sensitivities with respect to this development. In Italy, France and Germany, racism is increasingly open, and political reactions and violence against Arab and Turkish migrants have become more intense and more widespread since 1990.

On both sides the interaction between Islam and the West is seen as a clash of civilizations. The West's "next confrontation," observes M. J. Akbar, an Indian Muslim author, "is definitely going to come from the Muslim world. It is in the sweep of the Islamic nations from the Maghreb to Pakistan that the struggle for a new world order will begin." Bernard Lewis comes to a similar conclusion:

> We are facing a mood and a movement far transcending the level of issues and policies and the governments that pursue them. This is no less than a clash of civilizations—the perhaps irrational but surely historic reaction of an ancient rival against our Judeo-Christian heritage, our secular present, and the worldwide expansion of both.[2]

Historically, the other great antagonistic interaction of Arab Islamic civilization has been with the pagan, animist, and now increasingly Christian black peoples to the south. In the past, this antagonism was epitomized in the image of Arab slave dealers and black slaves. It has been reflected in the on-going civil war in the Sudan between Arabs and blacks, the fighting in Chad between Libyan-supported insurgents and the government, the tensions between Orthodox Christians and Muslims in the Horn of Africa, and the political conflicts, recurring riots and communal violence between Muslims and Christians in Nigeria. The modernization of Africa and the spread of Christianity are likely to enhance the probability of violence along this fault line. Symptomatic of the intensification of this conflict was the Pope John Paul II's speech in Khartoum in February 1993 attacking the actions of the Sudan's Islamist government against the Christian minority there.

On the northern border of Islam, conflict has increasingly erupted between Orthodox and Muslim peoples, including the carnage of Bosnia and Sarajevo, the simmering violence between Serb and Albanian, the tenuous relations between Bulgarians and their Turkish minority, the violence between Ossetians and Ingush, the unremitting slaughter of each other by Armenians and Azeris, the tense relations between Russians and Muslims in Central Asia, and the deployment of Russian troops to protect Russian interests in the Caucasus and Central Asia. Religion reinforces the revival of ethnic identities and restimulates Russian fears about the security of their southern borders. This concern is well captured by Archie Roosevelt:

> Much of Russian history concerns the struggle between the Slavs and the Turkic peoples on their borders, which dates back to the foundation of the

Russian state more than a thousand years ago. In the Slavs' millennium-long confrontation with their eastern neighbors lies the key to an understanding not only of Russian history, but Russian character. To understand Russian realities today one has to have a concept of the great Turkic ethnic group that has preoccupied Russians through the centuries.[3]

The conflict of civilizations is deeply rooted elsewhere in Asia. The historic clash between Muslim and Hindu in the subcontinent manifests itself now not only in the rivalry between Pakistan and India but also in intensifying religious strife within India between increasingly militant Hindu groups and India's substantial Muslim minority. The destruction of the Ayodhya mosque in December 1992 brought to the fore the issue of whether India will remain a secular democratic state or become a Hindu one. In East Asia, China has outstanding territorial disputes with most of its neighbors. It has pursued a ruthless policy toward the Buddhist people of Tibet, and it is pursuing an increasingly ruthless policy toward its Turkic-Muslim minority. With the Cold War over, the underlying differences between China and the United States have reasserted themselves in areas such as human rights, trade and weapons proliferation. These differences are unlikely to moderate. A "new cold war," Deng Xaioping reportedly asserted in 1991, is under way between China and America.

The same phrase has been applied to the increasingly difficult relations between Japan and the United States. Here cultural difference exacerbates economic conflict. People on each side allege racism on the other, but at least on the American side the antipathies are not racial but cultural. The basic values, attitudes, behavioral patterns of the two societies could hardly be more different. The economic issues between the United States and Europe are no less serious than those between the United States and Japan, but they do not have the same political salience and emotional intensity because the differences between American culture and European culture are so much less than those between American civilization and Japanese civilization.

The interactions between civilizations vary greatly in the extent to which they are likely to be characterized by violence. Economic competition clearly predominates between the American and European subcivilizations of the West and between both of them and Japan. On the Eurasian continent, however, the proliferation of ethnic conflict, epitomized at the extreme in "ethnic cleansing," has not been totally random. It has been most frequent and most violent between groups belonging to different civilizations. In Eurasia the great historic fault lines between civilizations are once more aflame. This is particularly true along the boundaries of the crescent-shaped Islamic bloc of nations from the bulge of Africa to central Asia. Violence also occurs between Muslims, on the one hand, and Orthodox Serbs in the Balkans, Jews in Israel, Hindus in India, Buddhists in Burma and Catholics in the Philippines. Islam has bloody borders.

CIVILIZATION RALLYING:
THE KIN-COUNTRY SYNDROME

Groups or states belonging to one civilization that become involved in war with people from a different civilization naturally try to rally support from other members of their own civilization. As the post-Cold War world evolves, civilization commonality, what H. D. S. Greenway has termed the "kin-country" syndrome, is replacing political ideology and traditional balance of power considerations as the principal basis for cooperation and coalitions. It can be seen gradually emerging in the post-Cold War conflicts in the Persian Gulf, the Caucasus and Bosnia. None of these was a full-scale war between civilizations, but each involved some elements of civilizational rallying, which seemed to become more important as the conflict continued and which may provide a foretaste of the future.

First, in the Gulf War one Arab state invaded another and then fought a coalition of Arab, Western and other states. While only a few Muslim governments overtly supported Saddam Hussein, many Arab elites privately cheered him on, and he was highly popular among large sections of the Arab publics. Islamic fundamentalist movements universally supported Iraq rather than the Western-backed governments of Kuwait and Saudi Arabia. Forswearing Arab nationalism, Saddam Hussein explicitly invoked an Islamic appeal. He and his supporters attempted to define the war as a war between civilizations. "It is not the world against Iraq," as Safar Al-Hawali, dean of Islamic Studies at the Umm Al-Qura University in Mecca, put it in a widely circulated tape. "It is the West against Islam." Ignoring the rivalry between Iran and Iraq, the chief Iranian religious leader, Ayatollah Ali Khamenei, called for a holy war against the West: "The struggle against American aggression, greed, plans and policies will be counted as a jihad, and anybody who is killed on that path is a martyr." "This is a war," King Hussein of Jordan argued, "against all Arabs and all Muslims and not against Iraq alone."

The rallying of substantial sections of Arab elites and publics behind Saddam Hussein caused those Arab governments in the anti-Iraq coalition to moderate their activities and temper their public statements. Arab governments opposed or distanced themselves from subsequent Western efforts to apply pressure on Iraq, including enforcement of a no-fly zone in the summer of 1992 and the bombing of Iraq in January 1993. The Western-Soviet-Turkish-Arab anti-Iraq coalition of 1990 had by 1993 become a coalition of almost only the West and Kuwait against Iraq.

Muslims contrasted Western actions against Iraq with the West's failure to protect Bosnians against Serbs and to impose sanctions on Israel for violating U.N. resolutions. The West, they alleged, was using a double standard. A world of clashing civilizations, however, is inevitably a world of double standards: people apply one standard to their kin-countries and a different standard to others.

Second, the kin-country syndrome also appeared in conflicts in the former Soviet Union. Armenian military successes in 1992 and 1993 stimulated

Turkey to become increasingly supportive of its religious, ethnic and linguistic brethren in Azerbaijan. "We have a Turkish nation feeling the same sentiments as the Azerbaijanis," said one Turkish official in 1992. "We are under pressure. Our newspapers are full of the photos of atrocities and are asking us if we are still serious about pursuing our neutral policy. Maybe we should show Armenia that there's a big Turkey in the region." President Turgut Özal agreed, remarking that Turkey should at least "scare the Armenians a little bit." Turkey, Özal threatened again in 1993, would "show its fangs." Turkish Air Force jets flew reconnaissance flights along the Armenian border; Turkey suspended food shipments and air flights to Armenia; and Turkey and Iran announced they would not accept dismemberment of Azerbaijan. In the last years of its existence, the Soviet government supported Azerbaijan because its government was dominated by former communists. With the end of the Soviet Union, however, political considerations gave way to religious ones. Russian troops fought on the side of the Armenians, and Azerbaijan accused the "Russian government of turning 180 degrees" toward support for Christian Armenia.

Third, with respect to the fighting in the former Yugoslavia, Western publics manifested sympathy and support for the Bosnian Muslims and the horrors they suffered at the hands of the Serbs. Relatively little concern was expressed, however, over Croatian attacks on Muslims and participation in the dismemberment of Bosnia-Herzegovina. In the early stages of the Yugoslav breakup, Germany, in an unusual display of diplomatic initiative and muscle, induced the other 11 members of the European Community to follow its lead in recognizing Slovenia and Croatia. As a result of the pope's determination to provide strong backing to the two Catholic countries, the Vatican extended recognition even before the Community did. The United States followed the European lead. Thus the leading actors in Western civilization rallied behind their coreligionists. Subsequently Croatia was reported to be receiving substantial quantities of arms from Central European and other Western countries. Boris Yeltsin's government, on the other hand, attempted to pursue a middle course that would be sympathetic to the Orthodox Serbs but not alienate Russia from the West. Russian conservative and nationalist groups, however, including many legislators, attacked the government for not being more forthcoming in its support for the Serbs. By early 1993 several hundred Russians apparently were serving with the Serbian forces, and reports circulated of Russian arms being supplied to Serbia.

Islamic governments and groups, on the other hand, castigated the West for not coming to the defense of the Bosnians. Iranian leaders urged Muslims from all countries to provide help to Bosnia; in violation of the U.N. arms embargo, Iran supplied weapons and men for the Bosnians; Iranian-supported Lebanese groups sent guerrillas to train and organize the Bosnian forces. In 1993 up to 4,000 Muslims from over two dozen Islamic countries were reported to be fighting in Bosnia. The governments of Saudi Arabia and other countries felt under increasing pressure from fundamentalist groups in their own societies to provide more vigorous support for the Bosnians. By the end of

1992, Saudi Arabia had reportedly supplied substantial funding for weapons and supplies for the Bosnians, which significantly increased their military capabilities vis-à-vis the Serbs.

In the 1930s the Spanish Civil War provoked intervention from countries that politically were fascist, communist and democratic. In the 1990s the Yugoslav conflict is provoking intervention from countries that are Muslim, Orthodox and Western Christian. The parallel has not gone unnoticed. "The war in Bosnia-Herzegovina has become the emotional equivalent of the fight against fascism in the Spanish Civil War," one Saudi editor observed. "Those who died there are regarded as martyrs who tried to save their fellow Muslims."

Conflicts and violence will also occur between states and groups within the same civilization. Such conflicts, however, are likely to be less intense and less likely to expand than conflicts between civilizations. Common membership in a civilization reduces the probability of violence in situations where it might otherwise occur. In 1991 and 1992 many people were alarmed by the possibility of violent conflict between Russia and Ukraine over territory, particularly Crimea, the Black Sea fleet, nuclear weapons and economic issues. If civilization is what counts, however, the likelihood of violence between Ukrainians and Russians should be low. They are two Slavic, primarily Orthodox peoples who have had close relationships with each other for centuries. As of early 1993, despite all the reasons for conflict, the leaders of the two countries were effectively negotiating and defusing the issues between the two countries. While there has been serious fighting between Muslims and Christians elsewhere in the former Soviet Union and much tension and some fighting between Western and Orthodox Christians in the Baltic states, there has been virtually no violence between Russians and Ukrainians.

Civilization rallying to date has been limited, but it has been growing, and it clearly has the potential to spread much further. As the conflicts in the Persian Gulf, the Caucasus and Bosnia continued, the positions of nations and the cleavages between them increasingly were along civilizational lines. Populist politicians, religious leaders and the media have found it a potent means of arousing mass support and of pressuring hesitant governments. In the coming years, the local conflicts most likely to escalate into major wars will be those, as in Bosnia and the Caucasus, along the fault lines between civilizations. The next world war, if there is one, will be a war between civilizations.

THE WEST VERSUS THE REST

The West is now at an extraordinary peak of power in relation to other civilizations. Its superpower opponent has disappeared from the map. Military conflict among Western states is unthinkable, and Western military power is unrivaled. Apart from Japan, the West faces no economic challenge. It dominates international political and security institutions and with Japan international economic institutions. Global political and security issues are effectively settled by a directorate of the United States, Britain and France, world economic issues by a directorate of the United States, Germany and Japan, all of which maintain extraordinarily close relations with each other to the exclusion of lesser and largely non-Western countries. Decisions made at the U.N. Security Council or in the International Monetary Fund that reflect the interests of the West are presented to the world as reflecting the desires of the world community. The very phrase "the world community" has become the euphemistic collective noun (replacing "the Free World") to give global legitimacy to actions reflecting the interests of the United States and other Western powers.[4] Through the IMF and other international economic institutions, the West promotes its economic interests and imposes on other nations the economic policies it thinks appropriate. In any poll of non-Western peoples, the IMF undoubtedly would win the support of finance ministers and a few others, but get an overwhelmingly unfavorable rating from just about everyone else, who would agree with Georgy Arbatov's characterization of IMF officials as "neo-Bolsheviks who love expropriating other people's money, imposing undemocratic and alien rules of economic and political conduct and stifling economic freedom."

Western domination of the U.N. Security Council and its decisions, tempered only by occasional abstention by China, produced U.N. legitimation of the West's use of force to drive Iraq out of Kuwait and its elimination of Iraq's sophisticated weapons and capacity to produce such weapons. It also produced the quite unprecedented action by the United States, Britain and France in getting the Security Council to demand that Libya hand over the Pan Am 103 bombing suspects and then to impose sanctions when Libya refused. After defeating the largest Arab army, the West did not hesitate to throw its weight around in the Arab world. The West in effect is using international institutions, military power and economic resources to run the world in ways that will maintain Western predominance, protect Western interests and promote Western political and economic values.

That at least is the way in which non-Westerners see the new world, and there is a significant element of truth in their view. Differences in power and struggles for military, economic and institutional power are thus one source of conflict between the West and other civilizations. Differences in culture, that is basic values and beliefs, are a second source of conflict. V. S. Naipaul has argued that Western civilization is the "universal civilization" that "fits all men." At a superficial level much of Western culture has indeed permeated the rest of the world. At a more basic level, however, Western concepts differ fundamentally from those prevalent in other civilizations. Western ideas of individualism, liberalism, constitutionalism, human rights, equality, liberty, the rule of law, democracy, free markets, the separation of church and state, often have little resonance in Islamic, Confucian, Japanese, Hindu, Buddhist or Orthodox cultures. Western efforts to propagate such ideas produce instead a reaction against "human rights imperialism" and a reaffirmation of indigenous values, as can be seen in the support for religious fundamentalism by the younger generation in non-Western cultures. The very notion that there could be a "universal civilization" is a Western idea, directly at odds with the particularism of most Asian societies and their emphasis on what distinguishes one people from another. Indeed, the author of a review of 100 comparative studies of values in different societies concluded that "the values that are most important in the West are least important worldwide." [5] In the political realm, of course, these differences are most manifest in the efforts of the United States and other Western powers to induce other peoples to adopt Western ideas concerning democracy and human rights. Modern democratic government originated in the West. When it has developed in non-Western societies it has usually been the product of Western colonialism or imposition.

The central axis of world politics in the future is likely to be, in Kishore Mahbubani's phrase, the conflict between "the West and the Rest" and the responses of non-Western civilizations to Western power and values. [6] Those responses generally take one or a combination of three forms. At one extreme, non-Western states can, like Burma and North Korea, attempt to pursue a course of isolation, to insulate their societies from penetration or "corruption" by the West, and, in effect, to opt out of participation in the Western-dominated global community. The costs of this course, however, are high, and few states have pursued it exclusively. A second alternative, the equivalent of "band-wagoning" in international relations theory, is to attempt to join the West and accept its values and institutions. The third alternative is to attempt to "balance" the West by developing economic and military power and cooperating with other non-Western societies against the West, while preserving indigenous values and institutions; in short, to modernize but not to Westernize.

THE TORN COUNTRIES

In the future, as people differentiate themselves by civilization, countries with large numbers of peoples of different civilizations, such as the Soviet Union and Yugoslavia, are candidates for dismemberment. Some other countries have a fair degree of cultural homogeneity but are divided over whether their society belongs to one civilization or another. These are torn countries. Their leaders typically wish to pursue a bandwagoning strategy and to make their countries members of the West, but the history, culture and traditions of their countries are non-Western. The most obvious and prototypical torn country is Turkey. The late twentieth-century leaders of Turkey have followed in the Attatürk tradition and defined Turkey as a modern, secular, Western nation state. They allied Turkey with the West in NATO and in the Gulf War; they applied for membership in the European Community. At the same time, however, elements in Turkish society have supported an Islamic revival and have argued that Turkey is basically a Middle Eastern Muslim society. In addition, while the elite of Turkey has defined Turkey as a Western society, the elite of the West refuses to accept Turkey as such. Turkey will not become a member of the European

Community, and the real reason, as President Özal said, "is that we are Muslim and they are Christian and they don't say that." Having rejected Mecca, and then being rejected by Brussels, where does Turkey look? Tashkent may be the answer. The end of the Soviet Union gives Turkey the opportunity to become the leader of a revived Turkic civilization involving seven countries from the borders of Greece to those of China. Encouraged by the West, Turkey is making strenuous efforts to carve out this new identity for itself.

During the past decade Mexico has assumed a position somewhat similar to that of Turkey. Just as Turkey abandoned its historic opposition to Europe and attempted to join Europe, Mexico has stopped defining itself by its opposition to the United States and is instead attempting to imitate the United States and to join it in the North American Free Trade Area. Mexican leaders are engaged in the great task of redefining Mexican identity and have introduced fundamental economic reforms that eventually will lead to fundamental political change. In 1991 a top adviser to President Carlos Salinas de Gortari described at length to me all the changes the Salinas government was making. When he finished, I remarked: "That's most impressive. It seems to me that basically you want to change Mexico from a Latin American country into a North American country." He looked at me with surprise and exclaimed: "Exactly! That's precisely what we are trying to do, but of course we could never say so publicly." As his remark indicates, in Mexico as in Turkey, significant elements in society resist the redefinition of their country's identity. In Turkey, European-oriented leaders have to make gestures to Islam (Özal's pilgrimage to Mecca); so also Mexico's North American-oriented leaders have to make gestures to those who hold Mexico to be a Latin American country (Salinas' Ibero-American Guadalajara summit).

Historically Turkey has been the most profoundly torn country. For the United States, Mexico is the most immediate torn country. Globally the most important torn country is Russia. The question of whether Russia is part of the West or the leader of a distinct Slavic-Orthodox civilization has been a recurring one in Russian history. That issue was obscured by the communist victory in Russia, which imported a Western ideology, adapted it to Russian conditions and then challenged the West in the name of that ideology. The dominance of communism shut off the historic debate over Westernization versus Russification. With communism discredited Russians once again face that question.

President Yeltsin is adopting Western principles and goals and seeking to make Russia a "normal" country and a part of the West. Yet both the Russian elite and the Russian public are divided on this issue. Among the more moderate dissenters, Sergei Stankevich argues that Russia should reject the "Atlanticist" course, which would lead it "to become European, to become a part of the world economy in rapid and organized fashion, to become the eighth member of the Seven, and to put particular emphasis on Germany and the United States as the two dominant members of the Atlantic alliance." While also rejecting an exclusively Eurasian policy, Stankevich nonetheless argues that Russia should give priority to the protection of Russians in other countries, emphasize its Turkic and Muslim connections, and promote "an appreciable redistribution of our resources, our options, our ties, and our interests in favor of Asia, of the eastern direction." People of this persuasion criticize Yeltsin for subordinating Russia's interests to those of the West, for reducing Russian military strength, for failing to support traditional friends such as Serbia, and for pushing economic and political reform in ways injurious to the Russian people. Indicative of this trend is the new popularity of the ideas of Petr Savitsky, who in the 1920s argued that Russia was a unique Eurasian civilization.[7] More extreme dissidents voice much more blatantly nationalist, anti-Western and anti-Semitic views, and urge Russia to redevelop its military strength and to establish closer ties with China and Muslim countries. The people of Russia are as divided as the elite. An opinion survey in European Russia in the spring of 1992 revealed that 40 percent of the public had positive attitudes toward the West and 36 percent had negative attitudes. As it has been for much of its history, Russia in the early 1990s is truly a torn country.

To redefine its civilization identity, a torn country must meet three requirements. First, its political and economic elite has to be generally supportive of and enthusiastic about this move. Second, its public has to be willing to acquiesce in the redefinition. Third, the dominant groups in the recipient civilization have to be willing to embrace the convert. All three requirements in large part exist with respect to Mexico. The first two in large part exist with respect to Turkey. It is not clear that any of them exist with respect to Russia's joining the West. The conflict between liberal democracy and Marxism-Leninism was between ideologies which, despite their major differences, ostensibly shared ultimate goals of freedom, equality and prosperity. A traditional, authoritarian, nationalist Russia could have quite different goals. A Western democrat could carry on an intellectual debate with a Soviet Marxist. It would be virtually impossible for him to do that with a Russian traditionalist. If, as the Russians stop behaving like Marxists, they reject liberal democracy and begin behaving like Russians but not like Westerners, the relations between Russia and the West could again become distant and conflictual.[8]

THE CONFUCIAN-ISLAMIC CONNECTION

The obstacles to non-Western countries joining the West vary considerably. They are least for Latin American and East European countries. They are greater for the Orthodox countries of the former Soviet Union. They are still greater for Muslim, Confucian, Hindu and Buddhist societies. Japan has established a unique position for itself as an associate member of the West: it is in the West in some respects but clearly not of the West in important dimensions. Those countries that for reason of culture and power do not wish to, or cannot, join the West compete with the West by developing their own economic, military and political power. They do this by promoting their internal development and by cooperating with other non-Western countries. The most prominent form of this cooperation is the Confucian-Islamic connection that has emerged to challenge Western interests, values and power.

Almost without exception, Western countries are reducing their military power; under Yeltsin's leadership so also is Russia. China, North Korea and several Middle Eastern states, however, are significantly expanding their military capabilities. They are doing this by the import of arms from Western and non-Western sources and by the development of indigenous arms industries. One result is the emergence of what Charles Krauthammer has called "Weapon States," and the Weapon States are not Western states. Another result is the redefinition of arms control, which is a Western concept and a Western goal. During the Cold War the primary purpose of arms control was to establish a stable military balance between the United States and its allies and the Soviet Union and its allies. In the post-Cold War world the primary objective of arms control is to prevent the development by non-Western societies of military capabilities that could threaten Western interests. The West attempts to do this through international agreements, economic pressure and controls on the transfer of arms and weapons technologies.

The conflict between the West and the Confucian-Islamic states focuses largely, although not exclusively, on nuclear, chemical and biological weapons, ballistic missiles and other sophisticated means for delivering them, and the guidance, intelligence and other electronic capabilities for achieving that goal. The West promotes nonproliferation as a universal norm and nonproliferation treaties and inspections as means of realizing that norm. It also threatens a variety of sanctions against those who promote the spread of sophisticated weapons and proposes some benefits for those who do not. The attention of the West focuses, naturally, on nations that are actually or potentially hostile to the West.

The non-Western nations, on the other hand, assert their right to acquire and to deploy whatever weapons they think necessary for their security. They also have absorbed, to the full, the truth of the response of the Indian defense minister when asked what lesson he learned from the Gulf War: "Don't fight the United States unless you have nuclear weapons." Nuclear weapons, chemical weapons and missiles are viewed, probably erroneously, as the potential equalizer of superior Western conventional power. China, of course, already has nuclear weapons; Pakistan and India have the capability to deploy them. North Korea, Iran, Iraq, Libya and Algeria appear to be attempting to acquire them. A top Iranian official has declared that all Muslim states should acquire nuclear weapons, and in 1988 the president of Iran reportedly issued a directive calling for development of "offensive and defensive chemical, biological and radiological weapons."

Centrally important to the development of counter-West military capabilities is the sustained expansion of China's military power and its means to create military power. Buoyed by spectacular economic development, China is rapidly increasing its military spending and vigorously moving forward with the modernization of its armed forces. It is purchasing weapons from the former Soviet states; it is developing long-range missiles; in 1992 it tested a one-megaton nuclear device. It is developing power-projection capabilities, acquiring aerial re-fueling technology, and trying to purchase an aircraft carrier. Its military buildup and assertion of sovereignty over the South China Sea are provoking a multilat-eral regional arms race in East Asia. China is also a major exporter of arms and weapons technology. It has exported materials to Libya and Iraq that could be used to manufacture nuclear weapons and nerve gas. It has helped Algeria build a reactor suitable for nuclear weapons research and production. China has sold to Iran nuclear technology that American officials believe could only be used to create weapons and apparently has shipped components of 300-mile-range mis-siles to Pakistan. North Korea has had a nuclear weapons program under way for some while and has sold advanced missiles and missile technology to Syria and Iran. The flow of weapons and weapons technology is generally from East Asia to the Middle East. There is, however, some movement in the reverse direc-tion; China has received Stinger missiles from Pakistan.

A Confucian-Islamic military connection has thus come into being, de-signed to promote acquisition by its members of the weapons and weapons technologies needed to counter the military power of the West. It may or may not last. At present, however, it is, as Dave McCurdy has said, "a renegades' mutual support pact, run by the proliferators and their backers." A new form of arms competition is thus occurring between Islamic-Confucian states and the West. In an old-fashioned arms race, each side developed its own arms to balance or to achieve superiority against the other side. In this new form of arms competition, one side is developing its arms and the other side is at-tempting not to balance but to limit and prevent that arms build-up while at the same time reducing its own military capabilities.

IMPLICATIONS FOR THE WEST

This article does not argue that civilization identities will replace all other iden-tities, that nation states will disappear, that each civilization will become a single coherent political entity, that groups within a civilization will not conflict with and even fight each other. This paper does set forth the hypotheses that differences between civilizations are real and important; civilization-consciousness is increasing; conflict between civilizations will supplant ideolog-ical and other forms of conflict as the dominant global form of conflict; inter-national relations, historically a game played out within Western civilization, will increasingly be de-Westernized and become a game in which non-Western civilizations are actors and not simply objects; successful political, security and economic international institutions are more likely to develop within civiliza-tions than across civilizations; conflicts between groups in different civilizations will be more frequent, more sustained and more violent than conflicts between groups in the same civilization; violent conflicts between groups in different civ-ilizations are the most likely and most dangerous source of escalation that could lead to global wars; the paramount axis of world politics will be the relations between "the West and the Rest"; the elites in some torn non-Western countries will try to make their countries part of the West, but in most cases face major obstacles to accomplishing this; a central focus of conflict for the immediate future will be between the West and several Islamic-Confucian states.

This is not to advocate the desirability of conflicts between civilizations. It is to set forth descriptive hypotheses as to what the future may be like. If these are plausible hypotheses, however, it is necessary to consider their implications for Western policy. These implications should be divided between short-term advantage and long-term accommodation. In the short term it is clearly in the interest of the West to promote greater cooperation and unity within its own civilization, particularly between its European and North American components; to incorporate into the West societies in Eastern Europe and Latin America whose cultures are close to those of the West; to promote and maintain cooperative relations with Russia and Japan; to prevent escalation of local inter-civilization conflicts into major inter-civilization wars; to limit the expansion of the military strength of Confucian and Islamic states; to moderate the reduction of Western military capabilities and maintain military superiority in East and Southwest Asia; to exploit differences and conflicts among Confucian and Islamic states; to support in other civilizations groups sympathetic to Western values and interests; to strengthen international institutions that reflect and legitimate Western interests and values and to promote the involvement of non-Western states in those institutions.

In the longer term other measures would be called for. Western civilization is both Western and modern. Non-Western civilizations have attempted to become modern without becoming Western. To date only Japan has fully succeeded in this quest. Non-Western civilizations will continue to attempt to acquire the wealth, technology, skills, machines and weapons that are part of being modern. They will also attempt to reconcile this modernity with their traditional culture and values. Their economic and military strength relative to the West will increase. Hence the West will increasingly have to accommodate these non-Western modern civilizations whose power approaches that of the West but whose values and interests differ significantly from those of the West. This will require the West to maintain the economic and military power necessary to protect its interests in relation to these civilizations. It will also, however, require the West to develop a more profound understanding of the basic religious and philosophical assumptions underlying other civilizations and the ways in which people in those civilizations see their interests. It will require an effort to identify elements of commonality between Western and other civilizations. For the relevant future, there will be no universal civilization, but instead a world of different civilizations, each of which will have to learn to coexist with the others.

NOTES

1. Murray Weidenbaum, *Great China: The Next Economic Superpower?*, St. Louis: Washington University Center for the Study of American Business, Contemporary Issues, Series 57, February 1993, pp. 2–3.

2. Bernard Lewis, "The Roots of Muslim Rage," *The Atlantic Monthly*, vol. 266, September 1990, p. 60; *Time*, June 15, 1992, pp. 24–28.

3. Archie Roosevelt, *For Lust of Knowing*, Boston: Little, Brown, 1988, pp. 332–333.

4. Almost invariably Western leaders claim they are acting on behalf of "the world community." One minor lapse occurred during the run-up to the Gulf War. In an interview on "Good Morning America," Dec. 21, 1990, British Prime Minister John Major referred to the actions "the West" was taking against Saddam Hussein. He quickly corrected himself and subsequently referred to "the world community." He was, however, right when he erred.

5. Harry C. Triandis, *The New York Times*, Dec. 25, 1990, p. 41, and "Cross-Cultural Studies of Individualism and Collectivism," Nebraska Symposium on Motivation, vol. 37, 1989, pp. 41–133.

6. Kishore Mahbubani, "The West and the Rest," *The National Interest*, Summer 1992, pp. 3–13.

7. Sergei Stankevich, "Russia in Search of Itself," *The National Interest*, Summer 1992, pp. 47–51; Daniel Schneider, "A Russian Movement Rejects Western Tilt," *Christian Science Monitor*, Feb. 5, 1993, pp. 5–7.

8. Owen Harries has pointed out that Australia is trying (unwisely in his view) to become a torn country in reverse. Although it has been a full member not only of the West but also of the ABCA military and intelligence core of the West, its current leaders are in effect proposing that it defect from the West, redefine itself as an Asian country and cultivate close ties with its neighbors. Australia's future, they argue, is with the dynamic economies of East Asia. But, as I have suggested, close economic cooperation normally requires a common cultural base. In addition, none of the three conditions necessary for a torn country to join another civilization is likely to exist in Australia's case

53

R O B E R T   D .   K A P L A N

THE COMING ANARCHY

Tyranny is nothing new in Sierra Leone or in the rest of West Africa. But it is now part and parcel of an increasing lawlessness that is far more significant than any coup, rebel incursion, or episodic experiment in democracy. Crime was what my friend—a top-ranking African official whose life would be threatened were I to identify him more precisely—really wanted to talk about. Crime is what makes West Africa a natural point of departure for my report on what the political character of our planet is likely to be in the twenty-first century.

SOURCE: *Atlantic Monthly* (Feb. 1994).

The cities of West Africa at night are some of the unsafest places in the world. Streets are unlit; the police often lack gasoline for their vehicles; armed burglars, carjackers, and muggers proliferate. "The government in Sierra Leone has no writ after dark," says a foreign resident, shrugging.

A PREMONITION OF THE FUTURE

West Africa is becoming *the* symbol of worldwide demographic, environmental, and societal stress, in which criminal anarchy emerges as the real "strategic" danger. Disease, overpopulation, unprovoked crime, scarcity of resources, refugee migrations, the increasing erosion of nation-states and international borders, and the empowerment of private armies, security firms, and international drug cartels are now most tellingly demonstrated through a West African prism. West Africa provides an appropriate introduction to the issues, often extremely unpleasant to discuss, that will soon confront our civilization. To remap the political earth the way it will be a few decades hence—as I intend to do in this article—I find I must begin with West Africa.

There is no other place on the planet where political maps are so deceptive—where, in fact, they tell such lies—as in West Africa. Start with Sierra Leone. According to the map, it is a nation-state of defined borders, with a government in control of its territory. In truth the Sierra Leonian government, run by a twenty-seven-year-old army captain, Valentine Strasser, controls Freetown by day and by day also controls part of the rural interior. In the government's territory the national army is an unruly rabble threatening drivers and passengers at most checkpoints. In the other part of the country units of two separate armies from the war in Liberia have taken up residence, as has an army of Sierra Leonian rebels. The government force fighting the rebels is full of renegade commanders who have aligned themselves with disaffected village chiefs. A pre-modern formlessness governs the battlefield, evoking the wars in medieval Europe prior to the 1648 Peace of Westphalia, which ushered in the era of organized nation-states.

As a consequence, roughly 400,000 Sierra Leonians are internally displaced, 280,000 more have fled to neighboring Guinea, and another 100,000 have fled to Liberia, even as 400,000 Liberians have fled to Sierra Leone. The third largest city in Sierra Leone, Gondama, is a displaced-persons camp. With an additional 600,000 Liberians in Guinea and 250,000 in the Ivory Coast, the borders dividing these four countries have become largely meaningless. Even in quiet zones none of the governments except the Ivory Coast's maintains the schools, bridges, roads, and police forces in a manner necessary for functional sovereignty. The Koranko ethnic group in northeastern Sierra Leone does all its trading in Guinea. Sierra Leonian diamonds are more likely to be sold in Liberia than in Freetown. In the eastern provinces of Sierra Leone you can buy Liberian beer but not the local brand.

In Sierra Leone, as in Guinea, as in the Ivory Coast, as in Ghana, most of the primary rain forest and the secondary bush is being destroyed at an alarming rate. I saw convoys of trucks bearing majestic hardwood trunks to coastal ports. When Sierra Leone achieved its independence, in 1961, as much as 60 percent of the country was primary rain forest. Now six percent is. In the Ivory Coast the proportion has fallen from 38 percent to eight percent. The deforestation has led to soil erosion, which has led to more flooding and more mosquitoes. Virtually everyone in the West African interior has some form of malaria.

Sierra Leone is a microcosm of what is occurring, albeit in a more tempered and gradual manner, throughout West Africa and much of the underdeveloped world: the withering away of central governments, the rise of tribal and regional domains, the unchecked spread of disease, and the growing pervasiveness of war. West Africa is reverting to the Africa of the Victorian atlas. It consists now of a series of coastal trading posts, such as Freetown and Conakry, and an interior that, owing to violence, volatility, and disease, is again becoming, as Graham Greene once observed, "blank" and "unexplored." However, whereas Greene's vision implies a certain romance, as in the somnolent and charmingly seedy Freetown of his celebrated novel *The Heart of the Matter,* it is Thomas Malthus, the philosopher of demographic doomsday, who is now the prophet of West Africa's future. And West Africa's future, eventually, will also be that of most of the rest of the world.

Because the demographic reality of West Africa is a countryside draining into dense slums by the coast, ultimately the region's rulers will come to reflect the values of these shanty-towns. There are signs of this already in Sierra Leone—and in Togo, where the dictator Etienne Eyadema, in power since 1967, was nearly toppled in 1991, not by democrats but by thousands of youths whom the London-based magazine *West Africa* described as "Soweto-like stone-throwing adolescents." Their behavior may herald a regime more brutal than Eyadema's repressive one.

The fragility of these West African "countries" impressed itself on me when I took a series of bush taxis along the Gulf of Guinea, from the Togolese capital of Lomé, across Ghana, to Abidjan. The 400-mile journey required two full days of driving, because of stops at two border crossings and an additional eleven customs stations, at each of which my fellow passengers had their bags searched. I had to change money twice and repeatedly fill in currency-declaration forms. I had to bribe a Togolese immigration official with the equivalent of eighteen dollars before he would agree to put an exit stamp on my passport. Nevertheless, smuggling across these borders is rampant. *The London Observer* has reported that in 1992 the equivalent of $856 million left West Africa for Europe in the form of "hot cash" assumed to be laundered drug money. International cartels have discovered the utility of weak, financially strapped West African regimes.

The more fictitious the actual sovereignty, the more severe border authorities seem to be in trying to prove otherwise. Getting visas for these states can be as hard as crossing their borders. The Washington embassies of Sierra Leone and Guinea—the two poorest nations on earth, according to a 1993 United

Nations report on "human development"—asked for letters from my bank (in lieu of prepaid round-trip tickets) and also personal references, in order to prove that I had sufficient means to sustain myself during my visits. I was reminded of my visa and currency hassles while traveling to the communist states of Eastern Europe, particularly East Germany and Czechoslovakia, before those states collapsed.

Ali A. Mazrui, the director of the Institute of Global Cultural Studies at the State University of New York at Binghamton, predicts that West Africa—indeed, the whole continent—is on the verge of large-scale border upheaval. Mazrui writes,

> In the 21st century France will be withdrawing from West Africa as she gets increasingly involved in the affairs [of Europe]. France's West African sphere of influence will be filled by Nigeria—a more natural hegemonic power. . . . It will be under those circumstances that Nigeria's own boundaries are likely to expand to incorporate the Republic of Niger (the Hausa link), the Republic of Benin (the Yoruba link) and conceivably Cameroon.

The future could be more tumultuous, and bloodier, than Mazrui dares to say. France *will* withdraw from former colonies like Benin, Togo, Niger, and the Ivory Coast, where it has been propping up local currencies. It will do so not only because its attention will be diverted to new challenges in Europe and Russia but also because younger French officials lack the older generation's emotional ties to the ex-colonies. However, even as Nigeria attempts to expand, it, too, is likely to split into several pieces. The State Department's Bureau of Intelligence and Research recently made the following points in an analysis of Nigeria:

> Prospects for a transition to civilian rule and democratization are slim. . . . The repressive apparatus of the state security service . . . will be difficult for any future civilian government to control. . . . The country is becoming increasingly ungovernable. . . . Ethnic and regional splits are deepening, a situation made worse by an increase in the number of states from 19 to 30 and a doubling in the number of local governing authorities; religious cleavages are more serious; Muslim fundamentalism and evangelical Christian militancy are on the rise; and northern Muslim anxiety over southern [Christian] control of the economy is intense . . . the will to keep Nigeria together is now very weak.

Given that oil-rich Nigeria is a bellwether for the region—its population of roughly 90 million equals the populations of all the other West African states combined—it is apparent that Africa faces cataclysms that could make the Ethiopian and Somalian famines pale in comparison. This is especially so because Nigeria's population, including that of its largest city, Lagos, whose crime, pollution, and overcrowding make it the cliché par excellence of Third World urban dysfunction, is set to double during the next twenty-five years, while the country continues to deplete its natural resources.

Part of West Africa's quandary is that although its population belts are horizontal, with habitation densities increasing as one travels south away from the Sahara and toward the tropical abundance of the Atlantic littoral, the borders erected by European colonialists are vertical, and therefore at cross-purposes with demography and topography. Satellite photos depict the same reality I experienced in the bush taxi: the Lomé-Abidjan coastal corridor—indeed, the entire stretch of coast from Abidjan eastward to Lagos—is one burgeoning megalopolis that by any rational economic and geographical standard should constitute a single sovereignty, rather than the five (the Ivory Coast, Ghana, Togo, Benin, and Nigeria) into which it is currently divided.

As many internal African borders begin to crumble, a more impenetrable boundary is being erected that threatens to isolate the continent as a whole: the wall of disease. Merely to visit West Africa in some degree of safety, I spent about $500 for a hepatitis B vaccination series and other disease prophylaxis. Africa may today be more dangerous in this regard than it was in 1862, before antibiotics, when the explorer Sir Richard Francis Burton described the health situation on the continent as "deadly, a Golgotha, a Jehannum." Of the approximately 12 million people worldwide whose blood is HIV-positive, 8 million are in Africa. In the capital of the Ivory Coast, whose modern road system only helps to spread the disease, 10 percent of the population is HIV-positive. And war and refugee movements help the virus break through to more-remote areas of Africa. Alan Greenberg, M.D., a representative of the Centers for Disease Control in Abidjan, explains that in Africa the HIV virus and tuberculosis are now "fast-forwarding each other." Of the approximately 4,000 newly diagnosed tuberculosis patients in Abidjan, 45 percent were also found to be HIV-positive. As African birth rates soar and slums proliferate, some experts worry that viral mutations and hybridizations might, just conceivably, result in a form of the AIDS virus that is easier to catch than the present strain.

It is malaria that is most responsible for the disease wall that threatens to separate Africa and other parts of the Third World from more-developed regions of the planet in the twenty-first century. Carried by mosquitoes, malaria, unlike AIDS, is easy to catch. Most people in sub-Saharan Africa have recurring bouts of the disease throughout their entire lives, and it is mutating into increasingly deadly forms. "The great gift of Malaria is utter apathy," wrote Sir Richard Burton, accurately portraying the situation in much of the Third World today. Visitors to malaria-afflicted parts of the planet are protected by a new drug, mefloquine, a side effect of which is vivid, even violent, dreams. But a strain of cerebral malaria resistant to mefloquine is now on the offensive. Consequently, defending oneself against malaria in Africa is becoming more and more like defending oneself against violent crime. You engage in "behavior modification": not going out at dusk, wearing mosquito repellent all the time.

And the cities keep growing. I got a general sense of the future while driving from the airport to downtown Conakry, the capital of Guinea. The forty-five-minute journey in heavy traffic was through one never-ending shantytown: a nightmarish Dickensian spectacle to which Dickens himself would never have given credence. The corrugated metal shacks and scabrous walls were coated with black slime. Stores were built out of rusted shipping containers, junked cars, and jumbles of wire mesh. The streets were one long puddle of floating garbage. Mosquitoes and flies were everywhere. Children, many of whom had protruding bellies, seemed as numerous as ants. When the tide went out, dead rats and the skeletons of cars were exposed on the mucky beach. In twenty-eight years Guinea's population will double if growth goes on at current rates. Hardwood logging continues at a madcap speed, and people flee the Guinean countryside for Conakry. It seemed to me that here, as elsewhere in Africa and the Third World, man is challenging nature far beyond its limits, and nature is now beginning to take its revenge.

Africa may be as relevant to the future character of world politics as the Balkans were a hundred years ago, prior to the two Balkan wars and the First World War. Then the threat was the collapse of empires and the birth of nations based solely on tribe. Now the threat is more elemental: *nature unchecked.* Africa's immediate future could be very bad. The coming upheaval, in which foreign embassies are shut down, states collapse, and contact with the outside world takes place through dangerous, disease-ridden coastal trading posts, will loom large in the century we are entering. (Nine of twenty-one U.S. foreign-aid missions to be closed over the next three years are in Africa—a prologue to a consolidation of U.S. embassies themselves.) Precisely because much of Africa is set to go over the edge at a time when the Cold War has ended, when environmental and demographic stress in other parts of the globe is becoming critical, and when the post–First World War system of nation-states—not just in the Balkans but perhaps also in the Middle East—is about to be toppled, Africa suggests what war, borders, and ethnic politics will be like a few decades hence.

To understand the events of the next fifty years, then, one must understand environmental scarcity, cultural and racial clash, geographic destiny, and the transformation of war. The order in which I have named these is not accidental. Each concept except the first relies partly on the one or ones before it, meaning that the last two—new approaches to mapmaking and to warfare—are the most important. They are also the least understood. I will now look at each idea, drawing upon the work of specialists and also my own travel experiences in various parts of the globe besides Africa, in order to fill in the blanks of a new political atlas.

THE ENVIRONMENT AS A HOSTILE POWER

For a while the media will continue to ascribe riots and other violent upheavals abroad mainly to ethnic and religious conflict. But as these conflicts multiply, it will become apparent that something else is afoot, making more and more places like Nigeria, India, and Brazil ungovernable.

Mention "the environment" or "diminishing natural resources" in foreign-policy circles and you meet a brick wall of skepticism or boredom. To conservatives especially, the very terms seem flaky. Public-policy foundations have contributed to the lack of interest, by funding narrowly focused environmental studies replete with technical jargon which foreign-affairs experts just let pile up on their desks.

It is time to understand "the environment" for what it is: *the* national-security issue of the early twenty-first century. The political and strategic impact of surging populations, spreading disease, deforestation and soil erosion, water depletion, air pollution, and, possibly, rising sea levels in critical, overcrowded regions like the Nile Delta and Bangladesh—developments that will prompt mass migrations and, in turn, incite group conflicts—will be the core foreign-policy challenge from which most others will ultimately emanate, arousing the public and uniting assorted interests left over from the Cold War. In the twenty-first century water will be in dangerously short supply in such diverse locales as Saudi Arabia, Central Asia, and the southwestern United States. A war could erupt between Egypt and Ethiopia over Nile River water. Even in Europe tensions have arisen between Hungary and Slovakia over the damming of the Danube, a classic case of how environmental disputes fuse with ethnic and historical ones. The political scientist and erstwhile Clinton adviser Michael Mandelbaum has said, "We have a foreign policy today in the shape of a doughnut—lots of peripheral interests but nothing at the center." The environment, I will argue, is part of a terrifying array of problems that will define a new threat to our security, filling the hole in Mandelbaum's doughnut and allowing a post–Cold War foreign policy to emerge inexorably by need rather than by design.

Our Cold War foreign policy truly began with George F. Kennan's famous article, signed "X," published in *Foreign Affairs* in July of 1947, in which Kennan argued for a "firm and vigilant containment" of a Soviet Union that was imperially, rather than ideologically, motivated. It may be that our post–Cold War foreign policy will one day be seen to have had its beginnings in an even bolder and more detailed piece of written analysis: one that appeared in the journal *International Security*. The article, published in the fall of 1991 by Thomas Fraser Homer-Dixon, who is the head of the Peace and Conflict Studies Program at the University of Toronto, was titled "On the Threshold: Environmental Changes as Causes of Acute Conflict." Homer-Dixon has, more successfully than other analysts, integrated two hitherto separate fields—military-conflict studies and the study of the physical environment.

In Homer-Dixon's view, future wars and civil violence will often arise from scarcities of resources such as water, cropland, forests, and fish. Just as there will be environmentally driven wars and refugee flows, there will be environmentally induced praetorian regimes—or, as he puts it, "hard regimes." Countries with the highest probability of acquiring hard regimes, according to Homer-Dixon, are those that are threatened by a declining resource base yet also have "a history of state [read 'military'] strength." Candidates include Indonesia, Brazil, and, of course, Nigeria. Though each of these nations has exhibited democratizing tendencies of late, Homer-Dixon argues that such tendencies are likely to be superficial "epiphenomena" having nothing to do with long-term processes that include soaring populations and shrinking raw materials. Democracy is problematic; scarcity is more certain.

Indeed, the Saddam Husseins of the future will have more, not fewer, opportunities. In addition to engendering tribal strife, scarcer resources will place a great strain on many peoples who never had much of a democratic or institutional tradition to begin with. Over the next fifty years the earth's population will soar from 5.5 billion to more than nine billion. Though optimists have hopes for new resource technologies and free-market development in the global village, they fail to note that, as the National Academy of Sciences has pointed out, 95 percent of the population increase will be in the poorest regions of the world, where governments now—just look at Africa—show little ability to function, let alone to implement even marginal improvements. Homer-Dixon writes, ominously, "Neo-Malthusians may underestimate human adaptability in *today's* environmental-social system, but as time passes their analysis may become ever more compelling."

While a minority of the human population will be, as Francis Fukuyama would put it, sufficiently sheltered so as to enter a "post-historical" realm, living in cities and suburbs in which the environment has been mastered and ethnic animosities have been quelled by bourgeois prosperity, an increasingly large number of people will be stuck in history, living in shantytowns where attempts to rise above poverty, cultural dysfunction, and ethnic strife will be doomed by a lack of water to drink, soil to till, and space to survive in. In the developing world environmental stress will present people with a choice that is increasingly among totalitarianism (as in Iraq), fascist-tending mini-states (as in Serb-held Bosnia), and road-warrior cultures (as in Somalia). Homer-Dixon concludes that "as environmental degradation proceeds, the size of the potential social disruption will increase."

Tad Homer-Dixon is an unlikely Jeremiah. Today a boyish thirty-seven, he grew up amid the sylvan majesty of Vancouver Island, attending private day schools. His speech is calm, perfectly even, and crisply enunciated. There is nothing in his background or manner that would indicate a bent toward pessimism. A Canadian Anglican who spends his summers canoeing on the lakes of northern Ontario, and who talks about the benign mountains, black bears, and Douglas firs of his youth, he is the opposite of the intellectually severe neoconservative, the kind at home with conflict scenarios. Nor is he an environmentalist who opposes development. "My father was a logger who thought about ecologically safe forestry before others," he says. "He logged, planted, logged, and planted. He got out of the business just as the issue was being polarized by environmentalists. They hate changed ecosystems. But human beings, just by carrying seeds around, change the natural world." As an only child whose playground was a virtually untouched wilderness and seacoast, Homer-Dixon has a familiarity with the natural world that permits him to see a reality that most policy analysts—children of suburbia and city streets—are blind to.

"We need to bring nature back in," he argues. "We have to stop separating politics from the physical world—the climate, public health, and the environment." Quoting Daniel Deudney, another pioneering expert on the security aspects of the environment, Homer-Dixon says that "for too long we've been prisoners of 'social-social' theory, which assumes there are only social causes for social and political changes, rather than natural causes, too. This social-social mentality emerged with the Industrial Revolution, which separated us from nature. But nature is coming back with a vengeance, tied to population growth. It will have incredible security implications.

"Think of a stretch limo in the potholed streets of New York City, where homeless beggars live. Inside the limo are the air-conditioned post-industrial regions of North America, Europe, the emerging Pacific Rim, and a few other isolated places, with their trade summitry and computer-information highways. Outside is the rest of mankind, going in a completely different direction."

We are entering a bifurcated world. Part of the globe is inhabited by Hegel's and Fukuyama's Last Man, healthy, well fed, and pampered by technology. The other, larger, part is inhabited by Hobbes's First Man, condemned to a life that is "poor, nasty, brutish, and short." Although both parts will be threatened by environmental stress, the Last Man will be able to master it; the First Man will not.

The Last Man will adjust to the loss of underground water tables in the western United States. He will build dikes to save Cape Hatteras and the Chesapeake beaches from rising sea levels, even as the Maldive Islands, off the coast of India, sink into oblivion, and the shorelines of Egypt, Bangladesh, and Southeast Asia recede, driving tens of millions of people inland where there is no room for them, and thus sharpening ethnic divisions.

Homer-Dixon points to a world map of soil degradation in his Toronto office. "The darker the map color, the worse the degradation," he explains. The West African coast, the Middle East, the Indian subcontinent, China, and Central America have the darkest shades, signifying all manner of degradation, related to winds, chemicals, and water problems. "The worst degradation is generally where the population is highest. The population is generally highest where the soil is the best. So we're degrading earth's best soil."

China, in Homer-Dixon's view, is the quintessential example of environmental degradation. Its current economic "success" masks deeper problems. "China's fourteen percent growth rate does not mean it's going to be a world power. It means that coastal China, where the economic growth is taking place, is joining the rest of the Pacific Rim. The disparity with inland China is intensifying." Referring to the environmental research of his colleague, the Czech-born ecologist Vaclav Smil, Homer-Dixon explains how the per capita availability of arable land in interior China has rapidly declined at the same time that the quality of that land has been destroyed by deforestation, loss of topsoil, and salinization. He mentions the loss and contamination of water supplies, the exhaustion of wells, the plugging of irrigation systems and reservoirs with eroded silt, and a population of 1.54 billion by the year 2025: it is a misconception that China has gotten its population under control. Large-scale population movements are under way, from inland China to coastal China and from villages to cities, leading to a crime surge like the one in Africa and to growing regional disparities and conflicts in a land with a strong tradition of warlordism and a weak tradition of central government—again as in Africa.

"We will probably see the center challenged and fractured, and China will not remain the same on the map," Homer-Dixon says.

Environmental scarcity will inflame existing hatreds and affect power relationships, at which we now look.

SKINHEAD COSSACKS, JUJU WARRIORS

In the summer, 1993, issue of *Foreign Affairs,* Samuel P. Huntington, of Harvard's Olin Institute for Strategic Studies, published a thought-provoking article called "The Clash of Civilizations?" The world, he argues, has been moving during the course of this century from nation-state conflict to ideological conflict to, finally, cultural conflict. I would add that as refugee flows increase and as peasants continue migrating to cities around the world—turning them into sprawling villages—national borders will mean less, even as more power will fall into the hands of less educated, less sophisticated groups. In the eyes of these uneducated but newly empowered millions, the real borders are the most tangible and intractable ones: those of culture and tribe. Huntington writes, "First, differences among civilizations are not only real; they are basic," involving, among other things, history, language, and religion. "Second . . . interactions between peoples of different civilizations are increasing; these increasing interactions intensify civilization consciousness." Economic modernization is not necessarily a panacea, since it fuels individual and group ambitions while weakening traditional loyalties to the state. It is worth noting, for example, that it is precisely the wealthiest and fastest-developing city in India, Bombay, that has seen the worst intercommunal violence between Hindus and Muslims. Consider that Indian cities, like African and Chinese ones, are ecological time bombs—Delhi and Calcutta, and also Beijing, suffer the worst air quality of any cities in the world—and it is apparent how surging populations, environmental degradation, and ethnic conflict are deeply related.

Huntington points to interlocking conflicts among Hindu, Muslim, Slavic Orthodox, Western, Japanese, Confucian, Latin American, and possibly African civilizations: for instance, Hindus clashing with Muslims in India, Turkic Muslims clashing with Slavic Orthodox Russians in Central Asian cities, the West clashing with Asia. (Even in the United States, African-Americans find themselves besieged by an influx of competing Latinos.) Whatever the laws, refugees find a way to crash official borders, bringing their passions with them, meaning that Europe and the United States will be weakened by cultural disputes.

Because Huntington's brush is broad, his specifics are vulnerable to attack. In a rebuttal of Huntington's argument the Johns Hopkins professor Fouad Ajami, a Lebanese-born Shi'ite who certainly knows the world beyond suburbia, writes in the September-October, 1993, issue of *Foreign Affairs,*

> The world of Islam divides and subdivides. The battle lines in the Caucasus . . . are not coextensive with civilizational fault lines. The lines follow the interests

of states. Where Huntington sees a civilizational duel between Armenia and Azerbaijan, the Iranian state has cast religious zeal . . . to the wind . . . in that battle the Iranians have tilted toward Christian Armenia.

True, Huntington's hypothesized war between Islam and Orthodox Christianity is not borne out by the alliance network in the Caucasus. But that is only because he has misidentified *which* cultural war is occurring there. A recent visit to Azerbaijan made clear to me that Azeri Turks, the world's most secular Shi'ite Muslims, see their cultural identity in terms not of religion but of their Turkic race. The Armenians, likewise, fight the Azeris not because the latter are Muslims but because they are Turks, related to the same Turks who massacred Armenians in 1915. Turkic culture (secular and based on languages employing a Latin script) is battling Iranian culture (religiously militant as defined by Tehran, and wedded to an Arabic script) across the whole swath of Central Asia and the Caucasus. The Armenians are, therefore, natural allies of their fellow Indo-Europeans the Iranians.

Huntington is correct that the Caucasus is a flashpoint of cultural and racial war. But, as Ajami observes, Huntington's plate tectonics are too simple. Two months of recent travel throughout Turkey revealed to me that although the Turks are developing a deep distrust, bordering on hatred, of fellow-Muslim Iran, they are also, especially in the shantytowns that are coming to dominate Turkish public opinion, revising their group identity, increasingly seeing themselves as Muslims being deserted by a West that does little to help besieged Muslims in Bosnia and that attacks Turkish Muslims in the streets of Germany.

In other words, the Balkans, a powder keg for nation-state war at the beginning of the twentieth century, could be a powder keg for cultural war at the turn of the twenty-first: between Orthodox Christianity (represented by the Serbs and a classic Byzantine configuration of Greeks, Russians, and Romanians) and the House of Islam. Yet in the Caucasus that House of Islam is falling into a clash between Turkic and Iranian civilizations. Ajami asserts that this very subdivision, not to mention all the divisions within the Arab world, indicates that the West, including the United States, is not threatened by Huntington's scenario. As the Gulf War demonstrated, the West has proved capable of playing one part of the House of Islam against another.

True. However, whether he is aware of it or not, Ajami is describing a world even more dangerous than the one Huntington envisions, especially when one takes into account Homer-Dixon's research on environmental scarcity. Outside the stretch limo would be a rundown, crowded planet of skinhead Cossacks and *juju* warriors, influenced by the worst refuse of Western pop culture and ancient tribal hatreds, and battling over scraps of overused earth in guerrilla conflicts that ripple across continents and intersect in no discernible pattern—meaning there's no easy-to-define threat. Kennan's world of one adversary seems as distant as the world of Herodotus.

Most people believe that the political earth since 1989 has undergone immense change. But it is minor compared with what is yet to come. The breaking apart and remaking of the atlas is only now beginning. The crack-up of the

Soviet empire and the coming end of Arab-Israeli military confrontation are merely prologues to the really big changes that lie ahead. Michael Vlahos, a long-range thinker for the U.S. Navy, warns, "We are not in charge of the environment and the world is not following us. It is going in many directions. Do not assume that democratic capitalism is the last word in human social evolution."

Before addressing the questions of maps and of warfare, I want to take a closer look at the interaction of religion, culture, demographic shifts, and the distribution of natural resources in a specific area of the world: the Middle East.

THE PAST IS DEAD

Built on steep, muddy hills, the shantytowns of Ankara, the Turkish capital, exude visual drama. Altindag, or "Golden Mountain," is a pyramid of dreams, fashioned from cinder blocks and corrugated iron, rising as though each shack were built on top of another, all reaching awkwardly and painfully toward heaven—the heaven of wealthier Turks who live elsewhere in the city. Nowhere else on the planet have I found such a poignant architectural symbol of man's striving, with gaps in house walls plugged with rusted cans, and leeks and onions growing on verandas assembled from planks of rotting wood. For reasons that I will explain, the Turkish shacktown is a psychological universe away from the African one.

To see the twenty-first century truly, one's eyes must learn a different set of aesthetics. One must reject the overly stylized images of travel magazines, with their inviting photographs of exotic villages and glamorous downtowns. There are far too many millions whose dreams are more vulgar, more real—whose raw energies and desires will overwhelm the visions of the elites, remaking the future into something frighteningly new. But in Turkey I learned that shantytowns are not all bad.

Slum quarters in Abidjan terrify and repel the outsider. In Turkey it is the opposite. The closer I got to Golden Mountain the better it looked, and the safer I felt. I had $1,500 worth of Turkish lira in one pocket and $1,000 in traveler's checks in the other, yet I felt no fear. Golden Mountain was a real neighborhood. The inside of one house told the story: The architectural bedlam of cinder block and sheet metal and cardboard walls was deceiving. Inside was a *home*—order, that is, bespeaking dignity. I saw a working refrigerator, a television, a wall cabinet with a few books and lots of family pictures, a few plants by a window, and a stove. Though the streets become rivers of mud when it rains, the floors inside this house were spotless.

Other houses were like this too. Schoolchildren ran along with briefcases strapped to their backs, trucks delivered cooking gas, a few men sat inside a café sipping tea. One man sipped beer. Alcohol is easy to obtain in Turkey, a secular state where 99 percent of the population is Muslim. Yet there is little problem of alcoholism. Crime against persons is infinitesimal. Poverty and illiteracy are watered-down versions of what obtains in Algeria and Egypt (to say nothing of West Africa), making it that much harder for religious extremists to gain a foothold.

My point in bringing up a rather wholesome, crime-free slum is this: its existence demonstrates how formidable is the fabric of which Turkish Muslim culture is made. A culture this strong has the potential to dominate the Middle East once again. Slums are litmus tests for innate cultural strengths and weaknesses. Those peoples whose cultures can harbor extensive slum life without decomposing will be, relatively speaking, the future's winners. Those whose cultures cannot will be the future's victims. Slums—in the sociological sense—do not exist in Turkish cities. The mortar between people and family groups is stronger here than in Africa. Resurgent Islam and Turkic cultural identity have produced a civilization with natural muscle tone. Turks, history's perennial nomads, take disruption in stride.

The future of the Middle East is quietly being written inside the heads of Golden Mountain's inhabitants. Think of an Ottoman military encampment on the eve of the destruction of Greek Constantinople in 1453. That is Golden Mountain. "We brought the village here. But in the village we worked harder—in the field, all day. So we couldn't fast during [the holy month of] Ramadan. Here we fast. Here we are more religious." Aishe Tanrikulu, along with half a dozen other women, was stuffing rice into vine leaves from a crude plastic bowl. She asked me to join her under the shade of a piece of sheet metal. Each of these women had her hair covered by a kerchief. In the city they were encountering television for the first time. "We are traditional, religious people. The programs offend us," Aishe said. Another woman complained about the schools. Though her children had educational options unavailable in the village, they had to compete with wealthier, secular Turks. "The kids from rich families with connections—they get all the places." More opportunities, more tensions, in other words.

My guidebook to Golden Mountain was an untypical one: *Tales From the Garbage Hills,* a brutally realistic novel by a Turkish writer, Latife Tekin, about life in the shantytowns, which in Turkey are called *gecekondus* ("built in a night"). "He listened to the earth and wept unceasingly for water, for work and for the cure of the illnesses spread by the garbage and the factory waste," Tekin writes. In the most revealing passage of *Tales From the Garbage Hills* the squatters are told "about a certain 'Ottoman Empire' . . . that where they now lived there had once been an empire of this name." This history "confounded" the squatters. It was the first they had heard of it. Though one of them knew "that his grandfather and his dog died fighting the Greeks," nationalism and an encompassing sense of Turkish history are the province of the Turkish middle and upper classes, and of foreigners like me who feel required to have a notion of "Turkey."

But what did the Golden Mountain squatters know about the armies of Turkish migrants that had come before their own—namely, Seljuks and

Ottomans? For these recently urbanized peasants, and their counterparts in Africa, the Arab world, India, and so many other places, the world is new, to adapt V. S. Naipaul's phrase. As Naipaul wrote of urban refugees in *India: A Wounded Civilization,* "They saw themselves at the beginning of things: unaccommodated men making a claim on their land for the first time, and out of chaos evolving their own philosophy of community and self-help. For them the past was dead; they had left it behind in the villages."

Everywhere in the developing world at the turn of the twenty-first century these new men and women, rushing into the cities, are remaking civilizations and redefining their identities in terms of religion and tribal ethnicity which do not coincide with the borders of existing states.

In Turkey several things are happening at once. In 1980, 44 percent of Turks lived in cities; in 1990 it was 61 percent. By the year 2000 the figure is expected to be 67 percent. Villages are emptying out as concentric rings of *gecekondu* developments grow around Turkish cities. This is the real political and demographic revolution in Turkey and elsewhere, and foreign correspondents usually don't write about it.

Whereas rural poverty is age-old and almost a "normal" part of the social fabric, urban poverty is socially destabilizing. As Iran has shown, Islamic extremism is the psychological defense mechanism of many urbanized peasants threatened with the loss of traditions in pseudo-modern cities where their values are under attack, where basic services like water and electricity are unavailable, and where they are assaulted by a physically unhealthy environment. The American ethnologist and Orientalist Carleton Stevens Coon wrote in 1951 that Islam "has made possible the optimum survival and happiness of millions of human beings in an increasingly impoverished environment over a fourteen-hundred-year period." Beyond its stark, clearly articulated message, Islam's very militancy makes it attractive to the downtrodden. It is the one religion that is prepared to *fight.* A political era driven by environmental stress, increased cultural sensitivity, unregulated urbanization, and refugee migrations is an era divinely created for the spread and intensification of Islam, already the world's fastest-growing religion. (Though Islam is spreading in West Africa, it is being hobbled by syncretization with animism: this makes new converts less apt to become anti-Western extremists, but it also makes for a weakened version of the faith, which is less effective as an antidote to crime.)

In Turkey, however, Islam is painfully and awkwardly forging a consensus with modernization, a trend that is less apparent in the Arab and Persian worlds (and virtually invisible in Africa). In Iran the oil boom—because it put development and urbanization on a fast track, making the culture shock more intense—fueled the 1978 Islamic Revolution. But Turkey, unlike Iran and the Arab world, has little oil. Therefore its development and urbanization have been more gradual. Islamists have been integrated into the parliamentary system for decades. The tensions I noticed in Golden Mountain are natural, creative ones: the kind immigrants face the world over. While the world has focused on religious perversity in Algeria, a nation rich in natural gas, and in

Egypt, parts of whose capital city, Cairo, evince worse crowding than I have seen even in Calcutta, Turkey has been living through the Muslim equivalent of the Protestant Reformation.

Resource distribution is strengthening Turks in another way vis-à-vis Arabs and Persians. Turks may have little oil, but their Anatolian heartland has lots of water—the most important fluid of the twenty-first century. Turkey's Southeast Anatolia Project, involving twenty-two major dams and irrigation systems, is impounding the waters of the Tigris and Euphrates rivers. Much of the water that Arabs and perhaps Israelis will need to drink in the future is controlled by Turks. The project's centerpiece is the mile-wide, sixteen-story Atatürk Dam, upon which are emblazoned the words of modern Turkey's founder: "*Ne Mutlu Turkum Diyene*" ("Lucky is the one who is a Turk").

Unlike Egypt's Aswan High Dam, on the Nile, and Syria's Revolution Dam, on the Euphrates, both of which were built largely by Russians, the Atatürk Dam is a predominantly Turkish affair, with Turkish engineers and companies in charge. On a recent visit my eyes took in the immaculate offices and their gardens, the high-voltage electric grids and phone switching stations, the dizzying sweep of giant humming transformers, the poured-concrete spill-ways, and the prim unfolding suburbia, complete with schools, for dam employees. The emerging power of the Turks was palpable.

Erduhan Bayindir, the site manager at the dam, told me that "while oil can be shipped abroad to enrich only elites, water has to be spread more evenly within the society. . . . It is true, we can stop the flow of water into Syria and Iraq for up to eight months without the same water overflowing our dams, in order to regulate their political behavior."

Power is certainly moving north in the Middle East, from the oil fields of Dhahran, on the Persian Gulf, to the water plain of Harran, in southern Anatolia—near the site of the Atatürk Dam. But will the nation-state of Turkey, as presently constituted, be the inheritor of this wealth?

I very much doubt it.

THE LIES OF MAPMAKERS

Whereas West Africa represents the least stable part of political reality outside Homer-Dixon's stretch limo, Turkey, an organic outgrowth of two Turkish empires that ruled Anatolia for 850 years, has been among the most stable. Turkey's borders were established not by colonial powers but in a war of independence, in the early 1920s. Kemal Atatürk provided Turkey with a secular nation-building myth that most Arab and African states, burdened by artificially drawn borders, lack. That lack will leave many Arab states defenseless against a wave of Islam that will eat away at their legitimacy and frontiers in coming years. Yet even as regards Turkey, maps deceive.

It is not only African shantytowns that don't appear on urban maps. Many shantytowns in Turkey and elsewhere are also missing—as are the considerable territories controlled by guerrilla armies and urban mafias. Traveling with Eritrean guerrillas in what, according to the map, was northern Ethiopia, traveling in "northern Iraq" with Kurdish guerrillas, and staying in a hotel in the Caucasus controlled by a local mafia—to say nothing of my experiences in West Africa—led me to develop a healthy skepticism toward maps, which, I began to realize, create a conceptual barrier that prevents us from comprehending the political crack-up just beginning to occur worldwide.

Consider the map of the world, with its 190 or so countries, each signified by a bold and uniform color: this map, with which all of us have grown up, is generally an invention of modernism, specifically of European colonialism. Modernism, in the sense of which I speak, began with the rise of nation-states in Europe and was confirmed by the death of feudalism at the end of the Thirty Years' War—an event that was interposed between the Renaissance and the Enlightenment, which together gave birth to modern science. People were suddenly flush with an enthusiasm to categorize, to define. The map, based on scientific techniques of measurement, offered a way to classify new national organisms, making a jigsaw puzzle of neat pieces without transition zones between them. "Frontier" is itself a modern concept that didn't exist in the feudal mind. And as European nations carved out far-flung domains at the same time that print technology was making the reproduction of maps cheaper, cartography came into its own as a way of creating facts by ordering the way we look at the world.

In his book *Imagined Communities: Reflections on the Origin and Spread of Nationalism*, Benedict Anderson, of Cornell University, demonstrates that the map enabled colonialists to think about their holdings in terms of a "totalizing classificatory grid. . . . It was bounded, determinate, and therefore—in principle—countable." To the colonialist, country maps were the equivalent of an accountant's ledger books. Maps, Anderson explains, "shaped the grammar" that would make possible such questionable concepts as Iraq, Indonesia, Sierra Leone, and Nigeria. The state, recall, is a purely Western notion, one that until the twentieth century applied to countries covering only three percent of the earth's land area. Nor is the evidence compelling that the state, as a governing ideal, can be successfully transported to areas outside the industrialized world. Even the United States of America, in the words of one of our best living poets, Gary Snyder, consists of "arbitrary and inaccurate impositions on what is really here."

Yet this inflexible, artificial reality staggers on, not only in the United Nations but in various geographic and travel publications (themselves by-products of an age of elite touring which colonialism made possible) that still report on and photograph the world according to "country." Newspapers, this magazine, and this writer are not innocent of the tendency.

According to the map, the great hydropower complex emblemized by the Atatürk Dam is situated in Turkey. Forget the map. This southeastern region of Turkey is populated almost completely by Kurds. About half of the world's 20 million Kurds live in "Turkey." The Kurds are predominant in an ellipse of territory that overlaps not only with Turkey but also with Iraq, Iran, Syria, and the former Soviet Union. The Western-enforced Kurdish enclave in northern Iraq, a consequence of the 1991 Gulf War, has already exposed the fictitious nature of that supposed nation-state.

On a recent visit to the Turkish-Iranian border, it occurred to me what a risky idea the nation-state is. Here I was on the legal fault line between two clashing civilizations, Turkic and Iranian. Yet the reality was more subtle: as in West Africa, the border was porous and smuggling abounded, but here the people doing the smuggling, on both sides of the border, were Kurds. In such a moonscape, over which peoples have migrated and settled in patterns that obliterate borders, the end of the Cold War will bring on a cruel process of natural selection among existing states. No longer will these states be so firmly propped up by the West or the Soviet Union. Because the Kurds overlap with nearly everybody in the Middle East, on account of their being cheated out of a state in the post–First World War peace treaties, they are emerging, in effect, as *the* natural selector—the ultimate reality check. They have destabilized Iraq and may continue to disrupt states that do not offer them adequate breathing space, while strengthening states that do.

Because the Turks, owing to their water resources, their growing economy, and the social cohesion evinced by the most crime-free slums I have encountered, are on the verge of big-power status, and because the 10 million Kurds within Turkey threaten that status, the outcome of the Turkish-Kurdish dispute will be more critical to the future of the Middle East than the eventual outcome of the recent Israeli-Palestinian agreement.

America's fascination with the Israeli-Palestinian issue, coupled with its lack of interest in the Turkish-Kurdish one, is a function of its own domestic and ethnic obsessions, not of the cartographic reality that is about to transform the Middle East. The diplomatic process involving Israelis and Palestinians will, I believe, have little effect on the early- and mid-twenty-first-century map of the region. Israel, with a 6.6 percent economic growth rate based increasingly on high-tech exports, is about to enter Homer-Dixon's stretch limo, fortified by a well-defined political community that is an organic outgrowth of history and ethnicity. Like prosperous and peaceful Japan on the one hand, and war-torn and poverty-wracked Armenia on the other, Israel is a classic national-ethnic organism. Much of the Arab world, however, will undergo alteration, as Islam spreads across artificial frontiers, fueled by mass migrations into the cities and a soaring birth rate of more than 3.2 percent. Seventy percent of the Arab population has been born since 1970—youths with little historical memory of anti-colonial independence struggles, post-colonial attempts at nation-building, or any of the Arab-Israeli wars. The most distant recollection of these youths will be the West's humiliation of colonially invented Iraq in 1991. Today seventeen out of twenty-two Arab states have a declining gross national product; in the next twenty years, at current growth rates, the population of many Arab countries will double. These states, like most African ones, will be ungovernable through conventional secular ideologies. The Middle East analyst Christine M. Helms explains,

Declaring Arab nationalism "bankrupt," the political "disinherited" are not rationalizing the failure of Arabism . . . or reformulating it. Alternative solutions are not contemplated. They have simply opted for the political paradigm at the other end of the political spectrum with which they are familiar—Islam.

Like the borders of West Africa, the colonial borders of Syria, Iraq, Jordan, Algeria, and other Arab states are often contrary to cultural and political reality. As state control mechanisms wither in the face of environmental and demographic stress, "hard" Islamic city-states or shantytown-states are likely to emerge. The fiction that the impoverished city of Algiers, on the Mediterranean, controls Tamanrasset, deep in the Algerian Sahara, cannot obtain forever. Whatever the outcome of the peace process, Israel is destined to be a Jewish ethnic fortress amid a vast and volatile realm of Islam. In that realm, the violent youth culture of the Gaza shantytowns may be indicative of the coming era.

The destiny of Turks and Kurds is far less certain, but far more relevant to the kind of map that will explain our future world. The Kurds suggest a geographic reality that cannot be shown in two-dimensional space. The issue in Turkey is not simply a matter of giving autonomy or even independence to Kurds in the southeast. This isn't the Balkans or the Caucasus, where regions are merely subdividing into smaller units, Abkhazia breaking off from Georgia, and so on. Federalism is not the answer. Kurds are found everywhere in Turkey, including the shanty districts of Istanbul and Ankara. Turkey's problem is that its Anatolian land mass is the home of two cultures and languages, Turkish and Kurdish. Identity in Turkey, as in India, Africa, and elsewhere, is more complex and subtle than conventional cartography can display.

A NEW KIND OF WAR

To appreciate fully the political and cartographic implications of postmodernism—an epoch of themeless juxtapositions, in which the classificatory grid of nation-states is going to be replaced by a jagged-glass pattern of city-states, shanty-states, nebulous and anarchic regionalisms—it is necessary to consider, finally, the whole question of war.

"Oh, what a relief to fight, to fight enemies who defend themselves, enemies who are awake!" André Malraux wrote in *Man's Fate*. I cannot think of a more suitable battle cry for many combatants in the early decades of the twenty-first century. The intense savagery of the fighting in such diverse cultural settings as Liberia, Bosnia, the Caucasus, and Sri Lanka—to say nothing of what obtains in American inner cities—indicates something very troubling that those of us inside the stretch limo, concerned with issues like middle-class entitlements and the future of interactive cable television, lack the stomach to contemplate. It is this: a large number of people on this planet, to whom the comfort and stability of a middle-class life is utterly unknown, find war and a barracks existence a step up rather than a step down.

"Just as it makes no sense to ask 'why people eat' or 'what they sleep for,'" writes Martin van Creveld, a military historian at the Hebrew University in Jerusalem, in *The Transformation of War*, "so fighting in many ways is not a means but an end. Throughout history, for every person who has expressed his horror of war there is another who found in it the most marvelous of all the experiences that are vouch-safed to man, even to the point that he later spent a lifetime boring his descendants by recounting his exploits." When I asked Pentagon officials about the nature of war in the twenty-first century, the answer I frequently got was "Read Van Creveld." The top brass are enamored of this historian not because his writings justify their existence but, rather, the opposite: Van Creveld warns them that huge state military machines like the Pentagon's are dinosaurs about to go extinct, and that something far more terrible awaits us.

The degree to which Van Creveld's *Transformation of War* complements Homer-Dixon's work on the environment, Huntington's thoughts on cultural clash, my own realizations in traveling by foot, bus, and bush taxi in more than sixty countries, and America's sobering comeuppances in intractable-culture zones like Haiti and Somalia is startling. The book begins by demolishing the notion that men don't like to fight. "By compelling the senses to focus themselves on the here and now," Van Creveld writes, war "can cause a man to take his leave of them." As anybody who has had experience with Chetniks in Serbia, "technicals" in Somalia, Tontons Macoutes in Haiti, or soldiers in Sierra Leone can tell you, in places where the Western Enlightenment has not penetrated and where there has always been mass poverty, people find liberation in violence. In Afghanistan and elsewhere, I vicariously experienced this phenomenon: worrying about mines and ambushes frees you from worrying about mundane details of daily existence. If my own experience is too subjective, there is a wealth of data showing the sheer frequency of war, especially in the developing world since the Second World War. Physical aggression is a part of being human. Only when people attain a certain economic, educational, and cultural standard is this trait tranquilized. In light of the fact that 95 percent of the earth's population growth will be in the poorest areas of the globe, the question is not whether there will be war (there will be a lot of it) but what kind of war. And who will fight whom?

Debunking the great military strategist Carl von Clausewitz, Van Creveld, who may be the most original thinker on war since that early-nineteenth-century Prussian, writes, "Clausewitz's ideas . . . were wholly rooted in the fact that, ever since 1648, war had been waged overwhelmingly by states." But, as Van Creveld explains, the period of nation-states and, therefore, of state conflict is now ending, and with it the clear "threefold division into government, army, and people" which state-directed wars enforce. Thus, to see the future, the first step is to look back to the past immediately prior to the birth of modernism—the wars in medieval Europe which began during the Reformation and reached their culmination in the Thirty Years' War.

Van Creveld writes,

In all these struggles political, social, economic, and religious motives were hopelessly entangled. Since this was an age when armies consisted of mercenaries, all were also attended by swarms of military entrepreneurs. . . . Many of them paid little but lip service to the organizations for whom they had contracted to fight. Instead, they robbed the countryside on their own behalf . . .

Given such conditions, any fine distinctions . . . between armies on the one hand and peoples on the other were bound to break down. Engulfed by war, civilians suffered terrible atrocities.

Back then, in other words, there was no "politics" as we have come to understand the term, just as there is less and less "politics" today in Liberia, Sierra Leone, Somalia, Sri Lanka, the Balkans, and the Caucasus, among other places.

Because, as Van Creveld notes, the radius of trust within tribal societies is narrowed to one's immediate family and guerrilla comrades, truces arranged with one Bosnian commander, say, may be broken immediately by another Bosnian commander. The plethora of short-lived ceasefires in the Balkans and the Caucasus constitute proof that we are no longer in a world where the old rules of state warfare apply. More evidence is provided by the destruction of medieval monuments in the Croatian port of Dubrovnik: when cultures, rather than states, fight, then cultural and religious monuments are weapons of war, making them fair game.

Also, war-making entities will no longer be restricted to a specific territory. Loose and shadowy organisms such as Islamic terrorist organizations suggest why borders will mean increasingly little and sedimentary layers of tribalistic identity and control will mean more. "From the vantage point of the present, there appears every prospect that religious . . . fanaticisms will play a larger role in the motivation of armed conflict" in the West than at any time "for the last 300 years," Van Creveld writes. This is why analysts like Michael Vlahos are closely monitoring religious cults. Vlahos says, "An ideology that challenges us may not take familiar form, like the old Nazis or Commies. It may not even engage us initially in ways that fit old threat markings." Van Creveld concludes, "Armed conflict will be waged by men on earth, not robots in space. It will have more in common with the struggles of primitive tribes than with large-scale conventional war." While another military historian, John Keegan, in his new book *A History of Warfare*, draws a more benign portrait of primitive man, it is important to point out that what Van Creveld really means is *re-primitivized* man: warrior societies operating at a time of unprecedented resource scarcity and planetary overcrowding.

Van Creveld's pre-Westphalian vision of worldwide low-intensity conflict is not a superficial "back to the future" scenario. First of all, technology will be used toward primitive ends. In Liberia the guerrilla leader Prince Johnson didn't just cut off the ears of President Samuel Doe before Doe was tortured to death in 1990—Johnson made a video of it, which has circulated throughout West Africa. In December of 1992, when plotters of a failed coup against the Strasser regime in Sierra Leone had their ears cut off at Freetown's Hamilton

Beach prior to being killed, it was seen by many to be a copycat execution. Considering, as I've explained earlier, that the Strasser regime is not really a government and that Sierra Leone is not really a nation-state, listen closely to Van Creveld: "Once the legal monopoly of armed force, long claimed by the state, is wrested out of its hands, existing distinctions between war and crime will break down much as is already the case today in . . . Lebanon, Sri Lanka, El Salvador, Peru, or Colombia."

If crime and war become indistinguishable, then "national defense" may in the future be viewed as a local concept. As crime continues to grow in our cities and the ability of state governments and criminal-justice systems to protect their citizens diminishes, urban crime may, according to Van Creveld, "develop into low-intensity conflict by coalescing along racial, religious, social, and political lines." As small-scale violence multiplies at home and abroad, state armies will continue to shrink, being gradually replaced by a booming private security business, as in West Africa, and by urban mafias, especially in the former communist world, who may be better equipped than municipal police forces to grant physical protection to local inhabitants.

Future wars will be those of communal survival, aggravated or, in many cases, caused by environmental scarcity. These wars will be subnational, meaning that it will be hard for states and local governments to protect their own citizens physically. This is how many states will ultimately die. As state power fades—and with it the state's ability to help weaker groups within society, not to mention other states—peoples and cultures around the world will be thrown back upon their own strengths and weaknesses, with fewer equalizing mechanisms to protect them. Whereas the distant future will probably see the emergence of a racially hybrid, globalized man, the coming decades will see us more aware of our differences than of our similarities. To the average person, political values will mean less, personal security more. The belief that we are all equal is liable to be replaced by the overriding obsession of the ancient Greek travelers: Why the differences between peoples?

THE LAST MAP

In *Geography and the Human Spirit,* Anne Buttimer, a professor at University College, Dublin, recalls the work of an early-nineteenth-century German geographer, Carl Ritter, whose work implied "a divine plan for humanity" based on regionalism and a constant, living flow of forms. The map of the future, to the extent that a map is even possible, will represent a perverse twisting of Ritter's vision. Imagine cartography in three dimensions, as if in a hologram. In this hologram would be the overlapping sediments of group and other identities atop the merely two-dimensional color markings of city-states and the remaining nations, themselves confused in places by shadowy tentacles, hovering overhead, indicating the power of drug cartels, mafias, and private security agencies. Instead of borders, there would be moving "centers" of power, as in the Middle Ages. Many of these layers would be in motion. Replacing fixed and abrupt lines on a flat space would be a shifting pattern of buffer entities, like the Kurdish and Azeri buffer entities between Turkey and Iran, the Turkic Uighur buffer entity between Central Asia and Inner China (itself distinct from coastal China), and the Latino buffer entity replacing a precise U.S.-Mexican border. To this protean cartographic hologram one must add other factors, such as migrations of populations, explosions of birth rates, vectors of disease. Henceforward the map of the world will never be static. This future map—in a sense, the "Last Map"—will be an ever-mutating representation of chaos.

The Indian subcontinent offers examples of what is happening. For different reasons, both India and Pakistan are increasingly dysfunctional. The argument over democracy in these places is less and less relevant to the larger issue of governability. In India's case the question arises, Is one unwieldy bureaucracy in New Delhi the best available mechanism for promoting the lives of 866 million people of diverse languages, religions, and ethnic groups? In 1950, when the Indian population was much less than half as large and nation-building idealism was still strong, the argument for democracy was more impressive than it is now. Given that in 2025 India's population could be close to 1.5 billion, that much of its economy rests on a shrinking natural-resource base, including dramatically declining water levels, and that communal violence and urbanization are spiraling upward, it is difficult to imagine that the Indian state will survive the next century. India's oft-trumpeted Green Revolution has been achieved by overworking its croplands and depleting its watershed. Norman Myers, a British development consultant, worries that Indians have "been feeding themselves today by borrowing against their children's food sources."

Pakistan's problem is more basic still: like much of Africa, the country makes no geographic or demographic sense. It was founded as a homeland for the Muslims of the subcontinent, yet there are more subcontinental Muslims outside Pakistan than within it. Like Yugoslavia, Pakistan is a patchwork of ethnic groups, increasingly in violent conflict with one another. While the Western media gushes over the fact that the country has a woman Prime Minister, Benazir Bhutto, Karachi is becoming a subcontinental version of Lagos. In eight visits to Pakistan, I have never gotten a sense of a cohesive national identity. With as much as 65 percent of its land dependent on intensive irrigation, with wide-scale deforestation, and with a yearly population growth of 2.7 percent (which ensures that the amount of cultivated land per rural inhabitant will plummet), Pakistan is becoming a more and more desperate place. As irrigation in the Indus River basin intensifies to serve two growing populations, Muslim-Hindu strife over falling water tables may be unavoidable.

"India and Pakistan will probably fall apart," Homer-Dixon predicts. "Their secular governments have less and less legitimacy as well as less management ability over people and resources." Rather than one bold line dividing the subcontinent into two parts, the future will likely see a lot of thinner lines and smaller parts, with the ethnic entities of Pakhtunistan and Punjab gradually replacing Pakistan in the space between the Central Asian plateau and the heart of the subcontinent.

None of this even takes into account climatic change, which, if it occurs in the next century, will further erode the capacity of existing states to cope. India, for instance, receives 70 percent of its precipitation from the monsoon cycle, which planetary warming could disrupt.

Not only will the three-dimensional aspects of the Last Map be in constant motion, but its two-dimensional base may change too. The National Academy of Sciences reports that

> as many as one billion people, or 20 percent of the world's population, live on lands likely to be inundated or dramatically changed by rising waters. . . . Low-lying countries in the developing world such as Egypt and Bangladesh, where rivers are large and the deltas extensive and densely populated, will be hardest hit. . . . Where the rivers are dammed, as in the case of the Nile, the effects . . . will be especially severe.

Egypt could be where climatic upheaval—to say nothing of the more immediate threat of increasing population—will incite religious upheaval in truly biblical fashion. Natural catastrophes, such as the October, 1992, Cairo earthquake, in which the government failed to deliver relief aid and slum residents were in many instances helped by their local mosques, can only strengthen the position of Islamic factions. In a statement about greenhouse warming which could refer to any of a variety of natural catastrophes, the environmental expert Jessica Tuchman Matthews warns that many of us underestimate the extent to which political systems, in affluent societies as well as in places like Egypt, "depend on the underpinning of natural systems." She adds, "The fact that one can move with ease from Vermont to Miami has nothing to say about the consequences of Vermont acquiring Miami's climate."

Indeed, it is not clear that the United States will survive the next century in exactly its present form. Because America is a multi-ethnic society, the nation-state has always been more fragile here than it is in more homogeneous societies like Germany and Japan. James Kurth, in an article published in *The National Interest* in 1992, explains that whereas nation-state societies tend to be built around a mass-conscription army and a standardized public school system, "multicultural regimes" feature a high-tech, all-volunteer army (and, I would add, private schools that teach competing values), operating in a culture in which the international media and entertainment industry has more influence than the "national political class." In other words, a nation-state is a place where everyone has been educated along similar lines, where people take their cue from national leaders, and where everyone (every male, at least) has gone through the crucible of military service, making patriotism a simpler issue. Writing about his immigrant family in turn-of-the-century Chicago, Saul Bellow states, " 'The country took us over. It was a country then, not a collection of 'cultures.' "

During the Second World War and the decade following it, the United States reached its apogee as a classic nation-state. During the 1960s, as is now clear, America began a slow but unmistakable process of transformation. The signs hardly need belaboring: racial polarity, educational dysfunction, social fragmentation of many and various kinds. William Irwin Thompson, in *Passages About Earth: An Exploration of the New Planetary Culture*, writes, "The educational system that had worked on the Jews or the Irish could no longer work on the blacks; and when Jewish teachers in New York tried to take black children away from their parents exactly in the way they had been taken from theirs, they were shocked to encounter a violent affirmation of negritude."

Issues like West Africa could yet emerge as a new kind of foreign-policy issue, further eroding America's domestic peace. The spectacle of several West African nations collapsing at once could reinforce the worst racial stereotypes here at home. That is another reason why Africa matters. We must not kid ourselves: the sensitivity factor is higher than ever. The Washington, D.C., public school system is already experimenting with an Afrocentric curriculum. Summits between African leaders and prominent African-Americans are becoming frequent, as are Pollyanna-ish prognostications about multiparty elections in Africa that do not factor in crime, surging birth rates, and resource depletion. The Congressional Black Caucus was among those urging U.S. involvement in Somalia and in Haiti. At the *Los Angeles Times* minority staffers have protested against, among other things, what they allege to be the racist tone of the newspaper's Africa coverage, allegations that the editor of the "World Report" section, Dan Fisher, denies, saying essentially that Africa should be viewed through the same rigorous analytical lens as other parts of the world.

Africa may be marginal in terms of conventional late-twentieth-century conceptions of strategy, but in an age of cultural and racial clash, when national defense is increasingly local, Africa's distress will exert a destabilizing influence on the United States.

This and many other factors will make the United States less of a nation than it is today, even as it gains territory following the peaceful dissolution of Canada. Quebec, based on the bedrock of Roman Catholicism and Francophone ethnicity, could yet turn out to be North America's most cohesive and crime-free nation-state. (It may be a smaller Quebec, though, since aboriginal peoples may lop off northern parts of the province.) "Patriotism" will become increasingly regional as people in Alberta and Montana discover that they have far more in common with each other than they do with Ottawa or Washington, and Spanish-speakers in the Southwest discover a greater commonality with Mexico City. (*The Nine Nations of North America,* by Joel Garreau, a book about the continent's regionalization, is more relevant now than when it was published, in 1981.) As Washington's influence wanes, and with it the traditional symbols of American patriotism, North Americans will take psychological refuge in their insulated communities and cultures.

54

YAHYA SADOWSKI

THE MYTH OF GLOBAL CHAOS

When the cold war ended in 1989, Americans were like a baby tasting its first mouthful of peanut butter: both delighted and confused. They felt triumphant about the rapid collapse of Soviet communism, but they could not quite swallow it. They could neither understand how it had happened so quickly nor figure out how to adjust to a world without the "red menace." For forty years, U.S. foreign policy had employed the Soviet threat as its centerpiece. When the Union of Soviet Socialist Republics (USSR) dissolved in 1991, Americans had to think about how they were going to deal with the world "from scratch."

Initially, the optimism of American society prevailed. The first vision of life after the cold war to capture the public imagination was the one artic ulated by Francis Fukuyama in his famous article "The End of History."[1] Fukuyama argued that the Soviet Union had been defeated not by the force of arms but by the universal allure of American values. Music videos, film noir, blue jeans, and other commodities had penetrated the iron curtain, carrying with them the romance of individualism, materialism, and liberty. The globalization of American values had convinced the Russians as well as the Poles and the Chinese and the Mozambicans of the superiority of the American way of life. Now the whole world was scrambling to emulate the democratic capitalism epitomized by the United States. And once done, capitalism would make the world more prosperous, and democracy would make it more peaceful.

But with the passage of time, the millennial hopes articulated by Fukuyama dimmed. The violent breakup of the USSR, the civil war in Somalia, the shocking genocide in Rwanda, all had a sobering effect. But the war in Bosnia in particular worked to reshape the national mood in America (and elsewhere) into one of pessimism. The Bosnian war was not only extremely violent, but it also appeared almost totally irrational. . . .

Many serious thinkers worried that what had happened to Bosnia seemed likely to spread elsewhere—and not just to neighboring Balkan states. The vicious hypernationalism that afflicted Bosnia was only one of several irrational ideologies that seemed to be sweeping the globe. Religious fundamentalism, ethnic bigotry, and plain old nihilism also seemed to be becoming more popular. The world seemed to be slipping over a precipice into an epoch of ethnic and

SOURCE: From *The Myth of Global Chaos*, by Yahya Sadowski, pp. 1–2, 4–5, 170–173, 176–177, 192, 205–206, 254, 257. Copyright 1998 Brookings Institute Press.

cultural violence. It seemed less like the end of history than like the revenge of history. A real danger seemed to exist that the atrocities in Bosnia were a harbinger of worse things to come globally.

Meditating on this prospect, a group of American thinkers began to develop similar ideas. Gradually they converged toward the same three frightening conclusions:

1. The current trend for the political, economic, and cultural institutions of the West to be spread around the world—what is called "globalization"—is forcing more and more people to confront alien values, whether in the form of glitzy television commercials or through resettlement in industrial shantytowns where tribes of different religions are forced to live cheek-to-jowl.

2. When the basic values of a culture are threatened, violence becomes more common and more savage. For some, the decay of rationality means an easing of the restrictions against theft, murder, and rape. Others seek to resist the threat to traditional values through a fanatic, angry reassertion of fundamentalist tradition. Either way, apparently irrational violence increases.

3. As a result of globalization and the way it threatens traditional values, the world is witnessing an explosion of irrational violence, manifest in the drug wars of Latin America, the tribal massacres of Africa, fundamentalist revolts in the Middle East, and ethnic cleansing in the Balkans. Crime, warfare, and genocide all seem to be not only proliferating but also spinning out of control. Thus, the same process of globalization that Fukuyama thought had destroyed communism might be planting the seeds for an epoch of global chaos.

Thinkers who shared these three convictions never adopted a single common moniker, preferring instead to market their own individual epigrams: "the coming anarchy," "the clash of civilizations," "jihad vs. McWorld," and so on. In some newspapers, their ideas were collectively called "chaos theory," but this was unfortunate, because the same name had already been applied to a movement of physical scientists who applied new techniques of nonlinear mathematics.[2] Yet, because the central thesis of the new foreign policy pessimists was that globalization spawns political chaos, "global chaos theory" may be an accurate label for their ideas.[3]

The architects of global chaos theory include some of the sharpest political strategists working in America today. They have erected a complex school of thought that deals with urbanization, narcoterrorism, immigration, humanitarian disasters, debates over military intervention, rogue states, collapsed states, the profusion of transnational organizations, terrorist networks, fundamentalism, ethnic conflict, and so on. Their edifice is still growing and evolving and continues to exert influence on American policymakers.

But on close inspection, most of the major claims of global chaos theory turn out to be false. The great majority of the conflicts in the world today are not "clashes of civilizations" but fratricides that pit old neighbors, often from similar or identical cultures, against each other. Most ethnic conflicts are not the irrational result of "ageless tribal rivalries" but recent and rational quarrels over the distribution of resources. Societies in the throes of globalization are not any more likely to suffer anomic social violence, culture clashes, or ethnic conflict than countries that are not. The culture conflicts that worry global chaos theorists are not any more violent—or any more frequent—than the "brushfire wars" that plagued the third world during the long cold war.

In the final analysis, the end of the cold war may have changed the world less than either optimists or pessimists imagined. . . .

Most of the available evidence suggests that global chaos theory is wrong about most of its major claims. Globalization does not seem to be a major cause of culture clashes. Conflicts among cultures seem to be fairly evenly distributed throughout human societies. Anomie or the collapse of values does not seem to be an important cause of collective violence (although it may play a role in disposing individuals to murder, suicide, and so on). Wars today appear to be caused by the same mixture of forces that have propelled combat throughout history: fear, desperation, want, arrogance, foolishness, and myriad other forces. Finally, neither the number of conflicts nor their savagery seems to have increased dramatically. This is not to say war is not a nasty business—but that is hardly news.

What lessons for the conduct of U.S. foreign policy can Washington draw from the shortcomings of global chaos theory? The most obvious lessons are negative. If global chaos theory fundamentally misunderstands the dynamics of contemporary politics, it is legitimate to treat its own policy recommendations warily. President Clinton would have been well advised not to base his Bosnia policy on a reading of *Balkan Ghosts*. Americans need not gird themselves for a looming clash of civilizations because battles of this kind are not the dominant form of conflict in today's world.

Some of the negative lessons that can be drawn from the critique of global chaos theory are more specific and concrete. For example, some chaos theorists have suggested that, because (they claim)- globalization causes culture conflict, everyone should be cautious about anything that promotes globalization. They argue that America should be cautious about rushing to encourage the development of democracy or free speech in other societies because this can breed nationalist backlash. They worry that immigration and multicultural education or anything else that forces alien values into contact may ignite tensions. Whether or not democratization or multicultural education are good ideas can be debated, but the evidence suggests that culture conflict ranks low among the problems they are likely to cause.

In balance, over the short term, globalization does appear to disrupt societies, and sometimes this can produce conflict. Yet over the long term globalization also seems to often promote prosperity, political legitimacy, and even greater intercultural understanding. Even if someone could figure out a way to hold back or reverse globalization, this approach would probably indirectly fuel more culture conflicts than it would suppress.

A second negative lesson that can be drawn from the critique of global chaos theory concerns America's pattern of alliances or engagement with other countries around the world. Samuel Huntington has called for Washington to construct a system of alliances that ensures the victory of "the West against the rest." Although few global chaos theorists have endorsed this slogan, they, too, generally favor an alliance of the industrial countries of the "zone of peace" to face the threats and trouble that seem to characterize the third world. Nothing in the critique suggests that anything is wrong with strong alliances among the Western or industrialized states—but to view this as directed against the bloc of less developed countries could be dangerous.

The countries of "the global South" are diverse. They include some of the world's fastest growing economies and some of the fastest decaying ones. They include states of great stability, some with impressive democratic credentials, and other states that either exist only on paper or are formed from the stuff of nightmares. About all these countries share in common is that they are industrializing later, historically, than the West. That has never been enough to make them a single bloc—and any effort to lump them all together and treat them as if they were the same will fail. Even the countries that seem to share a common culture or civilization cannot be pigeonholed together. For example, Malaysia and Indonesia, which have Muslim majorities, have a great deal more in common with other newly industrializing countries such as Singapore than they do with other Muslim nations such as Afghanistan or Egypt.

American stockholders have already discovered that some of the best investments in the world today are in "emerging markets." Potentially and in fact, some of Washington's best allies—loyal, strategically positioned, influential—can also be found in the third world. Differences of culture rarely prevent states from understanding when they have common interests. America can judge its allies on their merits, without worrying that differences of religion or lifestyle will inevitably drive a wedge between them.

A final negative lesson from the critique of global chaos theory concerns the organization and application of the U.S. military. Many chaos theorists thought that the fanaticism and bloodlust of combatants in culture conflicts made them impervious to normal calculations of deterrence, pressure, and force majeure. They argued that either America should avoid intervening in such battles wherever possible or, when it was forced to engage, it might need to deploy large numbers of troops and be prepared for a long frustrating battle with high casualties on both sides.

War is a grave, ugly business, but ethnic or cultural wars are not substantially different from ideological or venal wars. Some culture wars are fought by irregular or guerrilla combatants who are hard to distinguish from the civilian population and must be rooted out in protracted, often grotesquely violent campaigns. (Anyone who thinks that regular armies cannot defeat guerrilla fighters should study what the Iraqis did in Kurdistan during the 1980s—although this is an example one hopes few democracies will emulate.) Others are fought by regular armies, commanded from centralized capitals, that can be defeated by entirely conventional means. (The Bosnian Serbs fell into this category, despite their experience with guerrilla warfare during World War II.)

Nothing changed at the end of the cold war that, by itself, requires America to develop a new form of military organization. The enemies, threats, and nuisances Washington faces today resemble those it has dealt with in the past. Perhaps it can afford a smaller military (perhaps it never needed the huge one it fielded during the cold war). America (like other democracies) has some problems prosecuting guerrilla wars in which the Pentagon's insistence upon applying overwhelming force conflicts with the political interest in minimizing casualties among the civilians who live cheek-to-jowl with enemy troops—but this was as much of a problem in Vietnam as it was in Somalia. Ethnic or cultural wars are won by much the same means that lead to victory in other battles.

Perhaps the most egregious myth about ethnic conflict that global chaos theory helped to propagate was the idea that Washington will be generally powerless to deal with ethnic conflict. Clinton thought he had learned this lesson from reading *Balkan Ghosts*—that America could not bring peace to Bosnia unless it was prepared to obliterate the fanatics of Serb separatism and to absorb the massive casualties that mission would require. But ethnic wars are not markedly different from other types of warfare. Washington had at least as many different options about how to deploy U.S. power to end the conflict in Bosnia as it did in 1990 when it decided to "liberate" Kuwait.

Ethnic conflicts are much less chaotic than they often seem in Western press accounts. They often appear when economic competition increases and political institutions decay. They are not usually started or fought by sociopaths, victims of atavism, anomie, or other crazy people. Even the wildest fringe elements in most ethnic conflicts are more like Mafia dons than serial killers. They are good family men, as popular and respected within their own local community as they are feared and hated outside of it. And many of the worst atrocities in ethnic wars—as in nonethnic wars—are conducted by people who, for good or ill, resemble Lt. Col. Oliver North—people who think they are "doing their duty" or serving "a higher cause."

Chaos is not a strategic threat, certainly not in the way that global chaos theorists would have people believe. It cannot be legitimately invoked to justify maintaining the Pentagon's inflated budgets or compel European allies to keep their wagons in the circle of the Atlantic alliance's laager. Despite all the din to the contrary, a global explosion of new and menacing ethnic conflicts has not occurred. What ethnic conflicts do exist are not markedly more savage or deadly or less tractable than other types of warfare in the developing countries. . .

ASSESSING THE RISK OF STATE COLLAPSE

The absence of material prosperity and political stability seem to be the two major structural problems that are most closely associated with the outbreak of ethnic or culture wars. So to prevent such wars all one needs do is promote economic growth and good government. Simple, no?

No. Both economic and political development remain daunting tasks, and limited expert agreement exists about how to foster them. Perhaps, greater hope can be found that they are more widely attainable now than twenty years ago. The success of the green revolution in countries such as Bangladesh and of export-led industrialization in countries such as South Korea have penetrated the gloom of the "limits to growth" pessimists. The spread or revival of democratic institutions throughout Latin America and in parts of Asia and Africa holds out the prospect of more civil governance. But there is little reason to believe that economic growth and good government will become universal any time soon.

Yet, efforts in these two areas can make a contribution to reducing the number of ethnic and culture wars. Sometimes a culture war can be prevented by marginal improvements in an economy or by maintaining a minimal level of political order.[4] Even when no immediate means are available to influence the economic and political forces that may be breeding a culture clash in some country, appreciating their role may enable policymakers to better deal with the situation.

One consistent conclusion of analyses of ethnic and culture conflicts is that they are easiest to resolve when they are addressed early, before fear has dissolved intercommunity bonds and violent incidents have bred a desire for revenge. This has helped to fuel the recent vogue of "preventive diplomacy."[5] Even most of those who opposed military intervention in Bosnia agree that, if Washington and the West had acted more forcefully in 1990 or even 1991, the entire conflict could have been smothered before it got going.[6] Intervention is cheaper before anything resembling an act of ethnic cleansing has a chance to inflate passions on all sides. A focus on social structure can contribute by allowing one to anticipate where such conflicts are most likely, by providing some early warning of emerging "hot spots."

For example, the ability of Washington or the international community to deal with the crises in the former Yugoslavia and Somalia would have been greatly enhanced if the likelihood of state collapse could have been anticipated. Such a warning might have given policymakers a chance to prevent state collapse or, if that proved impossible, at least to make early preparations for the disorder that would follow.[7]

. . . States can take decades or centuries to fully establish their authority, to instill a degree of public trust or at least acceptance. Many of the newest states are only "quasi-states," bureaucracies with little reach beyond their capital cities, whose main claim to authority comes from their having a flag and a seat at the UN.[8]

Statemaking is not something that happens every day. It is a process that has occurred in waves, and some evidence is available that states that emerged from the same wave share common characteristics, imprinted upon them by the international environment at the moment of their birth. Thus, the Latin American states born during the Bolivar wave share a dedication to "order and progress," while those that emerged in Eastern Europe from the Leninist extinction share a common obsession with "civil society." However, longevity is hardly a guarantor of state survival. Many of the regimes and countries that disappeared during the Leninist extinction had respectable histories of survival. Old states can and do collapse. To anticipate the breakdown of political order, more sophisticated tools need to be deployed. . . .

GLOBAL COMPLEXITY

Grappling with the structural conditions that promote ethnic and culture conflict will be a learning process. Few policymakers (and fewer intellectuals) seem to appreciate that all policies are experiments. Given the limits of knowledge about society, they can be nothing else. Policymakers should imitate Napoleon, who said before battle, "On s'engage et puis s'on voit." ("We will engage the enemy and then see what happens.") Policies begin with a plan, which has to be ruthlessly revised as its strengths and shortcomings become clear.[9]

Tinkering with the structures that foster ethnic and culture conflict, policymakers will inevitably learn a great deal. Despite the current prevalence of the Washington consensus, understanding of the mechanisms of economic development is still crude. No subfield of economics is more prone to fashion or exhibits such lurching variations over time. The Washington consensus replaced an earlier international consensus that emphasized the need for planning and state intervention, which had replaced an earlier consensus, and so on.[10] Understanding of the process of state formation is not even this advanced. The academic literature on state formation is of high quality, but scarce and recent.[11] (America's own experience with state building is particularly alarming. Neither Liberia, the Philippines, nor South Vietnam testify well on behalf of its ability to export political institutions.)

Although many surprises will arise as understanding of these problems advances, one thing is already clear. "The world is not only queerer than we think it is, it is queerer than we can think it is."[12] The international environment is not chaotic (most of its behavior has structural underpinnings that make it rationally understandable if not exactly predictable), but it is certainly complex. Learning to recognize, acknowledge, and deal with complexity may be the hallmark of successful diplomacy in the coming years. . . .

NOTES

1. In the summer of 1947, "Mr. X"—a pseudonym for George Kennan, who had just become the first director of the policy planning staff at the Department of State—published an article entitled "The Sources of Soviet Conduct" in *Foreign Affairs*. This article laid out certain theses about Soviet behavior, American interests, and the character of international relations that, over the next few years, not only assumed the status of the "conventional wisdom" among pundits and intellectuals but also were enshrined as the foundation of America's grand strategy for dealing

with the Soviet Union. Kennan's strategy was soon dubbed "containment," and his philosophy was called "realism." See John Lewis Gaddis, *Strategies of Containment: A Critical Appraisal of Postwar American National Security Policy* (New York: Oxford University Press, 1982), pp. 25–53.

2. See the definitive account of this development in James Gleick, *Chaos: Making a New Science* (Viking Penguin, 1987). In the 1993 movie *Jurassic Park,* millions of Americans were exposed to a bastardized form of chaos theory that suggested the movement revolved around Murphy's Law: "Anything that can go wrong will go wrong." By this time, physical scientists had begun to rename their theories, calling it the study of "nonlinear dynamics" or "complexity." (See Roger Lewin, *Complexity: Life at the Edge of Chaos* (Macmillan, 1992); and George Johnson, "Researchers on Complexity Ponder What It's All About," *New York Times,* May 6, 1997, p. C1.) For one of the few direct attempts to apply chaos theory to the social sciences, see Bernice Cohen, *The Edge of Chaos: Financial Booms, Bubbles, Crashes, and Chaos* (London: John Wiley and Sons, 1996).

3. The choice of a name for a movement matters. The word "chaos" had become evocative by the early 1990s, so many different thinkers were laying claim to it. See Stephen S. Hall, "Scientists Find Catchy Names Help Ideas Fly," *New York Times,* October 20, 1992, p. C1. See also Al Kamen, "Counting on Chaos to Save the Day for Dole," *Washington Post,* September 16, 1996, p. A17.

4. This has been clear in the recent downturn of ethnic violence in Bulgaria, Northern Ireland, and Quebec. See Christophe Chatelot, "Bulgaria Learns to Live with Its Turks," *Guardian Weekly,* May 11, 1997, p. 17; Christopher Chipello, "Economy Saps Quebec's Separatist Ardor," *New York Times,* October 31, 1997, p. A18; and Nuala O'Faolain, "Good Fortune in Belfast," *New York Times,* April 12, 1998, p. A13.

5. Kevin M. Cahill, ed., *Preventive Diplomacy: Stopping Wars before They Start* (Basic Books, 1996); Michael S. Lund, *Preventing Violent Conflicts: A Strategy for Preventive Diplomacy* (Washington: U.S. Institute of Peace, 1996); and United Nations, *Agenda for Peace: Preventive Diplomacy, Peacemaking, and Peace Keeping* (New York: United Nations, June 1992).

6. Misha Glenny, *The Fall of Yugoslavia: The Third Balkan War* (New York: Penguin, 1992).

7. For a concrete proposal to construct similar systems, for monitoring the likelihood of ethnic conflict, see Ted Robert Gurr, "Early-Warning Systems: From Surveillance to Assessment to Action," in Kevin M. Cahill, ed., *Preventive Diplomacy: Stopping Wars Before They Start* (Basic Books, 1996), pp. 123–43; and David Garment, "The Ethnic Dimension in World Politics: Theory, Policy, and Early Warning," *Third World Quarterly,* vol. 15, no. 4 (1994), pp. 551–82.

8. Regarding the problems that afflict this group, see Robert H. Jackson, *Quasi-States: Sovereignty, International Relations, and the Third World* (Cambridge, England: Cambridge University Press, 1990).

9. Albert Hirschman seems to be one of the few policy intellectuals to have appreciated this.

10. See Paul Krugman, "Cycles of Conventional Wisdom on Economic Development," *International Affairs,* vol. 71 (October 1995), pp. 717–32; and Peter Evans and John D. Stephens, "Studying Development since the Sixties," *Theory and Society,* vol. 17 (1988), pp. 713–45.

11. The study of this subject began with Charles Tilly, ed., *The Formation of National States in Western Europe* (Princeton University Press, 1975). For a volume that cites

the developments in the field since then, see Charles Tilly, *Coercion, Capital, and European States,* (Cambridge, Mass.: Blackwell, 1990).

12. John Burdon Sanderson Haldane, *On Being the Right Size and Other Essays* (Oxford, England: Oxford University Press, 1985).

55

BRUCE HOFFMAN

TERRORISM TODAY AND TOMORROW

THE FUTURE: TERRORIST USE OF WEAPONS OF MASS DESTRUCTION

. . . New adversaries, new motivations and new rationales have emerged in recent years to challenge at least some of the conventional wisdom on both terrorists and terrorism. More critically, perhaps, many of our old preconceptions —as well as government policies—date from the emergence of terrorism as a global security problem more than a quarter of a century ago. They originated, and took hold, during the Cold War, when radical left-wing terrorists groups then active throughout the world were widely regarded as posing the most serious threat to Western security. Even such modifications or "fine-tuning" as have been undertaken since that time are arguably no less dated by now, having been implemented a decade ago in response to the series of suicide bombings against American diplomatic and military targets in the Middle East that at the time had underscored the rising threat of state-sponsored terrorism.

In no area, perhaps, is the potential irrelevance of much of this thinking clearer, or the critical lacuna more apparent, than with regard to the potential use by terrorists of weapons of mass destruction (WMD): that is, nuclear, chemical or biological weapons. Most of the handful of publications that have authoritatively addressed this issue are themselves now seriously dated, having been conceived and written in some instances nearly two decades ago when very different situations, circumstances and international dynamics existed. Indeed, much of the research on potential uses of WMD during the Cold War understandably concentrated on nuclear confrontation involving almost exclusively the two superpowers and their allies. Potential terrorist use of such devices was either

SOURCE: From *Inside Terrorism*, by Bruce Hoffman, pp. 196–212, 216–217. Copyright Columbia University Press.

addressed within the Cold War/superpowers framework or else dismissed, given the prevailing patterns of substate violence and the aims and objectives of violent non-state groups active at the time.

Today, the threat of a general war—nuclear and/or conventional—between the superpowers of the Cold War era and their respective alliances has faded. But it has been replaced by new security challenges of a potentially far more amorphous, less quantifiable and perhaps even more ominous character, that may also be far more difficult to meet. . . . The increasing salience of religious motives for terrorist activity has already contributed to the increasing lethality of international terrorism. Moreover, many of the constraints (both self-imposed and technical) which previously inhibited terrorist use of WMD are eroding. The particular characteristics, justifications and mindsets of religious and quasi-religious—as compared with secular—terrorists suggest that religious terrorists will be among the most likely of the potential categories of non-state perpetrators to use WMD.

THE CHANGING CHARACTERISTICS OF INTERNATIONAL TERRORISM

In the past, terrorist groups were recognizable mostly as collections of individuals belonging to an organization with a well-defined command and control apparatus, who had been previously trained (in however rudimentary a fashion) in the techniques and tactics of terrorism, were engaged in conspiracy as a full-time avocation, living underground while constantly planning and plotting terrorist attacks, and who at times were under the direct control, or operated at the express behest, of a foreign government (as, for example, in the case of Libya's sponsorship of JRA operations claimed in the name of the "Anti-Imperialist International Brigades"). Radical leftist organizations such as the JRA, RAF, RB, etc., as well as ethno-nationalist/separatist terrorist movements like the PLO, IRA and ETA, conformed to this stereotype of the "traditional" terrorist group. These organizations engaged in highly selective and mostly discriminate acts of violence. They targeted for bombing various "symbolic" targets representing the source of their hostility (e.g. embassies, banks, national airline carriers), or kidnapped and assassinated specific persons whom they considered guilty of economic exploitation or political repression in order to attract attention to themselves and their causes.

However, radical or revolutionary as these groups were politically, the vast majority were equally conservative in their operations. These types of terrorists were said to be demonstrably more "imitative than innovative," having a very limited tactical repertoire directed against a similarly narrow target set.[1] They were judged as hesitant to take advantage of new situations, let alone to create new opportunities. What little innovation was observed lay more in the terrorists' choice of targets (e.g. the 1985 hijacking of the Italian cruise ship *Achille Lauro* by Palestinian terrorists, as opposed to the more typical terrorist hijacking of passenger aircraft), or in the methods used to conceal and detonate explosive devices, than in their tactics or their interest in using non-conventional weapons—particularly chemical, biological, radiological or nuclear.[2]

Although various terrorist groups—including the RAF, RB and some Palestinian organizations–had occasionally toyed with the idea of using such indiscriminately lethal weapons, none had ever crossed the critical psychological threshold of actually implementing their heinous daydreams or executing their half-baked plots. Admittedly, in 1979 Palestinian terrorists poisoned some Jaffa oranges exported to Europe in hopes of sabotaging Israel's economy; and a police raid on an RAF safe house in Paris the following year discovered a miniature laboratory designed to be used for the culture of *clostridium botulinum*.[3] But these two isolated incidents represented virtually the total extent of either *actual* use or serious *attempts* at the use by terrorists of such non-conventional weapons and tactics. Instead, most terrorists seemed relatively content with the limited killing potential of their hand-guns and machine-guns, and the slightly higher casualty rates that their bombs achieved. Like most people, terrorists themselves appeared to fear powerful contaminants and toxins about which they knew little and which they were uncertain how to fabricate and safely handle, much less effectively deploy and disperse. Indeed, of more than 8,000 incidents recorded in the RAND–St Andrews University Chronology of International Terrorist Incidents since 1968, fewer than sixty offer any indication of terrorists plotting such attacks, attempting to use chemical or biological agents, or intending to steal or fabricate their own nuclear devices.[4]

There has also been a general acceptance of Brian Jenkins's . . . observation that "Terrorists want a lot of people watching and a lot of people listening and not a lot of people dead." Even after the events of the mid-1980s, when a series of high-profile and particularly lethal suicide car-and-truck-bombings were directed against American diplomatic and military targets in the Middle East (in one instance resulting in the deaths of 241 Marines), Jenkins still saw no need to revise his thinking, reiterating that "simply killing a lot of people has seldom been one terrorist objective. . . . Terrorists operate on the principle of the minimum force necessary. They find it unnecessary to kill many, as long as killing a few suffices for their purposes."[5] This maxim was further applied to the question of potential terrorist use of WMD, in respect of which it was used to explain the paucity of actual known plots, much less verifiable incidents. Within the context of potential terrorist use of radiological or nuclear weapons, for example, Jenkins had noted in 1975 that

> Scenarios involving the deliberate dispersal of toxic radioactive material . . . do not appear to fit the pattern of any terrorist actions carried out thus far. . . . Terrorist actions have tended to be aimed at producing immediate dramatic effects, a handful of violent deaths—not lingering illness, and certainly not a population of ill, vengeance-seeking victims. . . . If terrorists were to employ radioactive contaminants, they could not halt the continuing effects of their act, not even long after they may have achieved their ultimate political objectives. It has not been the style of terrorists to kill hundreds or thousands. To make hundreds or thousands of persons terminally ill would be even more out of character.[6]

IMPLICATIONS OF RELIGIOUS
TERRORISM FOR USE OF WMD

In recent years, however, these long-standing assumptions have increasingly been called into question by terrorist attacks that have either involved a weapon of mass destruction or caused large numbers of fatalities. Three incidents in particular. . . have generated heightened concern that terrorism may be entering a period of increased violence and bloodshed. They are:

- the March 1995 nerve gas attack on the Tokyo subway system;
- the bombing a month later of the Alfred P. Murrah Federal Building in Oklahoma City;
- the 1993 bombing of New York City's World Trade Center.

The connecting thread (although not necessarily the sole motivating factor) linking these otherwise unrelated incidents is religion. Indeed, in addition to these examples, some of the most serious terrorist acts—either in lethality or in their political implications—of the years 1995–7 have similarly had a salient religious element.

As the three incidents listed above demonstrate, the more "traditional" and familiar types of ideological, ethno-nationalist and separatist organizations which dominated terrorism from the 1960s to the 1990s—and upon which analysts like Jenkins based many of their most fundamental judgements about terrorists and their behaviour—have now been joined by a variety of rather different terrorist entities with arguably less comprehensible nationalist or ideological motivations. Many in this "new generation" of terrorist groups not only espouse far more amorphous religious and millenarian aims but are themselves less cohesive organizational bodies, with a more diffuse structure and membership. Even more disturbing is that in some instances their aims go far beyond the establishment of a theocracy amenable to their specific deity (e.g. the creation of an Iranian-style Islamic republic in Algeria, Egypt or Saudi Arabia) to embrace mystical, almost transcendental, and divinely inspired imperatives or a vehemently anti-government form of populism reflecting far-fetched conspiracy notions based on a volatile mixture of seditious, racial and religious dicta. In this respect, the emergence of obscure, idiosyncratic millenarian movements (such as the Japanese Aum Shinrikyo religious sect, which committed the March 1995 nerve gas attack on the Tokyo underground, and the militantly anti-government Christian white supremacist militias that have surfaced in the United States, implicated in the Oklahoma City bombing) alongside zealously nationalist religious groups (such as the Islamic extremists who carried out the World Trade Center bombing, the Algerian GIA and the Lebanese Hezbollah, with its links to various shadowy Egyptian and Saudi extremist groups) represents a very different and potentially far more lethal threat than the more familiar, "traditional" terrorist groups.

Indeed, while some observers point optimistically to the decline in the number of international terrorist incidents during the 1990s as an especially noteworthy and salutary development in the struggle against terrorism, at the same time the proportion of persons killed in terrorist incidents has paradoxically—and alarmingly—increased. According to the RAND–St Andrews Chronology, a record 484 international terrorist incidents were recorded in 1991, the year of the Gulf War, followed by 343 incidents in 1992, 360 in 1993 and 353 in 1994, falling to 278 incidents in 1995 (the last calendar year for which complete statistics are available). But while terrorists were becoming less active, they were also becoming more lethal. For example, at least one person was killed in 29 per cent of terrorist incidents in 1995: the highest ratio of fatalities to incidents recorded in the Chronology since 1968, and an increase of 2 per cent over the previous year's record figure.[7] By comparison, only 17 per cent of international terrorist incidents in the 1970s killed anyone, and just 19 per cent in the 1980s. Whether this development represents an enduring trend or not remains unclear. It nonetheless provides evidence for the assertion that international terrorism is more lethal today than it has been in the past and therefore raises the question: why this is so?

Among the various factors that account for terrorism's increasing lethality (including the terrorist's perennial quest for attention; the increased prevalence of state sponsorship and the greater resources thereby accorded terrorists; developments in terrorist weaponry, which is getting smaller, more easy to conceal and more powerful; and the increasing sophistication of professional terrorism), the most significant is perhaps the dramatic proliferation of terrorist groups motivated by a religious imperative. This suggestion is borne out by the pattern of international terrorism during 1995. As previously noted, although religious terrorists committed only 25 per cent of the recorded international terrorist incidents in 1995, they were responsible for 58 per cent of the total number of fatalities recorded that year. Looking at the data from another perspective, those attacks that caused the greatest numbers of deaths in 1995 (incidents that killed eight or more persons) were all perpetrated by religious terrorists.

We have already noted that since the mid-1980s it has been religious terrorists or members of either mainstream religious movements or smaller "cults" in the United States and Israel who have come closest to crossing the threshold of terrorist use of WMD, or evidence the traits and tactical abilities required to carry out such attacks. . . .

. . . Indeed, the Aum sect's nerve gas attack on the Tokyo subway arguably crossed an important psychological threshold so far as terrorist use and potential use of WMD is concerned: for this incident clearly demonstrated that it is possible to execute a successful chemical terrorist attack, and may conceivably have raised the stakes for terrorists everywhere. Terrorist groups in the future may well feel driven to emulate or surpass the Tokyo incident, either in levels of death and destruction caused or in the use of a non-conventional weapon of mass destruction in order to ensure the same, if not greater, media coverage and public attention as the 1995 attack generated.

The proliferation of religious terrorism also raises a number of other disquieting possibilities and consequences, given that the members of many of these groups, sects and cults are what might be described as "amateur" terrorists in contrast to the relatively small number of "professionals" who have dominated terrorism in the past. Previously, terrorism was not just a matter of having the will and motivation to act, but of having the capability to do so—the requisite training, access to weaponry and operational knowledge. These were not necessarily readily available, and were generally acquired through training undertaken in camps known to be run either by other terrorist organizations or in concert with the terrorists' state sponsors. Today, however, information on the means and methods of terrorism can be easily obtained at bookstores, from mail-order publishers, on CD-ROM or even over the Internet. . .

Terrorism has thus arguably become accessible to anyone with a grievance, an agenda, a purpose or any idiosyncratic combination of the above. . . We have also seen that the intention of the bombers of the World Trade Center in 1993 is believed to have been to bring down one of the 110-storey twin towers on top of the other and to release into the damaged tower a toxic cloud of sodium cyanide that allegedly would have killed any survivors of the initial blast. According to the judge who presided over the bombers' trial, had they succeeded, the sodium cyanide in the bomb would have been "sucked into the north tower," thus killing everyone there.[8] By comparison, there is no evidence that the secular or "professional" terrorists of the past—the persons once considered to be the world's arch-terrorists, such as the Carloses, Abu Nidals and Abul Abbases—ever contemplated, much less attempted, the complete destruction of a high-rise office building packed with people, let alone further enhancing such an attack by deploying a chemical weapon.

Not only is the information necessary to undertake WMD attacks relatively easily accessible, but the availability of critical *matériel* may already have been facilitated by the proliferation of fissile materials from the former Soviet Union and the putative illicit market in nuclear materials that is reportedly emerging in Eastern and Central Europe. While much of the material believed to be on offer in this black market cannot be classified as strategic nuclear material (SNM), that is, suitable for use in the construction of a fissionable explosive device, such highly toxic radioactive agents could be paired with conventional explosives and turned into a crude, non-fissionable atomic bomb (known as a "dirty" bomb). For example, a combination fertilizer truck-bomb with radioactive agents could have not only destroyed one of the World Trade Center's towers, but also rendered a considerable chunk of prime real estate in one of the world's financial nerve centres indefinitely unusable because of radioactive contamination. The prospect not only of the resulting disruption to commerce, but of the attendant publicity and enhanced coercive power of terrorists armed with such "dirty" bombs (arguably a more credible risk than terrorist acquisition of fissile nuclear weapons), is deeply disturbing.

The growth of religious terrorism and its emergence in recent years as a driving force behind the increasing lethality of international terrorism shatters some of our most basic assumptions about terrorists and the violence they commit. It also raises serious questions about the continued relevance of much of the conventional wisdom on terrorism—particularly as it pertains to potential future terrorist use of WMD. In the past, most analyses of the possibility of mass indiscriminate killing involving chemical, biological, radiological or nuclear terrorism tended to discount it, for reasons surveyed above. Few terrorists, it was argued, know anything about the technical intricacies of either developing or dispersing such weapons. Political, moral and practical considerations were also perceived as important restraints on terrorist use of such weapons. Terrorists, we assured ourselves, wanted more people watching than dead. Therefore we believed that terrorists had little interest in and still less to gain from killing wantonly and indiscriminately.

While some of these arguments may still have force in respect of most secular terrorists, incidents like the nerve gas attack on the Tokyo subway and the World Trade Center and Oklahoma City bombings in particular—alongside some of the other attacks perpetrated by religious terrorists and additional plots that went awry—appear to render them dangerously anachronistic. In sum, compelling new motives, notably those associated with religious terrorism, coupled with increased access to critical information and key components, notably involving WMD, leading to enhanced terrorist capabilities, could portend an even bloodier and more destructive era of violence ahead than any we have seen before.

A DISQUIETING TRAJECTORY

Events in Kenya and Tanzania, Afghanistan and the Sudan in August 1998 demonstrate clearly that terrorism is—and will remain—one of the main threats to international security as we approach the twenty-first century. The tragic embassy bombings in Nairobi and Dar es Salaam underscore with particular force that terrorism is among the most fluid and dynamic of political phenomena: one constantly evolving into new and ever more dangerous forms in order to evade existing security procedures and surmount the defensive barriers placed in its path. At the same time, the dramatic American cruise missile attacks on terrorist training camps in Afghanistan and a pharmaceutical factory alleged to be manufacturing chemical weapons in the Sudan serve as timely reminders of how difficult and complex a problem terrorism is, and how governmental responses must accordingly be both innovative and multi-faceted if they are to achieve any demonstrable effect. Any government's ability to craft an effective response to terrorist attack and provocation will inevitably depend on its ability fully to understand the fundamental changes that distinguish today's terrorists from their predecessors. Only in this way can the array of required countermeasures be first identified and then brought to bear with genuinely positive results.

The two embassy attacks conform to an emerging trend in international terrorism: the infliction of mass, indiscriminate casualties by enigmatic adversaries striking far beyond terrorism's traditional operational theatres in Europe and the Middle East. As we have seen, terrorism was formerly practised by distinct organizational entities with established chains of command and a defined set of political, social or economic objectives. These groups also often issued communiqués taking credit for—and explaining in great detail—their actions.[9] Hence, however disagreeable or distasteful their aims and motivations may have been, their ideology and intentions—albeit politically radical and personally fanatical—were at least comprehensible.

Most significantly, however, these more familiar terrorist groups engaged in highly selective and mostly discriminate acts of violence directed against a comparatively narrow range of targets. Moreover, only rarely did these groups venture outside their self-proclaimed operational area (in the main, their own or neighbouring countries, established international centres, or global crossroads of diplomacy and commerce) to carry out attacks: Palestinian and Lebanese terrorists frequently operated in Europe, and on occasion the IRA might strike in Germany or the ETA in France. Thus, for nearly three decades, the locus of *international* terrorism remained firmly entrenched in Europe and the Middle East. Only occasionally did it spill over into Asia and Latin America; Africa remained almost untouched.

Finally, these groups were often numerically small. According to the US Department of Defense, neither the Japanese Red Army nor the Red Army Faction ever numbered more than twenty to thirty hard-core members. The Red Brigades were only slightly larger, with a total of fewer than fifty to seventy-five dedicated terrorists. Even the IRA and ETA were unlikely to be able to call on the violent services of more than two hundred to four hundred activists, while the feared Abu Nidal Organization was limited to some five hundred men-at-arms at any given time.[10]

The two embassy attacks diverged dramatically from these established patterns. First, rather than attempting either to limit casualties or to strike specifically at the citizens of their self-proclaimed enemy state, the bombers were clearly prepared to inflict random, widespread collateral casualties among the hundreds of Kenyan and Tanzanian embassy employees and ordinary passersby in pursuit of their objective.

Second, the bombings occurred in a region of the world that had hitherto remained—mercifully—outside the maelstrom of international terrorism. Indeed, the masterminds behind the attacks probably regarded Kenya and Tanzania as irresistibly attractive operational environments for precisely this reason. Both countries, they doubtless believed, were unschooled in the vast array of counterterrorist measures routinely deployed in other parts of the world and were therefore unattuned to the need for eternal vigilance against the transnational terrorist threats so prevalent elsewhere. This factor alone must send disquieting reverberations to other parts of the globe as yet unaffected by international terrorism. *No* country can any longer feel completely secure. In 1992 and again in 1994, Argentina—another state located in a part of the world traditionally outside the ambit of international terrorism—became tragically enmeshed in far-distant struggles with the massive truck bombings of the

Israeli embassy in Buenos Aires and, two years later, of a Jewish community centre in the same city.

Third, the bombings themselves do not appear to have been undertaken by a specific existing or identifiable terrorist organization. Instead, the Kenyan and Tanzanian attacks are believed to have been financed by a millionaire Saudi Arabian dissident, Osama bin Laden, as part of his worldwide campaign against the United States. In the months before the bombings, bin Laden not only publicly declared war on the United States because of its support for Israel and the presence of American military forces in Saudi Arabia, but had issued a *fatwa*, thereby endowing his calls for violence with an incontrovertible theological as well as political justification. In the wake of this edict, an estimated four to five thousand individuals scattered throughout the Muslim world are reported to have pledged their loyalty to bin Laden and are allegedly prepared to follow his summons to battle.

Fourth, in contrast to the explicit, intelligible demands of the familiar, predominantly secular terrorist groups, most of which in the past claimed credit for and explained their violent acts, no credible claim of responsibility for the embassy bombings has ever been issued. To date, the only information that has come to light has been in the form of a vague message justifying the bombings in terms of defending the Muslim holy places in Mecca and Medina and promising to "pursue US forces and strike at US interests everywhere."[11] The resurgence of terrorism motivated by a religious imperative could hardly be more palpable.

Finally, this type of indiscriminate attack by an enigmatic adversary, accompanied by hazy claims and broad demands, is typical of a pattern of international terrorism observed increasingly in recent years, whereby an *ad hoc* gathering of like-minded individuals appears to be brought together for a specific mission—sometimes only a one-off—for which they emerge from obscurity and after which they are meant to vanish as suddenly into thin air. This trend represents a very different threat from that posed by the more familiar, traditional terrorist adversaries—and one potentially far more lethal.

The absence of any publicly identified central command authority may play a critical role in removing any inhibitions on the terrorists' intention to inflict widespread, indiscriminate casualties. Further, the anonymity intrinsic to this type of operation, coupled with the lack of a discernible organizational structure with a distinguishable command chain behind the attackers (as was common to terrorist groups in the past), is deliberately designed both to thwart easy identification and to facilitate the perpetrators' escape and evasion of detection. The main evidence linking bin Laden to the embassy bombings came in the first instance from a Palestinian or Jordanian man arrested in Pakistan, who arrived from Kenya on the day of the explosions travelling on a false Yemeni passport. Had it not been for a fortuitously alert immigration official in Karachi, even this tenuous connection might never have materialized.

These new types of adversaries impose new limits on the means and measures that the United States and other similarly afflicted nations can bring to bear in countering them. The so-called "privatization" of terrorism, encapsulated by bin Laden's allegedly pivotal role in funding and supporting anti-American terrorism worldwide and the East Africa bombings in particular, raises a new battery of problems that are certain to make combating terrorism even more difficult than it has been in the past. . . .

In countering and deterring these future terrorist threats, the most urgent and pressing need is continually to improve intelligence capabilities. Just as terrorism itself is dynamic and constantly evolving, so too must governmental capabilities and responses improve and adapt. In no area is this more critical than in the realm of HUMINT—human intelligence. Clearly, the controversy that has raged over whether the Sudanese factory was actually manufacturing the chemical precursors to VX nerve gas is testimony to the need for up-to-date, completely accurate intelligence of a type obtainable only from reliable, on-the-spot agents and sources.

Success in the struggle against terrorism will to a large extent depend also on continued, and continually strengthened, international cooperation—as evident in the helpful assistance provided by Kenyan, Tanzanian and Pakistani authorities to the FBI and other American investigators. While this is an especially positive and welcome development, like much counterterrorist activity it is inherently reactive in nature and, in the case of the embassy bombings, akin to closing the barn door after the horse has escaped. In the future, therefore, if governments are effectively to prevent and pre-empt other such attacks, increased and strengthened multinational intelligence sharing and law enforcement cooperation on a more regular and systematic basis will be critical. Given the transnational dimension of many of these threats—for example, bin Laden's alleged complementary global financial and terror networks; the Aum Shinrikyo sect's activities not only in Japan but in Russia and Australia; and the network of Algerian Islamic extremists operating across Europe as well as in Algeria itself—any response that is to yield results will have to involve enhanced binational and multinational intelligence exchange, cooperation over extradition, the enactment of more formal accords and treaties both between individual countries and on a more comprehensive basis, and the coordination of national policies to monitor, prevent, pre-empt and judicially resolve terrorist acts. The UN resolution passed in December 1997 that denned indiscriminate attacks on civilians, such as those caused by bombings, as terrorist acts is clearly a step in the right direction.

At the same time, perhaps the most sobering realization that arises from addressing the phenomenon of terrorism is that the threat and the problems that fuel it can never be eradicated completely. Their complexity, diversity and often idiosyncratic characteristics mean that there is no magic bullet, no single solution to be found and applied *pari passu*. This conclusion, however, reinforces the need for creative solutions if not to solve, then at least to ameliorate both the underlying causes and the violent manifestations. Only in this way will the international community be able prudently, effectively and productively to marshal its resources where and against whom they will have the greatest positive effect.

In sum, the emergence of this new breed of terrorist adversary means that nothing less than a sea-change in our thinking about terrorism and the policies required to counter it will be required. Too often in the past we have lulled ourselves into believing that terrorism was among the least serious or complex of security issues. We cannot afford to go on making this mistake. . . .

Notes

1. Brian Michael Jenkins, *International Terrorism: The Other World War* (Santa Monica, CA: RAND Corporation, R-3302-AF, November 1985), p. 12.

2. Radiological terrorism involves *contamination* with readily available radioactive materials, for instance those used in medicine and commerce, as compared with nuclear terrorism, which implies an explosion caused by the chain reaction created by fissionable materials.

3. From time to time additional reports have surfaced, for example, that in 1979 RAF terrorists were being trained at Palestinian camps in Lebanon in the use of bacteriological weapons and earlier threats by the group to poison water supplies in twenty German towns if three radical lawyers were not permitted to defend an imprisoned RAF member; suspicions that in 1986 terrorists in India may have contemplated poisoning drinking water tanks there; and the letters sent to Western embassies by Tamil guerrillas in 1986 claiming to have poisoned Sri Lankan tea with potassium cyanide.

4. Admittedly, these are only those incidents or plots that we *definitely* know about and that have also been reported in open, published sources.

5. Brian Michael Jenkins, *The Likelihood of Nuclear Terrorism* (Santa Monica, CA: RAND Corporation, P-7119, July 1985), p. 6.

6. Brian Michael Jenkins, *Will Terrorists Go Nuclear?* (Santa Monica, CA: RAND Corporation, P-5541, November 1975), pp. 6–7.

7. Terrorist trends for 1994 provide a particularly good illustration of this development not only in terms of the previous record-setting percentage of fatalities to incidents, but also in that the total of 423 fatalities recorded that year was the fifth highest annual figure in the Chronology since 1968 (RAND–St Andrews Chronology of International Terrorist Incidents).

8. Tom Hays and Larry Neumeister, "Trade Center Bombers Get Life in Prison," Associated Press, 25 May 1994; Richard Bernstein, "Chemist Can't Pinpoint Bomb Contents at Trial," *New York Times;* 21 January 1994. See also Matthew L. Wald, "Figuring What it Would Take to Take Down a Tower," *New York Times,* 21 March 1993.

9. Rachel Ehrenfeld, *Narco-terrorism* (New York: Basic Books, 1990), pp. ix, xiii.

10. Two particularly informative discussions about the myth of "narco-terrorism" and the political baggage the term carried with it can be found in Grant Wardlaw, "Linkages Between the Illegal Drugs Traffic and Terrorism," *Conflict Quarterly,* Vol. 8, no. 3 (Summer 1988), pp. 5–26, and Abraham H. Miller and Nicholas A. Damask, "The Dual Myths of 'Narco-terrorism': How Myths Drive Policy," *Terrorism and Political Violence*, vol. 8, no.1 (Spring 1996), pp. 114–31.

11. Peter Lupsha, "Gray Area Phenomenon: New Threats and Policy Dilemmas," unpublished paper quoted by Ambassador Edwin G. Corr, "Introduction," in Max G. Manwaring (ed.), *Gray Area Phenomena: Confronting the New World Disorder* (Boulder, CO: Westview, 1993), p. xiii.

56

ROBERT O. KEOHANE

THE GLOBALIZATION
OF INFORMAL VIOLENCE

THE GLOBALIZATION OF INFORMAL VIOLENCE AND THE RECONCEPTUALIZATION OF SPACE

The various definitions of globalization in social science all converge on the notion that human activities across regions and continents are being increasingly linked together, as a result both of technological and social change (Held *et al.*: 15). Globalism as a state of affairs has been defined as "a state of the world involving networks of interdependence at multicontinental distances, linked through flows of capital and goods, information and ideas, people and force, as well as environmentally and biologically relevant substances" (Keohane and Nye 2001: 229).

When globalism is characterized as multidimensional, as in these definitions, the expansion of terrorism's global reach is an instance of globalization (Held *et al.* 1999: 80; Keohane and Nye 2001: 237). Often, globalism and globalization have been defined narrowly as economic integration on a global scale; but whatever appeal such a definition may have had, it has surely disappeared after September 11. To adopt it would be to imply that globalized informal violence, which takes advantage of modern technologies of communication, transportation, explosives, and potentially biology, somehow threatens to *hinder* or *reduce the level of* globalism. But like military technology between 1914 and 1945, globalized informal violence strengthens one dimension of globalism—the networks through which means of violence flow—while potentially weakening globalism along other dimensions, such as economic and social exchange. As in the past, not all aspects of globalization go together.

I define informal violence as violence by non-state actors, capitalizing on secrecy and surprise to inflict great harm with small material capabilities. Such violence is "informal" because it is not wielded by formal state institutions and it is typically not announced in advance, as in a declaration of war. Such violence becomes globalized when the networks of non-state actors operate on an intercontinental basis, so that acts of force in one society can be initiated and controlled from very distant points of the globe.

SOURCE: From *The Globalization of Informal Violence*, by Robert O. Keohane, pp. 273–277. Copyright 2002 Routledge.

The implications of the globalization of *formal* violence were profound for traditional conceptions of foreign policy in an earlier generation, particularly in the United States, which had so long been insulated by distance from invasion and major direct attack. The great expositors of classical realist theories of foreign policy in the United States, such as Walter Lippmann, began with the premise that defense of the "continental homeland" is "a universally recognized vital interest." Before World War II, threats to the homeland could only stem from other states that secured territory contiguous to that of the United States or that controlled ocean approaches to it. Hence the Monroe Doctrine of 1823 was the cornerstone of American national security policy. As Lippmann recognized in 1943, changes in the technologies of formal violence meant that security policy needed to be more ambitious: the United States would have to maintain coalitions with other great powers that would "form a combination of indisputably preponderant power" (Lippmann 1943: 88, 101). Nevertheless, Lippmann was able to retain a key traditional concept: that of a geographically defined defensive perimeter, which can be thought of as a set of concentric circles. If the United States were to control not only its own area but the circle surrounding that area, comprising littoral regions of Europe and Asia, its homeland would be secure.

The American strategists of the 1950s—led by Bernard Brodie, Thomas Schelling, and Albert Wohlstetter—had to rethink the concept of a defensive perimeter, as intercontinental ballistic missiles reduced the significance of distance: that is, as formal violence became globalized. John Herz (1959: 107–108) argued that nuclear weapons forced students of international politics to rethink sovereignty, territoriality, and the protective function of the state:

> With the advent of the atomic weapon, whatever remained of the impermeability of states seems to have gone for good. . . . Mencius, in ancient China, when asked for guidance in matters of defense and foreign policy by the ruler of a small state, is said to have counseled: "dig deeper your moats; build higher your walls; guard them along with your people." This remained the classical posture up to our age, when a Western sage, Bertrand Russell, could still, even in the interwar period, define power as a force radiating from one center and diminishing with the distance from that center until it finds an equilibrium with that of similar geographically anchored units. Now that power can destroy power from center to center everything is different.

September 11 signifies that informal violence has become globalized, just as formal, state-controlled violence became globalized, for the superpowers, during the 1950s. The globalization of informal violence was not *created* by September 11. Indeed, earlier examples, extending back to piracy in the 17th century, can be easily found. But the significance of globalization—of violence as well as economically and socially—is not its absolute newness but its increasing magnitude as a result of sharp declines in the costs of global communications and transportation (Keohane and Nye 2001:243–45).

Contemporary theorists of world politics face a challenge similar to that of this earlier generation: to understand the nature of world politics, and its connections to domestic politics, when what Herz called the "hard shell" of the state (Herz

1959: 22) has been shattered. Geographic space, which has been seen as a natural barrier and a locus for human barriers, now must be seen as a carrier as well.

The obsolescence of the barrier conception of geographic space has troubling implications for foreign policy. One of the strengths of realism in the United States has always been that it imposed limitations on American intervention abroad. By asking questions about whether vital national interests are involved in a particular situation abroad, realists have sought to counter the moralistic and messianic tendencies that periodically recur in American thinking. For Lippmann, the key to a successful foreign policy was achieving a "balance, with a comfortable surplus of power in reserve, [between] the nation's commitment and the nation's power" (Lippmann 1943: 9). Going abroad "in search of monsters to destroy" upset that balance.[1] Realism provided a rationale for "just saying no" to advocates of intervening, for their own ideological or self-interested reasons, in areas of conflict far from the United States. It is worthwhile to be reminded that Lippmann, Hans J. Morgenthau and Kenneth N. Waltz were all early opponents of the war in Vietnam. Unfortunately, this realist caution, salutary as it has been, is premised on the barrier conception of geographical space. In the absence of clear and defensible criteria that American leaders can use to distinguish vital from non-vital interests, the United States is at risk of intervening throughout the world in a variety of conflicts bearing only tangential relationships to "terrorism with a global reach."

The globalization of informal violence, carried out by networks of non-state actors, defined by commitments rather than by territory, has profoundly changed these fundamental foreign policy assumptions.[2] On traditional grounds of national interest, Afghanistan should be one of the least important places in the world for American foreign policy—and until the Soviet invasion of 1979, and again after the collapse of the Soviet Union in 1991 until September 11, the United States all but ignored it. Yet in October 2001 it became the theatre of war. Globalization means, among other things, that threats of violence to our homeland can occur from anywhere. The barrier conception of geographical space, already anachronistic with respect to thermonuclear war and called into question by earlier acts of globalized informal violence, was finally shown to be thoroughly obsolete on September 11.

INTERDEPENDENCE AND POWER

Another way to express the argument made above is that networks of interdependence, involving transmission of informal violence, have now taken a genuinely global form. Using this language helps us to see the relevance for the globalization of informal violence of the literature on interdependence and power, which was originally developed to understand international political economy. In that literature, interdependence is conceptualized as mutual dependence, and power is conceptualized in terms of *asymmetrical interdependence*.[3] This literature has also long been clear that "military power dominates economic power in the sense that economic means alone are likely to be ineffective against the serious use of military force" (Keohane and Nye 2001:14).

September 11 revealed how much the United States could be hurt by informal violence, to an extent that had been anticipated by some government reports but that had not been incorporated into the plans of the government.[4] The long-term vulnerability of the United States is not entirely clear, but the availability of means of mass destruction, the extent of hatred for the United States, and the ease of entering the United States from almost anywhere in the world, all suggest that vulnerability may be quite high.

If the United States were facing a territorial state with conventional objectives, this vulnerability might not be a source of worry. After all, the United States has long been much more vulnerable, in technological terms, to a nuclear attack from Russia. But the United States was not *asymmetrically vulnerable.* On the contrary, the United States either had superior nuclear capability or "mutual assured destruction" (MAD) kept vulnerability more or less symmetrical. Russia has controlled great *force,* but has not acquired power over the United States from its arsenal.

With respect to terrorism, however, two asymmetries, which do not normally characterize relationships between states, favored wielders of informal violence in September 2001. First, there was an *asymmetry of information.* It seems paradoxical that an "information society" such as that of the contemporary United States would be at an informational disadvantage with respect to networks of individuals whose communications seem to occur largely through hand-written messages and face-to-face contacts. But an information society is also an open society. Potential terrorists had good information about their targets, while before September 11 the United States had poor information about the identity and location of terrorist networks within the United States and other Western societies. Perhaps equally important, the United States was unable coherently to process the information that its various agencies had gathered. Second, there is an *asymmetry in beliefs.* Some of Osama bin Laden's followers apparently believed that they would be rewarded in the afterlife for committing suicidal attacks on civilians. Others were duped into participating in the attacks without being told of their suicidal purpose. Clearly, the suicidal nature of the attacks made them more difficult to prevent and magnified their potential destructive power. Neither volunteering for suicide missions nor deliberately targeting civilians is consistent with secular beliefs widely shared in the societies attacked by al-Qaeda.

The United States and its allies have enormous advantages in resources, including military power, economic resources, political influence, and technological capabilities. Furthermore, communications media, largely based in the West, give greater weight to the voices of people in the wealthy democracies than to those of the dispossessed in developing countries. Hence the asymmetries in information and beliefs that I have mentioned are, in a sense, exceptional. They do not confer a permanent advantage on the wielders of informal violence. Yet they were sufficient to give the terrorists at least a short-term advantage, and they make terrorism a long-term threat.

Our failure to anticipate the impact of terrorist attacks does not derive from a fundamental conceptual failure in thinking about power. On the contrary, the power of terrorists, like that of states, derives from asymmetrical patterns of interdependence. Our fault has rather been our failure to understand that the most powerful state ever to exist on this planet could be vulnerable to small bands of terrorists due to patterns of asymmetrical interdependence. *We have overemphasized states and we have over-aggregated power.*

Power comes not simply out of the barrel of a gun, but from asymmetries in vulnerability interdependence—some of which, it turns out, favor certain non-state actors more than most observers anticipated. The networks of interdependence along which power can travel are multiple, and they do not cancel one another out. Even a state that is overwhelmingly powerful on many dimensions can be highly vulnerable on others. We learned this lesson in the 1970s with respect to oil power; we are re-learning it now with respect to terrorism.

NOTES

1. From a Fourth of July oration by John Quincy Adamas at the Capitol in 1821. Perkins 1993: 149–50.
2. A few pessimistic and prescient observers understood that terrorism could pose a threat to the United States homeland despite our dominance in military power. See Carter and Perry 1999, and the Hart–Rudman Report, Phase I, September 15, 1999, Conclusion 1.
3. In 1977 Joseph Nye and I distinguished between two types of dependence, which we labeled (following the contemporary literature on economic interdependence) sensitivity and vulnerability dependence. Sensitivity dependence refers to "liability to costly effects imposed from outside before policies are altered to try to change the situation." Vulnerability dependence, in contrast, refers to "an actor's liability to suffer costs imposed by external events even after policies have been altered." This language seems inappropriate in the contemporary situation, since in ordinary language, the attacks on an unprepared United States on September 11 demonstrated how vulnerable the country was. But the distinction between levels of dependence before and after policy change remains important. See Keohane and Nye 2001: 11; the text is unchanged from the 1st edition, 1977.
4. My colleague Ole Holsti has pointed out to me that in surveys conducted by the Chicago Council on Foreign Relations in 1994 and 1998, the public more often regarded international terrorism as a "critical" foreign policy issue than did leaders. Indeed, 69% and 84%, respectively, of the public regarded terrorism as a critical issue in those years, compared to 33% and 61% of the elites. See Holsti 2000: 21.

REFERENCES

Held, David and Anthony McGrew, David Goldblatt, and Jonathan Perraton, 1999. *Global Transformations.* Stanford: Stanford University Press.

Herz, John H. 1959. *International Politics in the Atomic Age.* New York: Columbia University Press.

Keohane, Robert O. and Joseph S. Nye. 2001. *Power and Interdependence. 3rd edition.* New York: Addison Wesley Longman.

Lippmann, Walter. 1943. *US Foreign Policy: Shield of the Republic.* Boston: Little, Brown.

57

JOHN ARQUILLA AND
DAVID RONFELDT

THE SHARPENING FIGHT
FOR THE FUTURE

If Osama bin Laden's al-Qaeda network is the principal adversary—as seems likely, although other possibilities, including sponsorship by a rogue state like Iraq, cannot be discarded yet—then it may prove useful to view the network from the perspective of the five levels of theory and practice . . . (organizational, narrative, doctrinal, technological, and social).[1] First, at the organizational level, we see a major confrontation between hierarchical/state and networked/nonstate actors. For the United States and its friends and allies, one challenge will be to learn to network better with each other. Some of this is already going on, in terms of intelligence sharing, but much more must be done to build a globally operational counterterror network. A particular challenge for the cumbersome American bureaucracy will be to encourage deep, all-channel networking among the military, law enforcement, and intelligence elements whose collaboration is crucial for achieving success. U.S. agencies have been headed in this direction for years—in the areas of counter-narcotics as well as counterterrorism—but interagency rivalries and distrust have too often slowed progress.

Regarding al-Qaeda, the organizational challenge seems to lie in determining whether this network is a single hub designed around bin Laden. If this is the case, then his death or capture would signal its defeat. However, the more a terrorist network takes the form of a multi-hub "spider's web" design, with multiple centers and peripheries, the more redundant and resilient it will be—and the harder to defeat.[2] In a somewhat analogous vein, it is worthwhile to note that since Napster's activities were curtailed by legal action in the United States, more free music is being downloaded and shared by loose peer-to-peer networks. Also, note that, despite the dismantling of the powerful Medellín and Cali cartels during the 1990s, drug smuggling by a plethora of small organizations continues to flourish in Colombia. The risk is that small, more nimble networks may spring up as successors to a defeated large network.

Second, at the narrative level, there is the broad contention of Western liberal ideas about the spread of free markets, free peoples, and open societies ver-

SOURCE: From *Networks and Netwars*, Ed. by Arquilla and Ronfeldt, pp. 364–369. Copyright 2001 The Rand Corporation.

sus Muslim convictions about the exploitative, invasive, demeaning nature of Western incursions into the Islamic world. To use Samuel Huntington's phrase, this conflict involves a "clash of civilizations." Also, at the narrative level it might be deemed a "time war" (term from Rifkin, 1987), in that this terrorist mindset is, in a sense, so tribal, medieval, absolutist, and messianic that it represents an effort to challenge the 21st century with 16th century (and earlier) ideals—as well as to ruin Americans' hopes about their future. Indeed, it may be advisable for U.S. strategy to approach this conflict more as a time war than as a clash of civilizations. Bin Laden is an Arab Muslim, but that is not the only context in which to view him. He resembles, in many respects, some of the more fanatical figures out of Norman Cohn's *The Pursuit of the Millennium* (1961)[3] and Eric Hoffer's *The True Believer* (1951).[4] Bin Laden is not clinically "insane," but he and his appeal are culturally and temporally perverse.[5]

To this basic imagery, the United States has made a point of adding that these terrorist attacks were "acts of war" against not only America but also against "the civilized world," and American public opinion has been quickly galvanized by the revival of the Pearl Harbor metaphor. Indeed, the disproportionate nature of the terrorists' use of force—including the mass murder of civilians—can only reinforce feelings of righteous indignation. Against this, the perpetrators are likely to exalt their own "holy war" imagery, which they will have trouble exploiting beyond the Islamic world—and they cannot do even that well as long as they remain concealed behind a veil of anonymity. But while the United States may have the edge in the "battle of the story" in much of the world, it will have to think deeply about how to keep that edge if U.S. forces are sent into action in any Middle Eastern countries. The development of the new field of "information strategy" is needed more than ever (see Arquilla and Ronfeldt, 1999, including the notion of creating "special media forces").

Third, in terms of doctrine, the al-Qaeda network seems to have a grasp of the nonlinear nature of the battlespace, and of the value of attack from multiple directions by dispersed small units. If this is indeed a war being waged by al-Qaeda, its first campaign was no doubt the bombing of the Khobar Towers in Saudi Arabia in 1996, followed by a sharp shift to Africa with the embassy bombings of 1998. In between, and since, there have been a number of other skirmishes in far-flung locales, with some smaller attacks succeeding, and others apparently having been prevented by good intelligence. Thus, bin Laden and his cohorts appear to have developed a swarm-like doctrine that features a campaign of episodic, pulsing attacks by various nodes of his network—at locations sprawled across global time and space where he has advantages for seizing the initiative, stealthily.[6]

Against this doctrine, the United States has seemingly little to pose, as yet. Some defensive efforts to increase "force protection" have been pursued, and missile strikes in Afghanistan and the Sudan in 1998 suggest that the offensive part of U.S. doctrine is based on aging notions of strategic bombardment. Needless to say, if our ideas about netwar, swarming, and the future of conflict are on the mark, the former is not likely to be a winning approach; a whole new doctrine based on small-unit swarming concepts should be developed. It is possible that the notion of "counterleadership targeting" will continue to be featured—this was tried against Moammar Qaddafi in 1986, Saddam Hussein in 1991, Mohamed Aidid in 1993, and against bin Laden himself in 1998. Every effort to date has failed,[7] but that may not keep the United States from trying yet again, as this seems a part of its doctrinal paradigm. Besides, if bin Laden is the only hub of the al-Qaeda network—possible, though unlikely—his death, capture, or extradition might turn the tide in this conflict.

Fourth, at the technological level, the United States possesses a vast array of very advanced systems, while al-Qaeda has relatively few—and has great and increasing reluctance to use advanced telecommunications because of the risks of detection and tracking. But this category cannot be analyzed quite so simply. The United States, for example, has extensive "national technical means" for gathering intelligence and targeting information—but perhaps only a small portion of these means have utility against dispersed, networked terrorists. Orbital assets—now the linchpins of American intelligence—may prove of little use against bin Laden. At the same time, al-Qaeda has access to commercial off-the-shelf technologies that may prove a boon to their operations.

Fifth, at the social level, this network features tight religious and kinship bonds among the terrorists, who share a tribal, clannish view of "us" versus "them." Al-Qaeda's edge in this dimension ties into its narrative level, with Islam being the pivot between the story of "holy war" against "infidels" and the network's ability to recruit and deploy hate-filled, death-bound strike forces who evince a singleness of mind and purpose. Against this, the United States faces a profound defensive challenge at the social level: How will the American people, despite the arousal of nationalism, react to the potential need to become a less open society in order to become, more secure? If the Pearl Harbor metaphor—key to the American narrative dimension—holds up, and if U.S. operations result in successful early counterstrikes, then there may be unusual public solidarity to sustain the "war against terrorism" at the social level. But something of a social divide may emerge between the United States and Europe over whether the response to the attack on America should be guided by a "war" or a "law enforcement" paradigm.

In summary, a netwar perspective on the various dimensions of the struggle with al-Qaeda—again, *if* this is indeed the key adversary, or one of the them—renders some interesting insights into both the context and conduct of this first major conflict of the new millennium. At present, bin Laden and al-Qaeda seem to hold advantages at the social and doctrinal levels, and apparently in the organizational domain as well. The United States and its allies probably hold only marginal advantages at the narrative and technological levels. In terms of strategy, there appears to be less room for al-Qaeda to improve. However, its sound doctrinal and solid social underpinnings might be further enhanced—and a vulnerability removed—if it moved further away from being a hub network revolving around bin Laden. Indeed, this may be an optimal strategy for al-Qaeda, since it is delimited from waging an open "battle of the story" at the narrative level, its one other apparent strategic option.

For the United States and its allies, there is much room for improvement—most of all at the organizational and doctrinal levels. Simply put, the West must start to build its own networks and must learn to swarm the enemy, in order to keep it on the run or pinned down until it can be destroyed. The United States and its allies must also seize the initiative—including by applying pressure on any states that harbor or sponsor terrorists. To be sure, the edge at the narrative level in the world at large must be maintained, but this should be achievable with an economy of effort. The crucial work needs to be done in developing an innovative concept of operations and building the right kinds of networks to carry off a swarming campaign against networked terrorists. Because, at its heart, netwar is far more about organization and doctrine than it is about technology. The outcomes of current and future netwars are bound to confirm this.

NOTES

1. Joel Garreau, "Disconnect the Dots," *Washington Post,* September 17, 2001, offers additional discussion, based an interviews with social network analysts, about how to attack a terrorist network.
2. A study with inputs from various researchers, "Special Report: Al-Qaeda," *Jane's Intelligence Review,* August 2001, pp. 42–51, provides an extensive analysis of al-Qaeda's organizational structure, history, and activities. The analysis views al-Qaeda as a kind of "conglomerate," with both formal vertical and informal horizontal elements, making it a partial hybrid of hierarchical and network forms of organization.
3. Consider this statement from Cohn (1961, pp. 314–315) about messianic religious fanaticism, known as chiliasm, that coursed through Europe in the Middle Ages:

   In the Middle Ages, the people for whom revolutionary Chiliasm had most appeal were neither peasants firmly integrated in the village and manor nor artisans firmly integrated in their guilds. The lot of such people might at times be one of poverty and oppression, and at other times be one of relative prosperity and independence; they might revolt or they might accept the situation; but they were not, on the whole, prone to follow some inspired *propheta* in a hectic pursuit of the Millennium. . . . Revolutionary Chiliasm drew its strength from the surplus population living on the margin of society—peasants without land or with too little land even for subsistence; journeymen and unskilled workers living under the continuous threat of unemployment; beggars and vagabonds. . . . These people lacked the material and emotional support afforded by traditional social groups; their kinship-groups had disintegrated and they were not effectively organized in village communities or in guilds; for them there existed no regular, institutionalized methods of voicing their grievances or pressing their claims. Instead, they waited for a *propheta* to bind them together in a group of their own—which would then emerge as a movement of a peculiar kind, driven on by a wild enthusiasm born of desperation.

4. Consider this statement by Hoffer (1951) (from a Harper Perennial edition of Hoffer's book issued in 1989, pp. 11–12) about "true believers" who enter into radical mass movements:

   For men to plunge headlong into an undertaking of vast change, they must be intensely discontented yet not destitute, and they must have the feeling that by the possession of some potent doctrine, infallible leader or some new technique they have access to a source of irresistible power. They must have an extravagant conception of the prospects and potentialities of the future. Finally, they must be ignorant of the difficulties involved in their vast undertaking. . . .

> On the one hand, a mass movement. . . appeals not to those intent on bolstering and advancing a cherished self, but to those who crave to be rid of an unwanted self. A mass movement attracts and holds a following not because it can satisfy the desire for self-advancement, but because it can satisfy the passion for self-renunciation.

5. A further comparison, drawn from Greek myth and tragedy, is that bin Laden aims to be the *Nemesis* of American *hubris*. This goddess of divine retribution is sent by Zeus to destroy mortals afflicted with this capital sin of pride, the pretension to be godlike. However, bin Laden may yet reveal that he has a "hubris-nemesis complex." For background, see Ronfeldt (1994).
6. For recent additions to the theoretical literature, see Johnson (2001) on "swarm logic," and Bonabeau and Meyer (2001) on "swarm intelligence." Swarming may benefit from advances in "peer-to-peer computing." On this, see Oram (2001).
7. The Russians succeeded in killing Dzhokhar Dudayev during the first (1994–1996) Chechen War—apparently triangulating on him while he used a cell phone—but the networked Chechens did quite well in that war, even without their "leader."

REFERENCES

Arquilla, John, and David Ronfeldt, *The Emergence of Noopolitik: Toward an American Information Strategy,* Santa Monica, Calif.: RAND, MR-1033-OSD, 1999.

Arquilla, John, David Ronfeldt, and Michele Zanini, "Information-Age Terrorism," *Current History,* Vol. 99, No. 636, April 2000, pp. 179–185.

Bonabeau, Eric, and Christopher Meyer, "Swarm Intelligence," *Harvard Business Review,* May 2001, pp. 107–114.

Cohn, Norman, *The Pursuit of the Millennium: Revolutionary Messianism in Medieval and Reformation Europe and Its Bearing on Modern Totalitarian Movements,* New York: Harper Torch Books, 1961.

Hoffer, Eric, *The True Believer: Thoughts on the Nature of Mass Movements,* New York: Harper & Row, 1951.

Johnson, Steven, *Emergence: The Connected Lives of Ants, Brains, Cities, and Software,* New York: Scribner, 2001.

Lesser, Ian O., Bruce Hoffman, John Arquilla, David Ronfeldt, Michele Zanini, and Brian Jenkins, *Countering the New Terrorism,* Santa Monica, Calif.: RAND, MR-989-AF, 1999.

Oram, Andy, ed., *Peer-to-Peer: Harnessing the Power of Disruptive Technologies,* O'Reilly & Associates, 2001.

Rifkin, Jeremy, *Time Wars: The Primary Conflict in Human History,* New York: Simon & Schuster, 1987.

Ronfeldt, David, *The Hubris-Nemesis Complex: A Concept for Leadership Analysis,* Santa Monica, Calif.: RAND, MR-461, 1994.

Ronfeldt, David, and John Arquilla, "Networks, Netwars, and the Fight for the Future," *First Monday,* October 2001, Vol. 6, No. 10, http://firstmonday.org/issue6_10/index.html.

58

THOMAS HOMER-DIXON

THE RISE OF COMPLEX TERRORISM

[Since September 11, 2001,] we've realized, belatedly, that our societies are wide-open targets for terrorists. We're easy prey because of two key trends: First, the growing technological capacity of small groups and individuals to destroy things and people; and, second, the increasing vulnerability of our economic and technological systems to carefully aimed attacks. While commentators have devoted considerable ink and airtime to the first of these trends, they've paid far less attention to the second, and they've virtually ignored their combined effect. Together, these two trends facilitate a new and sinister kind of mass violence—a "complex terrorism" that threatens modern, high-tech societies in the world's most developed nations.

Our fevered, Hollywood-conditioned imaginations encourage us to focus on the sensational possibility of nuclear or biological attacks—attacks that might kill tens of thousands of people in a single strike. These threats certainly deserve attention, but not to the neglect of the likelier and ultimately deadlier disruptions that could result from the clever exploitation by terrorists of our societies' new and growing complexities.

WEAPONS OF MASS DISRUPTION

The steady increase in the destructive capacity of small groups and individuals is driven largely by three technological advances: more powerful weapons, the dramatic progress in communications and information processing, and more abundant opportunities to divert nonweapon technologies to destructive ends.

Consider first the advances in weapons technology. Over the last century, progress in materials engineering, the chemistry of explosives, and miniaturization of electronics has brought steady improvement in all key weapons characteristics, including accuracy, destructive power, range, portability, ruggedness, ease-of-use, and affordability. Improvements in light weapons are particularly relevant to trends in terrorism and violence by small groups, where the devices of choice include rocket-propelled grenade launchers, machine guns, light mortars, land mines, and cheap assault rifles such as the famed

SOURCE: From *Foreign Policy*, No. 128, January/February 2002, pp. 52–62. Reprinted with permission of Foreign Policy. www.foreignpolicy.com.

AK-47. The effects of improvements in these weapons are particularly noticeable in developing countries. A few decades ago, a small band of terrorists or insurgents attacking a rural village might have used bolt-action rifles, which take precious time to reload. Today, cheap assault rifles multiply the possible casualties resulting from such an attack. As technological change makes it easier to kill, societies are more likely to become locked into perpetual cycles of attack and counterattack that render any normal trajectory of political and economic development impossible.

Meanwhile, new communications technologies—from satellite phones to the Internet—allow violent groups to marshal resources and coordinate activities around the planet. Transnational terrorist organizations can use the Internet to share information on weapons and recruiting tactics, arrange surreptitious fund transfers across borders, and plan attacks. These new technologies can also dramatically enhance the reach and power of age-old procedures. Take the ancient *hawala* system of moving money between countries, widely used in Middle Eastern and Asian societies. The system, which relies on brokers linked together by clan-based networks of trust, has become faster and more effective through the use of the Internet.

Information-processing technologies have also boosted the power of terrorists by allowing them to hide or encrypt their messages. The power of a modern laptop computer today is comparable to the computational power available in the entire U.S. Defense Department in the mid-1960s. Terrorists can use this power to run widely available state-of-the-art encryption software. Sometimes less advanced computer technologies are just as effective. For instance, individuals can use a method called steganography ("hidden writing") to embed messages into digital photographs or music clips. Posted on publicly available Web sites, the photos or clips are downloaded by collaborators as necessary. (This technique was reportedly used by recently arrested terrorists when they planned to blow up the U.S. Embassy in Paris.) At latest count, 140 easy-to-use steganography tools were available on the Internet. Many other off-the-shelf technologies—such as "spread-spectrum" radios that randomly switch their broadcasting and receiving signals—allow terrorists to obscure their messages and make themselves invisible.

The Web also provides access to critical information. The September 11 terrorists could have found there all the details they needed about the floor plans and design characteristics of the World Trade Center and about how demolition experts use progressive collapse to destroy large buildings. The Web also makes available sets of instructions—or "technical ingenuity"—needed to combine readily available materials in destructive ways. Practically anything an extremist wants to know about kidnapping, bomb making, and assassination is now available online. One somewhat facetious example: It's possible to convert everyday materials into potentially destructive devices like the "potato cannon." With a barrel and combustion chamber fashioned from common plastic pipe, and with propane as an explosive propellant, a well-made cannon can hurl a homely spud hundreds of meters—or throw chaff onto electrical substations. A quick search of the Web reveals dozens of sites giving instructions on how to make one.

Finally, modem, high-tech societies are filled with supercharged devices packed with energy, combustibles, and poisons, giving terrorists ample opportunities to divert such nonweapon technologies to destructive ends. To cause horrendous damage, all terrorists must do is figure out how to release this power and let it run wild or, as they did on September 11, take control of this power and retarget it. Indeed, the assaults on New York City and the Pentagon were not low-tech affairs, as is often argued. True, the terrorists used simple box cutters to hijack the planes, but the box cutters were no more than the "keys" that allowed the terrorists to convert a high-tech means of transport into a high-tech weapon of mass destruction. Once the hijackers had used these keys to access and turn on their weapon, they were able to deliver a kiloton of explosive power into the World Trade Center with deadly accuracy.

HIGH-TECH HUBRIS

The vulnerability of advanced nations stems not only from the greater destructive capacities of terrorists, but also from the increased vulnerability of the West's economic and technological systems. This additional vulnerability is the product of two key social and technological developments: first, the growing complexity and interconnectedness of our modem societies; and second, the increasing geographic concentration of wealth, human capital, knowledge, and communication links.

Consider the first of these developments. All human societies encompass a multitude of economic and technological systems. We can think of these systems as networks—that is, as sets of nodes and links among those nodes. The U.S. economy consists of numerous nodes, including corporations, factories, and urban centers; it also consists of links among these nodes, such as highways, rail lines, electrical grids, and fiber-optic cables. As societies modernize and become richer, their networks become more complex and interconnected. The number of nodes increases, as does the density of links among the nodes and the speed at which materials, energy, and information are pushed along these links. Moreover, the nodes themselves become more complex as the people who create, operate, and manage them strive for better performance. (For instance, a manufacturing company might improve efficiency by adopting more intricate inventory-control methods.)

Complex and interconnected networks sometimes have features that make their behavior unstable and unpredictable. In particular, they can have feedback loops that produce vicious cycles. A good example is a stock market crash, in which selling drives down prices, which begets more selling. Networks can also be tightly coupled, which means that links among the nodes are short, therefore making it more likely that problems with one node will spread to others. When drivers tailgate at high speeds on freeways, they create a tightly coupled system: A mistake by one driver, or a sudden shock coming from outside the system, such as a deer running across the road, can cause a chain reaction of cars piling onto each other. We've seen such knock-on effects in the U.S. electrical, telephone, and air traffic systems, when a failure in one part of the network has sometimes produced a cascade of failures across the country. Finally, in part because of feedbacks and tight coupling, networks often exhibit nonlinear behavior, meaning that a small shock or perturbation to the network produces a disproportionately large disruption.

Terrorists and other malicious individuals can magnify their own disruptive power by exploiting these features of complex and interconnected networks. Consider the archetypal lone, nerdy high-school kid hacking away at his computer in his parents' basement who can create a computer virus that produces chaos in global communications and data systems. But there's much more to worry about than just the proliferation of computer viruses. A special investigative commission set up in 1997 by then U.S. President Bill Clinton reported that "growing complexity and interdependence, especially in the energy and communications infrastructures, create an increased possibility that a rather minor and routine disturbance can cascade into a regional outage." The commission continued: "We are convinced that our vulnerabilities are increasing steadily, that the means to exploit those weaknesses are readily available and that the costs [of launching an attack] continue to drop."

Terrorists must be clever to exploit these weaknesses. They must attack the right nodes in the right networks. If they don't, the damage will remain isolated and the overall network will be resilient. Much depends upon the network's level of redundancy—that is, on the degree to which the damaged node's functions can be offloaded to undamaged nodes. As terrorists come to recognize the importance of redundancy, their ability to disable complex networks will improve. Langdon Winner, a theorist of politics and technology, provides the first rule of modern terrorism: "Find the critical but nonredundant parts of the system and sabotage . . . them according to your purposes." Winner concludes that "the science of complexity awaits a Machiavelli or Clausewitz to make the full range of possibilities clear."

The range of possible terrorist attacks has expanded due to a second source of organizational vulnerability in modern economies—the rising concentration of high-value assets in geographically small locations. Advanced societies concentrate valuable things and people in order to achieve economies of scale. Companies in capital-intensive industries can usually reduce the per-unit cost of their goods by building larger production facilities. Moreover, placing expensive equipment and highly skilled people in a single location provides easier access, more efficiencies, and synergies that constitute an important source of wealth. That is why we build places like the World Trade Center.

In so doing, however, we also create extraordinarily attractive targets for terrorists, who realize they can cause a huge amount of damage in a single strike. On September 11, a building complex that took seven years to construct collapsed in 90 minutes, obliterating 10 million square feet of office space and exacting at least $30 billion in direct costs. A major telephone switching office was destroyed, another heavily damaged, and important cellular antennas on top of the towers were lost. Key transit lines through southern Manhattan were buried under rubble. Ironically, even a secret office of the U.S. Central Intelligence Agency was destroyed in the attack, temporarily disrupting normal intelligence operations.

Yet despite the horrific damage to the area's infrastructure and New York City's economy, the attack did not cause catastrophic failures in U.S. financial, economic, or communications networks. As it turned out, the World Trade Center was not a critical, nonredundant node. At least it wasn't critical in the way most people (including, probably, the terrorists) would have thought. Many of the financial firms in the destroyed buildings had made contingency plans for disaster by setting up alternate facilities for data, information, and computer equipment in remote locations. Though the NASDAQ headquarters was demolished, for instance, the exchange's data centers in Connecticut and Maryland remained linked to trading companies through two separate connections that passed through 20 switching centers. NASDAQ officials later claimed that their system was so robust that they could have restarted trading only a few hours after the attack. Some World Trade Center firms had made advanced arrangements with companies specializing in providing emergency relocation facilities in New Jersey and elsewhere. Because of all this proactive planning—and the network redundancy it produced—the September 11 attacks caused remarkably little direct disruption to the U.S. financial system (despite the unprecedented closure of the stock market for several days).

But when we look back years from now, we may recognize that the attacks had a critical effect on another kind of network that we've created among ourselves: a tightly coupled, very unstable, and highly nonlinear psychological network. We're all nodes in this particular network, and the links among us consist of Internet connections, satellite signals, fiber-optic cables, talk radio, and 24-hour television news. In the minutes following the attack, coverage of the story flashed across this network. People then stayed in front of their televisions for hours on end; they viewed and reviewed the awful video clips on the CNN Web site; they plugged phone lines checking on friends and relatives; and they sent each other millions upon millions of e-mail messages—so many, in fact, that the Internet was noticeably slower for days afterwards.

Along these links, from TV and radio stations to their audiences, and especially from person to person through the Internet, flowed raw emotion: grief, anger, horror, disbelief, fear, and hatred. It was as if we'd all been wired into one immense, convulsing, and reverberating neural network. Indeed, the biggest impact of the September 11 attacks wasn't the direct disruption of financial, economic, communications, or transportation networks—physical stuff, all.

Rather, by working through the network we've created within and among our heads, the attacks had their biggest impact on our collective psychology and our subjective feelings of security and safety. This network acts like a huge megaphone, vastly amplifying the emotional impact of terrorism.

To maximize this impact, the perpetrators of complex terrorism will carry out their attacks in audacious, unexpected, and even bizarre manners—using methods that are, ideally, unimaginably cruel. By so doing, they will create the impression that anything is possible, which further magnifies fear. From this perspective, the World Trade Center represented an ideal target, because the Twin Towers were an icon of the magnificence and boldness of American capitalism. When they collapsed like a house of cards, in about 15 seconds each, it suggested that American capitalism was a house of cards, too. How could anything so solid and powerful and so much a part of American identity vanish so quickly? And the use of passenger airplanes made matters worse by exploiting our worst fears of flying.

Unfortunately, this emotional response has had huge, real-world consequences. Scared, insecure, grief-stricken people aren't ebullient consumers. They behave cautiously and save more. Consumer demand drops, corporate investment falls, and economic growth slows. In the end, via the multiplier effect of our technology-amplified emotional response, the September 11 terrorists may have achieved an economic impact far greater than they ever dreamed possible. The total cost of lost economic growth and decreased equity value around the world could exceed a trillion dollars. Since the cost of carrying out the attack itself was probably only a few hundred thousand dollars, we're looking at an economic multiplier of over a millionfold.

THE WEAKEST LINKS

Complex terrorism operates like jujitsu—it redirects the energies of our intricate societies against us. Once the basic logic of complex terrorism is understood (and the events of September 11 prove that terrorists are beginning to understand it), we can quickly identify dozens of relatively simple ways to bring modern, high-tech societies to their knees.

How would a Clausewitz of terrorism proceed? He would pinpoint the critical complex networks upon which modern societies depend. They include networks for producing and distributing energy, information, water, and food; the highways, railways, and airports that make up our transportation grid; and our healthcare system. Of these, the vulnerability of the food system is particularly alarming. . . . However, terrorism experts have paid the most attention to the energy and information networks, mainly because they so clearly underpin the vitality of modern economies.

The energy system—which comprises everything from the national network of gas pipelines to the electricity grid—is replete with high-value nodes like oil refineries, tank farms, and electrical substations. At times of peak energy demand, this network (and in particular, the electricity grid) is very tightly coupled. The loss of one link in the grid means that the electricity it carries must be offloaded to other links. If other links are already operating near capacity, the additional load can cause them to fail, too, thus displacing their energy to yet other links. We saw this kind of breakdown in August 1996, when the failure of the Big Eddy transmission line in northern Oregon caused overloading on a string of transmission lines down the West Coast of the United States, triggering blackouts that affected 4 million people in nine states.

Substations are clear targets because they represent key nodes linked to many other parts of the electrical network. Substations and high-voltage transmission lines are also "soft" targets, since they can be fairly easily disabled or destroyed. Tens of thousands of miles of transmission lines are strung across North America, often in locations so remote that the lines are almost impossible to protect, but they are nonetheless accessible by four-wheel drive. Transmission towers can be brought down with well-placed explosive charges. Imagine a carefully planned sequence of attacks on these lines, with emergency crews and investigators dashing from one remote attack site to another, constantly off-balance and unable to regain control. Detailed maps of locations of substations and transmission lines for much of North America are easily available on the Web. Not even all the police and military personnel in the United States would suffice to provide even rudimentary protection to this immense network.

The energy system also provides countless opportunities for turning supposedly benign technology to destructive ends. For instance, large gas pipelines, many of which run near or even through urban areas, have huge explosive potential; attacks on them could have the twin effect of producing great local damage and wider disruptions in energy supply. And the radioactive waste pools associated with most nuclear reactors are perhaps the most lethal targets in the national energy-supply system. If the waste in these facilities were dispersed into the environment, the results could be catastrophic. Fortunately, such attacks would be technically difficult.

Even beyond energy networks, opportunities to release the destructive power of benign technologies abound. Chemical plants are especially tempting targets, because they are packed with toxins and flammable, even explosive, materials. Security at such facilities is often lax: An April 1999 study of chemical plants in Nevada and West Virginia by the U.S. Agency for Toxic Substances and Disease Registry concluded that security ranged from "fair to very poor" and that oversights were linked to "complacency and lack of awareness of the threat." And every day, trains carrying tens of thousands of tons of toxic material course along transport corridors throughout the United States. All a terrorist needs is inside knowledge that a chemical-laden train is traveling through an urban area at a specific time, and a well-placed object (like a piece of rail) on the track could cause a wreck, a chemical release, and a mass evacuation. A derailment of such a train at a nonredundant link in the transport system—such as an important tunnel or bridge—could be particularly potent. (In fact, when the U.S. bombing campaign in Afghanistan began on October 7, 2001, the U.S. railroad industry declared a three-day moratorium on transporting dangerous chemicals.) Recent accidents in Switzerland and Baltimore, Maryland, make clear that rail and highway tunnels are vulnerable because they are choke points for transportation networks and because it's extraordinarily hard to extinguish explosions and fires inside them.

Modern communications networks also are susceptible to terrorist attacks. Although the Internet was originally designed to keep working even if large chunks of the network were lost (as might happen in a nuclear war, for instance), today's Internet displays some striking vulnerabilities. One of the most significant is the system of computers—called "routers" and "root servers"—that directs traffic around the Net. Routers represent critical nodes in the network and depend on each other for details on where to send packets of information. A software error in one router, or its malicious reprogramming by a hacker, can lead to errors throughout the Internet. Hackers could also exploit new peer-to-peer software (such as the information-transfer tool Gnutella) to distribute throughout the Internet millions of "sleeper" viruses programmed to attack specific machines or the network itself at a predetermined date.

59

STEPHEN D. KRASNER

PROBLEMATIC SOVEREIGNTY

The term *sovereignty* has been commonly used in at least four different ways: domestic sovereignty, referring to the organization of public authority within a state and to the level of effective control exercised by those holding authority; interdependence sovereignty, referring to the ability of public authorities to control transborder movements; international legal sovereignty, referring to the mutual recognition of states; and Westphalian sovereignty, referring to the exclusion of external actors from domestic authority configurations. These four meanings of sovereignty are not logically coupled, nor have they covaried in practice.

Domestic sovereignty involves both authority and control; interdependence sovereignty, only control; and Westphalian and international legal sovereignty, only authority. Authority is based on the mutual recognition that an actor has the right to engage in a specific activity, including the right to command others. Authority might, or might not, result in effective control. Control

SOURCE: From *Problematic Sovereignty*, Ed. Stephen D. Krasner, pp. 7–11. Copyright 2001 Columbia University Press.

can also be achieved through the use of force. If, over a period of time, the ability of a legitimated entity to control a given domain weakens, then the authority of that entity might eventually dissipate. Conversely, if a particular entity is able to successfully exercise control, or if a purely instrumental pattern of behavior endures for a long period, then the entity or practice could be endowed with legitimacy.[1] In many social and political situations both control and authority can affect the behavior of actors.[2]

DOMESTIC SOVEREIGNTY

The oldest usages of the term *sovereignty* refer to domestic sovereignty—the organization of authority within a given state and its effectiveness. Bodin and Hobbes wanted to establish the legitimacy of some one single source of authority within the polity. Later liberal theorists recognized that there need not be one single fount of legitimacy; indeed, the Founding Fathers in the United States wanted to divide authority among the different branches of the federal government and between the federal government and the states. The organization of domestic authority within the polity is irrelevant for international legal or Westphalian sovereignty.[3]

International legal and Westphalian sovereignty need not be affected by the level of domestic control that the political authorities within a polity can exercise. What are now termed failed states, essentially domestic governments that are incapable of regulating developments within their own borders, retain their international legal sovereignty. Both the state and its government continue to be recognized. They are members of international organizations, vote in the United Nations, and sign contracts with international financial institutions. The Westphalian sovereignty of such states might, or might not, be compromised by external actors. If powerful external entities were indifferent to the fate of a failed state, then there would be no external efforts to alter its domestic authority structures.

INTERDEPENDENCE SOVEREIGNTY

Many observers have claimed that new technological developments have undermined the ability of states to regulate movements across their own borders with regard to goods, capital, ideas, individuals, and disease vectors. Globalization is seen as threatening sovereignty, but sovereignty here is in the first instance entirely a matter of control rather than authority.[4] The fact that a state cannot govern a particular form of activity does not mean that some other authority structure will be developed or even that the authority of the state in that area, its right to regulate, will be challenged.

High levels of global interaction are not a new thing. Net capital flows were higher in the nineteenth century than at the end of the twentieth, although gross flows have dramatically increased. Ratios of trade to gross national product (GNP) increased from the Napoleonic Wars until World War I, declined in the interwar period, and grew again after 1950, and in some, but not all, countries surpassed the levels of the nineteenth century. In the Atlantic area migration was higher in the nineteenth century than has been the case more recently. Some areas have become more deeply enmeshed in the international environment, especially East Asia; others, notably most of Africa, remain much more isolated. What has changed is not so much the level of international interaction but the scope of government activities, the demands that have been placed on the state, and the range of constituencies to which governments in advanced industrialized countries must respond. In the nineteenth century countries could adhere to the gold standard, which facilitated international flows, because domestic economic performance could be sacrificed to international balance. In the late twentieth century, with the dramatic increase in the franchise, no regime could ignore questions related to domestic growth and employment.[5]

Regardless of whether interdependence sovereignty is more at risk today than in the past, the ability of states to regulate their transborder flows has no logical relationship to their status as independently recognized states, their international legal sovereignty, or their ability to exclude external authority structures (their Westphalian sovereignty). In practice, however, a loss of interdependence sovereignty might lead rulers to compromise their Westphalian sovereignty by entering into contractual arrangements to establish supranational authority structures better able to regulate activities beyond the control of any single state. Such treaties could be concluded only by international legal sovereigns, by political entities that mutually recognized each other's ability to freely enter into such contracts. . . .[6]

INTERNATIONAL LEGAL SOVEREIGNTY

International legal sovereignty involves the status of a political entity in the international system. Recognition of such sovereignty implies that a state has juridical equality, that its diplomats are entitled to immunity, and that its embassies and consulates have extraterritorial status. An international legal sovereign can enter into agreements with other entities.

The basic rule for international legal sovereignty is that recognition is extended to states with territory and formal juridical autonomy. The recognition of a specific government, such as the Communist government of China, has sometimes been separated from the recognition of the state itself. Historically, rulers have also invoked other conditions for recognition, such as the ability to defend territory and maintain order.[7] Recognition has been used as a political instrument; it has been withheld from some governments that met widely recognized criteria and extended to those with only tenuous or even no control over the territory they claimed to govern.

Even entities, as opposed to specific governments, that do not conform to the basic norm of appropriateness associated with international legal sovereignty, because they lack either formal juridical autonomy or territory, have been recognized. India was a member of the League of Nations and a signatory of the Versailles settlements even though it was a colony of Britain. The British Dominions were signatories at Versailles and members of the League even though their juridical independence from Britain was unclear. The Palestine Liberation Organization (PLO) was given observer status in the United Nations in 1974, and this status was changed to that of a permanent mission in 1988 coincident with the declaration of Palestinian independence, even though the PLO did not have any juridically accepted independent control over territory, although as Shibley Telhami points out, the organization did have de facto domestic sovereignty in Lebanon in the late 1970s Beyelo-Russia and the Ukraine were members of the United Nations even though they were part of the Soviet Union.[8]

Almost all rulers have sought international legal sovereignty because it provides them with both material and normative resources. Recognition facilitates contracting. Alliances can enhance security; membership in the World Trade Organization can increase access to markets; membership in the World Bank can provide financial resources.

Recognition may also enhance a ruler's domestic support. Recognition as a sovereign state is a widely, almost universally, understood construct in the contemporary world. A ruler attempting to enhance his own position by creating or reinforcing a particular national identity is more likely to be successful if his state or his government enjoys international recognition. In a situation in which domestic sovereignty is problematic, international recognition can enhance the position of rulers by signaling to constituents that a ruler may have access to international resources such as alliances and sovereign lending.

The absence of recognition, however, does not preclude activities that are facilitated by recognition. Lack of recognition has not prevented states from engaging in negotiating and contracting. American officials met their Chinese counterparts before they recognized the People's Republic of China (PRC) as the government of China. When Taiwan was de-recognized, . . . the United States took steps to provide Taiwan with something very much like the status that it had enjoyed before 1979. The Taiwan Relations Act stipulated that the legal standing of the Republic of China (ROC) in American courts would not be affected, that Taiwan would continue to control property that had been bought since 1949, and that the American Institute in Taiwan, a nongovernmental agency, would be created to, in effect, conduct the functions of an embassy.[9]

Recognition has not meant in practice that a state will respect the Westphalian sovereignty of its counterparts. The Soviet Union, for instance, not only established the communist regimes of the satellite states of Eastern Europe during the Cold War but intervened on an ongoing basis in their domestic political structures, organizing, for instance, their internal security services and their militaries. Recognition does not guarantee that domestic authorities will be able to monitor and regulate developments within the territory of their state or flows across their borders; that is, it does not guarantee either domestic sovereignty or interdependence sovereignty. Obviously, recognition does not guarantee that a state will not be invaded or even that its existence will not be extinguished. Conquest and absorption is not a challenge to rules of sovereignty but merely a redrawing of boundaries.

WESTPHALIAN SOVEREIGNTY

The basic rule of Westphalian sovereignty is that external authority structures should be excluded from the territory of a state. Sovereign states are not only de jure independent; they are also de facto autonomous. Rulers are always to some extent constrained by the external environment. Other states, markets, transnational corporations, or international financiers may limit the options available to a particular government, but that government is still able to freely choose within a constrained set. Moreover, the government of a Westphalian sovereign can determine the character of its own domestic sovereignty, its own authoritative institutions. Rulers might choose to establish an independent central bank because they believe that this would increase the country's attractiveness for international investors, a choice that would be completely consistent with Westphalian sovereignty. If, in contrast, another state or an international financial institution conditions a loan on the creation of an independent central bank, Westphalian sovereignty would be at risk. If the external actor is able to influence domestic decision-making processes through the appointment of officials or by altering the views of actors within the polity, Westphalian sovereignty would be even more challenged. And if the external actor could dictate the creation of an independent central bank, the Westphalian sovereignty of the state would be nullified, at least with regard to this particular issue area.

Domestic authority structures can be compromised both as a result of the coercive action of other states or through voluntary decisions. Poland would not have had a communist government in 1950 without the presence and threat of Soviet military forces. In contrast, the member states of the European Union have voluntarily created supranational institutions, such as the European Court of Justice, and pooled sovereignty through qualified majority voting, which compromises their domestic political autonomy. While coercion, or intervention, is inconsistent with international legal as well as Westphalian sovereignty, voluntary actions by rulers, or invitations, do not violate international legal sovereignty but can violate Westphalian sovereignty.

While autonomy can be compromised as a result of both intervention and voluntary choice, the former has gotten much more attention. Some observers have regarded nonintervention as the *grundnorm* of the sovereign state system.[10] Weaker states have always been the strongest supporters of nonintervention, which was first explicitly articulated by Wolff and Vattel during the latter part of the eighteenth century. During the nineteenth century Latin American leaders, who governed the weakest states in the system, vigorously defended the notion that coercion was unacceptable. The United States did not formally accept the principle of nonintervention until the seventh International Conference of American States held in 1933. After the Second World War nonintervention was routinely endorsed in major treaties, such as the Charter of the United Nations, although ethnic conflicts in the 1990s prompted Kofi Annan, the secretary-general of the United Nations, to argue at the fall 1999 General Assembly that sovereignty might have to be conditioned on respect for human rights.

Voluntary arrangements that compromise the domestic authority of a state have usually not been regarded as problematic. In part this is because such arrangements are consistent with international legal sovereignty, which requires only that agreements be entered into voluntarily, even if they violate Westphalian sovereignty. Rulers may choose to legitimate external authority structures for a variety of reasons including tying the hands of their successors, securing financial resources, and strengthening domestic support for values that they, themselves, embrace.

In sum, analysts and practitioners have used the term *sovereignty* in four different and distinct ways. The absence or loss of one kind of sovereignty does not logically imply an erosion of others, even though they may be empirically associated with each other. A state can be recognized, that is, have international legal sovereignty, but not have Westphalian sovereignty because its authority structures are subject to external authority or control; it can lose control of transborder movements but still be autonomous; it can have domestic sovereignty, a well-established and effective set of authoritative decision-making institutions, and not be recognized.

NOTES

1. In his discussion of evolutionary game theory Sugden (1989) suggests that a rule that is initially accepted for purely consequential reasons can over time come to be normatively binding and authoritative because it works and is generally accepted.
2. For further discussions of the discussion of the distinction between authority and control with reference to sovereignty, see, Wendt and Friedheim 1996: 246, 251; Onuf 1991: 430; Wendt 1992: 412–13; Shue 1997: 348.
3. An exception is a confederal structure in which the component entities in the federation, as well as its central government, have the legitimate right to engage in contracts with other states. Switzerland is one example. See Oppenheim 1992: 249–53.
4. Thomson 1995: 216.
5. O'Rourke and Williamson 1999; Obstfeld and Taylor 1997 and Krasner 1989; Eichengreen 1998.
6. Keohane 1984, 1995.
7. Fowler and Bunck 1995, ch. 2; Thomson 1995: 228; Oppenheim 1992: 186–90; Crawford 1996: 500.
8. Oppenheim 1992: 145–46.
9. Oppenheim 1992: 158–73; Peterson 1997: 107–8, 140, 148–52, 197; *Taiwan Relations Act.*
10. Jackson 1990: 6.

REFERENCES

Crawford, Beverly. 1996. "Explaining Defection from International Cooperation: Germany's Unilateral Recognition of Croatia." *World Polities* 48, no. 4: 482–521.

Eichengreen, Barry. 1998. *Globalizing Capital: A History of the International Monetary System*. Princeton: Princeton University Press.

Fowler, Michael Ross and Julie Marie Bunck. 1995. *Law, Power, and the Sovereign State: The Evolution and Application of the Concept of Sovereignty*. University Park: Pennsylvania State University Press.

Jackson, Robert H. 1990. *Quasi-States: Sovereignty, International Relations, and the Third World*. Cambridge: Cambridge University Press.

Keohane, Robert O. 1984. *After Hegemony: Cooperation and Discord in the World Political Economy*. Princeton University Press.

———. 1995. "Hobbes's Dilemma and Institutional Change in World Politics: Sovereignty in International Society." In Hans-Henrik Holm and Georg Sorensen, eds., *Whose World Order? Uneven Globalization and the End of the Gold War*. Boulder, Colo.: Westview Press.

Obstfeld, Maurice and Alan M. Taylor. 1997. *The Great Depression as a Watershed: International Capital Mobility Over the Long Run*. Working paper 5960, National Bureau of Economic Research, Cambridge, Mass.

Onuf, Nicholas Greenwood. 1991. "Sovereignty: Outline of a Conceptual History." *Alternative* 16: 425–46.

Oppenheim, L. 1992. *Oppenheim's International Law,* 9th ed. Edited by Sir Robert Jennings and Sir Arthur Watts. Harlow, Essex, U.K.: Longman.

O'Rourke, Kevin H. and Jeffrey G. Williamson. 1999. *Globalization and History: The Evolution of a Nineteenth-Century Atlantic Economy*. Cambridge: MIT Press.

Peterson, M. J. 1997. *Recognition of Governments: Legal Doctrine and State Practice*. New York: St. Martin's Press.

Shue, Henry. 1997. "Eroding Sovereignty: The Advance of Principle." In Robert McKim and Jeff McMahan, eds., *The Morality of Nationalism*. New York: Oxford University Press.

Sugden, Robert. 1989. "Spontaneous Order." *Journal of Economic Perspectives* 3:85–97.

Taiwan Relations Act. 1979. *U.S. Code*. Title 22, ch. 48, secs. 3301–16.

Thomson, Janice E. 1995. "State Sovereignty in International Relations: Bridging the Gap Between Theory and Empirical Research." *International Studies Quarterly* 39, no. 2: 213–33.

Thomson, Janice E. and Stephen D. Krasner. 1989. "Global Transactions and the Consolidation of Sovereignty." In Ernst-Otto Czempiel and James N. Rosenau, eds., *Global Changes and Theoretical Challenges: Approaches to World Politics for the 1990s*. Lexington, Mass.: D.C. Health.

Wendt, Alexander. 1992. "Anarchy Is What States Make of It: The Social Construction of State Politics." *International Organization* 46: 391–425.

Wendt, Alexander and Daniel Friedheim. 1996. "Hierarchy Under Anarchy: Informal Empire and the East German State." In Thomas J. Biersteker and Cynthia Weber, eds., *State Sovereignty as a Social Construct*, 240–72. Cambridge: Cambridge University Press.

60

STANLEY HOFFMANN

THE DEBATE ABOUT INTERVENTION

The shift from a license for intervention in defense of national self-determination to a justification for intervention in defense of human rights is part of the gradual shift from a liberalism of nation-states endowed by international law with rights and duties to a liberalism of rights and duties for both states and individuals, the rights of the states—including the right to sovereignty—being increasingly subordinated to their respect and promotion of the rights of the individuals.

COLLECTIVE, FORCIBLE INTERVENTIONS

We turn now to the contemporary debate and to the arguments in favor of collective, forcible interventions—or even unilateral ones in "egregious" cases (to use Rawls's adjective), when collective institutions are paralyzed or passive (we can think of India in Bangladesh or Tanzania against Idi Amin).

One argument is conspicuously absent, or subdued: it is that of the need to help national self-determination when it is being resisted. Even in the case of East Timor, the clamor for an external military interference was based on the atrocities committed by Indonesian military and paramilitary forces after the UN-sponsored referendum on independence rather than on a duty to enforce the results of this referendum given Indonesia's noncompliance. In Kosovo the Rambouillet document promised a referendum on the status of the territory after three years, but the agreement that put an end to the war in June 1999 referred only to an ill-defined autonomy. The focus throughout was on Serb atrocities, not on Kosovar demands for independence. (This had already been the case when the Security Council ordered Saddam Hussein to stop the massacres of Kurds and Shiites—there was no promise of self-determination for the Kurds.)

The Catholic doctrine of just war has been the traditional middle ground between Christian pacifism and theories justifying holy war to propagate a faith. It has developed in the context of interstate conflicts, but we find that today most of the justifications for interventions in domestic conflicts fall in the traditional categories of the *jus ad bellum*. These deal with just causes—self-defense and the vindication of rights; proportionality of values—the values destroyed

SOURCE: From *Turbulent Peace*, Ed. Chester A. Crocker, Fen Osler Hampson, and Pamela Aall, pp. 274–301. United States Institute of Peace Press.

should not exceed those that are being upheld; proper authority—who can legitimately decide the resort to force; reasonable chance of success; and last resort—the exhaustion of all efforts to save peace. The causes deemed important enough to require intervention can be divided into two categories. The first is the properly humanitarian one: the disinterested duty to put an end to or to reduce human suffering. This is the argument of Joelle Tanguy, speaking as an official of Doctors Without Borders. She makes a case for impartial aid agencies providing assistance to all the victims of humanitarian disasters and against linking it to "the kind of intervention carried out by political and military bodies," which condones the use of force. The latter will add to the suffering. "Both approaches are necessary, but in order to serve their purposes, we believe that they must be carried out independently."[1] In her view, politicizing humanitarian assistance makes it the hostage of political calculations and military priorities. Interference, yes; force, no. This is, obviously, the position of an NGO.

The second category of arguments addresses the right of states to use force inside the borders of other states. Usually, the "just cause" that is invoked is the defense of human rights when there are massive violations of them—in cases of genocide, brutal ethnic cleansing, or monstrous brutalities committed by rebel or rival gangs (as in Liberia or Sierra Leone). This is both clear enough and vague enough to leave room for argument: Was the level of violence in Kosovo before March 1999 high enough to vindicate military action? Was the latter justified, rather, by the violation of past agreements Milosevic had signed and the anticipation of further ethnic cleansing?

An elegant formulation comes from Kofi Annan: The UN Charter is "a living document, whose . . . very letter and spirit are the affirmation of . . . fundamental human rights," whereas sovereignty is being "redefined by the forces of globalization and international cooperation."[2] Less diplomatically, David Luban argues that "there is nothing regrettable about violating the statist order in order to protect human rights; the justice and injustice of war should be assessed along the dimension of human rights protection, not state sovereignty protection, and the social ontology that places states above individuals is indefensible.[3]

To the argument made by realists, that the pursuit of such altruistic aims contradicts the very logic of international relations—a logic of selfishness—and that the promotion of such values is not in the nature of "the game," which aims at promoting state interests, the advocates of a new international law reply that these are false distinctions, because the toleration of shocking or egregious atrocities is likely to lead either to chaos spreading through imitation or to regional destabilization through arms smuggling, massive flows of refugees, and self-interested interventions in support of feuding parties. (Of course, this does not address cases when such effects are not visible; paradoxically, East Timor was one such case. But here it could be argued that upholding the result of a UN-sponsored referendum was indeed both value and interest driven.)

The limitation, however vague, of causes of forcible intervention to particularly serious violations of rights is a way of dealing with the proportionality between values saved by force and values destroyed by it. Defenders of the war in Kosovo have replied to critics of the way in which it was waged—against civilian installations more than against Serb forces—by arguing that the damage was necessary to put an end to, and less horrendous than, the continuation of the ethnic cleansing of the Albanians.

On proper authority, the "intervenors" have been, on the whole, champions of the United Nations. But on the one hand they have become aware of its limitations (about which more will be said) and on the other they have deemed the cause more important than the procedure of the UN Charter, the substance more compelling than the formalities. This is why many (but not all) did defend the bypassing of the Security Council in the case of Kosovo, and the transformation of NATO from a military alliance (last used as a UN agent in Bosnia) into a regional organization, a "principal," substituting for a veto-ridden Security Council. Others would have preferred a resort to the council, followed by a resort to NATO or to a "coalition of the willing" if the council had been paralyzed by a Russian and/or a Chinese veto.

It is because of both proportionality and the need for a reasonable chance of success that the defenders do not seem bothered by the contrast between action against Serbia, or in Haiti, and inaction against Russia over Chechnya. Reasonable chance of success is, of course, a very iffy notion. Those who went beyond a purely humanitarian delivery of food and medicines in Somalia thought they had a good chance of eliminating the warlord Mohammed Farah Aideed; many believed that there was little chance of stopping the genocide in Rwanda after it began in the summer of 1994, despite later vehement arguments to the contrary. A reasonable chance of success requires a willingness to bear certain costs and to launch an effort sufficient to have such a chance. The United States had no such willingness in Somalia and in Rwanda; and despite British and Nigerian attempts, nobody was ready for a sufficient effort in Sierra Leone.

No less controversial is the last condition of *jus ad bellum:* that force be used only as a last resort. Not only can one think of cases in which force was used too late to save many victims (Bosnia, Haiti) and would, if used early, probably have been less destructive of "enemy" lives than protracted sanctions that hit innocent civilians over many years, but opponents of military intervention, it seems, will never be satisfied that all hopes for a peaceful resolution had been extinguished before force was used or that the efforts presented by officials as honest attempts at reaching an agreement had not been designed to be rejected. Defenders of NATO's actions in Kosovo insist that even after Rambouillet the Serbs refused any plan that would have allowed international forces into Kosovo. Critics point to provisions of the Rambouillet agreement (especially the right of NATO forces to move from Hungary to the disputed area) that, in their view, no self-respecting Serb government could have accepted. But if it could not accept this and yet was willing to accept outside "peacekeepers," Serbia surely could have made it clear.

The key, for the defenders of forcible intervention for humanitarian goals, is the vision of an international order in which state sovereignty is not an absolute but a set of attributes that can be curtailed when essential human rights are being violated, and in which the ban on aggression that has limited sovereignty since the Covenant of the League of Nations is completed by a ban on such internal atrocities as ethnic cleansing and systematic massacres of "enemies of the state." As in the Wilsonian view, or in that of Hans Kelsen, war is either a crime or a sanction enforced by the international society; but what constitutes a crime is no longer limited to transgressions across borders.

CRITICISMS OF INTERVENTION

The opponents or critics of intervention have deployed a formidable arsenal of arguments. Many of them raise questions about the "justness" of defending human rights abroad. The most sweeping attacks are of two kinds. One is legalistic, the other political. The legalistic stance proclaims the sanctity of the principle of national sovereignty as the cornerstone of the post-Westphalian world order and of its corollary, the principle of nonintervention. The latter is seen as protecting not only the state against outside interference and subversion, but also its citizens, for whom the state is the precondition of order and the focus of social identity. It is this crucial role of the state, even in an age of economic and technological globalization, which the World Court recognized when it gave an advisory opinion that refused to declare nuclear weapons illegal because of the right of states to defend themselves.

The political attack comes from the realists. They look at international relations from the viewpoint of the states and argue that a sound foreign policy is one that protects and promotes their essential interests. When they are in question, states need no human rights or humanitarian arguments to justify their interventions. When such interests are not involved, and even if one could argue in legal terms that there may be a right to intervene, say, against genocide—something, it must be added, these critics are not ready to concede—a distinction would still have to be made between such a right and an obligation to intervene. For military action to be an obligation, essential interests need to be at stake—as in the case of aggression. Risking lives "in the absence of any definable national interest" can only lead to overcommitment, to serious damage to relations with other, often far more important, governments, and to an erosion of domestic support.[4] There are too many dogs fighting in the world arena, and the United States has no dogs in most of those fights. Indeed, the truly vital interests—the protection of national security from foreign aggression, the preservation of U.S. world status and economic resources from challengers—are threatened by the external policies of rivals or rogues, not by their internal actions (which may be impossible, or far too risky, to try to stop).

A specifically military variant of this position, well stated by General Colin Powell, stresses that the purpose of U.S. armed forces is to fight and defeat enemies. The "other new missions that are coming along" are peripheral and must remain so.[5] Otherwise U.S. forces will be depleted by marginal operations and made unavailable and unfit for the real lurking dangers.

The neorealists, who look at international relations from the viewpoint of the system and of its stability, see internal wars as potentially destabilizing, at worst, when outsiders interfere and especially insofar as external intrusions can be interpreted as acts of disguised imperialism committed by a small coterie of Western powers, and, at best, as insignificant for structural change.

Thus, while the defenders of intervention are moved by a nightmare of human suffering spreading chaos if each state is left, so to speak, in possession of the people under its jurisdiction, the opponents are inspired by a nightmare of interstate chaos if the pillars of state sovereignty and nonintervention are torn down. They are also upset by the kinds of selectivity and inconsistency that crusades for good causes are bound to lead to. Responding to every "egregious" violation of human rights being physically and politically impossible, any criterion of choice other than the defense of essential national interests is likely to be morally shocking and politically embarrassing. Small states will be the targets but not the main powers; allies (such as the Turks) will be protected from "their" Kurds, but Iraq's Kurds will be favored. The Croats and the Bosnians will be allowed to have their states, but the Serbs will be barred from extending their control over Serbs in Croatia and in Bosnia. Kosovo will be encouraged to secede de facto, but Katanga's attempt to secede from Congo in the early 1960s was crushed. Ethnic atrocities in Europe will rouse to action states that will be far more indifferent to horrors in Sudan, or Rwanda, or Sri Lanka.

Selectivity and inconsistency in choosing whom to attack are not the only inevitable effects of the moralistic approach; there will also be constant doubt and debate about what rights are to be protected. What constitutes a genocide? (Remember the State Department's reluctance to call what happened in Rwanda genocide.) Do random massacres and mutilations on a grand scale amount to genocide? Are deliberate policies aimed at starving opponents as "egregious" as massacres? What acts can be seen as barbaric? (Many in Europe believe that U.S. capital punishment is uncivilized.) Is there any consensus on what constitutes an attack on human dignity? Is political persecution always less obnoxious than atrocities and group persecutions, because it attacks people for choices they have made or actions they have undertaken?

The conclusion is obvious: Get out of this morass and return to the verities of realism. There is only one problem with this: the definition of the national interest. A mild form of realism would recognize that all powers must heed the *imperatives* of physical and economic security, but also that many have sufficient resources to promote and *protect preferences,* especially about the kind of international milieu they would like to operate in; and among these preferences, the elimination of certain kinds of unacceptable behavior has every right to figure. Moving further away from orthodox realism, we might argue that certain important values constitute interests, both because, as moral persons, we have ethical interests about human behavior and because, as political persons, we have an interest in a certain kind of order that can no longer be limited to interstate relations, given the porousness of borders and the speed of communication and of communicable diseases, among which violence is one.

Is risking lives to save others abroad less essential than risking them for the defense of unessential bases or redundant resources? Are inconsistencies and selectivity on a global scale any worse than those one finds in the application of domestic punishments, tax laws, or educational policies?

Another criticism of the cause for which intervention occurs is that it presupposes a clear distinction between oppressors and victims, whereas in reality the victims of terror may themselves have practiced terrorism and engaged in provocations. This charge has been leveled particularly against the Kosovars and their Liberation Army and (by the Russians) against the Chechens. In a world of few angels, it remains nevertheless necessary to distinguish between mere sinners and true devils. There is little doubt that Bosnian Muslims were more often the victims of Serbs and Croats than the instigators of terror against them, or that Kosovars, since the revocation of their autonomy, had been grievously mistreated. War is often a contest between pure evil and part evil, as Arthur Koestler recognized about World War II. Indeed, this problem is not different from that of identifying an aggressor in interstate affairs.

Next comes the issue of the proper authority to wage a war of intervention. Here, the critics point out a dilemma. If—in true realist fashion—it is the United States that takes the lead (either unilaterally or as shaper of a coalition in the United Nations or NATO or the Organization of American States), it will risk both dissipating its resources and fomenting considerable resentment abroad, among foes, rivals, and even allies with little sympathy for the self-proclaimed "indispensable nation" and for the burdens borne by the "only superpower." If, in order to avoid all this, the United States turns the mess over to the United Nations, there is a grave risk of throwing away the required "chance of success," given the bureaucratic inefficiency of the organization (painfully evident in Bosnia) as well as its dependence on the political support of and guidance by a number of states with divergent concerns, different designs for the UN mission, and a tendency to dump on it more responsibilities than it can handle or to give it mandates that are unrealistic (such as the protection of free havens in Bosnia or the establishment of peace among armed factions in Cambodia, Angola, Somalia, and Sierra Leone).[6] Many of the critics conclude that the least objectionable formula would be entrusting the task to a regional organization. The problem, however, is that the Organization of African Unity, in the most troubled of continents, has shown it self both too divided and too devoid of resources to take the lead—hence its passivity vis-á-vis Sudan and its failure in Rwanda and the Democratic Republic of the Congo. The Organization of American States remains dominated by the United States, and the European Union has not reached the stage of strategic-diplomatic action so far. In the successful case of East Timor, where no intervenors used force, it was a combination of U.S. diplomatic and economic pressures and of a "coalition of the willing" led by Australia that obliged Indonesia to retreat. Thus there is indeed something Sisyphean about the problem of authorization

Critics also question whether military interventions respect the principle of proportionality of values. They emphasize the very high costs the intervenors often impose on the supposed beneficiaries. In the case of Kosovo, the immediate effect of the bombing operation was the massive expulsion of the Kosovars whose protection was the objective of the war, and the U.S. preference for the immunity of their combatants increased casualties among noncombatants, both Serbs and Kosovars. Conversely, in Bosnia the limits put by the Security Council on the mandate of the United Nations Protection Force (UNPROFOR) left the "safe havens" unprotected and Srebrenica at the mercy of its genocidal conquerors. These were two opposite ways of violating the old rule "Do no harm."

Another set of criticisms concerns the principle of last resort. Waiting too long in the hope that diplomacy will work and is not just used by the "guilty" party as a delaying tactic can allow the party to consolidate its forces and to begin to carry out its murderous designs. It can be argued persuasively that the United States should have intervened in Haiti when thugs opposed the arrival of U.S. ships, which turned around and left, or in Kosovo just after Milosevic's violation of the deal he had made with Richard Holbrooke in October 1998. In Bosnia's case it took more than three years to get to the "last resort." Critics point out that given the dangers of such delays, and the human costs of military intervention, preventive action would be preferable. There was practically none undertaken in Yugoslavia in the spring of 1991. In both Somalia and Rwanda, the UN presence had been withdrawn before the tragedies that hit those countries, whereas in Macedonia, where observers have been stationed for many years, peace has been preserved. The case for prevention has, however, one major flaw. Unless the Security Council decides under Chapter VII that a situation creates a threat to peace and security and orders a country to accept the stationing of an international force, the need for that country's consent can thwart the effort at prevention—as we saw in Kosovo; and not all countries are likely to obey UN "commands."

The most impressive critiques concern the "reasonable chance of success." In interstate wars the definition of success is the defeat of one side's forces and the acceptance by the loser of the conditions set by the winner (for instance, the restoration of Kuwait's independence and integrity in the Persian Gulf War, and that of South Korea's sovereignty over its territory in the Korean War). In internal wars defeating the violator of human rights is only the beginning of a long ordeal that often requires more from international society than it is willing to devote to areas that are not strategically or economically important. For what is at stake after military victory is, in these cases, the rebuilding or the building of a state, from the outside and by outsiders. The long experience of the United Nations in Cambodia has shown how difficult this is. Often the United Nations has not had the mandate and the means to disarm factions that can thus continue to make trouble, as in Angola, or else the mandate exists, but the members lack the will to carry it out, as in Somalia. When the objective of the operation is the establishment of democracy in a place that has not practiced it and where most of the preconditions for it are missing, the outsider has a choice between, so to speak, reducing democracy to a mere free election and actively and gradually setting up the institutions and inculcating the values and the procedures that breed democratic government. The former may be too little, and the latter is likely to provoke charges of neocolonialism. What the United States, Britain, and France did in post-1945 Germany was not done by the United States in Haiti after the return of President Jean-Bertrand Aristide. It is too soon to say whether a new, stable, Bosnia will emerge from the Dayton accords. This is because success has been defined, both there and in Kosovo, as the establishment of a peaceful multiethnic society—that is, the organized coexistence of ethnic groups that have just gone through traumatic violence. There seems to be an unhappy choice between trying to reach what, in the short term, is an unreasonable objective (whose lack of realism, as in Kosovo, fuels endemic violence against the remaining Serbs) and a partition that may look, so to speak, surgically sound now but would be likely to create new territorial claims, to reward the ethnic cleansers, and above all to promote balkanization. When, as in Kosovo, the hatreds are still incandescent, even the minimal objective—the elimination of ethnic violence—may require more of a military and of a policy presence than states are willing to contribute.

Thus, success after war requires the international fire brigade to spend a disproportionate amount of its resources on tasks that are unpleasant and difficult, in areas that, to quote John Kenneth Galbraith on Vietnam, ought to be allowed to return to the obscurity they so richly deserve. And success requires the outsiders to make extremely difficult choices: how far to go in enlisting the local political forces, whose objectives may be far different from those of the "liberators" or occupiers (as in Kosovo), versus how far to go in becoming the de facto rulers of a country, at the cost of fostering deep resentments and of perpetuating external tutelage. Another difficult choice is between encouraging a reconciliation of the previously warring factions or parties and insisting on the punishment of those guilty of war crimes and crimes against humanity. Such punishment turns out, in fact, to be a necessary prelude to reconciliation, but in the short run it may have the opposite effect, and it may be beyond the capacity of the outside intervenors to locate and detain the criminals.

A final charge needs to be mentioned. It is in the realm of the *jus in bello* and concerns the proportionality of the means used by the intervenors to their ends. In interstate wars often the military means have been excessive and violated the immunity of noncombatants. In internal conflicts the means have tended to be both insufficient and inadequate. Yugoslavia in 1992–94 is a clear case of insufficiency—Serbs and Croats pushed around and aside the hapless UN forces repeatedly. Somalia was another such case. Kosovo was a case of inadequacy: the "American way of war" ruled out ground forces for far too long and resulted in high-altitude bombing that inflicted little punishment on the Serb forces that were driving the Kosovars out of the country.

The essence of the critique of intervention in internal conflicts is the argument that the present nature of international society dooms such enterprises or ambitions. By having to concentrate on cases that do not involve the domestic turbulence in major powers, they oblige states to devote to secondary or inessential areas resources and attention that they are reluctant to provide, thus almost guaranteeing fiascoes: peacekeepers with no mandate to use force if the parties resume fighting (Angola, Cambodia, and Croatia in the spring of 1995), peacemakers who are far better at fighting than at the "social work" required after victory. States have to concentrate on essentials, for domestic as well as for geopolitical reasons, and international or regional organizations have neither sufficient autonomy (political and military) nor sufficient competence to be useful actors rather than parts of the problem.

NOTES

1. Berkeley Institute of Governmental Studies, *Public Affairs Report* (January 2000): 1
2. Kofi Annan, Secretary-General's Report to the General Assembly, UN Press Release SG/SM7136, GA/9596, September 20, 1999.
3. David Luban, "Intervention and Civilization" (unpublished paper), 10.
4. Henry Kissinger quoted in Ivo H. Daalder, "Knowing When to Say No: The Development of UN Policies for Peace-Keeping," in *UN Peace-Keeping, American Policy, and the Uncivil Wars of the 1990s,* ed. William J. Durch (New York: St. Martin's Press, 1996), 50.
5. Colin Powell quoted in ibid.,41.
6. Kissinger (quoted in ibid., 50) put it this way: "[I]f international consensus is the prerequisite for the employment of American power, the result may be ineffective dithering. If . . . international machinery can commit U.S. forces, the risk is American involvement in issues of no fundamental national interest."

61

M. ELAINE BUNN

PREEMPTIVE ACTION: WHEN, HOW, AND TO WHAT EFFECT?

What role should preemptive action play in U.S. national strategy? In the wake of the first public statements by President George W. Bush in June 2002, and in the buildup to military action against Iraq, the issue quickly became a lightning rod for controversy. While some commentators hailed preemption as a valuable concept whose time had come, others condemned it as a dangerous precedent that could damage American interests, strain our relations overseas, and make

SOURCE: "Preemptive Action: When, How and To What Effect," by M. Elaine Bunn, from *Strategic Forum*, No. 200, July 2003.

the United States a feared unilateralist in the international system. All the hue and cry has done little to clarify the issues and choices that policymakers face in weighing the utility and limits of the concept.

The National Security Strategy of the United States of America (September 2002) states that "the United States will, if necessary, act preemptively" to prevent rogue states or terrorists from threatening or using weapons of mass destruction (WMD) against the United States or its friends and allies (see page 677). Yet there is much misunderstanding and confusion about the administration's concept of preemption, which has led to a great deal of apprehension. Some of the confusion is self-inflicted, some is circumstantial, and some results from willful misreading.

While the administration was laying out a *general* concept, it did so against the backdrop of Iraq. It is not surprising, then, that some have failed to distinguish between the two. Iraq may be the first case study in the new policy—although some argue that action against Iraq was not preemption but a preventive war, while others argue it was a continuation of action from the 1991 Gulf War. In any event, Iraq is not the sum total of the policy.

In the popular mind, preemption is synonymous with the use of force, and specifically with military strikes. But the concept has a broader meaning and application, as implied by the administration's careful emphasis on preemptive *action*. To *preempt* is defined in Merriam-Webster's Collegiate Dictionary as "to prevent from happening or taking place: forestall; preclude." Many of the preemptive actions that the United States is likely to undertake will be nonmilitary. And the nonmilitary methods of preemptive action are likely to be less controversial than military preemption.

HISTORICAL ANTECEDENTS

There are a number of historical examples of the United States *contemplating* preemptive military actions including against WMD-armed adversaries (at least partially motivated by preemption or prevention, sometimes in addition to other motives), but only a small number of examples in which preemptive military action was actually taken.

U.S. Government deliberations in the late 1940s and early 1950s considered attacking Soviet nuclear capabilities while they were a fledgling force, and discussions in the early 1960s debated whether to take out Chinese nuclear capabilities.[1] In neither case did the United States go forward with preemptive strikes.

The Cuban Missile Crisis of October 1962 has been cited repeatedly by Bush administration officials as an example of preemptive action (as opposed to a preemptive strike); the quarantine or blockade of Cuba was intended to prevent any further buildup of offensive arms (medium-range ballistic missiles and nuclear warheads were already on the island, although the presence of nuclear warheads was not clear at the time).[2]

In 1989–1990, America threatened to take military action to shut down a Libyan chemical facility at Rabta, which the United States suspected was intended

Administration Statements on Preemption

- President Bush first explicitly discussed preemption in a speech at West Point on June 1, 2002: "If we wait for threats to fully materialize, we will have waited too long. . . . We must take the battle to the enemy, disrupt his plans, and confront the worst threats before they emerge . . . our security will require all Americans to be forward-looking and resolute, to be ready for preemptive action when necessary to defend our liberty and to defend our lives."
- In September 2002, the concept was elaborated in the National Security Strategy: "We must be prepared to stop rogue states and their terrorist clients before they are able to threaten or use weapons of mass destruction against the United States and our allies and friends. . . . The greater the threat, the greater is the risk of inaction—and the more compelling the case for taking anticipatory action to defend ourselves, even if uncertainty remains as to the time and place of the enemy's attack. To forestall or prevent such hostile acts by our adversaries, the United States will, if necessary, act preemptively."
- National Security Advisor Condoleezza Rice further clarified the strategy in an October 1, 2002, speech: "The number of cases in which it might be justified will always be small. Preemptive action does not come at the beginning of a long chain of effort."
- In December 2002, the Bush administration released its *National Strategy to Combat Weapons of Mass Destruction,* which states: "Because deterrence may not succeed, and because of the potentially devastating consequences of WMD use against our forces and civilian population, U.S. military forces and appropriate civilian agencies must have the capability to defend against WMD-armed adversaries, including in appropriate cases through preemptive measures. This requires capabilities to detect and destroy an adversary's WMD assets before these weapons are used."

to produce mustard or nerve gas. (This was against the backdrop of earlier tensions with Libyan leader Muammar Qadhafi and the 1986 U.S. bombing of Libyan leadership sites [Operation *El Dorado Canyon*] following the bombing of a Berlin night club that killed two Americans.) Qadhafi subsequently shut down the Rabta facility, claiming that a fire had destroyed it. U.S. officials in 1996 also threatened military strikes against a suspected chemical weapons plant that Qadhafi was building under a mountain near Tarhunah.[3]

In 1994, when North Korea threatened to remove fuel rods from the Yongbyon nuclear reactor, U.S. officials considered a preemptive strike on the reactor with conventional precision weapons. Former officials have recently testified that they were confident that such a strike would have eliminated the facilities at Yongbyon without causing any radioactive plume to be emitted downwind, but they also recognized that the result might well have been a very destructive North Korean conventional attack on South Korea. (Such a war was averted by the negotiation of the 1994 Agreed Framework.[4])

The United States is not the only country that has considered or carried out preemptive actions. The classic case is the 1981 Israeli attack on Iraq's Osirak nuclear facility because of concern that Iraq would use the reactor to produce highly enriched uranium for a weapons program. (Iran had previously bombed Osirak, in the opening days of the Iran-Iraq war in 1980, lightly damaging the facility.[5]) After its 1981 attack, Israel claimed it was exercising its inherent right of self-defense, consistent with Article 51 of the United Nations (UN) charter. The UN Security Council censured Israel, and the U.S. Ambassador to the UN spoke against Israel for its action.[6]

In these historical cases—none of which involved nonstate actors—the risk/benefit analysis of preemptive action was controversial. These examples point to the difficult choices associated with preemption and to the likelihood that, in the future, there will probably be relatively few situations where the risks of preemptive military action are worth the costs.

Though the option for preemption is not new, talking about it publicly and raising it (arguably) to the level of doctrine is new, which may be both helpful and harmful. Moreover, while the National Security Strategy sensibly refrains from setting down rigid criteria for when preemptive military action should be seriously considered or used, its reticence to elaborate the general conditions and circumstances, or the factors to be weighed in deciding on the preemptive use of force, has failed to resolve uncertainty regarding administration decisionmaking when faced with difficult future situations.

To better understand the issues at stake in the concept of preemptive action, consider the following questions: why the new focus on preemption; against whom and what; when, how, and to what effect preemptive action might be considered?

THE NEW FOCUS

The motivations underlying the Bush administration's emphasis on preemption spring from three strongly held assessments of the changing nature of international security and the heightened vulnerability of Americans to new-era threats.

The first, and foremost, perception is a growing nexus between transnational terrorism and WMD proliferation. It is hard to overestimate the impact of September 11, 2001, on administration thinking. In the months after the attacks, Congress and the public were asking what administration officials knew beforehand and whether they had done everything possible to prevent it. As the weight of responsibility for protecting the United States from an even worse occurrence—a potential September 11 with nuclear, biological, or chemical weapons—settled on the shoulders of administration officials, the need to act swiftly and firmly before threats become attacks is perhaps the clearest lesson they have drawn from that experience.

Second, there is a growing pessimism about deterrence. In the case of rogue state leaders, deterrence—while still applicable—may not always work. The perceived high-risk strategies of the former Iraqi and current North Korean leadership have added fuel to such arguments. In addition, some analysts have come to a working assumption that "deterring terrorists" is an oxymoron and that in the case of terrorists and WMD, possession equals use. While some believe that seeking to deny terrorists their objectives may have some (modest) long-term deterrent effect, many believe that terrorist organizations—which lack populations to protect or territory to safeguard and whose operatives may be willing to die for their cause—are essentially undeterrable, or at least very difficult to deter given international standards and political norms (for example, the unacceptability of threatening reprisals against innocent family members).

Third, there is a realization that if deterrence fails, defenses will never be perfect. Even if America had defenses of all types—ballistic missile defense, cruise missile and other air defenses, civil defense, detection, vaccines, port/border checks, and so forth—those defenses would not be 100 percent effective against WMD threats 100 percent of the time. As Secretary Donald Rumsfeld has stressed, "It is not possible to defend against every conceivable kind of attack in every conceivable location at every minute of the day or night. . . . The best, and in some cases, the only defense, is a good offense."[7]

Statements pointing to this administration's lack of confidence in traditional deterrence precede its statements on preemption. The President's May 2001 speech at the National Defense University addressed the need to broaden the concept of deterrence and put in new, more capable offensive and defensive elements to bolster this concept.[8] His campaign speech at The Citadel in September 1999 also sounded the theme that traditional deterrence is not sufficient in the new security situation.[9] However, the first explicit mention of preemption during the Bush administration was in the statement of the Chairman of the Joint Chiefs of Staff in the *Quadrennial Defense Review Report* issued September 30, 2001.[10] In recognizing that defense of the U.S. homeland is the highest priority for the Armed Forces, the report states that the United States "must deter, preempt, and defend against aggression" targeted at the United States.

WHAT TO PREEMPT?

Administration officials have consistently stated that the concept of preemption is focused on terrorists and rogue states—thereby presumably easing the minds of leaders in Russia and China, while potentially heightening concerns in Iraq (prior to the fall of Saddam), Iran, North Korea, and possibly Libya and Syria.

Rogue states. Though the President seems to have avoided the term "axis of evil" since he used it in his January 2002 State of the Union address, the National Security Strategy's characterization of rogue states appears to define the common traits of countries in the axis: those who brutalize their own people, display no regard for international law, threaten their neighbors, are determined to acquire weapons of mass destruction, sponsor terrorism around the globe, and reject basic human values. (Interestingly, the National Security Strategy applies this characterization and the phrase *rogue state* only to Iraq and North Korea— omitting Iran, the third country named in the axis of evil speech.)

Terrorists. The National Security Strategy defines *terrorism* as "premeditated, politically motivated violence perpetrated against innocents" and focuses as a priority on disrupting and destroying "terrorist organizations of global reach."

While the National Security Strategy lumps together rogue states and terrorists when discussing preemption, it is useful to consider them separately. There are important differences that may yield different preemptive options. In addition, the threshold for obtaining international support for preemptive action against a recognized sovereign state (even a rogue state) is likely to be significantly higher than against terrorist groups. In fact, many argue that because al Qaeda has attacked the United States (even before September 11), it is not "preemption" for America to seek to destroy al Qaeda infrastructure and leadership.[11]

Targets. The U.S. Government might want the option of taking preemptive action against a range of threats by rogue states and terrorists, including aggression of any kind, and particularly conventional attacks with mass effects, such as the September 11 attacks. However, American officials have focused their discussion almost exclusively on WMD—that is, chemical, biological, or nuclear weapons.

Even within the restricted subset of WMD, one might consider preempting the development of weapons-useable material, acquisition of weapons, or their use. Specific WMD targets might include:

- pre-capability components of weapons or precursor agents
- production sites, storage, deployment sites, launchers or other delivery systems
- military forces (of rogue states) or operatives (of terrorist networks) that might employ WMD
- command and control systems (which may be very different for terrorists than for rogue states), including leadership or a regime.

WHEN TO PREEMPT?

There has been considerable discussion of the distinction between *preemptive* action (when adversary use of force is imminent) and *preventive* action (for example, depriving an adversary of a capability that it might someday have or averting an action that it might someday contemplate). Some observers maintain that the issue being raised by the administration is not preemption but instead preventive military operations or *preventive war*—that is, taking preventive action *before* the need is certain and balancing the risks of acting against those of not acting. The threshold of a decision to take preventive action will be much higher than for preemptive action, for which there is actual, presentable intelligence of an imminent threat. However, from a practical standpoint, since the President and the National Security Strategy first used the phrases *preemptive action* and *preemption*, they have taken hold in public discussion. The debate really revolves, then, around the definition of *imminent*.

There are two ways to think about a preemption timeline: either the traditional peacetime-to-crisis-to-conflict-to-postconflict timeline, in which preemptive action is taken in peacetime or a building crisis; or, in the case of WMD, where an adversary is on the acquisition-to-use timeline. The points on the latter continuum range from just prior to the time at which an adversary has acquired a useable capability (for example, disrupting/interdicting delivery of the last item needed for a completed WMD capability, or in the terrorist case, interdicting the team before it infiltrates the WMD site, or before the handover of materials takes place), to the point where an adversary has the capability and generally hostile intent, to the point where there is a specific hostile intent and use is imminent.

At what point is danger imminent? Condoleezza Rice has noted, "new technology requires new thinking about when a threat actually becomes 'imminent' . . . We must adapt the concept of imminent threat to the capabilities and objectives of today's adversaries."[12] We can imagine a scenario in which preemption would be justified based on imminent danger. For instance, suppose that the United States had firm intelligence that a hostile rogue government was about to launch missiles with nuclear warheads that could kill millions of Americans (in the case of no or imperfect missile defenses). A President would at least have to consider the possibility of preemption in such a situation. If one is absolutely sure that a devastating attack is coming, preemption is an easier choice. That scenario is at one end of a WMD time continuum. At the other end is a nation with general hostile intentions and for which there is ambiguous intelligence regarding efforts to acquire WMD. Where along that spectrum is preemptive action justifiable? Presidents will likely hesitate to preempt when today looks quite a bit like yesterday, and they anticipate that tomorrow is going to look quite a bit like today. This raises the question of what U.S. thresholds will be and how to describe the action points.

Michael Waltzer, in his 1977 book *Just and Unjust Wars*, drew the line between legitimate and illegitimate first strikes *not* at the point of imminent attack but at the point of *sufficient threat*—a phrase he recognized as "necessarily vague." He meant it to cover three things: "a manifest intent to injure, a degree of active preparation that makes that intent a positive danger, and a general situation in which waiting, or doing anything other than fighting, greatly magnifies the risk."[13]

It is ironic that the closer to the "imminent use" end of the spectrum a situation falls, the easier preemption is to justify politically, but the harder it may be to be operationally decisive, because the adversary will likely have protected the intended targets of preemption through deception, hardening, burial, dispersal, or pre-delegation of release. Conversely, the farther from the imminent use end of the continuum a situation is, the less acceptable it is likely to be to world opinion, though preemptive strikes at that stage are more likely to be effective in eliminating or postponing the threat.

HOW TO PREEMPT?

Though most tend to think of preemption in terms of strike—kinetic weapons on target—the ways in which preemptive action can be carried out are much broader. Preemptive action also could employ a variety of nonmilitary, as well as military and intelligence, capabilities. The National Security Strategy states that the "United States will not use force in all cases to preempt emerging threats." Rice, in interviews shortly after the President's June 2002 West Point speech, made clear that preemptive action did not necessarily imply force. She stated, "It really means early action of some kind. It means forestalling certain destructive acts against you by an adversary."[14]

The National Strategy for Homeland Security, released in July 2002, has been little noticed in the preemption debate, although it addresses the issue extensively—in terms of "preventing and preempting future attacks."[15] It notes that:

> with advance warning, we have various federal, state, and local response assets that can intercede and prevent terrorists from carrying out attacks. These include law enforcement, emergency response, and military teams. In the most dangerous of incidents, particularly when terrorists have chemical, biological, radiological, or nuclear weapons in their possession, it is crucial that the individuals who preempt the terrorists do so flawlessly, no matter if they are part of the local SWAT team or the FBI's Hostage Rescue Team.[16]

Where preemptive action occurs will have implications for how it is done. Places might include international territory (such as interdicting capabilities, precursors, or terrorists at sea); the territory of a rogue state; the territory of a falling or failing state; or the territory of a friend or ally. Preemptive action in the latter case—that is, in nonmilitary ways with the cooperation of an ally—may be very different from that against rogue or failing states.

At times, military action will be required for preemption to be effective. Even in those cases, there are a variety of methods for applying military forces preemptively. While most people tend to focus on kinetic strike capabilities, there are also nonkinetic offensive means such as information operations (for example, disrupting command, control, and communications); special operations forces; or Coast Guard/Navy boarding ships, imposing blockades, or turning back/sabotaging shipments. The December 2002 interception of a North Korean ship at sea carrying 15 Scud missiles is an example of what that type of preemptive action—interdiction at sea as a kind of aggressive nonproliferation—might look like.[17]

When preemptive military action is required, there will likely be a need for decisive effect and the ability to act promptly for such action to be successful—not only to take advantage of potentially fleeting opportunities but also to allow the maximum amount of time for consultation, consideration, and deliberation of whether the United States will take action. America must be prepared to make investments in improving intelligence, surveillance, and reconnaissance capabilities; planning, including analysis of the effects of executing a plan (especially attacking WMD sites while trying to minimize collateral damage); and the military forces themselves (see box on page 684).

Complicating military options is the fact that adversaries, or the targets of preemption, are taking actions to constrain the U.S. ability to preempt. These enemy actions are designed to defeat the military effects of preemption, essentially eliminating the opportunity for surprise or raising costs to an unacceptable level. For example, adversaries may embed a target within commercial activities, cloak it in denial-deception operations, put it underground, conceal it, make it mobile, or embed it in populated areas that make it difficult to target without substantial collateral damage. Aided by the globalization of technology, adversaries are working to frustrate American precision-guided munitions. To be effective in such circumstances requires an extraordinary degree of precision, and precision strike requires intelligence collection on a scale that is extraordinarily difficult and very costly in terms of time and resources.[18]

Preemption sometimes is taken to mean nuclear preemption. This confusion is partly a holdover from Cold War usage and partly a result of recent developments. The 2002 Nuclear Posture Review (NPR)—which addressed not only nuclear issues but also nonnuclear strike as well as active and passive defenses—first came into public view through selective leaks of the classified *NPR Report* to Congress by critics who focused on its nuclear aspects. More recently, the discussion of preemption against Iraqi WMD coincided with the discussion of a new (or repackaged) nuclear weapon to target hard and deeply buried targets and chemical and biological weapons.

It is an understatement to say that the threshold of any Presidential decision for nuclear preemption would be higher than for conventional strike. It is difficult to imagine that a President would *preempt* with nuclear weapons in other than the most dire circumstances, with no other option to prevent massive American or allied casualties. The use of nuclear weapons would be among the most difficult decisions a President could make—given their destructiveness, the breaking of the 50-plus-year barrier to nuclear use, as well as the international opprobrium likely to follow. It would be hard enough for any President to make the decision to use nuclear weapons in response to the use of WMD; deciding to preempt with nuclear weapons would be far more difficult.

So why, some might ask, is the administration studying whether lower-yield, lower-collateral-damage, earth-penetrating nuclear weapons—either new or revamped—should be pursued? Administration officials argue that their purpose is (still) largely for deterrence—so that in the mind of a rogue state leader, it is credible that the United States might use nuclear weapons and thus the risks are not worth the gains.

Characteristics of Military Capabilities for Preemptive Action

To support preemptive options when military force is required, some portion of U.S. forces should have the following characteristics (not all forces need every attribute):

- *Stealth* to reach targets without forewarning.
- *Responsiveness* in striking targets (or boarding ships or setting up blockades) on short notice.
- *Long range* with no or minimal dependence on overflight, forward basing, or forward access.
- *Effectiveness* across the entire range of missions: blockades; embargoes; interdicting nuclear, biological, or chemical (NBC) components before they fall into terrorist or rogue state hands; defeating hardened or deeply buried facilities; and destroying NBC weapons or agents without dispersing them.
- *Precision and accuracy* to minimize collateral damage.
- *Reliability* to ensure effectiveness the first time, and, in some cases, sustainability.
- *Diversity of delivery* means and weapon effects.

Key Enablers

- *Exquisite intelligence (accurate, timely, persistent, and actionable)* is required for the mission and for after-action assessment.
- *Command, control, communications (C^3)* must be effective, timely, and responsive to senior decisionmakers.

TO WHAT EFFECT?

In any assessment of the effect preemptive action will have, both operational/military effect and political effect are important considerations.

On the operational/military side, the U.S. Government needs to think through the effectiveness of any preemptive operation in achieving its objectives and how to measure that effectiveness. If the overriding objective of preemption is *regime change*, the measure is fairly straightforward, though not necessarily easy to achieve. On the other hand, if the objective is to *disarm*, rather than to remove the leadership of the adversary, the measure of effectiveness is more temporal. Specifically, *for what period of time* would a particular preemptive action prevent or delay acquisition of a WMD capability? For example, the Israeli attack against the Osirak reactor may have set the Iraqi nuclear program back— it is unclear whether by several months or several years—but as the inspections after Operation *Desert Storm* in 1991 found, the attack did not end the Iraqi program. If anything, preemption may have led Iraq to take a much more expanded effort, pursuing several paths to nuclear capability in parallel.[19]

What level of confidence is required (in both the intelligence information and the U.S. ability to effectively carry out the mission) to make a decision to preempt? If, for example, the objective were to destroy WMD, how much must be destroyed for the preemptive action to be considered effective—all, most, or some? There is unlikely to be absolute confidence in the intelligence capability to locate all of an adversary's WMD, or in the capability to destroy it. Will preemption prompt the adversary to use the remainder? And is the United States better or worse off after such a preemptive action?

The answer depends fundamentally upon the assumption we make about the likelihood of use. Would a rogue leader use WMD in any event (either early, as a last chance to save the regime, or as the regime falls, in an effort to inflict as much pain as possible)? If he were going to use WMD anyway, and the United States destroys even some of it, preemption makes sense; but if it prompts adversary use of WMD capability that otherwise would not have been used, preemption would turn out to be a bad choice. The difficulty is in knowing the answer in advance. Are terrorists a different case? Does the assumption "possession equals use" apply? If so, the "better-or-worse-off" presumption in terrorist cases would be in favor of preemption.

Since preemptive action is unlikely to be 100 percent effective, the role defense plays in preemption must be considered. Should defenses of all types—ballistic missile defense, cruise missile and other air defense, defenses of borders and ports—be put on a higher state of alert or readiness prior to preemptive strikes? What effect would that have on tactical surprise? And is the U.S. Government more likely to consider preemption if it believes its defenses can be effective against any WMD capabilities that it fails to destroy? Conversely, do limited defenses reduce the pressure to preempt if U.S. leaders believe that the first few adversary WMD used could be neutralized?

With regard to the political effect, worldwide reaction to preemptive action by the United States would depend on a number of factors:

- What was the reason for preemptive action, its effectiveness, and the capability used?
- Was the level of force, if required, commensurate with the task, or was it perceived as excessive?
- How was the action viewed under international law?
- How effective was U.S. consultation and intelligence sharing as the crisis ramped up?
- What was the level of unintended damage (including the contaminating effects of partially destroyed WMD materials) to civilians and the territory of others?
- How effective was consequence management after the fact, and what was the American role in it?

- How effective was U.S. public diplomacy on the issues just mentioned (what proof was offered; how convincing was the case that preemption was the best of a number of bad options and that it was done in self-defense)?
- How effective was the public diplomacy by adversaries and others?

The reactions of allies and friends, conditioned as they would surely be by some or all of these factors, would have *consequences* for coalition building and cohesion as well as basing rights, access, and overflight.

The United States would also have to judge the policy effect of the message to the next potential adversary, as well as whether others—such as China versus Taiwan, or India and Pakistan—would see U.S. preemption policy as a green light for their own preemptive actions—or at least as rhetorical cover. The administration was obviously cognizant of the "precedent for other nations" criticism. National Security Advisor Rice has stated, "But this approach must be treated with great caution. . . . It does not give a green light—to the United States or any other nation—to act first without exhausting other means, including diplomacy. . . The threat must be very grave. And the risks of waiting must far outweigh the risks of action."[20] This statement implies that the bar is set high, but administration statements are vague about the conditions under which preemption would be undertaken and what the decision factors should be.

WHY TALK ABOUT IT?

Although preemption as an option is not new, the level of *public* discussion of it by American officials is. Previously, preemption had been discussed internally in defense or policy circles and very little externally. If other administrations have had the quiet option for preemption, why has this administration talked about it so publicly, and even written it explicitly into its National Security Strategy?

What effect does *public* discussion of preemption by U.S. officials—either generally or specifically, in peacetime and in crisis—have on friends as well as on potential adversaries? There are both advantages and disadvantages of U.S. officials talking publicly about preemption.

Discussion might signal a new seriousness in dealing with WMD and terrorism that will strengthen deterrence. Could discussion, for instance, have a deterrent effect on states that might let WMD fall into the hands of terrorists—especially if the weapons might be traced to them and they were held accountable? Might it make rogue states hesitate before an aggressive action that might be used to justify preemption? Might it send a message to rogue states that their continued existence depends on whatever WMD capabilities they may have not falling into the hands of terrorist groups, whether voluntarily or involuntarily?

While it may dissuade or deter rogue state brandishing of WMD, U.S. talk of preemption could, on the other hand, make rogue states more determined to *acquire or maintain* WMD, in order to make Americans think long and hard about the costs of preemption or regime change against them, as well as to work even harder to hide or disperse those capabilities or leaders against whom they think preemptive action might be taken. This concern appears to be animating North Korean determination to acquire nuclear weapons despite international opprobrium.

Public discussion of preemption may also be seen by the administration as opening a critical debate necessary to prepare the public for use of force in ways not previously thought to be consonant with the American sense of fairness. There is a public presumption (and even a military presumption) that "good guys don't preempt," which some believe, in the new security environment, stands as an inappropriate restraint on U.S. action. So the President or his advisors may have decided that it is necessary to engage in this public debate in order to prepare the intellectual groundwork (both internationally and domestically) that would otherwise make the use of preemptive options, if not impossible, then exceedingly difficult.

Secretary Rumsfeld has observed:

> It is difficult for all of us who have grown up in this country and believed in the principle that unless attacked, one does not attack . . . for the most part, our country has had a view that that was the way we do things. It was other countries that have attacked us for the most part and initiated conflicts. The question, though, is in the 21st century, with biological weapons, for example, that could kill hundreds of thousands of people, what does one do? Does one wait until they're attacked? . . . There is no doubt in my mind, but that the overwhelming majority of the American people would prefer that their government take the kinds of steps necessary to prevent that type of attack?[21]

Officials in other nations have also discussed the issue of preemptive action. Australian Prime Minister John Howard observed, "It stands to reason that if you believe that somebody was going to launch an attack on your country, either of a conventional kind or a terrorist kind, and you had a capacity to stop it and there was no alternative other than to use that capacity, then of course you would have to use it."[22] He also reportedly said that he would like to see the United Nations Charter changed to allow preemptive action against terrorists.

The French government document issued in January for its 2003–2008 military program addressed preemption as well: "We must . . . be prepared to identify and forestall threats as soon as possible. In this context, the possibility of preemptive action might be considered, from the time that an explicit and confirmed threatening situation is identified."[23]

In Japan, which has been reluctant since World War II even to contemplate taking actions except in self-defense, Japan Defense Agency Director General Shigeru Ishiba said in January:

> If North Korea expresses the intention of turning Tokyo into a sea of fire and if it begins preparations [to attack], for instance by fueling [its missiles], we

will consider [North Korea] is initiating [a military attack]. . . . Once North Korea declares it will demolish Tokyo and begins preparing for a missile launch, we will consider it the start of a military attack against Japan.[24]

Ishiba later stressed that, even with Japan's Peace Constitution, "Just to be on the receiving end of the attack is not what our constitution had in mind. . . . Just to wait for another country's attack and lose thousands and tens of thousands of people, that is not what the constitution assumes."[25]

Public discussion of American preemption may also alienate friends as well as warn enemies. Some have expressed concern that the public debate has a strategic consequence of complicating relationships with some allies and coalition partners. Talk of preemption may have exacerbated what some countries see as a U.S. tendency toward unilateralism and acting above the law and international norms. A German editorialist called the doctrine "immature, even dangerous . . . it is the law of the strongest."[26] Others have expressed concern that by stating the threat to take preemptive action, it sounds as if America is threatening to execute a "series of Pearl Harbors"—and that, if what the United States is trying to do is to create a consensus as to what is right and what is wrong, the result could be the opposite.

Much of the debate over preemption confuses *threats* of preemption with preemptive *operations*—that is, talking about it versus actually doing it. A preemptive threat may actually complicate a preemptive operation by undercutting the element of surprise. With regard to terrorist and rogue state adversaries, public talk of preemption may encourage them to redouble efforts to hide, disperse, or quickly use WMD capabilities that they anticipate may be the targets of preemptive action. Indeed, there may be a tradeoff between the operational pluses of surprise versus the political downsides of not having built the case and influenced public opinion before preemptive action (keeping in mind the distinction between tactical and strategic surprise). When the Defense Secretary was asked, "Is the United States contemplating preemptive strikes against other nations' WMD holdings?" Rumsfeld replied, "On the record. Why would anyone answer that question if they were contemplating it?"[27]

OPTION OR DOCTRINE?

An important issue for the national security community is whether preemption, which was treated as merely an option in the past, has been raised to the level of a doctrine by the Bush administration. The President himself said in remarks (perhaps impromptu) on June 14, 2002:

I was at West Point the other day and I was honored to give a graduation speech where I laid out a *new doctrine* [emphasis added] called preemption. . . . In the past, we used to have a doctrine called containment and deterrence. You can't contain a shadowy terrorist network. You can't deter somebody who doesn't have a country. And you're not going to be able—future Presidents won't be able to deter or contain one of these nations which harbors weapons of mass destruction, nations who hate America.[28]

This statement sounded like the death knell for previous doctrines. However, Secretary of State Colin Powell, responding to Congressional questions, observed that it is not "as if all other strategies and doctrines have gone away and suddenly preemption is the only strategy doctrine. That's just not the case."[29] Equally, Rice has made clear that "The National Security Strategy does not overturn five decades of doctrine and jettison either containment or deterrence. These strategic concepts can and will continue to be employed where appropriate."[30]

The question of "option or doctrine" is not purely a semantic distinction. To call preemption a doctrine implies that it is a central organizing principle for marshalling the instruments of national power in support of national objectives and that in relevant cases, action will be taken in accordance with established governing principles. Seen in this light, the recent use of force against Iraq may be the first application of a new doctrine of preemptive action.[31] On the other hand, preemption may have been an option employed in that specific situation, without its rising to the level of doctrine. With respect to North Korea, the administration has downplayed the idea that Pyongyang's recently disclosed nuclear program constitutes a crisis or that military force might be required, and it has insisted that a diplomatic solution is possible. This inconsistency could lead to the conclusion that since preemption has not been chosen in all cases where it conceivably applies, it must not be a doctrine. But the administration also reportedly moved B-52s and B-1s to Guam so that they would be available for military options in North Korea—one of which might be preemptive action. Probably only in hindsight, with historical perspective, will we be able to judge the administration's application of the concept of preemption.

CRITERIA

The National Security Strategy is notably silent on the issue of what, if any, decision criteria our national leadership would apply in considering the possibility of preemptive military action to counter WMD. Perhaps public elaboration of such criteria was too much to ask—given the sensitivity of the issue—but silence begs the question: Is there a roadmap that can be seriously considered or used?

Over a decade ago, Michèle Flournoy and Philip Zelikow, as part of the early debate on counterproliferation, developed a lengthy set of questions, which include the following points that still serve as a useful guide to decisions about preemption:

1. Do we have less than high confidence that we can deter a given country from using [nuclear, biological, or chemical] weapons against U.S., our allies, and our interests?

2. Do we believe that the country might transfer the capabilities to others who might use them?

3. Will the mere acquisition by this country of WMD significantly increase the danger of war or coercion or attack that would threaten our interests? If the answer to any of these three is yes, then the next question is:

4. Are we confident that these dangers can be significantly dealt with short of preemption? If not, then we go down the list.

5. Do the actions and behavior of the country ethically and legally justify offensive military action by the United States?

6. What kind of public reaction—domestic and foreign—can we anticipate? And if highly negative, would it be prohibitive, or is it something we'd be willing to weather criticism for?

7. Can military action contain or eliminate the danger without risking either retaliation or unintended consequences that would pose an even greater risk to our interests? Is preemption worth the risk of the response?

8. Do we know enough about the adversary's capabilities, their defenses, and their operations, to actually launch a strike that will be effective with high confidence of success and with acceptable levels of collateral damage?

9. Can we do it? Do we have the military and intelligence capabilities to pull it off?

10. Looking strategically at the long-term implications, what precedents does this action set? Do the anticipated benefits outweigh the costs and conversely, are we willing to live with not preempting in a given case? Are we willing to live with a given country having a capability that could be used in the future?[32]

These questions are as relevant today as they were 10 years ago. While the first several questions focus on countries—nonstate terrorists were not as great a concern then as now—they can be adapted to apply to terrorist groups as well as rogue states. The key question will be how great is the danger, but it is also important to ask whether the dangers can be dealt with in other ways, whether the actions ethically and legally justify U.S. military action, and whether the United States has the intelligence and military capabilities to be effective with high confidence of success and acceptable levels of unintended damage.

The 10 questions above are a starting point for decisionmakers and may also help the public think through preemption. Answers from today's perspective may differ from the day-after perspective; that is, if in fact WMD had already been used against the United States or American forces or allies with many thousands of casualties, would leaders and the public have a different perspective on the advisability and the desirability of preemption?

These points are geared to thinking about when military preemption might be appropriate, although they could be adapted to nonmilitary preemptive action as well. However, military preemption will be more difficult to justify than nonmilitary options. Adopting some version of these considerations as criteria for preemption might reduce the apprehension and misperceptions about administration policy, because when these factors are seriously weighed, there are likely to be few cases where the preemptive use of military strikes will be chosen as the best option.

Looking beyond Iraq, it is difficult to predict whether preemptive military action will be the doctrine of the future or a seldom-used option. The challenge here is somewhat like divining the future of case law, in which established practice is created step by step and can only be understood by looking backward, not forward.

Clearly, the United States is feeling its way carefully as it goes along. The recent U.S. focus on preemption was born of a defensive reaction in the face of emerging threats. If used too frequently, without good justification, and with ill effect, America is more likely to be increasingly viewed as an arrogant nation carrying out the "law of the strongest." Used judiciously, with good reason, and effectively—only in the toughest cases—preemption is likely to be accepted, if somewhat grudgingly, by the international community.

NOTES

1. William Burr and Jeffrey T. Richelson, "Whether to 'Strangle the Baby in the Cradle': The United States and the Chinese Nuclear Program, 1960–64," *International Security* 25, no. 3 (Winter 2000/2001), 54–99.
2. Anatoli I. Gribkov and William Y. Smith, *Operation ANADYR: U.S. and Soviet Generals Recount the Cuban Missile Crisis* (Chicago: Edition q, 1994).
3. Richard J. Newman, "The Qadhafi Question," *U.S. News and World Report,* April 15, 1996, 15.
4. Ashton B. Carter, "Three Crises with North Korea," prepared testimony before the Senate Foreign Relations Committee, February 4, 2003.
5. Rebecca Grant, "Osirak and Beyond," *Air Force Magazine,* August 2002, 74. Grant cites a statement issued by the official Iraqi news agency following the 1980 Iranian bombing of Osirak: "The Iranian people should not fear the Iraqi nuclear reactor, which is not intended to be used against Iran, but against the Zionist entity."
6. Anthony Clark Arend, "International Law and the Preemptive Use of Military Force," *The Washington Quarterly* 26, no. 2 (Spring 2003), 89.
7. Donald H. Rumsfeld, "21st Century Transformation of U.S. Armed Forces," presentation at the National Defense University, Washington, DC, January 31, 2002.
8. George W. Bush, remarks at the National Defense University, Washington, DC, May 1, 2001.
9. George W. Bush, remarks at The Citadel, September 23, 1999.
10. Department of Defense, *Quadrennial Defense Review Report* (Washington, DC: Department of Defense, September 30, 2001), particularly Chapter VIII: Statement of the Chairman of the Joint Chiefs of Staff.
11. See Walter B. Slocombe, "Force, Pre-emption and Legitimacy," *Survival* 45, no. 1 (Spring 2003), 123.
12. Condoleezza Rice, remarks on the President's National Security Strategy, Waldorf-Astoria Hotel, New York, NY, October 1, 2002.
13. Michael Walzer, *Just and Unjust Wars* (New York: Basic Books, 1977), 81.

14. David E. Sanger, "Bush to Formalize a Defense Policy of Hitting First," *The New York Times*, June 17, 2002.

15. The Office of Homeland Security, *The National Strategy for Homeland Security*, July 2002, accessed at <http://www.whitehouse.gov/homeland/book/nat_strat_hls.pdf>, 16.

16. *The National Strategy for Homeland Security*, 43.

17. In that case, it was determined the vessel was bound for Yemen. The Yemeni government asserted that the missiles were legally purchased, and the United States decided that there was no clear authority to hold the ship or prevent it from delivering the missiles.

18. See Slocombe, "Force, Preemption and Legitimacy," 126: "The problem with preemption, unfortunately, is not lack of legal legitimacy, but operational practicality . . . Precision weapons require precision intelligence, and pre-emption requires that intelligence be comprehensive as well as precise."

19. See Marc Dean Millot, "Facing the Emerging Reality of Regional Nuclear Adversaries," *The Washington Quarterly* 17, no. 3 (Summer 1994), 41. See also David A. Kay, "Denial and Deception Practices of WMD Proliferators: Iraq and Beyond," *The Washington Quarterly* 18, no. 1 (Winter 1995), 83.

20. Rice, remarks on the President's National Security Strategy, October 1, 2002.

21. Donald H. Rumsfeld, Department of Defense Regular News Briefing, January 29, 2003, accessed at <http://www.defenselink.mil/news/Jan2003/t01292003_t0129sd.html>.

22. John Shaw, "Startling His Neighbors, Australian Leader Favors First Strikes," *The New York Times*, December 2, 2002, A11.

23. LOI n° 2003–73 du 27 janvier 2003 relative à la programmation militaire pour les années 2003 à 2008 (1), section 2.3.1, accessed at <http://www.legifrance.gouv.fr/WAspad/Visu?cid=328577&indice=1&table=JORF&ligneDeb=1>.

24. "Ishiba: Japan to 'Counterattack' If N. Korea Prepares to Attack," *The Yomiuri Shimbun/Daily Yomiuri*, January 25, 2003.

25. James Brooke, "Japanese Official Wants Defense Against Missiles Expanded," *The New York Times*, April 17, 2003, 13.

26. Wolfgang Koydl, "The Law of the Strongest," *Sueddeulsche Zeitung*, June 3, 2002 (as translated by the Department of State "Foreign Media Reaction Early Report," June 13, 2002).

27. Donald H. Rumsfeld, meeting with the editorial board of *The Washington Post*, June 3, 2002, accessed at <http://www.defenselink.mil/news/Jun2002/t06042002_t0603edb.html>.

28. George W. Bush, remarks at Texans for Rick Perry Reception, Houston, TX, June 14, 2002, accessed at <http://www.whitehouse.gov/news/releases/2002/06/20020614-8.html>.

29. Hearing before the Senate Foreign Relations Committee on Treaty on Strategic Offensive Reductions, Washington, DC, July 9, 2002.

30. Rice, remarks on the President's National Security Strategy, October 1, 2002.

31. On the other hand, some argue that it was not preemption, but a continuation of the 1991 Gulf War that ended with a ceasefire and conditions that Iraq failed to meet.

32. Drawn from chapters by Michèle A. Flournoy and Philip Zelikow in *New Nuclear Nations: Consequences for U.S. Policy*, ed. Robert D. Blackwill and Albert Camesale (New York: Council on Foreign Relations Press, 1993), as well as more recent statements by Flournoy.

62

JOHN J. MEARSHEIMER
AND STEPHEN M. WALT

An Unnecessary War

In the full-court press for war with Iraq, the Bush administration deems Saddam Hussein reckless, ruthless, and not fully rational. Such a man, when mixed with nuclear weapons, is too unpredictable to be prevented from threatening the United States, the hawks say. But scrutiny of his past dealings with the world shows that Saddam, though cruel and calculating, is eminently deterrable. . . .

The deeper root of the conflict is the U.S. position that Saddam must be toppled because he cannot be deterred from using weapons of mass destruction (WMD). Advocates of preventive war use numerous arguments to make their case, but their trump card is the charge that Saddam's past behavior proves he is too reckless, relentless, and aggressive to be allowed to possess WMD, especially nuclear weapons. They sometimes admit that war against Iraq might be costly, might lead to a lengthy U.S. occupation, and might complicate U.S. relations with other countries. But these concerns are eclipsed by the belief that the combination of Saddam plus nuclear weapons is too dangerous to accept. For that reason alone, he has to go.

Even many opponents of preventive war seem to agree deterrence will not work in Iraq. Instead of invading Iraq and overthrowing the regime, however, these moderates favor using the threat of war to compel Saddam to permit new weapons inspections. Their hope is that inspections will eliminate any hidden WMD stockpiles and production facilities and ensure Saddam cannot acquire any of these deadly weapons. Thus, both the hard-line preventive-war advocates and the more moderate supporters of inspections accept the same basic premise: Saddam Hussein is not deterrable, and he cannot be allowed to obtain a nuclear arsenal.

One problem with this argument: It is almost certainly wrong. The belief that Saddam's past behavior shows he cannot be contained rests on distorted history and faulty logic. In fact, the historical record shows that the United States can contain Iraq effectively—even if Saddam has nuclear weapons—just as it contained the Soviet Union during the Cold War. Regardless of whether

Source: From "An Unnecessary War," by Mearsheimer, John J. and Walt, Stephen M. *Foreign Policy*: Jan/Feb 2003, Is. 134, p. 51, 10p, 6c. Reprinted with permission. www.foreignpolicy.com.

Iraq complies with U.N. inspections or what the inspectors find, the campaign to wage war against Iraq rests on a flimsy foundation.

IS SADDAM A SERIAL AGGRESSOR?

Those who call for preventive war begin by portraying Saddam as a serial aggressor bent on dominating the Persian Gulf. The war party also contends that Saddam is either irrational or prone to serious miscalculation, which means he may not be deterred by even credible threats of retaliation. Kenneth Pollack, former director for gulf affairs at the National Security Council and a proponent of war with Iraq, goes so far as to argue that Saddam is "unintentionally suicidal."

The facts, however, tell a different story. Saddam has dominated Iraqi politics for more than 30 years. During that period, he started two wars against his neighbors—Iran in 1980 and Kuwait in 1990. Saddam's record in this regard is no worse than that of neighboring states such as Egypt or Israel, each of which played a role in starting several wars since 1948. Furthermore, a careful look at Saddam's two wars shows his behavior was far from reckless. Both times, he attacked because Iraq was vulnerable and because he believed his targets were weak and isolated. In each case, his goal was to rectify Iraq's strategic dilemma with a limited military victory. Such reasoning does not excuse Saddam's aggression, but his willingness to use force on these occasions hardly demonstrates that he cannot be deterred. . . .

THE GULF WAR, 1990–91

But what about Iraq's invasion of Kuwait in August 1990? Perhaps the earlier war with Iran was essentially defensive, but surely this was not true in the case of Kuwait. Doesn't Saddam's decision to invade his tiny neighbor prove he is too rash and aggressive to be trusted with the most destructive weaponry? And doesn't his refusal to withdraw, even when confronted by a superior coalition, demonstrate he is "unintentionally suicidal"?

The answer is no. Once again, a careful look shows Saddam was neither mindlessly aggressive nor particularly reckless. If anything, the evidence supports the opposite conclusion.

Saddam's decision to invade Kuwait was primarily an attempt to deal with Iraq's continued vulnerability. Iraq's economy, badly damaged by its war with Iran, continued to decline after that war ended. An important cause of Iraq's difficulties was Kuwait's refusal both to loan Iraq $10 billion and to write off debts Iraq had incurred during the Iran-Iraq War. Saddam believed Iraq was entitled to additional aid because the country helped protect Kuwait and other Gulf states from Iranian expansionism. To make matters worse, Kuwait was overproducing the quotas set by the Organization of Petroleum Exporting Countries, which drove down world oil prices and reduced Iraqi oil profits.

Saddam tried using diplomacy to solve the problem, but Kuwait hardly budged. As Karsh and fellow Hussein biographer Inari Rautsi note, the Kuwaitis "suspected that some concessions might be necessary, but were determined to reduce them to the barest minimum."

Saddam reportedly decided on war sometime in July 1990, but before sending his army into Kuwait, he approached the United States to find out how it would react. In a now famous interview with the Iraqi leader, U.S. Ambassador April Glaspie told Saddam, "[W]e have no opinion on the Arab-Arab conflicts, like your border disagreement with Kuwait." The U.S. State Department had earlier told Saddam that Washington had "no special defense or security commitments to Kuwait." The United States may not have intended to give Iraq a green light, but that is effectively what it did.

Saddam invaded Kuwait in early August 1990. This act was an obvious violation of international law, and the United States was justified in opposing the invasion and organizing a coalition against it. But Saddam's decision to invade was hardly irrational or reckless. Deterrence did not fail in this case; it was never tried.

But what about Saddam's failure to leave Kuwait once the United States demanded a return to the status quo ante? Wouldn't a prudent leader have abandoned Kuwait before getting clobbered? With hindsight, the answer seems obvious, but Saddam had good reasons to believe hanging tough might work. It was not initially apparent that the United States would actually fight, and most Western military experts predicted the Iraqi army would mount a formidable defense. These forecasts seem foolish today, but many people believed them before the war began. . . .

Saddam undoubtedly miscalculated when he attacked Kuwait, but the history of warfare is full of cases where leaders have misjudged the prospects for war. No evidence suggests Hussein did not weigh his options carefully, however. He chose to use force because he was facing a serious challenge and because he had good reasons to think his invasion would not provoke serious opposition. . . .

History provides at least two more pieces of evidence that demonstrate Saddam is deterrable. First, although he launched conventionally armed Scud missiles at Saudi Arabia and Israel during the Gulf War, he did not launch chemical or biological weapons at the coalition forces that were decimating the Iraqi military. Moreover, senior Iraqi officials—including Deputy Prime Minister Tariq Aziz and the former head of military intelligence, General Wafiq al-Samarrai—have said that Iraq refrained from using chemical weapons because the Bush Sr. administration made ambiguous but unmistakable threats to retaliate if Iraq used WMD. Second, in 1994 Iraq mobilized the remnants of its army on the Kuwaiti border in an apparent attempt to force a modification of the U.N. Special Commission's (UNSCOM) weapons inspection regime. But when the United Nations issued a new warning and the United States reinforced its troops in Kuwait, Iraq backed down quickly. In both cases, the allegedly irrational Iraqi leader was deterred.

SADDAM'S USE OF CHEMICAL WEAPONS

Preventive-war advocates also use a second line of argument. They point out that Saddam has used WMD against his own people (the Kurds) and against Iran and that therefore he is likely to use them against the United States. Thus, U.S. President George W. Bush recently warned in Cincinnati that the Iraqi WMD threat against the United States "is already significant, and it only grows worse with time." The United States, in other words, is in imminent danger.

Saddam's record of chemical weapons use is deplorable, but none of his victims had a similar arsenal and thus could not threaten to respond in kind. Iraq's calculations would be entirely different when facing the United States because Washington could retaliate with WMD if Iraq ever decided to use these weapons first. Saddam thus has no incentive to use chemical or nuclear weapons against the United States and its allies—unless his survival is threatened. This simple logic explains why he did not use WMD against U.S. forces during the Gulf War and has not fired chemical or biological warheads at Israel.

Furthermore, if Saddam cannot be deterred, what is stopping him from using WMD against U.S. forces in the Persian Gulf, which have bombed Iraq repeatedly over the past decade? The bottom line: Deterrence has worked well against Saddam in the past, and there is no reason to think it cannot work equally well in the future.

President Bush's repeated claim that the threat from Iraq is growing makes little sense in light of Saddam's past record, and these statements should be viewed as transparent attempts to scare Americans into supporting a war. CIA Director George Tenet flatly contradicted the president in an October 2002 letter to Congress, explaining that Saddam was unlikely to initiate a WMD attack against any U.S. target unless Washington provoked him. Even if Iraq did acquire a larger WMD arsenal, the United States would still retain a massive nuclear retaliatory capability. And if Saddam would only use WMD if the United States threatened his regime, then one wonders why advocates of war are trying to do just that. . . .

If Saddam's use of chemical weapons so clearly indicates he is a madman and cannot be contained, why did the United States fail to see that in the 1980s? Why were Rumsfeld and former President Bush then so unconcerned about his chemical and biological weapons? The most likely answer is that U.S. policymakers correctly understood Saddam was unlikely to use those weapons against the United States and its allies unless Washington threatened him directly. The real puzzle is why they think it would be impossible to deter him today.

SADDAM WITH NUKES

The third strike against a policy of containment, according to those who have called for war, is that such a policy is unlikely to stop Saddam from getting nuclear weapons. Once he gets them, so the argument runs, a host of really bad things will happen. For example, President Bush has warned that Saddam intends to "blackmail the world"; likewise, National Security Advisor Condoleezza Rice believes he would use nuclear weapons to "blackmail the entire international community." Others fear a nuclear arsenal would enable Iraq to invade its neighbors and then deter the United States from ousting the Iraqi army as it did in 1991. Even worse, Saddam might surreptitiously slip a nuclear weapon to al Qaeda or some like-minded terrorist organization, thereby making it possible for these groups to attack the United States directly.

The administration and its supporters may be right in one sense: Containment may not be enough to prevent Iraq from acquiring nuclear weapons someday. Only the conquest and permanent occupation of Iraq could guarantee that. Yet the United States can contain a nuclear Iraq, just as it contained the Soviet Union. None of the nightmare scenarios invoked by preventive-war advocates are likely to happen.

Consider the claim that Saddam would employ nuclear blackmail against his adversaries. To force another state to make concessions, a blackmailer must make clear that he would use nuclear weapons against the target state if he does not get his way. But this strategy is feasible only if the blackmailer has nuclear weapons but neither the target state nor its allies do.

If the blackmailer and the target state both have nuclear weapons, however, the blackmailer's threat is an empty one because the blackmailer cannot carry out the threat without triggering his own destruction. This logic explains why the Soviet Union, which had a vast nuclear arsenal for much of the Cold War, was never able to blackmail the United States or its allies and did not even try.

But what if Saddam invaded Kuwait again and then said he would use nuclear weapons if the United States attempted another Desert Storm? Again, this threat is not credible. If Saddam initiated nuclear war against the United States over Kuwait, he would bring U.S. nuclear warheads down on his own head. Given the choice between withdrawing or dying, he would almost certainly choose the former. Thus, the United States could wage Desert Storm II against a nuclear-armed Saddam without precipitating nuclear war. . . .

WHAT ABOUT A NUCLEAR HANDOFF?

Of course, now the real nightmare scenario is that Saddam would give nuclear weapons to al Qaeda or some other terroist group. Groups like al Qaeda would almost certainly try to use those weapons against Israel or the United States, and so these countries have a powerful incentive to take all reasonable measures to keep these weapons out of their hands.

However, the likelihood of clandestine transfer by Iraq is extremely small. First of all, there is no credible evidence that Iraq had anything to do with the terrorist attacks against the World Trade Center and the Pentagon or more generally that Iraq is collaborating with al Queda against the United States. Hawks inside and outside the Bush administration have gone to extraordinary lengths over the past months to find a link, but they have come up empty-handed.

The lack of evidence of any genuine connection between Saddam and al Qaeda is not surprising because relations between Saddam and al Queda have been quite poor in the past. Osama bin Laden is a radical fundamentalist (like Khomeini), and he detests secular leaders like Saddam. Similarly, Saddam has consistently repressed fundamentalist movements within Iraq. Given this history of enmity, the Iraqi dictator is unlikely to give al Qaeda nuclear weapons, which it might use in ways he could not control.

Intense U.S. pressure, of course, might eventually force these unlikely allies together, just as the United States and Communist Russia became allies during World War II. Saddam would still be unlikely to share his most valuable weaponry with al Qaeda, however, because he could not be confident it would not be used in ways that place his own survival in jeopardy. During the Cold War, the United States did not share all its WMD expertise with its own allies, and the Soviet Union balked at giving nuclear weapons to China despite their ideological sympathies and repeated Chinese requests. No evidence suggests Saddam would act differently.

Second, Saddam could hardly be confident that the transfer would go undetected. Since September 11, U.S. intelligence agencies and those of its allies have been riveted on al Qaeda and Iraq, paying special attention to finding links between them. If Iraq possessed nuclear weapons, U.S. monitoring of those two adversaries would be further intensified. To give nuclear materials to al Qaeda, Saddam would have to bet he could elude the eyes and ears of numerous intelligence services determined to catch him if he tries a nuclear handoff. This bet would not be a safe one.

But even if Saddam thought he could covertly smuggle nuclear weapons to bin Laden, he would still be unlikely to do so. Saddam has been trying to acquire these weapons for over 20 years, at great cost and risk. Is it likely he would then turn around and give them away? Furthermore, giving nuclear weapons to al Qaeda would be extremely risky for Saddam—even if he could do so without being detected—because he would lose all control over when and where they would be used. And Saddam could never be sure the United States would not incinerate him anyway if it merely suspected he had made it possible for anyone to strike the United States with nuclear weapons. The U.S. government and a clear majority of Americans are already deeply suspicious of Iraq, and a nuclear attack against the United States or its allies would raise that hostility to fever pitch. Saddam does not have to be certain the United States would retaliate to be wary of giving his nuclear weapons to al Qaeda; he merely has to suspect it might.

In sum, Saddam cannot afford to guess wrong on whether he would be detected providing al Qaeda with nuclear weapons, nor can he afford to guess wrong that Iraq would be spared if al Qaeda launched a nuclear strike against the United States or its allies. And the threat of U.S. retaliation is not as far-fetched as one might think. The United States has enhanced its flexible nuclear options in recent years, and no one knows just how vengeful Americans might feel if WMD were ever used against the U.S. homeland. Indeed, nuclear terrorism is as dangerous for Saddam as it is for Americans, and he has no more incentive to give al Qaeda nuclear weapons than the United States does—unless, of course, the country makes clear it is trying to overthrow him. Instead of attacking Iraq and giving Saddam nothing to lose, the Bush administration should be signaling it would hold him responsible if some terrorist group used WMD against the United States, even if it cannot prove he is to blame.

VIGILANT CONTAINMENT

It is not surprising that those who favor war with Iraq portray Saddam as an inveterate and only partly rational aggressor. They are in the business of selling a preventive war, so they must try to make remaining at peace seem unacceptably dangerous. And the best way to do that is to inflate the threat, either by exaggerating Iraq's capabilities or by suggesting horrible things will happen if the United States does not act soon. It is equally unsurprising that advocates of war are willing to distort the historical record to make their case. As former U.S. Secretary of State Dean Acheson famously remarked, in politics, advocacy "must be clearer than truth."

In this case, however, the truth points the other way. Both logic and historical evidence suggest a policy of vigilant containment would work, both now and in the event Iraq acquires a nuclear arsenal. Why? Because the United States and its regional allies are far stronger than Iraq. And because it does not take a genius to figure out what would happen if Iraq tried to use WMD to blackmail its neighbors, expand its territory, or attack another state directly. It only takes a leader who wants to stay alive and who wants to remain in power. Throughout his lengthy and brutal career, Saddam Hussein has repeatedly shown that these two goals are absolutely paramount. That is why deterrence and containment would work.

If the United States is, or soon will be, at war with Iraq, Americans should understand that a compelling strategic rationale is absent. This war would be one the Bush administration chose to fight but did not have to fight. Even if such a war goes well and has positive long-range consequences, it will still have been unnecessary. And if it goes badly—whether in the form of high U.S. casualties, significant civilian deaths, a heightened risk of terrorism, or increased hatred of the United States in the Arab and Islamic world—then its architects will have even more to answer for.

63

STEPHEN G. BROOKS AND
WILLIAM C. WOHLFORTH

American Primacy in Perspetive

FROM STRENGTH TO STRENGTH

More than a decade ago, political columnist Charles Krauthammer proclaimed
. . . the arrival of what he called a "unipolar moment," a period in which one
superpower, the United States, stood clearly above the rest of the international
community ("The Unipolar Moment," America and the World 1990/91 [*Foreign Affairs*]). In the following years the Soviet Union collapsed, Russia's economic and military decline accelerated, and Japan stagnated, while the United
States experienced the longest and one of the most vigorous economic expan-
sions in its history. Yet toward the close of the century readers could find political scientist Samuel Huntington arguing . . . that unipolarity had already
given way to a "unimultipolar" structure, which in turn would soon become
unambiguously multipolar ("The Lonely Superpower," [*Foreign Affairs*],
March/April 1999). And despite the boasting rhetoric of American officials,
Huntington was not alone in his views. Polls showed that more than 40 percent of Americans had come to agree that the United States was now merely
one of several leading powers—a number that had risen steadily for several
years.

 Why did the unipolarity argument seem less persuasive to many even as
U.S. power appeared to grow? Largely because the goal posts were moved,
Krauthammer's definition of unipolarity, as a system with only one pole, made
sense in the immediate wake of a Cold War that had been so clearly shaped by
the existence of two poles. People sensed intuitively that a world with no great
power capable of sustaining a focused rivalry with the United States would be
very different in important ways.

 But a decade later what increasingly seemed salient was less the absence
of a peer rival than the persistence of a number of problems in the world that
Washington could not dispose of by itself. This was the context for Huntington's new definition of unipolarity, as a system with "one superpower, no significant major powers, and many minor powers." The dominant power in
such a system, he argued, would be able to "effectively resolve important

Source: "American Primacy in Perspective," by Brooks and Wohlforth, *Foreign Affairs*, July/August
2002. Copyright 2002 Council on Foreign Relations, Inc.

international issues alone, and no combination of other states would have the power to prevent it from doing so." The United States had no such ability and thus did not qualify.

The terrorist attacks last fall appeared to some to reinforce this point, revealing not only a remarkable degree of American vulnerability but also a deep vein of global anti-American resentment. Suddenly the world seemed a more threatening place, with dangers lurking at every corner and eternal vigilance the price of liberty. Yet as the success of the military campaign in Afghanistan demonstrated, vulnerability to terror has few effects on U.S. strength in more traditional interstate affairs. If anything, America's response to the attacks—which showed its ability to project power in several places around the globe simultaneously, and essentially unilaterally, while effortlessly increasing defense spending by nearly $50 billion—only reinforced its unique position.

If today's American primacy does not constitute unipolarity, then nothing ever will. The only things left for dispute are how long it will last and what the implications are for American foreign policy.

PICK A MEASURE, ANY MEASURE

To understand just how dominant the United States is today, one needs to look at each of the standard components of national power in succession. In the military arena, the United States is poised to spend more on defense in 2003 than the next 15–20 biggest spenders combined. The United States has overwhelming nuclear superiority, the world's dominant air force, the only truly blue-water navy, and a unique capability to project power around the globe. And its military advantage is even more apparent in quality than in quantity. The United States leads the world in exploiting the military applications of advanced communications and information technology and it has demonstrated an unrivaled ability to coordinate and process information about the battlefield and destroy targets from afar with extraordinary precision. Washington is not making it easy for others to catch up, moreover, given the massive gap in spending on military research and development (R&D), on which the United States spends three times more than the next six powers combined. Looked at another way, the United States currently spends more on military R&D than Germany or the United Kingdom spends on defense in total.

No state in the modern history of international politics has come close to the military predominance these numbers suggest. And the United States purchases this preeminence with only 3.5 percent of its GDP. As historian Paul Kennedy notes, "being Number One at great cost is one thing; being the world's single superpower on the cheap is astonishing."

America's economic dominance, meanwhile—relative to either the next several richest powers or the rest of the world combined—surpasses that of any great power in modern history, with the sole exception of its own position after 1945 (when World War II had temporarily laid waste every other major economy). The U.S. economy is currently twice as large as its closest rival, Japan. California's economy alone has risen to become the fifth largest in the world (using market exchange-rate estimates), ahead of France and just behind the United Kingdom.

It is true that the long expansion of the 1990s has ebbed, but it would take an experience like Japan's in that decade—that is, an extraordinarily deep and prolonged domestic recession juxtaposed with robust growth elsewhere—for the United States just to fall back to the economic position it occupied in 1991. The odds against such relative decline are long, however, in part because the United States is the country in the best position to take advantage of globalization. Its status as the preferred destination for scientifically trained foreign workers solidified during the 1990s, and it is the most popular destination for foreign firms. In 1999 it attracted more than one-third of world inflows of foreign direct investment.

U.S. military and economic dominance, finally, is rooted in the country's position as the world's leading technological power. Although measuring national R&D spending is increasingly difficult in an era in which so many economic activities cross borders, efforts to do so indicate America's continuing lead. Figures from the late 1990s showed that U.S. expenditures on R&D nearly equaled those of the next seven richest countries combined.

Measuring the degree of American dominance in each category begins to place things in perspective. But what truly distinguishes the current international system is American dominance in all of them simultaneously. Previous leading states in the modern era were either great commercial and naval powers or great military powers on land, never both. The British Empire in its heyday and the United States during the Cold War, for example, each shared the world with other powers that matched or exceeded them in some areas. Following the Napoleonic Wars, the United Kingdom was clearly the world's leading commercial and naval power. But even at the height of the Pax Britannica, the United Kingdom was outspent, outmanned, and outgunned by both France and Russia. And its 24 percent share of GDP among the six leading powers in the early 1870s was matched by the United States, with Russia and Germany following close behind. Similarly, at the dawn of the Cold War the United States was clearly dominant economically as well as in air and naval capabilities. But the Soviet Union retained overall military parity, and thanks to geography and investment in land power it had a superior ability to seize territory in Eurasia.

Today, in contrast, the United States has no rival in any critical dimension of power. There has never been a system of sovereign states that contained one state with this degree of dominance. The recent tendency to equate unipolarity with the ability to achieve desired outcomes single-handedly on all issues only reinforces this point; in no previous international system would it ever have occurred to anyone to apply such a yardstick.

CAN IT LAST?

Many who acknowledge the extent of American power, however, regard it as necessarily self-negating. Other states traditionally band together to restrain potential hegemons, they say, and this time will be no different. As German political commentator Josef Joffe has put it, "the history books say that Mr. Big always invites his own demise. Nos. 2, 3, 4 will gang up on him, form countervailing alliances and plot his downfall. That happened to Napoleon, as it happened to Louis XIV and the mighty Hapsburgs, to Hitler and to Stalin. Power begets superior counterpower; it's the oldest rule of world politics."

What such arguments fail to recognize are the features of America's post–Cold War position that make it likely to buck the historical trend. Bounded by oceans to the east and west and weak, friendly powers to the north and south, the United States is both less vulnerable than previous aspiring hegemons and also less threatening to others. The main potential challengers to its unipolarity, meanwhile—China, Russia, Japan, and Germany—are in the opposite position. They cannot augment their military capabilities so as to balance the United States without simultaneously becoming an immediate threat to their neighbors. Politics, even international politics, is local. Although American power attracts a lot of attention globally, states are usually more concerned with their own neighborhoods than with the global equilibrium. Were any of the potential challengers to make a serious run at the United States, regional balancing efforts would almost certainly help contain them, as would the massive latent power capabilities of the United States, which could be mobilized as necessary to head off an emerging threat.

When analysts refer to a historical pattern of balancing against potentially preponderant powers, they rarely note that the cases in question—the Hapsburg ascendancy, Napoleonic France, the Soviet Union in the Cold War, and so forth—featured would-be hegemons that were vulnerable, threatening, centrally located, and dominant in only one or two components of power. Moreover, the would-be hegemons all specialized in precisely the form of power—the ability to seize territory—most likely to scare other states into an antihegemonic coalition. American capabilities, by contrast, are relatively greater and more comprehensive than those of past hegemonic aspirants, they are located safely offshore, and the prospective balancers are close regional neighbors of one another. U.S. power is also at the command of one government, whereas the putative balancers would face major challenges in acting collectively to assemble and coordinate their military capabilities.

Previous historical experiences of balancing, moreover, involved groups of status quo powers seeking to contain a rising revisionist one. The balancers had much to fear if the aspiring hegemon got its way. Today, however, U.S. dominance is the status quo. Several of the major powers in the system have been closely allied with the United States for decades and derive substantial benefits from their position. Not only would they have to forgo those benefits if they tried to balance, but they would have to find some way of putting together a durable, coherent alliance while America was watching. This is a profoundly important point, because although there may be several precedents for a coalition of balancers preventing a hegemon from emerging, there is none for a group of subordinate powers joining to topple a hegemon once it has already emerged, which is what would have to happen today.

The comprehensive nature of U.S. power, finally, also skews the odds against any major attempt at balancing, let alone a successful one. The United States is both big and rich, whereas the potential challengers are all either one or the other. It will take at least a generation for today's other big countries (such as China and India) to become rich, and given declining birth rates the other rich powers are not about to get big, at least in relative terms. During the 1990s, the U.S. population increased by 32.7 million—a figure equal to more than half the current population of France or the United Kingdom.

Some might argue that the European Union is an exception to the big-or-rich rule. It is true that if Brussels were to develop impressive military capabilities and wield its latent collective power like a state, the EU would clearly constitute another pole. But the creation of an autonomous and unified defense and defense-industrial capacity that could compete with that of the United States would be a gargantuan task. The EU is struggling to put together a 60,000-strong rapid reaction force that is designed for smaller operations such as humanitarian relief, peacekeeping, and crisis management, but it still lacks military essentials such as capabilities in intelligence gathering, airlift, air-defense suppression, air-to-air refueling, sea transport, medical care, and combat search and rescue—and even when it has those capacities, perhaps by the end of this decade, it will still rely on NATO command and control and other assets.

Whatever capability the EU eventually assembles, moreover, will matter only to the extent that it is under the control of a statelike decision-making body with the authority to act quickly and decisively in Europe's name. Such authority, which does not yet exist even for international financial matters, could be purchased only at the price of a direct frontal assault on European nations' core sovereignty. And all of this would have to occur as the EU expands to add ten or more new member states, a process that will complicate further deepening. Given these obstacles, Europe is unlikely to emerge as a dominant actor in the military realm for a very long time, if ever.

Most analysts looking for a future peer competitor to the United States, therefore, focus on China, since it is the only power with the potential to match the size of the U.S. economy over the next several decades. Yet even if China were eventually to catch up to the United States in terms of aggregate GDP, the gaps in the two states' other power capabilities—technological, military, and geographic—would remain.

Since the mid-1990s, Chinese strategists themselves have become markedly less bullish about their country's ability to close the gap in what they call "comprehensive national power" any time soon. The latest estimates by China's intelligence agency project that in 2020 the country will possess between slightly more than a third and slightly more than half of U.S. capabilities. Fifty percent of China's labor force is employed in agriculture, and relatively little of its economy is geared toward high technology. In the 1990s, U.S. spending on technological development was more than 20 times China's. Most of China's weapons are decades old. And nothing China can do will allow it to escape its geography, which leaves it surrounded by countries that have the motivation and ability to engage in balancing of their own should China start to build up an expansive military force.

These are not just facts about the current system; they are recognized as such by the major players involved. As a result, no global challenge to the United States is likely to emerge for the foreseeable future. No country, or group of countries, wants to maneuver itself into a situation in which it will have to contend with the focused enmity of the United States.

Two of the prime causes of past great-power conflicts—hegemonic rivalry and misperception—are thus not currently operative in world politics. At the dawn of the twentieth century, a militarily powerful Germany challenged the United Kingdom's claim to leadership. The result was World War I. In the middle of the twentieth century, American leadership seemed under challenge by a militarily and ideologically strong Soviet Union. The result was the Cold War. U.S. dominance today militates against a comparable challenge, however, and hence against a comparable global conflict. Because the United States is too powerful to balance, moreover, there is far less danger of war emerging from the misperceptions, miscalculations, arms races, and so forth that have traditionally plagued balancing attempts. Pundits often lament the absence of a post—Cold War Bismarck. Luckily, as long as unipolarity lasts, there is no need for one. . . .

SO WHAT?

The first and most important practical consequence of unipolarity for the United States is notable for its absence: the lack of hegemonic rivalry. During the Cold War the United States confronted a military superpower with the potential to conquer all the industrial power centers of Europe and Asia. To forestall that catastrophic outcome, for decades the United States committed between 5 and 14 percent of its GDP to defense spending and maintained an extended nuclear deterrent that put a premium on the credibility of its commitments. Largely to maintain a reputation for resolve, 85,000 Americans lost their lives in two Asian wars while U.S. presidents repeatedly engaged in brinkmanship that ran the risk of escalation to global thermonuclear destruction.

Today the costs and dangers of the Cold War have faded into history, but they need to be kept in mind in order to assess unipolarity accurately. For decades to come, no state is likely to combine the resources, geography, and growth rates necessary to mount a hegemonic challenge on such a scale—an astonishing development. Crowns may generally lie uneasy, but America's does not.

Some might question the worth of being at the top of a unipolar system if that means serving as a lightning rod for the world's malcontents. When there was a Soviet Union, after all, it bore the brunt of Osama bin Laden's anger, and only after its collapse did he shift his focus to the United States (an indicator of the demise of bipolarity that was ignored at the time but looms larger in retrospect). But terrorism has been a perennial problem in history, and multipolarity did not save the leaders of several great powers from assassination by anarchists around the turn of the twentieth century. In fact, a slide back toward multipolarity would actually be the worst of all worlds for the United States. In such a scenario it would continue to lead the pack and serve as a focal point for resentment and hatred by both state and nonstate actors, but it would have fewer carrots and sticks to use in dealing with the situation. The threats would remain, but the possibility of effective and coordinated action against them would be reduced.

The second major practical consequence of unipolarity is the unique freedom it offers American policymakers. Many decisionmakers labor under feelings of constraint, and all participants in policy debates defend their preferred courses of action by pointing to the dire consequences that will follow if their advice is not accepted. But the sources of American strength are so varied and so durable that U.S. foreign policy today operates in the realm of choice rather than necessity to a greater degree than any other power in modern history. Whether the participants realize it or not, this new freedom to choose has transformed the debate over what the U.S. role in the world should be.

Historically, the major forces pushing powerful states toward restraint and magnanimity have been the limits of their strength and the fear of overextension and balancing. Great powers typically checked their ambitions and deferred to others not because they wanted to but because they had to in order to win the cooperation they needed to survive and prosper. It is thus no surprise that today's champions of American moderation and international benevolence stress the constraints on American power rather than the lack of them. Political scientist Joseph Nye, for example, insists that "[the term] unipolarity is misleading because it exaggerates the degree to which the United States is able to get the results it wants in some dimensions of world politics. . . . American power is less effective than it might first appear." And he cautions that if the United States "handles its hard power in an overbearing, unilateral manner," then others might be provoked into forming a balancing coalition.

Such arguments are unpersuasive, however, because they fail to acknowledge the true nature of the current international system. The United States cannot be scared into meekness by warnings of inefficacy or potential balancing. Isolationists and aggressive unilateralists see this situation clearly, and their domestic opponents need to as well. Now and for the foreseeable future, the United States will have immense power resources it can bring to bear to force or entice others to do its bidding on a case-by-case basis.

But just because the United States is strong enough to act heedlessly does not mean that it should do so. Why not? Because it can afford to reap the greater gains that will eventually come from magnanimity. Aside from a few cases in a few issue areas, ignoring others' concerns avoids hassles today at the cost of more serious trouble tomorrow. Unilateralism may produce results in the short term, but it is apt to reduce the pool of voluntary help from other countries that the United States can draw on down the road, and thus in the end to make life more difficult rather than less. Unipolarity makes it possible to be the global bully—but it also offers the United States the luxury of being able to look beyond its immediate needs to its own, and the world's, long-term interests.

64

JOSEPH S. NYE, JR.

LIMITS OF AMERICAN POWER

We cannot hope to predict the future, but we can draw our pictures carefully so as to avoid some common mistakes.[1] A decade ago, a more careful analysis of American power could have saved us from the, mistaken portrait of American decline. More recently, accurate predictions of catastrophic terrorism failed to avert a tragedy that leads some again to foresee decline. It is important to prevent the errors of both declinism and triumphalism. Declinism tends to produce overly cautious behavior that could undercut influence; triumphalism could beget a potentially dangerous absence of restraint, as well as an arrogance that would also squander influence. With careful analysis, the United States can make better decisions about how to protect its people, promote values, and lead, toward a better world over the next few decades. I begin this analysis with an examination of the sources of U.S. power.

THE SOURCES OF AMERICAN POWER

We hear a lot about how powerful America has become in recent years, but what do we mean by power? Simply put, power, is the ability to effect the out comes you want and, if necessary, to change the behavior of others to make this

SOURCE: From "Limits on American Power," by J. Nye, Jr. *Political Science Quarterly*, Vol. 117, No. 4, 2002–2003.

happen. For example, NATO's military power reversed Slobodan Milosevic's ethnic cleansing of Kosovo, and the promise of economic aid to Serbia's devastated economy reversed the Serbian government's initial disinclination to hand, Milosevic over to the Hague tribunal.

The ability to obtain the outcomes one wants is often associated with the possession of certain resources, and so we commonly use shorthand and define power as possession of relatively large amounts of such elements as population, territory, natural resources, economic strength, military force, and political stability. Power in this sense means holding the high cards in the international poker game. If you show high cards, others are likely to fold their hands. Of course, if you play your hand poorly or fall victim to bluff and deception, you can still lose, or at least fail to get the outcome you want. For example, the United States was the largest power after World War I, but it failed to prevent the rise of Hitler or Pearl Harbor. Converting America's potential power resources into realized power requires well-designed policy and skillful leadership. But it helps to start by holding the high cards.

Traditionally, the test of a great power was "strength for war."[2] War was the ultimate game in which the cards of international politics were played and estimates of relative power were proven. Over the centuries, as technologies evolved, the sources of power have changed. In the agrarian economies of seventeenth- and eighteenth-century Europe, population was a critical power resource because it provided a base for taxes and the recruitment of infantry (who were mostly mercenaries), and this combination of men and money gave the edge to France. But in the nineteenth century, the growing importance of industry benefited first Britain, which ruled the waves with a navy that had no peer, and later Germany, which used efficient administration and railways to transport armies for quick victories on the Continent (though Russia had a larger population and army). By the middle of the twentieth century, with the advent of the nuclear age, the United States and the Soviet Union possessed not only industrial might but nuclear arsenals and intercontinental missiles.

Today the foundations of power have been moving away from the emphasis on military force and conquest. Paradoxically, nuclear weapons were one of the causes. As we know from the history of the cold war, nuclear weapons proved so awesome and destructive that they became muscle bound—too costly to use except, theoretically, in the most extreme circumstances.[3] A second important change was the rise of nationalism, which has made it more difficult for empires to rule over awakened populations. In the nineteenth century, a few adventurers conquered most of Africa with a handful of soldiers, and Britain ruled India with a colonial force that was a tiny fraction of the indigenous population. Today, colonial rule is not only widely condemned but far too costly, as both cold war superpowers discovered in Vietnam and Afghanistan. The collapse of the Soviet empire followed the end of European empires by a matter of decades.

A third important cause is societal change inside great powers. Postindustrial societies are focused on welfare rather than glory, and they loathe high casualties except when survival is at stake. This does not mean that they will not use force, even when casualties are expected—witness the 1991 Gulf War or Afghanistan today. But the absence of a warrior ethic in modern democracies means that the use of force requires an elaborate moral justification to ensure popular support (except in cases where survival is at stake). Roughly speaking, there are three types of countries in the world today: poor, weak preindustrial states, which are often the chaotic remnants of collapsed empires; modernizing industrial states such as India or China; and the postindustrial societies that prevail in Europe, North America, and Japan. The use of force is common in the first type of country, still accepted in the second, but less tolerated in the third. In the words of British diplomat Robert Cooper, "A large number of the most powerful states no longer want to fight or to conquer."[4] War remains possible, but it is much less acceptable now than it was a century or even half a century ago.[5]

Finally, for most of today's great powers, the use of force would jeopardize their economic objectives. Even nondemocratic countries that feel fewer popular moral constraints on the use of force have to consider its effects on their economic objectives. As Thomas Friedman has put it, countries are disciplined by an "electronic herd" of investors who control their access to capital in a globalized economy.[6] And Richard Rosecrance writes, "In the past, it was cheaper to seize another state's territory by force than to develop the sophisticated economic and trading apparatus needed to derive benefit from commercial exchange with it."[7] Imperial Japan used the former approach when it created the Greater East Asia Co-prosperity Sphere in the 1930s, but Japan's post-World War II role as a trading state turned out to be far more successful, leading it to become the second largest national economy in the world. It is difficult now to imagine a scenario in which Japan would try to colonize its neighbors, or succeed in doing so.

As mentioned above, none of this is to suggest that military force plays no role in international politics today. For one thing, the information revolution has yet to transform most of the world. Many states are unconstrained by democratic societal forces, as Kuwait learned from its neighbor Iraq, and terrorist groups pay little heed to the normal constraints of liberal societies. Civil wars are rife in many parts of the world where collapsed empires left power vacuums. Moreover, throughout history, the rise of new great powers has been accompanied by anxieties that have sometimes precipitated military crises. In Thucydides' immortal description, the Peloponnesian War in ancient Greece was caused by the rise to power of Athens and the fear it created in Sparta.[8] World War I owed much to the rise of the kaiser's Germany and the fear that it created in Britain.[9] Some foretell a similar dynamic in this century arising from the rise of China and the fear it creates in the United States.

Geoeconomics has not replaced geopolitics, although in the early twenty-first century there has clearly been a blurring of the traditional boundaries between the two. To ignore the role of force and the centrality of security would be like ignoring oxygen. Under normal circumstances, oxygen is plentiful and we pay it little attention. But once those conditions change and we begin to miss it, we can focus on nothing else.[10] Even in those areas where the direct employment of force falls out of use among countries—for instance, within Western Europe or between the United States and Japan—nonstate actors such as terrorists may use force. Moreover, military force can still play an important political role among advanced nations. For example, most countries in East Asia welcome the presence of American troops as an insurance policy against uncertain neighbors. Moreover, deterring threats or ensuring access to a crucial resource such as oil in the Persian Gulf increases America's influence with its allies. Sometimes the linkages may be direct; more often they are present in the back of statesmen's minds. As the Defense Department describes it, one of the missions of American troops based overseas is to "shape the environment."

With that said, economic power *has* become more important that in the past, both because of the relative increase in the costliness of force and because economic objectives loom large in the values of postindustrial societies.[11] In a world of economic globalization, all countries are to some extent dependent on market forces beyond their direct control. When President Clinton was struggling to balance the federal budget in 1993, one of his advisers stated in exasperation that if he were to be reborn, he would like to come back as "the market" because that was clearly the most powerful player.[12] But markets constrain different countries to different degrees. Because the United States constitutes such a large part of the market in trade and finance, it is better placed to set its own terms than are Argentina or Thailand. And if small countries are willing to pay the price of opting out of the market, they can reduce the power that other countries have over them. Thus American economic sanctions have had little effect for example, on improving human rights in isolated Myanmar. Saddam Hussein's strong preference for his own survival rather than the welfare of the Iraqi people meant that crippling sanctions failed for more than a decade to remove him from power. And economic sanctions may disrupt but not deter nonstate terrorists. But the exceptions prove the rule. Military power remains crucial in certain situations, but it is mistake to focus too narrowly on the military dimensions of American power.

SOFT POWER

In my view, if the United States wants to remain strong, Americans need also to pay attention to our soft power. What precisely do I mean by soft power? Military power and economic power are both examples of hard command power that can be used to induce others to change their position. Hard power can rest on inducements (carrots) or threats (sticks). But there is also an indirect way to exercise power. A country may obtain the outcomes it wants in world politics because other countries want to follow it, admiring its values, emulating its example, aspiring to its level of prosperity and openness. In this sense, it is just as important to set the agenda in world politics and attract others as it is to force them to change through the threat or use of military or economic weapons. This aspect of power—getting others to want what you want–I call soft power.[13] It co-opts people rather than coerces them.

Soft power rests on the ability to set the political agenda in a way that shapes the preferences of others. At the personal level, wise parents know that if they have brought up their children with the right beliefs and values, their power will be greater and will last longer than if they have relied only on spankings, cutting off allowances, or taking away the car keys. Similarly, political leaders and thinkers such as Antonio Gramsci have long understood the power that comes from setting the agenda and determining the framework of a debate. The ability to establish preferences tends to be associated with intangible power resources such as an attractive culture, ideology, and institutions. If I can get you to *want* to do what I want, then I do not have to force you to do what you do *not* want to do. If the United States represents values that others want to follow, it will cost us less to lead. Soft power is not merely the same as influence, thought it is one source of influence. After all, I can also influence you by threats or rewards. Soft power is also more than persuasion or the ability to move people by argument. It is the ability to entice and attract. And attraction often leads to acquiescence or imitation.

Soft power arises in large part from our values. These values are expressed in our culture, in the policies we follow inside our country, and in the way we handle ourselves internationally. The government sometimes finds it difficult to control and employ soft power. Like love, it is hard to measure and to handle, and does not touch everyone, but that does not diminish its importance. As Hubert Védrine laments, Americans are so powerful because they can "inspire the dreams and desires of others, thanks to the mastery of global images through film and television and because, for these same reasons, large numbers of students from other countries come to the United States to finish their studies."[14] Soft power is an important reality.

Of course, hard and soft power are related and can reinforce each other. Both are aspects of the ability to achieve our purposes by affecting the behavior of others. Sometimes the same power resources can affect the entire spectrum of behavior from coercion to attraction.[15] A country that suffers economic and military decline is likely to lose its ability to shape the international agenda as well as its attractiveness. And some countries may be attracted to others with hard power by the myth of invincibility or inevitability. Both Hitler and Stalin tried to develop such myths. Hard power can also be used to establish empires and institutions that set the agenda for smaller states—witness Soviet rule over the countries of Eastern Europe. But soft power is not simply the reflection of hard power. The Vatican did not lose its soft power when it lost the Papal States in Italy in the nineteenth century. Conversely, the Soviet Union lost much of its soft power after it invaded Hungary and Czechoslovakia, even though its economic and military resources continued to grow. Imperious policies that utilized Soviet hard power actually undercut its soft power. And some countries such as Canada, the Netherlands, and the Scandinavian states have political clout that is greater than their military and economic weight, because of the incorporation of attractive causes such as economic aid or peacekeeping into their definitions of national interest. These are lessons that the unilateralists forget at their and our peril.

Britain in the nineteenth century and America in the second half of the twentieth century enhanced their power by creating liberal international economic rules and institutions that were consistent with the liberal and democratic structures of British and American capitalism—free trade and the gold standard in the case of Britain, the International Monetary Fund, World Trade Organization, and other institutions in the case of the United States. If a country can make its power legitimate in the eyes of others, it will encounter less resistance to its wishes. If its culture and ideology are attractive, others more willingly follow. If it can establish international rules that are consistent with its society, it will be less likely to have to change. If it can help support institutions that encourage other countries to channel or limit their activities in ways it prefers, it may not need as many costly carrots and sticks.

In short, the universality of a country's culture and its ability to establish a set of favorable rules and institutions that govern areas of international activity are critical sources of power. The values of democracy, personal freedom, upward mobility, and openness that are often expressed in American popular culture, higher education, and foreign policy contribute to American power in many areas. In the view of German journalist Josef Joffe, America's soft power "looms even larger than its economic and military assets. U.S. culture, lowbrow or high, radiates outward with an intensity last seen in the days of the Roman Empire—but with a novel twist. Rome's and Soviet Russia's cultural sway stopped exactly at their military borders. America's soft power, though, rules over an empire on which the sun never sets."[16]

Of course, soft power is more than just cultural power. The values the U.S. government champions in its behavior at home (for example, democracy), in international institutions (listening to other), and in foreign policy (promoting peace and human rights) also affect the preferences of others. America can attract (or repel) others by the influence of its example. But soft power does not belong to the government in the same degree that hard power does. Some hard power assets (such as armed forces) are strictly governmental, others are inherently national (such as our oil and gas reserves), and many can be transferred to collective control (such as industrial assets that can be mobilized in an emergency). In contrast, many soft power resources are separate from American government and only partly responsive to its purposes. In the Vietnam era, for example, American government policy and popular culture worked at crosspurposes. Today popular U.S. firms or nongovernmental groups develop soft power of their own that may coincide or be at odds with official foreign policy goals. That is all the more reason for the government to make sure that its own actions reinforce rather than undercut American soft power. All these sources of soft power are likely to become increasingly important in the global information age of this new century. And, at the same time, the arrogance, indifference to the opinions of others, and narrow approach to our national interests advocated by the new unilateralists are a sure way to undermine American soft power.

Power in the global information age is becoming less tangible and less coercive, particularly among the advanced countries, but most of the world does not consist of postindustrial societies, and that limits the transformation of power. Much of Africa and the Middle East remains locked in preindustrial agricultural societies with weak institutions and authoritarian rulers. Other, countries, such as China, India, and Brazil, are industrial economies analogous to parts of the West in the mid-twentieth century.[17] In such a variegated world, all three sources of power—military, economic, and soft—remain relevant, although to different degrees in different relationships. However, if current economic and social trends continue, leadership in the information revolution and soft power will become more important in the mix. . . .

Power in the twenty-first century will rest on a mix of hard and soft resources. No country is better endowed than the United States in all three dimensions—military, economic, and soft power. Its greatest mistake in such a world would be to fall into one-dimensional analysis and to believe that investing in military power alone will ensure its strength.

BALANCE OR HEGEMONY?

America's power—hard and soft—is only part of the story. How others react to American power is equally important to the question of stability and governance in this global information age. Many realists extol the virtues of the classic nineteenth-century European balance of power, in which constantly shifting coalitions contained the ambitions of any especially aggressive power. They urge the United States to rediscover the virtues of a balance of power at the global level today. Already in the 1970s, Richard Nixon argued that "the only time in the history of the world that we have had any extended periods of peace is when there has been a balance of power. It is when one nation becomes infinitely more powerful in relation to its potential competitors that the danger of war arises."[18] But whether such multipolarity would be good or bad for the United States and for the world is debatable. I am skeptical.

War was the constant companion and crucial instrument of the multipolar balance of power. The classic European balance provided stability in the sense of maintaining the independence of most countries, but there were wars among the great powers for 60 percent of the years since 1500.[19] Rote adherence to the balance of power and multipolarity may prove to be a dangerous approach to global governance in a world where war could turn nuclear.

Many regions of the world and periods in history have seen stability under hegemony—when one power has been preeminent, Margaret Thatcher warned against drifting toward "an Orwellian future of Oceania, Eurasia, and Eastasia—three mercantilist world empires on increasingly hostile terms. . . . In other words, 2095 might look like 1914 played on a somewhat larger stage."[20] Both the Nixon and Thatcher views are too mechanical because they ignore soft power. America is an exception, says Josef Joffe, "because the 'hyperpower' is also the most alluring and seductive society in history. Napoleon had to relay on bayonets to spread France's revolutionary creed. In the American case, Munichers and Muscovites *want* what the avatar of ultra-modernity has to offer."[21]

The term "balance of power" is sometimes used in contradictory ways. The most interesting use of the term is as a predictor about how countries will behave; that is, will they pursue policies that will prevent any other country from developing power that could threaten their independence? By the evidence of history, many believe, the current preponderance of the United States will call forth a countervailing coalition that will eventually limit American power. In the words of the self-styled realist political scientist Kenneth Waltz, "both friends and foes will react as countries always have to threatened or real predominance of one among them: they will work to right the balance. The present condition of international politics is unnatural."[22]

In my view, such a mechanical prediction misses the mark. For one thing, countries sometimes react to the rise of a single power by "bandwagoning"— that is, joining the seemingly stronger rather than weaker side—much as Mussolini did when he decided, after several years of hesitation, to ally with Hitler. Proximately to and perceptions of threat also affect the way in which countries react.[23] The Unites States benefits from its geographical separation from Europe and Asia in that it often appears as a less proximate threat than neighboring countries inside those regions. Indeed, in 1945, the United States was by far the strongest nation on earth, and a mechanical application of balancing theory would have predicted an alliance against it. Instead Europe and Japan allied with the Americans because the Soviet Union, while weaker in overall power, posed a greater military threat because of its geographical proximity and its lingering revolutionary ambitions. Today, Iraq and Iran both dislike the United States and might be expected to work together to balance American power in the Persian Gulf, but they worry even more about each other. Nationalism can also complicate predictions. For example, if North Korea and South Korea are reunited , they should have a strong incentive to maintain an alliance with a distant power such as the United States in order to balance their two giant neighbors, China and Japan. But intense nationalism resulting in opposition to an American presence could change this if American diplomacy is heavy-handed. Nonstate actors can also have an effect, as witnessed by the way cooperation against terrorists changed some states' behavior after September 2001.

A good case can be made that inequality of power can be a source of peace and stability. No matter how power is measured, some theorists argue, an equal distribution of power among major states has been relatively rare in history, and efforts to maintain a balance have often led to war. On the other hand, inequality of power has often led to peace and stability because there was little point in declaring war on a dominant state. The political scientist Robert Gilpin has argued that "*Pax Britannica* and *Pax Americana,* like the *Pax Romana,* ensured an international system of relative peace and security." And the economist Charles Kindleberger claimed that "for the world economy to be stabilized, there has to be a stabilizer, one stabilizer."[24] Global governance requires a large state to take the lead. But how much and what kind of inequality of power is necessary—or tolerable—and for how long? If the leading country possesses soft power and behaves in a manner that benefits others, effective countercoalitions may be slow to arise. If, on the other hand, the leading country defines its interests narrowly and uses its weight arrogantly, it increases the incentives for others to coordinate to escape its hegemony.

Pax Americana is likely to last not only because of unmatched American hard power but also to the extent that the United States "is uniquely capable of engaging in 'strategic restraint,' reassuring partners and facilitating cooperation."[25] The open and Pluralistic way in which U.S. foreign policy is made can often reduce surprise, allow others to have a voice, and contribute to soft power. Moreover, the impact of American preponderance is softened when it is embodied in a web of multilateral institutions that allow others to participate in decisions and that act as a sort of world constitution to limit the capriciousness of American power. That was the lesson the United States learned as it struggled to create an antiterrorist coalition in the wake of the September 2001 attacks. When the society and culture of the hegemon are attractive, the sense of threat and need to balance it are reduced.[26] Whether other countries will unite to balance American power will depend on how the United States behaves as well as the power resources of potential challengers.

NOTES

1. On the complexities of projections, see Joseph S. Nye, Jr., "Peering into the Future." *Foreign Affairs* (July–August 1994); see also Robert Jervis, "The Future of World Politics: Will It Resemble the Past?" *International Security* (Winter 1991–1992).

2. A. J. Taylor, *The Struggle for Mastery in Europe, 1848–1918* (Oxford, UK: Oxford University Press, 1954), xxix.

3. Whether this would change with the proliferation of nuclear weapons to more stats is hotly debated among theorists. Deterrence should work with most states, but the prospects of accident and loss of control would increase. For my views, see Joseph S. Nye, Jr., *Nuclear Ethics* (New York: Free Press, 1986).

4. Robert Cooper, *The Postmodern State and the World Order* (London: Demos, 2000), 22.

5. John Mueller, *Retreat from Doomsday: The Obsolescence of Major War* (New York: Basic Books, 1989).

6. Thomas Friedman. *The Lexus and the Olive Tree: Understanding Globalization* (New York: Farrar, Straus and Giroux, 1999), chap. 6.

7. Richard N. Rosecrance, *The Rise of the Trading State* (New York: Basic Books, 1986), 16, 160.

8. Thucydides, *History of the Pelopoanesian War,* trans. Rex Warner (London: Penguin, 1972), book I, Chapter 1.

9. And in turn, as industrialization progressed and railroads were built, Germany feared the rise of Russia.

10. Henry Kissinger portrays four international systems existing side by side: the West (and Western Hemisphere), marked by democratic peace; Asia, where strategic conflict is possible; the Middle East, marked by religious conflict; and Africa, where civil wars threaten weak postcolonial states. "America at the Apex," *The National Interest* (Summer 2001).

11. Robert O. Keohane and Josph S. Nye, Jr., *Power and Interdependence*, 3rd ed. (New York: Longman, 2000), chap. 1.

12. James Carville quoted in Bob Woodward, *The Agenda: Inside the Clinton White House* (New York: Simon and Schuster, 1994), 302.

13. For a more detailed discussion, see Joseph S. Nye, Jr., *Bound to Lead: The Changing Nature of American Power* (New York: Basic Books, 1990), chap. 2. This builds on what Peter Bachrach and Morton Baratz called the "second face of power" in "Decisions and Nondecisions: An Analytical Framework," *American Political Science Review* (September 1963): 632–42.

14. Védrine, *France in an Age of Globalization,* 3.

15. The distinction between hard and soft power is one of degree, both in the nature of the behavior and in the tangibility of the resources. Both are aspects of the ability to achieve one's purposes by affecting the behavior of others. Command power—the ability to change what others do—can rest on coercion or inducement. Co-optive power—the ability to shape what others want—can rest on the attractiveness of one's culture and ideology or the ability *to* manipulate the agenda of political choices in a manner that makes actors fail to express some preferences because they seem to be too unrealistic. The forms of behavior between command and co-optive power range along a continuum: command power, coercion, inducement, agenda setting, attraction, co-optive power. Soft power resources tend to be associated with co-optive power behavior, whereas, hard power resources are usually associated with command behavior. But the relationship is imperfect. For example, countries may be attracted to others with command power by myths of invincibility, and command power may sometimes be used to establish institutions that later become regarded as legitimate. But the general association is strong enough to allow the useful shorthand reference to hard and soft power.

16. Josef Joffe, "Who's Afraid of Mr. Big?" *The National Interest* (Summer 2001): 43.

17. See Cooper, *Postmodern State:* Bell. *The Coming of Post-Industrial Society.*

18. Nixon quoted in James Chace and Nicholas X. Rizopoulos, "Towards New Concert of Nations: An American Perspective." *World Policy Journal* (Fall 1999): 9.

19. Jack S. Levy, *War in the Modern Great Power System, 1495–1975* (Lexington: University Press of Kentucky, 1983), 97.

20. Margaret Thatcher, "Why America Must Remain Number One," *National Review,* 31 July 1995, 25.

21. Josef Joffe, "Envy," *The New Republic,* 17 January 2000, 6.

22. Kenneth Waltz, "Globalization and American Power," *The National Interest* (Spring 2000) 55–56.

23. Stephen Walt, "Alliance Formation and the Balance of Power," *International Security* (Spring 1985).

24. Robert Gilpin, *War and Change in World Politics* (New York: Cambridge University Press, 1981); 144–45; Charles Kindleberger, *The World in Depression, 1929–1939* (Berkeley: University of California Press, 1973), 305.

25. Ikenberry, "Institutions, Strategic Restraint," 47; also Ikenberry, "Getting Hegemony Right," *The National Interest* (Spring 2001): 17–24.

26. Josef Joffe, "How America Does It," *Foreign Affairs* (September–October 1997).